Cisco Digital Network Architecture

Intent-based Networking in the Enterprise

Tim Szigeti, CCIE No. 9794

David Zacks

Matthias Falkner

Simone Arena

Cisco Press

Cisco Digital Network Architecture

Tim Szigeti, David Zacks, Matthias Falkner, and Simone Arena

Published by:
Cisco Press

2 2023

Library of Congress Control Number: 2018959771

ISBN-13: 978-1-58714-705-0
ISBN-10: 1-58714-705-X

Warning and Disclaimer

This book is designed to provide information about Cisco Digital Network Architecture. Every effort has been made to make this book as complete and as accurate as possible, but no warranty or fitness is implied.

The information is provided on an "as is" basis. The authors, Cisco Press, and Cisco Systems, Inc. shall have neither liability nor responsibility to any person or entity with respect to any loss or damages arising from the information contained in this book or from the use of the discs or programs that may accompany it.

The opinions expressed in this book belong to the author and are not necessarily those of Cisco Systems, Inc.

Trademark Acknowledgments

All terms mentioned in this book that are known to be trademarks or service marks have been appropriately capitalized. Cisco Press or Cisco Systems, Inc., cannot attest to the accuracy of this information. Use of a term in this book should not be regarded as affecting the validity of any trademark or service mark.

Special Sales

For information about buying this title in bulk quantities, or for special sales opportunities (which may include electronic versions; custom cover designs; and content particular to your business, training goals, marketing focus, or branding interests), please contact our corporate sales department at corpsales@pearsoned.com or (800) 382-3419.

For government sales inquiries, please contact governmentsales@pearsoned.com.

For questions about sales outside the U.S., please contact intlcs@pearson.com.

Feedback Information

At Cisco Press, our goal is to create in-depth technical books of the highest quality and value. Each book is crafted with care and precision, undergoing rigorous development that involves the unique expertise of members from the professional technical community.

Readers' feedback is a natural continuation of this process. If you have any comments regarding how we could improve the quality of this book, or otherwise alter it to better suit your needs, you can contact us through email at feedback@ciscopress.com. Please make sure to include the book title and ISBN in your message.

We greatly appreciate your assistance.

Editor-in-Chief: Mark Taub

Alliances Manager, Cisco Press: Arezou Gol

Product Line Manager: Brett Bartow

Managing Editor: Sandra Schroeder

Development Editor: Marianne Bartow

Senior Project Editor: Tonya Simpson

Copy Editor: Bill McManus

Technical Editors: Roland Seville, Ramses Smeyers

Editorial Assistant: Cindy J. Teeters

Cover Designer: Chuti Prasertsith

Composition: codemantra

Indexer: Tim Wright

Proofreader: Jeanine Furino

About the Authors

Tim Szigeti, CCIE No. 9794, is a principal technical marketing engineer within the Cisco Enterprise Networking Business (ENB) team. In this role, he collaborates with customers, the field, engineering, Cisco IT, and third-party technology partners to drive the development of industry-leading network analytics solutions. In his more than 20 years with Cisco, Tim has authored/co-authored five generations of Cisco QoS Design Guides, four Cisco Press books, an IETF standard (RFC 8325), and multiple patents. Additionally, Tim has been inducted into the Cisco Distinguished Speaker Hall of Fame Elite, representing the Top 1 percent of Cisco speakers of all time.

Outside of Cisco, Tim's passion is on-track performance driving; as such, you may at times catch a glimpse of him taking corners at high speeds on the spectacular Sea-to-Sky Highway between his hometown of Vancouver and Whistler, British Columbia.

Additional information on Tim can be found on the Cisco Innovators website in the feature story "Cisco Innovators: Tim Szigeti," at https://newsroom.cisco.com/feature-content?type=webcontent&articleId=1845902.

Dave Zacks is a distinguished technical marketing engineer within the Cisco ENB team, focused on network architectures and fabrics, network hardware and ASIC design, switching, wireless, and the many and diverse technologies under the enterprise networking umbrella. Dave is based in Vancouver, Canada, and has been with Cisco for 19 years. Prior to his employment with Cisco, Dave traces his roots in computing to 1979, and has been involved in the datacomm and networking industry since 1985.

Dave is a Cisco Live Distinguished Speaker, having scored in the top 10 percent of all speakers at Cisco Live events worldwide as rated by the attendees. In addition, Dave is recognized as one of only a handful of such speakers to earn the Cisco Live Distinguished Speaker Elite designation, an honor awarded to speakers who have achieved Cisco Live Distinguished Speaker status ten times or more (Dave's total is currently 15).

In addition to his abiding focus on data communications, Dave maintains a deep and broad interest in many additional topic areas, including (but not limited to) particle and quantum physics, astrophysics, biology, genetics, chemistry, history, mathematics, cryptology, and many other topics. Dave has a special passion for rocketry, aeronautics, space travel, and advanced aircraft and spacecraft design, engineering, and operation.

Additional background on Dave can be reviewed on the Cisco Innovators website in the feature story "Cisco Innovators: Dave Zacks," at https://newsroom.cisco.com/feature-content?type=webcontent&articleId=1851941.

Dr. Matthias Falkner is a distinguished technical marketing engineer within the Cisco ENB team. He currently focuses on the evolution of enterprise and service provider network architectures, and in particular on end-to-end architecture solutions involving virtualization. Matthias is currently helping to drive the Cisco automation strategy for enterprise networks (including Cisco DNA Center). Matthias also holds responsibilities in branch virtualization and in the definition of the cloud exchange architecture. Prior to his role within ENB, Matthias was the lead TME architect for the Cisco ASR 1000 Series routers. He has also held positions in product management, and served as a product line manager for the Cisco 10000 Series routers. From 2000 to 2005, Matthias was a consulting systems engineer in the Deutsche Telekom account team with Cisco Germany. Matthias holds a PhD in Systems and Computer engineering from Carleton University, Canada, and an MSc in Operations Research & Information Systems from the London School of Economics and Political Science, UK. His technical interests are in the area of performance characterization of virtualized networks, high availability, and service chaining.

Simone Arena is a principal technical marketing engineer (TME) within the Cisco ENB team and is primarily focused on enterprise network architecture and on all things related to wireless and mobility. Simone is based in Italy and is a Cisco veteran, having joined Cisco in 1999. Throughout the years, Simone has covered multiple roles at Cisco, starting as a software engineer working with Catalyst switching platforms, to consulting system engineer in the field, to TME within different teams (Enterprise Solution Engineering, Wireless Business Unit, and now ENB).

Today Simone is the lead TME architect for Cisco DNA Wireless, and his time is split between helping customers and partners design the best solution that fits their needs and engineering and product management, trying to evolve and improve the products and solutions.

Simone is a Distinguished Speaker at Cisco Live and has spoken at Cisco Live events all over the world for several years. He consistently is rated as an excellent speaker by attendees for his deep technical knowledge and ability to impart this information in a meaningful way.

Besides wireless, Simone has two passions: his two daughters, Viola and Anita, and his hometown soccer team, Fiorentina.

In his spare time Simone enjoys listening to music, especially through his new tube amplifier (simply awesome!).

More information on Simone can be found on the Cisco Innovators website in the feature story "Cisco Innovators: Simone Arena," at https://newsroom.cisco.com/feature-content?type=webcontent&articleId=1849095

About the Technical Reviewers

Roland Saville is a technical leader within the Cisco ENB team, focused on developing best-practice design guidance for enterprise network deployments. He has more than 24 years of experience at Cisco as a systems engineer, product manager, consulting systems engineer, technical marketing engineer, technical leader, and architect. During that time, he has focused on a wide range of technology areas including routing, LAN switching, integration of voice and video onto network infrastructures, VoIP, network security, WLAN networking, RFID, energy management, Cisco TelePresence, Quality of Service (QoS), BYOD, Wi-Fi location, Cisco Connected Mobile Experiences (CMX), Software Defined Networking (SDN), Cisco APIC-EM, Cisco DNA, and cloud computing. He has also spent time focusing on the retail market segment. Prior to working at Cisco, Roland was a communications analyst for the Chevron Corporation. Roland holds a Bachelor of Science degree in Electrical Engineering from the University of Idaho and a Master of Business Administration (MBA) degree from Santa Clara University. He co-authored the book *Cisco TelePresence Fundamentals*, is a member of the IEEE, and has co-authored 13 U.S. patents.

Ramses Smeyers has been part of Cisco Technical Services since 2005 and currently works in the Solutions Support TAC organization as a principal engineer. Within this role he supports Cisco customers to implement and manage datacenter and campus solutions, with a focus on network automation and orchestration products. On a continual basis he creates training presentations and delivers them to Cisco technical teams across the world. He also takes a leading role on emerging technologies such as Cisco DNA, ACI, OpenStack, Ansible, and Docker.

For years Ramses has been a "customer" himself and hence perfectly understands how customers think and how to communicate with them. In his DNA, however, he's a geek, and that's the language he speaks to engineers. Ramses is very proficient in explaining complex messages to a variety of audiences and is a seasoned speaker at public events such as Cisco Live and Cisco PVT.

Dedications

Tim Szigeti:

To my family:

Senna, my pride: Has it really been nine years since you were born (and since I first dedicated a book to you)? I can hardly believe it! Every day you amaze, astonish, and inspire me with your inventiveness, resourcefulness, and creativity, whether you're designing cars of the future, building amazing structures from any type of construction material, or figuring out how to translate collecting chestnuts into a lucrative business venture. I don't know yet whether you will be an architect, an engineer, a scientist, a business magnate, or a full-time volunteer; but I do know that whatever you choose, you will be phenomenally successful at it! Always remember: the greatest rewards and satisfaction and joy come from serving others, and as such, may you ever be generous of your knowledge, your talents, and of yourself. Also may you ever be courageous, choosing the right path, even when an easier one is presented to you. And finally, may you ever be humble, bearing in mind that we can learn from every single person we meet.

Isla, my joy: Has it really been five years since you were born (and since I first dedicated a book to you)? I can hardly believe you're beginning *senior* kindergarten this year! What a lovely, intelligent, kind, and delightful young lady you're turning out to be! It's true, you still have me tightly wrapped around your little finger, but I don't mind; no, not at all. I wonder too what you will be when you grow up. Will you be a veterinarian? A dentist? A ballerina? An artist? An equestrian? A volunteer? I'm very excited to find out. I love that no matter what you do, you put your best and your all into your endeavors. When trying new things, remember to be patient, positive, and persistent: if things don't go quite right on the first try, dust yourself off, try to learn from what went wrong, and then give it another go. And another. And another... until you achieve your goal. I know you can do *anything* you set yourself to!

Lella, my love: Has it really been 19 years since we were married (and 14 since I first dedicated a book to you)? It's only when I stop and count the years that I begin to feel old; otherwise I still feel like the goofy nerd that you married a long, long time ago. For richer or for poorer, in sickness and in health, I consider myself blessed to have you beside me through our life journey. You're a true complement. You make me a better person, husband, and father. Without you, I'd be completely lost; with you, I just lose my keys, my socks, my patience, and sometimes my mind! But, you always manage to help me find everything that really matters. For this, and for a million other reasons, I love you forever.

Dave Zacks:

It is not often that you see a fundamentally new approach to network design and deployment begin to emerge and take hold. In a career, you may only get to see such a transition once or twice. It has been my privilege to be involved in just such an exciting journey with Cisco around the Cisco Digital Network Architecture—and my further privilege to work with a team of outstanding individuals as this transition takes place.

I dedicate this book to the multitude of people with whom I have shared this quest, and to the many friends I have made along the way.

Tim, Matt, and Simone—it has been a privilege to write this book with you, and to count you as my friends as well as co-workers.

Onward and upward! The adventure has really only just begun.

And for a bit of fun:

01001001 00100000 01100100 01100101 01100100 01101001
01100011 01100001 01110100 01100101 00100000 01110100
01101000 01101001 01110011 00100000 01100010 01101111
01101111 01101011 00100000 01110100 01101111 00100000
01100001 01101110 01111001 01101111 01101110 01100101
00100000 01110000 01100001 01110100 01101001 01100101
01101110 01110100 00100000 01100101 01101110 01101111
01110101 01100111 01101000 00100000 01110100 01101111
00100000 01100011 01101111 01101110 01110110 01100101
01110010 01110100 00100000 01110100 01101000 01101001
01110011 00100000 01100010 01100001 01100011 01101011
00100000 01110100 01101111 00100000 01000001 01010011
01000011 01001001 01001001 00100000 01110100 01100101
01111000 01110100 00101110 00100000 00100000 01000001
01110100 00100000 01110100 01101000 01100101 00100000
01100101 01101110 01100100 00100000 01101111 01100110
00100000 01110100 01101000 01100101 00100000 01100100
01100001 01111001 00101100 00100000 01101001 01110100
00100111 01110011 00100000 01100001 01101100 01101100
00100000 01101111 01101110 01100101 01110011 00100000
01100001 01101110 01100100 00100000 01111010 01100101
01110010 01101111 01110011 00100001

...And to everyone else, I hope you really enjoy this book!

Matthias Falkner:

More than three years ago Cisco embarked on a new era in enterprise networking by developing Cisco Digital Network Architecture. For many of us at Cisco—and probably for many of you networking geeks—this implied once again a completely new vocabulary of acronyms: Cisco DNA, ENFV, SDA, SDW, FB, FC, FE, NFVIS, VNF, LISP, VXLAN, VNID, PXGrid, ISE, etc. My family and friends were once again completely flabbergasted. I had just barely gotten over traditional networking acronyms (ATM and BGP took a few years) with them, and I now started to talk about Cisco DNA and all of its concepts with a renewed passion and excitement, completely confusing my non-networking audience in the process once again.

So I would like to dedicate this book to my wonderful wife Julia, my fantastic kids Amy, Caroline, Benjamin, and Christopher, my parents Renate and Kurt, as well as my extended family who had to endure this whole new wave of acronyms. Thank you for giving me the time and patience to contribute to this book with my awe-inspiring co-authors, Tim, Dave, and Simone. I could not have done this without all of you!

Simone Arena:

My favorite artist and rock legend Bruce Springsteen sings in the 1984 song "No Surrender": *We learned more from a three-minute record than we ever learned in school.*

It's the passion, the real-world experiences, the new perspective on things that a song can communicate that strikes the listener. Well, we have tried hard to put the same ingredients into this book, so I really hope you will enjoy it.

I would like to dedicate this book, and all the effort that went into it, to my whole family. I have a wonderful big Italian family, so I cannot name them all; but I do want to mention my wife Giulia, my two princesses Viola and Anita, my mom Laura, and my father Paolo (I am sure he will be reading the book from up there). They are my strength and inspiration.

A special thank you, from the bottom of my heart, goes to my wife Giulia because she simply knows how to deal with me, she has the right attitude and always the right word for me, at the right time...so that I never give up..."no retreat, baby, no surrender..."

Acknowledgments

Tim Szigeti:

First, I'd like to thank all the readers of our books, papers, design guides, and other collateral that we've collectively produced over the past 20 years. There is nothing more rewarding than when our readers close the feedback loop by sharing their first-hand stories of how they used our content to successfully deploy technology solutions to solve their business problems. These success stories fuel us to keep innovating, making the next generation of solutions even better, and when they are, we evangelize the latest and greatest of these all around the world, and finally, we put ink to paper and write another one of these books. It is your feedback that drives our passion to go through this process again and again, taking on greater challenges each time. So thank you!

I'd also like to thank the thousands of attendees at our collective Cisco Live sessions (likely tens of thousands by now). Even when we present brand new content for the first time, we see many familiar faces in the audience. We thank you for your trust and will continually strive to prove ourselves worthy of it. I was truly surprised at how many of you have already pre-ordered this book! Your willingness to join us on a journey over new ground is very humbling and deeply appreciated.

I'd like to start off my acknowledgments of individuals by thanking Rob Soderbery and Jeff Reed for launching Cisco's Enterprise Networking Business team on our digital networking journey. This represented a brand new direction and a major paradigm shift in enterprise networking. Nonetheless, you clearly articulated your vision and the broad strokes of the architecture, and then trusted your team to fill in the details. Thank you for your bold leadership.

Many thanks to Scott Harrell, Sachin Gupta, and Ravi Chandrasekaran for accepting the Cisco DNA torch and holding it high by driving the vision all the way to shipping reality. The products you launched marked milestones in the networking industry, including the UADP ASIC (the industry's first programmable ASIC), the Catalyst 9000 Series (the fastest ramping switch of all time), and Cisco DNA Center (the industry's first automation and analytics platform). It's no small feat to make dreams come true.

Thank you Ronnie Ray and Ramit Kanda for your leadership of the Cisco DNA Center and Cisco DNA Assurance teams; also thank you both for your support on this project.

Thanks too to Mark Montanez, both for your team leadership and your technical leadership. You kept us focused on the big picture, all the while dividing and conquering the many parts that had to come together to make Cisco DNA real. You played a multilevel game of chess throughout this entire process and showed us how it was done. Your example, encouragement, and guidance truly made all of us (Dave, Matt, Simone, and me) more effective in our roles as architects and engineers. Thank you too for being the catalyst for this book project; we never would have got it off the ground without your endorsement and support. Thank you, my friend!

Jason Frazier also deserves significant thanks, as he's arguably the world's leading hands-on expert of Cisco DNA. Thank you, Jason, for all the pioneering groundwork you did in your labs, piecing it all together and making everything work. Your brilliance, tirelessness, and sheer tenacity are the stuff of legends!

Thanks go out to Peter Jones, our resident expert in all things Doppler (i.e., UADP ASIC) and Cisco Multigigabit technology. Thank you, Peter, for taking me on a deep dive of the many layers of technical depth to be found in your ASIC by expertly navigating and summarizing multiple engineering documents (each between 10,000 and 19,250 pages in length), all without letting me drown.

Similar thanks go out to Michael Fingleton for taking me deep into the QFP ASIC, patiently breaking it apart and putting it back together again so that I could understand its inner workings.

Thank you, Jerome Henry, for always being available to share your immense knowledge, talents, and insights into wireless technologies, as well as many other related and even unrelated fields, such as advanced mathematics and statistics theories. You never hesitate to help, no matter what the ask, and you always deliver the highest quality of work. You're a true scholar and a true friend!

Thanks too to Tzahi Peleg, for always being willing to dig deep and go the extra mile to do the right things for Cisco DNA Center and Application Policy, in particular. Thanks, Tzahi, for sharing all your knowledge and passion with me. And thanks as always for tearing yourself away from the all-night discos in Tel Aviv to answer my many questions during Pacific Standard Time daytime meetings!

And thank you Guy Keinan for your talent and passion in making NBAR2 and SD-AVC the industry standard for application recognition technologies, and for taking the time to fully explain the inner workings of these to me in depth.

I'd like to also thank Michael Kopcsak and his team for challenging our status quo by helping us all to embrace design thinking philosophy and driving this into every product within Cisco Digital Network Architecture. Thank you too, Michael, for your contributions and permissions in the "Designing for Humans" chapter of this book.

Thank you, Zeus Kerravala, for your excellent and timely market and technical research, and for kindly granting us permissions for these to be incorporated into the text of this book. These clearly and specifically articulate the business value of Cisco DNA solutions.

I'd also like to thank the many members of the Cisco Press team, beginning with our executive editor Brett Bartow.

Brett: You gave us the opportunity to write this book back *before anyone had even heard of Cisco DNA*, and then you demonstrated the patience of Job in waiting for us to complete this work. Each of us has spent nearly 20 years working at Cisco, and were always used to working long and hard, but the past two years brought an unprecedented intensity to our "day jobs" that often resulted in pushing this extra-curricular effort to the backburner. Yet, you always brought us back to task and gave us whatever was needed to complete this project. Thank you for your unfaltering support in seeing this project through.

Thank you, Marianne Bartow, for doing the heavy lifting in editing and in the coordination of this entire process. You worked with us every step of the way, effortlessly solving big problems and small whenever we encountered them. We wish to express our appreciation for your efforts on our behalf and the outstanding unity and cohesion you brought to our work.

Thank you too, Tonya Simpson, for putting on the finishing touches by polishing up our content during the production phase. And thanks always to Cindy Teeters for all your administrative support during this entire project.

Next, I'd like to extend thanks to our technical reviewers Roland Saville and Ramses Smeyers.

Roland: You remain my favorite "philosopher engineer," as you can always identify the corner cases where any design recommendation breaks down and falls apart. Your technical knowledge, thoroughness, and attention to detail are second to none. I truly appreciate your comments and technical feedback. I don't even know how many books or papers you have reviewed over the years on my behalf, but I do know that I'd never write *anything* without asking for your review and input. It's not until content stands up to your technical scrutiny that I even dare to consider it good. Thank you!

Thank you too, Ramses, for coming into this project on short notice and diving right in and tackling the technical review of this extensive and diverse work.

Finally, I owe a huge debt of gratitude to my co-authors:

Thank you, Scott Harrell, for being willing to carve time out from your ultra-busy schedule of running a $20B business to write a foreword to this book! We're all very excited to see you putting your foot to the floor with Cisco DNA and the customer/market response from doing so. Thanks, Scott!

Many thanks and a shout-out to Kevin Kuhls for contributing your chapter on device programmability. This is an area that none of us has expertise in, despite listening to you present this content within our Cisco DNA Techtorial at Cisco Live after Cisco Live. We're tremendously glad (and honestly quite relieved) to have had a master write this chapter rather than fumbling through it ourselves. Thank you for patiently and expertly elucidating these important new concepts and protocols.

Grazie mille, Simone Arena! Your knowledge, expertise, and passion are off the charts! You're always willing to help others, often taking on more than you can comfortably carry, and never letting anyone down. Your work is amazing, and considering that you're writing all of this in your second language, you put us all to shame. I'm glad that with this project now closed, you'll have more time to spend with your lovely family. Go Fiorentina!

Words begin to fail me when I describe my respect, admiration, and gratitude for Matthias Falkner. Matt, you're one of the most educated and brilliant persons I've ever had the pleasure of working with; yet, at the same time, you're also one of the nicest and most down to earth. Thank you for steadfastly seeing this project through, beginning to end, when there were many times it would have been far easier to just let it go. It's always a true pleasure working with you and learning from you. I still want to be "Matt" when I grow up.

And my final words of thanks are for the incomparable Mr. Dave Zacks. Dave, I simply do not know how you do what you do. You're a master of virtually every subject, from networking to science to history to math to aircraft/spacecraft design to genetic engineering, etc. Your passion and pursuit of perfection in all your work is simply astounding, as is your sheer prolificacy. I remember thinking again and again: there's no way Dave is going to make this deadline, and then BAM! You send in chapter after chapter, hundreds of pages at a time, written as if off the top of your head, and all at a level of technical detail that is nothing short of astonishing! And even after chapters were sent to production, you called some back so as to make incremental changes to reflect the absolute latest status of development efforts, some of which were only a few weeks old. I cannot thank you enough for all you did on this project, Dave!

Dave Zacks:

It is always difficult to single out people for acknowledgments, since there are simply so many people that help you along the way, in big ways and small—sometimes without their ever realizing that they have helped you, or provided assistance that smoothed your path, or offered insights that helped you to reach the next level, and then strive for the one beyond that.

Tim did a great job of acknowledging not only the many individuals that we have the privilege to work with daily, but also so many of the people we have all worked with that helped in one way or another to make this book possible, and to make Cisco Digital Network Architecture real. Nevertheless, I have to double down on some of those acknowledgements, and include a few additional ones of my own as well.

First, Tim Szigeti himself. Tim helped all of us as authors create structure for our work, provided consistent and timely encouragement as the book progressed, and when necessary helped "herd the cats" to drive outcomes and deadlines. Tim is so precise, methodical, and insightful that he helps to set a strong example for all of us to follow. Thank you, Tim, from all of us as authors.

Next, to my co-authors along with Tim—Matt and Simone.

Matthias Falkner is one of the most thorough and structured individuals I know, and his insights are always a source of enlightenment in any conversation. Matt's ability to see "around" a problem always serves to provide me with an additional perspective, and his sense of humor makes him fun to work with. Matt, thank you for always being the "rock" that anchors our work to a solid foundation.

Simone Arena: Well, what can I say about Mr. Arena? Not only is Simone one of the premier wireless experts in Cisco (or anywhere else, for that matter), with an astounding depth of knowledge and a strong, focused work ethic, he is also someone I am happy to count as a good friend. As I discovered several years ago, Simone and I share a love of the music of "The Boss," Bruce Springsteen. Simone, my friend, "Talk about a dream, try to make it real…" That's what we do every day, and I am proud to work alongside you on that journey.

And a few more folks of note:

To our Enterprise Networks leadership team – Scott Harrell, Ravi Chandrasekaran, and Sachin Gupta, as well as the various Product Managers with whom I work daily (yes, I'm looking at you, Vikram Pendharkar)—thank you for your vision, the guidance you provide, and the structures you create that allow for creative execution of the Cisco DNA vision. The future success of Cisco depends on the foundation you—and all of us as a team—are laying down. Thank you for your insights, your energy, your influence, and your direction on this critical initiative for Cisco and our customers.

I'd also like to provide a big "Thank You" to my boss, Carl Solder, who has formed up the best TME team in Cisco, and I would argue, the best in the industry! You keep us all focused, charging ahead, and pulling in the same direction – no easy task! Thanks Carl for your constant support, your vision, your insights, and the inspiring example you provide.

Mark Montanez—friend, mentor, and my long-time close partner in all things Cisco. Mark, thank you for your encouragement over the years, and the many paths we have explored together—and the future paths as yet unexplored. Mark is one of those rare people who combines deep technical insights with the ability to see the "big picture," even when that picture is still forming. I have learned so very much from you over the years, my friend. Thank you, Mark, for all we have done together, and all we will collaborate on in the future.

Peter Jones—Peter is one of those individuals with whom you never can (or will) find the "bottom" of their knowledge. An inexhaustible store of information on UADP, ASIC hardware in general, and the current and future evolution of Ethernet, Peter is also able to see the larger ways in which technology impacts people, and how people can work together to make that technology more powerful. Peter has a persistent focus on how to make things better, simpler, and faster, and a relentless drive to get technical innovations adopted in the real world. A fellow fan of exceptional sci-fi, Peter is someone I am proud to count as a good friend, and someone from whom I have learned—and continue to learn—so very much. As always, look for Peter and me as co-presenters at Cisco Live, always contending for who can deliver the maximum amount of information in the minimum amount of time. Crank up the bit rates!

Shawn Wargo—When I switched over from a direct customer-facing role in Cisco into the product development teams several years ago, Shawn was already well known to me as a technical expert in Catalyst switching, as well as someone with a strong emphasis on practicality, clarity, and completeness. What I was pleased to find over the next several years is that Shawn and I have become not only closer co-workers, but also friends, with a common preference for hard-edged industrial music as well as a common focus on ASICs, hardware, and systems. Thank you, Shawn, for all the work we have done together, and all the work that remains ahead of us as we make Cisco DNA real!

There are just so many others to acknowledge that it is impossible here—it would take a book in and of itself. The Cisco Enterprise Network Business team is chock-full of brilliant minds and great people to work with, including Darrin Miller, Victor Moreno, Jason Frazier, Jerome Henry, Steve Wood, Muhammad Imam, Jeff McLaughlin, Sehjung Hah, and so many others from whom I have learned so much, and from whom I continue to learn every day. Thank you for the work we have collaborated on. And to anyone I omitted, know that our work together every day is what makes Cisco Digital Network Architecture possible.

Matthias Falkner:

Tim almost acknowledged everyone. However, the biggest acknowledgment for this book should go to Tim! He was instrumental in making this book happen. Thanks you, Tim, for being our rock at any stage in the writing process. I always felt that I could get sound advice about writing, technology, and process from you whenever I needed it. You provided me with so many doses of energy! I want to be "Tim" when I grow up!

I would also like to extend Tim's acknowledgments above to the group of Distinguished and Principal Engineers who have helped shape Cisco Digital Network Architecture. Thank you, Mark Montanez, Victor Moreno, Darrin Miller, Jean-Marc Barozet, Steve Wood, Marco Larivera, Craig Hyps, Jerome Henry, Shawn Wargo, Jason Frazier, as well as my co-authors Tim, Dave, and Simone, for all the stimulating discussions we had on defining the Enterprise Architecture Blueprint that lay the foundation for many chapters in this book. I feel truly privileged and honored to be able to learn from you. Every minute I spend on the phone or in discussions with you I learn. Thank you for helping me grow in my role as TME!

Simone Arena:

Wow! What a journey this book has been…a journey of learning, hard work, and passion. I would have never done it without my three fellow writers: Dave, Matt, and Tim. This dedication goes first to you, my friends: you inspire me with your work and made it possible for me to complete this book.

Tim, Matt, and Dave did a great job in mentioning all the people that were instrumental for this book, and I do a "plus one" on all of them; but a special mention from me goes to the following: Mark Montanez, you started it all, so it's all your fault! Jason Frazier, because every team should have a Jason. Roland Saville and Ramses Smeyers, thanks for the great work you have done reviewing this book! Talking about inspiring people, thank you, monsieur JP Vasseur: if I know a bit about analytics and machine leaning, it is because of you.

My gratitude goes also to all my colleagues at Cisco because they are the main reason for me to try and get better every day.

And finally, thank you, Carl Solder, because you believe in me and you always have my back.

Contents at a Glance

Foreword xxxiv

Introduction xxxvi

Part I Introduction to Cisco DNA

Chapter 1 Why Transform Your Business Digitally? 1

Chapter 2 The Business Value of Cisco DNA 19

Chapter 3 Designing for Humans 31

Chapter 4 Introducing the Cisco Digital Network Architecture 55

Chapter 5 The Cisco Digital Network Architecture Blueprint 87

Part II Cisco DNA Programmable Infrastructure

Chapter 6 Introduction to Cisco DNA Infrastructure 123

Chapter 7 Hardware Innovations 135

Chapter 8 Software Innovations 189

Chapter 9 Protocol Innovations 225

Chapter 10 Cisco DNA Infrastructure—Virtualization 267

Chapter 11 Cisco DNA Cloud 307

Part III Cisco DNA Automation

Chapter 12 Introduction to Cisco DNA Automation 325

Chapter 13 Device Programmability 337

Chapter 14 Cisco DNA Automation 361

Part IV Cisco DNA Analytics

Chapter 15 Introduction to Cisco DNA Analytics 397

Chapter 16 Cisco DNA Analytics Components 405

Chapter 17 Cisco DNA Analytics Engines 423

Part V Cisco DNA Solutions

Chapter 18 Cisco DNA Virtualization Solutions: Enterprise Network Functions Virtualization and Secure Agile Exchange 451

Chapter 19 Cisco DNA Software-Defined Access 497

Chapter 20 Cisco DNA Application Policy 569

Chapter 21 Cisco DNA Analytics and Assurance 631

Chapter 22 Cisco DNA Encrypted Traffic Analytics 711

Part VI Cisco DNA Evolution

Chapter 23 Cisco DNA Evolution 721

Index 725

Reader Services

Register your copy at www.ciscopress.com/title/9781587147050 for convenient access to downloads, updates, and corrections as they become available. To start the registration process, go to www.ciscopress.com/register and log in or create an account*. Enter the product ISBN 9781587147050 and click Submit. When the process is complete, you will find any available bonus content under Registered Products.

*Be sure to check the box that you would like to hear from us to receive exclusive discounts on future editions of this product.

Contents

Foreword xxxiv

Introduction xxxvi

Part I Introduction to Cisco DNA

Chapter 1 Why Transform Your Business Digitally? 1

Opportunities and Threats 1

Digitally Transforming Industries 3

Digital Advertising 3

Digital Media and Entertainment 3

Digital Finance 4

Digital Communications 4

Digital Transportation Services 5

Digitally Transforming Businesses 7

Transforming the Customer Experience 8

Burberry 8

Starbucks 9

UPS 11

Transforming the Employee Experience 11

Air France 12

RehabCare 13

Cisco 13

Transforming Business Operations 14

Boeing 14

Codelco 15

BC Hydro 16

Driving Digital Transformation with the Internet of Things 16

Are You Ready? 17

Summary 18

Further Reading 18

Chapter 2 The Business Value of Cisco DNA 19

Business Requirements of the Network Architecture 19

Cost Reduction 20

Risk Mitigation 20

Actionable Insights 21

Business Agility 22

Intent-Based Networking 23

Business Value of Cisco Digital Network Architecture 24
Reducing Costs Through Automation, Virtualization, and Programmable Hardware 25
Mitigating Risks with Integrated Security and Compliance 26
Revealing Actionable Insights Through Analytics 26
Accelerating Business Agility Through Open APIs 26
Adding It All Up 28
Summary 29
Further Reading 29

Chapter 3 Designing for Humans 31
Technology Versus User-Experience 31
Design Thinking Philosophy and Principles 33
Cisco Design Thinking Framework 34
Discover Phase 35
Opportunity Statement 36
Define Phase 37
Problem to Be Solved Statement 38
Explore Phase 39
The Cisco Design Thinking Journey for Cisco DNA 40
Cisco DNA Discovery Phase 41
The Front-Line Engineer 42
The Firefighter 44
The Expert 45
The Planner 48
Cisco DNA Definition Phase 49
Cisco DNA Exploration Phase 53
Summary 53
Further Reading 54

Chapter 4 Introducing the Cisco Digital Network Architecture 55
Requirements for Cisco DNA 56
Requirements to Reduce Complexity and Costs 57
Requirement to Increase Operational Flexibility 58
Flexibility 58
Intelligent Feedback Mechanism 59
Application, User, and Device Awareness 59
Security and Compliance Requirements 59
Cloud-Enablement Requirement 60

Architectural Principles 60
Openness 61
Extensibility 62
Programmability 62
Policy-based Networking 63
Security 63
Software Driven 64
Cloud Integrated 65
Conflicting Principles? 65
Overview of the Cisco DNA Components 66
Infrastructure 66
Cisco DNA Infrastructure Domains 67
Extending the Concept of Network Fabrics in Cisco DNA 69
Virtualization 70
Policy 72
Automation 73
Controllers 73
Orchestrators 75
Analytics Platform 77
Data Collection 77
Data Reporting 78
Cisco DNA Analysis 78
Feedback and Control 79
The Role of the Cloud in Cisco DNA 80
Cloud for Applications 81
Cloud for Automation and Management 82
Cloud for Analytics 82
Connecting the Building Blocks: APIs 83
Outcomes 84
Summary 85
Further Reading 86
Chapter 5 The Cisco Digital Network Architecture Blueprint 87
Cisco DNA Services 88
Cisco DNA Services—Transport 90
Cisco DNA Services—Policy 91
Relationship Between Cisco DNA Policies and Business Intent 92

Cisco DNA Infrastructure 93
Transport Functions 94
Supporting Network Functions 96
Fabrics 98
Automating Cisco DNA—Controllers 99
Automating Transport and Network Functions Infrastructure 99
Maintaining a View of the Infrastructure Functions and Connected Endpoints 100
Instantiating and Maintaining Cisco DNA Services 100
Relationships in Cisco DNA: Revisiting Domains, Scopes, and Fabrics 102
Cisco DNA Interfaces 105
Service Definition and Orchestration 107
Relationship Between the Controllers and the Service Definition and Orchestration Component 110
Analytics Platform 112
Data Collection 113
Data Extraction 113
Data Ingestion 114
Data Export 114
On-Premises and Off-Premises Agnosticism—Revisiting the Cloud 115
Application Hosting in the Cloud and the Evolution of the DMZ 116
Leveraging the Cloud for Cisco DNA Controllers and Analytics 118
Summary 120

Part II Cisco DNA Programmable Infrastructure

Chapter 6 Introduction to Cisco DNA Infrastructure 123
Picturing the Modern Network 124
Exploring Cisco DNA Infrastructure 125
The Evolving Network, and Why It Matters 126
Requirements: The Need for Change 126
Requirements: The Need for Speed (of Change) 127
Requirements: The Need for Simplicity 128
Requirements: The Need for Continuity 129
Cisco DNA Infrastructure Solutions 130
Flexible Hardware 130
Flexible Software 131
New and Evolving Protocols 132
The Emergence of Virtualization 133

Bringing It All Together 133

Summary 134

Chapter 7 Hardware Innovations 135

The Importance of Hardware in a Software-Defined World 135

The Making of a Chip 136

Delving Deeper: How Chips Are Designed and Built 136

Drivers of Chip Design and Density 143

When Good Chips Go Bad: What Can Go Wrong in Chip Design 145

When Good Chips Need to Get Better: Designing the Next Generation 146

Now We Speak the Same Language! 147

What's Happening in the World of Networks 148

How Traditional Network ASICs Process Packets 149

Traffic Handling with CPUs and FPGAs 150

Introducing Flexible Silicon 152

Flexible Switching Silicon: UADP 154

UADP Use Cases—Current, and Future 163

Introducing the Future: UADP 2.0 and 3.0 165

So What's Common Across All of These Variants of UADP? 171

UADP—Summing Up 172

Flexible Routing Silicon: QFP 173

QFP—An Introduction 174

QFP—Diving Deeper 176

QFP—Use in Platforms 180

UADP and QFP—Summing Up 181

Wireless: Providing Innovation for Mobility 182

Flexible Radio Assignment 183

Intelligent Capture 185

Summary 186

Further Reading 187

Chapter 8 Software Innovations 189

The Importance and Evolution of Networking Software 189

Cisco IOS: Origins and Evolution 190

Evolution of the Cisco IOS Data Plane 191

Evolution of the Cisco IOS Control Plane 194

Evolution of the Cisco IOS Management Plane 195

Evolution of Cisco Networking Software 196

The Evolution of Cisco IOS to IOS XE 198
Cisco IOS XE in a Nutshell 199
Cisco IOS XE: Delving Deeper 201
IOS XE Subsystems 202
IOS XE Database 203
Container Framework and Application Hosting 205
Cisco IOS XE: Bringing It All Together 207
Cisco IOS XE: Simplification with a Single Release Train 209
Cisco IOS XE: Software Maintenance Upgrades 209
The Issue with Software Upgrades 210
Types of SMUs—Cold, and Hot 211
Installing a SMU 211
Benefits of SMUs 212
Cisco IOS XE: Platform Support 212
Cisco IOS XE: Summary 213
Protecting Platforms and Networks: Trustworthy Systems 214
Trustworthy Systems: An Overview 215
Possible Attacks: IOS Modifications 215
Attack Mitigation with Trustworthy Systems 216
Defense: Image Validation and Signing 217
Defense: Runtime Defenses 217
Defense: Secure Boot 218
Understanding Boot Sequence Attacks 218
Protecting Device Integrity from the Ground Up with Secure Boot 219
Ensuring Device Identity with the Secure Unique Device Identifier 220
Cisco Secure Boot and Trust Anchor Module: Validating the Integrity of Software, Followed by Hardware 221
The Move to Intuitive Networking 222
Summary 223
Further Reading 223
Chapter 9 Protocol Innovations 225
Networking Protocols: Starting at the Bottom with Ethernet 226
Power Protocols: Power over Ethernet, to 60 Watts and Beyond! 227
The Future of Power over Ethernet 230
Multiple-Speed Protocols over Copper: Multigigabit Ethernet, Squeezing More Life Out of Existing Cabling Infrastructures 230

25G Ethernet—The New Kid on the Block 234
Ethernet Evolving: This Is Not Your Father's Ethernet! 235
Moving Up the Stack 235
Networking Protocols: Moving Up the Stack to Layer 2 235
Networking Protocols: Moving Up the Stack to Layer 3 237
First-Hop Reachability Protocols: HSRP and VRRP 237
Routing Protocols 238
Virtual Routing 240
Layer 2 over Layer 3 241
Networking Protocols Today: Summary 242
Networking Protocols for the New Era of Networking 242
VXLAN: A Next-Generation Encapsulation Technology 243
UDP Encapsulation 247
Virtual Network Support 248
Scalable Group Tag Support 248
Summary: Why VXLAN? 248
IS-IS: The Evolution of Underlay Routing 249
LISP: The Evolution of Overlay Host Reachability 249
The Need for Host Mobility 252
The Need for Host Scale 252
LISP to Address the Host Mobility and Scale Needs of the Next-Generation Network 253
Examination of LISP Roaming Operation 255
Summing Up: LISP As a Next-Generation Overlay Control Plane 257
Scalable Group Tags: The Evolution of Grouping and Policy 257
Scalable Group Tags for Group-Based Policies 261
SGT Transport End-to-End Across the Network 263
Bringing It All Together: What Next-Generation Protocols Within the Network Allow Us To Build 264
Summary 264
Further Reading 265

Chapter 10 Cisco DNA Infrastructure—Virtualization 267
Benefits of Network Function Virtualization 268
CAPEX Benefits of NFV 268
OPEX Benefits of NFV 270
Architectural Benefits of NFV 271

Use Cases for Network Function Virtualization 272
Control Plane Virtualization 272
Branch Virtualization 274
Virtualization to Connect Applications in VPCs 275
Virtualization of Multicloud Exchanges 276
Overview of an NFV System Architecture 278
Hypervisor Scheduling and NUMA 281
Input/Output Technologies for Virtualization 283
Challenges and Deployment Considerations of Network Function Virtualization 289
Performance 289
Oversubscribing the Physical Hardware Resources 290
Optimizing Server Configurations 290
Selecting the Right I/O Technique 291
VNF Footprint Considerations 292
Multi-tenancy and Multi-function VNFs 293
Transport Virtualization 296
Network Segmentation Architecture 297
Network Access Control 298
Network Path Virtualization 298
Network Services Edge 299
Policy-based Path Segmentation 299
Control Plane–based Segmentation 302
Multihop Path Isolation Techniques 302
Single-Hop Path Isolation Techniques 303
Summary 305

Chapter 11 Cisco DNA Cloud 307
Introduction to the Cloud 308
Cloud Service Models 311
Cloud Deployment Models 312
It's a Multicloud World! 313
Cisco DNA for the Cloud 315
Cisco DNA Cloud for Applications 316
Cisco DNA Cloud for Automation 318
Cisco DNA Cloud for Analytics 319
Summary 323
Further Reading 323

Part III Cisco DNA Automation

Chapter 12 Introduction to Cisco DNA Automation 325

Why Automate? 325

Reduce Total Cost of Ownership 326

Lower Risk 326

Move Faster 328

Scale Your Infrastructure, Not Your IT Department 328

Think "Out of the Box" 329

Simplify Like Never Before 330

Enable Applications to Directly Interact with the Network 330

Is Cisco DNA Automation the Same as SDN? 330

Centralized Versus Distributed Systems 331

Imperative Versus Declarative Control 331

The Cisco SDN Strategy 332

Automation Elements 332

Network Programmability 332

Network Controller 333

Network Orchestrator 334

Summary 335

Further Reading 336

Chapter 13 Device Programmability 337

Current State of Affairs 338

CLI Automation 338

SNMP 340

Model-Based Data 340

YANG 341

Protocols 344

Encoding 345

Network Protocols 346

NETCONF 347

RESTCONF 350

gRPC 351

Telemetry 352

gRPC Telemetry 353

Tools 354

Application Hosting 357
Summary 359
Further Reading 359

Chapter 14 Cisco DNA Automation 361

The Increasing Importance of Automation 362
Allow the Network to Scale 363
Reduce Errors in the Network 363
Time to Perform an Operation 363
Security and Compliance 364
Current Impediments to Automation 364
Classifying Network Automation Tasks 367
Infrastructure and Cisco DNA Service Automation 368
Standard and Nonstandard Automation Tasks 369
The Role of Controllers in Cisco DNA Automation 371
Leveraging Abstractions in Cisco DNA to Deliver Intent-Based Networking 372
Domain Controllers Versus Control Plane Protocols 375
Automating Your Network with Cisco DNA Center 377
Cisco DNA Center Basics 377
Device Discovery, Inventory, and Topology 380
Day 0 Operations—Standardizing on Network Designs 382
Standardizing Settings for Supporting Network Functions 384
Automating Device Credentials 384
Reserving and Managing IP Address Pools 385
Standardizing Service Provider QoS Profiles 386
Characterizing Wireless LAN Profiles 387
Standardizing on Network Designs 388
Automating the Deployment of Network Elements and Functions 390
Day N Operations—Automating Lifecycle Operations 394
Summary 395
Further Reading 396

Part IV Cisco DNA Analytics

Chapter 15 Introduction to Cisco DNA Analytics 397

A Definition of Analytics 397
Cisco DNA Analytics 398
Cisco DNA Analytics, Opportunities and Challenges 399
Brief History of Network Analytics 400

Why Cisco DNA Analytics? 401
The Role of Network Analytics in Cisco DNA 402
Summary 404

Chapter 16 Cisco DNA Analytics Components 405
Analytics Data Sources 405
Cisco DNA Instrumentation 407
Distributed Network Analytics 408
Telemetry 411
Why Telemetry? 412
The Cisco DNA Telemetry Architecture 413
Limitations of Today's Telemetry Protocols 413
The Evolution of Cisco DNA Telemetry: Model-Driven Telemetry 414
Analytics Engine 416
The Traditional Analytics Approach 416
The Need for Analytics Engines 418
Data Scalability 419
Analytics Efficiency 419
Application Development Simplification 420
The Role of the Cloud for Analytics 420
Summary 422
Further Reading 422

Chapter 17 Cisco DNA Analytics Engines 423
Why a Cisco DNA Analytics Engine? 425
Cisco DNA Analytics Engines 427
Cisco Network Data Platform 428
Telemetry Quotient 430
NDP Architecture 430
NDP Architecture Principles 430
NDP Architecture Layers 431
NDP Architecture Components 433
NDP Deployments Modes 436
On-Premises Deployments 436
Cloud Deployments 437
NDP Security and High Availability 438
Cisco Tetration Analytics 439
It's All About Quality of Data 440
Data Center Visibility with Cisco Tetration Analytics 442

Cisco Tetration Analytics Architecture 444
Data Collection Layer 444
Analytics Layer 445
Enforcement Layer 446
Visualization Layer 446
The Benefits of Cisco Tetration Analytics 446
Summary 448
Further Reading 449

Part V Cisco DNA Solutions

Chapter 18 Cisco DNA Virtualization Solutions: Enterprise Network Functions Virtualization and Secure Agile Exchange 451
The Cisco Strategy for Virtualization in the Enterprise 452
Cisco Enterprise Network Functions Virtualization 453
Details on Virtualization Hardware 455
NFVIS: An Operating System Optimized for Enterprise Virtualization 459
Virtualized Network Functions 463
Cisco Integrated Services Virtual Router 463
Cisco Adaptive Security Virtual Appliance 464
Cisco Firepower NGFW Virtual 464
Cisco Virtual Wide Area Application Services 464
Cisco Prime Virtual Network Analysis Module 465
Cisco Virtual Wireless LAN Controller 465
Third-party VNF Support 466
Service Chaining and Sample Packet Flows 468
Transparent Versus Routed Service Chains 471
Orchestration and Management 473
NFVIS GUI (Per System) 473
Cisco DNA Center (Network Level) 478
Configuring and Monitoring of an NFVIS Host Using Traditional Mechanisms 485
Virtualizing Connectivity to Untrusted Domains: Secure Agile Exchange 488
Motivation for the Cisco SAE Solution 489
Cisco SAE Building Blocks 492
Running Virtualized Applications and VNFs Inside IOS XE 493
Summary 496
Further Reading 496

Chapter 19 Cisco DNA Software-Defined Access 497
The Challenges of Enterprise Networks Today 497
Software-Defined Access: A High-Level Overview 499
SD-Access: A Fabric for the Enterprise 500
What Is a Fabric? 500
Why Use a Fabric? 501
Capabilities Offered by SD-Access 505
Virtual Networks 505
Scalable Groups 506
Stretched Subnets 508
SD-Access High-Level Architecture and Attributes 512
SD-Access Building Blocks 513
Cisco DNA Center in SD-Access 514
SD-Access Fabric Capabilities 515
IP Host Pools 515
Virtual Networks 516
Scalable Groups 517
SD-Access Device Roles 518
SD-Access Control Plane Nodes, a Closer Look 520
SD-Access Fabric Border Nodes, a Closer Look 523
SD-Access Fabric Edge Nodes 527
SD-Access Extended Nodes 531
SD-Access Wireless Integration 532
SD-Access Case Study 542
SD-Access Case Study, Summing Up 565
Summary 565
Further Reading 567

Chapter 20 Cisco DNA Application Policy 569
Managing Applications in Cisco DNA Center 570
Application Registry 570
Application Sets 574
Application Policy 576
Required Steps 576
Optional Steps 582
Queuing Profile 582
Marking Profile 583
Service Provider Profile 584

What Happens "Under the Hood"? 585
Translating Business Intent into Application Policy 586
Cisco DNA Infrastructure Software Requirements for Application Policy 589
NBAR2 589
NBAR2 Operation 592
QoS Attributes 594
"Holy Grail" Classification and Marking Policy 596
SD-AVC 599
Cisco DNA Infrastructure Platform-Specific Requirements for Application Policy 601
Routing Platform Requirements 602
Application Classification and Marking Policies 602
Queuing and Dropping Policies 603
Sub-Line Rate Hierarchical QoS Policies 605
Enterprise-to-Service Provider Mapping 606
Hardware Queuing 609
Internal System QoS 612
Switching Platform Requirements 613
Application Classification and Marking Policies 613
Hardware Queuing Policies 614
Internal System QoS 618
Wireless Platform Requirements 621
Application Classification and Marking Policies 621
DSCP-to-UP Mapping 622
Hardware QoS 624
Internal System QoS (Wireless Access Points) 626
Summary 628
Further Reading 629

Chapter 21 Cisco DNA Analytics and Assurance 631
Introduction to Cisco DNA Assurance 631
Context 633
Learning 638
The Architectural Requirements of a Self-Healing Network 639
Instrumentation 640
Distributed On-Device Analytics 641
Telemetry 642

Scalable Storage 643

Analytics Engine 643

Machine Learning 644

Guided Troubleshooting and Remediation 645

Automated Troubleshooting and Remediation 645

Cisco DNA Center Analytics and Assurance 647

Network Data Platform 647

NDP Contextual Correlation and Time Machine 649

NDP Complex Event Processing 650

NDP Time Series Analysis 650

NDP Architecture 650

NDP Operation 652

NDP Extensibility 653

Cisco DNA Assurance 653

Network Health 655

Client Health 663

Application Health 671

Path Trace 688

Sensor-Driven Tests 695

Intelligent Capture 697

Machine Learning 704

Summary 710

Further Reading 710

Chapter 22 Cisco DNA Encrypted Traffic Analytics 711

Encrypted Malware Detection: Defining the Problem 712

Encrypted Malware Detection: Defining the Solution 714

ETA: Use of IDP for Encrypted Malware Detection 714

ETA: Use of SPLT for Encrypted Malware Detection 715

Encrypted Malware Detection: The Solution in Action 716

Encrypted Malware Detection: Putting It All Together 719

Summary 720

Part VI Cisco DNA Evolution

Chapter 23 Cisco DNA Evolution 721

Index 725

Icons Used in This Book

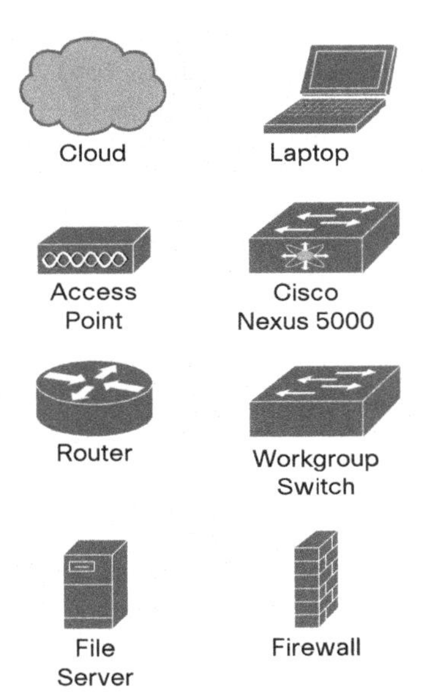

Command Syntax Conventions

The conventions used to present command syntax in this book are the same conventions used in the IOS Command Reference. The Command Reference describes these conventions as follows:

- **Boldface** indicates commands and keywords that are entered literally as shown. In actual configuration examples and output (not general command syntax), boldface indicates commands that are manually input by the user (such as a **show** command).
- *Italic* indicates arguments for which you supply actual values.
- Vertical bars (|) separate alternative, mutually exclusive elements.
- Square brackets ([ ]) indicate an optional element.
- Braces ({ }) indicate a required choice.
- Braces within brackets ([{ }]) indicate a required choice within an optional element.

Foreword

In the last 20 years, we've seen a new kind of business arise and grow: the digital native enterprise. Companies like Salesforce, Google, Amazon, Uber, eBay, and Airbnb have leveraged digitization as a disruptive force across a variety of industries. All of these companies rely on network connectivity for their businesses to flourish. For these companies, the network is the foundation of the business.

Fly by Wire

A reliance on the flow of data isn't limited to digital native companies, however. Nearly every large business or enterprise today relies on continued connectivity among employees, partners, suppliers, customers, databases, and software services to operate.

United Airlines can't put a plane in the air if there's a network outage: Electronic systems problems, when they arise, are well-publicized reasons for system-wide ground stops. Amazon is reported to be exposed to over a million dollars a minute of losses when its servers go offline. And when a cloud service goes down, critical business functions—like sales—can go with it across industries, as some customers of Salesforce discovered in a widely publicized outage in May 2016.

For thousands of companies of all kinds, the network is the foundation.

But the network is evolving.

There are converging trends—some technological, some business-driven—that put pressure on businesses' historically static network infrastructures. For example, the growing use of multiple cloud-based services for business-critical functions disrupts typically centralized security models (while it also enables the rapid provisioning of new applications). The influx of Internet of Things (IoT) devices into the workplace upends traditional security models and creates an endpoint environment that is constantly expanding and evolving.

Connectivity is now business-critical and the availability of modern campus and branch networks must grow to reflect this new reality. The resulting new systems will be, in many ways, more complex, and they simply cannot be managed the way networks, devices, and security were run just a few years ago.

Cisco DNA Center and the New Model of Networking

At Cisco, we saw this coming. We've known for years that the network architectures we've been using—that we helped build over the last 30 years, to be honest—were not what we would need for the next generation. As end devices and applications become more dynamic, so must the network. We need to be able to instantly reconfigure every node of the network the second a decision to utilize a new application in the cloud is made, or even more quickly, based on emerging threat conditions.

For this to work, we cannot expect network operators to continue to program each network device (each router and switch) separately, nor is it realistic to expect network managers of the near future to have to maintain complex access control lists (ACLs) and VLANs as the primary method of separating users and devices, and acting as the first line of defense for security breaches.

Telling network equipment *how* to do what we need it to do is getting less manageable by the day. Rather, we need to tell networks *what* we need them do, and then rely on them to handle the heavy lifting of configuring the equipment automatically.

This is what *intent-based networking* does, and what Cisco DNA Center is. It's the unified control system that lets IT managers set up and maintain an entire network fabric by defining rules that span network devices, and that move across the network with users as they and their devices are in motion.

Cisco DNA Center also provides a feedback loop—Assurance—that can use advanced analytics to make sure the network is doing what you intend for it to do. For security, for capacity planning, and especially for troubleshooting, this capability is invaluable, especially as enterprises' endpoint and application environments get more varied and dynamic.

Cisco DNA Center puts a coherent management interface on top of an entire network, including much of the network equipment we're using today. In other words, it's an abstraction layer on top of current systems. Network operators will be able to set up, maintain, and optimize business operations on networks without having to know every CLI on every device and be able to program every device by hand (just as business application programmers today rarely have to think about CPU-level microcode). But as we transition from traditional methods for running networks to a new, directed way to manage them, it's valuable to understand how the old and the new systems interact.

That's what I hope you get out of this book. Moving to intent-based network management is a big shift, and we know that networking experts need to learn to trust it before they learn to use it. We hope this book helps you understand the how and the why of intent-based networking in general, and Cisco DNA Center in particular, so you can take full advantage of this new capability.

The Network as Competitive Advantage

It is our sincere hope that by moving to intent-based network management, we will help network operators work more efficiently. We want you to spend less time programming multiple devices to do the same thing, less time chasing ACL configurations, and far less time troubleshooting.

With this time saved, we believe that network experts can apply their expertise to more strategic tasks. For every business running on a network (that is, nearly all of them), the people running the network can be a great lever in helping the business to run faster and be more dynamic. By focusing more on the value the network can unlock for businesses, and a little less on the minutiae of how it works, we'll be able to build more robust, more competitive, more agile, and more secure enterprises.

—Scott Harrell

SVP, Cisco and GM of Cisco's Enterprise Networking Business (ENB)

Introduction

Cisco Digital Network Architecture (Cisco DNA) represents the most fundamental change in enterprise networking in the past decade (possibly decades!).

To enable, facilitate, and accelerate the digital transformations of enterprises and to meet future business demands of networks (including multi-cloud, IoT, encrypted threats, etc.), Cisco has taken an entirely new approach to networking: intent-based networking. Thus, Cisco has re-engineered the enterprise network architecture, infrastructure, and solutions from the top down to align to this intent-based networking approach, the result of which is Cisco DNA.

Goals and Methods

The goal of this book is to introduce you to Cisco DNA, highlighting the current and future value propositions it offers to customers, the philosophy, tenets, and blueprints of the architecture, its hardware and software components, and the current solutions enabled by this architecture.

Who Should Read This Book?

This book has been written for four groups of readers:

- **Business decision makers (BDMs):** This book enables BDMs to see the impact that Cisco DNA can have on their business as a whole, to drive digital transformation and to gain competitive advantage.
- **Technical decision makers (TDM):** This book familiarizes TDMs with powerful emerging technologies and solutions that address their specific business needs.
- **Network architects:** This book provides technical details of cutting-edge technologies to network architects tasked with deploying these solutions, highlighting recommendations, interdependencies, limitations, and caveats.
- **Network operators:** This book provides guidance for network operators running Cisco DNA Center in their enterprise, showing them how to use this user-friendly interface to operate and benefit from powerful new networking solutions.

The authors of this book are principal and distinguished engineers who are leading the engineering efforts on Cisco DNA and are incredibly passionate about the work they are doing. As such, their motivation behind writing this book is their enthusiasm to share these latest and greatest breakthroughs in enterprise networking with any and all interested parties.

How This book Is Organized

This book is organized into 23 chapters in 6 parts.

Note The number of chapters in this book on Cisco DNA happens to correspond exactly to the number of chromosomes found in human Cisco DNA. As such, both happen to have 23 "chapters." This fact, however, is pure coincidence. Nonetheless, it makes for an interesting, albeit unintentional, parallel.

In Part I, "Introduction to Cisco DNA," readers are presented with business requirements, user requirements, and technical requirements of the enterprise network architecture. The five chapters in Part I are as follows:

- **Chapter 1, "Why Transform Your Business Digitally?":** The goal of this chapter is to understand the business opportunities and challenges that customers are facing in digital transformation, setting context for how Cisco DNA addresses these.
- **Chapter 2, "The Business Value of Cisco DNA":** This chapter introduces the concept of intent-based networking, and provides specific examples and data points of how Cisco DNA can reduce costs, mitigate risks, provide actionable insights, and increase business agility.
- **Chapter 3, "Designing for Humans":** This chapter serves as an intersection between business requirements and technical requirements by focusing on a third dimension of requirements: user requirements. It introduces the Design Thinking philosophy that Cisco employed in its top-down approach to Cisco DNA.
- **Chapter 4, "Introducing the Cisco Digital Network Architecture":** This chapter provides a technical introduction to Cisco DNA by outlining guiding architectural principles and tenets and introducing various components, including network infrastructure, network controllers, and network analytics platforms. (Note that the theme of the next three parts of the book are centered on these respective components.)
- **Chapter 5, "The Cisco Digital Network Architecture Blueprint":** This chapter "peels the onion" to expose the next level of architectural detail by showing how Cisco DNA components interact to connect users, devices, and applications. This chapter defines services in detail and explains concepts such as domains, scopes, and fabrics. It also offers an abstracted yet detailed blueprint to provide a framework for current and future elements of Cisco DNA.

Having introduced Cisco DNA in Part I, the next three parts are centered on key components of the architecture, specifically infrastructure, automation, and analytics. As such, Part II, "Cisco DNA Programmable Infrastructure," focuses on hardware, software, and protocol innovations within the infrastructure that provide the foundation for Cisco DNA. Part II is composed of six chapters:

- **Chapter 6, "Introduction to Cisco DNA Infrastructure":** This chapter presents evolving business needs of the network infrastructure, including the need for simplicity, continuity, and speed. Additionally, this chapter outlines how programmable hardware, flexible software, evolving protocols, and virtualization address these needs.
- **Chapter 7, "Hardware Innovations":** This chapter dives deep into hardware innovations for enterprise switching, routing, and wireless platforms. After an overview of application-specific integrated circuit (ASIC) design and production, this chapter provides in-depth details about the Cisco Unified Access Data Plane (UADP) ASIC, which represents the heart of Cisco DNA switching platforms, such as the Catalyst 9000 Series switches. A similar discussion follows on the Cisco QuantumFlow Processor (QFP) ASIC, which powers Cisco ASR routers. And finally, this chapter details wireless hardware to show how it enables new protocols, speeds, capabilities (like precision location and tracking), and analytics.
- **Chapter 8, "Software Innovations":** This chapter traces the evolution of Cisco IOS software (data plane, control plane, and management plane) and highlights the benefits of Cisco IOS XE software, in particular its cross-platform consistency, simplicity, flexibility, modularity, and support for containers for application hosting. This chapter also discusses trustworthy systems and the importance of secure infrastructure, as well as the move to controller-based networking via programmable interfaces.
- **Chapter 9, "Protocol Innovations":** This chapter outlines the evolution of networking protocols, beginning with Ethernet protocols and Power over Ethernet (PoE) and arriving at the movement toward Multigigabit Ethernet (mGig) over copper. It also provides an overview of the evolution of Layer 2 and Layer 3 protocols and next-generation networking protocols such as VXLAN, LISP, and TrustSec.
- **Chapter 10, "Cisco DNA Infrastructure—Virtualization":** This chapter complements the previous chapters by showing how the network functions enabled by hardware, software, and protocol innovations can be virtualized. Network function virtualization (NFV) enables network functions to run inside virtual machines on standard Intel x86–based hosting platforms; as such, NFV is inherently software driven. These functions can be quickly and easily deployed (even on an on-demand basis), providing network administrators flexibility, efficiency, and cost effectiveness.
- **Chapter 11, "Cisco DNA Cloud":** This chapter discusses how on-premises infrastructure can be extended to the cloud. It covers cloud service models, cloud deployment types and modes, multi-cloud challenges and solutions, and how Cisco DNA integrates with cloud-based service offerings.

Having laid a solid foundation at the infrastructure layer of the architecture, the discussion next proceeds to a higher layer of the architecture, beginning with Part III, "Cisco DNA Automation." The three chapters in this part highlight how network operations can be simplified and scaled using network controllers.

- **Chapter 12, "Introduction to Cisco DNA Automation":** This chapter explains the business reasons driving network automation, as well as the many operational benefits that can be realized by it. Also discussed are the differences between generic software-defined networking (SDN) and Cisco DNA Automation.

- **Chapter 13, "Device Programmability":** This chapter highlights the limitations of current tools used for programming—and gathering telemetry from—networks, and introduces new technologies that enable greater flexibility, efficiency, and capabilities than ever before. These technologies include the Network Configuration (NETCONF) protocol, Representational State Transfer Configuration (RESTCONF) protocol, Google Remote Procedure Call (gRPC) protocol, and Yet Another Next Generation (YANG) models for configuration and operational data.

- **Chapter 14, "Cisco DNA Automation":** This chapter discusses the importance of Cisco DNA automation as a major functional block in the architecture, drawing attention to how Cisco DNA automation goes well beyond the automatic configuration of individual network devices by allowing operators to treat their entire network as a single, cohesive, programmable system. This chapter explains how standardized network designs contribute to this objective, as well as how network functions are automated. The ongoing lifecycle management of Cisco DNA network elements is also addressed.

A key function that automation platforms provide is "talking" to the network—that is, taking the business intent expressed by the network operator, translating this into device-specific configurations, and then deploying these configurations at scale and end to end across the infrastructure. While this is an important function, it needs to be complemented by platforms that "listen" to the network, which is the key function performed by network analytics platforms, as discussed in Part IV, "Cisco DNA Analytics." Specifically, the Cisco DNA Analytics platform "closes the loop" by gathering telemetry data from the network and analyzing this data within the context of the expressed business intent so as to confirm either that the intent has indeed been delivered across the network or that it hasn't (in which case remediation actions can be triggered). Part IV is composed of three chapters:

- **Chapter 15, "Introduction to Cisco DNA Analytics":** This chapter introduces network analytics by examining the process of discovering, interpreting, and communicating meaningful information from raw network data and the business value that such actionable insights can present. Network analytics is broken down into its subcomponents, including infrastructure analytics, endpoint analytics, application analytics, user analytics, and policy analytics.

- **Chapter 16, "Cisco DNA Analytics Components":** This chapter explores the architectural components required to create an analytics solution, including instrumentation, distributed analytics, telemetry, and analytics engines. The roles and interrelationships of each component are examined, as well as how they come together to form a cohesive and comprehensive solution.

- **Chapter 17, "Cisco DNA Analytics Engines":** This chapter dives into detail on the analytics engine, highlighting how it can be used for network health monitoring, performance tuning, capacity planning, security analysis and threat prevention, and troubleshooting. To enable these use cases, network analytics engines need to perform data transformation, aggregation, and correlation, as well as time-series analysis and network baselining (via machine learning), all of which topics are discussed in this chapter.

Part V, "Cisco DNA Solutions" (arguably the most exciting part of the book), takes the concepts, principles, and components discussed thus far and shows how these are combined into cutting-edge architectural solutions that are significantly greater than the sum of their parts. The five chapters in Part V are as follows:

- **Chapter 18, "Cisco DNA Virtualization Solutions: Enterprise Network Functions Virtualization and Secure Agile Exchange":** This chapter presents two distinct use-case solutions of enterprise network function virtualization:
  - The virtualization of branch architectures, which focuses on the Cisco Enterprise Network Compute System (ENCS) and Cisco Enterprise Network Function Virtualization Infrastructure Software (NFVIS)
  - The virtualization of policy-based connectivity to external domains for multi-cloud architectures, namely the Cisco Secure Agile Exchange (SAE) solution, which combines virtualization with policy to allow network operators to define intent-based communication policies to connect employees, partners, customers, and/or guests to applications hosted in private, virtual private, or public clouds
- **Chapter 19, "Cisco DNA Software-Defined Access":** This chapter examines one of Cisco's newest and most exciting innovations in the area of enterprise networking: Software Defined Access (SDA). SDA presents an entirely new way of building—or even of thinking about and designing—enterprise networks. SDA revolutionizes networking by decoupling the IP address logical-addressing function from policy (IP ACLs have long been the traditional method of applying policy to users, groups, and applications, resulting in the IP address becoming overloaded with meaning, leading to brittle network designs and overwhelmingly complex network policies). SDA utilizes multiple components of Cisco DNA, including automation, assurance, and integrated security capabilities to deliver significantly increased simplicity, flexibility, security, mobility, visibility, and performance to enterprise networks.
- **Chapter 20, "Cisco DNA Application Policy":** This chapter presents a first-of-its-kind solution for intent-based application networking in the enterprise. Cisco DNA provides a comprehensive architecture to monitor, manage, provision, and troubleshoot applications. Specifically, Cisco DNA infrastructure provides powerful hardware and software capabilities to support granular application recognition—of even encrypted applications—as well as flexible and detailed application treatment capabilities. In turn, Cisco DNA Application Policy automates the deployment of intent-based application policies in an end-to-end manner over both brownfield and greenfield networks. Complementing these functions, Cisco DNA also includes application assurance (which is discussed in detail in Chapter 21) to monitor, report, and remediate (when necessary) how applications are being treated across the network.

- **Chapter 21, "Cisco DNA Analytics and Assurance":** This chapter discusses the role of analytics and assurance within the enterprise network architecture and introduces the Cisco DNA Analytics platform (an industry first), as well as the unprecedentedly powerful network monitoring and troubleshooting application that it enables: Cisco DNA Assurance. Most enterprises are bogged down by network monitoring and troubleshooting operations, and are challenged to collect data, replicate issues, resolve issues in a timely manner, and free the network from being blamed (which it often is, by default). To meet these challenges, Cisco DNA Assurance uses a time-series database (similar to a TV digital video recorder) to monitor the health of clients, network devices, and applications running on enterprise networks. Thus, IT support staff are freed from having to replicate issues; all they have to do is go "back in time" to whenever an issue was manifest, and see the entire state of the network at a given moment in time, allowing them to troubleshoot the root cause of the issue. Cisco DNA Assurance also expedites the troubleshooting and remediation process by leveraging contextual correlation, machine learning, and guided remediation.
- **Chapter 22, "Cisco DNA Encrypted Traffic Analytics":** This chapter presents a solution to what was (until recently) thought to be an unsolvable problem: how to identify threats in encrypted traffic. As the majority of enterprise traffic is now encrypted, cyber attackers seek to benefit from this lack of visibility by injecting malware and ransomware into the payloads of encrypted packets. However, Cisco DNA Encrypted Traffic Analytics (ETA) presents an architectural approach that combines programmable hardware, sophisticated software, automation, analytics, and cloud-based machine learning to produce a solution that has greater than 99 percent accuracy in detecting malware in encrypted traffic (with less than 0.01 percent false positives). This chapter examines two key use cases offered by ETA: encrypted malware detection and cryptographic compliance.

Cisco DNA is the Cisco long-term strategy for enterprise networking, and represents a journey that has only just begun. In the final part (and chapter) of this book, Part 6, "Cisco DNA Evolution," the authors share some of their prognostications (bounded by confidentially and intellectual-property restrictions) of future expressions of this architecture.

- **Chapter 23, "Cisco DNA Evolution":** In this final chapter, the authors (all of whom serve as Cisco DNA architects) wanted to share some of their thoughts on how they see Cisco DNA evolving over the next few years, thus presenting a sense of where Cisco DNA is heading (without giving away strategically competitive details). Also considered is the role of the network administrator and the skill sets that will maximize value in the transitions to come.

Figure Credits

Figure 1-3 copyright Worawee Meepian/Shutterstock

Figure 1-4 copyright Green Stock Media/Alamy Stock Photo

Figure 1-5 copyright maridav/123RF

Figure 1-6 copyright Newscast Online Limited/Alamy Stock Photo

Figure 1-7 copyright Nuttapol Sn/Shutterstock

Figure 1-8 copyright William Perugini/Shutterstock

Figure 1-9 copyright Andriy Popov/Alamy Stock Photo

Figure 1-10 copyright First Class Photography/Shutterstock

Figure 1-11 copyright Mario Ruiz/Epa/Shutterstock

Figure 14-7 (left) copyright Mladen Pavlovic/Shutterstock

Figure 14-7 (right) copyright Sergey Martirosov/123RF

Chapter 1

Why Transform Your Business Digitally?

The primary goal of Cisco Digital Network Architecture (Cisco DNA) is to accelerate the digital transformation of customers' businesses. Therefore, before diving into the technologies within this architecture, it's important to understand the business opportunities and challenges that customers are facing, thus setting relevant context for how Cisco DNA addresses these.

This chapter introduces and discusses the following:

- The opportunities and threats presented by digital transformation
- How digital technologies have transformed entire industries
- Case-study examples of how digital technologies are transforming key areas of business, including:
  - Customer experiences
  - Employee experiences
  - Operations
- Digital transformation and the Internet of Things (IoT)

Opportunities and Threats

Transform or die. It's really that simple when it comes to digital business. Provide your customers new experiences, delivering them greater value, personalization, convenience and satisfaction—or your competition will. Enable your employees new workplace experiences, empowering them to collaborate effectively, and effortlessly, improving their overall productivity and job satisfaction—or your opposition will. Leverage technology to reduce costs, make informed data-driven decisions, and reallocate resources from operation to innovation—or your rivals will.

Does that sound a bit dramatic? Not according to a 2015 study[1] of 941 companies around the world in 12 different industries done by the Global Center for Digital Business Transformation, which highlighted that roughly 40 percent of today's top ten incumbents (in terms of market share) in each industry will be displaced by digital disruption within the next five years. Furthermore, the same study showed that 43 percent of companies either do not acknowledge the risk of digital disruption or have not addressed it sufficiently, with nearly a third adopting a "wait and see" attitude. The industries most under threat of digital disruption are shown in Figure 1-1.

In contrast, companies that have mastered digital technology transformations have outperformed their industry peers by 9 percent in revenue generation and 26 percent in profitability, according to the Harvard Business Review Press book *Leading Digital.*

How real is digital transformation? To answer this, let's consider some examples of entire industries that were either significantly disrupted or completely transformed by various forms of digitalization.

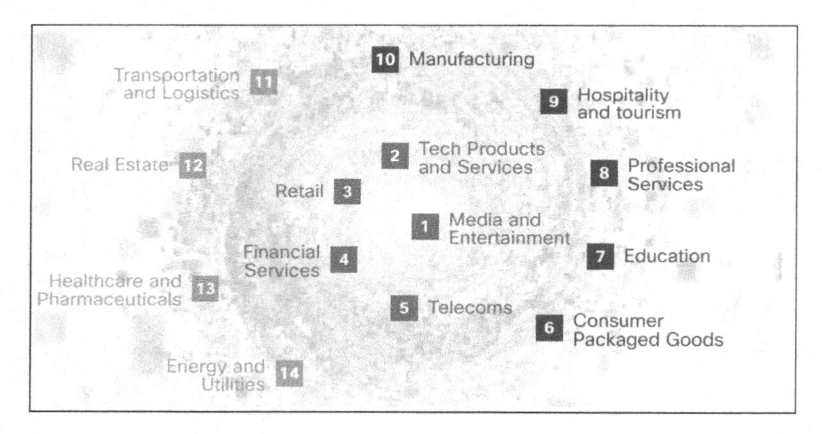

Figure 1-1 *Threat of Digital Disruption by Industry (Image Credit: Global Center for Digital Business Transformation, an IMD and Cisco Initiative https://www.imd.org/dbt/digital-business-transformation/)*

1 J. Bradley, J. Loucks, J. Macaulay, A. Noronha, and M. Wade, "Digital Vortex: How Digital Disruption Is Redefining Industries," Global Center for Digital Business Transformation, June 2015, https://www.cisco.com/c/dam/en/us/solutions/collateral/industry-solutions/digital-vortex-report.pdf.

Digitally Transforming Industries

Industries such as advertising, media and entertainment, finance, communications, transportation, and others have been radically transformed by the advent of digital technologies and processes. Incumbents that adopted "wait and see" attitudes were quickly displaced, while bold innovators grabbed market share at astonishing rates, as the following few examples demonstrate.

Digital Advertising

In 1995, Craig Newmark posed an email distribution list to friends, featuring local events in the San Francisco Bay Area. This list became a web-based service, called Craigslist, the following year and has since expanded to over 570 cities in 70 countries worldwide. As Craigslist steadily gained popularity, eventually becoming a top-100 website, it virtually single-handedly put the newspaper classified-advertising industry out of business in every city it entered, while earning itself nearly $700 million in annual revenues—all with only 50 employees!

Similarly, digital advertising for local businesses by applications like Angie's List, Yelp, and others have displaced paper-based "Yellow Pages" telephone directories, which held the monopoly for local business advertising for over 40 years.

Companies that have been slow to adapt to the shift from print advertising to digital have suffered similar fates. In sharp contrast, companies like Google, Facebook, and Baidu have embraced digital advertising and transformed themselves into industry leaders in this $187B[2] market, earning themselves $19B, $18B, and $10B (respectively) in 2016, and collectively garnishing 25 percent of the global market.

Digital Media and Entertainment

Apple complemented the release of the iPod in 2001 with its digital music iTunes Store in 2003. Within five years iTunes became the world's largest music vendor, earning over $6B per year in revenue. Concurrently, music retail stores like Virgin Megastores, HMV, Tower Records, and others closed up shop en masse.

In the video entertainment industry, scarcely a decade ago Blockbuster ruled as king, boasting 60,000 employees in over 9000 stores and nearly $6B in annual revenue. In one of the greatest instances of modern business irony, Blockbuster turned down an offer to purchase newcomer Netflix for $50M in 2000. Undaunted, Netflix transformed the video entertainment industry several times over: The first transformation digitalized the movie-selection process, enabling users to browse for movies online, rather than at a store (and the movies selected would be mailed to them on DVDs). The second, and more impactful transformation, was Netflix's digitalizing the delivery process as

2 Deepa Seetharaman, "Facebook Revenue Soars on Ad Growth," *Wall Street Journal*, April 28, 2016, http://www.wsj.com/articles/facebook-revenue-soars-on-ad-growth-1461787856.

well, enabling movies to be streamed to customers directly, anytime, anywhere, and on virtually any device. Yet another transformation saw Netflix become an original content producer, as well as distributor. The result of these digital transformations has made Netflix the world's leading Internet television network with over 125 million members in over 190 countries, earning over $11B in annual revenue. In 2018, Netflix, which was esteemed by Blockbuster as not being worth $50M, reached a market capitalization in excess of $144B.

Digital Finance

To facilitate the exploding demand of online purchases and transactions, PayPal digitalized the payment process. Sending checks and money orders through the mail seems like an artifact of the distant past now, in contrast to the flexibility, convenience, and speed of funds transferred via PayPal. Such customer benefits translate to significant bottom-line results for PayPal, who in 2017 processed over 5 billion transactions for 237 million users and earned $13B in revenue.

Digital Communications

With the advent of Voice over Internet Protocol (VoIP) technologies in the early 2000s, incumbent telecommunications providers were put under pressure to compete—which for many proved to be a new experience, having had the luxury of being geographic monopolies for decades. In the process they lost hundreds of billions of dollars. And the hemorrhaging continues. For example, a recent study estimates that the telecommunications industry will lose a further $386B between 2012 and 2018 to over-the-top (OTT) VoIP applications.[3]

In fact, a single application, WhatsApp, is threatening the short message service (SMS) market as a whole, as shown in Figure 1-2. WhatsApp provides users more flexibility and cost savings as compared to SMS, allowing users to send not only text messages, but also photos, videos, documents, and other media. And when users are connected to Wi-Fi networks, they can send and receive their messages and media for free, avoiding SMS data charges. The value of WhatsApp is recognized by many, including Facebook, which acquired it in 2014 for $19.3B. In 2016, WhatsApp surpassed 1 billion users.

Additionally, as the mobile messaging industry is becoming increasingly commoditized, regulatory changes (such as prohibiting roaming charges in certain markets) are putting even more pressure on classical business models utilized by telecom incumbents, further exacerbating their disadvantage to digital transformers, like WhatsApp.

3 Erik Heinrich, "Telecom Companies Count $386 Billion in Lost Revenue to Skype, WhatsApp, Others," *Fortune*, June 23, 2014, http://fortune.com/2014/06/23/telecom-companies-count-386-billion-in-lost-revenue-to-skype-whatsapp-others/.

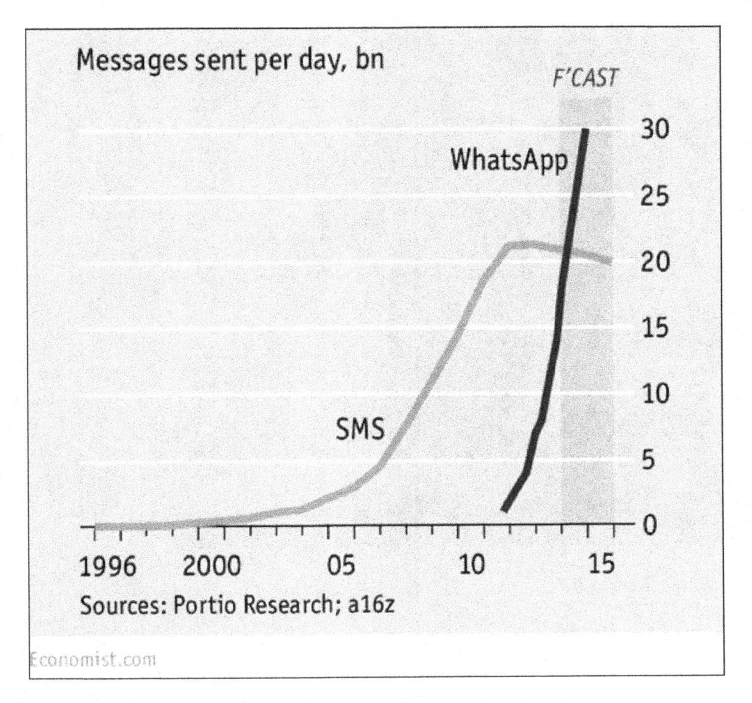

Figure 1-2 *WhatsApp Versus the SMS Industry*[4]

Digital Transportation Services

In San Francisco, New York, Chicago, and over 600 additional cities worldwide, hailing a cab is becoming a quaint memory, thanks to Uber, launched in 2011. In just a few short years, Uber completely transformed the taxi industry by leveraging digital technology. The Uber app, shown in Figure 1-3, allows customers with smartphones to submit a trip request, which is automatically sent to the nearest Uber driver, alerting the driver to the location of the customer, and vice versa. Customers know exactly how long they have to wait and can watch on a map as their driver is approaching their location. Drivers know exactly where their customers are and where they wish to go, and can receive Global Positioning System (GPS) directions to their destination. Transactions are cashless and paperless, with receipts being emailed to the customers (facilitating easier expense reporting for business travelers). Additionally, the Uber app also serves to prevent language barriers, as can often be the case when communicating with taxi drivers in foreign cities. Uber also benefits drivers, who for the most part are freelance and use their personal vehicles, saving them significant franchising fees and operating overhead commonly incurred by taxi operators. In 2017, Uber—still a private company—was valuated at nearly $70B.

4 Satoshi Kambayashi, "The Message Is the Medium," *The Economist*, March 26, 2015, https://www.economist.com/business/2015/03/26/the-message-is-the-medium.

Figure 1-3 *Uber Ride-Sharing Service*

Zipcar has had a similar impact on the traditional rental-car industry. Founded in 2000 in Boston, the car-sharing service operates 10,000 vehicles in over 500 cities in 9 countries serving over a million users. As such, Zipcar is one of the world's leading car rental networks in its own right. Members can reserve cars with Zipcar's mobile app, online, or by phone at any time—immediately or up to a year in advance. Members have automated access to Zipcars using an access card which works with the car's technology to unlock the door, where the keys are already located inside. The Zipcar mobile app also enables members to remotely honk the horn to locate their reserved Zipcar and unlock the doors (see Figure 1-4). As such, many urban residents find Zipcar to be a convenient and cost-effective alternative to buying, maintaining, and parking their own cars.

Note Avis acquired Zipcar in 2013 for $500M, providing a counter-example to Blockbuster, mentioned earlier. Specifically, Avis demonstrated foresight in adapting to digital transformation via a strategic acquisition.

Similarly, thanks to advances in digital technologies, bicycle-sharing services have exploded globally since the mid-2000s. As of June 2014, public bicycle-sharing systems were available in 712 cities, spanning 50 countries on five continents, operating approximately 806,200 bicycles at 37,500 stations. While implementations differ, bicycle-sharing companies often include wireless bike station terminals running on solar energy, radio-frequency identification (RFID) bike dock technology, and smartphone apps that locate and show the status of bike stations close to the users (see Figure 1-5). Bicycle-sharing systems aptly demonstrate the significant positive impact that digital technology can have on the environment as well as on the overall health of urban populations, by facilitating a greener and healthier transportation alternative.

Figure 1-4 *Zipcar Car-Sharing Service*

Figure 1-5 *Public Bike Sharing*

Digitally Transforming Businesses

While not every digitally transformed organization ends up reshaping its entire industry, such companies are—on average—26 percent more profitable than their industry peers, as has already been noted. This fact alone has encouraged many organizations to examine areas where they can digitally transform. Some of these key areas include

- Customer experience
- Employee experience
- Business operations

The following sections provide an overview of each of these areas, along with examples of industry leaders in each area.

Transforming the Customer Experience

Customer experience matters more than ever. And bad customer experiences can be fatal to a business.

For example, in 2011 Harris Interactive published a Customer Experience Impact Report that found that:

- 86 percent of customers will pay more for a better customer experience.
- 89 percent of consumers began doing business with a competitor following a poor customer experience (up from 68 percent in 2009).
- 79 percent of consumers who shared complaints about poor customer experience online had their complaints ignored.
- 50 percent of consumers give a brand only one week to respond to a question before they stop doing business with them.

Additionally, Forrester Research showed that a quarter of American consumers who had unsatisfactory service interactions in 2010 shared their experiences though social networks, which represented a 50 percent increase from the year before.[5]

Furthermore, an increasing number of customers are making purchasing decisions based on what their peers have to say, paying close attention to ratings, reviews, and testimonials on social-media and third-party sites and apps. As such, businesses have incentive like never before to leverage digital technology to provide superior customer service, as some of the following companies have demonstrated.

Burberry

In 2006 Burberry was lagging far behind its competitors. The high-fashion industry was growing at 12 to 13 percent per year, but Burberry was managing only 1 to 2 percent growth. Burberry's new CEO at the time, Angela Ahrendts, decided to rebrand the company and focus on a new market: millennials. As such, Burberry undertook an aggressive digital strategy to reach this new customer base. It revamped its website and included an "Art of the Trench" social-media element where anyone could post pictures of themselves in their classic Burberry coat. Burberry partnered with Twitter to broadcast live fashion shows, and likewise partnered with Google to develop advanced "lip detection technology" so that customers could send digital kisses to loved ones anywhere in the world.

---

5 www.forrester.com/North+American+Technologies+Customer+Experience+Online+Survey+Q4+2010+US/-/E-SUS805

Burberry also complemented its online digital presence with extensive digital technologies in its retail stores, such as giant external and internal video displays in all its stores and by arming all its sales associates with iPads. Burberry's fusion of digital and retail fashion is illustrated in Figure 1-6. Burberry even creatively combined RFID technology with its video displays, such that, for example, when a customer took a garment into a changing room to try it on, the RFID sensor recognized which garment(s) the customer was trying on and automatically signaled the video display in the changing room to begin playing a video of a fashion model wearing the same garment. This particular combination of digital technologies led to a significant increase in conversion rates to purchases. The net result of all these new digital customer experiences was the tripling of Burberry sales, as well as its share price, during Ahrendts' tenure.[6]

Figure 1-6 *Burberry—Fusing Digital and Physical Retail*

Starbucks

Starbucks has been well described as "a digital innovation machine."[7] It was one of the first coffee chains to recognize the value of offering its customers free Wi-Fi, along with content (delivered by partnering with the New York Times, The Economist, Spotify, and others), which dramatically increased the length of time its customers linger and relax at its stores, as well as the corresponding number of beverages they order. Starbucks

---

6 Yousef Khan, "How Burberry Embraced Digital and Transformed into a Leading Luxury Brand," Centric Digital, November 9, 2015, https://centricdigital.com/blog/digital-strategy/digital-transformation-in-traditional-fashion-burberry/.

7 Larry Dignan, "Starbucks' Digital Transformation: The Takeaways Every Enterprise Needs to Know," ZDNET, November 1, 2015, http://www.zdnet.com/article/starbucks-digital-transformation-the-takeaways-every-enterprise-needs-to-know/.

launched its MyStarbucks app in 2009, as shown in Figure 1-7. This morphed into a multi-purpose vehicle which includes the following:

- Personalized advertising and promotions.
- A digital replacement for a Starbucks card (and later fully integrated with both Apple Passbook and Apple Pay).
- A Starbucks Store locator.
- A reward-management system. The MyStarbucks Rewards program boasts over 20 million members and accounts for over 20 percent of transactions.
- A Mobile Order and Pay service that allows busy customers to "skip the line" by placing their order and paying for it while on their way to a Starbucks and then having their beverage and food ready and waiting for them to pick up and go. The Mobile Order and Pay customer experience resulted in a 17 percent increase in revenues in the first year after its release.

Figure 1-7 *Starbucks—Mobile Order and Pay*

UPS

United Parcel Service (UPS) is the world's largest package delivery company, delivering more than 19 million packages per day to over 8 million customers in more than 220 countries and territories around the world. However, customers were often frustrated to receive notices or emails to the effect that their packages would be delivered on a certain day between 8 a.m. and 6 p.m., as remaining at home for such a long window considerably inconvenienced most people.

In response to customer complaints, UPS began tracking each vehicle via GPS, not only to improve route optimizations (resulting in over 8 million gallons of fuel savings per year), but also to more accurately predict delivery windows, dramatically cutting these down to one- to two-hour slots. UPS also began enabling customers to monitor these reduced delivery windows via its mobile app. Customers now can elect to receive alerts when their delivery is imminent and can even provide the driver instructions directly from the app. These improvements in customers service via digital technologies have resulted in a dramatic increase in customer satisfaction and loyalty for UPS.

Transforming the Employee Experience

It's not only improved customer experiences that have a bottom-line impact on a business, but also improving the experience of their employees. Some of the challenges facing today's workforce include the following:

- **Information overload:** Information is still growing at exponential rates and employees can't find what they need, even with technology advances.
- **The need for speed:** With the rapid pace of today's work environment, employees increasingly need to work faster and collaborate more effectively to get their jobs done.
- **An aging workforce:** As baby boomers continue to retire, they are taking key knowledge with them, increasing the need to digitally capture their knowledge.

However, meeting these challenges with digital technologies can significantly improve the employee experience, as reported in a study by Deloitte[8] that showed increases in the following areas:

- **Employee productivity:** Organizations with strong online social networks are 7 percent more productive than those without.
- **Employee Satisfaction:** Organizations that installed social media tools internally found a median 20 percent increase in employee satisfaction.

8 Deloitte, "The Digital Workplace: Think, Share, Do," https://www2.deloitte.com/content/dam/Deloitte/mx/Documents/human-capital/The_digital_workplace.pdf.

- **Talent Attraction:** 64 percent of employees would opt for a lower-paying job if they could work away from the office.
- **Employee Retention:** When employee engagement increases, there is a corresponding increase in employee retention by up to 87 percent.

Some specific examples of companies that have harnessed digital technologies to improve employee experiences are overviewed next.

Air France

Prior to 2006, each Air France pilot, aircraft, and flight route required a unique set of on-board documentation that collectively added *60 pounds of paper* to each flight. Furthermore, critical decisions relating to safety and operations were delayed in the paper-based communications process, including the delays required to type and photocopy all the relevant information, as well as the delays in mailing these instructions and updates to each of the over 4000 pilots and 15,000 flight attendants within the organization. The collective daily operational information filled entire dedicated rooms at multiple airports that Air France serviced. To cope, Air France made the key decision to digitize all such communications. By 2013, all of the necessary information was delivered to pilots via an iPad app, dubbed Pilot Pad, as shown in Figure 1-8. Now, not only do pilots have far less to carry (as do the aircrafts, resulting in considerable fuel savings), but also whenever Air France updates a document in its library, 60 percent of affected pilots review the updates within 24 hours, thus increasing the safety and efficiency of the airline's operations.

Figure 1-8 *Air France Pilot Pad*

Additionally, pilots benefit by being able to take training via e-learning modules on their iPads, rather than trying to coordinate in-classroom training sessions, which traditionally has been very challenging, considering their extraordinary travel schedules. Also, the app allows pilots to complete non-flying duties whenever and wherever they want, making productive use of their time spent waiting in airports. The overall effect for Air France is the evolution of its flight operations into an efficient and user-friendly process, which has proved so popular with the pilots that Air France has subsequently rolled out a similar iPad-based solution for its in-flight cabin crews.

Other airlines have followed suit, such as Alaska Airlines, which estimates that its iPad-based system saves the company over 2.4 million pieces of paper overall and 25 pounds of paper per flight (which is critical in some of the remote locations serviced by the airline).

RehabCare

The 18,000 employees of RehabCare provide rehab and post-acute care services, in over 1200 hospitals and facilities across 43 states. In such an environment every minute counts and employees need to track and record every detail, including the diagnosis, treatment, and when the appointment began and ended. To meet these challenges, RehabCare equipped its staff with easy-to-use, process-driven applications on iPhone and iPad mobile devices to provide point-of-care information capture quickly and easily. Additionally, their cloud-based applications allow access to detailed patient information anytime, anywhere. RehabCare estimates it is saving millions per year, while enabling its employees to quickly capture and/or consult critical data in an intuitive manner. Benefits also extend to the patients, as the app significantly reduces patient pre-admission screening times.

Cisco

Cisco itself has been recognized for leading digital innovation in the workplace of its 70,000 employees worldwide. As a large and global organization, Cisco noticed the trends in collaboration and the need for an integrated workforce experience, and as such implemented various solutions to this effect. For example, it launched a Cisco video communication and collaboration platform to communicate more effectively, as well as enterprise social software to facilitate healthy collaboration with personalization and relevance. These programs include a connected workspace, wiki, and video blogs, expertise locator, and sales productivity, remote collaboration, and telecommuting applications.

As shown in Figure 1-9, these platforms connect to each other for an integrated and user-friendly experience. With the implementation of seven distinct collaboration programs, Cisco recorded a total of $1.052B in net benefits from collaboration solutions.

Figure 1-9 *Cisco Collaboration Tools*

Transforming Business Operations

While digital technologies can increase revenue by delivering new customer experiences and/or increasing employee productivity increases, profitability can also be increased by leveraging digitalization to streamline and economize business operations, as the following examples demonstrate.

Boeing

There are more than 6 million parts that make up a Boeing 747 aircraft, which all have to come together at precisely the right times in order to complete production. Furthermore, since these aircraft are assembled in the largest building in the world, namely Boeing's Everett Factory as shown in Figure 1-10, there's a lot of ground to cover when something goes missing. The bottom-line impact to Boeing of a misplaced or lost part, toolkit, machinery, or work-in-progress (WIP) inventory is greater than *$1 million per incident.* To reduce such losses, Boeing implemented RFID tracking along with Cisco wireless infrastructure location capabilities to instantly identify where any key part, tool, or WIP inventory is at any given time. This digital parts-tracking system reduced production delays, inventory expenses, and even government fines.

Figure 1-10 *RFID-Enabled Boeing 747 Assembly Line in Everett, Washington*

Codelco

Codelco, a Chilean state-owned mining company, is the world's largest producer of copper. Mining not only is dark, dirty, and labor-intensive process, but is also very dangerous, as was amply demonstrated by the events that captured the world's attention that unfolded in a (different company's) Chilean mine in 2010, where 33 workers were trapped underground for 68 days.

To make mining operations safer, Codelco equipped its immense mining trucks, shown in Figure 1-11, with digital technologies that allow them to drive autonomously, arriving at their destinations just-in-time and with fewer accidents than those with human drivers. Codelco then expanded the application of similar technologies to other mining equipment, making these autonomous as well. Now, many of Codelco's workers don't head down to the mine to work, but rather to the control center in the city. Mining via autonomous equipment not only improves safety, but also brings additional economic benefits to Codelco. For example, removing humans from underground mines allows Codelco to design them to different specifications, allowing Codelco to dig with less cost and with lower risk, thus opening up the possibility of exploiting ore caches that may not have been economically feasible otherwise.

Figure 1-11 *Codelco Autonomous Mining Trucks*

BC Hydro

BC Hydro is a Canadian electric utility in the province of British Columbia, and is the main electric distributor serving nearly 2 million customers. BC Hydro has installed 1.93 million smart meters since 2011 and more than 99 percent of customers now have a new meter.

Since the installation of these smart meters, BC Hydro has realized over $100 million in benefits, primarily from operational savings. Customers also benefit, as these meters have made their bills more accurate, due to reduced manual meter reads and bill estimates. Customers can also now view their hourly and daily energy use through their online account, providing them new tools to save energy and money. Furthermore, such new metering technology has laid the foundation for more widespread use of small-scale, green, distributed electricity generation including solar and wind power.

Driving Digital Transformation with the Internet of Things

With the advent of the Internet of Things (IoT), digital transformation is taking place in virtually every area of our lives. With billions of smart devices coming online every year, massive revolutions are taking place in the following fields:

- **Environmental monitoring:** IoT sensors are being used to monitor air and water quality, atmospheric and soil conditions, the movements of wildlife and their habitats, and even early warning-systems for earthquakes and tsunamis.
- **Infrastructure management:** IoT devices are being used to monitor infrastructure resources like bridges, railway tracks, wind farms, and even waste management systems. These devices can be used to monitor activity, measure structural conditions, schedule repairs and maintenance, and coordinate emergency response.

- **Manufacturing:** IoT intelligent systems are enabling the rapid manufacturing of new products, dynamic response to product demands, and real-time optimization of manufacturing production and supply chain networks. These systems can also optimize plant operations, energy operations, and health and safety.
- **Energy management:** IoT devices are being integrated into all forms of energy-consuming devices (switches, power outlets, bulbs, televisions, etc.) and are able to communicate with the utility supply company in order to effectively balance power generation and energy usage. Such devices also offer the opportunity for consumers to remotely control their devices, or centrally manage them via a cloud-based interface, and enable advanced functions like scheduling (e.g., remotely powering on or off heating systems, controlling ovens, changing lighting conditions, etc.).
- **Medical and healthcare:** IoT devices are being used to enable remote health-monitoring and emergency-notification systems. These health-monitoring devices range from blood pressure and heart rate monitors to advanced devices capable of monitoring specialized implants, such as pacemakers or advanced hearing aids. Additionally, consumer-oriented smart devices encouraging healthy living are proving very popular, such as connected scales, wearable heart monitors, step counters, etc.
- **Building and home automation:** IoT devices are being leveraged to monitor and control the mechanical, electrical, and electronic systems used in various types of buildings.
- **Transportation:** Smart devices are enabling inter- and intra-vehicular communication, smart traffic control, smart parking, electronic toll collection systems, logistics and fleet management, vehicle control, and safety and road assistance.
- **Smart cities:** There are several planned or ongoing large-scale deployments of "smart cities"—that is, cities that have nearly every element monitored and controlled by network-enabled smart devices. For example, Songdo, South Korea, the first of its kind, is a fully equipped and wired smart city, and is nearing completion. Nearly everything in this city is connected and is streaming data for machine-driven analysis, all with little or no human intervention. Also, Barcelona is a Cisco flagship smart city which integrates digital technologies to urban services (like smart parking, smart lighting, location-based analytics, etc.) and solutions (such as energy management, safety and security, and cloud exchange).

Are You Ready?

New market opportunities and business models, fast-moving disruptive threats, and an exploding IoT landscape are all driving digital transformation. As such, the relevant questions are no longer "What is digital transformation?" and "Why should you care?" but rather "Are you ready?"

The network not only is at the center of all the users, applications, and devices that are driving digital transformation, but is also the platform that can most effectively enable it. This is why Cisco has developed its new Cisco Digital Network Architecture to meet these dynamic, complex, and rapidly evolving business needs, as discussed in subsequent chapters.

Summary

This chapter discussed the "why?" behind Cisco Digital Network Architecture, which has as its goal the driving of digital transformation. The benefits of digital transformation were examined (including 9 percent greater revenues versus industry peers and 26 percent greater profits, according to Harvard Business Review), as were the threats facing businesses that are slow to transform digitally (approximately 40 percent of the top ten incumbents in each industry being faced with digital disruption within five years).

Various businesses that have transformed entire industries digitally were reviewed, including Apple, PayPal, WhatsApp, Uber, and others. Also businesses that excelled in transforming customer experience were discussed, including Burberry, Starbucks, and UPS. So too were businesses that transformed their employee experiences, including Air France, RehabCare, and even Cisco itself. Additionally, companies that digitally overhauled their operations were presented, including Boeing, Codelco, and BC Hydro.

Finally, the massive revolutionary impact of the Internet of Things was also overviewed, to illustrate that digital transformation extends far beyond the workplace and indeed is affecting virtually every area of our lives.

Thus, having discussed the business reasons supporting digital transformation, let's focus specifically on the business value of a Cisco Digital Network Architecture as the platform to enabling such transformation.

Further Reading

Bradley, J., J. Loucks, J. Macaulay, A. Noronha, and M. Wade. "Digital Vortex: How Digital Disruption Is Redefining Industries." Global Center for Digital Business Transformation. June 2015. https://www.cisco.com/c/dam/en/us/solutions/collateral/industry-solutions/digital-vortex-report.pdf.

Oracle Corporation. "2011 Customer Experience Impact Report: Getting to the Heart of the Consumer and Brand Relationship." 2012. http://www.oracle.com/us/products/applications/cust-exp-impact-report-epss-1560493.pdf.

Parker, G., M. Van Alstyne, and S. Choudary. *Platform Revolution: How Networked Markets Are Transforming the Economy and How to Make Them Work for You.* New York: W. W. Norton & Company; 2016.

Rogers, D. *The Digital Transformation Playbook: Rethink Your Business for the Digital Age.* New York: Columbia University Press; 2016.

Westerman, G., D. Bonnet, and A. McAffee. *Leading Digital: Turning Technology into Business Transformation.* Boston: Harvard Business Review Press; 2014.

Chapter 2

The Business Value of Cisco DNA

The network empowers digital transformation. After all, it is the network that tightly and pervasively connects users with business applications, enabling new experiences or streamlining operations, all while being actively protected from a constantly changing threat landscape. However, due to rapidly evolving business needs and trends, a traditional approach to networking cannot provide such benefits, and thus a new approach is needed. This new approach is referred to in the industry as *intent-based networking (IBN)*. Cisco Digital Network Architecture is an expression of intent-based networking for the enterprise route/switch/wireless network.

This chapter discusses the business value of Cisco DNA, including

- The business requirements of the network
- Intent-based networking
- Business-value propositions of Cisco DNA

Business Requirements of the Network Architecture

As discussed in Chapter 1, "Why Transform Your Business Digitally?," organizations across the world are engaged in digital transformations in order to gain or maintain competitive advantage. Since the network serves as a central interconnect between all elements of digital transformation, including users, applications, devices, and the Internet of Things (IoT), it offers the greatest platform toward digital transformation initiatives.

However, traditionally, the network also has been one of the biggest barriers to business evolution, being monolithic and disconnected from evolving business, user, and application requirements. Thus, to serve as an effective platform for digital transformation, the network must be secure, agile, flexible, intelligent, and simple to operate. These combined and evolving requirements necessitate a new intent-based, architectural approach to networking, one that offers considerable business value to the enterprise—this approach is discussed in this chapter.

The business requirements of a network as a platform to drive digital transformation are many, but can be organized into a few key areas, primarily including

- Cost reduction
- Risk mitigation
- Actionable insights
- Business agility

Each of these business requirements will be discussed in additional detail in the following sections.

Cost Reduction

According to a 2016 study by McKinsey, companies spend over $60B in network operations and labor. This is hardly surprising when considering that most enterprises have thousands of users, thousands of applications, and often tens of thousands of network-enabled devices. Furthermore, IP traffic is projected to more than double from 2016 to 2020 (per the Cisco Visual Networking Index forecasts); additionally, 20 billion more IoT devices are expected to come online within the same timeframe (per industry consensus). Managing all of these manually is becoming increasingly untenable for IT departments, a challenge that is exacerbated by the myriad of inconsistent and incompatible hardware and software systems and devices in the enterprise. Companies that can get a handle on these skyrocketing operational costs stand to gain considerable profitability and advantage.

More than operational costs can be reduced. For example, capital expenditures can also be economized by network infrastructures that are elastic, flexible, and agile. Such gains are realized when scalability is flexible and easily achieved, with seamless ability to make moves, adds, and changes as specific network demands shift. The network needs to operate at a capacity that comfortably supports its application environment, but also be agile enough to elastically align to changing needs, without needing expensive hardware installations to keep up with shifting demand. Networking hardware likewise needs to be flexible and adaptable, keeping up with the evolution of networking protocols, services, and policies as they continue to be defined, developed, and deployed.

Risk Mitigation

Emerging digital demands raise new security challenges that are best addressed through the network. Malicious actors that breach enterprise networks not only gain access to sensitive organizational and customer data but can also take down mission-critical systems and applications. In the past, security tools were often deployed and managed disparately from the underlying network infrastructure. For some organizations, this disparate management has led to gaps and misalignment between networking technologies and security coverage.

In addition, legacy network security solutions treated the enterprise network as an insular entity—assuming that as long as the network was sealed off from the outside, it was protected. This made sense in previous eras. However, with the proliferation of public cloud–hosted applications, Bring Your Own Device (BYOD), and mobile workers, threat vectors find pathways to the network from both the inside and the outside; it is therefore imperative for network security to take a 360-degree approach.

Given these factors, network security solutions need to be tightly intertwined with the network infrastructure in order to protect against today's internal and external threat vectors. Organizations that fail to do so sometimes make news headlines, as was the case with Target Corporation in 2013 when a data breach affected the personal data of over 70 million customers; similarly in 2017, Equifax suffered a breach that affected the personal data of 143 million customers. Such breaches can cause the loss of customers, and corresponding revenues, for years after the fact.

Additionally, an increasing number of organizations must conform with regulatory compliance demands, with harsh fines and penalties imposed when these are not met (as well as extensive productivity impacts incurred during any required remediation processes). Such organizations benefit greatly by having an automated and systematic approach to enforcing compliance through their architecture.

Actionable Insights

Typical enterprises are overloaded with data; however, in contrast, actionable insights are relatively rare. In this context, actionable insights refer to data-driven findings that can create real business value. Such insights are key catalysts to achieving digital business transformation.

For example, improving customer experience was discussed in the previous chapter. To provide effective new experiences for customers, it is vital to know the following:

- Who is buying your product or service?
- Where are they buying it?
- When are they buying it?
- Why are they buying it?
- What do they like about it?
- What don't they like about it?
- Is your product or service meeting their needs?
- Are there customer needs that your product or service doesn't meet?

Similarly, delivering beneficial new employee experiences depends on knowing the following:

- Are your employees able to achieve their work goals?
- What applications are your employees using to meet their goals?

- Where are they using these applications?
- Are these applications meeting their needs?
- Are there any needs that are not being met?
- What do they like about these applications?
- What don't they like about these applications?
- How well are these applications performing?
- How much does it cost to run these applications?

Such questions can also be posed for operational procedures, security threat analysis, compliance requirements, etc.

The point is that when companies have data points to answer these questions, rather than relying on opinions, anecdotes, or any other imperfect and/or biased form of information, they are much better poised to make the *right* decisions to meet their specific transformational objectives.

Furthermore, it is often the *correlation* of different data points that reveals key insights. For example, in recent years, market analysis done by cinema companies identified an underserved niche market: *parents* of young children, looking for a *relaxing* night out, but also desiring a *shared experience*. This insight has led to several cinema operators now offering child-free showings, alcohol, and theatres equipped with loveseats (i.e., paired seating). Such theatres are enjoying considerably higher revenues and profits than their less-tailored peers.

As another example, a few years ago Cisco IT began noticing significant amounts of traffic from an unknown application that was sourced from *within their campus* (i.e., not from within their data centers, where most internal applications are hosted). Further investigation revealed that the application in question was an internal *video-sharing* service (similar to YouTube), hosted *by employees*, and exclusively *for employees*. The information being shared helped to accelerate research and development, yet could not be posted to YouTube, as the material in question was proprietary and confidential. These insights led to the development of a Cisco IT–sponsored and maintained video-sharing service for employees, resulting in improved and secure information exchange.

Business Agility

Insights alone are not enough to capture new opportunities or to respond to threats—these must be coupled with the ability to take action. For example, application analytics may reveal a new security threat, but this insight needs to be acted on in order to serve any business value, such as quarantining infected hosts, dynamically adjusting firewall policies, rerouting flows for additional inspection, etc.

Business agility can span several layers. At the infrastructure layer it can include self-defending and self-healing networks. At the application layer it can include applications that can interact with the network in new ways, such as by dynamically requesting devices, services, and policies to be deployed on demand. At the operator layer, it can further include the reallocation of IT resources away from mundane operational tasks and toward the development of innovative and transformational projects. At the business and organizational layer, it can likewise include the morphing of entire business models and operations to deliver new products and services so as to capture new market opportunities.

At any dimension, however, delivering business agility requires an architecture that is flexible, extensible, and interoperable.

Intent-Based Networking

In 2017 a new buzz acronym was added to an already overcrowded IT lexicon that previously included SDN (software-defined networking), XaaS (Anything as a Service), AI/ML (artificial intelligence/machine learning), and 5G (5th-generation wireless systems); specifically IBN (intent-based networking).

While definitions of IBN vary (even as do definitions of SDN and other similar industry terms), some common elements are well agreed-on, including:

- Translation
- Validation
- Automation
- Analytics
- Assurance
- Remediation
- Learning

Let's briefly examine how these elements work together to form an intent-based networking system.

As the name implies, an intent-based network system begins with the expression of business *intent* by an operator. Examples of such expressions include

- "This group of users can access these services."
- "This application matters to my business."
- "Infected client devices should be quarantined."

> **Note** These expressions of intent are declarative, meaning that the objective is expressed (i.e., *what* you want to happen), but the underlying details of execution are not (i.e., *how* is it to happen). To illustrate, you might express your intent to a taxi driver by declaring, "Take me to the airport," but you may leave the specific details of the route up to him.

While operators speak the language of business, network devices do not. As such, expressions of business intent need to be *translated* into *validated* network device configurations.

Additionally, as business intent needs to be expressed across the network, the configurations of dozens, hundreds, or even thousands of network devices may need to be updated in order to deliver on the newly expressed intent. Therefore, to scale, expedite, and minimize errors, these configuration deployments need to be *automated*. Automation thus allows a network operator to treat thousands of network devices as a single software-enabled, programmable entity.

However, it is not enough to simply configure network devices and hope for the best, but rather, network telemetry must be ingested so as to determine the current state of the network. This network state must be *analyzed* in context of the expressed intent. Thus the system provides *assurance* via quantitative metrics that the intent was delivered OR triggers a *remediation* action in the event that it was not. Remediation may be guided, but ultimately it is the goal of IBN that this is completely automated—to achieve the vision of a "self-healing network."

Furthermore, the IBN system should be continually self-learning, so that it recognizes

- What is normal versus abnormal
- What are the most common root causes of issues
- What are the most effective remedial actions for a given issue

In this manner, the IBN system becomes not only smarter, but also more reliable, available, and adaptable to ever-evolving business requirements.

Cisco DNA is an IBN system for enterprise route/switch/wireless networks. Before examining the technical details of this architecture, let's first consider some of the business value propositions that it offers.

Business Value of Cisco Digital Network Architecture

To meet the business requirements of digital transformation, Cisco has reimagined the network architecture from the ground up, by:

- Custom-engineering programmable and flexible hardware application-specific integrated circuits (ASICs) that deliver the networking protocols, services, and policies—not only of today but also of tomorrow—at multigigabit speeds
- Rebuilding its operating systems with rich, model-driven, programmable application programming interfaces (APIs)
- Embedding network-wide security—across routing, switching, wireless, and the cloud—to help IT continuously detect and contain threats
- Automating network operations to enable IT to provision, orchestrate, adapt, and manage with simplicity at scale

- Providing network-wide deep visibility into user, application, and device information exposed through open APIs, which is centrally analyzed and correlated to reveal actionable insights
- Integrating with cloud services to provide IT on-demand scalability, flexibility, and faster time-to-value of anything as a service (XaaS), for public cloud, hybrid cloud (that is, public and private cloud), and multi-cloud environments

Before delving into the technology specifics, let's take a closer look at specific business benefits of Cisco DNA.

Reducing Costs Through Automation, Virtualization, and Programmable Hardware

The automation of provisioning and configuration tasks—previously done manually—saves tremendous amounts of time and money.

Consider the following examples:

- Day-zero automation has been shown to lower network deployment costs by as much as 79 percent.
- Automating the deployment of quality of service (QoS) across the enterprise has been shown to save customers between $200,000 and $1M, as well as three to six months' worth of time, *per deployment*.
- Customers have reported multimillion-dollar savings of WAN operational costs by deploying Cisco SD-WAN solutions, and the deployment of such solutions is 85 percent faster when automated.
- Studies have shown over 200 percent reduction in configuration times and over 50 percent reduction in troubleshooting times (due to fewer configuration mistakes) in IT departments that are automated versus manual (wherein the latter case, 70 percent of network violations and 35 percent of network downtime were attributable to human error).

Network virtualization also yields significant cost savings, which include the following:

- Virtualized platforms make more efficient utilization of hardware resources; for example, a single hardware device can function as a router, a firewall, a wireless LAN controller, and a container for third-party applications.
- Virtualized systems require less space, less power, and less maintenance than their physical counterparts.
- Virtualized systems can be deployed without a truck roll and can be updated, managed, and maintained centrally, reducing the need to dispatch technicians to remote locations for such operations.

Considerable capital-expenditure savings can also be realized by investing in hardware platforms built on flexible and programmable ASICs, as these have nearly double the average lifespan of their fixed ASIC counterparts.

Mitigating Risks with Integrated Security and Compliance

Next-generation network security is built upon the concept of "foundational security," meaning that security tools and functionalities are tightly integrated with every piece of the network infrastructure, evolving in lockstep with the network and arming the network to protect itself holistically in a digital era where the threat landscape is more dynamic.

Analytics capabilities allow security tools to establish baselines for a normal security environment and provide automated alerting and, in some cases, remediation when the network security environment shows an anomaly. This use of the network as a security sensor can reduce mean time to repair (MTTR), preventing disruption to the business.

Furthermore, pervasive and embedded security within Cisco DNA detects and deters over 99 percent of network breaches—by using the network as both a sensor and an enforcer.

Revealing Actionable Insights Through Analytics

As previously noted, manual provisioning and configuration tasks can be automated to save network administration tremendous amounts of time. These time savings are further enhanced by data-driven remediation.

Building on this, evolving capabilities in network analytics and machine learning enable increasingly automated remediation, setting the stage for greater levels of self-healing. Network analytics go beyond fixing problems with network performance—they also show great potential in detecting security anomalies and identifying customer behavior patterns that can drive customer experience initiatives.

For example, Intercontinental Hotel Group (IHG), which is the largest hotelier in the world, with 5200 properties in 100 countries, partnered with Cisco to build a new enterprise architecture to implement guest entertainment, engagement, and personalized marketing, based on the insights from precise metrics gathering. With this granular data integrated into loyalty programs and customer relationship management (CRM) systems, IHG is able to continuously personalize the guest experience—even anticipating guest needs—and thus continue to build satisfaction. This has resulted in double-digit growth in guest satisfaction for IHG, which is correspondingly being reflected in its revenue.

Accelerating Business Agility Through Open APIs

As previously noted, there are many dimensions of business agility, yet Cisco DNA can serve to innovate faster and drive transformation at any of these levels, including the following:

- **Infrastructure level:** Cisco DNA detects and contains threats up to 1000 times faster than the industry average by enabling threat-detection systems to deploy remediation and/or quarantining policies to the infrastructure in real time.

- **Application level:** Cisco DNA delivers applications up to 17 percent faster and drives better user experiences with analytics feedback. Additionally, Cisco DNA supports application policy integration with the infrastructure, such that applications can request services from the network in real time.
- **Operator level:** Cisco DNA increases IT time allocations to innovative projects by up to 600 percent, by saving time from network operations and troubleshooting; additionally, recent studies estimate networking staff teams to be 28 percent more efficient with Cisco DNA
- **Operations level:** Cisco DNA integrates with non-network systems via open APIs, including as lighting, heating ventilation and air-conditioning (HVAC), power, and other IoT systems, resulting in increased efficiency, improved experiences, and new possibilities. For example, the University of British Columbia leveraged mobile-user location analytics information from its 58,000 students, so as to determine which rooms students were in (and likewise which rooms were empty), and integrated these analytics with the university's HVAC systems so that the right rooms could be heated/cooled at the right time (rather than just every room all the time), resulting in 33 percent lower gas emissions and 5 percent energy savings ($200–400K per year).
- **Business and organizational level:** Cisco DNA enables business-level transformation, such that businesses can identify and capitalize on new opportunities, markets, and business models. For example, Quantium, an Australian data analytics firm, had the epiphany that location analytics data from mobile devices could be used not only to provide customer insights, but also to provide organizational behavior insights. For instance, volunteers (and it really needs to be stressed that all participants in this organizational behavior exercise were volunteers) offered to be tracked throughout their workday, so as to provide their leaders with organizational insights such as
  - Where are employees working?
  - How long are they in meetings?
  - How much time do employees get to spend with their managers?
  - Do employees work in teams or in silos?
  - Which teams work well together? Which don't?

Such insights were so valuable to Quantium internally that its quickly productized its methodology, becoming the first mover in a whole new market space.

Adding It All Up

In 2017, Cisco worked with International Data Corporation (IDC) to develop a five-state Digital Network Readiness Model, as shown in Figure 2-1.

Network Area	Stage: 1 Best Effort	2 Manual	3 Semi-Automated	4 Automated	5 Self-Driving
Architecture	Hardware and Device Centric				Open, Extensible, Software Delivered, and Cloud Enabled
Automation	Fragmented, Manual Management				Policy Driven, Automated, Self-Optimizing
Security	Perimeter-Focused Security				Rapid Networkwide Threat Detection and Containment
Service Assurance	Patchy Quality of Service (QoS)				Closed-Loop Automated Service Assurance
Analytics	Device-Specific Event Capture				Integrated IT, Business, and Security Data Analysis and Reporting

Figure 2-1 *Cisco Digital Network Readiness Model (Source: www.cisco.com/go/dnaadvisor)*

Additionally, IDC found that moving from one state of network readiness to the next results in reduced network infrastructure costs of $24,200 to $38,300 per 100 users per year, and that—on average—interviewed organizations were achieving benefits of $188,000 to $750,000 per 100 users per year by advancing their digital network readiness.[1] Some of these benefits are illustrated in Figure 2-2.

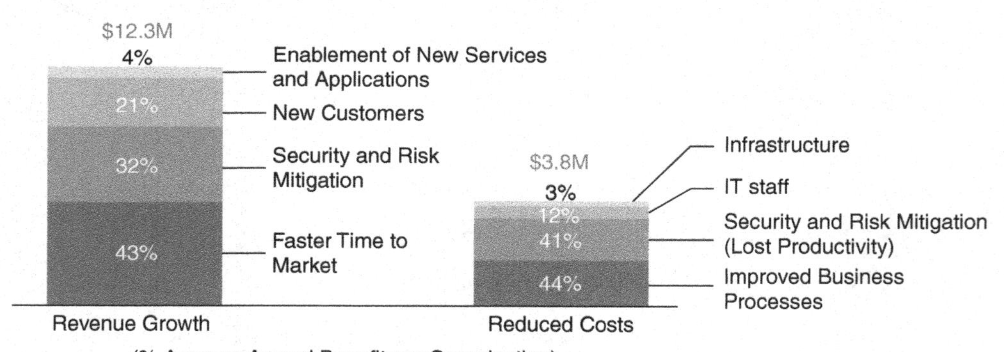

Source: IDC's Digital Network Business Value Research, 2016.

Figure 2-2 *Digital Network Readiness Model (Source: www.cisco.com/go/dnaadvisor)*

1 "Why a Digital-Ready Network Makes Business Sense," IDC White Paper, sponsored by Cisco, January 2017.

Summary

This chapter discussed the business value of Cisco Digital Network Architecture. The key business requirements of the network architecture as a platform for digital transformation were set out from the start, including: cost reduction, risk mitigation, actionable insights, and business agility. This discussion was continued by sharing data points from various analyst reports and customer case studies that illustrated both achieved and projected business values for each of these requirements.

Further Reading

Cisco Systems. "Cisco 2016 Midyear Cybersecurity Report." July 2016. https://www.cisco.com/c/dam/m/en_ca/never-better/assets/files/midyear-security-report-2016.pdf.

Cisco Systems. Cisco DNA Advisor. http://www.cisco.com/go/dnaadvisor.

Cisco Systems, Cisco ROI Calculator, https://dnaroi.cisco.com/go/cisco/dnaroi/index.html.

Cisco Systems. Cisco DNA Case Studies. https://www.cisco.com/c/en/us/solutions/enterprise-networks/network-architecture-customer-success-stories.html.

Cisco Systems. "Cisco Visual Networking Index: Forecast and Methodology, 2016–2021." Updated September 15, 2017. https://www.cisco.com/c/en/us/solutions/collateral/service-provider/visual-networking-index-vni/complete-white-paper-c11-481360.html.

IEEE Spectrum. "Popular Internet of Things Forecast of 50 Billion Devices by 2020 Is Outdated." August 2016. https://spectrum.ieee.org/tech-talk/telecom/internet/popular-internet-of-things-forecast-of-50-billion-devices-by-2020-is-outdated.

Greene, N., R. Mehra, M. Marden, and R. Perry. "The Business Value of Creating Digital-Ready Networks with Cisco DNA Solutions." IDC White Paper, sponsored by Cisco. November 2016. https://www.cisco.com/c/dam/en/us/solutions/collateral/enterprise-networks/digital-network-architecture/idc-business-value-of-dna-solutions-white-paper.pdf.

Greene, N., R. Parker, and R. Perry. "Is Your Network Ready for Digital Transformation?" IDC White Paper, sponsored by Cisco. January 2017. https://www.cisco.com/c/dam/en/us/solutions/collateral/enterprise-networks/digital-network-architecture/network-ready-digital-transformation.pdf.

Greene, N., R. Parker, and R. Perry. "Why a Digital-Ready Network Makes Business Sense." IDC White Paper, sponsored by Cisco. January 2017. https://www.cisco.com/c/dam/en/us/solutions/collateral/enterprise-networks/digital-network-architecture/digital-network-business-sense.pdf.

Schultz, E. "Calculating Total Cost of Ownership on Intrusion Prevention Technology." SANS Institute. February 2014. http://www.sans.org/reading-room/whitepapers/analyst/calculating-total-cost-ownership-intrusion-prevention-technology-34745.

ZK Research. "Digital Success Depends on Choosing the Right Network Vendor: Understanding the Hidden Costs of Not Choosing a Digital-Ready Network." December 2017. https://engage2demand.cisco.com/LP=8802.

Chapter 3

Designing for Humans

Cisco Digital Network Architecture was engineered to meet three distinct sets of requirements:

- Business requirements (which were discussed in the first two chapters)
- User requirements (which are discussed in this chapter)
- Technology requirements (which are discussed in depth in the chapters that follow)

When it comes to networking technology, it is not uncommon for user requirements to be an afterthought. However, with Cisco DNA, Cisco made a deliberate and conscious effort to consider user requirements at each step of the development process, by leveraging principles of design thinking. Since this design-centric approach is fundamentally different from those taken in the past, it bears explicit mentioning as a separate chapter.

As such, this chapter discusses

- Design thinking philosophy, principles, and framework
- The Cisco design thinking journey for Cisco DNA
- Cisco DNA user archetypes

Technology Versus User-Experience

In 2015, the executive team sponsoring Cisco Digital Network Architecture made an important decision: this new architecture was to be built by applying the principles of design thinking. *Design thinking* is a human-centric approach to innovation that was first taught by Stanford University in the early 1980s as "a method of creative action," and later adapted for business purposes at the design consultancy IDEO. Design thinking provides a framework to help teams build products that solve real problems for regular people. Specifically, design thinking is about discovering real human needs, and creating solutions that address those needs, with the overall goal being to "surprise and delight" users.

This design-centric approach was both new and radical for most of the Cisco architects and engineers working on Cisco DNA. In fact, the Cisco DNA architecture team was sent "back to school," specifically to the Stanford d.school (a.k.a. the Hasso Plattner Institute of Design), to become immersed in design thinking and culture, which they were then tasked with sharing across their respective teams.

As Cisco architects began their training at the Stanford d.school, one of the first and vitally important lessons impressed on them was that user experience is just as important as technology. This ran contrary to the genetic makeup of the engineers, who typically consider technology to be first and foremost. However, to make the point, the instructors cited a famous example: the GE magnetic resonance imaging (MRI) scanner.

Doug Dietz led the design and development of GE's MRI systems, which in every way were technologically superior to other medical imaging systems of their day, primarily because of their use of magnetic fields (versus the x-rays used by CT scans) to generate detailed internal images.

However, one day Doug was on hand at a hospital to see his new machine being put to use and was horrified to see a young girl reduced to tears as she was being prepared for an MRI scan. The young girl was so distraught that she had to be sedated by an anesthesiologist. It was only then that Doug found out that as many as 80 percent of pediatric patients required sedation when undergoing MRI scans. Clearly, the technological superiority of the MRI did little to assuage the terrifying user experience of most children.

Troubled, Doug attended the Stanford d.school and began studying design thinking. He also began observing and gaining empathy for young children in medical centers, speaking at length with them, as well as their doctors, volunteers, and staff, to better understand their needs, concerns, and challenges.

He soon hit on a key insight: these unfortunate sick children missed out on a lot of "adventures." This empathetic insight led him to develop a prototype of what became the "Adventure Series" scanner. While making no changes to the scanner itself, Doug and his ad hoc team applied colorful decals to the outside of the machine and every surface of the room to present an adventure to the young patient, complete with a script for the machine operators. These adventures include, for example, a pirate ship, as illustrated in Figure 3-1, where the operator tells the children they will be sailing inside of and have to lie completely still while on the boat, after which they get to pick a small treasure from a chest on the other side of the room. Some doctors also participated in the adventure, dressing up in full pirate costume, much to the delight of their pediatric patients. Doug and his team put together nine additional adventures centered on their MRI machines.

With the MRI redesign for kids, the number of pediatric patients needing to be sedated was reduced dramatically, to less than 5 percent in some hospitals. This lowered medical risk for these young children, as well as allowed more patients to be scanned each day. Overall patient satisfaction scores went up to 90 percent.

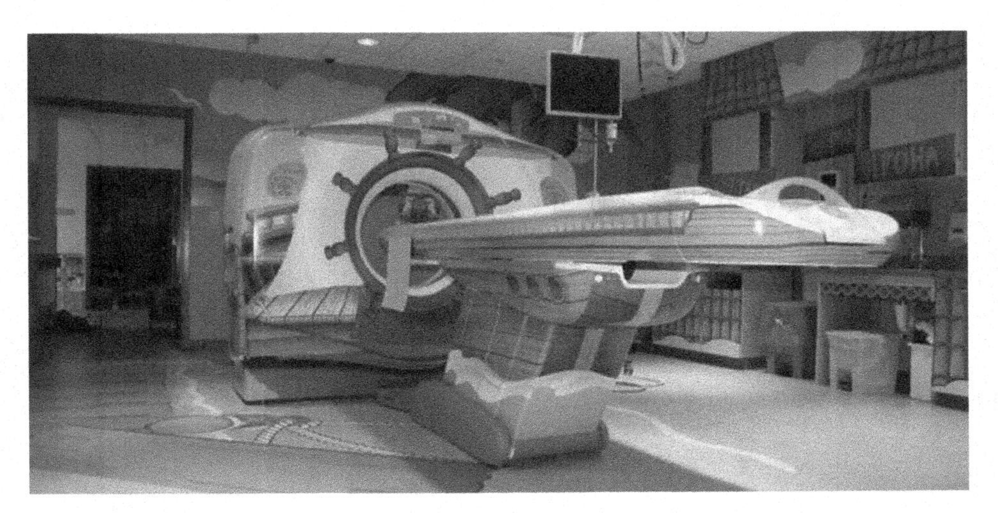

Figure 3-1 *GE Medical Scanner Transformed into a Pirate Adventure for Pediatric Patients*

They key takeaways of the case study were that superior technology in itself doesn't necessarily translate to a good user experience, and a poor user experience can actually prove to be a barrier to adopting superior technology. This lesson provided meaty food for thought to the Cisco DNA architecture team.

Design Thinking Philosophy and Principles

Technology, solutions, and data tend to change over time; however, intrinsic human needs do not. People, therefore, are the most constant variables in the design equation.

As a user, you don't always notice when design is done well, because when form meets function, you simply go about your task and then move on with your day. However, you do notice when something is designed poorly, because it *is* confusing or frustrating and it gets in the way.

As such, design thinking focuses on empathizing with users and understanding what they need up front, so as to build products they'll love to use—products that are both useful and usable.

This philosophy has historically been the domain of designers. But design thinking is a universal framework that helps everyone across the organization understand users, empathize with their needs, and collaborate to solve complex problems with confidence.

At its core, design thinking is about solving problems efficiently, effectively, and elegantly. Optimally, design thinking lives at the intersection of human needs, business requirements, and technology solutions, as is illustrated in Figure 3-2.

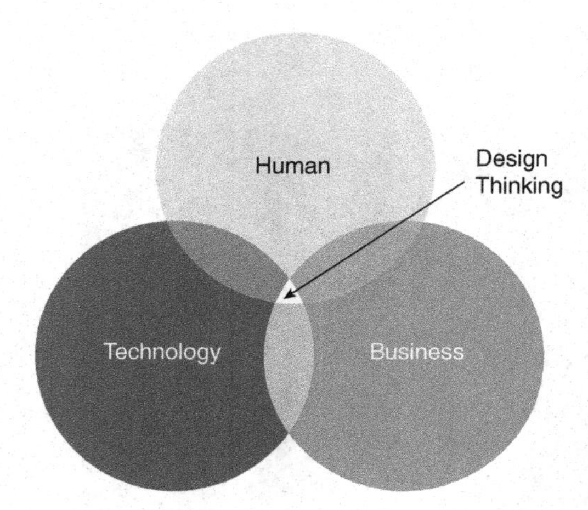

Figure 3-2 *Design Thinking "Sweet Spot"*

Design thinking includes a series of principles, such as

- **Put the user first:** To create better solutions, connect with users as often as you can. Their experience is your focus; improving it informs all that you do.
- **Keep it simple:** Strive to produce the most simple and effective product for your users.
- **Never stop evolving:** Evolve your products alongside users' needs.
- **Find proactive solutions:** Anticipate issues before they arise. Your solutions should provide just the right amount of attention, so they're never in the way but always around.
- **Dare to delight:** It's the little details that make the most impactful designs. Sweat the small stuff so that customers want to come back for more—and tell all their friends too.
- **Build together:** To do this effectively, teams must regularly come together to create each tool, platform, and product in alignment.

Cisco Design Thinking Framework

The Cisco Design Thinking framework adapts classic design thinking best practices to the unique context of Cisco's global workforce, heritage, technology portfolio, management culture, and partner and customer relationships. The result is an original Cisco Design Thinking framework that is innovative yet familiar, forward-looking yet approachable.

There are three phases to the Cisco Design Thinking framework, as illustrated in Figure 3-3 and described here:

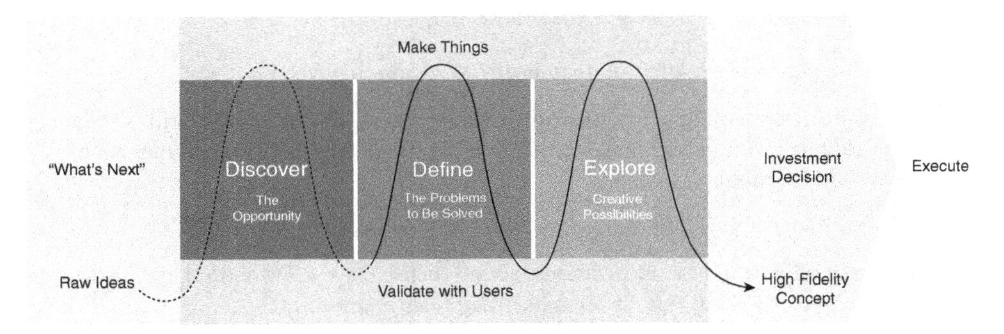

Figure 3-3 *Cisco Design Thinking Framework*

1. **Discover:** Strive to deeply understand your users and what they need, so you and your team can document a clear Opportunity Statement.
2. **Define:** Identify, document, and prioritize the problems to be solved based on the opportunity at hand and articulate a crisp Problem to Be Solved Statement.
3. **Explore:** Come up with a variety of potential solutions for the problems to be solved. Your objective is to identify one or more solutions to delight your target users, solve their core problems, and claim the opportunity.

These three core phases are contained by two guard rails that are fundamental tenets of the Cisco Design Thinking framework:

- **Validate with users:** You must constantly validate your ideas and your conclusions with real users. Anything worth acting on—and investing in—is worth gut checking with your target audience.
- **Make things:** It's not enough to explain your ideas to your users. You must make things to illustrate your ideas and give your users something to react to, validate, or reject.

The three phases of the Cisco Design Thinking framework are expanded in the following sections.

Discover Phase

In the first phase of Cisco Design Thinking, the priority is getting to know your users. By empathizing with users and truly understanding their core needs, current frustrations, and related pain points, you can uncover the valuable opportunities that drive true innovation.

The two main activities in this phase are data collection and insights synthesis. Once you gather information from your users, begin piecing together your observations in a way that starts to explain their behavior. Through user data, develop a clarifying narrative about your actual users and their everyday challenges.

The Discover phase seeks to answer the following questions:

- Who are your users? What do they need? What do they value?

  Try to learn something new about how they see themselves and the world. Validate your findings with users to ensure that you captured their needs and values accurately and thoroughly.

- What do your users need to accomplish?

  Dig in to understand the motivations behind their behavior. Why do they choose a particular tool? What does it seem like they really want to do?

- What is their experience today?

  Observe your users in action. Understand how your users currently deal with challenges, especially when completing specific workflows while using specific tools. When and where exactly do they get frustrated with the current experience? Why? How do current solutions fall short? By recognizing an unmet need or obstacle, you discover clear opportunities to make your users' lives better.

It's easy for biases in the Discover phase to alter the trajectory of the rest of the process. Therefore, it is important that the users being interviewed broadly represent the user base and that questions asked are open ended, so as to allow users to describe both their immediate and latent needs.

It's virtually impossible to predict where key insights will arise, and as such it's important to thoroughly document findings and data points, as they may allow insights to surface later through analysis. Always focus on user needs and problems. Invest in empathy rather than ideation, and to try formulate—and reformulate—needs and problems from the user's perspective.

Opportunity Statement

The Discover phase includes many valuable, and sometimes lengthy, conversations with customers. Although these conversations are very beneficial, they may be challenging to summarize. However, a distinct and concise result is needed from this phase in order to proceed to the Define phase. Specifically, the end result of the Discover phase is a crisp Opportunity Statement, which includes the following elements:

> [CORE USER] **needs to**
>
> [PRIMARY NEED] **because**
>
> [USER-VALIDATED INSIGHT].
>
> **Today,** [EXPLAIN HOW CURRENT SOLUTIONS FALL SHORT].

For example:

A *network engineer* [CORE USER] who responds to policy change requests in a complex security environment **needs to** *know how a policy change will affect and be affected by the rest of the security environment before it's deployed* [PRIMARY NEED], **because** even if they can easily write rules to capture the business intent, *they aren't confident the change will have the intended effect* [USER-VALIDATED INSIGHT] due to all the things that make their environment complex, including

- Residual policy that's built up over time (as they don't clean up rules unless someone puts in tickets to remove them)
- Out-of-band interactions with other parts of the security environment
- The need to keep adding policies because there are always new threats

Today, they perform human analysis, deploy changes, and rely on rollback to correct errors and unintended consequences. Best case, they proactively test and roll back. Worst case, they rely on their end users to report errors and negative results. This *error-prone process is expensive, risky, and often results in customer and user dissatisfaction* [HOW CURRENT SOLUTIONS FALL SHORT].

Define Phase

Once you have documented the opportunity, there are likely many problems that were identified and need to be solved. But which ones matter most to your users? The goal of the Define phase is to prioritize three—or fewer—clearly articulated problems that your solution will address on behalf of your users.

The Define phase seeks to answer the following questions:

- What are your users' biggest challenges?

  Document the main frustrations and pain points your users experienced and expressed in the Discover phase.

- What are some less obvious user challenges that can be inferred?

  People often have a hard time identifying the root causes of their challenges, because they tend to accept their current condition as unavoidable. How might you and your team reframe your approach to identify deeper, more insightful problems?

- What must our solution absolutely do?

  Here you hone in on your solution's top priority. There usually is a related secondary problem you need to solve as well. Is there anything else you should address?

- Have our users validated these problems?

  Review your problem statements with users to ensure you have captured them as completely as possible. This helps you and your team get clarity about how users would interact with your proposals.

The main activity in the Define phase is creating a validated Problems to Be Solved Statement. Progress toward articulating this statement may be done by telling a new story—one where the user's life has improved because they have your high-level, unspecified solution. By constructing and telling the user's before-and-after story, you're forced to consider their reaction to the new world and whether it matches your intention. Through the telling and retelling of this story, you'll quickly identify any holes or irrelevant details in your ideas. This helps determine what's necessary for your new concept to be successful.

Keep in mind that this high-level narrative is just an iteration meant to uncover which problems to prioritize. It will almost certainly be transformed in the Explore phase—if not completely reinvented.

Problem to Be Solved Statement

This statement directly relates to the Opportunity Statement from the Discover phase, helping you prioritize which key user problems your solution must address. You'll use this output to guide your creative ideation in the Explore phase—and as a gut check to make sure your concepts explicitly solve these problems.

Most often you will have only one or two problems to solve; in stretch-goal circumstances you may have three. However, attempting to tackle four or more problems at once is a formula for frustration—or worse.

A Problem to Be Solved Statement includes the following elements:

> **As a result of this, our solution absolutely must**
>
> [PRIMARY PROBLEM TO SOLVE],
>
> **while**
>
> [SECONDARY PROBLEM TO SOLVE],
>
> **plus if possible,**
>
> [TERTIARY PROBLEM TO SOLVE].

Continuing the previous network security opportunity, a Problem to Be Solved Statement can be defined as the following:

> **As a result of this, our solution absolutely must**
>
> [PRIMARY PROBLEM TO SOLVE]
>
> allow users to see how rules managed by one part of the security environment interact with other parts (such as firewall policies interacting with Internet policies),
>
> **while**
>
> [SECONDARY PROBLEM TO SOLVE]
>
> enabling them to understand rule behavior before it is deployed,

plus, if possible,

[TERTIARY PROBLEM TO SOLVE]

automatically generate the correct API scripts once the rule was verified and validated so it is easy to deploy across the network.

It's tempting to try to address each and every pain point in your Problems to Be Solved Statement. It's also tempting to be vague and open-ended in your Problems to Be Solved Statement. Both of these temptations result in vague, uninspiring prototypes in the Explore phase. As such, it is recommended to limit each solution to solve a few direct, focused problems, so as to facilitate the building of a direct, focused prototype. This way, you and your team focus on doing something important really well, rather than partially solving a broad range of less critical issues.

Explore Phase

At this point, you have a clear sense of who you're building for, the opportunity at hand, and the key problems to be solved. Now it's time for the team to start identifying creative solutions.

The key to the Explore phase is to ensure that the solutions developed explicitly solve the prioritized problems documented in the Define phase.

The Explore phase seeks to answer the following questions:

- How can you creatively solve the problems you've identified?

  Time to ideate. Perhaps have individuals come up with their own ideas first. Then share them with the group. Build upon each other's concepts. Then decide which solutions directly solve the user problems as a team.

- What's the quickest way to test each idea?

  After expansive concept generation, create tangible concepts or prototypes. Put these concepts out into the environment, measure response, and let the best concepts win. Aim to set up as many quick experiments as you can to help shape the end-state solution.

- Do you have evidence to support the chosen solution?

  Testing with real users is critical. If you don't validate prototypes with users, you run the risk of designing beautiful solutions that lack crucial elements that makes the solution impractical for real life use. Capture direct user quotes and interaction details that prove that your product does, in fact, solve their problems and satisfy their needs.

The main activities in the Explore phase involve ideation around solving your users' problems, and rapidly building and iterating until you validate the ideal solution. These activities include (but are not limited to)

- Brainstorming creative solutions
  - Brainstorm as many ideas as you can within a defined period of time
  - Share the ideas among the team
  - Build on these concepts together
  - Prioritize the best ideas or features
- Sketch low-fidelity concepts
  - Make your ideas tangible with quick sketches
  - Use sketches to begin validating ideas with your users
  - Pick the most promising idea to develop into a prototype
- Create interactive prototypes
  - Create a prototype that shows the key value for the user in a simple flow
- Validate with users
  - Meet the user one on one, ideally face to face
  - Watch the user walk through your prototype(s)
  - Validate whether or not the solution works
  - Note how to improve the solution in your next iteration

By the end of the Explore phase, your team has the opportunity to create high-fidelity prototypes of the proposed solution. This can be a wireframe, a clickable prototype, or a physical mockup. Identify precisely where the proposed user experience solves the problems you defined in the Define phase. And if it doesn't clearly and completely solve the problem for your users—iterate.

The most common struggle in the Explore phase is that many people are afraid of pitching "dumb ideas" in front of their colleagues. Others lose heart when users don't love their solutions right off the bat. Just remember, good ideas can come from anywhere. And when you fail fast, you learn even faster. Finding out what works—and what doesn't work—helps inform your decisions. So you can take significant steps toward a winning solution with more confidence. If you find you're getting off track, don't be afraid to pause, step back, look at the bigger picture, and reset.

The Cisco Design Thinking Journey for Cisco DNA

Having outlined design thinking principles and phases, the balance of this chapter focuses on how Cisco applied its Design Thinking framework to Cisco DNA, and the insights, opportunities, and key findings that were revealed along the way.

Cisco DNA Discovery Phase

Cisco began by conducting dozens of in-depth expert interviews with a wide cross-section of its customers, partners, and, in some cases, competitors. To maximize neutrality and minimize bias in the interviewing process, the majority of these interviewees were "blind" in that they were unaware of the party sponsoring the interview (in other words, the interviewees were being asked questions by a neutral third party rather than directly by a Cisco representative). During this phase, over 60 in-depth interviews were conducted by customers and partners representing some of the largest players in the following industry verticals:

- Banking and financial services
- Manufacturing
- IT companies
- Pharmaceuticals
- Retailers
- Service providers
- Universities and research centers

In addition to these interviews, Cisco regularly meets with its advisory boards of customers, including the Enterprise Technical Advisory Board (ETAB), Mobility Technical Advisory Board (MTAB), etc. These boards similarly represent Cisco's largest customers in various industry verticals and provide ongoing feedback and direction for product and technology development so as to meet their evolving business requirements.

Also, teams from Cisco spent time onsite at customer sites performing ongoing observations of how they design, build, and run their networks and the challenges they face in doing so.

Beyond onsite observations, the teams also performed extensive data analysis. For example, while working with Cisco IT, the Cisco DNA team analyzed and correlated over 1455 change management requests and 11,500 incident tickets opened during a six-month period.

During this Discovery phase, as Cisco sought to better understand who its users are along with their unmet needs and pain points, several network personality archetypes began to be manifest. These include (but are not limited to)

- The front-line (tier 1) network engineer (shown later, in Figure 3-4)
- The firefighter (tier 1–2) network engineer (shown later, in Figure 3-5)
- The expert (tier 3–4) network architect (shown later, in Figure 3-6)
- The planner (tier 3–4) network engineering manager (shown later, in Figure 3-7)

The point of this exercise was not only to identify the various roles within the networking department, but also to define the responsibilities, needs, motivators, and pain points of each role of network engineer, all backed up with direct customer quotes.

The Front-Line Engineer

The front-line engineer, as illustrated in Figure 3-4, is generally the first individual to handle a trouble ticket, and is usually the least experienced to do so. Front-line engineers typically have received very little training for their role, but at the same time are held under a lot of pressure to perform. Obviously, the more issues that are resolved at this entry-level tier the better, and resolution rates range from 10 percent to 75 percent of issues at this stage—illustrating that the customers who invest more in training, tools, and resources to support their front line reap corresponding benefits from doing so.

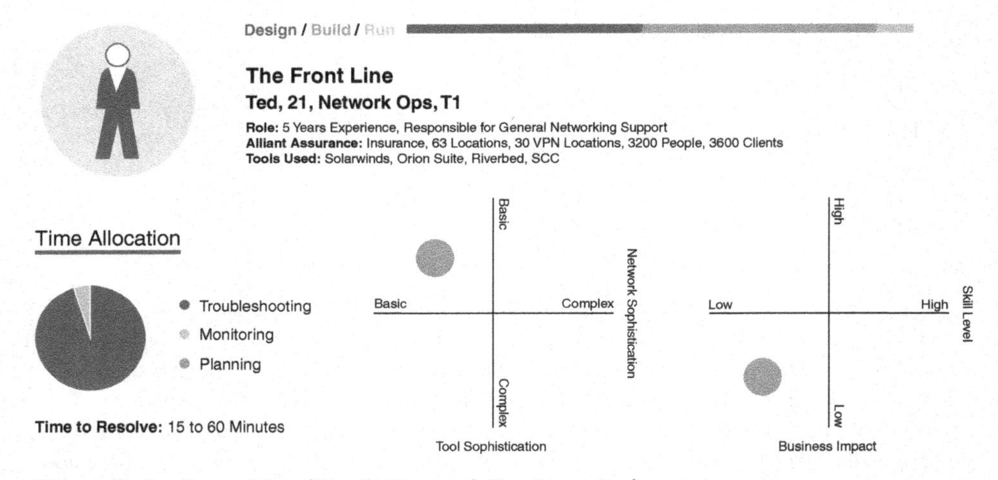

Figure 3-4 *Front-Line (Tier 1) Network Engineer Archetype*

Overview:

- Entry level
  - Starter salary
  - Less skilled
- Outsourced (sometimes)
- Remote (often)

Responsibilities:

- Entry-level support
- IT or network generalist
- Power user as remote hands (on site)
- Commonly outsourced support
- Rigidly follows a script
- Opens trouble tickets and routes to other teams

Needs & Motivators:

- I need a smarter ticketing system for which issues or alerts are routed.
- I'm motivated to interpret and document the reported issue with accurate content and context.
- I'm motivated to validate or re-create the issue to better understand the issue.
- I need a reliable knowledge base to resolve simple fixes.
- I need to trial and error some basic troubleshooting techniques to rule out issues.
- I need a proper escalation path based on business severity, impact of scale, and issue topic.
- I need a knowledge base to be connected to the alerts I'm getting from the tools.
- I'm motivated to resolve the issue call as quickly as possible.

Pain Points:

- I'm penalized if I don't put accurate content or enough context into a support ticket.
- I'm penalized if I miss symptoms or never get to the root cause.
- I'm penalized if I don't use the right tools (which I don't know how to use).
- I'm penalized if I don't escalate to the right expert due to misinformation or limited triage.
- I'm penalized if I don't escalate in a timely fashion.

Quotes:

- "Noise gets filtered by the network operations center."
- NOCs are "Typically trained monkeys looking for red lights"
- "Users always complain that it's a network problem, but 60 percent of problems end up being application and/or user issues."
- "~10 percent of issues are resolved at tier 1."—low-end quote
- "~75 percent of issues are resolved at tier 1."—high-end quote

Front-Line Engineer Opportunity Statement:

The front-line engineer **needs to** trial and error some basic troubleshooting techniques to rule out issues **because** "users always complain that it's a network problem, but 60 percent of problems end up being application and/or user issues." **Today**, front-line engineers aren't trained on how to use troubleshooting tools and they are penalized if they don't use the right tools or miss symptoms or don't get to the root cause.

The Firefighter

The firefighter, illustrated in Figure 3-5, represents the first level of escalation. When front-line engineers cannot solve a problem, firefighters are the next set of engineers who lay eyes and hands on the problem. They are typically better trained and have more experience than their front-line counterparts, but often share a common complaint that many of the issues they deal with should have been resolved at the first tier.

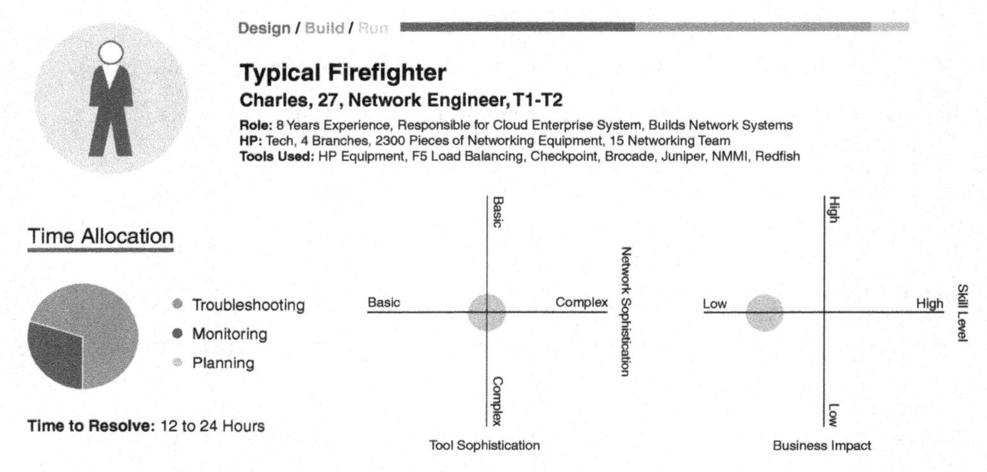

Figure 3-5 *Firefighter (Tier 1–2) Network Engineer Archetype*

Overview:

- More experienced
  - More training
  - Better compensation
- In house (more often)
- More responsibility, increased access

Responsibilities:

- Primary fixer for simpler T1–T2 issues
- Basic monitoring and troubleshooting tools
- Outside NOC (mostly)
- Most problems resolved at this level

Needs & Motivators:

- I need a smarter ticketing system that routes issues or alerts with the right context.
- I need tools to work out of the box without too much customization.

- I'm motivated to assess the issue severity, scale, and impact to escalate it to the right expert.
- I need faster communication and effective collaboration with the right experts for severity level 1–2 issues.
- I need a tool to allow me to drill down as deep as needed to resolve issues.
- I need a tool to provide an accurate topology picture to supplement documentation, which could be wrong.
- I need a tool that's customizable around summary views—a summary each for servers, routers, helpdesk, etc.
- Real-time status and events are important.

Pain Points:

- The severity filter is too loose and unreliable.
- The tools are fragmented and provide no correlation logic.
- I receive too much raw data and not enough insights.
- I have to deal with too many issues that should have been fixed at tier 1.

Quotes:

- "I don't want to be a data scientist, I'm a network analyst."
- "Documentation isn't always correct—I need tools to reliably discover and provide me with correct network view."
- "Tools must be multivendor; otherwise there are too many to touch."
- "Tell me if an event is normal."
- "~15 percent of issues are resolved at tier 2."—low-end quote
- "~70 percent of issues are resolved at tier 2."—high-end quote

Firefighter Opportunity Statement:

The firefighter **needs** tools to provide accurate, timely, and detailed information so as to allow him to drill down as deep as needed to resolve issues **because** network documentation is not always accurate and trustworthy. **Today**, firefighters have to make use of fragmented tools with no correlation logic, which provides them too much raw data and not enough insights.

The Expert

The next level of escalation is typically to the expert, illustrated in Figure 3-6. These architects have the most training, certifications, and experience, but are also the individuals who are trying to focus on forward-thinking planning and thus often resent the constant interruptions that these escalations present. An additional challenge is that much of their expert knowledge is "tribal knowledge" that would be helpful to disseminate to lower support tiers, but is often difficult/impossible to do, as it's largely undocumented.

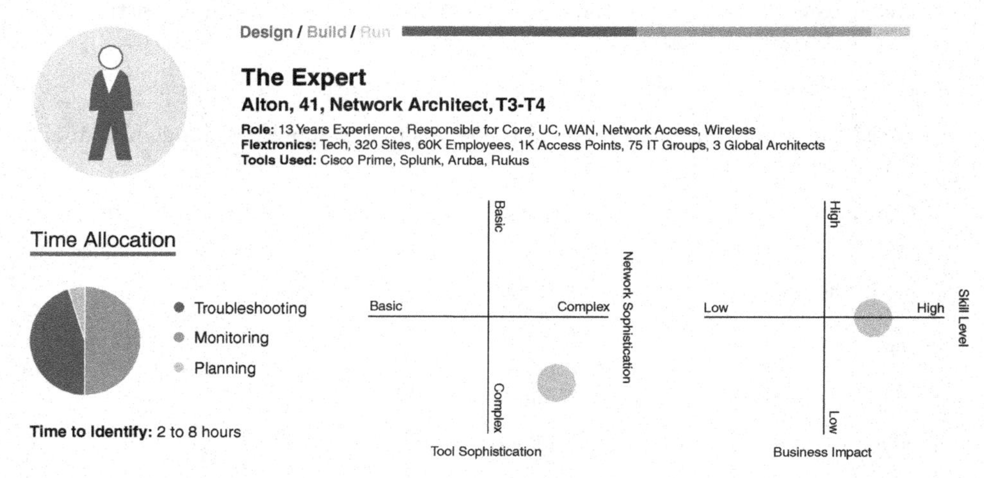

Figure 3-6 *Expert (Tier 3–4) Network Architect Archetype*

Overview:

- Most experience
  - Certifications
  - Most training/education
- In house (always)
- Most responsibility: network design and plan

Responsibilities:

- High-level alerts and business impacts
- Sophisticated tools and tribal knowledge
- Scenario planning for complex problems
- Big-picture and real-time monitoring
- Coordinating large-scale fixes
- Multivendor resolution
- End-to-end visibility
- "The buck stops here"

Needs & Motivators:

- I need to first confirm if it's indeed a network issue because it's often misrouted to our group.
- I need to simulate the problem with actual data points to assess the issue severity, scale, and impact.
- I need to interpret the surface symptoms and issues to get to the root cause.
- I need faster communication and effective collaboration with the right experts for severity 1–2 issues.
- I need a quick fix or permanent workaround for immediate needs.
- I need a good orchestration tool across multiple devices.
- I need better capacity planning, visibility, and prediction.

Pain Points:

- Too many issues that should have been fixed at tier 1 are coming to me.
- I'm constantly disrupted from my project work to do troubleshooting.
- I spend a large number of time proving it's not the network.

Quotes:

- "It would be great if you can take experience and bundle it into software."
- "What we're doing now is unsustainable and is tribal knowledge."
- "IT still needs expert eyes to look at tools together with the tribal knowledge to resolve issues."
- "The network operations team needs to spend money to understand the trends in order to do things proactively going forward."
- "At least 50 percent of my time is being spent proving it's not a network issue."
- "~15 percent of issues are resolved at tier 3."—customer average

Expert Opportunity Statement:

The expert **needs** to simulate the problem with actual data points to assess the issue, severity, scale, and impact **because** he spends a large amount of time proving it's not a network issue. **Today**, experts spend more time than they should troubleshooting issues (which approximately half of the time turn out not even to be network issues); their "tribal knowledge" would benefit lower tiers of engineers to root-cause or rule-out potential issues earlier in the process.

The Planner

A final role to consider is the network engineering manager, illustrated in Figure 3-7, primarily responsible for planning future network deployments. They spend considerably less time troubleshooting the network and are more interested in baselines, historical trends, analytics, and capacity planning.

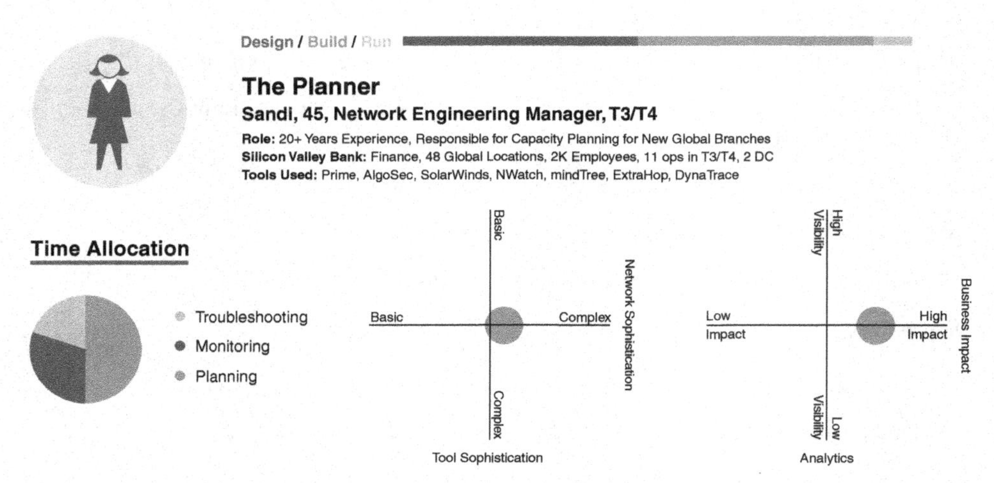

Figure 3-7 *Planner (Tier 3–4) Network Engineering Manager Archetype*

Responsibilities:

- Major capacity planning
- Network design and architecture
- Writing procedures
- Creating trainings for all tiers
- Daily health reports
- Historical trends and analytics
- Tools and process improvements
- Market trend research

Needs & Motivators:

- I need better visibility and analytics about my network performance, availability, and users to address issues proactively instead of just reactively.
- I need to stay ahead of market-leading products and case studies to evaluate what's applicable to us.
- I need to upgrade to more robust and correlated tools that enhance my company's network needs.

- I need a tool to audit that what has been implemented conforms to what was intended.
- I need better capacity planning tools that also do prediction.

Pain Points:

- I have to wait around a lot on other groups to get their pieces done.

Planner Opportunity Statement:

The planner **needs** better visibility and analytics about her network performance **because** she is looking to solve problems proactively (rather than reactively). **Today,** planners are forced to wait on other groups to get their respective work done, as they lack the tools and access to gather and analyze the needed information themselves.

Cisco DNA Definition Phase

Having identified key users and their needs, pain points, and opportunities, the Cisco DNA team proceeded to the Definition phase of the Design Thinking framework so as to identify the key problems to be solved.

Data soon revealed that the majority of budget and time being spent by network IT departments was on change management (~50 percent of both OPEX and network engineer time). Change management was a time-consuming process, where deploying a new service could easily take six months to a year, including six to eight weeks of testing before deployment. Furthermore, the change management process was identified to be highly prone to human error.

Change management was thus examined further, with the next step being to take inventory of change management requests and examine these to see where the most time was being spent. Specifically, 1455 change management tickets from Cisco IT were analyzed to this end, as summarized in Figure 3-8.

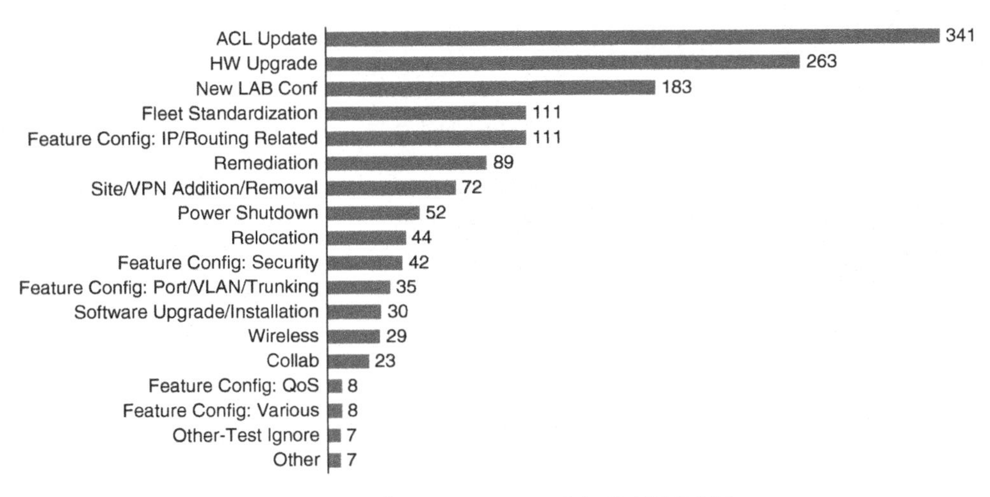

Figure 3-8 *Cisco IT Network Change Requests Q2–Q4 FY2016*

From the graph in Figure 3-8, it became evident that the majority of time and effort were spent on a very few tasks, specifically 55 percent of time was being spent on managing just three types of network changes:

- Access control list (ACL) updates
- Hardware upgrades
- New lab configurations

The data was further analyzed so as to be able to subdivide how many changes were standard versus how many were the result of new initiatives; the results are summarized in Figure 3-9.

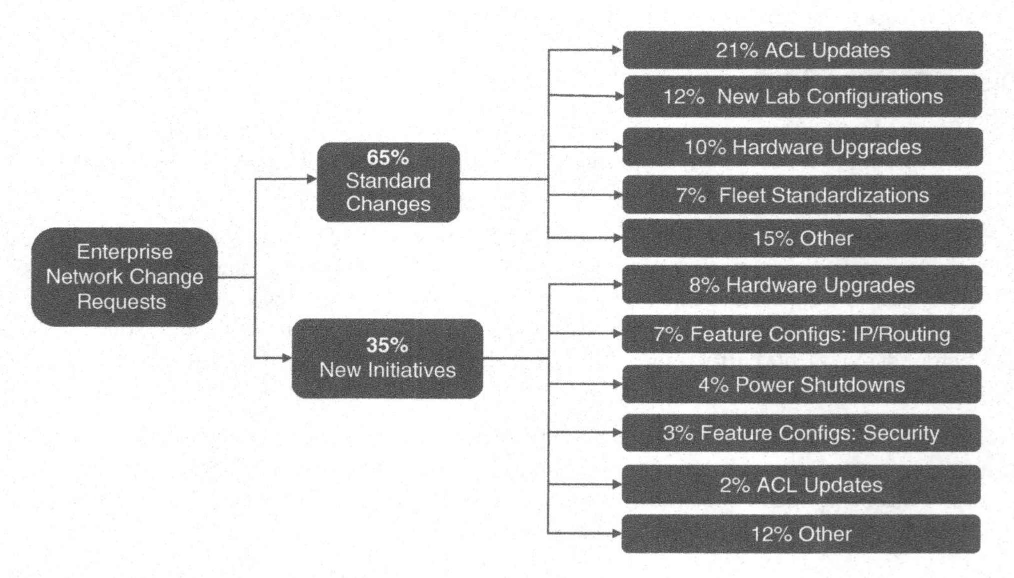

Figure 3-9 *Cisco IT Network Change Requests Q2–Q4 FY2016: Standard Versus New Initiatives*

As seen in Figure 3-9, nearly two-thirds of the changes made were standard changes and only about one-third of the changes were the result of new initiatives. This high degree of standardized changes presents a significant opportunity for automation to provide substantial operational savings to the networking department.

Standard changes (versus nonstandard) are also broken down further according to network platform type, as illustrated in Figure 3-10.

From this analysis, a Problem to Be Solved Statement evolved for base automation, specifically:

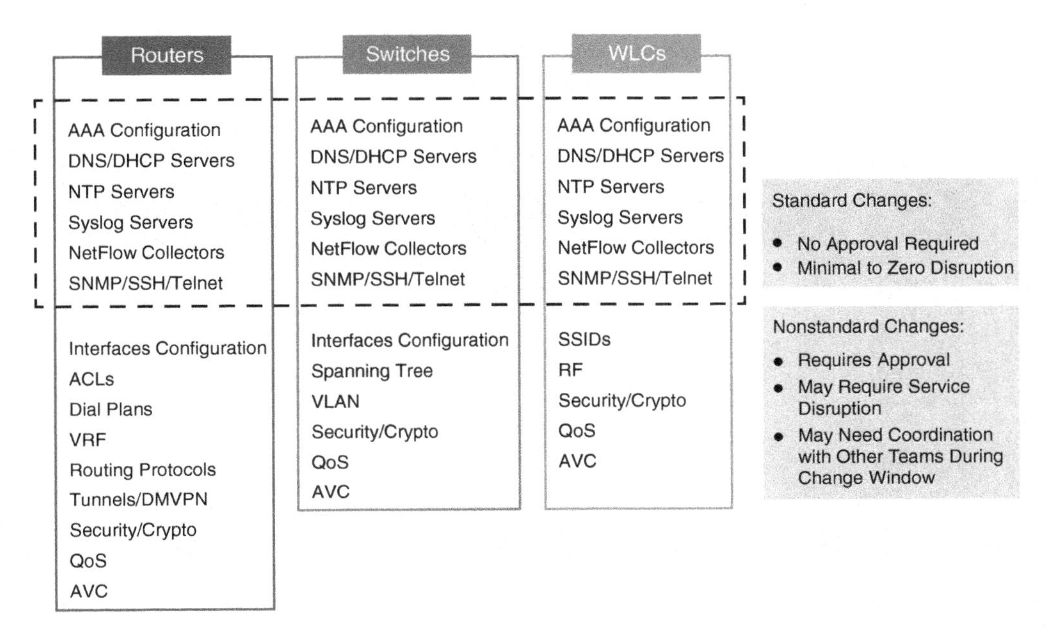

Figure 3-10 *Standard Versus Nonstandard Changes by Network Device Type*

As a result of this, our solution absolutely must automate standard changes, **while** supporting new initiatives, **plus if possible,** automate nonstandard changes, subject to an approval process.

Similarly, in the area of monitoring and troubleshooting, common needs kept surfacing and resurfacing, as summarized in Figure 3-11.

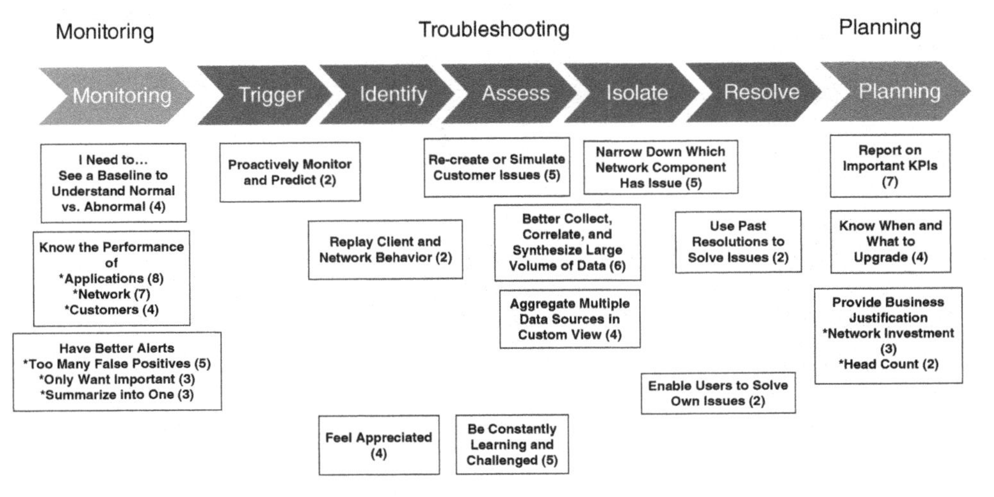

Figure 3-11 *Customer Clusters of Needs for Network Monitoring and Troubleshooting*

Not only were customer needs clustered together into common themes, but so too were customer pain points, as summarized in Figure 3-12.

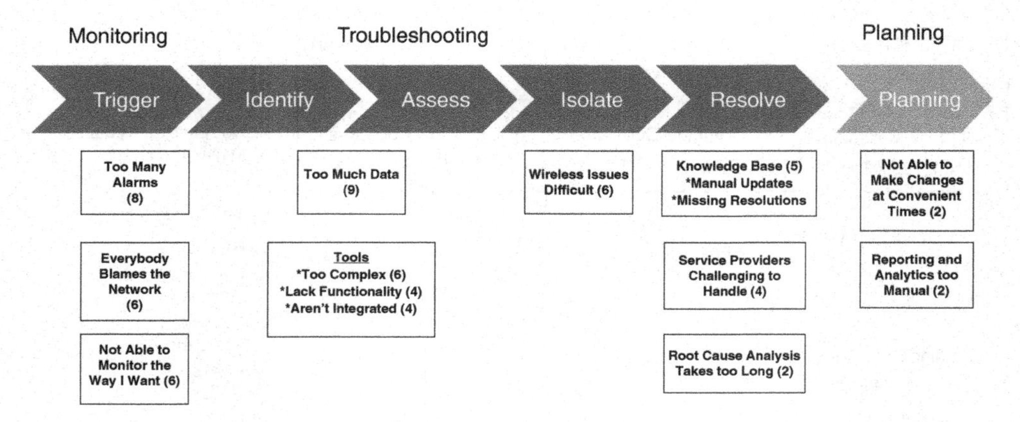

Figure 3-12 *Customer Clusters of Pain Points for Network Monitoring and Troubleshooting*

These needs and pain-point clusters were also correlated with Cisco IT case data, where over 11,500 trouble tickets were analyzed to see where typical IT departments spend their time troubleshooting, as shown in Figure 3-13.

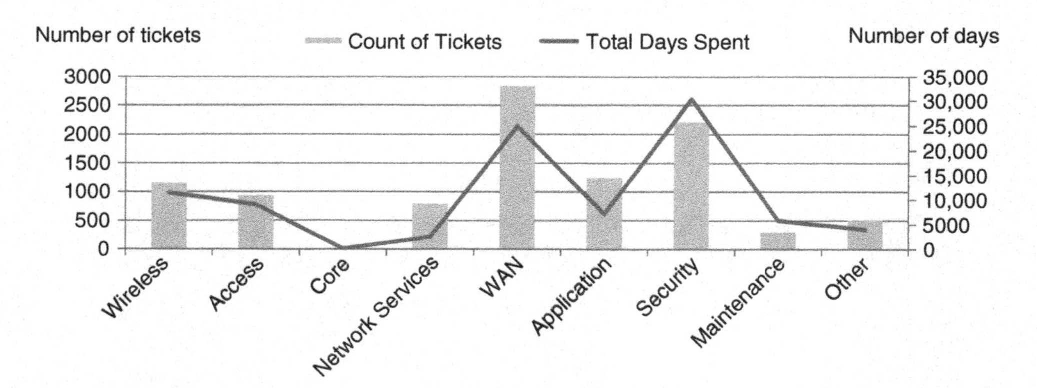

Figure 3-13 *Cisco IT Ticket Count and Time Spent on Network Troubleshooting Issues*

As shown in Figure 3-13, the top five areas where Cisco IT is spending time troubleshooting are

1. WAN
2. Security
3. Applications
4. Wireless
5. Access

With all these data points as guidance, the Problem to Be Solved Statement for network analytics emerged as:

As a result of this, our solution absolutely must know the performance of (wired and wireless) clients, network devices, and applications, **while** synthesizing and correlating large volumes of data, **plus if possible**, guiding/automating root-case analysis.

Cisco DNA Exploration Phase

As the Cisco DNA team progressed to the Exploration phase, they used a variety of techniques to continually gain customer feedback on their solutions. These included storyboards, mockups, workshops, and Early Field Trials.

Storyboards and evolving mockups were continually presented to customers for feedback, as well as Early Field Trial (EFT) software. At times there was quite a bit of internal resistance to sharing early software builds with customers (due to quality issues inherent to these early builds); however, the objective of receiving ongoing customer feedback overrode these concerns, and helped identify additional quality issues along the way.

Nonetheless, the Design Thinking exercise only helps the product teams to identify *what* the customers want them to build. The massive exercise of determining *how* to build out the architecture to support the overall solutions remains, and will now be covered in subsequent chapters.

Summary

This chapter introduced design thinking, emphasizing the need and value of addressing the human needs of users by showing empathy to the pain points they experience as they use products and services.

Cisco Design Thinking philosophies, principles, and framework were all introduced, including the Discover, Define, and Explore phases of the Design Thinking cycle. With the objectives of each phase outlined, the focus of the chapter then switched to Cisco's specific experiences in its application of Design Thinking for Cisco DNA.

Key user archetypes were explored, including the front-line engineer, the firefighter, the expert, and the planner. Similarly, the biggest problem areas to be solved were identified via data analysis, including the automation of standard networking changes and the monitoring of clients, network devices, and applications.

By using the Design Thinking framework, and continually looking to customers for input and guidance at each step of the way, Cisco has embarked on a new approach to engineering networking solutions. It's an approach that has certainly caused a fair share of discomfort within the product and engineering teams at Cisco, as it represents a considerable deviation from what had previously been the norm for decades. However, this new design-thinking approach is well worth the effort, as it positions Cisco to better meet the needs of its users by showing them more empathy at every stage in the design and engineering process.

Further Reading

Kelly, T., and D. Kelly. *Creative Confidence: Unleashing the Creative Potential Within Us All*. New York: Crown Publishing Group; 2013.

Getting Started with Cisco Design Thinking—A Practical Guide to Solving Complex Problems Together. Cutler, Matt and Rant Riley. c. 2017 Cisco.

Chapter 4

Introducing the Cisco Digital Network Architecture

Chapter 1, "Why Transform Your Business Digitally?," and Chapter 2, "The Business Value of Cisco DNA," provided the motivation to evolve the enterprise network architecture. They outlined why digitalization is transforming the business and how many enterprises are pursuing such a transformation. This chapter provides an initial introduction to Cisco Digital Network Architecture (Cisco DNA) in support of these digitalized business processes.

This chapter explains the following:

- Requirements for Cisco DNA
- Architectural principles
- Overview of the Cisco DNA components

The sections that follow lay the foundation for the Cisco Digital Network Architecture for the remainder of the book, starting off with the requirements that arise for the network as business operations and processes are digitalized. The principles driving the network architecture are also introduced in this chapter. These provide a guideline on what Cisco DNA aims to deliver—an architectural compass. The chapter then introduces the high-level components of Cisco DNA, which include the following:

- Network infrastructure
- Network functions
- Controllers
- Orchestrators
- Analytics platforms
- The cloud

The chapter concludes with a short section on the business outcomes that are supported by Cisco DNA.

Requirements for Cisco DNA

Over the last few years, the demands on network functionality have evolved significantly. Wireless is the dominant access method in enterprise networks, enabling the proliferation of endpoint types. According to the Cisco Visual Networking Index[1], non-PC devices will account for 71 percent of traffic generated by 2020, of which 30 percent is expected to come from smartphones.

Today, many employees can bring their own devices into the workspace, which requires the necessary functionality to authenticate, control, and audit these devices, as well as to shield corporate data from unwanted access. Multimedia communication has also increased dramatically, with video being the standard communication, whether for direct communication or for meetings.

What is more, many businesses are taking advantage of digitalization to transform their processes or disrupt an existing market. Think about the business models of Uber or Airbnb—based on interactive web applications that are easy to use, quick, and efficient. Entire market segments are being disrupted by digitalization!

Digitalized business processes require rapid service deployments to meet the ever-increasing demands and expectations of your customers, partners, and employees. Digitalization allows you to identify market opportunities and offer business services to your customers, and to capitalize on these opportunities by using rapid, agile application development. Cloud computing allows you to deploy such new services without requiring you to stand up your own compute infrastructure. This saves costs and makes application deployments more flexible. You can use cloud computing to collect rapid feedback from customers at a large scale (i.e., electronic surveys and business analytics) and to engage in shortened improvement cycles for the digitalized services to adapt business services according to such feedback. Application delivery is also accelerated by using existing software stacks based on open and agile principles and by drawing additional data from a multitude of information sources.

These digitalized business trends have led to a significant increase in not only overall IP traffic volumes but also network complexity. For example, in a digitalized world you need to manage an increasing number of end devices—especially a rising number of Internet of Things (IoT) devices like refrigerators, sensors, meters, etc. You need to reduce the time to enable new digitalized applications on the network to avoid being disrupted, ensure application service-level agreements (SLA) are met, and provide increasingly granular reports on the performance of networked applications, users, and devices. And to top it all, you need to guarantee security of the network and the integrity of the data to be accessed.

1 Cisco Systems. "Cisco Visual Networking Index: Forecast and Methodology, 2016–2021." Updated Sept. 15, 2017. https://www.cisco.com/c/en/us/solutions/collateral/service-provider/visual-networking-index-vni/complete-white-paper-c11-481360.html.

As a result of these digitalized business trends, the requirements for the enterprise network architecture have shifted significantly in the following four categories:

- Reduction of complexity and costs
- Increase of operational flexibility
- Security and compliance
- Cloud enablement

The remainder of this section explores these requirements in more detail.

Requirements to Reduce Complexity and Costs

As business processes are digitalized, the cost and complexity of the network and the applications are often becoming primary concerns for many enterprise operators. To keep both in check, simplicity and automation are critical requirements for the network.

The simplification of network operations and the deployment of new network transport services have become major requirements to offset the increased complexity caused by the increase in the number of devices, the proliferation of applications, and their increasingly dynamic usage. Simplicity extends throughout the network services lifecycle, from day 0 design and installation of the infrastructure components to day 1 service enablement and day 2 management and operations. Requirements for an evolved enterprise network include the following:

- Fast and error-free service deployment
- Consistent operations across different element types (routers, switches, access points, etc.)
- Automation of bootstrapping and configurations
- Automation of licensing and authentication
- Thorough reporting in case of failures

As the complexity of network operations increases with a growing number of end devices (e.g., from adding more and more IoT devices) and end users, so do operational expenses. As illustrated in Figure 4-1, operational expenses (OPEX) account for two thirds of all networking expenditures. Automation is a primary requirement to limit or even reduce the network OPEX. The requirement for network automation is to support the trends toward programmability, open application programming interfaces (API), standards-based protocols, and simplified network operations. Imagine if network services and operations were fully automated, deployable within minutes regardless of geography, and capable of providing instant feedback to the operator or users to reflect the state of the service, the network, or the application?

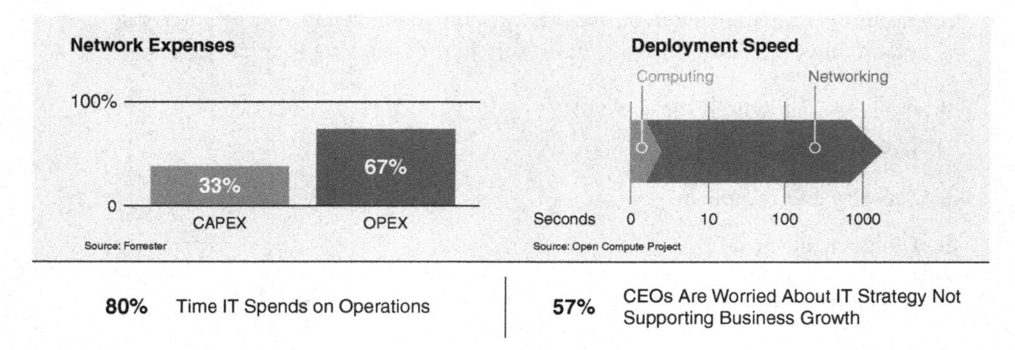

Figure 4-1 *CAPEX and OPEX in Digitalized Business Environments*

Requirement to Increase Operational Flexibility

In a digitalized business environment, the network must support fast innovation cycles. This requirement is especially critical in a digitalized world where market disruptions can happen overnight! The demand for Cisco DNA to support innovation includes the following:

- Flexibility
- A mechanism to provide intelligent feedback
- Application and user awareness

Flexibility

The number and types of endpoints seeking transport services from the enterprise network are expected to continue to grow. A fundamental requirement for an evolved enterprise network architecture, therefore, is to accommodate a wide variety of different endpoints, regardless of how they wish to connect. The same network and security services must be available to wired, wireless, mobile, and IoT hosts alike. Flexibility is also required from the network to support a variety of network and business applications that are increasingly dynamic in nature and no longer tied to a geographic location. As a result, the network must support network services and applications that can run anytime, anywhere.

The requirement for flexibility must be accompanied by speed of deployment. The previously discussed requirement for automation not only aims to reduce operational costs, but also aims to increase the speed of deployment of new functions. The requirement for speed of deployment goes hand in hand with the requirement for the network to be flexible. Both are important to foster business innovation and to ensure that the network supports a dynamic business environment.

Intelligent Feedback Mechanism

Significant improvements in network state feedback mechanisms have also become a main requirement. Instant feedback is already a characteristic of many business processes—think about all the applications on smartphones that report on service requests, from the location of your taxi request, to the status of an online purchase, to information about current traffic conditions. Such interactions also set the bar for network operations!

Traditional mechanisms like Simple Network Management Protocol (SNMP) and screen scraping are reaching limitations in Cisco Digital Network Architecture. SNMP is inefficient from a protocol perspective—it is based on polling rather than being event driven, which adds to the load of the underlying devices. SNMP thus lacks the required scalability and speed for a digitalized network. Operations based on the command-line interface (CLI) and screen scraping, on the other hand, are highly manual and prone to errors. Even seemingly minuscule changes in a vendor's screen output risk breaking custom scripts and wreaking operational havoc. These limitations raise the requirement for more state-of-the-art feedback mechanisms, such as Yet Another Next Generation (YANG) or event-based streaming telemetry. These mechanisms already have made successful advances in data center (DC) architectures.

The network must provide the correct metrics to support business-critical and transport policy decisions. Such data needs to support active troubleshooting, facilitate trending and health monitoring of network elements and applications, and be easily extendable. Analytics capabilities for the enterprise network are required to be at the user, application, or device granularity and, of course, support a myriad of device types that are expected in a network built to also accommodate the Internet of Things.

Application, User, and Device Awareness

In a digitalized world, applications are added in a matter of hours or days, especially if they are hosted in the cloud. The network therefore needs to keep pace with rapid application development cycles and offer the flexibility to introduce transport services for new applications in minimal time. Similarly, new users or devices (especially in a world of "things") can seek access to network services instantaneously.

As your enterprise network becomes more and more an integral part of every aspect of your business processes, it needs to become fully aware of the applications, users, and even devices to properly treat the traffic (e.g., prioritize traffic flows or apply the desired transport policies). The network must be able to identify users, applications, devices, and groups or combinations thereof. Awareness at this level of granularity even applies if encryption is enabled.

Security and Compliance Requirements

The digitalization of business operations also triggers important requirements for security, regulatory compliance, and availability. Malicious attacks on enterprise networks are evolving rapidly. In its Q3 2016 State of the Internet – Security Report, Akamai reports a 138 percent year-on-year increase in total distributed denial-of-service (DDoS) attacks over 100 Gbps in 2016.[2] Traditional approaches based on static signatures are not fulfilling the security requirements of today's businesses.

Security must keep pace with the dynamic application environment and the endpoint proliferation. The ability to segment traffic and users from each other is a challenge for any enterprise network architecture. The network should offer a single segmentation strategy that can be applied to different user groups and applications and be part of the operators' policy framework. The segmentation capabilities of the network should be complementary to the previously mentioned requirements of simplicity, application awareness, and endpoint flexibility. Segmentation, however, has to be augmented by tools that can baseline normal behavior, detect anomalous network states, and react to security breaches in real time while still complying with the security requirements of regulators.

A related requirement here is to also ensure high availability of the network itself. Some of the previously mentioned security breaches aim to deactivate the network in part or whole (e.g., a DDoS attack on DNS). Ensuring the availability of your network services thus continues to be a baseline requirement. Traditional high-availability mechanisms are expected to improve to offer better predictability and determinism. Any failure of a transport service must be graceful, with configurable orders of operations to prioritize applications according to their business priority. Again, the demands for simplicity, application awareness, and endpoint flexibility need to be supported by high availability.

Cloud-Enablement Requirement

The enterprise network needs to have the option to be fully integrated with the cloud to support rapid application development, prototyping, and hosting of digitalized applications. Cloud infrastructures must integrate seamlessly with the rest of the network from both an operations perspective and a transport perspective. Many enterprise network operators no longer wish to distinguish between applications hosted in their own data centers and applications hosted in the cloud. Network operations, analytics, and policy should apply with equal simplicity to either enterprise-hosted or cloud-hosted applications. Digitalized enterprise networks are able to take full advantage of the power of the cloud to speed the delivery of innovation and incremental services augmentation. Further, they are able to use cloud-based analytical analysis of crowd-sourced information (telemetry, utilization statistics, etc.) to facilitate rapid enhancement development and service augmentation.

Architectural Principles

All successful network architectures are based on sound principles that guide their logic and structure. For example, in the early 2000s, Cisco created the Architecture for Voice, Video, and Integrated Data (AVVID) to offer an enterprise-wide, open, and

---

2 https://content.akamai.com/PG7470-Q3-2016-SOTI-Security-Report.html?utm_source=GoogleSearch&gclid=CM7zsunN7NACFYSFswodxxwERw

standards-based architecture. More recently, the Cisco SAFE architecture provides a framework supported by Cisco Validated Designs (CVD) for end-to-end security across places in the network (PIN).[3]

Structured network architectures thus provide a compass to reach the "north star." A structured target architecture allows a planned evolution of the existing network architecture toward the north star, possibly in several controlled enhancement steps. The architectural principles in Cisco DNA are as follows:

- Openness
- Extensibility
- Programmability
- Policy-based networking
- Security
- Software driven
- Cloud integrated

Openness

Cisco DNA–based infrastructure is open by design. *Openness* in this context is defined as enabling customers and partners to guide and influence the operation of the network through the following:

- Allowing enterprise operators to integrate with existing or third-party operations support systems (OSS) for open management. An example of open management is the Cisco DNA controller, which enables you to develop custom applications to drive the operation of a Cisco DNA-based network.
- Allowing Cisco and third-party virtualized network functions (VNF), such as virtualized firewalls, virtualized deep packet inspection (DPI), or virtualized intrusion detection and intrusion prevention systems (IDS/IPS), to be integrated into the Cisco DNA architecture (open functionality).
- Relying on standards-based protocols for the operation of the fabrics and the underlay network, thus allowing third-party network elements or hosting servers to co-exist alongside Cisco products (open interoperability).
- Providing open and standards-based APIs so that the network elements can be controlled in a programmatic manner (open programmability).

3 Cisco SAFE Reference Guide, https://www.cisco.com/c/en/us/td/docs/solutions/Enterprise/Security/SAFE_RG/SAFE_rg/chap1.html.

Extensibility

Extensibility is another principle guiding Cisco DNA. It ensures that you can evolve a Cisco DNA network as technology progresses, or as your business requirements demand. The extensibility of Cisco DNA implies that Cisco as a vendor, an enterprise's business partners, or even you as a network operator can add functionality to the network. Such additions may be at the network control layer, for example, by developing applications that can be integrated with the network controllers. Alternatively, the extensibility may be at the infrastructure layer, via network elements that can be augmented in their functionality through a simple software upgrade, instead of mandating a forklift upgrade of hardware network elements just to support a new protocol header! The principal of extensibility guiding Cisco DNA also means that third-party software (even virtualized network functions) can become part of the architecture. In this case, extensibility is also tied to the principle of openness, previously introduced.

Programmability

Programmability is at the heart of Cisco DNA. It allows the network to be fully automated across all of its components, ready for machine-to-machine interactions. Gone are the days of skilled experts having to know all the hardware and software details about a particular network element, driving functionality into the network by logging into devices and configuring these using intricate CLI commands. Such practices have become major cost factors for network operators, being error-prone and slow. Allowing for disparate network elements adds complexity to the network.

Network automation is essential not only to reduce OPEX but also to increase the speed at which new network, business, or security services are introduced. Imagine a network where a new transport segment can be deployed for guest access at the click of a GUI button, triggering not only the instantiation of the required network segment, but also the associated access policies, firewall functions, or other functions you may wish to associate with this user group in your network. Programmability enables this capability to deploy within minutes, rather than weeks or months as is traditionally the case. Furthermore, compared to a more manually intensive deployment method, programmability, especially via a centralized Cisco DNA controller, is typically more accurate, less error-prone, and more tightly aligned to best practices for network deployment, operation, and use.

Chapter 14, "Cisco DNA Automation," introduces the components of the Cisco DNA controllers and orchestrators as key elements to facilitate this automation. Triggered by the orchestration applications, new digital services are deployed by the controller onto the relevant network elements at the right time. The controller offers a network abstraction layer to arbitrate the specifics of various network elements in this automation and toward the orchestration and analytics engines. Consistent, machine-based interfaces are being developed as an integral part of Cisco DNA to enhance automation techniques. These interfaces will also be used by Cisco DNA controllers to provide scale beyond what is available today. Speed and agility are critical requirements for service rollout and network operations, and a controller-based system helps to facilitate this. Network functions can also be instantiated by the controller.

Policy-based Networking

Policy-based networking is an important principle that is facilitated by the programmability just described. You have likely used policies in your network many times, configuring access control lists (ACL) to determine who can gain access to the network, to help classify traffic flows into the right quality of service (QoS) classes, or even to assist in Layer 4 firewall rules. But have these policies always been aligned with your business objectives, especially as they evolve over time? And are existing policy mechanisms scalable, easy to use and troubleshoot? There are plenty of anecdotes about ever-growing ACLs—operators are reluctant to remove entries at the risk of breaking existing behavior. And what is more, such policies are tightly coupled with the underlying segmentation/VLAN structure, and thus tied to the network topology.

In Cisco DNA, a key principle is to ensure that the business goals align with the services delivered by the network—services that are tied to users, applications, and devices, not topology. In other words, the network and the business are always fully coordinated to support the business objectives.

The Cisco DNA controller is vital to drive the *policies* associated with digitalized services consistently throughout the network infrastructure. It translates the business intent for the digital services into actionable and verifiable network policies at the user, application, or device level. Such business intent of a digital service may result in multiple network policies that need to be instantiated and monitored to deliver a service. The Cisco DNA controller, therefore, implements policy in any part of the network that a service instance reaches, such as the cloud or the campus, WAN, or data center domains, for all variants of policies, such as those governing access, transport, or path optimization.

Security

Security is another fundamental principle behind Cisco DNA. In a world of digitalized business processes and interactions between employees, customers, and partners, the communication channels need to be absolutely secure. Any security breaches in such an environment can challenge the very existence of your business.

In Cisco DNA, security functionality and components are pervasive throughout the infrastructure. As the architecture components are described in detail in later chapters, you will find that every building block considers the security implications of the functionality it provides for the architecture and includes the following:

- Securing all the communications/API calls that are used to integrate the building blocks into a coherent architecture. All programmatic interactions between components, both data plane and control plane, are authenticated and authorized. Extensive logs for authentication and authorizations need to be kept for logging and compliance.

- Deploying security services such as firewalls, intrusion prevention, or intrusion detection if and where needed—either using a physical appliance or using a virtualized network function.
- Offering secure and hardened infrastructure in the hardware-based network elements. Security hardening of the network needs to extend to the Cisco DNA network controller. When deployed as an appliance, the Cisco DNA Automation and Assurance capabilities run on a security-hardened server. Applications that run as part of the network control plane also need to be authenticated and properly authorized.
- Leveraging the Cisco DNA network infrastructure to support security detection by enhancing its sensor and security enforcement functions. Using the network as a sensor/enforcer can provide additional security capabilities that can significantly enhance the overall safety of the network. The typically highly distributed nature of an enterprise network can ensure that data can be collected anywhere in the network, and that attacks are mitigated close to their source.
- Automating the devices in the network based on a controller. This also adds to heightened security. Mistyped configuration commands are eliminated when network elements are provisioned from the controller. Furthermore, remnants of stale configurations are exposed to the controller and can thus be easily eliminated as security risks.

Software Driven

The principle of Cisco DNA being software driven is important to complement the extensibility, programmability, and openness of the architecture. New functionality in software can be developed in a fraction of time as compared to hardware—with new agile development methodologies often in months, weeks, or even days. An architecture that is software driven can thus react much quicker to changing business requirements. In Cisco DNA, this allows the alignment of the network and the business goals to always be in lockstep.

The majority of Cisco DNA functions are driven by software. Functions to forward and manipulate the IP traffic flows can be provided in a virtual form factor, allowing for a flexible separation of the packet-processing software from the underlying hardware, if desired. Control of the network elements has traditionally been a software-driven process, but is now being elevated in importance by enhancing this control plane with a centralized controller function that can run anywhere in your network (e.g., in your data center, in a virtual private cloud [VPC]). Because such a centralized control point of the network elements is responsible for the entire network infrastructure, additional intelligent algorithms can be developed to optimize the operation of the network. Such algorithms may even replace complex protocol interactions between the network elements and therefore contribute to the simplification of network operations. For example, a traffic-engineered path for a particular endpoint group can be algorithmically determined by software based on the full view of the network state. This can augment or replace protocol interactions to exchange state between network elements and the execution of a distributed traffic engineering algorithm.

Software also plays an increasing role in collecting telemetry data from the network, processing it, and presenting it to network operators or business applications in the right format at the right time. Software-driven functionality and network telemetry become particularly impactful with programmable application-specific integrated circuits (ASIC, specialized and sophisticated chipsets) when these are designed to scale and accelerate software-driven operations.

Cloud Integrated

Ensuring that Cisco DNA is fully cloud integrated is the last of the guiding design principles. Cloud computing in today's world already plays a fundamental role in changing the economics of networking. Using a cloud provider to host applications avoids capital costs to build up data center infrastructure and operational costs to run it. Using the cloud for management allows for a more ubiquitous access to the network for you as an operator. And finally, the cloud can also be used as a source of information by leveraging or connecting to applications that are outside your businesses operational responsibility—publicly available data such as traffic patterns, weather forecasts, population statistics, timetables, etc. can often be used to augment digitalized business processes.

In Cisco DNA different cloud models are fully integrated, including private clouds, virtual private clouds, hybrid clouds, and public cloud environments. This integration is designed both at the transport layer and the control layer of the network. At the transport layer, the various cloud environments can be fused into the enterprise network seamlessly by use of tunneling techniques. For example, a virtual IPsec gateway can be instantiated in a VPC and connected to the enterprise-operated fabric by means of an IPsec tunnel. Configuring the virtual router with similar policies and functions as the enterprise-operated branch environments then makes the VPC behave like other branches that are part of the network infrastructure. At the control layer, management and orchestration tools can be used to operate the network. Analytics and telemetry engines accessing and storing information in the cloud are also part of the cloud enablement aspect of Cisco DNA. By making the cloud an integral part of the enterprise network, Cisco DNA is addressing the requirement for cloud enablement to drive rapid application prototyping, fast application deployment, and continuous feedback loops to speed digitalized business processes.

Conflicting Principles?

The principles already discussed are guiding the architectural decisions behind Cisco DNA. They are the "compass" to evaluate architectural design alternatives. In some cases, these principles may seem to counter each other. For example, the desire for "openness" may imply full support of third-party hardware components in the architecture in the extreme case. This may lead to a significant increase in the systems integration effort, and thus impact speed and flexibility. The Cisco DNA architecture balances such conflicts based on feedback from operators and network architects, with an overarching goal to provide a cohesive, flexible, and powerful solution.

Overview of the Cisco DNA Components

Now that the higher-level architectural principles behind Cisco Digital Network Architecture are clear, this section provides an overview of the main architectural components: the Cisco DNA infrastructure, automation, analytics, and cloud integration. This section not only provides a high-level overview of these components, but also offers clear definitions of the main terms for any concepts that are used in the remainder of the book. Chapter 5, "The Cisco Digital Network Architecture Blueprint," elaborates on these building blocks and their functionality to described the architectural blueprint behind Cisco DNA.

The main tenets of Cisco DNA are shown in Figure 4-2, which illustrates how the principles of openness, extensibility, programmability, software driven, policy-based networking, security, and cloud integration (all discussed in the previous section) drive the overall architecture. Figure 4-2 also shows that the main components of Cisco DNA—infrastructure, automation, analytics platform, and cloud integration—collaborate as a system to deliver the requirements (outlined in the earlier section "Requirements for Cisco DNA") of reducing complexity and costs, increasing the operational flexibility, and enhancing security and compliance.

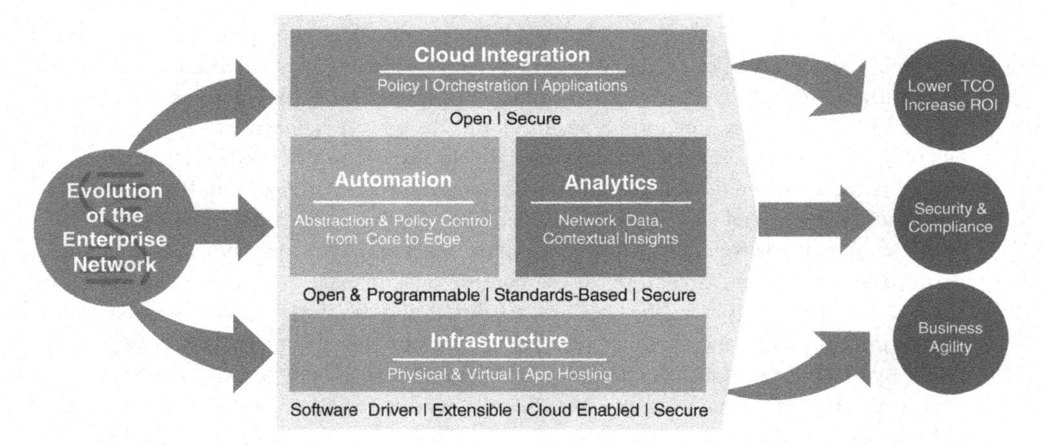

Figure 4-2 *Cisco DNA Concepts and Main Components*

Infrastructure

The infrastructure component in Cisco DNA represents all those functions that participate in carrying network traffic between users, devices, and applications. This building block corresponds to the traditional data plane and control plane functions needed to transport traffic across the network to connect users, applications, and devices with each other. Cisco DNA still relies on the proven distributed forwarding techniques that are successfully deployed in every network today! However, in a Cisco DNA infrastructure, these techniques also include significant enhancements that help to directly address and provide simplicity, security, and the shift toward policy-based networking.

The infrastructure component is made up of both hardware and virtualized network elements. Hardware-based network elements are enhanced in functionality to accommodate the Cisco DNA principles of software driven, programmability, and security. Network elements in Cisco DNA leverage programmable ASICs to this end. For example, transport protocol developments or packet formats such as the recent rise of the virtual extensible local area network (VxLAN) may not require the re-spin of ASICs, triggering a forklift upgrade of the installed base when you wish to introduce this technology into the network. While ASICs are continuing to improve in speed and functionality, the hardware-based network elements can also be uplifted by a software upgrade in Cisco DNA, extending the lifecycle of the installed base. Hardware-based network elements in Cisco DNA also allow high-bandwidth communication at speeds up to 100 Gbps and beyond.

VNFs are added to the functional components of the Cisco DNA infrastructure. They are integral to address the Cisco DNA principles of openness, software driven, programmability, and security. VNFs can perform infrastructure forwarding functions. For example, the Cisco Cloud Services Router (CSR) 1000V Series offers the same functionality as a hardware-based IOS XE router (the Cisco ISR 4000 Series or the Cisco ASR 1000 Series routers), but in a software-virtualized form factor. This provides both operational and functional consistency between the physical and virtual network infrastructures—significantly enhancing simplicity and operational consistency. Alternatively, Layer 4–Layer 7 functions such as firewalls, DPI, IPS/IDS, etc. can also be accommodated in Cisco DNA in a virtual form factor if and where desired. Such functions can even be provided by yourself or third-party vendors—for example, troubleshooting, monitoring tools, or even network functions from other vendors that have been certified in your organization.

The inclusion of VNFs as infrastructure components directly addresses the requirement of deploying functionality in the network with speed and agility, and keeps the network aligned with the business objectives.

Note that in Cisco DNA, applications can also be hosted within the infrastructure. In some situations, you may wish to deploy your own application workloads as a network operator (for instance, traffic generators, troubleshooting or monitoring tools, or even print servers or other business support functions). Such application workload could run efficiently in a container so as not to require an additional layer of operating system (which is the case in a virtual machine–based deployment). Cisco DNA fully recognizes the need to offer this level of flexibility.

Cisco DNA Infrastructure Domains

Traditionally, the enterprise infrastructure is composed of a campus, data center, and WAN/branch domains that connect users and devices to applications, along with their respective control functions. In Cisco DNA, while still helpful from a conceptual architecture perspective, the demarcations of these domains are less strict. But the concept of "domains" can be more flexible in Cisco DNA and be extended to "controller domains." The traditional separation of a network into campus, WAN/branch, and data center was partly motivated by different requirements, technologies, and organizational structures that characterized the domains. For example, the WAN domain traditionally had to contend with a variety of WAN technologies (serial, frame relay, ATM, etc.), secure connectivity to the Internet, provide access to mobile or nomadic users, and handle bandwidth-limited links to connect sites that are geographically dispersed. The campus's focus was on providing access ports to users and devices, and aggregating as many of these as possible efficiently—while dealing increasingly with user and device mobility, an increasing proliferation of device types, and bandwidth demands. Similarly, the DC architectures of the past were driven by connecting vast amounts of servers hosting applications to the network. In Cisco DNA however, a domain can also be created for all network elements in Campus and WAN, under the governance of a single controller instance.

Because these different network domains serve distinctly different needs, these domains are also present within a Cisco DNA network infrastructure. The pertinent domains in Cisco DNA are likely to remain the campus, the data center, the cloud, and the WAN (which includes WAN aggregation and branches), as illustrated in Figure 4-3. In the campus, multiple endpoints connect to the network using either wired or wireless access. The campus may also provide connectivity to the data center or WAN domains, helping endpoints to reach applications residing in the data center or to reach hosts located in branches, respectively. The WAN domain typically consists of many branches that are aggregated across an enterprise-managed or service provider–managed WAN into multiple WAN aggregation sites. The WAN aggregation sites connect into the campus domain. The data center domain provides the infrastructure to connect servers hosting enterprise applications to the network in the most efficient and flexible manner possible.

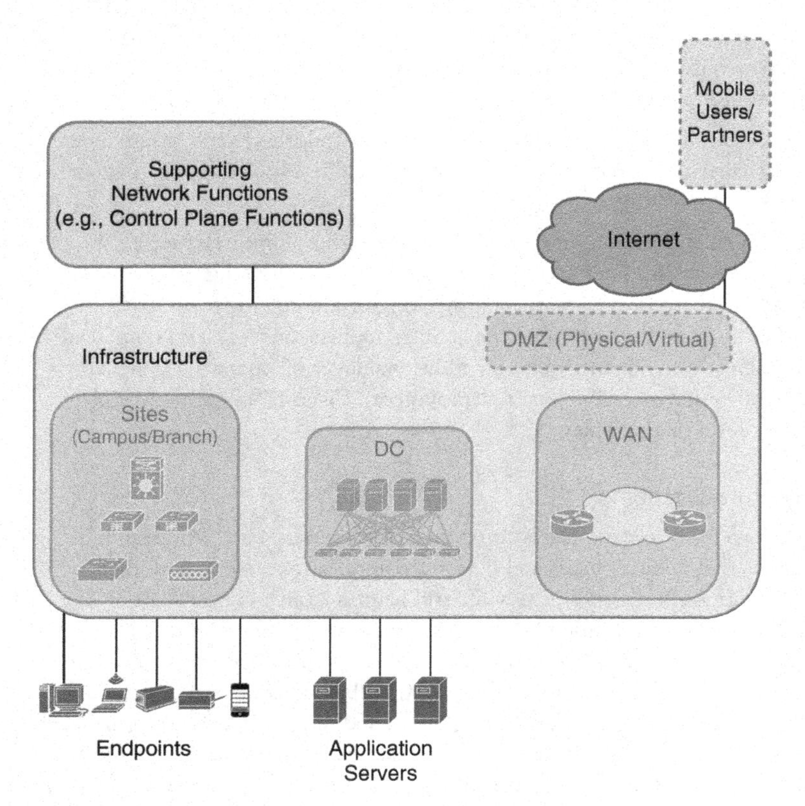

Figure 4-3 *Cisco DNA Infrastructure and Domains*

The forwarding infrastructure in Cisco DNA may be accompanied by additional functions that deserve calling out separately. For example, some control plane functions such as LISP Map-Servers/Map-Resolvers (MS/MR) may run in virtual machines (VM) to assist in determining the forwarding path. Other examples of such auxiliary functions are DNS servers or DHCP servers. Because these are often essential for the successful operation of the Cisco DNA infrastructure, they are called out separately in Figure 4-3.

Extending the Concept of Network Fabrics in Cisco DNA

The transport infrastructure in Cisco DNA is provided by the concept of an enterprise IP fabric. The Cisco DNA fabric refers to the infrastructure components in Cisco DNA, which include the following:

- A programmable underlay network consisting of both physical and virtual devices
- A logical overlay topology
- A controller and policy

The Cisco DNA fabric has the following characteristics:

- An any-to-any network connects forwarding functions based on an IP-based underlay infrastructure.
- Services can be deployed with flexibility to users, applications, or devices based on programmable overlays.
- Policy enforcement is primarily at the user or application level at the edge of the enterprise network.
- Localized encapsulation allows hosts and applications to connect to the network using a variety of Layer 2 protocols (i.e., different Ethernet encapsulation types).
- Location-independent forwarding helps to enable hosts and applications to move and decouples the IP address of the host or application from the underlying network infrastructure.
- Controller-based management simplifies network operations, in particular to make them network-wide instead of individual network-element based.
- High availability assures resilience of the network against failure of its network elements or software functions.
- Built-in infrastructure security assists in meeting the security and compliance requirements of Cisco DNA.

The data plane in the fabric is predominantly hardware based to offer high-speed transport at scale. Assuring low-latency packet transport, integrated security services, and/or QoS at high speeds typically requires sophisticated ASICs to be deployed in the network elements, such as Cisco Unified Access Data Plane or Cisco QuantumFlow Processor (discussed in more detail in Chapter 7, "Hardware Innovations"). Providing security in the fabric through encryption or imposition of security group tags is an important requirement driving the need for hardware support in Cisco DNA network elements. Furthermore, these ASICs are fully programmable in the Cisco DNA fabric, allowing for new software-based capabilities to be introduced into the network through a simple software upgrade. Finally, the requirement for a high volume of telemetry data to be collected and delivered to the analytics engine is also a reason for the use of high-speed ASICs in the fabric.

Virtualization

Virtualization plays another key role in the Cisco DNA infrastructure because it is a crucial mechanism to deploy services fast and with minimal dependencies on the underlying hardware infrastructure. The virtualization architecture that is part of Cisco DNA can be broken down into two main components:

- Transport virtualization (segmentation)
- Network function virtualization

The logical separation of traffic by means of VLANs or virtual routing and forwarding (VRF) is already a standard tool in enterprise network architectures. The network elements comprising the enterprise fabric are fully capable of logical separation of traffic at both Layer 2 and Layer 3. These concepts carry forward to Cisco DNA, but gain even more importance to ensure that services are associated with the right segmentation policies within the network. Recall that a service connects endpoints or endpoint groups; therefore, the service may be not only application aware but also user (identity) aware. The logical segmentation of groups of users and applications, then, is an essential component of the enterprise fabrics overlay architecture, augmenting (rather than replacing) the traditional concepts of VLANs and VRF.

Network function virtualization (NFV) is part of the architecture that can enable network functions to run anywhere in the network infrastructure based on the availability of x86-based compute resources. The virtualization of network functions that manipulate the IP traffic flows according to the policies is essential in Cisco DNA to provide a completely virtualized environment. Transport virtualization is extended in Cisco DNA by allowing these network functions to run in virtual machines or containers (for instance, LXC or Docker) on any available x86-based compute resources on the operator's policies. Network elements increasingly offer x86-based compute resources for this purpose, also allowing them to host specialized applications in a Cisco DNA network deployment. In cases where these resources are insufficient, dedicated x86-based servers may be co-located throughout the Cisco DNA infrastructure, as illustrated in Figure 4-4. The operating systems of the network elements in Cisco DNA are enhanced to support this virtualization, providing the ability to spin up or tear down network functions within minutes, to monitor their status, and to redeploy, restart, or even support their move from one location or server to the next.

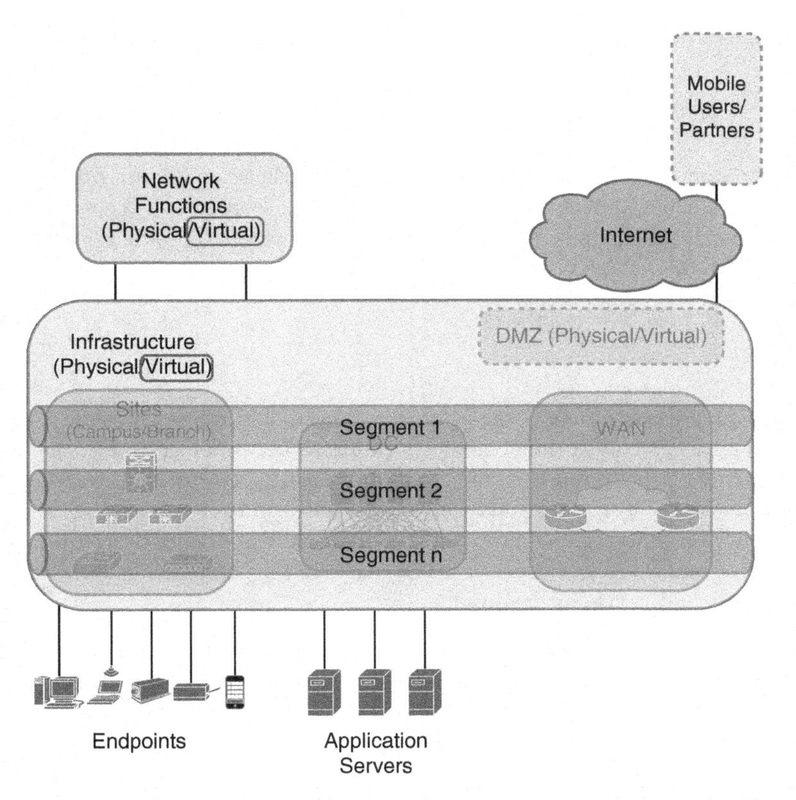

Figure 4-4 *Transport and Network Function Virtualization in Cisco DNA*

In this way, NFV allows for novel architectural approaches where the functions applicable to a service flow can be distributed in the infrastructure based on optimal placement policies. The functions no longer are tied to physical network elements, nor are they required to be executed in a single process on a network element.

The concept of chaining a service flow through multiple virtualized network functions based on policy is thus also supported by the Cisco DNA architecture. Virtualization allows for networking functions to be provisioned at a more granular level—even at the user, application, or device granularity, if desired—and to place those most optimally in the network: hosted within a network element, hosted in distributed x86-based resources, or centralized in the data center or the cloud. Service chaining helps to ensure that the right sequence of executing these functions is maintained while forcing a traffic flow through a path that "hits" each of the required functions. Traditionally architected using routing and VLANs, this paradigm is now enhanced using Service Function Chaining (SFC) based on a network services header (NSH). SFC not only decouples the chaining from the underlying topology constructs. It also allows for metadata to be passed between chained functions, such as the application type that a packet belongs to. For example, a flow may be passed through a DPI function identifying its application, and the application type can then be communicated to downstream functions that may leverage this information in processing the packet.

Note that virtualization in Cisco DNA is seamless between the different fabric domains. A virtualized network function such as DPI or a firewall may be deployed in a VM on a host connected to the campus, or it may be deployed in a VPC. The seamless extension of the enterprise fabric architecture into the cloud by means of encrypted tunnels carries forward to VNFs and gives the operator the flexibility to decide where to best instantiate a network function. Such flexibility is lacking in today's traditional enterprise network operations due to management complexity.

Policy

The drive toward policy is arguably one of the most important directional shifts that Cisco DNA brings to enterprise networking. In many traditional networks, network operations is not in lockstep with the business requirements. In an agile software application world, developing a new application might take only a few days—and yet onboarding the application onto the network may take months. Such discrepancies are the motivation for a shift toward policy and Cisco DNA services. The goal is to fully align the business objectives with network operations—at any point in time.

Policy is inherently tied to a Cisco DNA service, which is defined as any service that is offered to users, devices, and applications, consisting of transport in association with policies. The transport services define *how traffic is forwarded* through the network, with support of network functions. The policies define *how traffic is treated* by the network.

Policies in Cisco DNA are attributes of the service the network delivers to users, applications, or devices. Policy categories in Cisco DNA include the following:

- **Security:** Admission control, segmentation, and encryption
- **Traffic handling:** Quality of service, traffic engineering, and performance routing
- **Reporting:** Logging, accounting, and inspection

Note that the definition of policy in Cisco DNA is a lot more comprehensive, extending beyond simple security policies such as access control or ACLs. It encompasses all the characteristics of a service that is delivered to the users of the network to connect these or their devices to the applications: security policies, traffic handling policies, or reporting policies.

The focus on policy in Cisco DNA extends across all the building blocks of the architecture, not restricted to the infrastructure component alone. The role of the infrastructure component in delivering policy is to *instantiate* and *enforce* policy. Existing policy constructs such as ACLs are examples of relevant functions that carry forward from traditional networking. But these are also extended to include any mechanism or function that is required to implement the policy. For example, a virtualized firewall or a WAN optimization appliance becomes an instrument in Cisco DNA of policy—each are deployed to deliver on the policy aspects of a Cisco DNA service, and this association always couples the function to the services that rely on it.

For example, an extranet partner service in Cisco DNA specifies that selected partners (by policy) can access all those applications in your enterprise that are designated for partners, along with traffic treatment functionality such as "no security," "always log transactions," or that the extranet partners always have to go through a strict firewall function to enter your enterprise's network.

Automation

As shown earlier in Figure 4-2, automation is another main component of Cisco DNA. Automation helps deliver all the design principles previously identified, in particular the support for programmability, openness, and extensibility.

Automation is defined as the ability to externally manipulate network elements within a domain. It is a base capability provided via a controller in Cisco DNA.

This definition highlights the ability of a Cisco DNA-based network to be fully programmable—i.e., fully able to be manipulated by external elements such as a controller, using open APIs. The automation building block is broken down into two further subcomponents: controller and orchestrator. These are explored in detail next.

Controllers

The enterprise IP fabric in Cisco DNA is governed by a controller that oversees the configurations and operations of its network elements. As such, the controller has a domain-wide view of the state and the operations of the associated network elements. The Cisco DNA controller is responsible for the configuration of the network fabrics—the underlay communication and overlay services architectures. It configures the user- or application-visible network services (for example, applying a service policy to a particular IP flow, or applying one or more Layer 4–7 service functions to a user–application communication pattern). Most importantly, the controller is the element in the architecture to instantiate policy.

The controller is a mandatory component in Cisco DNA that defines and co-ordinates the instantiation of Cisco DNA services for a single domain. The principal function of a controller is to offer a layer where the network is viewed as a system and where network decisions can be made centrally, in particular to align the business intent. It configures the network elements using a set of well-defined south-bound interfaces, thus abstracting the network infrastructure and automating policy. The controller may also interact directly with applications via north-bound APIs, for example, Cisco Unified Communications Manager (CUCM). The controller may also communicate directly with the analytics engine to automate recommended data-driven actions.

As noted, a focus on policy and intent is one of the key architectural shifts supported by Cisco DNA. Recall that each service offered by Cisco DNA implements a business intent and is instantiated by a transport path with the associated policies.

The role of the controller to deliver policy-based services is to enable the actuation of policy. The underlying model in Cisco DNA is that policy can be expressed in the abstract with a terminology or syntax to align the network easily with the business intent (e.g., connecting a user group to a business-relevant application group with a high level of security). The Cisco DNA controller then possesses the intelligence to "translate" an abstract expression of policy into actual device configurations. This is performed in the controller with the assistance of a policy engine and associated application(s). The abstracted policy expressions are associated with concrete policies for the network elements that are under the controller's span of governance. The controller then instantiates the policy into the network elements (i.e., pushes the right device configurations). The network elements then execute the actual policies (i.e., they enforce the policies).

The benefits of the Cisco DNA controller's policy functionality can be illustrated by example of application-aware services. The network operator may specify in the policy application that a particular service applies only on a per-application basis. The controller must then translate this service policy into access policies to be applied at the policy enforcement points (PEP)—explicit points in the network where the policies are instantiated through device configuration. The PEPs ensure that the right applications are filtered out as users, applications, or devices access the network.

Such a filter may be based on standard DPI techniques, such as Cisco Application Visibility and Control (AVC). Alternatively, advanced mechanisms such as DNS as Authoritative Source (DNS-AS) can be deployed to create such filters. DNS-AS helps classify applications with the help of the DNS server, where the application type can be specified as part of the DNS record and returned to the requestor in the DNS response. The controller may also need to deploy policies between domains or within a particular fabric domain to effect the right treatment for the service, such as mapping the service to a QoS transport class. The domain-wide view of the controller, therefore, helps to instantiate the right policies in the right places of the network, and ultimately delivers on policy-based service delivery. Figure 4-5 depicts the main functionality of the controller: taking intent as an input from the orchestrator (more details following on this), computing the right policies and service constructs, and pushing those into the Cisco DNA fabric and NFV components using APIs.

Programmability is a critical supporting aspect of the Cisco DNA controller. Configuration of the underlay network, the overlay architecture, or even specific services is handled by a south-bound interface between the controller and the network elements and functions. This south-bound interface may rely on the CLI, or other standards-based mechanisms such as NETCONF interfaces, YANG data models, Representational State Transfer (REST), or REST Configuration Protocol (RESTCONF).

Supporting standards-based southbound interfaces contributes to the openness of Cisco DNA and also allows third-party vendors to participate in the network infrastructure, while supporting CLI lends to the ability for a controller to more readily be introduced into a brownfield environment in which not all of the network gear may yet support more advanced machine-to-machine protocols such as NETCONF/YANG. Toward the orchestration layer, the controller provides a level of network abstraction by exposing northbound APIs, which again may be standards based. The controller can enable a simplified operation of the domain fabric, and supports rapid and elastic provisioning of network services. The programmability aspect of the Cisco DNA controller is vital to delivering on the automation, as well as fast and flexible configuration, of Cisco DNA.

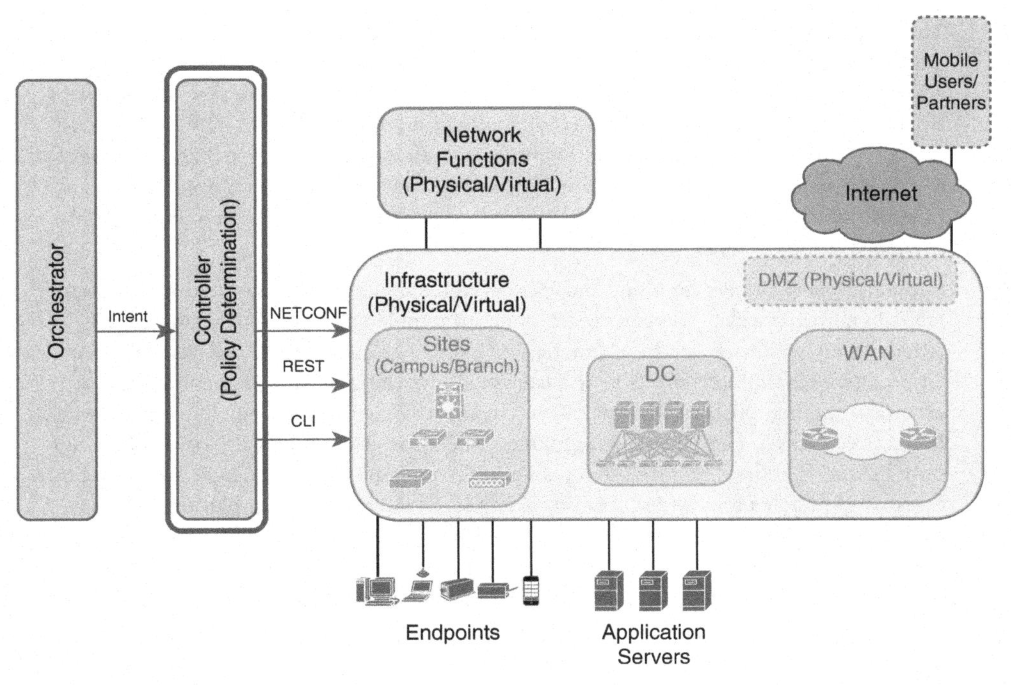

Figure 4-5 *Cisco DNA Controllers (Network Abstraction and Policy Determination)*

Orchestrators

The orchestrator in Cisco DNA plays the critical role of allowing the network operator to specify Cisco DNA services that cross multiple domains. Take for example the likely case of a service connecting applications in a data center to users and devices that are distributed throughout a global WAN with many campuses and branch locations. The different domains may be governed in this case by multiple controllers for administrative or scalability reasons. For example, one controller may be handling the data center (DC) environment, and another controller may be responsible for the campus and WAN. Such flexibility ensures that Cisco DNA can align with your organizational structures, and also allow for technology domain-specific controller functions to be leveraged. In the data center, the controller may focus on high availability and bandwidth, whereas in the campus the controller may focus on increased functionality to handle both wired and wireless clients consistently and with strong authentication. In such multidomain cases, a functional instance to coordinate services across domains and controllers is needed. This is the principle function delivered by the orchestrator.

The orchestrator is defined as an optional component that, if present, defines and coordinates the instantiation of the Cisco DNA services across different domains.

The orchestrator thus enhances the concept of network abstraction offered by the controller, abstracting from the details of network elements or virtualized network functions and providing the focus on the services. You as an operator can focus on the specification of the service details from the user, application, or device point of view, without having to know all the details of individual network elements or virtualized network functions. The orchestrator then interfaces to the controllers using standard APIs to instantiate the specified services at the right time in the right network element in the right sequence of operations.

Stipulating network services and their associated characteristics can be done in Cisco DNA in multiple ways. You can create standard templates for services using a GUI. Alternatively, a service can be characterized using a graphical tool. For example, the Cisco DNA branch orchestration application allows the customized specification of enterprise branch profiles. A network extension service (adding a new branch to extend the network reach) can be defined graphically, empowering you as the operator to not only list the functions required in a particular branch, but also influence their order and associated policies for the service. For example, a canvas-based templating approach allows you to drag an icon representing an x86-based host onto a work area, then graphically add the required virtualized network functions, interconnect them, and specify any parameters that may have to be provided for a particular instance of the template.

Model-based approaches to service declarations are also part of the orchestration architecture in Cisco DNA for those operators who seek further abstraction. Figure 4-6 shows the relationships between the Cisco DNA orchestrator and the controller(s).

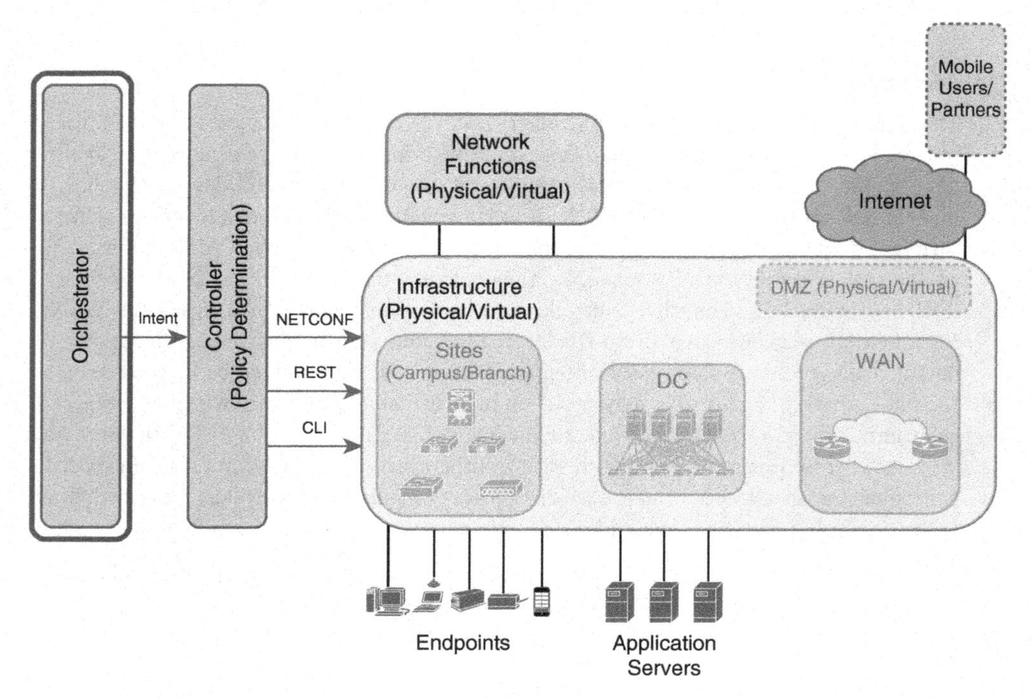

Figure 4-6 *Cisco DNA Orchestration (Cisco DNA Service Definition Across Domains)*

Analytics Platform

The third main component of Cisco DNA is the analytics platform (refer to Figure 4-2). Imagine a network where the operational state is continuously available, provided from throughout the network, and presented in a simple and graphical manner, without having to write custom scripts that screen-scrape outputs from multiple devices with different software versions deriving operational state with home-grown applications. The analytics engine is another element that significantly enhances the overall functionality of the enterprise network and supports the Cisco DNA principles of openness, policy based, security, and software based.

Analytics is defined as the process of correlating data and extracting meaning so as to identify anomalies, derive insights, and enable data-driven decisions.

The analytics platform is essential to provide feedback mechanisms—collecting data on an ongoing basis to offer continuous and relevant information about the operational state of the network. Such states can be harvested to optimize the network and security services (delivered to end users and applications). Alternatively, the states and data can be fed back to digitalized business applications, supporting the dynamic environment that these applications require, and fostering the cycle of continuous application development and improvement.

Analytics support is based on the following subcomponents:

- Data collection
- Data reporting (telemetry)
- Data analysis
- Feedback and control

Data Collection

The Cisco DNA network elements are enhanced to collect data about all aspects of the network, including the state of the network elements and the traffic flows pertaining to the services offered by the network. This data collection is not just restricted to the transport network elements (routers, switches, access points, etc.). It also extends to supporting network functions such as AAA servers and virtualized or physical Layer 4–Layer 7 functions. Network elements and virtual network functions in Cisco DNA are inherently designed to collect a vast amount of data. As an example, the network elements and functions provide statistics on user groups, in addition to the standard fields on source and destination IP addresses and ports; protocol types, bytes, or packets sent; or TCP flags. Furthermore, firewalls such as the Cisco Adaptive Security Appliance (ASA), authentication servers such as the Cisco Identity Services Engine (ISE), and URL filtering functions collect data at similar granularity. The continuous collection of such data always includes timestamps, allowing time-series analysis of all events. Data collection in Cisco DNA even extends to end-user and device information. Any telemetry data collected from the network or supporting network functions can be correlated with end-user or device identities to provide comprehensive reporting.

Data Reporting

The data reporting mechanisms (telemetry) in Cisco DNA allow for the collected data to be reported to a collector. *Telemetry* in Cisco DNA is defined as the export of instrumentation data to an analytics engine for further analysis.

This reporting mechanism leverages existing, well-established mechanisms such as SNMP, AAA, or Flexible NetFlow, but also extends now to REST or NETCONF. The telemetry in Cisco DNA supports an any-to-any model: data can be exported from any network element or function using multiple telemetry mechanisms, and to multiple collectors. Figure 4-7 shows a high-level representation of the Cisco DNA analytics components.

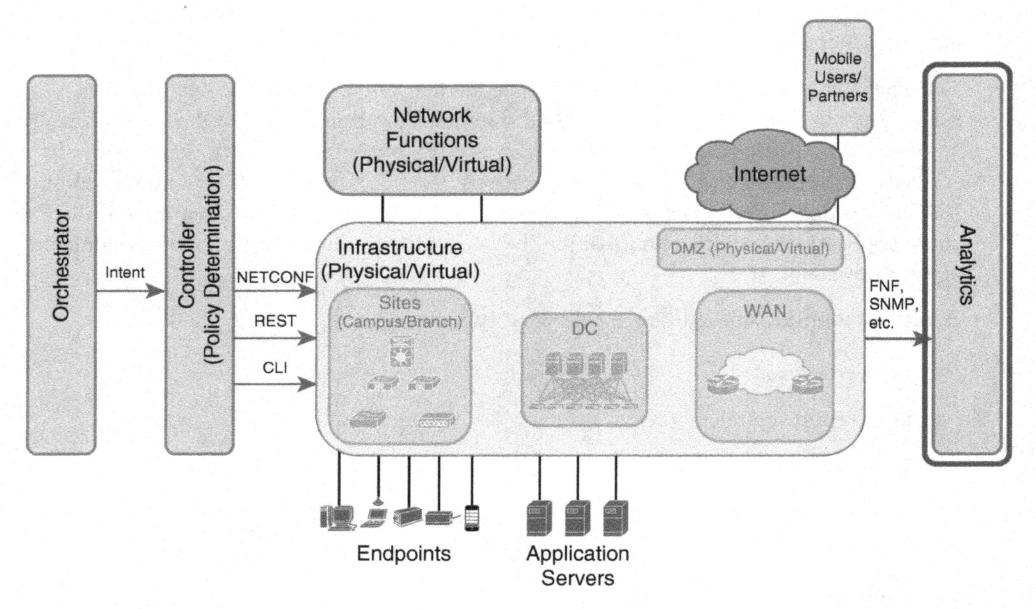

Figure 4-7 *Cisco DNA Analytics (Telemetry, Data collection, Analysis, and Reporting)*

Cisco DNA Analysis

Cisco DNA analytics engines normalize, analyze, and correlate the data that is collected and reported via telemetry. Data can be in different formats and thus may need to be normalized to the right timestamps and data formats to be automatically interpreted. Analysis of the data can come in multiple forms, and typically needs to consider the consumer of the data. An application developer wishing to leverage information about the network may be interested in a different data set than the data set a network operator responsible for hardware would be interested in. Consequently, multiple analytics engines may potentially co-exist to analyze the right data for the right consumer. In some cases data can even be correlated from different sources to draw meaningful inferences. For example, any public information on weather could be pulled into an analytics engine to enhance the capabilities for Cisco DNA services.

The analytics capabilities of Cisco DNA are illustrated in Figure 4-8 by example of Lancope's StealthWatch. In this solution the network acts as a security sensor and provides network anomaly-detection services to the operator. Data from various sources is correlated to make inferences about the security aspects of the network. The analytics engines within Cisco DNA offer the capability to not only analyze the events over time but also filter the relevant data collected from the network to the correct granularity or by correlating traffic flows (i.e., directionally). By looking at the events and data over time—both user specific and application specific—intelligent insights into the state of the network and the applications can be made. An example is detecting application or user behavior patterns that may be "out of profile" and which should be flagged for further analysis and/or upon which action should be taken (e.g., restrict, quarantine, or block) within the network infrastructure.

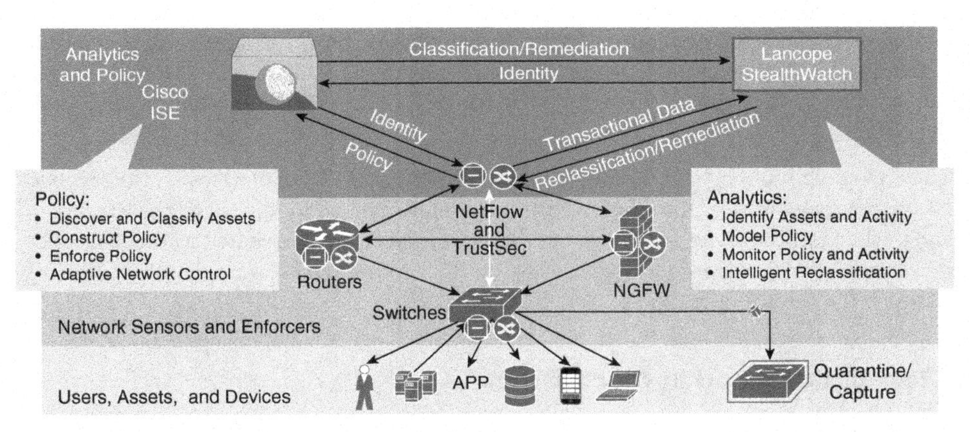

Figure 4-8 *Analytics Example Based on Lancope StealthWatch*

Such analytics capabilities can also be deployed in a virtualized form factor within Cisco DNA and, as such, be distributed in the infrastructure when and where appropriate, and where the required compute resources are available (for example, within a switch or router).

Feedback and Control

The insights gained by an analytics engine can be used to drive events and actions. Network or security services can be optimized based on the analytics results, for example, by instantiating new policies for particular applications or users, or by modifying existing policies. In Figure 4-8, the network functions work in unison with the identity engine, firewalls, and the Lancope StealthWatch Analytics engine to deliver continuous adjustments to the security policy.

The feedback and control in the analytics platform primarily target the implementation of a continuous feedback loop. Analytics results can be fed back to the controller to take action, for example, to optimize the operation of the network or the Cisco DNA services.

The analytics engine is thus vital in Cisco DNA to deliver service assurance. *Assurance* is defined as the coordination of automation with analytics to verify that the business intent has been delivered. If it has not, then assurance can automate the necessary changes to remediate.

Analytics and assurance thus deliver a continuous feedback cycle in Cisco DNA: network elements collect data on an ongoing basis. This data is reported via multiple mechanisms to one or more collectors, picked up by one or more analytics engines, and then reported back to the controller for further action. The controller can chose to present the results to the operator, or even trigger an automated optimization function to optimize the network configuration.

The Cisco DNA telemetry and analytics infrastructure does not just optimize available network services and operations. Analytics can also be exposed to the digitalized applications to enhance their operations or behavior. Information about user behavior on the network, such as their communication or location patterns, can enhance the applications riding on the network themselves, thus powering ever-improving and valuable client experiences.

The upcoming section "Connecting the Building Blocks: APIs" elaborates on the feedback loop from the controller into the orchestrator. Data collected by the network elements and pushed back into the controller can thus be analyzed and presented to the controller in a concise and condensed form, focusing on the relevant data sets required to optimize or refine the service operations.

The Role of the Cloud in Cisco DNA

Cloud computing has been perhaps the most disruptive trend in networking in recent years. Many enterprise applications are already running in a cloud environment to benefit from several advantages of the cloud. For starters, enterprise-operated data center infrastructure has often been underutilized, in some cases even running at below 20 percent capacity. Outsourcing data center operations to a cloud provider allows your organization to save both capital and operational costs to run servers and switches, as the cloud provider may be able to run its infrastructure with a higher degree of efficiency in terms of capacity usage than the organization itself could, thus lowering costs. The cloud provider offers network infrastructure as a service, for example in IaaS, PaaS, or SaaS models. The cloud provider can leverage techniques like virtualization to increase the utilization levels of the infrastructure, possibly even sharing the same physical infrastructure among multiple enterprises.

Secondly, the cloud model enables enterprises to be a lot more flexible. If you require additional capacity to run existing applications, or if you want to introduce a new application to customers, partners, or employees, a cloud-hosting model can significantly reduce the time to deployment. In these cases, you no longer need to engage in a lengthy product evaluation process, take the desired order through lengthy internal approval processes, then wait for delivery, and spend your own resources installing and deploying. The cloud provider pre-provisions capacity that can be sold to enterprises virtually on-demand.

In short, the cloud market is already an important tool for you as a network architect. But there is further room for improvement that Cisco DNA aims to address—making the cloud a fully integrated, principal building block of the architecture!

Cloud integration is the concept in Cisco DNA to fully incorporate the functionality offered by the cloud into the network architecture. How is this achieved in Cisco DNA? The different roles that the cloud can play in the architecture can be categorized into "cloud for applications," "cloud for management and orchestration," and "cloud for analytics." Let's explore these in more detail.

Cloud for Applications

Cloud for applications refers to the components in Cisco DNA to host applications in the cloud. In a public cloud model such as Microsoft Office 365, Cisco DNA provides secure connectivity (e.g., HTTPS) along with appropriate traffic handling and controls for such applications. In a private or hybrid cloud model, Cisco DNA provides virtualized network functions (e.g., the Cisco CSR 1000V with IPsec tunneling), allowing the VPC to become part of the network infrastructure.

The cloud is a fully integrated domain in Cisco DNA, particularly in a VPC model. When enterprise applications are hosted by a VPC provider, transport and network functions to connect the rest of the Cisco DNA network to the VPC are part of Cisco DNA operations. For example, a virtual router in the VPC provides connectivity to the WAN/DC/campus Cisco DNA domains. This virtual router can be configured such that the VPC behaves just like another branch. Additional virtualized network functions such as firewalls, IPS/IDS, or Cisco Wide Area Application Services (WAAS) can also be hosted in the VPC to support the transport of traffic to and from the enterprise applications. These auxiliary functions are configured to fully interoperate with the rest of the Cisco DNA network.

The cloud is now an important platform for innovation. Many an application has been developed based on resources in the cloud. Application developers no longer have to spend time and resources to maintain their own application development environments. These can simply be rented from a cloud provider. Gone are the days of having to upgrade basic system components. DevOps models allow for such development environments to be fully portable, such that the resulting applications run both in a cloud and in a self-hosted environment. In this way, cloud computing can become a vital factor to increase the speed of innovation for your enterprise.

The cloud is fully participating in and contributing to the principle of security in Cisco DNA. Applications hosted in the cloud can benefit from the security services offered by the cloud providers. The Cisco DNA network can be extended by an infrastructure-as-a-service model, where applications are hosted on dedicated and secured infrastructure by the cloud provider. Alternatively, the enterprise applications can be hosted in a software-as-a-service (SaaS) or platform-as-a-service (PaaS) model, supported by data encryption and security services of the cloud provider. In a VPC model, the integration of the cloud into the rest of the Cisco DNA network can also be fully secured. For example, the transport connection into the cloud can be either a private, dedicated circuit or encrypted. And additional security functions such as firewalls or intrusion prevention and detection functions can be deployed to augment the security of the network.

Cloud for Automation and Management

Cloud for automation refers to the automation components of Cisco DNA running in the cloud. Both the Cisco DNA controllers and the Cisco DNA orchestrators may be hosted in the cloud to benefit from its advantages—ubiquitous reachability from anywhere, scalable compute resources, etc.

The cloud is integrated not only from a transport perspective but, more importantly, from an automation and management perspective. The Cisco DNA orchestration component has full visibility into the available cloud hosting domains for applications. It can thus ensure that the Cisco DNA services can be instantiated into the cloud under the same pane of glass. Imagine seamlessly moving your enterprise applications to and from the cloud under the same orchestration umbrella! Moreover, the enterprise policies focusing on security, transport handling, and reporting that you have defined between user groups, device groups, and application groups can extend seamlessly into the cloud!

Cloud for Analytics

Cloud for analytics refers to the analytics platform of Cisco DNA running in the cloud. Note that such applications can support the data plane or the control plane (e.g., the platform to collect and process analytics data).

Using the cloud for analytics is a special case that deserves to be called out. In some sense, analytics in Cisco DNA can be viewed as "just another control application in my network." However, the sheer amount of data that is collected and the computational cycles required to perform the normalization, analytics, and correlations make cloud environments particularly attractive for this important Cisco DNA building block. The ability for the cloud to collect data from various sources—even those outside the Cisco DNA domain—may be beneficial for the correlation. Imagine how certain external events such as the weather can influence network usage patterns. A snow storm can entice employees to work from home and thus stress the VPN platform and Internet access infrastructure more. Figure 4-9 illustrates the relationship of private and public cloud hosting functions to the rest of the Cisco Digital Network Architecture building blocks.

Note that the full integration of the cloud into Cisco DNA for applications, automation, and analytics also allows for *multiple* cloud providers to become part of your enterprise Cisco DNA network. The cloud thus also extends the architectural flexibility that is required and provided by Cisco DNA. Applications can be hosted by multiple cloud providers, in multiple models—public or virtual private/hybrid cloud integration. Carrier-neutral facilities (CNF) or cloud interconnection fabrics (cloud "exchanges") can provide an efficient platform to integrate multiple cloud providers seamlessly into Cisco DNA.

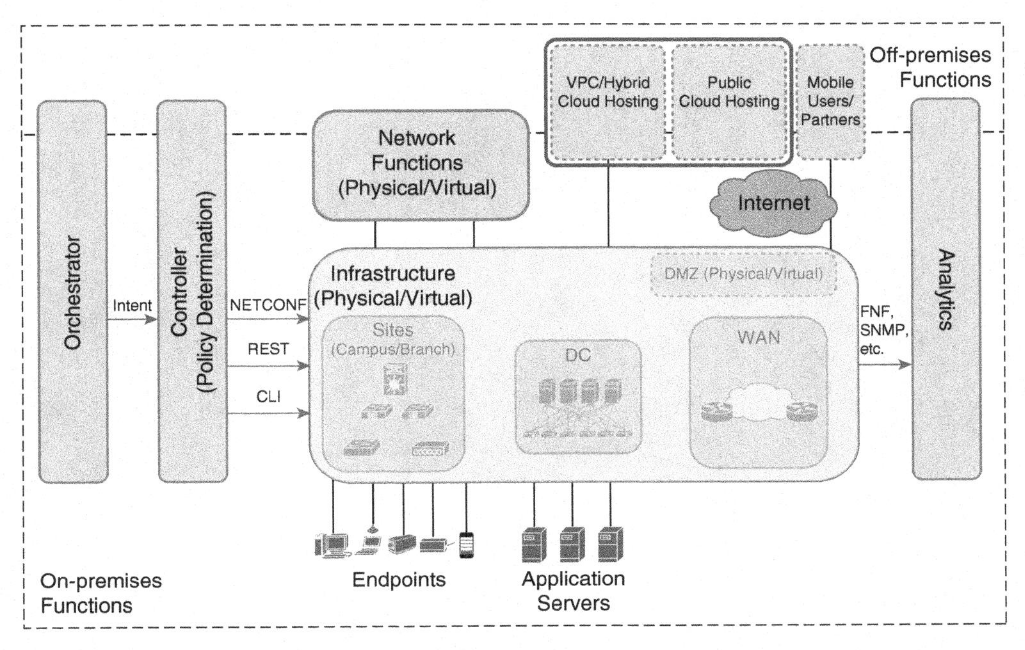

Figure 4-9 *Role of the Cloud in Cisco DNA—Location Independence of Cisco DNA Functions*

Connecting the Building Blocks: APIs

Now that the main components of the Cisco DNA architecture have been introduced, it's time to glue them all together. This "glue" in Cisco DNA is the open APIs. APIs enable better consistency and speed of development for machine-to-machine communications and, as such, form the necessary basis for automation. Each of the building blocks is programmable via the Cisco DNA APIs, and so all the components work together to deliver a coherent and integrated network architecture.

In conformance with the principles previously outlined, the APIs are open and standards based. API definitions—their names, input parameters, and outputs—are published. This provides full transparency of the functionality that can be driven by a building block, and also opens up the architecture for extensions. Recall that such programmability is essential to deliver speed and flexibility, underlining the importance of the APIs.

Furthermore, in many cases the interactions between the components are standards based. Technologies such as REST, NETCONF/YANG, and SNMP are examples of standards-based protocols that enable the APIs.

Figure 4-10 illustrates the importance of these APIs as a glue between Cisco DNA components. Moreover, it also shows the Cisco DNA closed-loop automation, because the APIs enable intelligence obtained through analytics and telemetry to be fed back into the Cisco DNA controller to optimize the network operations.

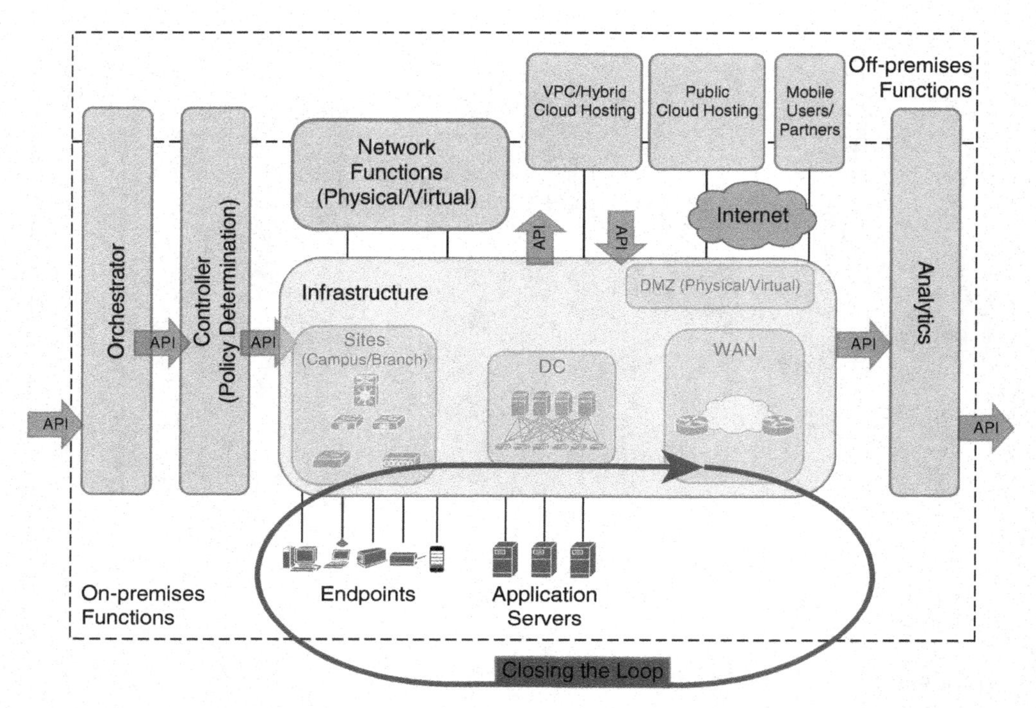

Figure 4-10 *Gluing the Components Together—the Role of APIs in Cisco DNA*

Outcomes

Motivated by the requirements and the guiding principles, the building blocks that were introduced integrate into a coherent architecture: Cisco Digital Network Architecture. The key goals of such an architecture are to support real business outcomes such as:

- Reducing costs to survive in an ever-dynamic and competitive business environment, where market disruptions are prevalent and where digitalization has lowered the barriers to entry into new and existing markets
- Increasing security and compliance in a world where your business's intellectual property is increasingly digitalized and where attacks are widespread
- Enhancing business agility to innovate continuously and to react quickly to market transitions

The support for those business outcomes is achieved in Cisco DNA through the following:

- Simplification and assurance
- Insights and experience
- Security and compliance

The building block approach of Cisco DNA, with clear functional responsibilities for each component and well-specified interfaces, makes the architecture easy to understand. This is essential to drive simplification into the network. Cisco DNA is designed to fully align with the business objectives—especially with the focus on policy—to ensure that the network delivers the services required to support your digitalized business processes in the most efficient and easy-to-use manner. No superfluous functions exist in the network that complicate its operations. All interactions are designed to support machine-to-machine communications that are fully automated, and that can be audited for service assurance.

The inclusion of the analytics platform as a key component is particularly helpful in Cisco DNA to deliver valuable insights into the network. You as an operator are aware of the state of the network at any point in time, enabling you to determine whether any provisioning steps you have initiated are successfully implemented, or whether unexpected failures or instabilities are emerging. Those insights ultimately improve the experience that Cisco DNA delivers, and allow you to focus on innovation to further your business, rather than spending valuable time "just keeping the network running."

A key outcome of the Cisco DNA approach is to raise compliance and security to new levels. The pervasive inclusion of security functions in every component and every API protects the network and the services that it delivers to your business. And the analytics capabilities of Cisco DNA again ensure that the integrity of the infrastructure is documented on an ongoing basis, and that any breaches are fully logged. Complying with regulatory requirements is thus also simplified, and again allows you to focus on what is important to you—your business—rather than manually performing sophisticated compliance audits or worrying about security leaks.

The bottom line is that Cisco DNA is designed to drive real business outcomes for you! The total cost of ownership of your enterprise network can be substantially reduced. A Cisco DNA network is simpler to operate through automation, offers full visibility at any point in time through service and network assurance, and can furthermore reduce both operational and capital expenditures through cloud integration.

Summary

This chapter provided initial insight into the architectural building blocks of Cisco DNA. It began by focusing on the requirements that arise from the digitalization of business processes. The digitalized business environments present new and enhanced requirements for the enterprise network, such as an increased focus on simplicity, automation, flexibility, intelligent feedback mechanisms, application, user, and device awareness, security and compliance, high availability, and the movement toward policy as a foundational component in networking. These requirements are taken into account in Cisco DNA by building the architecture on a set of sound principles that provide the architectural compass:

- Openness
- Extensibility
- Programmability

- Policy-based networking
- Security
- Software driven
- Cloud integrated

At a high level, Cisco DNA is then based on six main building blocks. The Cisco DNA infrastructure with supporting network functions provides connectivity between endpoints and allows traffic to be manipulated. This infrastructure is fully programmable and leverages both physical and virtualized network functions. The Cisco DNA controller provides an abstraction of the infrastructure to facilitate simplicity and also ensures that the right policies are determined and instantiated based on the business intent. The Cisco DNA orchestrator is the building block in the architecture where the business intent is defined at an abstract level, aligning the network to the business processes and operations. Complementing these components is an analytics building block to continuously collect data from the network, analyze it, and serve it up to network operators for network assurance, or even expose APIs for application developers to leverage network intelligence thus collected.

The outcomes of this architecture are to deliver on the requirements introduced here: a network that provides simplicity and assurance, that provides insights and experiences, and that meets the security and compliance requirements in a digitalized world.

Chapter 5 expands on each of these components. It examines the details of the infrastructure to intensify your understanding about relationships between components and functions, and thus deepen the architectural model behind Cisco DNA.

Further Reading

Akamai. "Q3 2016 State of the Internet–Security Report." Available for download at https://content.akamai.com/PG7470-Q3-2016-SOTI-Security-Report.html?utm_source=GoogleSearch&gclid=CM7zsunN7NACFYSFswodxxwERw.

Cisco Systems. *Cisco AVVID Network Infrastructure Overview*. 2002. https://www.cisco.com/web/offer/CAT4500/toolkit/comin_ov.pdf.

Cisco Systems. *Cisco Enterprise Network Functions Virtualization*. 2017. https://www.cisco.com/c/en/us/solutions/collateral/enterprise-networks/enterprise-network-functions-virtualization-nfv/white-paper-c11-736783.pdf.

Cisco Systems. *Cisco SAFE Reference Guide*. Updated Oct. 31, 2013. https://www.cisco.com/c/en/us/td/docs/solutions/Enterprise/Security/SAFE_RG/SAFE_rg/chap1.html.

Cisco Systems. "Cisco Visual Networking Index: Forecast and Methodology, 2016–2021." Updated Sept. 15, 2017. https://www.cisco.com/c/en/us/solutions/collateral/service-provider/visual-networking-index-vni/complete-white-paper-c11-481360.html.

Cisco Systems. *The Cisco Digital Network Architecture Vision–An Overview*. 2016. https://www.cisco.com/c/dam/global/ru_kz/solutions/enterprise-networks/digital-network-architecture/pdf/white-paper-c11-736842.pdf.

Chapter 5

The Cisco Digital Network Architecture Blueprint

So far this book has introduced the Cisco Digital Network Architecture philosophy and principles, in particular the fundamental goal of fully aligning your enterprise networks with the intent of your business operations. Chapter 4, "Introducing the Cisco Digital Network Architecture," introduced and defined the Cisco DNA building blocks at a high level, outlining their main purpose from a functional perspective and the relationships between each architectural component. This chapter provides further details on each of the building blocks, unpeeling the architectural "onion" to the next level of detail. This chapter covers the following:

- The Cisco DNA service definition in detail, intensifying the role of the enterprise network to connect users, applications, and devices to each other, and how policy is tightly coupled to a Cisco DNA service
- Details behind the Cisco DNA infrastructure, illustrating how segmentation is realized, as well as highlighting the role of supporting network functions such as Domain Name Service (DNS), Dynamic Host Configuration Protocol (DHCP), network address translation (NAT), firewalls, etc.
- The concepts of domains, scopes, and fabrics to provide structure in Cisco DNA
- The role of controllers in Cisco DNA to abstract the network infrastructure and to drive policy into the network
- The link between business intent and the Cisco DNA network services, providing functionality to define abstracted Cisco DNA services at a business level and automating the instantiation of these services based on orchestration to the Cisco DNA controller layer
- Further insights into how operational data is continuously extracted from the network, exploring the different data collection mechanisms available in Cisco DNA and explaining how telemetry and analytics offer meaningful and timely insights into Cisco DNA network state and operations

This chapter revisits the importance of the cloud in Cisco DNA to offer truly location-agnostic network functions. It expands on the role of the cloud to host applications, the Cisco DNA analytics platforms, and even the Cisco DNA automation layer.

Cisco DNA Services

The fundamental purpose of an enterprise network is to connect applications—application clients run on your notebook, tablet, or smartphone and connect to application servers in your enterprise data center. Applications may run in a sensor, such as a connected thermometer, alarm system, or a card reader, and connect to their peer applications operated by a partner. They may run in your data center and connect to a partner's applications. The role of the Cisco DNA-enabled network is to enable IP traffic to flow between any of those application pairs, regardless of who has operational responsibility for the devices or applications (the devices may be operated by your IT department, your employees, your partners, or even your customers).

Such application flows may become very sophisticated! Think about a Cisco Webex conference between your engineers, partners, and customers, connecting from worldwide locations. The connectivity between the Cisco Webex application clients is multipoint across the globe, most likely consumed on a myriad of devices ranging from PCs and notebooks to Apple iPhones/iPads and Android devices. Low-bandwidth voice streams and high-bandwidth video streams have to be synchronized and transmitted in real time. Some of the participants may be connected while being mobile in a car or train.

It's such applications that define your digitalized business, and the Cisco DNA-enabled network makes it real. Figure 5-1 illustrates this relationship between the Cisco DNA network and applications that run in a variety of host devices. The network provides the connectivity of applications that are identified, for example, by an application ID or an IP port number. The devices that the applications run on can be associated with an operator—whether that is your IT department, an employee, or a customer—and thus the device too can be identified by a user or operator ID and an endpoint type. It is the applications running on the devices that become the consumers of the Cisco DNA network services. Cisco DNA services are defined as "those services that are offered to users, devices, and applications, consisting of transport in association with policies." A Cisco DNA service has two main subcomponents:

1. Transport services define how traffic is forwarded through the network.
2. Policies define how traffic is treated by the network.

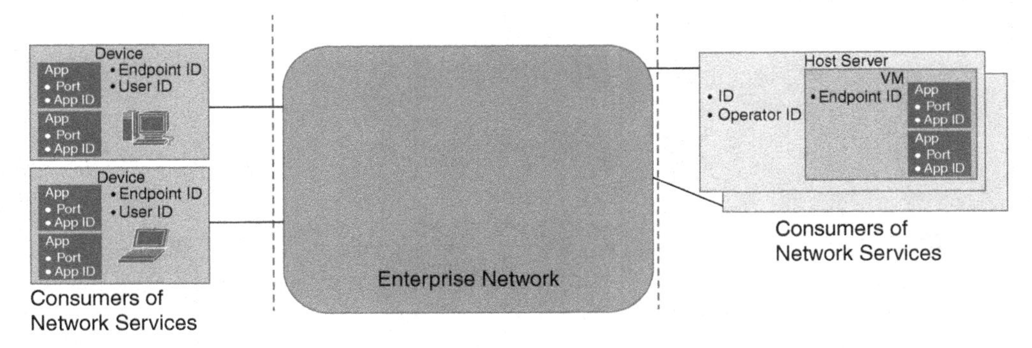

Figure 5-1 *The Enterprise Network Connects Users, Applications, and Devices*

From the perspective of the Cisco DNA network operator, it is useful to also differentiate between applications that are running on a particular device and applications that are under the control of a particular user (e.g., an employee), in particular because Cisco DNA is shifting toward policy-based networking. You may want to associate an access policy with a particular device type, in which case you would be interested in the set of all devices on the network of that type. Alternatively, you may want to associate a policy with a particular user or group of users, for example, to ensure that they can communicate with a particular application.

The Cisco DNA network therefore has to be aware of the users, applications, and devices connecting to it in order to deliver a transport service between them. Or, to be more precise, the network has to become aware of *groupings* of users, applications, and devices. For most enterprise networks, expressing the relationship between users, applications, and devices at the individual singleton level is impractical and simply not scalable. Instead, applications, users, and devices are typically grouped. The service that the network delivers for connectivity is typically associated with groups of applications, users, or devices. In the special case that an individual application, user, or device needs to be singled out, a group with that single member can be created and policy can be applied to it.

Figure 5-2 illustrates this user, application, and device awareness in Cisco DNA. Respective databases track users, devices, and applications or groupings, which allows you as a network operator to associate a Cisco DNA service between such groupings. These databases are populated in Cisco DNA by various means. For example, Cisco Identity Services Engine (ISE) is used to track users. Application registries are interfaced with to track applications. And, of course, you always have the option to explicitly create awareness of users, applications, and devices using an API or GUI.

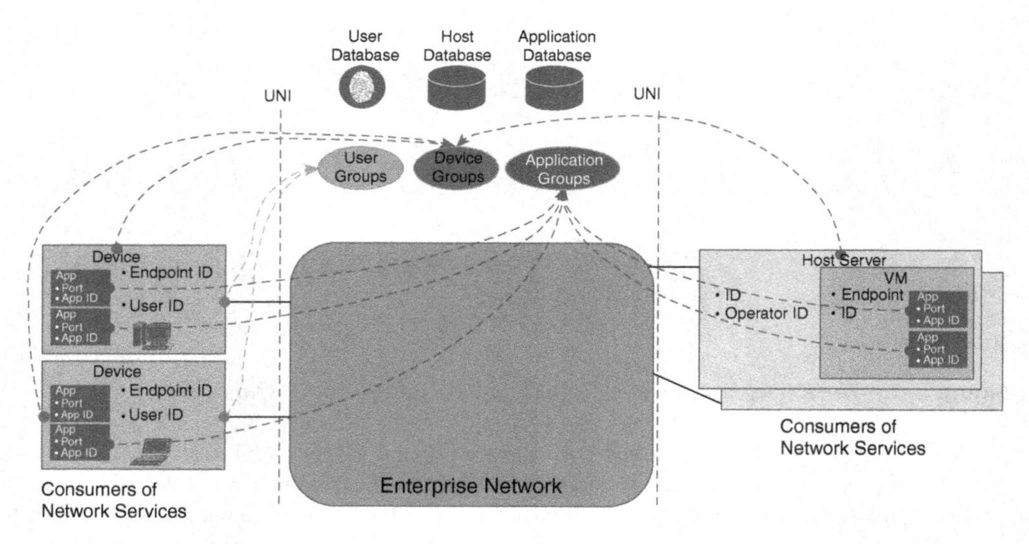

Figure 5-2 *User, Device, and Application Awareness in Cisco DNA*

The following subsections elaborate on the two parts of the Cisco DNA service: transport and policy.

Cisco DNA Services—Transport

The transport aspect of the Cisco DNA service definition highlights the fact that the primary purpose of offering a Cisco DNA service is to provide a communication path through the network between two or more users, applications, or devices (or groups).

At the network level, Cisco DNA service transport starts at an access interface (the ingress), which is either a physical interface or a logical interface. This ingress interface accepts IP packets as part of the service, and then ensures that the packets are transmitted to the remote end(s) of the service for delivery to the connected users, devices, or applications. The Cisco DNA network uses routing and switching as forwarding mechanisms. The Cisco DNA network may implement routing and switching to establish the path between ingress and egress. The transport may be based on a unicast service in the case where two endpoints are connected. Alternatively, the transport may be based on multicast if the relationship between the endpoints is point-to-multipoint. At the egress, the IP packets are then delivered to the recipients as part of the service.

The establishment of such communication paths in Cisco DNA may require support from additional functions. For example, network functions such as NAT, DHCP, Locator/ID Separation Protocol (LISP) Map Servers/Map Resolvers, or DNS may also come into play at the transport level to establish the communication path.

Both ingress and egress interfaces are defined by a user-to-network interface (UNI) to delineate the endpoint(s) of the Cisco DNA service. The UNI is the demarcation point of a Cisco DNA service between the Cisco DNA network and the users, applications, or devices (the "consumers").

Cisco DNA Services—Policy

The second part of a Cisco DNA service are the policies associated with the service. The Cisco DNA service policies describe how traffic that is associated with the service is treated by the network. For example, the service may be restricted to only certain types of traffic, and thus the associated policy may be to filter out unwanted traffic. Alternatively, the Cisco DNA service may be considered business critical, and thus the network has to ensure that this criticality is implemented from the ingress to the egress (for example, by associating the Cisco DNA service with high-priority queueing).

Policies in a Cisco DNA service fall into one of three categories:

- Access and security policies
- Transport handling policies
- Reporting policies

First, security policies govern all security aspects of the Cisco DNA service, such as which traffic can access the service. Access may be restricted to certain users, applications, or devices as described by a filter. All other nonconforming users, applications, or devices are restricted. The UNI previously described provides the demarcation point where such access policies are enforced. Traffic may then be segmented into virtual local area networks (VLAN) or virtual private networks (VPN) to ensure traffic separation between different user or application groups. Another example of a security policy that is associated with a Cisco DNA service is one that specifics its encryption level. For highly confidential Cisco DNA services, the security policy may require strong encryption end to end, preventing any unauthorized recipients to decipher the communication. Commonly, encryption is required as the service traverses untrusted devices (e.g., if a service provider network is used on the path from ingress to egress). For public Cisco DNA services, the security policy might not require encryption, allowing IP packets to be sent in the clear.

Second, transport handling policies govern how the IP packets are treated by the network from a transport perspective. These policies allow the network to manipulate the IP packet flow—for example, by applying compression, caching, adding metadata, or prioritizing on the forwarding path. Such policies may be critical to meet the service-level agreement (SLA) requirements associated with a Cisco DNA service, and hence to fulfill the right business intent.

Finally, reporting policies govern what data is collected for the IP flows of a Cisco DNA service. For some services, simple packet counts suffice. For other service, more stringent reporting is required, ensuring that full Cisco IOS NetFlow records, for example, are collected at every hop. Another example of a reporting policy is to duplicate/span the IP flows associated with a service based on an event trigger. For example, when an anomaly is detected on a particular port, such a duplication can be instantiated in the network to investigate the anomaly with an intrusion detection/prevention system (IDS/IPS). The IP packet flow associated with the Cisco DNA service is copied to the IDS/IPS, which performs a detailed anomaly detection without affecting the original packet flow.

Multiple policies can be applied to a Cisco DNA service, as depicted in Figure 5-3. The figure illustrates two examples of two-endpoint Cisco DNA services, where the ingress into each Cisco DNA service is at the UNI. Each Cisco DNA service may be associated with different security, transport handling, and reporting policies. Note that traffic associated with a Cisco DNA service is inherently assumed to be bidirectional, and so the network has to ensure that the policies associated with a Cisco DNA service in each direction align.

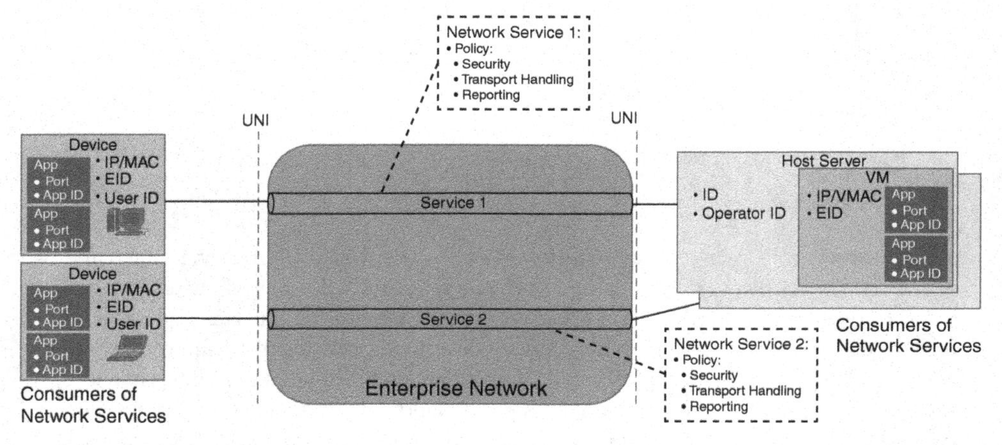

Figure 5-3 *Cisco DNA Services: Transport and Policy*

Relationship Between Cisco DNA Policies and Business Intent

Let's elaborate on the relationship between Cisco DNA policies and business intent in more detail. Recall that the main purpose of explicitly associating policy as a component of a Cisco DNA service is to ensure that the network fulfills the business intent, fully aligning with the business objectives.

Intent and policies can be expressed in various ways: an operator of a network element may express an access policy with a specific CLI command. An operator of the Cisco DNA service may express the access policy in more abstracted form, as a relationship between groups of users, applications, or devices, utilizing a generic syntax rather than a device-specific CLI.

This is where the service definition and orchestration component and the controller component of Cisco DNA come into play. Each offers a level of abstraction. The relationship between the business intent and a Cisco DNA service may be specified at an abstract level in Cisco DNA's service definition and orchestration building block. The business intent may be expressed at this level as, for example, "as a store manager, my store's point-of-sale traffic is business critical." Such a level of abstraction is helpful to align the Cisco DNA-enabled network with the business objectives.

The abstracted expression of business intent must be implemented in the various network elements and functions—and this is the role of the Cisco DNA controller component. As introduced in Chapter 4, the controllers provide an abstraction level of the network elements and functions, and this can be leveraged to instantiate policy. In Cisco DNA, the controller takes on the responsibility of "translating" or "mapping" the abstracted expressions of intent into device-specific configurations. The controllers may also have an abstracted notion of the Cisco DNA policy, likely with additional details and using a syntax that facilitates the ultimate instantiation of the Cisco DNA policy.

This relationship between business intent, Cisco DNA policies, and ultimate device configurations is illustrated in Figure 5-4.

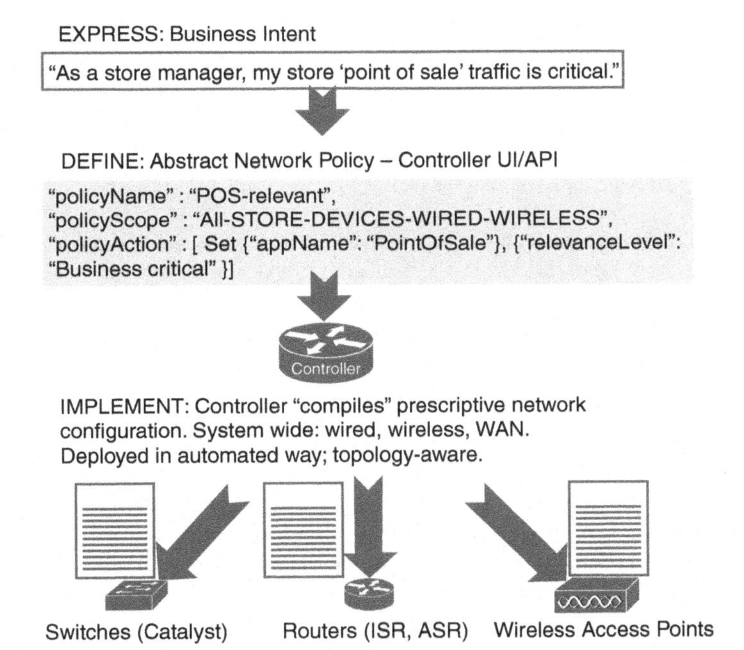

Figure 5-4 *Cisco DNA Services: Example of How Abstract Expression of Intent Is Transformed into Device Configurations By a Controller*

Now that we've covered the concept of a Cisco DNA service as consumed by users, applications, or devices, we'll elaborate on the structure of the Cisco DNA enterprise network in the subsequent sections.

Cisco DNA Infrastructure

Perhaps the most fundamental building block in a Cisco DNA-enabled network is the infrastructure. It consists of both physical and virtual network functions that are connected with each other to offer Cisco DNA services to users, applications, and devices. These functions are categorized as follows:

- **Transport functions:** Functions that participate in forwarding IP flows associated with Cisco DNA services from ingress to egress

- **Supporting network functions:** Functions that assist in the establishment of a forwarding path for a Cisco DNA service, as well as all functions that may manipulate the packet flows for the purpose of implementing Cisco DNA service policies
- **Fabrics:** Functions that enable logical overlays to be built on top of a programmable underlay network with the support of a controller.

This section elaborates on the Cisco DNA infrastructure components, highlighting their functional role in the architecture, as well as the relationships between components.

Transport Functions

The transport functions in a Cisco DNA-enabled network are provided by both physical network elements (such as routers and switches) and virtualized network functions (VNF). The principal functional roles these elements play in the architecture are

- **Network access:** The transport infrastructure provides the mechanisms for devices to access the network. This may be in the form of a dedicated physical port on an access switch. Access may be wireless based on wireless access points or other radio technologies. Regardless, devices are associated with either a physical or logical interface that represents the demarcation point of the network, and is specified by the UNI.
- **Policy enforcement:** In Cisco DNA, any device (and by implication, the applications that run on the device) seeking to consume a Cisco DNA service must traverse such a UNI. The UNI is a construct to enforce policy, even if this policy simply states "allow all traffic into the network." The Cisco DNA blueprint described here explicitly represents policy enforcement points (PEP) to highlight that functional component in Cisco DNA where policies are enforced. In most cases, the policies associated at the UNI are more sophisticated than a simple "allow all." As previously discussed, the Cisco DNA policies may involve additional security, traffic handling, and reporting policies. The PEPs are places where such policies are associated with a Cisco DNA service, for example, by associating an IP flow to a particular network segment, setting bits in packet headers to reflect policy aspects (think Differentiated Services Code Point [DSCP]!), or even pushing additional headers that can subsequently be used by the network to deliver according to the Cisco DNA policy.

  Note that the policy enforcement may also require the IP packet flows to be manipulated within the network. If the business intent is to provide an optimized Cisco DNA service, compression and caching may be applied to the IP flows, requiring again the manipulation of the packet flow and even possible redirection to L4–L7 network functions.
- **Packet transport:** An obvious function offered by the transport infrastructure is the transmission of packets associated with a Cisco DNA service from the ingress into the network to the egress. The transport infrastructure accepts packets across the UNI, then forwards these packets across the network, possibly traversing multiple geographically distributed network elements and functions, and finally delivers the packets to the recipient device. To do so, the Cisco DNA transport infrastructure must establish communication paths (for example, relying on well-established routing and switching mechanisms).

Note that security plays a special role in Cisco DNA. The transport infrastructure provides segmentation to delineate flows from different services. VLANs and VPN technologies provide the fundamental infrastructure here. Segmentation is complemented by encryption functions that are instantiated where required as per the Cisco DNA service policy. Finally, the IP flows associated with a Cisco DNA service can be subjected to additional security functions such as firewalls, anomaly detection, IPS/IDS, filtering, etc. The transport infrastructure provides security by design!

At this point it is also important to reiterate that the Cisco DNA architecture allows for network functions to be operated in the cloud. This is illustrated in Figure 5-5 by highlighting virtual private clouds (VPC). Applications may be hosted in a VPC, and a virtual routing function (e.g., using a Cisco CSR 1000V) may be used to provide the demarcation between the hosted applications and the Cisco DNA network. However, the UNI in this case is virtualized within the VPC, but exists none the less! The virtual router may be configured like any other branch router, for example with a software-defined wide-area network (SD-WAN) configuration, effectively rendering the VPC like just another branch. IP traffic generated by the cloud-hosted applications is received by a virtual interface and is still subject to a PEP representing the Cisco DNA service policy in the virtual router.

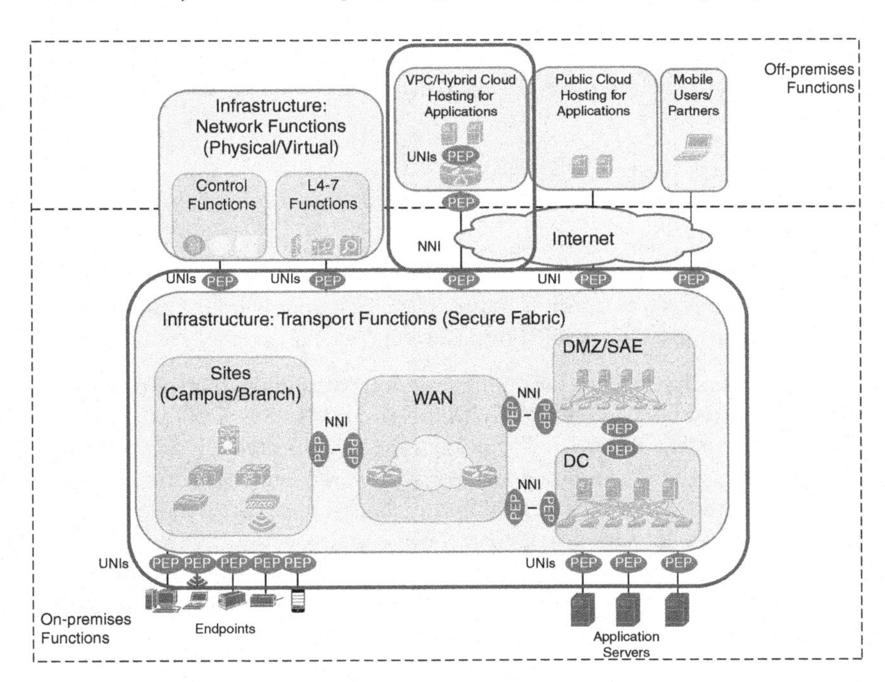

Figure 5-5 *Cisco DNA Infrastructure: Transport Functions*

The network elements in the Cisco DNA transport infrastructure may be grouped to provide structure and to facilitate the architectural understanding behind Cisco DNA. Network elements and functions may still be grouped into WAN, data center (DC), branch, and campus sites, or demilitarized zones (DMZ), as shown in Figure 5-5. Rather than focusing on the geographic location (or place in network, PIN), however, the motivation for such groupings is technical. All of these groupings are characterized by different technical requirements.

The WAN is still assumed to be characterized by lower bandwidth rates (as compared to campus/branch connections), and often relies on service providers offering carrier services for the interconnections. Campus and branch infrastructure in Cisco DNA can be grouped into sites, consisting of both routed and switched infrastructure. Sites mainly provide access into the Cisco DNA-enabled network for endpoints and to aggregate traffic. Policy enforcement points implementing the UNI are a particular feature of sites, in particular regulating which users, applications, or devices may gain access. The network elements representing the data center are similar in nature: they provide access into the network to applications. However, in this case, the x86-based hosts running the applications are typically operated by your IT department. Furthermore, the DC infrastructure in Cisco DNA typically needs to scale far beyond branches and campuses, both in terms of number of physical hosts and in terms of bandwidth. Network elements in the DMZ need to provide particular security functionality because they connect your Cisco DNA infrastructure with the outside world.

To disambiguate the term PIN from its common meaning of personal identification number, and to emphasize the increased focus on technological characteristics rather than a geographical placement, the WAN, DC, DMZ, and sites are also referred to as "technology scopes."

Supporting Network Functions

The transport infrastructure may rely on additional network functions to carry Cisco DNA service traffic from ingress to egress between applications. These supplementary network functions fall into two categories: control plane functions and Layer 4–Layer 7 functions, and they are realized in either a physical form factor or a virtual form factor.

Control plane functions help establish the communication paths in the transport infrastructure. For example, route reflectors or LISP Map Servers/Map Resolvers provide reachability information at the IP level and typically run in a dedicated physical appliance or as a VNF hosted on a generic x86-based server. Either way, control plane functions do not directly forward IP traffic but are essential for the transport infrastructure to achieve reachability. Other examples of supporting control plane functions are DNS servers and DHCP servers, which help endpoints to communicate in the network. The supporting Cisco DNA control plane functions, of course, complement any control plane processes that remain integrated into the transport infrastructure network elements.

The supporting Layer 4–Layer 7 network functions are typically in the data plane and, as such, may participate in manipulating the IP traffic flows of Cisco DNA services. Examples of such functions are NAT, Wide Area Application Services (WAAS), IDS/IPS, deep packet inspection (DPI), Cisco IOS NetFlow collectors, and firewalls. In most cases, such functions are instantiated in the Cisco DNA network to implement the policies for a particular consumer/producer relationship. Firewalls or IDS/IPS may be deployed to enforce a security policy. A pair of WAAS functions may be deployed to optimize the communication between two applications by using caching, data redundancy elimination, or optimizing TCP flows. Reporting policies may be enforced using DPI and Cisco IOS NetFlow collectors.

Both types of supporting network functions are treated like endpoint applications in Cisco DNA. This implies that they are connected to the transport infrastructure via a UNI and, as such, can also be associated with a PEP. Usually, reachability to such supporting network functions is universally granted, and so the access/reachability policy may simple state "allow all." In some cases though—especially for the supporting control plane functions—encryption or logging policies may also apply. In the case of the supporting L4–L7 network functions, the Cisco DNA service traffic may also be manipulated. For example, applying WAAS to an IP flow changes the packet arrival and payload distributions. The TCP flow optimization of WAAS influences packet-sending rates (e.g., by manipulating the exponential backoff timers). WAAS data redundancy elimination may compress traffic or even serve it out of a cache.

Figure 5-6 highlights this property of supporting network functions in Cisco DNA. The figure also points to the supporting network functions running either on premises or off premises. Both the control plane functions and the L4–L7 functions that may implement policy and manipulate the Cisco DNA service flows can be virtualized in the network. This also implies that these functions are already suitable to be run in a public cloud environment, a private cloud, or a hybrid cloud.

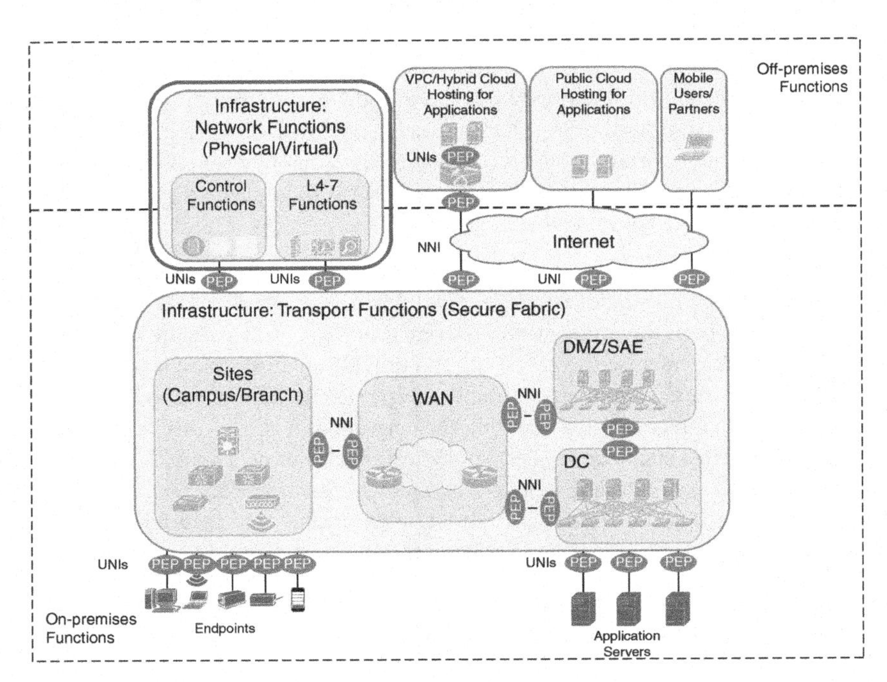

Figure 5-6 *Cisco DNA Infrastructure: Supporting Network Functions*

Fabrics

A key innovation in Cisco DNA on the transport infrastructure side is the use of network fabrics. Recall that in Chapter 4, the Cisco DNA fabric was defined as the infrastructure components in Cisco DNA, including a programmable underlay network, a logical overlay topology, and a controller and policy. The underlay network can be made up of both physical and virtual functions. The logical overlay networks help to deliver Cisco DNA services. The controller provides an end-to-end view of the network and an abstraction layer northbound.

Fabrics are fundamental in a Cisco DNA-enabled network for several reasons:

- The explicit separation of overlays from the network infrastructure is critical to the delivery of Cisco DNA services. Overlay networks allow the creation of virtual topologies built on top of arbitrary underlay topologies. This can create alternative forwarding characteristics that may not be present in the underlay. For example, endpoint mobility, flexible and programmable topologies, or state reduction in the core are benefits of overlay networks.
- In Cisco DNA, the primary overlay data plane encapsulation is based on virtual extensible LAN (VXLAN) supported by a LISP control plane. The VXLAN header offers bits to represent a scalable group tag (SGT) and a virtual network identifier (VNID). SGTs in the packet headers in Cisco DNA can be leveraged as policy anchors, using the SGT value to correlate a policy to the packet at transmission time. Traditionally, IP addresses or VLAN tags were used to implement policy as well as forwarding. These header fields are overloaded in their function, which complicated network architectures and operations. With a strict separation of the forwarding bits (Ethernet or IP headers) from the policy bits (SGTs and VNIDs), topology in Cisco DNA is cleanly separated from policy. This not only simplifies the virtual network topologies but, more importantly, allows a much expanded policy functionality—and recall, one of the key differentiators of Cisco DNA is to implement Cisco DNA service policies to reflect your business objectives!
- Fabrics, and by implication all the network elements that make up the fabric, are under the governance of a single controller. This allows the controller to have a fabric-wide view of both the underlay and overlay topologies and the state of the constituent network elements. The controller can provide an abstraction layer toward northbound architecture components (notably the service definition and orchestration building block), effectively representing the network as a single construct. Note that fabrics align with a single controller, but the reverse is not necessary. A single controller can still govern multiple fabrics. The following section elaborates further on the relationships between controllers, fabrics, and domains, and their relationships to the campus and branch sites, the WAN, the DC, and the DMZ.

The network elements of a fabric are further categorized by their function into border nodes, edge nodes, and intermediary nodes. Fabric border nodes connect the fabric to external L3 networks. They are similar in functionality to traditional gateways. Fabric edge nodes are responsible for connecting endpoints, which in Cisco DNA implies that they instantiate PEPs. Fabric intermediary nodes provide IP forwarding, connecting the edge and border nodes to each other.

The fabric control plane in Cisco DNA is based on LISP. LISP maintains a tracking database of IP endpoints (hosts) to provide reachability for the overlay networks. It essentially tracks the endpoints to their fabric edge nodes, and can thus serve the location (or particular edge node) for a destination host when requested from a source host.

From an architectural perspective, it is also helpful to differentiate network elements by their relationship to the fabric. Network elements are fabric enabled, fabric attached, or fabric aware.

A device is fabric enabled if it participates in, and communicates over, the logical fabric overlay topology. In other words, it interacts with both the fabric control plane and the data plane. Examples of fabric-enabled network elements are the border, edge, and intermediary nodes.

A device is fabric attached if it participates only in the fabric control plane and does not participate in the forwarding in the overlays. An example of a fabric-attached network element is a wireless LAN controller, which falls in the previously mentioned category of Cisco DNA supporting network functions.

Finally, a device is fabric aware if it communicates over the logical fabric overlay but does not participate in the fabric control plane. For example, wireless access points may not have the ability to participate in the fabric control plane unless they support LISP.

The second part of this book is dedicated to elaborating on the infrastructure components in Cisco DNA. The chapters in that section provide much more details on fabrics in Cisco DNA, so stay tuned!

Automating Cisco DNA—Controllers

The next major building block in the Cisco DNA blueprint is the controller layer. As introduced in Chapter 4, the controller constitutes a mandatory component in Cisco DNA that is responsible for all the network elements and functions under its span. In particular, the controller executes the following functions:

- Automating transport and network functions infrastructure
- Maintaining a view of the infrastructure functions and connected endpoints
- Instantiating and maintaining Cisco DNA services

Automating Transport and Network Functions Infrastructure

The controller assists with the automation and configuration of the transport infrastructure and its supporting network elements. For example, if the geographic reach of the network is to be extended, a new network element or virtual network function can be added to the infrastructure. Assuming the physical elements were installed, the controller then regulates the initial bring up (e.g., via plug and play) and configures the device to participate in the Cisco DNA infrastructure. Specifically, for network fabrics, the controller is responsible for creating the underlay configuration.

Maintaining a View of the Infrastructure Functions and Connected Endpoints

The controller plays a crucial role in delivering Cisco DNA services as per the business intent. A key function is thus to maintain awareness of the underlay infrastructure—i.e., the operational state and connectivity of the physical network elements. The controller is aware at any point in time about the hardware details (such as vendor, type, and linecard types) and software details (such as operating system version and firmware versions). The controller also needs to maintain awareness about user groups, application groups, and device groups that are configured in the network to enable the consumption of a Cisco DNA service.

This awareness allows the controller to have an up-to-date topological view of the infrastructure under its governance and the endpoint groups that exist in the network. Such a view is essential to offer a layer of abstraction to any north-bound Cisco DNA components (notably the service definition and orchestration layer). The Cisco DNA infrastructure under the span of a controller can be viewed as a system in itself. Any northbound building blocks do not need to know the details of the transport topology or specific information about individual network elements or functions.

Instantiating and Maintaining Cisco DNA Services

In addition to the creation (design, build, and run) of the underlay network, the controller is also responsible for the instantiation and maintenance of the Cisco DNA services. This is arguably its most important function—after all, the main pivot toward a Cisco DNA-enabled network is to align the network with the business intent, as defined by the Cisco DNA services and their associated policies.

The controller takes abstract expressions of such intent from the Cisco DNA service definition and orchestration component (discussed next) and drives the required functionality into the network elements. This implies the following:

- Creating or modifying the virtual overlay networks as required by the Cisco DNA service. For example, VLANs, VXLANs, or virtual routing and forwarding (VRF) instances are created throughout the network elements in the controller domain to achieve the desired segmentation policy.
- Creating or modifying PEPs in accordance with the policy. For example, if the Cisco DNA service associates a particular endpoint with a user group, the endpoint is classified at the PEP and put in the right Cisco DNA segment.
- Creating or modifying any VNFs that are associated with the supporting network functions building block. For example, a service may require WAN optimization, which may be realized using a virtualized Cisco WAAS VNF. The controller in this case creates the VNF and provides its initial configuration.

- Pushing relevant path information to force the traffic from a particular endpoint though a service chain as per the policy. For example, if an endpoint is associated with a policy that requires copying traffic to a traffic analysis module for reporting, the controller may push a network services header (NSH) to force the flow through a Cisco Network Analysis Module (NAM) VNF.

Figure 5-7 highlights the relationship between the controllers and the PEPs in Cisco DNA. PEPs may be instantiated throughout the network. PEPs are instantiated to regulate access to the Cisco DNA network. They are also created between different controller domains. Within a controller domain, the controller is fully aware and in charge of all PEPs to enforce the policy according to the Cisco DNA service definition.

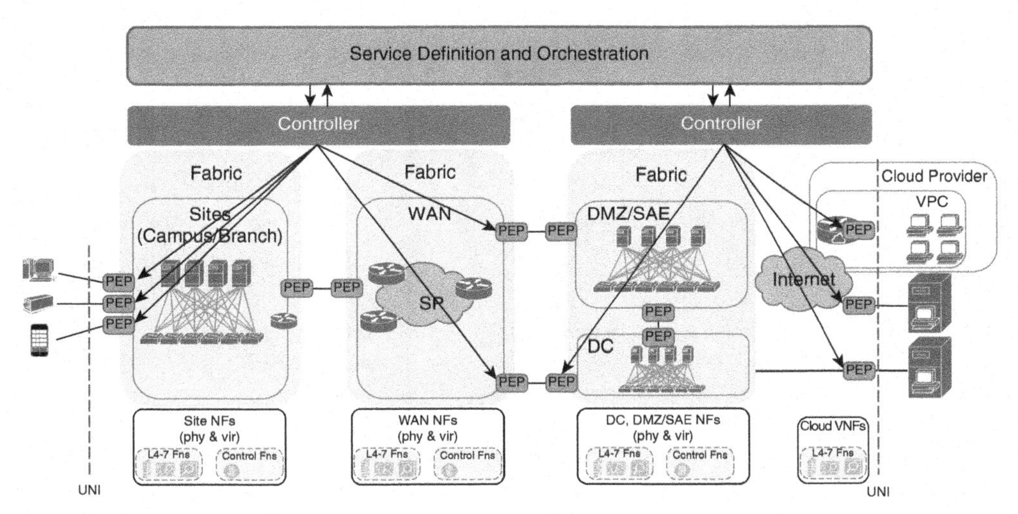

Figure 5-7 *Cisco DNA Controllers and Policy Enforcement Points*

Figure 5-8 shows the relationship between the controller and the other Cisco DNA functional building blocks. The controller has interfaces via APIs into the transport infrastructure, including the supporting network functions. These APIs allow the controller to programmatically interact with the network elements, creating the dynamic programmability that was introduced in Chapter 4. The controller also has APIs with the service definition and orchestration building block. As previously described, and also illustrated in Figure 5-4, these APIs allow Cisco DNA services created at an abstract level in the service definition and orchestrator component to be automatically communicated to the one or more controller domains.

By executing these functions, the Cisco DNA controller layer simplifies the end-to-end architecture through abstractions and ensures that the network is always fully aligned with the business intent—and most importantly that the business intent is always reflected by the instantiated network policies.

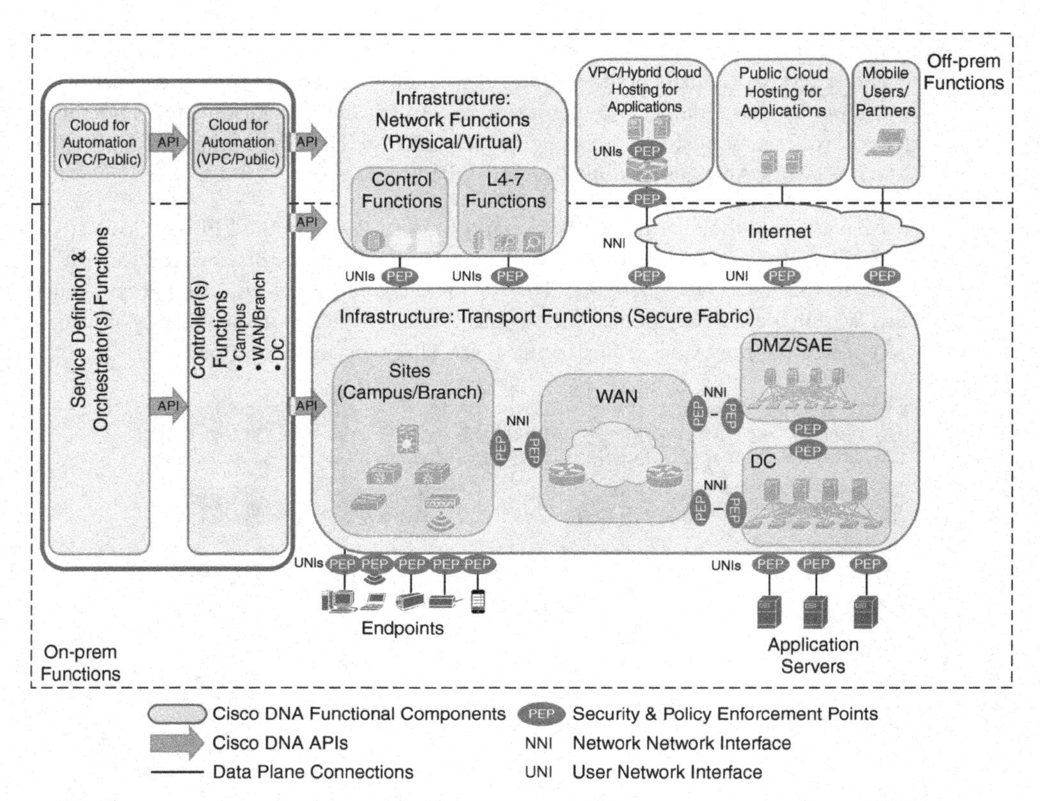

Figure 5-8 *Cisco DNA Controllers, Service Definition and Orchestration*

Relationships in Cisco DNA: Revisiting Domains, Scopes, and Fabrics

So far this chapter has introduced the concepts of network elements that are grouped into technology scopes (WAN, sites, DC, DMZ) based on their role in the Cisco DNA transport infrastructure. Also, you've seen that network elements can be grouped to form Cisco DNA fabrics with a common underlay network and one or more overlays, all under the direction of a single controller. Controller domains, however, may span multiple fabrics to provide a single abstraction layer.

From an architectural perspective, it is helpful to revisit the relationships in Cisco DNA between those concepts. The architectural structures in Cisco DNA based on controller domains, technology scopes, and network fabrics help simplify the architecture.

The principal relationships between controller domains, technology scopes, and network fabrics are as follows:

- The Cisco DNA transport infrastructure may consist of multiple network fabrics.
  - A network fabric may directly correlate to a technology scope (WAN, sites, DC, DMZ), but may also span multiple technology scopes.
- Each network fabric is under the governance of a single controller.
- A controller may govern multiple fabrics.
- The set of network elements under the direction of the same controller defines a controller domain.
- A network element may only be part of a single fabric network.
- The Cisco DNA infrastructure may be governed by multiple controllers.

Figures 5-9, 5-10, and 5-11 illustrate some examples of these relationships. In Figure 5-9, network fabrics correspond to technology scopes and are each under the direction of a controller instance. Figure 5-10 shows separate fabric networks that are instantiated for the WAN, DC, DMZ, and sites. However, a single controller instance directs the operations for the WAN and site fabrics. Another controller instance governs the DMZ, DC, and VPC. Figure 5-11 on the other hand depicts a Cisco Digital Network Architecture where a single network fabric spans both the WAN and the sites. In this case, a controller instance corresponds to that fabric. The DC and DMZ scopes are again under the direction of a second controller instance.

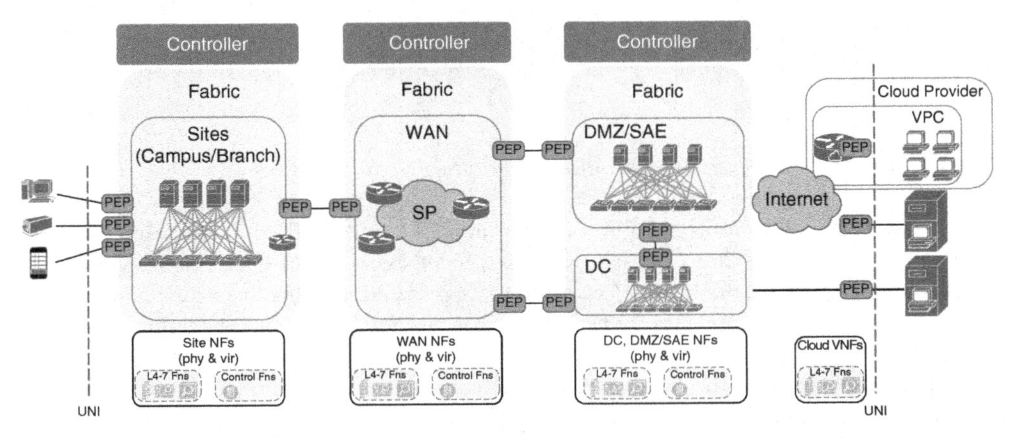

Figure 5-9 *Controller Domains Mapping to Fabric Networks and Technology Scopes*

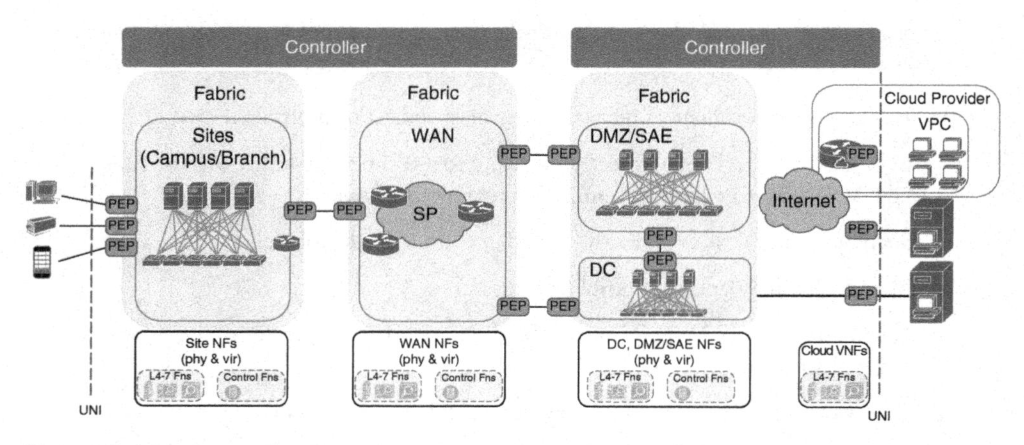

Figure 5-10 *Controller Domains Mapping to Multiple Fabric Networks*

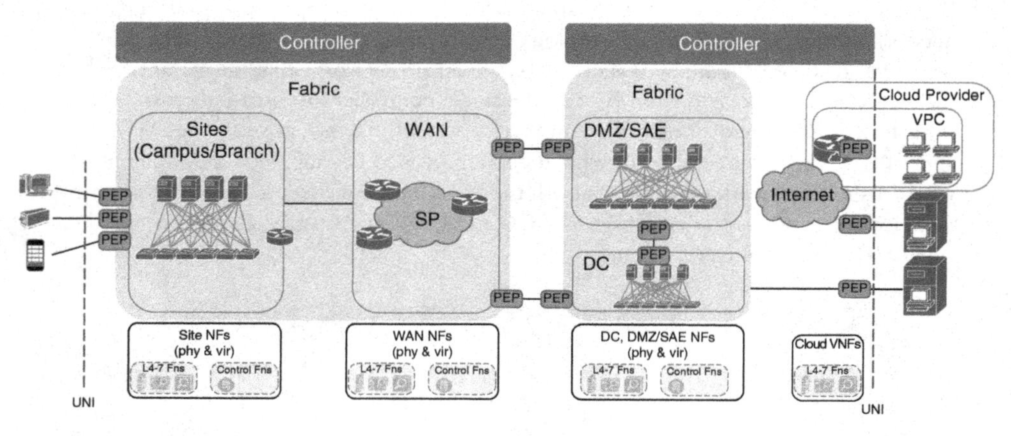

Figure 5-11 *Fabric Networks Spanning Technology Scopes*

In all the examples shown in Figures 5-9 through 5-11, a network-to-network interface (NNI) specifies how Cisco DNA services are carried between the different fabric network domains. Recall that the NNI in Cisco DNA is associated with the links connecting the border network elements in the adjacent fabric networks. The NNIs connecting fabrics must thus be enforcing policy on either side of the interface, as represented by a PEP icon in each fabric. In the case where a single controller instance governs more than one fabric network, the NNI for those fabric networks is configured by that single controller. In the case where fabric networks are governed by separate controller instances, the NNI configuration in each of the fabric border nodes needs to be coordinated between the two (or more) controllers.

Note that in Figures 5-9 through 5-11, the supporting network functions are outside of the network fabrics. They are assumed not to be fabric enabled, thus connecting to the Cisco DNA infrastructure via a UNI.

The statement "a Cisco DNA infrastructure may be governed by multiple controllers" offers you as a network architect an important trade-off: how finely granular to "slice" the network elements. For certain infrastructure sizes and organizational structures, a single controller instance directing a single fabric may suffice. This avoids multiple controllers and NNIs between the respective fabric networks. On the other hand, size and organizational structure may require you to arrange the infrastructure into multiple controller domains, thus increasing the number of controller instances (even if they are of the same type or the same vendor). The more network fabrics that are operated, the larger the number of NNIs in the architecture. These may be regulated from a single controller or from different controllers. The more fragmented the Cisco DNA infrastructure into network fabrics and possibly controller domains, the more NNIs are required.

Cisco DNA Interfaces

The network architecture structure described so far intends to increase the simplicity of a Cisco DNA-enabled network. To enable a complete end-to-end transport path for the connectivity of applications between devices, the fabrics and controller domains need to connect to each other—and these interconnections are specified in form of NNIs in Cisco DNA.

The concept of a user-to-network interface was already introduced. Any user, application, or device seeking to consume a Cisco DNA service—i.e., wishing to connect to applications in the data center or cloud, or communicate with an application running on a user device—must be admitted to the Cisco DNA infrastructure via a UNI. This even holds for the supplementary network services, which are viewed as applications supporting the network operation. The UNI is tightly coupled to the notion of a policy enforcement point. As traffic from endpoints enters the network, it is associated with a particular Cisco DNA service and, by definition, the respective policies (security, transport handling, and reporting) are applied.

Between the network fabrics, however, it is the NNIs that specify how traffic traverses through the various parts of the network. NNIs always exist when two controller domains are joined. For example, an NNI dictates how the network elements under a WAN controller domain connect to the network elements under the DC controller domain.

NNIs may also exist if multiple fabrics are under the governance of a single controller, as illustrated in Figure 5-11.

Recall that in either case, the NNIs are always associated on the links connecting the two groups of network elements. This is because each network element or virtual network function is only controlled by a single controller. The NNI is not instantiated by a single border element talking to neighbors in two or more different controller domains or fabric networks. In this case, such a border element would have to be configured by the respective controllers, violating the principle stated previously that a network element can participate only in a single fabric network.

The NNIs in Cisco DNA indicate the control plane relationships as two controller domains or fabric networks that are joined. They also stipulate the data plane specifics, e.g., which frame formats are admissible to carry traffic between them.

Figure 5-12 depicts the different UNI and NNI interfaces that exist in Cisco DNA. The figure assumes that fabric networks correspond to technological scopes (WAN, DC, sites, and DMZ) with a one-to-one relationship. Endpoints (devices) on the left and applications on the right are shown to always connect via a UNI, and are associated with a single PEP building block in the diagram. Similarly, the supporting network functions at the bottom of the figure are also shown to connect to the transport infrastructure via a UNI. NNIs are placed between fabric networks to connect the various transport fabrics together, providing an end-to-end infrastructure between the applications and the endpoints. Two PEPs are shown for each NNI to emphasize the point that the NNI between fabric domains is the link, not a single network element.

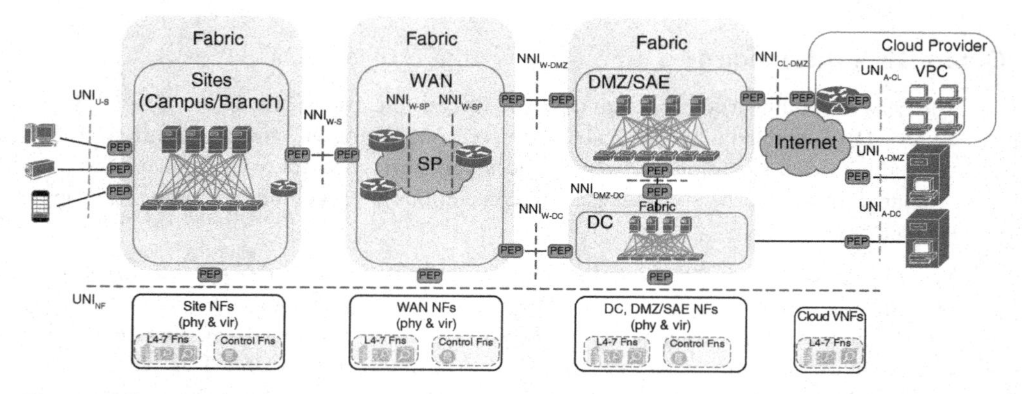

Figure 5-12 *Cisco DNA Network-to-Network Interfaces to Connect Different Fabric Domains*

Table 5-1 lists and describes the UNI and NNI interfaces shown in Figure 5-12.

Table 5-1 *UNI and NNI Interface Descriptions*

Interface Label	Description
$UNI_{U\text{-}S}$	Interface between users or devices and site; for example, users connecting wirelessly or wired into a branch or a campus. This interface is governed by a UNI PEP.
$UNI_{A\text{-}CL}$	Interface between applications and a cloud; for example, when the applications are hosted in a VPC and connected in the cloud environment to a network instance (VNF) for transport. This interface is governed by a UNI PEP.
$UNI_{A\text{-}DMZ}$	Interface between applications and DMZ; for example, if a host where the applications are running is directly connected to the access switch. This interface is governed by a UNI PEP.
$UNI_{A\text{-}DC}$	Interface between applications and the enterprise DC/private cloud; for example, when applications are running in the enterprise run DC. This interface is governed by a UNI PEP.

Interface Label	Description
UNI_{NF}	Interface between the infrastructure/fabric and the physical or virtual network functions. This interface is governed by a UNI PEP.
NNI_{W-S}	Interface between WAN and sites (campus, branch). This interface is governed by a pair of NNI PEPs.
NNI_{W-SP}	Interface between the WAN and the SP. This can be a managed or unmanaged WAN service that is contracted by the enterprise from the SP to connect branches with each other or with WAN aggregation sites. This interface is governed by a pair of NNI PEPs.
NNI_{W-DMZ}	Interface between the WAN and the DMZ/SAE. This interface is governed by a pair of NNI PEPs.
NNI_{DMZ-DC}	Interface between the DMZ/SAE and the DC/private cloud. This interface is governed by a pair of NNI PEPs.
NNI_{W-DC}	Interface between the WAN and the DC/private cloud. This interface is governed by a pair of NNI PEPs.
NNI_{CL-DMZ}	Interface between the cloud (VPC) and the DMZ. This interface is governed by a pair of NNI PEPs.

Service Definition and Orchestration

So far this chapter has built up the Cisco DNA architecture from the bottom up, explaining the role of the transport infrastructure with its supporting network functions. It also has offered details on the functions of the controller, particularly its value to abstract details of the network elements to simplify the network, and to drive policy into the network in accordance with the business intent. As already alluded to, the service definition and orchestration layer defines the business intent. This section provides additional details on this component of Cisco DNA.

The service definition and orchestration building block in Cisco DNA is the component in Cisco DNA that defines the Cisco DNA services at an abstract level in accordance with the business intent, offers a presentation layer to express the business intent, and coordinates the instantiation of the Cisco DNA service instances.

Let's look at each of these functions in turn.

First, the service definition and orchestration layer offers you as a network operator the capability to define Cisco DNA services. Recall that a Cisco DNA service expresses the relationship between applications, hosted on end-user devices or data center servers, and the associated policies. The Cisco DNA services layer thus is the place in the network where such a relationship is expressed at an abstract layer. Users, devices, and applications (or groups) are known at this level, learned from auxiliary sources such as Cisco ISE, your enterprises authentication, authorization, and accounting (AAA) servers, or application repositories, regardless of the controller domain that the endpoints are associated with. Policies are then formulated for those endpoint groups. These policies may govern the access to the network via authentication and authorization. For example, an access policy may state that users have to authenticate with a username/password combination or via IEEE 802.1X, or other authentication mechanisms. Associating a device or a user with a particular user or device group may also be stated in the access policy. The relationship between users, devices, and applications may also be governed by a policy expressed in this building block. For example, an access control policy may be specified to regulate that a user group may only communicate with one or more specified application groups. The other policy types in Cisco DNA—transport handling and reporting—are also characterized for a particular Cisco DNA service.

Table 5-2 illustrates an example of such a Cisco DNA service definition. User, application, and device groups are represented in a conceptual table, with the cell entries specifying the security (access, access control), transport handling, and reporting policies in the abstract.

Table 5-2 *Example of Abstracted Policies*

	Production Servers	Development Servers	Internet Access
Employee group (managed asset)	Permit Business critical Don't log Strong secure	Deny	Permit Business default
Employee group (BYOD)	Permit Business critical Don't log Strong secure	Deny	Permit Business default
Guests	Deny	Deny	Permit Log all Business irrelevant
Partners	Permit Business critical Log all Strong secure	Deny	Deny

Note that such policies are not necessarily expressed as pairs in all cases. A single-sided policy is thought of as a paired policy with one end being "any." For example, upon access to the network a device always undergoes a posture assessment, regardless of the intended subsequent communication relationship.

In Cisco DNA, services are typically expressed in terms of the groups of users, applications, and devices. This makes the policies manageable by reducing the combinations of pairings. Imagine having to specify policies at the user, application, and device level in an enterprise with thousands of users, multiple thousands of devices, and hundreds of applications! Specifying policies at the individual user, application, and device level can easily result in hundreds of thousands of policies—which for the most part are identical. Grouping significantly reduces complexity to express policies and assure their compliance. However, such grouped policies do not exclude user-, application-, or device-specific policies. These can always be thought of as groups with a single member. For example, you can always create a group for the CEO of your company, and then treat your CEO as a group with one member in the policy definitions.

Second, the Cisco DNA services and definition component offers a presentation layer for the expression of such policies. The presentation layer may be in the form of a GUI that allows you to graphically express abstracted Cisco DNA services and policies. Alternatively, the presentation layer may be in the form of APIs that are called by a northbound system. In either case, the syntax to describe the services is abstracted from the network element details to achieve simplicity. An example of such a syntax was given in Figure 5-4 where the policy "point-of-sale traffic is critical" was expressed to reflect the business intent. Such abstractions are provided by the presentation layer—either built into the GUI or defined in the APIs.

Third, the service definition and orchestration layer offers the capability to drive the Cisco DNA services into the network. It coordinates the instantiation of a Cisco DNA service into the different domains/fabrics via their specific controllers, and is critical to implement the Cisco DNA services across domains. The instantiation of the Cisco DNA services needs to be coordinated between multiple controllers (hence "orchestration"). Such coordination requires that the Cisco DNA service instantiation is driven into each of the controller domains in a timely manner. It also requires a feedback loop and rollback mechanisms from the controllers to the service definition and orchestration layer. If a Cisco DNA service is instantiated across domains, the possibility of a deployment failure exists. In this case, the Cisco DNA orchestration needs to either reverse the Cisco DNA service instantiation requests in the other controller domains and report a failure, or reattempt the Cisco DNA service instantiation in the controller domain where the instantiation failed, possibly with different parameters.

The service definition and orchestration component offers the capability to define and instantiate end-to-end Cisco DNA services that align with your business intent by leveraging abstractions.

Figure 5-8 already illustrated the relationship between the service definition and orchestration building block and the remaining Cisco DNA architecture components. APIs ensure that the abstracted Cisco DNA services defined are automatically and consistently driven into the Cisco DNA infrastructure via the controller layer.

Relationship Between the Controllers and the Service Definition and Orchestration Component

The relationship between the Cisco DNA service definition and orchestration component and the controllers is illustrated in Figure 5-13, showing a high-level workflow interaction between these components. The Cisco DNA service definition and orchestration layer learns about all users, applications, and devices and their groupings, regardless of which controller domain these are associated with. This is achieved by either interfacing directly with the respective endpoint management repositories or learning via the controllers.

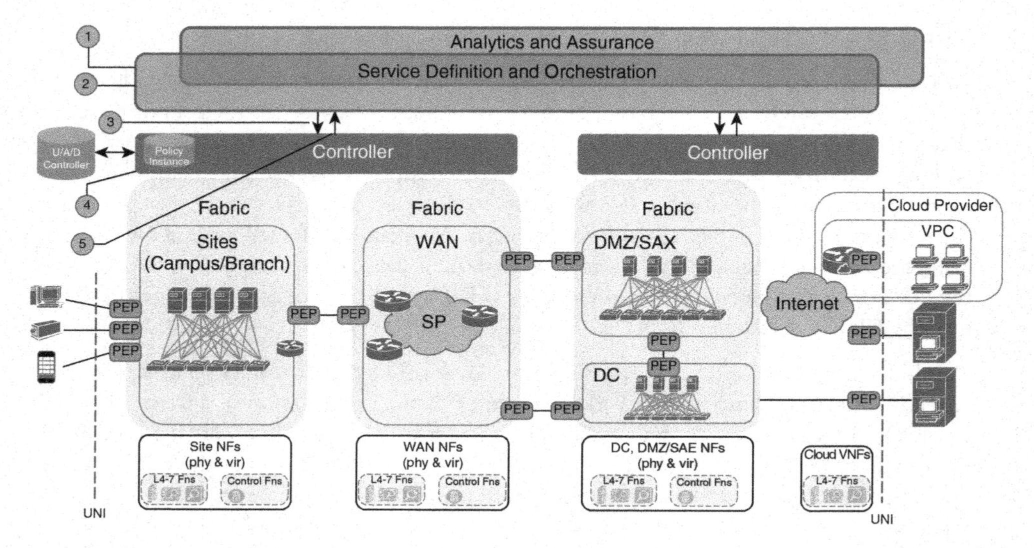

Figure 5-13 *Relationship Between the Cisco DNA Service Definition and Orchestration Component and the Controllers*

1. The service definition and orchestration learns about user groups, device groups, and application groups.
   - E.g., directly from ISE
   - E.g., via controllers
2. The service definition and orchestration defines the Cisco DNA service.
   - Cisco DNA services are abstract expressions of intent; for example, for application policies categorizing applications into relevant, default, or irrelevant
   - Access policies are abstracted into access/blocked/restricted
   - Cisco DNA services also contain details on monitoring
   - Cisco DNA services typically provide relationships between user groups, application groups, or device groups
   - Cisco DNA services may be scoped to a particular domain

3. The service definition and orchestration pushes the abstracted definition to the controller function.
   - Cisco DNA service scope is honored
4. The controller instantiates the Cisco DNA service.
   - Honoring Cisco DNA service scope
   - Controller decides how to realize the service and how to convert abstracted expressions of intent into device configurations
5. The controller provides feedback to the service definition and orchestration to report the outcome of the Cisco DNA service instantiation.

The service definition and orchestration layer then allows the abstract expression of a service, defining the policies (security, transport handling, and reporting) for individual endpoint groups or relationships. The Cisco DNA services may be associated with a particular scope to exclude certain controller domains. This may be helpful, for example, to prevent certain content from being accessed from outside the region, which may be the case if regulatory restrictions for applications apply.

Next, the Cisco DNA services are instantiated into the controllers by calling their respective APIs. The Cisco DNA services are typically created for the user/application/device groups at Cisco DNA service definition time. This may be independent of the time that users, devices, or applications come online. In this way, the Cisco DNA service instantiation is not tied to specific user/application/device access events in the network, which can be significantly more dynamic in nature than Cisco DNA service instantiations. The grouping of users, applications, and devices helps simplify the Cisco DNA services and makes these more manageable.

The respective Cisco DNA controllers then take the Cisco DNA service instantiation requests and drive the Cisco DNA services into the network. This implies computing the list of network elements that are required for the particular Cisco DNA service. In some cases, a VNF may need to be instantiated first to execute a particular policy function (such as WAN optimization). The controllers also translate the abstracted syntax of the Cisco DNA service that is specified at the Cisco DNA services and orchestration layer into specific device configurations. For example, a service expression that traffic is "business critical" may be translated into a priority queue configuration for some network elements, or may be translated into a class-based weighted fair queueing (CBWFQ) configuration for other network elements. Alternatively, an abstract expression of "highly confidential" may cause an IPsec configuration to be instantiated within a controller domain.

Finally, the controllers provide feedback to the Cisco DNA service definition and orchestration layer, again in form of API calls. This is important to ensure that any cross-domain Cisco DNA services are successfully instantiated in all domains. It also prevents controllers from having to communicate directly with each other, avoiding an any-to-any controller communication relationship.

Analytics Platform

The previous sections of this chapter examined how Cisco DNA services are defined and instantiated in the network. But this is only half of the Cisco DNA story—driving network functionality into the infrastructure to align with the business intent. The other half is about feedback, having the confirmation that the network has successfully instantiated a Cisco DNA service, that the Cisco DNA service aligns with the business intent. The other half is about having an instantaneous view of the state of the network whenever a user or an application manager complains about bad application performance. This section looks at the feedback mechanism that Cisco DNA offers to extract data from the network.

In Cisco DNA, the analytics building block is being defined here as "a component in Cisco DNA that gathers and normalizes operational data from the network elements and functions (data collection), exports data from network elements and functions (telemetry), facilitates the correlation of data from different sources to extract meaningful information for the purpose of reporting, optionally relying on machine learning (analysis), and provides APIs to feed the meaningful data back to the Cisco DNA controller or to other consumers of analytics data (reporting)."

Figure 5-14 illustrates the relationship between the analytics platform and the other Cisco DNA building blocks. APIs connect all the network elements and network functions to the analytics layer (southbound APIs) to collect telemetry data from the infrastructure. Northbound APIs from the analytics communicate back to the service definition and orchestration layer, and to the controllers to automate recommended data-driven actions. This ensures that the insights derived by analytics are acted upon in the network to optimize the operation and to ensure that the Cisco DNA services are at any point in time aligning with the business intent. These northbound APIs may also be leveraged to provide feedback to applications.

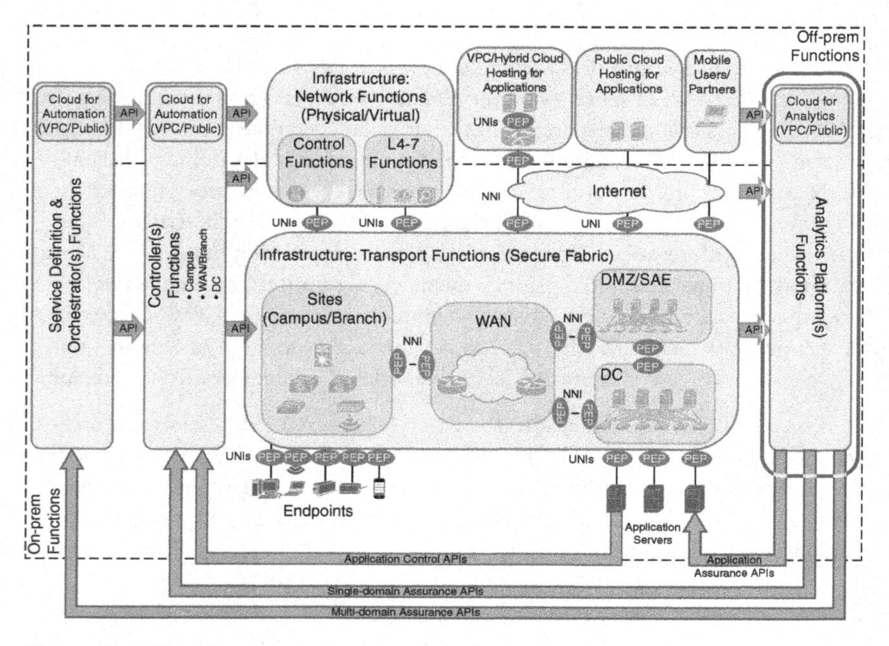

Figure 5-14 *Cisco DNA Analytics Platform*

Data Collection

A function of the Cisco DNA analytics platform is to collect data about the network. The data collected can come from multiple sources, be of multiple types, and be in multiple formats. In a Cisco DNA network, the principal data sources are the physical network elements and virtualized network functions. Secondary sources such as controllers or supporting network functions also provide meaningful data for the analytics platform. For example, logs from DNS or AAA servers can be exported to the analytics engine for correlation with data from other sources.

Data from network elements, VNFs, and secondary sources may be of different types:

- **Metrics:** Data about the operational state of the network elements and VNFs, such as system counts, connection counts (e.g., packet counters), timeouts, etc.
- **Events:** Data about incidents occurring in the network elements and VNFs, such as Syslog events, SNMP traps, event notifications, etc.
- **Streams:** Data that is continuously collected and streamed from, for example, network sensors

The different data types collected as part of the Cisco DNA analytics platform can be in different formats and have different granularity. For example, some data may pertain to the network elements and functions, while other data may provide information about applications or users.

Data Extraction

The Cisco DNA data collection function offers the flexibility of extracting such data in multiple ways. Several telemetry mechanisms help to extract data from the network elements and functions, such as Cisco IOS NetFlow, sFlow, IPFix, or NETCONF/YANG. The collected data may be directly exported to the data processing and analytics engine. Alternatively, the data may be first stored on premises in a local collector for a site. Not all of the raw data necessarily needs to be exported to the analytics engine. Local collectors allow the normalization of data arriving in different formats. Data may also be processed using a proxy engine (distributed analytics). The latter may be beneficial to optimize the data for transport, such as to reduce duplicate event data or to preprocess data to extract summary statistics. In this way, the centralized data processing and analytics engine may not need to absorb the raw data from a large number of sources.

Note that the extracted data may need to be supplemented with additional metadata—in particular with timestamps—before exporting. Also important in the data collection process is data accuracy. Important information may be lost if metrics are collected with insufficient precision (think decimal places), or if a preprocessing engine averages out data over too long a time period and loses an important outlier event that should be reported!

Data Ingestion

The data exported via telemetry from the network element and functions needs to be ingested into the Cisco DNA analytics engine. The analytics engine is the subcomponent of the Cisco DNA analytics platform that is responsible for analyzing the data and extracting meaningful information for various consumers of analytics data. The analytics engine has multiple constituents: a data ingestion process, one or more data processing engines, a data distribution logic (bus) to share incoming data with the various processing engines, and one or more storage repositories.

The data ingestion process is responsible for receiving the telemetry data from the various sources. For continuously streamed data, it maintains connections to the sources in the network elements, VNFs, on-premises collectors, or proxies. For data that needs to be pulled, the ingestion process implements the polling mechanism, periodically querying the sources for data.

The data distribution logic that is part of the Cisco DNA analytics platform allows the ingested data to be distributed to multiple analytics processing engines and multiple storage repositories. It implements a pub/sub messaging bus.

Multiple analytics engines process the data that was ingested and disseminated via the data distribution logic. Distributing the analytics processing load between multiple analytics algorithms allows the Cisco DNA analytics platform to scale. Also, it enables the processing to be targeted based on the type of data to be analyzed and reported. For example, an analytics process may specialize in computing information about network element data, whereas another analytics process may focus on correlating data from various sources on user or application data. Recall that data may come not only from the network elements and VNFs themselves, but also from auxiliary sources. This enables the analytics engines to correlate data from different sources and offer *meaningful* data, rather than just *raw* data, to the consumers of the analytics. Note that the analytics engines may rely on machine learning to do their job.

The data storage repositories that are part of the Cisco DNA analytics platform allow the ingested data or the post-processed data to be stored. This is extremely useful to offer time-series analysis—showing how the network, a Cisco DNA service, or a user experience evolves over time. It also allows the analytics engines to draw on historical data to make their inferences. Many machine learning algorithms that are based on artificial intelligence algorithms rely on such historical data to train the algorithms, or to continuously self-optimize the algorithms. A further functionality offered by the data storage repositories is support for text searches or keeping a database for information graphs—relationships between various kinds of objects (network topologies, user group information, policy graphs, etc.).

Data Export

The Cisco DNA analytics platform offers APIs to export the computed meaningful information to various consumers. First and foremost, analytics data can be fed back into the service definition and orchestration layer and controller layer of Cisco DNA.

This is extremely useful to provide Cisco DNA service assurance: guaranteeing that the Cisco DNA services that reflect the business intent are indeed operating as designed. Alternatively, if they are not, the controllers can leverage the analytics data to automatically drive changes into the infrastructure to bring the affected Cisco DNA services back into compliance.

The analytics data also serves to provide meaningful information back to other "consumers." A GUI, for example, can display analytics data to you as a network operator, to various levels of support staff, or even to the application owners directly. Similarly, application developers may query analytics data to optimize the behavior of their application. Think about the many applications that can leverage user location data from the network!

Figure 5-15 shows the detailed subcomponents of the Cisco DNA analytics platform previously discussed.

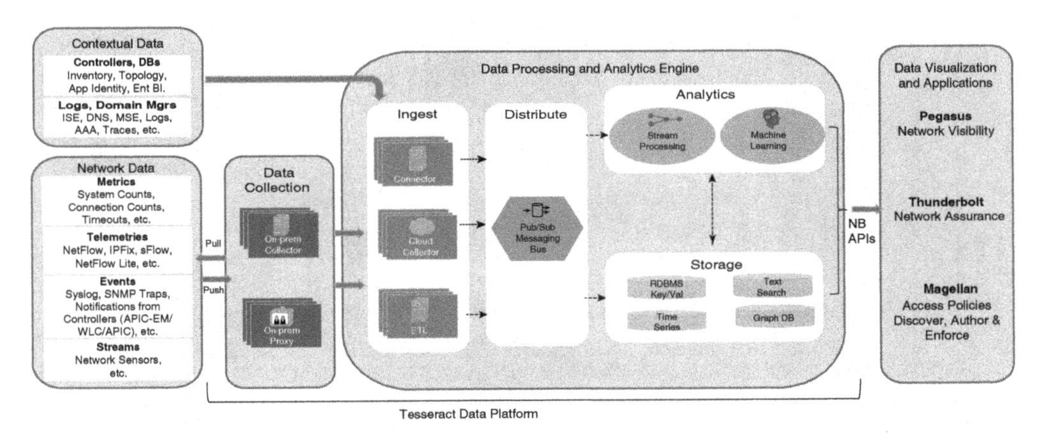

Figure 5-15 *Subcomponents of the Cisco DNA Analytics Platform*

On-Premises and Off-Premises Agnosticism—Revisiting the Cloud

One of the key enhancements of Cisco DNA is the full inclusion and support of the cloud in the enterprise network. As introduced in the previous chapter, this inclusion comes in three main forms:

1. Providing the ability to extend the enterprise network into the cloud for cloud-hosted applications.
2. Leveraging the cloud for hosting the Cisco DNA service definition and orchestration component and the controller component
3. Leveraging the cloud for hosting the Cisco DNA analytics platform

Figure 5-16 illustrates the relationship between the cloud-hosted components and the Cisco DNA building blocks introduced so far. This section is revisiting the role of the cloud in Cisco DNA to provide further details on how the cloud is fully integrated into the architecture.

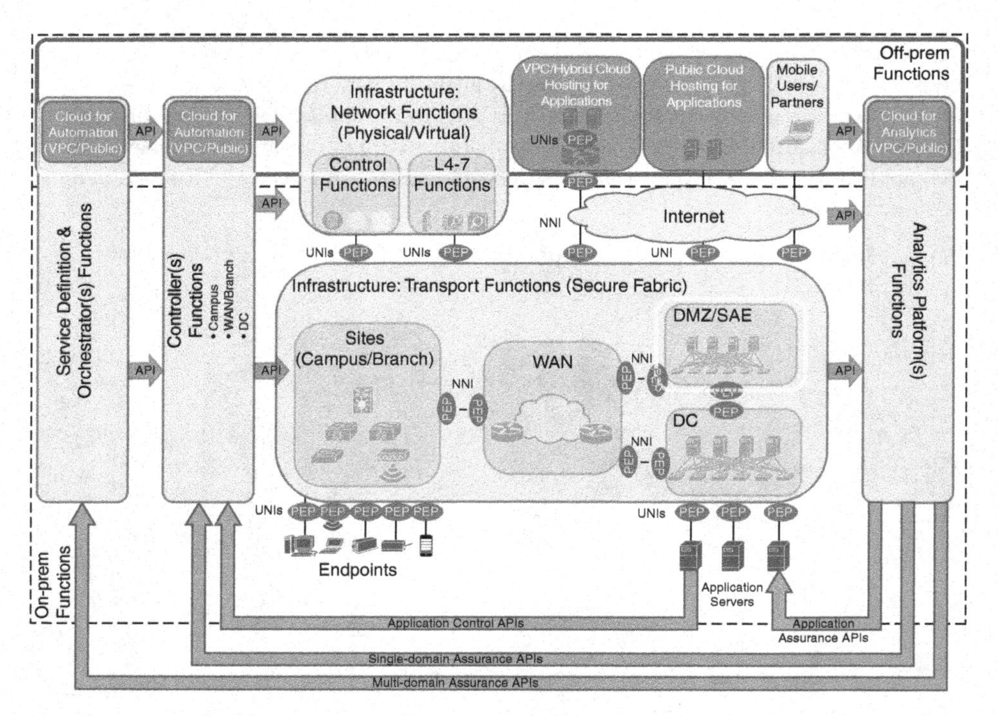

Figure 5-16 *Cisco DNA Cloud—On-Premises and Off-Premises Agnosticism*

Application Hosting in the Cloud and the Evolution of the DMZ

As enterprise applications are increasingly hosted in the cloud, the enterprise network architecture needs to ensure that connectivity is seamless to reach those applications. The connectivity options vary by the type of cloud that is consumed.

In the case of a virtual private cloud, such as Amazon AWS or Microsoft Azure, applications are hosted on the cloud provider's hosting infrastructure. This infrastructure may be physically shared between multiple enterprises, but it is strictly separated at a logical level to ensure privacy. From an enterprise architecture perspective, the applications are strictly separated from others and considered private.

Connectivity into a VPC environment is typically established by running a virtualized forwarding function such as a virtual router in the VPC. Such a virtualized forwarding function is often also responsible for encrypting the enterprise traffic flows across the Internet connecting the enterprise-managed Cisco DNA infrastructure to the cloud. Note that you own and control networking functionality within the VPC!

Toward the applications that are hosted in the VPC, traditional virtualization and segmentation techniques may be applied to ensure reachability.

Application hosting in a VPC is illustrated in Figure 5-16. Note that in such an architecture there are typically two types of PEPs: a PEP that regulates the access of the enterprise applications into Cisco DNA, and a PEP to enforce the policies of connecting a VPC domain to the remainder of the Cisco DNA infrastructure. The latter may, for example, postulate that traffic needs to be encrypted if the VPC is connected to the Cisco DNA DMZ across the Internet.

In the case of an application that is consumed as a service (SaaS), the connectivity of the application into the Cisco DNA architecture is typically over the Internet directly. In this case, you do not own any infrastructure or networking functions in the SaaS provider. Traffic to and from the hosted applications is secured at the application level.

SaaS traffic ingresses your Cisco DNA architecture in a gateway that is typically hosted in the DMZ. Additional security functions may be applied in the DMZ to protect your network against attacks. For example, the DMZ may be protected by a firewall. The SaaS traffic may have to traverse an application layer gateway. Functions such as intrusion prevention and intrusion detection may also be applied to protect against malicious traffic.

Note that in Figure 5-16 the SaaS and public cloud connectivity is also depicted. In this case, traffic is governed by a UNI PEP upon ingress into the Cisco DNA infrastructure.

In the case of applications being hosted in a hybrid cloud environment, they are hosted using a mix of on-premises hosts and private or even public cloud environments. A hybrid cloud is under a common orchestration platform to enable a seamless migration of your enterprise application between cloud environments. The previously described connectivity options apply to hybrid clouds as well.

As mentioned, a DMZ is needed in the architecture as an entry point into Cisco DNA. Because cloud connectivity in Cisco DNA is vital, the DMZ architecture is significantly enhanced to provide a secure and agile exchange infrastructure (SAE). SAE evolves a traditional DMZ along multiple fronts. First, it offers a place in the Cisco DNA architecture where traffic between multiple endpoint and application groups can be exchanged. Hosting applications in the cloud increases the diversity of traffic that leaves the enterprise-managed infrastructure. Extranet partners, customers, VPC applications, SaaS applications, and any Internet traffic originating from your enterprise can now be exchanged. Second, SAE extends a traditional DMZ architecture to be fully policy-based. The policies associated with a Cisco DNA service are brought forward and extended into the SAE domain of Cisco DNA. SAE focuses particularly on security functionality, because it primarily governs the connectivity to endpoints and applications that are not hosted on enterprise-managed infrastructure. Third, SAE leverages virtualization to implement Cisco DNA policies. Using VNFs allows such functions to be deployed more dynamically and potentially with a per-Cisco DNA-service granularity. This can have significant operational benefits. Think about upgrading the software on a shared firewall: a physical firewall shared among multiple applications is harder to upgrade. All the application owners need to coordinate their upgrade windows. Virtualized, per-application firewalls can be upgraded independently!

Figure 5-17 illustrates the concept of SAE, highlighting the domain as a central connectivity point for and between employee groups, partners, customers, mobile workers, and applications sitting in the private DC, a VPC, or consumed as a service. This exchange in SAE is fully policy-based under the same service definition and orchestration component or analytics component already described.

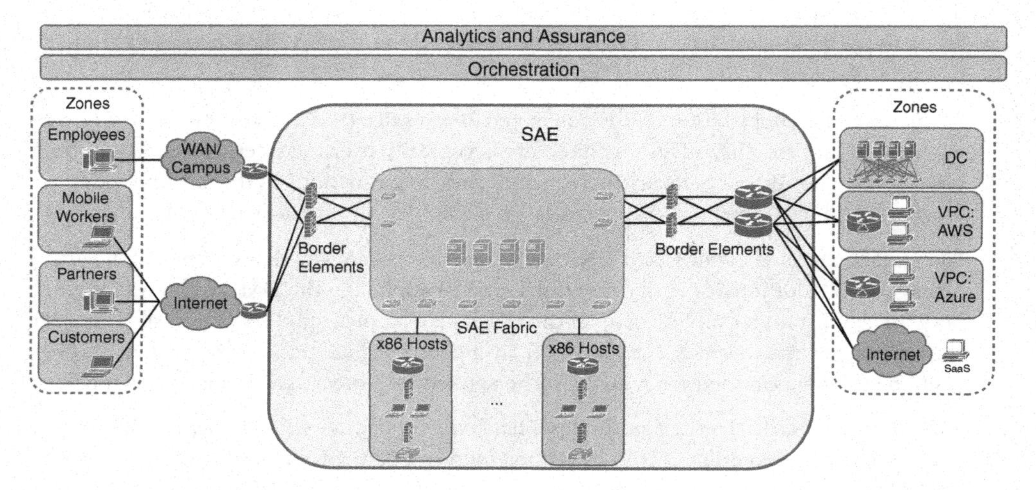

Figure 5-17 *Cisco DNA Secure Agile Exchange for Secure Policy-based Cloud Connectivity*

Leveraging the Cloud for Cisco DNA Controllers and Analytics

Connectivity into the cloud for Cisco DNA is, of course, important and relevant not only for enterprise applications. The Cisco DNA control plane applications also benefit from running in the cloud—after all, the Cisco DNA service definition and orchestration component, controller component, and analytics platform are all software functions! These functions are fully cloud enabled in Cisco DNA.

In the context of the Cisco DNA control functions (service definition and orchestration, controllers, and analytics platform), the benefits of cloud computing can be applied to Cisco DNA itself! Running these functions in a VPC, for example, alleviates the need to manage your own hosting infrastructure for Cisco DNA control. The cloud provider manages the complexities of operating server and storage infrastructures, power, cooling, etc. For the analytics functions in particular, this enables flexible scale-out of the Cisco DNA control infrastructure. As more analytics engines are deployed to extract meaningful information from your Cisco DNA infrastructure, additional compute and storage is simply consumed as a service. Also, the advantages of cloud hosting from a high-availability perspective can be leveraged. Your Cisco DNA control functions are always available—the cloud providers assume the responsibility of managing hardware failures. And from a software perspective, the Cisco DNA control functions are fully cloud enabled—leveraging virtualization and containers, as well as scale-out architectures in support. Finally, running the Cisco DNA control functions in the cloud allows you to manage your Cisco DNA services and infrastructure from anywhere.

Figures 5-18 and 5-19 show how the Cisco DNA service definition and orchestration component, controller component, and analytics platform run in a cloud environment respectively. A major difference in using the cloud for Cisco DNA control arises with the traffic patterns: for Cisco DNA services, traffic is segmented in the Cisco DNA infrastructure based on the relationships between users, applications, and device groups. The traffic uses overlays to traverse the Cisco DNA network. In the case of Cisco DNA control being hosted in a cloud environment, however, the traffic must reach the Cisco DNA infrastructure and components directly. As outlined in the previous sections, API calls are binding the service definition and orchestration component to the controller component, the controller component to the network elements and network functions, or to the analytics platform. These API calls allow for the various components to behave as one system. This is highlighted in the diagrams by the example of the controllers configuring the PEPs, or the analytics platform interfacing with the network elements to extract telemetry data.

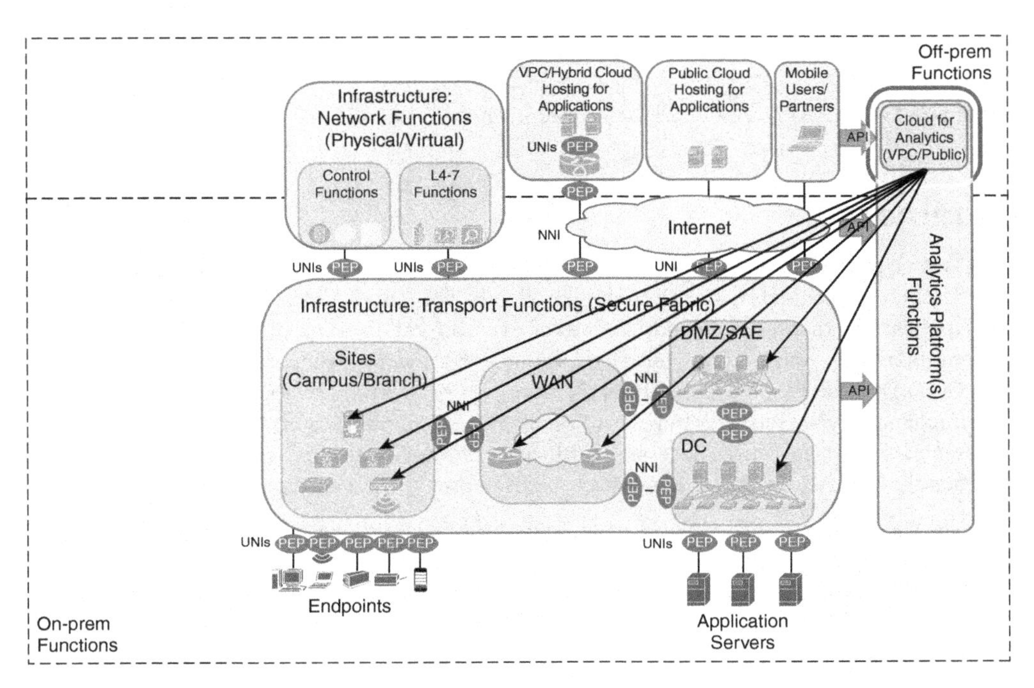

Figure 5-18 *Cisco DNA Cloud for Analytics*

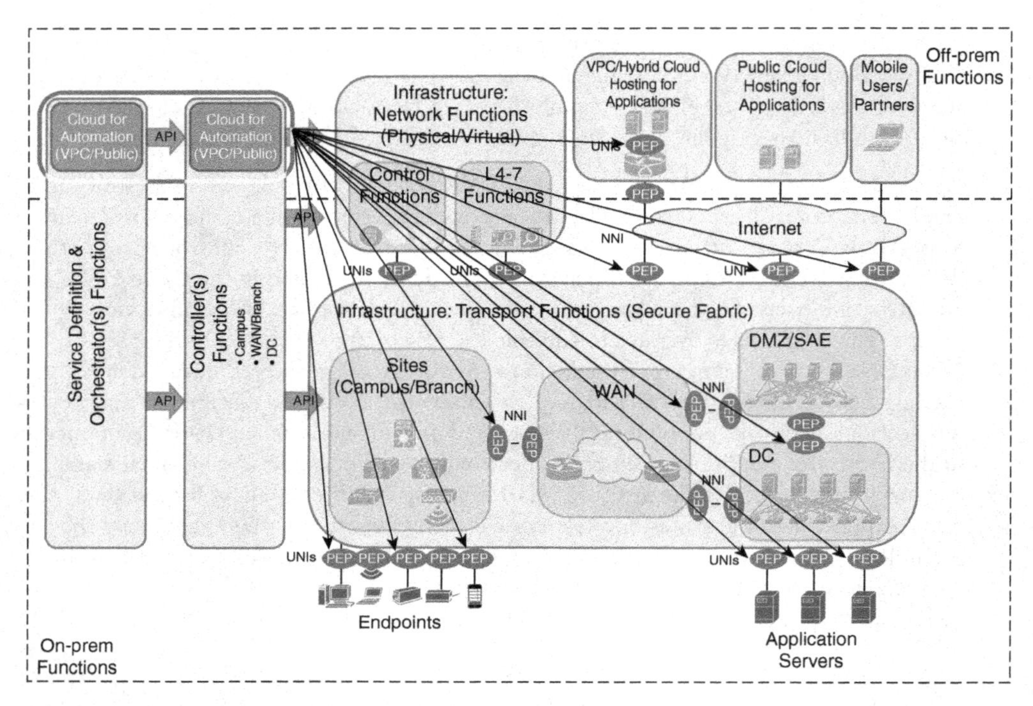

Figure 5-19 *Cisco DNA Cloud for Automation*

Summary

This chapter unpeeled the architectural onion another layer, looking at the architectural components of Cisco DNA in more depth. The key of Cisco DNA is to enable applications that reside in endpoints to talk to each other—regardless of whether these endpoints are operated by your IT department, by an employee, or by a partner. The Cisco DNA service not only offers the transport between these applications, but also implements your business policies to regulate the communication. The policies focus on security (authentication, access control, encryption), but also extend to govern transport handling (SLAs, quality of experience, traffic optimization) and reporting.

The Cisco DNA transport infrastructure in this blueprint consists of the traditional packet-forwarding elements arranged as a fabric. Supporting network functions provide the necessary infrastructure for the Cisco DNA control plane, as well as the capabilities to implement some of the policies required to instantiate a Cisco DNA service (e.g., firewalls, WAN optimization, etc.).

The controller layer in Cisco DNA plays a special role. Not only does this component abstract the complexities of diverse network elements and VNFs (possibly from multiple vendors), but, perhaps more importantly, the controllers offer an abstraction layer into the network, allowing Cisco DNA services (and policies in particular) to be expressed in the abstract. The controllers then perform the function of translating the abstract expression of intent into actionable device configurations, and driving these into the appropriate network elements. Controllers allow the Cisco DNA infrastructure to be structured into different controller domains, with well-defined interfaces between them.

The controllers in Cisco DNA work hand in hand with the service definition and orchestration building block, which is where Cisco DNA services are defined, expressing the relationships between users, applications, or devices. These are typically grouped in Cisco DNA for scalability. Cisco DNA services defined at this layer are expressed in a technology-abstracted syntax to facilitate the alignment with your business intent. The service definition and orchestration layer is responsible for driving the Cisco DNA services into all the different controller domains, making it the end-to-end building block. Controller domains, with their intricate knowledge of all network elements and functions, need not have a global view of the entire enterprise network. For a Cisco DNA service to be instantiated end to end across enterprise sites, the WAN, the DMZ, and various forms of the cloud, only the users, applications, and devices need to be globally known. The service definition and orchestration component in Cisco DNA thus contributes significantly to simplifying the architecture!

The analytics platform in Cisco DNA complements the mentioned building blocks to enable instantaneous and accurate information about the Cisco DNA network components. After all, one of the key goals in Cisco DNA is to guarantee that the network is at any time in full alignment with your business objectives as expressed by Cisco DNA services. Cisco DNA analytics provides the required functionality to collect various types of data from all over the network and from supporting sources, to normalize and feed this data up to the Cisco DNA analytics platform, and to correlate and run the data through multiple analytics engines to derive *meaningful* information. These results are then fed back into the controller and service definition and orchestration layers to deliver a closed-loop control cycle for Cisco DNA services. Alternatively, the insights derived from the analytics platform can be exposed to you as a network operator in a GUI, or to application developers who may also want to consume the data as part of their applications.

Last but not least, the Cisco DNA blueprint outlined in this chapter stresses the importance of the cloud in the architecture. Applications are assumed to run in the cloud—period. Whether the consumption model is in the form of a virtual private cloud, as a service, or a hybrid cloud, Cisco DNA services and their associated policies reach into the cloud. In case of a VPC, the Cisco DNA services are orchestrated into the cloud. In the case of SaaS or to allow access for mobile employees, customers, or partners over the Internet, the respective Cisco DNA services are instantiated in the DMZ. Due to the importance of the cloud, the DMZ is elevated in importance as a domain in Cisco DNA as a Secure Agile Exchange (SAE) point. In support of Cisco DNA services, SAE is fully policy aware and virtualized, critical to instantiate security functions on demand.

Figure 5-20 summarizes the Cisco DNA blueprint described in this chapter with all its principal components. We'll delve into the depths of each of these components in more detail in the subsequent chapters.

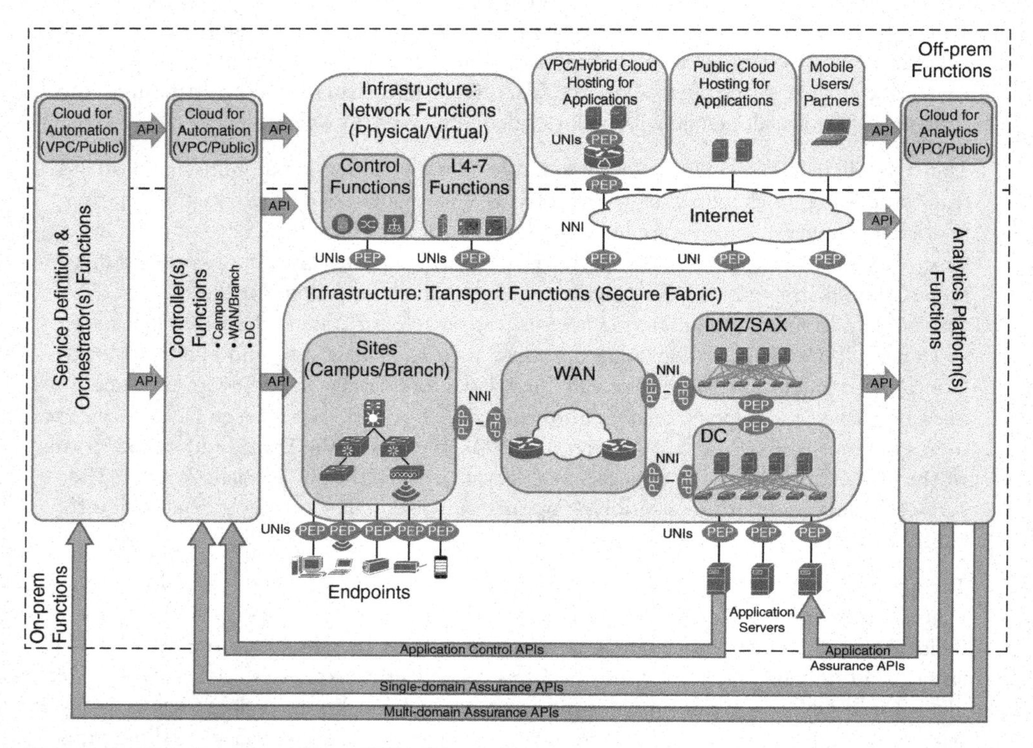

Figure 5-20 *Complete Cisco DNA Blueprint*

Chapter 6

Introduction to Cisco DNA Infrastructure

Network infrastructure is all around you. In any city, the tall buildings you see host anywhere from several to dozens or hundreds of networks—wired and wireless network infrastructures. They support all of the users, devices, things, and applications that organizations within those buildings use to drive and support daily activities.

The network is central to today's business infrastructure. It is an inextricable part of how business is conducted now and into the future. But how often do you stop to consider what actually makes up that network—the actual infrastructure in which the network is composed?

The next few chapters explore the hardware, software, and protocols that make up a modern network infrastructure, and the set of capabilities that these elements enable. These are the base components of the Cisco Digital Network Architecture (Cisco DNA). And just like the architecture of a building, the structure of Cisco DNA is only as strong as its foundation, which is introduced in this chapter. Cisco DNA has a very strong foundation in the flexible networking hardware and the powerful networking software on which it is fundamentally based.

This chapter presents the following:

- Picturing the modern network
- Exploring Cisco DNA infrastructure
- The evolving network, and why it matters
- Cisco DNA infrastructure solutions

The fundamental Cisco DNA hardware and software architectural components are examined in greater detail in Chapters 7 through 10.

You will learn the critical areas around Cisco DNA infrastructure that allow for a greater appreciation for the base underpinnings of Cisco DNA solutions and capabilities. It is important to understand the capabilities of Cisco DNA infrastructure, in order to better understand and appreciate the capabilities and solutions that this very functional, flexible, and future-proofed architecture supports.

Picturing the Modern Network

Imagine all the data that flows over all the networks used today, worldwide. According to "Cisco Visual Networking Index: Forecast and Methodology, 2016–2021,"[1] the estimated amount of all data transmitted over IP networks in 2015 totaled a staggering 72,571 exabytes per month. One exabyte equals a billion gigabytes (or a million terabytes). This is the total amount of all data flowing over IP networks that powers the world every month—data, voice, and video traffic. Assume a given month has 30 days and that the traffic is spread out equally all month long (which of course it isn't). This works out to a sum of 223,830 Gbps, which is 223 terabits per second, every second of every day. By the year 2020, these totals are projected to grow to 194,374 exabytes per month worldwide, which works out to the astounding sum of nearly 600,000 Gbps per second. This equates to a total traffic growth of 268 percent over a very short period.

Put another way, the total Internet traffic alone will account for almost 40 billion DVDs transmitted every month by the year 2020. Even just North America will account for 11 billion DVDs of Internet traffic within this timeframe. That's a whole lot of Netflix, Hulu, and all the rest.

Even if you just take the business portion of this traffic, and set aside the consumer-oriented traffic crossing the Internet (the majority of which is now video), in 2015, businesses worldwide transmitted 13,982 exabytes of IP-based data per month, equivalent to a continuous data rate of 43,154 Gbps. Furthermore, by 2020, business IP traffic is projected to grow to 32,165 exabytes per month, equating to 99,274 Gbps—accounting for 230 percent growth.

These numbers are astonishing and yet, this nets out to an average data rate per human being on this planet of just 32 Kbps in 2015, growing to 86 Kbps each by 2020. Of course, not everyone is online yet, and data flows are much lumpier than this, but things are rapidly trending with the growth in mobile networking, the huge growth in the Internet of Things (IoT), and increasing pervasiveness of the Internet and IP traffic flows.

Imagine in the near future when there are tens of billions of devices online along with billions of humans. The average data rates grow in the megabits per second per person, with the future growth of virtual reality, immersive videos, ever-more-realistic online gaming, and so on. Data will be flowing across the solar system with interplanetary probes and Mars rovers. The sky is not even the limit any more.

Bringing things more down to Earth, 5.6 million commercial buildings are estimated to exist in the United States. If you could see the totality of the network infrastructure that

1 Cisco Systems, June 6, 2017, https://www.cisco.com/c/en/us/solutions/collateral/service-provider/visual-networking-index-vni/complete-white-paper-c11-481360.pdf.

supports today's business environment for even a single building, the sum of it all might surprise you. It would amount to multiple tons of hardware.

Consider a 30-story downtown office tower. Assuming floor space dimensions of 150 feet × 100 feet, each floor of this office tower would host 15,000 square feet of space—or 450,000 square feet in total for the whole tower. Based on this square footage, estimate that each floor hosts 100 network cable drops (one drop per 150 square feet). This works out to 3000 cable drops in the building in total. Considering that each cable drop in such a building might be an average of 50 feet in length, and that a Category 6a cabling run of this length weighs approximately 2 pounds for the cabling itself, the twisted-pair networking cabling alone for such a building would weigh 3 tons—about the same as a GMC Hummer! This cabling would also stretch close to 30 miles if laid end to end.

Add in 50 access-layer switches at 20 pounds apiece, and a number of heavier distribution and core switches, and it could easily be close to 4 tons of network infrastructure. And that's not counting access points, wireless controllers, WAN routers, firewalls, patch panels, patch cabling, fiber-optic cabling in the risers, racks for equipment mounting, and air conditioning systems to keep the gear cool. In short, it takes a lot of physical hardware to move bits!

This network infrastructure—the largely "invisible" items—is what supports the modern world. Even though it might not be visible, it's critical to the operation of any modern organization or business.

This infrastructure creates networks that are designed and built for customers. Data flies over these networks at ever-increasing rates, and importance to business. People talk, send messages, and access mission-critical data over these networks. Devices, sensors, and things use the network to interact with providers, and each other.

Imagine taking away the network from your organization, or even impacting its operation in some significant way. It's very likely that the importance of the network will quickly become clear to everyone. Yet, many people never pause to reflect on the network infrastructure—the hardware and software elements that are so crucial or how the evolution of those elements is necessary to allow organizations to keep pace with their competitors.

This chapter and the ones that follow highlight the hardware and software items that make up the modern network. This group of chapters is designed to help you understand and appreciate the flexibility, power, and performance that these hardware and software elements provide to enable today's digital businesses. These elements comprise several key foundational underpinnings for the Cisco DNA infrastructure.

Exploring Cisco DNA Infrastructure

Let's explore Cisco DNA infrastructure by delving into the evolving network framework itself—the base components of the network, the hardware and software elements.

It is important to understand how hardware and software elements are able to adapt to support the growing and changing requirements of an organization.

Let's examine how a network infrastructure based on Cisco DNA principles is able to support the Cisco DNA vision. And let's see how it solves important problems for business, building a bridge to the future.

The Evolving Network, and Why It Matters

The next generation of hardware and software elements that make up the enterprise network must support both the rapid introduction and the rapid evolution of new technologies and solutions. These network elements must keep pace with the brisk changes in the business environment and support the capabilities that help drive simplification within the network.

Today's digitalized organizations face new challenges daily; the pace of change is only increasing. The network has to evolve. It's the lifeblood of the business. The next few chapters explore the hardware and software foundational elements of Cisco DNA that support this evolution. This is the technology that enables the next generation of enterprise networking deployments.

This section explores the capabilities and innovations that a network infrastructure enables and supports. It also examines some of the next-generation solutions now becoming available, and the impact of these innovations on networks and organizations.

Requirements: The Need for Change

Let's review changing organizational needs, extrapolating industry trends, and examine any shortcomings in today's network environments to predict what may be needed in the future. Today's network is changing more rapidly than ever. Fast-paced developments in business, academia, and our personal lives demand corresponding changes within the network.

As new protocols emerge, the network needs to be able to handle them. New security challenges arise that require a response from the organization. New applications are deployed that place new demands on the network to ensure proper access from employees. New devices are attached to the network, requiring appropriate access and traffic handling.

Note For additional information, check out the Cisco Systems report "Digital Vortex: How Digital Disruption Is Redefining Industries" (https://www.cisco.com/c/dam/en/us/solutions/collateral/industry-solutions/digital-vortex-report.pdf). This report contains numerous examples of digital processes that disrupted seemingly entrenched industries overnight.

A striking example of digital disruption is WhatsApp, purchased by Facebook in 2014 for $22 billion. Within the space of just a few years, WhatsApp's user base grew from a startup to an astonishing 1 billion users by February 2016. It grew by over 300 million users in the space of only 13 months. This phenomenal growth disrupted the SMS (Short Message Service) networking industry that had existed since 1996. It caused its growth to level off and even decline as WhatsApp and similar applications greatly increased in popularity. Yet what made WhatsApp possible?—the network. Benefitting from the "perfect storm" of pervasive smartphone use and widespread and speedy mobile IP data networks, WhatsApp upended the instant messaging marketplace and changed the industry's and users' expectations of instant messaging overnight.

There are many examples like this. Consider all the time spent today using the many communications, social media, and entertainment options, such as FaceTime for video calls, Webex for business meetings, iTunes and Spotify for music downloads and streaming, Netflix and Hulu for video, and so many others.

As the single thread that ties all of this technology together, the network is the backbone and support structure of today's "app economy" and also of your business. As an organization evolves and new applications are introduced, demands on the network change, and the network needs to adapt.

A Cisco DNA network infrastructure is ready for these changes. Is your network ready?

Requirements: The Need for Speed (of Change)

As increased demands are placed upon the network, the technologies that are used to establish, manage, and operate the network are also changing. The pace of this change is increasing.

New applications are spun up in a modern data center within a few minutes. But is the broader network ready to support those applications end to end? Demands on the network can, and do, change dynamically and unpredictably, as mobile users move and new applications are accessed, on premises or in the cloud. Access and security requirements are altered rapidly, based on organizational change, and the business environment and threat landscape is ever-changing. In short, the needs of the organization—and of the users, things, and applications leveraging the network—continue to evolve at an ever more rapid pace.

Again, let's revisit WhatsApp. As of November, 2016, the WhatsApp team indicated that it would expand from voice calling to video calling.[2] Imagine the increased data loads that such an addition might place on your network infrastructure overnight, with video calls typically consuming many tens of times the amount of bandwidth of traditional voice calls. Consider how rapidly users will likely adopt such features as they come along.

2 https://blog.whatsapp.com/10000629/WhatsApp-Video-Calling

Or take another example. Although 75 percent of the respondents in the Digital Vortex report previously noted indicated that digital disruption is a form of progress, and 72 percent indicated that they believe that it improves value for customers, only 54 percent indicated that they believe that it improves information security. This is a large gap, and indicates an area where improved robustness and security of the network infrastructure must help to fill the breach. How will the network keep up and drive these changes?

Cisco DNA infrastructure is designed for change, able to adapt rapidly from both a hardware and software perspective to support the ever-evolving needs of the business. The flexibility provided by the infrastructural components of Cisco DNA make it uniquely adaptable to face current and future organizational challenges, with a strong focus on speed, openness, and security.

The following chapters explore the details of Cisco DNA infrastructure; its hardware and software components and capabilities and how it provides the flexible, powerful, and adaptable base necessary to support the changing face of the network and the users, things, applications, and organizations it supports.

Requirements: The Need for Simplicity

If the Internet has proven anything in the last 20 years, it is that distributed systems work. The Internet is the world's largest distributed network. Domain Name System (DNS) is the world's largest distributed database. These are huge, distributed systems, under multiple administrative domains, and yet as a rule they work well, are robust, and have proven to scale.

The issue is not one of reaching the limits of distributed systems. Scale, as important as it is to address, is not the problem. The concerns faced by many organizations today is that distributed systems such as networks are, by nature, complex. The risk is that, if unaddressed, the increased pace of change in organizations, along with the need to deploy, manage, and troubleshoot large, distributed network systems, bring more complexity to the tasks of the solution architect and network manager, not less.

As part of the evolution toward a next generation of networking systems to support the organization, simplification and flexibility need to be part of the deployment model, and thus need to be baked into the infrastructure of the network system. As an example, think of the car you drive. Automobiles have an immense amount of mechanical and electrical complexity. Yet, as a driver, you are abstracted away from almost everything that the car does. When you sit in your car, you are presented with a steering wheel, a few pedals on the floor, a gear shifter, and a dashboard showing some basic indications of vehicle performance. You sit in your car, start it up, and drive. This is, of course, far from the experience of a network designer and administrator. However, it is the experience necessary to provide for next-generation networks.

Abstraction, which allows for automation, is the key. In the car example, the various capabilities presented to the driver—steering wheel, basic pedals, and a simple dashboard—are all abstractions of the underlying mechanical and electrical complexity of the car. These abstractions are key to making the car "consumable."

The value of abstractions in a network environment is equally clear. Abstractions provide simplification, enabling simplicity of operation and daily use even with upgrades and troubleshooting. To drive this simplification, the network infrastructure plays a key role.

How can we keep the sophisticated functionality of the network and build on it with new innovations while making things simpler? Again, the robust, flexible set of base infrastructural components that Cisco DNA provides is designed not only to deliver sophisticated functionality, but to do so in a simple, scalable fashion that supports the needs of current and future business models. This, of course, helps to enable new business models to flourish.

Requirements: The Need for Continuity

Networks are now ubiquitous. Users, devices, and applications expect a network that is readily available. Organizations increasingly depend on the network and, in many cases, cannot effectively operate without it.

Yet at the same time, organizational demands require change. How can you reconcile the need for business continuity with the need to implement innovative network capabilities to handle changing business functions? The answer is an evolutionary approach, which Cisco DNA's flexible hardware and software infrastructure adopts and embraces. This stands in contrast to the approaches taken by others within the industry, which may call for wholesale "forklift upgrades" necessary to adapt to some of these changes. The evolutionary approach adopted by Cisco DNA lowers risk, saves capital expenditures, and promotes operational continuity.

By providing many functions on top of existing hardware and software that you already own, and have deployed, Cisco DNA lets you easily, and incrementally, take the first steps into an evolved network world. The nature of Cisco DNA provides significantly better investment protection. It allows more value to be wrung out of existing Cisco infrastructure investments and new deployments to continue to add capabilities over time, which increases value to the organization.

At the same time, more advanced Cisco DNA capabilities may be realized with additional or newer network hardware and software platforms that can be deployed into your network. You can add in these functions and capabilities in a step-by-step fashion, as needed to accommodate changes in your business. These platforms can help to enable new, evolved functionality within the network architecture while supporting some of the key elements within Cisco DNA.

How is this accomplished? How do the needs for operational continuity and investment protection relate to the network infrastructure in place within your organization? Or the new upgrades to your network infrastructure you may be planning for your next network refresh? The following section explores these concerns.

Cisco DNA Infrastructure Solutions

This section discusses the hardware, software, protocol, and virtualization innovations that Cisco DNA offers. Specifically, the following sections provide an overview of the following:

- Flexible hardware
- Flexible software
- New and evolving protocols
- Virtualization

Flexible Hardware

In the most basic sense, networking hardware, such as a switch or router, moves data packets from location A to location B. Networking hardware examines packet headers transmitted by attached hosts such as IPv4 addresses, IPv6 addresses, Media Access Control (MAC) addresses, and so on. It communicates with adjacent network elements (using various Layer 3 routing protocols, Spanning Tree Protocol [STP] for Layer 2 connectivity, etc.) to determine how to forward traffic from those hosts to move it along to its destination. Conceptually, this is quite simple. And yet, there is so much more to it.

What happens when you need to handle new or evolved packet formats? What happens when support is necessary for segmentation such as Multiprotocol Label Switching VPNs (MPLS VPNs)? What if a need arises for a new application that demands IP subnet or Layer 2 extensions between areas of the network that have a full Layer 3 network infrastructure between them? What happens when new protocols are created, such as Virtual Extensible LAN (VXLAN), and modern network designs evolve to support these new technologies? What about the capabilities that such new protocols enable? In short, what happens when technology changes, as it inevitably will? Can the network adapt? Or will your network and organization get left behind?

Addressing these questions is critical to the adoption of new networking technologies, which include the following concerns:

- Capabilities that form the underpinning for new business processes
- Increased network security
- Support for simplified and streamlined business operations
- Providing operational cost savings
- Allowing for improved organizational responsiveness

The pace of innovation in the network, including the devices, users, and applications it supports, is not slowing down. In fact, it is accelerating faster than ever. In short, as business requirements change and improved sets of networking technologies emerge over time, the network needs to adapt to support them.

With traditional networking hardware, based on "hardwired" application-specific integrated circuit (ASIC) designs, the answer as to whether new network capabilities can easily be adopted to support ever-increasing requirements is generally "no," which is not a good answer for the needs of a modern business.

Chapter 7, "Hardware Innovations," examines ASICs in networking hardware, such as switches. Switches are typically designed for a certain set of functions and traffic handling, which they do at very high rates of speed. However, a typical switch may lack the flexibility to adapt to new network headers, functions, and protocols.

Need a new protocol? Require a new network function such as secure end-to-end segmentation or subnet extension to support a new or altered business process or a set of new network devices or services? Without a flexible hardware base such as the ones provided by Cisco DNA solutions, you may have to swap out major portions of the network infrastructure to support such new requirements, which can be a very disruptive and costly undertaking.

Alternatively, take a look at CPU-based network hardware designs, which are often seen in lower-end to midrange routers. They provide the flexibility to handle new network functions and protocols as they arise, but typically lack the performance to scale up to larger data rates, which may need to range from gigabits to tens or even hundreds of gigabits per second and beyond.

Other midrange options exist, such as field-programmable gate arrays (FPGA), which can scale up to higher data rates and provide a level of flexibility for traffic handling beyond what traditional hardwired network ASICs provide. However, the cost-per-bits-moved metric of FPGA-based solutions is often unattractive for large-scale network deployments.

So how can you provide the level of flexibility that the evolving network, and technology stack, demand as well as meet the performance and the cost goals of a next-generation enterprise network build? Chapter 7 explores in more detail the next generation of flexible hardware elements that are enabled by Cisco DNA for switching and routing infrastructures. It explains how Cisco DNA enables the rapid evolution of business and real-time network and policy enforcement that supports today's rapidly changing business and technology environment.

Flexible Software

Cisco IOS provides the most widely deployed software stack in the networking industry. The majority of network infrastructure elements in a typical enterprise network use IOS. Most network operators are well versed on IOS-based network designs, deployment, and troubleshooting.

As pervasive as IOS is, though, it is supplemented by adjacent software stacks for specific functions. Virtualization is becoming a key technology element in the arsenal of organizations, allowing them to deploy network-based services more flexibly and rapidly than ever before. Virtualized functions and containerized applications, whether on network elements themselves or on adjacent (and typically more powerful) server platforms, provide new, exciting, and ultimately necessary functions for business.

And so, the industry moves forward. Customer network deployments move forward. New norms emerge around network deployment, operation, and support. New requirements for virtualization of network functions and solutions arise. The pace of business continues to increase, and demands on the network continue to scale.

How can current and future software stacks keep pace in a way that embraces evolutionary change, in order to ultimately reap revolutionary results? The answer within Cisco DNA is through a combination of evolution of the world's most popular networking software, Cisco IOS, combined with new, enhanced capabilities.

IOS XE is Cisco's next generation of IOS, evolving the most successful networking software stack into the future. IOS XE enhances traditional IOS by adding in modularity, which allows for capabilities such as patching and enhanced high availability. IOS XE also adds in componentization, which allows for more rapid and accurate implementation of new features and capabilities, enhancing software reliability and easing troubleshooting. And, IOS XE supports containerization, allowing new capabilities to be hosted on Cisco platforms as "containerized" applications.

By evolving IOS onto a new software base that provides modularity, componentization, and containerization, new capabilities are delivered, and simplicity and flexibility are enhanced. The evolution of IOS XE is discussed further in Chapter 8, "Software Innovations."

New and Evolving Protocols

The intersection of flexible hardware and flexible software allows the creation and support of new protocols. The networking industry is in the midst of massive change. It is necessary to support the corresponding modifications in organizational requirements, capabilities, and expectations, which include the following:

- Evolving requirements for greater simplification
- Improved security
- Enhanced high availability
- Increased speed
- Increased accuracy of business operations

As new networking protocols emerge to support these changes such as VXLAN for Layer 2/Layer 3 overlays and LISP for next-generation routing, the combination of hardware and software flexibility provided by a Cisco DNA infrastructure allows these new protocols to be accommodated within existing network footprints. This is without necessarily requiring hardware replacement and churn in order to adopt such new technologies. This in turn allows for new solutions to be deployed on network hardware elements that may already be in place that support new capabilities for business. It also provides a significant level of investment protection while lowering total cost of ownership (TCO). New protocol support within Cisco DNA is discussed further in Chapter 9, "Protocol Innovations."

The Emergence of Virtualization

Physical network infrastructures are pervasive in today's world. However, the world around you is also virtualized in many ways. Bare-metal servers that previously ran only a single application now host multiple virtual machines (VM), each running its own app or apps. Applications are deployed within containers. Network-based functions that were previously deployed on-premises can now leverage the cloud. Data can reside locally, or located half a world away.

The networking industry is in the midst of massive change, and virtualization plays a key role. By integrating virtualized network functions (VNFs) into a Cisco DNA-based set of network infrastructure, new capabilities and new flexibility in deployment, operation, and management are realized.

Cisco Enterprise Network Function Virtualization Infrastructure Software (NFVIS) is intended to meet this goal, in a way that meets the requirements of a next-generation organization. NFVIS and related virtualization technologies within Cisco DNA are discussed in more detail in Chapter 10, "Cisco DNA Infrastructure—Virtualization."

Bringing It All Together

Whether functions are deployed locally on-premises or remotely in the cloud or whether they become virtualized or containerized, at the end of the day, they all need something physical to run on. When packets are moved across a desk or across the world, they might be accessing virtualized applications or attaching to virtualized functions in the cloud. However, they also need to cross a physical network of access points, switches, and routers to get there and back.

The network's physical infrastructure consists of multiple elements, hardware, software, and the methods used to access and interface with them. Based on the current and future evolution of the business (evolving and changing needs of users, applications, and devices within an organization), the trends within the industry, and the evolution of "the possible" in technology, network infrastructures are changing more rapidly than ever before.

There is always a physical underpinning to the network, even when it is combined with a virtualized deployment. The greatest functionality is extracted when both the virtual and physical infrastructure work together. Chapters 7, 8, and 9 examine the elements of the physical network infrastructure, hardware, software, and protocols. Chapter 10 examines the virtualized components that can layer on top of, and integrate with, the physical infrastructures that make up a network.

Chapter 11, "Cisco DNA Cloud," examines what a next-generation network infrastructure based on Cisco DNA principles looks like. It discusses the solutions it provides and how it directly supports the broader organizational goals of simplification, flexibility, investment protection, and lower TCO.

Summary

This chapter introduced the requirements of the modern enterprise network and provided an overview of the current state of the networking industry and future trends. It examined the evolving enterprise network and corresponding needs for (rapid) change, simplicity, and continuity.

This chapter also introduced the concepts and capabilities provided by the infrastructure supporting Cisco DNA, including the following:

- Flexible hardware
- Flexible software
- New and evolving protocols
- Virtualization

The following chapters explore the new innovations that Cisco is driving in the Cisco DNA network infrastructure—powerful, flexible hardware, software, and virtualization components—to benefit your business as it digitizes.

Let's get started! Turn the page to start diving into the first Cisco DNA infrastructure building block, focusing on hardware innovations, including the next generation of flexible hardware elements.

Chapter 7

Hardware Innovations

You don't normally think of hardware as flexible. The word *hardware* conjures up images of hulking pieces of "big iron," built to do a certain set of tasks, but inflexible to handle others. And while that has been the case in the past, network hardware has evolved—as it must to keep pace with the fast-changing world of organizational change and rapid business demands.

This chapter explains the following:

- Why hardware is important even in our software-defined world
- How networking hardware (ASIC silicon) is designed and built
- The importance of flexible hardware to support modern enterprise networks
- Examples of flexible hardware supporting Cisco DNA

The Importance of Hardware in a Software-Defined World

Why is hardware even important? After all, isn't everything in the world focused on software? In today's networks, isn't hardware just a commodity? The answer is "no"—hardware is not just a commodity, and the best value for a business is actually delivered by the appropriate fusion of hardware and software, working together to achieve the optimum set of outcomes, and providing maximum flexibility and investment protection in doing so.

The locus of maximum value for an organization is actually at the intersection of flexible hardware and software, especially in our current time of rapid technological and organizational change. Flexible hardware allows organizations to adapt their network over time to accommodate new functions, new protocols, and new solutions—all without compromising on performance, and with the ability to provide unparalleled investment protection, maximize the organization's return on investment (ROI) in their network infrastructure, and take full advantage of the latest networking innovations to benefit their business. In this way, flexible hardware is the ideal underpinning for the Cisco Digital Network Architecture and forms a perfect base for the entire Cisco DNA solution stack.

This chapter explores networking hardware, specifically the application-specific integrated circuits (ASICs) and other specialized silicon used in advanced communications. After covering details of chip design (so that we can speak a common language around silicon), this chapter examines some of the latest trends in networking that Cisco DNA addresses, and looks at how the specifics of today's and tomorrow's advanced and flexible hardware meet those challenges—always connecting it back to why the flexible, programmable hardware forms a base pillar for Cisco DNA—discussing why this flexible hardware matters, and what benefits it delivers for your business.

The Making of a Chip

To discuss networking hardware in a meaningful way, it is important to speak the same language. Let's review some of the terminology and processes related to making silicon chips—those tiny, but very powerful, pieces of ASIC technology that sit at the heart of sophisticated communications gear.

To begin with, what is an ASIC? A brief but concise description would be that an ASIC is an integrated circuit (IC) customized for a particular use or set of functions, rather than intended for general-purpose use.

While this accurately states what an ASIC is, let's expand on that. A piece of silicon (integrated circuit) designed for general-purpose use would be something like a CPU. You are familiar with these from manufacturers such as Intel, AMD, Qualcomm, and others. With the appropriate software, CPUs can be programmed to do almost anything. They may or may not perform at the level of speed that may be desirable, but a general-purpose CPU does offer flexibility.

By way of contrast, an ASIC typically is purpose-built for a specific task or set of tasks. With a more single-minded focus, and by leveraging hardware that is specifically designed for the tasks at hand, an ASIC typically is both faster and more cost-effective at executing a given set of well-defined tasks. Because network devices typically are set up for a common set of tasks (packet forwarding, traffic handling, etc.), ASICs have long been leveraged in network devices such as switches and routers.

Delving Deeper: How Chips Are Designed and Built

To really understand ASICs, you need to know how they are designed and built. This journey begins with defining what the ASIC in question needs to do.

What system will it be used in? What capabilities does it need to have? What speed does it need to operate at, and what scale does it need to provide? What timeframe will it appear in on the market? What's the state of the art of what's possible now—and what will be possible then? What are the technology trends that it will need to accommodate? These and many other questions need to be asked, and answered, when an ASIC is in the planning and design phase.

As summarized in Figure 7-1, the ASIC planning process typically begins with a definition from Marketing as to what a given system that the ASIC will support requires. What are customers asking for? What capabilities are required to serve the market? What market transitions are underway that the ASIC network hardware needs to support? What level of investment protection or backward compatibility is needed?

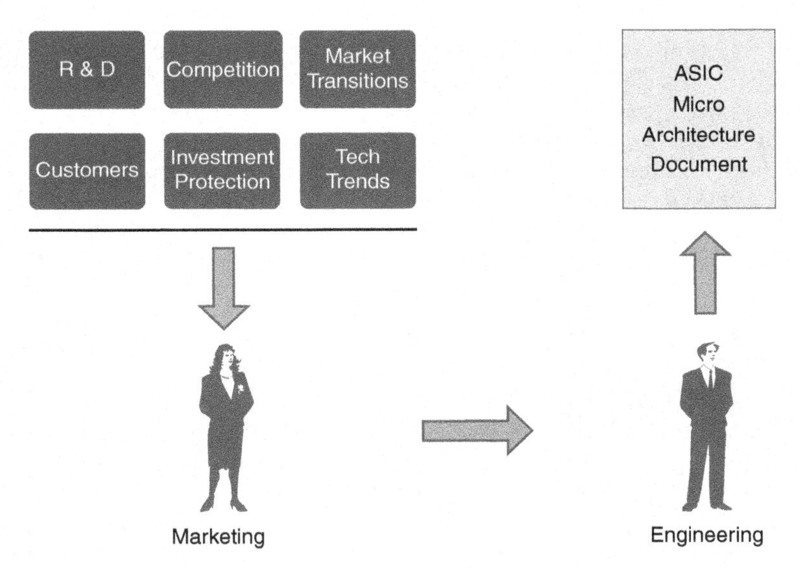

Figure 7-1 *ASIC Planning Process*

Once these questions are answered, an interaction between Marketing and Engineering takes place. Although it can be assumed this is a one-way street—Marketing asks, and Engineering delivers—it is often in reality more of a give and take, as the desires from Marketing come up against the reality of what's possible to achieve in silicon, given the current (and ever-evolving) state of the art, cost constraints, limitations on system board space, power consumption, heat dissipation, impacts on other elements of the planned system, and many other factors.

However, after the creative process is finished, what emerges is an ASIC specification: the ASIC micro-architecture document. This document summarizes what the chip in question will do, and details how those goals will be accomplished. It is, in fact, the "blueprint" for the chip. During the lifetime of the ASIC, which may be only one generation or an evolution over several generations, this micro-architecture document is revised and updated as needed. In effect, it is the "living document" reflecting the requirements and associated design of the chip.

Once the ASIC architecture is defined, it's time to start coding it. A present modern networking ASIC could have in excess of 1 to 3 billion transistors on it—or indeed, with the latest designs, close to 20 billion transistors. Transistors are the basic switching elements of digital circuitry—think of them as "on-off" switches for routing of electronic signals around a circuit—perfect for the binary transmissions used in computers and communications.

However, no longer are transistors visible to the naked eye. Today, a modern ASIC's transistors are etched into a silicon wafer with element sizes of 65, 45, 32, 28, 22, or even as low as 16, 14, 10, or even 7 nanometers—billions of a meter. To put that into perspective, a human hair is about 100,000 nanometers wide, so transistors are thousands of times smaller and thinner than a human hair.

Sizes this small are very hard to grasp. So, let's try to put that in perspective by creating our own scale. Let's say a single human hair in cross-section is the size of the Empire State Building, as shown in Figure 7-2. On this scale, we would have to zoom up on the bottom floors of the Empire State Building to start comparing to small things. A single red blood cell on this scale stretches up to about the tenth floor. Zoom in further, and a single bacterium stretches to the third floor of our Empire State Building-sized hair width. Zoom down still (much) further, and a single strand of protein (the basic building block of a cell) is about the size of a small dog on the sidewalk, next to that giant building-sized hair cross-section.

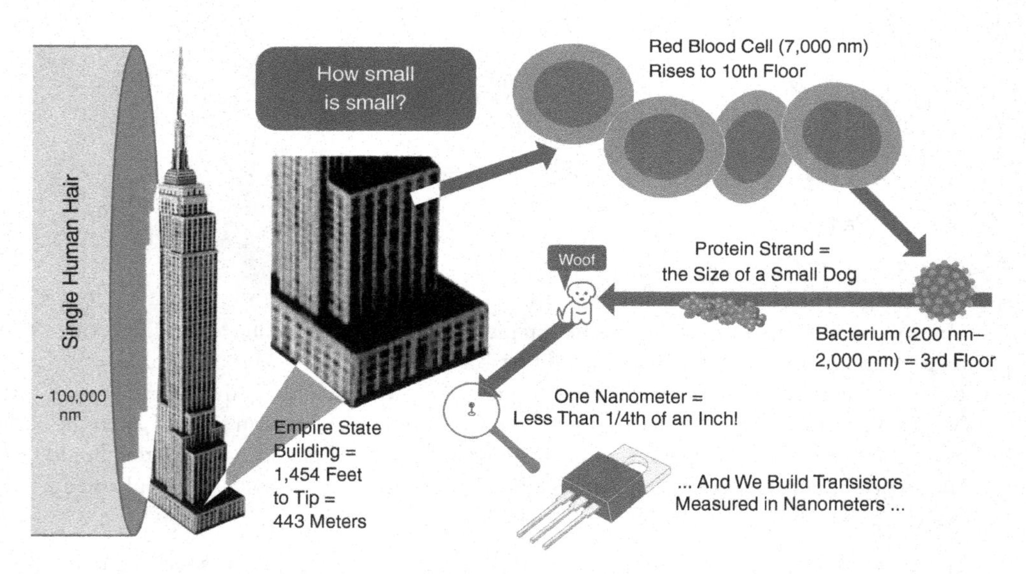

Figure 7-2 *ASIC Sizing in Perspective*

But we are still not in the realm of nanometers. To get down to that size we'd have to imagine three pennies stacked up one on top of the other, next to that Empire State Building-sized hair width. Three pennies next to that—less than 1/4th of an inch (about 6 millimeters) next to that massive Empire State Building-sized single cross-sectioned hair. That's the size of a single nanometer.

To put it into a different perspective, an individual silicon atom is about 2/10th of a nanometer wide, so in a modern ASIC, transistor elements are being built that are only a few dozen atoms wide. This provides the capability to pack literally billions of transistors onto a single silicon die, creating the ASICs that form the heart of today's powerful networking gear, and indeed the silicon that forms some of the most critical foundational elements in our modern technological society.

Now, here's an interesting fact: ASICs start out as code. That may seem counterintuitive at first—hardware actually starts out as software? However, stop and think about it for a second. Do you believe that any human, or team of humans, lays out billions of transistors on a chip? It's beyond human capability to do this, and has been for some time. ASICs actually begin their design process as software—specifically, software written in a specialized series of languages known as hardware description languages (HDLs). As indicated in Figure 7-3, two of the common HDLs that are in use within the industry are Verilog and VHDL.

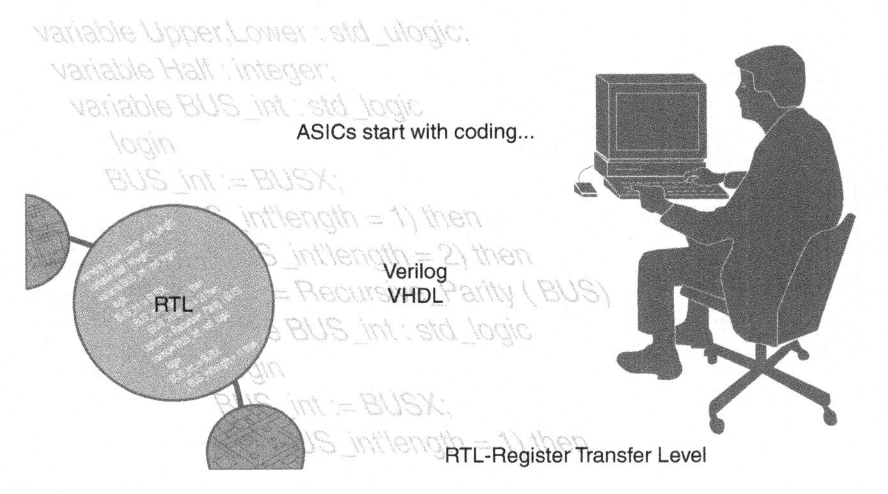

Figure 7-3 *ASICs Start Their Life As Code*

HDLs are different from standard software languages that you may be familiar with, such as C or C++, because HDLs need to incorporate things that matter at the hardware level, elements such as timing between hardware elements. ASIC designers are able to describe the actual circuits that make up various portions of the chip by coding them in a crisp and condensed form in the HDL (describing them at the hardware register level, hence the Register Transfer Level nomenclature used with HDLs).

When strung together, these portions of HDL code describe not only what the chip can do, but what form it will take when it is turned from software code into actual hardware instantiated into silicon. Basically, coding the chip takes all the items that Marketing and Engineering agreed that the ASIC needs to be able to do and expresses them as code required to drive those desired functions.

The process of synthesis is what then transforms the HDL code for the ASIC into the actual logic constructs—AND gates, OR gates, NAND gates, and the like—that make up the actual circuitry of the ASIC. Think of this as being similar to compiling a software program, only what pops out of the "compiler" in this case is not a piece of object code that you would run on your laptop computer or smartphone. Instead, the synthesis process produces what is called a *netlist*, which effectively is a description of what will ultimately become the physical blueprint for the chip. What starts out as software ends up as hardware. This is shown in Figure 7-4.

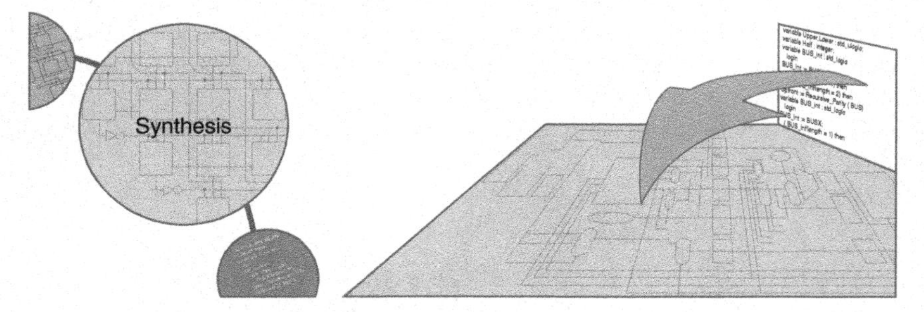

Figure 7-4 *ASIC Synthesis Process*

As it turns out, most ASICs today are of such a size and complexity that they are designed in functional blocks—one block may be for packet storage, another for processing, another for packet input/output from the chip to/from the outside world, or storage of networking policies such as security access controls lists (ACL) or descriptions of quality of service (QoS) handling, and the like. The process of arranging these functional blocks on the chip is called *floor planning and placement* and is shown in Figure 7-5.

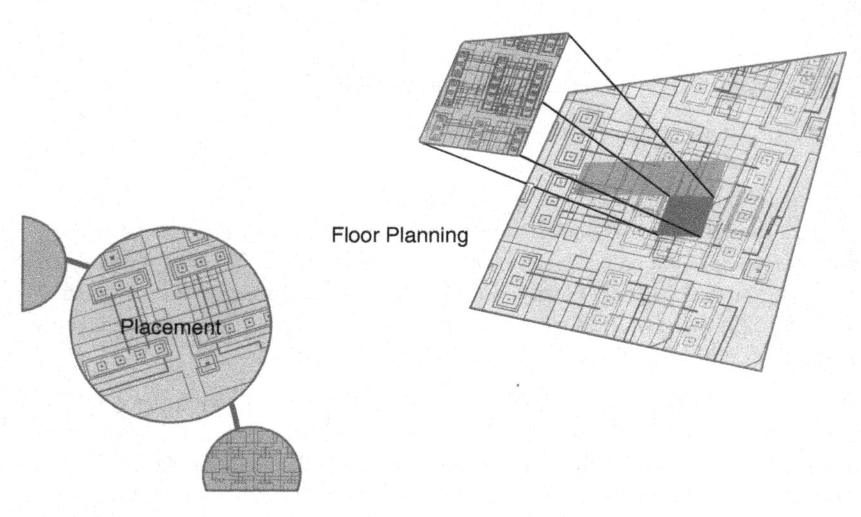

Figure 7-5 *ASIC Floor Planning and Placement*

The floor planning process for the ASIC is a process that is actually done by humans—placing the functional blocks around the chip in the optimum way, interconnecting them to power, and minimizing effects between various co-located blocks such as crosstalk (an effect generated by any rapidly varying electrical field, where the associated rapidly varying magnetic field may induce unwanted interference in adjacent blocks), among other tasks. As a combination of both art and science (due to the combination of digital and analog effects at play), this step is typically done by senior engineers on the ASIC design team, and is one of the final steps as the ASIC marches toward production.

Once the netlist has been produced and the floor planning for the chip has been completed, the actual physical ASIC construction can begin. This consists of the most commonly seen elements of silicon chip manufacturing: the etching of circuit designs into silicon wafers in large, high-tech "clean rooms." Basically (and simplifying somewhat), the chip design is physically laid out and etched using lithographic techniques onto a silicon wafer substrate, which essentially is an ultra-pure disk of silicon "doped," or infused, with impurities of various types to enhance the silicon's semiconductor nature in such a way as to best express the circuit's function. Silicon is used because, as a semiconductor, it is an ideal material for switching between, and storing, digital pulses of information—the binary 1s and 0s that make up computing and communications circuitry.

Using a combination of photolithographic and chemical techniques, the chip itself is laid out, or "photomasked," onto the silicon wafer—typically, in multiple layers—by exposure to a high-intensity electromagnetic radiation source. To maximize production, many chips of the same type are etched onto the same silicon wafer at once, as shown in Figure 7-6.

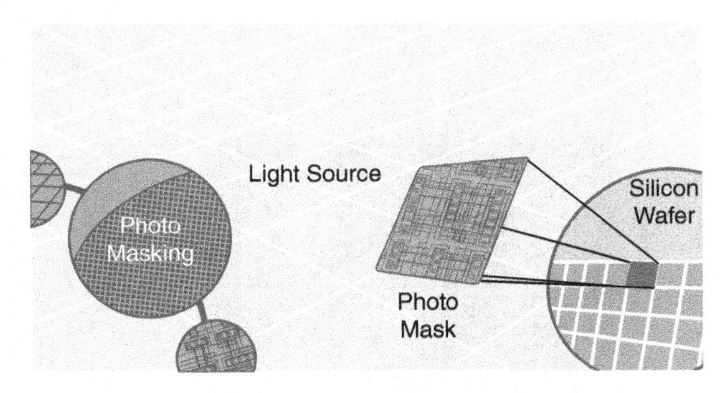

Figure 7-6 *ASIC Photomasking onto Silicon Wafer*

So now, there is a wafer with dozens or possibly hundreds of our ASIC designs imprinted on it. But, do they all work? That's the job of the next step: ASIC functional validation. The various ASIC dies now etched into the silicon wafer are individually tested. Think of this as somewhat akin to the Power-On Self-Test (POST) that your laptop undergoes when it boots up. Each silicon chip is "booted up" and run through a series of tests to determine if it is functional or not, at least at a basic level. Good chips are retained, and bad chips are marked and discarded (after the wafer is cleaved and the individual chips are apportioned out).

As shown in Figure 7-7, functional chips from the silicon wafer make it to the next stage, ASIC packaging, which places them into the more familiar flat, square or rectangular metal packages that we see ubiquitously on circuit boards. Again, once packaged, each ASIC is tested again, and some (which may fail during the packaging process) are discarded, while the others are retained. Figure 7-8 show the front and back of a typical packaged ASIC.

Figure 7-7 *ASIC Validation and Packaging*

Figure 7-8 *Typical Packaged ASIC—Front and Back*

On the front of the chip, you can see various markings indicating such things as its designer, type, and point of origin. On the back, notice the ball grid array (BGA), the series of hundreds of electrical contact points by which the chip communicates to and from the outside world. This is how the chip gets soldered to its host circuit board and becomes an integral part of the system—switch, router, or other network element—that it was designed for.

Drivers of Chip Design and Density

As you are likely aware, a "law" has existed in the technology industry for the past 40 years. Moore's law has underpinned many of the advances in technology and chip design and manufacture over the past four decades, and is thus at the fundamental root of the majority of technology advances across many diverse industries, not just computing and communications. Advances in silicon have revolutionized the world, and made possible many of the technologies used every day.

Simply stated, Moore's law outlines that the density of transistors that can be packed onto a silicon die will double every 18 to 24 months. This has held true, more or less, for the past 40 years—and of course, this is a geometric progression—rapidly leading to very high densities that we see in today's silicon, with billions of circuit elements.

Today, ASIC densities, as mentioned previously, may range from 65 nanometers to 45 nanometers, 32 nanometers, 22 nanometers, or even higher densities, leading to ever more complex and ever more capable chips. Basically, the smaller the transistor or circuit element, as shown in Figure 7-9, the more of them you can pack onto a chip and, hence, the more functionality the chip can provide.

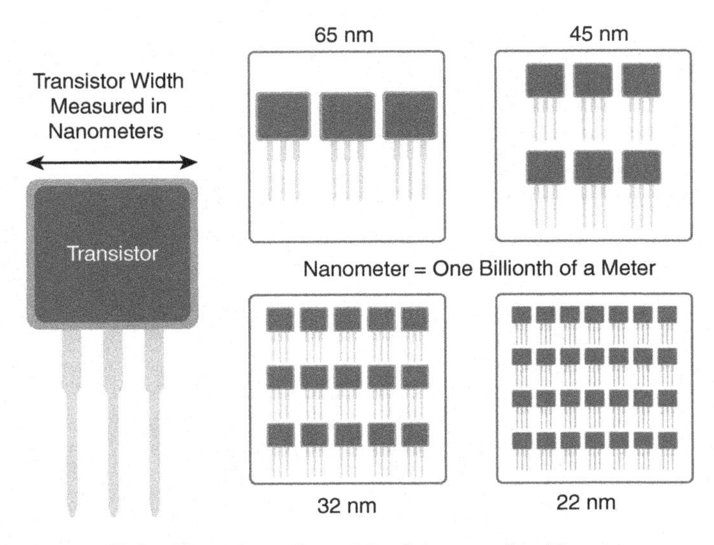

Figure 7-9 *Transistor Densities Measured in Nanometers*

However, creating higher circuit densities in a smaller amount of space to achieve ever-greater levels of device functionality is only part of the story. Some of the key additional drivers of ever-higher chip density are shown in Figure 7-10—namely, higher performance, lower power consumption (and thus less heat that is generated and has to be dissipated), and lower cost.

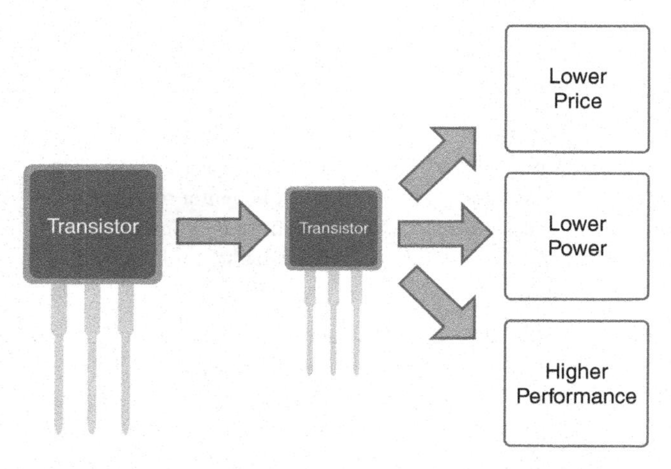

Figure 7-10 *Benefits of the Ever-Shrinking Transistor*

Now, at first this may seem counterintuitive. While some of the things associated with higher chip density make sense—smaller circuits consume less power, and smaller transistors and interconnections mean the electrons have less distance to travel, so speed and performance can increase—shouldn't the cost increase as we move to an increasingly higher-tech process?

The answer is "no," and the reason is increased yield.

Basically, all silicon wafers have impurities and imperfections associated with them. While the silicon wafer itself is ultra-pure, and great care is taken in its manufacture and use, undesired impurities or imperfections can always be present. These defects result in chips that may fail after the photomasking step, resulting in chips that have to be discarded after testing, as shown in Figure 7-11.

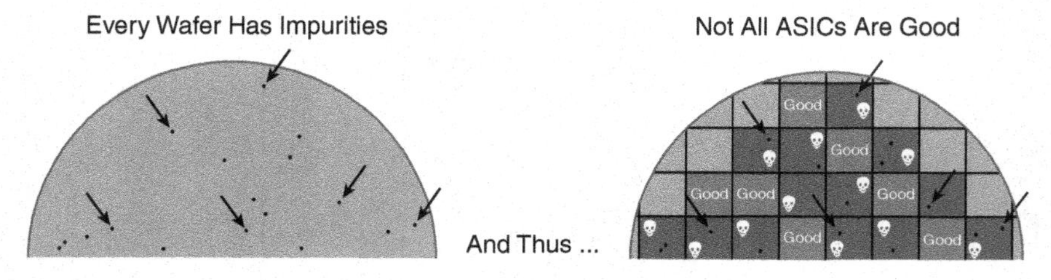

Figure 7-11 *Impurities in a Silicon Wafer, Resulting in Failed Chips*

The fraction of chips that are manufactured correctly and operate properly versus the failed ones is called the *yield* for the silicon wafer in question. The cost to manufacture a given chip is directly related (among other factors) to the yield achieved by the wafer manufacturing process. The higher the yield, the lower the per-chip cost. This makes sense intuitively when you consider that manufacturing a smaller version of the same chip (by going to a higher-density chip manufacturing process—45 nm versus 65 nm, say) makes it statistically less likely that any individual chip on the wafer will be masked over a "problem" area on the die, versus a larger version of the same chip design. An example of this is shown in Figure 7-12.

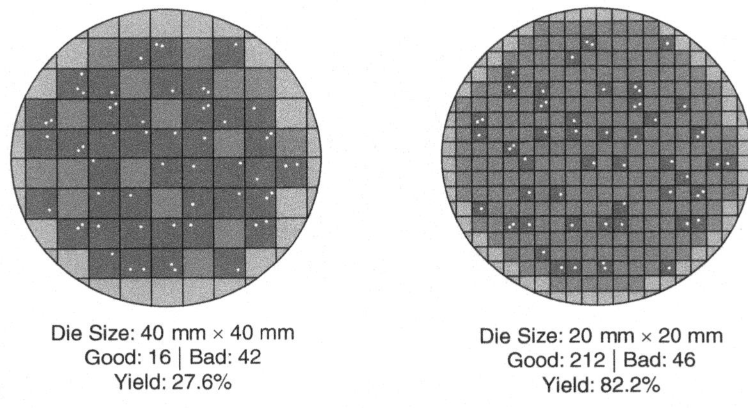

Figure 7-12 *Varying Yield with Different Silicon Densities and Associated Die Sizes*

Basically, the smaller the chip, the higher the typical yield. The higher the yield, the lower the per-chip cost (as there is a greater proportion of "good" chips that can be used versus "bad" ones that must be discarded). Of course, many other factors come into play concerning chip costs—the maturity of the given silicon "process node" (65 nm, 45 nm, 32 nm, 22 nm, 16 nm, 10 nm, etc.) being one—but all things being equal, smaller is typically better in terms of performance, power consumption, and cost.

As this book goes to press, the state-of-the-art in the industry is leading to the construction of chips at the 7 nm process node. Various additional factors, such as the capability to build up transistors on the silicon die in three dimensions rather than two, also lead directly to ever-greater transistor packing densities and efficiencies in chip design and manufacture. The technology involved is amazing, when you stop to think about it, and is the basis for many of our ever-greater technological capabilities and advances.

When Good Chips Go Bad: What Can Go Wrong in Chip Design

Remember that silicon hardware actually starts off as software? Well, like any software, chip designs can have bugs. The difference is, these bugs might get caught early in the design process—but on the other hand, they might not actually be found until the chip goes through the whole design and manufacture process, and you get the first chip back and place it onto a board to test it out.

This is a big moment for the ASIC team! The first batch of their ASIC comes back from the manufacturer, gets soldered onto the logic board, and the first load of software gets turned up to test not just that chip, but the system into which it is embedded, and of which it is a part. Does it work as intended? Does it meet all performance and functional specifications?

Figure 7-13 shows the whole lifecycle of an ASIC design process, from coding, synthesis, and floor planning, through manufacture and packaging, into system testing. If everything works, on to the next steps. But there is always the chance of a bug or unforeseen issue with the chip, which may only emerge during whole-system or unit testing.

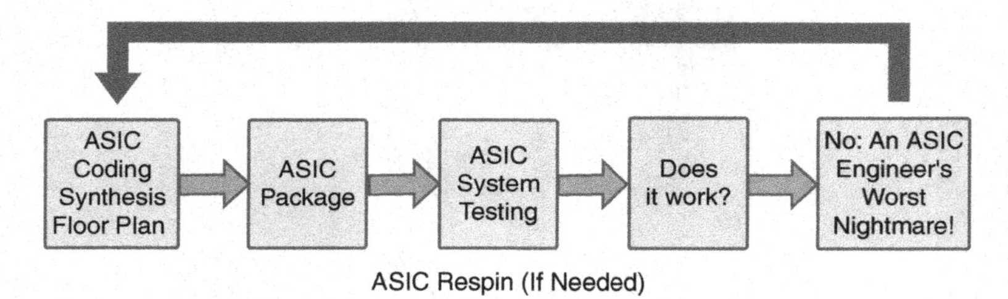

Figure 7-13 *ASIC System Test, and the Possibility of a Respin*

Depending on what is wrong, it may be possible to work around the issue in hardware or in software. If not, it's time for a respin. ASIC respins involve identifying the issue and then stepping back through the process to fix the problem, which may have been introduced, for example, at the coding or floor-planning stages. ASIC respins are as costly and time-consuming as you might expect, and are compounded by the fact that at this point in the project, other teams (software, system test, etc.) may be waiting on having a functional ASIC. While some issues can be found and fixed in simulation before the ASIC is physically produced, others may be possible to find only after production. Needless to say, ASIC respins are undesirable.

When Good Chips Need to Get Better: Designing the Next Generation

In addition to the respin scenario covered in the previous section, there are other reasons for an ASIC respin. After an ASIC has had a given period of time and success in the market, the ASIC designers may want to revisit the design of the ASIC and add or modify its underlying functionality. Maybe the market has changed, new protocols have come along, or customers want new functionality, capabilities, or scale that differs from what the initial ASIC offered.

When revisiting the ASIC design, depending on what's needed, the code for the ASIC typically is modified, and then the entire chip design process kicks off again, resulting in a new version of the ASIC in question. This process, sometimes also (somewhat confusingly) called a respin, ends up yielding the next generation of the ASIC involved.

If this is examined in Cisco switching, you can see this process playing out over many chip generations. One of the longest-lived switch ASIC families in Cisco history is the EARL series of ASICs—EARL being an acronym for Encoded Address Recognition Logic. As a chip design, EARL actually started its life in the Catalyst 5000/5500 Series switches—the precursor to the Catalyst 6500/6800—and has in fact made its way into the Nexus 7000/7700 Series switches as well.

As depicted in Figure 7-14, the EARL series of ASICs has now played out over eight generations—with each EARL generation increasing in density, functionality, and performance. Today, the EARL8 ASIC used in the Catalyst 6500, 6800, and Nexus 7000 M-Series line cards provides a wide range of advanced networking capabilities, including IPv4 and IPv6 forwarding, Multiprotocol Label Switching (MPLS), Virtual Private LAN Services (VPLS), Overlay Transport Virtualization (OTV), Generic Routing Encapsulation (GRE), Advanced IP Multicast, Encapsulated Remote Switched Port Analyzer (ERSPAN), NetFlow, Virtual Switching System (VSS), and a host of additional advanced functionality. With a lifespan approaching 20 years, and widespread customer acceptance of the platforms it is integrated into, Cisco's EARL technology represents one of the most prolific and widely used network fixed-function ASICs in the networking industry.

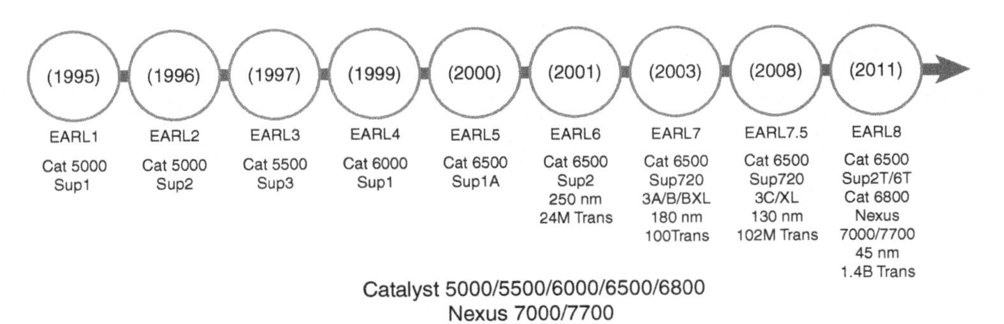

Figure 7-14 *Evolution of an ASIC—The EARL Family*

Now We Speak the Same Language!

Now you know how chips are made. Chip design is based on planning, synthesis, and manufacturing. You now have the basis for appreciating the differences between various types of networking silicon—and specifically to start understanding why flexible, programmable silicon plays such a big role in today's, and tomorrow's, network infrastructures.

Now, let's begin with the big trends in networking today, and how innovations in Cisco's advanced networking silicon—forming the foundation of Cisco Digital Network Architecture—are responding to those trends and creating the basis for the next big leaps in networking.

What's Happening in the World of Networks

Today, networking is changing faster than ever before. Why? Because business is changing faster than ever before.

This is a period of digital disruption. Long-established businesses are augmented (or obsoleted) seemingly overnight. New technologies spring up, opening up new possibilities that were previously infeasible, or even impossible. And all of this is happening at a pace that would have seemed unimaginable even a few years ago.

Look at Amazon. Consider Uber. And then think about the next area of our lives that might be headed for disruption in the new digital era.

What this means for networks is that they have to respond faster to the business, and not just in terms of megabits or gigabits. A network needs to be more adaptable—more agile—and more open to new innovations, be they in protocols, in capabilities, or in solutions.

An example of this is software-defined networking (SDN). Originally conceived at Stanford as part of its Clean Slate Program, SDN has since transmuted into many forms, including OpenFlow, overlays, and orchestration, among others. But whatever form SDN takes, or whatever set of capabilities it requires, chances are very good, as shown in Figure 7-15, that the resulting set of functional requirements needs to be expressed into network hardware—the silicon that powers the switching and routing infrastructure of the enterprise network.

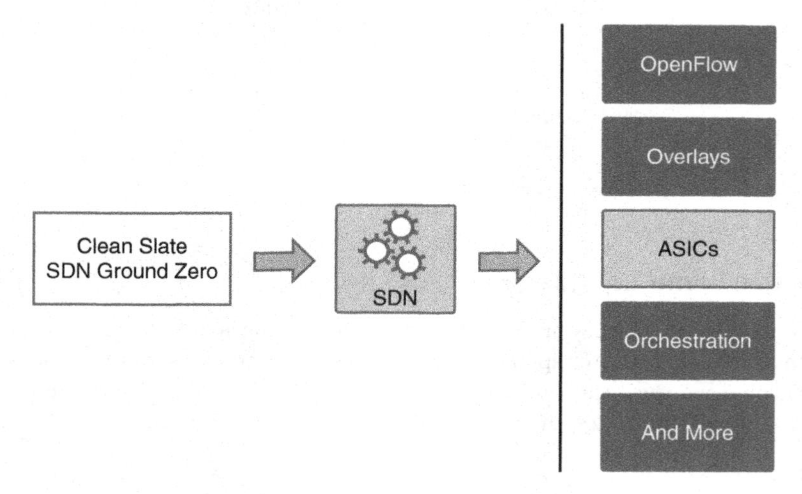

Figure 7-15 *ASICs As a Foundation for SDN Capabilities*

And yet this seems to be at odds with the areas just examined around the development of ASICs and silicon. The average amount of time from white-boarding out a new set of ASIC requirements to having that "first piece of silicon" that meets those requirements (the whole process just examined) is typically 18 to 24 months, and could be even longer. And yet, this is an era where requirements, capabilities, and technologies might morph in a period of months—and when new industry trends like SDN arise that need to be addressed.

How Traditional Network ASICs Process Packets

To examine how Cisco's innovative approach to flexible silicon with Cisco DNA addresses this issue, let's review how an ASIC (such as the ones examined earlier in this chapter) processes network packets.

A network ASIC is hard-coded (remember HDLs?) to perform a specific set of functions on packets it processes. These include the following:

- Parsing the packet (What kind of packet is this? IPv4? IPv6? MPLS? etc.)
- Layer 2 lookup
- Layer 3 lookup
- Policy actions such as filtering (ACLs) and QoS
- Packet modifications (Time to Live [TTL] decrement, L2 rewrite)
- Packet scheduling
- Statistics gathering

All packets that arrive at the network ASIC are handled in a processing pipeline, which applies the necessary steps in the correct order. It is this pipeline that is established by the network ASIC's HDL code, and laid down in its hard-wired silicon gates.

When a packet arrives at a network ASIC, the first step is to parse the packet to see what type of packet it is, so that the subsequent stages within the ASIC can process it appropriately. This involves examining the various packet headers, and creating internal "metadata" about the packet that can be passed from ASIC stage to ASIC stage as the packet gets processed and handled.

If a typical network ASIC needs to parse and process a type of packet it is not hard-coded to handle, it cannot. An example of this is the ASIC that powers a Catalyst 3750 switch. This ASIC parses IPv4 and IPv6 traffic, but has no capability to parse MPLS traffic. Lacking this hardware capability at the ASIC level, it is not possible to add MPLS support to a Catalyst 3750 switch. Sending all traffic that matches MPLS (unknown-to-the-switch protocol) up to the switch's control-plane CPU introduces such a processing burden, and results in such a poor level of throughput that this is not an option (think a few thousand packets per second [pps] at best, versus millions of pps the chip can process in hardware). So, protocols that are unknown to the switch (which the fixed parser block of the ASIC cannot understand) are typically simply dropped in hardware because they cannot be processed.

Thus, it can rapidly be seen, as depicted in Figure 7-16, that the traditional fixed processing pipeline of a network ASIC, while functional, lacks flexibility.

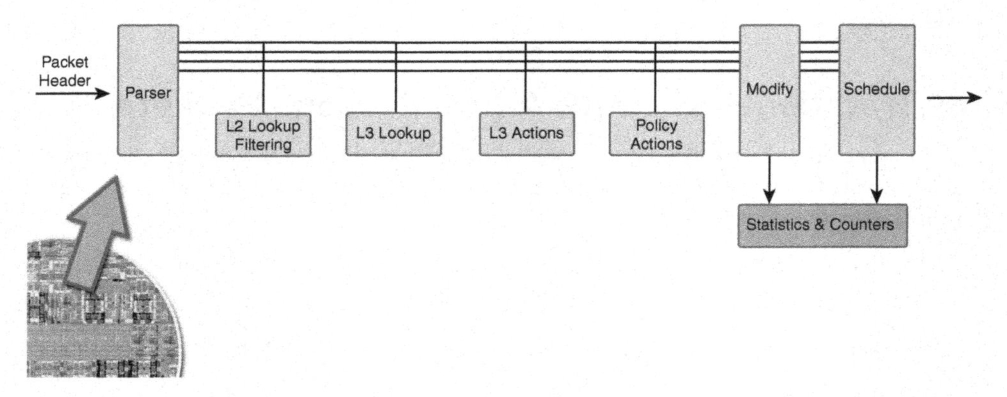

Figure 7-16 *Typical Fixed Network ASIC Processing Pipeline*

So how can today's organizations handle rapid network change? What happens when new protocols come along? What if the business needs to adopt new solutions, and those new solutions require new and different capabilities in the network?

Enter flexible silicon, a key component of Cisco Digital Network Architecture.

Beginning several years ago, Cisco pioneered the development and use of flexible network ASIC silicon with Unified Access Data Plane (UADP), the world's first fully flexible and programmable piece of switching silicon, and QuantumFlow Processor (QFP), a remarkable piece of flexible, programmable routing silicon.

The latter half of this chapter explores UADP and QFP in detail to help you understand the extraordinary capabilities that they provide, and why this set of capabilities matters for your business.

You might be saying to yourself, "What about CPUs? What about FPGAs? Don't they provide flexibility? Can't they be used for packet forwarding? How do they fit into this picture?"

So, let's cover that first.

Traffic Handling with CPUs and FPGAs

For lower-performance applications, you can certainly use a traditional CPU (x86 Intel or other) for processing packets. The flexibility a CPU provides for packet processing is excellent, and with the right software stack on top, a CPU can do almost anything for network traffic handling.

But the performance is limited. Why? Well, CPUs are not at all optimized for the types of things that get done every day—indeed, every microsecond—in networks. After a packet is parsed, it gets looked up in tables—all sorts of tables. Layer 2 lookups, Layer 3 lookups (including exact-match as well as Longest-Prefix match), ACL lookups for security and traffic filtering, QoS lookups for traffic classification, NetFlow table lookups...the list goes on and on. And every lookup has a different data structure, a different set of requirements, and a different possible outcome for the packet involved.

CPUs can certainly do this work. However, all the tables they are accessing exist "off-chip"—that is, in memory located outside of the CPU. Thus, every lookup incurs a performance penalty as data is shuttled between the CPU and the external memory. A single lookup for a packet could involve many memory accesses, and a single packet might incur many lookups. So, beyond a relatively modest performance level (typically, a few Gbps), CPU-based packet forwarding implementations tend to "top out" in the real world, where multiple packet-processing functions are required. The high-end CPUs required to obtain such performance levels also tend to be quite expensive, especially when examined through the lens of cost per bps moved. Larger CPUs also often involve higher levels of power consumption and heat generation/dissipation, issues that introduce additional challenges in system design for network devices.

So, as shown in Figure 7-17, CPUs get top marks for flexibility, but tend to not do so well at cost and performance.

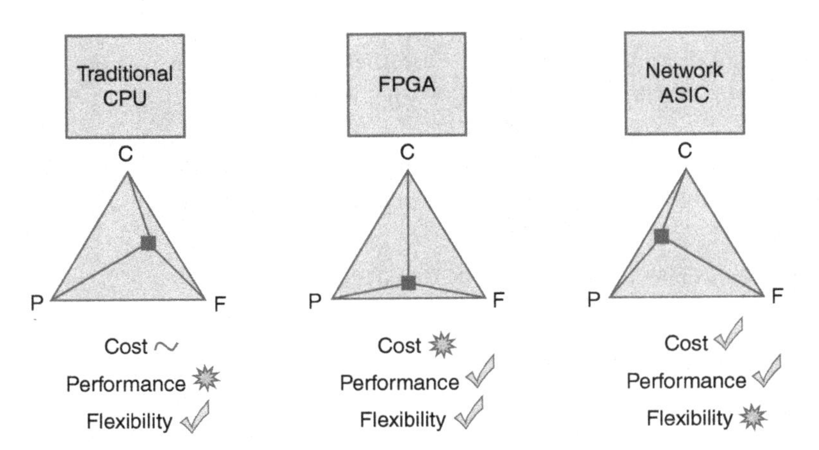

Figure 7-17 *Traffic Handling in CPUs, FPGAs, and Traditional Network ASICs*

Next up are field-programmable gate arrays (FPGA), specialized pieces of silicon that contain a number of programmable logic blocks, connected together by a set of reconfigurable logic elements such that an FPGA can, with the right software coding, be made to do many things that a traditional hard-wired ASIC could accomplish. FPGAs thus provide some of the same levels of flexibility that a CPU might, but at a higher performance level that is more comparable to the performance of a traditional network ASIC.

The downside to FPGAs is typically cost and complexity. On a cost-per-bps-moved basis, an FPGA tends to be an order of magnitude more expensive than a comparable network ASIC, because an FPGA is not optimized for any particular task, and again often lacks the on-chip memory needed for packet lookups (thus requiring augmentation with additional chips). Forming a middle ground between CPUs and ASICs, FPGAs are sometimes used as "gap fillers" in platform designs—helping to augment a traditional ASIC, which may lack one or two key functions, to fulfill a particular set of design objectives.

An example is Virtual Extensible LAN (VXLAN) support on the Catalyst 6800, where the EARL8 ASIC that forms the Catalyst 6800's forwarding engine supports many diverse protocols, but lacks support for VXLAN processing capability (as EARL8 was developed prior to VXLAN's debut into the market). In this case, front-ending the EARL8 ASIC complex with an FPGA to handle VXLAN can provide the required functionality—while the EARL8 chipset continues to process all other, non-VXLAN-encapsulated traffic flows (or traffic flows from which the VXLAN header has already been pushed/popped).

FPGAs are typically too expensive, however, to be used for the entire set of required packet-forwarding and traffic-handling functions in most platforms. Which brings us back to the traditional network ASIC, which provides excellent performance at a very reasonable cost (due to its fixed nature) but lacks the flexibility to handle new protocols and capabilities as they arise.

So, it seems like none of these are ideal for network traffic handling in our new, software-defined era...that there is no perfect answer, as shown in Figure 7-17.

Is there a better answer, one that provides the optimum balance between performance, flexibility, and cost? One that is ready to support the networking protocols and capabilities of today, and be flexible enough to handle the demands of tomorrow—even demands that may not be known yet?

Enter Cisco's flexible silicon to support Cisco DNA: UADP and QFP.

Introducing Flexible Silicon

The "holy grail" of flexible silicon is to provide all of the following:

- The programmability and flexibility approaching that offered by a CPU
- The performance equivalent to that of a hard-wired network ASIC
- The lowest possible cost

By correctly balancing all three of these factors, a truly flexible piece of silicon—a programmable network ASIC—can provide an unparalleled set of capabilities in today's (and tomorrow's) network infrastructures, as depicted in Figure 7-18.

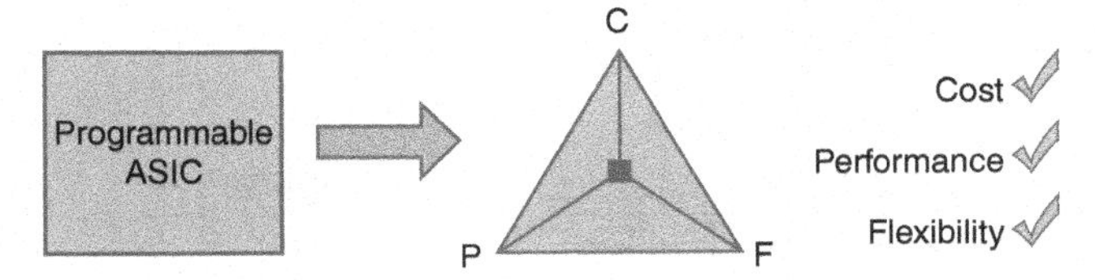

Figure 7-18 *The Right Balance—Benefits of Flexible Networking Silicon*

How can this balance be achieved? The key is by introducing microcode programmability and flexibility to the various stages in the network silicon processing pipeline. By doing so, these processing stages can be adapted over time to handle new protocols and new capabilities, in support of new network solutions.

The method used to adapt the flexible ASIC to these new capabilities as they arise is to download new microcode into the chip. This is typically done when the platform involved boots up, and the flexible network ASIC is programmed with the latest set of microcode (bundled as part of the platform's OS). As shown in Figure 7-19, the network operator can load a new version of software onto the box—reload—and get a whole new switching and routing functions on the platform involved. This is an excellent method of investment protection, allowing the network device to adapt to new needs and capabilities over time, and serves to illustrate the power of flexible hardware.

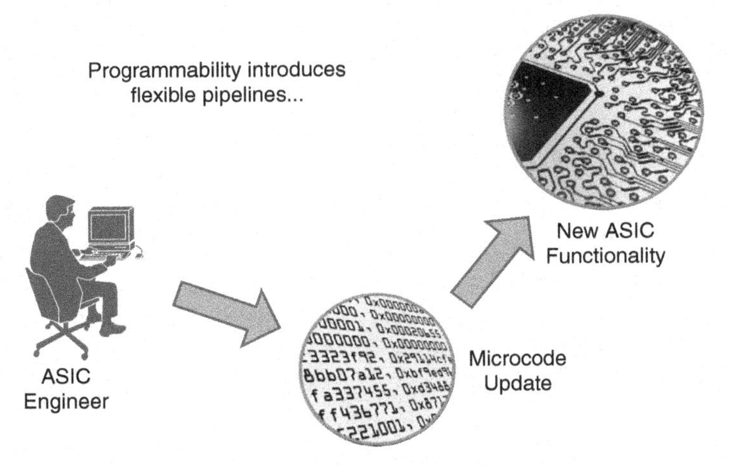

Figure 7-19 *Microcode Update—Key to a Whole New Set of Network ASIC Functionality*

Once the new microcode is loaded, some, most, or even all of the stages of the flexible network ASIC gain new levels of functionality—handling new protocols, providing new sets of capabilities—doing it all at a cost associated with a more traditional hard-wired network ASIC, thereby making these sophisticated functions available at price points that allow widespread and pervasive use within the network. Figure 7-20 shows an example of a flexible ASIC in action.

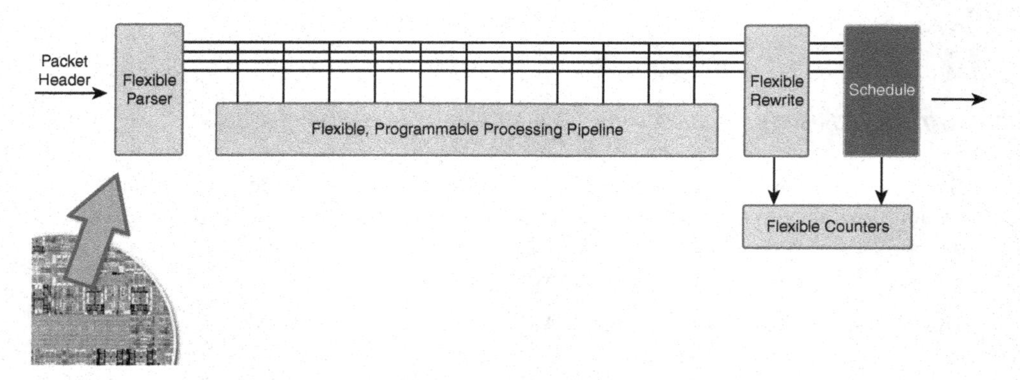

Figure 7-20 *Programmable ASIC Pipeline—Key to Flexibility*

The crucial distinction here is that a truly programmable ASIC provides this type of flexibility at a cost point that other technologies (such as FPGAs) cannot—and at a performance point well in excess of what any CPU could achieve.

Flexible ASIC technology is truly the key to the next generation of networking. Cisco pioneered the use of flexible ASIC technology in high-volume enterprise switching platforms when it introduced the Catalyst 3850 switch platform to the market in early 2013.

Flexible Switching Silicon: UADP

If you have ever used a Catalyst 3850, 3650, or 9000 Series switch, or passed traffic through one, you have used UADP.

The Cisco Unified Access Data Plane ASIC is a premier example of flexible switching silicon. Consisting of multiple generations of chips ranging from 1.3 billion to over 3 billion transistors—and now up to almost 20 billion transistors in its latest versions—UADP is one of the most complex, sophisticated, and impressive pieces of switching silicon anywhere in the world.

UADP began in 2013 as a key component in the then-brand-new Catalyst 3850 switch platform, and is the result of over five years of planning and design work prior to that, encompassing dozens of Cisco ASIC engineers and software and hardware designers. Today, UADP is used in the Catalyst 3850 and 3650 platforms, the Catalyst 4500 Supervisor 8-E and 9-E, and the Catalyst 9000 Series of fixed and modular switch platforms.

As a quick overview, some of the highlights of UADP are summarized in Figure 7-21 and examined in the subsequent list.

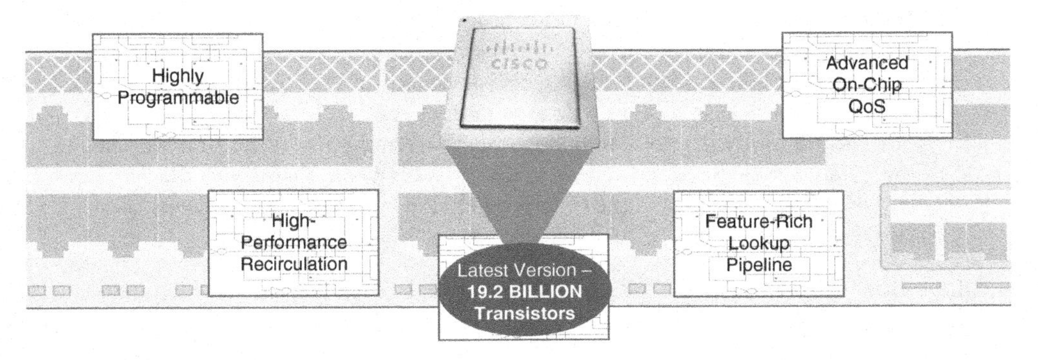

Figure 7-21 *UADP Overview*

UADP highlights are as follows:

- **Highly programmable:** UADP offers an unparalleled level of flexibility, by introducing a Flexible Parser block (capable of looking up to 256 bytes deep into the packet header), combined with a series of flexible, programmable packet-handling stages for handling the packet once parsed. With a total of 22 programmable stages (15 ingress, 7 egress) in the original UADP 1.0, and 25 programmable stages in the latest UADP 2.0 and 3.0 versions, UADP provides flexibility like no other ASIC in its class.
- **Advanced on-chip QoS:** Quality of Service is critical in enterprise networks, as the network strives to separate mission-critical, delay-sensitive traffic from other bulk traffic streams. UADP provides a set of comprehensive set of QoS capabilities, providing excellent traffic-handling flexibility.
- **High-performance recirculation:** All of the really interesting new capabilities in networking involve some sort of tunnel (defined as adding/removing a tunnel header in front of the existing packet header as provided by a user or device). Examples of such tunnels include MPLS, GRE, VXLAN, and many other protocols. UADP was created with tunneling in mind. Tunneling a packet involves a capability called recirculation—basically, feeding the newly encapsulated or newly decapsulated packet around for a "second pass" through the ASIC, necessary to handle the newly inserted or removed header for appropriate traffic handling and forwarding. As you will see, UADP is optimized for recirculation, and is thus primed for handling the newest and latest advances in networking as they arrive.
- **Feature-rich lookup pipeline:** All of the flexible, programmable stages in UADP can perform zero, one, or two lookups against a packet being processed—and all of the tables being referenced are on-chip, keeping performance consistently high. The result is a lookup pipeline that can provide many features to a packet in a single pass—and can provide multiple passes on a packet if required, for the maximum in feature processing as required by today's increasingly sophisticated network traffic handling.

- **High-density, powerful, flexible silicon:** 1.3 billion transistors per chip. Impressive in something that's smaller than your fingernail, isn't it? That was for the very first generation of UADP, version 1.0. The latest versions of the UADP ASIC now packs 3 billion transistors (UADP v1.1, as used in the Catalyst 3850/3650 Multigigabit Ethernet [mGig] switches), 7.46 billion transistors in the UADP 2.0 ASIC (as used in the Catalyst 9000 Series switches), or up to 19.2 billion transistors in the very latest UADP 3.0 ASIC (as used in the Catalyst 9000 25Gbps/100Gbps switches). And, all UADP ASICs are designed for flexibility as well as performance.

Let's examine UADP more deeply by first looking at a block diagram of the chip. Some of the key areas are shown in detail in Figure 7-22.

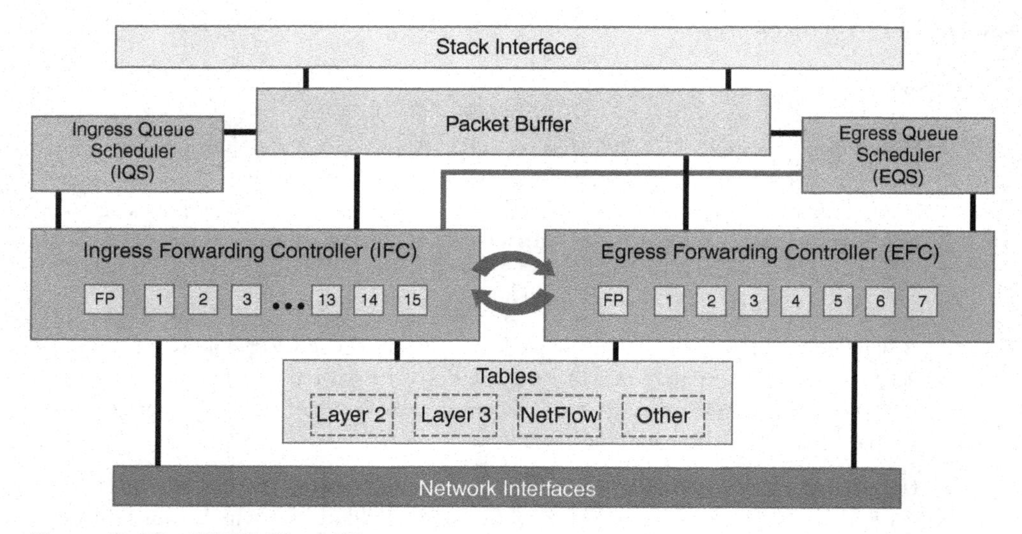

Figure 7-22 *UADP Block Diagram*

On the bottom of the diagram, the network interfaces are Ethernet ports (operating at various speeds) that you may attach devices to on the switch. These feed directly into the first key element of the UADP ASIC, the microcode-programmable Flexible Parser (FlexParser), as shown in Figure 7-23, housed within the UADP's Ingress Forwarding Controller (IFC).

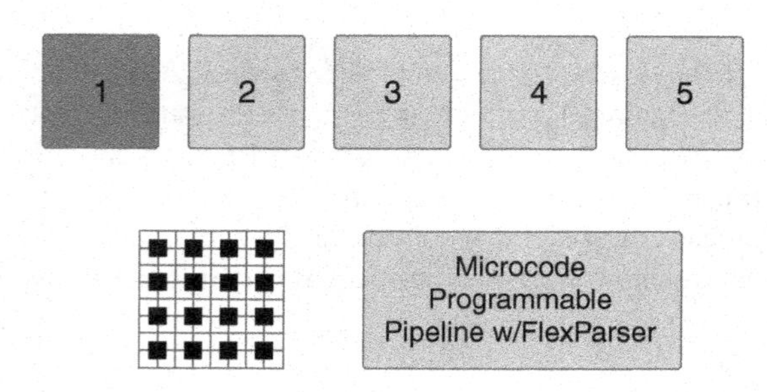

Figure 7-23 *First UADP Key Element—Flexible Parser (FlexParser)*

The FlexParser is key to the flexibility and adaptability to new protocols and functions that UADP provides. The FlexParser allows UADP to be adapted to understand, and allow to be processed, new protocols and new capabilities over time.

The FlexParser sits at the front of the IFC, which contains a total of 15 (UADP 1.0/1.1) or 17 (UADP 2.0/3.0) flexible, programmable stages for processing of packets identified and classified by the FlexParser block. This is shown in more detail in Figure 7-24.

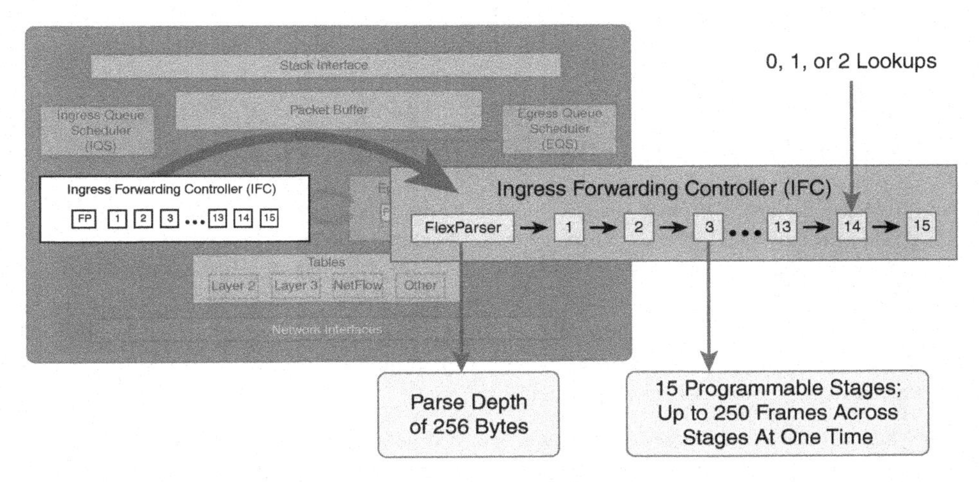

Figure 7-24 *UADP Ingress Forwarding Controller (IFC)*

The UADP ASIC's FlexParser can be programmed, via microcode, to handle many different packet types and encapsulations. At the time of writing, UADP has already been microcoded to handle the following key networking protocols, among others:

- IPv4
- IPv6
- GRE
- MPLS (L3 and L2 VPN)
- VXLAN

Critically, UADP can be programmed in the future for many other encapsulations, if and when the need for them arises. This includes encapsulations that have not necessarily even been invented yet. As of IOS-XE 16.3, the UADP ASIC in the Catalyst 3850, 3650, and 9000 Series switches handles VXLAN encapsulation. The VXLAN protocol, documented as RFC 7348, was invented after the UADP silicon was designed and built—and yet, the adaptable nature of UADP's FlexParser allows, via a simple software upgrade, for VXLAN traffic to be understood and processed, with high performance, in UADP's programmable hardware pipeline.

UADP's FlexParser can parse up to 256 bytes deep into the packet, allowing almost any protocol, current or planned, to be handled (requiring only the necessary microcoding, and associated higher-level software, for traffic handling). The ability in UADP to keep many packets in flight simultaneously (up to 250) keeps performance consistently high, and enables the impressive throughput numbers associated with succeeding generations of UADP as follows:

- UADP 1.0 (used in Catalyst 3850/3650 1G copper): 56 Gbps
- UADP 1.1 (used in Catalyst 3850 mGig and 10G fiber): 160 Gbps
- UADP 2.0 (used in Catalyst 9000 Series switches): 240 Gbps
- UADP 3.0 (used in the Catalyst 9000 Series 25G/100G switches): 1.6 Tbps

Once a packet makes it through the IFC, it's off to the Ingress Queue Scheduler (IQS). This is the portion of UADP that handles ingress packet queueing. The packet itself is placed into the packet buffer (6 MB on the original UADP, as used in the Catalyst 3850 and 3650 1G-copper platforms, and up to 16 MB and 32 MB/36 MB, respectively, in the Catalyst 3850 mGig/10G Fiber platforms and the Catalyst 9000 Series platforms). The IQS determines which packets receive priority for handling either into the stack interface (between switches) or to other front-panel ports.

Once the packet's turn arrives to be forwarded, it is sent along to the Egress Forwarding Controller (EFC), where it can undergo up to another seven programmable stages (UADP 1.0/1.1) or eight programmable stages of handling (UADP 2.0/3.0) on the egress side of the chip, for additional packet-processing flexibility. Once the packet passes the EFC, it is in turn scheduled out of the ASIC—and sped along into the outside world—via the Egress Queue Scheduler (EQS), ensuing appropriate traffic handling for all traffic flows.

All of the tables—Layer 2, Layer 3, NetFlow, etc.—that UADP needs to reference for traffic handing are located on-chip for maximum performance, which allows UADP to provide excellent performance even when many diverse functions and lookups are being performed on any given packet flow. Lookup bus bandwidths are up to 512 bits wide, meaning that lots of data can shuffle back and forth very rapidly and, when combined with the packet-handling rate of UADP, that the chip contains literally terabits' worth of internal bandwidth, as shown in Figure 7-25.

Along the way, all of the necessary packet-level and flow-level statistics, including counters, full-flow NetFlow, and other information, are gathered and logged. UADP includes the capacity for tens of thousands of NetFlow entries (with capacity varying by UADP version), tracking statistics and usage on every single packet traversing the platform—critically important in today's networks, where keeping close track of all traffic flows is important for new and emerging network security applications, as well as more traditional capacity planning and network usage accounting functions.

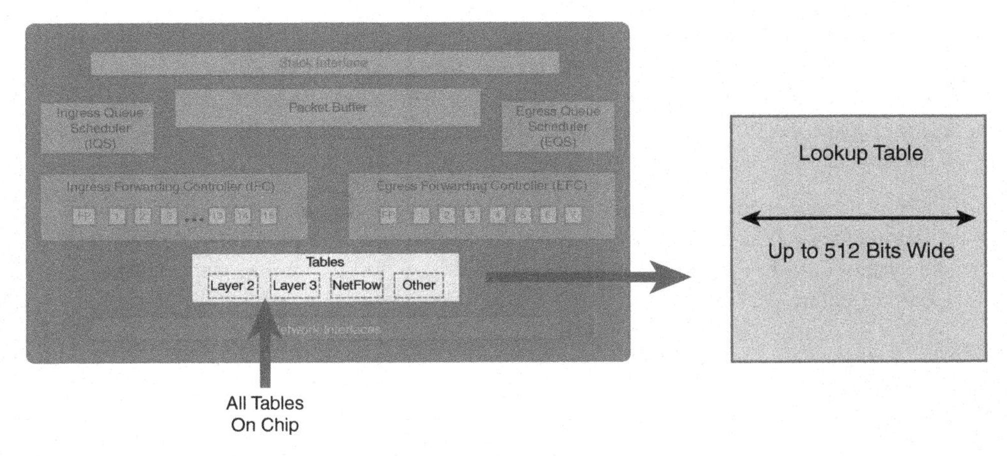

Figure 7-25 *UADP—On-Chip Tables and Bandwidth Capacities*

Should recirculation be required—which it will be if tunneling is involved—UADP performs exceptionally. Tunneling requires recirculation because, when a tunnel header is added or removed, the packet's destination has by definition changed, and so a recirculation (passing the packet through the ASIC's processing pipeline again) is necessary to forward the traffic to the "new" encapsulated or de-encapsulated destination, along with all the policies that need to apply to the packet.

The UADP's recirculation latency (the time required to get a packet off the end of the EFC's egress pipeline, and back to the front of the IFC's ingress pipeline) is sub-microsecond, clocking in at approximately 500 nanoseconds. That's 500-billionths of a second, or about 1/700,000th of the time it takes you to blink your eye. When combined with massive recirculation bandwidth (because bandwidth not being used by the front panel ports is available for recirculation, along with dedicated recirculation bandwidth as well), this means that traffic recirculation, when required, poses no issues for UADP. This is shown in Figure 7-26.

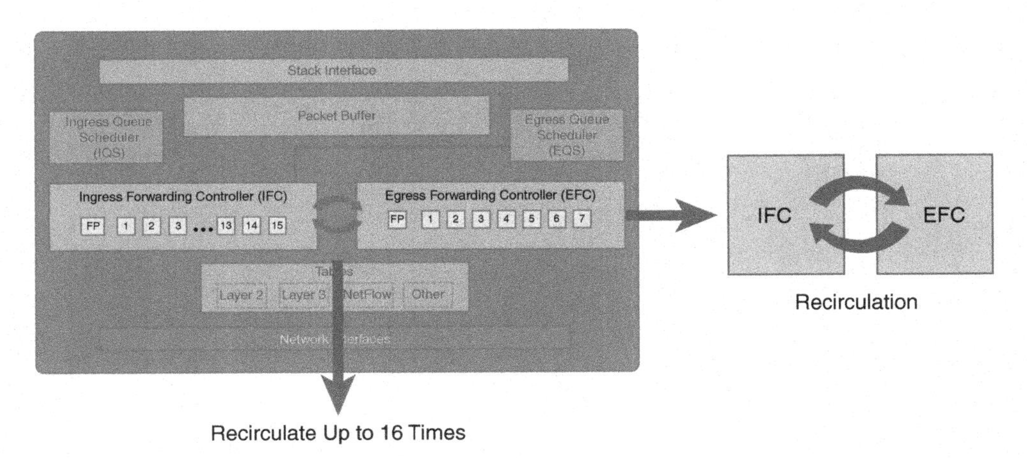

Figure 7-26 *UADP Recirculation*

For maximum flexibility, packets can be recirculated between the IFC and the EFC up to 16 times, allowing for any currently conceivable packet-handling requirements. At the present time, no use case exists for more than seven recirculations, but it's nice to know that the UADP hardware provides the flexibility for more in future, should this be required.

The second key element of UADP is the ability to connect to an extremely high-performance stacking interface, which is used to connect multiple UADP ASICs together in a system (multiple chips in one box and/or multiple boxes combined in a stack), as shown in Figure 7-27.

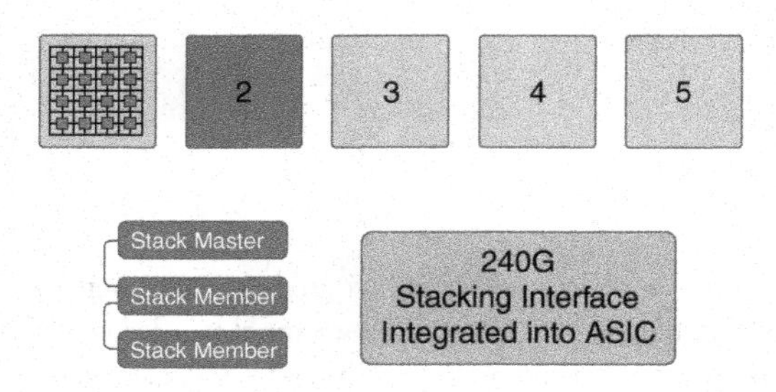

Figure 7-27 *UADP Stacking Interface*

The UADP stacking interface in the Catalyst 3850 operates at 240 Gbps and consists of three counter-rotating stack rings operating at 40 Gbps apiece. By incorporating a function known as Spatial Reuse (which allows recovery of unused bandwidth on the stack ring by destination stripping of unicast traffic from the ring), an effective doubling of stack ring bandwidth can be achieved, boosting stack performance up to 480 Gbps.

The Catalyst 3850 stack ring architecture (known as StackWise Plus) is shown in Figures 7-28 and 7-29, which depict multiple switches connected together in a stack; this architecture enables the stacked switches to behave as a single unit (that is, a single switch) for the purposes of configuration as well as network Layer 2/Layer 3 topology.

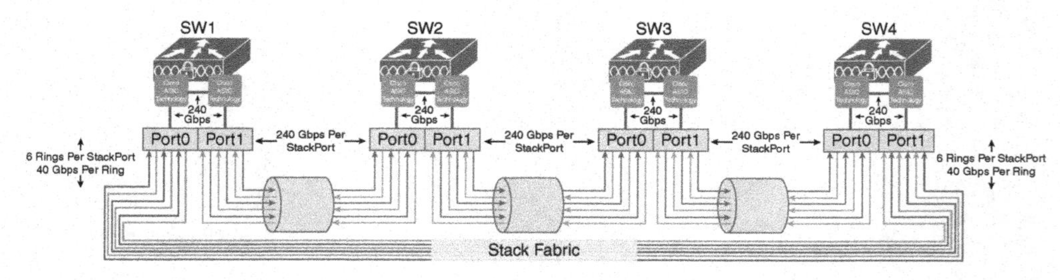

Figure 7-28 *Catalyst 3850 Stacking Ring—Using UADP*

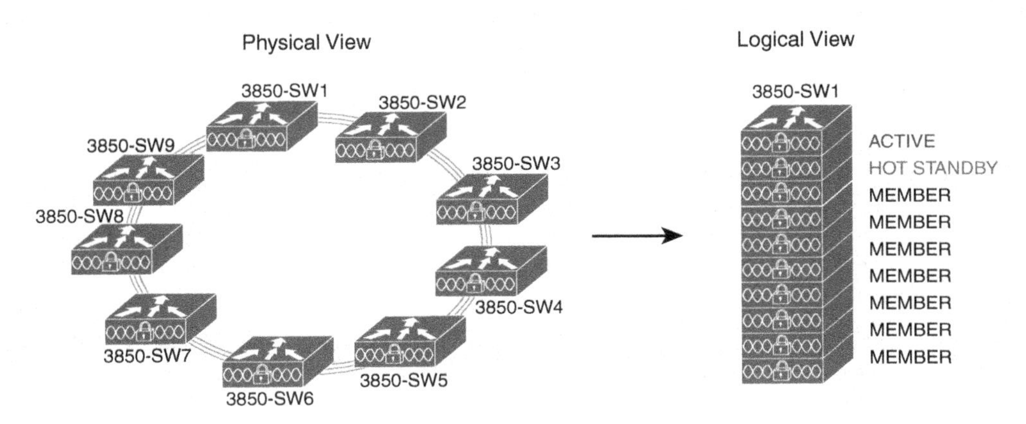

Figure 7-29 *Catalyst 3850 Switch Stack—Logical and Physical Views*

The Catalyst 3650 provides a "single lane" of stacking bandwidth, versus the Catalyst 3850's "three lanes," limiting 3650 stacking performance to a still very respectable 160 Gbps with spatial bandwidth reuse. The high performance of the Catalyst 3850/3650 stack, when combined with QoS which is stack-aware, ensures that inter-switch connections in a Catalyst 3850/3650 stack are never the bottleneck for traffic flows in the network.

This same stacking ring architecture is also present in the Catalyst 9300 Series switches, where it is used to connect up to eight Catalyst 9300 switches together in a StackWise Plus ring. In addition, this stacking architecture is also used on the Catalyst 9400 modular switch's Supervisor Engine, as well as on the Catalyst 9500 Series switches (where the ring is used to connect multiple ASICs together to provide forwarding for and across the entire switch). In these latter two cases (Catalyst 9400 and 9500), the internal stacking ring bandwidth between ASICs is increased to 720 Gbps for maximum performance.

Selected Catalyst 9000 Series switches also support StackWise Virtual capability, which allows for stacking interconnection of switches via front panel ports, providing enhanced flexibility and resilience.

The next major benefit of UADP is its integrated on-chip Micro Engines for fragmentation and for encryption/decryption, as shown in Figure 7-30.

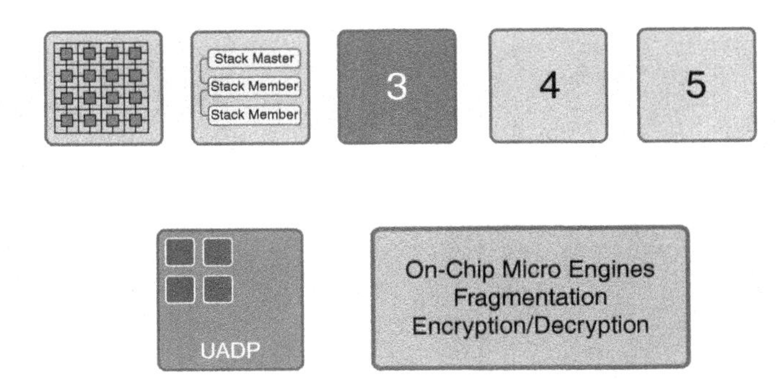

Figure 7-30 *UADP On-Chip Micro Engines*

Certain functions are always known to be common in networking, and at the same time known to be large consumers of processing power and bandwidth. These include fragmentation (common when any tunneling protocol is in use), as well as encryption and decryption.

By providing purpose-built areas within the UADP silicon dedicated to these functions, no cycles within the programmable pipeline are consumed for these processing-intensive capabilities. This preserves bandwidth and ensures that performance is kept consistently high, while also preserving microcode space within the UADP's programmable pipeline for other functions and capabilities.

Having high-performance fragmentation support—in hardware—on UADP is especially critical, considering how many of today's advanced networking functions leverage tunneling capability, and thus may need access to this high-performance packet fragmentation engine (for example, when the egress maximum transmission unit [MTU] size on an output interface is exceeded in the event that an encapsulation header is added to the packet involved).

In terms of encryption support, newer versions of the Catalyst 3850 platform (those with mGig ports) as well as the Catalyst 9000 Series switches also incorporate Media Access Control Security (MACsec) capability, for additional link-layer security. MACsec operates in these platforms at line rate and offers an excellent capability for port-level encryption of sensitive data, using robust encryption standards up to AES-256 with Galois Counter Mode (GCM).

The fourth key capability within UADP is high-performance packet recirculation. As mentioned previously when discussing the IFC and EFC, recirculation is a key element when handling tunneled traffic, which requires encapsulation/decapsulation, and this needs more than one pass through the ASIC prior to, or following, tunnel encapsulation/decapsulation. This is shown in Figure 7-31.

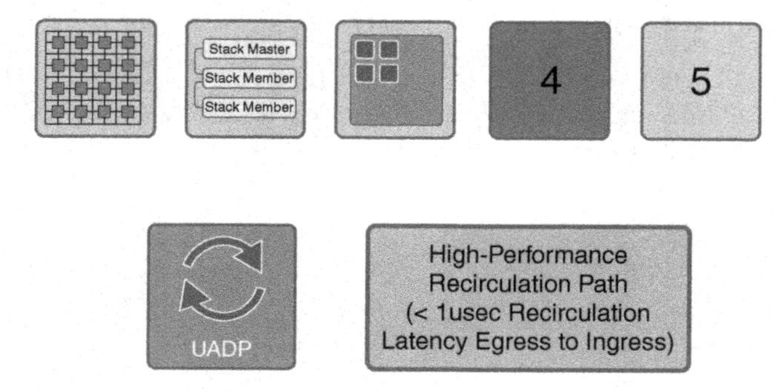

Figure 7-31 *UADP High-Performance Recirculation*

The extremely low recirculation latency, and highly optimized recirculation path, in UADP provides for excellent handling of tunneled traffic flows, and ensures that today's, and tomorrow's, tunneled protocols can be handled efficiently.

The fifth and final key element provided by UADP is integrated, on-chip full-flow NetFlow for traffic visibility, as shown in Figure 7-32.

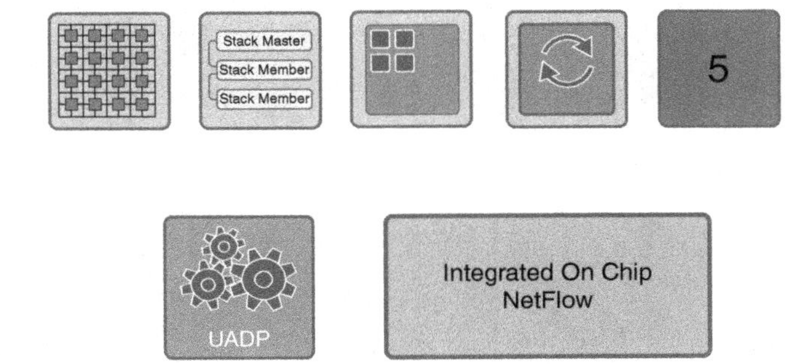

Figure 7-32 *UADP Integrated On-Chip NetFlow*

By providing NetFlow capability on every single packet that transits the switch, UADP provides excellent traffic visibility for accounting, capacity planning, security, and other purposes. The NetFlow table capacity offered by UADP—24,000 entries per UADP 1.0/1.1 ASIC, increased to higher capacities in following versions of UADP—is an excellent match for UADP's intended role within the switched network infrastructure of an organization.

Taken together, the five key capabilities of the UADP ASIC provide for unparalleled traffic-handling capability, flexibility, and power are as follows:

- Microcode-programmable FlexParser, with 15-stage programmable ingress pipeline and 7-stage programmable egress pipeline (increased to 17 ingress stages and 8 egress stages in UADP 2.0 and 3.0)
- Integrated extremely high-performance stacking capability
- On-chip Micro Engines for fragmentation and encryption
- High-performance recirculation (extremely low recirculation latency and high recirculation bandwidth)
- Integrated on-chip NetFlow (full-flow)

UADP Use Cases—Current, and Future

The UADP ASIC offers several key use cases, all implemented in currently available code. These include advanced QoS, support for MPLS VPNs, and support for VXLAN tunneling and Scalable Group Tags (SGT).

As shown in Figure 7-33, the advanced QoS capabilities of UADP include support for Approximate Fair Drop (AFD), an advanced QoS algorithm that ensures fairness among multiple competing sources for network traffic, especially when those traffic flows include low-bandwidth (mice) flows contending with high-bandwidth (elephant) flows in the network. AFD is designed to ensure appropriate QoS traffic handling to both types of flows, allowing them to coexist on the same network gracefully.

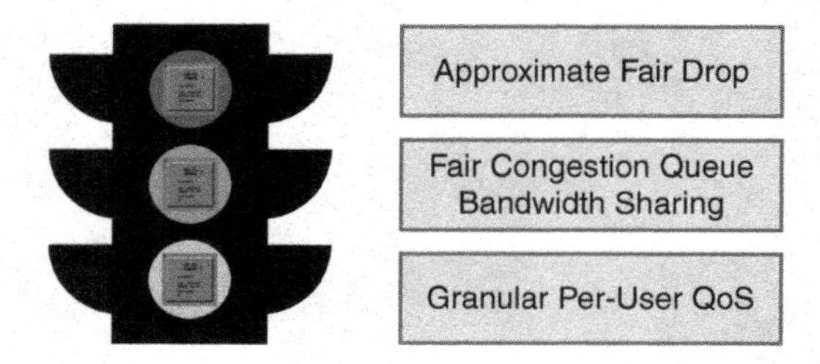

Figure 7-33 *UADP Advanced QoS Capabilities*

When combined with Fair Congestion Queue Bandwidth Sharing and Granular Per-User QoS, UADP offers excellent options for ensuring that traffic is handled in accordance with existing best practices as well as enterprise QoS policies.

Today, many organizations wish to avail themselves of the capability to introduce segmentation into their network topologies. This may be done, for example, to provide enhanced security by reducing the total network attack surface available to a malicious actor or rogue network device. With the requirement to support such advanced network segmentation on UADP, the ability to handle the appropriate network segmentation technologies such as MPLS VPNs for topology-oriented segmentation or SGTs for topology-less segmentation/micro-segmentation became key.

In addition, the use of newer technologies such as VXLAN serve to enhance the range of available network segmentation solutions available to the network designer and manager. Thanks to the flexible, programmable nature of the UADP ASIC, these capabilities were added via a simple IOS-XE software upgrade on the existing Catalyst 3850 and 3650 platforms, and are also available on Cisco's new Catalyst 9000 Series switches.

As mentioned, an excellent example of the flexibility provided by UADP is support for the VXLAN protocol. VXLAN is a key protocol for supporting the use of fabric-based network capabilities within the enterprise network, as provided by the Cisco Software-Defined Access (SD-Access) solution. The flexible nature of VXLAN encapsulation, which can support both Layer 2 and Layer 3 encapsulated payloads, is critical for use in tomorrow's flexible network fabric infrastructures.

A quick examination of the VXLAN protocol is provided in Figure 7-34.

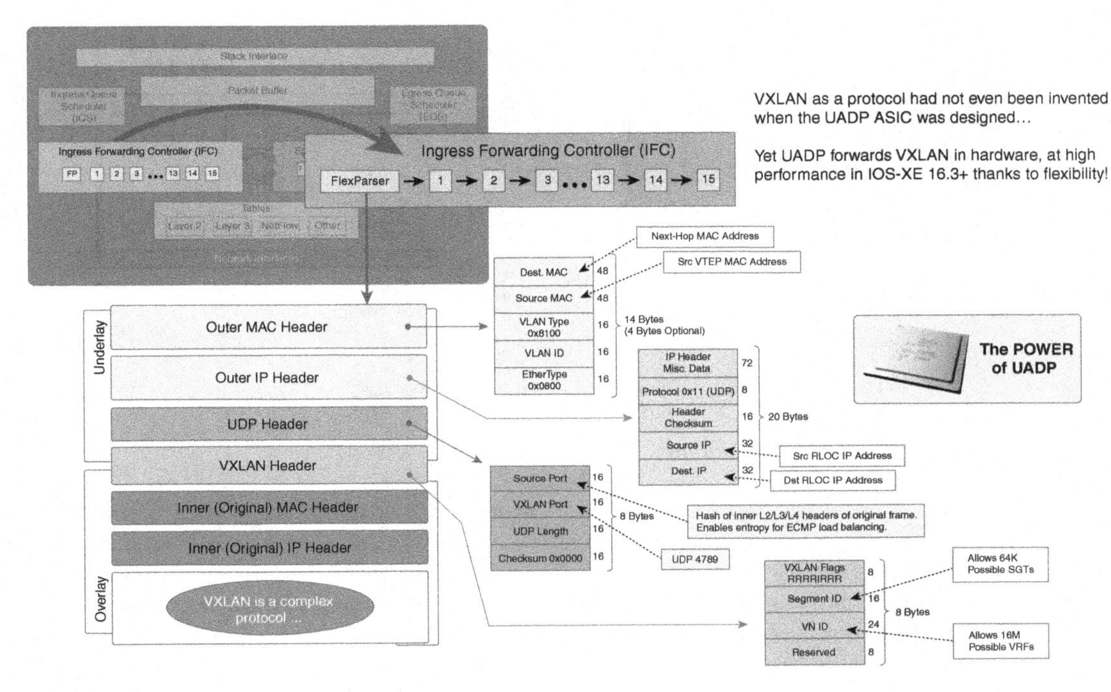

Figure 7-34 *UADP Support for VXLAN*

It is interesting to note that the UADP ASIC was designed before VXLAN as a protocol had even been invented, yet UADP forwards VXLAN traffic, in hardware, with high performance. Stop and think about that for a second. UADP was created before VXLAN was even invented, yet UADP supports VXLAN traffic forwarding and manipulation in hardware. This is the true power of flexible silicon—the ability to handle new protocols and new functions as they come along, flexibly adapting to new trends and requirements in the networking industry without having to replace the underlying hardware. This is an extremely powerful capability in the flexible silicon produced by Cisco, one which enables significant investment protection for customers, now and into the future.

Introducing the Future: UADP 2.0 and 3.0

UADP 2.0 and 3.0 are the latest and (so far) greatest member of the Unified Access Data Plane ASIC family. These new UADP versions continue the legacy of flexibility pioneered by the UADP versions that preceded them, and at the same time add critical new functionality and performance to enable the next generation of switching platforms, and the capabilities they provide.

A quick comparison of the various UADP models is provided in Figure 7-35.

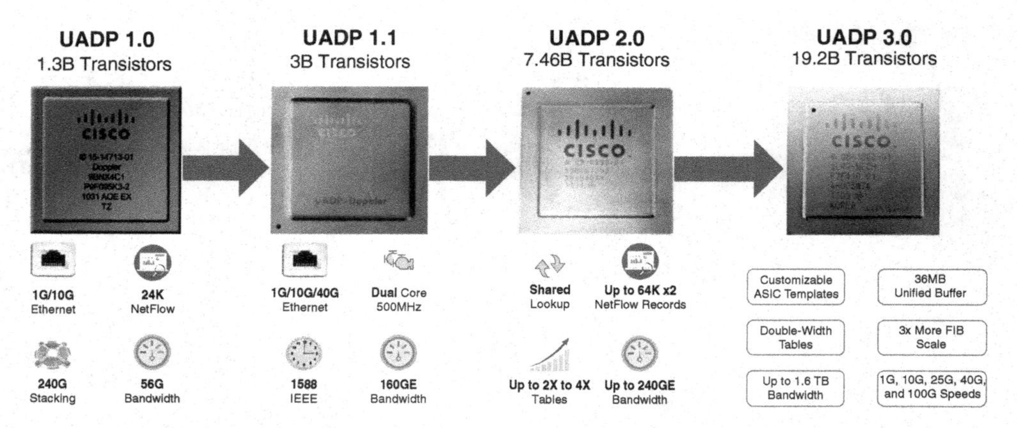

Figure 7-35 *The UADP Family*

The original UADP 1.0 ASIC was a very capable piece of silicon. Supporting 1G and 10G Ethernet, 56-Gbps processing bandwidth, an integrated 240-Gbps stacking interface, and up to 24,000 NetFlow records (full-flow, not sampled), UADP 1.0 formed the basis for the first Catalyst 3850 and 3650 platforms and offered great performance as well as flexibility. Produced in both 65-nm and 45-nm sizing, UADP 1.0 packaged all of this into 1.3 billion transistors' worth of packet-processing goodness.

UADP 1.1 built on top of the capabilities of 1.0, retaining UADP's hallmark flexibility and adding support for 40G Ethernet, IEEE 1588 precision timestamping, and up to 160 GB of total bandwidth. By moving to a 28-nm production process, UADP 1.1 squeezed two processing cores onto a single silicon die operating at a higher clock rate, further increasing performance—necessary to keep up with the vastly increased port densities and port speeds provided by the new Catalyst 3850 10G fiber switches and the Catalyst 3850/3650 mGig (100M/1G/2.5G/5G/10G) platforms.

UADP 2.0 and 3.0 are the latest variations of UADP. UADP 2.0 forms the foundation for the new Catalyst switching platforms—the Catalyst 9000 Series family, consisting of the Catalyst 9300 stackable switches, the Catalyst 9400 modular switches, and the Catalyst 9500 fixed-configuration core switches. UADP 3.0 is used in the higher-end Catalyst 9500 switch platforms—those employing integrated, high-density 25G and 100G Ethernet ports.

UADP 2.0 and 3.0 support a number of important additions to the set of capabilities already provided by the other UADP family members. These include an increase in bandwidth to 240 Gbps and 1.6 Tbps capacities, respectively (leveraging multiple cores at higher clock rates within a single ASIC to deliver higher overall capacity), an increase in the NetFlow table size supported, and an increase in other table sizes (Layer 2, Layer 3, etc.) anywhere from two to four times compared to previous UADP generations. As well, the total number of counters in the UADP 2.0 and 3.0 ASICs is substantially increased from previous generations, leading to a richer ability to generate statistics—very useful for next-generation analytics and related capabilities for traffic flow analysis.

In addition, one of the most important innovations provided by these latest generations of UADP is arguably their ability to provide flexible lookup table capability, enabling UADP 2.0 and 3.0 to flexibly reallocate these tables as needed for the particular job at hand, and share their packet-processing tables between the various areas within the UADP ASIC itself. This is shown in Figure 7-36.

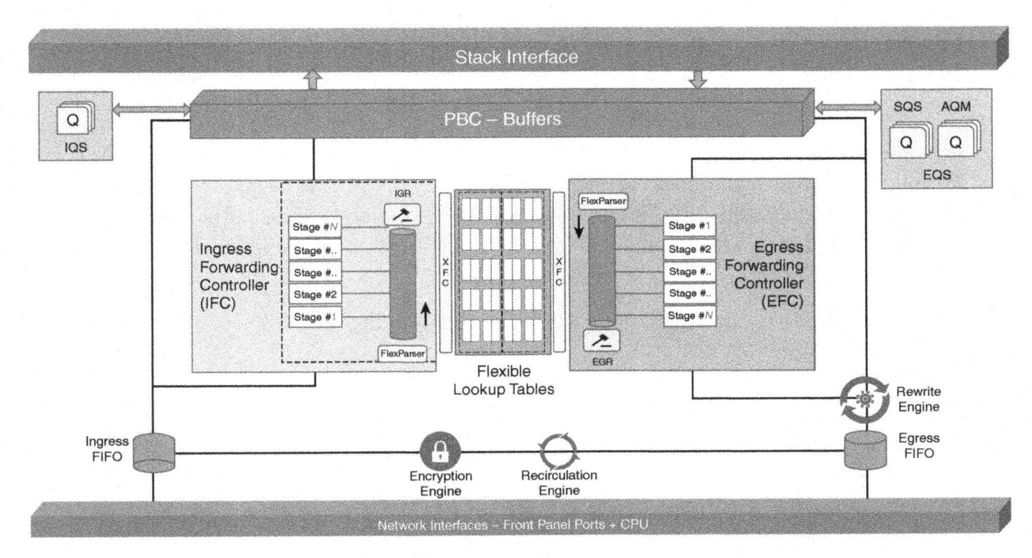

Figure 7-36 *UADP 2.0 and 3.0 Layout and Flexible Lookup Tables*

Why is this flexible lookup table capability important? Recall that everything in networking typically involves table lookups. However, the exact sizing of the lookup tables needs to vary according to the task at hand. For example, an access-layer switch may need more entries for MAC addresses (because it is Layer-2 adjacent to a large number of hosts), while a core switch may need more Layer 3 Forwarding Information Base (FIB) entries or NetFlow entries, because it is handling more traffic in aggregate and is exposed to a larger total routing domain.

UADP 2.0 and 3.0 are excellent for this use because their table sizing can be adjusted between various functions under software control. Depending on the platform and its network role, UADP 2.0 and 3.0 can be configured for a larger or smaller number of table entries for various given areas—unicast Layer 3, multicast Layer 3, Layer 2, NetFlow, security ACLs, QoS ACLs, and so forth. Within the chip, these are all handled as either ternary content-addressable memory (TCAM) or static random access memory (SRAM) resources, whose size can be modified as needed. This flexibility offers an excellent ability to customize the actual packet handling of the network switch incorporating UADP 2.0 or 3.0, in accordance with its role and placement within the network.

In addition, UADP 2.0 and 3.0 utilize shared lookup tables that can be accessed across both processing cores within the ASIC. This innovation conserves TCAM space by allowing both processing cores within the ASIC to access a single copy of a programmed table entry, thus avoiding having to program such an entry twice and providing maximum scalability without compromising performance.

As well, UADP 3.0 provides for double-width on-chip tables, thus allowing IPv4 and IPv6 entries to be stored in a single on-chip table entry, and providing for the same lookup performance for IPv4 and IPv6 traffic. Shared lookup tables and double-width table access are both excellent examples of how UADP 2.0 and 3.0, as used in the Catalyst 9000 Series switches, build upon the flexible legacy of the UADP architecture, while at the same time introducing new innovations that allow performance and functionality to scale to new levels.

The ability to share TCAM/SRAM lookup entries between the cores within the UADP 2.0 and 3.0 ASICs leads to much greater efficiency, as this avoids having to program the same entries redundantly across cores and across ingress and egress paths. In turn, this affords greater total performance and capacity, necessary for the expanded roles of the Catalyst 9000 Series platforms within the network.

The UADP packet-processing architecture is outlined in Figure 7-37.

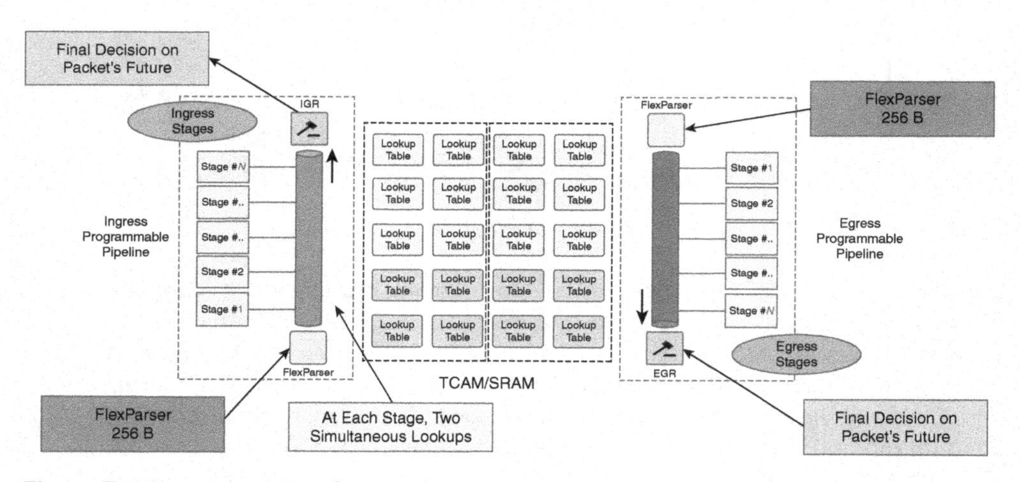

Figure 7-37 *UADP 2.0 and 3.0 Packet Processing*

Notice the ingress and egress pipeline structure of preceding UADPs is maintained, as is the ability to perform up to two simultaneous packet lookups in each stage of the multistage processing pipeline. UADP 2.0 and 3.0 actually increase the total number of stages on the ingress pipeline to 17 (from 15 previously), and also increase the total number of egress stages to 8 (from 7 previously)—yielding a total of 25 stages of fully programmable packet processing. The 256-byte deep packet header lookup capability of preceding UADPs is still retained, leading to an excellent ability to "look deep" into passing traffic.

Figure 7-37 also shows more detail on the Ingress Global Resolution (IGR) and Egress Global Resolution (EGR) stages of packet processing. All UADP ASICs incorporate the IGR and EGR logic outlined herein—however, let's delve a bit deeper into this now that we are examining the inner workings of the UADP 2.0 and 3.0 ASICs, in order to understand how this works.

The job of the IGR block in the UADP ASIC is to "sum up" and normalize the decisions made by each of the ingress programmable stages. For example, one stage may have said "Route the packet this way" while another stage may have said "Drop the packet due to matching a security ACL entry." The IGR resolves all of these various decisions and provides the "final decision" as to what the packet's fate, and further processing, will be. On the egress side of the chip, the EGR performs a similar function at the end of the egress pipeline. All UADP ASICs incorporate this IGR/EGR logic for their programmable pipelines, and Figure 7-37 shows this in more detail.

And what transistor count did all of this advanced capability on UADP 2.0 and 3.0 come with? An impressive 7.46 billion transistors on UADP 2.0, and a very impressive 19.2 billion transistors on UADP 3.0. Pretty striking for something you can hold in the palm of your hand!

Let's now examine the key platforms that the UADP 2.0 and 3.0 ASICs support. These are the Catalyst 9000 Series switches—the Catalyst 9300, 9400, and 9500, which together form the foundation for the next era of enterprise networking.

Figure 7-38 shows the Catalyst 9300 platform, the industry's new standard for advanced stackable access switches. The Catalyst 9300 is offered in 24-port and 48-port versions with Gigabit Ethernet front-panel ports, with both non-PoE (Power over Ethernet) and PoE-capable (PoE+/UPoE) models available. As well, a version of the Catalyst 9300 is offered with mGig-capable front-panel ports, offering connectivity of up to 1G/2.5G/5G/10G Ethernet with UPoE capability. All of the Catalyst 9300 models support modular fans, modular power supplies, and fully modular uplink capability, with 4 × 10G, 8 × 10G, and 2 × 40G uplink modules available. In addition, a new 2 × 25G uplink module is now available for the Catalyst 9300.

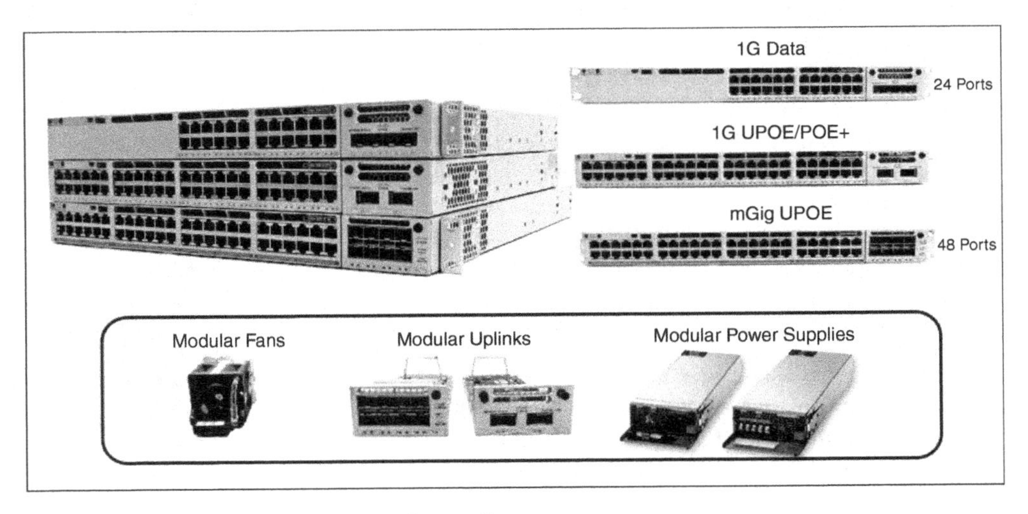

Figure 7-38 *Catalyst 9300 Switch Family*

Figure 7-39 shows the Catalyst 9400 platform, the industry-leading flexible, modular access switch family. The Catalyst 9400 is the first modular switch to be based on the UADP ASIC, and is offered in sizes ranging from four-slot through seven-slot and ten-slot varieties (although the Catalyst 4500 Supervisor-8E and -9E incorporated the UADP ASIC, they used this only for ancillary functions, whereas the Catalyst 9400 family uses the UADP ASIC as its primary forwarding chipset). All Catalyst 9400 switches offer two dedicated Supervisor slots for packet switching and processing redundancy, even in the smallest four-slot switch models, ensuring the highest levels of resiliency for demanding access-layer switch applications.

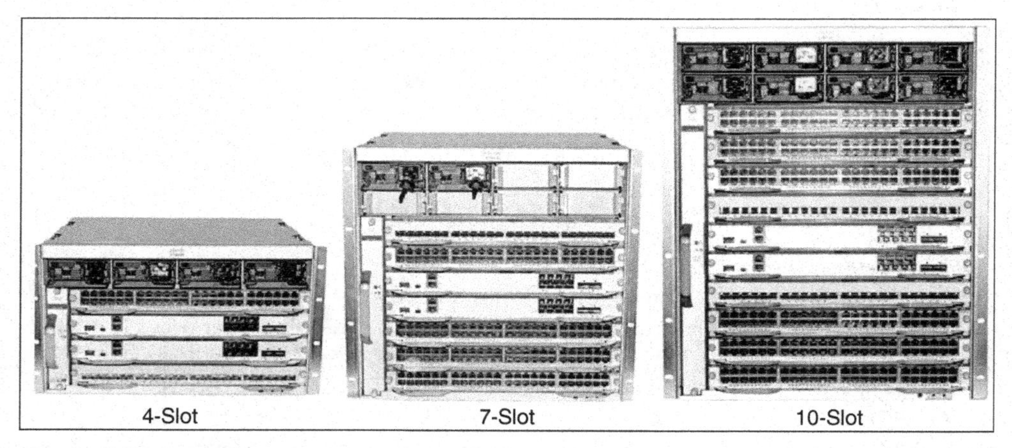

Figure 7-39 *Catalyst 9400 Switch Family*

The Catalyst 9400 family offers simple, functionally transparent line cards and centralized packet processing, building on the legacy of its predecessor platform the Catalyst 4500E, while offering a whole new set of packet-processing throughput and flexibility made possible by the use of the UADP 2.0 ASIC. The Catalyst 9400 also offers key hardware innovations such as a fan tray that is removable from both the front and the back side of the switch, as well as N+1 and N+N redundant power supplies. Along with the other Catalyst 9000 switch family members, the Catalyst 9400 platform boasts an ergonomic design that eases installation and use of the platform with such functions as blue beacon capability and RFID support to allow for easy identification of system components—showing the attention to detail and serviceability that is the hallmark of the Catalyst 9000 Series switch family.

Finally, Figure 7-40 shows the Catalyst 9500 switch family. Intended as a series of fixed-configuration core and aggregation switches, the Catalyst 9500 family provides a high level of port density for 10G, 25G, 40G, and 100G Ethernet in an extremely compact and powerful form factor, while also offering resiliency across important areas such as modularity for switch elements such as fans, uplinks, and power supplies.

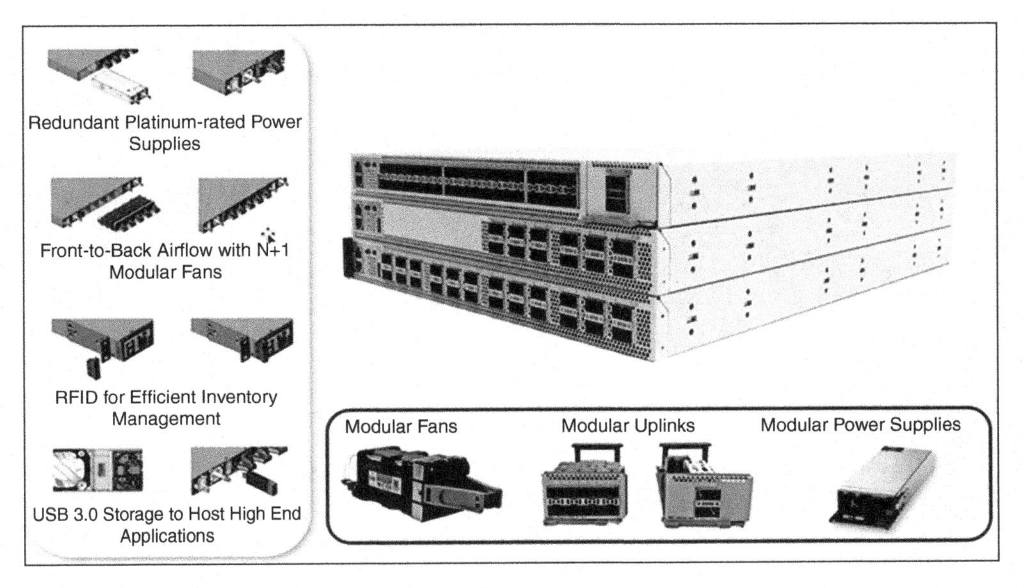

Figure 7-40 *Catalyst 9500 Switch Family*

For many modern enterprise network designs, sophisticated and high-performance functionality in a small package is critical. The Catalyst 9500 family of switches is designed to deliver against this need. With the capability to provide high-density 10-Gbps Ethernet, 40-Gbps Ethernet and now—with the latest additions to the Catalyst 9500 family based on UADP 3.0, high-density 25-Gbps Ethernet and 100-Gbps Ethernet—in a very compact form factor, the Catalyst 9500 leads the industry in terms of functionality and performance—all with the flexibility enabled by UADP.

So What's Common Across All of These Variants of UADP?

Flexibility is the common denominator among the UADP variants. Flexibility supports future growth in network design possibilities and provides investment protection as the network evolves, which is a critical element to support Cisco DNA. The only real constant in networking, as in life itself, is change. Cisco's UADP-based switch platforms are designed to deliver, with this need for flexibility and investment protection in mind.

In the future, the FlexParser and programmable pipeline capabilities of Cisco's powerful UADP ASIC make it possible to support many additional protocols and capabilities, based on market and customer demand, as indicated in Figure 7-41 (note, protocols marked with an asterisk in this figure are examples of potentially possible future capabilities, not currently committed features).

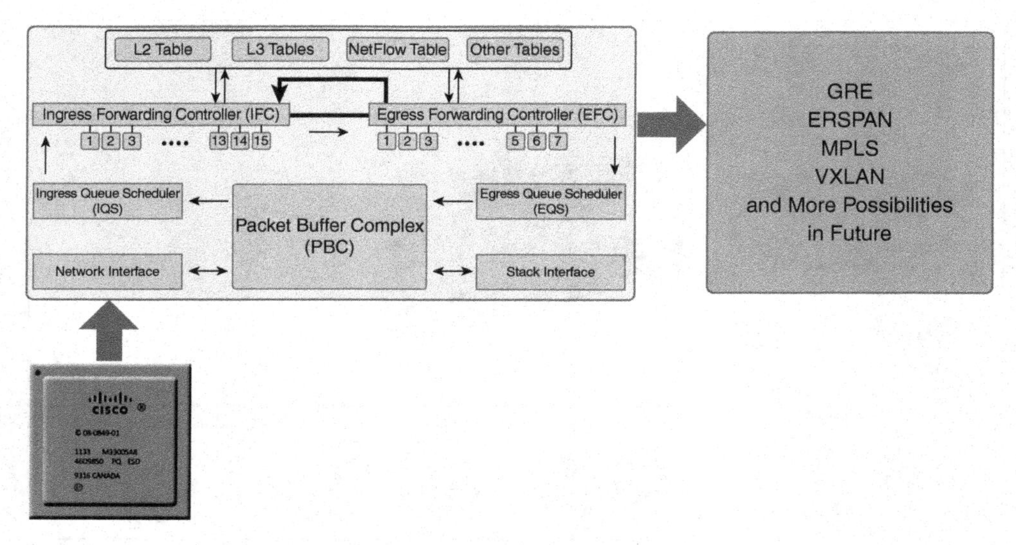

Figure 7-41 *Current, and Possible Future, UADP Use Cases*

The level of flexibility provided by Cisco's future-looking UADP ASIC is unparalleled in the industry, and is an absolutely critical underpinning for the evolution of the network with Cisco DNA.

UADP—Summing Up

Let's sum up what we've discussed about UADP.

Cisco's Unified Access Data Plane ASIC provides a level of robustness, flexibility, and capability unequaled by any networking silicon in the industry. Designed from the ground up for flexibility, and representing the intellectual capital and effort of over five years by Cisco in development, the UADP ASIC offers Cisco customers a level of investment protection that is second to none.

Cisco customers investing in platforms that leverage the UADP ASIC, as outlined in Figure 7-42, reap the benefits of the power and capability it provides today—and the flexibility that it provides to drive investment protection for the future.

Simply put, the UADP ASIC, and the platforms it powers, allows your network to continue to evolve as networking evolves, which is a crucial consideration given the pace of change in today's rapidly digitalizing world. Although there are always limits to any platform or chipset, UADP provides an excellent level of flexibility for network functions today and tomorrow.

The solid set of functionality provided by UADP, along with Cisco's other flexible networking silicon, forms a strong foundation for Cisco DNA, and an excellent foundation for the future of networking.

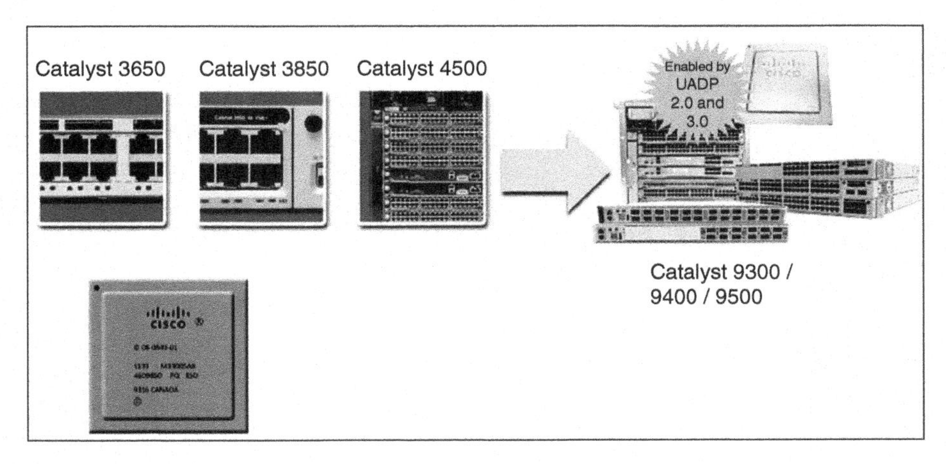

Figure 7-42 *UADP—Where Is It Used?*

Flexible Routing Silicon: QFP

The Cisco QuantumFlow Processor (QFP) forms the heart of the Cisco Aggregation Services Router 1000 (ASR 1000) product family. The ASR 1000 is designed to deliver on the inherent feature and scale requirements of enterprise routing as a premier WAN aggregation router, but to do so with the ability to evolve to current—and future—performance and capabilities.

WAN routers face very different scaling, performance, and feature requirements than LAN switches do. A router serving in the WAN aggregation role such as the ASR 1000 may be connecting in hundreds or even thousands of remote branch sites to a common WAN core or distribution location. In doing so, it must support key functions for all of these branches—QoS for connectivity and application prioritization, encryption for privacy and security, tunneling for use over multiple WAN carrier backbones and technologies, and more.

But with today's ever-increasing WAN speeds, the older, more traditional WAN routing platforms such as the venerable Cisco 7200 Series—long a workhorse of the fleet as a WAN aggregation router—were outstripped several years ago. As a traditional WAN router based on a CPU architecture for forwarding, the Cisco 7200 and its brethren offered excellent flexibility. However, their purely software-based forwarding approach couldn't scale above a few gigabits per second, which is an issue any CPU-based platform faces.

Scaling up by installing more and yet more such routers at a central site was not a sustainable solution for enterprise customers. What was needed was something that could support the three key routing attributes of performance, flexibility, and programmability, and do so at ever-increasing scale and density, as shown in Figure 7-43.

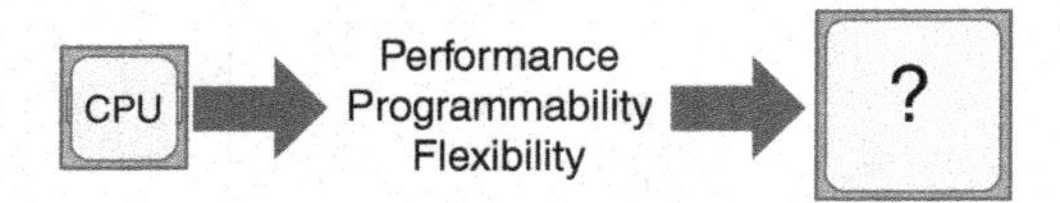

Figure 7-43 *Evolution of Routing*

So, what's the answer? Enter Cisco QuantumFlow Processor, a scalable and unique piece of flexible silicon designed specifically for the demanding requirements of the WAN aggregation role.

QFP—An Introduction

Cisco QFP is a powerful example of flexible silicon in action, designed for WAN routing and aggregation as shown in Figure 7-44.

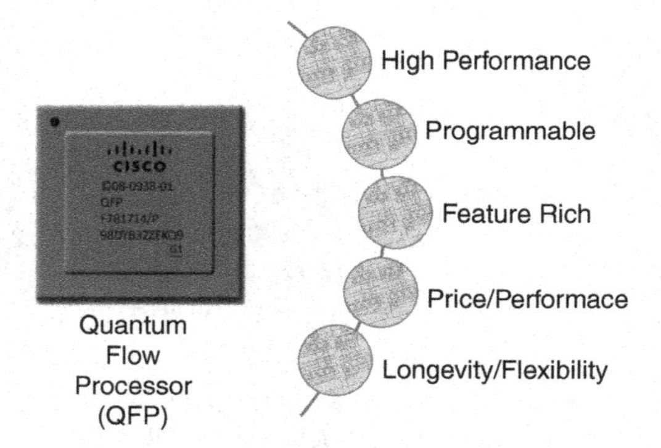

Figure 7-44 *Key Attributes of Cisco QuantumFlow Processor*

As such, QFP delivers on several of the key attributes that are needed for this role:

- **High performance:** In the ASR 1000 platform, QFP is scalable as high as 200 Gbps with the latest Embedded Services Processor engine (ESP-200), or as low as 2.5 Gbps for more entry-level solutions—spanning a huge range of WAN throughput needs with consistent features and performance. Integrated support for encryption also scale up as high as 78 Gbps with the ESP-200.
- **Programmable:** QFP is inherently flexible due to its multicore hardware architecture, which delivers extreme flexibility comparable to a more traditional CPU-based system, but with massively increased multidimensional scale.
- **Feature-rich:** The ASR 1000 by its nature and position in the network must deliver on all of the most critical features for a WAN aggregation device—not just raw throughput, but also enhanced services such as NAT, encryption, ACLs, NetFlow, and more. By offering hardware assist for many of the features, QFP enables the ASR 1000 to offer not only best-in-class performance, but also unparalleled feature richness—without scale or performance compromise.

- **Price/performance:** As a Cisco-designed piece of flexible silicon, QFP is targeted directly at offering the best price/performance ratio for the applications it is designed for, and deployed in. QFP offers the right blend of performance, features, and price that makes the platforms leveraging it, such as the ASR 1000, unique in the industry.
- **Longevity and flexibility:** These two attributes are key design goals for the QFP architecture, and are deeply intertwined. QFP was designed from the ground up as a chip architecture that could live a long time in the marketplace and be taken through several iterations. Central to this longevity in terms of lifetime in a customer network is the flexibility that QFP offers—through a simple software upgrade, a platform leveraging QFP can deliver a whole new, enhanced set of software functionality, delivered at hardware throughput speeds. The key to this capability is the hardware architecture of QFP.

Much like the UADP ASIC examined previously in this chapter, QFP is the result of a five-year design process. However, the outcome produced a markedly different chip than UADP—different because it was designed to achieve different goals, and to be placed at a different position in the network, with widely varying requirements compared to those desired from a LAN switch.

QFP is fundamentally based on a massively multicore processing design, with hardware assists for many key networking attributes and functions. As shown in Figure 7-45, the original QFP design was based on a 40-core processor design (with initial deliverables of 5 Gbps to 10 Gbps performance), which scaled up to today's total of 64 parallel cores and 200 Gbps of system performance.

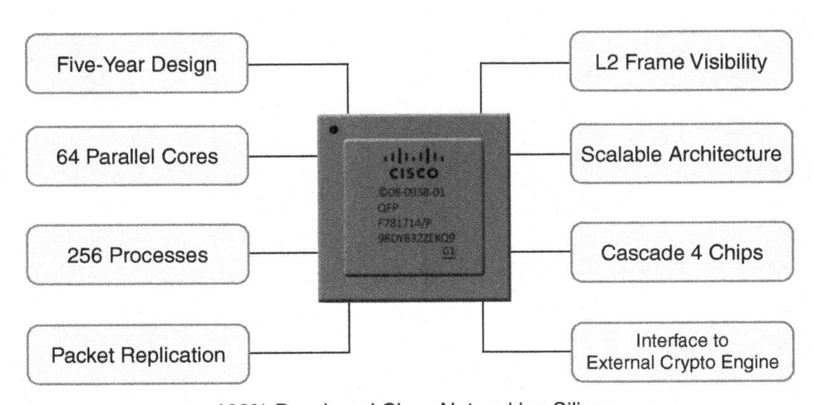

Figure 7-45 *QFP Overview*

Each processing core handles up to four threads of operation, allowing for up to 256 independent processes (such as packet forwarding and replication) to take place simultaneously within QFP. In addition, multiple QFPs (up to four) can be cascaded together in a system, and an interface is provided to allow attachment of an external encryption engine (a common requirement in WAN core routing).

The CPU in your laptop, desktop, or server might have two, four, or maybe even six or eight cores. The initial QFP hosted 40 cores, and today's QFP boasts 64 cores. Each processing core has roughly the performance of an entire Cisco 7200 router, so we are talking here about having a single chip with the power of 64 previous-generation routers, plus hardware assists for things like ACL lookups, QoS capabilities, encryption/decryption, etc., all shrunk down to a single chipset.

QFP was developed to deliver on next-generation routing needs, and its success can be judged by the wide acceptance that platforms leveraging QFP, such as the ASR 1000, have achieved in the marketplace.

QFP—Diving Deeper

Let's take a look inside QFP and see how it delivers some of its routing magic.

Figure 7-46 shows the basic block diagram of the QFP architecture. Notice that the packet-processing array shown at the top left is the collection of 40 or 64 processing cores noted previously—each with the equivalent processing capability to an entire Cisco 7200 router, and each with access to the full range of hardware assists offered by the QFP silicon, some of which are outlined in the functional block titled "General Resources."

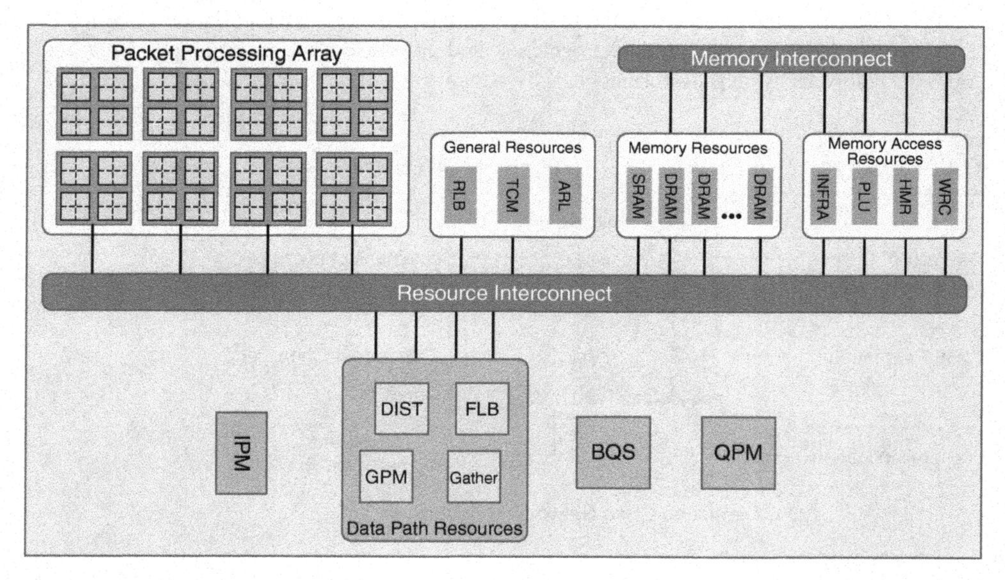

Figure 7-46 *Inside the QFP Architecture*

These include hardware-based TCAM for ACL lookups, routing table lookups, and packet replication. Another significant area of note is "BQS," the buffering, queueing, and scheduling functionality of QFP, which implements its advanced and unique QoS and packet-queueing architecture. Let's examine several of these key functional blocks.

First, it is important to understand how QFP handles traffic load balancing across its array of processing cores. This is highlighted as FLB in Figure 7-47.

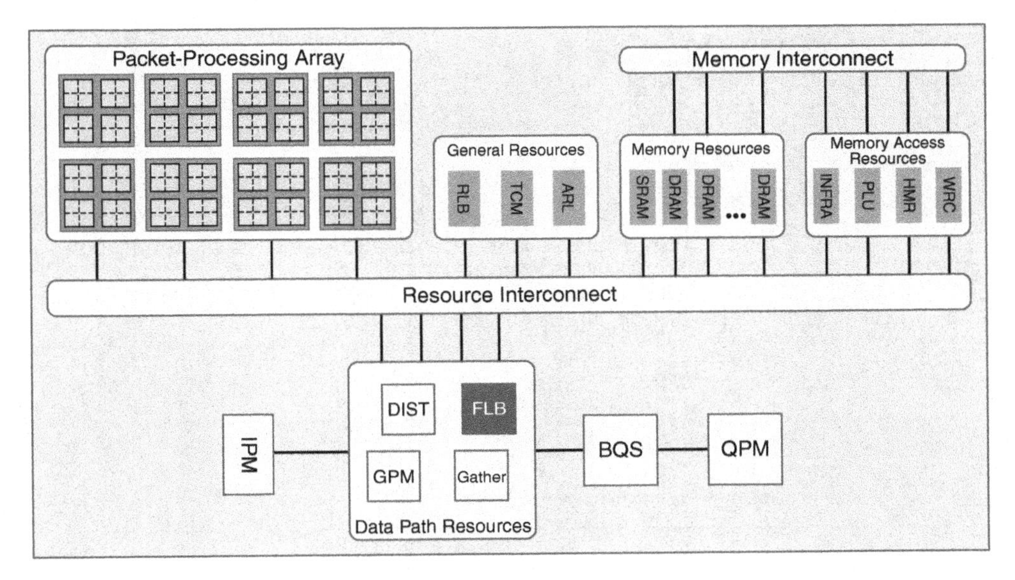

Figure 7-47 *QFP Packet Distribution Across Processing Cores*

It is necessary to ensure that as traffic is crossing a multicore processing array, such as that employed by QFP, that packets stay in order. Out-of-order packet delivery and packet reordering are typically pathological processes in a network, as TCP at the receiving node elsewhere in the network may sense out-of-order packet delivery as a sign that congestion exists in the network, and could trigger unnecessary delays or retransmissions that could slow down end-user data access and congest network pipes.

The designers of QFP were well aware of this possible issue. However, performing the trade-off of doing flow-based traffic load balancing across processing cores, such that any particular flow only used one processing core to ensure in-order packet delivery for that flow, would limit the performance of any one flow to the performance of a single processing core. This is an unacceptable outcome for high-performance network flows where the ability to harness the full throughput of QFP-based platforms is desired.

The job of the Flow Load Balancing (FLB) component within the QFP silicon is to assign each incoming packet to a free packet-processing element (PPE) within QFP's packet-processing array. Packets are "sprayed" across the array, leveraging the full throughput of the QFP design. Packets exiting the array are always reordered into their appropriate sequence, preventing out-of-order packet delivery. QFP does not reorder incoming packets, yet allows dozens of packets to be processed in parallel, including packets which may need more processing (NAT, etc.) than others do. The hardware-based lock capability within QFP ensures that traffic is handled and delivered optimally, and with consistent high performance.

Figure 7-48 highlights the packet-processing array.

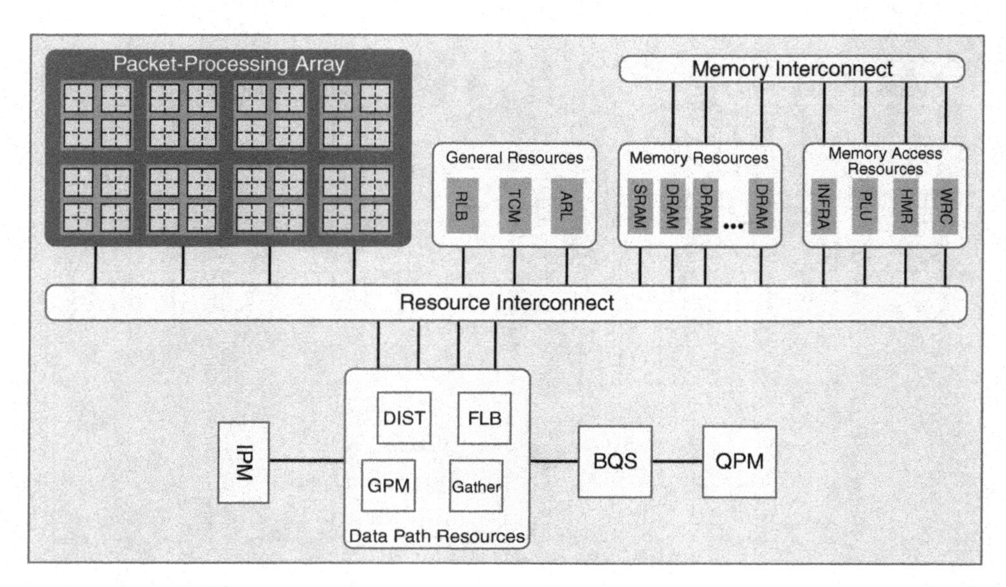

Figure 7-48 *QFP Packet-Processing Array*

QFP's packet-processing array is in many ways the "heart" of QFP, and the site where QFP's flexibility becomes manifest. This is because all of QFP's packet processors are just that—they operate as packet-processing engines, reprogrammable through software to deliver on the functions configured in the WAN routers they support. This is the key to delivering the flexibility demanded by WAN routing, married to the ever-increasing need for speeds and feeds that WAN aggregation routing is subject to.

Each packet processor within the QFP processing array can process up to four threads of operation in hardware (and because this is solely within the data plane of operation of the device, this equates to up to four packets in flight across any individual PPE at one time—or up to 4 × 64 = 256 packets in flight across a 64-core QFP at once). The operation of each PPE ensures that if a given thread is waiting for a particular function (such as a hardware lookup, for example), the other three threads operating on that PPE can continue to be processed unabated, ensuring consistent and optimal traffic handling.

In general, most functions can be handled in a single pass through the PPE, but in the event that recirculation is required (for example, with multicast), QFP handles this in a speedy and efficient fashion—ensuing that recirculated high-priority traffic continues to receive its appropriate level of treatment even when newer, incoming but lower-priority traffic may have arrived in the interim.

The PPEs themselves operate at a speedy 1.2 GHz and have access to a wide array of hardware-based assists. For example, ACL lookups are a common core WAN routing function. QFP does such lookups in TCAM for rapid resolution, as highlighted in

Figure 7-49. Likewise, lookups such as Weighted Random Early Detection (WRED) for QoS, flow locks, and the like are all handled in hardware, offloading these functions from the PPE processors and leading much better performance as well as more consistent sustained throughput.

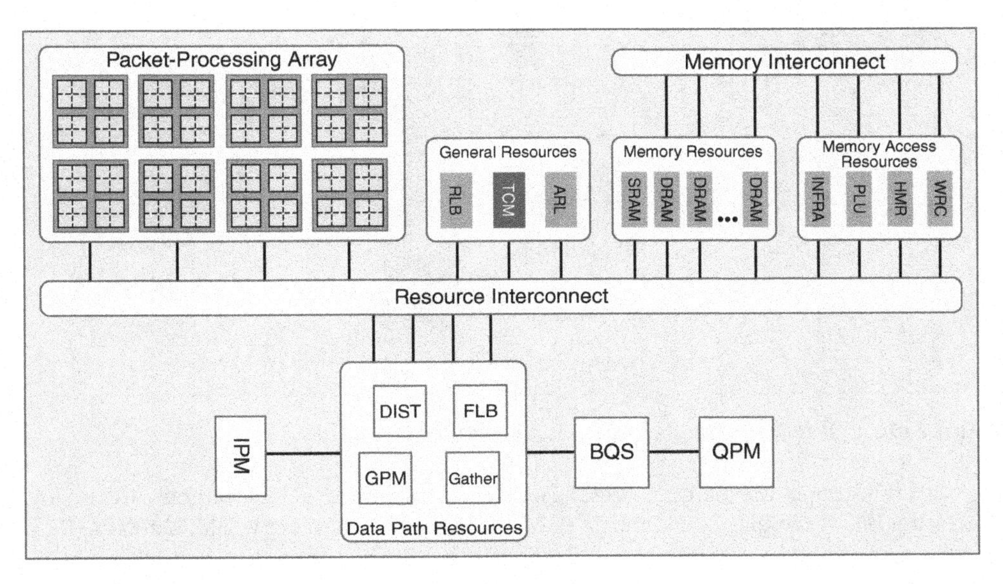

Figure 7-49 *QFP TCAM and Memory Resources*

With the ability to perform hundreds of millions of searches per second, QFP offers performance that is well matched to the needs of WAN aggregation routing, where packet rates reach extremely high values, and consistent high performance is needed. Layer 1 cache for each PPE individually and Layer 2 cache shared across all PPEs help to ensure that packet processing is always optimized. As a general rule, if many of the incoming packets all require the same or similar data-plane processing, as is often the case in many WAN routing scenarios, the cache and memory architecture of QFP ensures the speediest and most optimal handling for the traffic involved.

BQS, the buffering, queueing, and scheduling component within the QFP architecture, is highlighted in Figure 7-50.

QoS is a difficult task for any WAN router. Traffic must be recognized for what it is—various applications streams must be classified and sorted out one from another—and then traffic must be appropriately marked via Differentiated Services Code Point (DSCP) per the configured policies on the router, and queued appropriately out to the set of destinations involved. Of course, some applications are more important than others—again, per configuration by the network administrator—and bandwidth is always a constrained resource, so some applications must be given preferential access over others, with the use of multiple queues (priority and nonpriority), traffic policers, traffic shapers, etc.

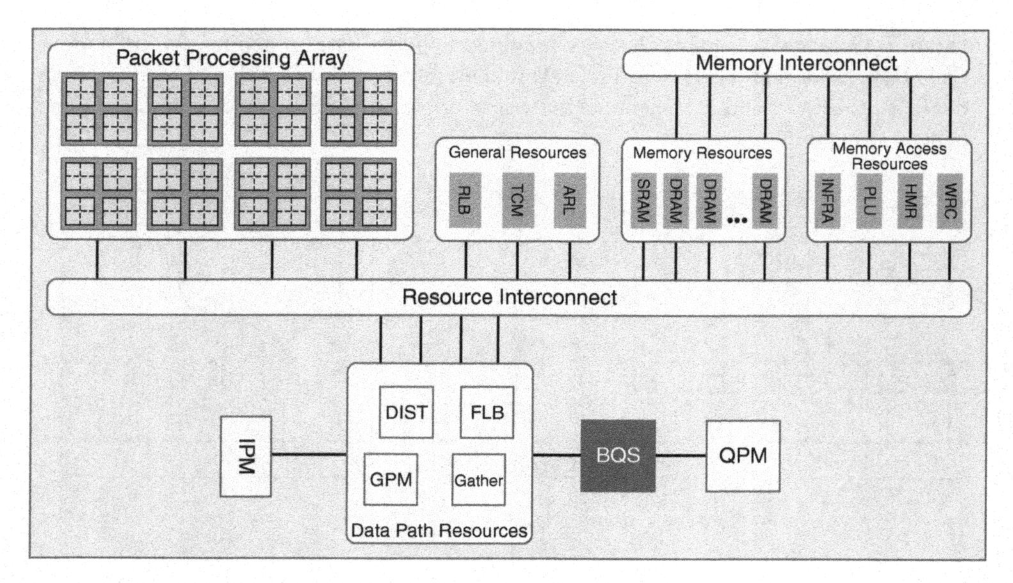

Figure 7-50 *QFP BQS—Buffering, Queueing, and Scheduling*

Now, think about the job that a WAN aggregation router has to do. It not only has to do this for one set of queues and traffic flows the way a branch router would, but has to do this in a head-end WAN routing role for literally hundreds or even thousands of downstream routers, which could be configured with multiple different bandwidths, multiple different policies, and widely varying anticipated traffic flows and application types.

Handling this daunting challenge within QFP is the job of the BQS portion of the silicon. BQS implements up to 128,000 queues in hardware (depending on the QFP version in use). QFP also offers up to five levels of queueing hierarchy for the richest set of QoS functions available on a midrange WAN aggregation router, providing flexible allocation of scheduling resources.

In a more traditional CPU-bound router, many of these QoS tasks would be very taxing for a processing core to accomplish. QFP does not expend any cycles within the PPE array to process such capabilities—the BQS portion of the QFP's flexible silicon performs all of these tasks, offloading the PPE cores for other tasks and ensuring consistent high performance for QoS-processed traffic flows.

QFP—Use in Platforms

QFP is used as the data plane for the Cisco ASR 1000 Series WAN aggregation routing platforms. These platforms now span a wide range of physical sizes and interface densities, as outlined in Figure 7-51.

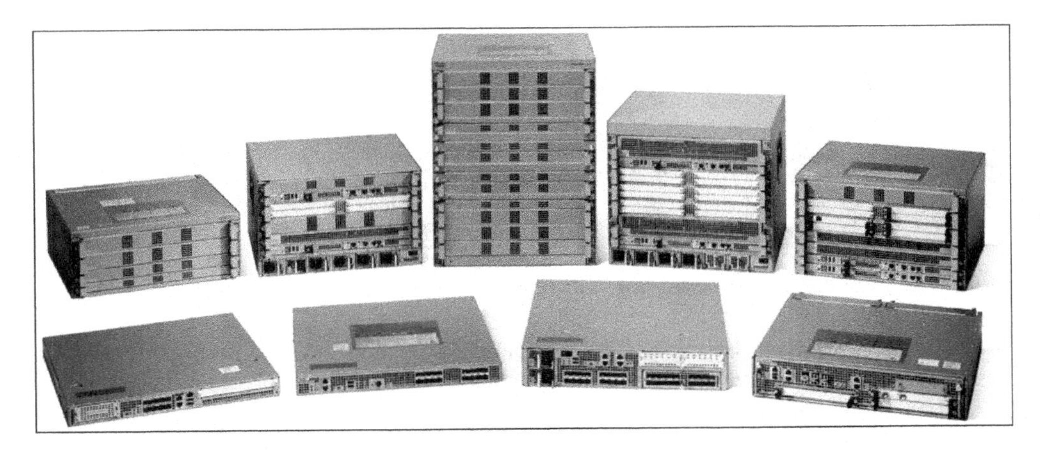

Figure 7-51 *Use of QFP in Platforms—Cisco ASR 1000 Series*

Offering scalability up to 8000 VRFs, 4 million IPv4 routes, 4 million IPv6 routes, 8000 IPsec tunnels, and 200 Gbps of throughput at the top of the product range, the ASR 1000 Series offers a set of WAN routing platforms to fill almost any need.

By separating the control plane functions of the router from data plane processing offered by QFP, and offering redundancy for both control plane and data plane functions within selected ASR 1000 models, the ASR 1000 Series platforms are custom-tailored to provide the right "fit" for many different places within the network, and for many different customer and traffic profiles.

UADP and QFP—Summing Up

UADP is a piece of Cisco flexible silicon, optimized for the growing and changing needs of the LAN switching role. QFP is a piece of Cisco flexible silicon optimized for the very demanding needs of the WAN aggregation routing role. The actual internal architecture of QFP is quite different from UADP, which was examined previously. Both sets of requirements, as well as the placement within the network, for platforms using QFP and UADP are quite different.

However, both chips have many similarities as well.

Observe that several important operational aspects are preserved across both UADP and QFP. The most important of these is flexibility. Both UADP and QFP offer silicon platforms that are inherently flexible and programmable, a vital attribute as Cisco DNA—especially as the capabilities that Cisco DNA must support continue to evolve over time. As shown in Figure 7-52, as new protocols, new functions, and new packet header formats and encapsulations come along, high-performance network hardware needs to be able to handle these without performance or traffic-handling issues.

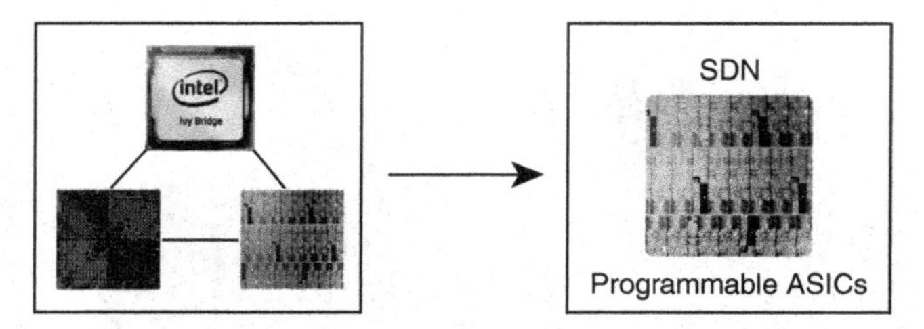

Figure 7-52 *Trend Toward Programmability Drives Flexibility Requirements*

UADP and QFP were designed from the ground up for this kind of flexibility—exactly the type of flexibility required in networks today, and tomorrow. It is a testament to Cisco's Engineering teams and their foresight that they saw these types of requirements for flexibility coupled with high performance coming years ago, and designed UADP and QFP to meet these needs, thus laying the solid hardware foundation for Cisco DNA.

Wireless: Providing Innovation for Mobility

Having examined the hardware innovations that Cisco is driving in the switching and routing areas with UADP and QFP, respectively, it is also important to note the hardware innovations that Cisco is providing in the area of wireless mobility. This is vital because wireless—and more specifically, 802.11 wireless—is now the primary "on-ramp" into the enterprise network in many organizations today.

While Cisco is driving many areas of innovation with respect to wireless, the following are a few critical ones to highlight in terms of flexible hardware:

- Integrated antenna arrays in Cisco Access Points (AP) to enable Cisco Hyperlocation, allowing for advanced location-tracking capabilities for associated wireless devices
- Advanced beam-forming technology in APs to maximize radio throughput for clients
- Flexible Radio Assignment (FRA) capability in APs to enable customized and optimized radio coverage
- Advanced packet capture capability (Intelligent Capture) in APs to enable sophisticated network analysis and troubleshooting

These capabilities, and more, are instantiated in Cisco's latest generation of APs, the Aironet 4800 Series, as illustrated in Figure 7-53.

The Aironet 4800 provide many advanced capabilities that allow network managers to optimize the available radio spectrum and RF environment in their wireless deployments, allowing the delivery of the best possible wireless network infrastructure, and wireless deployment, for their organization.

To see why this is the case, let's examine two key areas of innovation in the Aironet 4800 wireless platform: Flexible Radio Assignment and Intelligent Capture.

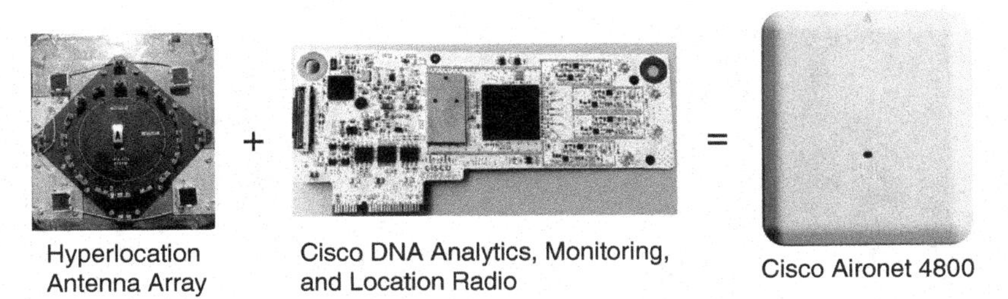

Figure 7-53 *Cisco Aironet 4800—Advanced Wireless Capabilities*

Flexible Radio Assignment

Flexible Radio Assignment (FRA) enables the Aironet 4800 to be designed and deployed with a macro-cell/micro-cell architecture, if so desired by the network manager. Normally, the multiple radios in the Aironet 4800 are deployed with one radio handling the 2.4-GHz band, and another handling the 5-GHz band. While functional, this does not necessarily lead to the optimum coverage for a given area and set of clients. Today, many clients support the 5-GHz spectrum, and this wireless band tends to be less "polluted" with interferers (other non-802.11 devices) than the 2.4-GHz band. The 5-GHz band also offers many more non-overlapping radio channels as opposed to the 2.4-GHz band, due to its use of higher frequency transmission.

The nature of 802.11 wireless communications is such that each wireless channel (and the clients using it) operates as a shared medium, so that when one user is transmitting, others have to defer and wait for the channel to become free (with Multi-In, Multi-Out [MIMO] techniques, this is improved somewhat, but the basic principle remains). The radio link speed at which any given client associated to a particular AP is affected (among other factors) by its distance from the AP's radio—all things being equal, the farther away the client is from the AP, the fainter the radio signal is, and thus the lower the data rate the client will associate to that AP at.

With many clients associated to the same AP, and using a shared radio medium for transmission, it can readily be seen that the performance (that is, the actual throughput) of a higher-speed (closer-in) wireless client can be affected by the presence of lower-speed (farther-away) clients on the same radio, and on the same channel.

As a result, you might want to optimize your deployment by choosing to have two radios in the AP operating in the 5-GHz band: one operating on one 5-GHz wireless channel with a lower power setting, and the other radio operating on a second 5-GHz (non-overlapping) channel with a higher power setting. This is illustrated in Figure 7-54.

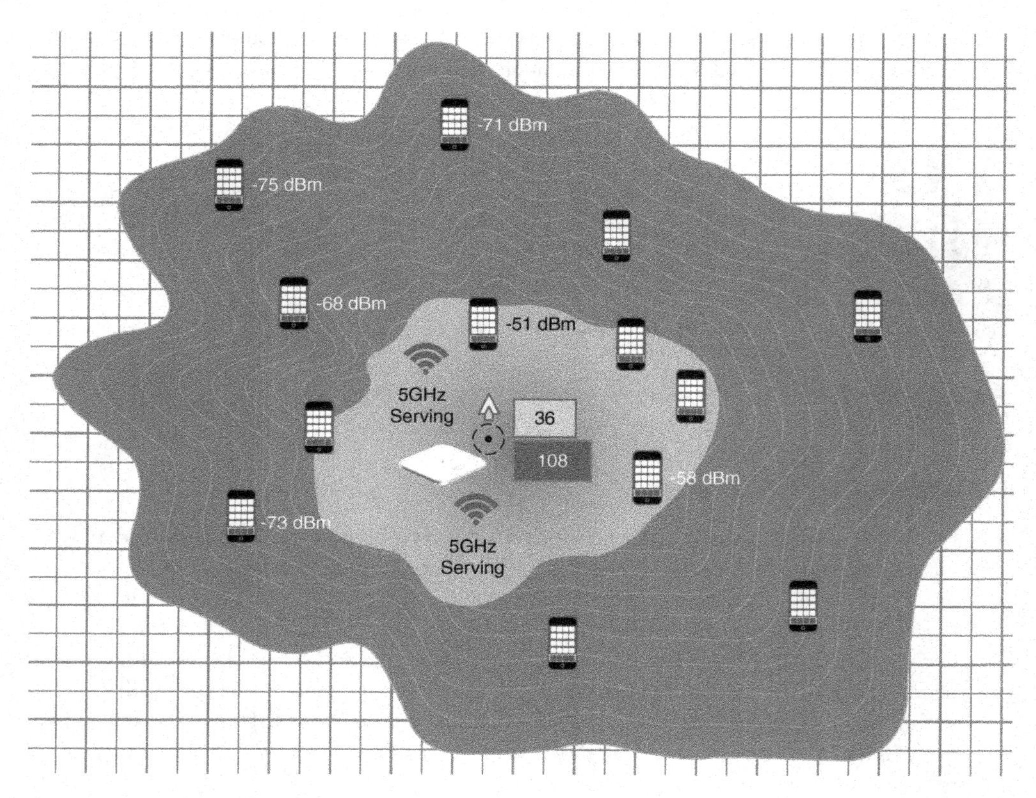

Figure 7-54 *Flexible Radio Assignment*

This is exactly what Flexible Radio Assignment (FRA) with the Aironet 4800 can accommodate. By allowing the individual radios within the Aironet 4800 to be reprogrammed to operate in either the 2.4-GHz band or 5-GHz band, a macro-cell/micro-cell architecture such as that shown in Figure 7-54 can be instantiated.

This consists of having both flexible radios operate in the 5-GHz band, one with a lower power setting (and thus associating only closer-in clients, typically at a higher data rate), and the other with a higher power setting (and thus offering longer reach, but potentially associating farther-away clients at a lower data rate). By combining this with other adjacent APs that continue to offer service in the 2.4-GHz band for devices that are not 5-GHz capable, an optimized wireless deployment can be arrived at that offers holistic coverage for all clients, with optimized and seamless performance. Closer-in clients get faster throughput, and farther-away clients get maximized wireless coverage.

Key to the ability to provide advanced capabilities such as FRA is the use of software-programmable radio hardware in platforms such as the Aironet 4800. By including hardware that allows the radios within the platform to be reprovisioned between bands, and with the ability to provide flexible power and channel assignment, Cisco is able to offer a unique solution that allows organizations large and small to optimize their wireless deployments and maximize throughput for their users—all in a seamless fashion.

Given the ever-increasing importance of wireless in enterprise network deployments, the use of flexible radios in platforms such as the Cisco Aironet 4800 is critical, and provides yet another proof point as to why flexible hardware is so important in modern network implementations.

Intelligent Capture

A second area of network innovation worth noting in the Aironet 4800 is Intelligent Capture. This unique and powerful capability allows for full packet capture and analysis of user traffic traversing the Aironet 4800—even when the user or device involved may be roaming from AP to AP within the network infrastructure.

Intelligent Capture leverages the multiple radios within the Aironet 4800 platform to be able to "listen while talking" over the radio bands involved. By leveraging the powerful and flexible hardware in this wireless platform, Intelligent Capture allows for the network operator to capture a designated subset of user traffic—for example, the traffic from a user who called into the Help Desk with a problem—and pull that traffic (including full packet copies) back to the Cisco DNA Center platform for analysis, without impacting other users on the same AP.

By then providing advanced analytics for the traffic involved, common issues (such as those associated with device attachment, logon, or access) are readily diagnosed, and suggested remediation actions are presented to the network operator—all in near real time.

Intelligent Capture is an excellent example of leveraging the power of the flexible hardware provided by the Aironet 4800 platform with its multiple radios, combined with the centralized and intuitive analytics provided by Cisco DNA Center, to assist in solving real-world network issues that arise in wireless network deployments.

Only with providing the fusion of advanced, custom-designed hardware functionality with software flexibility can such results be achieved. Cisco, in being able to provide the entire hardware and software "stack" in the network—including advanced analytics with Cisco DNA Center—is uniquely positioned to deliver on this important need.

It is important to note, however, that Intelligent Capture is not possible without the advanced and flexible hardware that Cisco enables in advanced wireless platforms such as the Aironet 4800—another example of why hardware continues to be so important, even in our software-defined age.

Summary

So, what does flexible hardware truly deliver? Why is it fundamentally important for Cisco Digital Network Architecture, and for your evolving network?

The two key attributes that Cisco's programmable network hardware delivers are flexibility and investment protection. Flexibility to handle new capabilities. New protocols. New functions. And the things that haven't been invented yet. Flexible silicon provides the opportunity to adapt to these changes, embrace them, and use them to further your business and organizational goals by evolving your network to the next level—thus providing the investment protection today's businesses need in order to adapt to rapid change.

This chapter examined

- How ASICs are designed and built
- Why flexible ASICs are key to the evolution of networking
- The inner workings of two of Cisco's key elements of flexible silicon
  - UADP—Unified Access Data Plane
  - QFP—QuantumFlow Processor
- How UADP and QFP provide flexibility and investment protection, allowing a smooth migration to present and future network technologies
- How Cisco is enabling advanced functionality for wireless deployments in the Aironet 4800 platform, using Flexible Radio Assignment and Intelligent Capture with Cisco DNA Center analytics

And why are ASICs themselves important? Why spend so much time to understand them, appreciate them, and realize how they impact your business?

As outlined in Figure 7-55, ASICs are the fundamental foundation upon which products are built. Those products form the basis for the network solutions that you can build out of them. And those solutions are the basis for the benefits that you deliver to your organization every day, through the enterprise networks that you design, build, and manage.

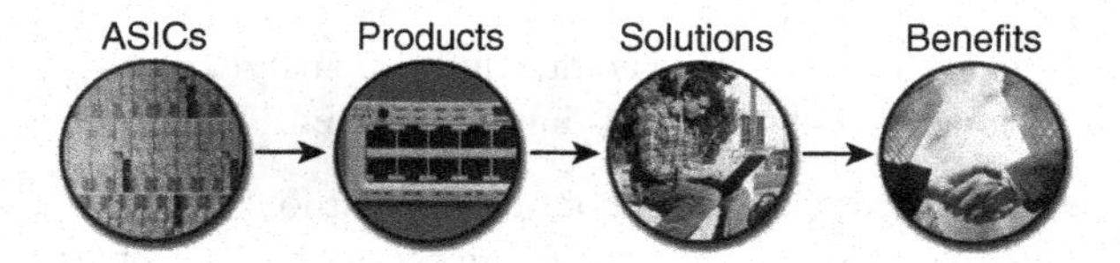

Figure 7-55 *ASICs As the Foundation for Products, Solutions, and Benefits*

With Cisco DNA, the power of flexible silicon allows your business to adapt and thrive in changing times. That is why so much time and focus was spent on the flexible silicon underpinnings of Cisco DNA.

Now, onward and upward as we begin to examine the Cisco flexible software offerings in the next chapter.

Further Reading

Harrel, Scott. "New Frontiers: Anti-Aging Treatment for Your Network." Cisco Blog. June 19, 2017. https://blogs.cisco.com/enterprise/new-frontiers-anti-aging-treatment-for-your-network.

Sayle, B., et al. *Cisco Catalyst 9000: A New Era of Intent-based Networking.* Cisco Systems eBook. https://www.cisco.com/c/dam/en/us/products/collateral/switches/nb-06-cat9k-ebook-cte-en.pdf

Cisco Systems. "Cisco QuantumFlow Processor: Cisco's Next Generation Network Processor Solution Overview." Updated Jan. 1, 2014. https://www.cisco.com/c/en/us/products/collateral/routers/asr-1000-series-aggregation-services-routers/solution_overview_c22-448936.html.

Cisco Systems. *Cisco Enterprise Wireless: Intuitive Wi-Fi Starts Here.* https://www.cisco.com/c/dam/en/us/products/collateral/wireless/nb-06-wireless-wifi-starts-here-ebook-cte-en.pdf

Chapter 8

Software Innovations

Just as network hardware and silicon innovations have been advancing, so have innovations in networking software. As the network infrastructure evolves, and greater and greater demands are placed on the network, the software that helps to define and shape the network also continues to evolve. This chapter examines that evolution, and peers more deeply into how Cisco's networking software infrastructure is changing to adapt to the ever-growing demands placed upon it.

This chapter explains the following:

- Networking software innovations with Cisco IOS XE
- Cisco trustworthy systems and the importance of secure infrastructure
- The move to intuitive networking

The Importance and Evolution of Networking Software

So often today, you hear about software-defined architectures and capabilities. And in many ways, the movement toward systems that are defined by software—and which can evolve at the speed of software—has taken the industry by storm. Software-defined systems offer many solutions to the problems faced by network managers, and help the network infrastructure to take on new challenges and rapidly adapt, assisting organizations large and small to enable new network functionality to help drive their businesses forward.

And yet, networking software always existed as a core foundation of the success of the networking industry, and has long served as the foundation upon which the achievements of the network infrastructure—and the organizations that leverage that infrastructure—have been based.

Let's examine the origins of the software foundation upon which today's modern network infrastructures are built, and how that software foundation is evolving.

There are many places today that networking software is deployed. Few if any, however, are as ubiquitous, or as critical for the proper operation of the enterprise network, as the code running in network devices themselves—the network operating system. As the most ubiquitous network operating system in use globally, Cisco IOS is a critical element of hundreds of thousands of networks worldwide, and forms an underpinning of the overall network infrastructure both of organizations and of the Internet itself. From its origins with Cisco in 1984 to the modern day, IOS evolved to serve the needs of many organizations—in healthcare, manufacturing, education, government, and every industry large and small.

Figure 8-1 shows the evolution of Cisco IOS, along with an approximate timeline of IOS deployment, and several of the key enterprise platforms that have leveraged Cisco IOS over the years.

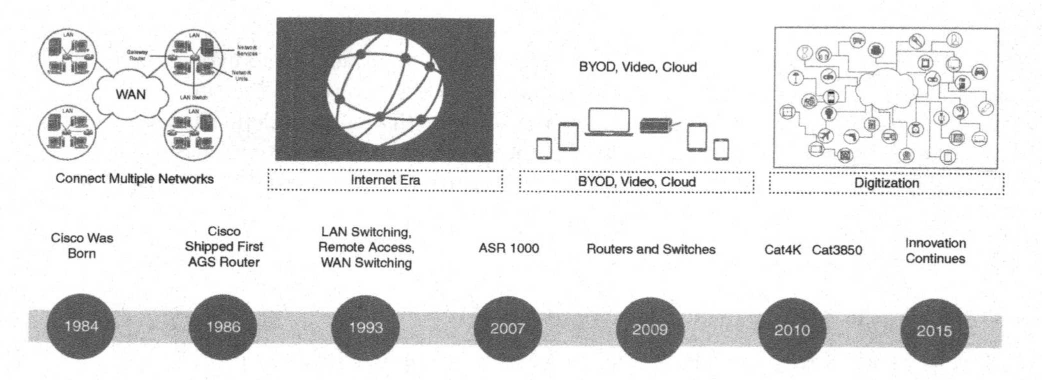

Figure 8-1 *Evolution of Cisco IOS*

Cisco IOS: Origins and Evolution

Initially, IOS was created to run on a single-CPU system, in products such as the Cisco 2500 and 4000 Series routers. Within these platforms, which were fundamentally software based, that CPU served to operate all three "planes of existence" which any networking device must accommodate:

- **Data plane:** The data plane deals with the basic movement, and forwarding, of data packets through the device. In the initial Cisco IOS software–based router implementations, each packet was handled solely by software. An incoming packet generated an interrupt to the CPU when it arrived, and the CPU suspended whatever other tasks it was doing, serviced the packet (forward, drop, remark, etc.), and then resumed its former tasks.

- **Control plane:** Any networking device must interact with other devices in the network to form a system. This interaction takes place at Layer 2, using protocols such as Spanning Tree Protocol (STP) or Per-VLAN Rapid Spanning Tree (PVRST+), and/or at Layer 3, using protocols such as Open Shortest Path First (OSPF), Enhanced Interior Gateway Routing Protocol (EIGRP), Intermediate System to Intermediate System (IS-IS), or Border Gateway Protocol (BGP). The purpose of these protocols is to establish the forwarding path along which traffic is sent once it arrives at the network devices involved, to rapidly resolve new forwarding paths when changes in the network topology might arise (from device or link failures, for example), and to avoid uncontrolled network loops which could interrupt or interfere with network operation.
- **Management plane:** It is critical that the network is both manageable and able to be monitored for correct operation. Traditionally, this was done using the command-line interface (CLI) for human interaction and scripting, as well as protocols such as Simple Network Management Protocol (SNMP) for network monitoring.

Cisco IOS was created to provide excellent capabilities at all three of these layers of network operation.

With the initial implementation of Cisco routers with lower-speed interfaces and less total interface density (for example, with a single 10-Mbps Ethernet port and single or dual T1 ports on a Cisco 2500 router), a single CPU handled all of these tasks—forwarding data, running the appropriate control plane protocols as designated by the network manager, and allowing for monitoring and control of network operations.

However, as network capabilities, and speeds and feeds, evolved, the Cisco IOS software managing the network had to evolve as well. Let's examine the evolution of all three planes of operation within Cisco IOS, and illustrate how they changed over time.

Evolution of the Cisco IOS Data Plane

The efficiency of forwarding packets in the data plane—the ability of a routing device to handle ever-greater interface speeds as well as ever-increasing interface densities—required improvement as network systems continued to evolve.

This fostered the evolution of what became known as Cisco Express Forwarding (CEF), an innovative solution where the common manipulations that a router was taking for a given packet (rewrite MAC address, select forwarding interface, etc.) were precomputed into a table, allowing for more rapid packet manipulation and dramatically speeding up the forwarding process, while making it more efficient and reducing total CPU processing load. CEF was a key innovation when introduced, enabling Cisco routers to adapt to the increasing performance of network systems and link speeds.

Another change that came about due to the necessity to accommodate higher-speed router interfaces was the movement from centralized to distributed forwarding as an option. This involved the movement of the data plane away from a single-CPU architecture, and the deployment of distributed forwarding systems within the router platform.

This was seen on the Cisco 7000 and 7500 Series routers, and later on the Cisco 12000 Series platforms, among others, which employed specific line cards with distributed forwarding capabilities.

These enabled the line cards to provide local CPUs (and later, custom application-specific integrated circuits [ASICs]) to operate the data plane locally—with the central router CPU running the control plane to determine the network topology (and adapt to changes in that topology), and then in turn programming the CEF forwarding tables on the line cards for distributed traffic forwarding. While lower-end routers continued to use a single central CPU for all tasks (as long as that CPU was sized accordingly for the interfaces it needed to handle), higher-end routing platforms typically moved to a distributed forwarding model.

The move to distributed forwarding required Cisco IOS to evolve. Now it was necessary to coordinate the function of packet forwarding across multiple line cards in the system, continuously monitor the state of those line cards, and manipulate the distributed forwarding model across those line cards as the network infrastructure was established by the network manager, and as it operated autonomously throughout the lifetime of the network device. This is a far more complex task than performing all actions within a single CPU, yet the basic design of Cisco IOS was robust enough to accommodate this change—and accommodate it, it did.

In the mid-1990s, Cisco made the move into switching, rounding out its routing portfolio with devices that could scale to much higher speeds, and to much greater density of interfaces. Some of the companies that Cisco initially acquired to move into the switching arena included Crescendo (basis of the Catalyst 5000 switch family), Kalpana (precursor to the Catalyst 3000 and later 3*x*50 switch families), and Grand Junction (forerunner of the Catalyst 1900 and later the 29*x*0 switch families).

As this move into switching was made, Cisco IOS had to adapt again. Switches handle many interfaces—initially dozens, and as switching evolved, scaling into hundreds—and even a distributed-forwarding CPU-based model was unable to keep pace. Switches rapidly demanded the evolution, first of field-programmable gate arrays (FPGAs), and later of custom ASICs, to perform the data plane packet-forwarding functions of the device. No longer could any CPU-based system—even with distributed forwarding—keep pace with the demands that switches placed on the network data plane.

Once again, this required Cisco IOS to evolve. IOS had to adapt to interface with, and properly program, silicon-based forwarding, where the actual packet manipulation was taking place in hardware, and the switch's CPU was instead involved with calculating the forwarding tables, and then in turn programming the underlying forwarding hardware to drive the actual processing of network packets as they arrived at the device.

Initially, switches operated in hardware at Layer 2 only, with routing tasks (forwarding traffic between subnets) still taking place on a CPU. The switch hardware recognized any packet with a destination of a router MAC or virtual MAC address (in the case of Hot Standby Router Protocol [HSRP] or Virtual Router Redundancy Protocol [VRRP], for example), and forwarded that frame to the software-based portion of the switch for packet forwarding or handling. This was the case, for example, with the Catalyst 5000 switch when used with a Route Switch Module (RSM). The RSM was a line card installed into one of the slots of the Catalyst 5000 switch, allowing the platform to perform Layer 3 routing tasks via the RSM, in addition to the Layer 2 switching tasks performed in hardware by the installed Supervisor module.

While effective, this was cumbersome as well as limited in performance. Initial switch platforms such as the Catalyst 5000 (and later its successor, the Catalyst 5500) ran a Layer-2-oriented operating system descended from Crescendo lineage (Catalyst OS, or CatOS), with the RSM running IOS. This presented the network manager with two CLI-based user interfaces he or she had to interact with, complicating the task of network deployment and management.

In addition, the linkage between the RSM and the Catalyst 5000 backplane was only 400 Mbps (2 × 200-Mbps channels), thus underperforming the 1.2-Gbps backplane of the Catalyst 5000 switch platform, and as well the RSM was CPU-based and thus limited in the total performance it provided.

Over time, CatOS was phased out in favor of Cisco IOS as the single operating system operating on switches (this change happened on the successor platforms to the Catalyst 5500—namely, the Catalyst 4500 in the Supervisor 4 timeframe, and the Catalyst 6500 with the Supervisor 2 and Supervisor 720). This not only made the network easier to deploy and manage, it also opened the door to more rapid innovation on a single network operating system. Some switch platforms, such as the Catalyst 3500 Series switches, were introduced with only IOS as a software option, simplifying their deployment and use.

Also over time, the ever-increasing speeds and feeds involved with switching, and the increasing use of Layer 3 for network segmentation, required the movement away from software-based routing solutions into true hardware-based packet forwarding, for both Layer 3 and Layer 2.

An example of this is seen with the evolution of the Catalyst 6500 switch platform. Initially introduced to the market in early 1999 as the Catalyst 6000, the switch initially was Layer 2 only, much like its Catalyst 5500 precursor, and employed a software-based Layer 3 routing module known as the Multilayer Switch Module (MSM) in conjunction with the switch's Supervisor 1 module (which handled all Layer 2 tasks). However, this was a short-term solution only, because the Catalyst 6000 with its 32-Gbps backplane (as opposed to the single 1.2-Gbps backplane of the Catalyst 5000, or a 3 × 1.2-Gbps backplane of the Catalyst 5500) easily outclassed the performance of the MSM.

Accordingly, Cisco developed the Policy Feature Card (PFC), an ASIC-based daughter-card that sat on the Catalyst 6500's Supervisor 1A module, and which handled all Layer 3 routing tasks. Leveraging Cisco IOS, the PFC employed a new switching mode called Multilayer Switching (MLS), in which the first packet of any given traffic flow (as tracked by a hardware-based NetFlow table) was punted to the switch's central CPU, and routed in software. The CPU then installed an entry in the switch's hardware NetFlow table, allowing all subsequent packets matching that flow to be forwarded in hardware by the PFC, including all packet manipulations required by Layer 3 routing.

In addition, the matching of traffic for functions such as access control lists (ACL) was done now in hardware, using ternary content-addressable memory (TCAM), allowing ACL matches for functions such as packet filtering for security, or the application of packet remarking for quality of service (QoS) entries, to be done in hardware. Finally, the speed of Layer 3 routing and Layer 2 forwarding on the data plane could match up. Now, network managers were free to design their networks according to the way they desired traffic to be routed and manipulated, not according to the restrictions imposed by Layer 2 and Layer 3 boundaries and the associated performance limits in network devices.

Of course, Cisco IOS had to evolve to meet these needs. The split between functions that ran on the control and management planes of the device—and thus ran on the device's CPU—and the functions that ran on the device's data plane were becoming ever more clear.

This trend continued as the limits of what was possible with the MLS switching model were reached. Sending the first packet of each flow to the device's CPU, and having to route that packet in software—along with the limited size of the NetFlow hardware cache table (nominally 32K flows on PFC1A)—required switching technology to move forward once again, and required IOS to keep pace.

This led directly to the development of Cisco forwarding hardware for switches that employed CEF switching directly in hardware. On the Catalyst 6500, this was first seen with the Supervisor 2 module, and was employed with all subsequent Supervisors on that platform, as well as all other Layer 3 switches within Cisco's product lineup. Now, it became necessary for Cisco IOS to compute both the Routing Information Base (RIB) and the Forwarding Information Base (FIB), and then process and program the corresponding CEF table directly into the switch hardware. Now, the separation between the data plane (packet forwarding in hardware) and the control and management planes in software was complete.

The evolution of Cisco IOS (and the described innovations it drove along the journey) was key not only in moving the state of networking forward but also in allowing the networking industry—and all the industries that depend on networking as their "life blood" for operation—to evolve and grow. In the world today, data moves around with dizzying speed, zipping across 10-Gbps and 100-Gbps interfaces around the globe, across networks that are constantly growing in terms of breadth and depth. Cisco IOS, and the data plane innovations, continues as one of the key linchpins of the network infrastructure that allows this growth to happen.

Evolution of the Cisco IOS Control Plane

Just as the data plane of Cisco IOS evolved to keep pace with, and drive, changes in the network infrastructure, so has the IOS control plane needed to evolve.

Over the years, Cisco has developed a rich evolution of the control plane options made available to network managers, and this evolution continues today. Beginning with simple protocols such as basic Spanning Tree Protocol (STP) for Layer 2 and Routing Information

Protocol (RIP) for Layer 3, Cisco IOS now supports a broad range of control plane protocols to adapt to a wide variety of different network requirements and topologies.

At Layer 2, Spanning Tree began as a simple way to avoid loops in Layer 2 networks. Because a frame at Layer 2 is not altered as it is forwarded (unlike routed packets, which have a TTL [Time To Live] value decremented at each hop), uncontrolled loops in a Layer 2 network can become very destructive to network operation. Spanning Tree is of course designed to prevent such events (known as broadcast storms) from occurring, by blocking links as needed to establish only a single "tree" for Layer 2 packet forwarding—a tree rooted at the STP root node and radiating outwards, with redundant links leading back to the root blocked as needed, and with the ability to unblock such links if and as a change in the Layer 2 topology occurs.

The capabilities for handling Layer 2 networks, and the continuing evolution of the protocols involved with this, are addressed in more detail in Chapter 9, "Protocol Innovations."

Likewise, Layer 3 networks evolved over the years. Beginning with RIP, routing quickly developed the need for more advanced networking protocols—ones that could handle classless addressing (i.e., routing based on more than just the traditional Class A (/8), Class B (/16), and Class C (/24) network boundaries), that could handle network address summarization, and that could provide much faster reconvergence as well as be used for routing between, and within, independent routing domains. This drove the evolution of routing protocols such as OSPF, EIGRP, IS-IS, and BGP—all of which Cisco IOS was key to driving, and providing to the broad marketplace of networking solutions available to the modern network manager.

The control plane solutions provided by Cisco continue to evolve even today. Again, this evolution is examined in more detail in the next chapter.

Evolution of the Cisco IOS Management Plane

As with the data plane and control plane operation of a network device, the needs of the device's management plane—and the corresponding needs of the network management systems—continued to evolve markedly over time.

Cisco IOS needed to keep pace with this evolution, and help drive it.

Beginning with the basics of the CLI, Cisco established one of the most widely recognized and used interfaces in the networking industry. The Cisco IOS CLI is known to hundreds of thousands of network managers worldwide, and is the basis of network management and operation in countless deployments. The Cisco IOS CLI is used not only for manual operation of network devices, but with scripting solutions for driving automation.

Likewise, SNMP as used within Cisco IOS is the basis for many network management solutions, serving to allow the remote monitoring of network device health, traffic handling and forwarding, and overall network operation in many deployments worldwide.

And yet, for all their utility, the use of the device CLI and protocols such as SNMP also introduces many issues. These include complexity in device operation (due to many CLI variations and many commands necessary for device operation) and excessive CPU loading of the device for network monitoring and management.

In response, the industry, and Cisco IOS, evolved solutions to meet these needs, going well beyond what the traditional CLI + SNMP approach to managing the device—and the network—provide. These capabilities, and this evolution, are examined in greater detail in Chapter 13, "Device Programmability."

Evolution of Cisco Networking Software

So far, this chapter has examined how Cisco IOS evolved to address the continuing and ever-growing requirements of the data plane, control plane, and management plane of the network. An additional important consideration is how Cisco's networking software overall needed to evolve to tackle the various, and very distinct, markets that it serves.

Broadly, these markets are divided into three major categories:

- **Enterprise:** This category is the most all-encompassing, spanning everything from small businesses to major, globe-spanning organizations, and including both private businesses and many public and governmental bodies. While this set of organizations is often subcategorized into Commercial, Small Enterprise, Large Enterprise, Global Enterprise, Public Sector, and the like, as a whole these organizations share several important characteristics. They all employ networks that are defined, implemented, and operated by a single holistic organization, usually by a single network team focused on the outcomes that the network involved helps to drive for that organization—be it small, large, or global in nature.

- **Service Provider (SP):** This category is focused on organizations that build a network to service the needs of other organizations (as well as themselves). Typically, SPs are focused on providing network functionality that other organizations can leverage, typically at a cost. This includes providing connectivity services as well as a possible range of ancillary services (for example, content distribution, security services, or other related functions). Over the years, SPs evolved to much more than just providers of basic connectivity for wide-area networks. Nevertheless, they are broadly categorized as organizations that build networks for others to leverage.

- **Data Center (DC):** Both enterprises (of all sizes) and service providers need to operate data centers, which house the multitude of servers and services that the network provides access to for the organization. Data centers have a unique set of requirements in terms of scale, performance, functionality, and fault tolerance that set them apart from a traditional enterprise or service provider network, and often require a separate and distinct network design, created to service the precise needs of the data center environment.

While examples certainly exist of "cross-overs" between these three broad categories—a common example being the WAN backbone of a large, multi-departmental enterprise organization that may actually begin to resemble more of a service provider deployment model—the preceding major categories define three distinct and unique sets of use cases, each corresponding to a particular associated set of network requirements around (among other variables) speeds and feeds, resiliency and fault tolerance, expansion requirements, Layer 2 and Layer 3 traffic handling, and more.

Accordingly, Cisco's network operating system software strategy evolved over the years to address these three unique markets as follows:

- **Enterprise:** The Enterprise market is largely served by Cisco IOS, which has now evolved into Cisco Open IOS XE (more details following). Open IOS XE (often abbreviated to simply IOS XE) is the direct evolution of Cisco IOS, building on this legacy and set of capabilities while evolving to support a next generation of enterprise-focused network designs, solutions, and outcomes. Given the focus of this text on examining Cisco Digital Network Architecture (Cisco DNA) and its impact on the evolution of the enterprise network, special attention is paid here to Cisco IOS XE and its capabilities and evolution. Open IOS XE is called "Open" because it embraces, and enables within the enterprise network, several attributes of open networking, including YANG data models, open industry-standard interfaces such as NETCONF and RESTCONF, and the ability to deploy containerized applications onto distributed network devices.

- **Service Provider (SP):** While Cisco IOS (and now, IOS XE) is certainly used in various places in SP networks, Cisco's SP-focused network operating system software is IOS XR. Designed with the unique scale, performance, and functionality needs of SPs in mind, IOS XR powers some of the largest and most complex SP networks in the world. Built from the ground up to provide the capabilities that SPs demand most, IOS XR sheds many of the diverse protocols and capabilities that need to be supported in enterprise environments for a more focused set of capabilities that are designed to service the world's largest networks. While some very large enterprises (especially those resembling SPs in some aspects, as previously mentioned) also deploy IOS XR–based platforms, the primary focus of IOS XR remains the core SP market.

- **Data Center (DC):** The demanding environment of the modern data center drives several unique requirements. These include (but are not limited to) widespread use of Layer 2 for server-to-server intra-DC connectivity, very rapid network failover and recovery requirements, and the need to accommodate very high (and ever-growing) performance needs, typically pushing the boundaries of what is possible for network connections. To meet these demands, Cisco created NX-OS, focused on the needs of the modern—and ever-evolving—data center. Because both enterprises and service providers deploy their own DCs, or host DCs for others, NX-OS is used in both types of deployments, within the data center and focused on the outcomes that data centers require.

The evolution of these various operating systems—IOS XE, IOS XR, and NX-OS—is illustrated in Figure 8-2.

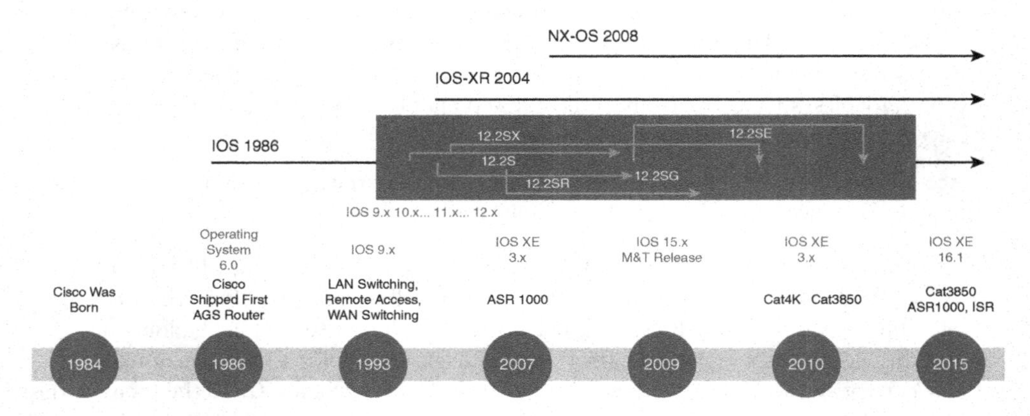

Figure 8-2 *Network Operating Systems—Origins and Evolution*

The Evolution of Cisco IOS to IOS XE

While Cisco IOS has served many tens of thousands of customers worldwide well for over three decades, an evolution of the basic architecture of Cisco IOS was undertaken several years ago to help IOS continue to adapt to an every-changing world, and an ever-evolving set of network requirements.

What factors came into play as the evolution of Cisco IOS was undertaken?

First, the need to provide a level of modularity for IOS was desirable. Traditionally, Cisco IOS was implemented and operated as a single, monolithic code base, with direct access to the underlying hardware of the platform on which it ran. While this model evolved over the years (for example, to address the separation of data plane and control plane detailed previously in this chapter) the basic structure of Cisco IOS was maintained—a single software code base, running on a device CPU, with direct access to the underlying network hardware.

For most enterprise network tasks, this worked very well over the years. Nevertheless, changes in network and device operational practices made some modifications in Cisco IOS desirable. As well, the ever-changing "state of the art of what's possible" made such changes more practical to realize than they were in the past. As well, the continuing evolution of network designs made alterations to what IOS needed to be capable of more urgent than had previously been the case.

Taken together, all of these elements created the necessity for Cisco IOS to evolve. IOS XE is the result of that evolution.

Cisco IOS XE in a Nutshell

Fundamental shifts have occurred in the enterprise networking landscape. These include the move from networks that only had to concern themselves with moving data, voice, and video, to more modern networks that have to encompass mobility, the deployment of ever-increasing types and numbers of IoT devices and applications, and the accommodation of cloud capabilities, all while also addressing the manifold security requirements of the modern enterprise. Taken together, these constitute a new era of networking, as illustrated in Figure 8-3.

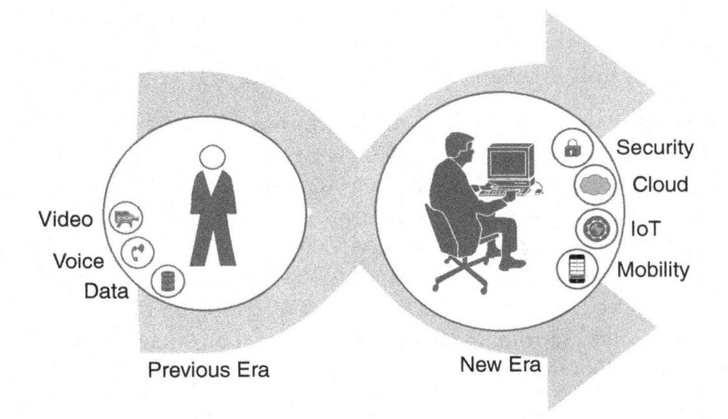

Figure 8-3 *New Era of Networking*

This is the era, and the trends, that Cisco IOS XE was created to address.

IOS XE set out to evolve the IOS infrastructure. The fact that this is an evolution is critical. There are tens of thousands of network professionals that know Cisco IOS inside and out—and many more networks that they support that depend on Cisco IOS, and the features and capabilities it provides, every day. Thus, one of the first goals of IOS XE was to provide an evolutionary path both for these networks and for the network managers and operators that implement and support them, while allowing the introduction of network technologies, new capabilities, and new network deployment modes and operating paradigms.

To evolve IOS to the next level of functionality and capability, it was important to set IOS XE on a strong foundation. IOS XE is implemented on top of a Linux kernel, providing a robust foundation that allows for extensibility, supports the use of multicore CPU processing, and sets the stage for hosting of additional applications and containers on the same platform that operates the core IOS XE set of processes and functions.

On top of that foundation, the core IOS XE functions operate within the context of IOSd, the IOS daemon that runs the core set of networking capabilities that Cisco IOS users and network managers depend on. Over the many years during which Cisco IOS evolved, IOS implemented hundreds of different capabilities, functions, and protocols that network managers use to create, define, operate, and manage their networks. You name a function provided by IOS, and somewhere in the world there is a network that leverages it, and a network manager that depends on it.

While not every function provided by traditional Cisco IOS is necessarily supported in IOS XE, most functions and capabilities are. This provides an important bridge in terms of functionality that network managers require to support business continuity and maintain operational discipline and control in their network infrastructures.

IOS XE is also designed to leverage the evolving hardware platforms that are in use in today's—and tomorrow's—network infrastructures. IOS XE is flexible enough to be implemented on CPU-only architectures (as often found in lower-end routers), as well as to leverage the heavily ASIC-based, silicon forwarding infrastructures found in many higher-end routing platforms (and virtually all switching platforms), including such advanced capabilities as multiswitch stacking, in which multiple switches are connected together to operate as a single, unified system, such as with StackWise-480 on the Catalyst 3850, 3650, and 9300 switch platforms and StackWise Virtual on selected versions of the latest Cisco Catalyst 9000 Series switch platforms.

IOS XE is also designed to be able to leverage the multicore CPU architectures and capabilities that are often employed in platforms today, distinct from the single-core CPU platforms of yesteryear. Leveraging such multicore CPU capabilities, where needed, required a fundamental rework of many Cisco IOS software capabilities and processes. The move to Cisco IOS XE provided this capability.

Overall, IOS XE set out to ultimately be a single OS that drives consistency in enterprise network deployments and, at the same time, drives simplified network administration, enabling an accelerated software lifecycle management capability with a similar CLI to older IOS variants, but enabling a whole new set of additional capabilities with modern interfaces such as NETCONF, RESTCONF, and Python scripting capabilities—thus moving IOS device and network management into the 21st century, and beyond.

Figure 8-4 illustrates this consistency. Cisco IOS XE enables the rapid deployment of new solutions, allows for simplified network administration, and provides streamlined software lifecycle management capabilities and ease of scripting, all while providing a familiar IOS CLI and allowing for a rapid adoption and learning curve.

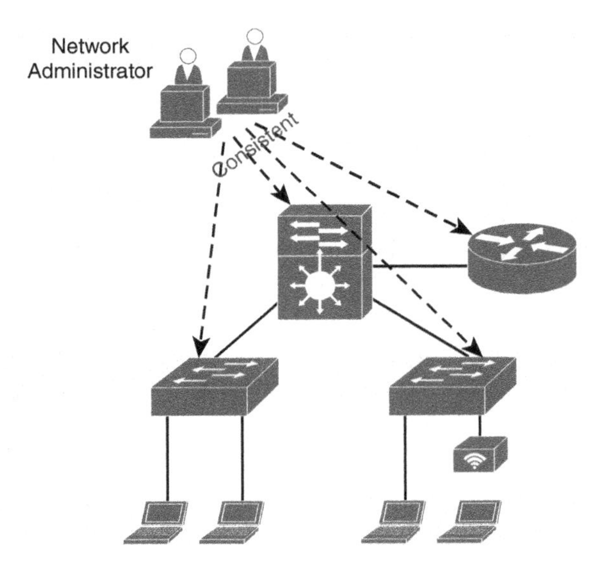

Figure 8-4 *Cisco IOS XE Across the Enterprise Network*

Cisco IOS XE: Delving Deeper

To deliver on some of the key goals of IOS XE, an evolution of the IOS architecture was required. This actually took place over several IOS variants over a period of a few years, as illustrated in Figure 8-5.

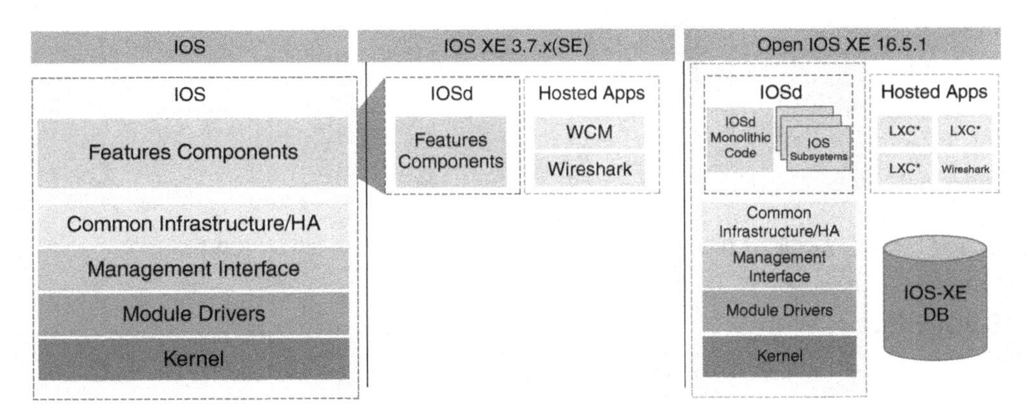

Figure 8-5 *Evolution of IOS to IOS XE*

Starting with the basics of Cisco IOS operating as a single monolithic code base, an evolution began with the first variants of IOS XE (the 3.6.*x* and 3.7.*x* train), which separated out the various feature components of IOS into IOSd, and allowed for the co-hosting on the IOS XE platform of other applications, such as Wireless Control Module (WCM) and Wireshark.

Continuing and accelerating this evolution, the IOS XE 16.*x* train introduced several key new capabilities for IOS XE. These included the separation of several key functions from the IOS XE monolithic code base (allowing these to operate as separate threads of execution on top of the IOS XE underlying kernel) and providing an in-built database function against which IOS XE processes could checkpoint their various data structures as they were created and used.

In addition, IOS XE expands the application hosting ecosystem to include a framework for support of container-based applications to operate and be co-hosted on the IOS XE platform involved.

Figure 8-6 outlines these three key architectural enhancements enabled with IOS XE 16.*x*—namely, IOS subsystems, the IOS XE Database, and support for containers for application hosting.

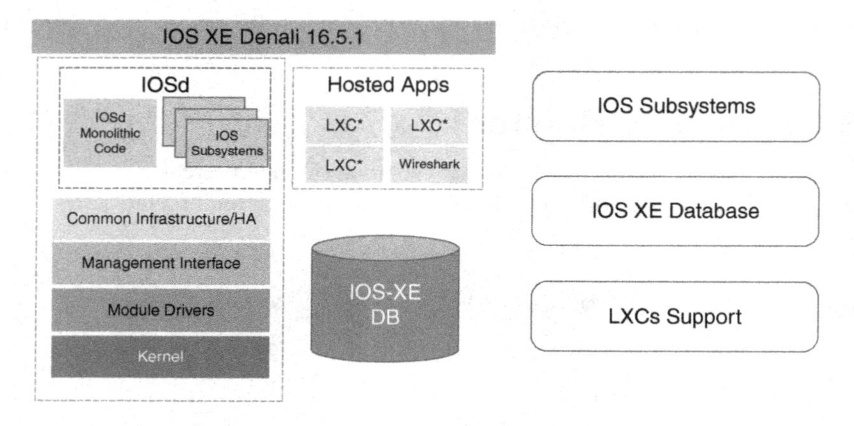

Figure 8-6 *IOS XE—Key Architectural Enhancements*

Let's examine each of these architectural enhancements provided by IOS XE.

IOS XE Subsystems

By separating out the code from the overall IOSd monolithic code base for key functions within Cisco IOS XE, several important benefits are realized. Perhaps the most critical among these from an operational perspective is the ability to provide greater process-level resiliency.

Once portions of the IOS XE code are modularized into separate subsystems, a failure of one of the subsystems leaves the rest of the system, and the other portions of code executing on it, intact. This is illustrated in Figure 8-7.

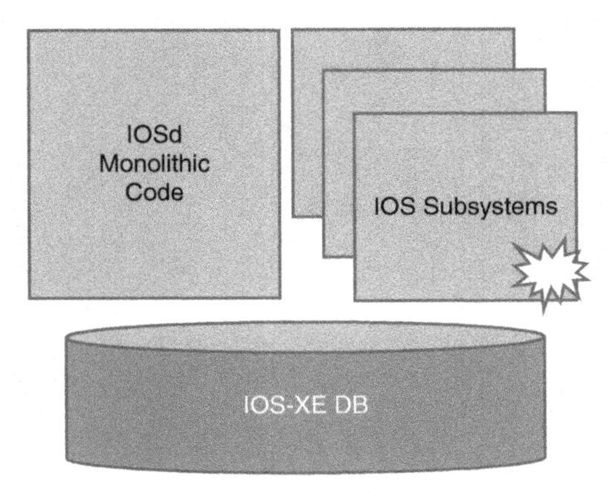

Figure 8-7 *IOS XE Subsystems*

Although individual processes within IOS XE have to be rewritten or altered to operate as separate subsystems (which takes time to do), IOS XE provides a strong foundation upon which various pieces of networking code can be altered—in an evolutionary way—to adopt these subsystem capabilities. As the evolution of IOS XE progresses, more and more subsystems can be broken out from the IOSd monolithic code base, allowing these functions—and the network managers that use these capabilities—to leverage the benefits of the modularized subsystem approach.

An additional benefit of the separation of code into subsystems is that these subsystems are equipped with well-defined interfaces, thus allowing alterations to areas of the code base to have less chance of disruption to other code areas. Over time, this leads to a more stable code base, and one that can be more rapidly altered to meet new network needs.

IOS XE Database

Previously in IOS, all the various pieces of code that might execute in IOS retained their own configuration and operational state in their private and separate memory areas. For example, OSPF, EIGRP, BGP, and Spanning Tree each retain their own separate sets of operational data, with no common method being used for data storage. Although this met the needs as they existed in the network, it did not allow for retention of this data across (for example) a process restart, meaning that this data was lost and had to be relearned when the process restarted.

In a device environment that hosts modularized subsystem processes, a more advanced capability was needed for process state retention, as well as data exchange between independent processes. This was the rationale behind the creation of the IOS XE Database function, which is illustrated in Figure 8-8.

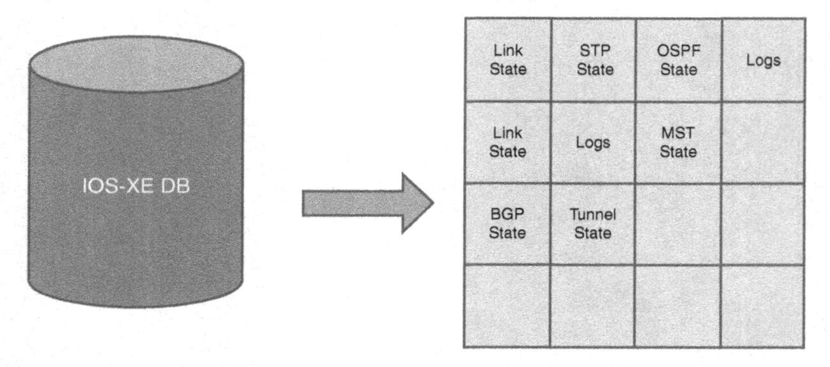

Figure 8-8 *IOS XE Database*

Various processes running under IOS XE are able to store their operational state and configuration data within the IOS XE Database, allowing it to be retained across process restarts, as well as to be more readily exchanged with, and examined by, other IOS XE processes operating within the platform. Although processes have to be recoded or altered to use the database functionality provided by IOS XE, this provides a strong foundational component for the evolution and use of next-generation networking capabilities—a key focus of IOS XE.

The decoupling of code and data provided by the IOS XE Database provides several key advantages: namely, the ability to provide higher application uptime, quicker recovery from network outages (because the operating state prior to the outage can more readily be recovered from the database rather than having to be relearned via the network), and an overall improvement in network reconvergence times (a key attribute in the modern network deployment, where so many business-critical functions all rely on the underlying network and its operational characteristics).

The use of the database approach in IOS XE also allows much easier access to common data models, such as those provided by YANG, accessed by open and programmable interfaces such as NETCONF and RESTCONF. This is illustrated in Figure 8-9.

By retaining data from various processes in a common database structure, this information is more readily extracted and used by various data-modeling approaches and access methods. The use of these approaches and data models is explored further in Chapter 13 and is further illustrated in Figure 8-10.

By leveraging a common database for storage of configuration and operational states, a more robust environment is provided both for making this data available to external functions running off-box (via standardized interfaces and data models) and for use by the container-based application hosting framework created by IOS XE—the third key architectural pillar provided by the IOS XE environment.

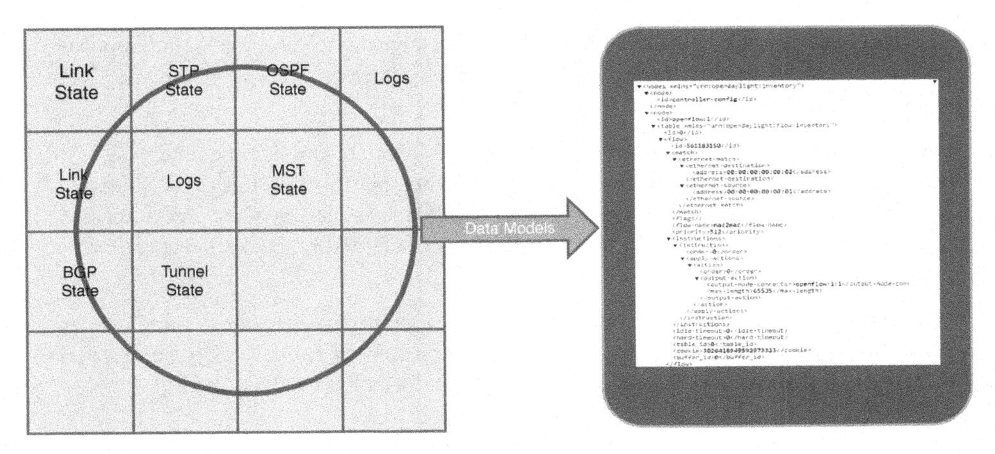

Figure 8-9 *IOS XE Database—Enabling Common Data Modeling*

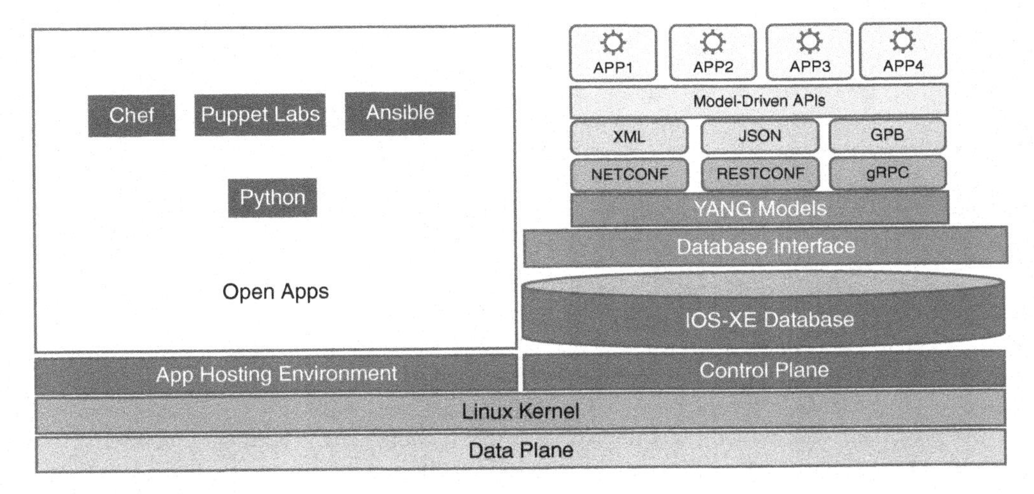

Figure 8-10 *IOS XE Database—Enabling Programmability*

Container Framework and Application Hosting

Today, the network is the key enabler of many functions by the modern enterprise. Network gear, including switches and routers, are located at key points of information flow within, and between, enterprise networks. As such, there is often a desire to run additional functions on a given piece of network gear.

In the past, this capability was very limited, or even nonexistent. Older versions of IOS (prior to IOS XE) ran, as mentioned previously, as a single piece of monolithic code which directly interfaced with the underlying network hardware. While this provided simplicity, and utilized those hardware resources very concisely (an important consideration when such resources were very scarce), it did not provide any way to "co-host" other application on the same piece of network hardware. The very infrastructure of IOS did not previously allow for this.

Starting with the earliest versions of IOS XE, Cisco began to provide the ability to host certain designated functions on a router or switch platform, alongside IOSd itself. These included WCM—the Wireless Control Module leveraged by Converged Access deployments—as well as Wireshark, leveraged to provide on-box packet-level capture of traffic flows transiting the network node.

While functional, a desire existed to broaden this capability to encompass more use cases. Thus was born the capability to provide a more general framework to support containerized applications, co-hosted on an IOS XE platform. This is illustrated in Figure 8-11.

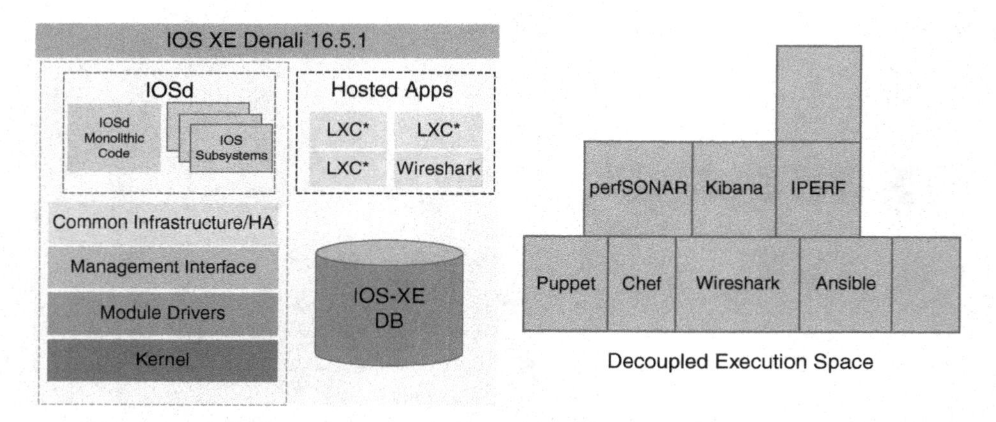

Figure 8-11 *IOS XE Container Framework Support*

By providing a decoupled execution space in which containerized apps can operate, the framework to host applications on a given IOS XE switch or router platform is provided.

Resources (storage space, memory, processing CPU cycles, etc.) on such a platform still need to be carefully husbanded in order to preserve network stability (after all, this same base of resources is operating the network as well). Accordingly, the apps to be containerized and operated on the network platform involved must be selected on the basis of working within the constraints inherent to a network-based platform. The app-hosting framework provided by Cisco IOS XE allows for the provision of containerized applications which can operate on an IOS XE platform, leading to many possible exciting future capabilities for deployment and use within the network. These might include application performance monitoring, network analysis, and other unique examples of network-integrated functionality.

Cisco IOS XE: Bringing It All Together

They say that the whole is often greater than the sum of its parts. This is certainly true of IOS XE.

One of the major benefits of, and goals for, IOS XE is the capability called Run Any Feature Anywhere (RAFA). Because IOS XE is designed to be utilized at many points in the enterprise network, and across many platforms (switches, routers, etc.), the ability exists to create a feature once and then deploy it at many locations, and across multiple platforms, within the enterprise network.

When intersected with the capability, as described in Chapter 7, "Hardware Innovations," of using the same flexible, programmable ASIC hardware (for example, UADP, Unified Access Data Plane) across multiple platforms, this creates the ability to achieve much faster deployment times for new features across platforms, enabling greater feature velocity as well as feature consistency, without the need to touch platform-independent items of code when bringing new capabilities onto a given platform. This is illustrated in Figure 8-12.

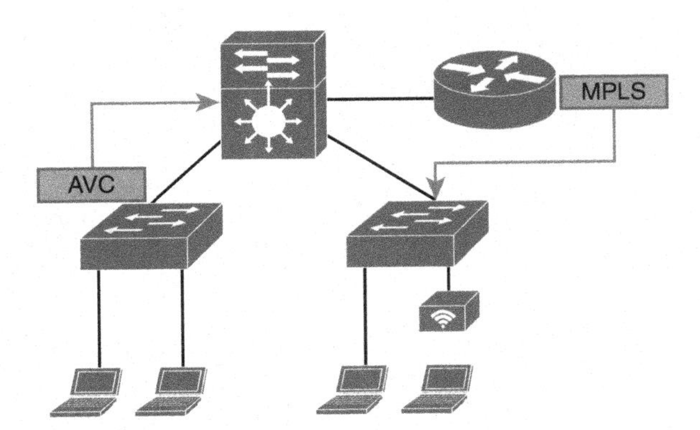

Figure 8-12 *Run Any Feature Anywhere (RAFA)*

With this capability, only the platform-dependent portions of the code base need to be modified as a function is made available across multiple platforms. And because IOS XE software, and flexible hardware forwarding elements such as UADP and QuantumFlow Processor (QFP), are more and more common across multiple platforms using IOS XE, the ability to provide functionality more broadly, and more quickly, to the marketplace becomes very apparent—and to do so in a more operationally consistent manner.

Take, for example, the function of Multiprotocol Label Switching (MPLS). MPLS has long been deployed in service provider networks to provide network segmentation, and is increasingly deployed in sophisticated enterprise networks that also require separation of communications across network segments within the enterprise, at scale. Some of the most common use cases for MPLS within the enterprise are illustrated in Figure 8-13.

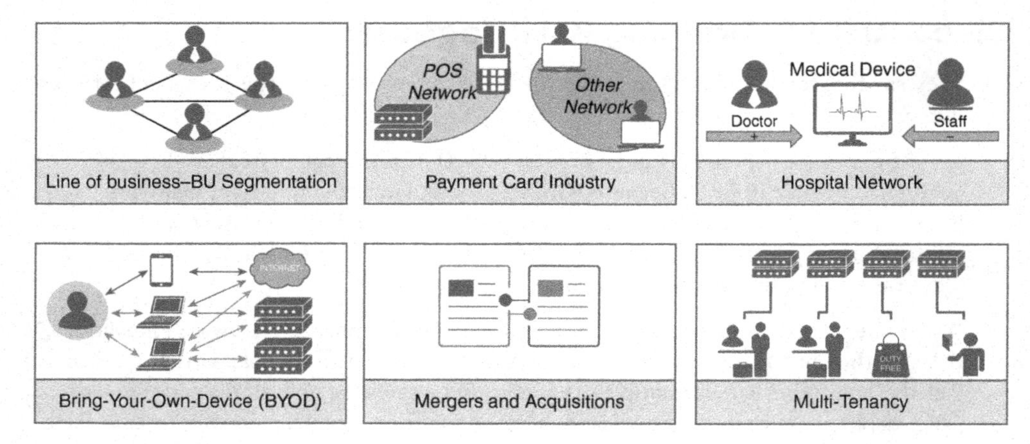

Figure 8-13 *Enterprise Use Cases for MPLS*

In the past, MPLS platform-independent (PI) code was created as part of a base set of IOS functionality, but it had to be adapted not only to every platform to couple it to that platform's unique data plane hardware (which may or may not even have the capability to support MPLS in hardware), but also to that platform's unique IOS train and infrastructure set. The net result of this is that promulgating a function such as MPLS across a wide set of enterprise devices (best case) took a long time, or (worst case) was limited to only a subset of network devices, due to hardware limitations within the device (for example, the Catalyst 6500/6800 supports MPLS in hardware using the EARL7/EARL8 ASIC set, but the Catalyst 4500-E/4500-X using the K10 chipset, or the Catalyst 3750 and older switches, cannot).

Now, by having both a common ASIC set across enterprise platforms (UADP for switching, QFP for routing) and a common set of IOS XE software, the implementation and broad deployment of a given feature set is far more rapid than in the past. This in turn allows customers to use these features and functionality more rapidly in their networks to solve real business problems and drive competitive advantage. In addition, the familiarity and continuity provided by the IOS experience means that staffing levels and expertise are better leveraged as the network grows and expands—thus helping to control long-term costs, and at the same time supporting an increased pace of innovation.

While there will always be platform-level differences driven by scale, market focus, and other considerations, the ability to provide greater network design and deployment consistency, driven by IOS XE, is a key advantage for organizations large and small.

Several important new innovations in network protocols are examined in Chapter 9, "Protocol Innovations." How those protocols in turn serve as the basis for powerful new solutions are explored in Chapter 19, "Cisco DNA Software-Defined Access." As we explore further, we will consistently see the power of IOS XE, combined with Cisco's flexible hardware infrastructure, in action.

Cisco IOS XE: Simplification with a Single Release Train

One of the major goals of IOS XE is to reduce the number of IOS release trains, and releases, with which customers have to contend. By creating a common code base to be leveraged across multiple platforms, IOS XE allows for simplified network operation and use by providing the following:

- Simplified and more consistent network administration
- Simplified and more consistent software lifecycle management
- The same CLI across multiple platforms for common features
- The ability to leverage platform capabilities in a consistent manner

Within hardware platforms that share many common components, this can go so far as the same binary image running across multiple platforms. For example, with the Catalyst 9000 Series switches, the exact same binary image (not just the same software version, but the exact same binary image) is deployed across the Catalyst 9300, 9400, and 9500 switch platforms—the first time ever that a single image was used across a Cisco stackable access switch, a modular access switch, and a fixed-configuration core/aggregation switch.

This ability to use the exact same binary image across multiple platforms makes it possible to qualify the image once (a process undertaken by many larger enterprise organizations, and one which can consume a great deal of time and resources for image qualification), and then reuse this image, and the capabilities it provides, across multiple places in the enterprise network. This reduces the time and effort required for such image and function qualification, and increases the speed with which enterprises test, deploy, and use sophisticated network functions across multiple platforms.

Cisco IOS XE: Software Maintenance Upgrades

Another example of the flexibility provided by IOS XE is the new capability known as Software Maintenance Upgrades, or SMUs.

SMUs are pieces of deployable code, typically small in size, that are intended as urgent point fixes for particular issues that may arise, allowing for an expedited delivery of that fix to customers in case of challenges that might include network-down or potentially revenue-affecting scenarios.

In the past, when a critical issue arose, it was often possible to address this via an updated version of software. However, that fix would have to be embedded within a larger binary image, one which would often have the fix for that particular issue, but additional code as well (addressing particular issues that the deployment involved may not have faced, or even code that implemented new features or capabilities). The enterprise thus might have had to accept, in an expedited fashion, a new software version to gain access to the fix needed—and accept everything else that came with that new release, including perhaps even bugs not present in their previous release. In any case, to access the fix to relieve the issue it was experiencing, the enterprise had to accept a new software image that it may not have had time to properly qualify.

SMUs are designed to address this situation. In particular, SMUs are designed to be

- **Quick to deploy:** SMUs are able to deliver point fixes much faster than by waiting for a new IOS XE release
- **Effective:** SMUs do not require an entire binary IOS XE code upgrade
- **Focused:** SMUs target the particular area of code that has the issue, and no other

In effect, SMUs are like a medication, in that:

- They address the issue involved effectively.
- In theory, there is no limit to the number you can take.
- In practice, you want to be selective when employing SMUs.

The Issue with Software Upgrades

In general, software upgrades are challenging for enterprise networks, across several dimensions of operation. These challenges include the following:

- **Cost:** Network software upgrades are expensive to plan, test, and deploy. Properly testing code prior to deployment is challenging, and many enterprises (especially smaller ones) lack the resources to do this effectively (as this might include the creation and use of a separate lab environment, the need to provide simulated application and user loads, etc.). In addition, each device upgrade causes a network outage as it is deployed, and so the rollout of the code upgrade must be carefully planned to minimize impact to the production network.
- **Time:** Many organizations today are faced with the challenge of doing more with less, or at best with the same amount of resources. Thus, the personnel required to maintain the network must also be the ones to upgrade it. The reduced number of staff available to many organizations today makes software upgrades and rollouts even more challenging to plan and execute. In addition, the network outages (or potential for them) associated with large, monolithic software upgrades often make a physical, onsite presence required, or at least desirable, during the upgrade process, at least at critical nodes within the network.
- **Scope:** As mentioned previously, new code typically requires a level of certification and analysis (often known as a "bug scrub"). The greater the potential scope of impact for a given code upgrade, the greater the need for such analysis becomes.

The use of SMUs with IOS XE can assist in addressing these points, by providing focused "point fixes" which reduce the cost, time, and scope of a given software fix deployment.

Types of SMUs—Cold, and Hot

SMUs with IOS XE come in two flavors: cold and hot.

- **Cold patches:** The simplest type of SMU, these are small pieces of code that are loaded onto an IOS XE platform, integrated with the existing release, and then require a reload of the device software to activate them. However, unlike a code upgrade to the entire box, the SMU in this case only affects the particular focused code that it patches—the larger IOS release running on the platform is unaltered (and thus, the operation and use of non-patched portions of the code is not affected). Due to the nature of how they are applied (device restart), cold SMUs are traffic-affecting. As of this writing, all SMUs available for IOS XE are of the cold variety.
- **Hot patches:** These allow for the "hot" restart of a patched process within IOS XE, and do not require a device reload. Such processes also typically leverage the database capability of IOS XE to checkpoint their state prior to such a restart (if applicable), thus allowing a faster recovery once the newly patched process comes back up. As of this writing, no hot SMUs are yet available for IOS XE. However, the architecture of the system allows for this capability to be delivered in the future.

Installing a SMU

Installation and activation of SMUs follows a three-step process, as detailed in Figure 8-14.

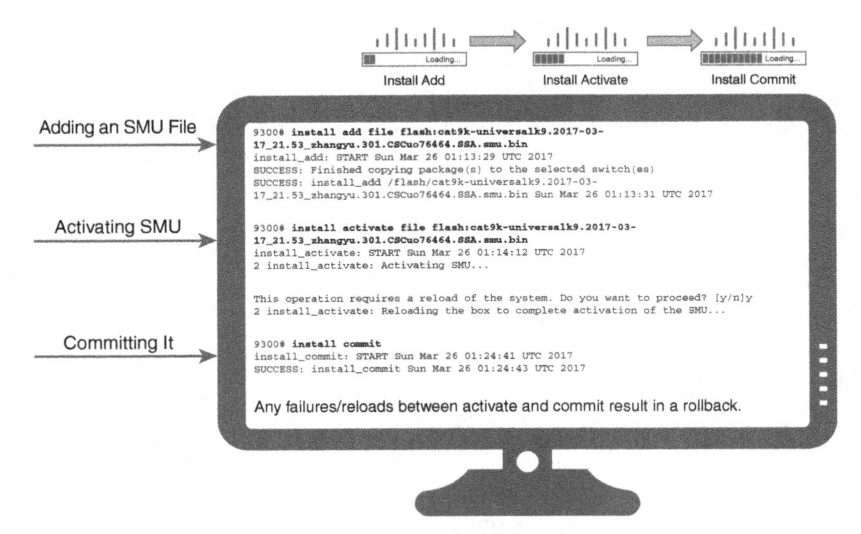

Figure 8-14 *Installing an SMU*

The steps are as follows:

Step 1. **Add the SMU file:** This basically consists of loading the SMU (delivered as a small, packaged binary file) onto the platform in the normal way (say, FTP or TFTP), and running the **install add** command to point to it.

Step 2. **Activate the SMU:** Running the **install activate** command activates the SMU and (in the case of a cold SMU) performs a device reload. When the device reloads, the new SMU becomes activated, integrated with the IOS XE code running on the device.

Step 3. **Commit the SMU:** Running the **install commit** command is used to commit, and keep, the patched SMU on the device. In the event of any failures between the **activate** and **commit** commands, an automatic rollback backs the SMU out of operation, thus providing a "safety net" for the deployment.

Benefits of SMUs

Even with the use of cold SMUs that require a device reload, the actual code that is targeted and patched to fix the particular point issue involved is much smaller than the amount of new code that an enterprise typically has to accept with a full IOS image upgrade. This makes SMUs—even cold ones—of significant benefit to enterprises, because they reduce the time, and the risk, associated with validating and deploying a code upgrade for a given point issue.

With the advent of hot SMU deployment capability in the future, this functionality will become even more valuable to network managers, because they will be able to deploy fixes for selected point-fix issues without even having to do a device reload.

Cisco plans to prioritize the availability of SMU point fixes for the most critical issues, based on the technical feasibility of delivering a SMU patch for a particular problem, a risk analysis of the impact of the issue involved in customer networks, and the benefits to customers from delivering such a method for a particular point fix versus including the fix in a broader Cisco IOS XE release vehicle. Although some additional complexity may exist in terms of keeping track of which SMUs a given device has installed over time, this is likely to be outweighed by the flexibility that the IOS XE SMU infrastructure provides. The use of SMUs does not eliminate the need for integrating code fixes into new IOS XE releases, which will continue to happen, but SMUs do allow for a new, innovative method of "point-fix" delivery for critical code issues in IOS XE—an important factor in the always-on, always-operational network environment of today, and tomorrow.

Cisco IOS XE: Platform Support

Cisco IOS XE is available across multiple switch and router platforms, including many of the most common platforms deployed in enterprise networks today. These include:

- Cisco Catalyst 3850 and 3650
- Cisco ASR 1000 platforms

- Cisco ISR 4000 platforms
- Cisco CSR (Cloud Services Router)
- Cisco Catalyst 9300—stackable access switch
- Cisco Catalyst 9400—modular access switch
- Cisco Catalyst 9500—fixed aggregation/core switch

The timeline of IOS XE releases across the platforms is summarized in Figure 8-15.

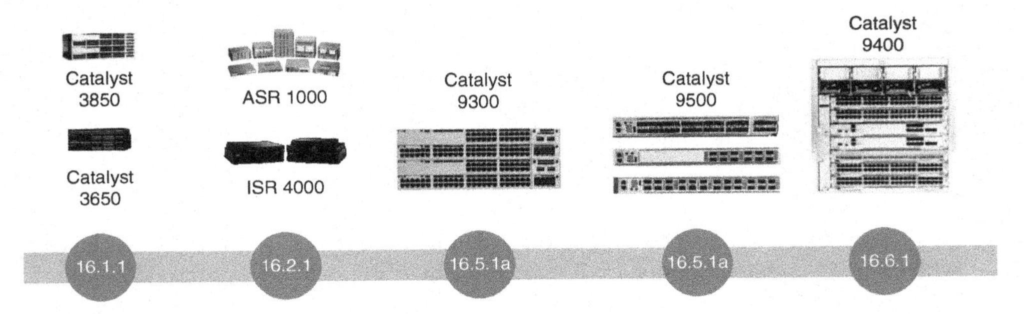

Figure 8-15 *Cisco IOS XE, Platform Support*

In particular, note that all of the Catalyst 9300, 9400, and 9500 platforms shown in Figure 8-15 use the exact same binary image, further simplifying the qualification, testing, and deployment of IOS XE across an end-to-end Catalyst 9000–based switched infrastructure, and marking a significant departure from the past in which multiple different software images, with disparate capabilities, might need to be deployed across the various switched infrastructure layers within a campus or branch network infrastructure.

Cisco IOS XE: Summary

In summary, IOS XE provides a strong foundation upon which to build the next generation of enterprise networks: a modern operating system for a new era of networking. Figure 8-16 summarizes the benefits that IOS XE provides, including better resiliency and high availability through modular subsystems and patchability, open programmability via standardized YANG data models and access methods such as NETCONF and RESTCONF, and the ability to host containerized apps.

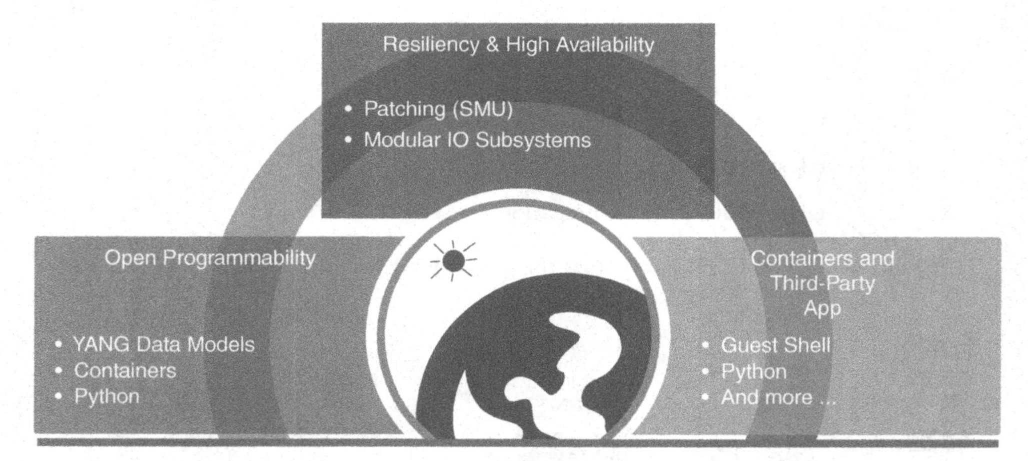

Figure 8-16 *Cisco IOS XE: A Modern OS for the New Era of Networking*

As Cisco and its customers embark on the evolution of enterprise network deployments with Cisco DNA—an evolution explored throughout this book—having a solid base upon which to build is critical. Cisco IOS XE provides that base, and when combined with Cisco's flexible, programmable hardware infrastructure, provides an unmatched capability to take on the most significant network challenges of today, and tomorrow, enabling a new set of capabilities for the next generation of network deployments and solutions. Some of these solutions are explored later in this book, such as critical new capabilities like Cisco Software-Defined Access, which leverage Cisco IOS XE and Cisco's programmable hardware to the hilt.

Now that we have reviewed some of the latest innovations with IOS XE, let's see some of the other areas where Cisco is driving important innovations for enterprise network deployments. Let's continue by examining an area of concern to many network administrators today, the security of the devices that make up their networks.

Protecting Platforms and Networks: Trustworthy Systems

With so much riding on the network infrastructure—often, the entire operation of an organization—it is important to pay close attention to protecting that infrastructure. IOS XE, along with other elements in Cisco's software and hardware portfolio, provides this via a mechanism known as trustworthy systems.

There are many elements that must be considered when properly securing a network infrastructure. Some common ones are firewalls, encryption, and ACLs. These are vitally important, with the majority of them focused on securing the data plane for data in flight—after all, that's what a network does, move data from point A to point B, and securing the data involved in between those points is critical.

However, in addition, an equally critical, yet often overlooked, area is the protection of the network device itself. It is vital to protect the integrity of the network platform from unwanted interference and outright attacks. Unless the network device is known to be secure, how can the network it supports be secure? Good security needs to start at the device foundation. This is the bedrock of the concept of the Cisco trustworthy systems initiative.

Trustworthy Systems: An Overview

Cisco trustworthy systems are designed to provide checks and balances that help validate network device platform integrity and provide alerts of any out-of-profile conditions and limit their impact.

Figure 8-17 outlines some of the capabilities that are intended to be addressed by Cisco trustworthy systems focused around platform integrity.

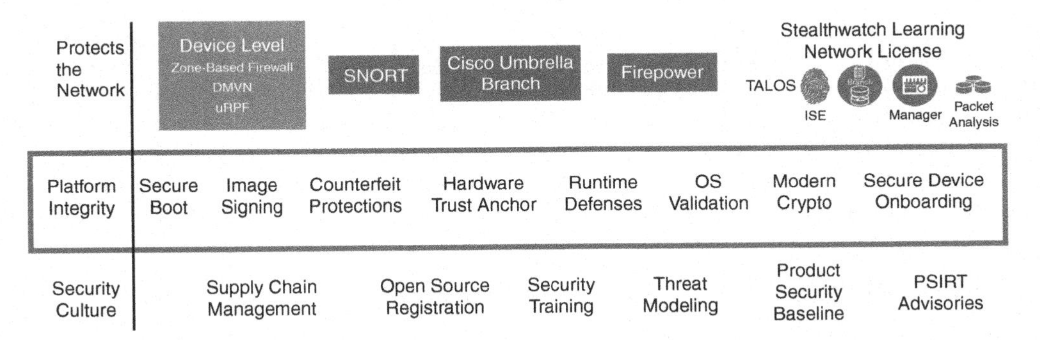

Figure 8-17 *Trustworthy Systems Capabilities*

Possible Attacks: IOS Modifications

First, let's examine some of the potential attacks that could be launched against a network device. For now, ignore attacks focused on bringing down the network, such as denial-of-service (DoS) attacks, as they are more well known, as are the mitigation techniques used to defeat them. Instead, let's focus on attacks that attempt to compromise the integrity of the network device platform itself.

Over the years, various attacks have been observed that attempt to modify the IOS software running on a device, with the intention of being able to compromise that device, or even take over the operation of the device, modify some aspect of the device's operation, or extract data from it.

Figure 8-18 outlines some of these attacks, along with a rough timeline corresponding to when these have been observed "in the wild."

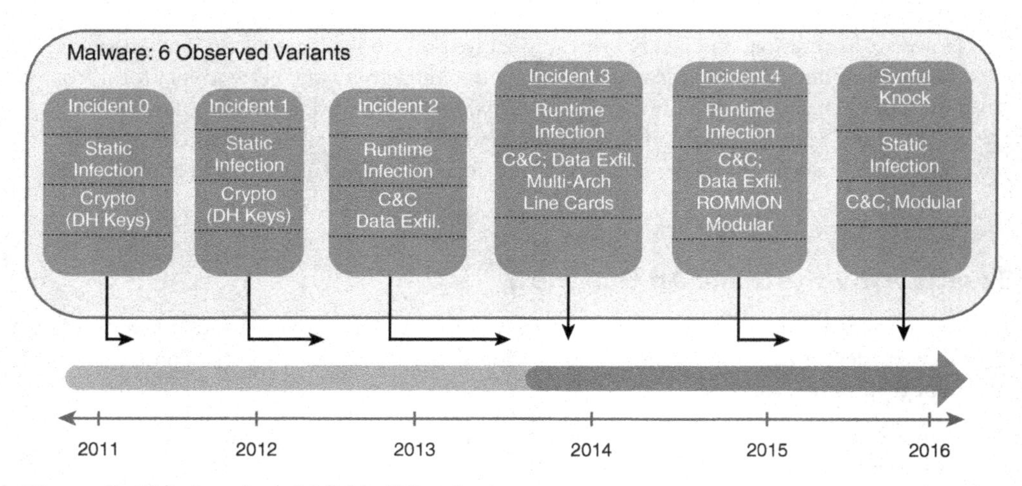

Figure 8-18 *Attacks—IOS Modifications*

Ranging across static and runtime infections, these attempts to inject malware into Cisco network devices tried to install command and control (C&C) systems, exfiltrate critical data, and compromise or alter crypto keys used for data privacy. All of these types of attacks are of great concern to the network administrator. Perhaps of even greater concern is the *next* attack—the one that nobody knows about yet because it has not yet been invented.

Attack Mitigation with Trustworthy Systems

What can be done to address these various types of attacks, and to help secure the network infrastructure and the various devices within it? This is where the Cisco trustworthy systems initiative comes in.

Cisco created the concept of trustworthy systems as a multilayered defense against such attacks on network device integrity. Accordingly, there are several areas of defense against such attacks, and several techniques and capabilities that are employed as part of the Trustworthy Systems approach. These are outlined in Figure 8-19, which also indicates which defense method is most appropriate at addressing which attack vector.

Each of the attack mitigation techniques, and explanations of the attack vectors that they are designed to contain are examined next.

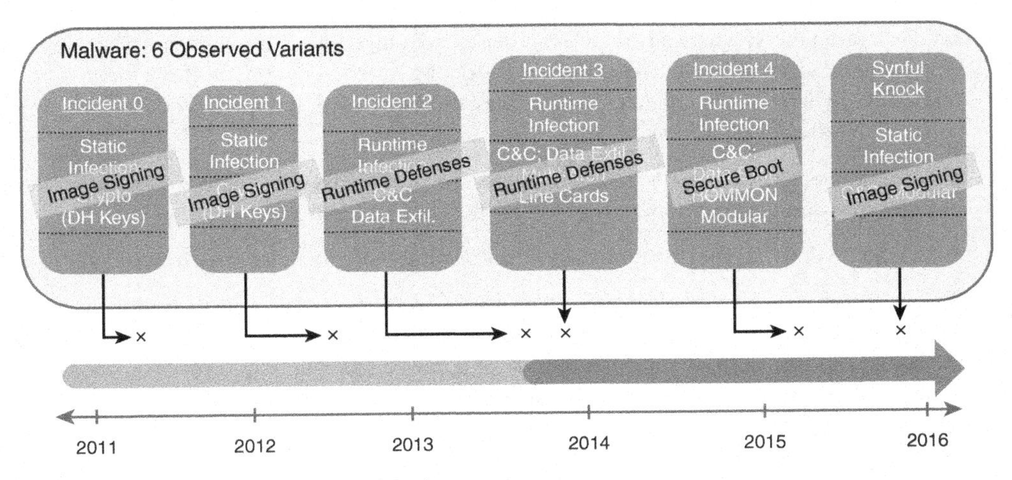

Figure 8-19 *Attack Mitigation Techniques*

Defense: Image Validation and Signing

Perhaps the easiest set of techniques to understand is image validation and signing. Every Cisco IOS image that employs image validation protection (including all Cisco IOS XE images) has an MD5 hash from the binary contents of the image provided by Cisco, which allows for the comparison of this MD5 hash as computed on the device to the corresponding MD5 value as posted on the Cisco.com website. Any tampering with the image (that is, altering the binary image to insert unwanted code) causes the MD5 hash used to sign the image to fail to validate, thus alerting the network manager that the image involved was compromised, and to take corrective action. As of 2015, Cisco uses SHA-512 hashes to validate images posted to Cisco.com.

In addition, some platforms and software versions also support digitally signed images, providing an ability to validate not only that the Cisco IOS image was not tampered with, but that the image originates from a trusted source (because it is signed with Cisco's private key, and verified with Cisco's public key, using asymmetric cryptography).

As shown in Figure 8-19, image signing is effective at defeating a number of attack vectors. Many static device infections or attack attempts can be detected, and defeated, with this widely deployed method. Image signing is thus an important foundational element of device-level security and validation. However, this does not by itself address all of the possible attack vectors that may be targeted at a network device.

Defense: Runtime Defenses

Once a network device boots up and is operating in the network, it may sometimes be possible to insert code into the device during runtime that could cause unwanted access or control of the device. For example, this may be done via a buffer overflow attack or similar attack vector, where advantage can be taken to insert code into a memory space in the device adjacent to a buffer space for traffic, by overflowing this buffer with an unexpectedly large or long data entry that may not be properly range-checked by the software on the device involved.

This technique is not limited to network devices, and has been used across many different device types and disparate operating systems for the insertion of malicious code.

What can be done in a networking device, such as a switch, to address such an attack?

An important capability implemented by some Cisco platforms, such as the Catalyst 9000 Series switches, is Address Space Layout Randomization (ASLR). ASLR randomizes the layout of code across the memory space of a device, making traditional attack techniques such as buffer overflow attacks much harder to execute because the same code is not laid down in the same place in memory every time. This is an example of how run-time defenses help defeat attempts to subvert a given network device.

Defense: Secure Boot

Despite all other attempts made to protect the integrity of the network device, most or all of them may be rendered invalid if control is gained by the attacker over the boot sequence of the device itself. If the boot process of the network device is subverted, many or all of the other checks that the network device might perform to verify the device's integrity can be defeated, because control early enough in the boot sequence effectively provides "root" control of the device—and does so in a way that is not easily detected or defeated. Even swapping out the software image on a device does not defeat such an attack if it occurs early enough in the boot sequence.

Protecting the integrity of the boot sequence is critical to secure device operation. This is the impetus behind Cisco's development of the Secure Boot process, and the hardware underpinnings that enable it. Let's proceed to understand Secure Boot as part of the Cisco trustworthy systems set of capabilities.

Understanding Boot Sequence Attacks

You need to understand how a network device boots up in order to understand the measures that need to be taken to protect this process.

Figure 8-20 shows, at a high level, what happens when a network device, such as a switch or router, boots up, and serves as a base to understand what means an attacker might use to subvert that boot sequence.

Basically, when powered on or restarted, a network device activates its BIOS (Basic Input/Output System) code, a process that loads up the operating system (typically from local flash storage). The OS begins to enable the operation of the network device—data plane, control plane, and management plane functions.

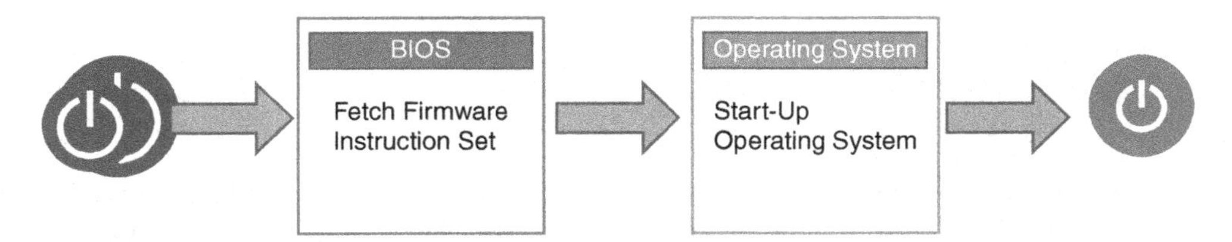

Figure 8-20 *Attacking the Boot Sequence*

An attacker can compromise this process by changing various parameters—the boot interface or device, bypassing the integrity checks on the code, or inserting persistent code into the device. While the OS integrity checks help to validate whether the OS image was tampered with, what about the integrity of the BIOS itself? What if an attacker managed to modify the BIOS, or bypass it? In other words, who guards the guardians?

Protecting Device Integrity from the Ground Up with Secure Boot

This is where Cisco Secure Boot comes in—by creating an immutable (nonmodifiable) hardware-based trust-anchor in a network device, one whose integrity can be cryptographically verified, and creating a "chain of trust" that allows the integrity of a network device to be ensured to a far greater degree than was possible in the past.

The process involved in Cisco Secure Boot is outlined in Figure 8-21.

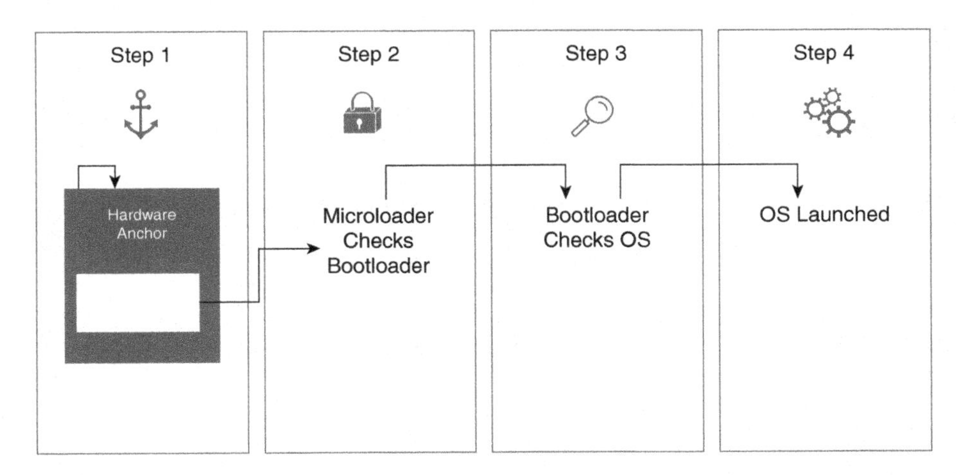

Figure 8-21 *Cisco Secure Boot—Anchors Secure Boot in Hardware to Create a Chain of Trust*

Secure Boot provides the following important items to check for software authenticity:

- Only authentic signed Cisco software images are able to boot up on a Cisco platform leveraging Secure Boot.

- The boot process stops if any step fails to authenticate.
- The Cisco IOS command **show software authenticity** is used to illustrate the results of the secure boot process.

Verifying results of the boot process also relies on the hardware trust anchor, TAm. This is a tamperproof piece of hardware that is built into the Cisco network device and implements an anti-tamper and anti-theft chip design. The hardware trust anchor uses built-in crypto in the form of a secure X.509 certificate, creating an immutable identity. This also serves as a secure repository for certificates and objects used for device authentication, and provides a certifiable entropy source for random number generation.

The purpose of the trust anchor as part of the Secure Boot process is to instantiate and start the microloader. Because this microloader originates in tamper-proof hardware, it is not modifiable, and is cryptographically verified for integrity. The microloader, being very small and simple, then loads up the bootloader, verifying its integrity. The bootloader loads up the main software image for the platform, again verifying the integrity of that image.

Because the trust at each stage in this process is based in trust on the prior stage, beginning with a hardware-based, non-modifiable, cryptographically secure microloader from the Trust Anchor module, a chain of trust is established that renders the entire boot process secure. If any stage in the boot process fails to verify, the boot process stops at that point, preventing the compromised network device from gaining access to, or becoming part of, the enterprise network involved.

Secure Boot is a critical element in creating a secure and tamper-resistant network environment. Many modern Cisco devices, such as the Catalyst 9000 Series switches, provide a hardware-based Trust Anchor module as the basis for the Secure Boot system that they offer.

Ensuring Device Identity with the Secure Unique Device Identifier

An additional important integrity check on many networks is ensuring that the devices are identified in a secure way and are well known to the network and to the network administrator and his or her network monitoring systems. For example, if an attacker swaps out a known-good network device with one that was modified to subvert its operation, or inserts a compromised network device into the network without detection, that device could be used to compromise network traffic flows. Detecting and defeating such attacks is also an important part of a trustworthy systems deployment.

Protecting against such an insertion of an unwanted network device is done by verifying the network device's Secure Unique Device Identifier (SUDI). The SUDI is a hardware-based cryptographic identifier that is embedded into the device during manufacturing and serves as a unique "fingerprint" for the device.

By inspecting the SUDI of the device, and matching that against devices expected to be (and authorized) in the network, the network administrator can quickly identify rogue devices if they are attached to the network, and block such devices from participating in the network infrastructure.

The SUDI supports multiple functions:

- Provides a tamperproof ID for the device
- Allows for authentication of connections with the device using the SUDI credential
- Binds the hardware identity to a key pair in a cryptographically secure X.509 certificate PID during manufacturing

Cisco Secure Boot and Trust Anchor Module: Validating the Integrity of Software, Followed by Hardware

Now, let's bring it all together to better understand the Secure Boot process, as well as sum up the Cisco trustworthy systems initiative overall.

Figure 8-22 illustrates how Cisco Secure Boot and the Cisco Trust Anchor module operate together to ensure the integrity of the network device, from initial power-on, through boot-up, and verifying the integrity of the network hardware.

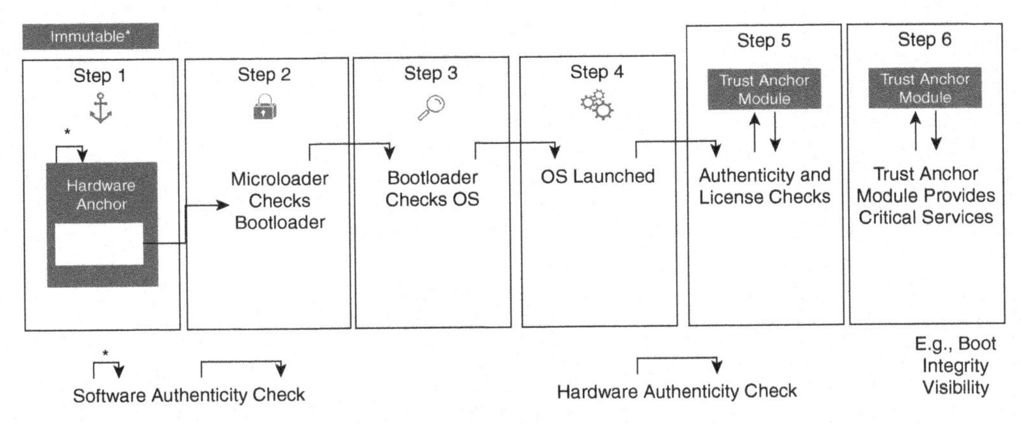

Figure 8-22 *Cisco Secure Boot and TAm—Operation*

Taken together with image signing and runtime defenses, this combination forms a powerful combination to assist in defeating many attacks that aim to subvert network devices. The Cisco trustworthy systems initiative, and the capabilities it encompasses, is a critical element in securing the integrity of the network devices, and is an important element in any organization's end-to-end security strategy.

Given the importance of the information flowing across networks in today's organizations, such protection of the integrity of the network devices that make up the network infrastructure is of vital importance. Cisco trustworthy systems helps validate such device—and network—integrity.

The Move to Intuitive Networking

We've spent a lot of time in this chapter examining Cisco IOS XE, which is appropriate because Cisco IOS is the most widely deployed network operating system in the world, and IOS XE is the next stage in the evolution of this critical software asset. However, there are many other areas of software innovation that Cisco is also driving. These include both the move toward intuitive network infrastructures and the move toward rapid, automated, programmatic change within network deployments using network controllers.

Cisco began the move toward the use of network controllers within the infrastructure a few years back, with the creation and deployment of the Cisco Application Policy Infrastructure Controller Enterprise Module (APIC-EM). Not the catchiest of names, perhaps, but what it may have lacked in naming it made up for in functionality. APIC-EM was the first true enterprise-class controller for Cisco network deployments, created with the goal of being an application platform that provided network discovery, automated the deployment of critical functions within the enterprise provided network, and allowed for simplified network troubleshooting.

As time moved forward, APIC-EM gave way to the next generation of intuitive networking—namely Cisco DNA Center. Building upon the initial goals of APIC-EM in terms of network discovery and automation, Cisco DNA Center also added the capability to provide Assurance, the ability to continuously monitor the underlying network infrastructure, report on errors or out-of-profile network conditions that might require a network operator's attention, and suggest the appropriate course of action to correct the issue.

The overall capabilities of Cisco DNA Center are outlined in Figure 8-23.

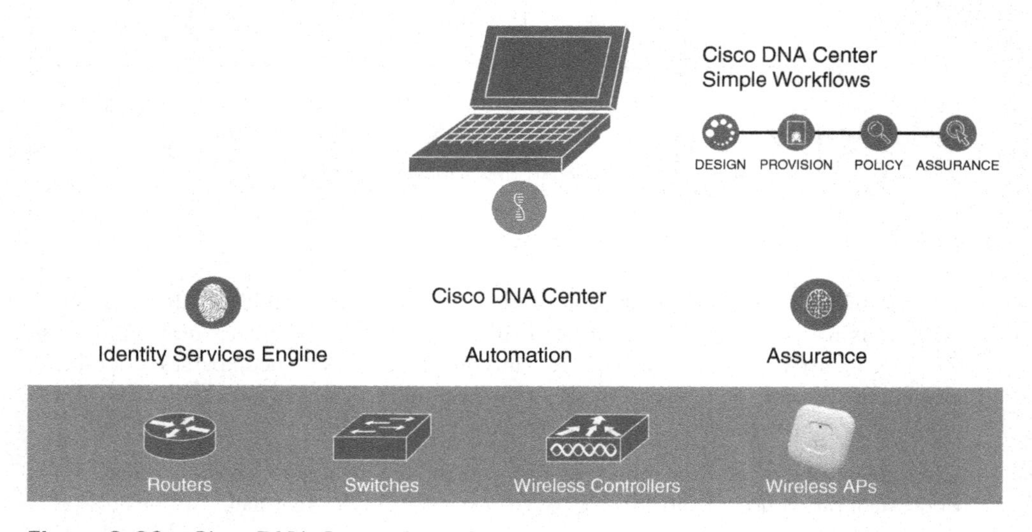

Figure 8-23 *Cisco DNA Center Overview*

The capabilities of Cisco DNA Center are examined in much more detail in the following chapters covering Network Automation and Assurance. For now, suffice it to say that Cisco DNA Center and the movement that it embodies toward truly intuitive networking are key cornerstones of future network deployments, allowing the capabilities delivered by Cisco IOS XE, Cisco's flexible hardware platforms, and solutions such as Software-Defined Access to be realized, and maximized, in enterprise network deployments in a simple and scalable manner.

Summary

This chapter explored the evolution of networking software, and the various "planes of operation" in a network—data plane, control plane, and management plane—and how these have evolved over time. It also explored the evolution of Cisco IOS, the most popular and widely deployed networking software in the world, and discussed Cisco IOS XE in detail. You read how IOS XE, in conjunction with the Cisco flexible, programmable hardware components (discussed in the preceding chapter), evolved to address the networking challenges of today, and tomorrow.

This chapter also described some of the attacks against network devices and reviewed advanced techniques deployed in modern network devices to detect, and defeat, such attacks using Cisco trustworthy systems.

Finally, this chapter discussed how networks are evolving with controller-based approaches and the future of intuitive networking with network automation and assurance capabilities, using Cisco DNA Center.

Going forward, let's explore how the protocols used to construct networks are also evolving as networking continues to progress. This evolution of network protocols, and the new innovations being driven there, is the subject of the next chapter.

Further Reading

Cisco IOS XE At-A-Glance: https://www.cisco.com/c/dam/en/us/products/collateral/ios-nx-os-software/ios-xe/nb-09-ios-xe-secure-open-flex-aag-cte-en.pdf

Cisco Trustworthy Systems FAQ: https://www.cisco.com/c/dam/en_us/about/doing_business/trust-center/docs/cisco-trustworthy-systems-faq.pdf.

Chapter 9

Protocol Innovations

Let's discuss protocols. Specifically, network protocols, and how they are evolving as the future of networking takes shape.

To begin with, what is a protocol? And more specifically, what is a communications protocol?

In a nutshell, communications protocols basically govern how systems, including devices, users, and applications, talk to each other. Networking protocols govern how the network is created, how it is maintained, and how systems communicate using it.

Networking protocols date back to the very dawn of the network age. The very first modern computer network created was ARPAnet, in 1969. It used a series of protocols (1822 and NCP) to deliver datagrams between hosts. As time progressed, the ARPAnet moved to TCP/IP (in 1982), and the seeds of the modern Internet, and the networks used today, were laid.

Networking protocols create the network, bind it together, allow it to operate seamlessly, and enable it to recover from outages and communications interruptions. This chapter examines how new protocol innovations are changing the face of how the modern network operates—and provide network users and network managers with advanced new capabilities.

This chapter explains the following:

- Networking protocols from the ground up, starting with Ethernet
- The evolution of Power over Ethernet (PoE)
- The movement toward Multigigabit Ethernet (mGig) over copper
- The evolution of Layer 2 and Layer 3 protocols
- Networking protocols for the next era of networking: VXLAN, LISP, and TrustSec

Let's begin with a review of the common protocols in use in today's networks so that you can compare and contrast what is possible in networks with the protocols used today with the new capabilities becoming available with the latest crop of protocols driving the next generation of networking.

Networking Protocols: Starting at the Bottom with Ethernet

You may not think of Ethernet as a networking protocol. However, it is—one that operates at the lowest layers within the network infrastructure, Layers 1 and 2. In fact, Ethernet is one of the most ubiquitous networking protocols in use today. Starting from its roots in 10-Mbps Ethernet running over thickwire coaxial cabling (10BASE-5…anyone remember vampire taps?), moving on from there to thinwire coax (10BASE-2…don't remove the terminating resistors!), and finally into twisted-pair cabling (starting with 10BASE-T) and fiber optics, Ethernet has transitioned through a number of physical media types over the years.

Ethernet is standardized as IEEE 802.3, with the "802" portion referring to the initial year and month the committee first met to begin standardizing this group of protocols (February 1980). The IEEE standards process defines all the elements of Ethernet. And as you will see, ongoing Ethernet development for future capabilities is still very much alive and well!

Ethernet has branched out in many directions since its inception, starting from humble beginnings to become one of the most prevalent networking standards in the world. It makes for interesting reading if you want to see all the various directions Ethernet has gone into over the many years since its invention.

The performance of Ethernet has seen a series of huge increases over time. Again starting with its roots in 10-Mbps speeds (IEEE 802.3i on twisted-pair copper media), Ethernet made the jump to 100 Mbps (802.3u—Fast Ethernet), 1000 Mbps (802.3z over fiber, 802.3ab over twisted-pair copper—Gigabit Ethernet), 10 Gbps (802.3ae over fiber, 802.3an over twisted-pair), and 100 Gbps (802.3ba over fiber and short-haul coax) speeds. In general, each generation of Ethernet increased the performance by ten times versus the prior generation, with the goal stated as being "ten times the performance for three times the price"—with that price differential decreasing over time as the newer, faster standard took hold in the marketplace, and product volumes ramped up accordingly. It's worth noting that there are over 4 billion 100BASE-T/1000BASE-T ports installed worldwide currently!

However, something interesting happened on the way from 10-Gbps to 100-Gbps Ethernet. An intermediate standard emerged, 40-Gbps Ethernet, running over multimode and single-mode fiber. This was the first time in Ethernet's development, beginning with 10 Mbps, that Ethernet did not increase by ten times in speed. Why did 40-Gbps Ethernet emerge? Two mains factors contributed to this: technical capability and cost. At the time, it was easier, and much less costly, to create 40-Gbps transceivers than to make the jump directly to 100 Gbps. Because some users needed more performance than 10-Gbps Ethernet provided, and could not wait for 100-Gbps Ethernet (and the associated switches and routers equipped with it) to become more cost effective, 40-Gbps Ethernet took root as an intermediate stepping-stone speed level. 40-Gbps Ethernet also offered some interesting capabilities with bidirectional (BiDi) optics, allowing for the more rapid adoption of this technology and providing investment protection, especially in data centers.

And, as you see, intermediate (i.e., between 10× jumps) speeds in Ethernet now offer some interesting options, which are reviewed later in the chapter in the discussion of Multigigabit Ethernet (IEEE 802.3bz) and 25-Gbps Ethernet.

Over 35 years, the basic frame format of Ethernet has remained intact: a 1500-byte frame with a 14-byte header and a 4-byte trailer, for a total of 1518 bytes on the wire. Of course, new capabilities such as 802.1Q have added extensions for virtual local area networks (VLAN), adding an additional 4 bytes to the header, in between the Source Media Access Control (MAC) value and the EtherType/Length field. The use of jumbo frames to grow Ethernet frames (up to a typical maximum of 9216 bytes) for more efficient data transfer was also added. Overall, though, the basic Ethernet frame format has proven to be very robust, and is now the single most common data frame format in use worldwide.

And yet, Ethernet continues to evolve. Let's review a few of the most common solutions used with Ethernet today in enterprise network designs.

Power Protocols: Power over Ethernet, to 60 Watts and Beyond!

The Power over Ethernet standard arose from the idea to have a single cable to a network device that provided both data *and* power to that device. Cisco pioneered the use of Power over Ethernet, or PoE, with a proprietary solution (called Inline Power) that offered 7 watts of total power to a given device, operating over the same Ethernet cable that connected that device to the network. This was first implemented using the Catalyst 3500 and 3550 PoE switches, and supported by Cisco IP Phones as one of the first types of devices to leverage this important new capability.

As PoE as a concept started to take hold, an effort was undertaken in IEEE 802.3 to standardize this capability. The first PoE standard was IEEE 802.3af, which provided for 15.4 watts of power at the power sourcing equipment (PSE—typically, an Ethernet switch) for delivery over up to 100 meters of twisted-pair copper cabling to the powered device (PD—typically, an IP phone, wireless access point, or another device that provided PoE support). This was really where PoE entered the mainstream, and very soon PoE devices and solutions began to proliferate.

The need for more power for some situations became apparent. Examples of this included multiradio access points, IP phones with integrated video, high-resolution IP cameras, and the like. To address this, the PoE standard was cranked up to 30 watts of power at the PSE (switch port), as IEEE 802.3at (also known as PoE+). Once again, this allowed for the creation of even more diverse PoE applications and uses.

As the demand for PoE power increased, Cisco provided a capability for up to 60 watts of power per PoE port, a capability known as Universal PoE (UPoE). Although not every application and use of PoE requires this much power, it's nice to know there is more power on tap if needed—and some applications (such as graphical terminals, for example) do use this extra power capability that UPoE can supply.

In the future, a new Ethernet power standard now on the horizon is 802.3bt, which will allow for up to 90 watts of PoE power at the PSE (Ethernet switch), again allowing a new generation of PoE-powered devices and applications to emerge.

Cisco is proud to have played a significant role in helping to define and evolve the PoE standard over time, and move it to new levels of capability. The evolution of Power over Ethernet is illustrated in Figure 9-1.

Another area that uses PoE power—and one that is seeing increasing adoption—is LED lighting. With this application of PoE, the actual lighting fixtures in a building are powered via PoE from a switch port. Because LED lighting is much more power-efficient than incandescent lighting, this is now both possible and very power-efficient. And in addition, since low-voltage copper twisted-pair cabling is much easier, and less costly, to install than traditional electrical wiring, major savings can be reaped in new installations if planning for PoE-powered lighting fixtures.

Many modern building projects are now taking advantage of this trend.

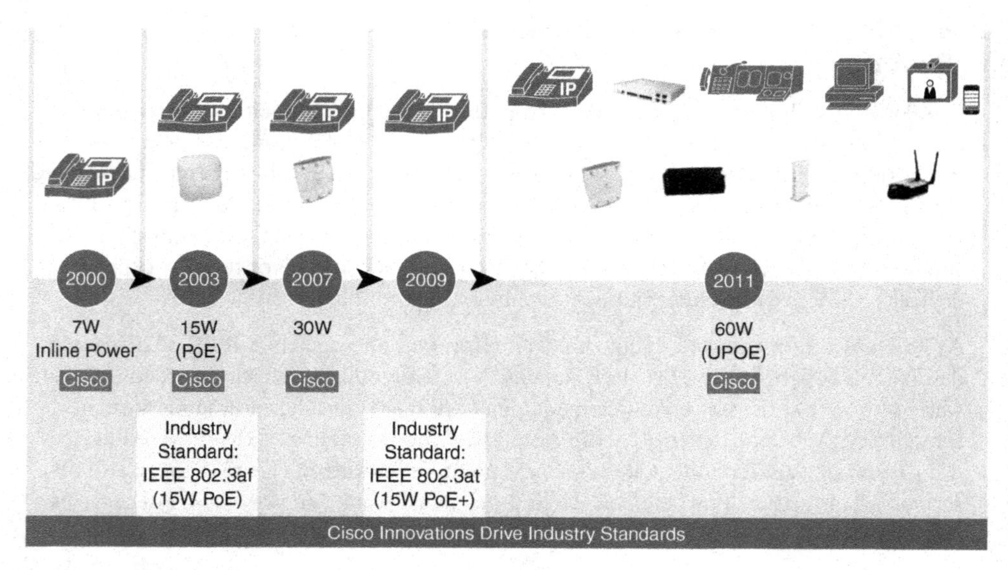

Figure 9-1 *Power over Ethernet Evolution Timeline*

And, because the connection to the powered device now supports data as well, expect these lighting devices, and other devices in the digital ceiling, to get "smarter" and much more multifunction over time. This includes things like HVAC systems, thermostat controls, and many other elements within the digital ceiling. Intelligent lighting panels, anyone?

Building on this trend (no pun intended), Cisco introduced the Digital Building Switch, a small-form-factor switch designed to be installed into plenum-rated spaces (such as the space above the ceiling tiles in a typical office deployment). This offers eight ports of 15.4 W (PoE) or 30 W (PoE+) capability for attached devices, and is ideal for deployment with PoE-powered lighting fixtures, digital controls, and other elements within a modern digital building system. This switch is shown in Figure 9-2.

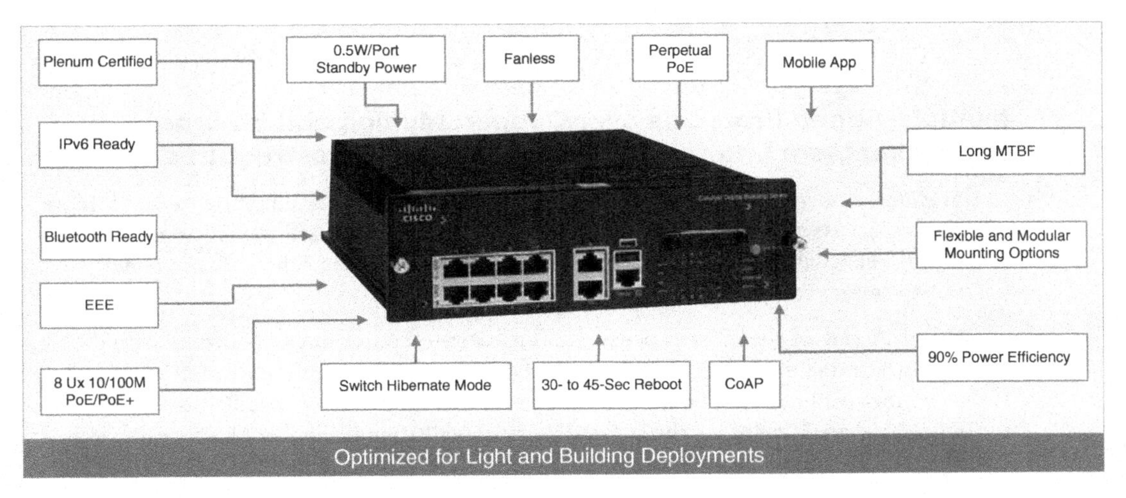

Figure 9-2 *Cisco Digital Building Switch*

As this trend toward the PoE-powered building accelerates, it also becomes important to ensure that the power stays on constantly. To this end, Cisco has engineered two impressive innovations. The first of these, Perpetual PoE, ensures that PoE power always stays up to the powered device, even if the switch in the wiring closet is reloaded (i.e., control plane reboot). This is important because you don't want the lights going out during a code upgrade on a switch! Likewise, Perpetual PoE capability is extremely useful for applications such as PoE-powered physical access/security devices, such as door entry systems and video surveillance cameras, which must remain powered up even if their attached switch reloads.

The second innovation is Fast PoE. This ensures that, if a switch is completely powered down, it asserts PoE power on the necessary switch ports within approximately 30 seconds of powering up. In other words, there is no need to wait for the switch to entirely boot up (which could take a few minutes) in order to power up PoE devices such as lighting fixtures. This capability ensures rapid recovery from events such as power outages.

The Future of Power over Ethernet

Power over Ethernet has now come of age. It's used for a lot more today than just IP phones!

Going into the future, the IEEE has now standardized 802.3bt, which supplies up to 90 watts of power per PoE switch port. Innovative new uses for these increased PoE power levels will no doubt emerge, including higher-powered versions of the PoE applications already discussed, as well as new functions not yet imagined.

So, there is no danger of running out of power in our Power over Ethernet implementations anytime soon. And as you can see from looking around the rich ecosystem of devices that leverage it, Power over Ethernet has proven to be extremely useful since it was invented over 15 years ago.

Multiple-Speed Protocols over Copper: Multigigabit Ethernet, Squeezing More Life Out of Existing Cabling Infrastructures

The lifetime over which organizations change out their network infrastructures (switches, routers, access points, etc.) varies between industries, individual companies, and even departments within an organization. Typically, lifetimes for an Ethernet switch might be five to seven years, or for an AP three to four years.

However, one of the most expensive and hardest-to-swap-out assets owned by an organization might not be one that you think about a lot—but it's absolutely critical to your overall network build. This is the cabling infrastructure installed within a building. More specifically, it's the twisted-pair copper cabling installed between a switch located in a wiring closet and the device located at the user's desktop or other device location.

And, there's a lot of this cabling out there! Current estimates indicate that over 70 billion meters of copper network cabling has been installed worldwide. That's 10 meters of copper network cabling for every person on Earth!

Installing this horizontal-run cabling in a building is expensive—and in some buildings (especially older ones), is very expensive and time-consuming. And once installed, this horizontal cable plant tends not to be swapped out or upgraded for many years, typically 10 to 15 years or more. Yet, at the same time, standards for this cabling have evolved. From the Category 5e cabling that was installed years ago, to the newer Category 6/6a cabling installed today, the quality of this cabling—and its ability to reliably transmit signals with less distortion and interference—has increased dramatically over time.

Think of this cabling as a transmission channel, because that's what it is: a channel (or conduit) for bits between the end-user network device and the upstream switch port. This channel consists of up to 100 meters of cabling for Ethernet—typically defined as up to 90 meters of solid copper twisted-pair cabling and up to 10 meters of stranded patch cable—along with patch panels being used in between. This is illustrated in Figure 9-3.

The number of bits squeezed into that channel depends on two things—the quality of the channel, and the method used for encoding the bits over the channel.

When 10-Gbps Ethernet over copper cabling was invented, it was necessary to move beyond the encoding methods used for Gigabit Ethernet to allow ten times as many bits per second to be sent over the twisted-pair cabling medium involved. 10-Gbps Ethernet over copper required the best-quality copper cabling available at that time (Cat6a), and used a new encoding method which allowed more efficient use of the bandwidth this cabling offered. When combined, it became possible to transmit 10 Gbps of data over up to 100 meters of Cat6a copper cabling.

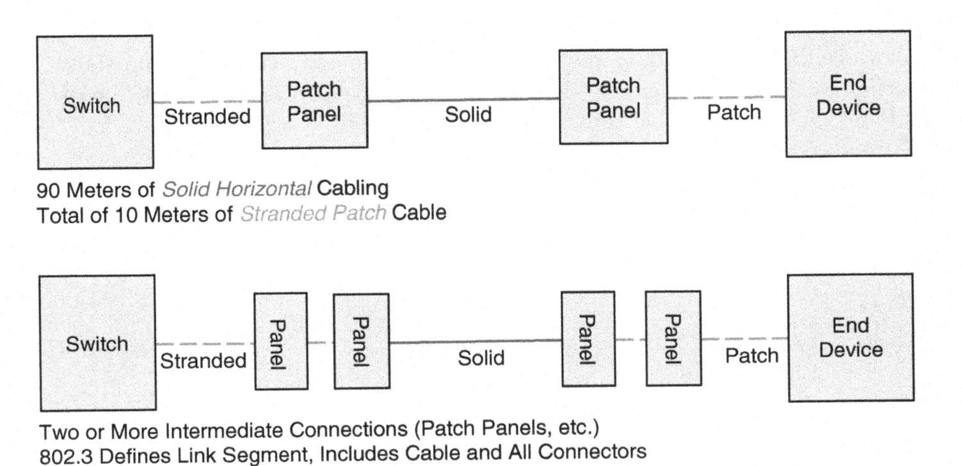

Figure 9-3 *Ethernet Cabling, Channel, and Link Segment*

The challenge is that cabling, once installed, is often never replaced, or is replaced only when a major building renovation project is underway. Due to this, adoption of 10-Gbps Ethernet over copper took hold fairly rapidly in the data center—where new cabling installations are more common as servers are added and moved—but adoption in the campus and branch areas of the enterprise network was slow. With the large amount of older (non-Cat6a) cabling installed in many buildings worldwide, 10-Gbps Ethernet out to 100 meters remained a distant dream for many organizations stuck with older Cat5e and Cat6 cabling in their horizontal cabling plants.

This is where Multigigabit Ethernet (mGig) comes in. Standardized as IEEE 802.3bz, mGig offers the capability to operate at two intermediate speeds over Cat5e and Cat6 cabling:

- Up to 2.5 Gbps over up to 100 meters of Cat5e cabling
- Up to 5 Gbps over up to 100 meters of Cat6 cabling

In addition, mGig is able to support speeds of 100 Mbps and 1000 Mbps over this same cabling. And, if Cat6a cabling is available, speeds of up to 10 Gbps can be realized with a compatible mGig-capable switch port. (Note that some mGig ports may only support lower speeds, such as 2.5 or 5 Gbps.)

How does mGig accomplish this? By taking the more sophisticated encoding techniques created for use with 10-Gbps Ethernet and downshifting these to a lower bitrate, an optimum use is made of the available bandwidth of a Cat5e or Cat6 cable—allowing more performance (2.5× or 5×) to be squeezed out of the same cable plant. Not bad for something you can get just by upgrading a switch or a line card!

Note that many capabilities are shared between 1000BASE-T, 10GBASE-T, and mGig. These include the use of an RJ-45 connector, the use of four-pair cabling, the provision for full-duplex communication (allowing transmission and reception of data on the same wires simultaneously), and support for PoE. As illustrated in Figure 9-4, the lessons learned and the technologies employed with 10GBASE-T were leveraged to allow mGig to encode more than 1 Gbps of data onto a Cat5e/Cat6 cabling infrastructure with mGig—scaling up performance without requiring a costly (and in some cases, impractical) cabling upgrade.

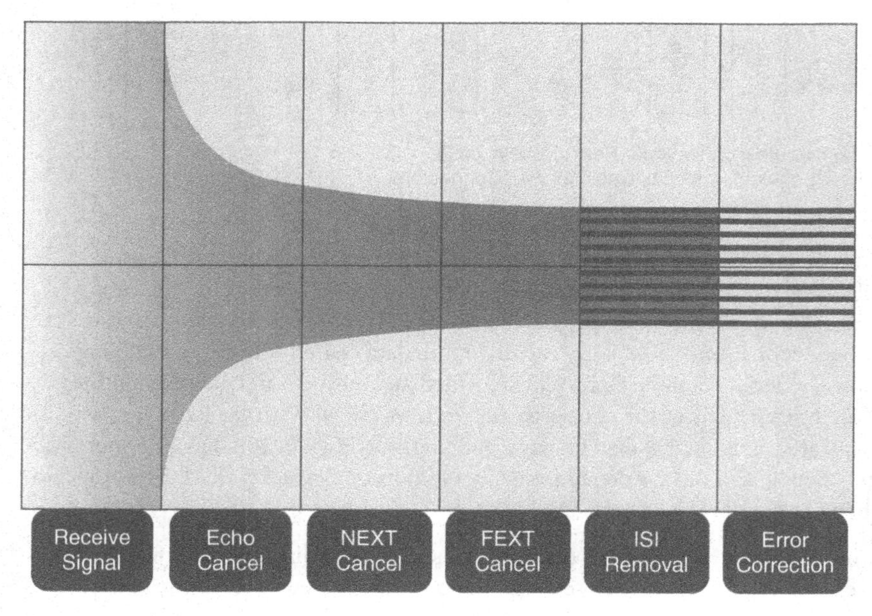

Figure 9-4 *Leveraging 10GBASE-T Technologies for Multigigabit Ethernet*

In addition, PoE support on PoE-capable switch platforms (up to 30 watts per port with PoE+, or up to 60 watts per port with UPoE) ensures that mGig-capable devices attached to such switches can also be powered devices—no need to choose between speed and power.

What are some of the applications of mGig?

One of the first and still one of the most important uses for mGig is supporting the evolution of wireless. As Wi-Fi has matured over the years, the performance available to wireless users has increased. From 11 Mbps with 802.3b, to 54 Mbps with 802.11a/g, to up to 450 Mbps (three spatial streams) or 600 Mbps (four spatial streams; not widely deployed) with 802.11n, the data rates available for wireless APs was well matched to the available backhaul performance from that AP to the wired infrastructure (100 Mbps or 1 Gbps).

However, when the transition was made to 802.11ac Wave 1, the maximum wireless performance available grew to 1.3 Gbps, slightly outpacing the performance of Gigabit Ethernet. At the time, this raised some eyebrows, but the half-duplex nature of much of wireless communications, and its operation as a shared medium, typically limited actual throughput from 802.11ac Wave 1 APs below 1 Gbps in any case.

However, as illustrated in Figure 9-5, with the advent of 802.11ac Wave 2, the total maximum performance (under ideal conditions) available via radio frequency (RF) grew to approx. 6.8 Gbps. Even when factoring in the inherent nature of wireless, and less-than-ideal operating parameters and distances for client-to-AP communications, it is now possible to see how sustained throughputs above 1 Gbps can be achieved in the real world. And yet, with only a single 1-Gbps uplink from an AP to a switch, this wired backhaul connection can now become the bottleneck to performance. Solutions such as running two cable drops to the AP are in many cases impractical due to expense or cabling difficulty, and offer challenges with proper link utilization via load balancing in any case.

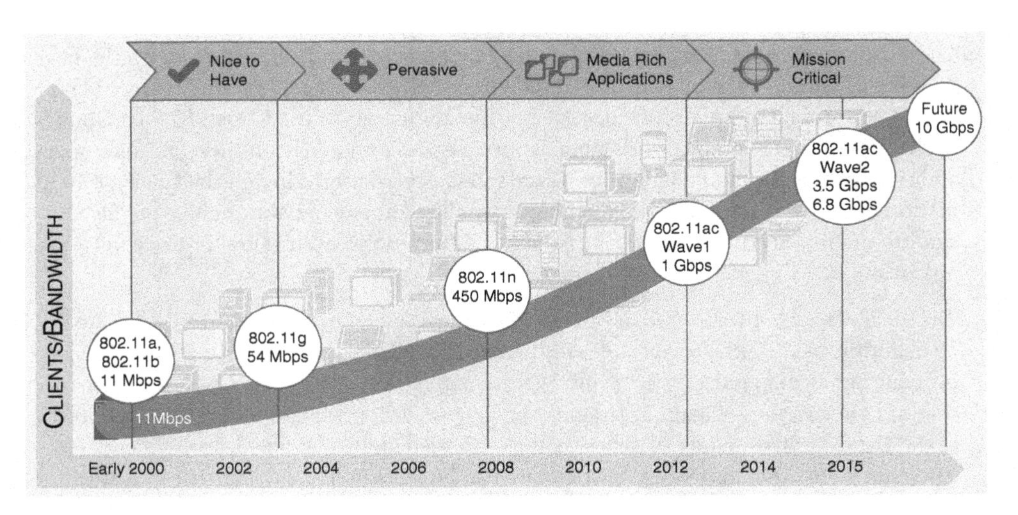

Figure 9-5 *Evolution of Wireless Standards—Past, Present, and Future*

This is where mGig helps. By offering a 2.5-Gbps (with Cat5e cabling) or 5-Gbps (with Cat6 cabling) connection out to an access point over a single cable drop, backhaul bandwidths are offered that are a great match for the performance needs of modern 802.11ac Wave 2 APs. And with the high-efficiency 802.11ax wireless standard on the horizon, total wireless throughputs will no doubt increase again—making mGig even more important for the wired network builds that support the wireless network infrastructure.

Additional uses for Multigigabit Ethernet include high-performance desktops and workstations (for example, Apple's iMac Pro now comes with 802.3bz support built in) and devices that send or receive massive amounts of data, such as CAD/CAM workstations, file servers, medical imaging systems, scientific instruments, and the like. As mGig switch ports begin to be more ubiquitously deployed in organizations, it is anticipated that the ingenious uses found for mGig will multiply even further.

25G Ethernet—The New Kid on the Block

One of the newest standards to emerge for the enterprise network is 25G Ethernet. This is a new technology that largely operates over the same fiber types and distances as 10G Ethernet, but which operates at 2.5 times the data rate. As a "single lane" technology, 25G Ethernet operates using a single optical transmitter and receiver over the fiber cabling involved, making it simpler and generally less costly than other alternatives such as 40G Ethernet.

It is widely anticipated that 25G Ethernet will be rapidly adopted in enterprise network deployments as products begin to come to market that support this new standard. The latest crop of Catalyst 9000 switch platforms and associated uplink modules now support options for 25G Ethernet, making this very practical to deploy in enterprise networks.

These additions to the Catalyst 9000 switch family introduced support for both the new 25-Gbps Ethernet standard and 100-Gbps Ethernet. By offering 25-Gbps Ethernet in an SFP28 form factor—equivalent in size to the ubiquitous SFP 1-Gbps/SFP+ 10-Gbps optics so well known to network administrators—and providing "on-the-wire" interoperability between 10G and 25G optics, Cisco's 25G Ethernet offering on the Catalyst 9000 platforms provides not only a compelling capability for new network builds, but also a smooth migration path for the reuse of existing fiber-optic cabling and in-place network migration.

The ideal placement for 25-Gbps Ethernet in a campus deployment is at the access-to-distribution layer links, replacing 10G Ethernet in this role and offering 2.5 times the performance at a comparable price point. When coupled with 100-Gbps links from distribution to core switches—again, leveraging the new small-form-factor QSFP28 100G optics in the Catalyst 9000 family of switches for simplified and streamlined deployments—a true next-generation network infrastructure can be put into place...one that leverages the next generation of Ethernet technologies and is not only well matched to the performance needs of today, but suitable to support the high-bandwidth needs of tomorrow's applications and devices. And all of this comes with the plug-and-play simplicity and cost effectiveness that has always been Ethernet's hallmark.

Ethernet Evolving: This Is Not Your Father's Ethernet!

This chapter has barely scratched the surface of how Ethernet evolved, and yet, notice how Ethernet matured, and proliferated, in the enterprise network: 10 Gbps, 25 Gbps, 40 Gbps, and 100 Gbps over fiber; 100 Mbps, 1 Gbps, 2.5 Gbps, 5 Gbps, and 10 Gbps over copper; PoE power ranging from 15.4 W to 30 W, 60 W, and in future up to 90 W per switch port. And all of this with the plug-and-play simplicity that has always been a hallmark of Ethernet, and something that users have come to expect—and rely on.

So what's next? As shown in the Ethernet Alliance website (https://ethernetalliance.org/ea/), there's a lot going on. Some of the more interesting projects underway from an enterprise network perspective are speed expansions to 200 Gbps and beyond that, up to 400 Gbps (802.3bs). Ranging beyond the enterprise network, Ethernet is also making its way into many new exciting and "nontraditional" areas, such as automobiles and factory plant applications (with the 802.3bp 1000BASE-T1 single-pair standard and the 802.3bu Power over Data Lines standard, among others).

And it does not stop there! Expect Ethernet, as the most ubiquitous networking protocol in the world for data transmission, to stay relevant and keep evolving for many years to come.

Moving Up the Stack

Thus far this chapter has examined how Ethernet as a protocol has evolved. Let's move up the stack to Layer 2 and Layer 3 protocols to really appreciate some of the new advances that have taken place in networking. Let's do this by first examining the existing Layer 2 and Layer 3 protocols that we use today to build networks—their uses, their shortcomings, and both the capabilities and challenges they bring for today's network deployments.

Only after exploring these for a short while can you really appreciate and "put into context" what the latest protocol and solution advances in the new era of networking bring.

Networking Protocols: Moving Up the Stack to Layer 2

As shown when examining the evolution of Ethernet, there was (and continues to be) a huge evolution underway regarding the physical layer of network deployments. Now, let's move up the stack to Layer 2. Let's shift the focus from how you physically connect networks together to how to use networking protocols to build out network designs as logical constructs over those physical connections, and create discrete network forwarding topologies.

As every network engineer knows, Spanning Tree Protocol (STP) exists as a protocol to eliminate loops in a Layer 2 network system. This is critical because Layer 2 Ethernet frames that are forwarded by a switch are not modified in any way—and thus, no inherent capability exists in an Ethernet network to avoid endless broadcast propagation in looped network designs (and loops and redundant paths are almost always created in network designs, to allow for fault tolerance and failover for device/link outages).

Spanning Tree exists to detect and block redundant paths within the network, ensuring that a loop-free Layer 2 topology is always created, and is maintained by reactivating blocked links in the event that failures or outages occur.

Although Spanning Tree is effective, it was created in an era where only a single network topology existed (one big LAN). As VLANs began to proliferate, Spanning Tree had to adapt. To allow maximum flexibility, Cisco created Per-VLAN Spanning Tree (PVST+), which allowed for separate STP instances per VLAN. Taking a different approach, IEEE standardized 802.1s, which created STP instances which could span multiple VLANs. Overall, many Cisco customers ended up deploying PVST+, which became very common in Cisco switched network deployments for enterprises.

Both approaches had advantages and drawbacks, but both shared some of the key challenges of Spanning Tree overall—slow reconvergence (typically, 30 seconds or more to reconverge after an outage), inefficient Layer 2 topologies with many blocked links (and thus wasted bandwidth), and in many cases, a divergence between the Layer 2 forwarding topology and the Layer 3 forwarding topology that ran over it (making understanding network traffic flows for traffic planning and troubleshooting more difficult).

Over time, technologies became available that resolved (or at least minimized) some of the more objectionable traits associated with Spanning Tree. One of the most important of these was the move to more rapid reconvergence (from subsecond to a few seconds, depending on topology and network size). This was a significant improvement from the 30 seconds or more reconvergence with standard STP, and was generally welcomed by the networking community. This took the form of Per-VLAN Rapid Spanning Tree (PVRST+) for many Cisco deployments, and 802.1w as the IEEE-standardized approach.

Although this helped to address some of the concerns with Spanning Tree, many other considerations continued to plague large-scale Layer 2 designs. Widespread broadcast propagation, inefficient use of available network links and bandwidths, and the disconnect between the Layer 2 and Layer 3 forwarding topologies were not so easily solved.

Broadcasts were contained by the use of more VLANs to create isolated broadcast domains, but at the expense of additional complexity and the increased need to create more and more IP subnets aligned to these VLANs. Although strategies were adopted to make the Layer 2 and Layer 3 forwarding topologies congruent to each other, this involved much manual effort, and was complex both to design and to implement and properly maintain.

Over the years, many network managers and engineers came to dislike large-scale Layer 2 network designs—a dislike which only intensified when faced with a network "meltdown" (for example, a broadcast storm) incurred if an uncontrolled loop formed in such a design with wide-spanning VLANs.

Such VLANs that span across large areas (or all) of a large campus deployment may sometimes be considered desirable, or even mandated, for certain applications. And yet, their use places the entire network at risk in the event that an uncontrolled Layer 2 loop occurs. A large, wide-spanning Layer 2 network design essentially places the network into a single, large "failure domain"—meaning that the area of the network that could be deleteriously affected, or even taken offline, with such an event as a broadcast storm could propagate across the entire campus site. Any network manager that has ever lived through such a large-scale, campus-spanning broadcast storm situation likely has little desire to ever relive the experience.

A large Layer 2 deployment also typically suffers from traffic inefficiency even when operating normally. Because a given VLAN only has one IP default gateway for the subnet involved, and that default gateway must be located on a given switch somewhere in the deployment, traffic from an end-user device on that subnet going to a device located on another subnet may have to traverse a long distance across the widely spanned VLAN to reach this gateway—only to be turned around and sent back to this second host, which may be physically quite near to the first one. For example, think about a user in one widely spanned subnet printing to a printer that is located down the hall but in another subnet, with the default gateway for the widely spanned VLAN located halfway across the campus. This obviously is inefficient, but is a consequence of using widely spanned VLANs in a traditional network deployment.

Large numbers of VLANs, if trunked everywhere in the network, also tend to lead to a very large CPU load for the necessary maintenance of all of the Spanning Tree processing on the network nodes involved, often leading to high CPU conditions on such critical network devices, as well as slow network reconvergence on failure or, in the worst cases, complete network outages.

And so, network engineering "best practices" tended to emphasize the increased use of Layer 3 in network designs, the maxim being "Route where you can, bridge where you must." And yet, this approach also was not problem-free, as discussed next.

Networking Protocols: Moving Up the Stack to Layer 3

Layer 3 traditionally uses two primary types of network protocols to influence traffic flow: first-hop reachability protocols such as Hot Standby Routing Protocol (HSRP) and Virtual Router Redundancy Protocol (VRRP), and routing protocols such as Open Shortest Path First (OSPF), Enhanced Interior Gateway Routing Protocol (EIGRP), and Border Gateway Protocol (BGP). They are briefly examined in turn. Let's consider what they accomplish, and the challenges they continue to face.

First-Hop Reachability Protocols: HSRP and VRRP

First, consider network-attached hosts that cannot route. This includes most desktops and laptops, most servers, printers, and in fact almost any device attached to a user subnet within the network. If you are building out the network using the most common traditional network deployment model—a Layer 2 access switch or switch stack, dual attached to two separate distribution switches for redundancy, with the Layer 2/Layer 3 boundary deployed at these distribution switches—how can the non-routing, end-user device know which distribution switch to pick to take traffic off of its subnet in such a case, when two paths exist?

HSRP and VRRP fulfill this task by assigning a common virtual MAC address to the distribution switch pair on the end-user subnet in question, with a common virtual IP address also shared between these two distribution nodes. The non-routing devices attached to the end-user subnet involved then simply direct the off-subnet traffic to this virtual MAC/IP combination as the default gateway, and the distribution node acting as the HSRP or VRRP master (as negotiated between the distribution nodes) then routes the traffic off-subnet as needed.

HSRP is commonly deployed in Cisco network environments, as it has existed for a long time and most Cisco network administrators are very familiar with it. VRRP is an alternative approach, standardized by the IETF, that performs a similar function. Both approaches make default gateway redundancy for non-routing devices possible, but introduce an increasing amount of control plane processing load between the HSRP or VRRP peer nodes as the number of subnets involved increases, or as first-hop redundancy protocol timers are reduced to provide for faster failover times. In larger networks with a large number of subnets and/or with reduced timers for faster reconvergence, this processing load can become burdensome.

In addition, the network manager for such a deployment must also take into account that their Layer 2 topology (created by Spanning Tree) and their Layer 3 topology (created by HSRP or VRRP) may not be congruent—the path that you might imagine would be followed by a host to reach its virtual default gateway at Layer 3 might not be the actual path as dictated by the blocking and forwarding ports in Spanning Tree at Layer 2. While not insurmountable, this makes both understanding and troubleshooting the network more complex (example: differences between MAC and Address Resolution Protocol [ARP] aging timers causing unexpected flooding of unicast traffic flows), and is an area often overlooked by many otherwise-conscientious network administrators.

Routing Protocols

The purpose of a routing protocol is to exchange routes for IP subnets between network devices, so that end-to-end reachability is established across an enterprise. Any routing protocol must perform this task.

Early routing protocols such as Routing Information Protocol (RIP) were based on the distance-vector approach and only considered hop count between devices as the routing metric, not taking into account factors such as link speed or bandwidth. In addition, the early versions of RIP only handled classful IP subnetting, and did not take advantage of classless IP addressing, which became very common over time. Although this was corrected with RIPv2, RIP as a protocol lacked flexibility and was discarded over time by most enterprises in favor of more sophisticated approaches.

Two protocols that emerged to replace RIP in many enterprise deployments were OSPF and EIGRP.

OSPF and EIGRP

Open Shortest Path First was standardized by the IETF and is a link-state protocol. It essentially builds a graph of the nodes within a network, and each node calculates its shortest path to other nodes within the topology. OSPF is designed to produce a stable, loop-free Layer 3 topology, and incorporates the ability to create separate OSPF areas that are used for route summarization, allowing for greater scalability and enhancing network stability. Although OSPF was very popular, the plethora of area and link types in OSPF rendered the protocol somewhat inflexible and complex for some.

Enhanced Interior Gateway Routing Protocol, a Cisco-proprietary protocol, adopts a hybrid approach between the distance-vector and link-state methods. EIGRP uses an algorithm called Diffusing Update Algorithm (DUAL) to produce a stable, loop-free topology. Unlike OSPF, EIGRP allows summarization at any network location (not just area boundaries), and tends to be simpler to plan and implement than an OSPF network design. However, the proprietary nature of EIGRP historically has limited deployments to Cisco-only routed network environments. It is worth noting, though, that EIGRP is now part of the IETF RFC process as RFC 7868 (https://tools.ietf.org/html/rfc7868).

Both EIGRP and OSPF were enhanced over time to support IPv6 as well as IPv4 addressing. Both are considered to be interior gateway routing protocols, meaning that they are designed to be deployed by organizations wherein the entire network is under a single administrative control.

BGP

Border Gateway Protocol is widely used as an inter-domain (or exterior) routing protocol—a routing protocol used to exchange routes between two or more routing domains administered by separate organizations. The design and capabilities of BGP excel at this task, being oriented to allow the controlled distribution of routing information, and providing for the fine-tuning of controls over the flow of data across administrative and organizational boundaries. BGP is also by far the most scalable of routing protocols, as evidenced by the fact that it is the sole routing protocol used within the Internet backbone, where many hundreds of thousands of routes exist. Like OSPF and EIGRP, BGP handles both IPv4 and IPv6 addressing.

However, while BGP is very capable, the number of available controls and capabilities within BGP render it somewhat complex for the typical enterprise network administrator to tackle. Thus, in any but the largest enterprise network backbones that need the scalability and control that BGP offers, BGP is used in most enterprise networks today (if at all) as a protocol for interfacing to the Internet, and possibly to exchange routes directly with other partner organizations (such as with an extranet configuration, where the fine-grained route control and filtering capabilities of BGP are very valuable).

Virtual Routing

OSPF, EIGRP, and BGP were also extended over time to support multiple virtual routing and forwarding instances (VRF). VRFs are an important consideration for many modern network deployments because they allow the segmentation of what would otherwise be a single, massive IP routing table for the entire enterprise into smaller, separate routing tables (VRFs). This has the very beneficial effect of allowing the network designer to separate out one IP routing spaces from another—for example, providing segmentation of Employees from Contractors, Guests from Staff, IoT devices from mission-critical systems, and many other examples.

Many enterprises found network segmentation using VRFs to be extremely beneficial to them—allowing them to more directly integrate security into their network designs, reducing the attack surface available to malware and other issues that might arise in the network, and allowing for the more direct control of traffic flows via firewalls between VRFs when so dictated by the organization's network and security policies.

VRFs are also very useful when, for example, two organizations merge, as the same IP address space (same subnets) can exist in two different VRFs without direct conflict, although network address translation (NAT) is still necessary if end devices in the two VRFs need to communicate with each other.

And yet, virtualized routing, network segmentation, and VRFs did not come without a price. That price was complexity.

Each VRF typically requires its own routing instance or address family to be configured and maintained on each network node. In addition, because the IP packet header has no place within the data plane to store the VRF information, it is necessary to tag the packets traveling between devices such that the receiving node knows which VRF context to route (and constrain) the packet within. Two approaches are commonly used for this: VRF-lite and MPLS.

The first approach is VRF-lite, which employs 802.1Q trunks between all network nodes and which uses distinct VLAN tags on each trunk, with one VLAN per trunk attached to each VRF instance. This has the benefit of being relatively simple to understand, but suffers from a large penalty in that it does not scale well. As the number of VRFs increases, so does the number of VLANs needed on trunks—often exponentially.

Consider, for example, a network node faced with 30 uplinks and downlinks and 20 VRFs. In this example, the network manager would need to create and maintain 600 unique VLANs (and associated subnets) on this one node alone, just to link it to its adjacent routed nodes in the network (i.e., unique VLANs and subnets per VRF, per link). Multiply this by a large number of routers across the network, and you can see how impractical this rapidly becomes to design, implement, and maintain. In addition, the creation of a new VRF in this model would necessitate reconfiguring every network device to connect the VRF end to end—hardly practical in a large, complex, and mission-critical enterprise network build.

Due to these limitations, VRF-lite deployments are not generally recommended above five to ten VRFs at a maximum, as they rapidly become far too cumbersome to deploy and manage beyond this limit (and may not even be practical below this). In those deployments which may not need more than a handful of VRFs, VRF-lite deployments are practical, and widely used in smaller implementations. However, as mentioned, scaling becomes an issue fairly rapidly if and when the number of VRFs grows, especially in environments without extensive configuration automation capabilities.

The other traditional option is Multiprotocol Label Switching (MPLS) or, more specifically, MPLS VPNs. Originally developed as a service provider technology, MPLS VPNs found a home with larger enterprise networks wishing to deploy network segmentation at a greater scale than can be easily accommodated by VRF-lite. MPLS VPNs do away with the per-hop VLAN/subnet tagging approach used by VRF-lite to sort out VRF traffic between nodes, leveraging instead a 4-byte MPLS label appended to all packets within the MPLS domain, and using a two-level MPLS tagging technique (i.e., two MPLS labels stacked together) between switches and routers in the network path for VRF separation and scalability.

However, again this comes at a price in terms of complexity. Network managers wishing to deploy MPLS VPNs must be ready to understand, deploy, and manage Multiprotocol Border Gateway Protocol (MP-BGP), Label Distribution Protocol (LDP), and MPLS-based quality of service (QoS), at a minimum, along with BGP-specific considerations such as route reflectors and the proper placement of customer edge (CE), provider edge (PE), and provider (P) routers. Although not insurmountable, this does represent a fairly steep learning curve for many enterprise organizations, and has proven over time to be a significant barrier to adoption of MPLS VPNs within enterprise network infrastructures. As well, careful planning is needed in an MPLS VPN build-out because not all network equipment supports MPLS tagging, and if additional capabilities such as multicast or IPv6 are in use, further device-level considerations and additional protocol and implementation complexities apply.

Due to these challenges and the considerable complexities involved, many enterprise organizations that may want what network segmentation can do for them—secure compartmentalization of different areas of the network from each other, reduction of network attack surfaces, and separation of discrete user communities, applications, and risk levels—have shied away from deploying network segmentation techniques end to end across their network environments currently.

Layer 2 over Layer 3

To add even more options, and more complexity, some organizations opt to tunnel Layer 2 traffic across their Layer 3 network—keeping the network segmented into separate VLANs and subnets, but selectively tunneling Layer 2 traffic between different areas over top of a Layer 3 transport. Various options exist, with the most common being deployed over top of an MPLS network transport. Capabilities include point-to-point Ethernet over MPLS (EoMPLS) pseudowires, and multipoint Virtual Private LAN Service (VPLS).

Although these allow Layer 2 traffic to be transported across a network backbone that is otherwise only routed in nature, they do nothing to alleviate the penalties associated with large, campus-spanning Layer 2 domains—STP processing loads on device CPUs, widespread broadcast propagation, inefficient looped topologies with blocking ports, and the ever-present risk of network outages caused by uncontrolled Layer 2 loops. And again, challenges with proper placement of the IP default gateway in such deployments often lead to traffic hairpinning at Layer 3, rendering traffic flows even more inefficient and difficult to understand and troubleshoot.

Thus, while Layer 2 tunneling techniques over Layer 3 can be employed, most network managers use these capabilities sparingly, if at all. Again, the users and applications in the network might call for such connectivity options, but most network managers deflect these requirements due to the compromises and potential risks they introduce into the network design as a whole.

Networking Protocols Today: Summary

One of the first observations to make about networks today is that they are complex. There are many choices to make—which STP protocol to select, how widely to span VLANs, whether and how to deploy network segmentation at Layer 3, which routing protocol to use, how to design the subnets across the organization—and many of these choices intersect with each other, often in complex (and sometimes nonobvious) ways. Optimizing for one layer often means compromising at another.

What's a network manager to do?

The various issues and challenges set forth in the preceding pages spurred the invention of some key new networking protocols and technologies—protocols to be explored in the subsequent pages of this chapter. These new capabilities offer novel approaches to network design that, when taken together, provide the basis for the new era of networking that the Cisco Digital Network Architecture offers.

Networking Protocols for the New Era of Networking

Now that we have examined the evolution of network protocols and capabilities—at Layer 1 with Ethernet, and Layer 2 with Spanning Tree, and at Layer 3 with various first-hop redundancy and routing protocols—you are better positioned to appreciate some of the new advances in networking that have recently become available and the options they offer for the further advancement and simplification of network design and deployment.

As described in the previous sections, the protocols that often are used to build many networks are functional but come with some significant limitations. Layer 2 network designs suffer from severe challenges concerning scale, broadcast propagation, and fragility when enabled over a wider area. Layer 3 network designs suffer from complexity driven by a proliferation of VLANs and subnets, complex routing protocol designs, and potential disparities between the Layer 2 and Layer 3 topology that make understanding traffic flows and troubleshooting more complex.

And, network segmentation adds further complexity with the use of multiple VRFs, the transport of these VRFs end to end across the network, and the intricacies involved with the design and support of VRF-lite or MPLS VPN solutions. In addition, it may still be necessary in some cases to transport Layer 2 across the Layer 3 network, necessitating even more complexity for Layer 2 tunneling technologies. While Ethernet at Layer 1 moved ahead over the years and provided many more connectivity options, the standard Layer 2 and Layer 3 protocols that are used to build networks have not changed significantly in several years.

Or have they? Let's look at some of the newest protocol developments and innovations, and start to explore how they can be used to address some of the shortcomings in network design today.

VXLAN: A Next-Generation Encapsulation Technology

Virtual Extensible LAN (VXLAN) encapsulation offers a new method of data encapsulation in modern network deployments. *Encapsulation* simply refers to "wrapping" one packet format inside another. Many network technologies such as Generic Routing Encapsulation (GRE), MPLS, etc. use encapsulation for data transport. So, what is different and new about VXLAN?

VXLAN is powerful in that, with a single encapsulation type, it supports the transport of both Layer 2 and Layer 3 packet information. This allows VXLAN to be used to encapsulate and transport any type of packet across the network—distinct, for example, from MPLS, which uses different methods to transport Layer 3 packets (MPLS VPN) and Layer 2 packets (VPLS or EoMPLS).

But, why do you even want to encapsulate data at all? In a word, flexibility. The use of encapsulation technologies allows you to build "overlays" within the network. The concept of overlays and underlays is explored further in Chapter 19, "Cisco DNA Software-Defined Access," because overlays are a crucial part of the SD-Access solution, but overlays are explored here first to outline the power that VXLAN encapsulation brings to network design.

An overlay is simply a virtual network topology, built on top of the underlying physical network (known as the underlay). Overlays might at first seem like a new concept. However, overlay technologies have been used for many years. For example, anyone using a Cisco centralized Wireless LAN Controller (WLC) deployment (one in which the APs all tunnel their data back to a central WLC) is using an overlay. In this case, the overlay is using the Control and Provisioning of Wireless Access Points (CAPWAP) protocol, running between the APs and the central WLC.

One of the things that many network managers appreciate about the centralized WLAN model is the simplicity it brings to wireless network design, deployment, and use. Much of this simplicity (smaller groups of larger IP address pools used for end-user provisioning, for example) is brought about because this WLAN deployment approach uses, and leverages, an overlay model. In the case of the centralized WLAN model, this involves tunneling all wireless user data, as well as all WLC and AP control plane communications, over the top of the underlay network, using CAPWAP encapsulation, back to the centralized WLC.

The concept of an overlay network is illustrated in Figure 9-6.

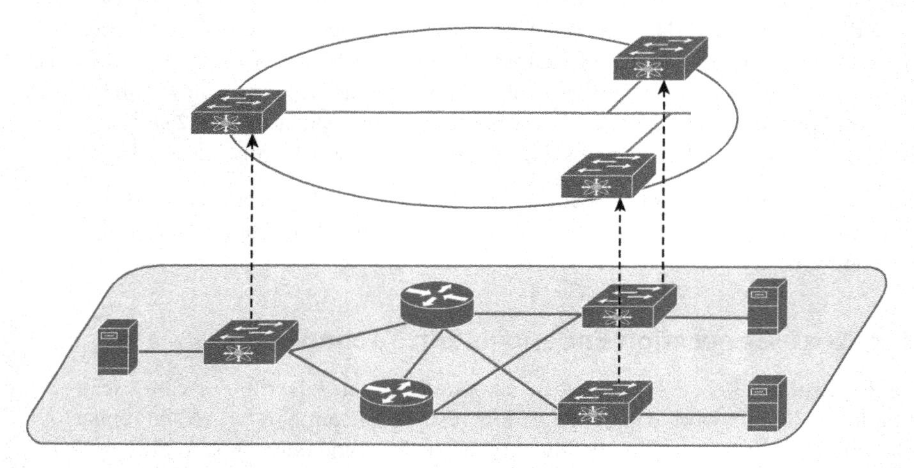

Figure 9-6 *Network Overlays—Overview*

Essentially, an overlay creates a logical topology used to virtually connect devices built on top of the arbitrary physical network topology (the underlay). Examples of network overlays include

- GRE or Multipoint GRE (mGRE)
- MPLS or VPLS
- IPsec or Dynamic Multipoint Virtual Private Network (DMVPN)
- CAPWAP
- VXLAN
- LISP (Location/ID Separation Protocol)
- Cisco Overlay Transport Virtualization (OTV)
- Cisco Application Centric Infrastructure (ACI)

With an overlay, the logical topology built within the overlay is distinct from that used by the underlying network infrastructure (the underlay). This allows the overlay to be designed separately from the underlay network, and to provide functions that the underlay network by itself may not be able to accommodate.

For example, the underlay network may be designed as a fully routed topology (i.e., routing all the way down to the wiring closet). This type of network design, known as a routed access design, has many desirable properties. It is very stable, scales nicely, reconverges very quickly around network outages, and provides excellent traffic load balancing by using Equal Cost Multipath (ECMP) for all routed traffic flows. Many organizations choose this fully routed network topology for these very reasons.

However, choosing this deployment method comes with trade-offs. With such a design, there is no way to extend a VLAN at Layer 2 between any two or more wiring closets—limiting flexibility for some types of applications which may need, or desire, a subnet to appear in more than one place in the campus.

This type of design also necessitates the generation, use, and ongoing support of a large number of subnets (at least one or more per wiring closet). In a large deployment, this can quickly become onerous to manage, and potentially wastes a large amount of IP address space (because each subnet needs to be sized to the maximum it might grow to in terms of the number of hosts it needs to support, which inevitably results in wasted IP address space during deployment and use).

Enter overlays. With an approach that leverages a VXLAN overlay, it is possible to get the best of both worlds: an underlay transport network that is entirely routed (and thus very stable, scalable, fast-reconverging, and with excellent traffic load-balancing capabilities) and an overlay network that provides more flexible services (such as the "stretching" of overlay IP subnets across wider areas, without having to incur the traditional issues associated with the wide-scale use of Spanning Tree and large, looped Layer 2 designs).

In essence, with an overlay-based network design, the network devices (switches and routers) attach to the underlay network, and the hosts (end users, devices, etc.)—the actual users of the system—attach to the overlay network. This has the hugely beneficial property that the underlay network is kept very static and stable (promoting higher availability, and thus supporting business continuity), while the constant change and churn of adding new users, devices, and services to the network takes place in the overlay (promoting rapid deployment and operation of new network functionality for the organization, without placing the network at risk).

This is illustrated in Figure 9-7, which illustrates the separation of the "forwarding plane" (underlay) from the "services plane" (overlay) within the network.

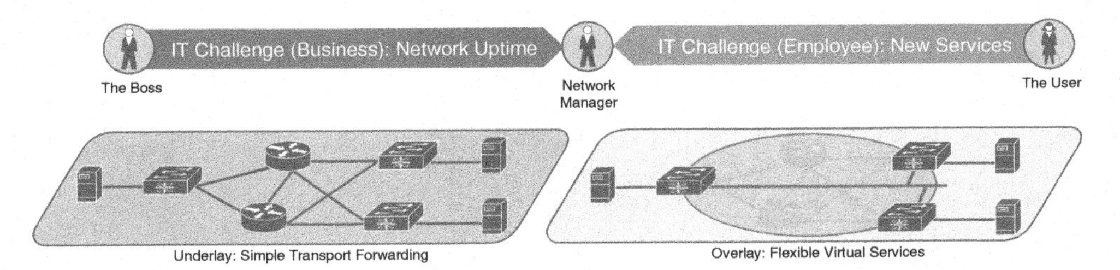

Figure 9-7 *Underlay and Overlay Separation*

Once you grasp the importance of the separation of functionality illustrated in the preceding figure, you will truly grasp the power and the importance of overlay networks, and why they have an ever-increasing place within modern network designs. The ability to create overlay networks such as this is why VXLAN is such an important tool in the network practitioner's toolkit.

And in fact, the use of VXLAN for the creation of an overlay network topology brings with it another important benefit. The VXLAN packet header contains space within it to store two pieces of additional data about the encapsulated packet it contains. This information, often called "metadata" (data about the data), is crucial, as it helps to provide additional context data about the transported packet—for the proper handling of the encapsulated packet itself within the overlay.

To best understand this, let's take a look at the VXLAN packet encapsulation format. Figure 9-8 outlines the VXLAN header.

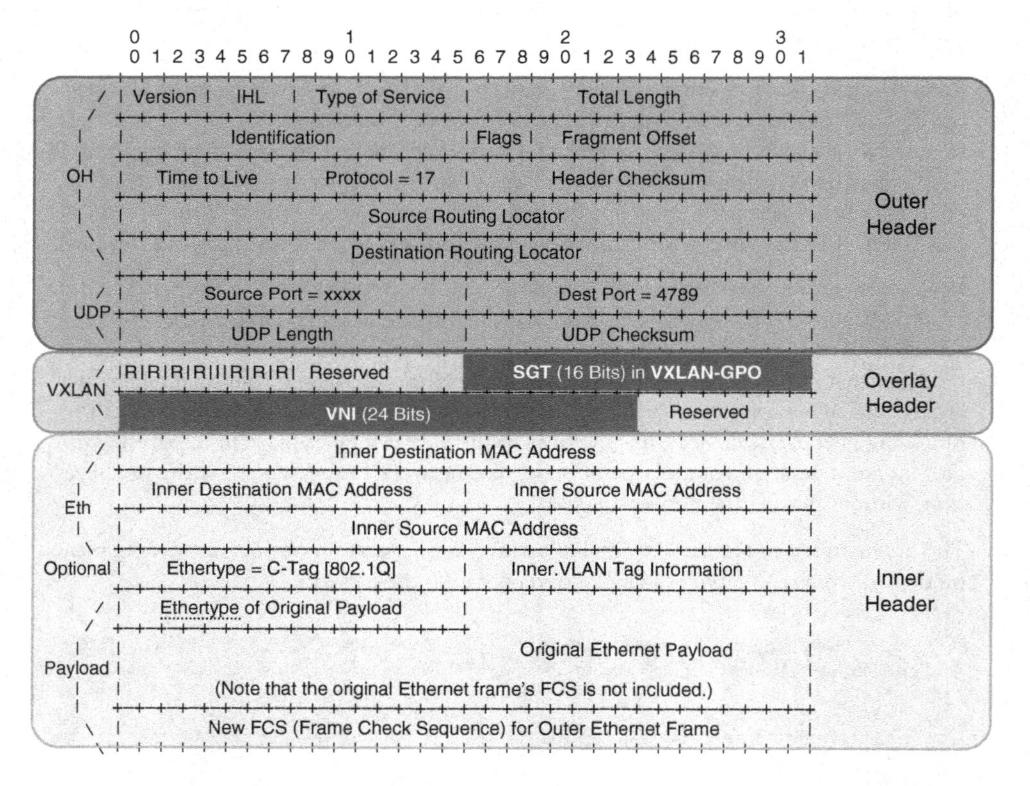

Figure 9-8 *VXLAN Packet Header Format*

By inspecting the preceding figure, a number of items quickly become apparent:

- VXLAN is a User Datagram Protocol (UDP)-based encapsulation. The outermost portion of the packet is a standard UDP format, and thus is routable by any IP-speaking device.
- The inner, encapsulated packet is an entire Ethernet Layer 2 frame, including the original source MAC, destination MAC, and original Ethernet header, in addition to the IP packet contained within it. This is critical because it means that VXLAN as a technology can be used to support both Layer 2 and Layer 3 overlay solutions.

- The VXLAN header, in between the outer UDP header and the inner encapsulated packet, provides areas within this header that are used to transport two very important pieces of packet metadata: a scalable group tag (SGT) value and a virtual network identifier (VNI) value. Taken together, as shown in the following text, these provide sufficient context about the inner, encapsulated packet to provide some very interesting and extremely useful additional capabilities for use within a VXLAN-based overlay network, especially around integrated network segmentation.

It should be noted that the VXLAN packet format outlined in Figure 9-8 constitutes the VXLAN-GPO (Group Policy Option) header format, as defined in the IETF Internet-Draft document located at https://tools.ietf.org/html/draft-smith-vxlan-group-policy-04. The VXLAN-GPO format is distinct from the more "basic" or generic VXLAN encapsulation because it also allows for the transport of the SGT value for the encapsulated packet in the VXLAN header. Additional information on VXLAN-GPO and its use in advanced solutions such as Cisco Software-Defined Access can be reviewed in the Cisco SD-Access white paper

> https://www.cisco.com/c/dam/en/us/solutions/collateral/enterprise-networks/software-defined-access/white-paper-c11-740585.pdf

A number of variations exist on the basic VXLAN header as defined in RFC 7348 (https://tools.ietf.org/html/rfc7348). The VXLAN-GPO header format is examined here in more detail, as this is the format used for the Cisco Software-Defined Access (SD-Access) solution, and outlined in more detail in Chapter 19. For brevity, "VXLAN" is used to refer to the VXLAN-GPO header format noted above, unless otherwise specified.

Let's examine the importance of each of the three points previously noted in terms of the provided value for a VXLAN-based overlay.

UDP Encapsulation

By using a standard UDP encapsulation as the outer packet header, any IP-speaking node can route a VXLAN-encapsulated packet. The source IP address in this outer VXLAN header is the node that is encapsulating the packet into VXLAN (known as a source VXLAN Tunnel Endpoint [VTEP] in data center nomenclature, or a source Routing Locator [RLOC] in Software-Defined Access), and the destination IP address in this outer UDP header is the node that decapsulates the packet out of VXLAN (destination VTEP/RLOC) for ultimate delivery to the end host involved.

By leveraging UDP in this way, intermediate network nodes (those between the source and destination RLOCs) do not need to know about, understand, or interpret the inner VXLAN packet headers. This is what allows VXLAN to operate as an overlay on top of the underlying, IP-based network infrastructure (the underlay). Of course, the outer UDP packet header also contains a Differentiated Services Code Point (DSCP) value, which can be copied from the inner (encapsulated packet) DSCP value, so intermediate nodes can still properly handle QoS even without having to understand VXLAN, or "look into" the inner encapsulated packet, to do so.

Virtual Network Support

The ability to embed a 24-bit VNI value in the VXLAN header is of tremendous value because it provides a method within the VXLAN overlay to transport the Virtual Network Identifier end to end across the network. This VNI corresponds to a VRF value, and with this capability, the VXLAN overlay provides end-to-end VRF transport, allowing packets entering one end of the overlay to be tagged with their correct VRF designation as they are encapsulated, and for that VRF value to be derived at the decapsulating VXLAN node and used to determine which VRF context to forward the inner packet within upon egress from the VXLAN overlay.

With the ability to transport VRFs end to end across the network as an inherent property, VXLAN provides an overlay transport that is aware of network segmentation and capable of supporting highly secure network infrastructures. This is hugely significant because it opens the door for many enterprises to build out a network segmentation solution end to end across their network, without having to touch every intermediate network node in the underlay to do so. As discussed in Chapter 19, network segmentation is one of the key pillars of the SD-Access solution, and one of the major benefits SD-Access provides.

Scalable Group Tag Support

As noted in a subsequent discussion in this chapter, SGTs provide a powerful method of "grouping" similar users and devices in the network for the purposes of policy application. By grouping similar users and devices together based on their authentication or device profile, enterprise-level policies (such as which group of users or devices is permitted to talk to another group, or blocked from such access) are easily defined, in a way that is separate from the IP addresses or subnets assigned to those users and devices.

This essentially provides a "level of abstraction" for defining access and other policies within the network infrastructure, making the definition and use of group-based policies a much more natural, and vastly simplified, capability for enterprises to deploy. By being able to carry the SGT value for a user or device end to end within the overlay packet header, VXLAN makes the use of group-based policies far more practical within an organization than ever before. As you'll read in Chapter 19, group-based policies are another key cornerstone capability offered by SD-Access, and when combined with network segmentation using VRFs, or virtual networks, offer a unique and compelling set of solutions for enterprise network deployments.

Summary: Why VXLAN?

As noted, VXLAN provides a set of data plane encapsulation functionalities that are critically important to be able to define an overlay network. These include the ability to transport both Layer 2 and Layer 3 data end to end across the network in the overlay (providing flexibility) and the ability to embed metadata attributes within the VXLAN header (VNI and SGT) that enable more context to be derived for the inner, transported packet (including context that supports network segmentation use cases and the provision and enforcement of group-based policies).

However, as important as VXLAN is, it is only part of the set of new protocols to be examined to support the next-generation evolution of network designs. VXLAN provides only the new basis for data plane encapsulation in an evolved network. In addition to this, three more areas equally important for next-generation network protocols:

- The evolution of underlay routing (IS-IS)
- The evolution of end-device reachability in the overlay (LISP)
- The evolution of device grouping for policy application (SGTs)

IS-IS: The Evolution of Underlay Routing

As a network routing protocol, Intermediate System to Intermediate System (IS-IS) has existed for a long time. Within service provider networks, IS-IS has had a substantial level of deployment and success over the years. Within the enterprise network, OSPF and EIGRP traditionally have been more widely used.

However, when beginning to build out the next-generation vision for enterprise network design and operation, IS-IS is worth another look, as it has some powerful attributes that make it a worthy contender for deployment as the routing protocol within the underlay portion of a network design.

Due to its simplified design and protocol-independent nature, IS-IS is very useful as a "bootstrap" routing protocol to initially bring devices up in the network—a critical consideration for simplified network deployments. IS-IS is also an extensible routing protocol, being able to utilize Type, Length, Value (TLV) attributes for propagation of routing information between nodes. This ability makes IS-IS ideal for the extension of new data types and routing information attributes in a next-generation network design because it can be used to transport additional routing data for current, or future, applications in building out the underlay network.

The Software-Defined Access solution does not mandate the use of IS-IS as the routing protocol in the underlay portion of the SD-Access network build. However, it is the protocol of choice should the network manager choose to let that underlay be built automatically using Cisco DNA Center. (This is discussed when SD-Access is examined in Chapter 19.) Doing so allows all of the previously mentioned advantages that accrue to IS-IS to be reaped within the network design.

LISP: The Evolution of Overlay Host Reachability

Cisco Location/ID Separation Protocol (LISP) offers a very significant advancement to the state of the art for routing and device reachability in networks. In the Cisco Software-Defined Access solution, LISP operates as the overlay control plane for user and device reachability, coordinating device access and allowing for user and device mobility within the overlay network infrastructure.

The basic functionality of LISP is easy to understand. Just as Domain Name System (DNS) provides the ability to resolve a human-readable name to an IP address (resolving the "who is?" question for a host or service), LISP provides the ability to resolve an IP address to a destination (i.e., what network device [switch or router] that user or device currently is located behind—resolving the "where is?" question for a host or service).

The basic operation of LISP is outlined in Figure 9-9.

DNS resolves **IP addresses** for a queried **name**.

Answers the "**who is**" Question

Who is lisp. cisco. com?

Host

DNS Server

Address is 153.16.5.29, 2610:D0:110C:1::3.

DNS
Name-to-IP
URL Resolution

LISP resolves **locators** for a queried **identity**.

Answers the "**where is**" Question

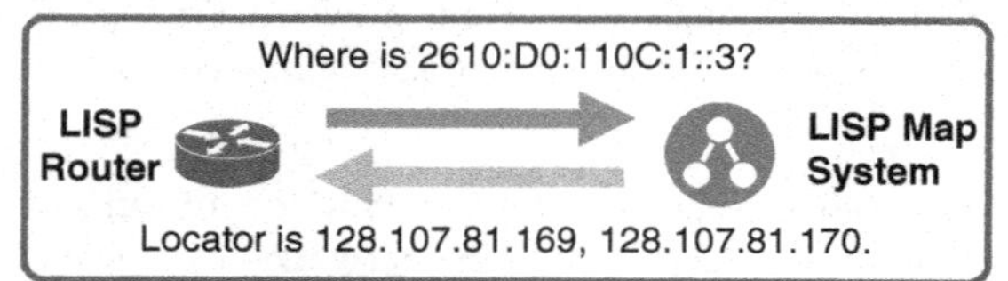

LISP
ID-to-Locator
Map Resolution

Figure 9-9 *LISP Overview*

As shown, LISP implements a mapping system (essentially, a database) containing information on all the hosts and end devices attached to the network, and noting their IP addresses, MAC addresses, or other information about them as needed, in addition to their location (i.e., which network device, such as a switch or router, they are located behind). Endpoints added to the LISP system in this way are known as Endpoint IDs (EIDs) and consist of individual hosts as well as entire subnets (for aggregation). This LISP database is built and maintained on a network device (such as a switch or router) or provided by a dedicated server.

As any end-user device connects to the network, the LISP-speaking device to which it attaches (such as a switch in the SD-Access solution, for example) populates the information about that device into the LISP mapping system database. Any other LISP-speaking node (for example, another switch) that has end-user traffic to deliver to that end-user device then simply queries the LISP mapping system and determines which LISP Routing Locator (RLOC, such as a switch or router) that end-user device is located behind.

Essentially, the LISP mapping system acts as a "single source of truth" about where any hosts or subnets are located at any point in time within the LISP-based infrastructure, and can always be consulted to determine the location of any endpoint. This behavior is outlined in more detail in Figure 9-10.

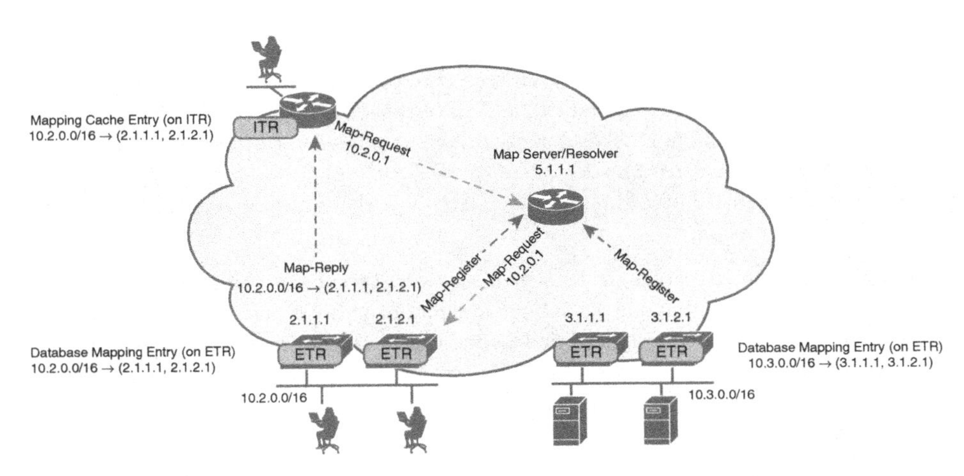

Figure 9-10 *LISP Operation*

Notice that LISP introduces a few new pieces of terminology, but these are easy to understand. An Ingress Tunnel Router (ITR) encapsulates incoming packets into an overlay, and an Egress Tunnel Router (ETR) decapsulates packets from the overlay and forwards them along to their destinations. Because most routers attached to the overlay perform both ingress and egress tunnel routing, these are commonly known as xTRs.

Also central to LISP is the concept of Map-Registration, as shown in Figure 9-10. In this example, the RLOCs involved (ITRs and ETRs) registered the subnets and hosts that are behind them into the LISP mapping database (Map-Server/Resolver) as these come online.

Any node that wants to talk to hosts in those subnets then simply queries the LISP database to determine how to reach hosts in these subnets—the Map-Request and Map-Reply shown in Figure 9-10. The Map-Request indicates which host or subnet is being looked up, and the Map-Reply indicates which RLOC, or set of RLOCs, can be used to reach that host or subnet.

Note that Figure 9-10 shows the "non-proxy" mode of operation of LISP, where LISP queries (Map-Requests) are sent from the ingress LISP-speaking switch or router to the LISP Map Server/Resolver node, and then forwarded along to the actual RLOC (switch or router) behind which the host lives, with that destination RLOC then replying to the source RLOC with the required location information. LISP also supports a "proxy" mode of operation in which the Map Server/Resolver responds directly back to the initial RLOC query on behalf of the destination, which simplifies the overall transaction somewhat. This proxy mode of LISP Map Server/Resolver operation is the mode that is used in SD-Access, which is examined in Chapter 19.

So why use LISP for reachability in the overlay? Why not use a traditional routing protocol? There are two primary advantages to the use of LISP for device reachability in the overlay: mobility and scale. Let's explore these and examine why LISP is ideal as a control plane protocol for use in current and future overlay network environments.

The Need for Host Mobility

It's a highly mobile world. The average user in an enterprise network has two to three devices (laptop, mobile phone, and tablet), and all of these are typically Wi-Fi equipped and used in a mobile fashion. Likewise, many other examples exist of mobile devices, such as handheld scanners, card readers, medical devices, mobile video cameras, and much more. Mobility is a fact of life. It is a key attribute that must be considered in an enterprise network design.

Traditional routing protocols do not lend themselves well to host mobility, however. Most routing protocols assume that a given subnet, and all of the hosts and devices contained within it, are fixed at a given location (tied to one wiring closet, for example). For traditional wired networks, where all the attached hosts are cabled back to a switch located within 100 meters, this assumption holds true. For wireless networks, and for highly mobile users, not so much.

To accommodate host mobility, wireless networks often tunnel all of the data from a user or device back to a central location (using a CAPWAP overlay, for example). This makes the user or device mobile in the RF domain (i.e., it can roam from AP to AP on that WLC as required), but at the same time the user or device stays fixed from a wired network perspective (i.e., to the wired network, that mobile user or device is always seen to be located on the other end of the link—likely an 802.1Q trunk—leading from the wired aggregation switch down to the WLC it services).

Although this is effective today, consider how wireless networks are evolving. Even with 802.11ac Wave 2, performance per access point scales above 1 Gbps (as mentioned in the preceding discussion of Ethernet evolution and mGig technology). In the future, these per-AP performance levels will scale even higher with 802.11ax and other technologies. How does a centralized WLAN solution—one that might be aggregating data from hundreds or even thousands of APs—keep up? Although larger and faster centralized WLCs are an option, sooner or later these may be outstripped by the growth in both the performance offered by individual APs and the sheer number of APs deployed in ever-proliferating wireless networks. When the limits of a centralized approach are reached, an alternative is needed.

The answer in networking is to allow the option to move to a distributed forwarding system, where data is routed farther out toward the edge of the network rather than all being trunked, and handled, centrally. Distributed data plane termination allows the network to scale, as compared to a purely centralized data plane approach.

As you will see, the use of LISP, with its mapping system used to track host locations as hosts move around the network environment, is ideally suited to this task as the data plane becomes distributed.

The Need for Host Scale

However, within the concept of a distributed data plane lies a problem—specifically, a challenge around scaling for mobile hosts. If mobile hosts and devices are moving around in the network, they will want to retain their IP address in many cases, and not change this address as they roam from an AP in one wiring closet to an AP in another (consider the impact on an IP-based phone call, for example, if the IP address changes midstream—the call will be dropped).

However, if an end user or device is to retain its IP address as it moves, it then becomes necessary to track that IP address across the network to determine reachability. Propagating the end device's IP addresses (/32 IPv4 or /128 IPv6) via a traditional routing protocol rapidly becomes impractical. Why? Consider the number of hosts that could exist (for example) in a university campus or other large site. With a midsized university hosting 40,000 students, faculty, and staff, and each of those users having three devices on average, and most or all of those users and devices being mobile, a routing protocol would have to carry approximately 120,000 items of information (/32 host routes) to track where all the users and devices are. Of course, add in IPv6 with multiple addresses per node and allow the network to scale over time, and the number of addresses balloons further.

Because the job of any routing protocol is to propagate all reachability information everywhere, and /32 or /128 hosts addresses by their nature are not summarizable in a mobile environment, this rapidly outruns the capacity of any network equipment's hardware tables (ternary content-addressable memories, or TCAMs)—especially the smaller edge devices often seen at the edge of network infrastructures (wiring closet switches). Never mind the very considerable control plane load that all of this mobility in such a campus would generate into any routing protocol trying to track it!

How can LISP help to address these two issues of host mobility and scale? Let's examine LISP further to find out.

LISP to Address the Host Mobility and Scale Needs of the Next-Generation Network

So how can LISP help? As noted previously, LISP works on the basis of separating location (host location) from identity (host IP). This is illustrated in Figure 9-11.

Because LISP separates the identity of a device from its location, it allows the host to retain the same IP address, even if it is mobile within the overlay portion of the network. When the host moves in a LISP-based system, only its locator IP (the IP address of the network node it is currently located behind) changes; the host's ID (its host IP address) remains unaltered. This overlay IP address for the host is then tracked in the LISP mapping system. And to aid in scalability, RLOCs (switches and routers) speaking LISP do not need to track the location of every device in the network all of the time as they would with a routing protocol—they only query for destinations *for which they have actual traffic*, which is typically only a small subset of all the devices in the network overall.

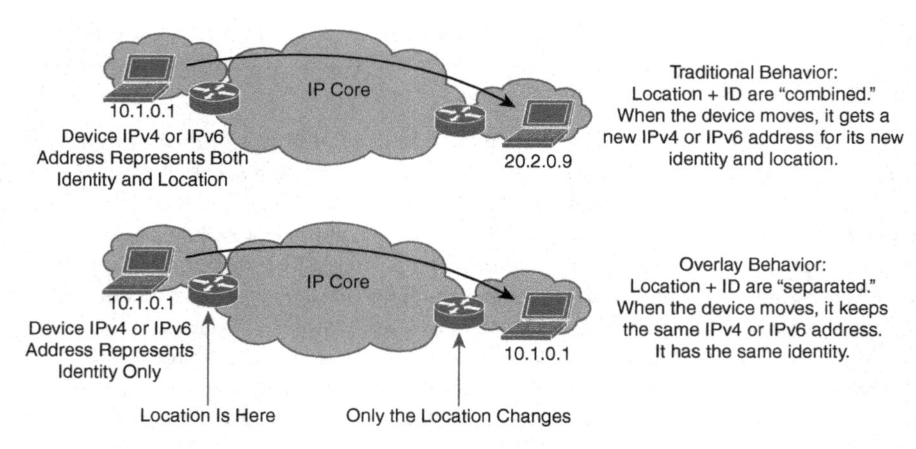

Figure 9-11 *LISP—Location and Identity Separation*

Also, once queried with LISP, this reachability information is then cached on the source RLOC, reducing its need to query the LISP mapping system database again for this information for subsequent traffic to that same destination.

The comparison between a traditional routing protocol approach and the LISP approach is illustrated in Figure 9-12.

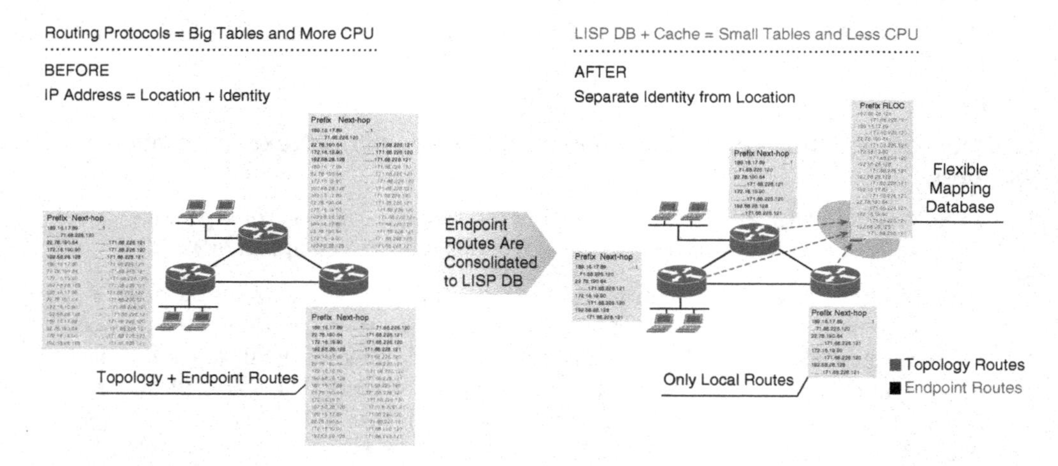

Figure 9-12 *LISP Versus Traditional Routing Protocols*

As shown, LISP scales much better for the demanding task of mobile host tracking than a traditional routing protocol. The task of a routing protocol is to flood all information (in this case, hosts) everywhere and ensure that all nodes have a consistent "picture" of the network at any point in time (i.e., that the routing protocol is "converged"). Although this makes sense with a smaller collection of aggregated and relatively stable subnet routes (which is what routing protocols handle), it is not necessarily a good match of a large collection of rapidly changing, mobile host routes.

It is also important to note that the task of flooding the host information to all of the switches and routers involved, in the manner that a traditional routing protocol would, could easily exhaust hardware resources (TCAM space and CPU utilization) in edge network devices, as previously noted. A traditional routing protocol approach would flood this information to all network nodes, even when many of the network devices involved may not have any traffic destined for many of the hosts in that network.

By way of contrast, LISP, with its on-demand host lookup capabilities from a centralized mapping system and its ability to cache host information on edge network nodes once it is so looked up, is a much better match for the demanding task of keeping track of a large number of mobile hosts in the network. By avoiding the flooding of host information, and allowing the destination host's location to be looked up only when traffic is actually traversing an edge network node to a given destination, LISP provides a more scalable solution for host mobility than a traditional routing protocol.

LISP operates with much more economy of resource utilization on edge network devices, due to its on-demand lookup nature, which retrieves and uses destination host information from the LISP mapping system only when traffic is actually presented for that destination host by a user or device. This economy of network device resource utilization is a key consideration, given the relatively constrained amount of TCAM space and CPU resources typically available on smaller edge campus switches.

So how does LISP work to support a highly mobile network environment? Let's explore this by walking through how an individual host is handled as it roams within a LISP-based infrastructure.

Examination of LISP Roaming Operation

Referring back to Figure 9-10, image we have a host with the IP address 10.2.0.1, which is located behind the RLOC (switch loopback address) 2.1.1.1 (for now, we will ignore the second switch in the diagram, noted as 2.1.2.1, because this is not critical to understanding how basic roaming works in LISP).

Initially, this 10.2.0.1 host is located in its "home subnet" (10.2.0.0/16), which is the subnet normally defined as attached to the 2.1.1.1 switch. The LISP Map Server/Resolver (abbreviated to MS/MR—a software function running on a switch, router, or server somewhere in the infrastructure) is notified by the 2.1.1.1 RLOC that this host is in fact attached and active. This is done when this host first "comes up" on the network, by way of a LISP Map-Register notification from the 2.1.1.1 RLOC to the LISP MS/MR. In this way, the LISP MS/MR knows where this host is, and can resolve requests for the host's location that may come in from other RLOCs in the system, allowing such RLOCs to forward data to this host appropriately.

Now, let us suppose that the 10.2.0.1/32 host roams over to the right-hand-side RLOC shown in Figure 9-10, the switch noted as 3.1.1.1 (again, we will ignore the second RLOC noted as 3.1.2.1 to clarify the description of roaming here). Such a roam could occur, for example, with a wireless host that is using a distributed wireless data plane termination approach (which, as will see later, is what SD-Access employs). In this case, the wireless host wishes to keep its existing IP address—but this address does not match the destination subnet present on the 3.1.1.1 RLOC (which is the 10.3.0.0/16 subnet).

How can LISP track this roaming host and continue to provide reachability? It's actually quite straightforward.

The roamed-to RLOC, upon sensing the device roam, sends a new Map-Register notification to the LISP MS/MR, which updates its mapping table to indicate that this roaming host (10.2.0.1/32) is now located behind the 3.1.1.1 RLOC. Subsequent to this, the LISP MS/MR also sends an update to the roamed-from RLOC to indicate that this host (i.e., this individual /32 IP address, 10.2.0.1) has roamed and is now located behind the 3.1.1.1 RLOC.

The 2.1.1.1 RLOC then updates its tables to indicate that this host has roamed, and what its new location (i.e., new RLOC, 3.1.1.1) is in the system, caching this information for future use. Caching reduces the load on the LISP MS/MR, because previously queried-for destinations can simply be satisfied out of the local cache, avoiding an unnecessary lookup. After this has transpired, the 2.1.1.1 RLOC now knows where this host (10.2.0.1/32) roamed to, so it realizes that the host is no longer local to itself, and therefore sends any required traffic along to this new destination as needed (encapsulating this via a VXLAN overlay if this is in use—which, as you will see in Chapter 19, is the approach used by the SD-Access solution).

So, as you can see, mobility and roaming in LISP are very efficient and a natural part of how the protocol operates. This is why LISP is ideal for handling host reachability in highly mobile environments—like most enterprise networks—and why LISP is used as the reachability control plane for the overlay in SD-Access.

But, you may be asking yourself, with all of this caching going on, what happens if a node ends up with a stale cache entry that points to the wrong destination (i.e. what would happen if the top-left RLOC in Figure 9-10 had an older cached entry for 10.2.0.1/32 that pointed to the 2.1.1.1 RLOC, even after this host had roamed over to the 3.1.1.1 RLOC)?

LISP handles this situation easily. If the 2.1.1.1 RLOC received traffic from the top-left RLOC in Figure 9-10 for the 10.2.0.1/32 (roamed) host, it would send a Solicit Map Request (SMR) message back to this top-left RLOC (the one with the stale cache entry). This SMR message tells the originating RLOC that the cached information it has is out of date, and forces this RLOC to re-query the LISP MS/MR for up-to-date mapping information. The originating top-left RLOC in this picture will then re-query the LISP MS/MR database to learn where the roamed host has moved to (RLOC 3.1.1.1, in this example), and then update its own local LISP map cache accordingly. This then allows the top-left RLOC to forward traffic along to the correct 3.1.1.1 RLOC from that point forward for this roaming host. Problem solved!

To complete the connectivity picture, there are a few additional complexities to deal with around the use and extension of the default gateways to the various RLOCs in the system, but as we will see in Chapter 19, SD-Access solves this with the employment of the Distributed Anycast Default Gateway capability inherent in an SD-Access deployment.

There is a lot more to LISP than the brief overview provided here, but this should serve to provide an introduction into how LISP operates. For further details, please refer to the soon-to-be-published *The LISP Network: Evolution to the Next-Generation of Data Networks* (Cisco Press, 2018).

Summing Up: LISP As a Next-Generation Overlay Control Plane

LISP makes an ideal control plane for host reachability as the network moves toward overlays. LISP checks all of the right boxes—lightweight in nature (similar to a DNS lookup), simple to understand, rapid in operation, and very conservative with its use of scarce hardware resources such as TCAM tables and CPU cycles in network devices—thus making LISP ideal for host mobility in today's distributed, highly dense, highly mobile workplaces.

This is why LISP is used as the protocol of choice for host reachability in the SD-Access overlay—which is examined further in Chapter 19.

Now, let's move on to the last evolved network protocol that is examined in this chapter, Scalable Group Tags (SGTs), which are part of the larger Cisco solution set known as TrustSec.

Scalable Group Tags: The Evolution of Grouping and Policy

Scalable Group Tags (SGT) help to address one of the other really significant challenges facing enterprise networks: the creation and application of network policies.

"Policy" may seem to be one of those very abstract words for which it is hard to pin down the meaning. However, it's actually quite simple. Policies are used in networks constantly. Do you have ACLs deployed in network devices for traffic filtering? If so, then you have an access policy. Maybe you have QoS deployed and sorting traffic into different queues to prioritize transmission? You have a QoS policy. Matching traffic to different profiles to send it over one WAN transport versus another? You have a traffic engineering policy. There are many examples of how policies are used in networks today.

And yet, what is one of the key challenges with defining and rolling out policies? In existing networks, policies are all tied to IP addresses. Think about the policies you may have deployed in network devices. In one way or another, they all reference the "5-tuple" used in IP packet headers—source IP address, destination IP address, source port, destination port, and protocol (TCP, UDP, etc.)—those 104 bits in the IPv4 header, when combined with the 6 bits used for DSCP, are what are used to craft policies, which reference devices and endpoints by these items.

These IP-based 5-tuple values are the only "transitive attributes" that survive end to end with the packet as it moves from source to destination over the network, and so policies in use today are coupled to them. Think about that for a second: when you are writing a security ACL, you are directly transcribing your IP subnet structure into the ACL definition and deployment. This is because there are no fields in the IP header that directly contain user or device identity or group information—so IP addresses are used as a proxy for this, as illustrated in Figure 9-13.

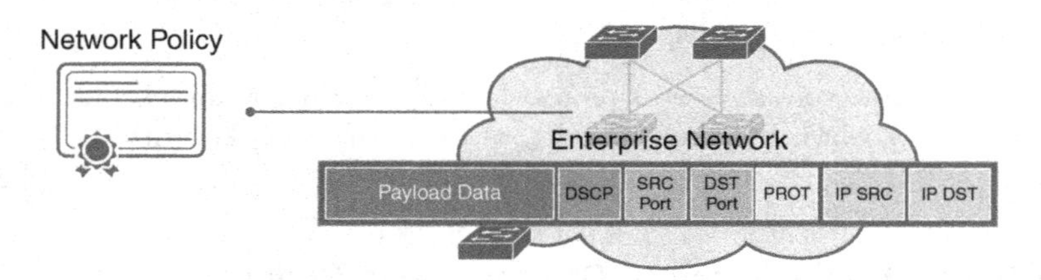

Figure 9-13 *Policy in Networks Today—Based on the IP "5-Tuple"*

So, what's the issue with defining policies this way? In a word, complexity.

Basically, because the IP address is the only transitive element that moves with the packet end to end, it is overloaded with meaning today. As illustrated in Figure 9-14, an IP address today is "overloaded" to provide the following:

- **Location:** Subnets are directly tied to fixed network locations.
- **Identity:** On a first-hop device, or on a firewall ten hops away, the IP address is inspected and directly used as a proxy for identity to apply policy (pass/drop, for example).
- **Drive traffic treatment:** Inspection of the IP address/subnet is directly tied to policy on how the traffic will be treated (path selection or QoS, for example)

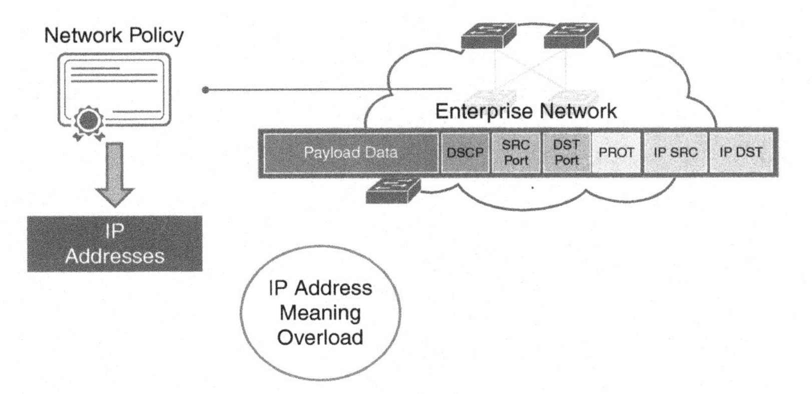

Figure 9-14 *Policy in Networks Today—Overloaded Meaning with IP Addresses*

And importantly, the use of subnets also drives inherent constraints. Ask most network managers if they ever get requests to extend a subnet between multiple wiring closets in a campus for custom applications. They will often say yes. Then, ask if they fulfill such requests, and most will say no, they do not stretch subnets like this on request—due to all the issues noted previously in this chapter with large-scale Layer 2 networks and the risks these pose to the network infrastructure. So, there is an implicit policy (no subnet stretching) associated with many large-scale enterprise network designs, again directly tied to the IP subnet/VLAN structure.

So, what's the outcome of all this "overloading" of IP addresses in the network for policy? Again, in a word, complexity. Lots of subnets. A proliferation of wireless service set identifiers (SSID). Longer and ever longer and more complex ACLs that have to enumerate all of these subnet structures for traffic filtering.

Many network managers are faced with ACLs in network devices and firewalls that are hundreds, or even thousands, of lines long—and that are so large and complex in many cases that no one really understands the totality of what all of the ACL entries do any more, or why these ACL entries were placed there in the first place (remember, you might be managing this ACL, but it may have first been created by someone else, possibly years earlier, possibly someone who is not even with the organization any more).

The result: when new security requirements come along, it's likely that more new ACL entries might just get tacked onto the end of the ACL, and old ACL entries are never deleted (because the effects of deleting such entries may not be well understood, and could cause a network outage, or a security breach).

All of this is illustrated in Figure 9-15.

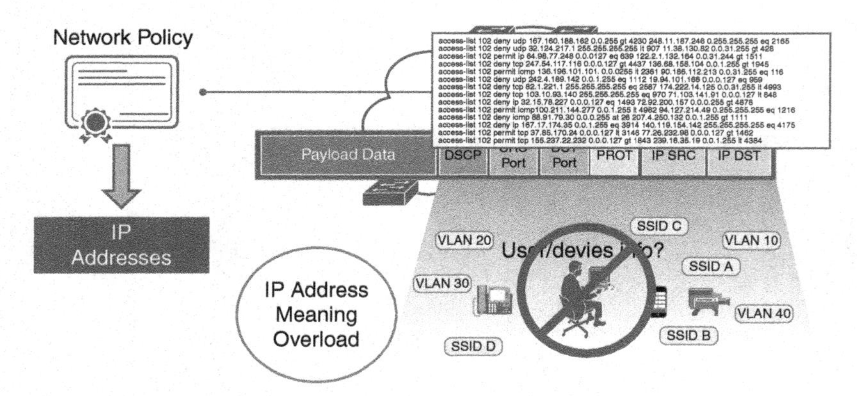

Figure 9-15 *Policy in Networks Today—Outcomes and Challenges*

Essentially, in networks you end up using VLANs and SSIDs as grouping methods to apply policy. Adding voice to your network? Carve out a bunch of voice VLANs, and the subnets associated with them. Adding in Internet of Things (IoT) devices? More VLANs, more subnets. Add in IP-based video systems, door locks, badge readers, cameras, and all of the other current (and future) additions to our IP networks—and then consider properly securing them from each other, and from the outside—and you begin to see the enormity of the problem, as illustrated in Figure 9-16.

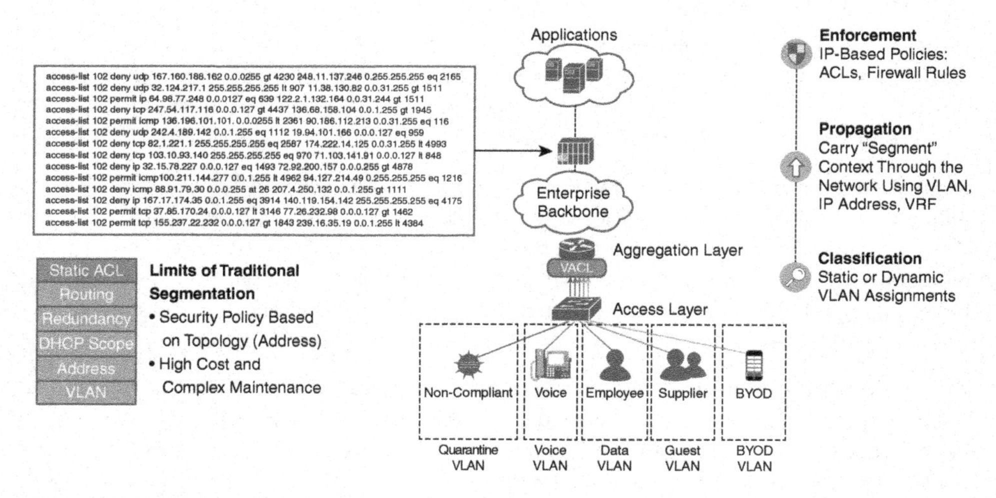

Figure 9-16 *Complex Security Policy Definition and Application Today*

This is why networks can have thousands of VLANs and subnets in them—coupled with very large and complex ACLs to secure all of these VLANs. VLANs and ACLs are often used as policy tools. And when the only tool you have is a hammer, everything looks like a nail. Net result: many organizations find it very cumbersome, error prone, and time consuming to roll out new network-based services and secure them properly (and securing the network is a necessity, given the ever-increasing number of cyber threats present in current, and future, network environments).

What if there was a better way to group users and devices to apply policy? There is. This is where Scalable Group Tags come in.

Scalable Group Tags for Group-Based Policies

Scalable Group Tags, or SGTs, are small, 16-bit tags assigned to users and devices as they connect to, and authenticate into, the network.

This authentication can be very simple and static (example: plug into this switch port or associate to this SSID, and you are assigned to tag X) or can be more sophisticated and dynamic (example: use 802.1X for dynamic validation of username/password or other device credentials on wired or wireless mediums, and get assigned into groups X, Y, or Z based on that authentication, or be profiled as a device of a particular type, and get assigned to groups Q, R, or S based on what type of device it happens to be). To assist with these authentication requirements, an authentication, authorization, and accounting (AAA) server such as Cisco Identity Services Engine (ISE) is often used.

This SGT tag value is assigned to the user's traffic on ingress at the first-hop network device, based on their authentication, and carried across the network to the last-hop network device, where (for example) an access-control policy in place on that device decides whether to forward or drop the packet involved based on whether those two groups (source and destination) were allowed to, via defined enterprise network policy, communicate with each other. This is illustrated in Figure 9-17.

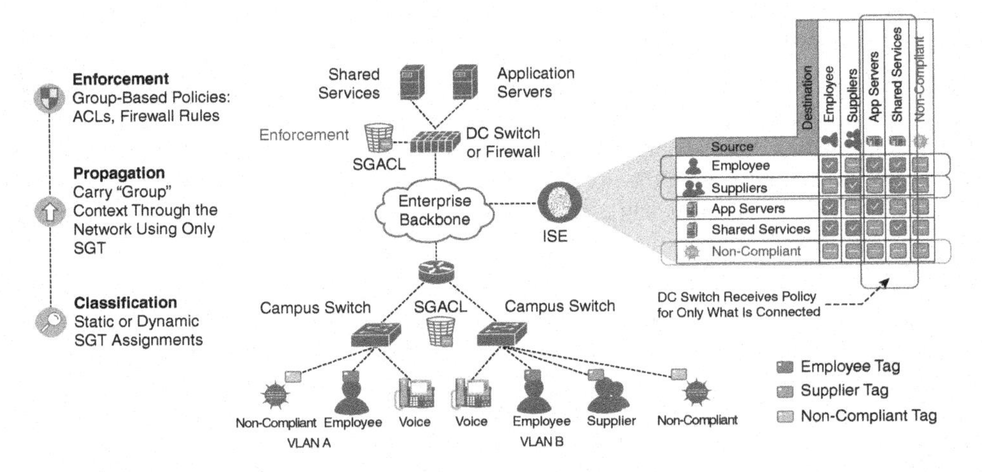

Figure 9-17 *SGT—Segmentation Based on Groups*

As illustrated, the SGT tags, and their definitions, are defined on the central authentication authority for the network—Cisco Identity Services Engine—along with the policies of which group interactions are permitted or denied. These policies are then dynamically downloaded to network devices, which apply the policies locally for enforcement.

For security policies based on SGTs, enforcement is typically done on egress, using Scalable Group Access Control Lists (SGACL), as illustrated in Figure 9-18. This has the beneficial property that it is then not necessary to insert policies for every possible egress destination at every ingress point to the network—a property that massively aids in the ability to scale policy enforcement in highly distributed network architectures.

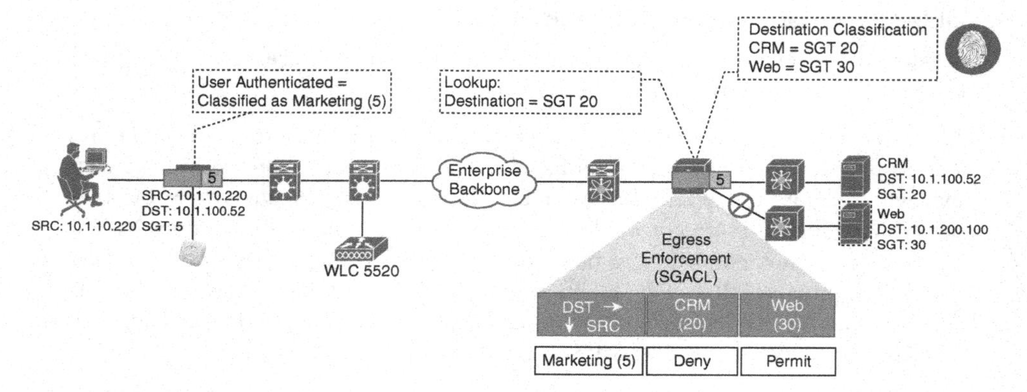

Figure 9-18 *Ingress Classification with Egress Enforcement*

Unlike traditional ACLs, which contain references to IP addresses, SGACLs contain references only to group information (SGTs) and Layer 4 port information (for applications). This makes SGACLs more compact, and easier to understand and maintain, than their IP-based counterparts. The exact meaning of the enterprise policies involved—this group can talk to that group, but not to this other one—is concisely coded into the SGACLs and is very easy to parse and understand.

Effectively, SGTs and SGACLs provide a level of "abstraction" for the grouping of devices and users in the network, allowing for a much more natural way to group similar devices and users together, and to apply policy to them and between these as discrete groups, in a way that is decoupled from the device's underlying IP address. This level of abstraction provided by SGTs is an extremely useful and powerful concept.

If you ask network managers what they want to accomplish when securing their network environments, they will always say, in effect, "I want to allow this group of users and things to have access to that group of users and things, and block access between these other sets of groups." Today, a network technologist then has to take this desired outcome for the business and translate it into the language of VLANs, subnets, and IP-based ACLs—an inherently complex and fragile method of policy expression, and one that has definite scaling, management, and ongoing policy maintenance challenges that most network managers are only too familiar with.

By way of contrast, the use of Scalable Group Tags and SGACLs allows for a far more natural way of expressing and transporting group membership in the network, and expressing the policies to be used for traffic flow between groups—in a way that is decoupled from (i.e., not dependent on) the IP address of the devices involved. This in turn makes expressing and implementing network policies a far more natural outcome in the network, and one that addresses the scaling and complexity concerns that otherwise arise in many of today's network deployments.

SGT Transport End-to-End Across the Network

SGTs as a technology have existed for some years as part of the Cisco TrustSec initiative. However, they have had only limited deployment in the past, due to the difficulty of carrying the SGT tag metadata end to end in the data plane, across the heterogeneous network environments often deployed in enterprises, with a mixture of old and new hardware and software versions (as some older hardware and software versions in platforms cannot handle or propagate SGTs). This is illustrated in Figure 9-19.

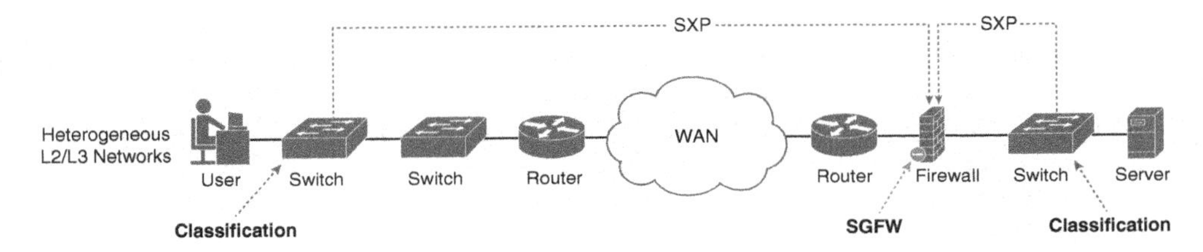

Figure 9-19 *Challenges with SGT Propagation in a Heterogeneous Network*

As illustrated, various capabilities such as SGT Exchange Protocol (SXP, a TCP-based protocol used to map individual IP addresses to SGT tags) exist for environments that cannot carry an SGT tag end to end in the data plane (which many enterprise networks cannot). However, such capabilities can be challenging to deploy and manage at scale.

The ideal situation is to transport the SGT tag inline with the data packet as it moves across the network, but in a traditional network environment, this means that every network device, and every network link, between any two (possibly widely separated) points on the enterprise network needs to be SGT capable (i.e., each device and each link must be capable of inserting, transporting, and/or removing SGT tags). Unfortunately, this is often not the case, due to the plethora of network gear of different vintages often deployed across many enterprise networks.

But wait! Now that the ability to build out overlay networks with VXLAN is possible, you can carry the SGT end to end in the VXLAN packet header—and only the ingress nodes and the egress nodes for the overlay (not the intermediate nodes) need to be able to handle and interpret the SGT tag metadata information contained within the VXLAN header.

This vastly simplifies the problem, and makes the use of SGTs for group-based policies far more practical in many enterprise network designs, as illustrated in Figure 9-20.

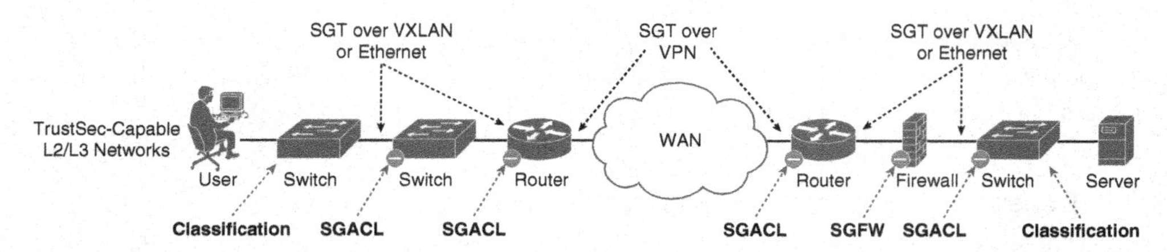

Figure 9-20 *SGT Propagation and Enforcement with an Overlay Network*

Bringing It All Together: What Next-Generation Protocols Within the Network Allow Us To Build

It's all starting to gel together, isn't it?

If you stop and think about it, the evolved network protocols just examined—VXLAN as an evolved data plane, IS-IS as an evolved underlay routing protocol, LISP as an evolved overlay reachability protocol, and SGTs and SGACLs as an evolved method of providing grouping and policy—when taken together, really allow an entirely different—in fact, a radically novel and innovative—approach to be taken for next-generation network design, implementation, and support.

This is an approach that is focused on solving the most important issues facing enterprise networks: complexity, security, speed of deployment, ease of management, and rapidity and accuracy in policy definition and enforcement.

This is the exact approach adopted by the Cisco Software-Defined Access solution. And as you will see in Chapter 19, SD-Access leverages many of these next-generation network protocols to help build out the solution. That's why so much time was spent talking about these protocols here, and explaining their operation and benefits!

But before you examine SD-Access in detail, you'll be introduced to other key areas of Cisco DNA. Automation, assurance, and virtualization all play vital roles in laying the groundwork for next-generation network design, implementation, deployment, and support. These topics are discussed in the next several chapters.

Congratulations! You made it through flexible hardware, evolved software, and next-generation protocols. Now, onward and upward with virtualization!

Summary

This chapter introduced and explored the following topics:

- The use of existing network protocols today, and the challenges associated with them
- The evolution of physical layer protocols such as Ethernet, as well as the evolution of Layer 2 and Layer 3 networking

- The movement toward underlay and overlay separation in enterprise network designs, and the benefits of this approach
- The use of VXLAN as an evolved overlay data plane
- The use of IS-IS as an evolved underlay routing protocol
- The use of LISP as an evolved overlay reachability protocol
- The use of SGTs as an evolved grouping mechanism for simplified policy application

Further Reading

Cisco TrustSec—White Papers, At-a-Glance documents, Case Studies, Design Guides, Presentations, and Solution Overviews. https://www.cisco.com/c/en/us/solutions/enterprise-networks/trustsec/white-paper-listing.html.

Cisco TrustSec Accelerates and Simplifies Network Security Solution Overview. https://www.cisco.com/c/en/us/solutions/collateral/enterprise-networks/trustsec/solution-overview-c22-737173.html

Segment Your Network for Stronger Security. https://www.cisco.com/c/dam/en/us/products/collateral/security/stealthwatch/network-segmentation-ebook.pdf

Farinacci, D., and V. Moreno. *The LISP Network: Evolution to the Next-Generation of Data Networks.* Indianapolis: Cisco Press; 2018.

RFC 6830. "The Locator/ID Separation Protocol (LISP)." January 2013. https://tools.ietf.org/html/rfc6830.

RFC 7348. Virtual eXtensible Local Area Network (VXLAN): A Framework for Overlaying Virtualized Layer 2 Networks over Layer 3 Networks. August 2014. https://tools.ietf.org/html/rfc7348.

Chapter 10

Cisco DNA Infrastructure—Virtualization

The previous chapters focused on the hardware and software innovations that Cisco DNA offers: the flexibility of introducing new protocol and feature innovations into the Unified Access Data Plane (UADP) or the QuantumFlow Processor (QFP) as new technologies emerge, and the functional and operational consistency that Cisco IOS XE provides across all parts of the architecture, including switching and routing. This chapter adds another tool to the Cisco DNA toolbox—virtualization. It focuses on the virtualization of those functions that manipulate and forward packets—that is, on Cisco Network Function Virtualization (NFV)—instead of virtualizing application workloads. This chapter also discusses *transport virtualization*, the segmentation of the transport network to offer virtual networks.

Network Function Virtualization allows you to run network functions inside virtual machines on standard Intel x86–based hosting platforms. Many of the tenets of Cisco DNA outlined in Chapter 5, "The Cisco Digital Network Architecture Blueprint," are supported by virtualization. NFV is inherently *software driven*. These functions are typically much easier to deploy, especially when combined with *programmability*. A *virtualized network function (VNF)* is spun up within minutes, triggered by a REST, RESTCONF, or NETCONF call. This also allows you to *extend* the network services in Cisco DNA easily. Many of the VNFs under consideration provide additional security functionality, supporting the tenet of *security* in Cisco DNA. Furthermore, the virtualization architecture in Cisco DNA is fully *open*, offering application programming interfaces (APIs) at all software layers to partners or customers, and even allowing the instantiation of third-party VNFs to give you even more deployment flexibility. NFV is thus a prime example of how Cisco DNA changes the architecture to align the network with your business intent.

Transport virtualization has been a standard tool in building enterprise networks for many years now. User traffic is segmented from each other by means of virtual LANs (VLANs), Virtual Extensible LAN (VXLAN), or virtual routing and forwarding (VRF) instances. More recently, concepts like Cisco TrustSec Security Group Tagging (SGT) gained popularity as enhanced policy-based mechanisms for segmentation.

This chapter explains the following:

- Benefits of virtualizing network functions
- Use cases for virtualization
- The building blocks of a virtualized system architecture
- Challenges and deployment considerations
- Transport virtualization

The chapter begins by reviewing some of the benefits that virtualization offers, organizing these around architectural, operational expenditure (OPEX), and capital expenditure (CAPEX) benefits. The following section then describes the use cases that emerge in the enterprise today: virtualizing control plane functions, simplifying branch architectures with virtualization, virtualizing the connectivity to multiple cloud environments, and virtualizing network functions in the cloud. The subsequent section then delves into the overall system architecture of an x86-based host running multiple VNFs. Particular attention is given here to the various input/output (I/O) mechanisms that are available to share physical interfaces among multiple VNFs, since this is often a bottleneck in the overall architecture. This chapter then elaborates on the dominant challenges that Network Function Virtualization introduces, such as understanding the attainable performance when running multiple VNFs side by side, or deciding the granularity with which VNFs should be deployed from a multitenancy and multifeature perspective. The latter part of this chapter then reviews transport virtualization in detail, highlighting different methods for segmentation of the data plane (e.g., TrustSec, VLANs, VxLANs, VRFs) as well as the control plane segmentation.

Benefits of Network Function Virtualization

Virtualization of application workloads has been extremely successful for IT departments over the past decade. Prior to application virtualization, many servers were dedicated to host a small number of applications, the servers often running at single-digit utilization levels and thus incurring a lot of costs. Application workload virtualization proved that a common x86-based hosting platform can be shared to use the underlying host hardware resources more efficiently. This proof point inspired the idea of virtualizing network functions to reap similar cost benefits. In addition to total cost of ownership (TCO) benefits related to OPEX and CAPEX, NFV can also be leveraged to change the overall network architecture.

The following sections discuss the CAPEX, OPEX, and architectural benefits of NFV in detail

CAPEX Benefits of NFV

NFV promises to reduce capital expenditures by deploying standard Intel x86–based servers instead of dedicated hardware appliances. In an appliance-based model, specialized networking appliances are deployed to deliver networking functions, in particular so-called Layer 4—Layer 7 functions (WAN optimization, intrusion detection and prevention, network or port address translation, etc.). Such appliances are often more expensive than x86-based server platforms. Furthermore, a standard x86-based server can host multiple virtualized network functions, allowing for the same hardware architecture to be used for multiple purposes. This promises to deliver CAPEX benefits on two fronts:

- **Economies of scale:** Leveraging the same hardware platform for multiple functions may allow for larger-volume discounts from server vendors. This is especially the case if the same server platform used in your data centers for application workload hosting is leveraged.
- **Reduction in hardware purchases:** Consolidation of multiple virtualized network functions into the same hosting platform can reduce the total number of hardware devices that need to be acquired and operated.

Table 10-1 outlines the CAPEX benefits of NFV.

Table 10-1 *CAPEX Benefits of Network Function Virtualization*

CAPEX Benefit of NFV	Description
Deployment of standard x86-based servers	Servers considered cheaper than routers/appliances. Servers already deployed in branch, data center (DC), or points of presence (PoP).
Deployment of best-of-breed services	Separation of network functions allows best-of-breed (virtualized) services. Eliminates vendor lock-in. Encourages openness and competition among software vendors. CAPEX reduction through competition.
Cost reduction through economies of scale	Deployment of huge server farms in DCs leads to better resource utilization.
Simplified performance upgrades	Capability to increase performance without forklift upgrades.

These benefits should also be examined critically on a case-by-case basis. For example, comparing only the cost of the hardware portion of an Intel x86–based platform (without the associated software functionality) to an appliance priced for both hardware and software can be misleading. Intel x86–based hosts may have shorter depreciation cycles as purpose-built appliances and may require more frequent upgrades. Although the CAPEX for an x86-based host may be cheaper, replacement costs may be incurred more frequently. It is thus important in a TCO comparison between an appliance-based architecture and a virtualized architecture to apply the same timeframe for the comparison, and include *all* aspects of the costs—software and hardware—needed to deliver the functionality.

OPEX Benefits of NFV

From an OPEX point of view, NFV also promises cost reductions. Consolidating multiple network functions from dedicated appliances into a single server platform promises to simplify hardware management. Gone are the days when the hardware architecture for each network function had to be fully understood to be managed. In a virtualized world, functions run on standard x86-based server platforms—and the latter are typically very well understood from a management perspective.

Specifically, this triggers OPEX savings on multiple fronts. Hardware element management is now common regardless of which virtualized network function is instantiated on top of it. Furthermore, in highly distributed network environments (think thousands of branches), such a reduction in the hardware platforms can also pull through additional OPEX savings, for example, by reducing site visits. Multiple hardware-based appliances in the branch increases the likelihood of one failing. Today, such a failure often requires specialists to visit the site for replacement. Collapsing multiple network functions into a single host reduces such failure occurrences, and thus the need for onsite support.

Using the same type of hardware in the data center for application workload hosting and in the network for NFV also promises additional OPEX savings. Synergies can be achieved by combining the workforce to look after the x86-based servers—regardless of whether these are hosting application workloads or VNFs. In the long run, organizational efficiencies are even achieved by merging L4–L7 network function operations teams with the application hosting teams.

From a flexibility perspective, NFV also simplifies the deployment of a function and thus further reduces OPEX. In an appliance-based model, deployment of a new network function typically implies acquisition of the hardware, testing, staging, shipment, etc. Since NFV is based on software running on standard x86-based servers, the deployment of a new function is typically simpler. Spare x86 CPU, memory, and storage resources may already be deployed, eliminating the need to test and stage new hardware. The deployment of a new function may thus reduce to testing the software aspects of the new function. And, of course, this benefit extends to future software upgrades as well. Gone are the days of hardware end-of-life announcements triggering a cycle of replacement hardware selection, testing, staging, shipment, and deployment. If an x86-based host becomes obsolete, a new server (with the same architecture) is easily deployed.

Table 10-2 outlines the OPEX benefits of NFV.

Table 10-2 *OPEX Benefits of Network Function Virtualization*

OPEX Benefit of NFV	Description
Reduction of branch visits	Changes/upgrades in the service can be made in software. No longer need to swap appliances onsite for service upgrades or appliance failures.
Automated network operations	Virtualization places focus on automation and elasticity, particularly for the initial deployment of a network function.

OPEX Benefit of NFV	Description
Flexible VNF-based operation	Software upgrades are done independently per VNF. VNFs are placed flexibly in branch, DC, or PoPs.
Elimination or reduction of organizational boundaries	IT and network operations align.

Architectural Benefits of NFV

In addition to CAPEX and OPEX savings, NFV also offers potential architectural simplifications. Take for example direct Internet access in branches. A common Internet access architecture is to backhaul all traffic destined outside of the enterprise to a centralized or regional data center. Connectivity to the untrusted Internet is protected by a demilitarized zone (DMZ) in those locations, where firewalls, intrusion detection and prevention (IDS/IPS), or similar security functions are deployed. With NFV, such functions may be deployed in the branches themselves, offering a *direct* breakout to the Internet instead of backhauling to a DMZ. Such an architectural change offers reduction of WAN bandwidth. The increased scale in managing hundreds or possibly thousands of security VNFs in this model is addressed by automation. In the distributed VNF model, the configuration and management of VNFs is highly automated and programmable, deploying identical security policies in each branch and thus addressing the concern of network operators of running highly distributed environments.

Another example for a potential architecture shift enabled by NFV revolves around high availability (HA). Many current high-availability architectures are designed to recover from failures within 50ms (a timeframe that originated from voice and SONET/SDH requirements). The designs typically embrace full redundancy at many layers. Redundant hardware complemented by software redundancy protects against respective hardware and software failures. Aggressive liveliness protocols such as Bidirectional Forwarding Detection (BFD) are deployed to detect failures within milliseconds. For stateful functionality like network address translation (NAT) or firewalls, session state redundancy is deployed to duplicate the state databases in redundant systems. In an architecture with VNFs, some network operators may choose to simplify network redundancy by deploying standby VNFs, which may be spun up only (cold standby), or even preconfigured (hot standby) on redundant servers. For applications that tolerate a failover time longer than 50ms, such alternative HA architectures may be acceptable and lead to further TCO savings.

Yet another example of an architectural option revolves around capacity expansion. In a hardware appliance–based architecture, additional capacity requirements trigger the deployment of extra hardware, or a replacement of the lower performing appliance by a higher performing model. In a virtualized architecture, additional capacity is deployed by either instantiating a VNF with more associated CPUs or by horizontally scaling additional VNFs next to the existing VNF. Again, this simplifies the overall network architecture and brings about cost savings. Table 10-3 summarizes the architectural benefits of NFV.

Table 10-3 *Architecture Benefits of Network Function Virtualization*

Architecture Benefit of NFV	Description
Reduction of the number of network elements to manage and deploy	Integration of network functions into a single system. reduces the number of appliances/network elements (NE) to manage and configure. Fewer hardware types to deploy and plan for.
Service elasticity	Deployment of VMs much faster than appliances. Easy scale up and scale down of services. Flexible service portfolio (mixing VNFs).
Operational efficiencies through virtualization	Leverages virtualization advantages from data center (vMotion, dynamic resource scheduling, power management, etc.) also for VNFs.
Reduced complexity for high availability	Virtual machines (VM) have a smaller failure domain. Stateless deployments become more acceptable, so less complexity through stateful redundancy deployments. In-service Software Upgrade (ISSU) simplified by deploying a NEW VM and failing over.

Not all of the examples listed so far may apply to your environment. Enterprise networks are highly diverse and often particular to each organization. But the point is simple: with NFV, you as an operator have another tool available to design and run your enterprise network. If you find the cost of embracing and adopting NFV acceptable, add this tool to your toolbox and benefit from the advantages described in this section.

Use Cases for Network Function Virtualization

Let's now take a look at the imminent use cases for NFV that emerged in the enterprise market. In general, these use cases are categorized into four main buckets:

- Virtualization of control plane functions
- Deploying VNFs in a virtual private cloud (VPC) for reachability
- Virtualizing branch transport and Layer 4–7 functions
- Leveraging virtualization to connect to public clouds

Control Plane Virtualization

The first use case for NFV centers on control plane functions. Today, all networks require such functions to exchange state information to achieve a successful transport path from the source to the destination of IP flows. Three examples of such control plane functions are as follows:

- **Route reflectors (RR):** Route reflectors are often already implemented as an appliance, learning prefixes and forwarding information from, for example, Border Gateway Protocol (BGP) neighbors and distributing the relevant forwarding information back to such neighbors. In large networks, deployment of such control plane appliances increases the scalability by avoiding a full mesh of neighbor sessions.
- **LISP Map-servers/Map-resolvers:** Map-servers and -resolvers in the Locator/ID Separation Protocol (LISP) perform the function of storing information about endpoints in a distributed database. The Map-Server/Map-Resolver (MS/MR) accepts prefixes identifying endpoints in the network and responds to queries from LISP Egress and Ingress Tunnel Routers (xTR) seeking information about an endpoint.
- **Wireless LAN controllers (WLC):** WLCs are responsible in the network to manage the operations and behavior of the access points under their governance. Examples of functions performed by a WLC include authentication of clients and access point configuration (e.g., for radio resource management). Deployment of a virtualized WLC becomes particularly effective when wireless traffic is not tunneled back to the WLC; that is, when the WLC operates the wireless control plane only.

Of course, there are many more such examples. In various network appliances, such functions already run on x86 CPUs. Take for example the Cisco Aggregation Services Router (ASR) 1000 Series routers. In an ASR 1000, a powerful processor—QFP—delivers the data plane forwarding performance. Packets forwarded between interfaces are sent to this processor and treated there by applying the relevant forwarding plane features (including NAT, firewall, routing, etc.), and are then sent on toward the destination IP address on an egress interface. Control plane packets, however, are processed by the x86 CPU that also is part of the overall ASR 1000 system architecture. Routing protocols (BGP, Open Shortest Path First [OSPF], Enhanced Interior Gateway Routing Protocol [EIGRP]), and multicast control plane functions are all examples of processes that are executed in the onboard x86 CPU of an ASR 1000. Control plane packets do not benefit from the hardware acceleration offered by QFP.

Any control plane software processes that leverage x86 compute resources are thus prime candidates to virtualize in an NFV-enabled architecture. VNFs like the Cisco CSR 1000v are already deployed as virtualized BGP route reflectors. The Cisco Virtual Wireless LAN Controller (vWLC), or a Performance Routing virtualized Master Controller (vMC) are other examples of where control plane functionality is deployed as a VNF. And in many cases, the attainable performance in such a virtualized environment can be at par with the performance of the appliance-based deployments. Figure 10-1 illustrates the architecture of placing virtual control plane functions in a shared services area in a campus network.

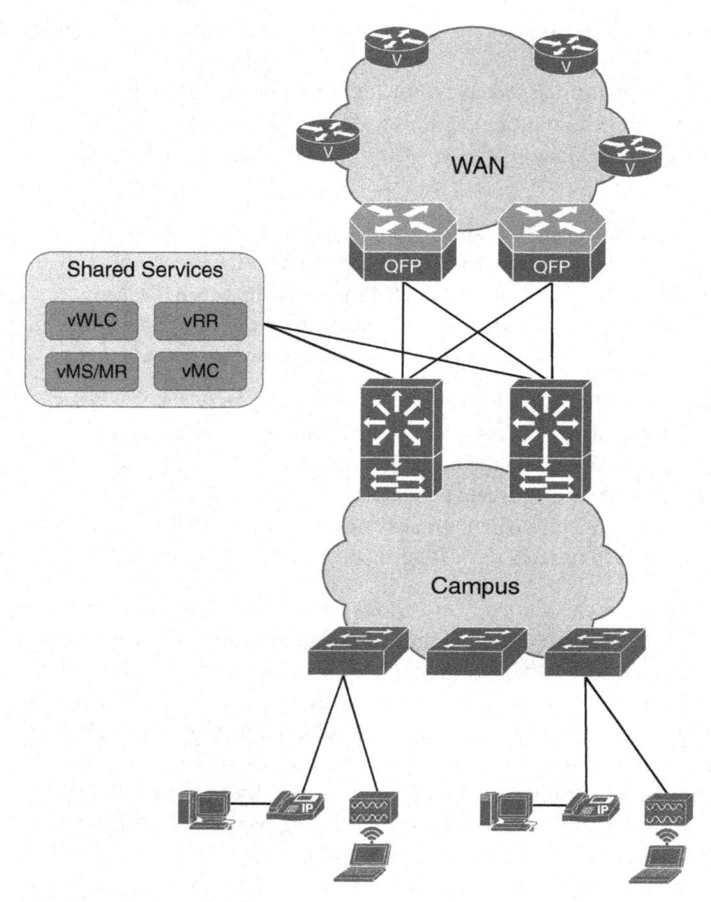

Figure 10-1 *Virtualization of the Network Control Plane*

Branch Virtualization

The second use-case category for NFV is targeting branch environments. In many branches, multiple appliances are deployed. Routers provide connectivity to the rest of the enterprise network, possibly using a service provider's virtual private network (VPN) or Internet service. WAN optimization appliances may be installed to optimize the traffic over the WAN. WLC appliances may be deployed in larger branches to configure access points. Voice or security appliances are often also part of the branch architecture. Throw in a switch for connectivity! It is thus not uncommon to have numerous dedicated appliances in branches. And redundancy is often a requirement, so the number of deployed systems can immediately double.

All of these hardware systems must be maintained, operated, and managed. New software functionality or patches may be required. Hardware failures may occur, triggering an onsite visit by a skilled engineer. Vendors may run out of parts for a system and be forced to announce the end of sale, and ultimately support, for one of the deployed systems. Such events trigger network-wide fleet upgrades of the deployed system. None of this may contribute significantly to the TCO if these costs are incurred a single time. But many organizations are operating enterprise networks with hundreds or even thousands of branches, typically spread over a wide geographic area. Any single operation, any cost incurred for a single branch, is thus immediately multiplied by the number of branches in the organization's network.

The virtualization of network functions promises to make a significant impact on the TCO in such an environment. Imagine that your branches consist of an x86-based server (or two for redundancy) where routing, WAN optimization, WLC, and other functions are collapsed into a single chassis. This significantly simplifies the hardware landscape of the branch. When coupled with automation enabled by increasing programmability of the VNFs, and multiplied by the number of branches in your network, significant TCO savings is achieved. This is what makes the branch virtualization use case so attractive for many enterprise network architects! Figure 10-2 shows the concept of collapsing multiple appliance-based functions into an x86-based host and running the functions as virtual machines.

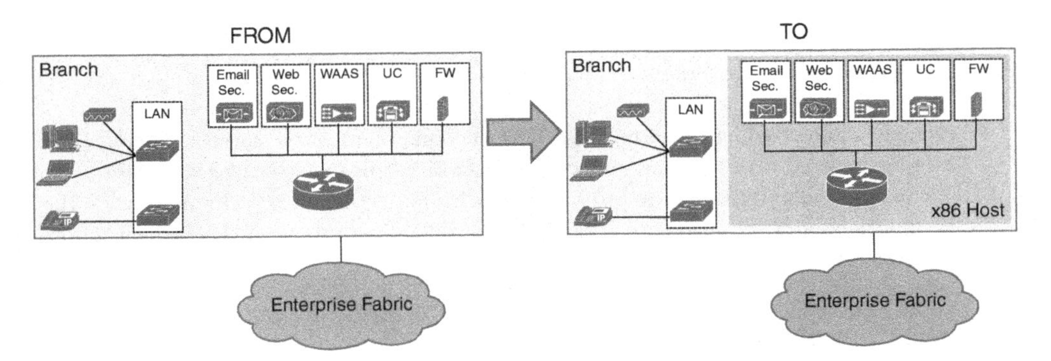

Figure 10-2 *Virtualization of the Enterprise Branch Architectures*

Virtualization to Connect Applications in VPCs

The third use case that is also already widely deployed centers on connectivity to applications running in virtual private cloud environments. Many of you are embracing services by Amazon, Microsoft, Google, or the like to host enterprise applications in a virtual private cloud (VPC) environment. The benefits of a VPC are by now well apparent for many enterprises: you can deploy an application without lengthy and costly investments in server infrastructures. You consume the infrastructure—servers and their OS—as a service. You don't have to worry about backups or server failures. The list goes on. But how to get your traffic to such a VPC environment? By now the answer should be obvious: run virtualized network functions in the VPC.

Figure 10-3 illustrates this use case. A virtual router such as the Cisco CSR 1000v is deployed inside the VPC as a VNF, and configured to provide connectivity to the rest of your enterprise network. Of particular importance are encrypted tunnels and WAN optimization functionality. By connecting the virtual router in the VPC with your enterprise network environment, the VPC effectively becomes a natural part of your overall architecture—just like a branch that is connected over an untrusted provider. The same security functionality, the same WAN optimization functionality, and the same firewall or IPS/IDS functionality are applied in the VPC as in your branch architectures—albeit deployed as virtual machines.

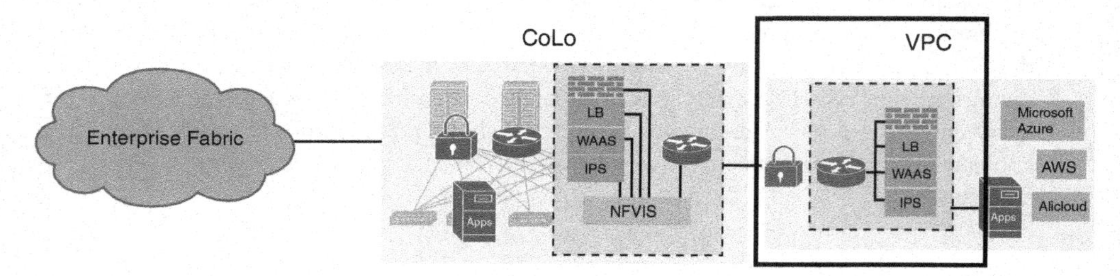

Figure 10-3 *Virtualized Network Functions Running in Public Clouds*

For many cloud providers, offering such VNFs becomes part of the service catalog. The VNFs are ordered from the marketplace and instantiated in an automated way. APIs into the cloud providers allow you to program the behavior of these VNFs. In most cases, the consumption model of such networking VMs is aligned with the overall VPC consumption model, for example by offering term-based licenses.

Virtualization of Multicloud Exchanges

The move of applications into cloud environments also motivates the fourth use case that is currently considered by many enterprises: virtualizing the DMZ. In many cases, the discussion about hosting applications in the cloud has already progressed beyond a single VPC architecture. Applications hosting is being designed for hybrid and multicloud environments. They can be hosted by multiple VPC providers and be migrated from one environment to the other, including back into an enterprise-operated cloud. Applications are also increasingly being consumed as a service over Internet connections.

As a result, the traditional security perimeter that motivated traditional DMZ architectures is changing significantly. The security perimeter in a cloud-first architecture is required to cover all of the above application hosting environments. These are also likely to be much more distributed in the enterprise architecture than traditionally centralized DMZs.

And this is where virtualization comes in! NFV helps in this use case to build security perimeters that are customized based on the type of external connectivity. For applications hosted as a service, you can choose to deploy one type of a chain of VNFs. For applications hosted in a VPC, another type of VNF chain can be instantiated. All other external connectivity—for example, to the Internet or extranet partners—also receives a customized network treatment by instantiating the appropriate and relevant VNFs.

This use case is illustrated in Figure 10-4. VNF service chains can be deployed depending on where the traffic comes from and where it is going. In today's use cases, the VNFs focus on applying the appropriate security functionality (e.g., firewalls, IPS/IDS, web filtering, etc.), but other VNFs can, of course, also be chained in. NFV enables this use case by allowing such deployments to be flexible, granular, on-demand, and automated. In many cases, the functional components of such an virtualized security perimeter are hosted in carrier-neutral facilities. The resulting architecture therefore is typically described as a *cloud exchange*, rather than an evolved DMZ. The idea may have started with "let's virtualize DMZ functions" but has evolved to much more by combining virtualization, carrier-neutral facilities, automation, and virtualized service chains that are instantiated on a per-source-destination-pair basis.

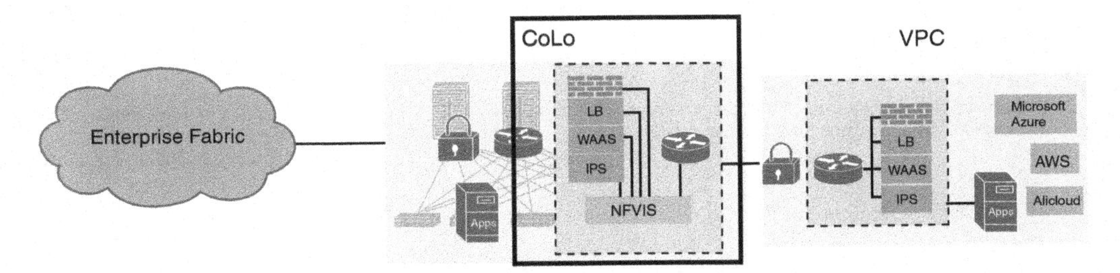

Figure 10-4 *Virtualizing Multicloud and Internet Edge Zones*

The mentioned use-cases are examples of where virtualization already plays a role in many network architectures. They are also great examples of how virtualization is not simply a replacement of an appliance chassis with an x86-based host. The use cases emerged because they address a particular problem or are offering architectural benefits that could not be addressed in the same way with a hardware-based appliance. The key learning from these use cases is: virtualization is a great *additional* tool in your toolbox, but it does not replace hardware based systems!

Overview of an NFV System Architecture

Now that we have explored the business benefits of NFV and examples of compelling use cases, let's dig into the solution architecture in this section. The four main components of a virtualized system architecture are as follows:

- An x86-based hosting platform offering the hardware resources (CPU, memory, storage, interfaces, etc.)
- The x86-based operating system with virtualization support (e.g., KVM)
- One or more virtualized network functions; the software processes that treat the IP flows, perform forwarding decisions, and apply networking features as configured
- The automation and programmability platform.

In a basic virtualized system architecture, hardware resources (CPU, memory, and storage) based on standard server technologies such as Intel x86 processors are being abstracted by a hypervisor layer to present virtual CPU/memory/storage to virtual machines or applications that run on top of the hypervisor. The focus of NFV is to run networking functions inside a virtual machine, as opposed to running VNFs in a container or running applications directly on the host OS.

Figure 10-5 shows the main differences between a type 1 hypervisor, a type 2 hypervisor, and Linux containers. Type 1 hypervisor operating systems directly control the hardware and offer a virtualization environment to present virtual compute resources (memory, storage, CPU, I/O, etc.) to one or more virtual machines. An example of a type 1 hypervisor is VMware ESXI.

Containers share the OS kernel of the host and thus are lightweight; however, each container must have the same OS kernel.

Containers are isolated but share OS and, where appropriate, libs/bins.

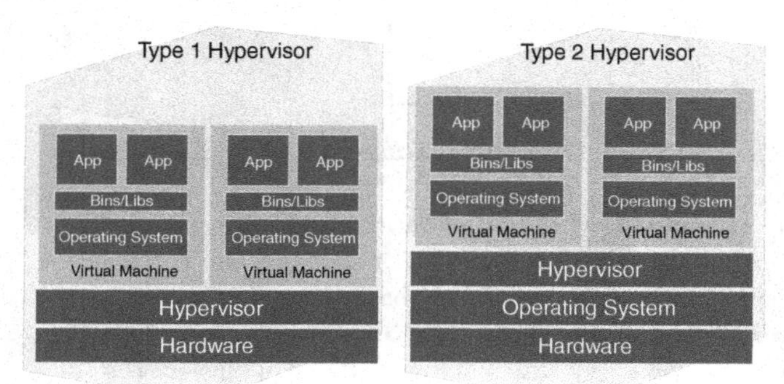

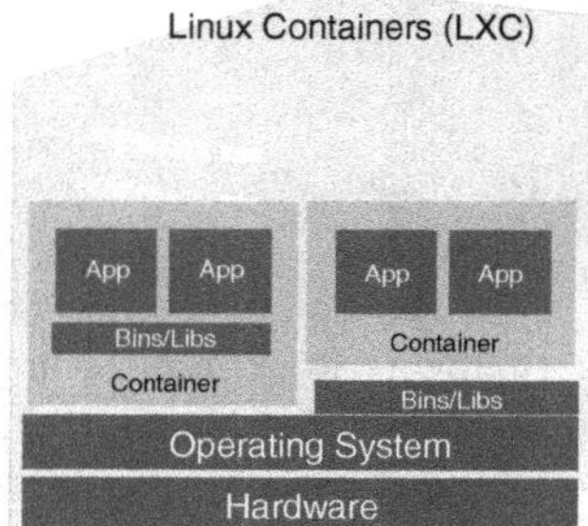

Figure 10-5 *Virtual Machines and Containers*

In a type 2 hypervisor, a standard operating system such as Linux controls the server hardware, and the hypervisor runs on top of the host OS to perform hardware abstraction toward the virtual machines. An example of a type 2 hypervisor is Kernel-based Virtual Machine (KVM) for Linux.

In both cases, an additional operating system is running inside the virtual machines to accommodate the application workloads. In some cases, this additional VM OS may be beneficial; for example, if the application is supported on an OS that differs from the underlying hardware OS. Applications with different OS support can thus run on the same host.

Linux containers run applications in segregated environments on top of the host operating system kernel directly. No additional OS inside the container is required. The segregation consists of separating the name spaces, isolating the operating environment of the containerized applications. Resources can also be isolated between containerized applications and the kernel, and can also be prioritized (c.f. Linux cgroups). Libraries are shared where appropriate.

For networking VNFs, one or more software processes are running inside the VM to perform packet processing (e.g., firewall, routing, IPS/IDS, etc.). These software processes are associated with the virtualized CPUs allocated to the VM, and this association is either static or floating and depends on the software architecture of the VNF. For example, for the Cisco CSR 1000v virtual router, the Cisco IOS XE networking software runs multiple processes (representing data plane, control plane, and middleware communication functions) that are now executed inside a VM. These IOS XE software processes are statically mapped to virtual CPUs (vCPU) within the virtual machine. Some of the VNF internal software processes have strict timing requirements to ensure a successful operation. Processes can be monitored by watchdog timers to verify their liveliness.

In addition to the vCPU threads configured for a VM, numerous VM system threads are also generating processing loads. Examples are the VM kernel process, virtual network interface card (vNIC) processes, or interrupt processes. The aggregate of all vCPU processes from the set of VMs as well as the VM-specific processes are presented to the hypervisor layer for scheduling onto physical CPU cores. Additional software processes, such as those for virtual switching in the operating system, may also request CPU resources. The hypervisor scheduler is responsible for allocating all these processes in its process queue to the physical CPUs for a time slice, as well as to manage memory or storage access. A simplified representation of a virtualized system architecture focusing on the CPU resources (both physical and virtual) is depicted in Figure 10-6.

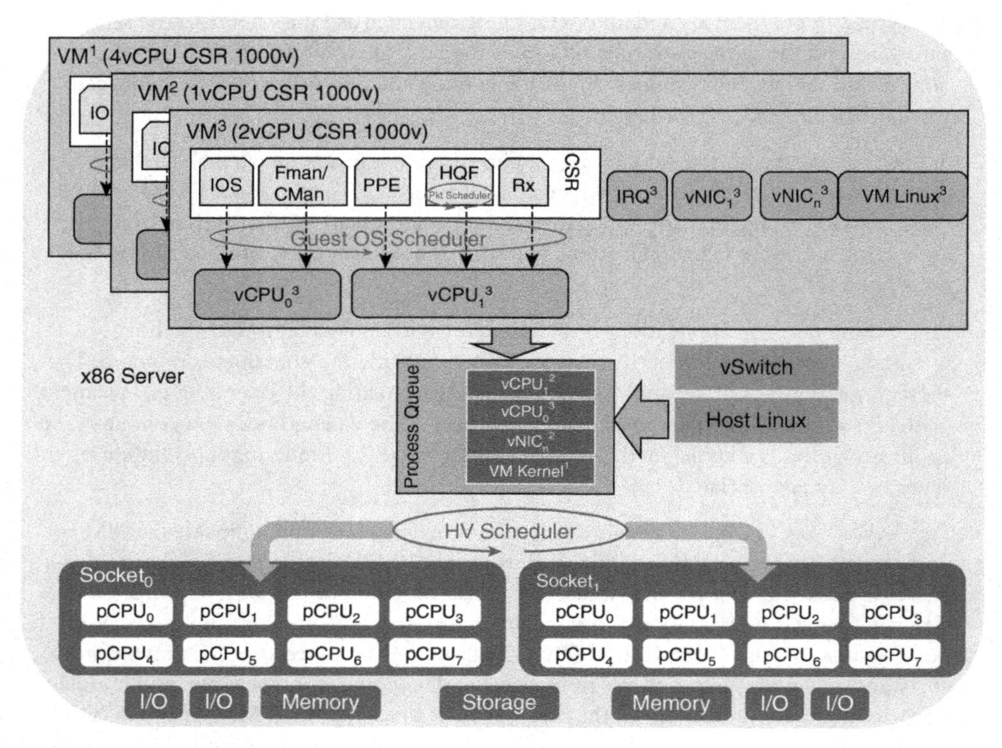

Figure 10-6 *Virtualized System Architecture Running Multiple Virtual Machines*

A virtualized system architecture may expose various throughput bottlenecks, as shown in Figure 10-7. For example, the physical port density and speed of the server may constrain the amount of traffic that is processed. The set of networking VMs running on the server may be capable of processing more traffic than the servers' physical ports. Another bottleneck may be the hypervisor scheduler, in particular if a large number of processes need to be allocated CPU cycles with strict timing. The VNF typically has a maximum packet processing capacity that may also limit its throughput. Perhaps the most important bottleneck to understand in I/O-bound networking environments is the packet path from the physical NIC (pNIC) into the VMs. A variety of technology options exist to pass packets from a physical interface into a virtual machine: in KVM, Open vSwitch (OVS), with or without Intel's Data Plane Development Kit (DPDK) support, is available. An open source virtual switch project called Fast data – Input/Output (FD.io) is another alternative. Virtual machines are even bound more tightly to a physical interface, for example, by configuring a direct Peripheral Component Interconnect (PCI) pass-through mode, or by deploying single-root I/O virtualization (SR-IOV). These different techniques are explained in more detail later in the chapter.

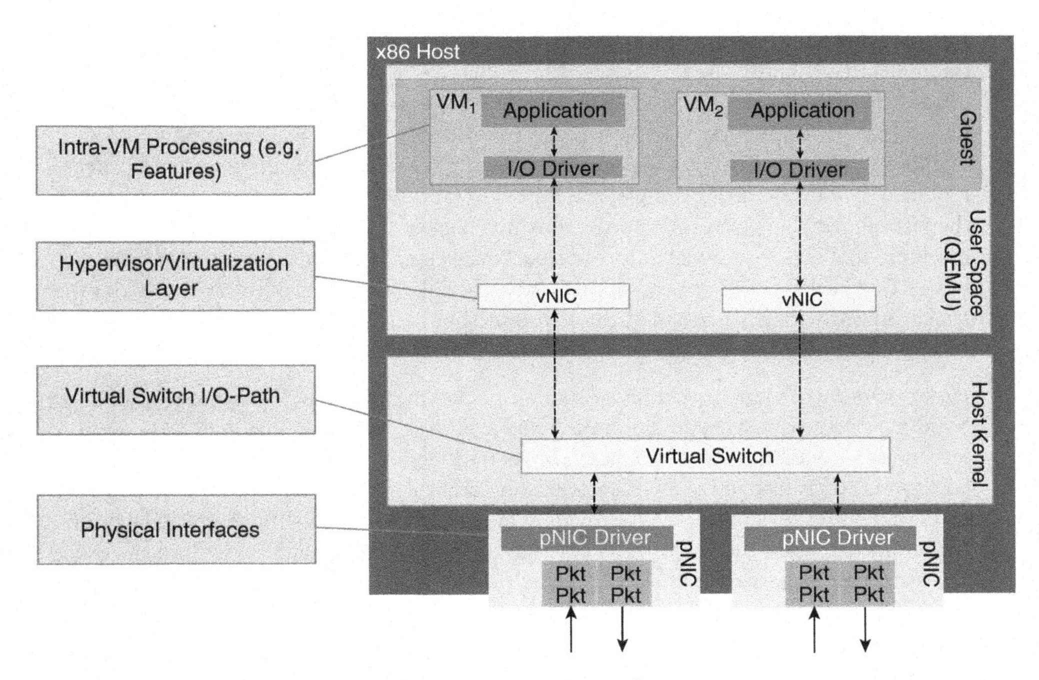

Figure 10-7 *Bottlenecks in a Virtualized System Architecture*

Hypervisor Scheduling and NUMA

The hypervisor scheduler can implement fairness to regulate the processing of the workloads. For example, KVM implements a standard Linux Completely Fair Scheduler (CFS) that time-slices between processes, supporting dynamic process priorities and pre-emption. VMware's ESXi scheduler typically allocates equal shares to each vCPU, but allows vCPU processes to have scheduling entitlements. Related vCPU processes can also be co-scheduled to avoid synchronization latencies. To optimize the utilization levels of the individual cores or to improve the power efficiency of a socket, the scheduler may move processing threads from one physical CPU to another. The processing thread is moved either in the same CPU socket or in another socket. This results in thrashing the instruction and data caches (that is, resulting in CPU caches that may need to be repopulated). Such scheduling activities can thus impact the processing of the software workloads, and even lead to sporadic packet losses. Translating the virtual memory addresses used by a VM into the underlying physical memory addresses is another important function performed by the hypervisor.

It is important to note that the hypervisor scheduler has no awareness of the VM internal software processes or its software architecture. The VM abstracts its internals toward the hypervisor via the vCPU and vNIC processes. In a networking environment this implies that the hypervisor scheduler, for example, has no awareness of a packet queuing process that needs to be executed, or if a VM internal watchdog timer process requires CPU cycles. For example, the Egress Quality of Service (QoS) scheduler within the virtual machine governs the order in which packets are egressed out of the virtual machine. It allows for low-latency voice packets to gain preferential treatment over best-effort packets. The system's hypervisor scheduler, however, is not aware of or even synchronized with the actions of the VM internal QoS scheduler, as depicted as HQF in Figure 10-6.

Figure 10-8 reveals further details of a single-socket multicore architecture. Non-uniform Memory Access (NUMA) architectures enhance the performance in a multicore architecture by providing separate memory for each processor core and thus enabling these cores to hit their respective memory banks in parallel.[1] An x86-based server is typically equipped with two sockets, each providing multiple CPU cores. A hierarchical layer of caches accompanies the cores. Each core has its own L1 cache with very fast memory access. A pair of cores shares the L2 cache, which is bigger in size. The third layer in the cache hierarchy is the L3 cache, which is shared among all cores on a socket. The scheduling algorithm of the hypervisor determines which software process (e.g., vCPU) gets scheduled onto which core. NUMA also provides a bus to allow data to move between the different memory banks and to access data residing in memory associated with other cores. Ensuring that related software processes are scheduled onto the same socket and, ideally, close onto cores sharing the same L1/L2 caches may positively impact performance. If related processes are scheduled onto cores sharing the same L1/L2 cache, the memory state (e.g., packet buffer) does not need to be repopulated. On the other hand, if related processes requiring the same memory state are scheduled onto cores that only share the L2 cache or are even scheduled onto different sockets, memory state needs to change, leading to cache trashing that can impact the overall performance of the software processes. NUMA also provides a QuickPath Interconnect (QPI) bus to allow data to move between the different memory banks and to access data residing in memory associated with other cores. Memory access bandwidth across this QPI link is slower than accessing memory on the same socket.

Note that the Cisco Enterprise Network Compute System (ENCS) and the Cisco Cloud Services Platform CSP2100 offer some of these optimizations out of the box. For example, vCPUs assigned to VNFs are typically pinned to particular physical CPUs. Similarly, memory management is configured in the Cisco Enterprise Network Function Virtualization Infrastructure Software (NFVIS) to be optimized for the VNFs.

1 M. Falkner, A. Leivadeas, I. Lambadaris, G. Kesidis, "Performance Analysis of virtualized network functions on virtualized systems architectures," *IEEE 21st International Workshop on Computer Aided Modelling and Design of Communication Links and Networks (CAMAD)*, 2016: 71–76.

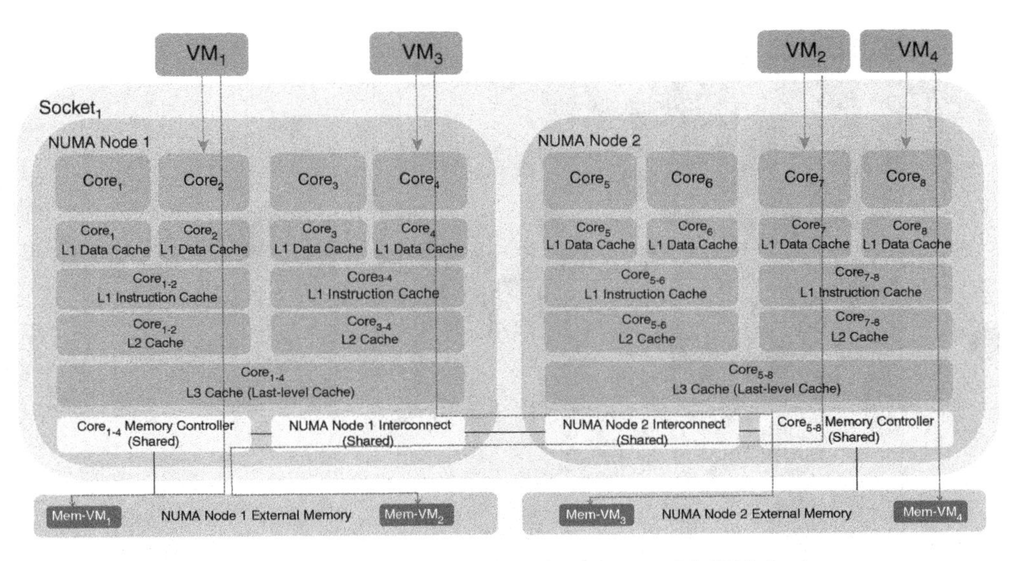

Figure 10-8 *Non-Uniform Memory Access in Multicore x86 CPU Socket*

Input/Output Technologies for Virtualization

Virtualization of network functions differs from application virtualization. In the former case, the I/O workload generated by packet flows dominates. By definition of a VNF and its purpose being to process networking traffic, packets are continuously arriving into the server and need to be passed to its respective VM for processing. Networking VMs are thus generating high I/O workloads for the hypervisor and, as such, are referred to as I/O bound. Other VNFs may also be storage or memory bound, especially for L4–7 networking operations where the entire payload of a packet needs to be processed. In contrast, many non-networking applications receive only a limited number of external inputs. Their requirement for CPU cycles is predominantly for algorithmic computations, possibly also with intensive memory and storage access. Such applications or networking functions consequently become compute bound. Understanding the resource demands from either VNFs or applications mixed on a particular general-purpose server is important to maximize its utilization.

In general, packets arrive on the physical NIC and are copied into memory via two direct memory access (DMA) operations. Along with the packet copy, a descriptor specifying the buffer location (memory address and length) is also copied into memory. The pNIC then sends an interrupt to indicate the arrival of the packet, as shown in Figure 10-9.

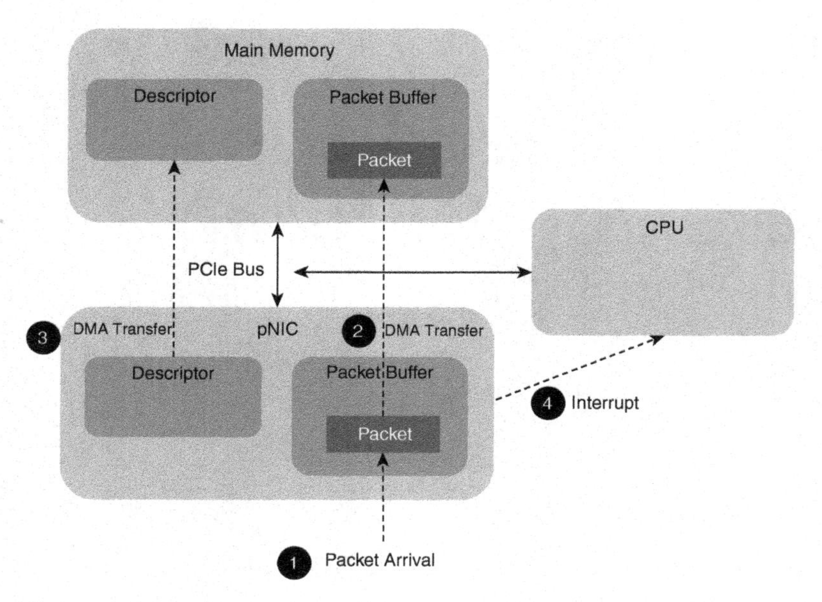

Figure 10-9 *Details of a Packet Arrival into a pNIC*

The size of the packet buffers, the descriptors, as well as the number of interrupts are further examples of bottlenecks that may ultimately impact the throughput. The packet is then processed by the virtual switch or a Linux bridge process such as OVS, OVS-DPDK, FD.io VPP, SR-IOV, direct PCIe pass-through, or an OpenStack I/O path. The different system configurations are illustrated, respectively, in Figures 10-10 through Figure 10-15.

In the case of OVS-DPDK, packets are passed to the virtual switch for distribution to the destination VNFs (Cisco CSR 1000V instances), assisted by the DPDK libraries for fast packet processing. The DPDK libraries offer a poll mode driver (PMD) that allows packets to pass from the physical interface to the virtual switch (user space) directly, thus avoiding the networking stack of the kernel. OVS-DPDK offers enhanced switching functionality, supporting, among others, jumbo frames, link bonding, native tunneling support for VXLAN, Generic Route Encapsulation (GRE) or Generic Network Virtualization Encapsulation (GENEVE), Multiprotocol Label Switching (MPLS), or ingress/egress policing. From a CPU resource perspective, OVS-DPDK is relying on CPU cycles from the host's x86 core to switch packets, thus stressing the hypervisor scheduler in a system where multiple VNFs are also contending for the same CPU cycles. Any CPU core associated for switching to OVS-DPDK becomes unavailable to process VNFs. OVS-DPDK can, however, be configured to use multiple CPU cores for packet switching to increase its throughput toward the VNFs. Note that Figure 10-10 and Figure 10-11 highlight the pertinent queues in these setups. Such internal queues are set up to pass packets on their path from the virtual switch into the VNFs, and their depths can become a bottleneck with high data rates. For OVS-DPDK the pertinent queues are in the DPDK driver in the guest user space.

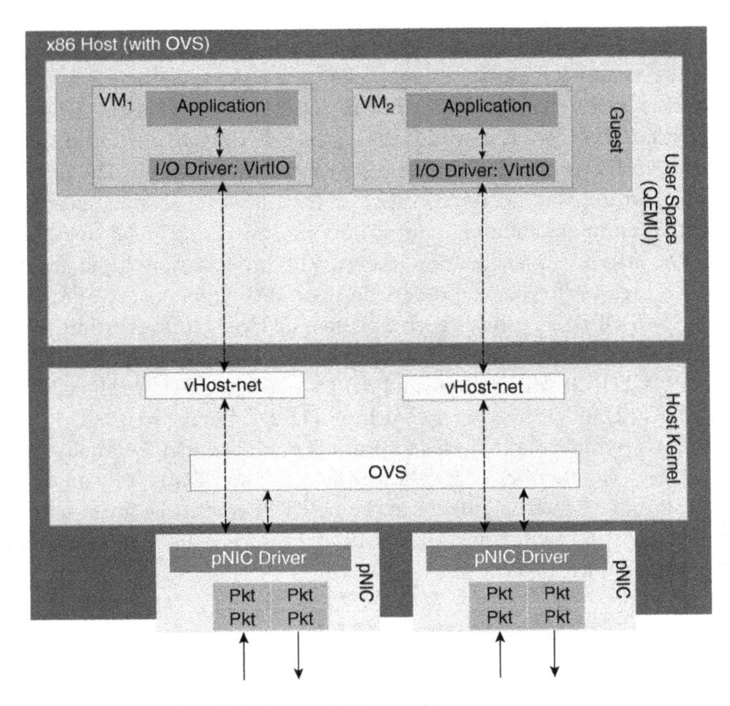

Figure 10-10 *OVS-based I/O Architecture*

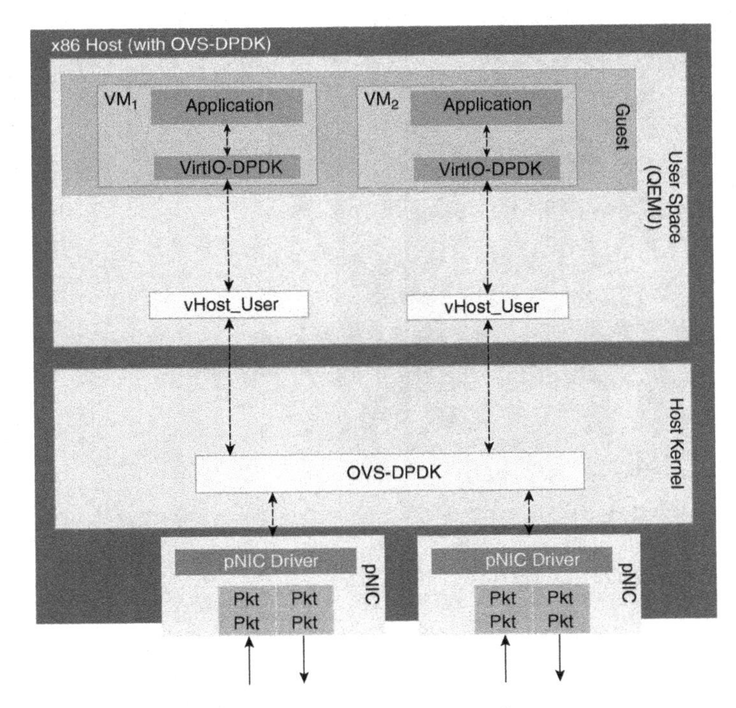

Figure 10-11 *OVS-DPDK-based I/O Architecture*

FD.io VPP (vector pocket processing) is an open source alternative solution to optimize the I/O path in a virtualized system.[2] Running as a Linux user-space process, the FD.io VPP drivers enable NIC access over PCI. FD.io processes multiple packets with similar characteristics (called vectors). Packets are removed from the receive rings of the interface and are formed into a packet vector, to which a processing graph is then applied. The processing graph represents the features that need to be applied (e.g., IPv4 forwarding, classification, multicast, etc.). This approach minimizes interrupts and traversing a call stack and thus also thrashing of the instruction caches and misses. VPP processes multiple packets at a time, making it a high-performance processing stack that supports even more networking functions than OVS-DPDK. Features such as Dynamic Host Configuration Protocol (DHCP), segment routing, Address Resolution Protocol (ARP), Layer 2 Transport Protocol version 3 (L2TPv3), VRFs, IPv6, and MPLS-over Ethernet are all supported. Similar to OVS-DPDK, FD.io VPP makes use of Intel's DPDK library to accelerate packet processing, and thus requires CPU cycles to process packets which become unavailable for VNF processing. The number of CPU cores assigned to FD.io VPP can be configured. FD.io VPP also leverages internal queues in the DPDK driver in the guest user space to pass packets from the virtual switch into the VNFs. An FD.io-based virtualized system architecture is shown in Figure 10-12.

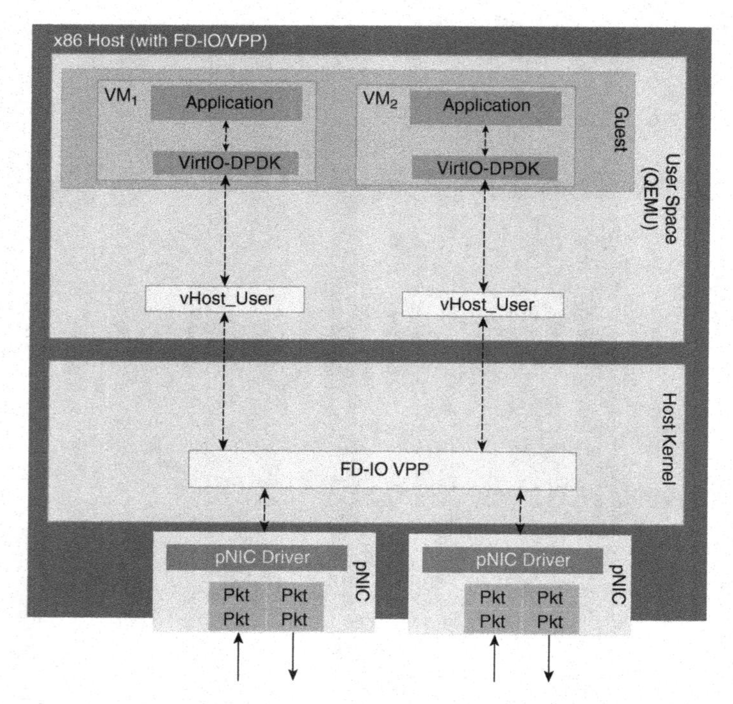

Figure 10-12 *FD.io VPP–based I/O Architecture*

2 M. Konstantynowicz, "FD.io: How to Push Extreme Limits of Performance and Scale with Vector Packet Processing Technology," https://www.ietf.org/proceedings/96/slides/slides-96-bmwg-10.pdf.

SR-IOV, in contrast, offers a virtualized Peripheral Component Interconnect Express (PCIe) pass-through mechanism that does not rely on the hypervisor to pass packets between the NIC to the individual VNFs. SR-IOV virtualizes PCIe, creating PCIe physical functions (PF) and virtual functions (VF). This allows a physical port to be shared among multiple VNFs. The processing of features in an SR-IOV setup is entirely done inside the VNF, requiring the VNF to support the appropriate drivers. Features such as VXLAN, MPLS, policing, etc. previously mentioned for OVS-DPDK and FD.io VPP now have to be applied to packets inside the VNFs. SR-IOV has some functional limitations due to its dependency on the underlying hardware and software. The server's NIC cards and the BIOS have to support the technology. Further caveats are, for example, the number of VFs that can be configured for a physical NIC, currently limiting the number of VFs to 128 on an Intel Fortville NIC, but the practical limit can be as low as 64. Depending on the hardware and the driver implementation, other caveats may exist such as packet mirroring, VLAN filtering, multicast addresses, or promiscuous unicast.

After processing by the virtual switch, the packet is fetched by the vNIC to be handed off to the actual VM I/O driver (for example, Virtio). In case of SR-IOV, the packets are directly fetched by the SR-IOV driver inside the VM. Note that packets may thus be copied several times as they are passed from the virtual switch to the application, using a vNIC as well as the virtual machine's I/O driver. Such packet copy operations place additional requests onto the hypervisor scheduler, and may limit the throughput and cause additional delay or even packet losses. All of the above I/O paths can thus also have throughput limitations.

Figures 10-13, 10-14, and 10-15 illustrate a virtual system architecture with SR-IOV, direct PCIe pass-through, and OpenStack, respectively.

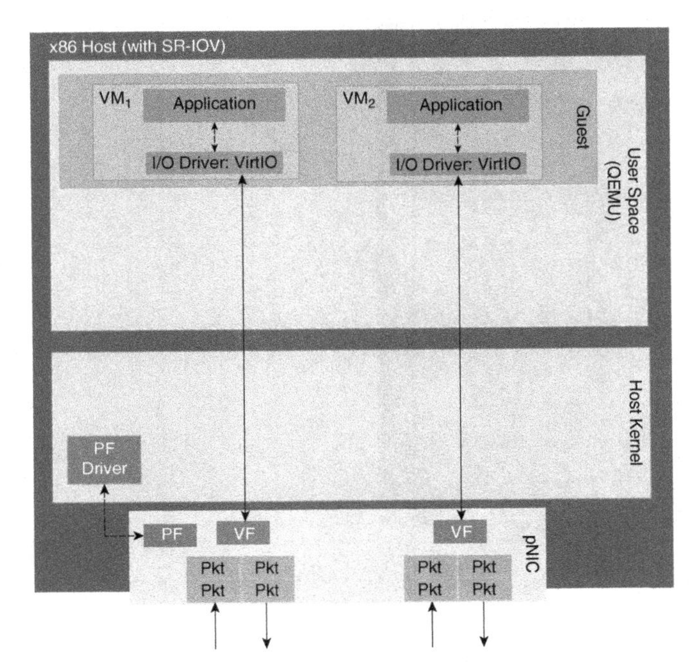

Figure 10-13 *SR-IOV-based I/O Architecture*

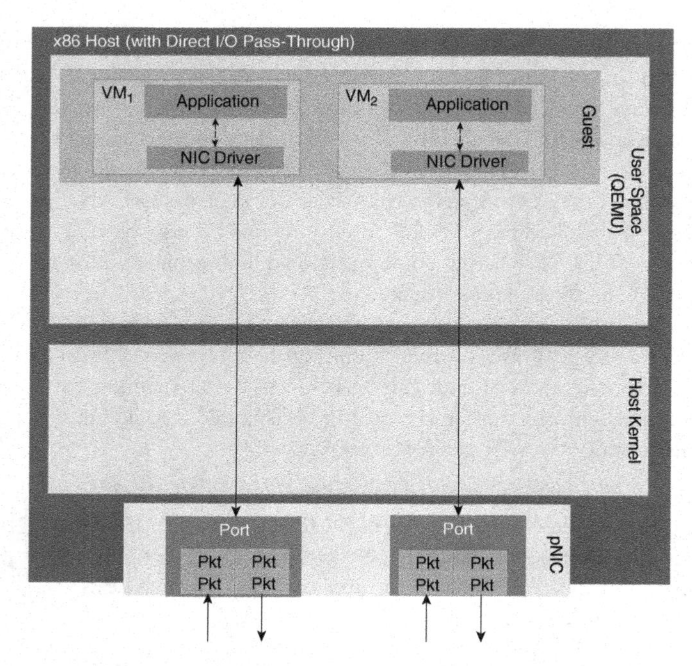

Figure 10-14 *Direct PCIe Pass-through I/O*

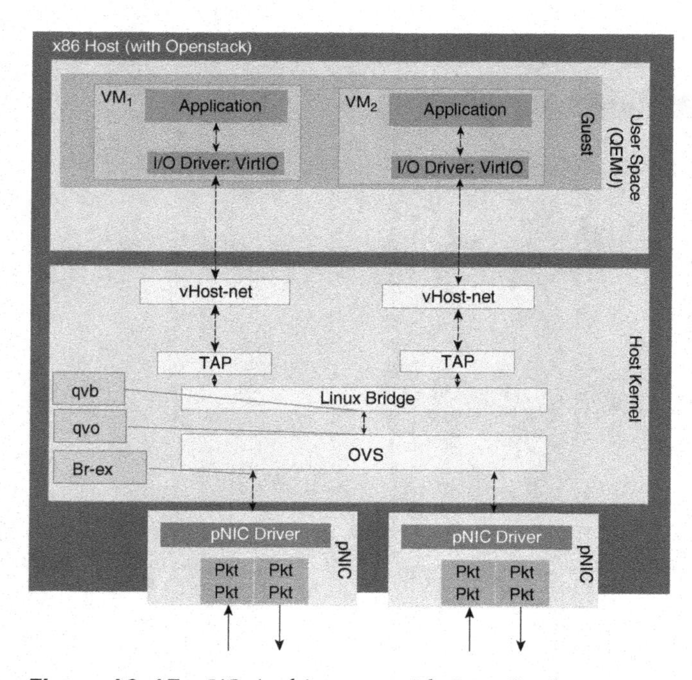

Figure 10-15 *I/O Architecture with OpenStack*

Challenges and Deployment Considerations of Network Function Virtualization

As you can imagine, virtualizing network functions also has implications on how you deploy and operate your network. Consider performance. What are the performance characteristics of virtualized network functions as compared to physical appliances? Another aspect revolves around deployment models: how many VNFs should you deploy on an x86-based host, and should they be configured analogous to a physical appliance? These topics are the focus of the next section.

Performance

The previous section highlighted the major components of a virtualized system architecture: a hardware host based on a standard x86 architecture, with shared CPU, memory, storage, and I/O resources, and running a *standard* operating system (e.g., Linux in many cases) to schedule software processing requests and managing the system. Such a system architecture deviates significantly from specialized hardware appliances such as routers, switches, firewalls, etc. that were optimized for decades from both a hardware and software perspective.

Take for example a Cisco ASR 1000 Series router. Its forwarding plane is based on the QuantumFlow Processor, which is optimized to forward packets while applying a broad set of features. The I/O path in the ASR 1000 connects the physical interfaces to the QFP, and is wired to ensure no packet loss, allowing for priority lanes and XON-XOFF feedback loops to ensure that backpressure is applied and that the system behaves in a predicable manner. Sophisticated hardware assists ensure that encrypted traffic is handled with high performance, or that classification lookups (e.g., for ACLs or QoS) support the desired throughput rates.

Many of the optimizations that are embedded in dedicated networking appliances are missing in general-purpose x86-based hosts. Underlying hardware resources are shared typically between many VNFs and applications. Traffic destined to different VNFs or applications shares common physical interfaces. CPU cycles are pooled to serve all of the processes installed on the host. Memory and storage are also not dedicated to particular processes. And by virtue of deploying off-the-shelf x86-based hosts, any hardware optimizations that appliances offer for efficient transport and processing of network traffic are also absent. As discussed previously, the fact that the operating system scheduler is not optimized for packet processing may also affect the throughput, latency, and jitter of a virtualized system architecture.

Compared to networking systems that incorporate hardware acceleration and were optimized for packet forwarding, running a VNF on top of a virtualized system architecture may not reach the same performance envelope today. But remember, one of the key benefits of NFV is to reduce the number of hardware systems to operate in your network by using a single x86-based standard host for a variety of functions. And the attainable throughput of VNFs is often more than sufficient for many use cases.

You need to be aware of a number of design and deployment decisions, discussed in the following sections, that may impact the performance you get out of a virtualized system architecture.

Oversubscribing the Physical Hardware Resources

First, consider the number of VNFs to host on the server. With a single VNF, the underlying OS can allocate all of its hardware resources to the processes of that one VNF. Assuming that the VNF requires less virtual resources (vCPU, vMem, vStorage) than available physically, the OS scheduler typically successfully manages to satisfy all requests for hardware. This contrasts with a system configuration where the sum of all offered hardware resource requests (that is, requests for CPU cycles, requests for memory access, or requests for storage from many VNFs) exceeds the available hardware resources. In this case the OS scheduler must time-slice resource allocations between VNF processes. The behavior of one VNF may have adverse effects on the behavior of other VNFs. Instantiating many VNFs implies that the hypervisor has to switch between more processes presented from the VNFs (as depicted earlier in Figure 10-6). This can lead to a situation where process switching overhead is incurred in the host OS, and where the CPU caches need to be repopulated, possibly leading to cache trashing. If OVS is used to send and receive packets to and from physical interfaces, the I/O processing intensity may also conflict with process switching.

A rule of thumb is to avoid oversubscribing the underlying physical hardware resources. The sum of all vCPUs associated with all of the instantiated VNFs should not exceed the number of physical cores available in the system. Similarly, the sum of all memory or storage associated with the deployed VNFs should be below the available memory or storage resources. And, of course, the CPU, memory, and storage requirements for the host itself (that is, the OS's requirements for CPU, memory, and storage) should be factored into this equation!

Optimizing Server Configurations

Many x86-based host operating systems have a myriad of tuning parameters that positively affect the performance of VNFs. Some examples include the following:

- **CPU pinning:** The vCPUs presented by VNFs can be statically pinned to physical cores.
- **Hyperthreading:** Hyperthreading allows a single physical core to behave as two logical cores, for example, by exploiting the fact that during a memory access period of one processing thread another thread can take advantage of the available CPU cycles[3]. For many VNF use cases, disabling hyperthreading has shown to improve performance.

3 If a processing thread has to wait for a memory access to complete, the CPU is idling. Hyperthreading allows the CPU to process another thread in the meantime.

- **Tuning interrupt handling:** Pinning interrupt request (IRQ) processes to particular physical cores also improves the determinism of the system and observable performance.
- **Optimizing packet queue length configurations:** Since VNFs are typically I/O intensive, sending and receiving packets to and from interfaces, the internal queue lengths for the I/O path can impact performance. Setting the queue length to a higher value is shown to improve performance, albeit at the cost of increased latency.

Other examples of OS performance tuning under Linux/KVM are TCP Segmentation Offload (TSO), generic segmentation offload (GSO), influencing memory ballooning that allows guest memory to be adjusted dynamically, kernel shared memory (KSM), or influencing the NUMA behavior.

While any or all of the mentioned tuning knobs positively impact the amount of traffic to be forwarded in a virtualized environment, there is a cost: the server configurations must be modified at the operating system level. For example, in case of a Linux KVM, to pin virtual CPUs to physical CPUs, you may need to issue multiple Linux commands such as

```
sudo virsh vcpupin test 0 6
```

Editing of Linux scripts or VNF configuration files may also be necessary to reap the benefits of such performance tuning. While some of the tuning steps are automated, it does take a special skill set and adds to operational complexity that virtualization is aiming to simplify!

Selecting the Right I/O Technique

By far the biggest bang for your buck to increase performance is to select the right I/O technique. As shown in [1] , direct PCIe pass-through or SR-IOV allows you to achieve higher overall system throughput levels than virtual switching based techniques such as OVS or OVS-DPDK.

Figure 10-16 shows an example of such a performance comparison. The graph illustrates the total system throughput of an x86-based server when multiple networking VNFs (1..10) are instantiated. The VNFs are configured to forward IPv4 Internet mix (IMIX) traffic without applying additional features. Four I/O technologies are compared side-by-side: OVS, OVS-DPDK, FD.io, and SR-IOV. The former three are based on virtual switching, and thus require CPU cycles to be allocated for the switching process. SR-IOV bypasses the scheduler by offering a virtualized PCIe channel directly into each of the VNFs, but requires NICs with the appropriate support. The throughput obtained as additional VNFs are added for each of the I/O technologies is compared to a benchmark. The benchmark assumes ideal behavior of the host by mathematically extrapolating the measured throughput of the first VNF with SR-IOV. (Under ideal conditions, each additional VNF contributes the same amount of throughput to the total system throughput again as the very first VNF measured with SR-IOV, limited by the physical interface capacity of the server.)

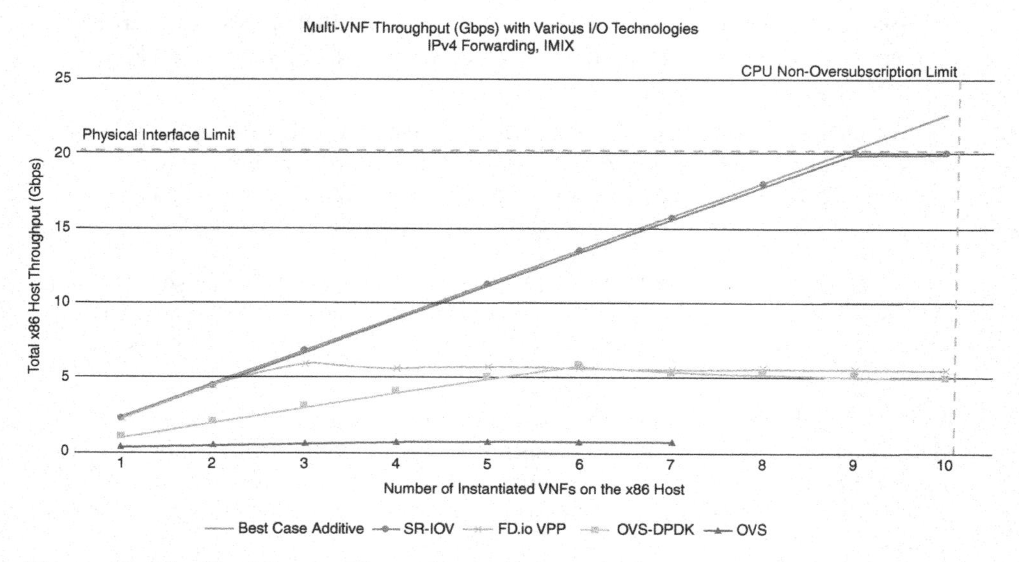

Figure 10-16 *Total System Throughput of an x86-based Host as a Function of the Number of Instantiated VNFs*

The results in Figure 10-16 highlight the current superiority of SR-IOV from a throughput perspective. For the other three techniques that are based on CPU-based switching, the total system throughput reaches a plateau, with FD.io and OVS-DPDK outperforming OVS. Note that a flattening of the total system throughput as VNFs are added implies that the *average* throughput per VNF in fact declines. This may again be operationally undesirable! Adding VNFs to the server impacts the throughput of the existing VNFs that are already passing traffic, and furthermore, the decline may not always be deterministic and predictable.

Figure 10-16 also shows that the attainable throughput per VNF is very respectable. In case of IPv4 forwarding only, multiple Gbps worth of throughput are forwarded by each VNF. In aggregate, the x86-based server is capable of delivering 10 Gbps of traffic or more depending on the number of VNFs and the chosen I/O technology. For the use cases described earlier in this chapter (branch virtualization or cloud connectivity in particular) this may be more than sufficient.

VNF Footprint Considerations

Many virtualized networking functions are configured in multiple ways in terms of number of vCPUs, virtual memory, virtualized interfaces, etc. The Cisco CSR 1000v, for example, is marketed with footprints of 1vCPU, 2vCPU, 4vCPU, and 8vCPU. Adding vCPUs to a VNF resource profile, however, does not imply that its throughput is scaling linearly. The internal VNF software architecture should be considered to assess the impact on the overall throughput and performance. In the case of the CSR 1000v, IOS XE running inside a VM only uses a single vCPU for the control plane process. So, increasing the number of vCPUs per VM in this case improves the processing that is allocated to the data plane, and for higher footprints for QoS and receive packet processing. But it does not scale the control plane in proportion to the data plane. Consider for example a comparison between a single 4vCPU CSR deployment and two 2vCPU CSR 1000v. In the former case, a single vCPU is being used for the control plane and three vCPUs are being used for the data plane processes. In the latter case, on the other hand, the total number of control plane threads generated by the two VMs is two, as is the number of data plane threads. Hence in the 2x2vCPU VNFs scenario, the control plane scales in proportion to the data plane, whereas the 1x4vCPU deployment scales only the data plane. Note however that a single control plane process for a 4vCPU deployment is sufficient for many deployments.

Multi-tenancy and Multi-function VNFs

A distinction can be made not only in how many features are executed together in a VNF, but also how many tenants (customers, departments, and partners) are configured to be processed within. This gives rise to four possible generic categories of deployment models:

- **Multi-feature multi-tenant (MFMT):** VNFs are configured to execute multiple features on a given traffic flow. Furthermore, multiple tenants share a single VNF. This model, shown in Figure 10-17, is closest to the current physical edge infrastructure deployments.
- **Multi-feature single-tenant (MFST):** In this model, shown in Figure 10-18, each tenant is allocated a (ideally) single VNF, and all of the features applied to the tenant's traffic flow are configured in this VM. Service chaining is no longer required.
- **Single-feature single-tenant (SFST):** As shown in Figure 10-19, each tenant receiving services is allocated dedicated VNFs (that is, the VNFs are not shared or multi-tenanted between multiple customers). Furthermore, in case multiple networking services are applied to the tenant's traffic streams, multiple VNFs are instantiated and the packet flow is chained between them. Note that not all VNFs are instantiated on the same server or even in the same geographical location. The service chains can span multiple servers distributed throughout the network.
- **Single-feature multi-tenant (SFMT):** As shown in Figure 10-20, separate VNFs are instantiated to deliver a single service, but each VNF can serve multiple customers at the same time. For example, a single firewall VNF could be configured to protect multiple customers, each of these even requiring a different set of firewall rules. To apply multiple services to a tenant's traffic flow, service chaining is again required, in this case even with multitenant awareness. Per-tenant service chains between the multi-tenant VNFs, IEEE 802.1ad (QinQ) VLAN trunks, or Network Services Header (NSH) based service chaining are possible options in this case.

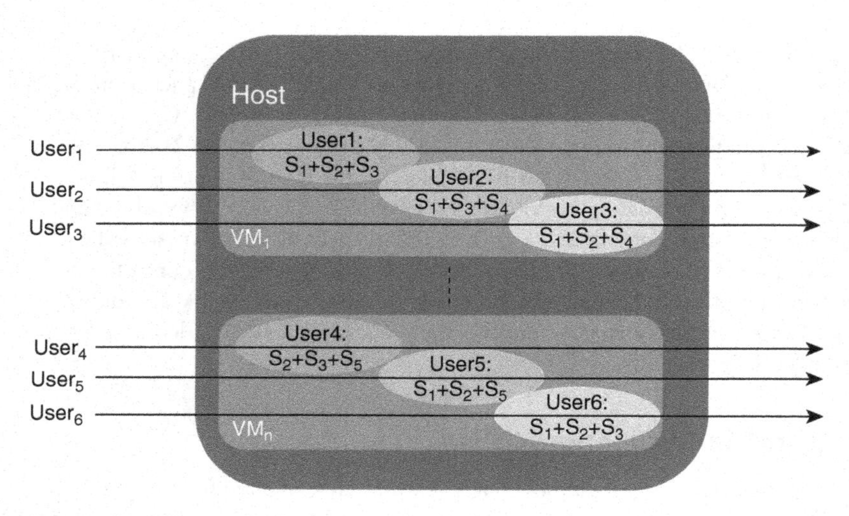

Figure 10-17 *MFMT Chaining: Each VNF Executes Multiple Features per Tenant and Serves Multiple Tenants*

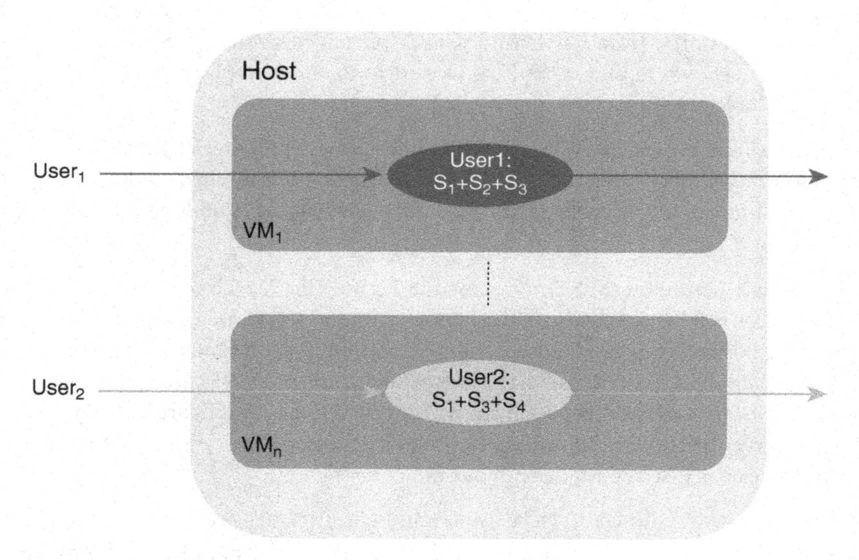

Figure 10-18 *MFST Chaining: Each VNF Executes Multiple Features but Serves Only a Single Tenant*

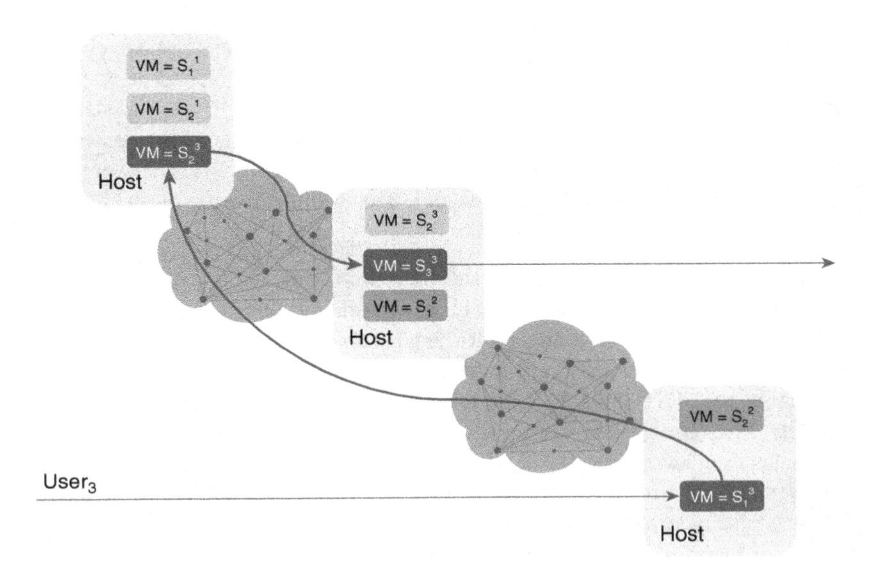

Figure 10-19 *SFST Chaining: Each VNF Executes a Single Feature and Serves Only a Single Tenant*

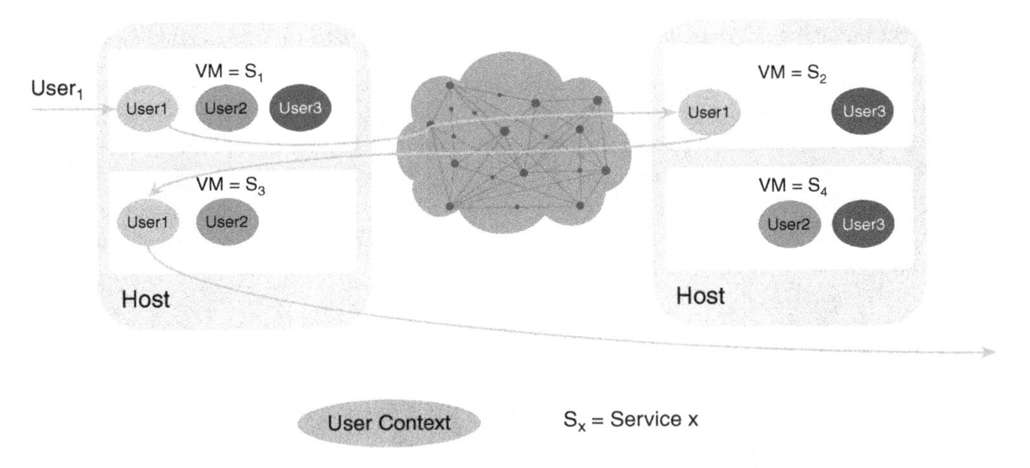

Figure 10-20 *SFMT Chaining: Each VNF Executes a Single Feature but Serves Multiple Tenants*

These deployment models are evaluated across different criteria, such as the number of VNFs required, whether service chaining is required or not, or the operational complexity of provisioning and monitoring the services.

In terms of the number of VMs required, the single-service single-tenant model requires the highest number of VNFs. The number required is the product of the number of tenants multiplied by the number of services per tenant. In some service provider use cases, the required number of VNFs in the SFST model may explode the TCO calculation. A multi-tenant multi-service model requires the least number of VNFs to be instantiated. The total number depends on the multi-tenancy capacity of the VNFs, and also assumes that the VNF is technically capable of executing all (or multiple) functions at the same time. The number of VNFs required in the remaining two models is between both extremes, with the number of VNFs of the single-tenant multi-feature model likely exceeding the multi-tenant single-feature model.

However, in terms of operational complexity, a different picture arises. Instantiation of single-tenant VNFs is typically simpler, since it only requires finding the hardware resources for the VNF(s) to be applied. In a multi-tenant deployment, onboarding an additional user requires the identification of an existing VNF with sufficient capacity. From this perspective, the SFST and MFST models offer more simplicity than the SFMT and MFMT models. Attributing orchestration complexity also to the task of instantiating the service chains then favors overall the MFST model. Failure detection and recovery models are also very different for these deployment models. Detecting the failure of an individual VNF is typically straightforward. However, the recovery complexity depends on the statefulness of features. Stateless features can more easily be failed over with mechanisms such as Hot Standby Routing Protocol (HSRP). A standby VNF takes on the traffic previously sent to the failed VNF. In a stateful environment, the flow state (e.g., for NAT sessions) must be kept synchronized between the active and the standby VNFs, which is difficult to achieve in real time, especially if VNFs are service chained across different data centers. Rebuilding the service chain also adds to the recovery complexity.

The preceding categorization illustrates the trade-offs that different deployment models offer. Consider many hybrid models in terms of multi-feature deployments. For example, NAT and firewall functions are often correlated, so they could be instantiated in a single VNF. Some features are also tenant agnostic, such as filtering globally blacklisted URLs. A VNF in this case does not need to have user awareness, and can be provisioned in a tenant-agnostic manner. This eliminates the need for tenant-aware VNFs for such services and reduces the total number of VNFs.

Transport Virtualization

Virtualization in Cisco DNA is not only relevant from an NFV perspective. Transport virtualization is crucial to allow the underlying physical network resources to be shared between many segments. Network segmentation is the capability of splitting a physical network into multiple logical partitions to keep the traffic from different groups of users/devices separated. The need for network segmentation in the enterprise is not new, but is becoming more important driven by the following recent interesting trends:

- Internet of Things (IoT) and Bring Your Own IoT (BYOI)
- Mobility in the context of the next-generation workspace

Take IoT as an example. IoT means a lot of traditionally non-IP "things" (such as healthcare instruments, HVAC and lighting apparatus, etc.) becoming IP-enabled and connected to the network. The enterprise infrastructure needs network partitioning to keep these different systems, and their administrative and security policies, completely separated. Guest access and user/device mobility is another simple but important use case where role-based access to internal resources needs to be guaranteed independently of where endpoints connect. Other common use cases for network segmentation are focused around security:

- **Security for multi-tenant dwelling:** For example, airports with multiple airlines, a public-sector building with multiple agencies, or an enterprise building where departmental separation is required (e.g., engineering, sales, and human resources).
- **Regulatory compliance:** For example, HIPAA in healthcare, PCI DSS in retail, Sarbanes-Oxley in finance, and many others.
- **Security for mergers and acquisitions:** For example, keeping policy differentiation while dealing with overlapping IP addresses.
- **Cloud computing security:** In a multi-tenant private or public cloud environment.

In order to satisfy new customer requirements and provide a solution to these important industry trends, network segmentation and virtualization is built into Cisco DNA to create logical separation of services at Layer 2 (L2) and Layer 3 (L3).

Network Segmentation Architecture

The Cisco segmentation architecture is based on three main components: network access control, network path isolation, and service edge, as illustrated in Figure 10-21.

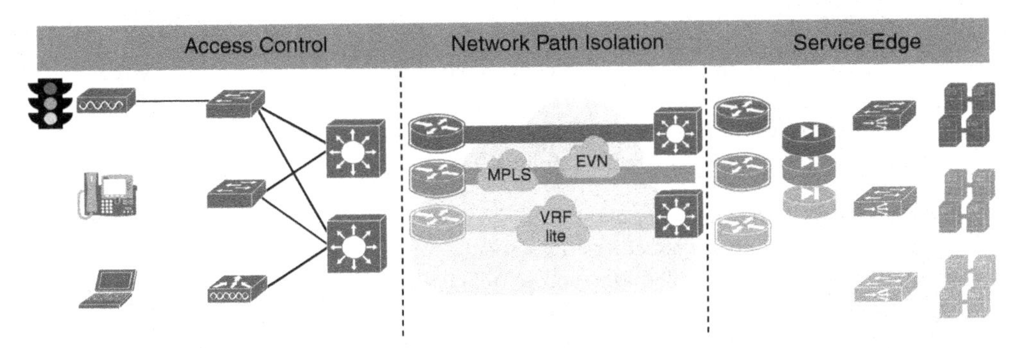

Figure 10-21 *Overall Network Segmentation Architecture*

The components and functions of the architecture are listed in Table 10-4.

Table 10-4 *Functions of Transport Segmentation Components*

Access Control	Network Path Isolation	Service Edge
Policy-based access control	Map VRFs to VLANs in access and service edge	Shared or dedicated services
Device authentication and authorization	VRF segmentation and transport	Inter VRF routing
Classification and VLAN, SGT, and ACL enforcement	Traffic isolation	Isolated application environment

Network Access Control

The access control function assigns an identity to the users/things connecting into the network so they are successfully assigned to a corresponding group. A group is used as a pointer to a set of permissions to allow for client/device differentiating access. In the context of network segmentation, the identity also provides the linkage to path isolation and virtualization techniques so that the permission is enforced throughout the network and not only at the access network device. Access control is composed of three main subfunctions:

- **Authentication:** Authentication governs who (device/users) is trying to access the network. Authentication is done dynamically via IEEE 802.1X, via Web-Auth, or via network-based classification through network sensors. Alternatively, authentication is also done statically.
- **Authorization:** Authorization defines the policies associated with the authenticated endpoint.
- **Policy enforcement:** Policy enforcement associates a parameter to identify the endpoint in the rest of the network. This parameter could be a VLAN, a VRF, an ACL, or a security group tagging (SGT). It also enforces the policy in Cisco DNA by means of the policy enforcement point (PEP).

The Cisco Identity Services Engine (ISE) is the central platform for policy definition and management; it gathers advanced contextual data about who and what is accessing the network and then defines role-based access policies.

Network Path Virtualization

The term *network path virtualization* (or *network virtualization* for short) refers to the creation of multiple logical network partitions overlaid on top of a common physical network infrastructure. Each partition is logically isolated from the others and must appear to the end device/user as a fully dedicated network and provide all forwarding, security, and services expected from a physical network. Virtualization of the transport layer must address the virtualization both at the device level and at the interconnection level:

- **Device forwarding virtualization:** The creation of VLANs for a switch and VRF for a router are both examples of creating multiple separated control and data planes on top of the same physical device.
- **Data path virtualization:** The virtualization of the interconnection between devices. This is either a single-hop or multihop interconnection. For example, an Ethernet link between two switches provides a single-hop interconnection that is virtualized by means of IEEE 802.1Q VLAN tags. When an IP cloud is separating two virtualized devices, a multihop interconnection is required to provide end-to-end logical isolation and usually is implemented through tunneling.

The solutions to implement network path virtualization are classified in two main categories: policy based and control-plane based. These are elaborated in detail to follow.

Network Services Edge

The service "edge"' is the place (central or distributed) where an enterprise deploys shared (DHCP, DNS, Internet access, etc.) or protected resources (that is, human resources databases). By default, the different logical networks (VPNs) built on top of the physical infrastructure are totally isolated from each other, so a mechanism to break this behavior is needed to allow for such shared resources.

The technical solutions to implement such shared services across virtualized networks include "prefix leaking" between routing tables using BGP or Easy Virtual Network (EVN) route replication and the use of a multicontext firewall. Providing a separate firewall per VPN allows the application and management of security policies for each virtual network independently, and it is hence the recommended deployment model. The analysis and discussion of the different deployment models of protecting access to shared services is out of the scope of this document.

Policy-based Path Segmentation

Policy-based path segmentation restricts the forwarding of traffic to specific destinations based on a defined policy and independently of the information provided by the forwarding control plane.

A classical example of policy-based segmentation is the use of VLANs and related ACLs assigned to a switch port or to a service set identifier (SSID) for wireless users. Groups of devices or users are assigned to VLANs and ACLs by static configuration or as a result of the authentication via IEEE 802.1X or other technologies. Although very common for use cases such as guest access, the main limitation of this Layer 2 virtualization solution is scalability: every time a VLAN is added, a series of parameters needs to be configured on the network devices (subnet, DHCP pool, routing, etc.).

Also, the logical isolation provided by VLANs ceases to exist at the boundary between Layer 2 and Layer 3 domains (the distribution layer devices). To extend the propagation beyond the access device, define and map a VRF to the VLAN. Figure 10-22 shows how different SSIDs can be mapped to VLANs and VRFs at the access layer.

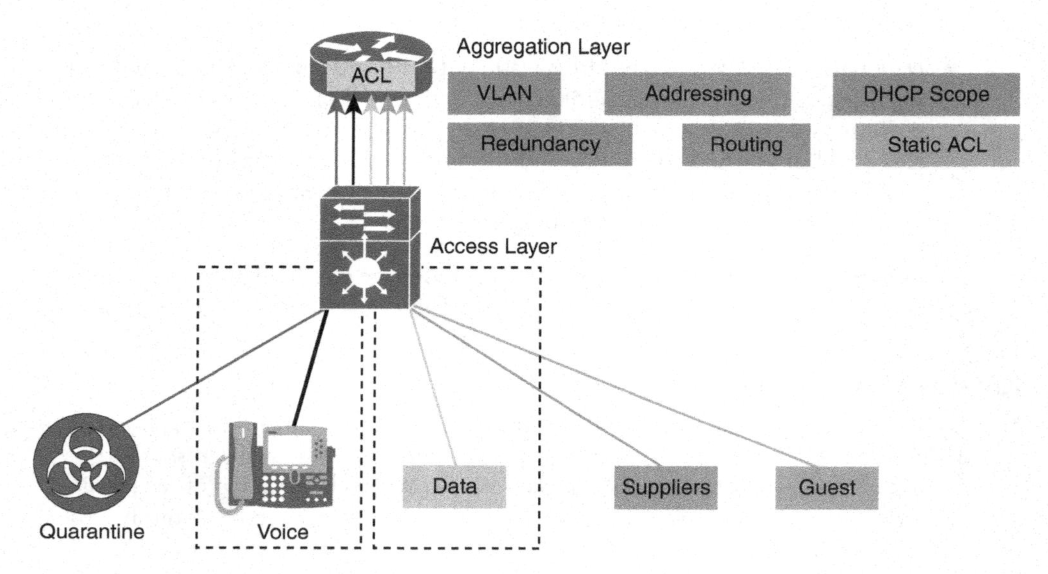

Figure 10-22 *Segmentation Example in the Campus Using Different SSIDs, VLANs, and VRFs*

Specific to wireless users, peer-to-peer blocking allows for a simple segmentation to control traffic between users connected to the same SSID by either dropping it or forwarding to the core network (the forwarding option is available only for traffic switched centrally at the WLC). Peer-to-peer blocking is used primarily for the guest wireless LAN (WLAN) and is configured at the SSID level.

For Wi-Fi access, customers in the example use the Control and Provisioning of Wireless Access Points (CAPWAP) protocol to tunnel wireless traffic from APs to a centralized WLC on top of an IP cloud and to provide the desired segmentation. SSIDs broadcast over the air interface are mapped at the WLC to different VLANs as traffic enters the wired network. To add virtualization at Layer 3, the VLANs are also mapped to a separate VRF on the first hop layer device as shown in Figure 10-23.

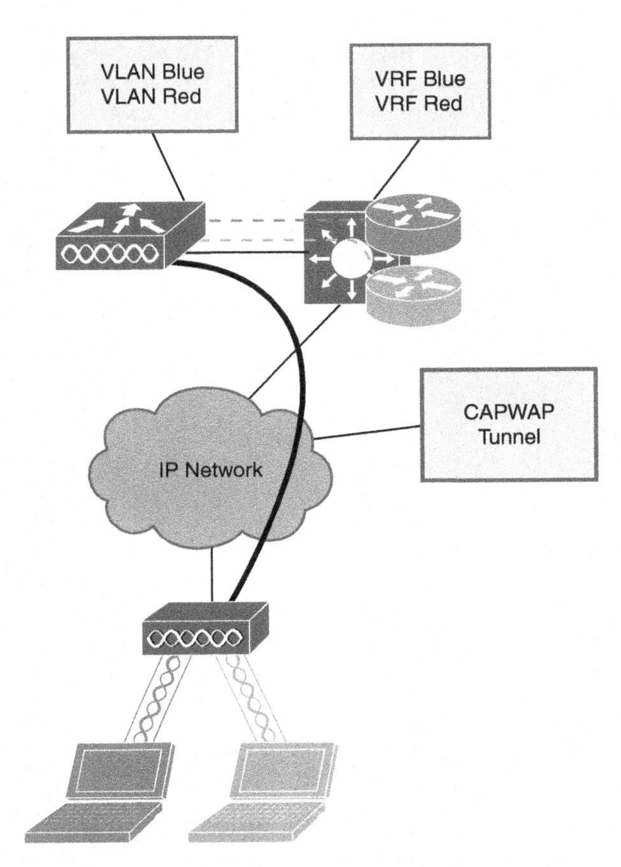

Figure 10-23 *CAPWAP Tunnel to Segment Wireless Traffic*

The Cisco TrustSec solution overcomes the previously described limitations of solutions based on VLANs and ACLs and brings role-based access control (RBAC) to the network (to all devices in the network and not just the access device). TrustSec does not require changes in VLANs and subnets and works with the existing design. It is based on three functions:

- **Classification:** SGT is assigned dynamically as the result of a Cisco ISE authorization. Alternatively, it can be assigned via static methods to map the SGT to a VLAN, subnet, or IP address.
- **Propagation:** SGT information is either propagated inline (hop by hop) or via the SGT Exchange Protocol (SXP).
- **Enforcement:** The network device enforces the policy via SGT ACLs dynamically downloaded from ISE.

A TrustSec SGT tag is inserted at L2 in the Ethernet frame in the Cisco Meta Data (CMD) field. For inline propagation, every node in the network must be able to interpret the TrustSec SGT rag and act on it. If the customer deployment does not require any-to-any segmentation, TrustSec can be used with the SXP protocol that allows the propagation of SGT information across a network that is not TrustSec enabled, as illustrated in Figure 10-24.

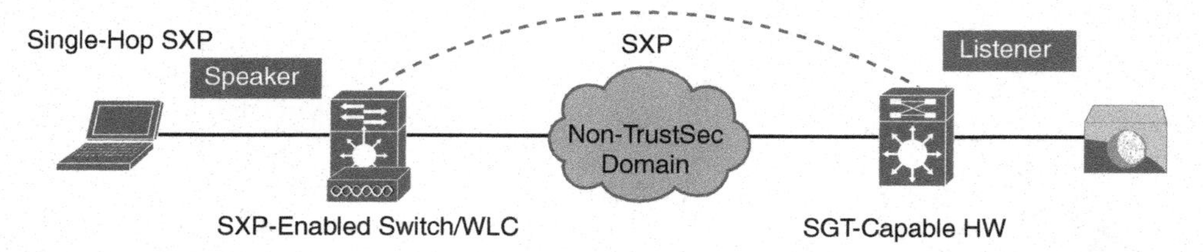

Figure 10-24 *Cisco TrustSec Solution*

In summary, policy-based technologies do not rely on a control plane to transport the virtualization information and, in order to provide any-to-any segmentation, they are hop-by-hop in nature. This can result in more deployment and management complexity and limited scalability.

Control Plane–based Segmentation

Control plane–based techniques achieve path isolation by restricting the propagation of routing information to only subnets that belong to a VPN. To achieve control plane virtualization, a Layer 3 device must use the VRF technology that allows for the virtualization of the forwarding plane. Path virtualization technologies are classified based on how virtualization info is transported across the underlying network infrastructure:

- **Multihop path isolation:** The virtualized devices are not directly connected and the virtualization info is carried across a network that is not virtualization-aware by the use of some Layer 3 tunneling technology. VRF-lite with GRE and MPLS VPN are examples of multihop solutions.
- **Single-hop path isolation:** The VRF information in carried hop-by-hop and all the devices in the path need to be VRF-aware. VRF-lite and EVN are part of this category.

Multihop Path Isolation Techniques

VRF-lite with GRE is the simplest multihop technology, where a GRE tunnel is built between the routers that are part of the same virtual network and the VRFs are mapped to the GRE header. The implication is that GRE peering sessions need to be established among all the routers that are part of the virtual network, and if a router is added in a new site, all the existing routers need to be reconfigured. This can introduce scalability limits in the architecture. In addition, GRE tunneling may not be implemented in hardware (e.g., lower-end switches), further adding caveats to the architecture from a throughput perspective. For these reasons, VRF-lite with GRE did not see a big adoption among customers and is recommended only if deployed in a hub-and-spoke topology typical of guest access scenarios.

In an MPLS VPN design, the exchange of VPN routes is achieved by using an additional control plane element called Multiprotocol BGP (MP-BGP), which is an extension of the existing BGP-4 protocol. The MPLS core is made up of provider edge (PE) and provider (P) routers. At the PE level MP-BGP is used to exchange VRF routes. This is represented in Figure 10-25. MPLS VPN uses two sets of labels. The outer label represents the PE destination and is used by the PE routers to forward the packet through the network. The inner MPLS label is the VPN label and carries the VRF information. Only the destination PE interprets this VPN label and forwards the original packet on to the associated VRF.

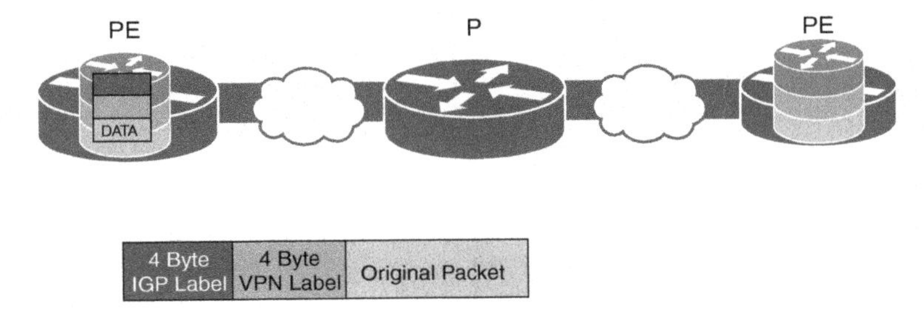

Figure 10-25 *VRF-based Segmentation*

Similar to a GRE tunnel overlay architecture, MPLS VPN based on BGP requires that a full-mesh neighbor relationship is established. The added configuration and management complexity of such full meshes are mitigated by the deployment of BGP route reflectors (RR) to relay the BGP information to other PEs in the network.

In case of an MPLS core, Virtual Private LAN Services (VPLS) is also used to provide an L2 pseudo wire service across the core network. VPLS mitigates the Spanning Tree Protocol (STP) problems that arise from the extensions of VLANs across multiple switches. However, VPLS also requires a full mesh of control plane communication and may result in MAC scalability limitations.

In summary, multihop segmentation techniques have the advantage to touch and virtualize only the devices at the edge of the network; the rest of the network ignores the VPN information. MPLS-VPN solutions scale very well and are suited to support any-to-any connectivity, relying on an underlay MPLS network based on BGP. This increases the learning curve and hence the deployment time and cost.

Single-Hop Path Isolation Techniques

An example of a single-hop (or hop-by-hop) isolation technique is VRF-lite. In this case, each and every network device is virtualized, together with all their physical interconnections. From a data plane perspective, the same concept of VLAN tags is used to provide logical isolation on each point-to-point link interconnecting the Layer 3 virtualized network devices. VRF-lite does not rely on MP-BGP or MPLS labels to carry the network segmentation information. Instead it requires the setup of hop-by-hop path isolation. Separate interfaces or subinterfaces must be provisioned for each virtual network on core-facing interfaces on an end-to-end virtualized path.

Multi-VRF is manageable for networks with a limited number of VRFs and hops in a virtual network path. As the number of virtual networks grows, new interfaces/subinterfaces and related IP addresses and routing need to be added. This increases planning and provisioning overhead, and that's the reason why Cisco introduced Easy Virtual Network (EVN).

With Cisco EVN, path isolation is achieved by using a unique tag for each virtual network (VN). This tag is called the VNET tag and is operator assigned. An EVN device on the virtual path uses the tags to provide traffic separation among different VNs. This removes the dependency on physical/logical interfaces to provide traffic separation. VLAN-based segmentation with VRF-lite is illustrated in Figure 10-26.

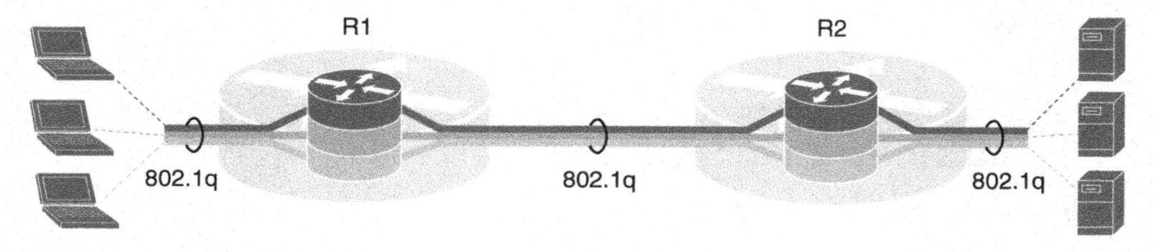

Figure 10-26 *VLAN-based Segmentation with VRF-lite*

As illustrated in Figure 10-27, only a single trunk interface is required to connect a pair of EVN devices and instead of adding a new field to carry the VNET tag in a packet. The VLAN ID field in IEEE 802.1Q is repurposed to carry a VNET tag.

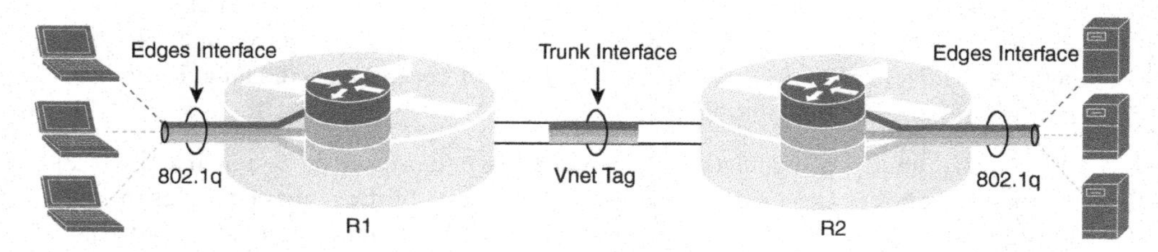

Figure 10-27 *VLAN-based Segmentation with Cisco EVN*

In summary, VRF-lite and EVN are IP-based solutions that reuse familiar technologies like IEEE 802.1Q and Interior Gateway Protocol (IGP) routing protocols to provide virtualization. This provides a straightforward migration from existing campus architecture and a shorter learning curve (for example, because complexities arising from BGP are no longer needed).

Summary

This chapter discussed virtualization as an increasingly valuable tool in the network architect's toolbox for building Cisco DNA. Both Network Function Virtualization (NFV) and transport virtualization (segmentation) fall into this category. The key takeaways in this chapter are as follows:

- Network Function Virtualization allows you to deploy networking functions—be they control plane or data plane—in your network as virtual machines running on standard x86-based hosts. This reduces the overall TCO in your network by consolidating a number of appliances into a single x86-based server, diminishing operational overheads associated with running many hardware components. Possibly more importantly, the virtualization of network functions allows you to deploy network functionality within minutes when supported by the appropriate automation mechanisms.
- VNFs can be dispatched per user group or segment, or even at an application-level granularity. They can be shared between multiple tenants, or dedicated to a single tenant. NFV thus offers increased deployment flexibility in your network!
- The attainable performance of a single VNF is currently below the performance that is achieved with a dedicated hardware device, especially if the focus is on top-line throughput. Look at NFV as complementary to your hardware-based forwarding elements rather than as a replacement!
- It is crucial for you to have a good understanding of the x86 hardware components, the operating system, and which components are shared among multiple VNFs. Understand the importance of the I/O path, since in many networking use cases the focus is on forwarding packets between the physical interfaces of the host. Understanding how the addition of a VNF to the host may affect already deployed VNFs is important to reach an acceptable operational model.
- Segmentation of the data plane and control plane functions in the network is crucial, especially as IoT use cases are considered in Cisco DNA. Policy-based segmentation is enabled in Cisco DNA with Cisco TrustSec, where tags are applied to a packet flow based on the identity and authentication of a device or a user.

Together, NFV and transport virtualization provide you with a complete set of tools to virtualize your Cisco DNA network infrastructure even down to the application or user group level! The ride continues in the next chapter.

Chapter 11

Cisco DNA Cloud

Cloud. When you read this term, you might immediately think of the advantages that the cloud offers to your business: flexibility, scalability, cost reduction...just to mention a few. It's evident that today cloud computing is considered a key ingredient of any digital transformation strategy; your company might have already embraced or started looking at the cloud as a strategy to innovate and differentiate from competitors. As a result, you likely are considering new ways to allow for faster service creation, easier experimentation, and more customer engagement without reducing the security and compliance of your network. The cloud can provide this for you.

Cloud adoption is expanding, and IT architects are growing more sophisticated in how they think about cloud computing. A lot of market research confirms this trend. For example, IDC CloudView reports that cloud adoption is accelerating rapidly in recent years, as shown in Figure 11-1.

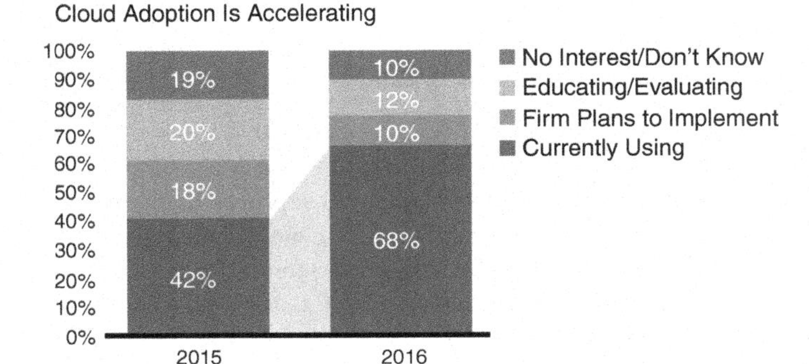

Figure 11-1 *Cloud Adoption*

As of 2017, enterprise adoption of cloud computing has truly moved into the mainstream, with 68 percent currently using a public or private cloud for more than one to two small applications, a 61 percent increase over the previous year's figure.

The trend toward cloud adoption is clear and the advantages are well understood, but if your organization hasn't already embraced cloud integration, answers that may be less obvious to you are how to integrate the cloud into your existing enterprise network, the challenges it might introduce, and how to overcome them.

The goal of this chapter is to describe how Cisco Digital Network Architecture brings together networking, security, analytics, and management components to simplify, secure, and optimize the way your organization integrates and works with the cloud.

The chapter starts with a quick introduction to the cloud as it pertains to cloud networking so that you are familiar with the terminology used. The rest of the chapter explains the following:

- Cloud service models
- Cloud deployment models
- Multi-cloud
- Cisco DNA for the cloud

The "Cisco DNA for the Cloud" section examines how Cisco DNA enables the cloud for three distinct domains: applications, network automation, and analytics and assurance.

Introduction to the Cloud

The National Institute of Standards and Technology (NIST) Special Publication 800-145 defines cloud computing as "a model for enabling ubiquitous, convenient, on-demand network access to a shared pool of configurable computing resources (e.g., networks, servers, storage, applications, and services) that can be rapidly provisioned and released with minimal management effort or service provider interaction."[1]

From this definition and having the enterprise customer in mind, it is clear that adopting the cloud is much more than just moving some applications from a private data center to a cloud service provider. Cloud computing is really a new architectural approach that considers the transport layer, the networking aspects, the security, and the analytics components. This is the main reason why in the Cisco DNA architecture the cloud is considered as another "domain," in addition to the campus, WAN, and data center, that must be fully integrated to provide the advertised advantages.

1 https://nvlpubs.nist.gov/nistpubs/Legacy/SP/nistspecialpublication800-145.pdf

Let's consider some of the main advantages of embracing the public cloud:

- **Flexibility:** The cloud offers the capability to spin up a service when needed without having to provision the required software and hardware in advance.
- **Elasticity:** You get a potentially endless pool of resources at your disposal and you can configure your solutions to dynamically increase or decrease the amount of resources needed. If built correctly, a cloud application or service easily scales vertically (same instance with more or less processing power) or horizontally (dynamically increase or reduce the number of instances to cope with a change in service demand).
- **Reliability and availability:** Most cloud providers offer a service-level agreement (SLA) that guarantees 99.99 percent availability. If a server fails, hosted applications and services are automatically moved to any of the available servers in another availability zone. Imagine if you were required to build this capability with your in-house IT infrastructure; doable but not easy or inexpensive.
- **Utility pricing:** The end user pays only for the resources it consumes.
- **From CAPEX to OPEX:** There is a shift from a capital expenditure (buying up front) model to an operational expenditure (pay as you go) model. If done correctly, adopting the cloud provides a cost reduction in operating your business. It allows you to save substantial CAPEX costs by reducing the network and server infrastructure on site. This also removes associated operational costs in the form of power, air conditioning, and administration costs.
- **Metering:** Cloud systems automatically control and optimize resource use by leveraging a metering capability at some level of abstraction appropriate to the type of service (e.g., storage, processing, bandwidth, and active user accounts). Resource usage is monitored, controlled, and reported, providing transparency for both the provider and consumer of the utilized service.

Let's consider a scenario to see how these advantages may apply in the real world. Suppose your company is an innovative market analysis and research firm called DA13. You, as the chief IT architect, are in charge of designing and implementing the infrastructure to support a machine learning (ML) application to analyze business data for a new service that the company will be launching.

The first thing you need to do is prototype the solution and decide what type of computing infrastructure you need to run the application effectively and reliably. From a quick analysis of server specifications, if you want to run this solution on premises, you need to purchase and test multiple different physical flavors of the server (with different CPU, memory capacity, type of memory, etc.) to choose the one that gives you the best results. This process is not optimal in multiple ways:

- You have to purchase all the servers in advance.
- You have to wait for the time it takes to deliver the physical hardware, to install and cable it in the rack, and to install and upgrade the related software and patches.
- Once the tests are done, the unused server becomes redundant.

Compare this process to provisioning a server in the public cloud from a cloud service provider (CSP) such as Amazon Web Services (AWS), Microsoft Azure, or Google Cloud Platform (GCP), which enables you to do the following:

- Provision the servers in minutes
- Change the server specs dynamically
- Pay only for the time you have used the servers
- Deprovision the instances that you don't need

Continuing the scenario, suppose your ML application is now in production and it's becoming evident that the server you have chosen isn't capable of handling the amount of data it needs to process. If your firm has chosen to run the solution on premises with its own server, it now must add processing power (scale up) in order to have better performance.

Suppose that a few months later, DA13 decides that there is another important use for this ML solution and another team needs to leverage it. This means that you have to add additional servers. If you run the solution in the cloud, it's fairly simple to spin up another instance of the same server and put a load balance in front and just scale horizontally (scale out in this case). If the demand decreases you can always scale down (reduce the resources per instance) and scale in (reduce the number of instance) to save money.

It's becoming pretty clear from this scenario that for most enterprise customers, the greater the adoption of the cloud, the greater the benefits may be. But sometimes people forget that cloud computing poses challenges as well, and it's important to call them out in order to have an informed decision on whether to move to the cloud and, if so, how to plan this move.

Some of the challenges of cloud computing are as follows:

- **Reduced control:** The infrastructure and services may be completely owned by the CSP; this can pose challenges when, for example, the enterprise customer has some internal strict policy for certifying and upgrade software.
- **Regulation and privacy:** Although CSPs usually implement the best security standards and industry certifications, organizations that are subject to regulations such as the Payment Card Industry Data Security Standard (PCI DSS) or the Health Information Portability and Accountability Act (HIPAA) must consider data privacy issues that may make use of a public cloud more challenging. The global availability of the services that CSPs provide makes them an attractive target for hackers.
- **Legacy environment:** For start-up companies, adopting cloud services usually is a very easy decision because they can start from scratch. For a typical enterprise, applications and services are usually written and deployed using a traditional approach and hence tightly coupled to local hardware resources (storage and network), local firewall, local load balancers, etc. It's not easy to move the applications to the cloud.
- **New IT skills:** Adopting cloud technologies requires specific skills that might not be already present in your organization. Acquiring these skills takes time and investment.

It's important to note that there are many other factors an enterprise likely would need to consider for a complete analysis when looking into selecting the right cloud solution. For example, when it comes to data backup, factors such as service-level objective (SLO), recovery point objective (RPO), and recovery time objective (RTO) are important to understand and take into consideration. But a complete analysis of the many possible factors is beyond the scope of this book and would unnecessarily complicate things.

To be successful in adopting the cloud, the most critical decision is which cloud service model and type of deployment (public, private, or hybrid cloud) to choose, a decision that is based on a combination of business, technology, and internal organizational factors. The cloud model is composed of three service models and four deployment models, and it's very important to understand them very well when deciding which combination best fits your needs.

The next two sections discuss the three different cloud service models and the four cloud deployment models.

Cloud Service Models

There are three cloud service models commonly available, as described by NIST SP 800-145:

- Software as a Service (SaaS)
- Platform as a Service (PaaS)
- Infrastructure as a Service (IaaS)

Figure 11-2 shows a representation of the service models, highlighting the most important stack components and the areas of responsibility between the cloud provider and you, the consumer.

The SaaS model provides the highest level of abstraction and simplification. The whole "service" stack, from the infrastructure to the application level, is provided by the cloud service provider. As the customer, you directly access the service through an application running on the cloud infrastructure. The application typically is accessible through a user web interface or an application programming interface (API). On the other side, the consumer does not manage or control the underlying cloud infrastructure, including the network, servers, operating systems, storage, or even individual application capabilities, with the possible exception of limited user-specific application configuration settings.

In the PaaS model, the cloud service provider provides all the components of the platform needed to run your own applications. This includes the underlying cloud infrastructure with networking devices, servers, operating systems, and storage. As a user you enjoy more control over the applications and possibly configuration settings for the application-hosting environment.

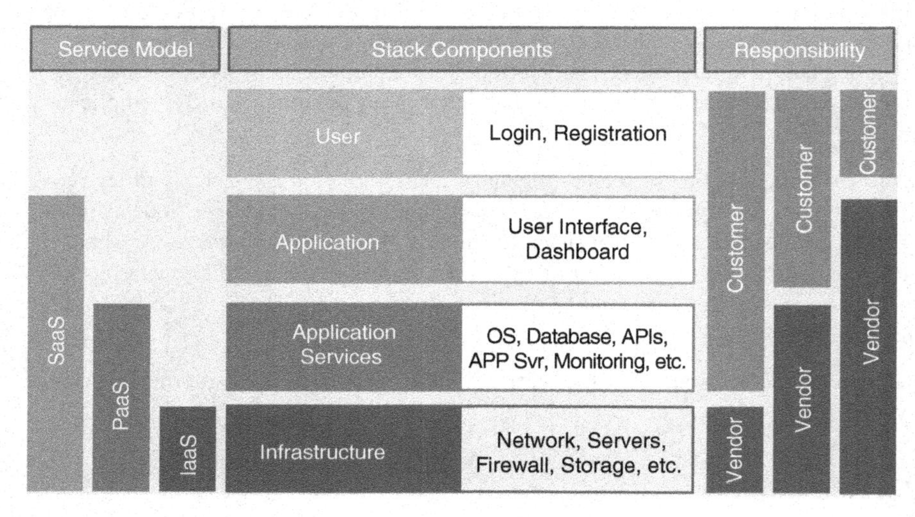

Figure 11-2 *Cloud Service Models*

Finally, in the IaaS model, you have the highest level of control and lowest degree of abstraction. The cloud service provider provides the building blocks for the infrastructure but it's up to you to put them all together into a working solution. In other words, the IaaS model provides the computing resources, the storage, and networking components (e.g., routers, firewalls, etc.) and leaves you to deploy the applications. This translates into a lot of flexibility but also additional work for the integration required.

As discussed a bit later in the chapter, Cisco DNA plays a role in helping you to deploy one or a combination of these models. The reality is that, based on your company business and internal organization, any of these models may be effective, and quite often a combination of models provides the ideal solution.

Cloud Deployment Models

Most people immediately associate the cloud with a public cloud deployment. In reality there are four different cloud deployment types and usually the success of an enterprise cloud adoption strategy is dependent on leveraging a mix of these. The four deployment types as defined by NIST SP 800-145 are as follows:

- Private cloud
- Community cloud
- Public cloud
- Hybrid cloud

Private cloud means that the infrastructure is provisioned for exclusive use by a single organization comprising multiple consumers (e.g., business units). It may be owned, managed, and operated by the organization, a third party, or some combination of them, and exists either on or off premises.

In the case of the *community cloud*, the infrastructure is provisioned for exclusive use by a specific community of consumers from organizations with shared concerns (e.g., mission, security requirements, policy, and compliance considerations). It is owned, managed, and operated by one or more of the organizations in the community, a third party, or some combination of them, and it exists either on or off premises.

In a *public cloud* the infrastructure is provisioned for open use by the general public. It is owned, managed, and operated by a business, academic, or government organization, or some combination of them. It exists on the premises of the cloud provider.

Finally, for *hybrid cloud* the infrastructure is a composition of two or more distinct cloud infrastructures (private, community, or public) that remain unique entities, but are bound together by standardized or proprietary technology that enables data and application portability (e.g., cloud bursting for load balancing between clouds).

For a startup company that is starting to build its services from scratch, leveraging the public cloud is usually a natural choice. For an enterprise that has legacy applications that were not written for the cloud, often the winning strategy is adopting a hybrid model that leverages the ease of deployment of some public cloud services with the more controlled environment of the private cloud. So, most of enterprise customers end up with what is called a multicloud.

It's a Multicloud World!

Cloud. You say cloud, but probably you should say multicloud.

There is no one cloud model or deployment type that meets your requirements. Customers today live in a multicloud world: you may use Cisco Webex as a collaboration tool and Salesforce.com for your enterprise resource planning (ERP) application, all of which are consumed via a SaaS model. But you may also leverage the Microsoft Azure Active Directory service for implementing single sign-on (SSO) to your cloud applications, and this is Platform as a Service. You may also have a Cisco Cloud Services Router 1000v (CSRv) deployed in AWS to implement Infrastructure as a Service and connect securely hundreds of branches to your applications in the cloud.

So, a hybrid cloud strategy is seen as critical by many organizations, and working with multiple clouds from multiple providers is the new normal. International Data Corporation (IDC) in April 2017 conducted a study called "IDC CloudView"[2] which covered 31 countries and reached 8188 respondents. The results of this survey, presented in Figure 11-3, confirm the growing trend toward adopting both cloud and multicloud computing.

2 IDC CloudView: https://www.idc.com/getdoc.jsp?containerId=IDC_P37198

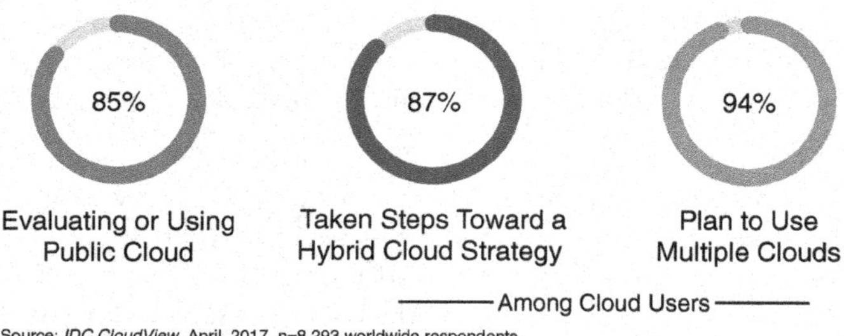

Figure 11-3 *Multicloud World*

Let's look at the numbers: 85 percent of respondent are using or considering a cloud strategy, and 94 percent of current cloud users plan to use multiple clouds. And the latter number is up from 85 percent the previous year. This increase is the result of different cloud models serving different needs, as explained before, but it's also due to the fact that cloud computing has become a strategic initiative for transforming and digitizing the business. What's even common is multiple business entities within the same organization adopting the cloud in different ways that fit their needs but may result in an unclear company cloud strategy.

This is to say that there is no single cloud. It's common to see an enterprise customer using multiple public service providers such as AWS, Azure, and Google for IaaS or PaaS services and the same customer also leveraging SaaS providers such as Salesforce and Workday. And of course, let's not forget the customer's own private clouds.

Sum it all up and the result is a network that extends to multiple private and/or public cloud services from multiple providers, a network that, contrary to the premise of cloud computing being a great simplifier, might be pretty complex to manage, control, and secure.

That's the reason the Cisco cloud strategy and solutions[3] focus on delivering a level of independence and consistency across multiple clouds. The Cisco Multicloud Portfolio brings together networking, security, analytics, and management, from the infrastructure to any application and across your network, to

- Simplify your multicloud operations
- Secure your adoption of any cloud model
- Optimize performance and agility across your clouds

Of course, there are many aspects of this multicloud strategy. In the next section, the focus is on how Cisco DNA integrates the cloud for applications, automation, and analytics and assurance.

3 For more about Cisco cloud solutions, go to https://www.cisco.com/c/en/us/solutions/cloud/overview.html.

Cisco DNA for the Cloud

Cisco DNA is the architecture blueprint for the enterprise network that connects users and things to applications in support of the digitalized enterprise business processes. Where these applications reside, it doesn't really matter: they can be in your data center, in a private cloud, or moved to a public cloud. Cisco DNA treats the cloud as another domain of the enterprise network, allowing a smooth integration with the existing areas of branch, campus, WAN, and data center, as shown in Figure 11-4.

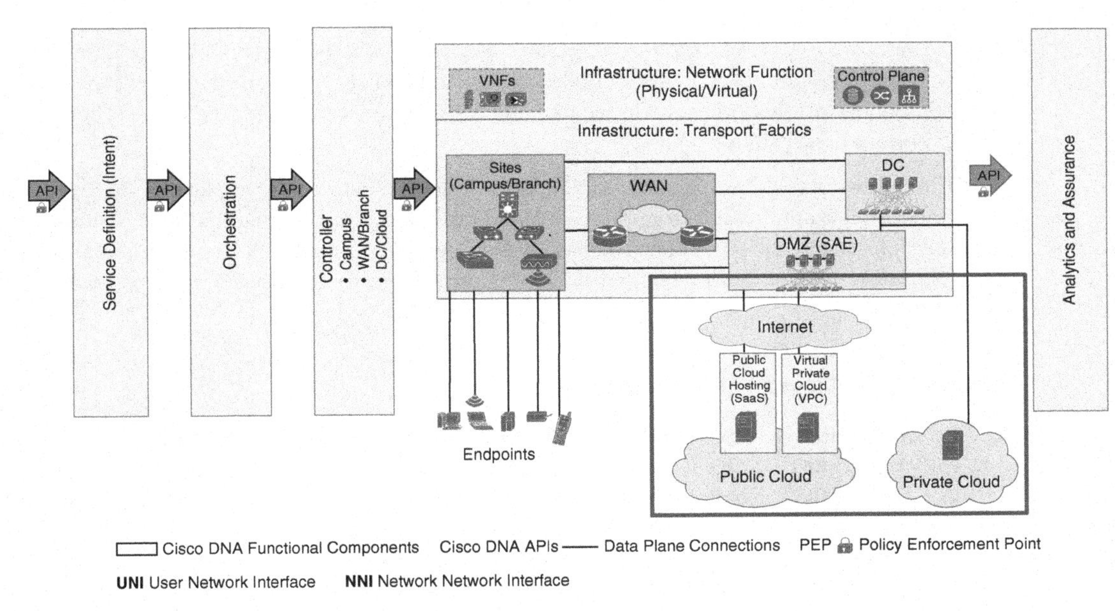

Figure 11-4 *Cloud as a Network Domain in Cisco DNA*

The Cisco DNA platform fully integrates different cloud models, including private clouds, virtual private clouds, hybrid clouds, or public cloud environments. This integration is designed both at the transport layer and the control layer of the network.

At the transport layer, the various cloud environments are fused into the enterprise network seamlessly by use of tunneling techniques. For example, a virtual IP Security (IPsec) gateway can be instantiated in a virtual private cloud (VPC) and connected to the enterprise-operated fabric by means of an IPsec tunnel. Configuring the virtual router with similar policies and functions as the enterprise-operated branch environments then makes the VPC behave like other branches that are part of the network infrastructure. For example, if the virtual router in the VPC has SD-WAN capabilities, path optimization could also be leveraged for architectures where multiple connections to the VPC are available.

The cloud becomes an essential tenet in Cisco DNA for orchestration and management, allowing Cisco DNA services and the network infrastructure to be governed by using cloud technologies. At the control layer, management and orchestration tools are deployed in the cloud to operate the network at scale and are reachable from anywhere. Analytics and telemetry engines accessing and storing information in the cloud are also part of the cloud service management aspect of Cisco DNA. By making the cloud an integral part of the enterprise network, Cisco DNA is addressing the requirement for cloud enablement to drive rapid application prototyping, fast application deployment, and continuous feedback loops to speed digitized business processes.

In summary, in Cisco DNA all architecture functions—whether control plane or data plane related—are cloud enabled: orchestration, automation, network transport functions, and analytics either run in the cloud or are able to interact with the cloud. This is an important Cisco DNA principle.

The following sections explain how Cisco DNA helps connect your application to the cloud, enable automation from the cloud, and provide a scalable Analytics and Assurance solution. This is a journey that you have just started, but Cisco DNA lays the foundation for securely and smoothly integrating your enterprise network with the cloud of your choice.

Cisco DNA Cloud for Applications

Let's revisit the scenario with the DA13 market analysis and research firm introduced earlier. Assume that, thanks to the public cloud, you have conducted a quick prototyping exercise and have decided to leverage an IaaS solution to install a server and the related storage in the cloud and run the machine-learning application there. This choice gives you the advantages of lowering the entry budget to deploy the solution while being fast to market and enabling DA13 to start providing the service within the aggressive Marketing department timelines. Also, leveraging the cloud allows the service to scale both vertically and horizontally in case the market analysis service turns out to be a success and you are asked to dynamically provide more performance and scale according to user demand.

Now you need to decide how to allow internal consumers to connect to the application. Your company has multiple locations and employees should be able to access the service from anywhere. Also, the data analyzed in the cloud is very sensitive customer data and hence you need a secure solution to provide a connection to upload the data.

Based on these requirements, you decide to extend your data center in the cloud by building a VPC and providing a secure connection to it. You also want to maintain all the advanced network services you have today on your head-end routers where you connect your branches to the main company data center: enterprise-class routing features, flexible virtual private networks (VPN), a stateful firewall, and application inspection, all integrated in your on-premises routers.

The solution that meets your requirement leverages a Cisco CSRv router in the public cloud VPC. By deploying this virtual router in Amazon AWS, for example, every branch office, campus, and data center location can directly access your application in the AWS VPC securely. You can choose from a wide variety of VPN technologies supported on the Cisco CSR 1000V, including point-to-point IPsec, Cisco FlexVPN, Cisco Dynamic Multipoint VPN (DMVPN), and Cisco Easy VPN. Your IT staff is familiar with the Cisco Aggregation Services Router (ASR) and hence with the same Cisco IOS XE software and VPN configuration used with the CSRv. This allows IT to quickly integrate an Amazon AWS VPC into the existing enterprise VPN topologies.

The Cisco CSR 1000V also includes advanced software security features, including access control lists (ACLs) and a stateful zone-based firewall (ZBFW). You can extend the enterprise security policies to access the ML service into the public cloud using a familiar platform and configuration syntax and providing the same security you have on premises.

As shown in Figure 11-5, from a Cisco DNA architecture perspective, the VPC becomes an extension of your data center.

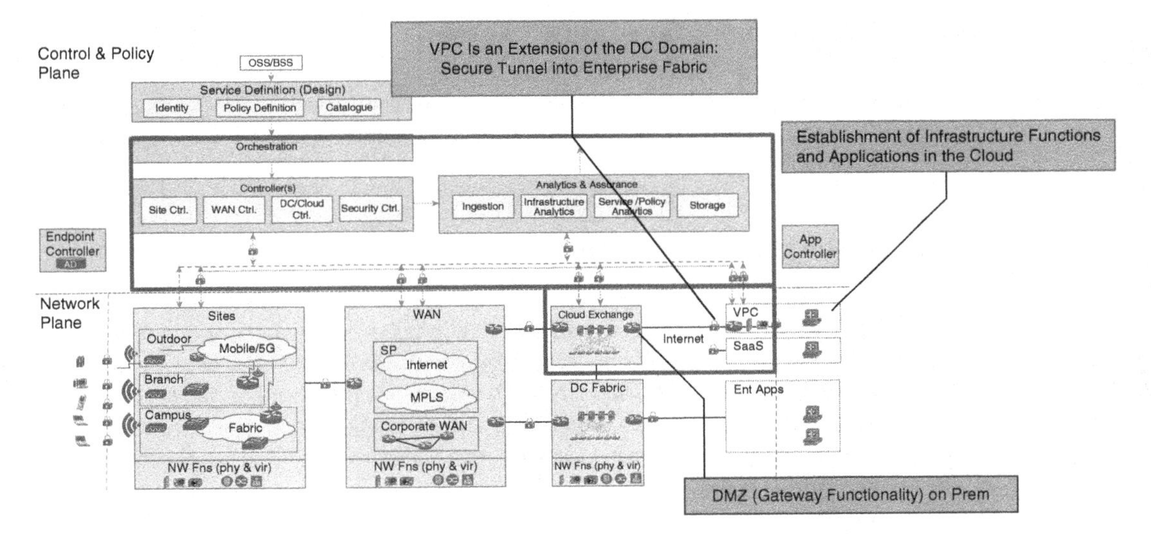

Figure 11-5 *Extending the DC to the Public Cloud*

Last but not least, Cisco DNA Center automates the whole instantiation of the CSRv router in the cloud and the VPN integration with your physical router on premises. This is done via a new Cisco DNA Center application called Cloud Connect. You simply create a Cisco DNA Center profile with your public cloud provider account and credentials, and then an automated provisioning flow guides you through the setup. You select the site and the router you want to connect to the cloud. You specify the cloud provider (AWS, Azure, etc.) and the VPC you want to connect to. You pick the type of router based on the desired performance, and then Cisco DNA Center takes care of the whole process of creating the CSRv instance in the cloud and configuring the VPN. Figure 11-6 is a screenshot of Cisco DNA Center showing the instantiation.

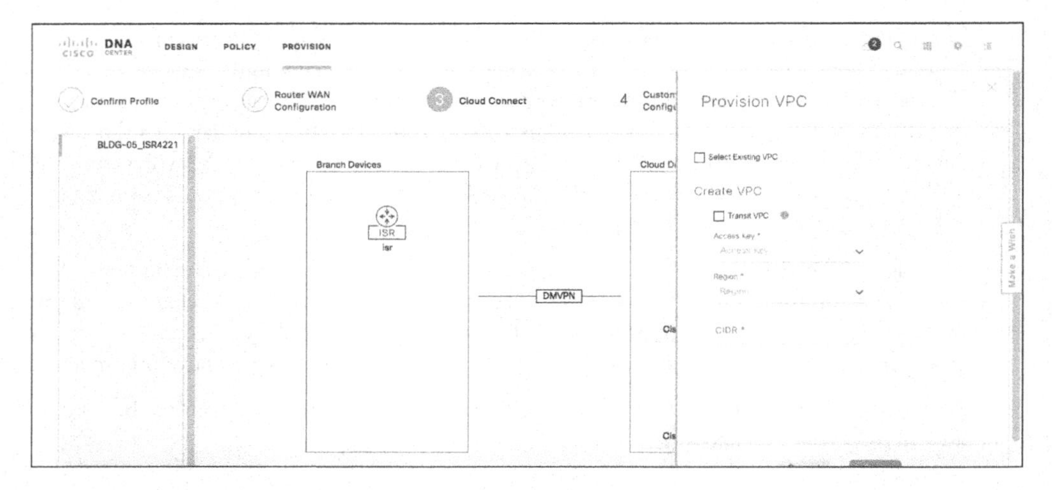

Figure 11-6 *Cloud Integration in Cisco DNA Center*

This is a great example of how Cisco DNA helps you automatically and securely integrate your application regardless of whether it's located on premises, in a private cloud, or even in a public cloud.

Cisco DNA Cloud for Automation

Cisco DNA automation provides the necessary abstraction layer to implement your business intent in an easy way, without dealing with all the underlying network configuration complexity. This is what provides the simplicity you need to make your deployment fast, secure, and reproducible. Cisco DNA automation is represented by the Cisco DNA Center platform that embeds the Cisco DNA controller and provides a single pane of glass to design your network, define network policy, provision your network, and ensure it is continuously available.

In the Cisco DNA architecture, the automation layer can be either on premises or in the cloud; it orchestrates network functions and resources that can be either on premises or in a private or public cloud, as demonstrated in the previous section with the automation of a CSRv router in the public cloud VPC.

From an architecture point of view, placing the automation layer in the cloud requires the proper security to be in place to ensure reachability into the network infrastructure from the cloud-based automation. In Cisco DNA this is done by defining the relative policy enforcement point (PEP). The PEP is either a secure Transport Layer Security (TLS) or Datagram Transport Layer Security (DTLS) tunnel initiated from the device on premises to the cloud, or a secure Restful API. It really depends on what function or service you need to manage. This is represented in Figure 11-7.

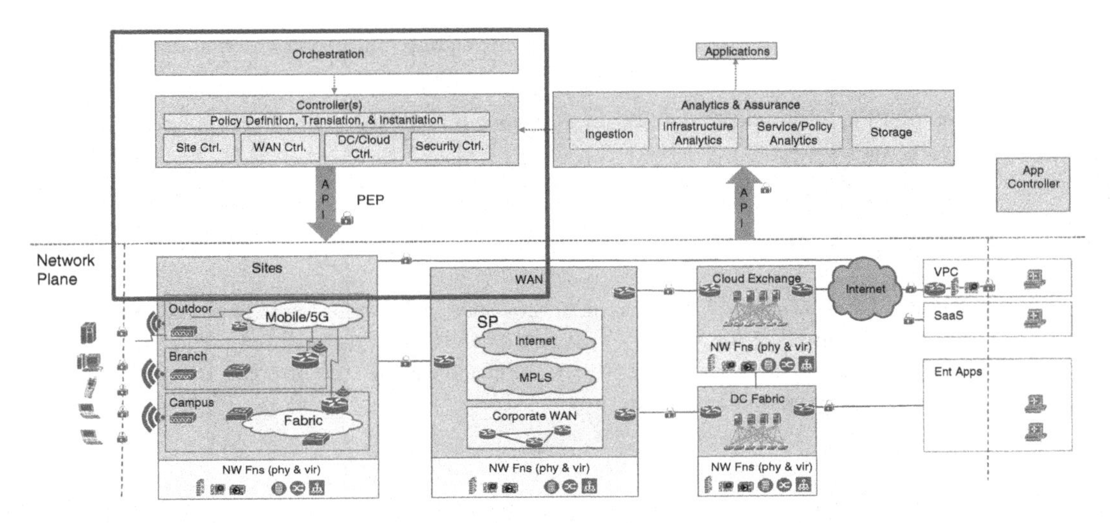

Figure 11-7 *Policy Enforcement Points in Cisco DNA*

Cisco has multiple network automation solutions in the cloud that apply to different network domains: Meraki Dashboard[4] allows the lean enterprise to automate from the cloud the deployment of a whole network stack, including wireless, switching, routing, and security. Meraki is consumed as a SaaS model and the integration in Cisco DNA is through Cisco DNA Center, which is capable of managing your Meraki devices.

Another example is the Cisco SD-WAN[5] solution, which is orchestrated from the cloud. The automation component deploys an overlay WAN architecture capable of meeting SLA requirements for business-critical and real-time applications and providing end-to-end segmentation for protecting critical enterprise compute resources.

At the time of writing, Cisco DNA Center is not available in the cloud…yet. Cisco DNA Center was built from the ground up as a platform based on modern cloud technologies, so it's not hard to imagine that Cisco strategy is oriented to provide this important automation and orchestration component directly from the cloud.

Cisco DNA Cloud for Analytics

Analytics is a major building block of Cisco Digital Network Architecture. It's main functions are

- Gathering operational telemetry from the underlying network via southbound APIs.
- Ingesting, normalizing, and de-duplicating the telemetry data.

4 Learn more about Meraki at https://meraki.cisco.com.

5 Learn about SD-WAN solutions at https://www.cisco.com/c/en/us/solutions/enterprise-networks/sd-wan/index.html.

- Extracting meaningful information by correlating multiple contextual data. This process may include leveraging machine learning.
- Sharing insights with applications via northbound APIs. One such application is Assurance.
- Communicating directly with the Cisco DNA controller to automate recommended data-driven actions. This is what is referred to as the "Cisco DNA circle of life" or closing the automation loop.

Figure 11-8 shows how Analytics fits in the Cisco DNA architecture and highlights all the different communication interfaces that are established in the architecture to integrate Analytics. Most of these leverage secure APIs and thus are independent from where the actual function runs, on premises or in the cloud.

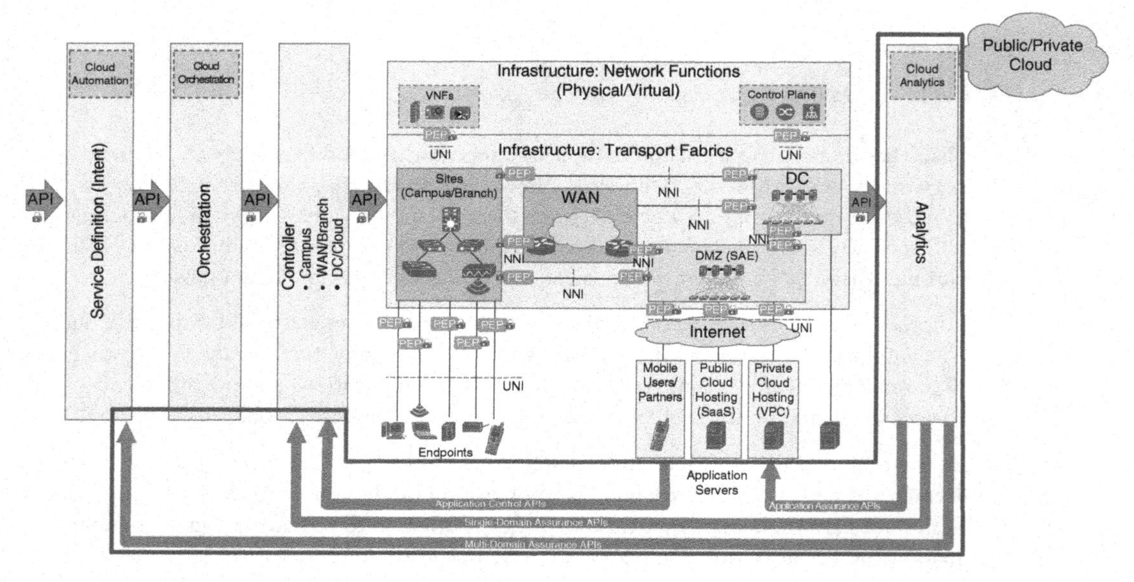

Figure 11-8 *Cisco DNA Distributed Analytics*

As explained in Chapters 15 to 17, to perform the tasks described earlier, the Cisco DNA architecture leverages an enterprise analytics engine, Network Data Platform, that is one of the services provided by the Cisco DNA Center common application infrastructure framework.

This software infrastructure platform is built with the latest big data cloud technologies and provides an abstraction layer to deploy the different Cisco DNA services (Cisco DNA controller, Cisco DNA Analytics, Assurance, etc.) on premises, in the cloud, or in multiple deployments. In other words, it gives you the flexibility to deploy the services where it makes sense. Other advantages of the Cisco DNA Center common application framework layer are

- Built-in operational capabilities to manage and monitor the infrastructure
- Cluster and node management

- Services management
- Multitenancy (roadmap)

The Analytics engine may ingest and analyze data from different sources (syslog, SNMP, NetFlow v9/IPFIX, Cisco Identity Service Engine [ISE] for contextual user/device info, IP address management [IPAM], AND CMX for Location). Cisco DNA Center is designed to scale and leverages built-in collectors to interface with the different information sources to optimize the data ingestion and transform it in common data models for all types of telemetry for easier application consumption.

Considering the huge amount of data that a network generates and the fact that the analytics engine is designed to keep a long-term state of this data to continuously validate and correlate it, it's pretty clear that the analytics component is a perfect candidate to be deployed in the cloud.

The cloud gives Analytics important benefits:

- **Elastic scale and performance:** The platform scales horizontally to adapt to the amount of data being received. Also, if more processing power is needed the platform scales vertically to the desired performance
- **Global footprint:** For a distributed enterprise, the public cloud, with its global presence, represents a great way to have a data repository closest to where data is generated.
- **Machine learning:** ML implies running complex algorithms against billion of data records per day to find and highlight traffic patterns and compute models to detect anomalies. This is done effectively only in the cloud.
- **Ongoing cross learning:** Again for ML, when it comes to building network behavioral models, using anonymized data sets covering a broad range of deployment models from different customers is a huge plus.
- **Cost effectiveness:** The installation costs and infrastructure requirements for the customer are reduced and hence time to production is expedited.

Today, Cisco DNA already has examples of running Analytics in the cloud. For example, the Cognitive Threat Analytics component of Stealthwatch for Encrypted Traffic Analytics (ETA)[6] runs completely in the cloud and leverages machine learning to process huge amounts of data received from the Cisco DNA network to gain insight into threats in encrypted traffic with real-time analysis correlated with user and device information. The platform analyzes information such as Sequence of Packet Lengths and Times (SPLT) and Initial Data Packet (IDP) to obtain packet data from the first packet of a flow and extract interesting data such as an HTTP URL or Domain Name System (DNS). It also looks at the byte distribution, analyzing the probability that a specific byte value will

6 To learn more about ETA, check out Chapter 22 and https://www.cisco.com/c/en/us/solutions/enterprise-networks/enterprise-network-security/eta.html.

appear in the payload of a packet within a flow. Finally, it processes TLS-specific information found in the TLS handshake, which can reveal interesting, unencrypted metadata used to extract data elements, such as cipher suite, TLS version, and the client's public key length. This is done for every interesting flow. Actually, the extraction is done in hardware, in the Catalyst 9000 innovative ASICs, but the data processing is done in the Cognitive Threat Analytics engine; how could it scale if not deployed in the cloud?

Another great example of how Cisco DNA is running analytics in the cloud is the Cisco Connected Mobile Experiences (CMX) Operational Insights, part of the Cisco DNA Spaces solution.[7] This is a cloud-enabled platform for managing, monitoring, and optimizing your enterprise assets, such as Internet of Things (IoT) sensors. The solution uses a wide range of tags and sensors, including Wi-Fi, Bluetooth Low Energy (BLE), and radio-frequency identification (RFID) to continually integrate, monitor, and manage your connected operations, as shown in Figure 11-9. Again, potentially you are dealing with an incredibly large amount of data that needs to be processed in order to classify, categorize the data, and extract business-relevant information.

CMX Operational Insights leverages the power of the Cisco DNA infrastructure to collect and transport the information, but the Operational Insights service is provided using a SaaS model to leverage the power and ease of deployment in the cloud.

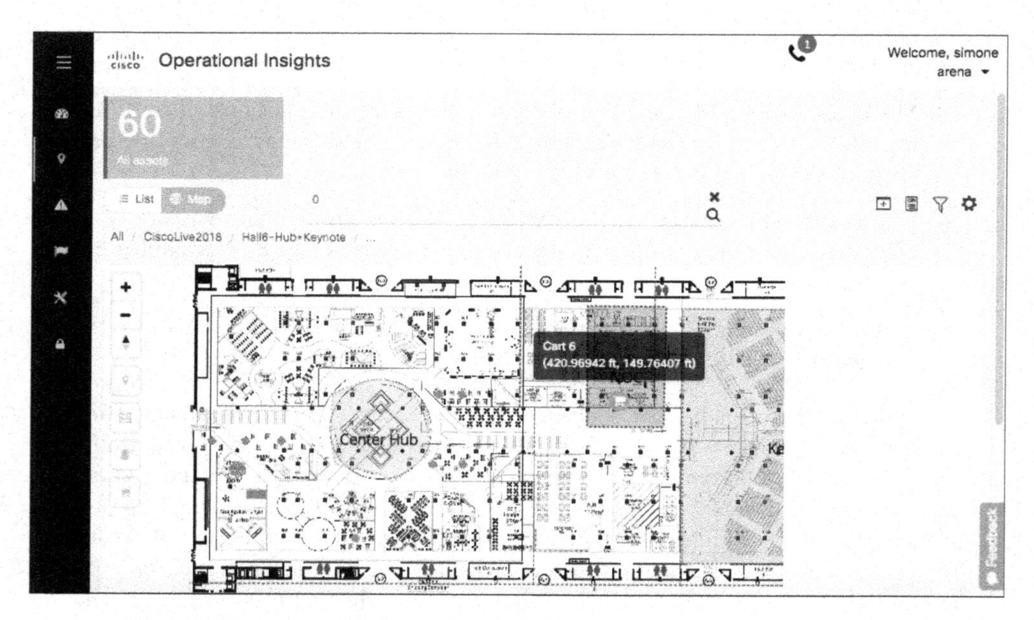

Figure 11-9 *CMX Operational Insights*

7 To learn more about CMX Operational Insights, go to https://www.cisco.com/c/en/us/solutions/enterprise-networks/connected-mobile-experiences/operational-insights.html.

Summary

The cloud is a critical enabler of any enterprise network digitization strategy. Cisco DNA embraces the cloud as a main component of the network blueprint and helps customers fully exploit the benefits the cloud gives in terms of flexibility, agility, high availability, and scale.

This chapter provided an introduction to cloud computing and reviewed the Cisco DNA solution for the cloud, including

- An overview of the different cloud service models (SaaS, PaaS, IaaS) and deployment models (private, public, hybrid cloud) available today
- The Cisco DNA architecture for cloud integration
- A overview of the specific domains of Cisco DNA in the cloud: applications, automation, and analytics and assurance

Further Reading

Cisco Multicloud Portfolio: https://www.cisco.com/c/en/us/solutions/cloud/overview.html

Cisco DNA Center: https://www.cisco.com/c/en/us/products/cloud-systems-management/dna-center/index.html

Chapter 12

Introduction to Cisco DNA Automation

The speed of change in application and compute technologies has increased rapidly in recent years through the use of controllers and DevOps models. New instances of applications are spun up in minutes as underlying compute platforms are scaled out on demand. However, network agility has not kept pace with IT agility and, as such, is often proving to be a gating constraint to innovation and time to market. IT departments are spending more than ever just to *maintain* their networks, leaving them little budget and few cycles (if any) to *transform*, thus perpetuating an ultimately self-defeating cycle.

This chapter explains the following:

- The reason it is critical to automate network operations and the many business and operational benefits that may be realized by doing so
- The difference between generic software-defined networking (SDN) and Cisco Digital Network Architecture (Cisco DNA) Automation
- The key elements to Cisco DNA Automation and their respective roles

Why Automate?

Traditional network management is performed on a "box-by-box" basis, which is a highly manual, time-consuming, repetitive, and error-prone process. Automation addresses all of these challenges by abstracting network hardware and software complexity from the network operator. Furthermore, automation provides unprecedented functionality, such as allowing applications to *directly interact* with the network infrastructure (i.e., without any manual administrative intervention). Thus, automation is a key component of intent-based networking, and enables the IT department to

- Reduce total cost of ownership (TCO)
- Lower deployment risk
- Move faster

- Scale your infrastructure, not the IT department
- Think "out of the box"
- Simplify like never before
- Enable applications to directly interact with the network

Each of these benefits of automation are discussed in turn next.

Reduce Total Cost of Ownership

According to a recent study[1], almost 68 percent of the TCO of the network is attributable to operational costs; furthermore, 83 percent of this budget is being used simply to maintain the current network environment (which, incidentally, is up 75 percent from five years ago). Put another way, businesses are spending the majority of their IT networking budget just to stand still (i.e., to maintain the status quo). If such businesses take no strategic action to alleviate this growing operational burden, within the next decade they will have zero budget for innovation and will be completely unable to meet shifting market demands.

A network controller, on the other hand, can reduce operational load by automating time-consuming, repetitive processes. The time savings can be substantial.

Figure 12-1 shows a summary of a Forrester Research study comparing Current IT time allocations versus Fast IT (i.e., IT departments which are automated). Notice the increase in time allocations to "Other" projects, which are innovations and new initiatives, under the Fast IT (automated) model.

Lower Risk

The "box by box" approach to network management is fraught with human error, which is the largest cause of network downtime, as shown in Figure 12-2.

Human error is often exacerbated when time is of the essence, such as when trying to restore network availability as soon as possible. Thus, there is an implicit trade-off between how quickly changes can be made and the inherent risks of making these changes manually.

In contrast, a Cisco DNA controller deploys Cisco Validated Designs (CVD), which are prescriptive stress-tested, scale-tested, widely deployed best-practice configurations. This reduces deployment risk on the front end (by not having to perform exhaustive lab testing of network configuration permutations to meet a specific business requirement, thus facilitating deterministic results), as well as on the back end (by eliminating typos and other human errors that may be introduced during the actual configuration deployment process).

---

1 "Cisco APIC Enterprise Module Simplifies Network Operations" by ZK Research http://www.cisco.com/c/dam/en/us/products/collateral/cloud-systems-management/application-policy-infrastructure-controller-apic/white-paper-c11-730846.pdf

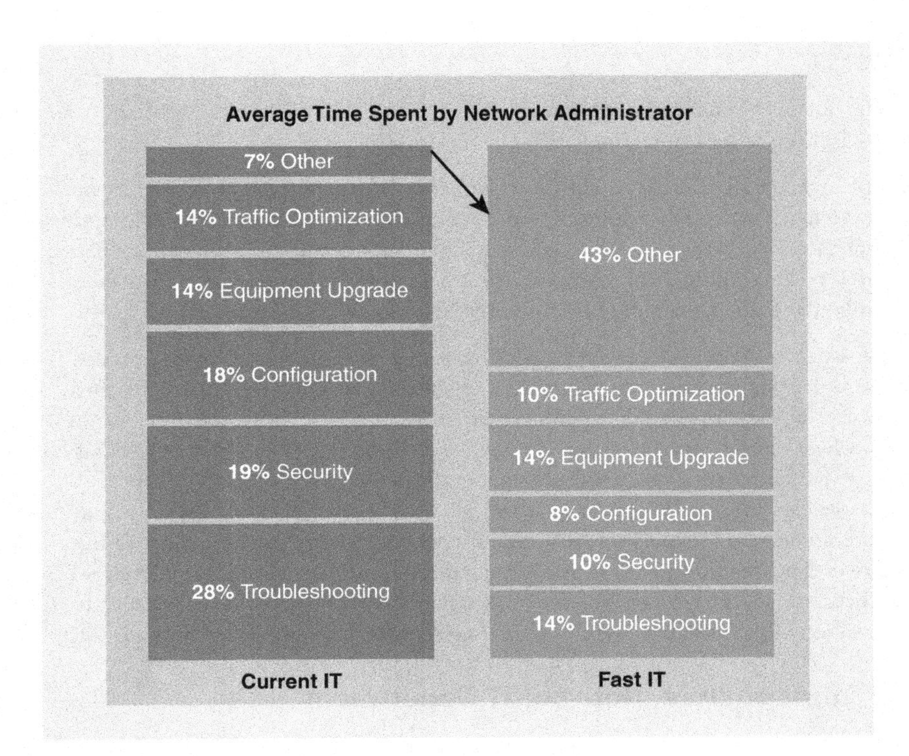

Figure 12-1 *Current IT Time Budgets Versus Fast IT (Automated IT) Time Budgets*

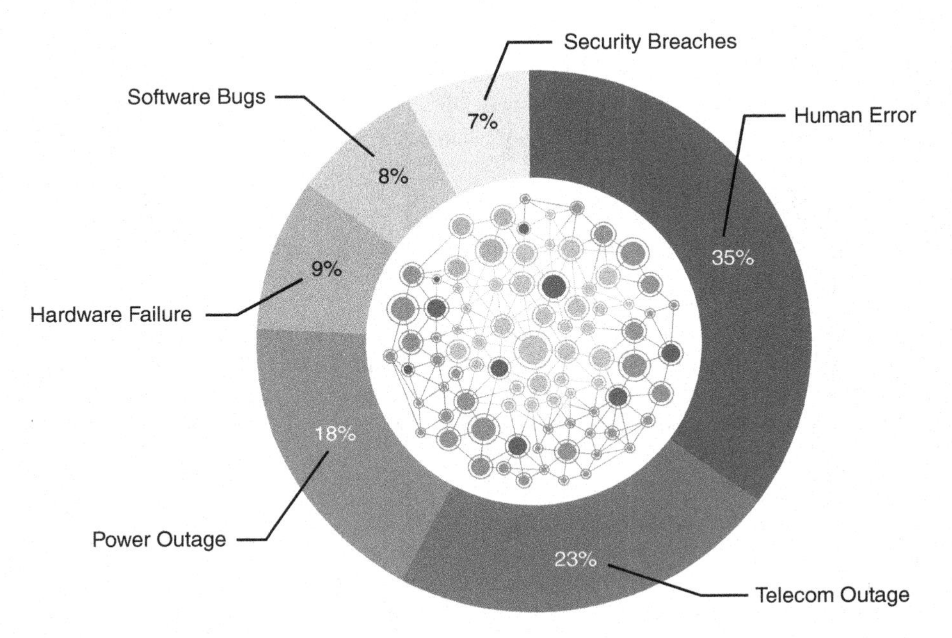

Figure 12-2 *Causes of Network Downtime*

Move Faster

Saving time not only benefits TCO but also allows you to shift focus from routine (but necessary) operations to strategic and innovative projects.

For example, when Cisco IT rolled out Cisco Jabber as its primary collaborative application, it had to make a two-line configuration change across 10,000 network devices; this deployment took over three months to complete. Similarly, some Cisco customers have reported that pushing out policy changes across their global infrastructures costs them over $1 million and takes them over four months to complete.

In contrast, when network changes are automated, then new applications are on-boarded in minutes, rather than months, which increases organizational agility and allows for businesses to adapt quickly and nimbly to new requirements. This also keeps the network well aligned to deliver on current business needs. Such was the case with Symantec Corporation, which found that automating its QoS deployments allowed it to roll out services to business-critical applications in minutes, rather than the six months it took previously. Furthermore, freeing up IT resources from operational tasks and reassigning these to business initiatives that are more strategic to the organization, such as research and development, has been shown not only to increase job satisfaction in IT departments, but also to foster innovation in digitalization, which often translates to competitive business advantage.

Scale Your Infrastructure, Not Your IT Department

About 15 years ago, wireless LAN vendors began to realize the value of controllers to manage wireless access points. Following this lead, compute vendors too began to leverage the concept of controllers in the data center, allowing them to manage exponentially more devices with fewer people. For example, in 2009 Amazon had a device-to-admin ratio of 200:1; however, by 2013 this ratio was 10,000:1. Put another way, Amazon was able to manage 50 times more devices per admin within a four-year period. The key to this massive increase in scaling efficiency? Automation.

Note In contrast to Amazon, the 2009 device-to-admin ratio in IT networking departments was 50:1 and remained at more or less that same level for several years thereafter.

Industry trends, such as mobility, Bring Your Own Device (BYOD), and the Internet of Things (IoT), continue to place exponentially increasing demands on the network infrastructure. For example, in 2017 Gartner estimated that there were 8.4 billion devices connected to the Internet, and that by 2020, these would exceed 20 billion.[2] However, other industry analysts predict closer to 30 billion.[3]

2 Gartner, "Gartner Says 8.4 Billion Connected 'Things' Will Be in Use in 2017, Up 31 Percent from 2016," February 7, 2017, https://www.gartner.com/newsroom/id/3598917.

3 IEEE Spectrum. "Popular Internet of Things Forecast of 50 Billion Devices by 2020 Is Outdated." August 2016, https://spectrum.ieee.org/tech-talk/telecom/internet/popular-internet-of-things-forecast-of-50-billion-devices-by-2020-is-outdated

As devices increase, so does the network infrastructure. However, IT budgets do not typically increase at the same rates (if at all), creating a "complexity chasm" between the number of devices being added to the network and the number of devices that the IT department can effectively manage, as is shown in Figure 12-3.

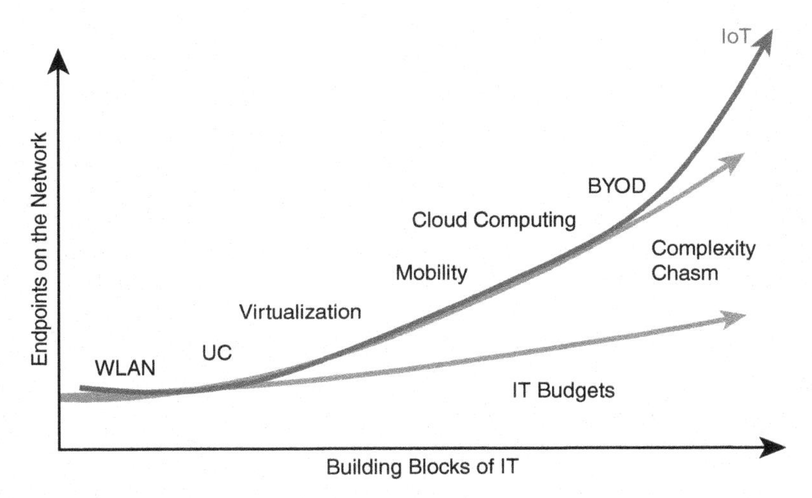

Figure 12-3 *Widening IT "Complexity Chasm"*

To keep up with such industry trends to avoid getting stuck in a complexity chasm, IT departments need to work smarter than ever, by automating.

Think "Out of the Box"

Box-centric network management forces a network administer to instantiate a business requirement on each network device manually and manage these independently. For example, many enterprise network devices have access lists that are thousands (if not tens of thousands) of lines long; often these are poorly documented and many entries therein may no longer even be relevant (yet most administrators wouldn't dare remove suspected stale or legacy entries, and would rather just leave these be, "just in case"). Furthermore, it may be difficult to compare and correlate if every policy enforcement point (PEP) in the network infrastructure has a consistent view of the overall enterprise policy.

In contrast, a controller-based approach allows you to view policy as a holistic network-wide expression of intent. You only need to express your business intent once, and the controller ensures that this intent is instantiated consistently at every PEP in the network. Should a policy change, or a specific rule no longer be needed, such incremental changes are similarly abstracted and efficiently managed by the controller.

Simplify Like Never Before

The biggest barrier to technology adoption in the enterprise network architecture is complexity, especially the complexity that results from platform-specific differences, whether these be hardware or software inconsistencies. For example, less than 10 percent of the over 3000 features in Cisco IOS software are deployed in production networks by the majority of customers, who cite complexity as the biggest barrier to deployment.

One of the single greatest benefits provided by the network controller in a Cisco DNA architecture is simplicity through abstraction. Specifically, you (as a network operator) no longer have to be a CCIE to deploy Cisco Enterprise Network Function Virtualization (ENFV), Software-Defined Access (SDA), Software-Defined Wide Area Networks (SD-WAN), or any other complex technology solution over your infrastructure. The controller abstracts all platform-specific capabilities, constraints, syntax, and caveats from you. All you need to do is express business-level intent, and the controller does the rest. First it translates your intent into Cisco Validated Design device-specific configurations; then it deploys these configurations end to end across your infrastructure.

Enable Applications to Directly Interact with the Network

Automation via network controllers also presents entirely new capabilities, such as allowing applications to interact directly with the network infrastructure—without any manual intervention. For example, a collaborative application can inform a controller of a proceeding voice or video call, allowing the controller to deploy the necessary QoS policies—end to end—in real time. Continuing the example, when the call has terminated, the controller is also informed of this event and can then remove any dynamically added policies, thus freeing up networking resources for future requirements. Such capabilities are not limited to collaboration applications, but are completely open to any application. Specifically, controller northbound application programming interfaces (API) allow applications to interact directly with the network controller to make real-time requests of the infrastructure.

Is Cisco DNA Automation the Same as SDN?

Since the term "software-defined networking" (SDN) was coined around 2009, it has morphed into many different expressions. The original SDN concepts focused on a separation of the infrastructure control plane from the data plane, such that control plane functions would be centralized. In such a centralized system, the network controller has at times been referred to as a "god box," as it handles all control-plane decisions. However, such a fully centralized system comes at the cost of the many advantages realized by distributed systems.

Centralized Versus Distributed Systems

Centralized systems, where decisions are made at a central node, are the antithesis of distributed systems, where component devices are enabled and empowered to make autonomous decisions. While there are attractive advantages to centralizing certain functions, such as policy, the advantages offered by distributed systems should not be dismissed lightly.

For instance, the effectiveness of distributed systems is evident in the design and evolution of the Internet itself: the original purpose of the Internet was to provide a communication system with no single point of failure, where network devices could make independent and dynamic decisions of how to get information from point A to point B. Such decisions could be coordinated—via routing protocols—but ultimately network devices make these decisions autonomously. The Internet has proven itself to be the most robust telecommunications system the world has ever known because of its distributed nature.

Similarly, DNS has proven itself to be the world's largest and most dynamic database, and it too is a distributed system. Likewise BGP, which is based on distributed autonomous systems, has proven itself to be the most effective policy-routing protocol ever.

The point of these examples is that there are many extremely well-proven advantages to distributed systems, including resiliency, scalability, flexibility, etc. As such, it would be unwise to discard these many advantages in favor of a fully centralized system.

Optimally, a network architecture should merge the advantages of both centralized and distributed systems, which is a goal of Cisco DNA; this goal is realized by declarative control, which is discussed next.

Imperative Versus Declarative Control

Cisco DNA combines the advantages of both centralized and distributed systems by making an important distinction in the *type of control* that the network controller wields over the infrastructure, which may be either imperative or declarative.

Imperative control focuses on the details of *how* a specified objective is to be realized. In other words, each step to realize the objective is broken down in explicit detail, and then the controller sends these step-by-step instructions to the network device, which follows these implicitly. All intelligence and decision-making capabilities are thus handled by the controller; the role of the device is relegated to following instructions and reporting back. An analogy of imperative control is a GPS device that provides a driver explicit turn-by-turn directions to get to a particular destination.

Declarative control, in contrast, focuses on *what* should be accomplished rather than *how* it is to be accomplished. For example, "treat Cisco WebEx with priority" is an example of what should be accomplished. On some platforms, this may mean assigning WebEx audio to a hardware priority queue, while on others this may mean assigning it to a software low-latency queue. The controller doesn't care either way, as long as the result is achieved. As such, intelligence and decision making are shared between the controller and the network device(s), with the device being enabled and empowered to make implementation decisions of the expressed intent. A corresponding analogy of declarative control is getting in a taxi and telling the driver your intended destination (versus following a GPS-calculated turn-by-turn route); you don't particularly care which route the driver takes, as long as you get to your destination.

The Cisco SDN Strategy

The Cisco approach to Cisco DNA Automation is not to make the controller a "god box", but rather to continue to harness the power, speed, scalability, and flexibility of distributed systems in the infrastructure while also coordinating their management and policy via a centralized network controller, using a declarative model of control. For example, path selection, QoS, and security policies can all be centrally managed by the Cisco DNA controller, but distributed network devices still make routing, scheduling, and dropping decisions independently.

Thus, utilizing a declarative control model, the advantages of both centralized and distributed systems are combined into a powerful yet simple-to-manage Cisco Digital Network Architecture.

Automation Elements

Deploying intent across the network infrastructure, rather than on a box-by-box basis, requires key functional components. Three key components to Cisco DNA Automation include

- Network programmability
- Network controller
- Network orchestrator

Network Programmability

Customers have expressed a clear preference against "homogenous networks"; that is, a network infrastructure composed exclusively of one vendor's products. Most customers are averse to homogenous networks for fear of being "locked in" to a single vendor's architecture, support system, product direction, strategy, pricing, etc. As such, "heterogeneous" or multivendor networks are far more common. However, while heterogeneous networks sidestep the previously mentioned concerns, they do so at an additional cost of management complexity, as now the IT department has to support disparate hardware and software products, with different capabilities and features, and they must do so via different operating systems, syntax, and management tools. As such, having a common, open, and standards-based interface to programming network devices would abstract and alleviate the additional complexity inherent to heterogeneous networks.

Another advantage that network programmability protocols offer is execution speed. For instance, interfaces such as the command line interface (CLI) were never intended to handle real-time operations, as they were designed on the assumption that a human would be typing the commands that the network device would then execute. That being the case, it's not uncommon for some platforms to take several hundred milliseconds to execute a given command. For manual configuration, such delays are barely noticeable, as generally it takes much longer to type the command than to execute it. Furthermore, most manual changes are done during scheduled change windows anyway, and as such, the millisecond at which the commands begin being executed doesn't particularly matter (as no traffic is typically flowing through the box during such a scheduled network downtime). However, to realize the vision of applications interacting directly with the network, new interfaces for network programmability need to be supported by network devices, as delays of even a few hundred milliseconds are often unacceptable to meet such real-time application requirements.

Additionally, network programmability can be combined with data models, like YANG (which is a tongue-in-cheek acronym standing for "Yet Another Next Generation"; YANG is defined in IETF RFC 6020). Data models are very powerful constructs, as they facilitate abstraction between the network controller and the infrastructure and present a uniform method to describe data across multivendor platforms. The data being described can include configuration capabilities and options, as well as counters and other metrics being instrumented by the device. As such, data models can be leveraged both by network controllers (for configuration) and by analytics engines (for telemetry).

Network programmability is discussed in detail in Chapter 13, "Device Programmability."

Network Controller

The network controller is the heart of Cisco DNA Automation. The controller provides these key functions:

- Solicits business intent from the network operator
- Interfaces directly with applications, via northbound APIs, to capture real-time application requirements of the network
- Defines the Cisco DNA services at an abstract level to align with the business intent
- Translates the policy into network element configurations
- Interfaces directly with network devices, via southbound APIs, to program these network devices to instantiate the business intent and/or application requirements
- Instantiates and programs network functions (L2–L7) that support Cisco DNA services
- Keeps track of host/user/network element databases
- Assists in the setup and configuration of the transport infrastructure
- Provides programmatic interfaces to the network orchestrator, analytics platform, infrastructure, and network functions
- Hosts both Cisco and third-party controller applications
- Provides the necessary API infrastructure to host local or remote controller applications

Some of these key functions are illustrated in Figure 12-4.

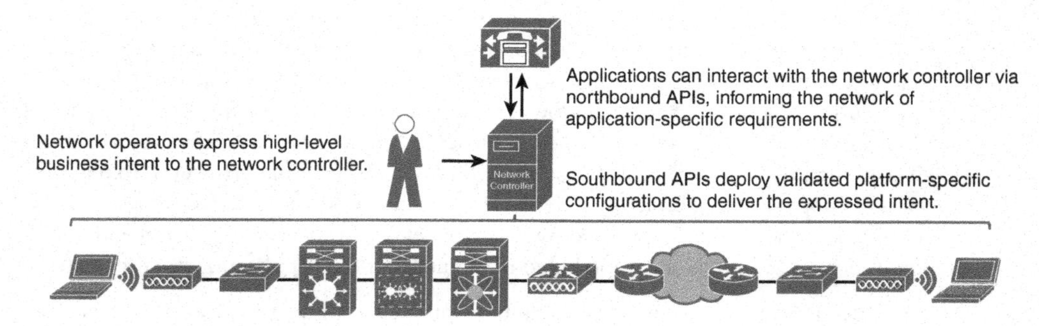

Figure 12-4 *Key Functions of the Network Controller*

As such, the controller can be likened to a mediator between the operator, the applications, and the network. It speaks the languages of all three parties, allowing for efficient communication without the burden of each party having to learn the vocabulary, language, and communication style of the other.

Network controllers are discussed in detail in Chapter 14, "Cisco DNA Automation."

Network Orchestrator

As the merits of centralizing policy and management via a network controller are well understood, it's hardly surprising that multiple network controllers were developed in parallel for respective places in the network, so as to capitalize on time to market.

For example, the Cisco Data Center Network Manager (DCNM) controller was developed for managing DC fabrics on Nexus platforms. Similarly, the Cisco Application Policy Infrastructure Controller (APIC) was developed to harness the Cisco Nexus 9000 Series switches' unique capabilities to deploy Cisco Application Centric Infrastructure (ACI). Following this lead, a controller was likewise developed for the enterprise infrastructure (beyond the data center), namely the Cisco Application Policy Infrastructure Controller Enterprise Module (APIC-EM). APIC-EM, in turn, evolved into a software function within the Cisco DNA Center appliance, internally referred to as the Network Controller Platform (NCP).

The challenge presented by having multiple controllers is to coordinate policy across the domains that each controller administers. This is the role of the network orchestrator; specifically, to coordinate cross-domain policy.

In other words, when multiple network controllers are present, the following occurs:

- The function of soliciting business intent shifts from the network controller to the network orchestrator
- The network orchestrator ensures that the business intent is conveyed to each network controller

Each network controller, in turn, continues to be responsible for expressing and instantiating the intent to the individual network devices. As such, it can be said that the network orchestrator is a "controller of controllers."

Note Some may object to the effect of: "Wouldn't it just be easier and simpler to have a single controller of everything?" This is a valid objection, at least in theory. In practicality, though, the challenge of developing a single controller for every type of network device would likely serve only to excessively delay automation solutions. Additionally, different places in the network have different characteristics, needs, and constraints. For example, data centers typically have highly uniform topologies (such as spine-and-leaf), while enterprise networks typically have much greater diversity in their topologies. Conversely, enterprise networks need to support device mobility; however, this is not a requirement in a data center, where servers are fixed and hard-wired. As such, controllers are optimized and tailored to their respective domains.

Summary

This chapter introduced the many benefits of automating the network infrastructure, which include the following:

- Reducing TCO, by allowing IT departments to reallocate expensive operational resources toward innovation
- Lowering risk, by minimizing the main cause of network downtime, which is human error
- Moving faster, by allowing new applications to be on-boarded in minutes rather than months
- Simplifying operations, by abstracting network complexity from the operator
- Providing new capabilities, such as allowing applications to interact directly with the network

Following this, Cisco DNA Automation was compared with centralized software-defined networking (SDN) architectures. The merits of distributed systems were reviewed, as were the imperative versus declarative models of control. This discussion concluded with how Cisco DNA Automation combines the advantages of both centralized and distributed systems via a declarative model of control.

Finally, the principle elements of Cisco DNA Automation were reviewed, including the following:

- Network programmability, which provides an open and real-time interface between a network controller and heterogeneous network devices

- Network controller, which serves a mediator between the operator, applications, and the network
- Network Orchestrator, which is a "controller of controllers" in a multidomain network

Each of these elements are discussed in additional detail in the chapters that follow.

Further Reading

"Cisco APIC Enterprise Module Simplifies Network Operations" by ZK Research http://www.cisco.com/c/dam/en/us/products/collateral/cloud-systems-management/application-policy-infrastructure-controller-apic/white-paper-c11-730846.pdf

Greene, N., R. Parker, and R. Perry. "Why a Digital-Ready Network Makes Business Sense." IDC White Paper, sponsored by Cisco. January 2017. https://www.cisco.com/c/dam/en/us/solutions/collateral/enterprise-networks/digital-network-architecture/digital-network-business-sense.pdf.

Chapter 13

Device Programmability

A fully automated network is a lofty but challenging goal to realize with traditional interfaces and methods. Today the vast majority of network changes are performed manually. The mistakes and policy violations that are inherent to such manual processes are what lead to the majority of operational expenditures on network visibility and troubleshooting. Network engineers are simultaneously an organization's greatest resource and its biggest source of risk. In contrast to the growth of rapid provisioning and configuration management in other areas of IT, the network has fallen behind. In an attempt to assist and accelerate adoption of network automation, attention must be given to not only the network controller but also the individual network element.

Device programmability describes the capability to extend configuration management, operational state, and traffic engineering through application programming interfaces (API) and open protocols. These APIs for the network element extend direct access to business support systems (BSS) and operational support systems (OSS). In addition, they can offload some level of effort from the network controller or configuration manager through model-based data abstractions to simplify configuration and provide consistency across platforms and new protocols, allowing a modern web-like interface to provide get and set transactions.

This chapter explains the following:

- The current tools for network programmability, including their benefits and shortcomings
- Model-based configuration and operational data in YANG
- NETCONF, RESTCONF, and gRPC protocols
- How telemetry leveraging YANG can expose normalized operational data
- Tools to leverage programmability
- New capabilities available via application hosting on IOS-XE platforms

Current State of Affairs

Traditional network engineers focused on learning command-line interfaces (CLI) across many platforms and vendors. It is a human skill that does not translate well to machines. However, engineers are by definition a resourceful bunch, and network engineers are no exception.

Many, if not most, engineers use Microsoft Notepad or spreadsheets leveraging Find/Replace as "configuration management" and then Copy/Paste the text into a console. This practice has been around for years and evolved using versioning tools to control release management of updating templates or adding new features or adding templates for different device types. In addition, the practice of documenting methods of procedure (MOP) as an ordered list of commands to enter and steps to verify is commonplace.

CLI Automation

Scripting configuration changes in Perl or Python is quite common; however, this is a very crude form of automation. While it solves some of the problems generated by "finger-defined networking" (i.e., manual typing of commands), it falls victim to an interface intended for human interaction, as CLI presents many syntax changes, modes, and prompts. Tools were painstakingly generated and shared by the open community in an attempt to mask some of the complexity.

The majority of CLI automation is based on Python Expect. A session is created to the network element and characters are interpreted by the script instead of passed to the screen. It is called Expect because the script waits for some expected characters to return before running the next line in the script. In the case of configuring a Cisco router, the script must be able to establish a connection over Secure Shell (SSL), handle encryption negotiation, determine whether the characters received are for a login prompt, a user mode prompt, an exec mode prompt, a configuration mode prompt, an interface configuration mode prompt, and the list goes on. The Expect script must know what characters it should receive from the remote device. This is usually a prompt, but all cases must be accounted for. If the session has a question or confirmation step before returning to the prompt, that must be accounted for as well. If a script receives something it did not expect, it continues waiting until it times out and ends in a failure with only the subset of intended commands prior to the unexpected result entered. If this sounds complex and painful, that's because it is.

Fortunately, the open source community has created libraries and functions to assist in this effort. Paramiko is a Python (2.7+, 3.4+) implementation of the SSHv2 protocol, providing both client and server functionality. Netmiko took this a step further and is an implementation geared specifically for interacting with several network device types across vendors. These tools dramatically simplify configuration automation, but have some drawbacks. Because they are based on automating the interaction with the human interface, they are sensitive to the list of expected characters. Therefore, if there is a new configuration mode or some new command that requires a confirmation or additional response like yes/no before returning to the prompt, then those additional cases must be added by the user within their script or by the open source community in a newer version of the library. Additional shortcomings are that the errors or warnings sent by the network element are ignored or some logic must be added to interpret the text of the warning and react accordingly. Also, the error may be simply inadequate to respond to, such as

```
Invalid input detected at '^' marker.
```

There are even more advanced tools to help with CLI automation. These tools look to abstract the configuration as a description of the intended function, and include

- Cisco Application Policy Infrastructure Controller Enterprise Module (APIC-EM), which leverages CLI automation for interacting with Cisco networking devices (while Cisco DNA Center is evolving to model-based programmability, as will be discussed later in this chapter).
- Cisco Network Services Orchestrator (NSO), which utilizes the CLI in the Network Element Driver (NED) for communicating with devices that do not support modern programming interfaces.
- NAPALM (Network Automation and Programmability Abstraction Layer with Multivendor support) is a Python library that implements a set of functions to interact with different network device operating systems using a unified API. Each device type has a driver to interpret the device specifics and convert to the unified API.
- Ansible is an automation framework built in Python that uses data structures to represent the intended state of IT assets. It includes modules and plug-ins developed to abstract the communication with networking devices over SSH and present the user with a simple interface.

Although APIC-EM, NSO, NAPALM, and Ansible have masked considerable complexity of CLI automation (through considerable effort by their engineering staffs and the open source community), they still are built upon a brittle foundation of interpreting and sending text over a session to the network element. Therefore, each has, or is building, capabilities upon modern APIs and model-driven data, as discussed shortly.

Configuration is only a small part of managing a network. The vast majority of interactions with the network element are for gathering operational data. This can be accomplished via regular queries such as **show processes cpu** to monitor CPU utilization, **show ip route** to validate the current best path(s) to a destination, **show inventory** to conduct asset management, or **show interface** to troubleshoot individual network interfaces. Each of these commands has one thing in common—the output is intended to be viewed on a screen. The spacing is designed to present data visually in the most efficient and easy-to-consume manner for humans. How, then, can a script return data from a **show** command? By default, the response is returned as a single string, where all the whitespacing turns it into a mess. Regular expressions (regex) must be leveraged to pull out the interesting information from the response. This can be taken a few steps further by converting the text into a programming object such as a list or a set of key-value pairs as in a Python dictionary. For the regex savvy, this is not a problem, but those individuals are in short supply. Again, the open source community has come to the rescue with libraries of regex templates to use in conjunction with textfsm, an open source Python text parsing engine. However, these libraries are incomplete, subject to requiring update if a **show** command changes its output (this happens more often than you think) and require programming expertise to properly utilize.

SNMP

Simple Network Management Protocol (SNMP) is leveraged widely today for gathering data from the network elements and is generally regarded as reasonably suitable for device monitoring. However, SNMP is not without issues. Although it can be used for configuring devices, it is rarely used in this capacity by network administrators. This is at least in part due to the lack of writeable Management Information Base (MIB) elements, which makes it incomplete, and the fact that there is no concept of rollback or replay for SNMP writeable objects. A MIB Object Identifier (OID) is a string of numbers that uniquely identifies the specific item for which some data is retrieved, but it is hardly self-describing, nor is it obvious which OID relates to which item in the device configuration. In addition, SNMPv3 is the only version that includes security features such as authentication and encryption, but many devices are not SNMPv3 capable and, as such, it has not been widely adopted among network engineers. MIBs are nontrivial to develop and are relatively inflexible. SNMP also requires the running of an application on a server. RFC 3535[1] breaks down the shortcomings of SNMP for configuration and highlights the need for new methods for network management.

CLI automation is the symptom, not the disease. The issue lies with dependence upon configuration and operational data in unstructured text format. The modern tools do a lot to enable automation and, considering the CLI is the only method to reach the majority of devices in production networks, it isn't going away anytime soon. Likewise, SNMP was initially developed back in 1988 and still is an invaluable tool for network monitoring.

Model-Based Data

Given the lessons learned from CLI automation and SNMP, and borrowing concepts from other segments of IT led to a new method for representing data in a structured way. Instead of textual representation of information, the information is stored and transmitted

1 "Overview of the 2002 IAB Network Management Workshop"; https://tools.ietf.org/html/rfc3535

in a machine-friendly format. Automation is run by machines and therefore the data that is sent or collected should be in a proper format. For example, consider how humans determined location and directions before smartphones. Maps were an excellent visual representation of geography for thousands of years. However, a map is a terrible input format for a machine. A machine cannot simply look around at landmarks or street signs and determine location. A program to convert a map to a digital format is a massive undertaking. Therefore, a new model was created with the machine perspective in mind. It represented the same location information, but instead in global positioning coordinates, a simple set of numbers to represent location exactly. From that simple concept, there now is Global Positioning System (GPS) capability on most mobile phones, leading to on-demand location awareness and all kinds of integration opportunities. Following this analogy, model-based data represents the networking device configuration in computer programming data structures that are easy for a machine to consume and share with other machines or applications. Figure 13-1 demonstrates this in a layered approach of model-based data as an abstraction of device configuration and operational data. These models are the basis of the payload that protocols transmit.

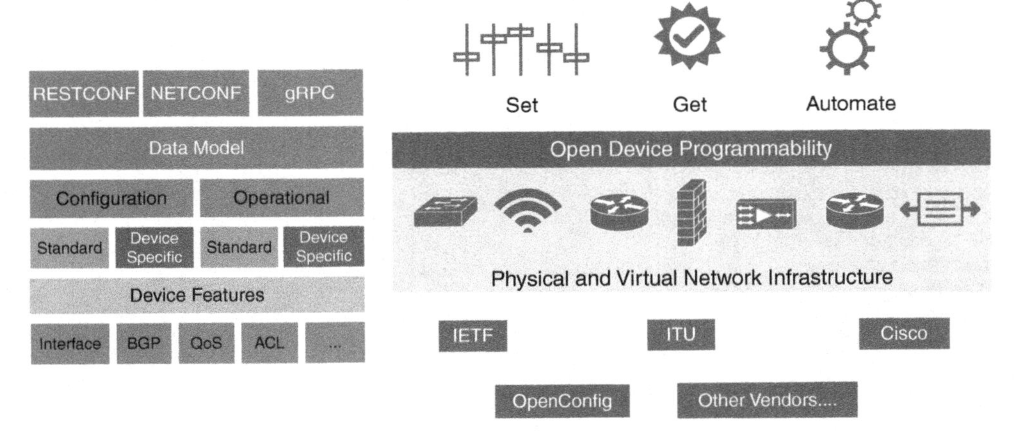

Figure 13-1 *Model-Based Interfaces*

YANG

In the case of representing configuration of a network device, models are more flexible and abstract, which makes these better suited to the needs of the evolving and innovating field of networking. In addition, there must be strict rules to follow to allow the industry to collaborate and interoperate. Models explicitly and precisely define data structure, syntax, and semantics. Yet Another Next Generation (YANG) models look to create a mold for which the relevant network element data is stored in programming data structures. YANG was built with the following requirements:

- Human readable
- Hierarchical configuration

- Extensible through augmentation
- Formal constraints for configuration validation
- Reusable types and groupings
- Modularity through modules and submodules
- Defined versioning rules

YANG is a programming language to model data. Its hierarchical tree structure is intended to organize the functionality of the device or service as nodes. Each node has a name and either child nodes or a value if it is a leaf in the tree. As seen in Figure 13-2, although it is built with programming data structures, it is still human readable and, in many cases, is recognizable compared to CLI configuration. YANG is structured in modules and submodules. Data is imported from external modules and is organized into model libraries to enable extensibility by augmentation by another module. YANG expresses constraints around data to match the constraints of the platform. For example, on Cisco switches, a user can configure a virtual local area network (VLAN) identifier (ID) between 1 and 4094, with the exception of 1002–1005 (which are reserved for token ring and Fiber Distributed Data Interface [FDDI]). This is represented as

```
type uint16 {
                  range "1..1001 | 1006..4094";
              }
```

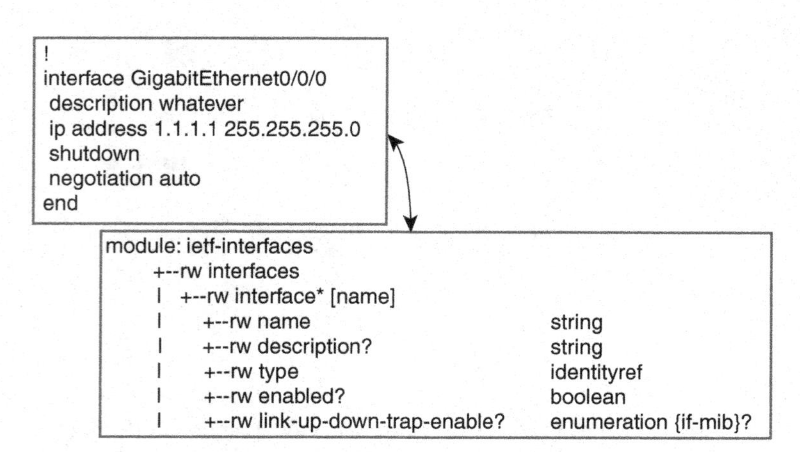

Figure 13-2 *An Example YANG Model*

Concepts such as **typedef** and groupings allow for reuse of code. For example, a percent type can be limited to just reasonable values (0–100) and that type reused throughout the model. Groupings such as the common portion of an interface—name, description, and whether enabled—can be coded once and reused for interface definitions, as shown in Example 13-1.

Example 13-1 *Programming Common Portions of Interface Configurations*

```
grouping interface-common-config {
    description
      "Configuration data nodes common to physical interfaces and subinterfaces";
    leaf name {
      type string;
    }
    leaf description {
      type string;
    }
    leaf enabled {
      type boolean;
      default "true";
    }
}
```

YANG was created with flexibility in mind to allow models to be augmented or extended to add new features or functionality easily. YANG models are commonly used to configure devices or to deploy services. Also, YANG is not limited to networking devices or functions; the same concepts apply to representing the configuration of a hypervisor or server or even multiple systems all working together to deploy a service.

There are two sets of relevant data for network devices: configuration data (what the device is told to do) and operational data (what the device is doing and the state of its components). SNMP had both types together in MIBs and there was no way to easily separate them. With these states clearly distinguished, it is easier to set finer controls on what data is sent where or who is permitted access. It is also clearer to the consumer (of the data) what can be manipulated and what is simply feedback from the device. As shown in Example 13-2, the read/write (rw) components are configuration data, while the read-only (ro) components are operational data.

Example 13-2 *YANG-Modeled Configuration (rw) and Operational (ro) Interface Data*

```
(linuxhost)$ pYANG -f tree -p ietf-interfaces.YANG

module: ietf-interfaces
   +--rw interfaces
   |  +--rw interface* [name]
   |     +--rw name                        string
   |     +--rw description?                string
   |     +--rw type                        identityref
   |     +--rw enabled?                    boolean
   |     +--rw link-up-down-trap-enable?   enumeration {if-mib}?
```

```
+--ro interfaces-state
   +--ro interface* [name]
      +--ro name                string
      +--ro type                identityref
      +--ro admin-status        enumeration {if-mib}?
      +--ro oper-status         enumeration
```

There are also two classes of YANG models, Open and Native, as illustrated in Figure 13-3. Native is specific to the vendor implementation; Open is created by the standards body (Internet Engineering Task Force [IETF]) or community (OpenConfig) to represent vendor-agnostic abstractions. Thus far, it seems the IETF models have wide coverage from a vendor perspective but minimal functional coverage of configurable items, whereas OpenConfig models have higher feature velocity as they are driven by the people who want to use them. Native models are generated directly by the vendor and cover all configuration and operational data available on the platform. Thanks to the modular and flexible nature of YANG, vendors can map the Open models to their Native model as opposed to directly coding the Open model into its operating system or configuration database.

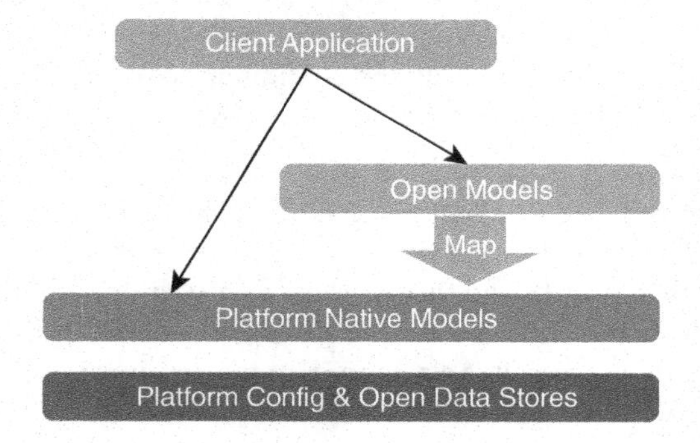

Figure 13-3 *Open and Native Model Mapping*

Models are commonly written for a specific technology or service, which means there are models for interfaces, quality of service (QoS), routing protocols, MIB implementations, etc. With all the Open models and Native models, a device could support hundreds of models. Therefore, the versioning and maintenance of models is paramount to their usefulness. YANG models have strict rules for versioning to protect backward compatibility. Also, YANG model mapping and importing promote inclusion of new modules.

Protocols

With just the data model, there is no real improvement other than on the device itself. Protocols are introduced to take action and "do stuff" with the data. Using protocols and API applications together presents solutions that are more than the sum of their parts. To borrow from the map versus GPS analogy presented earlier, being aware of location is only minimally interesting. But with applications working together, the calendar app communicates with the mapping app and consumes input from the traffic feed app to warn the user when it's time to leave for an important meeting, or even deviate a trip home based on a message requesting a stop by the grocery store. In the networking world, more data is available than ever before. But it's the sharing of this data between applications (via open APIs) that allows for entirely new communication possibilities. Some examples are devices reporting new equipment directly to the asset management system; IT service management (ITSM) applications requesting relevant information from devices as a ticket is routed through queues; and adding information such as Border Gateway Protocol (BGP) peering states and interface statistics directly into the ticket automatically for better situational awareness and decision making. The protocols provide the transport to exchange the model-based data in an efficient, reliable, and globally consistent manner.

Encoding

YANG is just a representation of what can be configured on the device. Therefore, there must be a way to fill in the blanks with the intended configuration or operational data in the payload of the protocol's transport. That is where the encoding comes into play. In this context, "encoding" describes the format to convert structured data to a serialized format for transmission. Because YANG is a tree structure, the encoding must provide a representation of data in a tree structure as well.

The following are the three most common encoding types in network programmability, as shown in Figure 13-4:

- Extensible Markup Language (XML)
- JavaScript Object Notation (JSON)
- Yet Another Markup Language (YAML)

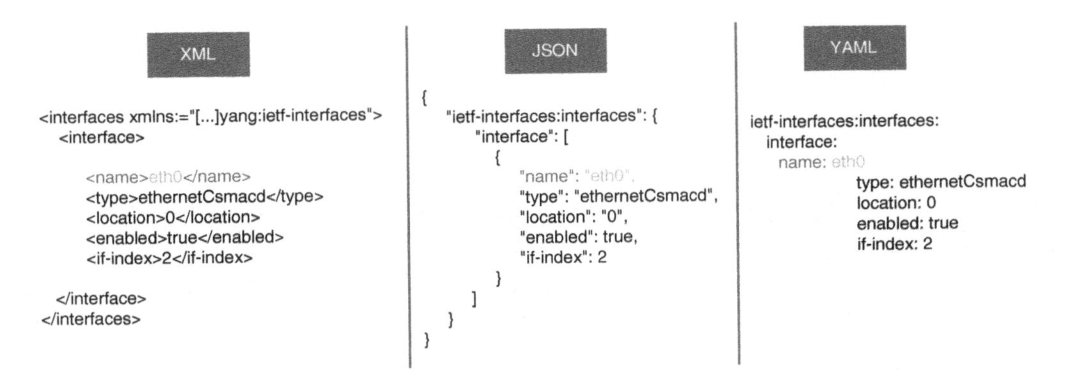

Figure 13-4 *Encoding Formats*

XML is the oldest encoding method and looks familiar to Hypertext Markup Language (HTML) coders and is a markup language that defines a set of rules for encoding documents in a format that is both human-readable and machine-readable. XML represents key-value pairs where the value is surrounded by <key> and </key> tags to organize the data.

JSON is the current de facto standard encoding for web applications. It represents data objects as key-value pairs and common programming special characters such as [] to represent a list or array and {} to represent a dictionary object.

YAML is a favorite in situations in which humans must interact with the encoded data. It is the simplest, usually requires the least typing, and has multiple options to represent data. It leverages Python-style indentation to indicate nesting or leverages [] and {} characters like JSON. All three encoding types are supported by several programming languages and have conversion libraries to and from each format.

Google Protocol Buffers (protobufs or GPB) is a relatively new entry to the encoding landscape. A protobuf is a binary encoding of the data to transmit. Just like XML, JSON, and YAML, the objective is to represent structured data to be transmitted serially. However, protobufs offer two options, self-describing or compact. Self-describing is similar to the other encodings as the key-value pairs are maintained. However, with compact mode, only a key index and value are encoded. It achieves this by separating the data definition from the data itself by uniquely numbering the fields like an index. When compiling a protobuf, the generated .proto file represents the structure of the data, and from then on only the data is transmitted. Because only the data is transported with indexed fields and values versus the key-value pairs, a protobuf doesn't lend itself to human readability. For example, if the field number 1 represents the device hostname, then only 1:RouterA is sent. However, the goal of using protobufs is speed, which is easily achieved because it is roughly 20 to 100 times faster than XML and 3 to 10 times smaller. Given its size and speed, it fits perfectly for use cases of streaming data. As such, protobufs is examined again later in the "Telemetry" section.

Network Protocols

Now that you are familiar with the model and encoding, next to consider is the transport. How does the data get from client to the server (i.e., the network device)? And vice-versa? That is the role of the protocols. Protocols such as Network Configuration Protocol (NETCONF), Representational State Transfer Configuration Protocol (RESTCONF), and Google Remote Procedure Call (gRPC) are built leveraging many years of lessons learned in IT and networking. The goal of exposing all configuration and operational data to nearly any application is now within grasp.

NETCONF

NETCONF, Network Configuration Protocol, was born from the networking community to specifically address shortcomings in available mechanisms for network management. The 2002 IAB Network Management Workshop outlined in RFC 3535 (previously cited) several requirements for a design for the next-generation network management protocol, including the following:

- Distinction between configuration and state data
- Multiple configuration datastores (candidate, running, and startup)
- Configuration change transactions
- Configuration testing and validation support
- Selective data retrieval with filtering
- Streaming and playback of event notifications
- Extensible procedure call mechanism

NETCONF was built to support these requirements in RFC 4741[2] (which in turn was updated and obsoleted by RFC 6241[3]), as illustrated in Figure 13-5. In addition, wherever possible, it leveraged common and best practices instead of creating new capabilities.

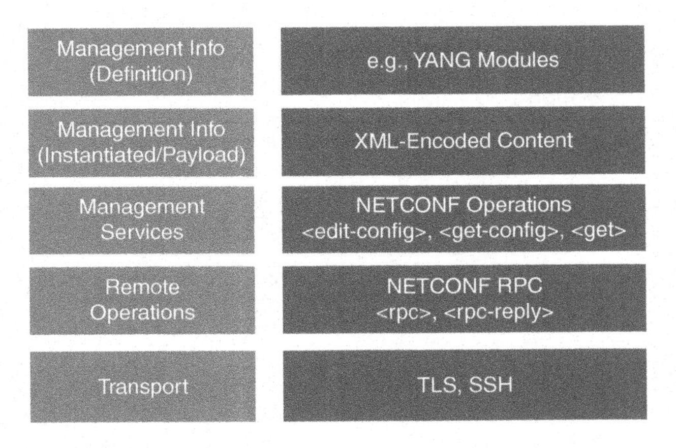

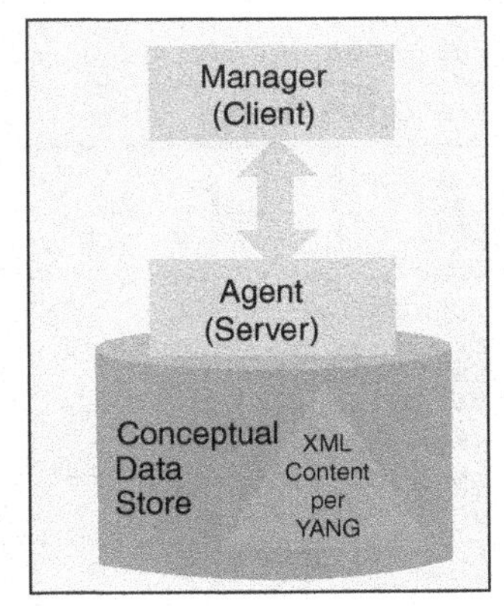

Figure 13-5 *NETCONF Overview*

As with many protocols, it is easiest to start at the bottom. NETCONF Transport relies on SSH or Transport Layer Security (TLS). SSH is the most common implementation and is in use on Cisco devices supporting NETCONF. NETCONF is a session-oriented protocol and allows for multiple messages and responses. As SSH is very common and

2 "NETCONF Configuration Protocol"; https://tools.ietf.org/html/rfc4741

3 "Network Configuration Protocol (NETCONF)"; https://tools.ietf.org/html/rfc6241

understood, it makes validating service availability a single step of **ssh** to port 830 with the **netconf** flag:

```
ssh -p 830 cisco@172.20.20.20 -s netconf
```

NETCONF uses Remote Procedure Call (RPC) for the Messages layer encoded as RPC messages and ensures responses to RPC as rpc-reply. The entire message, including the RPC message, is encoded in XML. The Operations layer describes the operations to edit or retrieve data as follows. The **get** operation retrieves both operational and configuration data, where the **get-config** is exclusive to configuration data. Similarly, **edit-config** only manipulates configuration data; operational data cannot be edited because it represents the state of the network device and its components. All RPC messages receive a response to indicate success or failure of the call. NETCONF operations are summarized in Table 13-1.

Table 13-1 *NETCONF Operations Summary*

Main Operations	Description
<get> (close to **show**)	Retrieves running configuration and device state information
<get-config> (close to **show running config**)	Retrieves all or part of specified configuration datastore
<edit-config> (close to **configure terminal**)	Loads all or part of a configuration to the specified configuration datastore
Other Operations	**Description**
<copy-config>	Replaces an entire configuration datastore with another
<delete-config>	Deletes a configuration datastore
<commit>	Copies candidate datastore to running datastore
<lock> / <unlock>	Locks or unlocks the entire configuration datastore system
<close-session>	Gracefully terminates NETCONF session
<kill-session>	Forces termination of NETCONF session

The concept of a datastore is also critical to understanding NETCONF. There are three possible configuration datastores:

- Running
- Startup
- Candidate

The running configuration datastore is the configuration currently applied, similar to running-config on Cisco devices, and is the only one required.

The startup configuration datastore, as the name implies, is the configuration to be applied at the next boot, similar to startup-config in Cisco devices.

The candidate configuration datastore may be a new concept for individuals who have been exposed only to Cisco IOS or IOS-XE platforms. It is a temporary "scratchpad" for configuration. It allows for configuration to be entered to the device and committed to the running configuration completely, not line by line. NETCONF capability of a network device does not imply candidate store availability, because in some cases only the running store is available and saving configuration is via save-config RPC. In addition, not all datastores are writeable. In some cases, the running datastore is not writable. In these cases, the candidate datastore is the writeable datastore and the commit or copy RPC takes the action to move configuration to the running datastore.

The Content layer of the message holds the configuration to be edited in the case of an edit-config RPC or the operational or configuration data in a get or get-config RPC respectively. The scope of an RPC is filtered to limit the data returned in the rpc-reply or to describe where the edit-config data is applied.

The NETCONF stack, including the Messages (RPC), Operations, and Content layers, is illustrated in Figure 13-6.

```
<get-config>

<rpc message-id='101' xmins="urn:ietf:params:xml:ns:netconf:base:1.0">
 <get-config>
  <source>
   <running/>
  </source>
  <filter>
   <interfaces xmins="urn:ietf:params:xml:ns:yang:ietf-interfaces">
    <interface>
     <name>GigabitEthernet0</name>
    </interface>
   </interfaces>
  </filter>
 </get-config>
</rpc>
```

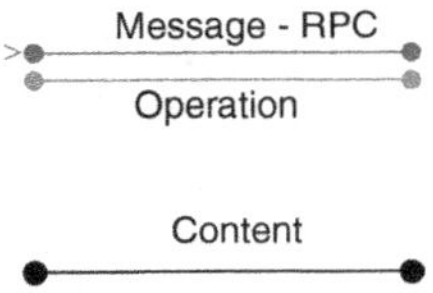

Message - RPC

Operation

Content

Figure 13-6 *NETCONF Stack*

Thus far there has been no mention of content conforming to a YANG model, and that is because NETCONF does not require YANG; in fact, NETCONF was created years before YANG was developed. Some devices are NETCONF 1.0 capable, which means conformance with RFC 4741, but RFC 6241 describes NETCONF 1.1, which leverages YANG for the data model.

One major advantage to NETCONF for configuration of network devices is transactionality. As per the RFC 3535 design requirements, transactions are paramount for configuration management. This allows all or none of a configuration to be applied; no in between. Therefore, if there is a syntax error or invalid entry in the edit-config, an error rpc-reply is returned describing the issue and no change is made. This differs dramatically from CLI automation. If a syntax error or some invalid entry is sent, all of the commands before the error are accepted, the invalid line is likely skipped, and some or all of the commands after the error may be applied. This creates an unknown and possible failed configuration.

With all the different NETCONF capabilities, supported RPCs, datastores, XML filtering options, and YANG models, there must be a way for a client to quickly determine the device capability. NETCONF includes a capability exchange included in the initial session handshake to share capabilities and supported YANG modules. In addition, a get-schema RPC is used to download the specified YANG module for the client to inspect the module directly.

NETCONF also supports subscribing and receiving asynchronous event notifications. This is discussed in the upcoming "Telemetry" section.

RESTCONF

RESTCONF, Representational State Transfer Configuration Protocol, is a method for interacting with YANG data as defined in NETCONF, but over the most common transport in the world: Hypertext Transfer Protocol (HTTP). RESTCONF was recently ratified in RFC 8040.[4] RESTCONF is not a replacement for NETCONF, but rather a supplement to provide an alternative web-like interface to the underlying YANG data.

REST is a framework for stateless client-server communications that is the de facto standard among web services. It is an architectural style that specifies constraints to support consistent performance, scalability, and modifiability. For example, web browsers are able to explore complex server content with no prior knowledge of the remote resources. It is the server's responsibility to supply locations of resources and required data. One key tenant is that the client and server must agree on media used. In the case of the Internet that content is HTML. REST content types range from JSON, XML, and HTML. Because REST most commonly is implemented in HTTP, it supports a set of operations or verbs: GET to retrieve data, POST to create an object, PUT to change content, POST to merge a change, and DELETE to remove an object. Another fundamental tenet of REST is the use of return codes. Each message receives an HTTP return code to provide information, success, redirection, or error information. Table 13-2 presents a comparison between RESTCONF and NETCONF.

Table 13-2 *Comparison of RESTCONF and NETCONF*

RESTCONF	NETCONF	
GET	<get-config>, <get>	
POST	<edit-config>	(operation="**create**")
PUT	<edit-config>	(operation="**create/replace**")
PATCH	<edit-config>	(operation="**merge**")
DELETE	<edit-config>	(operation="**delete**")

4 "RESTCONF Protocol"; https://tools.ietf.org/html/rfc8040

RESTCONF is described as REST-like, as it does not conform strictly to REST; this is because the media type is not application/json, but instead is a JSON or XML representation of the YANG model. This means the RESTCONF Uniform Resource Identifier (URI) and JSON or XML payload is based on the YANG model. The RESTCONF URI is illustrated in Figure 13-7.

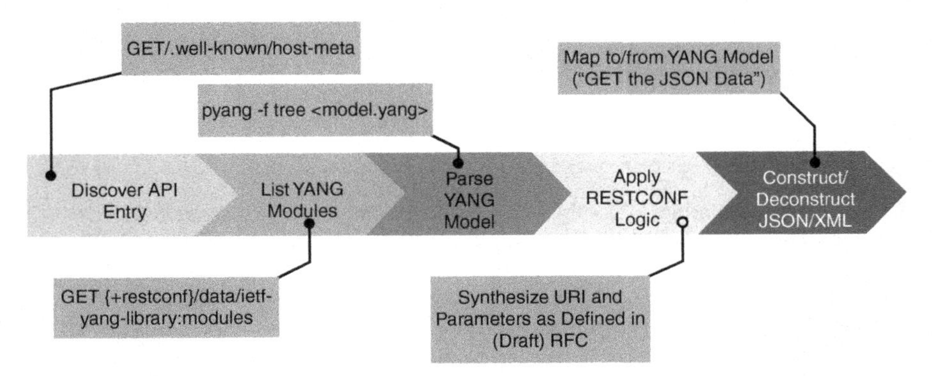

Figure 13-7 *RESTCONF URI Format*

Not every client application supports NETCONF, but nearly any web-based service can leverage a REST-like interface. RESTCONF is a clientless, stateless, uniform protocol. Each communication is a single transaction to gather information or modify the state of the server. Similar to NETCONF, RESTCONF validates the entire message before editing any configuration data. RESTCONF supports familiar web operations such as these:

- GET operations retrieve configuration data and state data; for example, getting current interface counters.
- POST operations create new configuration data; for example, adding a loopback interface.
- PUT operations perform a destructive replacement of configuration data (like a configuration replace); for example, changing the IP address of a given interface.
- PATCH operations perform a configuration merge, similar to traditional copy and paste configuration changes; for example, adding interface descriptions to multiple interfaces.
- DELETE operations remove an object; for example, removing a loopback interface.

gRPC

Remote Procedure Call (RPC) provides services that can be remotely called by clients. RPC specifies methods or functions with defined parameters and return types. Essentially RPC is running commands on a remote server without the hassle of automating SSH, Virtual Network Computing (VNC), or Remote Desktop Protocol (RDP) to run commands and return data. gRPC (Google Remote Procedure Call) is a flavor of RPC client-server application, where the remote services appear as a local object. gRPC creates objects on the client like classes and methods in C, Go, Java, Python, or Ruby that include "getters" (functions to return data) and "setters" (functions to set variables) that are remotely executed on the server.

There are four types of RPC:

- **Unary:** A single request and response
- **Client streaming:** A set of requests with a single response
- **Server steaming:** A set of requests with several responses
- **Bidirectional streaming:** A combination of client and server streaming, suited for multiple requests with multiple responses, where each stream is independent

Deadlines and timeouts are leveraged to terminate sessions. The server may wait to respond with its stream or the client can build the next request on the previous server response. A concept of channels is leveraged to modify the default client-server session by client specifying channel arguments.

The gRPC server listens on a port in either HTTP/2 or a raw Transmission Control Protocol (TCP) socket. HTTP/2 has slight overhead but offers built-in encryption and authentication of TLS. A raw TCP socket allows for flexibility and simplicity. gRPC authentication is quite flexible. It allows simple credentials, Secure Sockets Layer (SSL) with or without Google token-based authentication (used when communicating with Google services), or an external authentication system via code extension.

By default, gRPC leverages protobufs as the interface definition language (IDL) to describe the format of the messages and payload to properly interact with the services and data available on the remote server. These protobufs, as described earlier in the "Encoding" section, can be self-describing or compact. The efficiency, flexibility, and language bindings of protobufs make gRPC an attractive choice for interacting with a wide range of devices and services. gRPC is commonly used by large cloud computing environments and provides high-performant, scalable methods. The popularity of protobufs compute and container environments continues to pour over into networking use cases, and thus the list of networking devices that support gRPC continues to grow.

Telemetry

Today's network devices create a wealth of state information, and analytics platforms perform impressive reporting, visibility, root cause analysis, and anomaly detection in our networks. Telemetry is the practice of gathering and storing that operational data and presenting it to the analytic platforms. In most networks today, that is commonly achieved by gathering system logs, SNMP polling and traps, and flow data (usually in the form of NetFlow). Unfortunately, these data-gathering methods are incomplete, inefficient, or have inconsistent formatting. SNMP MIBs may be structured independently and thus interpreted differently across vendors or even business units within vendors. Syslogs, while consistent in eight severity levels (from debug to emergency), are inconsistent in the formatting and content of messages across products as well. Efforts are underway to deliver products and services to normalize this data and present the analytics platforms with a consistent format, such as the Common Information Model (CIM). While CIM is a laudable initiative, it serves to solve only part of the problem, and requires constant updating (as new MIBs are created or as Syslog messages change from device version to version, etc.). At best CIM server to mask the inadequacies of these legacy mechanisms, and as such, only goes so far toward addressing messaging inconsistency.

Consider though: What if there was no need for normalization? Why not instead leverage model-based definitions in YANG? That way the data is self-describing, complete, extensible, and standardized. In addition, it makes sense to provide additional transport features such as low-latency, high-speed throughput, nonrepudiation, and a multi-destination subscription model. That's exactly what NETCONF and gRPC telemetry streaming have set out to do, so as to meet the needs of network telemetry requirements.

There are several options and details to describe a specific telemetry stream, also known as a sensor group. Network devices support multiple streams, each with its own parameters such as direction, destinations, encoding, sample-interval, and paths. There are two types of transmission directions, dial-in and dial-out. These refer to who is the initiator of the conversation, the server or the client. This does not mean dial-in is polling of data. Once the initial session is established, the network device transmits telemetry data for the desired path at the designated interval. The set of stream destinations is configured statically by some means such as CLI or NETCONF for dial-out, but the subscription details are dynamic for dial-in mode, allowing clients to subscribe without configuration change. Encoding is also statically configured on the network device for the sensor group. Encoding for telemetry streaming options are JSON, self-describing gRPC, or compact gRPC. The sample interval is how often to gather statistics and transmit. Paths describe the YANG model path of interest that the particular sensor group transmits telemetry data per sample interval.

Collecting data—by itself—is not the end goal for telemetry, as the client needs to forward the data via telemetry to a data analytics stack, either directly or by leveraging a data bus to distribute the data. Projects such as Pipeline receive raw telemetry and transform it for data analysis before forwarding to a data bus, such as Kafka, to publish relevant streams to data analytics engines or big data platforms. In addition, there are collection stacks capable of directly consuming telemetry, such as ELK Stack (Elasticsearch, Logstash, and Kibana) or Splunk, to receive, store, and display data in a massively scalable and rich GUI to provide near-real-time situational awareness, historical trending, auditing, and powerful queries to correlate and search operational data.

gRPC Telemetry

As previously mentioned, using protobufs is dramatically more efficient in serializing data for transport. gRPC, by default, leverages those protobufs. There are two methods to represent YANG in protobufs. A .proto can be created to describe each model or a single

.proto can describe all models. The single .proto cannot adequately index all models and therefore is self-describing (include key with value, not just index), and therefore is less efficient. Conversely, the unique .proto per model leverages compact mode. There are trade-offs to be made. There are operational advantages to a single .proto to maintain on the client, and human-readable key-value pairs of data in transit assist in troubleshooting and are easier to integrate. However, the compact protobuf encoding is about three times faster than self-describing.

gRPC's HTTP/2 transport supports both dial-in and dial-out, while TCP supports only dial out.

Tools

While NETCONF, RESTCONF, gRPC, and YANG are quite interesting, they are limited in functionality without tools to harness their power. Fortunately, vendors and the open source community have created several projects and products to leverage the power of model-driven configuration, data, and telemetry.

Pyang is an open source project to validate a YANG module for correctness, convert it to additional formats, and even generate code in relation to the module. Pyang ensures syntax, module references, and conformance with standards. Common uses are to create a skeleton XML instance, convert to JSON, or display the graphical representations of the module as a simple tree or even a Unified Modeling Language (UML) diagram. Pyang also creates code in several languages, such as Python and Java, to build classes with similar structure to the module. Its ability to integrate plug-ins allow for the majority of features.

Ncclient is an open source Python NETCONF client. It is a Python library with an intuitive API to simplify interaction with XML whose goal is to make scripting NETCONF easier. It is an exhaustive client capable of all capabilities included in the NETCONF RFC (RFC 6241): edit-config, get-config, copy-config, delete-config, validate, get, discard-changes, commit, lock, unlock, confirmed-commit, rollback-on-error, datastore capabilities, url, xpath, etc. NCCLIENT is a commonly used NETCONF client and is leveraged in many open source tools and custom scripts and is integrated into some other NETCONF tools.

ConfD is a Cisco-developed tool (via its Tail-f acquisition) that models management interfaces in YANG. The underlying mechanism to communicate with devices can be NETCONF, RESTCONF, CLI, REST, web, or SNMP. Abstracting a non-model-driven configuration device in YANG provides significant advantages to integration with automation systems, as demonstrated in the "NETCONF" and "YANG" sections. While ConfD is not open source, it does offer a basic distribution at no cost. ConfD includes netconf-console, a command-line NETCONF client to communicate with devices.

NCC is a Python-based NETCONF client to facilitate communicating with devices. It includes edit-config and get-config and is an open project to allow extension. The same project includes Python scripts to poll, perform filtered get, and even download all schemas (YANG modules) to determine missing sources for import or include statements.

YANG-explorer is an open source project to visualize YANG modules and communicate with network elements. It loads in a web browser to give a simple interface to interact and explore YANG modules. It is an extensive multiuser client to build device profiles for multiple network elements, browse a YANG tree and drill down to properties, upload YANG modules from files or devices, build and execute RPCs against devices, save RPCs for later use, and even generate Python.

YANG Catalog is a recent addition to open source YANG tools thanks to the efforts of contributors and IETF Hackathons. There have been many YANG modules developed in recent years and YANG Catalog seeks to be a reference of the modules for developers to validate and add modules to the community, and a searchable library for operators to find the correct module to use. For example, it assists in finding the right module for the specific use case based on module type (service model or not), maturity level, if the module is implemented, vendor or equipment type, the contact, and if there is open source code available. It also validates YANG modules and visualizes dependencies or bottlenecks. It also integrates with YANG-explorer to test the YANG module against a device.

There are many common REST clients with similar features and capabilities, including Postman, PAW, Cocoa, Insomnia, and many more. Some clients are open source, some are free, and some require purchase. For example, Postman was created to help build, test, and document APIs faster. It has a simple and intuitive GUI to interact with a REST API. It includes a history of prior requests to make it easy to resend or modify a previously sent request. In addition, it includes collections as a feature to organize a set of REST calls for reuse or sharing. In addition, it supports variables for the same calls against different devices or environments. It also includes scripting capability to react based on responses, such as to save data in variables.

Ansible, an open source community project sponsored by Red Hat, is an automation platform for configuration management, software provisioning, and task automation. It uses data structure abstractions to represent the intended state of IT assets. It has broad acceptance among system administrators, where it is a mainstay in DevOps and hybrid IT environments. In the past few years Ansible has grown to include powerful network automation capabilities. Ansible represents a configured state in an easy-to-read YAML format as a set of tasks called a playbook. It provides looping and acts as a script manager across several devices. It is *idempotent*, which is to say if the element is found in the intended state already, such as a loopback exists and is configured with a given IP address, then nothing is done. However, if the element is in another state, the task leverages the code in the module to bring the element to the desired state, Ansible is commonly leveraged for networking to create configurations based on a template, deploy initial configurations to devices, deploy service-based configurations to devices individually or in a list, or gather facts about devices as a seed for later tasks or to return data to the user. As previously mentioned, Ansible leverages SSH, but it also has plug-ins and modules to utilize NETCONF as a method to interact with devices. In addition, Ansible is developing more functions and tools to abstract and simplify network configuration through its development team and the open source community. Ansible also includes a product called Ansible Tower to extend Ansible's capability with a centralized point of job execution, GUI, dashboard, log aggregation, and workflow management for multiple playbooks. Ansible use has grown significantly due in part to the low barrier of entry from a skill and system requirements perspective and from an active community delivering rapid features.

Puppet is an open source software configuration management tool that inspects and operates IT infrastructure. Puppet leverages a declarative manifest to describe the intended state of a device or system of devices. Puppet clients regularly check in with the master to monitor devices to determine if they are in the desired state or take action upon the device. Puppet uses a resource abstraction of types and providers. A type is a human-readable model of a resource that includes a set of attributes as parameters or variables. A provider is a method with which to manipulate the resource described by the type. For example, a type may be an interface with several attributes such as name, encapsulation, IP address, etc., while the provider may be code with methods such as SSH to manipulate the endpoint. Puppet follows a pull model from the agent. The agent regularly checks in with the Puppet master to share relevant data. The Puppet server maintains a database of resources and interdependencies and displays them graphically. This presents a transactional behavior where the result of any requested configuration change is reported back to the server. Traditionally, Puppet requires an agent installed on the devices under management. Puppet developed agents for Nexus devices and types/providers to configure many tasks and provides a unique capability to Puppet users. However, most Cisco devices do not support agents and therefore require a different approach. YANG modules describe the configuration and operational data in a similar fashion to Puppet types. Leveraging the similarity, the Puppet engineering team and user community developed types based on the YANG module and providers via NETCONF transport. These efforts are underway and will provide a capability to manage IT infrastructure to include NETCONF 1.1-capable network devices all from a single platform.

YANG Development Kit (YDK) is an open source project created to ease and encourage network programmability using data models.

YDK has two components:

- YDK-gen, which creates APIs in a variety of programming languages (including Python, Ruby, Go, C++, and C#)
- The APIs that are generated from YDK-gen (such as YDK-Py or YDKcpp)

For the majority of relevant modules, such as IETF, OpenConfig, and native Cisco modules, the APIs are already created and available via the Python Package Index (PyPI). Additional APIs for modules not present, such as service models or other vendor models, are also created via YDK-gen.

Within the APIs there are three elements: models, services, and providers.

- *Models* are a mirror of the YANG module. They take advantage of the similar structures and capabilities to create data structures within them. For example, YANG containers, lists, and leafs (of various types, such as integer, string, Boolean, enumeration, etc.) are analogous to Python classes, lists, and variables of various types (that can be extended to similar constructs as YANG).

- *Services* are classes to perform the actions, including implementing the RPCs themselves—i.e., representing create, read, update, and delete (CRUD) actions, management protocols, direct access to the protocols, and a service to encode and decode data transmitted to/from the device.
- *Providers* are classes to implement a service; for example, creating the NETCONF session or encoding in XML.

Depending on the situation, a single provider could implement multiple services or multiple providers may be required to implement a service. YDK was created for the programmer looking to control a network device. It creates a set of libraries to import into scripts or programs to abstract YANG directly to the programming language of choice with no need for XML or JSON payload, as in the case with ncclient or similar tools. YDK is open source and is an active project with regularly updated functionality and models. In addition, efforts are underway to integrate or leverage YDK within network automation platforms to accelerate their feature delivery.

Cisco Network Services Orchestrator (NSO) is a flexible and extensible network orchestration platform. It was designed for the entire service automation lifecycle from deploy, validate, and update/redeploy through decommission. It is another product developed by the Tail-f team within Cisco and is a superset of ConfD capability. Not only does NSO present a YANG abstraction to nearly any networking service or downstream device or system API (NETCONF, RESTCONF, CLI, REST, web, or SNMP) via Network Element Driver (NED), but it includes a GUI and comprehensive northbound API for system integration. In addition, the network service models integrate data from outside systems such as Internet Protocol Address Management (IPAM), operational support systems (OSS), or service provisioning systems like business support systems (BSS) to allow business data integrated to the service deployment automation. Also, the services may include advanced logic and programming in Java or Python to provision flexible services templates. NSO maintains a Configuration Database (CDB) that represents the state of the entire network. As such, configuration changes are committed in a "dry run" to determine the impact to the configuration without sending a single command to a device. Service instantiation is deployed as a single atomic transaction across the entire network or system. Therefore, if a single managed endpoint fails to accept the change, the entire system returns to the prior state. NSO provides an incredibly powerful and flexible automation framework, but such power leads to a higher learning curve or Advanced Services driven deployment. Common use cases are service providers deploying services across multiple devices within their network and network function virtualization (NFV) service provisioning.

Application Hosting

With the advancements in multiple cores and hypervisor support in modern processors and the industry shift toward microservices and containerization, opportunities now exist to extend compute resources throughout the enterprise leveraging the network infrastructure, as shown in Figure 13-8. Cisco traditionally has offered container or agent support on Nexus and service provider platforms and this capability is now available on enterprise networking devices as well via IOS XE. Primary concerns of application hosting and service containers are the impact to the network devices' performance and security considerations. It is paramount that the container environment not negatively impact the management, control, and data planes of the network element. Therefore, performance and security is controlled via Linux container (LXC) technologies to isolate guest applications such as unprivileged containers or Linux kernel control groups (cgroups) for namespace isolation and resource limitation.

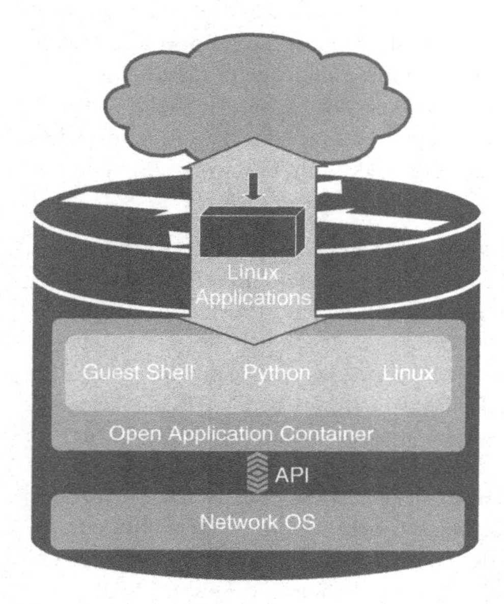

Figure 13-8 *Network Device Containerization for Application Hosting*

There are several use cases for application hosting on the network devices. Built into the IOS-XE software release is a Guest Shell to present a Linux environment to the user based on CentOS or Montavista Linux (depending on platform). This Guest Shell enables a Linux shell for scripting and Python environment with libraries for communication with network devices via traditional IP-based or backend CLI APIs. This environment allows for installing Linux applications and tools to extend scripting capability to the device. For example, a log parser could filter messages in search of prospective issues or Embedded Event Manager (EEM) tracking resource threshold transitions may call Python scripts to react or remediate problems locally. In addition to Guest Shell, application containers could be installed to support a myriad of use cases from network probes, distributed telemetry processing, data collection for bulk transport for devices with limited upstream connectivity, configuration management agents, asset management applications, or a customer-built application container. The options are nearly limitless as more and more services and applications provide container support.

Summary

This chapter discussed the many aspects of network device programmability and how the network element exposes additional functionality and abstract functions from the network controller. This chapter introduced the following:

- **Model-driven architecture:** A structure of configuration and operational data built for machines avoids conversion of text or CLI input to data structures and presents an opportunity for integration with external applications and services.
- **Device APIs:** These are the vehicles to transmit the model-based data. Leveraging industry-standard encoding and protocols, nearly any application can get or set data on the network element via RESTCONF. NETCONF was built by network management experts to address the needs of a network management protocol.
- **Telemetry:** Device telemetry solves the problem of exporting data to analytics platforms by providing multi-destination, low-latency, model-based data transport.
- **Tools:** A wide range of tools is available to leverage both legacy CLI methods and modern model-based APIs from both vendors and the open source community.
- **Application hosting:** Multicore processors and Linux kernel features, container-based applications, and Linux guestshell can reside directly on the network device to extend capability and distribute workloads.

Leveraging these features extends networking capabilities to DevOps environments, rapid, reliable configuration deployment, and ubiquitous availability of operational data to OSSs and BSSs. Network device programmability facilitates machine-to-machine communications, adding value, capability, and scalability to the network operator. Network programmability is not a threat to network engineers, but rather is an enabler, as it minimizes mundane and repetitive tasks and lets the engineer work "up the stack" to more complex, interesting, and challenging projects like new technology adoption and building capabilities on top of programmability. Programmability reallocates network engineering efforts from operations and troubleshooting to engineering, testing, and development.

Further Reading

Tischer, R., and J. Gooley. *Programming and Automating Cisco Networks: A Guide to Network Programmability and Automation in the Data Center, Campus, and WAN.* Indianapolis: Cisco Press; 2016.

Chapter 14

Cisco DNA Automation

As outlined in Chapter 13, "Device Programmability," device programmability lays the foundation for more sophisticated network automation. Device programmability allows you to interact with physical and virtual network elements using a machine-to-machine paradigm in a predictable and deterministic manner. The desired functionality is automated into the network layer using APIs. Cisco DNA automation, however, goes well beyond network element automation via the device level. It allows you to treat your network "as a system" in itself, to operate on multiple network elements simultaneously with consistency. Network controllers play a crucial role in Cisco DNA, providing capabilities to standardize configuration and common network settings and drive these into the infrastructure using device programmability. Controllers also allow for the creation and maintenance of a detailed device inventory of your network that once created can offer a visualization of the network topology. Controllers also enable operators to carry out management functions on multiple network devices at the same time with consistency.

This chapter discusses the importance of Cisco DNA automation as a major functional block in the architecture. The following section reviews the need for sophisticated automation functions in general—whether automating device-by-device operations or using network controllers. The section highlights the business benefits at a high level. It then examines some impediments to automation. What stops network operators from increasing the level of automation? A large part of this chapter is devoted to the automation capabilities that are offered by a network controller. It emphasizes the difference between device-by-device automation and network-controller automation, exploring the different stages of Cisco DNA automation in subsequent sections.

This chapter explains the following:

- Standardizing network designs
- Automating the deployment and configuration of network functions
- Ongoing lifecycle management of the Cisco DNA network elements

This chapter finishes with a deep dive into the functional architecture for automation in Cisco DNA, in particular the role of a network controller for automation.

The Increasing Importance of Automation

Automating network operations is not new. Anybody starting to learn the capabilities of routers, switches, access points, or other networking elements in a lab or training course is traditionally exposed to configuring features using the command-line interface (CLI). Students quickly realize the shortcomings of this approach. You mistype a command but get insufficient feedback on what the proper syntax should be. You enter a valid syntax for a command but misinterpret its behavior and do not obtain the desired functionality. And to understand and verify the operation of the network element, you again issue CLI-based commands to show its state, and are returned sometimes multiple screen-lengths of data that you subsequently have to scan and interpret to find the statistic that you were looking for.

Imagine then that you are an operator of even a small network with a few routers, switches, wireless access points, and firewalls. The manual and cumbersome process that you tried in the lab now has to be repeated for all the different types of network elements (routers, switches, wireless access points, firewalls, IPS/IDS, WAN optimization, deep-packet inspection appliances, etc.). A multivendor environment often further complicates the operational procedures because every vendor has its own operational models for its systems. And for larger networks, such a manual, CLI-based approach is simply not sustainable.

The benefits of using automated network operations have thus been apparent for a long time for any operator of even small networks. Mechanisms such as standardizing a configuration for a particular device type, automating the deployment of the standardized configurations into the network devices and status verification, and even automating the extraction of relevant data points from the **show** commands have been common practices for many years. Some operators use network management tools to assist in the task of network automation. Others rely more on self-developed scripts to accommodate unique automation scenarios. Combinations of tool-based and scripted automations are common in many operational networks.

The recent trends in networking in a digitalized world described in Chapter 4, "Introducing the Cisco Digital Network Architecture," motivate a heightened interest in sophisticated automation functions. The principal underlying driver for this evolution is cost reduction. Automating network operations procedures promises in particular the potential to keep operational expenditures (OPEX) in line as architectures evolve to support digitalized business processes. The benefits of automation in Cisco DNA are viewed from several aspects, which include the following:

- Allow the network to scale
- Reduce errors in the network
- Time to perform an operation
- Security and compliance

Allow the Network to Scale

Cisco DNA is designed to scale to accommodate an ever-increasing number of endpoints. Individual users increasingly attach to the network with multiple devices at the same time. More and more Internet of Things (IoT) devices are also deployed and need to be networked, with a wide variety of requirements on the network. Some IoT endpoints are geographically co-located with users, but generate and consume high-bandwidth streams. At the other end of the spectrum are highly distributed sensors, deployed in huge numbers but each generating small amounts of traffic.

The growth in endpoints typically needs to be complemented by a growth in the network infrastructure. More access points and switches are needed to connect the endpoints to the network, which in turn triggers increases at the various aggregation layers. Also, supporting network functions such as firewalls, IPS/IDS, or unified threat management (UTM) systems is likely required in larger numbers to meet these demands. Automating the deployment, configuration, and ongoing operations of the network is crucial in this environment to allow the number of endpoints to scale.

Reduce Errors in the Network

One of the main advantages of automation is to introduce predictability and determinism. By its very definition, automation is "the controlled operation of an apparatus, process, or system by mechanical or electronic devices that take the place of human labor."[1] If you have an automation script to drive a predetermined configuration into a router, say, the execution of the script must always yield the same result. Under the assumption that the initial state of the target network element is well known and stable, and that the automation procedure was tested and validated, its execution should always produce the same target end state.

Automation helps reduce the errors in network configurations that are often incurred by manual operations. The execution of an automation script should bring about the same end result every time. Ideally, automation also helps bring the entire network into a well-known state, where the configuration and operational status of each network device is deterministic at any point in time. And this helps reduce operational expenses: once the automation procedure is validated, you spend less time troubleshooting and correcting configuration errors. And the same procedure can be applied across many network elements at the same time, rather than executing a sequential manual process that may break in different ways each time a manual operation is executed.

Time to Perform an Operation

Many systems are measured also in "time to *X*." Your network operations team may be measured by the time taken to *deploy* a new network element. IT operators may be measured by the time taken to *onboard a new user*. Similarly, the network support team may be measured by the time to *troubleshoot and resolve* a misconfiguration. One of the

1 https://www.merriam-webster.com/dictionary/automation

key benefits of automation is the ability to reduce the time it takes to perform an operation. Imagine you have a graphical operations environment (such as Cisco DNA Center) that allows you to upload a new configuration to enable a new service (e.g., a new security function) in the network. You provide the configuration snipped as part of the design phase, select the domains and devices where this new capability should be deployed, and click a button. An automated procedure is able to leverage machine-to-machine communications to drive the functionality into the desired network element within minutes. Ideally, the automation also reports on the outcome to confirm the successful execution of the operation, or to flag any unforeseen conditions that prevented the operation from succeeding.

One of the key benefits of automation is to reduce the time to execute an operation. This enables you to deploy new Cisco DNA services for end users or new network functions much faster. It also allows you to reduce the time to troubleshoot issues, leading to a greater operator and user experience.

Security and Compliance

Automation also has significant benefits to meet the security and compliance needs required in a digitalized network. As the network becomes increasingly vital for digitalized business processes, it is a prime target for security attacks. Recent reports of attacks, such as the malicious lockout of hotel guests from their rooms at a ski resort highlight the vulnerability of many networks and the negative business impact caused. Controller-based automation in particular not only helps to detect an attack using various mechanisms (e.g., anomaly detection), but also installs remedies to a particular attack throughout the entire network almost immediately after the safeguard was devised.

Automating security operations does not apply only to special events such as an attack. It should be leveraged to comply with internal or regulatory compliance procedures. A network controller can automate the instantiation of configurations that were approved by your compliance team, run audit checks to verify that these configurations are effective, and offer proof of compliance by logging all events.

Current Impediments to Automation

Despite the apparent benefits of automation discussed in the previous section, many enterprises still face obstacles to fully automate their network and security operations. A study by Gartner reported on the percentage of network changes that are automated in today's enterprise networks. Over 50 percent of enterprises still do not automate network changes, and 37 percent of all respondents automate up to 25 percent of all changes. According to a Gartner Blog Network blog entry referencing this study[2] and as illustrated

---

2 Andrew Lerner, "Network Resolutions for 2017," Gartner Blog, Dec. 20, 2016, https://blogs.gartner.com/andrew-lerner/2016/12/20/network-resolutions-for-2017/

in Figure 14-1, "Multiple surveys and client interactions indicate that 80+% of network changes are manually driven." Note that these data points do not distinguish between device-level automation and controller-based automation. The results report on the state of automation for network changes in general, and highlight the significant potential that any level of automation can still offer.

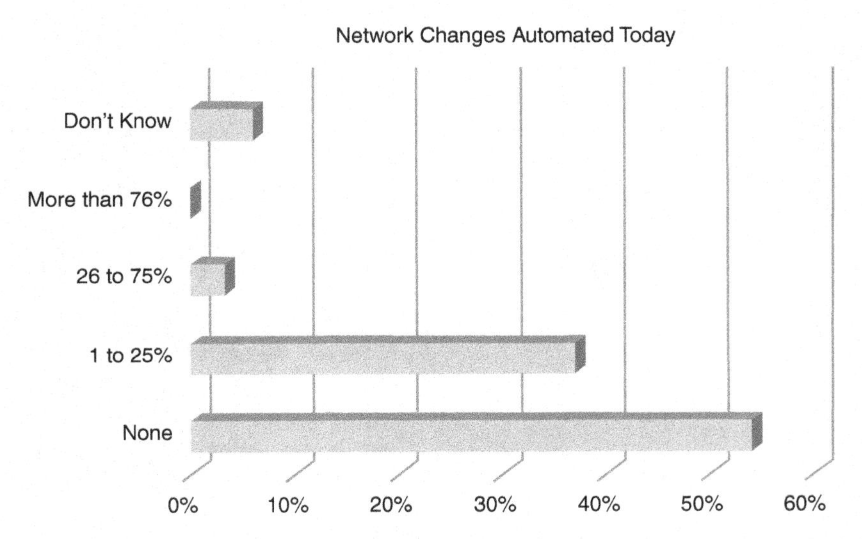

Source: http://blogs.gartner.com/andrew-lerner/2016/12/20/network-resolutions-for-2017/

Figure 14-1 *State of Automation in Enterprise Networks*

A recent internal study by Cisco complements these findings by Gartner. The study analyzed over 1500 cases for network changes and categorized these into standard and nonstandard changes. Standard changes were defined to be those that have well-defined procedures and workflows, that are repetitive, and thus are prime candidates to be automated. Examples of cases in this category are access control list (ACL) updates, hardware upgrades, standardizing deployments to corporate specifications, or even configuring laboratory environments with well-known connectivity parameters. Of the 1500 cases analyzed, about 65 percent of all changes fell into this category.

The remaining 35 percent of cases were classified to be nonstandard, defined to require procedures and workflows that were not encountered before, or where a highly skilled network engineer is required for the solution. Some of the hardware upgrade cases were associated with this category. Other examples include special routing configurations, security or ACL changes, or dealing with power shutdowns. Figure 14-2 provides the detailed categorization of the analyzed cases.

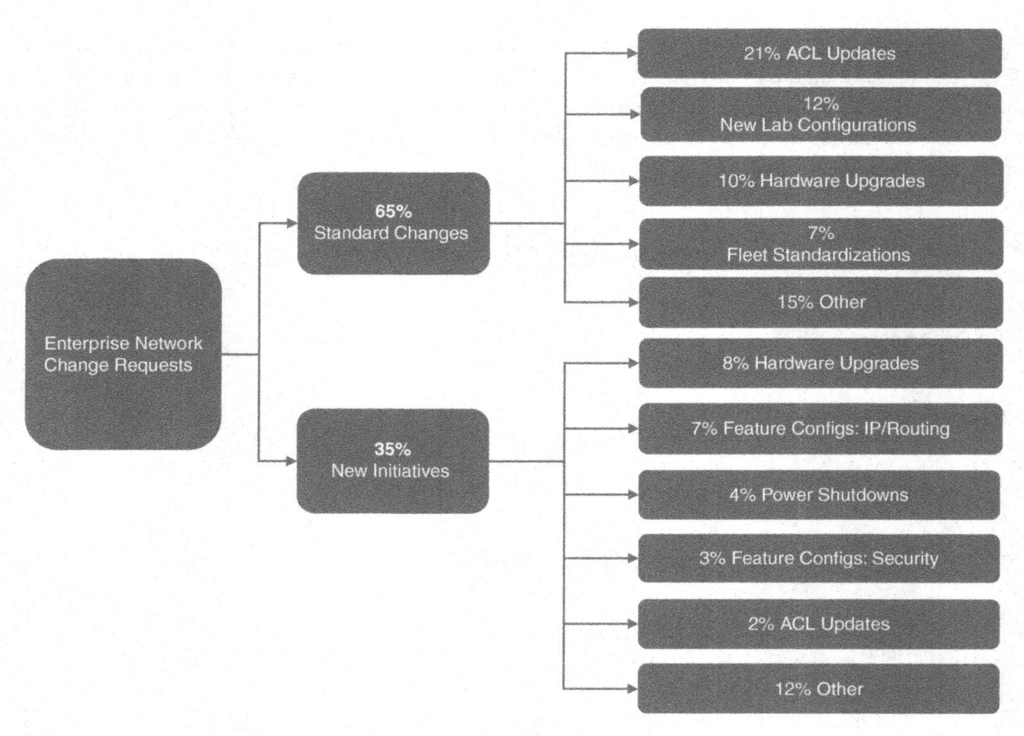

Figure 14-2 *Standard and Nonstandard Network Changes*

So what is stopping many enterprises from increasing the level of automation in their networks? In addition to the mentioned finding that not all operations and changes can be automated, there are often historical and organizational reasons for the lack of automation.

First on the list of obstacles are "snowflakes." Many networks have evolved over time, resulting in a wide variety of network element generations and architectures that are operated concurrently. Technologies introduced years ago may still be operated to save costs. Depreciated assets continue to run where possible to delay replacement costs. At the same time, newer network elements are introduced to satisfy new demands for connectivity, or to fulfill growth when the existing network element types can no longer be purchased due to vendor end-of-sale lifecycles.

Mergers and acquisitions are another reason resulting in a highly diverse networking landscape. The networks from different companies that are merging are likely very different. Building a coherent standardized network architecture after a merger or acquisition can be very hard and disruptive, so different networks based on multiple vendors are allowed to coexist. As enterprises evolve, so do their networks, and the results are often snowflakes—none of which are alike—where in the extreme many disparate networks coexist, with network elements that all seem to have individual configurations. Automating snowflakes is impossible, because automation assumes that the *same* procedure or configuration is applied multiple times. Standardizing on network operations, procedures, configurations, and hardware elements is thus a fundamental requirement to benefit from automation.

Second, organizational structures often also inhibit automation and standardization. In some enterprises, individual departments operate their own network infrastructures. For example, manufacturing may have its own network, separate from the sales and finance departments. For global enterprises, the network in Asia and Europe may be architected and run separate from the Americas network. Large enterprises may thus have multiple networking departments aligning to the organizational structure. And each network department is likely implementing different operational procedures, with possibly different suppliers for networking equipment than the other, resulting in multiple 'standards' even within the same enterprise.

Third on the obstacles list is employee behavior. For some employees, automation is perceived as a threat to their job. Many directors of IT and networking departments encounter resistance of their staff to automate. Statements such as "I am concerned that automation will put me out of a job" or "If I automate my job, I will become redundant in the organization" are not uncommon sentiments by many IT employees. As a result, many an automation project may not progress as planned or succeed.

Last, some enterprises may not choose to standardize, especially when a multivendor environment is desired by corporate policy. Full standardization may be hard to achieve in such an environment. Normalizing the set of functions deployed in your network among multiple vendors often takes more time, as vendors support functionality at a different development pace. Full standardization may sometimes come at the cost of deployment flexibility and speed of innovation in such environments.

None of these obstacles are insurmountable! Standard network architectures and procedures can be enforced. Concerns by IT staff can be addressed by demonstrations that the individuals become more productive for the organization through automation, rather than being replaced by automation. They are able to do more with less. But you have to be aware that such concerns exists and are real, and address them appropriately if you want to successfully automate your network operations.

Classifying Network Automation Tasks

The problem of automating network operations can be dissected from several angles. The target network operations can be subclassified into those that touch the network infrastructure and those that touch the clients of the network (users, devices, or applications). Automation operations can also be classified into standard and nonstandard changes. In the former category are mainly routine operations that are repetitive in nature. The latter class of changes may be more sophisticated, requiring networking experts and more elaborate workflows to complete. This section elaborates on these classifications to deepen your understanding of network automation.

Infrastructure and Cisco DNA Service Automation

In a Cisco Digitalized Network Architecture, automation is categorized into two main sets of activities:

1. Systematically configuring the network infrastructure (such as routers, switches, access points, and auxiliary network functions)
2. Provisioning Cisco DNA services connecting users, devices, and applications with each other, leveraging software interactions between a network controller and the network infrastructure

Automated configuration of the network infrastructure focuses on getting the network up and running. Network elements must be deployed and configured to form a network architecture, rather than remain a disjointed set of physical boxes or virtual machines. Examples of infrastructure automation are the programmatic deployment of a virtual router, or the configuration of the routing algorithms in all the switches and routers forming a software-defined access network.

Once the architecture is set up, it also must be maintained to continue to operate. Configurations may need to be updated, software images may need to be upgraded, and licenses for network software may need to be renewed. All of these operations center on the network infrastructure, rather than providing a transport service that is exposed to and consumed by endpoints that connect to the network. The concept of Cisco DNA infrastructure automation is illustrated in Figure 14-3.

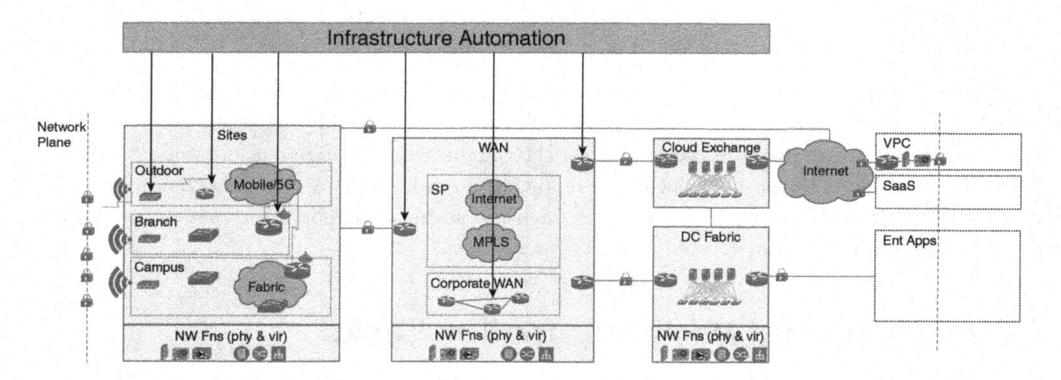

Figure 14-3 *Cisco DNA Infrastructure Automation*

The second set of automation activities are those that allow endpoints—users, applications, or devices—to use the network for their communication requirements. New users must be authorized to consume Cisco DNA network services. Devices and applications may need to be segmented to implement security policies. You may have received an alarm about a malicious user or an unusual traffic pattern and consequently forced traffic from the suspected origin to be redirected for further analysis. All of these are examples of processes touching endpoints, where the network infrastructure is consumed to transport IP traffic from a source to a destination. In many cases, these activities often have an element of policy associated with them. Access policies are automated to grant or deny access to a user, device, or application. Access control policies or application policies are instrumented to automatically regulate the communication between endpoint groups or the treatment of specific application flows, respectively. The concept of Cisco DNA service automation is illustrated in Figure 14-4.

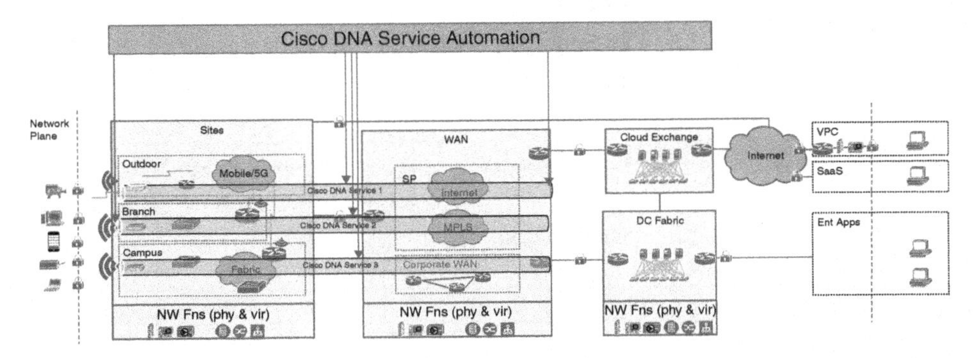

Figure 14-4 *Cisco DNA Service Automation*

Standard and Nonstandard Automation Tasks

Cisco DNA infrastructure automation revolves around the everyday tasks for many network operations teams: performing standard or nonstandard changes to keep the network infrastructure up and running.

Standard changes are defined as those that are repetitive, require no approvals, and typically have minimal or no disruption to network operations. They are often mundane in nature. Examples of standard network changes are

- Deploying and managing auxiliary network functions, such as
  - DHCP/DNS servers
  - NTP servers
  - Syslog servers
  - NetFlow collectors
- Configuring and managing authentication, authorization, and accounting (AAA) for the network infrastructure elements, including some Secure Shell (SSH)/Telnet or Simple Network Management Protocol (SNMP) configurations, or their password management

In contrast, nonstandard changes typically are more disruptive to network operations, often requiring approvals from senior architects or experts. They also often require cooperation of multiple operations teams to implement, such as the data center team or the security operations teams. Nonstandard changes often have a device-specific aspect, differing for routers, switches, or wireless LAN controllers (WLC). Table 14-1 lists some examples of nonstandard network changes by device type.

Table 14-1 *Examples of Nonstandard Network Infrastructure Changes*

Routers	Switches	WLCs
Interface configurations	Interface configurations	Service set identifier (SSID)
ACLs	Spanning tree	Radio frequency (RF) configurations
Voice dial plans	Virtual local area networks (VLAN)	Security/crypto
Virtual routing and forwarding (VRF) configurations	Security/crypto	QoS
Routing protocols	QoS	Deep packet inspection
Tunnel configuration	Deep packet inspection	
Security/crypto		
Quality of service (QoS)		
Deep packet inspection		

Both standard and nonstandard operations benefit from automation. Standard network changes are low-hanging fruit for automation. They are typically common across the different types of network element, needing to be operated on routers, switches, wireless LAN controllers, etc. Nonstandard changes, on the other hand, may require more elaborate support from the automation environment. For example, a flexible notion of a workflow process can help with a chain of approvals that is often required in nonstandard changes, or allow different experts in your team to perform parts of the automated nonstandard changes.

Figure 14-5 illustrates an example of such a workflow, designed to help a network architect to design a new virtualized enterprise branch topology template. To create a new branch template, you have to be aware of the overall geographic network hierarchy consisting of sites, buildings, and floors. From a networking perspective, IP pools are associated with network elements in the sites, becoming an attribute of the site profile. Other attributes could be the list of certified images to be deployed in the network elements of that site, or the characteristics of the WAN connectivity that is typically contracted out to a service provider. The site template also characterizes the types of network elements to be deployed, as well as their prescribed configurations.

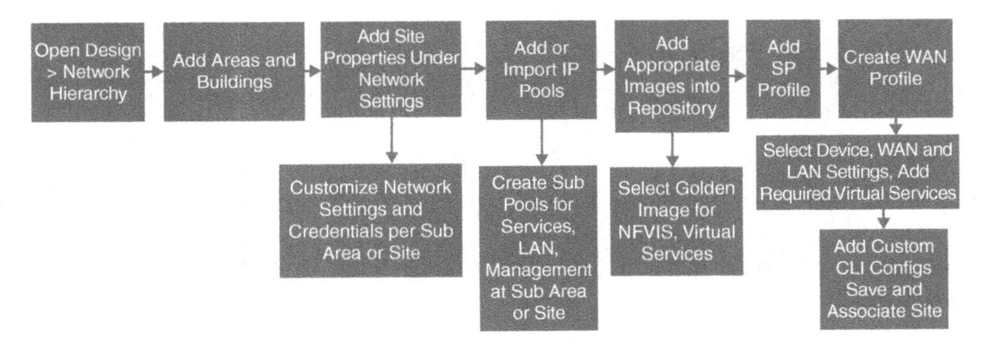

Figure 14-5 *Example of a Nonstandard Network Operation Workflow*

The later section "Automating Your Network with Cisco DNA Center" elaborates on such automated workflows.

The Role of Controllers in Cisco DNA Automation

Chapter 5, "The Cisco Digital Network Architecture Blueprint," introduced the concept of network controllers as an architectural building block. Network controllers become an essential component for automation. They allow you to operate on the network as a system in itself.

Imagine your network as a loosely coupled collection of network elements of different types. Today, many enterprise operators manipulate such individual network elements. To enable Layer 3 reachability in the WAN, routing configurations are pushed into routers one system at a time. Similarly, to establish Layer 2 connectivity in the campus, switches are configured with the appropriate VLAN, spanning tree, or security functions.

But element-by-element operations do not guarantee that the desired end-to-end behavior is successful. A single misconfiguration of a router can potentially break end-to-end reachability. A wrongly applied bridge priority can have detrimental effects on the switching topology. Even if automation is applied on a device-by-device basis, device-specific configurations have to be taken into account. Every network device likely has its own specific parameters such as device IP addresses, or possibly different QoS configurations that are a function of the device's place in the network. Such device-specific parameters are often a cause of error in manual or automated device-by-device configurations. The network remains a loosely coupled set of individual network elements, rather than a coherent system on its own.

The benefit of the controllers in Cisco DNA is to provide a domain-wide view of your network architecture and to operate on it coherently as a system. The controller allows network architects to standardize the network topology for the constituent sites and for the network domain under the controller's governance. For network operators, the controller enables the execution of configuration changes consistently throughout the network, ensuring that the integrity and cohesiveness of the network is maintained. It is this domain-wide view of your network architecture that makes the Cisco DNA controller an invaluable element in the architecture to

- Create the transport and network functions infrastructure
- Maintain a view of the infrastructure functions and connected endpoints
- Instantiate and maintain Cisco DNA services

Leveraging Abstractions in Cisco DNA to Deliver Intent-Based Networking

Another main advantage of the controller for automation is the introduction of an abstraction layer for network operations. By governing a particular network domain as a system, you can describe the intended behavior in a more abstract, network-wide manner, instead of specifying a set of very detailed configuration commands requiring sophisticated parameter details. Higher-level expressions of network behavior are the fundamental building blocks of intent-based networking (IBN), which aims to put the spotlight of network operations on describing the desired behavior using abstractions.

Consider for example that you as a network operator want to prioritize an application. Current network operations focus on automating the instructions on how network elements execute their functionality. In Cisco IOS configuration, you specify a set of class map commands to filter the traffic of your application. This requires intricate knowledge about the characteristics of the application, possibly the IP address of the application server, or maybe specifics about the port numbers that the application rides on. You then proceed to configure a policy map to determine the actions that a specific network element should execute on the filtered traffic. Again, this configuration step requires knowledge about detailed parameters, as well as a cross-reference to a class map. Finally, you apply the policy map to one or more interfaces to control the scope of the QoS configuration.

And then you repeat this process for every network element that the application traffic may traverse, taking into account device specifics at every hop because not all of your collection of routers, switches, and access points are likely going to have the same QoS capabilities. In this traditional approach, you are effectively using your knowledge and skills as a network operator to translate the desired intent into device configurations—typically a nontrivial mental exercise! Figure 14-6 illustrates such an example of providing application QoS end-to-end with varying device types and capabilities.

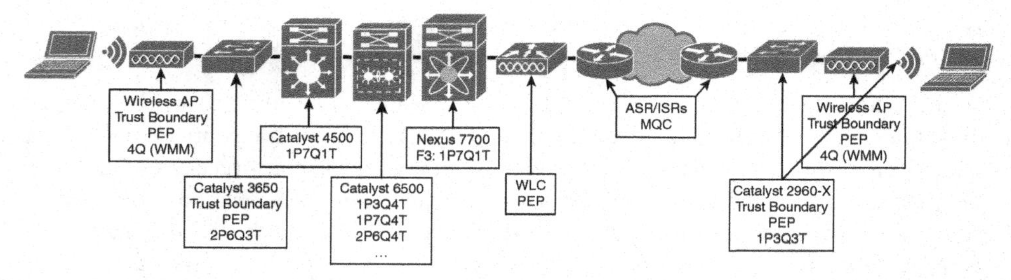

Figure 14-6 *Example of a Traditional, Non-Intent-Based Application Prioritization QoS Configuration Path*

Figure 14-7 shows an example of an abstraction for drivers of cars. The left picture illustrates the steering wheel of a Formula 1 driver. The driver is given a myriad of controls to influence the detailed operation of many elements of the car while driving, such as the braking systems, traction controls, communications with the pits, etc. This is an example of imperative control of a system.

Figure 14-7 *Example of Imperative Versus Declarative Control*

In contrast, the right picture depicts the controls of a regular vehicle. Notice that the driver is presented with the basic controls to operate the vehicle as a whole, not its constituent parts. The steering wheel allows the driver to influence its direction. Pedals are used to determine the speed and displays provide feedback on the car's current status. This is an example of a declarative control system.

In intent-based networking, the controller's knowledge of all the devices under its governance is leveraged to help achieve the desired behavior. The goal of providing priority for an application can be reduced to an abstract expression such as "Application X is business critical in my domain." Such an abstract expression of intent can be interpreted by the controller based on its knowledge of the network. The controller knows all of the network elements under its governance and the network topology. The QoS capabilities of the devices are therefore also known, such as

- QoS configuration syntax
- Queueing scheduling details (number or priority queues, Weighted Fair Queues (WFQ), Scheduler details)
- Possible limitations regarding number of queues, Weighted Random Early Detection (WRED), syntax, etc.

This complete knowledge of the device types, topology, and device capabilities allows the controller to derive the appropriate device configurations automatically. The controller translates the desired behavior into actual device configurations. The derived configurations can then be pushed to the relevant network elements automatically using the southbound APIs described in Chapter 13. Figure 14-8 shows an example of how an abstract expression of intent is expressed to classify an application—a far cry from the current device-centric mode of configuring QoS policies requiring in-depth knowledge of the devices, software, CLI commands, etc.

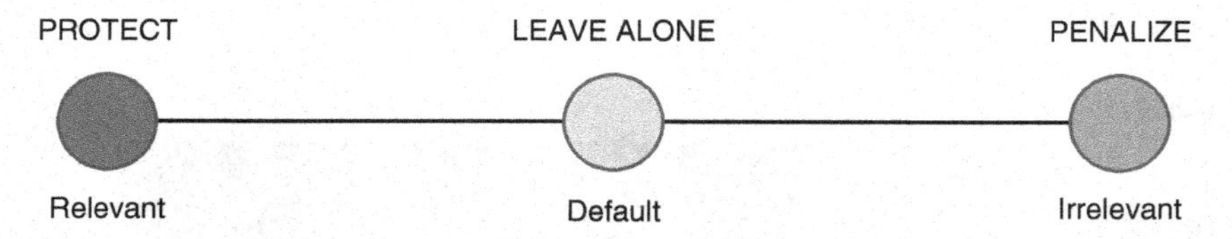

Figure 14-8 *Expressing Application Intent in the Abstract*

The three application categories are detailed as follows:

- **Relevant:** These applications directly support business objectives. Applications should be classified, marked, and treated marked according to industry best practice recommendations. (RFC 4594)
- **Default:** These applications may/may not support business objectives (e.g., HTTP/HTTPS/SSL). Applications of this type should be treated with a default forwarding service. (RFC 2474)
- **Irrelevant:** These applications do not support business objectives and are typically consumer-oriented. Applications of this type should be treated with a "less-than best effort" service. (RFC 3662)

Note that the application categories have also been standardized by the Internet Engineering Task Force (IETF), as indicated by the RFC references in the list. These standards assist in achieving an industry-wide classification for applications.

The abstractions empowered by the Cisco DNA controller in the architecture allow a much simpler method of operating the network. You as a network operator or network architect can focus on determining the desired behavior of the network (the "what") rather than worrying about the mechanics of configuring network elements (the "how").

Other examples of such simplified expressions of intent, as well as the anticipated operational group, are listed in Table 14-2.

Table 14-2 *Examples of Expressed Network, Security, or IT Intent*

Expressed Intent	Operational Group	Execution
Application *X* is business critical.	IT	Create filters for application *X*. Configure QoS for application *X* on all relevant network elements.
User-group *X* should receive preferred network access.	IT	Configure filters for user-group *X*. Configure QoS for user-group *X* on all relevant network elements.

Expressed Intent	Operational Group	Execution
All IoT devices and applications should be isolated from all enterprise applications, devices, and users.	Security	Create a segment for IoT devices. Configure an access control policy for all IoT devices. Associate IoT devices with the IoT segment.
User *X* is blocked from network access.	Security	Create a filter for user *X*. Configure an ACL to block user *X* from network access on all relevant network elements.
All routers must have a minimum software version *X*.	Network	Create an inventory of running software versions. Initiate an upgrade procedure for all routers to software version *X* for all noncompliant routers.

Notice that none of these statements of intent contain network element specifics. They express a desired behavior for the network as a system, for a subset of all network element types, or for the services delivered to users, devices, and applications.

Domain Controllers Versus Control Plane Protocols

The previous discussions introduced the value of network domain controllers to govern the operation of the network as a cohesive system. So what is the relationship between such domain controllers and existing control plane protocols? Do domain controllers replace traditional distributed control plane protocols like Border Gateway Protocol (BGP), Enhanced Interior Gateway Protocol (EIGRP), Open Shortest Path First (OSPF), Protocol-independent Multicast (PIM), Spanning Tree Protocol (STP), and the like?

In Cisco DNA, a distinction is made between the Cisco DNA domain controller functions and network control plane functions. As discussed earlier, the Cisco DNA controller functions govern the operation of a network domain as a whole, instantiating network functions and elements and pushing device configurations using APIs to instantiate expressed intent. The Cisco DNA domain controllers, however, do not replace traditional control plane protocols. Specifically, a domain controller in Cisco DNA does not establish and control real-time forwarding or session state information. This job still remains with network control protocols.

In contrast, the network forwarding control planes focus on the establishment and maintenance of dynamic state—whether this is at Layer 2 for switching, Layer 3 for routing, or even at a higher layer for session-based traffic such as IPsec. These distributed control plane protocols create and maintain state within the network elements for both unicast and multicast traffic. Distributed forwarding or session databases are effectively created and maintained by such control plane protocols. For all routers in a routing domain, a routing protocol creates a distributed Layer 3 forwarding database and ensures that updates are propagated as the state of the network changes. For all switches in the network, a similar forwarding database is created based on Media Access Control (MAC) addresses. For example, STP ensures that such Layer 2 topologies do not create any forwarding loops. Again, the protocol offers an update mechanism to maintain a correct forwarding state as the topology changes (for example, when switches are added or fail).

Note that the network control plane functions no longer need to run based on protocols between a set of network elements. Figure 14-9 illustrates some recent examples in the networking industry of control plane architecture evolutions. The traditional architecture based on protocol exchanges between network elements is shown as model 1. Models 2 and 3 illustrates the concept of off-box network control planes. In model 2, the individual network elements no longer run the protocols required to determine forwarding or session states. These computations are completely centralized in an off-box function that may also have visibility of multiple network elements. Algorithms based on graph theory determine an optimal forwarding state and push this state via APIs into the network elements. Model 3 is a variant of such a centralized forwarding control plane, where only a subset of the computation is centralized off-box, supported by some on-box computations. The third model pertains to overlay networks, where both the virtual data plane and control plane are created on demand, decoupled from the hardware-specific capabilities of the individual network elements. Multiple overlay networks with their respective forwarding and control planes are established in parallel. The fourth model illustrates the approach taken in an IBN architecture. The distributed or centralized forwarding control planes are complemented by policy agents that may aid in the translation and instantiation of policy.

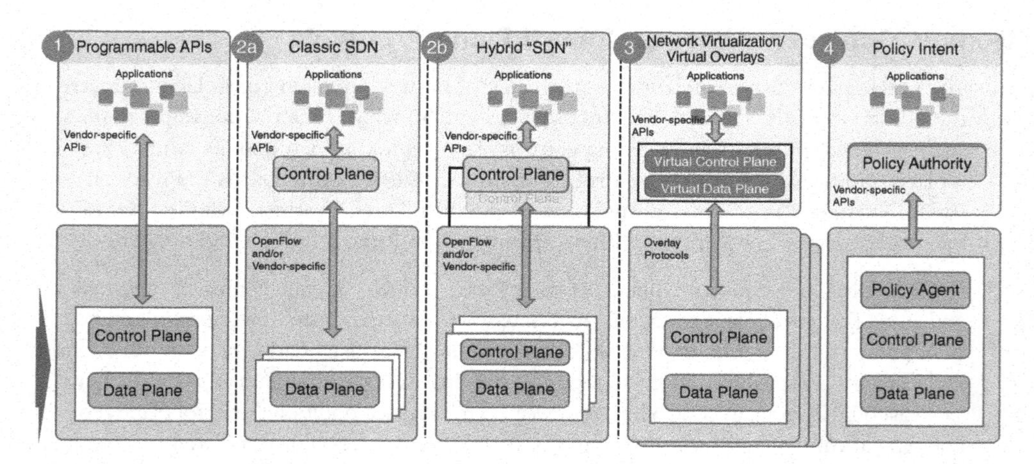

Figure 14-9 *Options for Centralized and Distributed Network Control Planes*

The approach taken in Cisco DNA is model 4. Forwarding and session control plane protocols are not replaced by the Cisco DNA domain controllers. Instead, they are leveraged to continue with the determination of the computation of the dynamic forwarding state. The Cisco DNA controller focuses on the instantiation and configuration of the network elements, as well as governing the behavior of the network elements as constituent components in the overall architecture. Note that as part of this determination, the Cisco DNA domain controllers may govern the control plane functions. For example, upon instantiation of a network element, a configuration with the initial routing protocol configuration may be pushed. But the Cisco DNA controllers do not participate in or execute the dynamic computations of forwarding or session states.

Automating Your Network with Cisco DNA Center

So far this chapter introduced the topic of network automation to augment the capabilities offered by device programmability. It highlighted the need for network-wide automation capabilities in a network supporting digitalized business processes, and some of the challenges that operators face to increase their level of automation.

Network domain controllers provide the capabilities to operate on the network as a system, rather than as a loose collection of individual physical or virtual network elements of different types. The abstractions offered by a network controller function enables expressions of intent, where you can describe at a network level what the network's behavior should be, rather than worrying about the technicalities of programming individual devices and functions.

This section delves into the details that the Cisco DNA Center platform offers in the overall architecture, in particular from an automation perspective. This section explores base controller capabilities, such as keeping an inventory of all devices with all relevant metadata, or maintaining a topology model. It also demonstrates how Cisco DNA Center simplifies your network operations by offering software image management functions and assisting in license management. Finally, it explores in detail functions automating the deployment of network elements, as well as ongoing lifecycle management.

Cisco DNA Center Basics

The Cisco DNA Center platform allows you to manage all aspects of operating your enterprise network domain, including routers, switches, wireless access points, and their supporting network functions (WLAN controllers, DNS, DHCP, etc.). The platform is designed around workflows and Automation and Assurance tools.

Cisco DNA Center workflows allow you to automate the full lifecycle of your enterprise network, including the following phases:

- Design
- Provision
- Assurance
- Policy (Intent)

Automation and Assurance tools offer the capability to execute standard automation functions, such as discovering devices in the network, maintaining an inventory of all network elements and functions, viewing the network topology, and managing licenses. Figure 14-10 illustrates the overall software architecture of Cisco DNA Center. The platform is built on a state-of-the-art software architecture. Its capabilities and applications are implemented as microservices running on top of a container scale-out architecture. The Cisco DNA Center platform infrastructure offers common capabilities such as support for role-based access control (RBAC), Datagram Transport Layer Security (DTLS) secure channel communication, common database repositories for state data, and resource management. The Cisco DNA controller and analytics/assurance functions are the main components sitting above the Cisco DNA Center platform infrastructure.

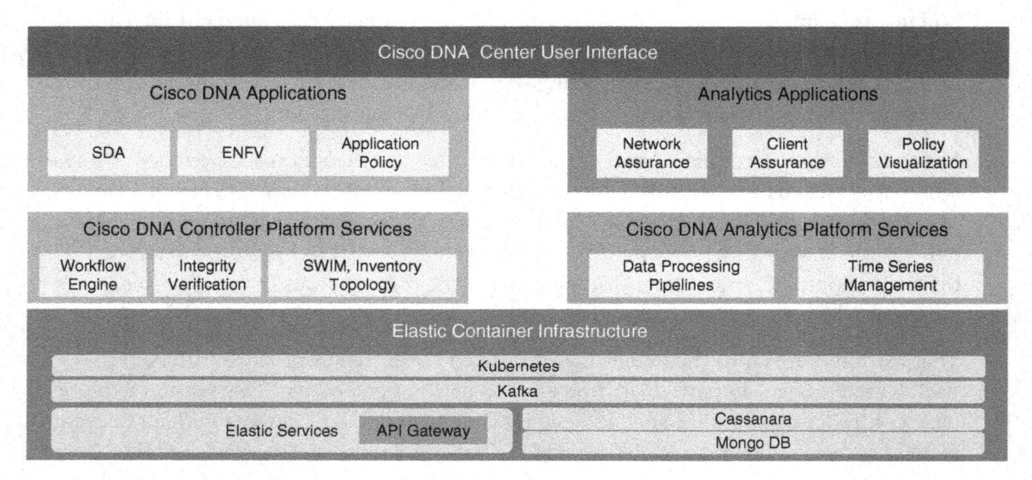

Figure 14-10 *Cisco DNA Center Architecture*

On the automation side, a common service automation framework offers the capability to create network services orchestration applications. The intent expressed via the GUI is internally mapped to a customer-facing service (CFS) model. Such models representing the intent are abstracted for the end-to-end network. The workflow engine has the capabilities to break this internal end-to-end CFS model into individual abstracted device models, referred to as resource-facing service (RFS) models. These RFS models are still abstracted. They do not reflect specific capabilities of a particular device, but rather express the service in a device-type agnostic model. Finally, the automation infrastructure provides the capabilities to convert the device-type agnostic RFS models into actual device-specific models and commands that can be programmed into each participating device using the device programmability APIs.

An example of such a Cisco DNA Center internal model transformation is as follows:

- **User intent:** Application X is business critical throughout my network.
- **CFS:** Application X gets higher priority than best-effort applications.
- **RFS:**
  - **Routers:** Place traffic from Application X into a Low-latency Queue (LLQ).
  - **Switches:** Place traffic from Application X into a WFQ and implement WRED.
- **Device models:** Provide device-specific commands/APIs based on the platform type and software version to instantiate the RFS in the particular device.

Figure 14-11 illustrates the advantages of the underlying scale-out architecture that Cisco DNA Center is based on. Application microservices for automation and analytics run on a Cisco DNA Center appliance. In case the demand for a particular micro-service increases, the platform has the capability to instantiate additional containers.

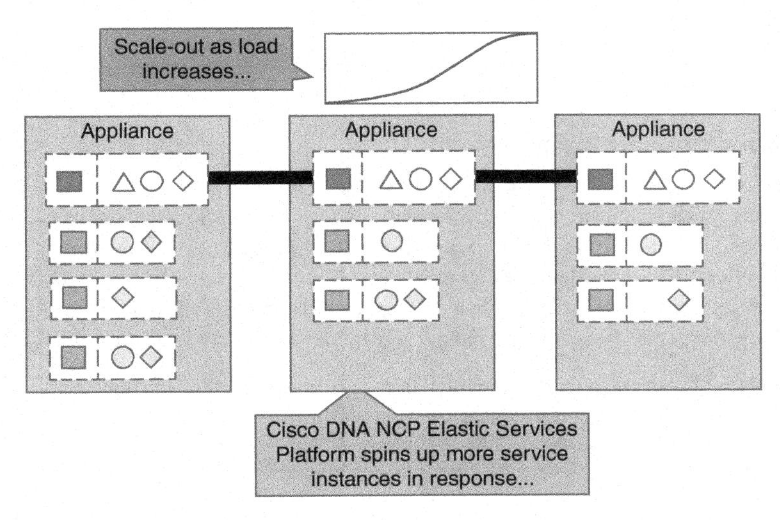

Figure 14-11 *Cisco DNA Center Scale-out Architecture Based on Microservices*

The user interface is the component in the Cisco DNA Center architecture that exposes these capabilities to the operator. Figure 14-12 shows the initial Cisco DNA Center landing screen from which you can control your enterprise network domain.

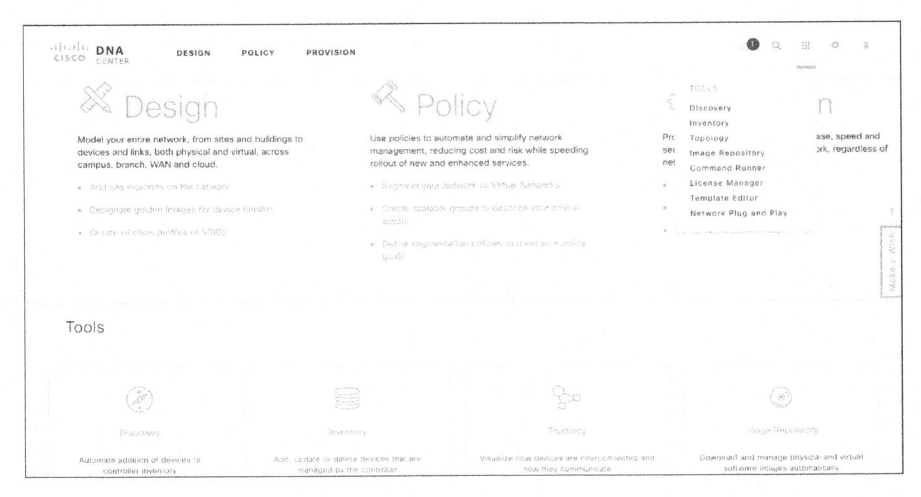

Figure 14-12 *Cisco DNA Center Landing Screen with Workflows and Applications*

The remainder of this section focuses on the automation-related capabilities: standard applications such as Discovery, Inventory, and Topology (shown in the Tools menu in Figure 14-12), as well as the Design and Provision workflows. The Assurance workflow (not shown in Figure 14-12) and Policy workflow are discussed in detail in Chapter 19, "Cisco DNA Software Defined Access," Chapter 20, "Cisco DNA Application Policy," and Chapter 21, "Cisco DNA Assurance."

Note that Cisco DNA Center supports both physical and virtual network elements.

Device Discovery, Inventory, and Topology

At the heart of the Cisco DNA Center platform are the device Discovery, Inventory, and Topology applications. Recall that the goal of automation is to perform standard and non-standard operations consistently on a set of network elements simultaneously. The controller function of Cisco DNA Center needs to become aware of all the devices that exist in the network under its governance. The first task in the operation is to establish an inventory of all network elements and functions by executing the device Discovery application.

Figure 14-13 shows the Discovery user interface to discover the devices in your network and add them to the Cisco DNA Center inventory.

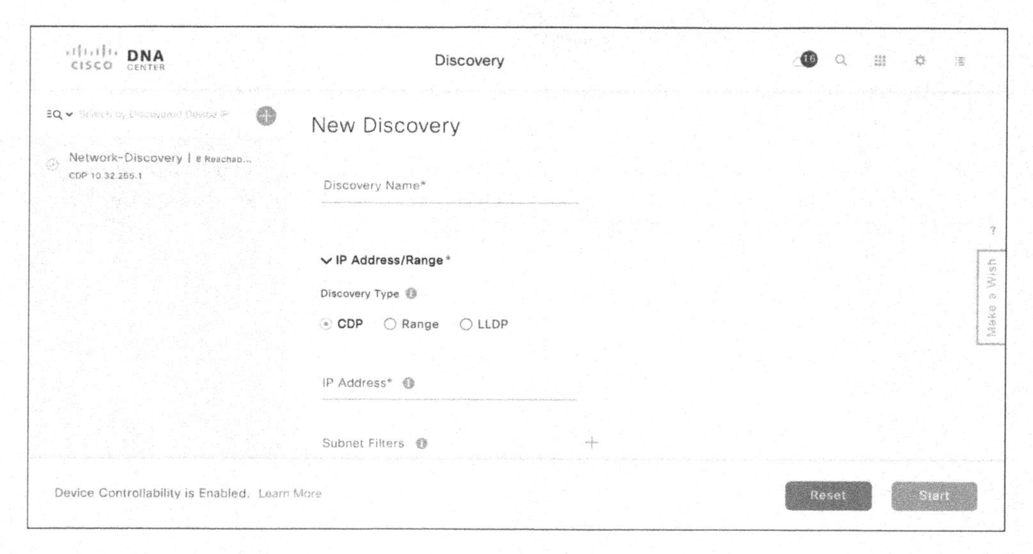

Figure 14-13 *Discovering Devices Using the Device Discovery Application*

Device discovery operates based on either

- Cisco Discovery Protocol (CDP)
- IP address range
- Link Layer Discovery Protocol (LLDP)

Both LLDP and CDP are protocols to share information about directly connected devices. Both protocols offer the capability to advertise a device's identity, its capabilities (e.g., operating system or IP address), and neighbors. Using the IP Address/Range option allows you to perform a similar discovery based on a range of IP addresses that you enter in the GUI. Cisco DNA Discovery then sweeps across the entered range, querying each device in the range for its details.

Devices that are discovered using the Discovery application or those that were provisioned by Cisco DNA Center as part of the Provision workflow are then tracked in the Inventory application. The Inventory application gives you insights into all of the devices known to Cisco DNA Center, forming the basis for many of the subsequent operations. The Inventory application summarizes the pertinent information of all known devices in its initial screen, illustrated in Figure 14-14.

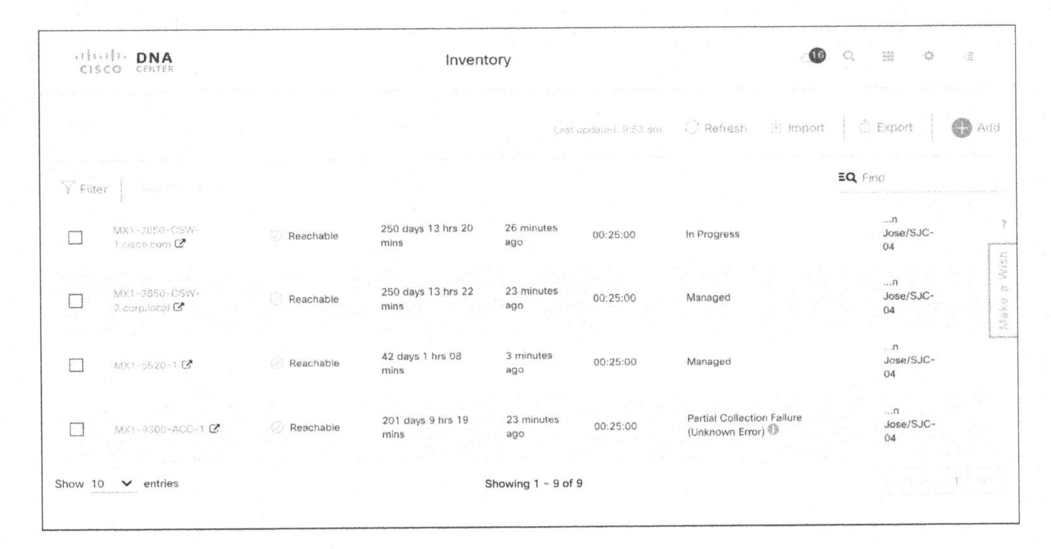

Figure 14-14 *Cisco DNA Center Inventory*

Details such as device name, management IP address, reachability status, operational uptime, and location are tracked for each device. You can also select one or more elements in the inventory list and perform basic operations such as

- Update the device credentials
- Update the resync interval
- Resynchronize the device with the inventory
- Delete the device from the inventory
- Launch the Command Runner application to execute CLI commands

A filter function allows you to view a subset of all devices in the inventory based on any of the metadata fields. For example, you can filter out a subset of elements based on the device name, MAC address, IP address, reachability status (reachable, unreachable), IOS/firmware version, platform, serial number, uptime, last update time, resync interval, last inventory collection status, device role, location, device family, or device series. Wildcards can be used in the filter specifications. The filter function is particularly useful to automate a large network with possibly thousands of devices, allowing you to select the appropriate subset of devices for the desired operation.

The Topology application in Cisco DNA Center then allows you to view the network topology of your enterprise routers, switches, access points, and supporting devices. This is particularly helpful to understand the structure of your Cisco DNA architecture. It also helps you to verify that the actual state of the architecture matches your intent. The topology is thus an integral part of the Assurance functionality of Cisco DNA Center discussed in Chapter 21. Having a solid understanding of the topology also helps in troubleshooting issues.

Figure 14-15 illustrates an example of the network Topology application of Cisco DNA Center. The different device types—routers, switches, access points, and hosts—are represented by respective icons. A set of multiple elements is represented in collapsed mode, with the caption indicating the number of network devices that are actually in the topology (16 in this example). Alternatively, an expanded view allows you to see all the devices and their links to adjacent devices individually. Again, a filter option is available to zoom in on a particular subset of devices based on VRF, VLAN, or routing protocol. Selecting a device in the Topology application reveals its metadata details, such as the management IP address, software version, device family, MAC address, or platform.

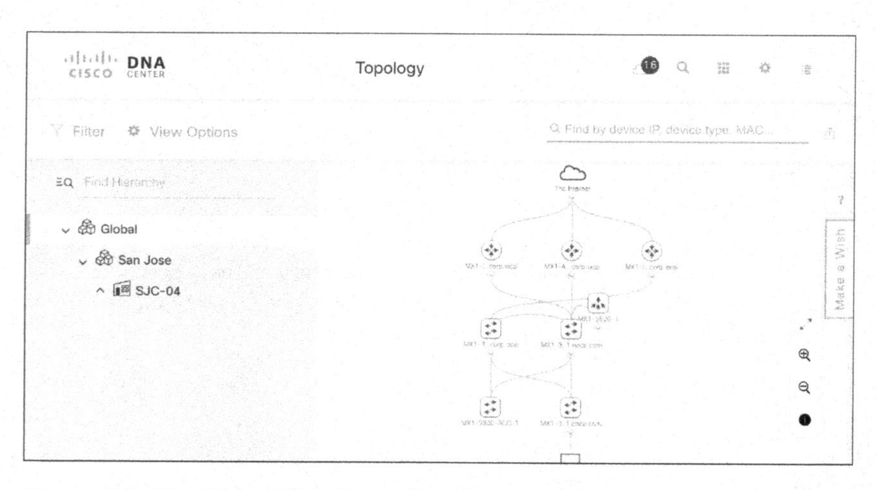

Figure 14-15 *Cisco DNA Center Topology*

Day 0 Operations—Standardizing on Network Designs

Recall from the previous discussion that the fundamental prerequisite to automation is standardization. Cisco DNA Center provides support to drive standardization into your architecture starting with the Design workflow.

The Design workflow allows you to express your intended enterprise network architecture, starting with the geographical characterization of the topology. The Network Hierarchy screen allows you to specify the structure of your architecture in terms of sites, buildings, and floors. A site or area is associated with a geographic location, allowing for a map-based view in addition to a list view. Sites may have one or more buildings. A building can consist of one or more floors, a property that is particularly relevant for the wireless automation and assurance functions.

The concepts of sites, buildings, and floors are fundamental to the Cisco DNA Center design phase. The purpose of the Design workflow is to allow a network architect to specify a network architecture template. For example, a small site may be defined in your enterprise to contain a single WAN router to which two access switches connect. Wired hosts or wireless access points in turn connect to the access switches. Such a simple design with associated parameters (device types, initial device configurations, IP addresses, etc.) can be stored in an architecture design template, and subsequently associated with a site or a building. Furthermore, standard settings can be applied at any level of the hierarchy and inherited down to lower levels. For example, settings applied to a site are by default inherited into buildings.

Representing your network in such a hierarchy also allows for the flexibility to accommodate site- or location-specific differences. For example, you may want to operate a separate DNS or DHCP server in different regions of your network. A hierarchical representation of your architecture also allows for the default inheritance to be overridden. A different set of standards can be applied to different parts of the network hierarchy if desired. Figure 14-16 shows the Network Hierarchy screen with a geographical map of the network sites and a list of the site hierarchy on the left.

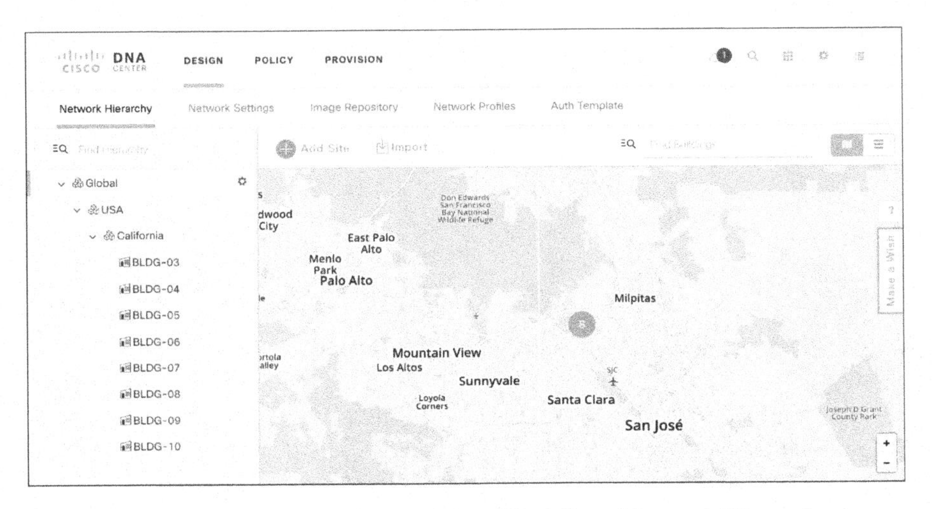

Figure 14-16 *Cisco DNA Center Design Workflow: Network Hierarchy*

Standardizing Settings for Supporting Network Functions

An example of such standard network settings are the details to reach auxiliary network functions such as Network Time Protocol (NTP), DHCP, DNS, Syslog, or other servers. Reachability to these network functions is critical for the operation of the network, and hence even the slightest misconfiguration can have disastrous effects on the network. Often, these functions are operated on a regional basis, administered by different teams.

The Network Settings screen in the Cisco DNA Center Design workflow allows you to standardize and automate reachability to such auxiliary network functions. Figure 14-17 shows the details of the parameters to standardize on such network settings. The IP addresses of primary or secondary servers are entered, as well as the time zone and message-of-the-day banners. Note that the network hierarchy concept outlined here provides the flexibility to apply settings on a network-wide basis, or to override them if regional or even site-specific parameters apply. The green bar on the network hierarchy navigation pane on the right indicates the current scope of the parameters. By default, settings entered in the global scope are inherited down to sites and buildings. Selecting a particular lower-level hierarchy allows you to overwrite the global settings, breaking the inheritance if desired.

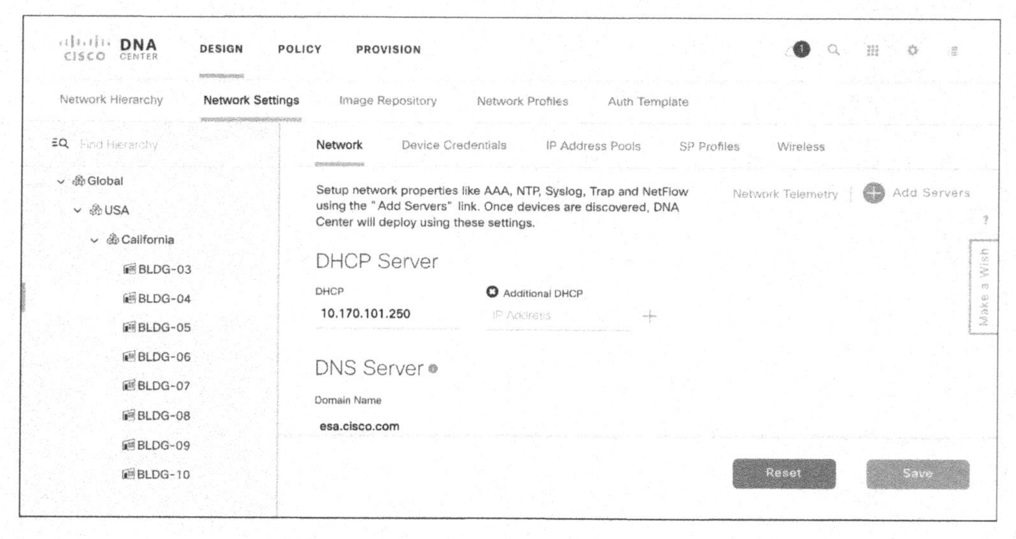

Figure 14-17 *Cisco DNA Center Design Workflow: Network Settings*

Automating Device Credentials

Another example of seemingly mundane settings that may have disastrous effects if misconfigured are device credentials. These are critical for the Cisco DNA controller to continuously monitor the devices' state and configurations. After all, for the Cisco DNA controller to function it requires a full view of all the network elements and functions under its governance. The Cisco DNA controller periodically verifies that the state and configuration it has in its device and topology model database still reflects the current state in the devices themselves. Being able to log in and monitor the device states is thus critical.

Figure 14-18 illustrates the parameters to control the device credentials. CLI, HTTP(S), and SNMP credentials are currently supported.

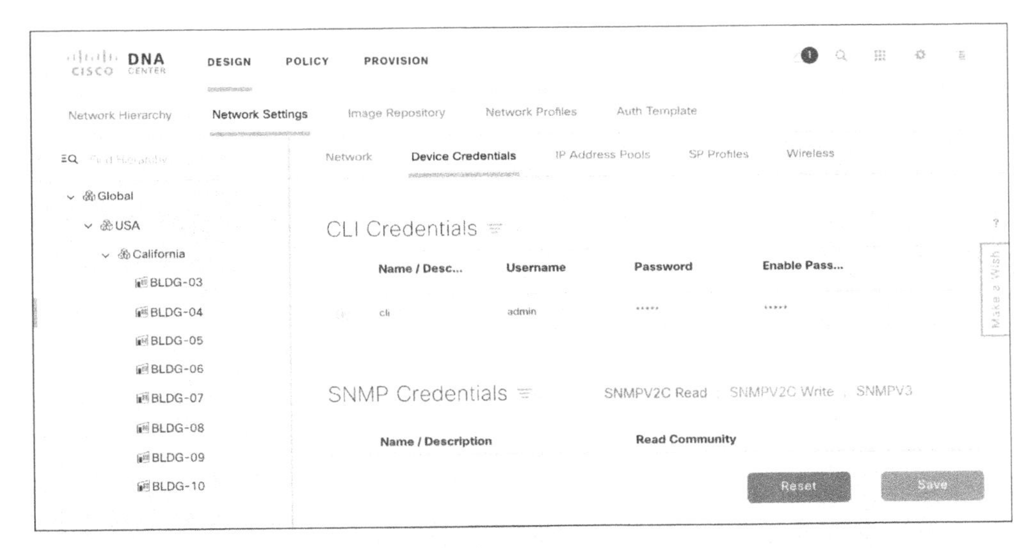

Figure 14-18 *Cisco DNA Center Design Workflow: Device Credentials*

Reserving and Managing IP Address Pools

Another example of a standard that can be enforced in the Cisco DNA Center controller is the use of IP addresses. Again, misconfigurations of IP addresses in devices or overlapping use of IP addresses can be major causes for disruptions in the IP communication patterns, especially if these addresses pertain to network elements as opposed to end hosts.

Cisco DNA Center allows you to reserve IP address pools and associate them with particular deployments, such as sites or in network design templates, in the corresponding design workflows.

Figure 14-19 shows the Cisco DNA Center user interface to reserve IP address pools for specific uses. Each reserved pool is associated with a label, a subnet mask to characterize its size, the gateway IP address for the pool, and optional DNS/DHCP server addresses. The user interface also reflects the current usage of the pool, indicating how many of the IP addresses were already allocated during provisioning activities.

Figure 14-19 *Cisco DNA Center Design Workflow: IP Address Pool Reservations*

Note that Cisco DNA Center also allows integration with an external IP address management (IPAM) system such as Infoblox or BlueCat. The *Cisco Digital Network Architecture Center User Guide*[3] provides additional details on how to import an address pool from an external IPAM system.

Standardizing Service Provider QoS Profiles

Yet another example of settings that Cisco DNA Center helps to standardize across your infrastructure are the quality of service (QoS) settings used for site connectivity provided by service providers. Navigating within the Design workflow Network Settings screen to the SP Profiles QoS tab allows you to template different QoS models that you contracted from one or more service providers in your network. The SP Profiles tab allows you to store different templates, identified by a name and a tag representing the SP, and characterizing the number of queues that the QoS profile implements.

These templates are subsequently referred to when you design your site profiles. For example, creating a virtualized system architecture for a branch requires you to characterize the SP that provides the WAN connectivity. The SP Profile entered in this step of the Design workflow is referenced in subsequent Cisco DNA Center configuration workflows (e.g. the Routing and NFV network profile workflow). This allows you to ensure greater consistency across all sites being served by the same SP in your network from a QoS perspective. Figure 14-20 shows how SP QoS settings can be added as templates into Cisco DNA Center.

---

3 https://www.cisco.com/c/en/us/td/docs/cloud-systems-management/network-automation-and-management/dna-center/1-1/user_guide/b_dnac_ug_1_1.html

Figure 14-20 *Cisco DNA Center Design Workflow: SP Profiles QoS Settings*

Characterizing Wireless LAN Profiles

Finally, the Network Settings tab allows you to template the WLAN settings that are applied in the wireless deployments in your network. Settings such as the SSID or RF profiles can again be stored in a template repository, to be referenced against in the later deployment workflow when a wireless AP is provisioned.

Figure 14-21 illustrates some of the options to standardize wireless settings.

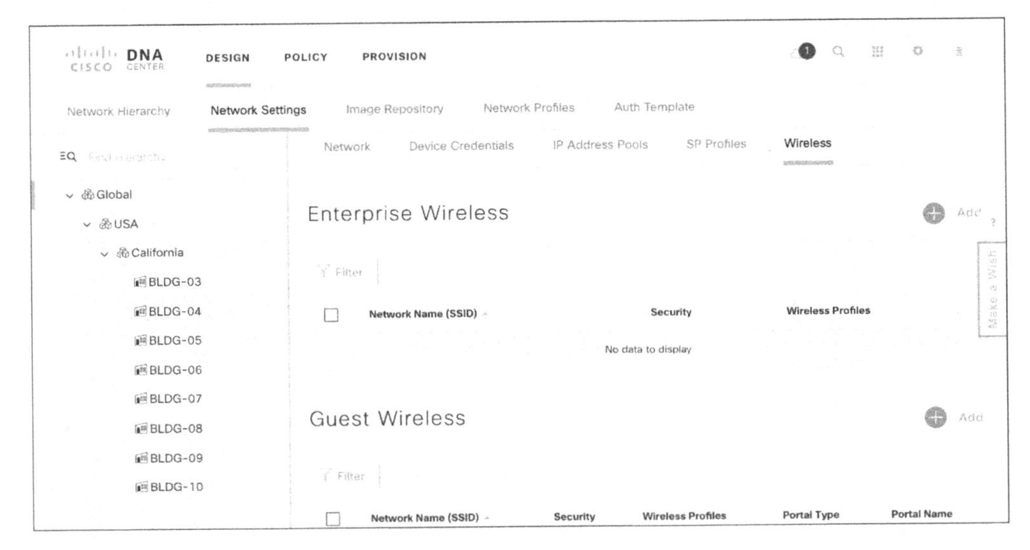

Figure 14-21 *Cisco DNA Center Design Workflow: WLAN Profiles*

Standardizing on Network Designs

The beginning of this chapter outlined the complications that can arise in operating a network from nonstandard site architectures and device configurations. The Cisco DNA Center Design workflow Network Profiles screen allows you as an architect to create standardized templates for your network elements and site topologies. As in the case with standard network settings, these can be applied during the Provision workflow to devices in your various sites as they are deployed.

The Network Profiles screen starts with the inventory of all template designs. This allows you to see all the templates that are stored in the Cisco DNA Center library, identified by template name. The inventory also lists the type of profile. Currently, network profiles can be of type routing and virtualization, switching, and wireless. The inventory also provides an indication of the deployment of a particular profile. The association of the intended design to an actual deployment is done via a site. Once you have added an architecture template to the inventory, you can associate it with one or more sites. During the Provision workflow, devices are also associated with a site. Sites are thus common anchors to which both design templates and actual devices are associated, allowing for the templates to be applied in all the devices of a site. An example of a network profile library in Cisco DNA Center is illustrated in Figure 14-22.

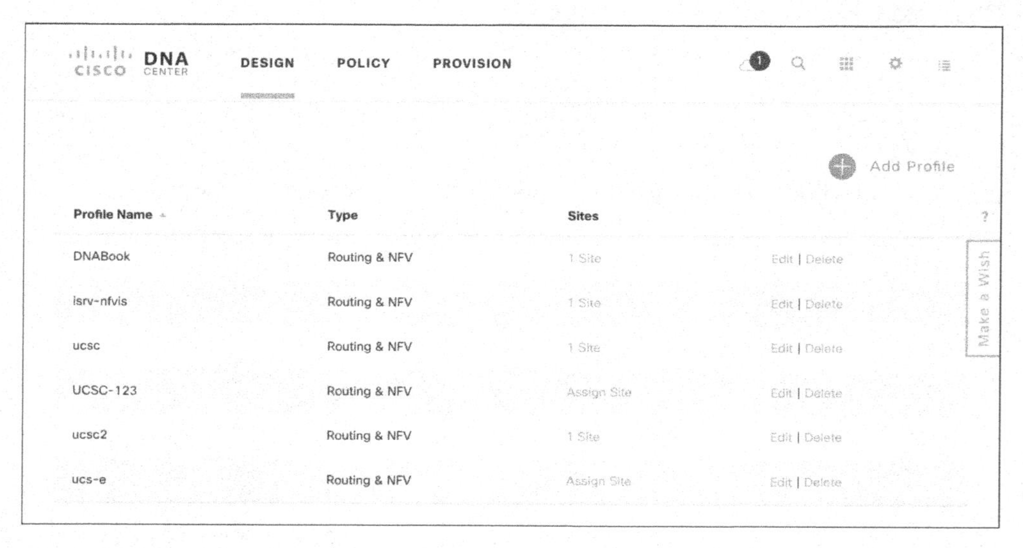

Figure 14-22 *Cisco DNA Center Design Workflow: Network Profiles*

Additional site architecture profiles are added by clicking the Add Profile option. This initiates the Cisco DNA Center Profile Design workflow for routing and NFV, switching, or wireless. In the example of a virtualized branch, the initial workflow screen shown in

Figure 14-23 is displayed. The generic branch architecture is specified, with options for a single or dual WAN router deployment, as well as a selection of the WAN router type. Notice that you can apply the SP Profile specified in an earlier step of the network design workflow, characterizing the QoS profile that is to be applied toward the WAN.

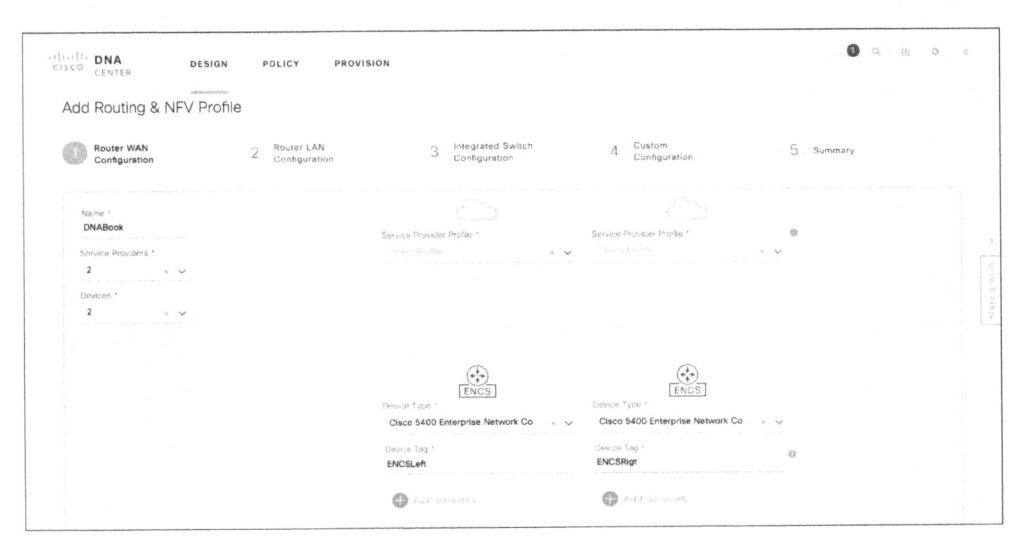

Figure 14-23 *Cisco DNA Center Design Workflow: Network Profile Workflow for NFV*

In the case of a virtualized branch, additional virtual network functions (VNF) are added to the template. This is achieved by clicking the Add Services option in the workflow. A canvas appears, allowing you to select among the known VNF types. In the case of a virtualized branch, the internal VLAN connectivity between the VNFs is built in based on validated designs. The canvas represents a segment connecting the LAN ports to the LAN network, the WAN ports to the WAN network, and any inter-VNF segments to the service network. The DIA option allows for a VNF of type Firewall to front-end the WAN connection, instead of a virtual WAN router.

For each type of VNF added to the design, you can select an actual product. For example, if you select a virtual router in your design, you can subsequently specify for a Cisco Integrated Services Virtual Router (ISRv) to be instantiated. An additional parameter allows you to determine some of the profile characteristics for the VNF. The VNF profiles define how many resources are associated with the virtual machine in terms of vCPUs, virtual memory, or virtual storage. These are important parameters to validate the total resource demand against the x86-based host capacities when the device is brought to life. Figure 14-24 shows a sample canvas for specifying a virtual branch template with different VNFs in Cisco DNA Center.

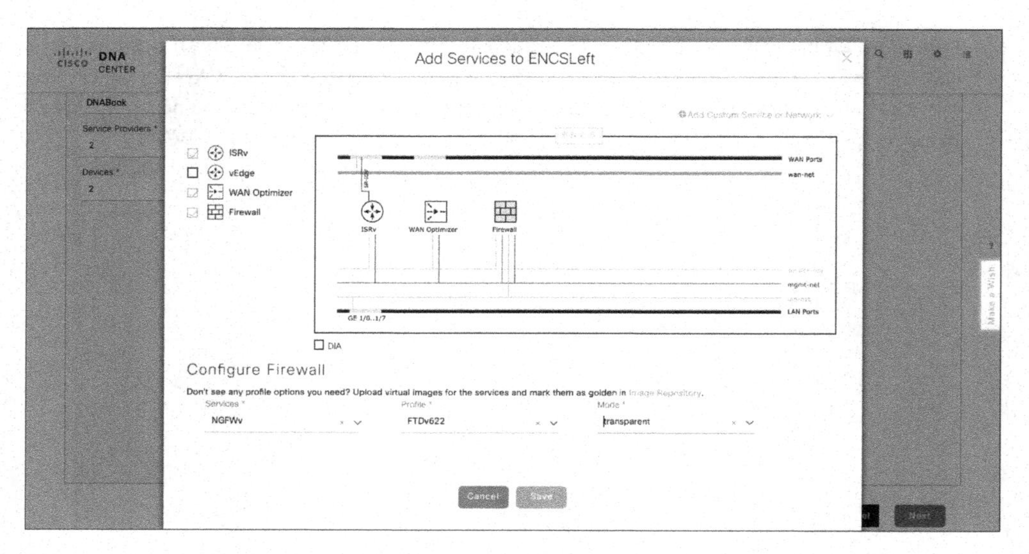

Figure 14-24 *Cisco DNA Center Design Workflow: Network Profile Workflow—Selecting Virtualized Network Functions on the Canvas*

At this stage in the design process, not all parameters can be completely determined. Any site-specific variables, such as IP addresses, cannot be built into the template by definition. Such parameters are completed during the Provision workflow, where the template is applied to a particular site deployment.

The Network profile workflow allows for additional parameters to be associated with the template. For example, whether the LAN ports are to be configured as access or trunk ports, VLAN settings on the physical interfaces, parameters for the internal virtual switch in Cisco Enterprise NFV Infrastructure Software (NFVIS), or even if a particular configuration snippet should be applied upon device instantiation. Details of these steps are found in Chapter 18, "Cisco DNA Virtualization Solutions: Enterprise Network Function Virtualization and Secure Agile Exchange."

At the end of the Network profile workflow, Cisco DNA Center validates the template to ensure that all parameters are correctly specified. In the case of Enterprise Network Function Virtualization (ENFV), a guidance is offered to ensure that the resource requirements of all the VNFs in terms of virtual CPUs (vCPU), memory, and storage, do not exceed the capacity of the specified x86-based host type.

Automating the Deployment of Network Elements and Functions

The Design workflow described in the previous section is a fundamental prerequisite to enable network automation in a digitalized network architecture. The next step in the automation journey is to leverage Cisco DNA Center workflows to automatically deploy new network elements. This step is covered by the Provision workflow.

As briefly introduced, the concept of sites is critical to associate an actual deployment with a site architecture profile to increase the level of standardization in your network. A particular network design profile is associated with one or more sites. Similarly, as you provision a device, you also select the site in which the device is located. The association of both the device to be provisioned and the design template to a site allows Cisco DNA Center to correlate the two. At a high level, the workflow follows this sequence of events:

1. One or more devices are shipped to a site for deployment.
2. A local operator (not necessarily CCIE qualified!) performs the physical deployment of the device(s)—cabling of power and physical connections.
3. The devices are powered on.
4. The Network Plug and Play Client function is automatically activated upon power-up. This process sends a message to Cisco DNA Center with the device's details, such as its serial number and type.
5. Cisco DNA Center adds the device to its unclaimed inventory.
6. The Cisco DNA Center Provision workflow is performed by a network operator.
   - The unclaimed device is selected for provisioning.
   - The unclaimed device is associated with a site in Cisco DNA Center.
   - Cisco DNA Center finds the corresponding site template, checks that the device types match, and if successful pushes the device configuration using Representational State Transfer (REST) API calls to the device.
7. The device on site then executes the configurations pushed by Cisco DNA Center.
   - In the example of an x86-based host configured for ENFV, the VNFs specified in the ENFV template are instantiated and networked as per the design template.

Various options are supported to perform the plug-and-play capability of a device. First, the device leverages DHCP with Option 43. In this case, the DHCP server returns the details of the Cisco DNA Center controller acting as the Plug and Play (PnP) server in the DHCP response. The device thus learns from DHCP which Cisco DNA Center instance to contact to complete its provisioning process. Second, DNS may be leveraged to obtain the required information. In this case, the DNS server maps the URL pnpserver.localdomain to the IP address of the PnP Server running in Cisco DNA Center. The third option to perform zero-touch provisioning of a device involves contacting a Cisco cloud service. In this option, the URL https://devicehelper.cisco.com/device-helper again is redirected to the IP address of the Cisco DNA Center instance. Notice that the URL is in the domain cisco.com. Fourth, a local operator leverages the USB port on a physical device to be provisioned to provide a bootstrap file, again providing the required details to contact the PnP server. And last, Cisco also offers an installer app for onsite operators. This application runs on a hand-held device, and again provides the details of the PnP server running in Cisco DNA Center.

After the device registers itself with the PnP server running in Cisco DNA Center, it is placed in an unclaimed device inventory list. This is the basis for the subsequent provisioning step: providing the required variables and site-specific details for the final deployment.

Figure 14-25 illustrates the initial provisioning screen for unclaimed devices. Select one or more devices in the workflow. The option Assign Device to Site creates the association of that device with a particular site in your network hierarchy. This allows Cisco DNA Center to also create the correlation to the design template for the specified site. The option Provision then kicks off the provisioning step, where the design profile is applied and the device is provisioned using the REST API calls from Cisco DNA Center to the device to be provisioned.

DNA CENTER DESIGN POLICY PROVISION

Refresh Network Telemetry Upgrade Readiness Update Status

Filter | Actions | Tag Device | LAN Automation

Assign Device to Site
Provision
Resync
Delete Device
Update OS Image

De Na	...ss	Site	Serial Number	Uptime	OS Version	OS Image	Last Sync Status	Credential Status	Last Provisioned Time
	169.234	...ornia/BLDG-03	FGL210710QX		3.7.1-FC2	Cisco NFV Inf...	Managed	Not Provisioned	-
	97.88	...ornia/BLDG-03	FOC20090MNY		3.8.1-FC3	Enterprise NF...	Managed	Not Provisioned	-
NFVIS	172.25.220.70	...ornia/BLDG-03	FCH1910V061	114 days, 14:44:00.00	3.8.1-FC3	Cisco NFV Inf...	Managed	Not Provisioned	Aug 15 2018 00:44:05
NFVIS	172.20.114.228	...ornia/BLDG-03	FGL210311EL		3.7.1-FC2	Cisco NFV Inf...	Managed	Not Provisioned	Aug 15 2018 19:30:03
NFVIS	172.28.169.232	...ornia/BLDG-03	FGL21071051	1 days, 11:48:00.00	3.8.1-FC3	Cisco NFV Inf...	Managed	Not Provisioned	-
		...ornia/BLDG-		284 days,			Wrong	Not	Aug 14

Figure 14-25 *Cisco DNA Center Provision Workflow: Network Profile Workflow—Selecting Virtualized Network Functions on the Canvas*

Recall that not all parameters can be determined at the design stage. Some variables in a design are site-specific. Part of the Provision workflow is thus to allow you to enter those site-specific parameters. Figures 14-26, 14-27, and 14-28 illustrate some examples of such parameters in the case of a virtual branch deployment, allowing you to verify the profile to be applied to the device in question, to provide the details for the WAN interface to the service provider at the site, and to specify IP addressing details of a virtual router (as an example). Other site-specific variables follow similar templates to allow the site or device provisioning to complete.

Figure 14-26 *Cisco DNA Center Provision Workflow: Confirming the Profile to Be Applied to a Device*

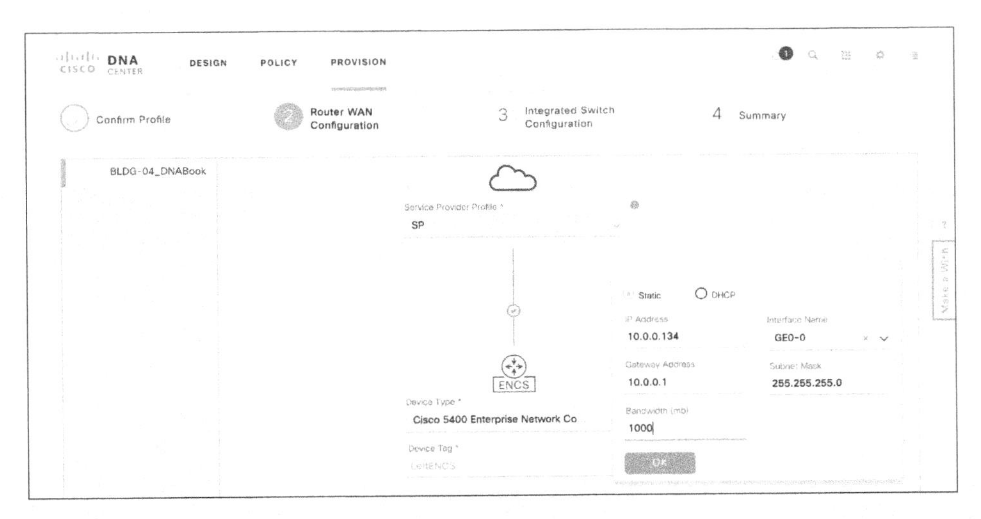

Figure 14-27 *Cisco DNA Center Provision Workflow: Specifying Site-Specific WAN Interface Parameters*

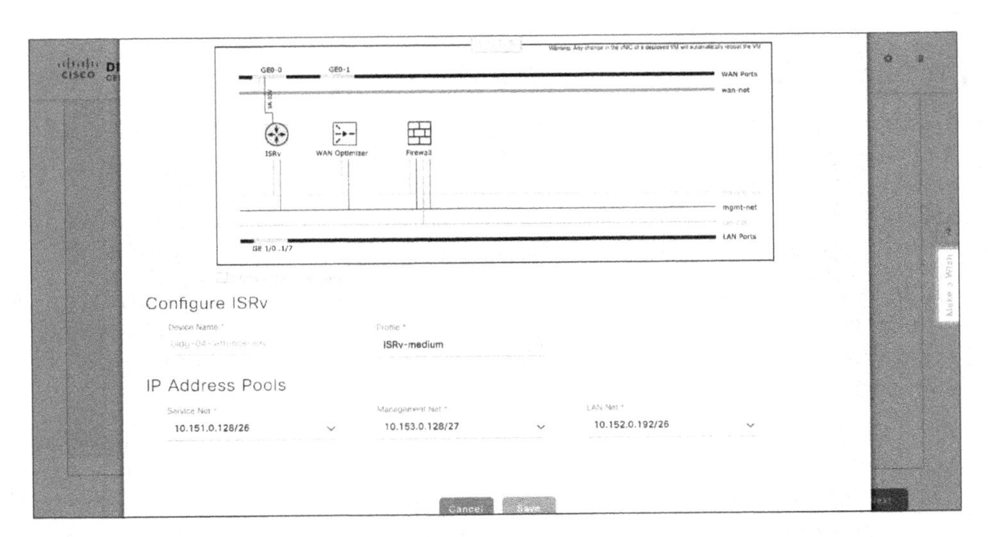

Figure 14-28 *Cisco DNA Center Provision Workflow: Specifying Virtual Router IP Address Pools*

At the end of the Provision workflow, the operator initiates the actual provisioning process. This triggers a set of API calls from Cisco DNA Center to the device to be provisioned. The sequence of events is monitored from within Cisco DNA Center to ensure that the automated process proceeds as intended. Figure 14-29 shows an example of the deployment steps, with details of each activity and the associated timestamps. The actual payload of the API call from Cisco DNA Center to the device is also displayed for verification purposes.

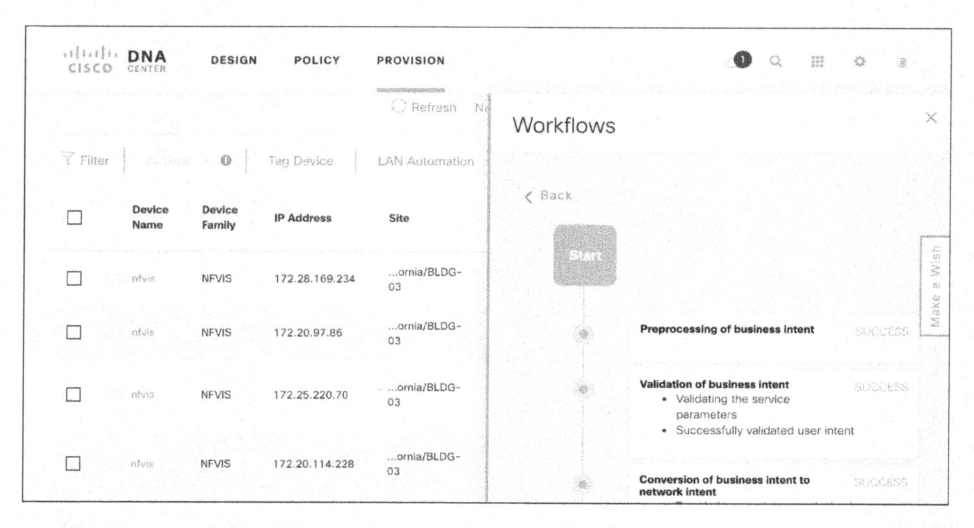

Figure 14-29 *Cisco DNA Center Provision Workflow: Viewing Details of the Provision Workflow*

Day N Operations—Automating Lifecycle Operations

The last leg in the Cisco DNA automation journey is the ongoing maintenance and update of the deployed devices. The tools and functions previously described—Inventory, Topology, Design templates—also play a role in this phase. They allow you to push updates to your configurations or template architectures to one or more devices in your network hierarchy.

Two applications are worth mentioning for day N operations: software image management and license management. As previously indicated, these are applications that run as part of Cisco DNA Center to allow you to perform ongoing management of your software images and licenses, respectively.

Figure 14-30 shows the capabilities of the Software Image Management (SWIM) application. Software images for the various devices in your network are added to Cisco DNA Center's Image Repository. This is done from a local machine with which the operator connects to Cisco DNA Center. Alternatively, software images are uploaded from a specified URL. Once uploaded, the software image is associated with a device family (routers, switches, access points, for example) and also marked as "golden." Golden images are those images that you have certified for deployment in your network, or that you wish to standardize on throughout your infrastructure.

A day N software image upgrade process is then initiated from the Image Repository application by selecting the option Update Devices. You as an operator can select one or more devices as a target for the software upgrades. The Cisco DNA Center SWIM application then performs a number of checks to validate the upgrade. For example, memory and hard disks are verified for sufficient space to perform the software upgrade. If the pre-checks are successful, the new software images are pushed to the selected devices and activated. Finally, a set of post-checks are executed to ensure that the software upgrade was successful. At any stage in this process, a rollback procedure is activated in case a particular step in the upgrade fails.

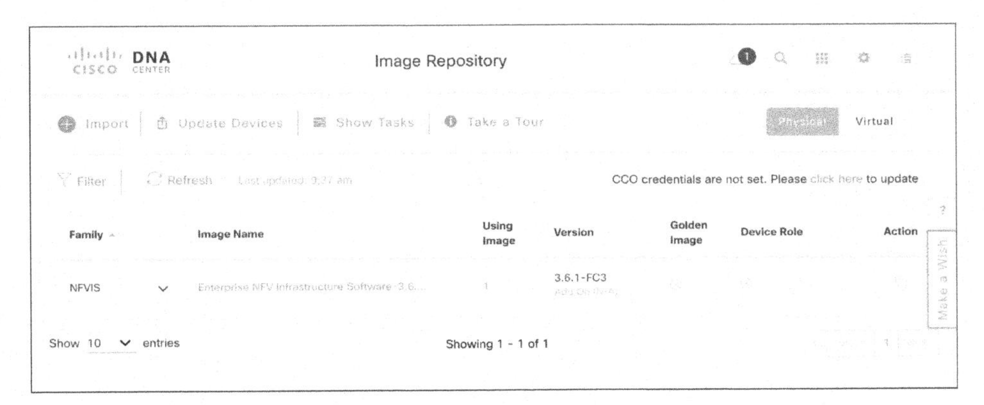

Figure 14-30 *Cisco DNA Center Software Image Management*

The License Manager application running on top of Cisco DNA Center allows you to perform similar day N operations for licenses. The application is linked to the Cisco Smart Licensing capability. View the purchased licenses by device type, how many devices are in your network of a particular type that require a license, as well as how many licenses out of the purchased pool are currently in use. The License Manager application also provides you compliance details, such as the expiration dates for time-based licenses in your pool.

Summary

This chapter explored the topic of network automation as a main capability of the Cisco Digital Network Architecture. While many enterprises realize the potential and necessity to automate their network operations, multiple challenges still create roadblocks for an increased level of automated operations. Examples of such roadblocks include non-standard "snowflake" deployments from the historical evolution of many networks, and reservations of IT and network operations staff that they may become obsolete.

The topic of *network* automation extends the capabilities offered by device programmability to the network level. Rather than operating on a device-by-device basis, network automation aims to treat the network as a coherent system in itself. Operations are applied to the network to achieve a desired behavior, rather than pushing configurations to individual devices. This subtle but important distinction forms the basis for intent-based networking, where network operators are encouraged to describe the intended behavior of the network, rather than configuring devices one by one. Intent-based networking focuses on *what* the network should do for users, devices, and applications, rather than *how* the individual elements are configured. The chapter introduced the Cisco DNA controller as a fundamental element in the overall Cisco Digital Network Architecture to enable intent-based networking and the supporting abstraction levels. The key takeaways of this chapter are as follows:

- Standardization is a prerequisite to any automation paradigm. Both standard and nonstandard operations are addressed in Cisco DNA Center, the platform in Cisco DNA to enable network-wide automation.
- Cisco DNA Center supports automation tools for standard processes (Inventory, Discovery, Topology, Network Plug and Play). In addition, Cisco DNA Center supports sophisticated workflows to operate all stages of your Cisco DNA network: Design, Policy, Provision, and Assurance.
- The Cisco DNA Center Design workflow is particularly important to drive standards into your Cisco DNA network. Settings such as IP addresses of common network functions (DNS, DHCP, Syslog, and NTP servers, for example) can be standardized and automated. The Design workflow also accommodates the creation of standard site and device templates that are stored in a library to be applied in the provisioning phase of the network.
- The Cisco DNA Center Provision workflow supports Network Plug-and-Play, allowing you to ship network elements to your sites and automatically provision them. Once a device calls home to the Cisco DNA Center plug-and-play server using one of multiple mechanisms, the appropriate design template can be applied.

While automation is an important and even essential capability of an intent-based network architecture, it must be complemented by the corresponding analytics and assurance functions. These allow you to verify that the intended and automated capabilities are indeed deployed and operational in your network at any point in time. The topic of network analytics and assurance is thus the next milestone in the journey to enable the Cisco Digital Network Architecture. You may not be surprised that Cisco DNA Center again plays a major role!

Further Reading

Cisco Systems. *Cisco Digital Network Architecture Center User Guide, Release 1.2.1.* Updated August 13, 2018. https://www.cisco.com/c/en/us/td/docs/cloud-systems-management/network-automation-and-management/dna-center/1-2-1/user_guide/b_dnac_ug_1_2_1.html.

Staffing Industry Analysts (SIA). "IT Employers to Add Staff but Facing Tech Skills Shortage, Hays Reports." Feb. 1, 2018. https://www2.staffingindustry.com/row/Editorial/IT-Staffing-Report/Feb.-1-2018/IT-employers-to-add-staff-but-facing-tech-skills-shortage-Hays-reports?.

Gartner, "IT Budget: Enterprise Comparison Tool", http://www.gartner.com/downloads/public/explore/metricsAndTools/ITBudget_Sample_2012.pdf

Chapter 15

Introduction to Cisco DNA Analytics

Cisco Digital Network Architecture (Cisco DNA) analytics is the discovery and communication of business insights through the exploration of data from various sources that attach to the network.

Are you looking to find answers to questions such as the following?

- How can I leverage the information that traverses the network to improve my user experience?
- Is my network secure and compliant with the applicable regulations?
- What is the "normal" behavior for my applications?
- What are the performance levels of my network end to end?

If so, then you need to collect, correlate, and analyze a lot of data and present it in such a way that that it makes it useful and actionable. This is what analytics helps you to achieve.

This chapter introduces network analytics in the context of Cisco DNA. This chapter explains the following:

- The definition of analytics
- The value of analytics
- Network analytics as a Cisco DNA component

A Definition of Analytics

The term "analytics" is overused and applies to different disciplines besides IT and networking. It's becoming a buzzword and means different things to different people. So let's start by defining "analytics" to set a common ground and eliminate ambiguity.

Analytics is commonly defined as the discovery, interpretation, and communication of meaningful patterns in data.

Analytics is definitely about the data and may actually involve a lot of it, to the point that it is often presented as a Big Data problem; but that is not enough to fully describe it.

Analytics is first of all the *discovery* of data, because you cannot measure what you don't see.

Analytics is also the *interpretation* and *correlation* of data: digging through the information from different data sources and correlating it in a way that makes you discover the embedded value.

How many times have you looked through hundreds of lines of syslog output and were not able to identify the relevant messages you were really looking for? Or maybe your network is experiencing a peak in Dynamic Host Configuration Protocol (DHCP) requests and AAA login sessions; this could be a symptom of a security attack or an issue in the network, but if this happens in a university at 8 a.m., then it's absolutely normal and you should not get a notification. A famous 19th-century American mathematician, John Tukey, explains it very well: "The greatest value of a picture is when it forces us to notice what we never expected to see."[1] This is exactly what analytics is supposed to do: extracting the value from the data.

Finally, analytics is about the *communication* of the discovered meaningful patterns. It is about presenting the data in such a way that it becomes useful and actionable. Giving you access to the information you want is a first great step, but making that same data actionable is the main goal of analytics. This is how analytics ultimately enables assurance to verify that the business intent has been conveyed. If it has not, then assurance automates the necessary changes to remediate.

Cisco DNA Analytics

The general definition of analytics is now clear. More specifically focusing on IT and networking, *network analytics* is the process of extracting data from the network and correlating it to identify anomalies, derive insights, and enable data-driven decisions.

Referring to an IT industry definition and considering how the derived information can be used, network analytics may be represented by three different categories:

- **Operations analytics:** Applying analytics to large data sets for IT operations to extract unique business insights. Examples are security threat detection and compliance, network performance, and user and application profiling.
- **IoT analytics:** The processing and analyzing of data from multiple IoT sensors that attach to the network.
- **Business analytics:** The use of the network information combined with social media and business-relevant data to extract business and customer insights.

1 John Tukey, *Exploratory Data Analysis* (Reading, MA: Addison-Wesley, 1977).

If you consider the possible sources of information, network analytics is also defined through the following extended set of categories:

- **Infrastructure analytics:** This refers to the analysis of the information extracted from the network devices themselves (switches, router, firewall, access points, etc.).
- **Endpoint analytics:** Gaining information from the end devices (IoT sensors, video cameras, badge readers, etc.) attached to the network contributes greatly to the overall knowledge of the network and its performance.
- **Application analytics:** Application profiling information is crucial to verify, for example, that SLAs are being met or to characterize traffic patterns.
- **User analytics:** This is about gaining visibility on the user context, including authentication, authorization, and movements information and correlating it with traffic patterns.
- **Policy analytics:** This involves gaining insights into how the Cisco DNA policies get applied throughout the network.

Cisco DNA Analytics is the Cisco implementation of network analytics that leverages the Cisco network as an incredible source of information. Just think about it, the network connects everything (users, devices, applications, and processes) and transports all the information that these assets produce. The network is the ideal place to get insights.

Cisco DNA Analytics gathers data from all the categories just mentioned. Single data source visibility and reporting is good, but not adequate for solving complex problems. Most of the analytics solutions available today just look at one of these data sets and provide a silo solution. The real value-add of Cisco DNA Analytics is the correlation of the multiple data sources; this is what transforms network data into actionable insights that help customers make business decisions, reduce operating expenses (OPEX), and create accurate forecasts.

Cisco DNA Analytics, Opportunities and Challenges

Analytics represents both opportunities and challenges, as represented in the following scenarios:

- The new connection of people, process, data and things—The Internet of Everything (IoE)—is dramatically changing the role of information in today's organizations and represents a tremendous opportunity: examining this data can yield critical insights into user behavior, security risks, capacity consumption, network service levels, fraudulent activity, customer experience, and much more.
- On the other side, the IT infrastructure, the user devices, and the applications generate massive streams of data every second of every day, in an array of unpredictable formats that are difficult to process, analyze in a timely manner, and secure by traditional methods.

That's why network analytics is an extremely interesting topic in the IT world today and a central component of Cisco DNA architecture. How to leverage the benefits of network analytics while overcoming the related challenges is made clear in this and subsequent chapters of the book dedicated to Analytics.

Brief History of Network Analytics

Networks are changing very rapidly with the adoption of new technologies and solutions to support always-new customer requirements. Similarly, network analytics has undergone a fast evolution represented by the following three phases:

- Network analytics 1.0
- Network analytics 2.0
- Network analytics 3.0

Back in the 1990s, the initial phase (1.0) performed the network analysis on well-known structured data such as Simple Network Management Protocol (SNMP) Management Information Base (MIB) or NetFlow records. The data was stored in traditional data warehouses and the business intelligence was extracted and consumed in terms of hours or days.

As analytics entered the 21st century, a new phase emerged (2.0) where unstructured data was added to the collection of information. Unstructured data includes, for example, information in the form of syslog messages from a network device or a raw stream of metrics from multiple sensors attached to the network. This phase involves hauling large amounts of data to a back-end infrastructure, where that data is analyzed and processed. In general, the larger the volume, the better, as more data may yield more insights than less data. Much of the research and development in this phase was focused on making sure data processing scales well and can keep up with the volume of information. This is the phase of Big Data platforms where important technologies such as MapReduce algorithms[2], Hadoop[3], Hive[4], and Kafka[5] have made it possible to retrieve business insights in terms of minutes.

Starting from 2010, phase 3.0 represents the introduction of distributed network analytics where the analysis is conducted closer to the source of the data, which is often at the edge of the network. In some cases (imagine an oil platform in the middle of the ocean, for example), moving massive amounts of data to centralized data stores requires huge bandwidth and hence is unpractical. Also, changes are happening very fast and data loses

2 https://hadoop.apache.org/docs/r1.2.1/mapred_tutorial.html

3 http://hadoop.apache.org/

4 https://hive.apache.org/

5 http://kafka.apache.org/

value over time, so the analysis needs to be performed as close to the source as possible. This phase is characterized by the need for a very quick access to data: insights need to be available in terms of milliseconds.

Historically there have been two main approaches to adopting analytics:

- Reactive analytics
- Proactive analytics

Reactive analytics is the basic approach. When something happens, you get the data, analyze it, and then take action. This is "after the fact" analysis and it's the typical methodology of a technical assistance service.

Proactive analytics has a different approach to analytics. You use multiple sources of data to analyze a particular problem and correlate them to gain insights. This correlation allows you to gain more valuable information and help you better identify the root cause of the problem. For example, one thing is to have information about a particular network flow (source and destination IP addresses); adding to this the user credential, the time of the day, and the location from which the flow was generated gives a much clearer picture of what's happening in your network.

Proactive analytics may also mean running sophisticated algorithms (machine learning) to build models of the network behavior and predict what can happen and take preemptive actions. An example is studying the traffic patterns over multiple WAN links on a router and preemptively configuring a traffic-shaping rule to avoid network congestion. Another important use case is analyzing the end-to-end user throughput: leveraging machine learning, traffic is modeled and a baseline is created so that deviation from this "normal traffic" is detected and notified. Based on this information, the network administrator can take action to anticipate the problem or prevent it for happening again. Given its capability of implementing correcting action before the problem actually happens, this approach is also preemptive. Cisco DNA Analytics refers to this approach simply as "proactive" to differentiate it from a reactive one.

Today customers are mostly using a reactive approach, but they need to shift to more advanced analytics if they want to extract knowledge from the collected data and support their business strategy. This is what Cisco DNA Analytics provides.

Network analytics also evolved to become more and more critical to the business processes. The next section addresses two very simple but important questions: Why implement Cisco DNA Analytics? What is the value from a business prospective?

Why Cisco DNA Analytics?

As customers embark on a transformational journey to building a digital business, their networks need to evolve to respond to new requirements. Cisco DNA Analytics is a key enabler for this evolution and a critical component of any modern network architecture.

Let's examine the main customer business requirements and how Cisco DNA Analytics contributes to fulfill them:

- **Faster innovation:** The network needs to enable faster innovation by delivering deep insights into users' behaviors, applications, and security threats, so that the business can take immediate action to optimize factors such as network performance, employee productivity, customer experience, and daily processes.
- **Lower TCO:** IT is being asked to sustain the increasing demand in terms of devices joining the network, applications, and services, while reducing cost and complexity. Cisco DNA Automation and Assurance come to the rescue. Through the Cisco DNA Controller, Automation allows IT to define the business intent and automatically deploy it in the network. But it's then Cisco DNA Analytics that extracts the right telemetry from the network and enables Assurance to verify that the business intent was delivered. If it did not, then Assurance automates the necessary changes to remediate.
- **Security and compliance:** The network may act as a sensor and analyze all the traffic flowing through the network devices to rapidly detect and mitigate threats. Once again, Analytics plays a key role in providing the necessary information to then take the right action.

Cisco DNA Analytics also helps to overcome main technical challenges for IT with the following elements:

- **Data discovery:** Over time the network has grown complex, and just using SNMP-based analytics is no longer sufficient. IT administrators need more data and they need it fast.
- **Data interpretation:** As industry embraces software-defined networking (SDN) and moves to a centralized, software-defined network control, IT needs holistic and accurate data to make centralized decisions.
- **Data communication:** Because mobility and cloud technologies increase the attack surface of businesses, eliminating the network perimeter, IT needs the security insights from the network to detect anomalies and mitigate possible threats.

In a nutshell, to respond to all the challenges of a digitized business, you need information; more specifically, you need a lot of data, you need the data to be accurate, and you need it fast. This is what Cisco DNA Analytics delivers and that's why it's a critical component of Cisco DNA.

The Role of Network Analytics in Cisco DNA

Cisco DNA provides the foundation for digital transformation and Cisco DNA Analytics is a key building block of the architecture that allows fulfilling the customer business requirements described earlier.

Cisco DNA analytics achieves this by enabling three important benefits of the Cisco DNA architecture: closing the Cisco DNA Assurance loop, gaining critical network insights, increasing security by real-time and dynamic threat defense. As illustrated Figure 15-1, Analytics plays an important and horizontal role in Cisco DNA by providing the necessary telemetry to Cisco DNA Center and Assurance in order to verify if the business intent was met. Second, it extract important information about the wired and wireless devices and the user experience end to end, which helps the administrator to effectively monitor and troubleshoot the network. Last but not least, Cisco DNA Analytics provides relevant data that enables the network itself to behave as a sensor and hence increase the visibility of possible security threats.

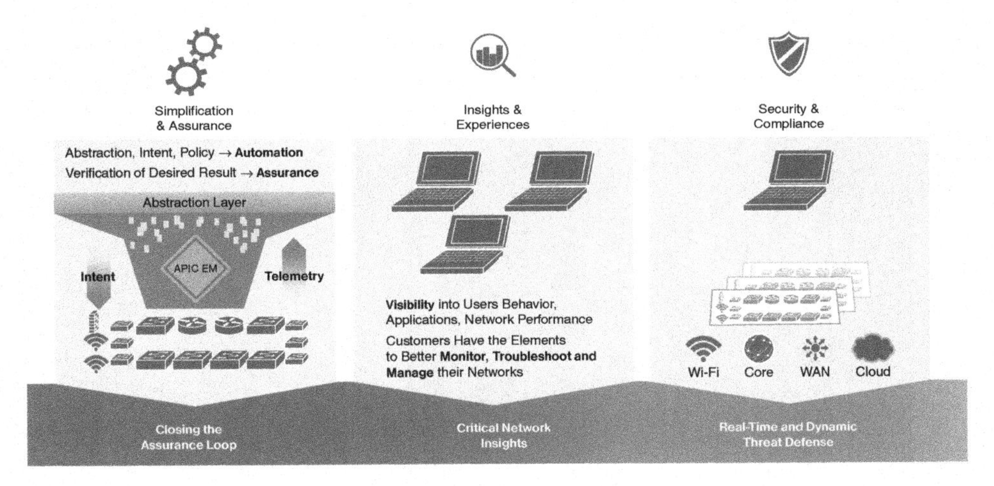

Figure 15-1 *The Role of Analytics in Cisco DNA*

The chapters that follow go into the details of the different components of Cisco DNA Analytics. Chapter 16, "Cisco DNA Analytics Components," discusses the different Analytics components, including Instrumentation and Telemetry, so it explains how to extract information from the network (Instrumentation), and how to efficiently send it to a remote platform for further processing (Telemetry). Chapter 17, "Cisco DNA Analytics Engines," introduces and describes how Cisco DNA Analytics leverages unsupervised machine learning, behavior analysis, and intelligent algorithms to provide smarter data.

Cisco DNA Analytics is a critical component of the Cisco DNA architecture as it enables other important functions like Assurance. Later in the book, Chapter 21, "Cisco DNA Analytics and Assurance," explains how important Cisco DNA Assurance is to "close the loop": with Cisco DNA Automation you are able to express business intent and apply it to the network. Analytics extracts the relevant information from the network and enables Assurance to verify that the business intent has been delivered. This is the "circle of life" of the Cisco DNA architecture, and this is what brings value to the customers.

Summary

Cisco DNA Analytics is the process of correlating data and extracting meaning to identify anomalies, derive insights, and enable data-driven decisions. Analytics enables Assurance to verify that the business intent, implemented through Automation, has been actually conveyed.

The chapter introduced the following:

- The concept of analytics, starting with a common definition
- A brief history of analytics and its evolution
- Introduction to Cisco DNA Analytics: the reasons why Analytics is important in any modern network architecture and the role it plays as a key component of Cisco DNA

Chapter 16

Cisco DNA Analytics Components

Chapter 15, "Introduction to Cisco DNA Analytics," presented Cisco DNA analytics as a key building block of Cisco Digital Network Architecture. Now let's examine the different elements of Cisco DNA Analytics.

This chapter explains:

- The sources of useful analytics information
- Instrumentation
- Distributed network analytics
- Telemetry and analytics engine
- How these components come together to form a complete solution

Analytics Data Sources

Analytics is about data. Data is defined as any valuable information carried by the network, such as

- User context
- Device and application information
- Network device–related data
- Environmental information from sensors

The data may be consumed by multiple "users": network administrators for monitoring, application developers, etc.

When considering Network Analytics, data is gathered from different sources; potentially everything that connects to the network is a source of information, as represented in Figure 16-1.

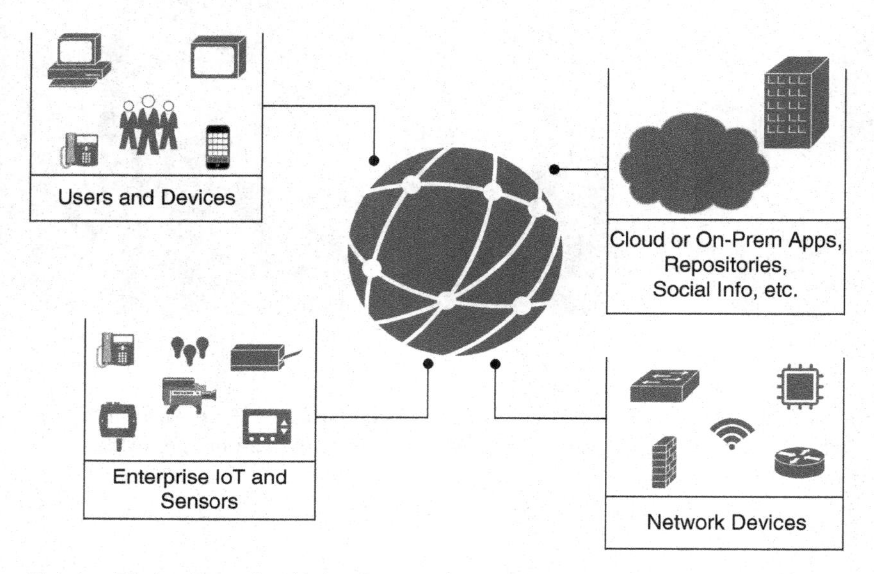

Figure 16-1 *Data Analytics Sources*

Network elements, sensors and Internet of Things (IoT) devices, servers and related applications (on premises and/or in the cloud), and user identity servers and external repositories are only a few examples of possible data sources for Analytics.

Analytics is about collecting information and correlating it to obtain additional insights. Each data source shown in Figure 16-1 brings a lot of information independently, but imagine the added value that could be gained by correlating them. For example, what if you could leverage an external repository like the Cisco Technical Assistance Center (TAC) database to compare known customer issues with the actual network devices' configuration and topology? This analysis could show inconsistency of a feature implementation and point out hardware or software incongruencies.

Another simple example of the value of correlation is that users' traffic data can be related with the information gathered from the policy server (such as Cisco Identity Services Engine) to add a user context to the traffic profile and answer questions such as "Who is consuming all my expensive WAN bandwidth at my branch location?"

The challenge of dealing with multiple sources is multifold. First, you need to cope with the large amount of data that these sources may produce and that could saturate a low-bandwidth WAN link (think about a remote location) and/or stress the CPU and memory resources of the collecting platform. Second, this data usually comes in multiple different formats, so it's not easy for the collectors and applications to consume it and extract valuable information. Additionally, all this data arrives at different time intervals; it's not synchronized, which makes correlation even more challenging.

This is a typical "big data" problem, but before diving into the different aspects of scalability (covered later in the "Telemetry" section), let's first focus on accuracy as another critical aspect of dealing with data. The information collected from the network needs to be accurate if you want to base business decisions on it. So the first step for Cisco DNA Analytics is to make sure that the right information is extracted from the network devices. This is what Instrumentation is all about.

Cisco DNA Instrumentation

"Not everything that counts can be counted and not everything that can be counted counts." This simple quote from Albert Einstein explains why Instrumentation is a key aspect of the Cisco DNA Analytics solution.

Instrumentation is defined here as the process of *extracting the relevant data* from the network and making it available for further analysis.

Networks offer rich sets of telemetry data that include the following:

- NetFlow records
- Device statistics (CPU and memory utilization, interface counters, etc.)
- Simple Network Management Protocol (SNMP) data
- Internet Protocol Service Level Agreement (IP SLA) performance measurements
- System event (syslog) records

Collecting data from the network is not the hard part. Making use of it, doing something interesting with it and gaining insights, is more challenging. In other words, how do you go from data to information, and then to knowledge?

Imagine you are gathering analytics on a wireless network. Most of the management tools available in the market provide information such as top access points in terms of client count, the so-called "hot zones." That's important information, but what about "cold zones," or wireless access points (AP) that are indicating zero clients associated while historically they were serving users normally? Which information would be more indicative of a problem in the wireless network? Probably it's the latter because it can indicate that something is wrong with the AP's radios. The point is: you need to make sure you get the right information, the information that counts.

Gathering data can be expensive in terms of local resources on the network device (mainly CPU and memory) and bandwidth consumption to transport the data to a remote destination for further analysis. So you cannot simply take *all* the data; it would be too much.

What's then the real meaning of "extracting the relevant data" in the Instrumentation definition? Mainly two things:

- **Information accuracy and relevancy:** The data needs to show what you, as network administrator or data analyst, are looking for.
- **Efficient transport:** Simply put, the collection process should neither overwhelm the device nor saturate the uplink to the centralized collectors.

Imagine polling some interface statistics on a router through a SNMP Management Information Base (MIB). What is the right polling interval? Is it five minutes, one minute, or one second? If you are looking for information on a stable network, a five-minute interval probably is a good compromise in terms of getting an average view of the network without stressing the device. Sometimes, though, you need to poll every few seconds to really catch what's going on. Setting the right polling interval greatly influences the accuracy of the information gathered and the ability to transport that information.

A big focus of Cisco DNA Instrumentation is making sure that the information needed is available through software and represented by some sort of counters. This is key because you cannot measure what you don't see. Cisco expertise in networking comes as an added value here: Cisco designed and implemented most of the protocols that run today's networks and hence Cisco more likely knows what is the relevant data and where to find it.

Finally, Instrumentation is greatly improved with Cisco hardware programmability. As explained in chapter 13, "Device Programmability," if the network device leverages programmable application-specific integrated circuits (ASIC) such as the Unified Access Data Plane (UADP) ASIC, then Instrumentation can change and evolve over time. This means that, if needed, a new piece of information or parameter is extracted at the hardware level for further software processing without requiring hardware respin of the ASIC. This is also a great investment protection story.

Distributed Network Analytics

Traditional analytics involves hauling large amounts of data to a back end, where that data is analyzed and processed. In general, the larger the volume the better, as more data may yield more insights than less data. This is the reason why, in recent years, much of the research and development in analytics have been focusing on making sure the back-end infrastructure scales well and can keep up with large volumes of data; important tools have been made available to address the scalability challenges of the back-end platforms, the so called big data technologies, which include Map Reduce algorithms, Hadoop, and Hive, for example.

Something is changing in the way network information is produced and analyzed, and today the focus of analytics is on optimizing the data collection, processing, and transmission of data. If you think about it, in an enterprise lots of data originates directly on the network devices that connect IoT sensors, video cameras, or other end users' devices. Considering where the data is generated, the edge of the network, and where data is processed, usually servers in a data center, the traditional analytics approach of sending all possible information to a centralized location is probably not the most efficient approach.

If you are generating data within the data center, it is absolutely valuable to also process it directly there. But in the enterprise, data generation is much more distributed at the edge of the network and may include remote locations; in this case, the approach of distributing some of the analytics functions is much more effective.

With distributed analytics, the idea is to perform the right amount of processing and analysis where it makes more sense. Instead of relying on data generated and collected from many devices and locations to be made centrally available for processing, part of the analytics is performed right at the edge of the network, closer to the source. This is more efficient for multiple reasons:

- It may *save time* because it helps to quickly identify the anomalies as they arise at the edge and enable decisions to be made faster. In situations such as a malware attack where timing is critical, delays caused by centralized processing can cause serious problems.
- It *saves upstream bandwidth* in the transport because the data is pre-analyzed, and instead of sending raw data, the device streams "smart" data in smaller volumes.
- It *saves money* because it optimizes the whole analytics process.

At the time of writing Cisco was actively investing in distributed analytics solutions embedded in the Cisco DNA network as a new and effective way of processing data. An interesting use case for distributed analytics is security and anomaly detection. Malware software is becoming everyday more sophisticated and hence hard to detect with a traditional signature-based approach. Cisco is investigating a solution that uses distributed advanced analytics to model traffic patterns, detect anomaly behavior, and then close the loop with mitigation actions; the whole processing is done right at the edge of the network, without sending all the traffic to a centralized repository for processing.

The idea is to leverage software agents that perform distributed analysis within the scope of an individual networking device or multiple standalone analytics engines. The agent is a piece of software that may run in a container, in a virtual machine (VM), or directly integrated in the Cisco IOS software on the network device as depicted in Figure 16-2.

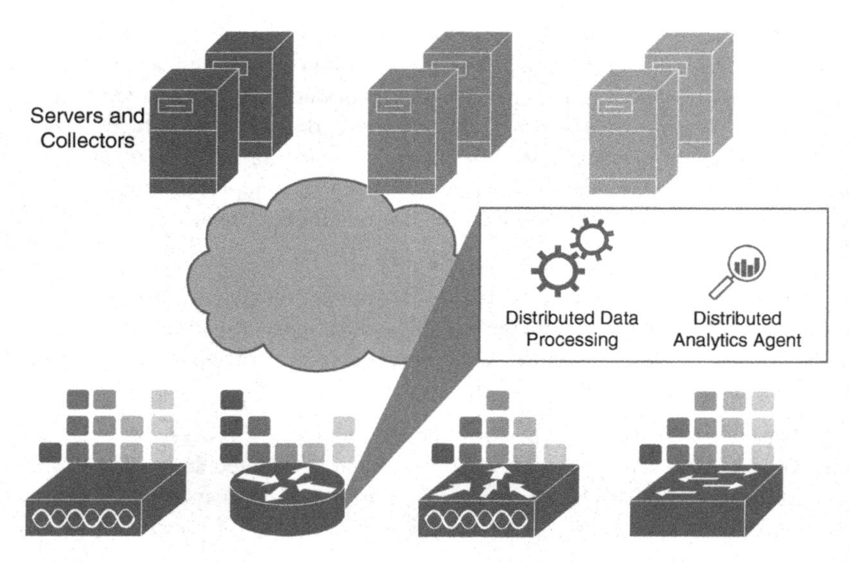

Figure 16-2 *The Cisco DNA Distributed Analytics Concept*

The distributed analytics model may leverage either a dedicated hardware device or a VM/Container that performs a subset or all the following functions:

- **Data collection:** It collects information from multiple local sources such as Cisco NetFlow, Cisco Network-Based Application Recognition (NBAR), local metrics, SNMP MIBs, etc. It dynamically extracts information depending on current network conditions.
- **Data normalization:** As a general design principle, as data is natively represented in different formats by different data sources, it is up to the agent to ensure that the data is rendered and normalized in a way that is easily consumed upstream.
- **Data analytics:** Advanced analytics and machine-learning algorithms may run closer to the network device in order to get the relevant data directly, filter it, and process it in a distributed fashion.
- **Data actions:** As a result of the analytics, traffic can be modified and an action applied directly at the network edge. A typical example is applying quality of service (QoS) policy on certain traffic to provide a specific treatment. This results in traffic getting different priority, as shown with the different shaded coding in Figure 16-2.
- **Data telemetry:** Streaming "smart" data to an upstream collector. The term "smart" is used here to highlight that the data may be pre-analyzed and prefiltered to add context and optimize it, before it is sent to a collector.

What does "dynamically" mean in the data collection process described at the beginning of the preceding list?

Let's go back for a second to the example about SNMP instrumentation mentioned earlier: choosing the correct SNMP polling interval for a specific interface counter is critical for that information to be relevant. Choosing a large polling interval, such as five minutes, provides an average representation of the behavior of that interface and doesn't overwhelm the device itself. But what if there is a problem (traffic spike) that happens only for a few seconds: a five-minute interval would average out the results and probably miss the spike. This is graphically represented in Figure 16-3.

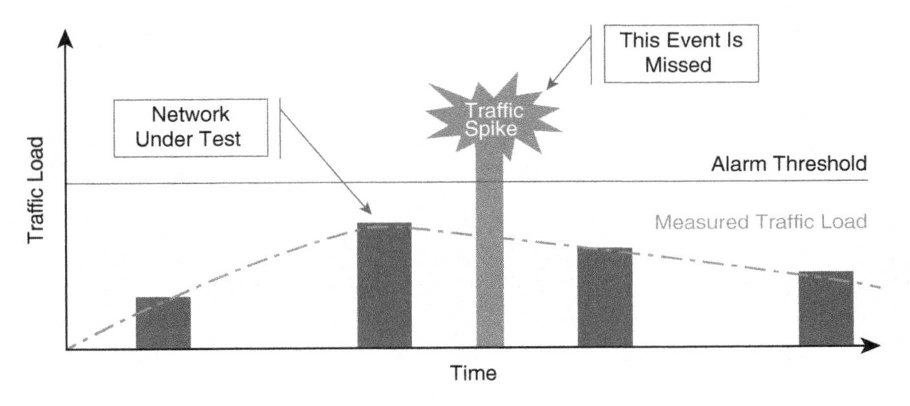

Figure 16-3 *SNMP Polling Limitations*

Reverting to one second for the polling interval on all interfaces in your network would most probably kill the boxes, so it's a no go. So you need to have dynamic thresholds and change them according to network behavior. This is done today in a traditional manner by implementing a combination of SNMP traps and SNMP polling, but it's not efficient. Polling is not efficient because, again, you need to decide on a polling interval. With dynamic data collection based on a push model, the agent may change the polling interval from a larger default value to a smaller one if some conditions apply (for example, the traffic exceeds a defined threshold on the interface).

Telemetry

Telemetry derives from the Greek words "tele" (= remote) and "metron" (= measure). Telemetry is about data collection and its efficient transport to a remote location.

Telemetry is not new in networking. SNMP has been around since 1998, so for more than 30 years network administrators have been using different types of methods to gather information from the network. Syslog, NetFlow, and so forth are all examples that are referred to as telemetry. Today these traditional approaches have problems keeping up with the scale and speed of modern networks. New approaches such as streaming telemetry are promising to answer today's challenges. This section first explains the need for telemetry, then describes telemetry in the context of Cisco DNA, highlighting the limitations of traditional approaches, and wraps up by introducing the new Model-driven Telemetry (MDT).

What is the role of telemetry in the Cisco DNA architecture? The Cisco DNA circle of life represents how Cisco DNA brings together automation, analytics, and assurance to provide a closed feedback loop to the customer. The network administrator expresses the business intent; the Cisco DNA controller translates it and deploys it in the network using automation; then Cisco DNA analytics extracts the relevant information from the network and feeds it back to the assurance module to verify that the intent has been met. Telemetry is the component that is responsible for extracting and transporting this key information, as represented in Figure 16-4.

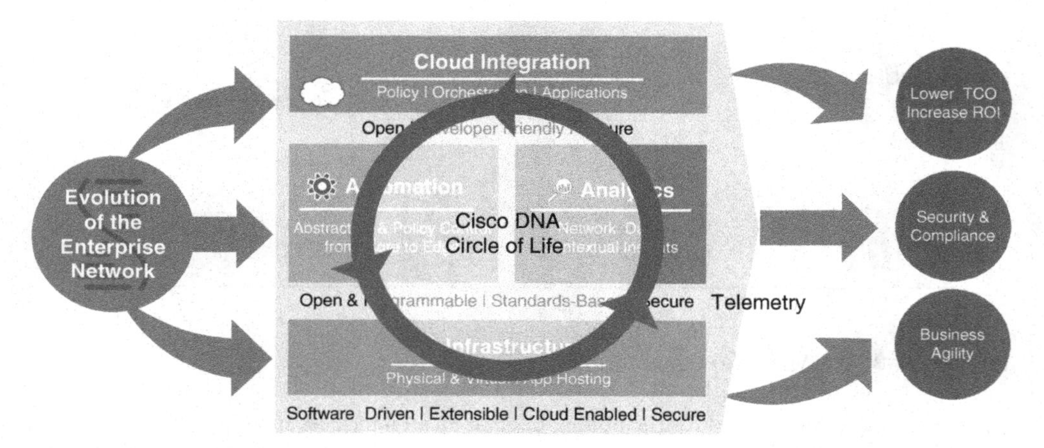

Figure 16-4 *Cisco DNA Circle of Life*

Why Telemetry?

Before getting into the details of the architecture, let's start by understanding why Telemetry is necessary. Here are few simple questions:

- Do people complain about the network and you don't understand why?
- Do you often hear that the network is impacting your organization's ability to achieve its business goals?
- Do you know if the QoS policy you have just applied has actually produced the wanted results?

If you have answered yes to any of these questions, chances are you need a solution to monitor and analyze data from your network. And when it comes to network monitoring, everything is based on Telemetry because the data is generated in the network devices that are usually physically separated from where the information is stored and analyzed.

The Cisco DNA Telemetry Architecture

Figure 16-5 shows a graphical representation of Telemetry architecture in Cisco DNA.

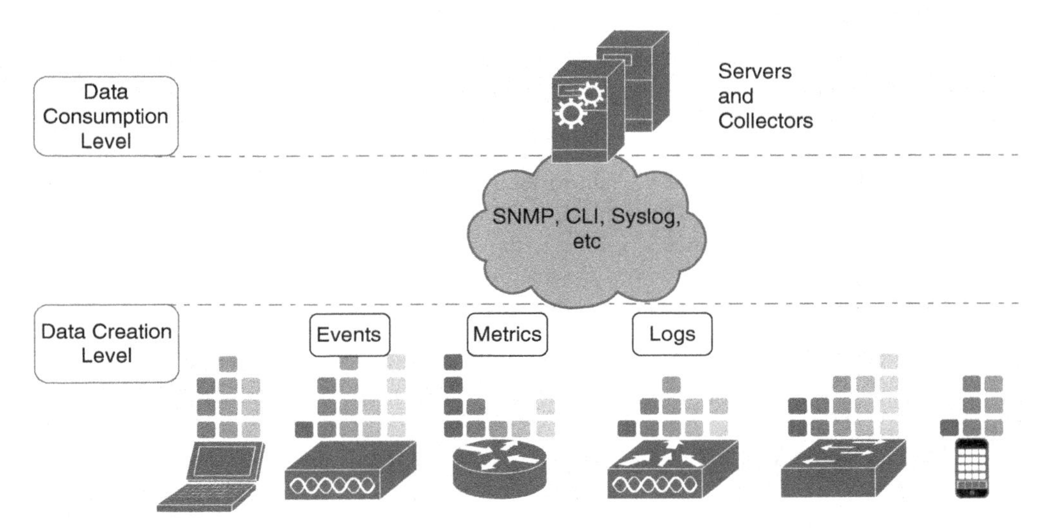

Figure 16-5 *Telemetry Architecture*

Data is generated at the device level. You can have hardware sensors (network devices or dedicated sensors) or software sensors (software agents on user devices and servers) streaming information to an upstream collector. The information comes in multiple types and formats: events (like the ones generated by SNMP), logs (like syslog or AAA), or metric data (like the different counters on a network device).

On the other end of the network, the data consumption layer is where the telemetry data is actually stored, analyzed, visualized, and used as the basis for meaningful actions; usually there are multiple collectors and servers utilizing multiple types of interfaces/APIs toward the network.

Connecting the two layers, today you have many different ways and protocols that visualize and transport the telemetry data: Command Line Interface (CLI), SNMP, syslog, NetFlow, and Radius, just to mention a few. This is a problem for a Telemetry solution because the upper layer has to deal with multiple data formats, with often-redundant information and with the risk of receiving too much data. Let's explore some of the limitations of the current protocols and how Cisco DNA Telemetry changes the game in terms of transport efficiency.

Limitations of Today's Telemetry Protocols

With networks growing in size and complexity, more and more data is generated from the network. So the first challenge for a Telemetry solution is mainly scaling and dealing with the amount of information that needs to be transported.

Most of the protocols today are based on polling mechanisms: the server opens a connection and requests a set of values, and the devices process the request and returns the data. If there are multiple polling servers, multiple connections need to be opened and processed in parallel.

This is exactly how SNMP works: to retrieve large amounts of data, SNMP polling relies on the GetBulk operation. Introduced in SNMPv2, GetBulk performs a continuous "get" operation that retrieves all the columns of a given table (e.g., statistics for all interfaces). The device being queried returns as many columns as can fit into a packet. If the polling server detects that the end of the table has not yet been reached, it does another GetBulk operation, and so on. If you have multiple SNMP servers, the network device has to process each request independently even if both polling servers requested the same MIB at more or less the same time. As you can imagine, this is not optimized from a device prospective and SNMP scale is a known issue.

Another problem is data formats. Not to pick on SNMP, which has been around for more than 30 years and still does the job for most networks, but this is another limitation typical of this protocol.

SNMP imposes a very specific format when it comes to indexing and exporting data. And this model is different from how the information is stored in the network device itself. So for every SNMP call, the device needs to convert the internal data structure into the one used for SNMP. This is highly inefficient and may affect performance when you need to retrieve a lot of data.

Another limitation of traditional approaches comes from the lack of completeness of information: a syslog that misses a key piece of data, a MIB that isn't complete or available, or a piece of information that is only available via CLI.

Other times the issue is machine-friendliness: CLI and syslog are human-readable strings that are inefficient for any automation software. In other words, many of the protocols used today for getting information out of a device are meant to be used and interpreted by humans; but what is good for humans is usually not good for machines, and this may lead to inefficiencies, especially when you want to retrieve a lot of information.

What if the network device could push telemetry data at a certain interval and could directly transmit the bulk data as stored internally? Add what if the format used was machine-friendly? Cisco DNA Analytics brings a new approach to telemetry called Model-driven Telemetry (MDT) or Streaming Telemetry.

The Evolution of Cisco DNA Telemetry: Model-Driven Telemetry

As networks grow in size and complexity, the demand for monitoring data increases. Whether the goal is better analytics, troubleshooting, proactive remediation, or security auditing, an IT operator needs more and more data quickly from the network.

To respond to these IT challenges, Cisco DNA Analytics adopts a model-driven, streaming approach to Telemetry.

The first challenge is how to get as much data off a network device as fast as possible, in a way that makes consuming it easy. This brings two requirements for Telemetry:

- Getting rid of the inadequacies of the polling mechanism, highlighted earlier in the discussion of SNMP.
- Using as much raw data as possible and using a standard model-driven data structure. By using its native format, accessing the data is very quick and efficient; by using a model-driven approach, external access to the data is greatly simplified.

Network operators poll for information at regular intervals, so why not just embrace a "push" model and send them the data they need? This is the idea behind the streaming aspect of Telemetry: it's the device that sends the data to a receiver at regular intervals or upon a triggering event. This is also important to optimize the transmission in presence of multiple receivers; in this case, when requested the same information from multiple servers, the device simply has to duplicate the data and send it twice.

Second, what does Model-driven Telemetry really mean and why is it important? Well, as described in Chapter 12, "Introduction to Cisco DNA Automation," network programmability is an efficient way to manage the scale and complexity of today's large networks. Gone are the days when a network engineer can manage the network by typing CLI commands and manually analyzing the results.

Programmability requires the data to be in a machine-friendly format to make it easy for tools to ingest. The good news is that the networking industry has converged on Yet Another Next Generation (YANG)[1] data modeling language for networking data, making it the natural choice for Cisco DNA Telemetry.

Model-driven Telemetry leverages models in two ways. First, MDT is fully configurable using telemetry YANG models. You can turn it on, specify where to stream, and specify with what encoding and transport mechanism to stream, all by using just YANG models (no CLI required).

Also, MDT leverages YANG in the specification of what data to be streamed: the network device measures a staggering number of parameters all the time, so how do you tell which subset you want? When working from the CLI, you have to use memorized **show** commands. With SNMP, you request a MIB. With MDT, you specify the YANG model that contains the preferred data.

Also, as Cisco DNA moves to an automated and centralized control approach of managing networks, there is the need for a lot of information to be sent upstream so that the Cisco DNA Controller can make informative decisions. This means that telemetry is becoming a big data problem. So, in addition to being fast and comprehensive, telemetry data must be tailored to the needs of big data analytics tools.

1 For more info on YANG, see RFC 6020 at https://tools.ietf.org/html/rfc6020.

For this reason Cisco DNA Telemetry adopts well-known encoding technologies like JSON and Google Protocol Buffers (GPB) to transfer data to software applications and make it easy for them to manipulate and analyze the data.

Is streaming telemetry going to replace traditional approaches? There is probably room for both as some data lends itself well to telemetry-based models while other data is still well suited to an occasional poll-based model. Interface counters, interface rates, and other traffic-based info are a good fit for a push model because a real-time view of the environment is critical in this case. Physical device metrics, such as temperature and power, could be poll based. The key to Telemetry is to provide relevant data without overwhelming the devise and the network link to the collector, and that's what Cisco DNA Analytics is focused on.

In summary, Cisco DNA embraces programmability and Model-driven Telemetry as a building block of the architecture blueprint, and this is an important and clear indication for new product development across routing and switching wireless. Is MDT adopted across all the Cisco products? There are a lot of existing devices out there that do not support YANG models and telemetry, so the traditional approach not only is still valid but is the only option that you have. Cisco DNA is an architecture that brings value not only in greenfield environments but also in existing customers' networks where you still need to enable traditional telemetry via syslog, SNMP, NetFlow, and so forth to get the information you need. In this case the focus of Cisco DNA is to make Telemetry more efficient, and that's one of the main reasons for introducing an Analytics Engine.

Analytics Engine

The Analytics Engine is a critical building block of the Cisco DNA Analytics architecture. This section describes the role and functions of the Analytics engine as a big data platform, while Chapter 17, "Cisco DNA Analytics Engines," details the two Cisco Analytics engines: Cisco DNA Network Data Platform for the enterprise and the Tetration Analytics platform for the data center.

The Traditional Analytics Approach

Analytics is not new in networking; IT administrators have long been using multiple tools and applications to collect and analyze data to gain some sort of insights from their network. Figure 16-6 illustrates a traditional architecture for Analytics.

A traditional approach to Analytics is characterized by the use of different protocols to transport data back to multiple servers and collectors residing either on premises or in the cloud (public or private). Northbound of the collectors you usually have a series of independent monitoring, security, and management applications that access the data through different interfaces. This architecture presents multiple limitations. Let's describe a few and introduce how an Analytics Engine can make the solution much more efficient.

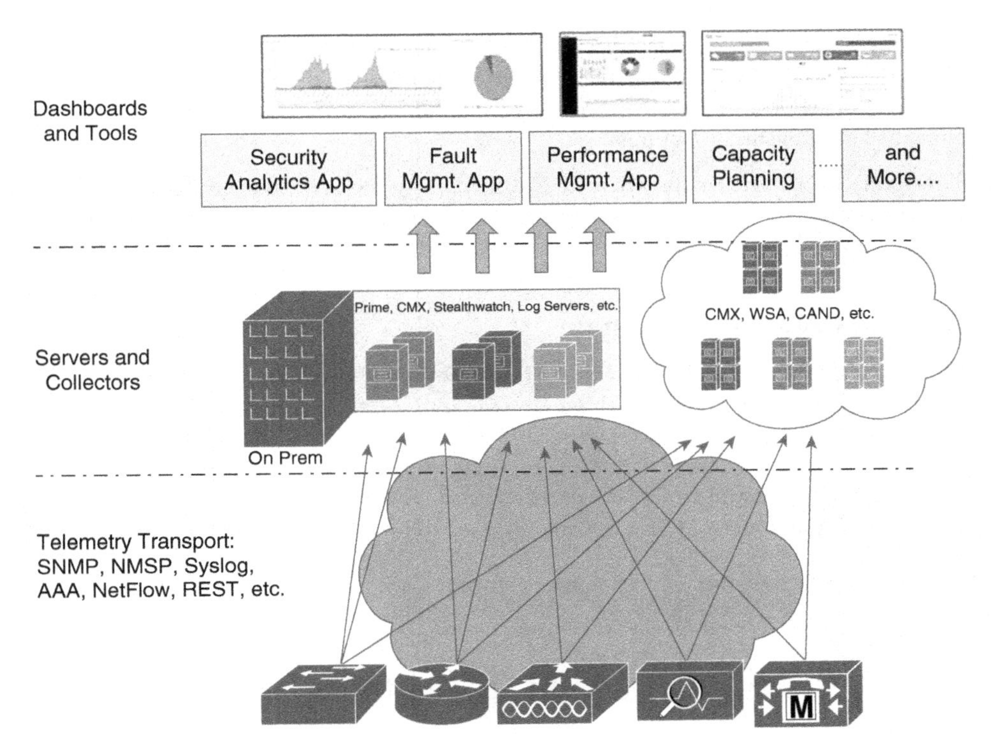

Figure 16-6 *Traditional Architecture for Analytics*

One of the most important shortcomings of a traditional approach is around Telemetry and it's due mainly to two factors:

- **Inconsistency of data export:** Many protocols are used (SNMP, NetFlow, syslog, etc.), each with a different data format. This makes it harder to use the data across different platforms and correlate them.
- **Inefficiency of transport protocols:** As described earlier in the "Telemetry" section, traditional telemetry protocols such as SNMP are based on a pull mechanism that limits the scalability and the performance of these protocols.

Another problem is related to the fact that in traditional analytics, applications and tools usually live in silos. This means that if you need a comprehensive view of your network, including devices and application performance, security information, and user insights, you probably have to deal with a lot of different dashboards. This makes it very hard to cross-correlate information and also adds operational cost of deploying and managing multiple independent systems.

Last but not least, the data sets that can be retrieved from a traditional system are usually preset and static, with little or no possibility for cross correlation. This truly limits the amount of business insights gained from the network data. Think about it: it's one thing to get the information about a particular flow from a NetFlow collector; it's a completely different story to able to identify the user and the application that generated that flow and the time and location where it was generated. Adding contextual information leads to more insightful business decisions.

How to make Analytics more efficient? Fix the data by providing the analytics tools and applications with data that is normalized, deduplicated, and correlated. In other words, analytics needs high-quality data, and providing that is the role of the Analytics Engine.

The Need for Analytics Engines

An Analytics Engine is a big data platform that provides high-quality and contextualized data to northbound applications. This allows the transformation of raw network data into knowledge and business insights. Figure 16-7 shows a high-level representation of the Analytics Engine interactions with the other solution components. "Analytics App" refers to any network management, IT service management, or assurance application that leverages the analytics data from the network.

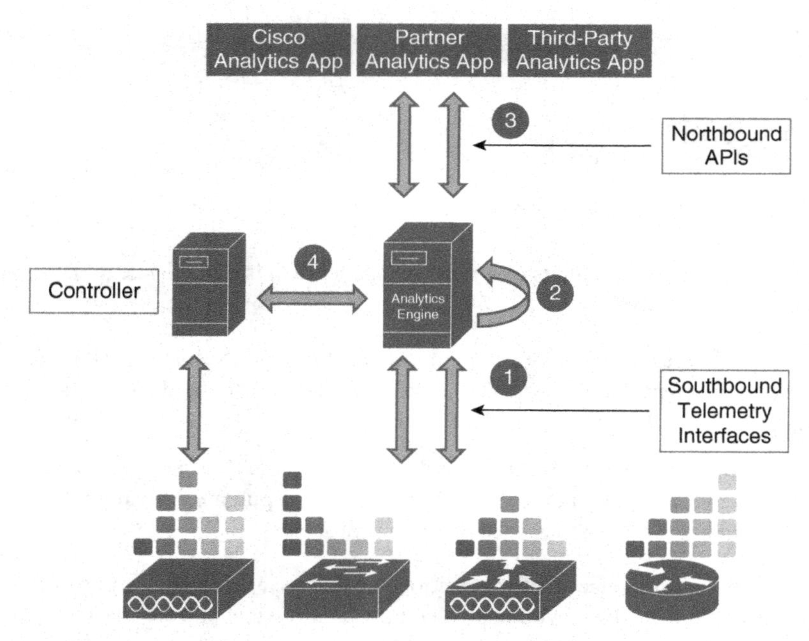

Figure 16-7 *Analytics Engine High-Level Interaction Diagram*

This simple diagram explains the main functions and architecture relationships of the Analytics Engine:

1. Gathers Telemetry data from multiple sources (network devices, sensors, user devices, servers); it does so by abstracting the telemetry operation from the underlying network elements via southbound interfaces.

2. Normalizes the information, as it may come from multiple sources using different formats.
3. Correlates data to extract and presents meaningful insights about the networks, its applications, and its users. This process may leverage machine-learning algorithms.
4. Exposes Analytics information to Cisco and third-party applications and tools via APIs.
5. May also communicate directly the Controller to receive information on the network (topology, for example) and to automate recommended data-driven decisions.

Leveraging the preceding functionalities, the Analytics Engine provides the following advantages to an Analytics network solution:

- Data scalability
- Analytics efficiency
- App development simplification

Data Scalability

With today's scale and performance, monitoring and controlling the network requires more and more data. Also, IT is being asked to increase the speed of service deployment and associated infrastructure changes; Automation plays a big role in making networks simpler to deploy and let IT focus on services and the business intent. The shift to a centralized and automated control of the network, though, requires accurate information. IT needs visibility end to end and the telemetry from network devices, sensors, and user devices can easily overwhelm traditional data warehouses; again, this translates into more data. That's the reason why scaling of the back-end systems is a major concern of Analytics.

The Analytics engine solves the scaling problem because it is built upon big data technologies like Hadoop, Hive, Kafka, and others that allow the platform to ingest data at a fast rate, to store it at a very granular level, and to efficiently present it to the upper application layer.

From an architecture point of view, the Analytics Engine can leverage the cloud to scale horizontally or use a distributed approach where the Analytics functions are deployed in multiple places in the network, closer to the data sources. Chapter 17 introduces the Cisco DNA Analytics platforms and covers the analytics engine architecture in more details.

Analytics Efficiency

The second advantage of leveraging an analytics engine is efficiency. Current analytics solutions are very fragmented and live in silos. The result is that collecting all the required data and extracting useful information is very difficult and inefficient.

First of all, the Analytics Engine needs to provide telemetry efficiency. As described in the previous sections, telemetry data is generated from multiple sources, leveraging different protocols and different formats, and information is often redundant because the same parameter is transported multiple times.

The Analytics Engine is the component that filters data to reduce the redundant information, normalizes the data to a common format based on a model-driven approach, and stores the data in a way that is much more efficient to either retrieve it for further processing or to present it to upper layers.

The Analytics Engine also increases the effectiveness of the analytics solution by enriching the value of the information and providing more quality data. This is performed with the following:

- **Data correlation:** The analytics engine receives information from multiple sources and is the ideal component to cross-correlate this data to gain additional insights. If you want to correlate flow information with user data, you must access multiple tools and perform the correlation manually.
- **Contextual metadata:** The analytics engine may add contextual information from many different sources, such as user and location databases and external repositories, in the form of metadata.
- **Cognitive analytics:** The analytics engine runs sophisticated machine-learning algorithms that first draw a baseline of the network behavior and then may predict and anticipate possible problems or anomalies.

Application Development Simplification

Analytics developers struggle to get the information that they need from the network. The data is fragmented, exposed through various protocols, in different formats, and requires the data analyst to have a deep network knowledge that is often unavailable.

The role of the Analytics engine is to abstract all the underlying network details and provide a simplified and normalized access to network data through openly defined APIs. In this way the developer or data analyst doesn't need to spend time and resources to know the topology of the underlying network or decide what protocols to use to retrieve the necessary information.

An Analytics Engine allows simplification of the development process and hence fosters innovation at the application and service levels.

The Role of the Cloud for Analytics

The cloud (either public or hybrid) is an integral part of Cisco DNA and provides a deployment option for many Cisco DNA functions. Chapter 11, "Cisco DNA Cloud," introduces the cloud as a component of Cisco DNA and describes in details, the cloud service models, the deployment mode, and how Cisco DNA considers the cloud one of the network domains. This section specifically describes how the cloud plays a critical role for analytics.

Running the analytics engine in the cloud brings multiple advantages to analytics both in terms of streamlining operations and providing deeper insights. The advantages include the following:

- **Scale and performance:** The analytics platform needs to accommodate vast amounts of data, and a cloud model makes it easier to add storage or computing resources to scale horizontally or to increase performance.
- **Historical data and trends:** More scalability means being able to store more data and for a longer period, which is critical in order to produce meaningful reports and provide the baseline trends.
- **Painless upgrades:** As enterprise customers are looking at developing Analytics in the cloud, this approach usually provides a simpler way to do software and hardware upgrades when compared to an on-premises distributed system. This is simpler because of the automation and orchestration tools that are used to build a cloud service.
- **High Availability:** Similarly, running a platform in the cloud makes it easier to add physical and virtual redundancy to increase the service uptime.
- **Effective correlation:** Converging more data sources and information into a centralized location brings the possibility of performing more insightful correlation. Think about a cloud-sourcing analytics approach that compares telemetry data from a specific location (for example, "client authentication failures") with other locations in your company; the comparison adds context to the information and helps the network to make the right decision regarding whether to further investigate or categorize it as "Normal" behavior.
- **Extensibility:** Running the analytics engine in the cloud also enables the inclusion of data sources from other domains (like third-party engines, applications, and repositories), offering an interesting aspect of extensibility.

Many applications benefit from the advantages of moving workloads to the cloud. For Analytics, being so data and resource intensive, the scalability and flexibility you gain makes the decision of adopting the cloud a natural and easy one.

But, to be fair, working with the cloud poses some challenges in terms of security and data privacy that may prevent or delay customer adoption. Cisco DNA architecture provides ways to adopt the cloud without compromising the security and confidentiality of your data. In the specific case of Analytics, Cisco DNA provides a solution for Cisco DNA Spaces and Assurance, just to mention two cloud-enabled services, to securely transport a big quantity of data from your network to the Cisco cloud. It does this by encrypting the communication between the on-premises collector and the data ingestor in the cloud, but also by anonymizing the data before sending it. The data is then processed and analyzed in a completely anonymous way in the cloud, and the results of the analysis are transported back to the customer network and de-anonymized before showing it to the data owner, the customer. More details are provided in Chapter 11.

Summary

The chapter introduced the main components and features of the Cisco DNA Analytics solution, which include the following:

- The variety of analytics data sources
- Instrumentation and the importance of extracting the relevant information from the network
- Distributed network analytics as a new approach to analytics
- Telemetry, the limitation of current approaches and the advantages of Model-driven Telemetry
- The role and benefits of the Analytics Engine
- The role of the cloud in Analytics

Further Reading

YANG RFC: https://tools.ietf.org/html/rfc6020

Cadora, S. "What's So Special About Model-Driven Telemetry?" Cisco Blog. Aug. 24, 206. http://blogs.cisco.com/sp/whats-so-special-about-model-driven-telemetry.

Vasseur, JP. "Internet Behavioral Analytics (IBA) Using Self Learning Networks." 2015 Cisco Live. https://clnv.s3.amazonaws.com/2015/usa/pdf/BRKSEC-3056.pdf.

Chapter 17

Cisco DNA Analytics Engines

What do most of the IT network managers have in common today, besides the need for more people and a bigger budget? They all want to extract more data from their network and they need more information on what the network transports. And they want it faster.

The use cases for network analytics and extracting useful insights from the network are not significantly different from 20 years ago when the IT manager started using tools like Simple Network Management Protocol (SNMP). Network analytics can help with

- Monitoring the network health
- Troubleshooting user and application issues
- Performance tuning
- Capacity planning
- Security analysis and prevention

But a few things have changed dramatically when it comes to gathering data from the network in the recent years:

- The speed at which the information is needed, going from "some" minutes interval to real time; this has to do with the velocity of application deployment and associated infrastructure changes as well as the need to protect those applications and the associated business data against a rapidly evolving set of security threats.
- The scale of the problem. Today's networks are more and more complex and connect an ever-increasing number of devices and "things" that generate an ever-increasing amount of data. And this is only going to get more interesting with the adoption of the Internet of Things (IoT).
- The trend toward software-defined networking; in other words, the need to export accurate information in a centralized place where the analysis takes place and decisions are made.

So, it's easy to understand how in the recent years network analytics has become a "big data" problem. You need that back-end infrastructure to scale horizontally and dynamically so that you can store and process huge amounts of data. Previous chapters examined how technologies such as Hadoop, Hive, Kafka, and other open source frameworks for processing big data have come to the rescue and have made it possible to process and analyze petabytes of data with relative ease and affordable economics.

Raw data is important. As a matter of fact, a principle of big data is to always rely on raw data because it's lossless and you never know what information will be required. And this is the reason why data scientists love raw data.

In network analytics, the same rule applies: if you can extract and transport raw data, do it. This is the case of most data centers, which usually have plenty of bandwidth and have the data sources (servers and network devices) and data repositories co-located.

But if you have an enterprise with multiple locations geographically distributed, IT has to consider the cost of transporting bytes back to a centralized location or to the cloud, in which case simply grabbing raw data is typically not an option. And with increasing east-west traffic, it is no longer sufficient to limit telemetry collection to central border network elements; it needs to be extended to every edge node, which again increases the amount of data. In these scenarios, it becomes crucial to find ways to reduce the data that is sent up, which means performing some distributed data processing at the edge by filtering, deduplicating, and compressing the raw data.

For both data center and enterprise, IT is interested in gaining insights from their network, rather than analyzing the raw data. As a matter of fact, getting the data is not the hard part and IT is already overwhelmed by numbers and figures today; the real value lies in processing the raw data and doing something valuable with it, extracting some actionable data.

Let's consider another key point of view: automation and the move to intent-based networking has given the network operator a completely new level of flexibility in deploying cost-effective, scalable, and maintainable networks. However, with this approach, the operator loses a direct relationship with the underlying device hardware. Given the abstraction that comes with most automation, as well as configuration that is in many cases generated by controllers (and perhaps is not in human-readable form), how do administrators verify that their intent has been actually deployed and that it provides the results expected? Without an automated method to extract the relevant data from the network and validate what is actually happening, this is basically impossible.

Given these considerations, it's clear that network analytics cannot be considered just a big data problem; there is a need for "something" to process the raw data and transform it in quality information in order to optimize the transport but also to enrich the data and provide useful insights. This is the role of the Cisco Digital Network Architecture (Cisco DNA) analytics engine.

Why a Cisco DNA Analytics Engine?

Everything connects to the network: users, devices, servers, printers, sensors, and all sort of IoT devices. A huge amount of data is transported by the network every second. This makes the network infrastructure itself a great source of big data.

Every business is realizing that unlocking the power of the information embedded in the network and deriving business insights is very critical. Historically, however, IT has not been very successful in creating value from this data and has dealt with multiple challenges, as described in Chapter 18, "Cisco DNA Virtualization Solutions: Enterprise Network Functions Virtualization and Secure Agile Exchange." The challenges are shown in Figure 17-1 and explained in the following list:

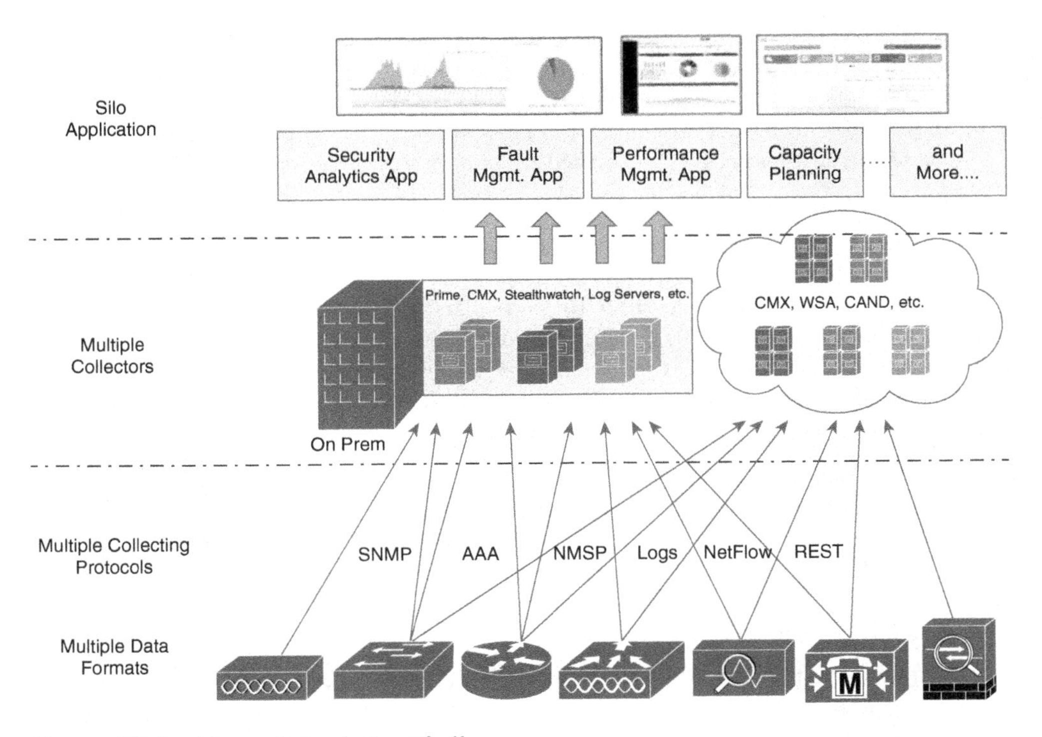

Figure 17-1 *Network Analytics Challenges*

- **Network data inefficiencies:** There is little consistency in the data gathered from network devices. Also, this information sometimes is redundant and overwhelming, and some other times is not enough. There are also inefficiencies related to the way information is stored and extracted from the devices: different network OSs, different data formats, and lack of data models.

- **Telemetry inefficiencies:** These are related to the way information is exported out of the devices. Multiple telemetry protocols are not designed with stream and large-scale processing in mind and use inefficient pull or poll mechanisms.
- **Analytical inefficiencies:** Existing analytics systems tend to be built in silos and for a specific purpose. As a result, telemetry from network elements needs to be sent out to multiple systems, putting load both on network elements and the bandwidth of a WAN link, for example; furthermore, the network operator lacks an end-to-end view of the network and no easy way exists to correlate the information across platforms.
- **Developer inefficiencies:** Building analytics on top of raw network data requires deep knowledge of the underlying network. As a result, analytics developers tend to spend most of their time in data collection and normalization as opposed to the analytics logic, their core competency.

Beyond addressing the mentioned challenges, a Cisco DNA analytics engine is key to bringing additional value in the analytics process. Some of the important functions of the Cisco DNA analytics engine and related advantages are as follows:

- **Data transformation:** The network delivers tremendous volumes of information, and often this can be filled with irrelevant noise rather than signal. Data transformation functions within the analytics engine allow developers to reduce the incoming stream to include only data relevant to the particular application. These are usually referred to as traditional extract, transform, load (ETL) functions. An example is a filtering function that may filter logs according to a specific location. For instance, if you are troubleshooting a problem in your company's Italian branches, you may want to drop all the messages coming from the French ones.
- **Data aggregation:** An analytics application almost always combines data from multiple sources. Aggregation/correlation of data allows network operators to easily combine multiple streams of information into one stream in order to gain more insights. For example, a performance monitoring application may need to link incoming flow records from multiple customer profiles in order to determine if the service level agreement (SLA) is met.
- **Data correlation:** This refers to the capability of an analytics engine to provide additional context, and hence value, by pulling in and correlating data from various sources. For example, a NetFlow stream of information could be augmented with the user authentication information coming from the AAA server or with location information coming from Cisco Mobility Services Engine (MSE).
- **Time analysis:** Network data flows continuously, but network operators often need a snapshot of the stream over an arbitrary time period. Cisco DNA analytics engines have the capability to store data efficiently and allow an operator to define a time period and the streaming data to include in the "window." For example, a time window could show all interfaces in the last five minutes that exceeded a certain amount of megabits per second.

- **Network baselining through machine learning:** How does an operator know if the network is behaving normally? What is normal? Machine-learning algorithms analyze the network flows and establish a baseline from which anomalies are detected easier. Consider client onboarding: what is the "normal" behavior at 9 a.m. when all the employees get connected and leverage DHCP services is very different from what is normal at 10 a.m. The analytics engine can take these factors into consideration before flagging a problem with "too many DHCP request per second." A deep analysis of the different machine-learning algorithms (supervised, unsupervised and deep learning, etc.) is out of the scope of this book, but it's important to state here that the Cisco DNA analytics engine provides infrastructure support for leveraging multiple machine-learning algorithms in a scalable fashion.

To address the IT challenges and provide the additional advantages described in the preceding list, Cisco DNA introduces two analytics engines, Cisco Network Data Platform (NDP) for the enterprise and Cisco Tetration tailored to the needs of the data center.

Cisco DNA Analytics Engines

Why are there two analytics engines in Cisco DNA, NDP for the enterprise and Tetration for the data center? The main reasons for this choice are mostly technical and originate in the fundamental differences of these two network domains. The most important are as follows:

- **Scale:** To address the data center use cases, Tetration needs to process millions of flows per second, capture and store hundreds of billions of telemetry records, apply intelligent algorithms, and provide actionable insight in minutes; for this you need scale. That's why this platform comes equipped with multiple servers and multiple switches to connect them. Such scale is usually not needed in the enterprise, so a lot of this capacity would be wasted and the cost would not be justified.

- **Data sets:** Each analytics platform has been optimized for the extraction, processing, and analysis of the data common to the specific domain. The data center is all about applications, whereas for the enterprise the operators care more about users and devices.

- **Brownfield support:** Given the distributed nature of the enterprise, support of older equipment is a must. Therefore, NDP has been built to support all the existing legacy southbound protocols to communicate with the network devices.

- **Analytics scope:** The Tetration engine is very focused on a critical analytics function—application dependency mapping within a data center. NDP is a broader data collection, processing, and analytics engine because it needs to serve broader use cases in the enterprise, ranging from network analytics to client and application insights. NDP relies on APIs and Cisco and third-party analytics applications to provide specific actual business insight based on the data that is collected. Cisco Network Assurance is an example of integration with an internal application whereas ServiceNow[1] represent a third party app.

Why did Cisco decide to build its own analytics engine instead of leveraging open source or commercial products available in the market? The answer lies in the importance of quality of data.

When it comes to network analytics, quality of data means different things. Yes, it is about accuracy, precision, and contextualized data, but this is true for any analytics solution. Specifically, in network analytics, data quality means that the data is optimized for the final user, in this case the data analyst and developer that are writing the analytics applications. In other words, it includes the following:

- **Model-driven data:** Having a common, known, standard model for data representation that you can leverage is critical for network analytics because each platform and operating system would otherwise stream data in a proprietary format. Make sure that the data you receive gets formatted in the right way before it's exposed to the application layer. Who better than Cisco to understand the data coming from network devices?
- **Network-aware data:** Data could be structured or unstructured, but in a received stream there could be empty values, which is an indication that something is not right and you should raise an alert. For example, if you receive a Flexible NetFlow (FNF) stream from a Cisco device, the Cisco analytics platform knows exactly what each field should contain and can measure the quality of the data received and act upon it.

Bottom line, Cisco as a networking vendor understands network protocols and network information gathering and hence is in a unique position to build an analytics platform that processes and analyzes the data built by those protocols.

Let's take a deeper look at each of the Cisco DNA analytics engines.

Cisco Network Data Platform

Cisco Network Data Platform (NDP) is the Cisco DNA network analytics platform for the enterprise. The goal of NDP is to simplify network analytics and enable Assurance by hiding complexities of network infrastructure data collection and analysis.

NDP is a real-time distributed analytics platform that provides a 360-degree granular view of the network and associated services. It's built from the ground up to be secure, multitenant, and cloud enabled; it scales from small networks to large enterprise infrastructures with thousands of nodes. NDP is integrated in Cisco DNA Center.

---

1 For more information, see https://www.cisco.com/c/dam/en/us/products/collateral/data-center-analytics/network-assurance-engine/solution-overview-c22-740224.pdf.

NDP is also flexible and can be used in multiple use cases. The initial focus is on IT Operations Analytics (ITOA) and Network Performance Monitoring and Diagnostics (NPMD) where customers are particularly concerned with the following:

- **Network assurance:** Very relevant to the Cisco DNA controller-based approach, network assurance leverages the analytics data from NDP to get insights into the network for troubleshooting and root cause analysis. Network assurance gives IT the possibility to measure the performance of the network, identify issues, go back in time to analyze network performance, see trends, and even suggest corrective actions. From an architecture point of view, assurance closes the automation loop: the user expresses a business intent (a network-wide QoS policy to treat Skype as business relevant, for example), this intent gets automated by the Cisco DNA controller, and then network assurance gets the telemetry data from NDP and verifies that the intent has been correctly implemented and has given the expected outcomes.
- **User and network behavior analysis:** What is your network's and applications' "normal" behavior? Are they performing up to the users' or customers' expectation? NDP gives you the tools establish a baseline and then monitor deviation from it.
- **Security assessment and policy violations:** If you have a baseline, you not only can monitor the performances but also can determine the anomalies in your traffic that could be caused by a security attack.

To deliver on these use cases, NDP interacts with other components of the Cisco DNA architecture. Figure 17-2 represents these interactions.

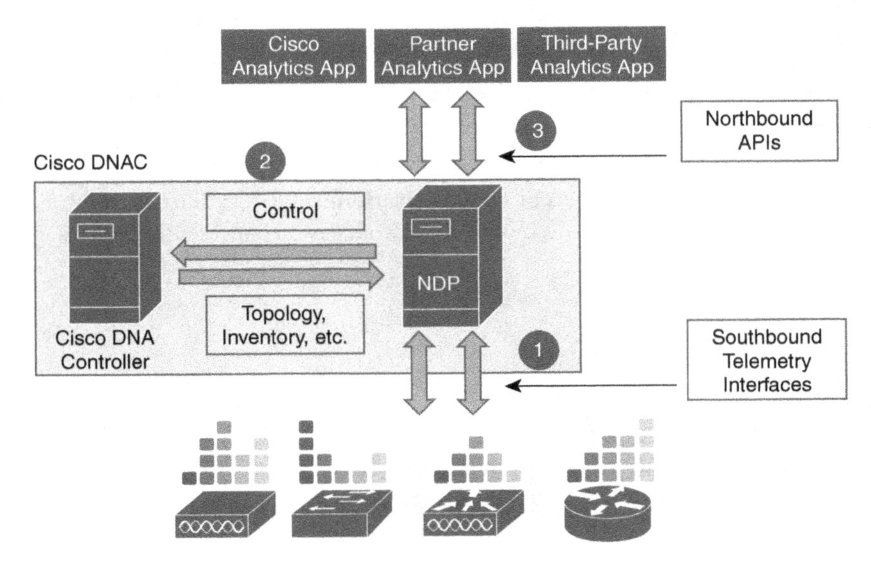

Figure 17-2 *NDP Interactions*

Specifically, NDP interacts with the following:

1. **Network elements:** Southbound, NDP collects telemetry data related to services deployed in the network from the network devices and end-hosts.
2. **Cisco DNA Controller:** NDP interacts with the Cisco DNA Controller to collect context information (such as inventory, device capabilities, topology, sites, locations, etc.) and also to configure the network elements for telemetry-related settings (control).
3. **Applications:** Northbound, NDP interfaces with the Analytics applications that leverage the NDP capabilities through open APIs.

Let's consider an example of how these interactions are important by introducing the Telemetry Quotient.

Telemetry Quotient

One of the innovations that NDP introduces in network analytics is the Telemetry Quotient (TQ), a measure of the network "readiness" for telemetry and hence analytics. A higher TQ means that the devices in the network support good telemetry capabilities (for example, FNF is supported on all the access devices) and these have been turned on.

The TQ also represents a great example of the importance of the integration of NDP with the Cisco DNA Controller. The TQ is exposed to the network operator via NDP and, based on the value, the operator might receive a recommendation to perform some configuration changes to increase the TQ. These changes on the network, although instructed by NDP, are automated through the Cisco DNA controller to keep a coherent interaction between the different components.

NDP Architecture

This section gives an overview of the NDP architecture and the principles behind it. It describes the main components/layers of the NDP platform, how they interact with each other, and the different deployment modes, and it touches on important security aspects.

NDP Architecture Principles

As the Cisco Network analytics engine for the enterprise, NDP has been built from the ground up according to the following principles:

- **Simplify analytics applications development:** NDP focuses on network analytics and on enabling common network use cases. The important principle here is that NDP hides the network details from the app developer and provides access to standard model data via open APIs. The developer doesn't need to deal with the underlying technologies and can focus on processing and analyzing the data for the desired use case.

- **Technology framework abstraction:** NDP architecture is built with a modular and flexible approach so that the chosen framework is not locked to a particular technology in a way that prevents the innovation and adoption of future better choices. NDP also takes care of the scaling and management of the infrastructure (compute, network, and data-related) resources.
- **Distributed analytics and advanced telemetry:** As discussed in Chapter 16, "Cisco DNA Analytics Components," Cisco DNA analytics leverages distributed analytics, and advanced telemetry protocols are key to an optimized analytics solution. NDP is built to exploit these protocols when available.
- **Platform extensibility:** Although the core NDP platform provides the base building blocks of a data platform, it is possible to extend NDP in different ways: new data models, collector plug-ins for adding new data sources, analytic logic pipeline, data storage, etc.
- **Multitenant and cloud enabled:** NDP is architected to be multitenant at the platform level from day one. It also leverages the cloud or can be implemented directly in a private cloud or public cloud. So, single-tenant and on-premises deployments are special cases of the general multitenant and cloud-ready deployments.
- **Cloud tethered:** NDP may be deployed with a link to a Cisco-managed cloud. This primarily brings benefits to the customer in terms of hot patches, optimizations, newer capabilities, and seamless upgrades with zero downtimes, all of which are easily adopted. But it's also beneficial to Cisco in terms of gathering anonymized data that can be leveraged to improve the product and develop new innovations.

NDP Architecture Layers

From a functionality point of view, NDP has multiple layers, each performing a specific job. Figure 17-3 shows a high-level representation of the building blocks of the NDP engine and the view of the related NDP architecture layers.

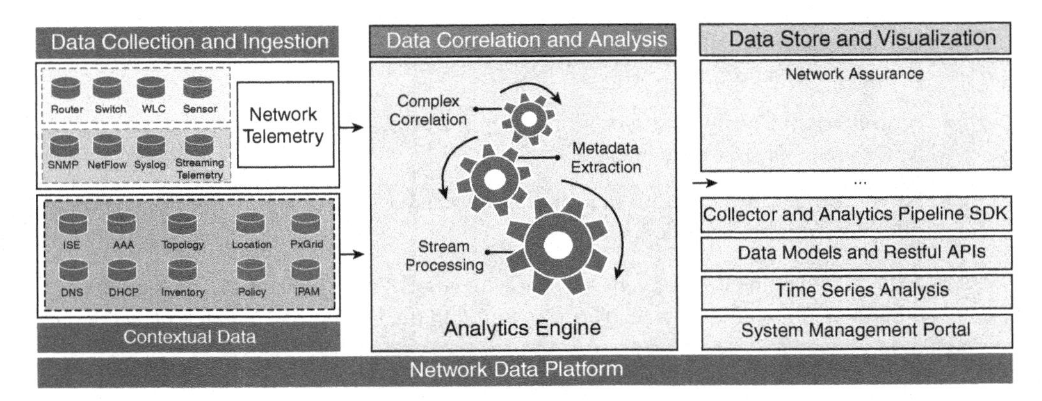

Figure 17-3 *NDP Engine and the Architecture Layers*

On the left side of Figure 17-3 are the analytics sources. These can be the network devices themselves for network-related data or the servers, controllers, and repositories for the contextual data. The right side of the figure represents the consumers of the analytics platforms, the applications and analytics tools that leverage the open APIs to access the data.

Figure 17-3 shows the different building blocks of the NDP platform as they relate to the logical layers or functions that the platform delivers. The first logical layer is the data collection and ingestion layer. This layer employs NDP collectors that are responsible for gathering data from different data sources/telemetry protocols. There are two type of collectors:

- **Data collectors:** Extract data from network devices, hosts, network applications, etc. Each collector knows how to communicate with the data source and understands the data formats associated with that protocol. They implement either a push model or a polling model, depending on the telemetry protocol. Examples of data collectors are the Flexible NetFlow, syslog, and SNMP collectors.
- **Context collectors:** Derive context data from network controllers and management systems (such as Cisco DNA Controller, Prime, etc.), identity services such as Identity Services Engine (ISE), and user data repositories such as MSE. Context data also includes aspects such as network inventory and topology.

The collector is also responsible for performing multiple types of optimization, which include the following:

- **Deduplication:** Deduplication reduces the amount of duplicate info received. For example, in NetFlow, packets passing through several exporter devices will result in NetFlow receiving the same flow multiple times, one for each exporter device. Here, deduplication can be used to avoid duplicate counts of the same packets, and the same type of optimization can be done across multiple network devices, across multiple flows from a single user, or across similar flows from multiple users.
- **Compression:** Existing compression techniques reduce the amount of data exchanged or stored.
- **Aggregation:** Data aggregation can be applied across contexts, such as users, applications, etc., or over time intervals.
- **Filtering:** Filtering techniques can be made available if certain data matching certain rules needs to be discarded.

When the NDP engine is deployed as a standalone node, the collector layer functions are embedded in the engine itself. This is clarified in the next section, which presents the NDP components.

After the collector function has gathered and optimized the data from the respective sources, it publishes the information to the ingestion processing. This layer is primarily responsible for accepting incoming data as fast as possible, so that the collector doesn't have to drop any single byte and all the info is retained. The data is then made available to "consumers" in a scalable fashion. In other words, ingestion layer provides a publish-subscribe (pub-sub)[2] message exchange mechanism where the collection layer is the publisher and the analytics layer is the subscriber. The ingestion layer provides two important services: persistence of messages, which ensures that messages are not lost in case the ingestion service is restarted, and replay of messages, which allows replay of messages from a particular point. The pub-sub architecture is used for building real-time data pipelines and streaming apps. It is horizontally scalable, fault-tolerant, and really fast.

The data correlation and analysis layer enables developers to build analytics pipelines using a single framework for both streaming and batch processing. An analytics pipeline represents a specific sequence of steps involving various transformations such as filtering, grouping, splitting and joining, windowing, aggregation etc. In practice, this layer allows the developer to build the analytics logic.

The data store and visualization layer provides multiple types of data repositories for storing raw and processed data. These are provided for the following data models:

- **Column/Key-Value store:** For key-based results, aggregated data, etc.
- **Time series store:** For processing and storing time series data
- **Graph store:** For processing and storing graph data models
- **Unstructured data store:** For processing textual data like syslogs

The data store function within NDP handles the sharding[3], scaling, and management of the data and data stores.

Finally, the data visualization function within this layer provides the interface for data externalization. It defines different language software development kits (SDK) and APIs to access analytics data from the different stores. It abstracts the data capabilities without exposing the semantics of individual data stores.

NDP Architecture Components

NDP is built on a distributed and flexible architecture to deliver scalability and extensibility in the different deployment modes supported: cloud, on-premises, and hybrid.

2 For more information on the pub-sub mechanism, see https://kafka.apache.org/.

3 Shard is a database construct; for more info, see https://www.cisco.com/c/en/us/solutions/collateral/data-center-virtualization/unified-fabric/white-paper-c11-730021.html.

The NDP architecture consists of three main components as represented in Figure 17-4.

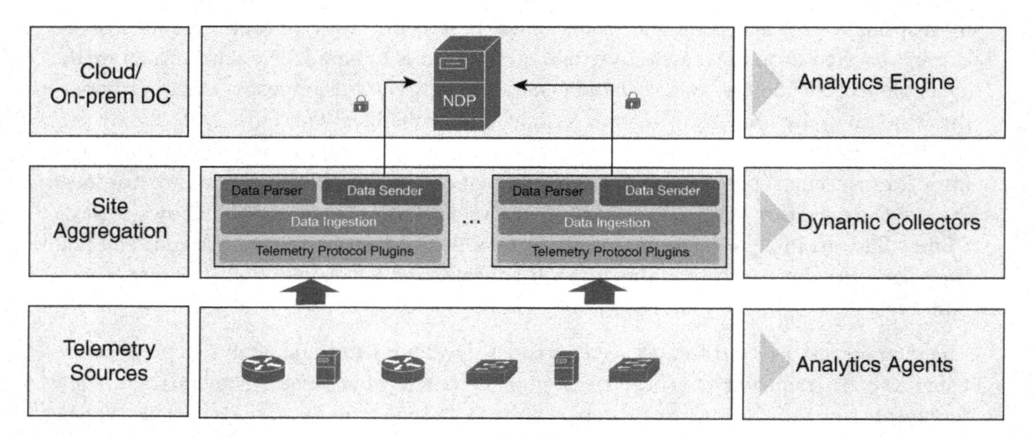

Figure 17-4 *NDP Architecture Components*

Each component is as follows:

- **NDP analytics engine:** This represents the main analytics platform and is typically deployed in the data center (on-premises or cloud). Most of the analytics processing happens in this component. For smaller deployments, it can run as a single standalone node (up to 50,000 devices) and hence collapse the other components. It can be deployed with multiple nodes/engines for scalability and high availability. Each NDP Engine implements all the layer functionalities represented in Figure 17-3. External applications and the Cisco DNA Controller interface only with the main NDP engine and not with the other components below.
- **NDP collector:** As the name suggests, the main job of the NDP collector is to optimize the data gathering and parsing functions. It does this through specific plug-ins written for the specific data being collected. The NDP architecture is flexible and the collector can either be embedded in the NDP engine or distributed as a standalone function. The distributed NDP collector has not been released at the time of writing.
- **NDP analytics agent:** An optional component that is embedded in the network device or in another analytics source. The main function of the agent is to extract optimized telemetry from the device, and aggregate and secure this data directly from the device.

Let's analyze a bit further the collector and its functions. This component, as previously noted, can be embedded in the NDP engine itself or it can be deployed as an external appliance when it's necessary to distribute the collection function. Figure 17-5 illustrates the NDP collector's function building blocks.

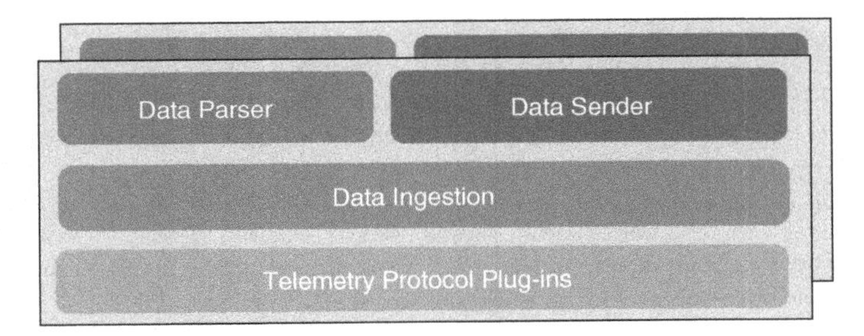

Figure 17-5 *NDP Collector Function Building Blocks*

Starting from the bottom block, the functions are as follows:

- **Protocol plug-ins:** The pieces of software that interact with a specific telemetry protocol. There is a plug-in for each standard protocol, such as SNMP, Radius, NetFlow, etc., but also for new/custom streaming telemetry protocols. Remember the extensibility principle for NDP? The collector has been designed to be easily extended to support new telemetry protocols developed by Cisco or third parties.
- **Data ingestion:** Same functions as previously described in the data ingestion layer of the main analytics engine. It collects the data from the different plug-ins and makes it available for other blocks to process.
- **Data parser:** The use of a data parser depends on the use case. If the use case requires raw data to be sent to the central engine, then this component is not involved. But it might be useful to parse the data to reduce the duplicated information (for example, you could have multiple NetFlow collectors in the network analyzing the same flow) or to apply some filters and metadata (such as the location from where the packets originated). In this case, it makes sense to have this processing locally at the site.
- **Data sender:** This block acts as a consumer of messages from the local ingestion layer, establishes a secure session with the counterpart, the Data Receiver in the NDP engine, and transfers the messages securely.

There are three main reasons why external NDP collectors would be beneficial:

- An NDP collector helps to scale the data collection. Instead of sending the telemetry data from the network devices/sources directly to the centralized analytics engine, the NDP collector distributes the data-gathering process and optimizes the transport by deduplicating and filtering the data locally onsite; by doing so, it reduces the amount of traffic sent upstream. This is critical when you have distributed locations connected to the analytics engine through slow and costly WAN links.
- When the analytics engine is deployed in cloud mode, then the collector is a mandatory component to securely connect the enterprise domain with the cloud.
- The collector makes the data processing more efficient by getting closer to the source of data. This is in accordance with the concept of distributed analytics, discussed in Chapter 16.

NDP Deployments Modes

In accordance with the Cisco DNA principle of flexibility and to meet the possible different customer requirements, NDP supports multiple deployment modes: on-premises, cloud, and hybrid (which is simply a mix of the other two). Let's examine the details of the on-premises and cloud options.

Even if the NDP architecture has been developed to be able to support multiple mode, at the time of writing the on-premises model is the only one supported by Cisco DNA.

On-Premises Deployments

In on-premises deployments, the NDP engine is usually installed in the data center, part of the Cisco DNA Center appliance. This is either the enterprise data center (DC) or a private cloud data center. Optionally, external NDP collectors can be deployed to scale the telemetry collection in branch offices and/or aggregation locations or even inside the campus.

When the NDP engine is deployed as a standalone node (i.e., without external NDP collectors), the mode is called centralized and all the data collection and analysis happens inside the engine itself. Figure 17-6 shows a centralized deployment.

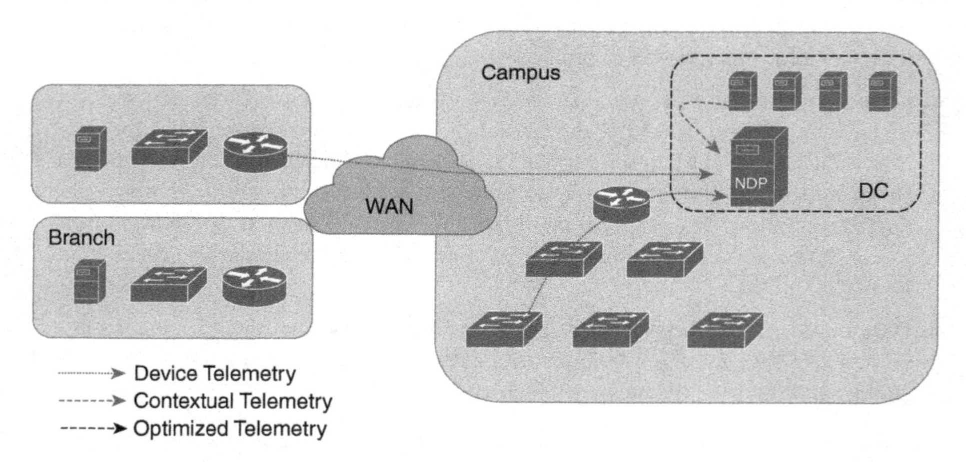

Figure 17-6 *NDP Centralized On-Premises Deployment*

The blue dashed arrow in Figure 17-6 represents the telemetry data (Flexible NetFlow, for example) coming from one or more network devices. The dotted line arrow represents the contextual telemetry gathered from contextual sources and repositories such as controllers, AAA servers, etc. In this mode all telemetry data is sent directly to the centralized NDP engine. At the time of writing the standalone centralized mode is the only one supported.

This deployment is recommended for campus networks or large branches where the standalone NDP can be deployed onsite in a data center. When it comes to a distributed enterprise with locations across a WAN, you need to consider the available WAN bandwidth, as all telemetry data is sent to the central NDP in this deployment. The NDP engine could be deployed as a single node or multiple nodes for better high availability and/or horizontal scaling.

To increase the collector flexibility and optimize the transport of telemetry data across the WAN, Cisco is also delivering a distributed deployment where the telemetry-gathering function is distributed to multiple local NDP collectors, as shown is Figure 17-7.

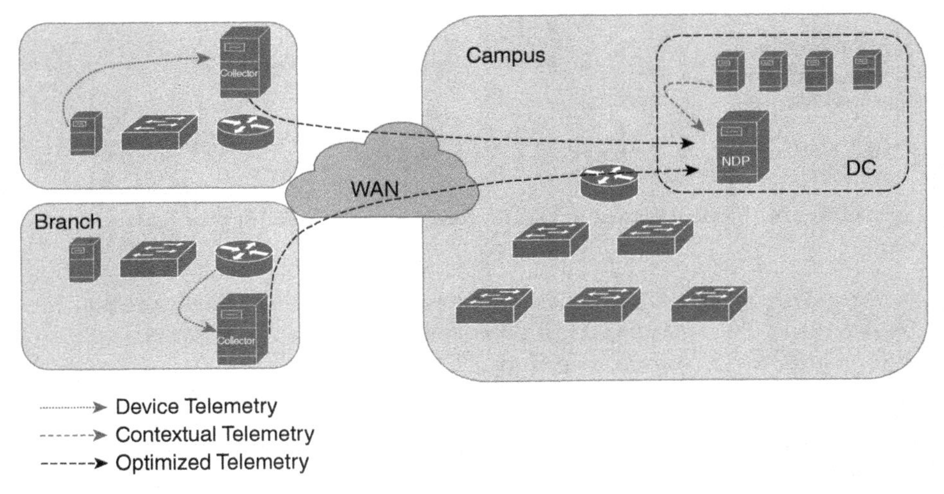

Figure 17-7 *NDP Distributed On-Premises Deployment*

By offloading the telemetry collection function to the NDP collectors, if deployed across the WAN, the normalization and filtering of data happens locally and hence optimizes the amount of data sent to the central NDP engine. This is represented by the black dashed arrow in Figure 17-7.

The deployment mode is flexible, and the NDP collector shown in Figure 17-7 at a single branch, in reality, can be deployed at a regional office level to collect data from multiple branches and aggregate the telemetry traffic.

Cloud Deployments

In cloud deployments, the NDP Engine is hosted in the cloud. In this case NDP collectors are recommended, as sending the data directly to the cloud is not efficient. Also, legacy devices are not able to perform streaming telemetry and hence there is a need for an on-premises collector.

Figure 17-8 shows the diagram of the interactions for an NDP cloud deployment.

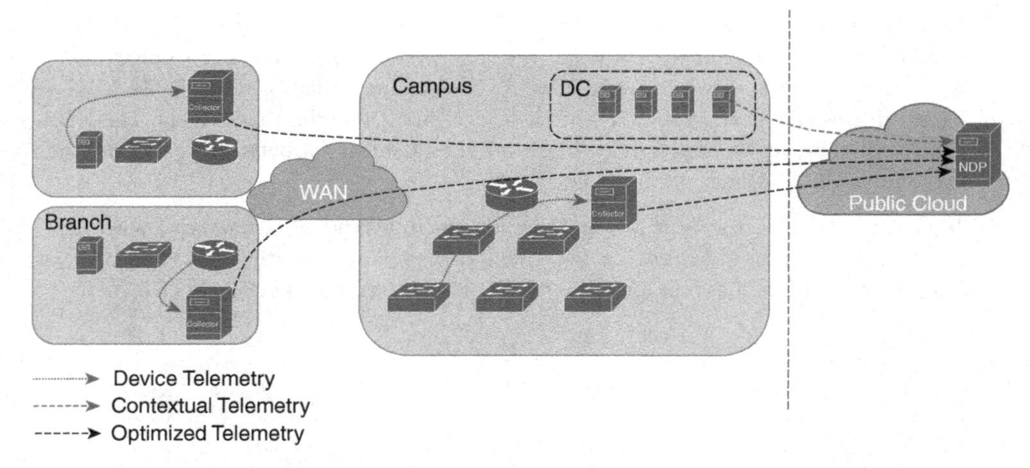

Figure 17-8 *NDP Cloud Deployment*

The advantages of this deployment are typical of a cloud-delivered service and are as follows:

- **Scale and performance:** The analytics platform needs to accommodate vast amounts of data, and a cloud model makes it easier to add storage or computing resources to scale horizontally or to increase performances.
- **Historical data and trends:** More scalability means being able to store more data and for longer periods. This is critical in order to produce meaningful reports and provide the baseline trends.
- **Painless upgrades:** As enterprise customers are looking at developing analytics in the cloud, this approach usually provides a simpler way to do software and hardware upgrades when compared to an on-premises distributed system. This is because of the automation and orchestration tools that are used to build a cloud service.
- **High availability:** Similarly, running a platform in the cloud makes it easier to add physical and virtual redundancy to increase the service uptime.

At the time of writing, Cisco DNA Center and NDP engine were not available in the cloud yet, but Cisco considers this a natural evolution of the Cisco DNA architecture.

NDP Security and High Availability

The analytics engine deals with a lot of critical network and user data. It's mandatory to provide protection and confidentiality for the information managed by the NDP platform and also guarantee that the platform is highly available.

Let's consider security first. The NDP platform provides security at the following levels:

- **Transport security:** NDP provides northbound APIs access for other applications to interact with the platform. All these APIs are protected using open standards such as Hypertext Transfer Protocols (HTTPs), Secure Sockets Layer/Transport Layer Security

(SSL/TLS), OAuth, etc. The communication between the NDP engines and the distributed collectors is protected with a secure tunnel such as Internet Protocol Security (IPsec) or Diagram Transport Layer Security (DTLS). Finally, most NDP collectors need to communicate with data sources using respective telemetry protocols. These collectors implement the security standard required by those telemetry protocols.

- **Data security:** NDP Engine uses role-based access control (RBAC) to provide controller and fine-granular access to data. This is true for all the APIs exposed by the platform in a single- or multitenant environment. NDP provides also a secure credential store service to store key material required for the transport security aspects already mentioned.

High availability is a key characteristic of NDP and is implemented at different levels. Both the NDP Engine and the NDP collectors are built on top of a Cisco-developed Infrastructure as a Service (IaaS) that provides the support for application/service restartability in case of failures of a software component. So, for example, if the SNMP collector within an NDP collector engine fails, it is automatically restarted without compromising the overall functionality of the NDP collector itself.

At a system level, NDP collectors can be deployed in a 1:1 active–active deployment where the entire node is backed up by another node that can take over in case of failure.

For the centralized NDP engine, the system supports an N+1 active–active deployment; this means that NDP can be deployed in a cluster and any node can fail without compromising the functionality of the platform. The cluster function is also used for scalability.

Cisco Tetration Analytics

Modern data centers have evolved in a brief period of time into the complex environments seen today, with extremely fast, high-density switching networks pushing large volumes of traffic, and multiple layers of virtualization and overlays. Data centers typically handle millions of flows a day, and are fast approaching billions of flows. On average, there are 10,000 active flows per rack at any given second.[4] The result is a highly abstract network that can be difficult to secure, monitor, and troubleshoot.

The type of workload deployed is changing in nature as well. The popularization of microservices has caused development of containerized applications that exhibit entirely different behavior on the network than traditional services. Their lifecycles often can be measured in milliseconds, making their operations difficult to capture for analysis. The same effect can be seen with hybrid cloud and virtualized workloads, which move between hypervisors as needed. Furthermore, highly scaled data centers are challenging Transmission Control Protocol (TCP) to meet their high-performance needs, including the need to handle multiple unique conversations within the same long-lived TCP session.[5]

4 T. Benson, A. Akella, and D. Maltz, "Network Traffic Characteristics of Data Centers in the Wild," *Proceedings of the 10th ACM SIGCOMM Conference on Internet Measurement* (2010): 267–280.

5 L. Qiu, Y. Zhang, and S. Keshav, "Understanding the Performance of Many TCP Flows," *Computer Networks* 37, no. 3 (2001): 277–306.

At the same time, IT architects are faced with two significant challenges:

- Increasing the speed of service deployments and associated infrastructure changes
- Gaining security insights on the applications and associated data to protect them against a rapidly evolving set of security threats

It's clear that to be able to efficiently and confidently respond to these changes, you need a complete understanding of the applications flow in your data center, meaning you need complete visibility.

The Cisco Tetration Analytics platform is designed to address these challenges using comprehensive traffic telemetry data collected from both servers and Cisco Nexus switches. The platform performs advanced analytics using unsupervised machine-learning techniques and behavioral analysis and enforces a consistent whitelist policy for applications. The platform provides a ready-to-use solution that includes the following:

- It provides complete visibility into application components, communications, and dependencies to enable implementation of a zero-trust model in the network.
- It performs real-time asset tagging, allowing administrators to associate specific characteristics with traffic telemetry data and workloads.
- It automatically generates whitelist policy based on application behavior.
- It provides a mechanism for including any existing security policy based on business requirements.

Based on the information provided, IT organizations can enforce consistent policy across heterogeneous infrastructure and apply application segmentation.

Let's dive deeper and understand how Cisco Tetration works and how it all starts with the quality of data you analyze.

It's All About Quality of Data

As stated in the introduction, to be able to efficiently and confidently respond to changes, you need a complete understanding of the applications that are present on your network. The problem is that in data centers, it can be almost impossible to manually catalog and inventory the myriad applications that are running at any one time, and doing so usually requires extensive and often challenging manual collaboration across a number of separate groups. And even if an organization performs manual application dependency mapping, it is not a one-time operation. Mappings must be maintained as living documents—otherwise, the source of information will increasingly diverge from the source of truth (the actual application traffic).

It's clear that in order to manage your data center securely and efficiently, you need correct and up-to-date information about the applications. The question is how to get it.

Historically, three approaches are usually used for application mapping:

- **Manual approach:** The network team attempts to manually collect application information across groups that have deployed applications on top of the network infrastructure.
- **Simple automated approach:** Simple automated tools are run in an attempt to collect application dependency mapping information.
- **Outsourced approach:** An external agency combines the manual and native approaches and then evaluates the collected information and compiles it into a report.

Most organizations find the manual approach labor and cost intensive, and from a technical perspective it is too rigid. Manual application dependency mapping is feasible only at a very small scale. The network team also should have a strong relationship with the application teams, who must gather the required data. This process is prone to human error and mistakes, and the probability of accurately mapping the applications in the data center is low. The collected data is usually compiled into a static report that diverges from reality as soon as it is published.

Businesses may be tempted by the simple automated option. It appears to incur only the low capital costs needed to purchase software that claims to be able to map applications, and to require only a small operations team to run the application dependency mapping tool. However, current simple software implementations of application dependency mapping are notoriously ineffective at truly mapping the application landscape. Often, the application dependency mapping software is not to blame. The problem instead is the source data ingested. With poor or incomplete input data, the application dependency mapping tool cannot make accurate observations, however revolutionary the mapping algorithm may be. Therefore, to complete the mapping process, the low-quality automated recommendations must be supplemented by human input, increasing the long-term costs of using this approach. Traditional application dependency mapping software usually does not learn from this human supervision, causing staff to have to repetitively help the tool. Traditionally, capturing enough high-quality source input data at data centers at scale has been a task that only few organizations with huge resource pools and equipment have been able to achieve.

The outsourced approach has the problems of both approaches, and it adds a layer of cost and complexity. It also does not usually provide any more actionable or insightful mapping than the other two techniques.

To efficiently map all the applications in your data center, you need the raw information and you need it fast. For this, Cisco has introduced a new approach to network analytics: Cisco Tetration.

Data Center Visibility with Cisco Tetration Analytics

To perform accurate application dependency mapping, a huge breadth of high-quality input data is critical to be able to make relevant observations. To achieve this, the Cisco Tetration Analytics architecture was designed from the foundation to capture high-quality data.

The Cisco Tetration Analytics platform consists of next-generation Cisco switches that have flow-capturing capabilities built in to the application-specific integrated circuit (ASIC), small-footprint OS-level agents, and a next-generation analytics cluster that incorporates big data technology that can scale to billions of recorded flows, as shown in Figure 17-9.

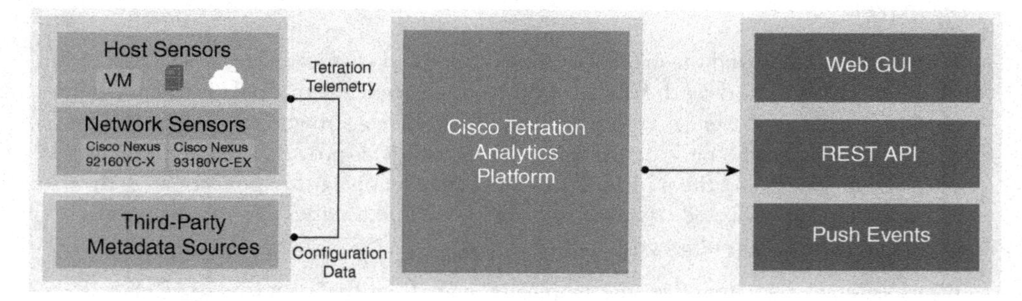

Figure 17-9 *Cisco Tetration Analytics Architecture*

Because data is exported to the Cisco Tetration Analytics cluster every 100 ms, the detail of the data is much finer.

Cisco Tetration Analytics is much less likely to miss so-called mouse flows, which often are missed by NetFlow collectors, with an export rate set to 60 seconds. Because the flow table is flushed so often, Cisco Tetration Analytics sensors are unlikely to be overwhelmed and therefore unlikely to need to drop flow records because of lack of available memory. This is a significant change in the architectural model: the flow-state tracking responsibility is transferred from the sensor to the collector, allowing hardware engineers to design smaller, more efficient, and more cost-effective ASICs.

Not only does Cisco Tetration Analytics allow you to analyze a huge amount of data at one time, it keeps a detailed historical record without archiving or losing any resolution in the data. This look-back feature allows the system to understand more than a single snapshot in time, and to show trends for an application. For example, many businesses have applications that have a seasonality about them, with additional capacity or dependencies pulled in dynamically at moments of extreme load or at the end of a fiscal quarter. Understanding this behavior is important because the application may have hidden dependencies that are not visible during quiet periods. Without this knowledge, traditional application dependency mapping tools may recommend policies that do not truly map an application's full requirements across its entire lifecycle. This is the quality of data you need.

After this high-quality and comprehensive input data has been ingested by the analytics cluster, it is available for analysis by application insight algorithms within the Cisco Tetration Analytics platform. Whereas traditional application dependency mapping tools use a top-down approach because they do not have access to such data, Cisco Tetration Analytics is designed with a bottom-up approach in which recommendations are made from actual application traffic.

Because the Cisco Tetration Analytics architecture delivers such high-quality data, the platform can make use of unique mapping algorithms that take advantage of this capability, generating far more accurate and complete application dependency maps and recommendations. The mapping algorithm computes a unique profile about every endpoint to be mapped. The profile is based on a large number of data points, including detailed network flow information mapped to the originating process within the endpoint operating system. This information is then combined with information from external data sources such as domain name, load-balancer configuration, and geolocation information. The machine-learning algorithm then iteratively compares each profile to the other profiles until a best fit is achieved.

An example of this mapping is shown in Figure 17-10.

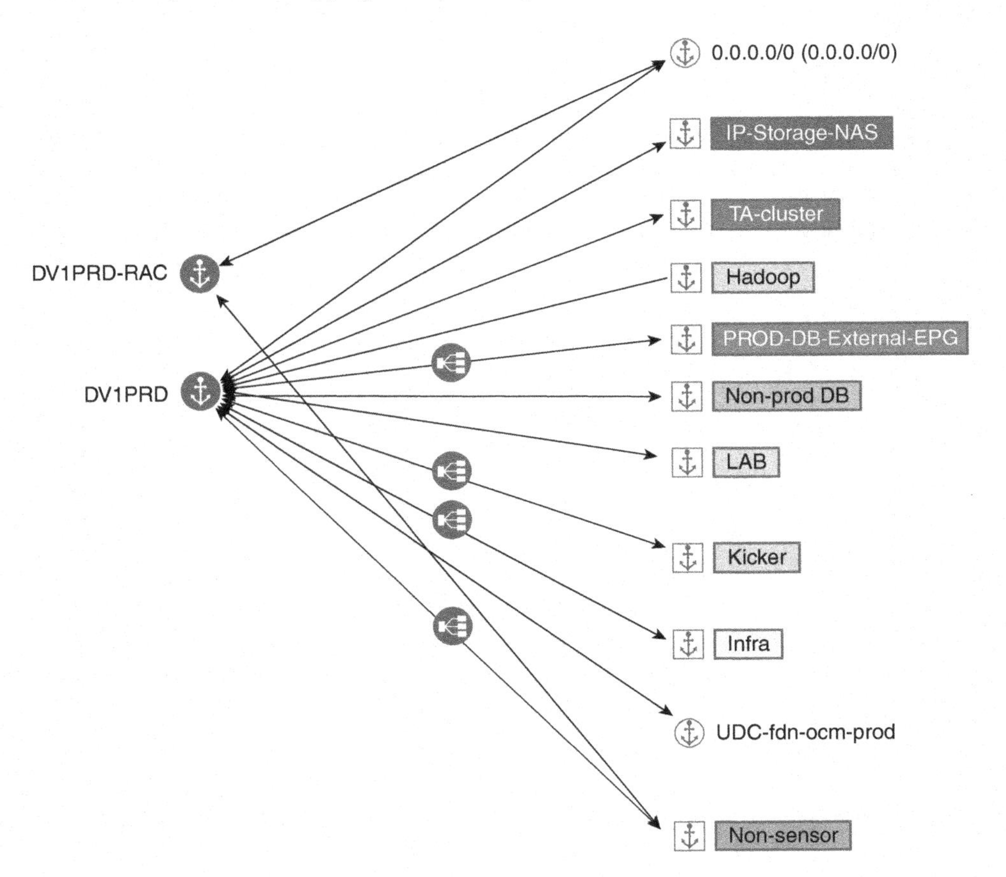

Figure 17-10 *Cisco Tetration Analytics Application Insight Map*

Any recommendations that the application dependency mapping makes are accompanied by a confidence score. Confidence scores indicate how sure the algorithm is that the grouping is correct. This score allows human operators to prioritize their time when providing any additional input: they can start with the recommendations about which the tool is least confident. As the system learns, the confidence score is likely to go up for a given grouping as the tool starts to understand the patterns that group particular endpoints together in your data center. The recommendations that the application insight feature makes can then be confirmed by a human supervisor. However, unlike traditional application dependency mapping tools, Cisco Tetration Analytics understands the instructions from the operator and learns from the experience. The next time the application dependency mapping tool is run, it factors in the human guidance, saving valuable time for the operator.

Let's examine the architecture of the Cisco Tetration solution.

Cisco Tetration Analytics Architecture

The Cisco Tetration Analytics platform has four main functional layers.

Data Collection Layer

This layer consists primarily of sensor functions. Sensors are the eyes and ears of the analytics platform. Two types of sensors are used:

- **Software sensors:** These lightweight sensors run as user processes and can be installed on any server (virtualized or bare metal). Two types of software sensors are used: full-visibility sensors and limited-visibility sensors. Limited-visibility software sensors are designed to collect connection information to support specific Cisco Tetration Analytics use cases. These sensors are not designed to provide comprehensive telemetry data.
- **Hardware sensors:** These sensors are embedded in Cisco Nexus 92160YC-X, 93180YC-EX, and 93108TC-EX Switches.

Figure 17-11 shows the Telemetry that Cisco Tetration extracts from both hardware and software sensors.

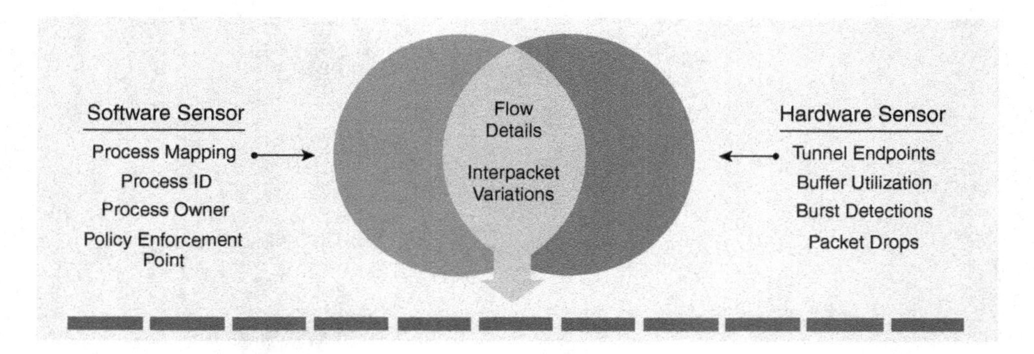

Figure 17-11 *Telemetry Data: Hardware Sensors and Software Sensors*

The full-visibility software sensors and the hardware sensors collect three types of telemetry information:

- **Flow information:** This information contains details about flow endpoints, protocols, and ports; when the flow started; how long the flow was active; etc.
- **Inter-packet variation:** This information captures any inter-packet variations seen within the flow. Examples include variations in the packet's time to live (TTL), IP/TCP flags, and payload length.
- **Context details:** Context information is derived outside the packet header. In the case of a software sensor, this information includes details about the process, including which process generated the flow, the process ID, and the user associated with the process.

Sensors do not process any information from payloads, and no sampling is performed. Sensors are designed to monitor every packet and every flow. In addition to the sensors, this layer includes configuration information from third-party sources, such as load balancers, Domain Name System (DNS) server records, the IP address management database, etc. This configuration data is used to augment the information provided by the analytics platform.

Analytics Layer

Data from the sensors is sent to the Cisco Tetration Analytics platform, which is the brain that performs all the analyses. This multi-node big data platform processes the information from the sensors and uses unsupervised and guided machine learning, behavior analysis, and intelligent algorithms to provide a ready-to-use solution for the following use cases:

- Accurate insight into application component communications based on observed behavior
- Automated grouping of similar endpoints (for example, web server clusters and database clusters)
- Consistent whitelist policy recommendations for applications and monitoring for compliance deviations in minutes
- Policy impact analysis to test a policy before enforcing it in the network
- Automated policy enforcement that enables a zero-trust model
- Monitoring to track policy compliance deviations and update policy in near-real time
- Pervasive visibility in real time across data center infrastructure

- Long-term data retention for historical analysis without loss of detail
- In-depth forensics using powerful search filters and visual queries

Enforcement Layer

Full-visibility software sensors act as the enforcement point for the detailed application policy generated by the platform, helping enable application segmentation. Using the data from the sensors, the Cisco Tetration Analytics platform provides consistent enforcement across public, private, and on-premises deployments. This layer also helps ensure that policy moves along with the workload, even when an application component is migrated from a bare-metal server to a virtualized environment. In addition, the enforcement layer helps ensure scalability, with consistent policy implemented for thousands of applications spanning tens of thousands of workloads.

Visualization Layer

The Cisco Tetration Analytics platform enables consumption of this data through an easy-to-navigate and scalable web GUI and through Representational State Transfer (REST) APIs. In addition, it provides Apache Kafka–based push notification to which northbound systems can subscribe to receive notifications about policy compliance deviations, flow anomalies, etc. Advanced users have access to the Hadoop data lake and can write custom applications using programming languages such as Python and Scala that are run on the platform using the powerful computing resources available.

The Benefits of Cisco Tetration Analytics

Cisco Tetration Analytics application insight has the intelligence to truly map your data center's application landscape, helping address a wide range of problems in the data center.

During the mapping process, the platform captures and tracks the consumers and providers of services for an application. Correctly identifying the provider of a service is achieved using degree analysis: tracking the number of inbound connections and, if possible, who initiated the TCP session. With this information, you can apply whitelist security policies across the data center. Whitelists are usually expensive to implement and difficult to maintain because they usually take a lot of ternary content-addressable memory (TCAM) space in network devices and they are complex to deploy and maintain. With Cisco Tetration Analytics application dependency mapping, this task is substantially easier.

Application whitelisting is a core concept of the next-generation Cisco Application Centric Infrastructure (ACI) data center networking solution.

To deploy a data center network that implements application whitelisting, application dependency must be fully mapped before migration; otherwise, you risk cutting off legitimate communications to a given workload. Cisco Tetration Analytics mapping results are used to ease the migration path. In fact, the platform has a policy compliance tool that uses the results of application dependency mapping to simulate what-if whitelist scenarios on real application traffic, displaying detailed information about what traffic would have been permitted, mistakenly dropped, escaped, or rejected.

Data centers are living entities that change constantly. Often applications need to update, change configuration, or scale. If you have application dependency mapping data for reference before and after an application change, you can verify the success of an update, check the results of a change, or monitor the stability of an application at the network level.

For example, an update to an application might cause it to incorrectly launch with development settings that point at a test database server, causing a critical application to fail in minutes. Application dependency mapping can detect that the application is now incorrectly connecting to a test database server and alert staff. Disaster recovery is a minimum requirement for most production data centers.

In fact, most IT leaders have a disaster-recovery plan in place. But how can you validate your disaster-recovery plan at the network level, especially when application whitelisting is applied and may affect the effectiveness of your disaster recovery plan?

Because of the long look-back period, Cisco Tetration Analytics helps to make sure that any policy it recommends is aware of disaster-recovery dependencies that it has detected from any tests.

Some other benefits of an accurate application dependency map are as follows:

- **Facilitate mergers and acquisitions (M&A):** Get a clear understanding of which applications need to be migrated as part of the M&A process, and which application components and services are redundant and can be phased out. This information is critical and can accelerate the integration of the two entities.

- **Migrate applications to other infrastructure or the cloud:** Now you can migrate applications to a new infrastructure or a public cloud with confidence, knowing exactly which components are required and what network services each application is dependent on.

Figure 17-12 shows the traffic patterns discovered between neighboring endpoint clusters. The thickness of a chord indicates the number of ports that are exposed between neighboring clusters.

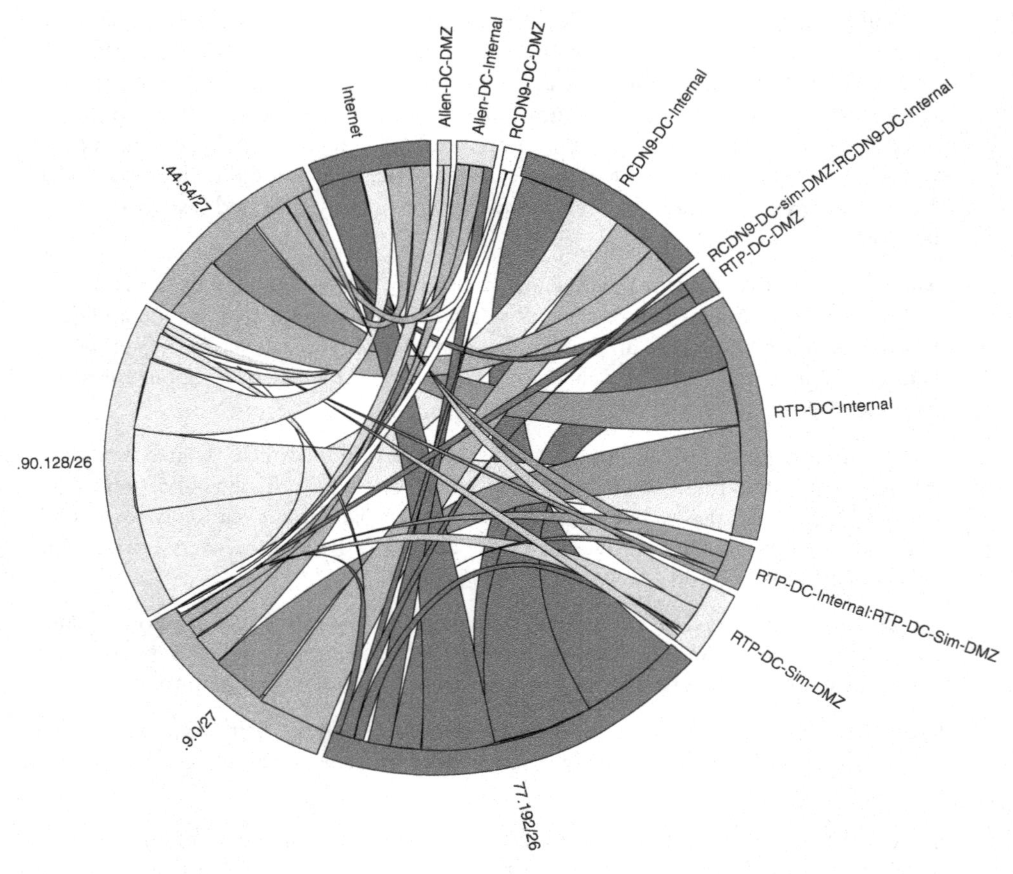

Figure 17-12 *Application Traffic Dependency Diagram*

Summary

IT managers need complete visibility into the behavior of their networks, users, and applications to make informed decisions and move to intent-based networking and embrace full automation of their network.

The network, whether in the enterprise or in the data center, is getting ever more complex and transporting ever more data. The challenge becomes how to extract the relevant insight from all this data.

To cope with complexity of today's networks, with the speed and scale at which data needs to be processed, Cisco DNA leverages the functions of the Cisco DNA Analytics Engine. This chapter introduced Cisco Network Data Platform (NDP), the enterprise Network Analytics Engine, and Cisco Tetration, the Analytics platform for data centers. The problems they solve were analyzed. This chapter also provided a description of the architecture of each and the benefits it brings.

Further Reading

Cisco DNA Center Analytics: https://www.cisco.com/c/en/us/solutions/enterprise-networks/dna-analytics-assurance.html

Cisco Tetration Analytics: https://www.cisco.com/c/en/us/products/data-center-analytics/tetration-analytics/index.html.

Cisco Tetration White Papers: https://www.cisco.com/c/en/us/products/data-center-analytics/tetration-analytics/white-paper-listing.html

Chapter 18

Cisco DNA Virtualization Solutions: Enterprise Network Functions Virtualization and Secure Agile Exchange

Virtualization has been introduced throughout this book so far as one of the key tenets in Cisco Digital Network Architecture. Chapter 10, "Cisco DNA Infrastructure—Virtualization," laid the foundation with an in-depth explanation of the technologies, highlighting both transport virtualization (segmentation) and the virtualization of network functions (NFV). This chapter elaborates on how Cisco offers virtualization *solutions* that leverage this technology to deliver the business benefits of aligning the network with your enterprise's intent, of offering fast and flexible deployments for Cisco DNA services, and of lowering the total cost of ownership (TCO) in your network (e.g., through reduced branch site visits). This chapter explains the following:

- Virtualization of branch architectures based on the Cisco Enterprise Network Functions Virtualization solution
- Virtualization of policy-based connectivity to external domains in support of multicloud architectures

This chapter is thus organized around these two solutions. The section on Enterprise NFV builds on the technology foundation of Chapter 10 but applies these technologies in the context of solution and product details. Particular focus is given in this section on the system architecture details of the Cisco Enterprise Network Compute System (ENCS), which plays a crucial role in branch virtualization. The relevance of the Cisco Enterprise Network Functions Virtualization Infrastructure Software (NFVIS) is also introduced as an example of an operating system supporting NFV. The section on Enterprise Network Functions Virtualization (ENFV) also goes into details of service chaining in a branch virtualization context, and touches on the orchestration options for the Cisco ENFV solution.

The subsequent section in this chapter then concentrates on virtualizing external connectivity in Cisco DNA. The supporting Cisco solution for this use case is Secure Agile Exchange (SAE), which aims to combine virtualization with policy to allow you to define intent-based communication policies as you connect employees, partners, customers, or guests to applications hosted in your own private clouds, virtual private clouds, or even public clouds (i.e., consumed as a service).

There is also a section devoted to virtualization based on Cisco IOS XE. The Linux OS–based nature of IOS XE running on physical routers and switches also allows for the deployment of virtualized network functions (VNF) and containers directly within IOS XE. Details of this architectural variant of virtualization, are described toward the end of this chapter.

The Cisco Strategy for Virtualization in the Enterprise

In the Cisco vision, x86-based compute resources are available throughout the network wherever needed. x86-based hosts are already deployed across the network, in the access network, the core, or in distributed data centers. x86-based compute resources are also consumed by cloud providers. They are even already in the Cisco ASR 1000 Series routers, the Cisco ISR 4000 Series routers, and the Cisco Catalyst 9000 Series switches. Consequently, Cisco's strategy for virtualization in the enterprise is to leverage these resources where available and necessary. Virtualization is not restricted to a single place in the network (PIN)!

The Cisco vision is to virtualize and automate the deployment of software-based services anywhere in the network, on any platform, to achieve simplicity, agility, and cost reductions. Virtualization needs to support an architecture that is

- Secure, through the deployment of security VNFs where needed, as well as through a fully hardened virtualization solution.
- Open, programmable and extensible, supporting VNFs not just from Cisco, but also from partners or third-party vendors. Published APIs are required to make the solution open and programmable, based on standards-based protocols such as REST, NETCONF, or RESTCONF at both the virtualization OS and the VNF level.
- Policy-based, allowing for the alignment of the Cisco DNA enterprise network with your business intent, where VNFs are deployed in support of these policies at the user, application, or device level of granularity.
- Cloud integrated, allowing you to consume resources in various cloud consumption models (private, virtual-private, public), with seamless and consistent deployment and operations.

In other words, virtualization needs to support the key tenets of Cisco DNA! Any network function (security, WAN, wireless, etc.) should be a candidate to run virtually, anywhere in the network (branch, campus, service provider points of presence [SP PoPs], data center, cloud), on any host that has x86-based compute resources available (x86, router, switch, cloud). In Cisco's vision, you as a network architect or operator should have the ultimate choice of how to deploy a network function: both physical and virtual deployment options should be available to you with the same functionality and operational model. Finally, the solutions need to support flexible deployment models for enterprises and managed service providers (MSP).

Figure 18-1 illustrates the main use cases for virtualization. As introduced in Chapter 10, *branch virtualization* brings about significant TCO reductions, by collapsing the number of hardware appliances to operate in the branch onto a single (or redundantly deployed) x86-based host. *Data center/private cloud virtualization* complements the flexibility of deploying application workloads as virtual machines (VMs) or containers by also applying the relevant network functions in a virtual form factor. Because such applications are increasingly hosted in *public or virtual private clouds*, virtualization also applies to those pins in an analogous manner. Public or virtual private cloud (VPC) connections can increasingly lead you to adopt a multicloud strategy, and motivate *virtualization in a co-location facility* where connections to several cloud providers and environments are consistently underpinned with policy-based virtualized service chains. Virtualization in Cisco DNA is not restricted to your own operations. Service providers also offer virtualized network functions; for example, *virtualized customer premises equipment (CPE)* that runs in distributed SP PoPs or in centralized SP data centers, and allow for functionally reduced "thin" CPE to be deployed in your enterprise sites. Such a consumption model also may bring about overall cost reductions for both the enterprise and the MSP.

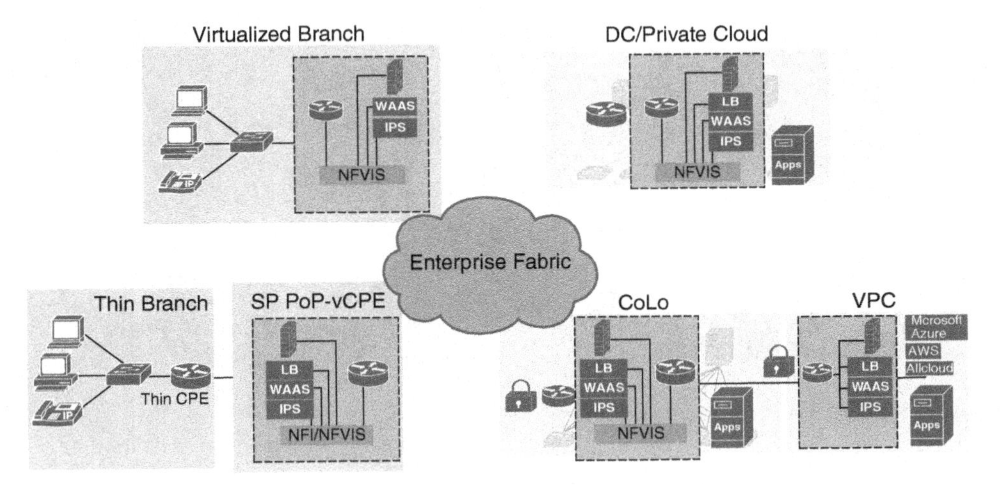

Figure 18-1 *The Cisco Strategy for Enterprise Virtualization*

Cisco Enterprise Network Functions Virtualization

Let's now delve into the details of the Cisco Enterprise Network Functions Virtualization (ENFV) solution.[1] This solution offers a full solution stack to virtualize enterprise branch environments. The stack consists of four main building blocks:

- An orchestration environment to allow easy automation of the deployment of virtualized network services, consisting of multiple VNFs. The orchestration environment for ENFV is integrated into Cisco DNA Center.

1 https://www.cisco.com/c/en/us/solutions/enterprise-networks/enterprise-network-functions-virtualization-nfv/index.html

- The VNFs that provide the desired network functionality, or even non-networking software applications, required at a deployment location.
- The Network Functions Virtualization Infrastructure Software (NFVIS) platform to facilitate the deployment and operation of VNFs and hardware components. NFVIS is based on a standard Linux operating system distribution, but enhances this with additional NFV-optimized functions. For example, a lifecycle management function facilitates the instantiation of VNFs, and the coupling of them into a service chain.
- x86-based compute resources to provide the CPU, memory, and storage required to deploy and operate VNFs and run applications.

The stack is illustrated in Figure 18-2.

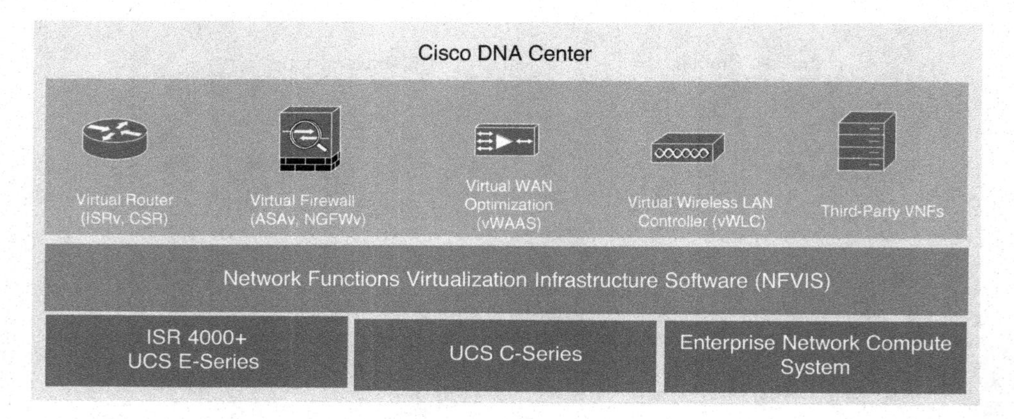

Figure 18-2 *Cisco ENFV Solution Stack*

The Cisco ENFV solution offers a fully systems-integrated environment to virtualize branch functions, while also providing a variety of deployment options. For example, from an orchestration perspective, ENFV is an integral part of the Cisco DNA automation and assurance functions offered by Cisco DNA Center. All the layers in the ENFV solution stack are fully solution tested. Similarly, functional flexibility is provided by

- Offering Cisco VNFs that are consistent with the physical network elements[2]
- Supporting third-party VNFs and application workloads
- Allowing the solution to run on a variety of Cisco hardware hosts

2 The Cisco ISRv offers the same functions as the physical Cisco ISR 4000 Series routers. Both are based on IOS XE. Similarly, the Cisco ASAv has functional and operational consistency with the Cisco ASA appliances. This consistency applies to other virtualized Cisco offers as well.

The following sections provide details on each of these layers in the Cisco ENFV solution, starting in a bottom-up manner from the hardware layer all the way to the orchestration layer.

Details on Virtualization Hardware

Three platform options currently form the basis of ENFV by providing the necessary compute resources: the Cisco ISR 4000 Series routers equipped with Cisco Unified Computing System (UCS) E-Series compute blades, Cisco UCS C-Series servers, and the Cisco Enterprise Network Compute System (ENCS). These hardware options, depicted in Figure 18-3, allow you to choose the right platform for your branch virtualization environment.

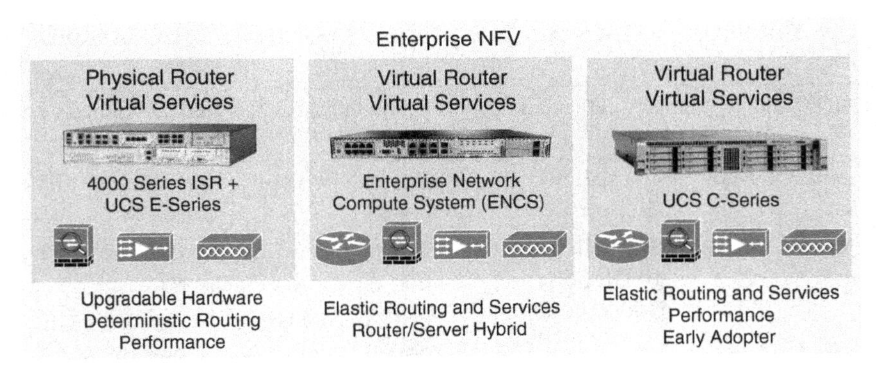

Figure 18-3 *Cisco ENFV Hardware Options*

The first option based on the Cisco ISR 4000 Series routers installed with a Cisco UCS E-Series compute blade is optimized for deployments where either a Cisco ISR 4000 Series router is already installed (i.e., a brownfield environment) or your operational model has a preference for a physical router. In this deployment option, the NFVIS operating system is installed on the Cisco UCS E-Series compute blade, whereas the Cisco ISR 4000 Series host is operating on the Cisco IOS XE software. Cisco Enterprise Network Functions Virtualization (ENFV) concentrates on the UCS E-Series compute blade, where Layer 4–7 functions such as firewall, WAN optimization, and intrusion prevention system/intrusion detection system (IPS/IDS) are virtualized using the Cisco Adaptive Security Virtual Appliance (ASAv) Series, the Cisco Virtual Wide Area Applications Services (vWAAS), or the Cisco Firepower Threat Defense Virtual (FTDv) software solutions, respectively, on top of NFVIS. Virtualization of the routing functionality is not required in this option because it is performed by Cisco IOS XE in the Cisco ISR 4000 Series host. This hardware option in the Cisco ENFV portfolio also allows you to leverage the Cisco ISR 4000 Series voice capabilities that come with Cisco IOS XE. Table 18-1 provides specific hardware details on the various Cisco UCS E-Series blades for the Cisco ISR family of routers.

Table 18-1 *Cisco UCS E-Series Hardware Details*

	UCS-E104S M2	UCS-E160S M3	UCS-E160D M2	UCS-E180D M2
Processor	Intel Xeon (Ivy Bridge) E3-1105C v2 (1.8 GHz)	Intel Xeon Broadwell DE processor D-1528 (1.90 GHz)	Intel Xeon (Ivy Bridge) E5-2418L v2 (2 GHz)	Intel Xeon (Ivy Bridge) E5-2428L v2 (1.8 GHz)
Core	4	6	6	8
Memory	8 to 16 GB DDR3 1333 MHz	8 to 32 GB VLP DDR4 RAM	8 to 48 GB DDR3 1333 MHz	8 to 96 GB DDR3 1333 MHz
Storage	200 GB to 2 TB (2 HDD) SATA, SAS, SED, SSD	200 GB to 4 TB (2 HDD) SATA, SAS, SED, SSD	200 GB to 3 TB (3 HDD) SATA, SAS, SED, SSD	200 GB to 5.4 TB (3 HDD) SATA, SAS, SED, SSD
RAID	RAID 0 and 1	RAID 0 and 1	RAID 0, RAID 1, and RAID 5	RAID 0, RAID 1, and RAID 5
Network port	Internal: two GE ports External: one GE port	Internal: two GE ports External: two 10 GE ports (1000/10000)	Internal: two GE ports External: one GE port PCIE Card 4 GE or one 10 GE Fibre Channel over Ethernet (FCoE)	Internal: two GE ports External: two GE ports PCIE Card 4 GE or one 10 GE FCoE

In some cases, your branch deployments may already have a data center–grade Cisco UCS C-Series server installed. For example, in a retail environment, enterprise applications supporting point-of-sale, video surveillance, or voice communications may already be hosted on an x86-based platform. The same Cisco UCS C-Series server can be leveraged in this case to also run virtualized network functions. In this model, the server's operating system is upgraded to run NFVIS, giving you the flexibility to run VNFs alongside the enterprise application workloads. Note that a virtual routing function may be required in this case to provide transport connectivity across the WAN. An instantiation of the Cisco Integrated Services Virtual Router (ISRv) (or the CSR 1000v) is typical in this model. Deployment of a DC-grade server in the branch offers the advantage of significantly more compute resources. A standard Cisco UCS C-Series server offers up to 44 compute cores, with hundreds of gigabytes of configurable memory. On the other hand, the power and cooling requirements of DC-grade servers are often higher than for branch-optimized network elements, especially when considering a redundant deployment option with two or more servers.

The Cisco ENCS Series offers an attractive alternative. The Cisco ENCS Series is purpose-built for branch virtualization. It offers x86-based compute resources to run multiple VNFs, but in a form factor that is optimized for the branch from a size, power, and cooling perspective. Like the previous hardware options, the Cisco ENCS Series is also powered by Cisco NFVIS. NFVIS is thus a common convergence layer abstracting a variety of hardware options and providing common operating system functions optimized for branch virtualization. The Cisco ENCS Series hosts come in two main variants: the Cisco 5100 Series and the Cisco 5400 Series. The Cisco 5100 Series is cost-optimized for smaller branch virtualization use cases. The four-core AMD processor offers the ability to instantiate up to two VNFs (depending on the VNFs resource requirements). This model has reduced interface capabilities; for example, it does not provide the Cisco Network Interface Module (NIM) slot and has no integrated L2 switch. The Cisco 5400 Series hosts come in three variations offering from 6 to 12 CPU cores. The Cisco 5406 provides 6 CPU cores clocked at 1.9 GHz. The Cisco 5408 offers 8 CPU cores clocked at 2.0 GHz. The Cisco 5412 has the highest number of CPU cores—12 in total—clocked at 1.5 GHz. Table 18-2 summarizes the various Cisco ENCS hardware models and their resource capacities from a core and memory perspective.

Table 18-2 *Cisco ENCS Hardware Details*

	5100 Series	5400 Series
CPU vendor/model	AMD Merlin, Falcon, RX-421ND	Intel Xeon Broadwell D-1500 Series
CPU cores/frequency	4-core @ 3.4 GHz	6-, 8-, 12-core with Hyperthreading @ 1.5–2.0 GHz
CPU L2 cache size	2 MB	1.5 MB per core
Memory	16–32 GB	16–64 GB
Storage (M.2 SATA)	64–400 GB	64–400 GB
Storage (SFF)	—	Two disks with RAID (SATA, SAS, SED, SSD)
Dimensions	12.7" × 10" × 1RU	17.5" × 12" × 1RU
WAN options	4 × GE, Cellular	2 × GE, Cellular, T1, DSL, Serial
LAN	—	8-port switch with optional PoE
Hardware offload	—	Supported for VM to VM Traffic
Lights-out management	—	Built-in CIMC

Figure 18-4 reveals more details about the Cisco ENCS running Cisco NFVIS as its operating system.

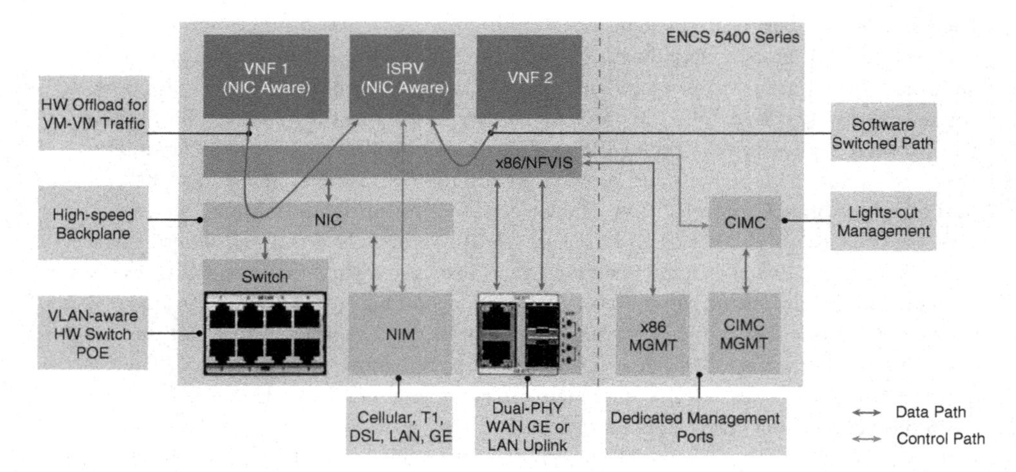

Figure 18-4 *Cisco ENCS Building Blocks by Example of the Cisco ENCS 5400*

The hardware provides various physical interfaces:

- A console port.
- A Cisco Integrated Management Controller (CIMC) port for lights-out management. CIMC provides access to boot-level functions, allowing configuration of the hardware below the operating system layer, as well as associated monitoring.
- A management port providing direct access to the NFVIS operating system.
- Up to four Ethernet uplink ports (WAN or LAN), two of which are RJ-45 based and two of which are small form-factor pluggable (SFP) based.
- Up to eight Ethernet LAN ports connected to a physical integrated switch
- A single NIM slot for connectivity other than Ethernet

The NIM slots in the Cisco ENCS deserve particular attention: they allow you to connect the Cisco ENCS to the WAN using standard Cisco NIM modules, such as the 3G/4G NIM or the T1/E1 NIM. Although the Cisco ENCS is fundamentally an x86-based host, it still satisfies non-Ethernet WAN interfaces. This makes the Cisco ENCS particularly useful for branches that still have non-Ethernet WAN interfaces provisioned, or if media diversity is required for uplink redundancy. Note that the NIM slot is controlled by the Cisco ISRv directly. The driver software for the NIM interfaces is embedded in the Cisco ISRv routing VNF, not in the Cisco NFVIS software. This implies that the NIMs can only be leveraged in conjunction with the deployment of a Cisco ISRv VNF.

Figure 18-4 also shows the built-in network interface card (NIC) in the Cisco ENCS. This NIC provides a built-in, high-speed backplane to which all VNFs and application workloads can be connected. The NIC supports single-root I/O virtualization (SR-IOV, discussed in Chapter 10), and offers a hardware-assisted path to pass traffic between VNFs. For example, if traffic needs to traverse two or more VNFs with SR-IOV support, the NIC is provisioned to forward the packets in hardware instead of utilizing NFVIS for software-based service chaining. Such a hardware-based VNF-to-VNF path does not use the x86 cores for switching. With SR-IOV-supported VNFs, the available x86-based compute resources are dedicated to VNF processing, rather than having to spend CPU cycles for software switching. In other words, the built-in NIC gives you greater deployment flexibility not only by offering a faster hardware-assisted service chaining path, but also by providing the ability to deploy *more* VNFs onto the host.

The integrated switch is controlled by the NFVIS Linux operating system. It thus offers standard functionality that you may expect at this level, such as specifying the hardware configuration (RAID, boot order, BIOS settings), monitoring and troubleshooting at the hardware layer, power-cycling the platform, or performing disaster recovery. The physical switch is not governed by IOS XE (e.g., by the ISRv directly) and thus does not provide extended switching functionality that is common in physical IOS XE–based switches (e.g., the Cisco Catalyst 9000 Series switches).

NFVIS: An Operating System Optimized for Enterprise Virtualization

The second major building block in the Cisco ENFV solution stack is the operating system for the various x86-based hosts. Cisco Network Functions Virtualization Infrastructure Software (NFVIS) is based on a standard Linux operating system with Kernel-based Virtual Machine (KVM). KVM extends Linux to VMs to run with unmodified operating systems (i.e., KVM is an example of a type-2 hypervisor). KVM offers core virtualization infrastructure to present the VMs with virtual CPU, virtual memory, virtual storage, or virtual interfaces. Each VM is associated with private virtualized hardware—network cards, disks, or even graphics adapters. Linux with KVM also includes Quick Emulator (QEMU), Libvirt, and other associated processes.

Particularly noteworthy is the additional software switching capability that KVM offers to the solution. The Open vSwitch (OVS) that is part of the Linux KVM environment provides connectivity for the VNFs to the underlying physical interfaces or to each other. OVS is the default switching path in all NFVIS-based systems if SR-IOV is not supported. For example, if physical interface models in Cisco UCS-C servers or if the VNFs do not support SR-IOV, packets are switched using OVS. This is illustrated in Figure 18-4 as the "Software switched path."

Virtualizing the underlying host resources using KVM, however, is not sufficient to optimize the virtualization of network functions. To optimize your experience for the branch virtualization use case targeted by ENFV, NFVIS offers additional functions such as:

- **Zero-Touch Provisioning (ZTP):** Imagine you want to virtualize all the branches in your enterprise network—possibly ranging in the hundreds or even thousands. The ZTP functionality embedded into NFVIS allows an NFVIS-based system (Unified Compute System UCS E-Series, Unified Compute System UCS C-Series, ENCS) to automatically call home to a plug-and-play server to complete its bootup process and obtain site-specific configurations. Upon completion of the power-on sequence, the NFVIS-based system boots a minimal configuration that has the necessary Plug and Play (PnP) details to find the PnP server. The PnP server information is either statically configured, learned via DHCP Option 43 through the DHCP process, obtained via DNS, or default to a cloud-based redirection tool from Cisco. The NFVIS-based host then establishes a highly secure connection to the PnP server, authenticating against credentials based on the device's hardware serial number. This prevents rogue devices from automatically connecting to your network. The orchestration system (Cisco DNA Center) then provides further device configurations for the x86-based host, or even instantiates the actual VNFs that are associated with the site by association with the host's serial number.

- **Lifecycle management and VNF health monitoring:** VNF lifecycle management functions are essential for the use case of branch virtualization. This capability in NFVIS allows for the automatic instantiation and ongoing monitoring of the VNFs in your branch. The NFVIS Lifecycle Manager (LCM) loads VNFs based on the profile that is associated with the host. It subsequently monitors the liveliness of each instantiated VNF as well as the communication path (service chain). In case of failures, it attempts to stop and restart (reboot) the affected VNFs, or performs additional remedial actions such as raising syslog alarms. The lifecycle management functionality can also be leveraged to insert additional VNFs into the service chain as part of a day N operations change.

  The LCM functionality in NFVIS is fully automated based on REST API calls from the Cisco DNA Center orchestration system.

- **Service chaining:** One of the key benefits of branch virtualization is that multiple network functions are collapsed inside a single x86-based host in VNF form factors. This of course implies that the traffic is steered within the system through these various VNFs—i.e., traffic is associated with a service chain. NFVIS instantiates the desired service chains based on the profile that is designed for the system at the orchestration and management layer.

  The service chaining functionality within NFVIS currently leverages bridges. Traffic is forced to traverse a number of VNFs in sequence by association of the interfaces with different bridges. Further details are provided a bit later in the section "Service Chaining and Sample Packet Flows."

- **Open APIs:** Many of the operations previously outlined are assumed to be driven from a centralized management and operations system—Cisco DNA Center. The overall ENFV solution is integrated based on open APIs. At the host layer, NFVIS exposes APIs for all the functions previously outlined, supported by the associated API transport mechanisms. The NFVIS APIs are called from northbound systems (such as Cisco DNA Center) via REST or NETCONF. APIs are offered to register VNF images, deploy VNFs, start and stop VNFs, create and manage software bridges, monitor host resources (CPU, memory, storage, I/O), log details, manage users, manage the NFVIS configuration, etc. Full details about the NFVIS APIs are available in the *API Reference for Cisco Enterprise Network Functions Virtualization Infrastructure Software.*[3]

3 https://www.cisco.com/c/en/us/td/docs/routers/nfvis/user_guide/b-api-reference-for-cisco-enterprise-nfvis/b-api-reference-for-cisco-enterprise-nfvis_chapter_00.html

- **Web server:** NFVIS also has an embedded web server to allow connectivity to a particular NFVIS host through HTTP Secure (HTTPS). This is particularly useful if you want to manage a system through a local management tool or locally through APIs.
- **Device management:** NFVIS packages tools in support of x86 management (for example, a resource manager).
- **Statistics:** Statistics collection in NFVIS is also enhanced above the standard Linux functionality. Tools like syslogd, snmpd, and collectd assist in statistics collection and reporting.

A final noteworthy point that differentiates NFVIS from a standard Linux operating system concerns security. NFVIS supports secure boot to authenticate, for example, an ENCS system using the secure unique device identifier (SUDI).

Figure 18-5 illustrates the key functional building blocks of NFVIS, and highlights the additional functionality above and beyond the standard Linux OS.

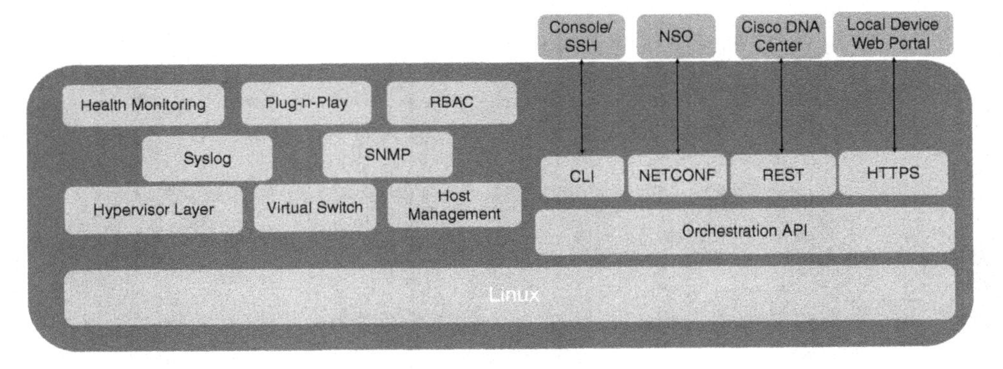

Figure 18-5 *Cisco NFVIS Functional Building Blocks*

After booting, NFVIS automatically sets up an internal network infrastructure to prepare the system for communication between its different components. The virtual software switching path is used for this purpose to create a bridge and a VLAN for the WAN ports (WAN-br and WAN net respectively), for the LAN ports (LAN-br, LAN net), and for the internal management network (Mgmt-br, Mgmt net). The latter is particularly critical to subsequently monitor the VNFs from NFVIS. This management network is not intended for exterior reachability of the VNFs—it is for internal NFVIS monitoring only. External reachability of instantiated VNFs is provided via port forwarding of one of the host's IP address (NFVIS Management IP or WAN IP). Figure 18-6 illustrates the internal networking connectivity for the Cisco ENCS 5400 Series.

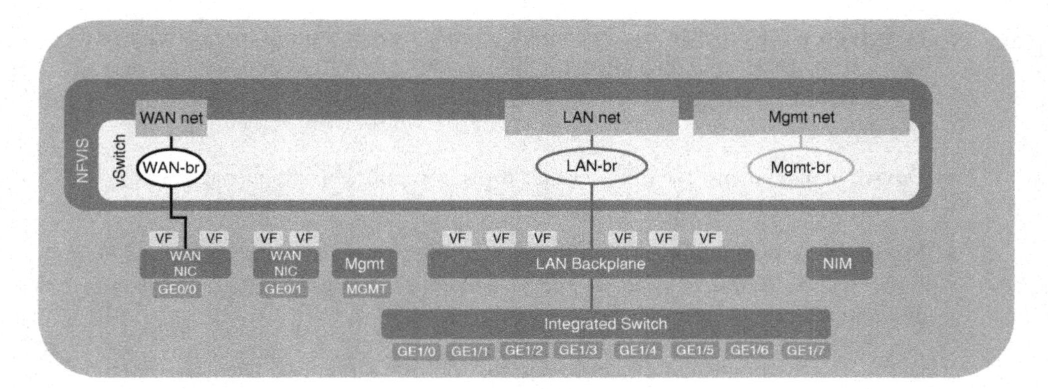

Figure 18-6 *Default Internal Network Connectivity for the ENCS 5400 Series*

Figure 18-7 shows the corresponding default network setup for the UCS E-Series blade. Note that in this case an internal NIC connects the blade to the ISR 4000 Series host. This internal NIC has two configurable internal Gigabit Ethernet (GE) interfaces. The single GE0 is connected to the WAN ports of the ISR 4000 Series host using the default NFVIS-controlled WAN bridge. The single GE1 connects to the ISR 4000 Series LAN ports. The NFVIS-created LAN bridge connects the local physical ports on the UCS E-Series blade (GE2 and higher) to the internal LAN GE (GE1), allowing traffic to reach the VNFs through either the local UCS E-Series ports or through the ISR 4000 Series LAN ports.

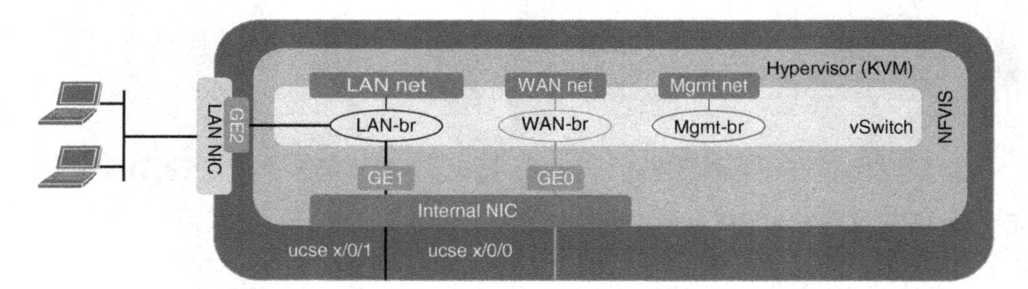

Figure 18-7 *Default Internal Network Connectivity for the UCS E-Series*

NFVIS consumes one of the x86-based hosts CPU cores, as well as 2 GB of RAM and 10 GB of storage. Take this into account when deciding on which hardware platform to use. A four-core ENCS 5104 has three cores available for VNF onboarding, sufficient for one instance of Cisco ISRv plus an additional one-vCPU VNF or application workload of your choice. The Cisco 5412, on the other hand, has 12 physical cores available, leaving you more flexibility to onboard a variety of VNFs. More details on NFVIS are available in the *Cisco Enterprise Network Functions Virtualization Infrastructure Software Configuration Guide*.[4]

4 https://www.cisco.com/c/en/us/td/docs/routers/nfvis/user_guide/nfvis-config-guide/nfvis-user-guide_chapter_0110.html

Virtualized Network Functions

The third major building block in the Cisco ENFV solution are the VNFs and application workloads. The solution accommodates any commercially available VNF, such as the Cisco Integrated Services Virtual Router (ISRv), Cisco Adaptive Security Virtual Appliance (ASAv), Cisco Firepower Threat Defense Virtual (FTDv), and Cisco Virtual Wide Area Application Services (vWAAS). VNFs from third-party vendors can also be onboarded and chained into a service. Similarly, because NFVIS is based on a standard Linux OS with KVM, any application workload can also be hosted on an NFVIS-based system. This is particularly useful if you want to run some application workloads locally in your branch, such as Cisco Unified Survivable Remote Site Telephony (SRST), print servers, packet generators, etc.

Cisco Integrated Services Virtual Router

The dominant network function in any branch environment is routing for connectivity to the WAN. Here, the Cisco ISRv provides the same functionality as physical IOS XE–based routing platforms (ISR 4000 Series, ASR 1000 Series). The Cisco ISRv leverages the same IOS XE software architecture, just in a virtualized form factor. You can therefore leverage all of the extensive routing features, such as Open Shortest Path First (OSPF), Enhanced Interior Gateway Protocol (EIGRP), Intermediate System to Intermediate System (IS-IS), and Border Gateway Protocol (BGP), quality of service (QoS) mechanisms, security functionality (ACLs), encryption (IPsec-based VPNs), or even features such as zone-based firewalls, network address translation (NAT), and deep packet inspection (Cisco Application Visibility and Control [AVC]). IOS XE has over 3000 features, so it is truly a Swiss Army knife for networking, and with the Cisco ISRv also in a virtual form factor.

The ISRv is available in different form factors to accommodate varying resource and throughput requirements.[5] Two-vCPU and four-vCPU versions are available, typically consuming two and four physical CPU cores respectively,[6] allowing for throughputs up to 1 Gbps of forwarding. Of course, this throughput is dependent on feature configuration, but is more than sufficient for most of today's branch use cases. Cisco ISRv throughput is licensed in different throughput limits; 50 Mbps, 100 Mbps, 250 Mbps, and 1 Gbps licenses are available. The license is enforced inside the VNF by means of an egress shaper. The aggregate egress bandwidth leaving the Cisco ISRv VM out of *any* port is monitored, and shaped to the licensed bandwidth limit.

---

5 Cisco Integrated Services Virtual Router Data Sheet, https://www.cisco.com/c/en/us/solutions/collateral/enterprise-networks/enterprise-network-functions-virtualization-nfv/datasheet-c78-736768.html

6 Hyperthreading is not recommended in ENFV, hence the virtual CPU requirement directly correlates to physical CPU cores.

Cisco Adaptive Security Virtual Appliance

The Cisco ASAv offers virtual firewall capabilities for branch deployments. Again, the software is carrying forward the functionality from the corresponding hardware-based appliance. With the exception of clustering and multicontext support, all of the stateful firewall inspection capabilities are available inside a Cisco ASAv virtual machine. Examples are flow- or connection-based inspections, high-speed NAT support, unicast and multicast routing (including IPv6), Authentication Authorization, and Accounting (AAA) functionality, Cisco TrustSec, mobile network inspection (Diameter, Stream Control Transmission Protocol [SCTP], GPRS Tunneling Protocol [GTPv2]), remote-access VPNs, etc.

The Cisco ASAv also comes in various footprints. At the low end, one vCPU and 1 GB of RAM are required to deliver up to 100 Mbps of forwarding. The one-vCPU/2-GB Cisco ASAv10 and four-vCPU/8-GB Cisco ASAv30 offer intermediary footprints for throughputs of up to 1 Gbps and 2 Gbps respectively. At the high end, the Cisco ASAv50 forwards up to 10 Gbps of traffic, requiring eight vCPUs and 16 GB of RAM.

For further details on the Cisco ASAv, see, for example, the ASAv data sheet.[7]

Cisco Firepower NGFW Virtual

The Cisco Firepower NGFW Virtual (NGFWv) extends the firewall capabilities of the Cisco ASAv to also offer a stateful next-generation firewall, supporting IPS/IDS capabilities. URL Filtering, Cisco Advanced Malware Protection (AMP), and Cisco Application Visibility and Control (AVC) are some of the key capabilities that NGFWv offers above and beyond the standard firewall functions. Network traffic is inspected with content awareness (files and file types) and correlated with context, such as user or applications, to detect malware or other intrusions.

The Cisco NGFWv is available in a four-vCPU footprint requiring 8 GB of RAM and 50 GB of disk space.

As you might expect, the functionality is also aligned with the corresponding physical appliance to allow you to seamlessly choose between a virtual or physical deployment.

Further details on the Cisco NGFWv are available in the Cisco Firepower NGFW data sheet.[8]

Cisco Virtual Wide Area Application Services

The next VNF that is popular in branch deployments is the WAN optimization function provided by Cisco vWAAS VNF. Cisco vWAAS offers WAN acceleration techniques such

---

7 https://www.cisco.com/c/en/us/products/collateral/security/adaptive-security-virtual-appliance-asav/datasheet-c78-733399.html

8 https://www.cisco.com/c/en/us/products/collateral/security/firepower-ngfw/datasheet-c78-736661.pdf

as TCP flow optimization, data redundancy elimination (DRE) and caching, and payload compression.

Cisco vWAAS is offered in multiple models with different vCPU, RAM, and storage requirements. For example, Cisco vWAAS-750 requires two vCPUs, 4 GB of RAM, and 250 GB of storage for up to 8 Mbps of WAN bandwidth; Cisco vWAAS-6000 requires four vCPUs, 8 GB of RAM, and 500 GB of storage for up to 90 Mbps of WAN bandwidth; and Cisco vWAAS-12000 requires four vCPUs, 12 GB or RAM, and 750 GB of storage to deliver up to 310 Mbps of WAN bandwidth.

Additional technical details on Cisco vWAAS are provided at Cisco.com.[9]

Cisco Prime Virtual Network Analysis Module

The Cisco Prime Virtual Network Analysis Module (vNAM) is another type of VNF that proves beneficial in a virtualized branch deployment. It allows you to inspect traffic and gain Layer 4 through Layer 7 visibility into traffic flows. It provides detailed information and visibility on how applications in your branch are performing. Cisco vNAM leverages the Network-based Application Recognition (NBAR) engine to identify applications and obtain specific statistics. Cisco vNAM provides capabilities to view short- and long-term network usage on a per-application, per-host, per-conversation basis. It integrates with Cisco TrustSec to learn about user and application groups. In combination with Cisco vWAAS, a vNAM VNF demonstrates the effectiveness of the WAN optimization functionality.

The Cisco vNAM VNF requires two vCPUs, 3 GB of RAM, and 100 GB of disk space.

The Cisco vNAM data sheet offers additional technical details.[10]

Cisco Virtual Wireless LAN Controller

Virtualizing the Wireless LAN Controller (WLC) in a branch environment is another popular candidate of VNFs in the Cisco branch virtualization solution. For deployments that today see a redundant pair of physical WLCs at a branch, virtualization of the WLC function may reduce overall costs for licensing and operation of appliances.

The Cisco Virtual Wireless LAN Controller (vWLC) provides functional consistency with the physical WLC appliance. It offers control, management, and troubleshooting capabilities for wireless access points, supporting the Cisco FlexConnect solution. Management of the radio frequencies (RF) is one of its important capabilities. Additional functions of the Cisco vWLC include securing the Configuration and Provisioning of Wireless Access Points (CAPWAP) tunnel between the AP and the vWLC, supporting voice communications, or allowing for fault tolerance to a backup controller.

---

9 Cisco Virtual WAAS Technical Overview, https://www.cisco.com/c/en/us/td/docs/app_ntwk_services/waas/vwaas/vwaas-623/vwaas-install-config/v-intro.html

10 https://www.cisco.com/c/en/us/products/collateral/cloud-systems-management/prime-virtual-network-analysis-module-vnam/data_sheet_c78-723214.html

The Cisco vWLC comes in two form factors: the small version requires one vCPU, 2 GB of RAM, and 8 GB of disk space. This version scales to 200 access points and up to 6000 clients. The large version increases the scale to 3000 access points and 32,000 clients, and consumes two vCPUs, 8 GB of RAM, and also 8 GB of disk space.

Further details on the Cisco vWLC are found in its data sheet.[11]

Note that a key advantage of maintaining the same software architecture between physical networking appliances and their virtualized counterparts previously mentioned is operational consistency. Once you have instantiated a Cisco ISRv, ASAv, NGFWv, vWAAS, or vWLC features are configured in exactly the same manner as on the physical platforms. This also makes the VNFs easily integrated into any existing backend management system. After the VNFs are reachable via IP, any logging, statistics collection, and troubleshooting procedures remain the same. This facilitates the introduction of Cisco ENFV into your existing enterprise environment. Remember that it should not matter whether a network function is deployed in a physical appliance or virtually. This should be *your* choice based on the architectural and business requirements.

Third-party VNF Support

The Cisco VNFs covered thus far are currently at the top of network functions deployed in a branch, but they are by no means the only candidates! After all, the key benefit of virtualization in the branch is that it gives *you* as the network architect or operator the flexibility to deploy any VNF or even application workload...provided it is supported under a Linux KVM environment! The Cisco ENFV solution stack is fully supportive of this principle. It has been designed from the ground up to run third-party VNFs or application workloads on top of Cisco NFVIS.

Support for third-party VNFs comes in two forms. First, the requirements that any VNF has to fulfill to be compliant with the NFVIS OS are well documented and specified. Just as you have OS requirements to run applications on a Microsoft Windows or an Apple iOS system, the NFVIS VNF Specification[12] describes the details for third-party VNFs. For example, it requires compliance with the NFVIS's Linux and KVM versions, chipset support, and API or OVS version numbers. Table 18-3 provides insight into the basic OS requirements that third-party VNFs need to be compliant with.

11 https://www.cisco.com/c/en/us/products/collateral/wireless/virtual-wireless-controller/data_sheet_c78-714543.html

12 https://developer.cisco.com/site/nfv/#the-ecosystem-program

Table 18-3 *Cisco NFVIS Requirements for VNFs*

Requirement Category	Requirement
Max vCPU per VNF	NFVIS: Function: ((Number of platform physical cores – 1) × 2) Explanation: NFVIS requires one core. CSP-2100: MaxBMvCPU = (number of physical cores) – 1 Hyperthreading is disabled on CSP-2100.
Minimum number of vCPUs	1
Maximum vMemory allowed per VNF	NFVIS: Function: MaxVNFvMem = Physical memory – 2 GB Explanation: NFVIS needs 2 GB of RAM. CSP-2100: MaxVMvMem = Physical memory – 4 GB Explanation: CSP 2100 needs 4 GB of RAM.
Maximum vHDD	NFVIS: Function: MaxVNFvHDD = Available-SSD/HDD – 15 GB Explanation: NFVIS needs disk to store images, logs, etc. CSP-2100: CSP 2100 Function: MaxVMvHDD = Available-SSD/HDD – 16 GB Explanation: CSP 2100 needs disk to store images, logs, etc.
Storage controller supported	VirtIO 1.0 or IDE
Maximum disk size volume per VNF	NFVIS: Function: Available SSD/HDD – 15 GB CSP-2100: Hardware needs to be RHEL 7.3 certified.
Hyperthreading	On/Allowed
Chipset support	Hardware needs to be CentOS 7.2 certified.
64-bit hardware	Required
Hypervisor support	NFVIS: KVM CentOS 7.2 CSP-2100: KVM RHEL 7.3
Virtualization	NFVIS: Libvirt 1.2.8 or higher CSP-2100: Libvirt 2.0.0 or higher
API	QEMU 1.5.3 or higher
vSwitch	NFVIS: OVS 2.3.2 or higher CSP-2100: OVS 2.4.0 or higher

A VNF manifest file in XML format can be accommodated to inform the Cisco NFVIS about all the files in a third-party VNF package: VNF properties file, image files, or one or more bootstrap files. The VNF properties file is also in XML format, and describes the type of VNF (router, firewall, etc.), name, version, disk-bus types, and root disk image format, among other properties. Perhaps most importantly, the VNFs resource requirements in terms of minimum and maximum number of vCPUs required, memory requirements, support for SR-IOV, bootstrap configurations, etc. can also be itemized in this file.

The second form of support for third-party VNFs and application workloads is provided through the Cisco NFV Open Ecosystem. This is a certification program for partners and interested parties to certify interoperability of candidate VNFs with Cisco NFVIS. Third-party VNFs can be qualified by a partner following the NFVIS VNF Test plan.[13] This test plan offers a workflow to test the loading of a candidate VNF into the NFVIS image repository, file format compliance and packaging, interface onboarding, VNF boot, management connectivity, software upgrades, etc.

Service Chaining and Sample Packet Flows

Spinning up network functions in virtual machines to replace physical network appliances is only half of the story in Network Functions Virtualization. The other half is how to connect VNFs with each other—in other words, how to "internalize" the physical connectivity that used to exist between the hardware-based network elements inside an x86-based host. This topic is often captured under the label "service chaining."

In a purely physical network architecture, you establish connectivity between devices using cables (typically Ethernet) within a branch. You also set up the corresponding Layer 2 and Layer 3 configurations to steer user traffic to the desired devices and to enable connectivity at both of these respective layers.

As multiple VNFs are hosted on the same x86-based system, physical connectivity between them may no longer be required. The hypervisor environment on top of which the VNFs are riding provides a *virtual* switching capability, as discussed in Chapter 10. And the Layer 2 connectivity between VNFs is now configured at the hypervisor layer by means of virtual bridges and virtual networks. Virtual bridges create a Layer 2 domain between the virtual NICs of the VNFs. The vNICs are associated with a range of MAC addresses. Virtual networks inside the host specify a Layer 2 segment that is typically associated with VLAN range.

Figure 18-8 shows the default internal connectivity of an NFVIS host by example of a Cisco ENCS. The physical WAN interfaces of the host are connected by default to a virtual WAN bridge, leveraging the virtual switch of the KVM hypervisor. Associated with this bridge is also a network (wan-net). Both the WAN bridge and the WAN network have DHCP enabled by default. Also, the Gigabit Ethernet interface GE0/0 is by default associated with the WAN bridge.

The physical LAN interfaces are also connected to a virtual bridge (lan-br) and an associated VLAN network. Note that all of the physical LAN interfaces that are exposed on the front panel of the ENCS share the same bridge.

13 https://pubhub.devnetcloud.com/media/nfv/docs/ThirdPartyNFVEcosystemCertificationTestPlanv1_6.pdf

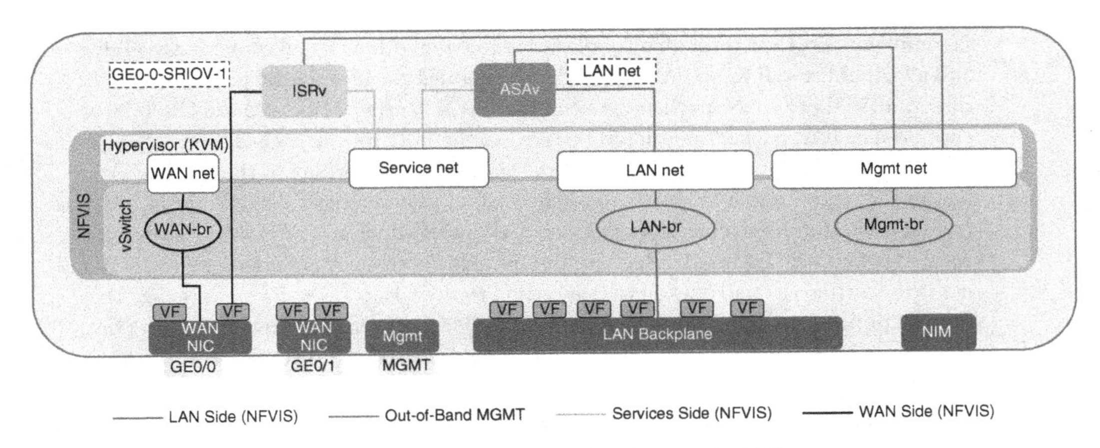

Figure 18-8 *Default Internal Network Connectivity for an ENCS System*

VNFs are by default connecting to one (or both in case of a single VNF in the system) of these internal bridges to receive traffic from the physical interfaces. In the virtual branch use case described herein, a virtual router typically receives traffic from the WAN interfaces via the virtual WAN bridge. Alternatively, if the virtual router instance supports SR-IOV, a direct virtual Peripheral Component Interconnect Express (PCIe) connection can be established to the SR-IOV virtual function (VF), bypassing the KVM hypervisor for virtual switching. Recall that SR-IOV relieves the hypervisor from having to switch packets in software between the physical interface and a virtual interface of a VNF. However, this technology requires support both of the physical interface (which is a given in Cisco ENCS, for example) and of the particular virtual routing VNF (such as the Cisco ISRv).

Traffic from the physical LAN interface is typically connected to one of the L4–L7 VNFs using the LAN bridge. (If the virtual router is the only VNF hosted on the system, it may be connected to *both* the physical LAN and WAN interfaces via the virtualized LAN and WAN bridges.) The "trick" in a virtualized system architecture is to leverage virtual bridges and virtual networks to now steer traffic between the desired VNFs. To this end, one or more bridges are created in the switch with their associated VLAN networks, as illustrated in Figure 18-8. Anchoring VNFs in different VLAN networks (and their associated bridges) then forces traffic to traverse the various VNFs in the desired order for processing.

Figure 18-8 also illustrates an internal management bridge. This bridge is created by default in NFVIS to allow the ongoing monitoring of the instantiated VNFs. It is not accessible from the outside. The physical management port shown in Figure 18-8 represents the connectivity to the NFVIS host itself, which is used to access and mange NFVIS. The physical CIMC and console ports for ENCS are not represented in the figure.

A sample packet flow through a simple service chain with a virtual router (Cisco ISRv) and a virtual firewall (Cisco ASAv) is illustrated in Figure 18-9. In the packet flow direction WAN to LAN, packets arrive in the WAN interface. Because the Cisco ISRv supports SR-IOV, packets are directly passed to the ISRv for processing. The VNF internal ISRv configuration manipulates the traffic flow according to the configured features (e.g., routing, QoS, NAT, etc.). The Cisco ISRv then has a virtual interface that is connected to the service network (service-net) out of which traffic is then forcibly forwarded toward the LAN side. Because the only downstream VNF connected to service-net is the virtual firewall, packets are switched to the Cisco ASAv for processing. The firewall policies configured in the ASAv are applied to the traffic flow. Again, the firewall VNF has a VLAN network configuration that forces traffic to egress toward lan-net, and thus ultimately allows packets to egress the ENCS system on a physical LAN port.

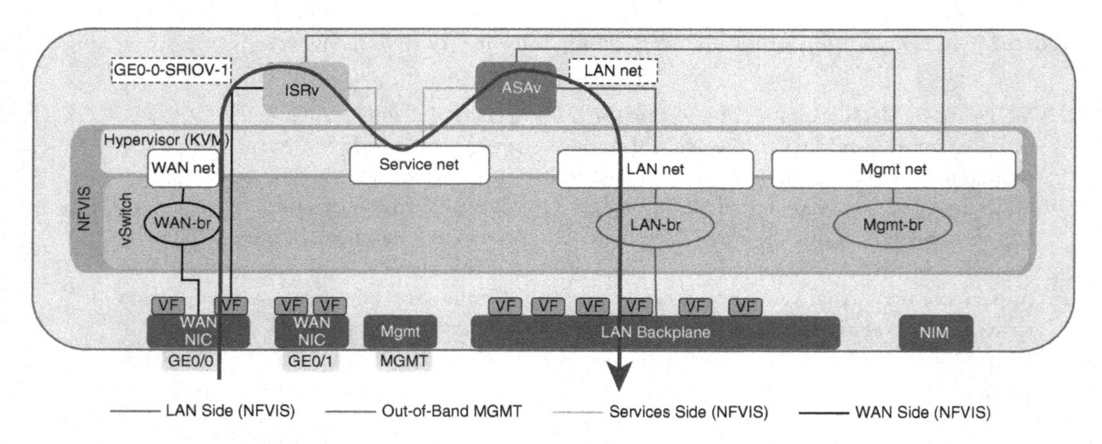

Figure 18-9 *Sample Packet Flow with a Two-VNF Service Chain*

In this configuration, the fact that each VNF is anchored in different VLAN networks and that each VLAN connects "only" two VNFs creates a service chain.

A slightly more complex example is shown in Figure 18-10. In this case, a virtual WAN optimization VNF in the form of Cisco vWAAS is also instantiated. Cisco vWAAS cooperates with the Cisco ISRv by means of an efficient protocol (AppNav) to optimize WAN traffic. The Cisco ISRv performs the redirection function for traffic, allowing for application of redirection filters. The Cisco vWAAS VNF performs WAN optimization on the traffic flows, including Transmission Control Protocol (TCP) flow control optimizations, caching, and data redundancy elimination. The AppNav control protocol running between Cisco vWAAS and the Cisco ISRv communicates the state of the WAN optimization engine to the ISRv, such as session state and configured WAN optimization services that are applied by a particular vWAAS instance. This tight, optimized coupling between the Cisco ISRv and Cisco vWAAS affects the packet flow. In the packet flow direction WAN to LAN, packets arrive from the WAN interface at the Cisco ISRv. The Cisco ISRv by its AppNav configuration filters traffic to be redirected to Cisco vWAAS.

Traffic is optimized by Cisco vWAAS, returned to the Cisco ISRv, and forwarded to the virtual firewall (ASAv). In the return direction, traffic from the LAN interface is first processed by the Cisco ASAv in the example. From there, packets are forwarded to the Cisco ISRv, where the AppNav filter and redirection are once again determining which flows need to be optimized by the Cisco vWAAS VNF. Note that the service VLAN network (and its associated bridge) provides connectivity between all three of these VNFs. The service chain in this case is enforced by a combination of the AppNav protocol and the configured VLANs.

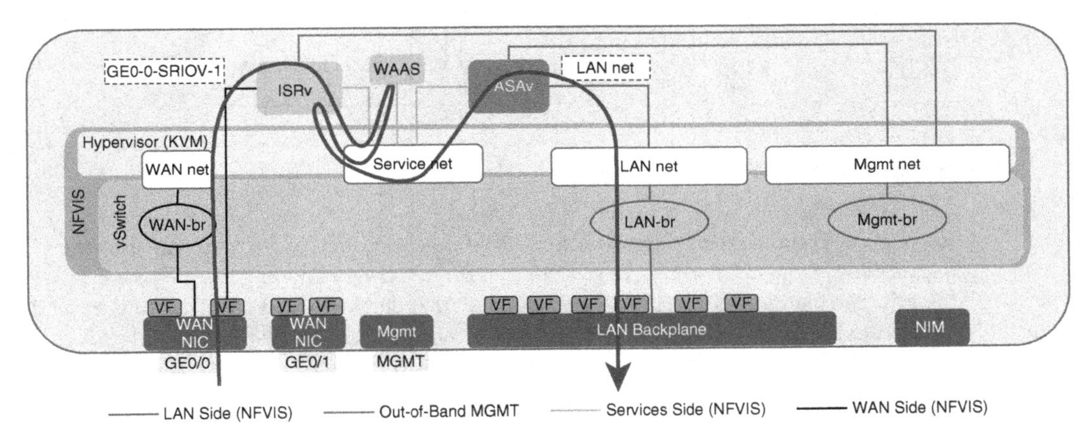

Figure 18-10 *Sample Packet Flow with a Three-VNF Service Chain with WAAS and AppNav*

Transparent Versus Routed Service Chains

A further distinction in service chaining can be made based on the configuration of the participating VNFs. The two options are

- Routed service chains
- Transparent service chains

In a routed service chain, each VNF in the chain has its own IP address, and the VNFs may use IP routing to direct traffic toward the next VNF in the chain. This is also the case when VNFs are addressed directly by the clients or server endpoints—that is, when the VNF becomes the actual destination of a traffic flow. Consider for example a Wireless LAN Controller (WLC) running in a virtual machine. In this case, the access points communicate with the vWLC directly via IP. Access points learn the IP address of the vWLC via the usual mechanism, Address Resolution Protocol (ARP), and subsequently send packets with that address as the destination IP. This is illustrated in Figure 18-11.

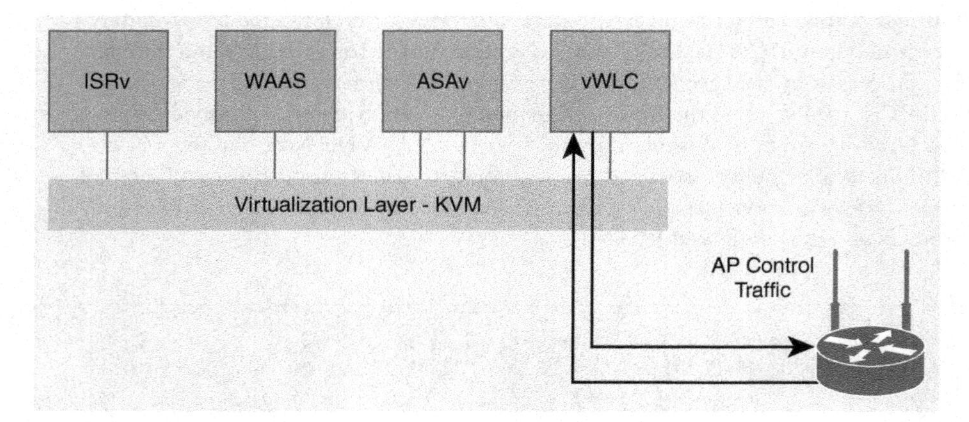

Figure 18-11 *Routed Service Chain*

In contrast, in transparent (inline) mode, VNFs are configured to be transparent to the packet flows from an IP perspective. The clients and servers do not generate packets directly destined to a VNF. The VNF is not the final destination of a traffic flow. Instead, VNFs provide a network function that operates on the packet flow transparently to the client and the server. When a client or a server is trying to reach an IP address on the opposite side of such a VNF, packets flow through this VNF transparently. Even operations like ARP broadcasts are forwarded through the VNF so that another device can respond to the ARP requests. Clients are not required to know about the presence of a VNF, and thus do not require specific configurations. Figure 18-12 illustrates an example of a virtual Cisco ASAv firewall. Direct Internet access (DIA) traffic must pass through a firewall before it is forwarded. The Cisco ASAv is configured in transparent mode, eliminating the need of the source or the destination to know about its existence. Traffic is nonetheless forced through the virtual firewall by the service chain architecture, albeit unbeknown to the endpoints.

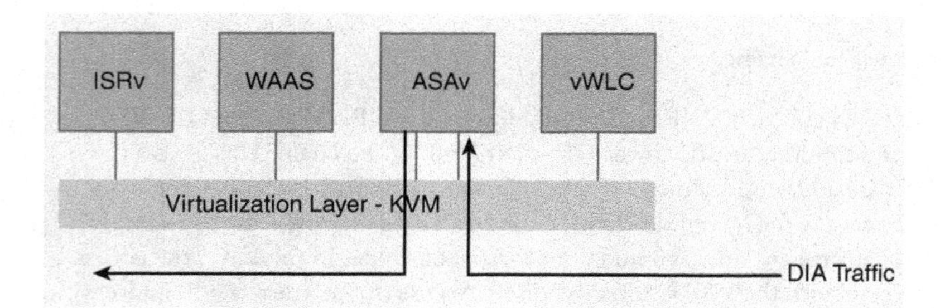

Figure 18-12 *Transparent Service Chain*

Orchestration and Management

Virtualizing the branch infrastructure presents a different orchestration and management situation to you as an operator: functions that were dedicated to a particular hardware appliance now are running in a virtual machine, and multiple of such virtual machines share the same underlying hardware resources, potentially impacting each other.

First, from an orchestration and automation perspective, you therefore need to deploy a *generic* x86-based host for VNFs—in all of your (possibly thousands) branch locations. In contrast to standard data-center x86-based workload hosts, the NFV server platform may be configured to optimize the execution of *network functions*, rather than application workloads. Monitoring functions of generic x86-based hosts may also be new to your organizational unit to understand the behavior of the hosts as it processes multiple VNFs. For the Cisco ENFV solution, the options for automating and orchestrating an NFVIS-based server are as follows:

- Device level (individual system)
  - Web-based graphical user interface for an individual NFVIS system
  - Traditional mechanisms (command-line interface, APIs)
- Network level (multiple systems)
  - Centralized network-wide automation based on Cisco DNA Center

Second, once you have the VNFs instantiated, you need to configure, monitor, and manage them. Luckily, in most cases the fact that many VNFs are derived from their physical brethren implies that the same (or very similar) orchestration and management tools and procedures apply. For example, for Cisco vWAAS VNF or the NGFWv VNF, the WAAS Central Manager (WCM) or the Firepower Management Center (FMC) is leveraged, respectively, to also help you manage already instantiated VNFs. Also, traditional monitoring mechanisms like SNMP, NetFlow, CLI **show** commands, or Embedded Event Manager (EEM) scripts can also be leveraged if supported by the particular VNF.

The remainder of this section focuses on the NFVIS host management and monitoring options in the Cisco ENFV solution.

NFVIS GUI (Per System)

Let's start with the operator portal provided with NFVIS and illustrate various samples of operations that you can perform on a particular system. Recall from the functional overview of NFVIS that one of the components added on top of the standard Linux (with a KVM hypervisor) environment is a web server. This capability is leveraged in Cisco ENFV to allow you to manage and monitor an NFVIS-based host locally. Figure 18-13 shows the initial landing screen (Home) when you log into the NFVIS host using a standard browser.

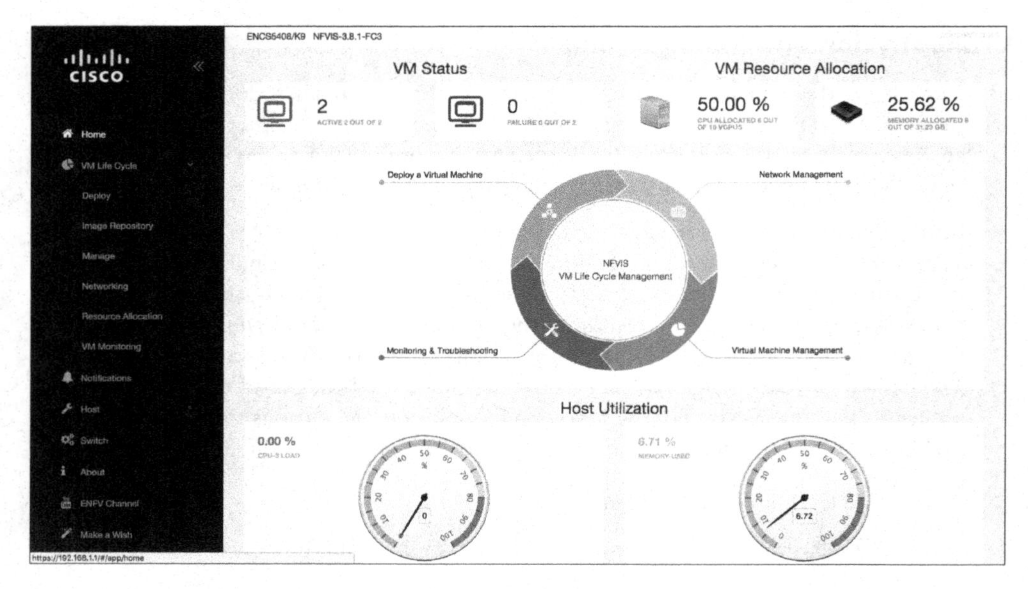

Figure 18-13 *NFVIS Local Management Portal Landing Screen*

The Home screen provides information on the main state of the host, such as the number of active VNFs, failure summaries, and resource utilizations for the CPU cores and memory. The circle in the center of the landing screen represents the workflow lifecycle to allow you to drill into various actions: deploying a VNF on the local system, managing the network interfaces and internal software switches, managing virtual machines, or performing monitoring and troubleshooting activities.

These respective workflows are also accessible from the menu on the left of the landing page. You are presented with options to perform virtual machine lifecycle management, monitor notifications, configure and diagnose the x86-based host, observe and configure the internal switch settings, display information about the NFVIS system itself, or access the help videos (ENFV channel).

One of the important actions you may want to perform on the NFVIS host is to deploy a virtual machine. To do so, expand the VM Life Cycle menu on the left and choose the Deploy option. The VM Deployment screen, shown in Figure 18-14, allows you to see the existing VNFs deployed on the system on a canvas, as well as a list of VNF images that are registered with the host. Dragging and dropping a registered VNF type from the top onto the canvas allows you to trigger the instantiation of an additional VNF on the system. You can also manipulate the internal network settings by dropping a network onto the canvas and graphically controlling the connections to the instantiated VNFs.

Note that the VNF of type OTHER allows you to deploy a generic workload VM (e.g., Linux or Windows).

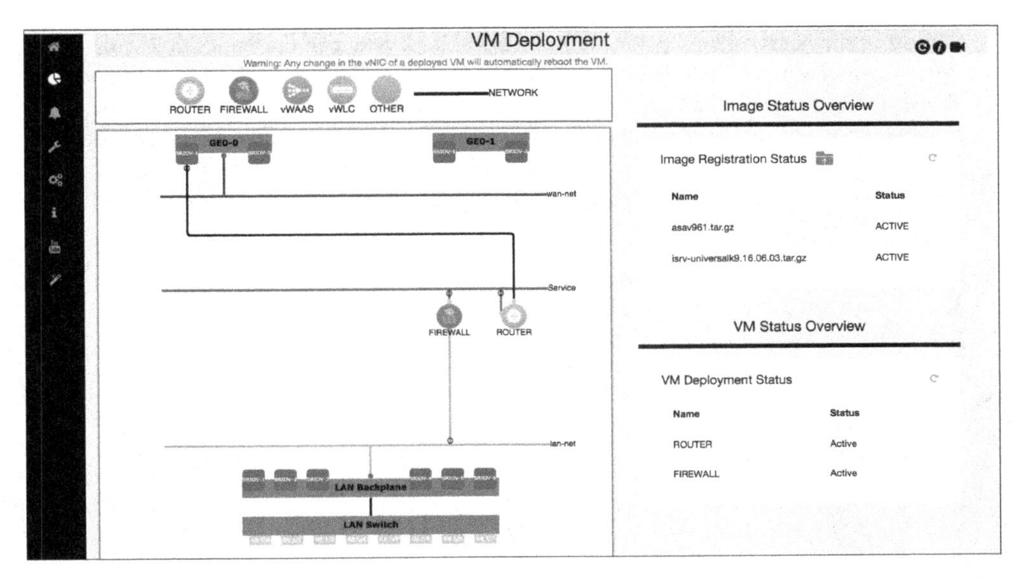

Figure 18-14 *NFVIS GUI: VNF Deployment Canvas*

Choosing Image Repository from the VM Life Cycle menu allows you to register different VNF types in the system, such as different virtual routers, firewalls, WAN optimization VNFs, etc., as shown in Figure 18-15. The generic VNF software images are uploaded (e.g., in .tar or .qcow2 format) and then used to create VNF profiles. In this step, you can take a generic VNF image to generate an actual VNF instance with a specific number of vCPUs, memory reservations, or disk storage capacity.

NFVIS
ENCS5408/K9 NFVIS-3.8.1-FC3
Thu Aug 16, 12:51:59 AM

Image Registration | Browse Datastore | USB Upload | Image Packaging

Images

Image Name	State	Type	Version	Action
asav961.tar.gz	ACTIVE	FIREWALL	961	
isrv-universalk9.16.06.03.tar.gz	ACTIVE	ROUTER	16.06.03	

Showing 1 to 2 of 2 entries
Previous 1 Next

Profiles

Profile	CPU	Memory (MB)	Disk (MB)	Source Image	Action
ASAv10	1	2048	8192	asav961.tar.gz	
ASAv30	4	8192	16384	asav961.tar.gz	
ASAv5	1	1024	8192	asav961.tar.gz	

Figure 18-15 *NFVIS GUI: VNF Image Repository*

Choosing the Networking option from the VM Life Cycle menu provides you with options to view and manipulate the network interface and internal bridge settings, as shown in Figure 18-16. Notice the internal bridges that connect VNFs to the physical interfaces and to each other. You can create additional networks and edit (or even delete) existing networks. The status and settings of physical interfaces and the virtualized SR-IOV networks are also displayed on this screen.

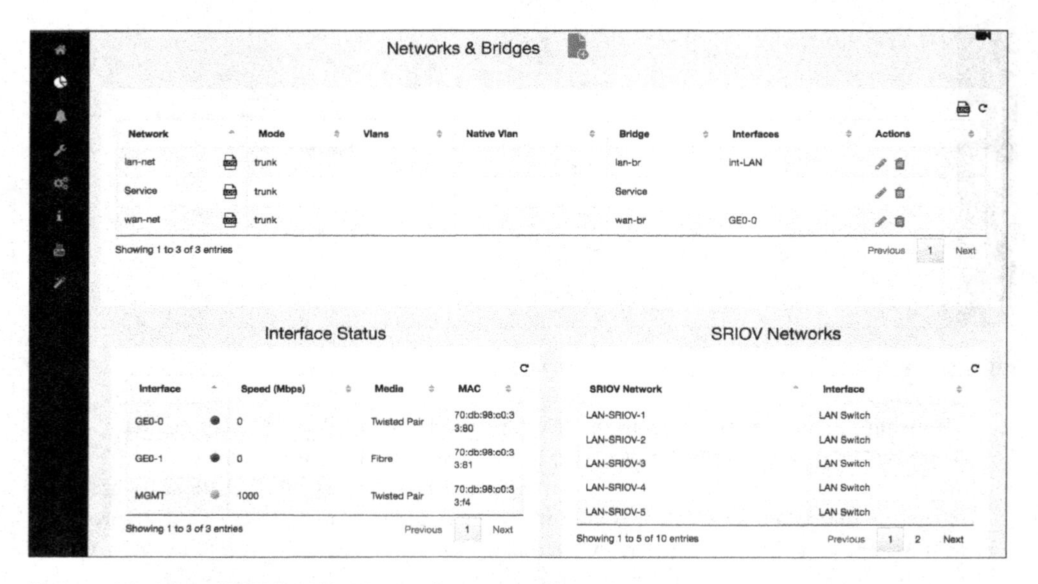

Figure 18-16 *NFVIS GUI: Networking Details*

Another example of the operations that are performed locally on an NFVIS system using the portal is shown in Figure 18-17, the Resource Allocation screen. The physical resources allocated in the system are displayed for the CPUs, memory, and disk. This allows you to correlate the shared hardware resources to the actual VNFs that are instantiated. For example, you can see which VNF instance is running on which CPU core (and socket), and how much of the available total memory or disk is consumed by a particular VNF instance.

You can observe the resource utilization from a host perspective by expanding the Host menu and choosing Monitoring, as shown in Figure 18-18. Whereas the last example showed you the correlation of the physical resources to the instantiated VNFs, in this view the actual CPU, memory, network interface, and disk utilizations are displayed over time. In combination, both of these views allow you to better understand what is happening on the NFVIS host both from an overall system perspective and from a particular VNF perspective.

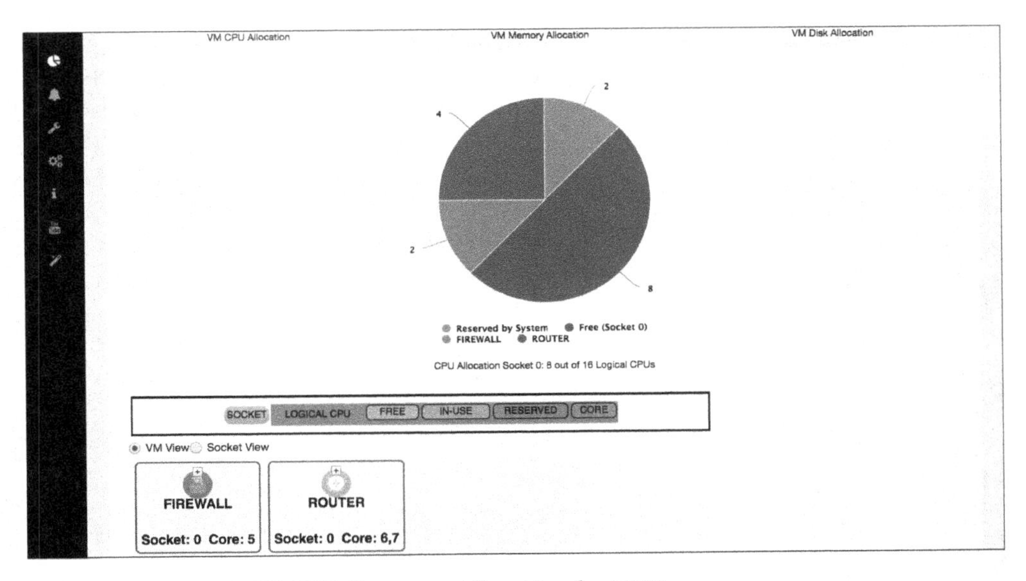

Figure 18-17 *NFVIS GUI: Resource Allocation by VNF*

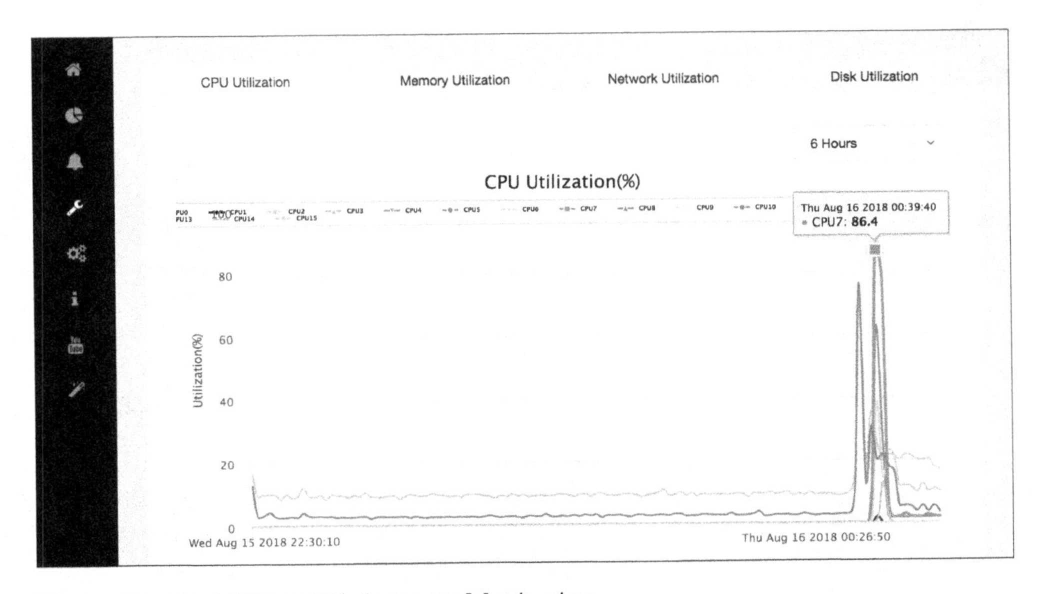

Figure 18-18 *NFVIS GUI: Resource Monitoring*

The final example of operations you can perform on a per-NFVIS-system basis is shown in Figure 18-19, the Switch Settings screen. Recall from the hardware options overview that an ENCS host provides an integrated physical switch that is leveraged to connect multiple physical interfaces to the VNFs, as well as to perform VNF-to-VNF switching in hardware. In this portal screen, you can monitor and manipulate the details of these physical interfaces and switches. You can enter the switch's Spanning Tree settings, VLAN configuration, and Link Aggregation Control Protocol (LACP) parameters. Packet statistics by port for unicast, multicast, and broadcast packets in both directions (in and out) are also displayed.

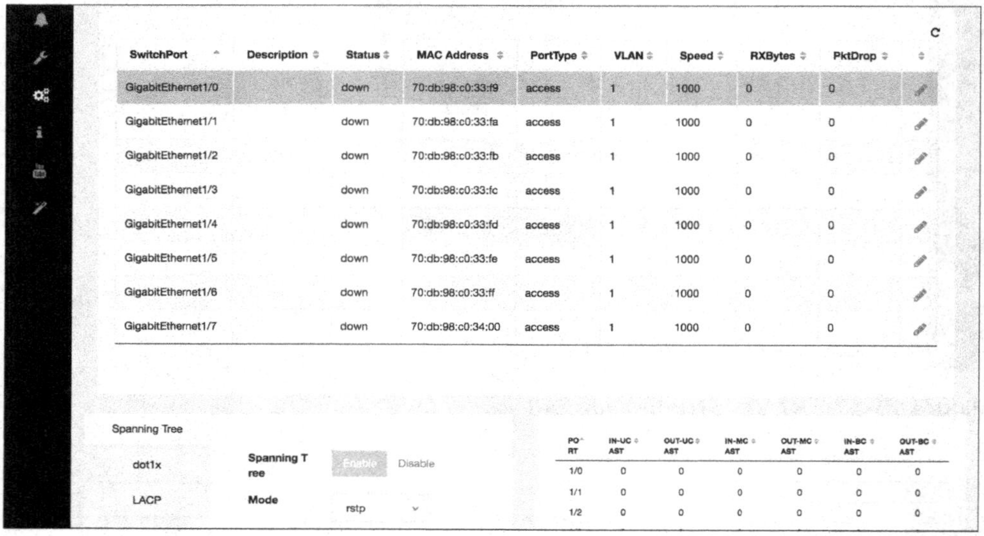

SwitchPort	Description	Status	MAC Address	PortType	VLAN	Speed	RXBytes	PktDrop
GigabitEthernet1/0		down	70:db:98:c0:33:f9	access	1	1000	0	0
GigabitEthernet1/1		down	70:db:98:c0:33:fa	access	1	1000	0	0
GigabitEthernet1/2		down	70:db:98:c0:33:fb	access	1	1000	0	0
GigabitEthernet1/3		down	70:db:98:c0:33:fc	access	1	1000	0	0
GigabitEthernet1/4		down	70:db:98:c0:33:fd	access	1	1000	0	0
GigabitEthernet1/5		down	70:db:98:c0:33:fe	access	1	1000	0	0
GigabitEthernet1/6		down	70:db:98:c0:33:ff	access	1	1000	0	0
GigabitEthernet1/7		down	70:db:98:c0:34:00	access	1	1000	0	0

Spanning Tree

dot1x

LACP

Spanning Tree Enable Disable

Mode rstp

PORT	IN-UCAST	OUT-UCAST	IN-MCAST	OUT-MCAST	IN-BCAST	OUT-BCAST
1/0	0	0	0	0	0	0
1/1	0	0	0	0	0	0
1/2	0	0	0	0	0	0

Figure 18-19 *NFVIS GUI: Switch Settings*

Cisco DNA Center (Network Level)

The second option to automate the deployment and operation of VNFs in the branch is provided by Cisco DNA Center. This platform allows you holistic operations of multiple devices in your enterprise network from a single pane of glass. Cisco DNA Center supports all stages of the enterprise network operations lifecycle.

Cisco DNA Center allows you as a network designer to standardize the network designs of your branch, campus, and WAN environments. Cisco DNA Center offers workflows to specify the desired network architecture and functionality, and save the resulting profiles in a library for subsequent deployment. This allows you to increase the conformity of your network to standardized network designs—an absolute MUST to automate network operations across hundreds or even thousands of sites and devices.

For your network deployment teams, Cisco DNA Center offers support to automate the roll-out and instantiation of network functions (both physical and virtual), for example by leveraging zero-touch deployment (network plug-and-play, PnP) to add network elements to the network. Of course, Cisco DNA Center helps you to ensure that the deployments conform to the intended architecture prescribed in the design phase. The Cisco DNA controller platform enables the automation of the network infrastructure as a whole system, rather than network element by network element.

Cisco DNA Center also enables you to operate your network based on policies. The respective Policy workflows allow you to specify policies pertaining to user groups, device groups, and even application groups. Supported by Cisco Identity Services Engine (ISE), access policies can regulate which users, devices, or applications are granted access to your network. For all admitted endpoints, access control policies can be authored to further regulate the relationship between user groups, application groups, or device groups. Moreover, application policies can govern how traffic between users, devices, and applications is to be treated by the network.

Finally, Cisco DNA Center provides assurance tools and mechanisms to understand the ongoing behavior of your network. The Cisco DNA Assurance capabilities provide you with an in-depth understanding on how users, devices, or applications experience the network. Any issues that the Cisco DNA assurance engine detects is flagged, and can also be traced back over time. This is where the network-wide view of Cisco DNA Center proves extremely valuable. Rather than analyzing any issues on a per-network-element basis and correlating events between network elements yourself, the Cisco DNA Assurance capabilities allow you to understand the behavior of the network as an entity. For example, a connectivity issue for wireless clients is viewed from the wireless client to the application, including diverse functions like DNS, DHCP, the Wireless LAN Controller (WLC), etc. that may play a role in the end-to-end communication path. Of course, key performance indicators (KPIs) for individual network elements are also collected and available for you to fully grasp the state of your enterprise network.

Figure 18-20 shows the initial landing page of Cisco DNA Center, showing the principal workflows for network design, policy, provisioning, and assurance. Supporting tools to perform network discovery, list the inventory of devices, display the topology, manage software images or licenses, or authoring CLI templates are also shown.

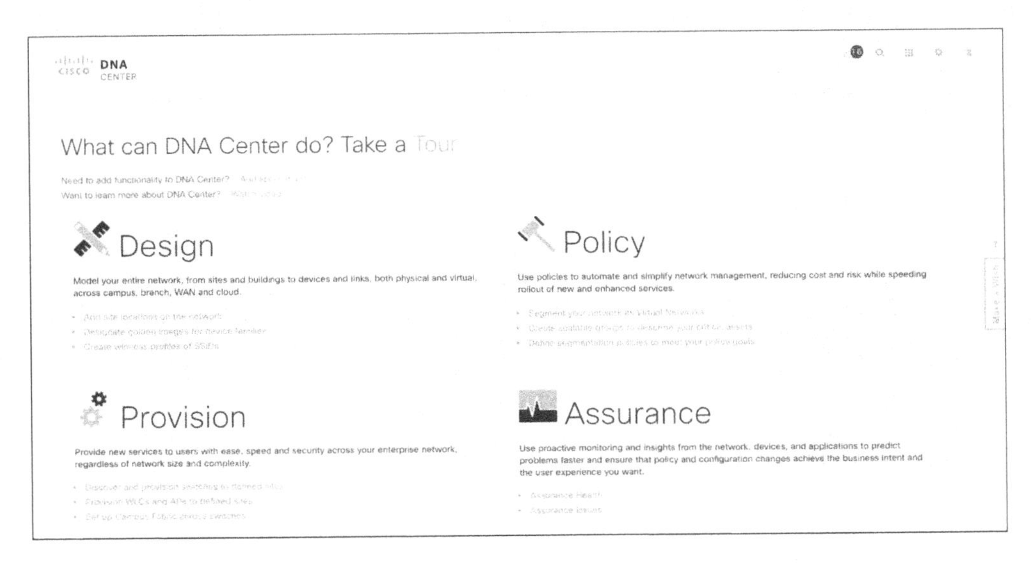

Figure 18-20 *Cisco DNA Center Landing Page*

From an ENFV perspective, the Cisco DNA Center workflows for network design and provisioning are particularly relevant. The workflows are mostly generic from a network function perspective, allowing you to focus on the deployment and operation of network functions regardless of whether these are deployed as a physical appliance or in a virtual form factor. For example, as illustrated in Figure 18-21, the Cisco DNA Center Design workflow allows you to view the network hierarchy in terms of sites and buildings, which of course also pertains to the deployed VNFs. Similarly, generic network settings (details about DNS, DHCP, Network Time Protocol [NTP], and AAA servers, for example), device software image management, or license management are functions that Cisco DNA Center offers that apply to either physical or virtual network functions.

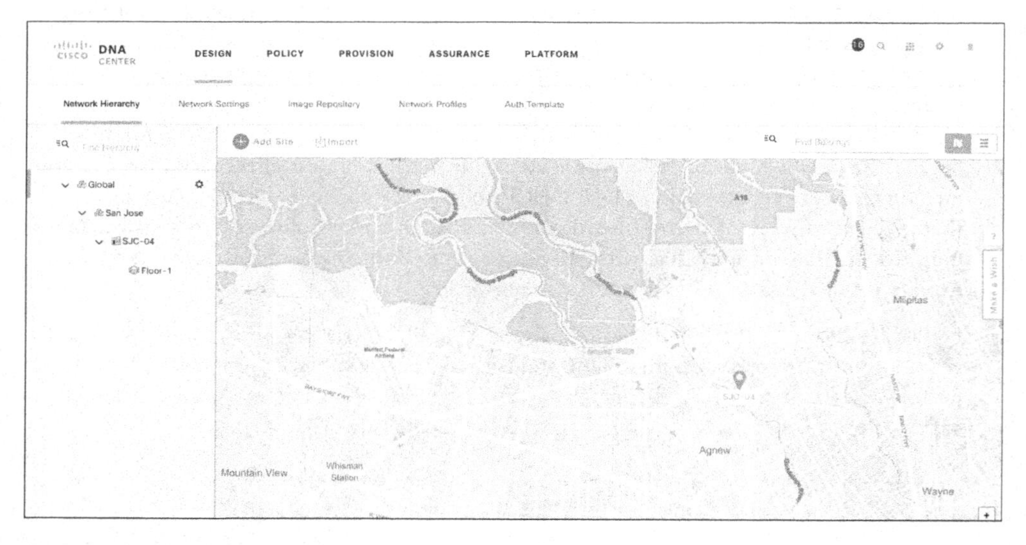

Figure 18-21 *Cisco DNA Center Network Hierarchy by Geography*

The capability to specify the desired network architecture from a routing perspective is entered in the Cisco DNA Center Design workflow under Network Profiles. Figure 18-22 illustrates the current library of specified designs, with metadata details such as the name of the profile, its type (routing & NFV, switching, wireless), the sites that this profile is associated with, as well as options to edit its details or even delete the profile from the library. Adding a new profile is achieved by clicking Add Profile in the upper-right side. Note that the site attribute is particularly important for the deployment of profiles. Sites, as created in the network hierarchy, provide the common anchor to link the desired network architecture with devices that are actually deployed. The network designer specifies a network profile and details the list of sites to which this profile pertains. When devices are dispatched for deployment, they are also associated with a site.

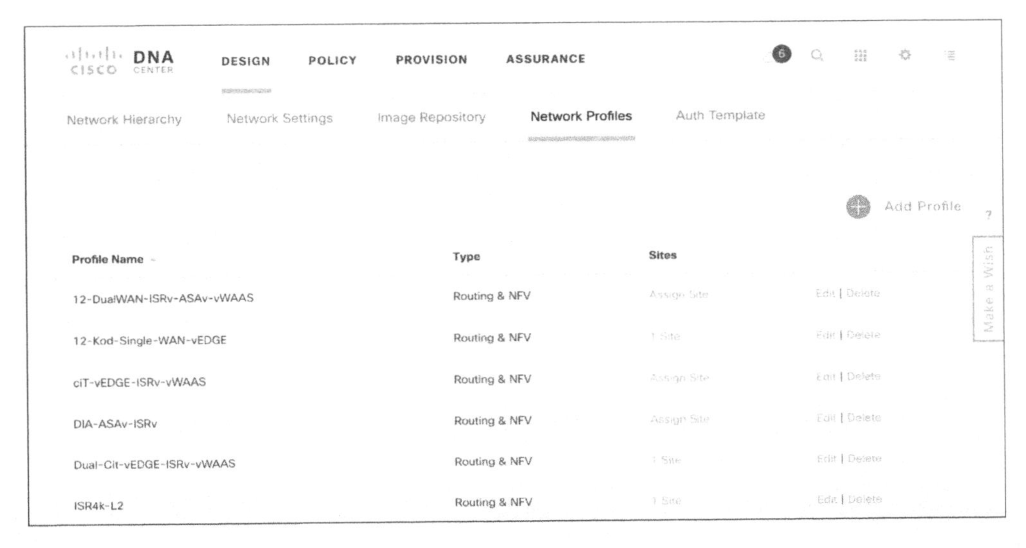

Figure 18-22 *Cisco DNA Center Network Profile Library*

Because both network elements (physical or virtual) and network profiles are associated with a site, Cisco DNA Center correlates the two and ensures

- That the right device is deployed at the right site (and flags if a discrepancy occurred), as learned from the PnP process.
- Application of the appropriate configuration for the network element that the designer has prescribed in the network profile. In the case of ENFV, Cisco DNA Center instantiates the desired VNFs as per the profile, and creates the necessary virtual switching connectivity between them. It also pushes an initial VNF configuration if specified for in the profile during the design phase.

Adding a network profile for routing allows you to describe the intended WAN architecture. Prescribe the details of the WAN connectivity to the service providers in the initial screen of the ENFV Design workflow. Figure 18-23 illustrates the various options for the WAN connectivity: single router or redundant router configuration to one or more SPs. In this step of the workflow, the hardware platform is selected from a list of registered devices. For example, for ENFV you can select among the ISR 4000 Series router with a UCS E-Series compute blade, an ENCS system, or a UCS C-Series server—all of which support NFVIS. Selection of one of these devices then allows you to describe the intended virtual system architecture as the workflow continues.

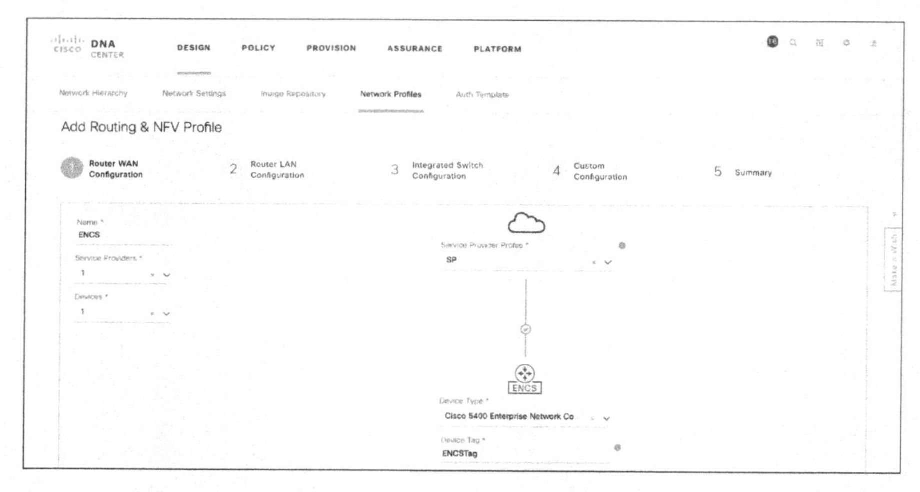

Figure 18-23 *Cisco DNA Center Routing Profile*

Cisco DNA Center recognizes that the selection of a Cisco ENCS as a hardware platform implies the additional specification of a virtualized system profile, and thus presents you with different options than if a physical Cisco ISR 4000 Series router were selected.

Figure 18-24 shows the canvas that appears for virtualized profiles. You can choose to characterize not only the (virtual) routing function, but also one or more additional Layer 4–Layer 7 VNFs or application workloads. The Cisco DNA Center ENFV canvas thus allows you to select among the registered VNF types (e.g., router, firewall, WAN Optimization), and shows you the prescribed connectivity from an NFVIS perspective between the VNFs and to the physical interfaces of the underlying host (both LAN and WAN interfaces).

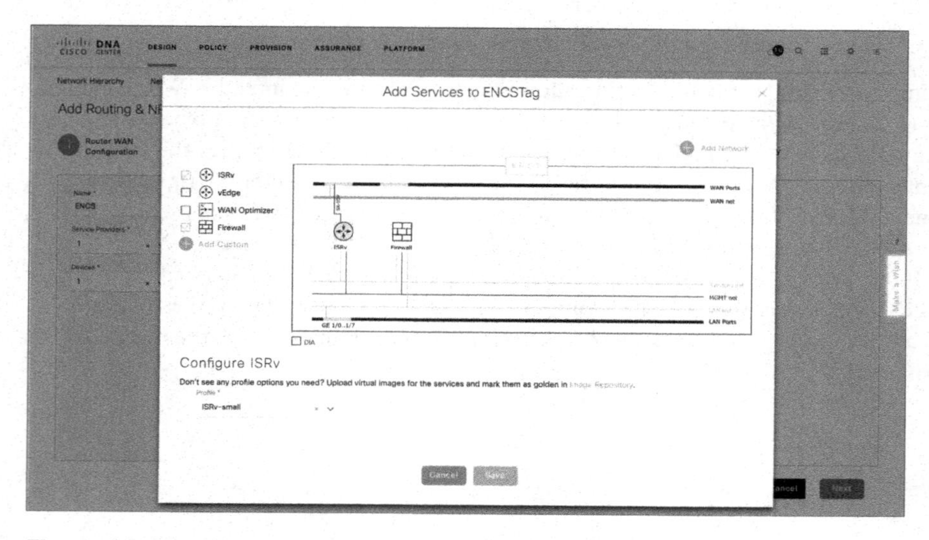

Figure 18-24 *Cisco DNA Center ENFV Design Canvas*

For each of the VNFs in the profile, you can specify details about a particular VNF—for example, select a Cisco ISRv virtual router, with resource profile "small." The resource profiles determine the amount of hardware resources required for the specific VNF in terms of vCPUs, virtual memory, or virtual storage. Cisco DNA Center uses this information both during the design phase and during the deployment phase to ensure that sufficient hardware resources are actually available to run the network function, or flag an issue in case they are not.

Proceeding through the Cisco DNA Center Design workflow for ENFV then allows you to provide details on the desired LAN configuration, the specifics for the built-in switch in case the hardware is a Cisco ENCS, or even to provide custom configuration details for the system. For example, under the Router LAN Configuration step, shown in Figure 18-25, you place interfaces into either L2 or L3 mode by type and, in case of the former, restrict the range of allowed VLANs.

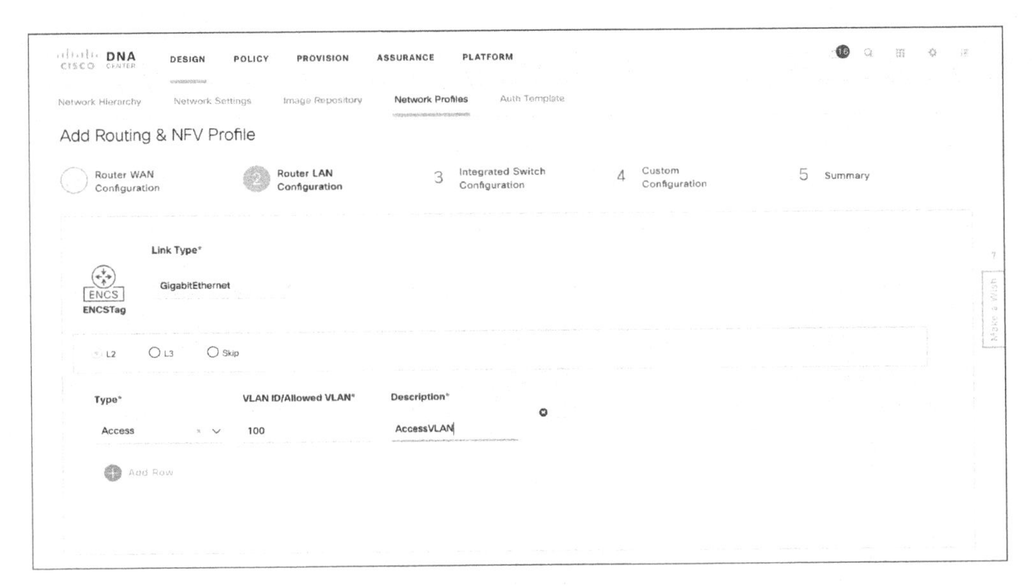

Figure 18-25 *Cisco DNA Center ENFV LAN Configuration Details for ENCS*

At the end of this Design workflow, Cisco DNA Center summarizes the profile on a single screen, showing routing connectivity to the WAN SP, the type of NFVIS host selected, and the VNFs, LAN configuration, etc. that have been specified under the profile as well as their details. Cisco DNA Center also summarizes the total physical CPU, memory, and storage requirements for the profile to ensure that the selected hardware type offers sufficient resources. The Summary screen of the ENFV Design workflow in Cisco DNA Center is shown in Figure 18-26.

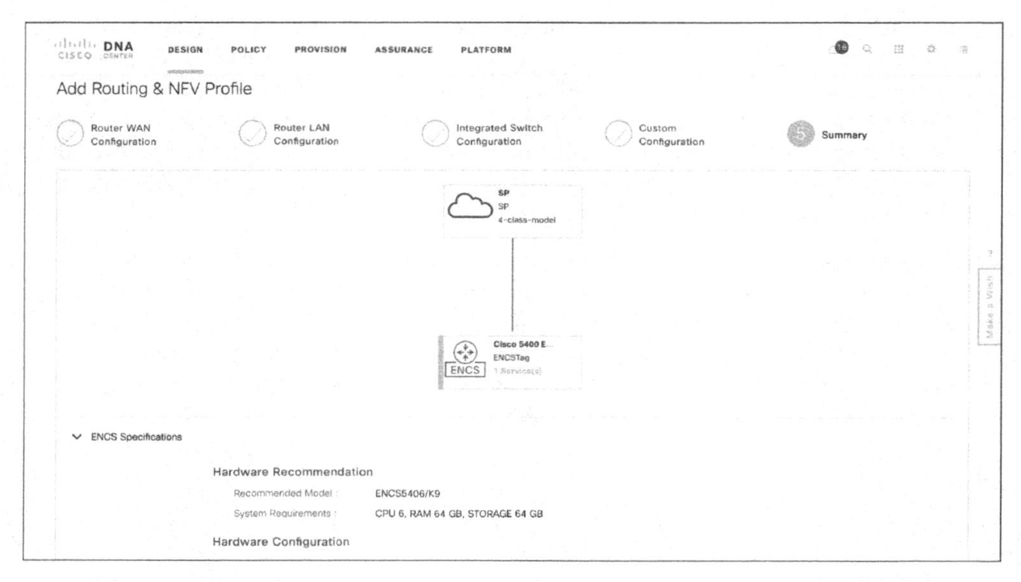

Figure 18-26 *Cisco DNA Center ENFV Profile Summary*

The deployment of physical and virtual network functions in a site is assumed to happen in an independent workflow. The Provision workflow assumes that you have acquired the hardware and shipped it to a particular site. In the example of ENFV, a Cisco ISR 4000 Series router with a UCS E-Series compute blade, an ENCS system, or a UCS C-Series server is assumed to be installed in the desired location, connected to a power source and the relevant LAN and WAN connections, and powered up. The PnP process of NFVIS then ensures that the device registers with Cisco DNA Center. Upon successful completion of this process, the device appears in Cisco DNA Center's inventory as an "unclaimed" device.

The Provision workflow of an NFVIS-based system, as shown in Figure 18-27, enables you to associate the deployed device with a site—and this is really all that is required to then continue the provisioning of the NFVIS-based system as per the profile! Recall that the site-specific architecture is characterized by the designer in the Design workflow, and stored in a profile that associates to a site. By also associating an NFVIS system to a site, Cisco DNA Center finds the correct profile to apply, and thus learns about the VNFs or application workloads to be instantiated on the virtualized system. The rest is history! Cisco DNA Center communicates with the NFVIS host using REST APIs, brings up the VNFs as per the profile with their optional day 1 configuration files, creates the internal connectivity (VLANs, bridges, etc.) as per the profile, and establishes the connectivity to the physical LAN and WAN ports. Done!

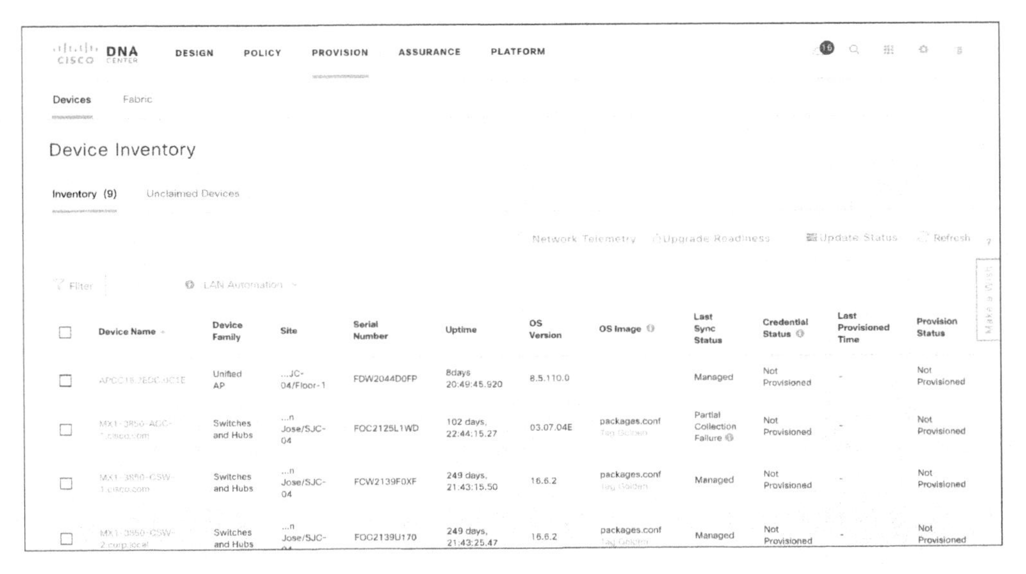

Figure 18-27 *Cisco DNA Center ENFV Provision Workflow*

Configuring and Monitoring of an NFVIS Host Using Traditional Mechanisms

The previous two sections illustrated, respectively, how an individual NFVIS-based host is managed and operated using a per-system GUI and how Cisco DNA Center is leveraged to automate the deployment of ENFV from a network-wide single pane of glass. The third option briefly discussed here is to leverage traditional monitoring and management mechanisms: the command-line interface (CLI), Management Information Bases (MIBs), or the Cisco Integrated Management Controller (CIMC).

Any NFVIS-based hosts can be configured and monitored using CLI commands by, for example, using the NFVIS's physical management port or the physical WAN ports. On a Cisco ENCS system, the management port is assigned a default IP address of 192.168.1.1 for access to NFVIS. In fact, any operation that is executed by the local GUI or the centralized Cisco DNA Center has a corresponding NFVIS command. As listed in the *Cisco Enterprise Network Functions Virtualization Infrastructure Software Command Reference*,[14] the command categories at the NFVIS host level are as follows:

- Banner and Message Commands
- System and IP Configuration Commands
- PnP Commands

14 https://www.cisco.com/c/en/us/td/docs/routers/nfvis/command/b-nfvis-command-ref.html

- Resource Commands
- Networks and Bridges Commands
- VM Lifecycle Management Commands
- Internal Management IP Commands
- System Monitoring Commands
- System Operations Commands
- System Time Commands
- System Portal Commands
- System Routes Commands
- System Log Commands
- Span Session and Packet Capture Commands
- Upgrade Package Commands
- Factory Default Reset Command
- Syslog Commands
- SNMP Commands
- RADIUS Commands
- TACACS Commands
- User Management Commands
- Secondary IP and Source Interface Commands
- Ports and Port Channel Commands
- Support Commands

As an example, the statistics for the physical host resources are displayed using the **show system-monitoring host** command:

```
show system-monitoring host [cpu | disk | memory | port] stats
```

Similarly, the VNF-specific statistics are shown using the **show system-monitoring vnf** command:

```
show system-monitoring vnf [cpu | memory] stats
```

Recall that VNFs are accessed by NFVIS via the internal management network and bridge. These are specifically created for such internal system monitoring activities. The NFVIS CLI commands are not only useful to display the system state for monitoring. They are used to set parameters as well, as illustrated in the following command sequence. The **system settings** commands allow you to specify the IP address of the NFVIS host and to set the default gateway, as shown in Example 18-1.

Example 18-1 *Configuration Example for the WAN IP Address in the NFVIS CLI*

```
nfvis# configure terminal
nfvis(config)# system settings wan ip address 10.192.133.11 255.255.255.0
nfvis(config)# system settings default-gw 10.192.133.1
nfvis(config)# end
```

NFVIS also supports a wide range of MIBs that are queried using SNMP. The following list gives you a sample of the available MIBS:

- CISCO-UNIFIED-COMPUTING-EQUIPMENT-MIB
- CISCO-UNIFIED-COMPUTING-FAULT-MIB
- CISCO-UNIFIED-COMPUTING-MIB
- CISCO-UNIFIED-COMPUTING-MEMORY-MIB
- CISCO-UNIFIED-COMPUTING-NOTIFS-MIB
- CISCO-UNIFIED-COMPUTING-PROCESSOR-MIB
- CISCO-UNIFIED-COMPUTING-STORAGE-MIB
- CISCO-UNIFIED-COMPUTING-TC-MIB
- ITU-ALARM-TC-MIB
- ENTITY-MIB
- IF-MIB
- SNMPv2-MIB
- SNMPv2-CONF-MIB
- SNMPv2-SMI-MIB
- SNMPv2-TC-MIB
- SNMP-FRAMEWORK-MIB
- INET-ADDRESS-MIB
- CISCO-SMI
- CISCO-TC
- CISCO-PROCESS-MIB

As you would expect, SNMP GET commands (GET, GETNEXT, GETBULK) are issued by a network management system (NMS) to gather data from the NFVIS host. SNMP SET commands allow you to modify the value of an object variable, and SNMP notifications generate unsolicited notifications for trap events. SNMPv1, SNMPv2c, and SNMPv3 are supported.

Finally, for the Cisco x86-based hosts, the Cisco Integrated Management Controller capabilities are also available to perform low-level hardware-centric management operations. CIMC allows you to configure and view hardware-related parameters, such as setting the management IP address, viewing and upgrading BIOS versions, manipulating the boot sequence, power-cycling the server, monitoring the health of the hardware components, or even accessing the KVM console.

Figure 18-28 summarizes the various management and operations options at the x86-based host, NFVIS, and VNF level. Recall that this section focuses on the NFVIS system aspects, and not on the management and operations of the VNFs. Of course, once these are up and running, traditional mechanisms to operate the VNF internals are applicable. This is also illustrated in Figure 18-28 by calling out the VNF syslog, SNMP, CLI, NetFlow, or EEM script capabilities.

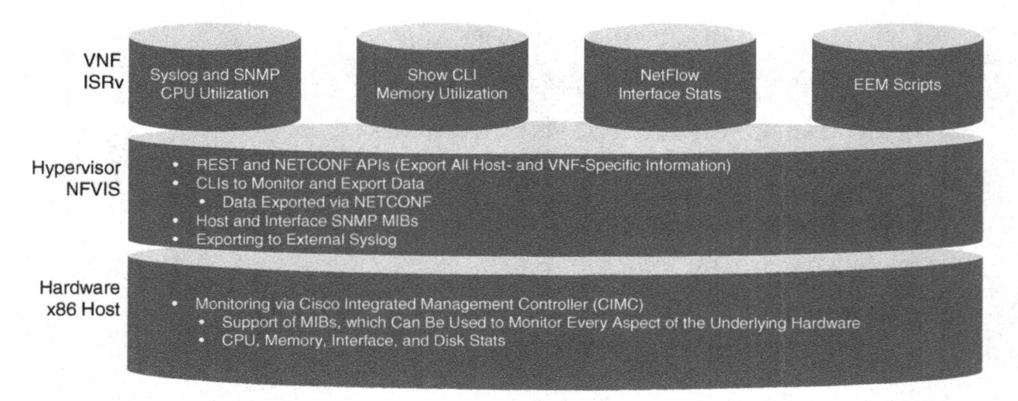

Figure 18-28 *Summary of Various Management and Operations Options of an NFVIS x86-based Host and VNFs*

Virtualizing Connectivity to Untrusted Domains: Secure Agile Exchange

The concept of branch virtualization is also generalized and applied to secure the connectivity from your enterprise network to untrusted domains. The Cisco Secure Agile Exchange (SAE) solution extends the concepts of branch virtualization to apply VNFs and service chaining based on policies between "consumers" of application traffic and "providers" (that is, where applications are hosted). Relationships between consumers and providers are expected to become increasingly complex as

- Applications move into the cloud (VPC) or are consumed as a service (for example, SaaS)
- Enterprises partner with more and more external organizations to participate in the delivery of digitalized business services

- Customers and employees become increasingly more mobile, wishing to consume services from anywhere on any device

The Cisco SAE solution leverages virtualization and service chaining with a focus on securing such increasingly complex communication relationships. The following section motivates the Cisco SAE solution, followed by a section detailing the solution building blocks.

Motivation for the Cisco SAE Solution

Consider a traditional demilitarized zone (DMZ) architecture in the data center. Typically, connections from the outside world are gathered to arrive in a DMZ, where security functions such as firewalling, intrusion detection and prevention, web security, etc. are applied to protect the enterprise assets from unwanted attacks.

Today, this part of your network infrastructure is predominantly relying on hardware-based appliances that are shared among many different types of external connectivity and for many different application flows. Managing a common infrastructure appliance for many different connections to the Internet (or partners) for tens or even hundreds of applications may cause operational complexities. For example, a software upgrade for a firewall appliance in the DMZ impacts all of the applications and connections that it protects against, and thus has to be coordinated among all the application owners. Such coordination becomes increasingly complex as the number of applications grows.

Virtualizing a traditional DMZ architecture offers the advantage of being able to deploy security network functions at a finer granularity, possibly for groups of like applications. The virtualized network functions are applied to a traffic flow based on its requirements. For example, traffic between a trusted partner and your enterprise applications may not require the same level of protection (i.e., the same security functions and rules) as connectivity between your engineering department and the Internet. Security VNFs are applied in the DMZ more dynamically, based on the source and destination relationship of the traffic. Also, network functions are deployed as needed, following a usage-based consumption model. If you establish a new relationship to a partner organization, the applicable security VNFs can be instantiated if and when needed. In contrast, in a hardware appliance–based environment, you have to plan for such relationships long term to ensure that sufficient infrastructure resources are available also for future growth in terms of partners or traffic. Virtualization in this context thus again enables a dynamic consumption model, where costs are incurred if and when needed (operational expenditures, or OPEX), rather than built out with anticipated capacity (capital expenditures, or CAPEX). The architectural shift from hardware-based appliances to VNFs is illustrated in Figure 18-29.

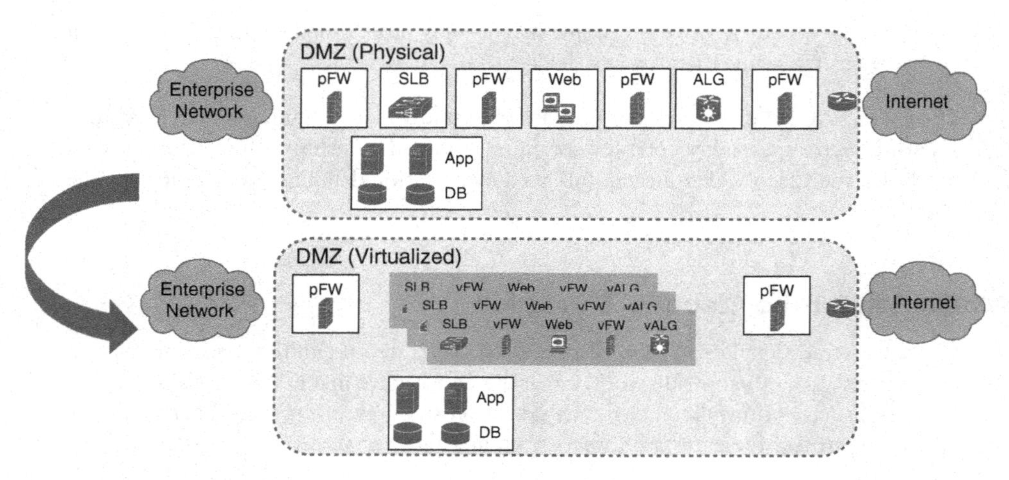

Figure 18-29 *Virtualizing a DMZ Infrastructure*

The consumer and provider landscape also becomes increasingly more dynamic. More and more applications are hosted in hybrid cloud environments, in virtual-private cloud infrastructures managed by your own networking department (e.g., Amazon AWS, Google GPC, Microsoft Azure), consumed as a service (e.g., Microsoft Office 365, Salesforce), or even in your own private cloud environments to meet regional or regulatory requirements. Similarly, the number of consumers becomes increasingly more sophisticated: digitalized business processes foster easier relationships with partner organizations. The number of partners wishing to interact with your applications grows steadily. Employees are also no longer restricted to work in an office environment, but are increasingly connecting from home or from the road. Both of these trends imply that traffic patterns are becoming increasingly fluid and dynamic—the old traffic patterns of all traffic being directed to your data centers is breaking up. These trends lead to the discussions on where to architect connectivity to external domains. The two principal options are

- Direct Internet access (DIA)/direct cloud access (DCA) from the branch
- A set of more centralized breakout points, possibly hosted by a carrier-neutral facility (CNF) provider

DIA/DCA in the branch requires a security perimeter to be established in every branch. This is an attractive option from an architectural perspective for a smaller number of branch locations and if the security functions can be highly automated. For example, assuming that x86-based compute resources are available, a virtual firewall can be automatically deployed in each branch, and governed with a standardized set of firewall rules to regulate and protect traffic to and from untrusted domains. This is the ENFV use case described in the previous section.

A more centralized approach (not necessarily fully centralized in a single location!) is often more cost effective for larger numbers of branches and as the network functions that need to be applied to the consumer–provider relationships varies. In this case, connecting several branches to a more central facility using an enterprise WAN, grouping consumers and providers from a policy perspective, and then applying virtualized security functions in a service chain becomes more attractive.

Branches are connected to such a facility using traditional WAN mechanisms (such as MPLS VPN) or even Internet-based mechanisms (software-defined WAN [SD-WAN]). The decision whether to centralize or distribute a network function is often determined by an enterprise architecture cost analysis. Centralizing functions may allow you to use more efficient transport mechanisms. For example, connecting to a cloud provider using a high-quality direct link (e.g., Amazon AWS Direct Connect or Microsoft Azure ExpressRoute) may be economically attractive from a few centralized locations, but becomes overly costly for a large number of branches. In some cases, compute and networking resources are utilized more efficiently in a more centralized location serving multiple branches, rather than distributing those resources and underutilizing them in each.

Grouping of consumers and providers by similar characteristics reduces the variability in the policies to be applied. Without such groupings, the number of possible relationships between application consumers and application providers grows exponentially (the n^2 problem).

Carrier-neutral facilities (co-location) can be leveraged to host these functions to further save on costs. CNFs offer a marketplace where multiple service providers, cloud providers, and enterprises are present and can "meet." This gives you additional benefits from an enterprise network architecture perspective:

- Your architecture becomes independent of the SP WAN provider. Any of the SPs present at the co-location facility can be leveraged to connect branches to your cage in the CoLo. You can choose an architecture with multiple WAN providers for redundancy, or more easily switch between providers when the WAN services no longer meet your requirements from a technical or cost perspective.
- Your architecture also becomes independent of the cloud provider. As multiple cloud providers connect to the CoLo facility, your architecture is no longer tied to host applications with a single provider. This becomes increasingly important for hybrid cloud environments, where some applications may reside in your own data centers, other are hosted in VPCs, and yet others are consumed as a service. Again, if a particular cloud provider no longer meets your business requirements, you can more easily switch to another provider without significant changes to your enterprise architecture.

Figure 18-30 illustrates the co-location/CNF aspects of the Cisco SAE solution, highlighting the increasing number of connections to untrusted domains and cloud providers. Note that enterprise applications may still remain in parts in your own data centers.

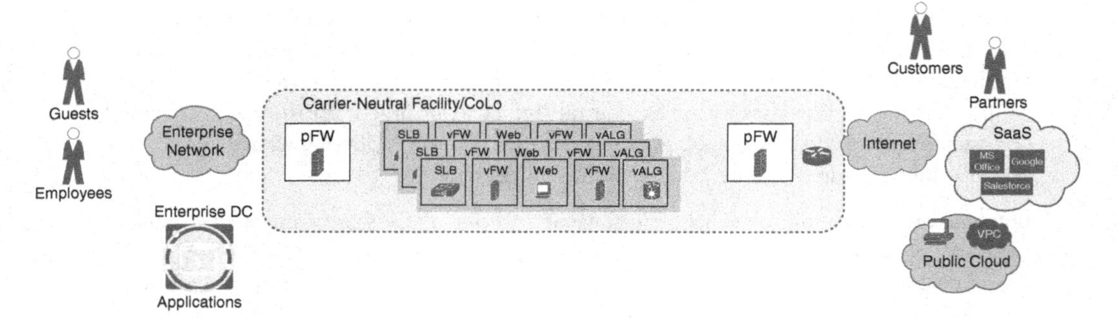

Figure 18-30 *Increasing Partner and Consumer Relationships Motivates SAE in Carrier-Neutral Facilities*

The Cisco SAE solution thus offers much more than just virtualizing a DMZ. The benefits and changes with virtualization and service chaining applied to dynamic consumer–provider relationships in centralized co-location facilities constitute a novel architectural approach. Cisco SAE allows your enterprise to be future-proof and ready for a network architecture supporting digitalized business processes.

Cisco SAE Building Blocks

Let' s examine Cisco SAE from an architectural building block perspective. As previously indicated, the concepts of virtualizing network functions and chaining them also applies to this use case. The main differences between virtualizing connectivity to untrusted domains centrally and virtualization in branches are severalfold:

- **Scale:** In SAE, due to the anticipated large number of dynamic consumer–provider relationships, the number of service chains in the architecture is larger. The Cisco ENFV solution accommodates a small number of VNFs and, consequently, service chains anchored against physical LAN and WAN interfaces. In the more centralized Cisco SAE solution, multiple service chains are instantiated to be applied to consumer–provider traffic flows anchored against logical interfaces, and even based on the desired business policies.
- **Types of VNFs:** Due to the nature of Cisco SAE providing connectivity to external, untrusted domains, service chaining focuses on *security* VNFs. Virtual firewalls, IPS/IDS, deep packet inspection (DPI), antimalware, antivirus, and data-loss prevention functions become standard components in SAE service chains.
- **Service chain dynamics:** In Cisco SAE, service chains are expected to be created and removed based on the consumer–provider relationships. These may change more often than in a branch environment as new partners and cloud providers are added, or as applications are moved from enterprise-operated data centers to single-cloud or multicloud environments.

From an architectural building block perspective, there are thus strong synergies between Cisco ENFV and Cisco SAE. The same four-layer architecture previously introduced also applies. Standard x86-based hosts provide the hardware resources to run virtualized network functions. The Cisco NFVIS operating system provides an optimized Linux-based environment to deploy and operate the VNFs, offering support for plug-and-play, local management and operations, lifecycle management, and open APIs. The VNF layer in case of Cisco SAE focuses on (but is not restricted to) virtualized security functions. Third-party VNFs are also supported. And the automation and orchestration functions in Cisco SAE support the dynamic nature of the use case and simplify ongoing operations of the solution.

To accommodate the scale requirements expected for a more centralized virtualization solution, hardware platforms with a larger number of cores than available in the Cisco ENCS are recommended in Cisco SAE. The Cisco Cloud Services Platform (CSP) 2100 offers an NFVIS-based appliance akin to the Cisco ENCS for this purpose. Both 1 RU (rack unit) and 2 RU versions are available offering up to 44 cores per chassis, and up to 768 GB of RAM—a lot of horsepower to run VNFs! More details on the Cisco CSP 2100 are provided in its data sheet.[15]

Running Virtualized Applications and VNFs Inside IOS XE

The solutions already described to virtualize network functions are based on the Cisco NFVIS operating system as described earlier in this chapter. An alternative hosting environment also exists *within* IOS XE for limited hosting of applications or VNFs. The IOS XE software architecture is actually based on a Linux environment, as depicted in Figure 18-31. All of the IOS XE–based hardware platforms are equipped with a multicore x86 processor that is first and foremost used to execute the IOS XE control plane. With IOS XE–based virtualization, the same Linux environment can be leveraged to also run containerized applications or even VNFs. Both KVM and Linux Containers (LXC) are supported.

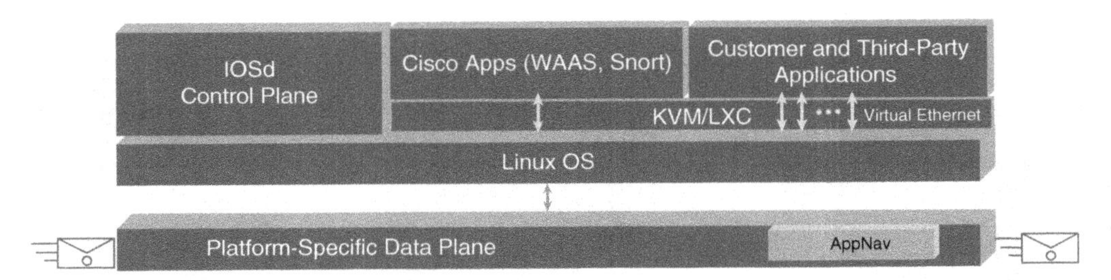

Figure 18-31 *IOS XE Software Architecture Based on Linux*

15 https://www.cisco.com/c/en/us/products/collateral/switches/cloud-services-platform-2100/datasheet-c78-735317.html

The number of physical CPU cores available on the ISR 4000 Series router or the ASR 1000 Series routers, for example, are sufficient to run lightweight applications or VNFs. The typical use cases fall into four main categories:

- **Troubleshooting:** Deploy a virtual machine inside IOS XE to run customized troubleshooting tools. Examples are Wireshark and Speedtest applications.
- **Supporting network applications:** The IOS XE virtualization capability is leveraged to run file servers, print servers, domain controllers, or similar applications.
- **Analytics:** Virtualized network analysis and application performance monitoring functions are also hosted within an IOS XE–based network element. For example, the IPERF tool falls into this category.
- **Device customization:** The standard LXC and KVM environments can be used in any generic manner to augment the capabilities of the host platform. Customizations such as the deployment of custom encryption functions or business policy–based routing could be provided by your network operations team or a partner.

The physical resource requirements for IOS XE–based virtualization again pertain to CPU cores, memory, and storage. On the ISR 4000 Series routers, up to three cores with varying clock speeds (depending on the model) are available for containers. Any containerized application of VNF that fits this profile can thus be instantiated directly on top of the IOS XE Linux OS. For a fully virtualized branch this may not be sufficient, in which case the Cisco ENFV solution may be more appropriate. But for the lightweight use cases summarized, IOS XE–based virtualization provides additional flexibility without dispatching new hardware into your branches.

To accommodate the additional containerized applications or VNFs, additional memory and storage has to be available in the IOS XE–based platforms. A minimum of 4 GB of additional dynamic RAM (DRAM), 50 GB of solid-state drive space, and 1 TB of hard disk drive space are required for this capability. Table 18-4 lists the available physical CPU cores for the ISR 4000 Series router platforms, as well as the additional (on top of IOS XE itself) memory and storage requirements.

Table 18-4 *Cisco ISR 4000 Series Compute Resources for IOS XE Virtualization*

Platform	Service Cores	Speed (GHz)	Min Additional DRAM	Min Additional SSD	Min Additional HHD
ISR4451	3	2	4GB	200GB	1TB
ISR4431	3	1	4GB	200GB	1TB
ISR4351	3	2.4	4GB	50GB	1TB
ISR4331	3	2.0	4GB	50GB	1TB
ISR4321	1	2.4	4GB	50GB	1TB

The capabilities of the containerized applications or VNFs are expected to be described in a Yet Another Markup Language (YAML) descriptor file. This file specifies how many virtual CPUs (vCPU) and CPU cycle shares are required, how much memory and disk space needs to be reserved, as well as the virtual NIC descriptions or console and AUX port connectivity.

The actual container or VNF must be provided in one or more disk image files of type ISO, RAW, or QEMU Copy On Write (QCOW2). ISO disk image files are appropriate for read-only file systems such as a CD-ROM. RAW image files are supported for read and write file systems. QCOW2 image files are applicable for read and write file systems with compression. In the latter case, the file sizes may be significantly smaller at the expense of longer install times.

A manifest file and a version file in simple text format provide, respectively, the SHA1 hash for all files in the Open Virtual Appliance (OVA) and the application's version number.

Containerized applications and VNFs are instantiated within IOS XE by use of the **virtual-service** commands. For example, the command

```
virtual-service install name testapp package bootflash:testapp.ova
```

installs a container called testapp provided in the OVA file testapp.ova. To enable packets to be directed to the container, a virtual port group with its associated IP address must be configured in the device's IOS XE configuration. This allows the IOS XE data plane to direct traffic destined to the container app's IP address, as illustrated in Figure 18-32. The creation of the virtual port group also activates the virtual switching capabilities via OVS at the Linux level, thus allowing connectivity between the IOS XE data plane and the application container or VNF.

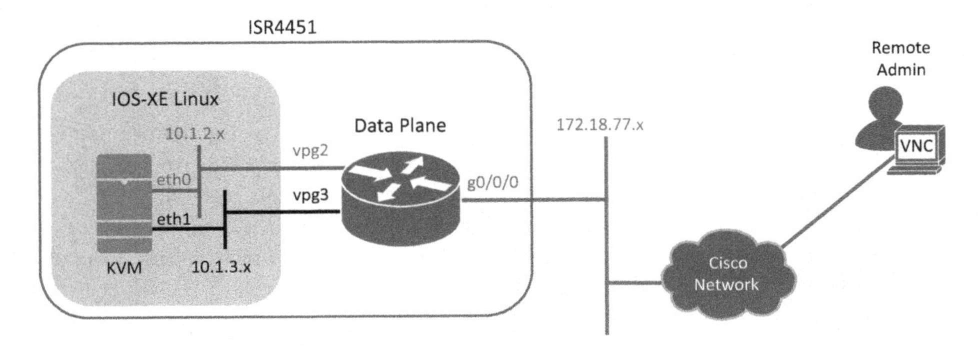

Figure 18-32 *Networking Details for IOS XE Based on Linux*

Details on how to configure application containers in IOS XE are available from Cisco.com.[16]

16 https://www.cisco.com/c/en/us/td/docs/switches/lan/catalyst3850/software/release/37e/b-openflow-37e-3850-and-3650/b-openflow-37e-3850_chapter_010.pdf

Summary

Virtualization of enterprise branch environments is one of the key initial use cases for NFV. The Cisco Enterprise NFV solution allows you to collapse multiple L4–L7 networking appliances into an x86-based hosting system without loss of functionality. This promises to reduce the complexity both from an architectural perspective and from an operational perspective of your branch environments. The following are some major points covered in this chapter:

- The Cisco ENFV solution consists of four main building blocks. Various different hardware models give you the flexibility of selecting the appropriate x86-based hardware resources for your branch environment.
- Cisco Network Functions Virtualization (NFVIS) offers the required hypervisor and virtualization OS with additional advantages. NFVIS also retains the flexibility and openness of the underlying Linux OS.
- From a VNF perspective, the Cisco ENFV solution leverages both Cisco VNFs and support for third-party VNFs. Most Cisco VNFs are functionally equivalent to their hardware-based siblings, allowing you to embark on the journey of virtualization without fearing a loss of functionality. The Cisco ENFV solution allows you to run third-party VNFs or application workloads as long as they match the underlying NFVIS (Linux) requirements.
- Cisco ENFV offers a centralized toolset embedded in the Cisco DNA Center solution. Any NFVIS system can also be managed using a local GUI. For the die-hard operators among you, using traditional mechanisms such as CLI, syslog, or MIBs is an option.

This chapter also discussed how the ENFV solution is extended to cover the use case of virtualizing connectivity from your enterprise network to untrusted and multicloud domains. All the preceding building blocks are carried forward in the Cisco SAE solution, but with additional scalability required to host many service chains, and with a particular focus on security VNFs.

For modest virtualization requirements, the chapter also reviewed the capabilities that exist within Cisco IOS XE. Any Cisco IOS XE–based hardware platform leverages x86 processors to execute the control plane functions. With today's multicore x86 CPUs, a limited number of cores remain available in the IOS XE–based switches and routers to also run limited application workloads or even additional network functions not covered by IOS XE.

Further Reading

Cisco UCS E-Series Data Sheets, https://www.cisco.com/c/en/us/products/servers-unified-computing/ucs-e-series-servers/datasheet-listing.html

Cisco Enterprise Whitepaper, https://www.cisco.com/c/en/us/solutions/collateral/enterprise-networks/enterprise-network-functions-virtualization-nfv/white-paper-c11-736783.pdf

Chapter 19

Cisco DNA Software-Defined Access

This chapter examines one of Cisco's newest and most exciting innovations in the area of enterprise networking—Software-Defined Access. SD-Access brings an entirely new way of building—even of thinking about and designing—the enterprise network. SD-Access embodies many of the key aspects of Cisco Digital Network Architecture, including such key attributes as automation, assurance, and integrated security capabilities.

However, to really appreciate what the SD-Access solution provides, we'll first examine some of the key issues that confront enterprise network deployments today. The rest of the chapter presents the following:

- Software-Defined Access as a fabric for the enterprise
- Capabilities and benefits of Software-Defined Access
- An SD-Access case study

The Challenges of Enterprise Networks Today

As capable as the enterprise network has become over the last 20-plus years, it faces some significant challenges and headwinds in terms of daily operation as well as present and future growth.

The enterprise network is the backbone of many organizations worldwide. Take away the network, and many companies, schools, hospitals, and other types of businesses would be unable to function. At the same time, the network is called upon to accommodate a vast and growing array of diverse user communities, device types, and demanding business applications.

The enterprise network continues to evolve to address these needs. However, at the same time, it also needs to meet an ever-growing set of additional—and critical—requirements. These include (but are not limited to) the need for:

- **Greater simplicity:** Networks have grown to be very complicated to design, implement, and operate. As more functions are mapped onto the network, it must accommodate an ever-growing set of needs, and has become more and more complex as a result. Each function provided by the network makes sense in and of itself, but the aggregate of all the various functions, and their interaction, has become, for many organizations, cumbersome to implement and unwieldy to manage. Combined with the manually intensive methods typically used for network deployments, this complexity makes it difficult for the enterprise network to keep pace with the rate of change the organization desires, or demands.
- **Increased flexibility:** Many enterprise network designs are relatively rigid and inflexible. The placement of Layer 2 and Layer 3 boundaries can, in some cases, make it difficult or impossible to accommodate necessary application requirements. For example, an application may need, or desire, a common IP subnet to be "stretched" across multiple wiring closets in a site. In a traditional routed access design model (in which IP routing is provisioned down to the access layer), this requirement is not possible to accommodate. In a multilayer design model, this need could be accommodated, but the use of a wide-spanning Layer 2 domain in this model (depending on how it is implemented) may expose the enterprise to the possibility of broadcast storms or other similar anomalies that could cripple the network. Organizations need their networks to be flexible to meet application demands such as these, when they arise. Today's network designs often fall short. Although such protocols and applications can be altered over time to reduce or eliminate such requirements, many organizations face the challenge of accommodating such legacy applications and capabilities within their networks. Where such applications can be altered or updated, they should be—where they cannot be, a network-based solution may be advantageous.
- **Integrated security:** Organizations depend on their networks. The simple fact is that today, the proper and ongoing operation of the network is critical to the functioning of any organization, and is foundational for the business applications used by that organization. Yet, many networks lack the inherent security and segmentation systems that may be desired. Being able to separate corporate users from guests, Internet of Things (IoT) devices from internal systems, or different user communities from each other over a common network has proved to be a daunting task for many enterprise networks in the past. Capabilities such as Multiprotocol Label Switching Virtual Private Networks (MPLS VPNs) exist, but are complex to understand, implement, and operationalize for many enterprise deployments.
- **Integrated mobility:** The deployment and use of mobile, wireless devices is ubiquitous in today's world—and the enterprise network is no exception. However, many organizations implement their wireless network separate from and "over the top" of their existing wired network, leading to a situation where the sets of available network services (such as security capabilities, segmentation, quality of service [QoS], etc.) are different for wired and wireless users. As a consequence, wired and wireless network deployments typically do not offer a simple, ubiquitous experience for both wired and wireless users, and typically cannot offer a common set of services with

common deployment models and scale. As organizations move forward and embrace wireless mobile devices even further in their networks, there is a strong desire to provide a shared set of common services, deployed the same way, holistically for both wired and wireless users within the enterprise network.

- **Greater visibility:** Enterprise networks are carrying more traffic, and more various types of traffic, across their network backbones than ever before. Being able to properly understand these traffic flows, optimize them, and plan for future network and application growth and change are key attributes for any organization. The foundation for such an understanding is greater visibility into what types of traffic and applications are flowing over the network, and how these applications are performing versus the key goals of the organization. Today, many enterprises lack the visibility they want into the flow and operation of various traffic types within their networks.
- **Increased performance:** Finally, the ever-greater "need for speed" is a common fact of life in networking—and for the devices and applications they support. In the wired network, this includes the movement beyond 10-Gigabit Ethernet to embrace the new 25-Gbps and 100-Gbps Ethernet standards for backbone links, as well as multi-Gigabit Ethernet links to the desktop. In the wireless network, this includes the movement toward 802.11ac Wave 2 deployments, and in future the migration to the new 802.11ax standard as this emerges—all of which require more performance from the wired network supporting the wireless devices. By driving the performance per access point (AP) toward 10 Gbps, these developments necessitate a movement toward a distributed traffic-forwarding model, as traditional centralized forwarding wireless designs struggle to keep pace.

Cisco saw these trends, and others, beginning to emerge in the enterprise network space several years ago. In response, Cisco created Software-Defined Access (SD-Access). The following sections explore

- A high-level review of SD-Access capabilities
- What SD-Access is—details of architecture and components
- How SD-Access operates: network designs, deployments, and protocols
- The benefits that SD-Access provides, and the functionality it delivers

So, let's get started and see what SD-Access has in store!

Software-Defined Access: A High-Level Overview

In 2017, Cisco introduced Software-Defined Access as a new solution that provides an automated, intent-driven, policy-based infrastructure with integrated network security and vastly simplified design, operation, and use.

SD-Access, at its core, is based on some of the key technologies outlined previously in this book:

- **Cisco DNA Center:** Cisco DNA Center is the key network automation and assurance engine for SD-Access deployments. When deployed in conjunction with Cisco Identity Services Engine (ISE) as the nexus for policy and security, Cisco DNA Center provides a single, central point for the design, implementation, and ongoing maintenance and operation of an SD-Access network.
- **Cisco DNA flexible infrastructure:** The flexible infrastructure of Cisco DNA was covered in depth in Chapter 7, "Hardware Innovations" and Chapter 8, "Software Innovations." By levering these flexible, foundational hardware and software elements within a Cisco network, SD-Access is able to offer a set of solutions that allows an evolutionary approach to network design and implementation—easing the transition to the software-defined, intent-driven networking world, and providing outstanding investment protection.
- **Next-generation network control-plane, data-plane, and policy-plane capabilities:** SD-Access builds on top of existing capabilities and standards, such as those outlined in Chapter 9, "Protocol Innovations," including Location/ID Separation Protocol (LISP), Virtual Extensible Local Area Network (VXLAN), and Scalable Group Tags (SGT). By leveraging these capabilities, expanding upon them, and linking them with Cisco DNA Center to provide a powerful automation and assurance solution, SD-Access enables the transition to a simpler, more powerful, and more flexible network infrastructure for organizations of all sizes.

SD-Access: A Fabric for the Enterprise

The SD-Access solution allows for the creation of a fabric network deployment for enterprise networks. So, let's begin with examining two important areas:

- What is a fabric?
- What benefits can a fabric network deployment help to deliver?

What Is a Fabric?

Effectively, a fabric network deployment implements an overlay network. Overlays by themselves are not new—overlay technologies of various flavors (such as CAPWAP, GRE, MPLS VPNs, and others) have been used for many years. Fundamentally, overlays leverage some type of packet encapsulation at the data plane level, along with a control plane to provision and manage the overlay. Overlays are so named because they "overlay," or ride on top of, the underlying network (the underlay), leveraging their chosen data plane encapsulation for this purpose. Chapter 9 introduced overlays and fabrics in more detail, so this will serve as a refresher.

Figure 19-1 outlines the operation of an overlay network.

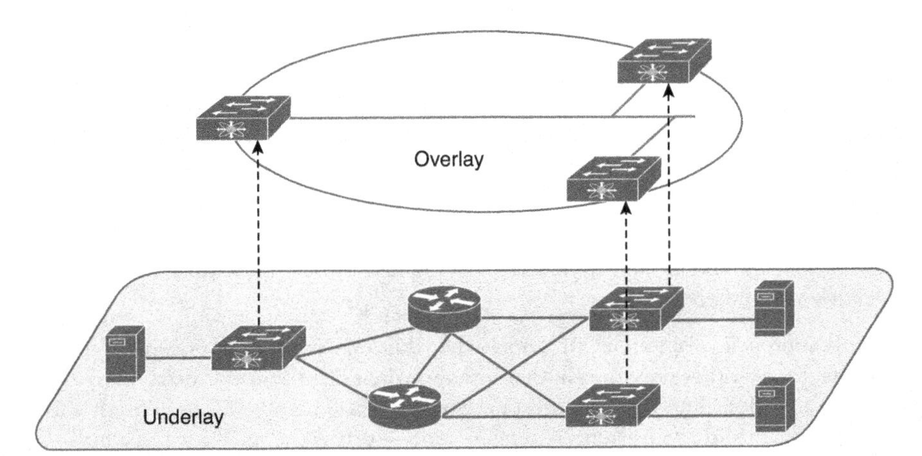

Figure 19-1 *Overlay Network Operation*

Overlay networks provide a logical, virtual topology for the deployment, operating on top of the physical underlay network. The two distinct "layers" of the network—logical and physical—can and often do implement different methods for reachability, traffic forwarding, segmentation, and other services within their respective domains.

A network fabric is the combination of the overlay network type chosen and the underlay network that supports it. But before we examine the type of network fabric created and used by SD-Access, we need to answer an obvious question: why use a fabric network at all for enterprise deployments?

Why Use a Fabric?

Perhaps the clearest way to outline why a fabric network is important within the enterprise is to quickly recap the main issues facing enterprise networks, namely:

- The need for greater simplicity
- The need for increased flexibility
- The need for enhanced security
- The requirement for ubiquitous mobility
- The need for greater visibility
- The need for simplified and more rapid deployment
- And the ever-growing need for more performance

These various demands place network managers into an awkward position. As stewards of one of the most critical elements of an organization—the enterprise network—one of their primary tasks is to keep the network operational at all times: 24/7/365. How best to accomplish this is broken down into a few simple, high-level steps:

Step 1. Design the network using a solid approach.

Step 2. Implement that design using reliable, proven hardware and software, leveraging a best-practices deployment methodology.

Step 3. Implement a robust set of change-management controls, and make changes only when you must.

Essentially, this means "build the network right in the first place—then stand back and don't touch it unless you need to."

Although this approach is functional, it ignores the additional realities imposed upon network managers by other pressures in their organizations. The constant demand to integrate more functions into the enterprise network—voice, video, IoT, mission-critical applications, mergers and acquisitions, and many more—drives the need for constant churn in the network design and deployment. More virtual LANs (VLANs). More subnets. More access control lists (ACLs) and traffic filtering rules. And the list goes on.

In effect, many network managers end up getting pulled in two contradictory directions, as illustrated in Figure 19-2.

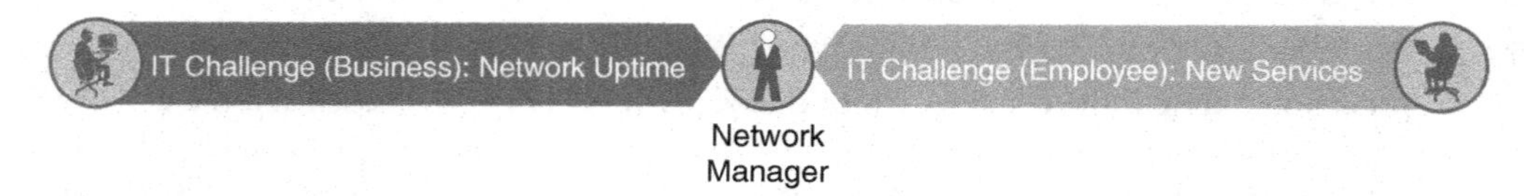

Figure 19-2 *The Dilemma of Today's Network Manager*

Essentially, many networks undergo this tension between these two goals: keep the network stable, predictable, and always on, and yet at the same time drive constant churn in available network services, functions, and deployments. In a network that consists of only one layer—essentially, that just consists of an underlay, as most networks do today—all of these changes have to be accommodated in the same physical network design and topology.

This places the network at potential risk with every design change or new service implementation, and explains why many organizations find it so slow to roll out new network services, such as (but not limited to) critical capabilities such as network-integrated security and segmentation. It's all a balance of risk versus reward.

Networks have been built like this for many years. And yet, the ever-increasing pace of change and the need for new enhanced network services are making this approach increasingly untenable. Many network managers have heard these complaints from their organizations: "The network is too slow to change." "The network is too inflexible." "We need to be able to move faster and remove bottlenecks."

So, how can a fabric deployment, using Software-Defined Access, help enterprises to address these concerns?

One of the primary benefits of a fabric-based approach is that it separates the "forwarding plane" of the network from the "services plane." This is illustrated in Figure 19-3.

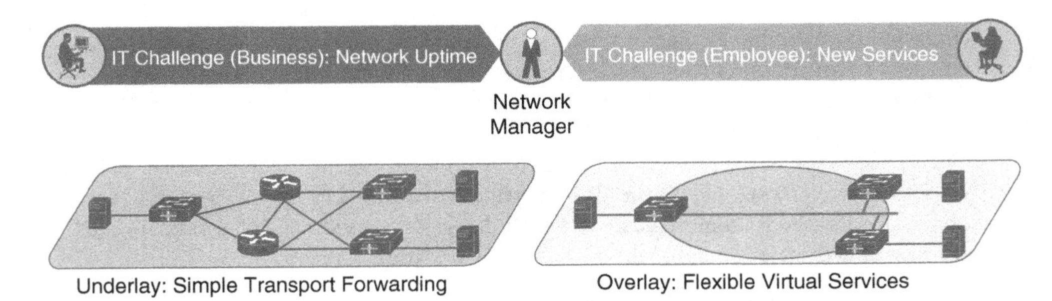

Figure 19-3 *Separation of Forwarding and Services Planes—Using an Overlay*

In this approach, the underlay provides the basic transport for the network. Into the underlay are mapped all of the network devices—switches and routers. The connectivity between these devices is provided using a fully routed network design, which provides the maximum stability and performance (using Equal Cost Multipath [ECMP] routing) and minimizes reconvergence times (via appropriate tuning of routing protocols). The underlay network is configured once and rarely if ever altered unless physical devices or links are added or removed, or unless software updates need to be applied. It is not necessary to make any changes to the underlay to add virtualized services for users. In a fabric-based design, the underlay provides the simple, stable, solid foundation that assists in providing the maximum uptime that organizations need from their network implementations.

The overlay, on the other hand, is where all of the users, devices, and things (collectively known as endpoints) within a fabric-based network are mapped into. The overlay supports virtualized services (such as segmentation) for endpoints, and supports constant change as new services and user communities are added and deleted. Changes to one area of the overlay (for example, adding a new virtual network, or a new group of users or devices) do not affect other portions of the overlay—thus helping to provide the flexibility that organizations require, without placing the network overall at risk.

In addition, because the overlay provides services for both wired and wireless users, and does so in a common way, it assists in creating a fully mobile workplace. With a fabric implementation, the same network services are provided for both wired and wireless endpoints, with the same capabilities and performance. Wired and wireless users alike can enjoy all of the virtualization, security, and segmentation services that a fabric deployment offers.

And speaking of security, an inherent property of a fabric deployment is network segmentation. As outlined in Chapter 9, next-generation encapsulation technologies such as VXLAN provide support for both virtual networks (VNs) and SGTs, allowing for both macro- and micro-segmentation. As you will see, these two levels of segmentation can be combined within SD-Access to provide an unprecedented level of network-integrated segmentation capabilities, which is very useful to augment network security.

Finally, a fabric deployment allows for simplification—one of the most important areas of focus for any organization. To find out why, let's explore this area a bit further.

Networks tend to be very complex, in many cases due to the difficulty of rolling out network-wide policies such as security (ACLs), QoS, and the like. Many organizations use a combination of security ACLs and VLANs to implement network security policies—mapping users, devices, and things into VLANs (statically or dynamically), and then using ACLs on network devices or firewalls to implement the desired security policies. However, in the process of doing so, many such organizations find that their ACLs end up reflecting their entire IP subnetting structure—i.e., which users in which subnets are allowed to communicate to which devices or services in other subnets ends up being directly "written into" the ACLs the organization deploys.

If you recall, this was examined in some detail back in Chapter 9. The basic fact is that the IP header contains no explicit user/device identity information, so IP addresses and subnets are used as a proxy for this. However, this is how many organizations end up with hundreds, or even thousands, of VLANs. This is how those same organizations end up with ACLs that are hundreds or thousands of lines long—so long and complex, in fact, that they become very cumbersome to deploy, as well as difficult or impossible to maintain. This slows down network implementations, and possibly ends up compromising security due to unforeseen or undetected security holes—all driven by the complexity of this method of security operation.

A fabric solution offers a different, and better, approach. All endpoints connecting to a fabric-based network such as SD-Access are authenticated (either statically or dynamically). Following this authentication, they are assigned to a Scalable Group linked with their role, as well as being mapped into an associated virtual network. These two markings—SGT and VN—are then carried end to end in the fabric overlay packet header (using VXLAN), and all policies created within the fabric (i.e., which users have access to which resources) are based on this encoded group information—not on their IP address or subnet. The abstraction offered by the use of VNs and SGTs for grouping users and devices within an SD-Access deployment is key to the increased simplicity that SD-Access offers versus traditional approaches.

All packets carried within an SD-Access fabric contain user/device IP address information, but this is not used for applying policy in an SD-Access fabric. Polices within SD-Access are group-based in nature (and thus known as group-based policies, or GBPs). IP addresses in SD-Access are used for determining reachability (where has a host connected from or roamed to) as tracked by the fabric's LISP control plane. Endpoints are subject to security and other policies based on their flexible groupings, using SGTs and VNs as their policy tags—tags that are carried end to end within the SD-Access fabric using the VXLAN-based overlay.

Now you are beginning to see the importance of the protocols—LISP, VXLAN, and SGTs—that were covered in Chapter 9. If you skipped over that section, it is highly recommended to go back and review it now. These protocols are the key to creating network fabrics, and to enabling the next generation of networking that SD-Access represents. They serve as the strong foundation for a fabric-enabled network—one that enables the simplicity and flexibility that today's organizations require—while also providing integrated support for security and mobility, two key aspects of any modern network deployment.

Capabilities Offered by SD-Access

Now that you understand the power that the separation of IP addressing and policy offered by Software-Defined Access provides, let's delve a bit deeper and see what advanced, next-generation, network-level capabilities SD-Access offers for organizations.

Virtual Networks

First and foremost, SD-Access offers macro-segmentation using VNs. Equivalent to virtual routing and forwarding instances (VRF) in a traditional segmentation environment, VNs provide separate routed "compartments" within the fabric network infrastructure. Users, devices, and things are mapped into the same, or different VNs, based on their identity. Between VNs, a default-deny policy is implemented (i.e., endpoints in one VN have no access to endpoints in another VN by default). In effect, VNs provide a first level of segmentation that, by default, ensures no communications between users and devices located in different VNs. This is illustrated in Figure 19-4.

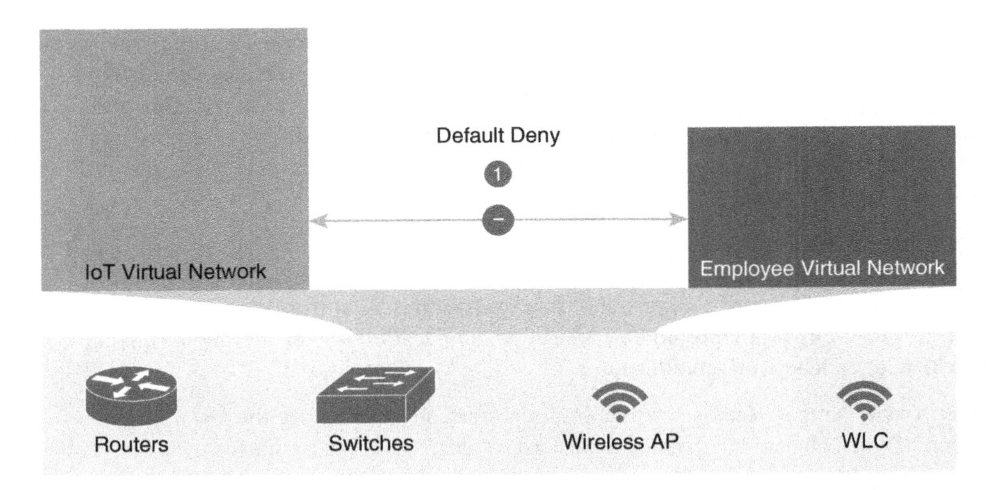

Figure 19-4 *Virtual Networks in SD-Access*

In this example, IoT devices are placed into one VN, and employees into another. Because the two VNs are separate and distinct routing spaces, no communication from one to the other is possible, unless explicitly permitted by the network administrator (typically via routing any such inter-VN traffic via a firewall, for example).

VNs provide a "macro" level of segmentation because they separate whole blocks of users and devices. There are many situations where this is desirable—examples include hospitals, airports, stadiums, banks...in fact, any organization that hosts multiple different types of users and things, and which needs these various communities sharing the common network infrastructure to be securely (and simply) separated from each other, while still having access to a common set of network services.

However, as useful as VNs are, they become even more powerful when augmented with micro-segmentation, which allows for group-based access controls even *within* a VN. Let's explore this next.

Scalable Groups

The use of Scalable Groups within SD-Access provides the capability for intra-VN traffic filtering and control. Scalable Groups have two aspects: a Scalable Group Tag (SGT), which serves as the group identity for an endpoint, and which is carried end to end in the SD-Access fabric within the VXLAN fabric data plane encapsulation, and a Scalable Group ACL (SGACL, sometimes also previously known as Security Group ACL), which controls what other hosts and resources are accessible to that endpoint, based on the endpoint's identity and role.

Group-based polices are far easier to define and understand than traditional IP-based ACLs because they are decoupled from the actual IP address structure in use. In this way, group-based ACLs are much more tightly aligned with the way that humans think about network security policies—"I want to give this group of users access to this, this, and this, and deny them from access to that and that"—and, as such, group-based policies are far easier to define, use, and understand than traditional access controls based on IP addresses and subnets.

Group-based policies are defined using either a whitelist model or a blacklist model. In a whitelist model, all traffic between groups is denied unless it is explicitly permitted (i.e., whitelisted) by a network administrator. In a blacklist model, the opposite is true: all traffic between groups is permitted unless such communication is explicitly blocked (i.e., blacklisted) by a network administrator.

In Software-Defined Access, a whitelist model is used by default for the macro-segmentation of traffic between VNs, and a blacklist model is used by default for the micro-segmentation of traffic between groups in the same VN. In effect, the use of groups within SD-Access provides a second level of segmentation, allowing the flexibility to control traffic flows at a group level even within a given VN.

The use of these two levels of segmentation provided by SD-Access—VNs and SGTs—is illustrated in Figure 19-5.

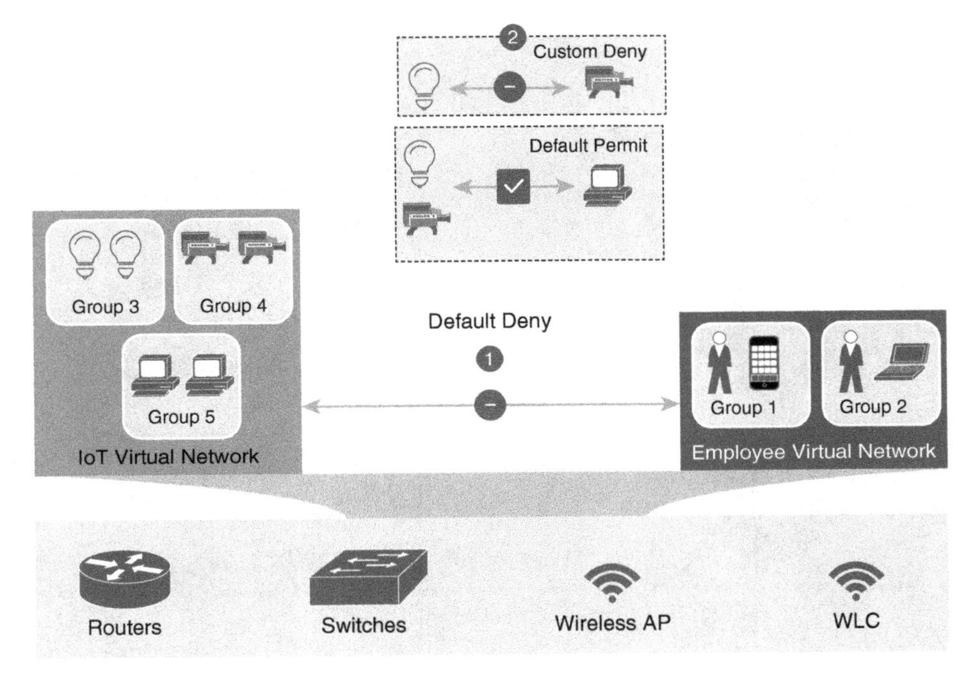

Figure 19-5 *Groups and Virtual Networks in SD-Access*

By providing two levels of segmentation, macro and micro, SD-Access provides the most secure network deployment possible for enterprises, and yet at the same time the simplest such approach for such organizations to understand, design, implement, and support. By including segmentation as an integral part of an SD-Access fabric deployment, SD-Access makes segmentation consumable—and opens up the power of integrated network security to all organizations, large and small.

Using Cisco DNA Center, SD-Access also makes the creation and deployment of VNs and group-based policies extremely simple. Policies in SD-Access are tied to user identities, not to subnets and IP addresses. After policies are defined, they seamlessly follow a user or device as it roams around the integrated wired/wireless SD-Access network. Policies are assigned simply by dragging and dropping groups in the Cisco DNA Center user interface, and are completely automated for deployment and use, as illustrated in Figure 19-6.

Before SD-Access, policies were VLAN and IP address based, requiring the network manager to create and maintain complex IP-based ACLs to define and enforce access policy, and then deal with any policy errors or violations manually. With SD-Access, there is no VLAN or IP address/subnet dependency for segmentation and access control (as these are defined at the VN/SGT grouping levels). The network manager in SD-Access is instead able to define one consistent policy, associated with the identity of the user or device, and have that identity (and the associated policy) follow the user or device as it roams within the fabric-based network infrastructure.

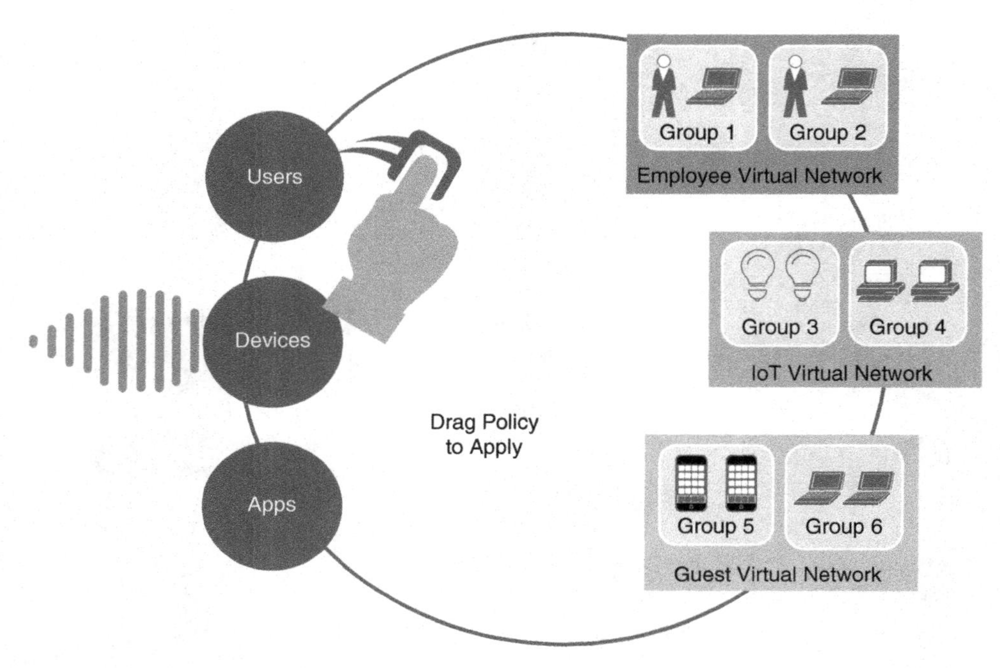

Figure 19-6 *Groups and Virtual Network Assignment with SD-Access*

As you will see, policies within SD-Access are based on contracts that define who, or what, the user or device has access to in the network. Such contracts are easily updated via Cisco DNA Center to reflect new policy rules and updates as these change over time—with the resulting network-level policies then pushed out to the network elements involved in an automated fashion. This massively simplifies not only the initial definition of network policies, but also their ongoing maintenance over time.

In summary, simplified, multilevel network segmentation based on virtual networks and group-based policy is an inherent property of what SD-Access offers, and is an extremely important and powerful part of the solution.

Let's continue on and explore what else SD-Access has in store.

Stretched Subnets

Most organizations at one time or another have faced the need to provide a single IP subnet that spans across—i.e., is "stretched between"—multiple wiring closets within a campus deployment. The reasons for such a need vary. They might involve applications that need to reside within a single common subnet, or older devices that cannot easily employ subnetting (due to the higher-level protocols they employ).Whatever the reason, such deployment requests pose a quandary for the typical network manager. Providing this capability in a traditional network deployment means extending a VLAN between multiple wiring closets—connecting them all together into a single, widely spanned Layer 2 domain. Although this is functional to meet the need, acceding to such requests places their network at overall risk.

Because all modern networks employ redundant interconnections between network devices, such wide-spanning Layer 2 domains create loops—many loops—in a typical enterprise network design. The Spanning Tree Protocol "breaks" any such loops by blocking ports and VLANs on redundant uplinks and downlinks within the network, thus avoiding the endless propagation of Layer 2 frames (which are not modified on forwarding) over such redundant paths.

However, this wastes much of the bandwidth (up to 50 percent) within the network due to all of the blocking ports in operation, and is complex to maintain because now there is a Layer 2 topology (maintained via Spanning Tree) and a Layer 3 topology (maintained via routing protocols and first-hop redundancy protocols) to manage, and these must be kept congruent to avoid various challenges to traffic forwarding and network operation. And even when all of this is done, and done properly, the network is still at risk because any misbehaving network device or flapping link could potentially destabilize the entire network—leading in the worst case to a broadcast storm should Spanning Tree fail to contain the issue.

Essentially, the use of wide-spanning Layer 2 VLANs places the entire network domain over which they span into a single, common failure domain—in the sense that a single failure within that domain has the potential to take all of the domain down, with potentially huge consequences for the organization involved.

Due to these severe limitations, many network managers either ban the use of wide-spanning VLANs entirely in their network topologies or, if forced to use them due to the necessity to deploy the applications involved, employ them gingerly and with a keen awareness of the ongoing operational risk they pose.

One of the major benefits provided by SD-Access, in addition to integrated identity-based policy and segmentation, is the ability to "stretch" subnets between wiring closets in a campus or branch deployment in a simple manner, and without having to pay the "Spanning Tree tax" associated with the traditional wide-spanning VLAN approach.

Figure 19-7 illustrates the use of stretched subnets within SD-Access.

With SD-Access, a single subnet (10.1.0.0/16, as shown in Figure 19-7) is stretched across all of the wiring closets within the fabric deployment. By doing so, any endpoint attached within any of these wiring closets can (if properly authenticated) be mapped into this single, wide-spanning IP subnet, which appears identical to the endpoint (same default gateway IP and MAC address), regardless of where the endpoint is attached—without having to span Layer 2 across all of these wiring closets to provide this capability.

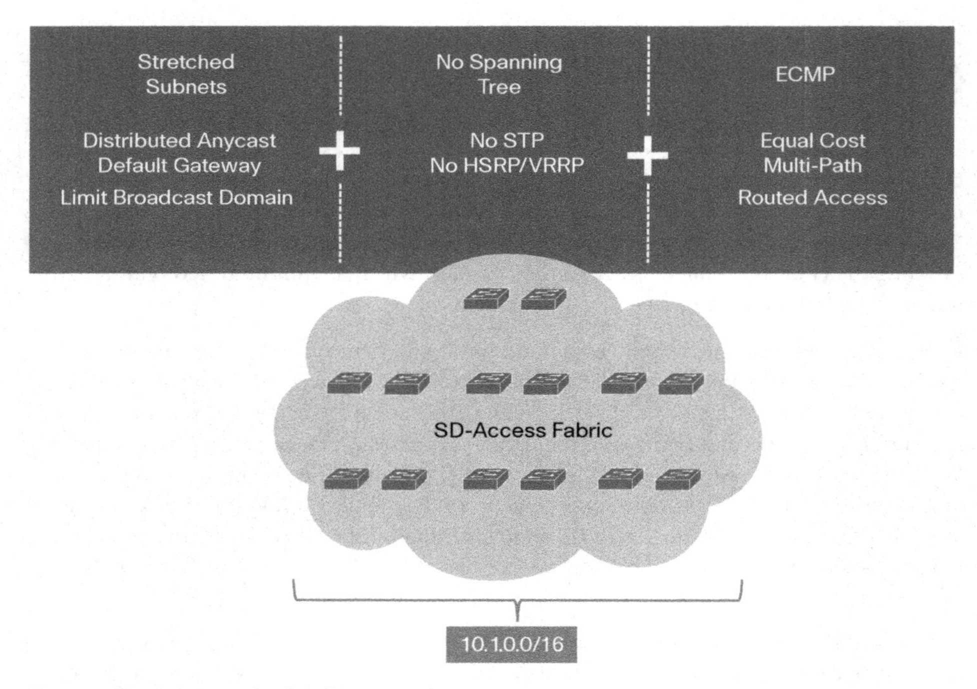

Figure 19-7 *Stretched Subnets with SD-Access*

This is accomplished by the use of the Distributed Anycast Default Gateway function within SD-Access. No matter where a device attaches to the subnet shown, its default gateway for that subnet is always local, being hosted on the first-hop switch (hence, distributed). Moreover, it always employs the same virtual MAC address for this default gateway (thus, anycast). The combination of these two attributes makes the SD-Access fabric "look the same" no matter where a device attaches—a critical consideration for roaming devices, and a major factor in driving simplification of the network deployment.

In addition, it is vital to note that SD-Access provides this stretched subnet capability without actually extending the Layer 2 domain between wiring closets. Spanning Tree still exists southbound (i.e., toward user ports) from the wiring closet switches in an SD-Access deployment—but critically, Spanning Tree and the Layer 2 domain are not extended "northbound" across the SD-Access fabric. SD-Access makes it possible to have the same IP subnet appear across multiple wiring closets, without having to create Layer 2 loops as a traditional wide-spanning VLAN approach does.

In this way, SD-Access provides the benefits of a stretched IP subnet for applications and devices that may need this capability, but eliminates the risk otherwise associated with doing so. Broadcast domains are limited in extent to a single wiring closet, and no cross-network Layer 2 loops are created.

SD-Access also provides several additional key attributes with the approach it employs for stretched subnets.

First, because SD-Access instantiates the default gateway for each fabric subnet always at the first-hop network switch, traditional first-hop gateway redundancy protocols such as Hot Standby Router Protocol (HSRP) or Virtual Router Redundancy Protocol (VRRP) are not required. This eliminates a major level of complexity for redundant network designs, especially because maintaining congruity between the Layer 2 and Layer 3 first-hop infrastructures—a significant task in traditional networks—is not needed. SD-Access stretched subnets are very simple to design and maintain. In fact, all subnets (known as IP host pools) that are deployed within an SD-Access fabric site are stretched to all wiring closets within that fabric site by default.

Secondly, since SD-Access is deployed on top of a fully routed underlay network, ECMP routing is provided across the fabric for the encapsulated overlay traffic. This ensures that all links between switches in the fabric network are fully utilized—no ports are ever placed into blocking mode—offering vastly improved traffic forwarding compared to traditional Layer 2/Layer 3 designs.

To ensure that traffic is load-balanced over multiple paths optimally, the inner (encapsulated) endpoint packet's IP five-tuple information (source IP, destination IP, source port, destination port, and protocol) is hashed into the outer encapsulating (VXLAN) packets' source port. This ensures that all links are utilized equally within the fabric backbone by providing this level of entropy for ECMP link load sharing, while also ensuring that any individual flow transits over only one set of links, thus avoiding out-of-order packet delivery.

The use of a routed underlay also ensures rapid recovery in the event of network link or node failures, because such recovery takes place at the rapid pace associated with a routing protocol, not the relatively more torpid pace associated with Layer 2 reconvergence.

The use of a routed underlay for SD-Access results in a more stable, predictable, and optimized forwarding platform for use by the overlay network, and the ability to then deploy stretched subnets in the SD-Access overlay network provides a flexible deployment model without the trade-offs (i.e., inability to deploy a stretched-subnet design) that such a fully routed network deployment incurs in a traditional (non-fabric) network system.

Finally, the use of stretched subnets with SD-Access allows organizations to massively simplify their IP address planning and provisioning. Because subnets within the SD-Access fabric site are by default stretched to all wiring closets spanned by that fabric site, a much smaller number of much larger IP address pools can be provisioned and used for the site involved. This not only greatly simplifies an organization's IP address planning, it leads to much more efficient use of the IP address pool space than the typical larger-number-of-smaller-subnets approach used by many enterprise network deployments. This simplicity and efficient use of IP address space in turn allows organizations to be speedier to adapt to the support of new devices and services that need to be mapped into the network infrastructure.

Now that we've examined some of the key network-level benefits of an SD-Access deployment, let's continue and explore the components that combine to create an SD-Access solution.

SD-Access High-Level Architecture and Attributes

This section reviews the high-level architecture of SD-Access, outlines some of the major components that make up the solution, and examines the various attributes associated with these components.

SD-Access as a solution is composed of several primary building blocks:

- **Cisco DNA Center:** This serves as the key component for implementation of the automation and assurance capabilities of SD-Access. Consisting physically of one or more appliances, Cisco DNA Center provides the platform from which an SD-Access solution is designed, provisioned, monitored, and maintained. Cisco DNA Center provides not only the design and automation capabilities to roll out an SD-Access fabric network deployment, it also provides the analytics platform functionality necessary to absorb telemetry from the SD-Access network, and provide actionable insights based on this network data.
- **Identity Services Engine:** ISE provides a key security platform for integration of user/device identity into the SD-Access network. ISE allows for the policy and segmentation capabilities of SD-Access to be based around endpoint and group identity, allowing the implementation of network-based policies that are decoupled from IP addressing—a key attribute of an SD-Access deployment.
- **Network infrastructure (wired and wireless):** The SD-Access solution encompasses both wired and wireless network elements, and provides the ability to create a seamless network fabric from these components. A review of which network elements make up an SD-Access fabric is outlined later in this chapter. A unique and powerful capability of SD-Access is the capacity to reuse many existing network infrastructure elements—switches, routers, access points, and Wireless LAN Controller (WLCs)—and repurpose them for use in a powerful new fabric-based deployment model.

By delivering a solution that embodies the best aspects of software flexibility and rapid development, with hardware-based performance and scale, SD-Access provides "networking at the speed of software."

The high-level design of an SD-Access solution is shown in Figure 19-8, along with callouts concerning some of the key attributes of SD-Access.

Now, let's dive into the details and examine how SD-Access is built, review the components that are part of an SD-Access solution, and detail the benefits SD-Access delivers.

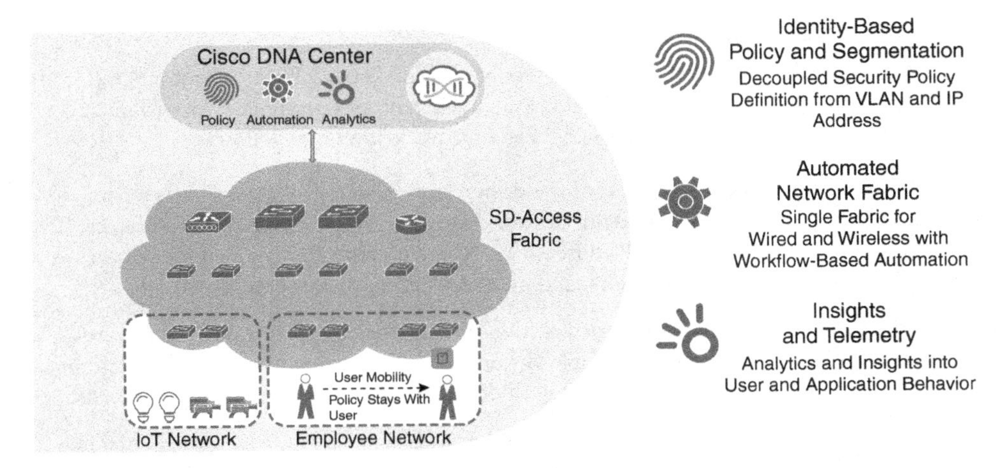

Figure 19-8 *SD-Access High-Level Architecture and Key Attributes*

SD-Access Building Blocks

As mentioned, the SD-Access solution leverages several key building blocks: namely, Cisco DNA Center, ISE, and the network infrastructure elements which form the SD-Access fabric. Figure 19-9 illustrates these key building blocks of SD-Access:

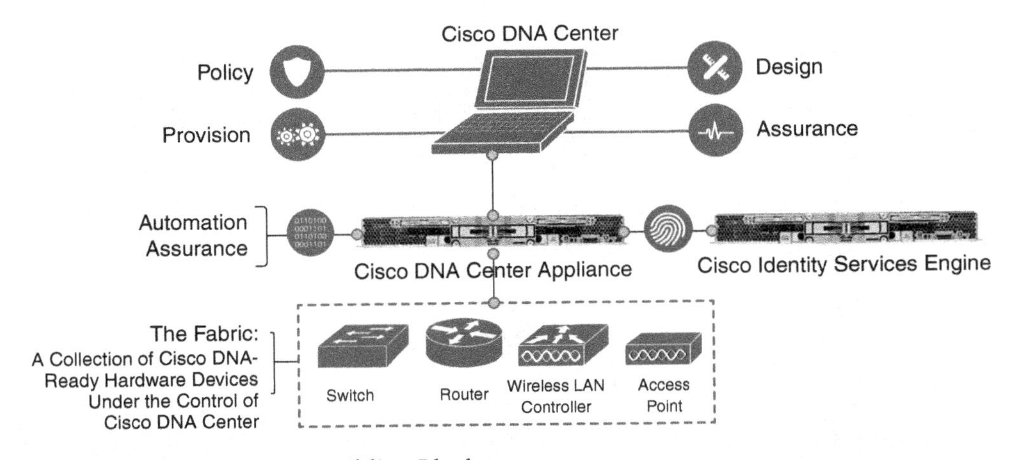

Figure 19-9 *SD-Access Building Blocks*

Let's begin by examining Cisco DNA Center, with a focus on how this supports an SD-Access deployment.

Cisco DNA Center in SD-Access

Cisco DNA Center's support of the SD-Access solution set is focused on a four-step workflow model. These four major workflows consist of Design, Policy, Provision, and Assurance. The major focus of each of these four workflows is as follows:

- **Design:** This workflow allows for the design of the overall system. This is where common attributes such as major network capabilities (DHCP and DNS services, IP host pools for user/device IP addressing, etc) are created and enumerated, as well as where network locations, floors, and maps are laid out and populated.
- **Policy:** This workflow allows the creation of fabric-wide policies, such as the creation of Virtual Networks, Scalable Groups, and contracts between groups defining access rights and attributes, in line with defined organizational policies and goals.
- **Provision:** Design and policy come together in this workflow, where the actual network fabrics are created, devices are assigned to various roles within those fabrics, and device configurations are created and pushed out to the network elements that make up the SD-Access overlay/underlay infrastructure.
- **Assurance:** The final workflow allows for the definition and gathering of telemetry from the underlying network, with the goal of analyzing the vast amounts of data which can be gathered from the network and refining this into actionable insights.

These four workflows in Cisco DNA Center are outlined in Figure 19-10.

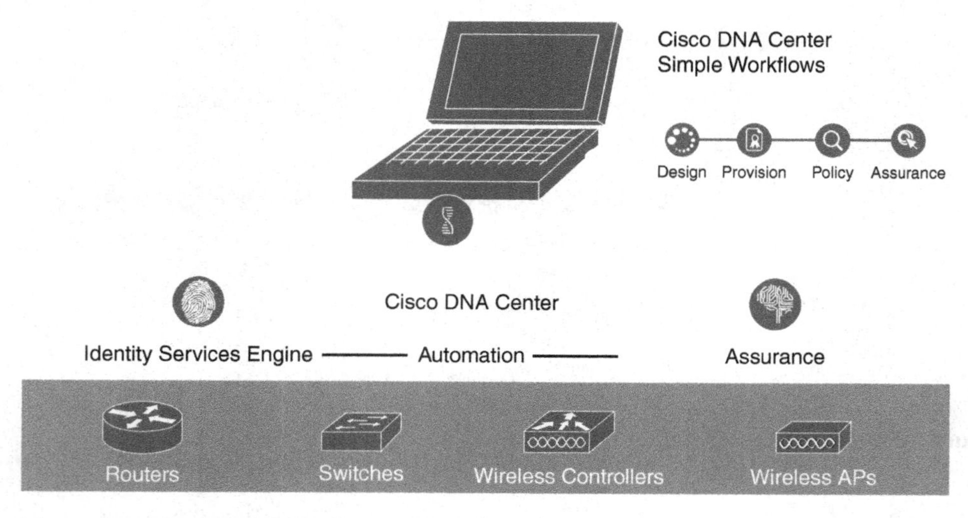

Figure 19-10 *Cisco DNA Center Workflow*

As the central point for defining, deploying, and monitoring the SD-Access network, Cisco DNA Center plays a key role in any SD-Access implementation. A single Cisco DNA Center instance can be used to deploy multiple SD-Access fabrics.

Many of the key attributes and capabilities of Cisco DNA Center were outlined previously as we examined the Automation and Assurance functionality of Cisco DNA. Any SD-Access deployment leverages Cisco DNA Center as the core element for the definition, management, and monitoring of the SD-Access fabric.

Now, let's examine a few of the key elements that Cisco DNA Center provisions in an SD-Access fabric deployment.

SD-Access Fabric Capabilities

Three of these key elements which are defined in Cisco DNA Center and then rolled out into the SD-Access fabric for deployment are IP Host Pools, Virtual Networks, and Scalable Groups. Let's double-click on each of these areas to gain a better understanding of the role they play in an SD-Access implementation.

IP Host Pools

IP host pools are created within Cisco DNA Center, and are the IP subnets which are deployed for use by users, devices, and things attached to the SD-Access fabric. Host pools, once defined within a fabric deployment, are bound to a given Virtual Network, and are rolled out by Cisco DNA Center to all of the Fabric Edge switches in the fabric site involved. The subnets defined in the Host Pools are rolled out onto all the network edge switches within that fabric site (same virtual IP and virtual MAC at all locations at that site), thus driving network simplification and standardization.

Each IP host pool is associated with a distributed anycast default gateway (as discussed previously) for the subnet involved, meaning that each edge switch in the fabric serves as the local default gateway for any endpoints (wired or wireless) attached to that switch. The given subnet is by default "stretched" across all of the edge switches within the given fabric site deployment, making this host pool available to endpoints no matter where they attach to the given fabric at that site.

Figure 19-11 illustrates the deployment and use of IP host pools within an SD-Access fabric deployment.

Endpoints attaching to the SD-Access fabric are mapped into the appropriate IP host pools, either statically, or dynamically based on user/device authentication, and are tracked by the fabric control plane, as outlined in the following text concerning fabric device roles. To provide simplicity and allow for easy host mobility, the fabric edge nodes that the endpoints attach to implement the distributed anycast default gateway capability, as outlined previously, providing a very easy-to-use deployment model.

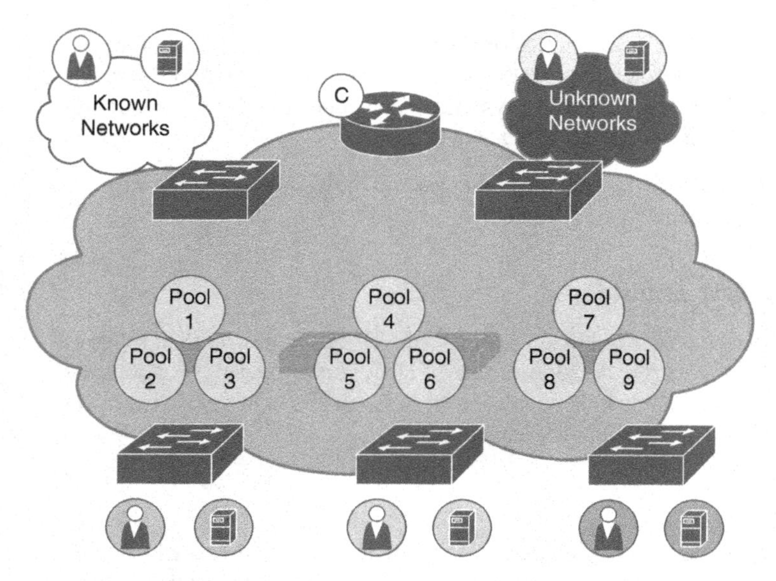

Figure 19-11 *Cisco DNA Center—Provisioning of IP Host Pools*

Virtual Networks

Virtual networks are created within Cisco DNA Center and offer a secure, compartmentalized form of macro-segmentation for access control. VNs are mapped to VRFs, which provide complete address space separation between VNs, and are carried across the fabric network as virtual network IDs (VNIs, also sometimes referred to as VNIDs) mapped into the VXLAN data plane header.

An illustration of VNs within an SD-Access deployment is shown in Figure 19-12.

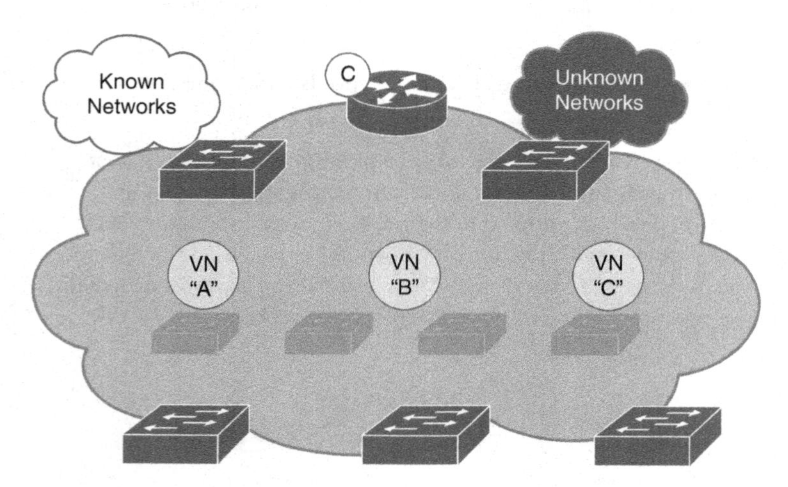

Figure 19-12 *Cisco DNA Center—Provisioning of Virtual Networks*

Every SD-Access fabric deployment contains a "default" VN, into which devices and users are mapped by default (i.e., if no other policies or mappings are applied). Additional VNs are created and used as desired by the network administrator to define and enforce the network segmentation polices that the administrator may wish to use within the SD-Access fabric. An additional VN that exists by default within an SD-Access deployment is the INFRA_VN (Infrastructure VN), into which network infrastructure devices such as access points and extended node switches are mapped.

The scale for implementation of additional VNs depends of the scalability associated with network elements within the fabric, including the border and edge node types involved. New platforms are introduced periodically, each with its own scaling parameters, and as well the scale associated with devices may also vary by software release. Please refer to Cisco.com, as well as resources such as the *Software-Defined Access Design Guide* outlined in the "Further Reading" section at the end of this chapter (https://www.cisco.com/c/dam/en/us/td/docs/solutions/CVD/Campus/CVD-Software-Defined-Access-Design-Guide-2018AUG.pdf) for the latest information associated with VN scale across various device types within an SD-Access fabric deployment.

Scalable Groups

Scalable Groups (SG) are created within Cisco DNA Center as well as ISE, and offer a secure form of micro-segmentation for access control. SGs are carried across the SD-Access fabric as SGTs mapped into the VXLAN data plane header. Scalable Group ACLs (SGACLs) are used for egress traffic filtering and access control with an SD-Access deployment, enforced at the fabric edge and/or fabric border positions in the fabric.

For additional details on the use the SGTs and SGACLs, please refer to Chapter 9, where this is covered in greater depth.

The use of SGTs within an SD-Access deployment is illustrated in Figure 19-13.

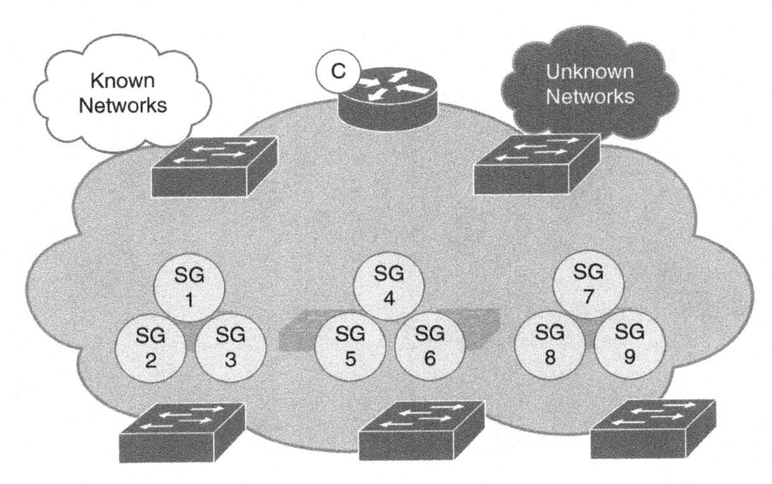

Figure 19-13 *Cisco DNA Center—Provisioning of Scalable Groups*

The combination of VNs and SGTs within the SD-Access solution, along with the automated deployment of these capabilities by Cisco DNA Center, provide an extremely flexible and powerful segmentation solution for use by enterprise networks of all sizes.

The ability to easily define, roll out, and support an enterprise-wide segmentation solution has long been a desirable goal for many organizations. However, it has often proved to be out of reach for many in the past due to the complexities (MPLS VPNs, VRF-lite, etc.) associated with previous segmentation solutions.

SD-Access and Cisco DNA Center now bring this powerful capability for two levels of segmentation—macro-segmentation using VNs, and micro-segmentation using SGTs—to many enterprise networks worldwide, making this important set of security and access control capabilities far more consumable than they were previously.

Now that you've been introduced to some of the higher-level constructs that Cisco DNA Center assists in provisioning in an SD-Access fabric deployment—IP host pools, virtual networks, and Scalable Groups—let's delve into the roles that various network infrastructure devices support within the fabric.

SD-Access Device Roles

Various network infrastructure devices perform different roles within an SD-Access deployment, and work together to make up the network fabric that SD-Access implements.

The various roles for network elements with an SD-Access solution are outlined in Figure 19-14.

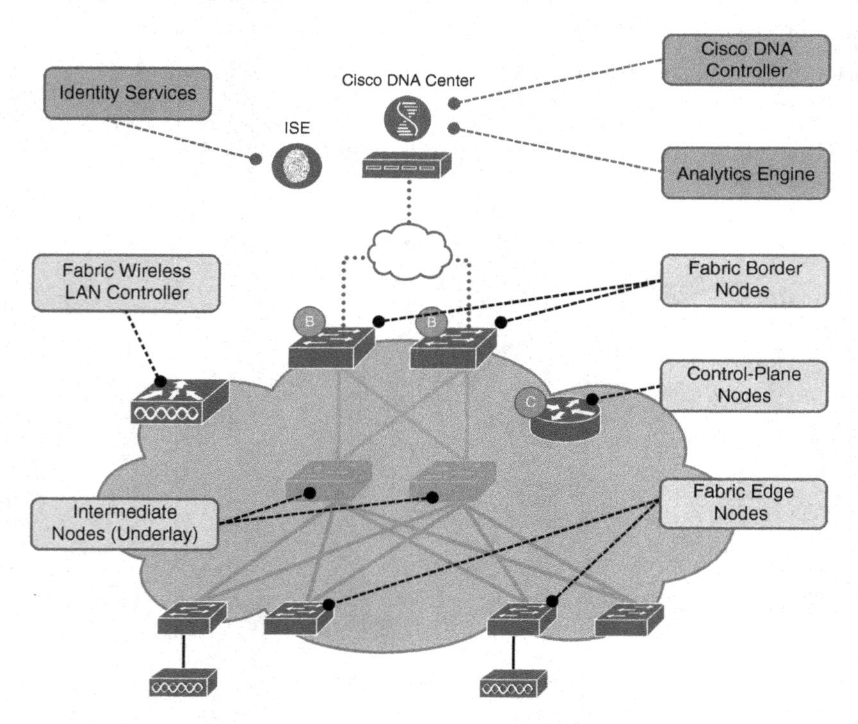

Figure 19-14 *SD-Access—Device Roles and Terminology*

These various device roles and capabilities are summarized briefly as follows:

- **Cisco DNA Center:** Serves as the overall element for designing, provisioning, and monitoring the SD-Access deployment, as well as for providing network monitoring and assurance capabilities.
- **Identity Services Engine:** Serves as the primary repository for identity and policy within the SD-access deployment, providing dynamic authentication and authorization for endpoints attaching to the fabric. ISE also interfaces with external identity sources such as Active Directory.
- **Control plane nodes:** One or more network elements that implement the LISP Map Server/Map Resolver (MS/MR) functionality. Basically, the control plane nodes within the SD-Access fabric "keep track" of where all the users, devices, and things attached to the fabric are located, for both wired and wireless endpoints. The control plane nodes are key elements within the SD-Access fabric architecture, as they serve as the "single source of truth" as to where all devices attached to the SD-Access fabric are located as they connect, authenticate, and roam.
- **Border nodes:** One or more network elements that connect the SD-Access fabric to the "rest of the world" outside of the fabric deployment. One of the major tasks of the border node or nodes is to provide reachability in and out of the fabric environment, and to translate between fabric constructs such as virtual networks and Scalable Group Tags and the corresponding constructs outside of the fabric environment.
- **Edge nodes:** Network elements (typically, many) that attach end devices such as PCs, phones, cameras, and many other types of systems into the SD-Access fabric deployment. Edge nodes serve as the "first-hop" devices for attachment of endpoints into the fabric, and are responsible for device connectivity and policy enforcement. Edge nodes in the LISP parlance are sometimes known as Routing Locators (RLOCs), and the endpoints themselves are denoted by Endpoint IDs (EIDs), typically IP addresses or MAC addresses.
- **Fabric Wireless LAN Controller (WLC):** Performs all the tasks that the WLC traditionally is responsible for—controlling access points attached to the network and managing the radio frequency (RF) space used by these APs, as well as authenticating wireless clients and managing wireless roaming—but also interfaces with the fabric's control plane node(s) to provide a constantly up-to-date map of which RLOCs (i.e., access-layer fabric edge switches) any wireless EIDs are located behind as they attach and roam within the wireless network.
- **Intermediate nodes:** Any network infrastructure devices that are part of the fabric that lies "in between" two other SD-Access fabric nodes. In most deployments, intermediate nodes consist of distribution or core switches. In many ways, the intermediate nodes have the simplest task of all, as they are provisioned purely in the network underlay and do not participate in the VXLAN-based overlay network directly. As such, they are forwarding packets solely based on the outer IP address in the VXLAN header's UDP encapsulation, and are often selected for their speed, robustness, and ability to be automated by Cisco DNA Center for this role.

It is important to note that any SD-Access fabric site must consist of a minimum of three logical components: at least one fabric control plane, one or more edges, and one or more borders. Taken together, these constructs comprise an SD-Access fabric, along with Cisco DNA Center for automation and assurance and ISE for authentication, authorization, and accounting (AAA) and policy capabilities.

Now, let's explore a few of these device roles in greater detail to examine what they entail and the functions they perform. As we examine each role, a sample overview of which devices might typically be employed in these roles is provided.

SD-Access Control Plane Nodes, a Closer Look

The role of the control plane node in SD-Access is a crucial one. The control plane node implements the LISP MS/MR functionality, and as such is tasked with operating as the single source of truth about where all users, devices, and things are located (i.e., which RLOC they are located behind) as these endpoints attach to the fabric, and as they roam.

The SD-Access control plane node tracks key information about each EID and provides it on demand to any network element that requires this information (typically, to forward packets to that device's attached RLOC, via the VXLAN overlay network).

Figure 9-15 illustrates the fabric control plane node in SD-Access.

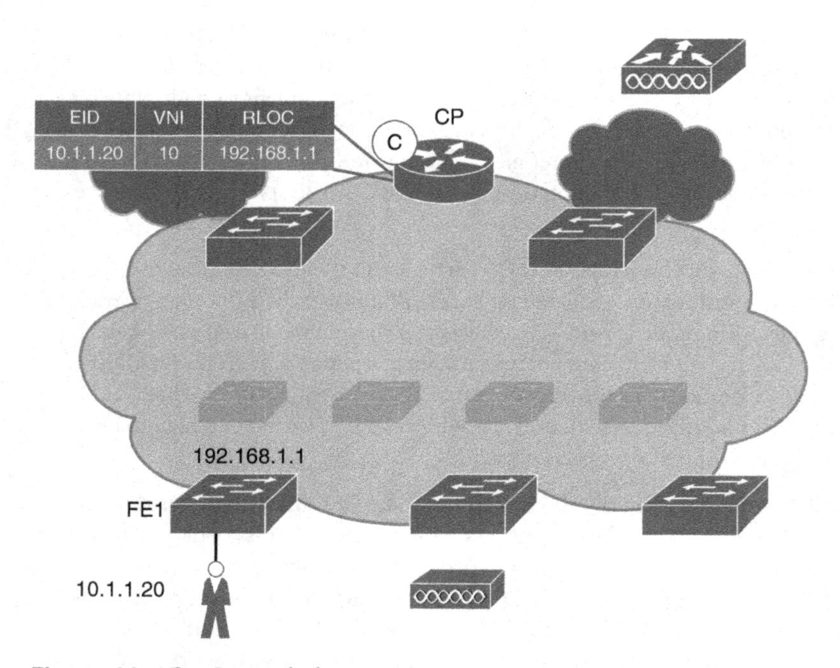

Figure 19-15 *Control Plane Nodes*

The fabric control plane node provides several important functions in an SD-Access network:

- Acts as a host database, tracking the relationship of EIDs to edge node (RLOC) bindings. The fabric control plane node supports multiple different types of EIDs, such as IPv4 /32s and MAC addresses.
- Receives prefix registrations from edge nodes for wired clients, and from fabric-mode WLCs for wireless clients.
- Resolves lookup requests from edge and border nodes to locate endpoints within the fabric (i.e., which RLOC is a given endpoint attached to and reachable via).
- Updates both edge and border nodes with wireless client mobility and RLOC information as clients roam within the fabric network system, as required.

Effectively, the control plane node in SD-Access acts as a constantly updated database for EID reachability. More than one control plane node can be (and would in most cases be recommended to be) deployed in an SD-Access fabric build.

If more than one control plane node is employed, they do not require or use any complex protocol to synchronize with each other. Rather, each control plane node is simply updated by all of the network elements separately—i.e., if two control plane nodes exist in a given fabric, an edge node, border node, or WLC attached to that fabric is simply configured to communicate with both control plane nodes, and updates both of them when any new device attaches to the fabric, or roams within it. In this way, the control plane node implementation is kept simple, without the complexity that would otherwise be introduced by state sync between nodes.

It is important to note that the control plane node is updated directly by an edge node (for example, an access switch) for wired clients attached to that switch, while for wireless clients the WLC (which manages the wireless domain) is responsible for interfacing with, and updating, the control plane node for wireless clients. The integration of wireless into an SD-Access fabric environment is examined in more detail later in this chapter.

A key attribute that it is critical to note about LISP as a protocol is that it is based on the concept of "conversational learning"—that is to say, a given LISP-speaking device (source RLOC) does not actually learn the location of a given EID (i.e., which destination RLOC that EID currently resides behind) until it has traffic to deliver to that EID. This capability for conversational learning is absolutely key to the LISP architecture, and is a major reason why LISP was selected as the reachability protocol of choice for SD-Access.

The task of a traditional routing protocol, such as Border Gateway Protocol (BGP), is essentially to flood all reachability information everywhere (i.e., to every node in the routing domain). Although this is workable when the number of reachability information elements (i.e., routes) is small—say, a few thousand—such an approach rapidly becomes impractical in a larger deployment.

Imagine, for example, a large campus such as a university that hosts on a daily basis (say) 50,000 to 75,000 users, each of whom may be carrying two or three network devices on average. Using an approach with a traditional routing protocol that attempted to flood the information about 150,000 to 200,000+ endpoints to all network devices would present a huge scaling challenge. Device ternary content-addressable memories (TCAMs) and routing tables would need to be enormous, and very expensive, and tracking all the changes as devices roamed about using the flooding-oriented control plane approach of a traditional routing protocol would rapidly overwhelm the CPU resource available even in large routing platforms—let alone the relatively much smaller CPU and memory resources available in (say) an access switch at the edge of the network.

Rather than use this approach, the LISP control plane node, operating in conjunction with LISP-speaking devices such as edge and border nodes, provides a conversational learning approach where the edge and border nodes query the control plane node for the destination RLOC to use when presented with traffic for a new destination (i.e., one that they have not recently forwarded traffic for). The edges and borders then cache this data for future use, reducing the load on the control plane node.

This use of conversational learning is a major benefit of LISP, as it allows for massive scalability while constraining the need for device resources, and is one of the major motivations for the use of LISP as the control plane protocol for use in SD-Access.

For further details on the operation of LISP, please refer to Chapter 9, which provides a description of the LISP protocol itself, as well as how roaming is handled within LISP.

SD-Access Control Plane Nodes: Supported Devices

Multiple devices can fulfill the task of operating as a fabric control plane node. The selection of the appropriate device for this critical task within the fabric is largely based on scale—in terms of both the number of EIDs supported and the responsiveness and performance of the control plane node itself (based on CPU sizing, memory, and other control plane performance factors).

Figure 19-16 outlines some of the platforms that, as of this writing, are able to operate as control plane nodes within the SD-Access fabric.

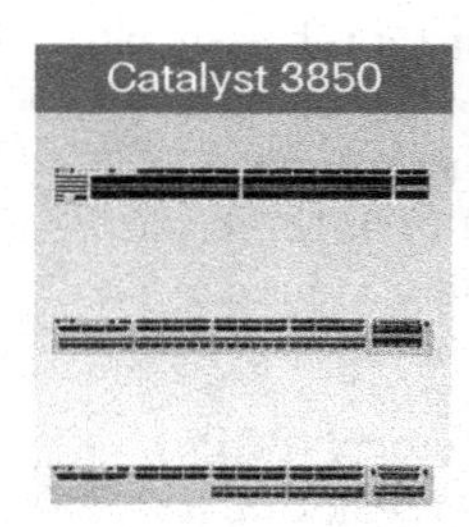

Catalyst 9500

Catalyst 6K

ASR1K/ISR4K and CSR1Kv

- Catalyst 3850
- 1/10G SFP
- 10/40G NM Cards
- IOS-XE 16.6.1+

- Catalyst 9500
- 10/40G SFP/QSFP
- 10/40G NM Cards
- IOS-XE 16.6.1+

- Catalyst 6800
- Sup2T/6T
- 6880-X or 6840-X
- IOS 15.5.1SY+

- CSRv
- ASR 1000-X/HX
- ISR 4430/4450
- IOS-XE 16.6.1+

Figure 19-16 *Control Plane Nodes, Device Support*

For many deployments, the fabric control plane node function is based on a switch platform. This is often very convenient, as such switches often exist in the deployment build in any case.

The control plane function is either co-located on a single device with the fabric border function (outlined in the following section) or implemented on a dedicated device for the control plane node. Typically, dedicating a device or devices to the control plane role, rather than having them serve dual functions, results in greater scalability as well as improved fault tolerance (because a single device failure then only impacts one fabric role/function, not both simultaneously). Nevertheless, many fabrics may choose to implement a co-located fabric control plane/border node set of functions on a common device, for the convenience and cost savings this offers.

Typically, the Catalyst 3850 platform (fiber based) is selected as a control plane node only for the smallest fabric deployments, or for pilot systems where an SD-Access fabric is first being tested. The amount of memory and CPU horsepower available in the Catalyst 3850 significantly restricts the scalability it offers for this role, however.

Many fabric deployments choose to leverage a Catalyst 9500 switch as a fabric control plane node. The multicore Intel CPU used in these platforms provides a significant level of performance and scalability for such fabric control plane use, and makes the Catalyst 9500 an ideal choice for many fabric control plane deployments. For branch deployments that require a fabric control plane, the ISR 4000 platforms are also leveraged for this task, with their CPU and memory footprint making them well suited to this task for a typical branch.

The very largest fabric deployments may choose to leverage an ASR 1000 as a fabric control plane node. This offers the greatest scalability for those SD-Access fabric installations that require it. It is worth noting that some control plane node types offer more limited functionality than others.

Please refer to Cisco.com, as well as resources such as the *Software-Defined Access Design Guide* outlined in the "Further Reading" section at the end of this chapter, for the exact details of the scalability and functionality for each of these control plane options, which vary between platform types. The control plane scale associated with these platforms may also vary between software releases, so referring to the latest online information for these scaling parameters is recommended.

Because new platforms are always being created, and older ones retired, please also be sure to refer to Cisco.com for the latest information on supported devices for the SD-Access fabric control plane role.

SD-Access Fabric Border Nodes, a Closer Look

Now, let's examine further the role of a fabric border node in SD-Access fabric.

As previously mentioned, the task of a border node is twofold: to connect the SD-Access fabric to the outside world, and to translate between SD-Access fabric constructs (VNs, SGTs) and any corresponding constructs in the outside network.

Figure 19-17 depicts fabric border nodes (marked with a B) in an SD-Access deployment.

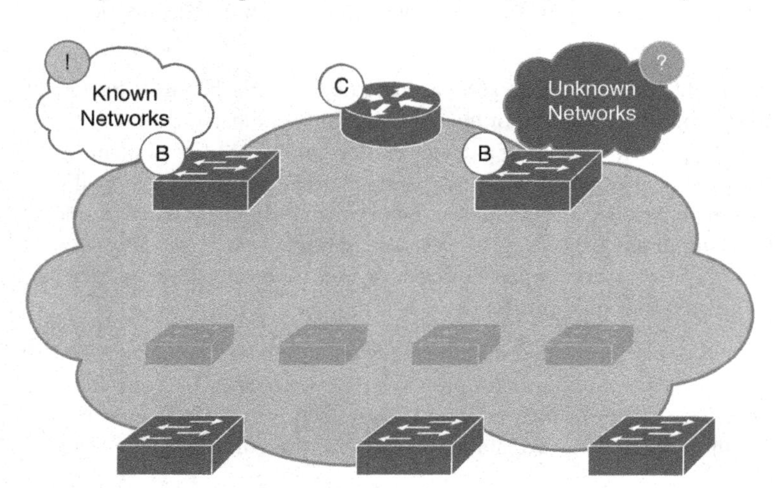

Figure 19-17 *SD-Access Border Nodes*

An important item to note is that SD-Access defines two basic types of border node: a fabric border and a default border. Let's examine each one of these in turn, after which we'll look at the devices supported.

SD-Access Fabric Border Nodes

Fabric border nodes (i.e., ones that are not default border nodes) connect the SD-Access fabric deployment to external networks that host a defined set of subnets (in Figure 19-17, this is the border attached to the cloud marked Known Networks). Examples of these are fabric border nodes attaching to a data center, wherein lie a set of defined server subnets, or a fabric border node attaching to a WAN, which hosts a defined set of subnets leading to, and hosted at, branch locations. For this reason, fabric borders are also sometimes referred to as *internal borders* because they border onto defined areas typically constrained within the enterprise network.

The fabric border node advertises the subnets (IP host pools) located inside the fabric to such external-to-the-fabric destinations, and imports prefixes from these destinations to provide fabric reachability to them. In LISP nomenclature, the fabric border node performs the role of an Ingress/Egress Tunnel Router (xTR).

The tasks performed by a fabric border node include

- Connecting to any "known" IP subnets attached to the outside network(s)
- Exporting all internal IP host pools to the outside (as aggregates), using traditional IP routing protocols
- Importing and registering known IP subnets from outside, into the fabric control plane
- Handling any required mappings for the user/device contexts (VN/SGT) from one domain to another

An SD-Access deployment implements one or more fabric border nodes for a given fabric deployment, as needed. Each fabric border node registers the IP subnets that are located beyond it into the LISP mapping database as IP prefixes (with the exception of the default border type, as noted in the next section), allowing the LISP control plane to in turn refer any other nodes needing reachability to those prefixes to the appropriate fabric border node for forwarding. More than one fabric border may be defined and used for redundancy, if required.

Once the traffic arrives at the fabric border node from a fabric node (such as an edge switch), the VXLAN encapsulation for the incoming packet is removed, and the inner (user) packet is then forwarded on the appropriate external interface, and within the appropriate external context (for example, if multiple VRFs are in use in the outside network connected to the fabric border, the packet is forwarded in the correct one as per the border's routing policy configuration).

When traffic arrives from the external network, the fabric border reverses this process, looking up the destination for the traffic from the fabric control plane node, then encapsulating the data into VXLAN and forwarding this traffic to the destination RLOC (typically, an edge switch).

SD-Access Fabric Default Border Nodes

As mentioned, fabric border nodes lead to "known" destinations outside of the fabric. However, there is often the need to reach out to destinations beyond the fabric for which it is impractical, or even impossible, to enumerate all possible subnets/prefixes (such as the Internet, for example). Borders that lead to such "unknown" destinations are known as fabric default borders.

The fabric default border node advertises the subnets (IP host pools) located inside the fabric to such external destinations. However, the fabric default border does not import any prefixes from the external domain. Rather, the fabric default border node operates similarly to a default route in a traditional network deployment, in that it serves as a forwarding point for all traffic whose destination inside or outside the fabric cannot otherwise be determined. When the LISP mapping system supporting a fabric domain has a "miss" on the lookup for a given external destination, this indicates to the system doing the lookup to forward traffic to the fabric default border node (if so configured). In LISP nomenclature, the fabric default border node performs the role of a proxy xTR (PxTR).

The tasks performed by a fabric default border node include

- Connecting to "unknown" IP subnets (i.e., Internet)
- Exporting all internal IP host pools to the outside (as aggregates), using traditional IP routing protocols
- Handling any required mappings for the user/device contexts (VN/SGT) from one domain to another

Note that a fabric default border node does *not* import unknown routes. Instead, it is the "default exit" point if no other entries are present for a given destination in the fabric control plane.

An SD-Access deployment may implement one or more fabric border nodes and/or default border nodes for a given fabric site, as needed (the exact number depending on the deployment needs involved, as well as the fabric border platforms and software releases in use—refer to resources such as the *Software-Defined Access Design Guide* outlined in the "Further Reading" section at the end of this chapter for more details).

The actual operation of a fabric default border node is largely identical to that of a non-default border node for such actions as packet encapsulation, decapsulation, and policy enforcement, with the exception that outside prefixes are not populated by the default border into the fabric control plane. It is worth noting that it is also possible to provision a border as an "anywhere border," thus allowing it to perform the functions of an internal border as well as a default border.

SD-Access Fabric Border Nodes: Supported Devices

Multiple devices can fulfill the task of operating as a fabric border node or default border node. As with the fabric control plane node, the selection of the appropriate device for this critical task within the fabric is largely based on scale—in terms of both the number of EIDs supported and the performance and sizing of the border node itself. By its nature, a border node must communicate with all devices and users within the fabric, and so is typically sized in line with the fabric it supports.

However, in addition, because the fabric border node is, by virtue of its role and placement within the network, inline with the data path in and out of the fabric, sizing of the fabric border node must also take into account the appropriate device performance, including traffic volumes, link speeds, and copper/optical interface types.

Figure 19-18 outlines some of the platforms that, as of this writing, operate as border nodes within the fabric.

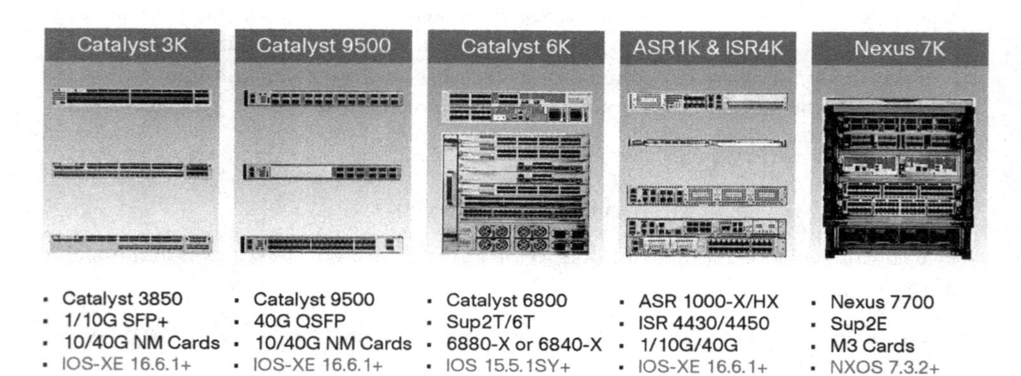

Figure 19-18 *Border Nodes, Device Support*

A wide range of fabric border exists, as shown, with a wide range of performance and scalability available. Again, the appropriate choice of fabric border node depends on the scale and functionality requirements involved.

As mentioned previously, a fabric border is implemented either as a dedicated border node or co-located with a fabric control plane function. While some deployments choose the co-located option, others opt for dedicated borders and control planes to provide greater scalability and to lessen the impact of any single device failure within the fabric.

Again, the Catalyst 3850 platforms (fiber based) are typically selected as a border node only for the smallest fabric deployments, or for pilot systems where an SD-Access fabric is first being tested. The amount of memory and CPU horsepower available in the Catalyst 3850, as well as the hardware forwarding performance it offers, may restrict the scalability it offers for this role, however.

Many fabric deployments choose to leverage a Catalyst 9500 switch as a fabric border node. The higher overall performance offered by this platform, both in terms of hardware speeds and feeds and in terms of the multicore Intel CPU used, provides a significant level of performance and scalability for such fabric border use, and makes the Catalyst 9500 an ideal choice for many fabric border deployments.

For branch deployments, the ISR 4000 platforms are also leveraged for this fabric border task, with their CPU and memory footprint making them well suited to this task for a typical branch. The very largest fabric deployments may choose to leverage an ASR 1000 as a fabric border node. This offers the greatest scalability for those SD-Access fabric installations that require this.

When selecting a border platform, please note that not all fabric border functions and capabilities are necessarily available across all of the possible border platforms available.

Please refer to Cisco.com, as well as resources such as the *Software-Defined Access Design Guide* outlined in the "Further Reading" section at the end of this chapter, for the exact details of the scalability and functionality for each of these fabric border options. The border node scale associated with these platforms varies between platform types, and may also vary between software releases, so referring to the latest online information for these scaling parameters is recommended.

Because new platforms are always being created, and older ones retired, please also be sure to refer to Cisco.com for the latest information on supported devices for the SD-Access fabric border role.

SD-Access Fabric Edge Nodes

Fabric edge nodes serve to attach endpoint devices to the SD-Access fabric. When endpoints attach to the fabric, the edge node serves to authenticate them, either using static authentication (i.e., static mapping of a port to a corresponding VN/SGT assignment) or dynamically using 802.1X and actual user/device identity for assignment to the correct VN/SGT combination, based on that user's or device's assigned role.

For traffic ingressing the edge node from attached devices, the fabric edge node looks up the proper location for the destination (RLOC, switch or router) using the fabric control plane node, then encapsulates the ingress packet into VXLAN, inserting the appropriate VN and SGT to allow for proper traffic forwarding and policy enforcement, and subsequently forwards the traffic toward the correct destination RLOC. In LISP nomenclature, the fabric edge node operates as an xTR.

For appropriate QoS handling by the fabric edges as well as intermediate nodes and border nodes, the inner (user) packet DSCP value is copied into the outer IP/UDP-based VXLAN header, and may be used by any QoS policies in use within the fabric network.

Figure 19-19 illustrates the use of fabric edge nodes in SD-Access.

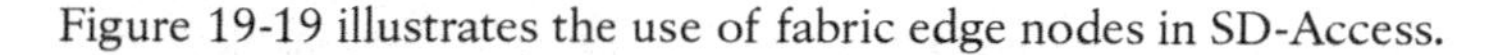

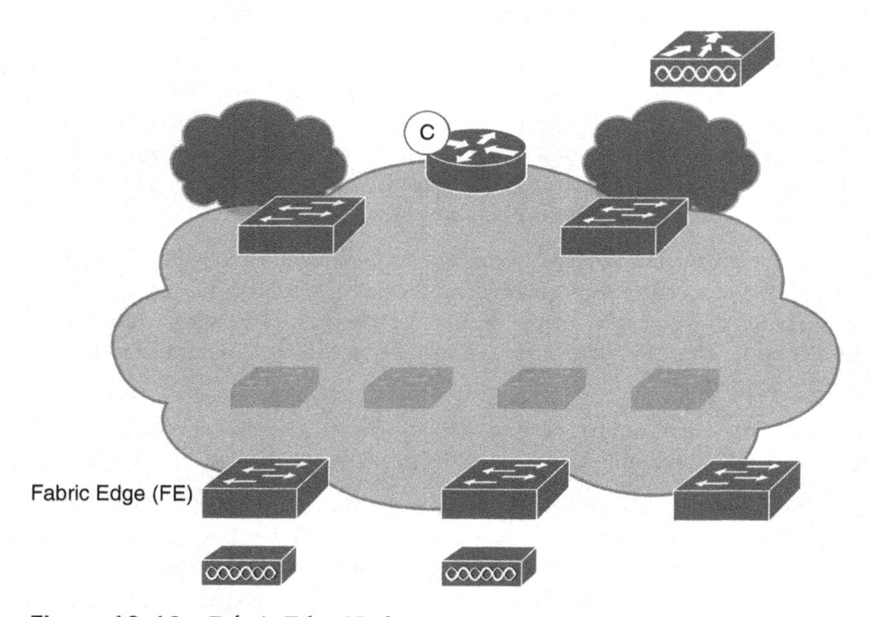

Figure 19-19 *Fabric Edge Nodes*

A summary of some of the important functions provided by fabric edge nodes includes

- Identifying and authenticating attached wired endpoints
- Registering endpoint ID information with fabric control plane nodes
- Providing anycast Layer 3 gateway services for attached endpoints
- Onboarding users and devices into the SD-Access fabric
- Forming VXLAN tunnels with attached APs

As noted, the fabric edge node provides authentication services (leveraging the AAA server provided in the network, such as ISE) for wired endpoints (wireless endpoints are authenticated using the fabric-enabled WLC). The fabric edge also forms VXLAN tunnels with fabric-enabled access points. The details of wireless operation with SD-Access are covered later in this chapter.

A critical service offered by the fabric edge node is the distributed anycast Layer 3 gateway functionality. This effectively offers the same IP address and virtual MAC address for the default gateway for any IP host pool located on any fabric edge, from anywhere in the fabric site. This capability is key for enabling mobility for endpoints within the SD-Access fabric, and is illustrated in Figure 19-20.

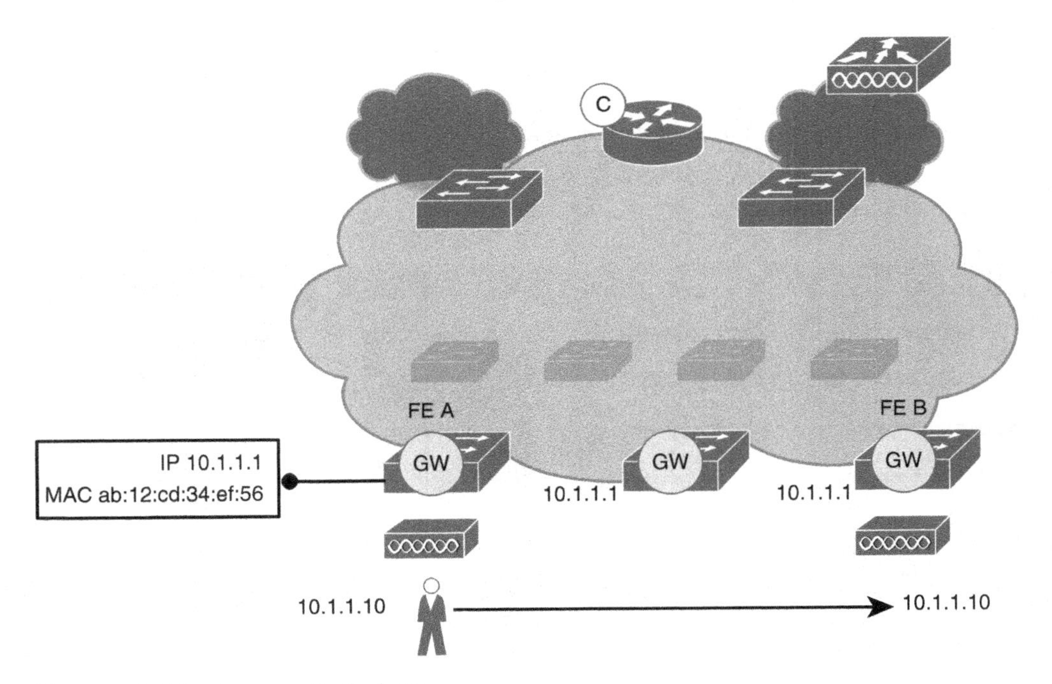

Figure 19-20 *Anycast Default Gateway*

The following are important items of note for the distributed anycast default gateway functionality provided by SD-Access:

- It is similar principle to what is provided by HSRP/VRRP in a traditional network deployment (i.e., virtual IP gateway).
- The same Switch Virtual Interface (SVI) is present on every fabric edge for a given host pool, with the same virtual IP and virtual MAC address.
- If a host moves from one fabric edge to another, it does not need to change its Layer 3 default gateway information (because the same virtual IP/MAC address for the device's default gateway is valid throughput the fabric site).

This anycast gateway capability is also critical for enabling the overall simplicity that an SD-Access-based deployment offers because it supports the "stretched subnet" capability inherent in SD-Access, as outlined previously in this chapter. This in turn allows enterprises, as noted previously, to vastly simplify their IP addressing planning and deployment.

Organizations deploying SD-Access now reap many of the benefits long enjoyed with wireless overlays for IP addressing—smaller numbers of larger subnets, and more efficient use of IP address space—for both their wired and wireless endpoints attached to their fabric edge switches.

SD-Access Edge Nodes: Supported Devices

Multiple devices can fulfill the task of operating as a fabric edge node. The selection of the appropriate fabric edge node is typically driven by the port densities, uplink speeds, port types (10/100/1000, mGig, PoE or non-PoE, etc.) and edge functionality required.

Figure 19-21 provides an overview of some of the platforms that may be employed in the fabric edge role.

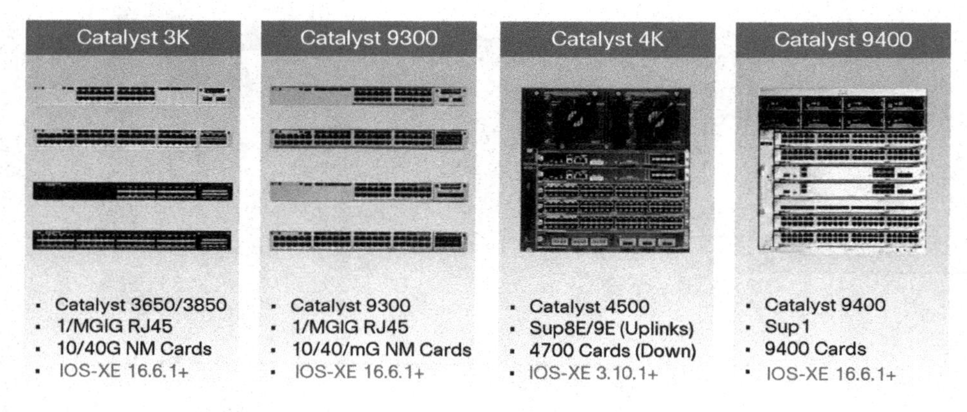

Figure 19-21 *Edge Nodes, Device Support*

A very important aspect to note with the fabric edge node support in SD-Access is the inclusion of both the Catalyst 3850 and 3650 platforms. This capability to support the fabric edge capability on these platforms is a direct result of the outstanding capability provided by the flexible, programmable Unified Access Data Plane (UADP) chipset they employ.

Every Catalyst 3850 and 3650 ever produced, since the introduction of the platform, can (with the appropriate software load and licensing) be provisioned into an SD-Access fabric and operate as a fabric edge node. As one of the leading access switch platforms in the industry, deployed by many thousands of Cisco customers worldwide, this opens up the ability to deploy VXLAN-based SD-Access fabrics to many networks that would otherwise have to wait for a multiyear hardware refresh cycle before the migration to a next-generation network design could be considered.

The ability to leverage these widely deployed enterprise switches as fabric edge nodes in SD-Access is a direct result of Cisco's inclusion of programmable ASIC hardware into these platforms. This provides an outstanding level of investment protection for Cisco customers using these platforms, and highlights the importance of the flexible, programmable UADP ASIC that was examined in detail in Chapter 7.

In addition, the Catalyst 4500 using Supervisor 8/9 (for uplinks to the rest of the fabric network) and 4700-series linecards (for downlinks to attached devices) can be employed as an SD-Access fabric edge switch, thus providing outstanding investment protection for those sites that prefer a modular access switch architecture.

Please refer to Cisco.com, as well as resources such as the "Software-Defined Access Design Guide" outlined in the "Further Reading" section at the end of this chapter, for the exact details of the scalability and functionality for each of these fabric edge options as shown. The fabric edge scale associated with these platforms varies between platform types, and may also vary between software releases, so referring to the latest online information for these scaling parameters is recommended.

Because new platforms are always being created, and older ones retired, please also be sure to refer to Cisco.com for the latest information on supported devices for the SD-Access fabric edge role.

SD-Access Extended Nodes

In some types of deployments, it might be desirable to connect certain types of network devices below the fabric edge. These may be devices that are specific types of Layer 2 switches, such as switches that provide form factors other than those supported by the fabric edge node, or that are designed to work in environments too hostile or demanding for a standard fabric edge node to tolerate.

In an SD-Access deployment, such devices are known as extended nodes. These plug into a fabric edge node port and are designated by Cisco DNA Center as extended nodes. Operating at Layer 2, these devices serve to aggregate endpoints attached to them into the upstream fabric edge node, at which point the traffic from these extended nodes is mapped from their respective Layer 2 VLANs into any associated VNs and SGTs, and forwarded within the SD-Access fabric. For this purpose, an extended node has an 802.1Q trunk provisioned from the fabric edge node to the attached extended node.

Because extended nodes lack all the capabilities of a fabric edge node, they depend on the fabric edge for policy enforcement, traffic encapsulation and decapsulation, and endpoint registration into the fabric control plane.

Supported extended nodes for an SD-Access fabric deployment as of this writing include the Catalyst 3560-CX compact switches, as well as selected Cisco Industrial Ethernet switches. Only these specific types of switches are supported as extended nodes, as they are provisioned and supported by Cisco DNA Center as an automated part of the SD-Access solution overall.

The ability to "extend" the edge of the SD-Access fabric using these switches allows SD-Access to support a broader range of deployment options, which traditional Cisco edge switches might not otherwise be able to handle alone. These include such diverse deployment types as hotel rooms, cruise ships, casinos, factory floors, and manufacturing sites, among others.

Please refer to Cisco.com, as well as resources such as the *Software-Defined Access Design Guide* outlined in the "Further Reading" section at the end of this chapter, for the exact details of the scalability and functionality for each of these fabric extended node options. The extended node scale associated with these platforms varies between platform types, and may also vary between software releases, so referring to the latest online information for these functionality and scaling parameters is recommended.

Because new platforms are always being created, and older ones retired, please also be sure to refer to Cisco.com for the latest information on supported devices for the SD-Access fabric extended node role.

Now that we've examined the options available for the SD-Access fabric wired infrastructure, let's move on to examine wireless integration in an SD-Access fabric deployment.

SD-Access Wireless Integration

Wireless mobility is a fact of life—and a necessity—for almost any modern organization. Almost all devices used in an enterprise network offer an option for 802.11 wireless connectivity—and some devices, such as smartphones and tablets, are wireless-only, offering no options for wired attachment. Today's highly mobile workforce demands secure, speedy, reliable, and easy-to-use access to wireless connectivity.

SD-Access offers a sophisticated new mode for wireless deployment, allowing for direct integration of wireless capabilities into an SD-Access fabric, and allowing wireless endpoints and users to access all of the benefits that a fabric deployment provides—including macro- and micro-segmentation, group-based policy enforcement, and stretched subnets, as well as full distributed traffic forwarding.

Segmentation, group-based policies, and stretched subnets were examined earlier in this chapter, and elsewhere in this book, in some detail, including their benefits, so in this section we'll focus on the distributed traffic forwarding that fabric offers and see how this provides significant benefits for wireless deployments.

One significant trend in 802.11 wireless over recent years has been the move to ever-greater speeds offered by APs for endpoint attachment over RF. From the early days of 11-Mbps 802.11b, to 54 Mbps with 802.11a/g, it is now common to see enterprises deploying 802.11ac Wave 1 and Wave 2 APs that offer well over 1 Gbps of real-world wireless bandwidth to endpoints and users. In the future, the new 802.11ax standard will push this limit closer to 10 Gbps, while at the same time increasing the efficiency of usage of the wireless medium.

Figure 19-22 depicts the evolution of wireless from a "nice-to-have" capability to its present, and future, status as a mission-critical capability for many organizations worldwide.

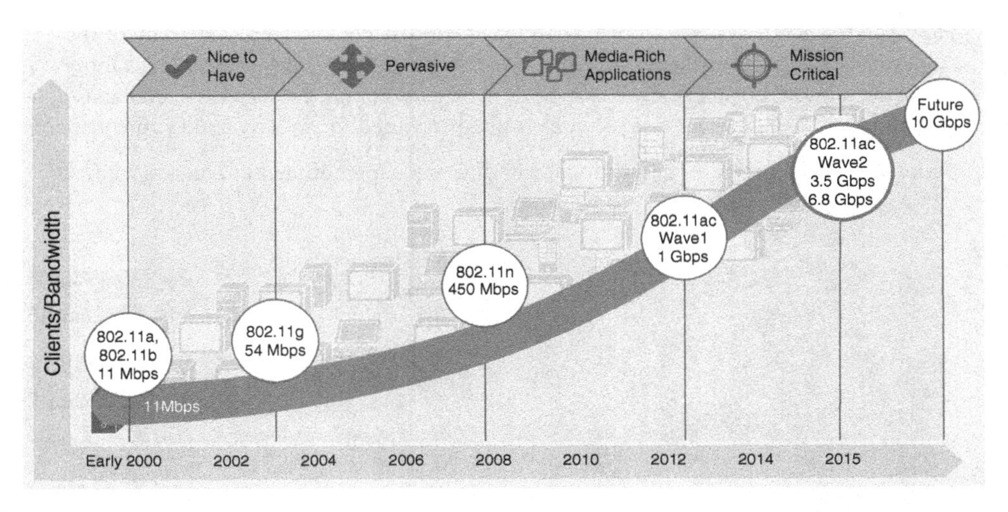

Figure 19-22 *Wireless Standards Evolution*

As wireless bandwidths increased, they placed ever-greater pressures on the traditional centralized method of wireless LAN deployment. Many organizations deploy centralized wireless, in which APs form Control and Provisioning of Wireless Access Points (CAPWAP) tunnels back to a central WLC, or cluster of WLCs, and forward all wireless client data, as well as control plane traffic, over these CAPWAP tunnels.

This method of wireless deployment (known as Cisco Unified Wireless Network, or CUWN) has several important benefits, including simplified deployment and operation (because all IP addressing and policy enforcement is handled at the WLC) and integrated secure guest access. Some of these benefits are outlined in Figure 19-23.

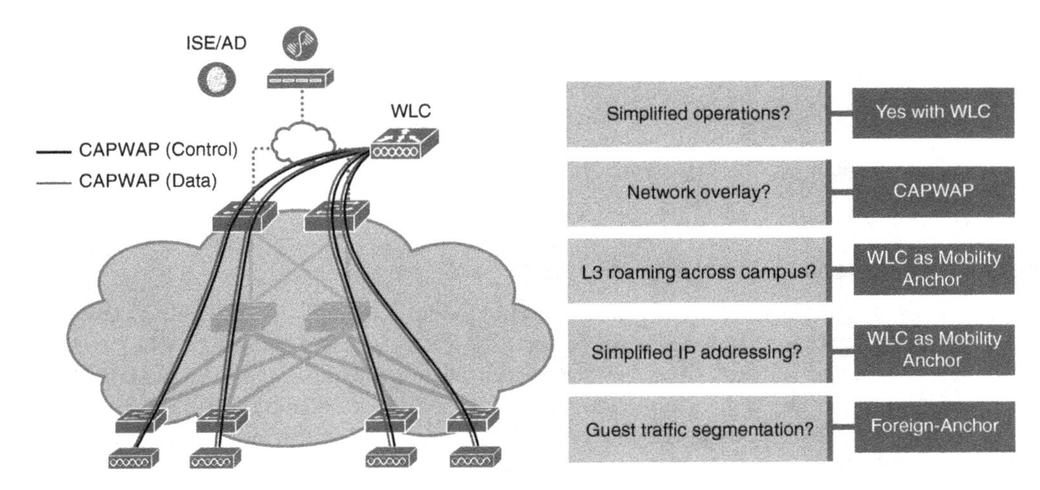

Figure 19-23 *Traditional Cisco Unified Wireless Network—Strengths*

However, this method of traditional centralized wireless deployment lacks some of the strengths that typically accrue to a Cisco wired network deployment, including support for segmentation, greater scalability and capability for complex policies for QoS and security, and the scalability that comes with a fully distributed forwarding and feature plane.

Some of these benefits for a traditional wired network are outlined in Figure 19-24.

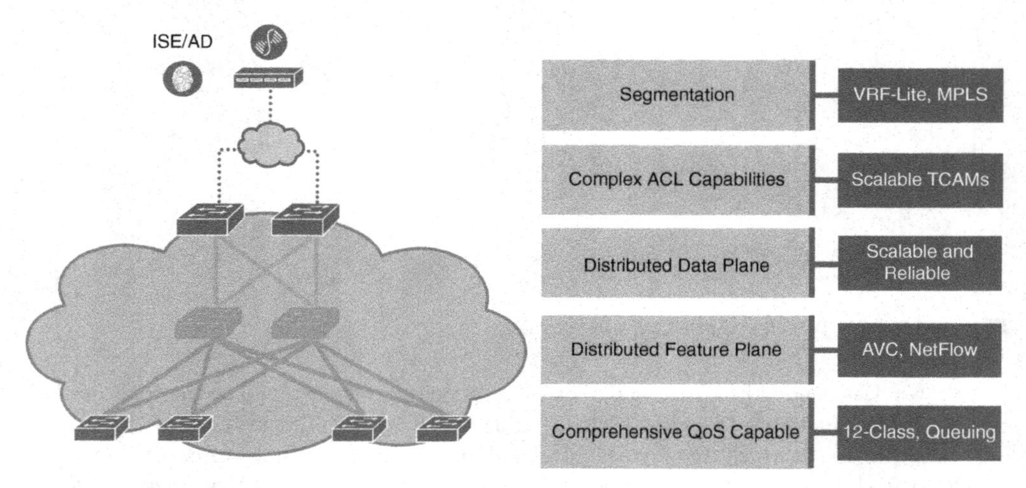

Figure 19-24 *Traditional Cisco Wired Network—Strengths*

An SD-Access wireless deployment provides the best of both of these worlds, offering:

- The *simplicity* of a traditional centralized wireless deployment (retained by using the WLC as the primary point for wireless control)
- The *scalability* of a traditional wired deployment (by employing a fully distributed data plane, leveraging the switched network infrastructure for traffic forwarding).
- The *feature richness* of a traditional wired deployment (by providing integrated functionality for secure segmentation and policy enforcement)

Let's examine how SD-Access wireless integration works, to see these capabilities in action.

SD-Access Simplified Wireless Control Plane

SD-Access wireless retains and builds upon the traditional simplicity of wireless deployments, by continuing to leverage the feature-rich Wireless LAN Controller (WLC) as the central point for wireless AP deployment and RF management. In an SD-Access fabric, the WLC continues to be used to onboard clients, manage APs, and control the RF domain, retaining the simplicity and operational paradigm that wireless network managers have become accustomed to over many years.

However, the fabric-enabled WLC is integrated with the SD-Access fabric control plane, such that when a wireless client attaches or roams, an update is always sent to the fabric control plane node, noting which switch (RLOC) the wireless client is located behind (based on which AP it is associated with). This ensures that, in a fabric deployment, the SD-Access control plane node always serves as a single point of reference for where any endpoint is located in the fabric network—wired or wireless.

Figure 19-25 illustrates the basic functions performed by a WLC that is integrated into an SD-Access fabric.

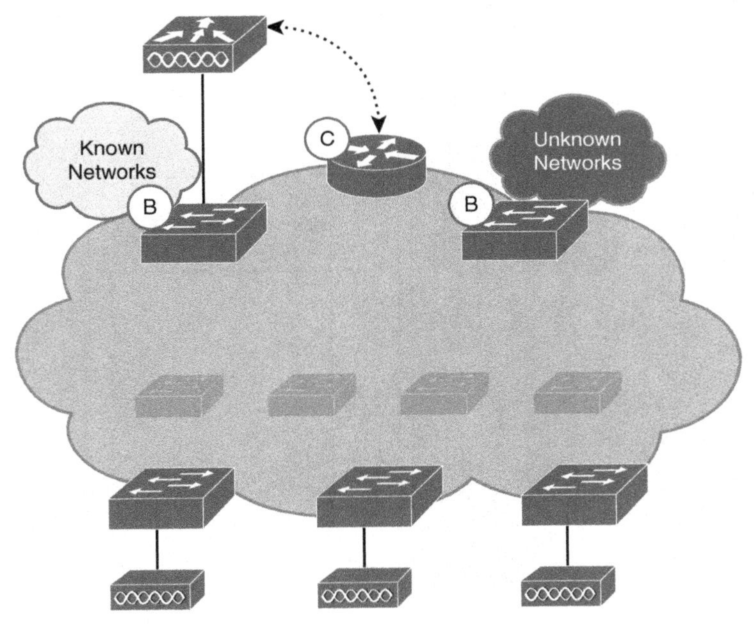

Figure 19-25 *SD-Access Wireless Integration—Fabric-Enabled WLC*

There are several important items to note concerning the operation of a WLC within a fabric-enabled wireless system:

- The fabric-enabled WLC connects outside of the fabric, accessing the SD-Access fabric via the fabric border, in the underlay network.
- The fabric-enabled WLC registers wireless clients with the fabric control plane (indicating which RLOC [fabric edge switch] they are attached to).
- Fabric-enabled APs are provisioned in a dedicated IP host pool within the fabric (in the VXLAN overlay).
- SSIDs (to which wireless clients attach) use regular IP host pools for traffic forwarding and policy application.

With the use of a fabric-integrated WLC, any endpoint within the SD-Access fabric domain can query the fabric control plane for any endpoint—wired or wireless—and always forward traffic within the fabric overlay to the correct destination, thus enabling seamless connectivity across the fabric to and from any endpoint.

The integration between the WLC and the fabric control plane node is illustrated Figure 19-26.

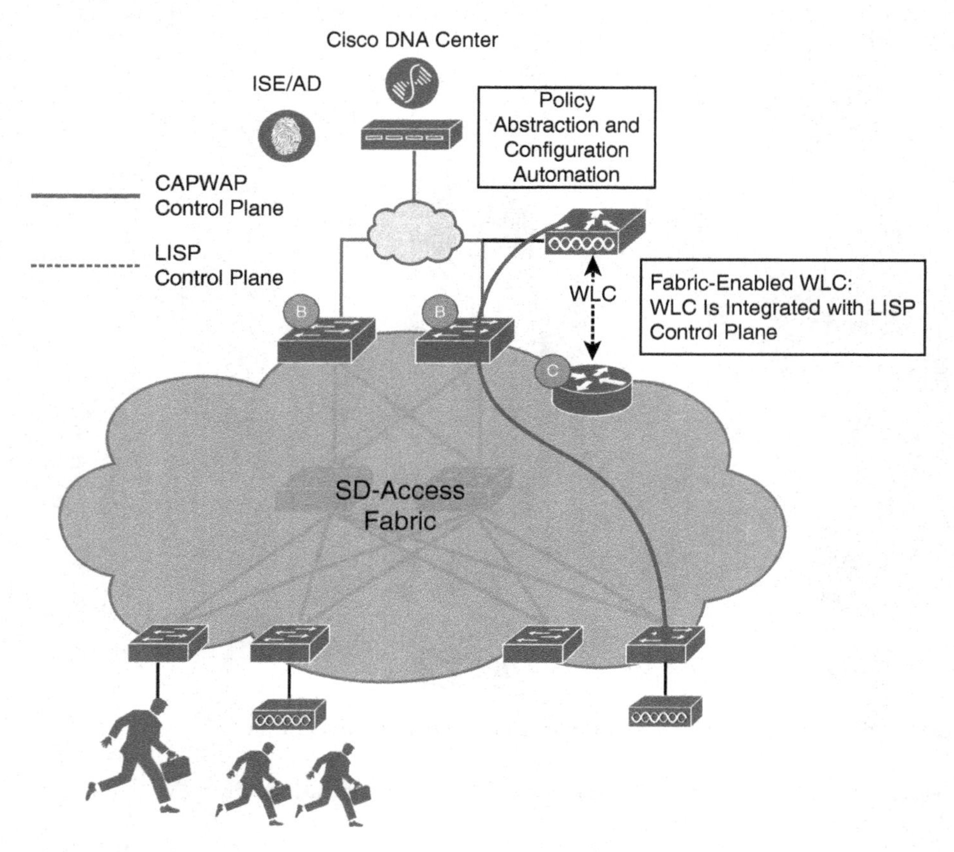

Figure 19-26 *SD-Access Wireless Integration—Control Plane*

There are several important items to note concerning the control plane integration of wireless with the SD-Access fabric:

- **Automation:** Cisco DNA center simplifies the overall fabric deployment, including the wireless integration components.
- **Centralized wireless control plane:** The WLC still continues to provide wireless client session management, AP management, Radio Resource Management (RRM), and overall mobility functions.
- **Integration with the LISP control plane:** Operating with AireOS 8.5 or above, the fabric-enabled WLC integrates with the LISP control plane to provide updates to the

LISP control plane nodes for wireless clients as they attach and roam. Thanks to this integration, wireless mobility is incorporated into the fabric deployment.

Each fabric-enabled access point retains a control plane CAPWAP tunnel back to its associated WLC for management. This retains the simplicity of management and operation that wireless operators are accustomed to and eases the migration path toward a fabric-integrated wireless deployment.

However, unlike in a traditional CUWN deployment, this CAPWAP tunnel is *not* used for data plane forwarding—it is purely a control plane tunnel only between the AP and WLC. In SD-Access, the wireless data plane is entirely distributed, as outlined in the following section.

A more detailed review of the integration between the fabric-enabled WLC and the SD-Access fabric control plane is provided in Figure 19-27.

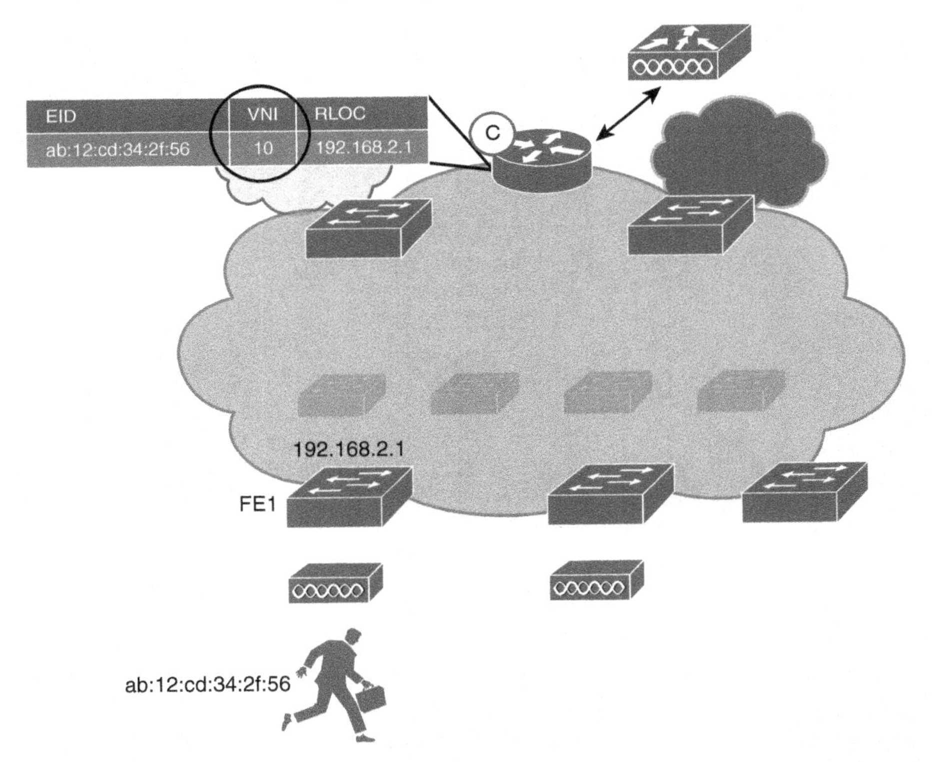

Figure 19-27 *SD-Access Wireless Integration—Control Plane Operation*

There are several important items to note concerning wireless integration with the SD-Access fabric. First, for wireless clients, the client's MAC address is tracked and is used as the EID. Second, because wireless roams are handled as Layer 2 roams within the fabric—enhancing deployment efficiency—a Layer 2 VNI is employed within the fabric for this use. And finally, it is necessary that the WLC and the APs be co-located at the same site (i.e., not separated over a WAN), due to the tight timing constraints driven by the integration of the WLC with the fabric control plane.

Overall, the method used for integrating wireless with SD-Access fabric retains the traditional simplicity of the wireless control plane, while ensuring seamless operation in a fabric deployment model.

Now, let's move on to examining how SD-Access wireless provides data plane integration, and the benefits this provides.

SD-Access Optimized Wireless Data Plane

SD-Access wireless helps to address the ever-increasing needs for both bandwidth and sophisticated services for wireless traffic by leveraging a fully distributed data plane approach. With the move to 802.11ac Wave 2 and, in future, 802.11ax, the necessity for a distributed data plane forwarding option for wireless traffic becomes ever more apparent.

With SD-Access wireless, each fabric-enabled AP, in addition to the CAPWAP control plane tunnel it uses to the fabric-enabled WLC, forms a VXLAN data plane tunnel to its adjacent fabric edge switch, and uses this VXLAN tunnel for forwarding of all endpoint data plane traffic. This is illustrated in Figure 19-28.

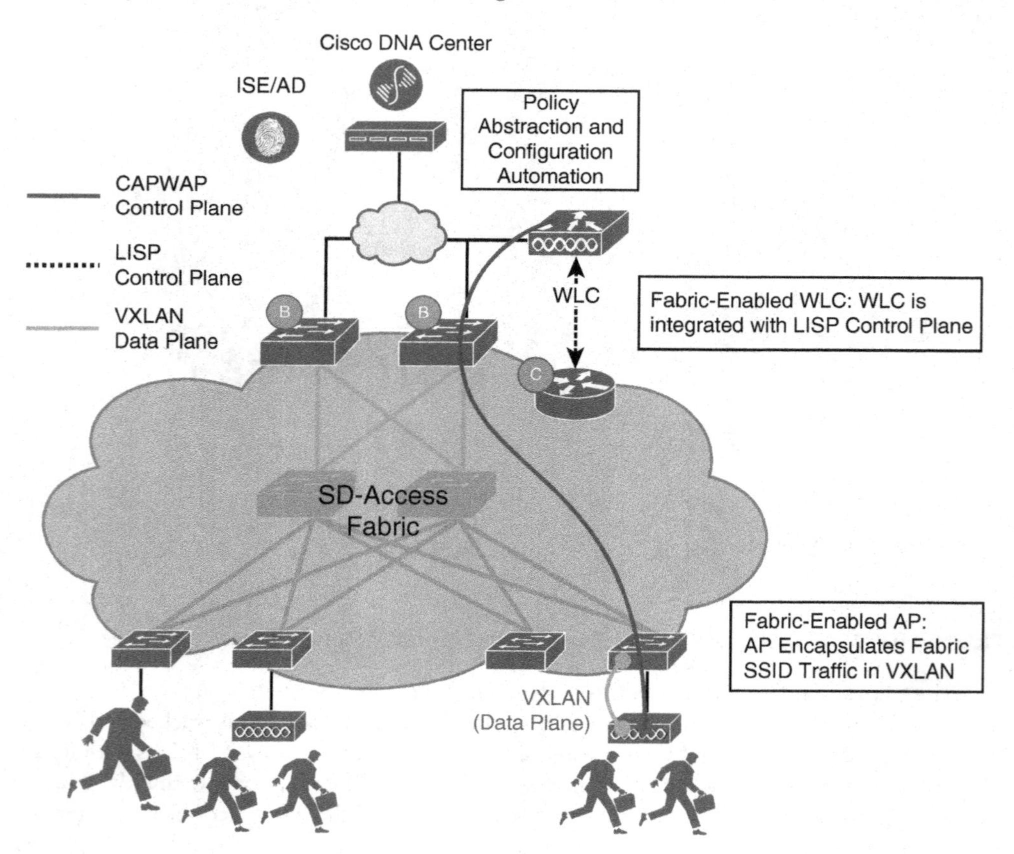

Figure 19-28 *SD-Access Wireless Integration—Data Plane*

Important items to note here include the following:

- **Optimized distributed data plane:** By leveraging the fabric overlay with its distributed anycast default gateway and associated stretched subnet functionality, the ability to provide a single IP subnet for all attached wireless devices for a given SSID is provided, without complications. All roams within the fabric-enabled wireless deployment are handed as Layer 2 roams.
- **VXLAN from the AP:** Allows hierarchical user/device policy and segmentation capabilities (based on VN/SGT groupings) to be provided for wireless clients, in exactly the same manner as wired clients, right from the AP—thus allowing for a truly unified enterprise access policy.

The use of VXLAN for the data plane tunnel between the AP and its adjacent fabric edge switch ensures that all of the VN and SGT information associated with the wireless clients is passed to this adjacent wired switch and used for policy enforcement.

At the same time, the use of a one-hop VXLAN tunnel ensures that the adjacent switch is always seen by the SD-Access fabric control plane as the RLOC for other devices to forward traffic to within the fabric, avoiding an "RLOC explosion" that might otherwise accrue if the fabric control plane had to track every fabric-enabled AP directly.

By decapsulating, inspecting, and then re-encapsulating all wireless traffic within the fabric at the wired access switch, the scalability and feature set of the switched infrastructure is leveraged to the greatest extent possible, while still retaining seamless mobility and ease of operation, deployment, and use. And thanks to the performance offered by the flexible, programmable UADP ASIC, with its high-speed recirculation functionality optimized for tunneling (as examined in Chapter 7), this capability is offered with very high throughput.

A further depiction of the integration between the fabric-enabled AP and its adjacent fabric edge switch is illustrated in Figure 19-29.

A few items of note here are that the AP operates in Local mode and is directly adjacent to the fabric edge switch. (APs can also be attached to an extended node switch, if these are in use.) Also, APs apply policies such as Cisco Application Visibility and Control (AVC) and QoS locally on the AP itself to distribute these functions as far as possible toward the network edge and thus further increase scalability.

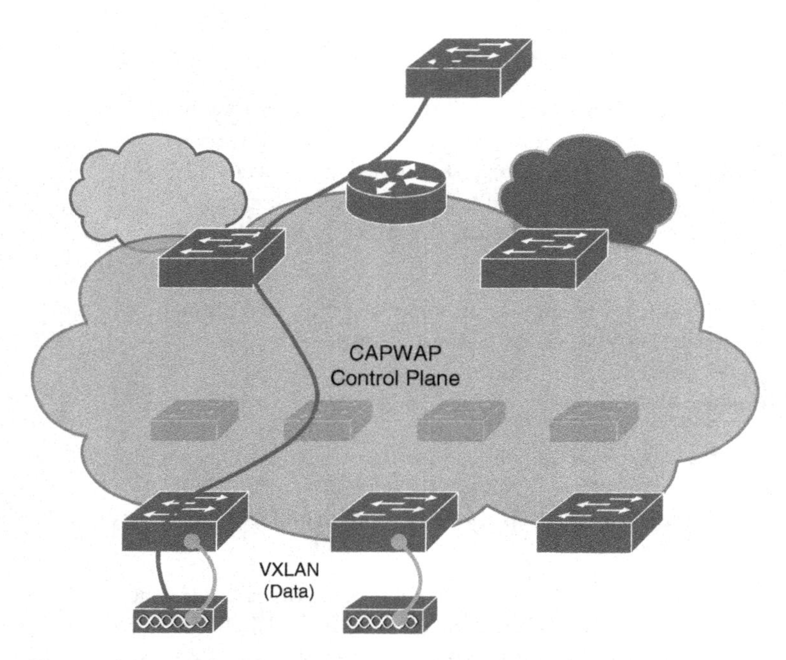

Figure 19-29 *SD-Access Wireless Integration—Data Plane Operation*

SD-Access Over-the-Top (OTT) Wireless Support

For completeness, it should be noted that that wireless deployments in SD-Access can also be accommodated in an Over-the-Top (OTT) deployment mode, in which the existing CAPWAP tunnels (for both data plane and control plane) are retained from the APs to the WLCs, just as they are today—using the SD-Access fabric only for transport (i.e., not integrated directly as with fabric-enabled wireless).

This capability for OTT wireless use is valuable as a stepping-stone to an SD-Access deployment, especially in cases where the existing deployed wireless network equipment does not support the use of fabric-enabled wireless operation, or in the event that the organization involved simply wishes to deploy a more traditional wireless environment while upgrading its wired deployment to SD-Access.

Also note that OTT wireless does not provide all of the benefits of a fabric-integrated SD-Access wireless deployment. A truly integrated SD-Access wireless deployment provides support for integrated two-level segmentation (macro and micro, based on VN and SGT), greater scalability via the use of a distributed data plane, and consistent policy for both wired and wireless users. Although an OTT wireless deployment lacks these capabilities, it remains an option in the event that a fabric-integrated wireless deployment cannot be undertaken for any reason.

SD-Access Wireless: Supported Devices

Multiple devices are used within a fabric-enabled wireless deployment, including many existing WLCs as well as 802.11ac Wave 2 and (with certain caveats) 802.11ac Wave 1 APs.

Figure 19-30 provides an overview of some of the platforms that are employed in an SD-Access fabric-enabled wireless deployment.

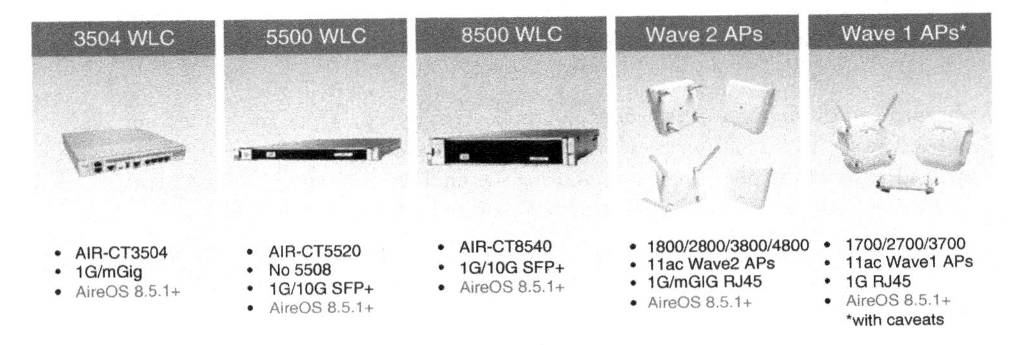

Figure 19-30 *Fabric Wireless, Device Support*

The ability to reuse the existing WLCs and APs, as shown, in a fabric-enabled wireless deployment assists in easing the migration to SD-Access, and provides a significant level of investment protection for existing Cisco wireless deployments.

Please refer to Cisco.com, as well as some of the references noted at the end of this chapter, for the exact details of the scalability and functionality for each of these wireless options as shown, as well as for the caveats associated with the use of 802.11ac Wave 1 APs in a fabric deployment.

The scale associated with these various wireless platforms varies between platform types, and may also vary between software releases, so referring to the latest online information for these scaling parameters is recommended.

Because new platforms are always being created, and older ones retired, please also be sure to refer to Cisco.com for the latest information on supported devices for SD-Access wireless capability.

The benefits that accrue to an integrated wireless deployment with SD-Access—seamless and simple control plane integration, the use of a distributed data plane, and the ability to leverage the strengths of SD-Access for segmentation and security in a common way for both wired and wireless users—all serve to assist in driving wireless networking toward a more-scalable and feature-rich future, a future that offers consistent and powerful capabilities for wired and wireless users alike.

SD-Access Multicast Support

Finally, an important aspect of many enterprise network deployments is the use of IP multicast. Multicast is supported in an SD-Access fabric deployment. The method of multicast replication used is known as "head-end" replication, meaning that multicast traffic ingressing an SD-Access fabric node (edge or border) will be replicated by that device into multiple unicast VXLAN-encapsulated copies of the original (inner) multicast packet, with one copy sent to each RLOC that is receiving the multicast stream. Once these unicast VXLAN-encapsulated copies reach each destination RLOC, they are then decapsulated (revealing the inner, original IP multicast packet), which is then locally replicated by that RLOC to any attached multicast receivers.

This method of multicast forwarding and replication thus provides end-to-end multicast capability across the SD-Access fabric, in a simple and straightforward fashion. This method also has the benefit of not requiring the underlay network to be multicast-enabled, in order to support IP multicast capability in the overlay fabric.

A future version of SD-Access is planned to provide "native" IP multicast replication, meaning that rather than having the head-end (ingress) RLOC replicate out multiple unicast-encapsulated copies of the multicast traffic, an underlay multicast group will be used to provide the replication capability between the RLOCs involved. This has the benefit of distributing the multicast replication load across the underlay network and its many devices, at the cost of having to configure IP multicast support in the underlay network. However, because configurations are automated within Cisco DNA Center, this should impose little extra burden on the network administrator once available.

SD-Access Case Study

Now that we have examined all the basics of Software-Defined Access, let's delve into a case study and examine how to use Cisco DNA Center to define, deploy, and manage the various components that make up an SD-Access fabric.

Let's start in Cisco DNA Center. As detailed in other chapters of this book, Cisco DNA Center offers a next-generation solution for network definition, deployment, and ongoing maintenance and operation. As noted previously, when you first log into Cisco DNA Center, you are offered a four-step workflow—namely, Design, Policy, Provision, and Assurance. Let's start this journey into the SD-Access case study with Design, where you provide all the basic information that is necessary as you begin to build out your fabric solution.

Please note that this is necessarily an abbreviated description of building out and operating an SD-Access fabric with Cisco DNA Center, due to space limitations inherent with a single chapter within this larger volume. More complete and detailed explanations of building out an SD-Access fabric are contained within the "Further Reading" references at the end of this chapter. However, this case study provides a good overview of the major steps involved and serves to illustrate how simple, powerful, and flexible Cisco DNA Center makes building out an entire fabric-based network solution.

With that said, let's get started!

In the Cisco DNA Center GUI, click Design to access the Network Hierarchy screen displayed in Figure 19-31. This shows an overall map, indicating the various positions where sites were already defined, and where new sites can be defined prior to deployment. In this example, we are reviewing an educational system with sites scattered across various locations in the United States.

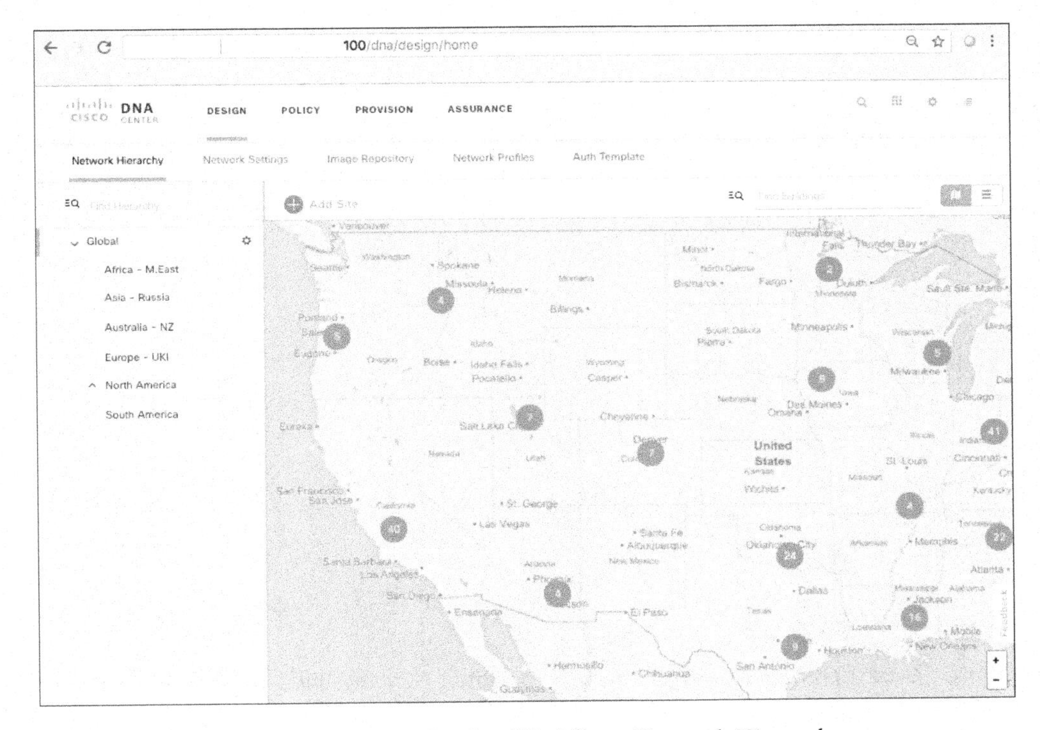

Figure 19-31 *Cisco DNA Center Design Workflow: Network Hierarchy*

As you can see, the previously defined sites are located across the United States. The bubbles indicate the number of sites within each region, and by mousing over an area and clicking it, a zoomed-in view is obtained, all the way down to the individual site level. Sites are also organized into a hierarchy, as you can see on the left side, allowing for easy access to the various defined sites. A new site is added simply by clicking the blue plus sign icon next to the Add Site text—a common paradigm within Cisco DNA Center. Sites contain one or multiple buildings, each of which contains floors complete with floor maps and layouts.

In this case, let's zoom into an already-defined site in San Jose and start examining the network definition for the site.

Figure 19-32 shows some of the basic network definitions for the site, noting the common deployment items for the site including DNS servers, DHCP servers, syslog servers, and the like.

> **Note** IP addresses in the figures have their leading octets deliberately obscured to ensure the security of the site involved.

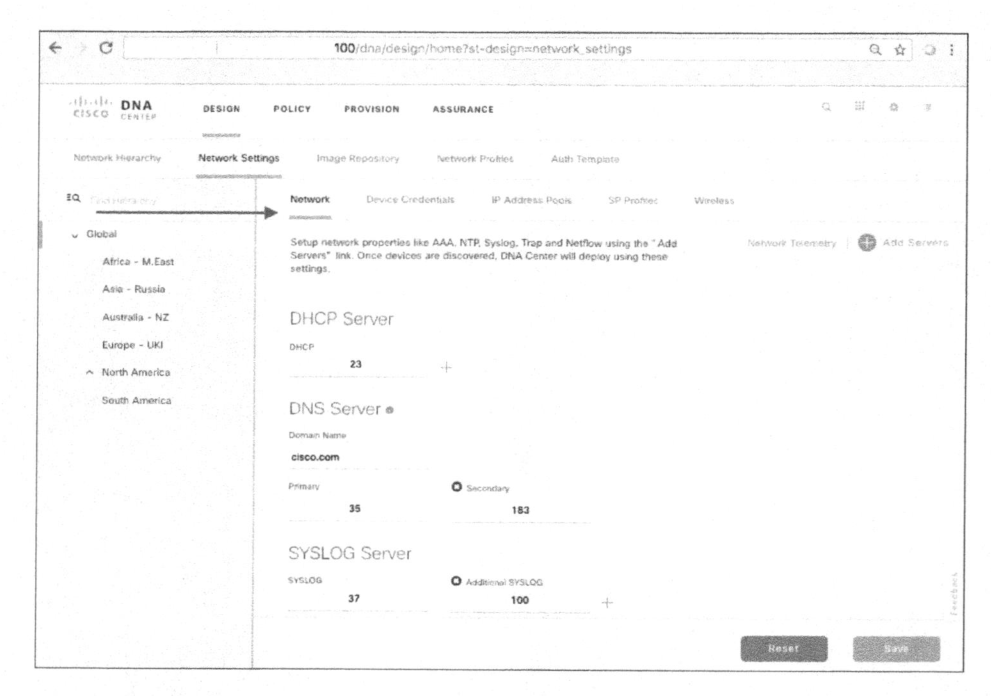

Figure 19-32 *Design Workflow: Network Settings, Network Tab*

Note that many network settings can be defined at a higher site hierarchy level and then inherited to sites below that in the hierarchy. In fact, what you are viewing in Figure 19-32 is the Global settings for the items noted, which a lower-level site such as the San Jose site could inherit, or override with more site-specific settings if and as needed. This ability to provide higher-level inheritance with site-specific override capability makes defining new sites within Cisco DNA Center very easy.

In addition to the settings shown in Figure 19-32, additional elements that can be defined for the network settings for a site include definitions for the AAA servers in use, the SNMP servers in use, the NetFlow collectors server to use, and the NTP server in use, as well the local time zone and message of the day for the site.

Additional important elements of defining a site are the IP host pools (subnets) which are defined for, and made available, at the site. These are the IP subnets provided for use by users, devices, and things at the sites involved. Figure 19-33 illustrates how an IP address pool is defined for the site involved; observe in the background that several other IP address pools already have been defined. Note that to get to this screen we navigated to Design > Network Settings and clicked Edit next to an existing IP host pool.

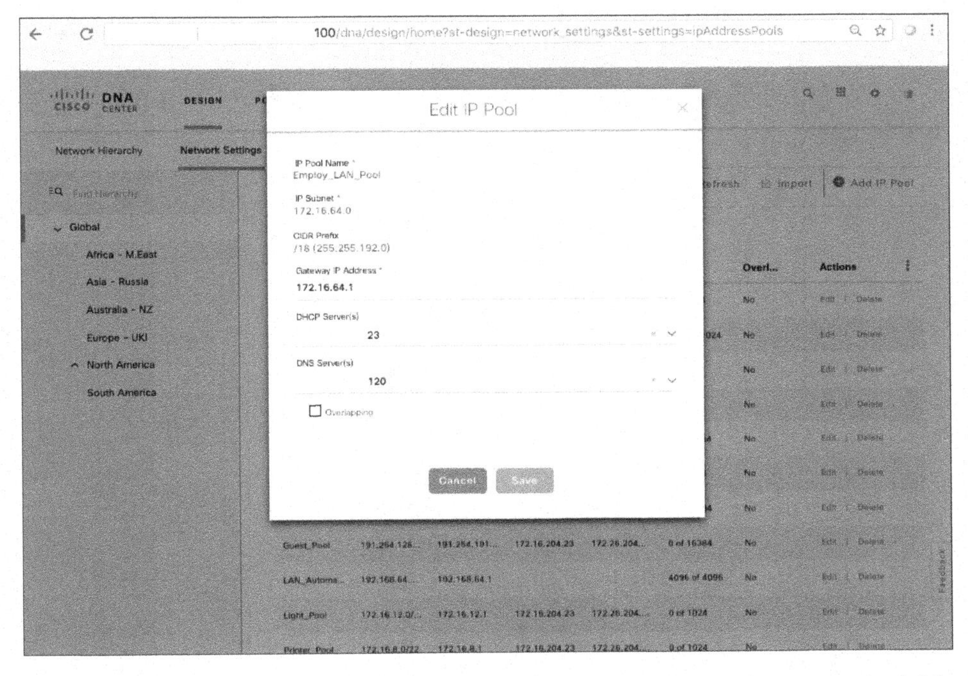

Figure 19-33 *Edit IP Pool Dialog Box Opened from the Network Settings, IP Address Pools Tab*

For each IP host pool, a subnet range is defined, complete with the assignment of a gateway IP address (which is used as the distributed anycast default gateway for the subnet). DHCP and DNS servers are also assigned from those previously defined in the Network Settings area.

With the critical servers and services assigned for a site, it is now timely to review the status of the various devices that may end up being used for establishing the fabric at the site involved, as shown in Figure 19-34. These devices are discovered by Cisco DNA Center by pointing at a given "seed device" to which Cisco DNA Center has connectivity. Cisco DNA Center then logs into that device (using credentials supplied by the network administrator) and proceeds to "walk" across the network, discovering devices, adding them into the Cisco DNA Center inventory, and noting the network topology interconnecting them.

As you see, devices so discovered and added into the inventory are analyzed and shown with their software versions, device types, and revisions noted for easy review. Any software images standardized on by the organization can be denoted as "golden" images, making it simpler to determine at a glance whether devices are in compliance with organizational standards for software deployment. Note that the arrow as shown is not part of the Cisco DNA Center GUI; instead, we are using it simply as an aid to where to look on the screen.

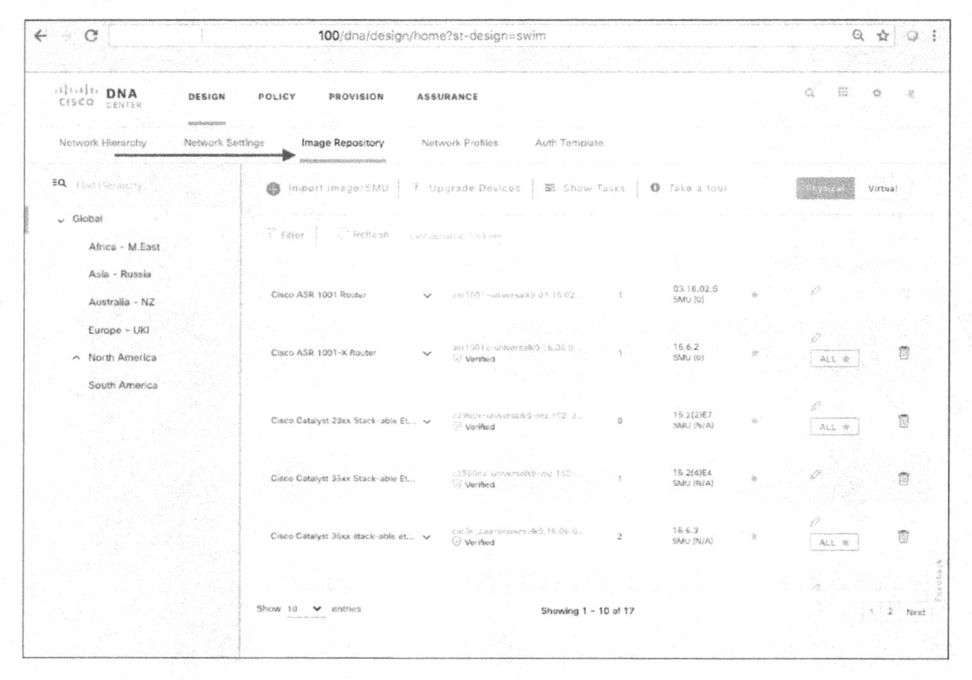

Figure 19-34 *Design Workflow: Image Repository Tab*

Cisco DNA Center also provides a tool that can be used to automate the deployment of the network itself—namely, LAN Automation. This capability again employs a seed device, and starting from that device can "walk out" up to two layers within the network hierarchy and automate the deployment of new devices it so discovers. This automation includes, and is intended to support, the deployment of an automated underlay suitable for the later overlay of an SD-Access fabric.

If deployed with LAN Automation, this underlay is built using the routed access deployment model (i.e., routing all the way down to the access layer), using Intermediate System to Intermediate System (IS-IS) as the routing protocol. Alternatively, if the network already exists, or the organization prefers to deploy its own underlay with its own chosen IGP routing protocol, this can also be accommodated. Further details are available in some of the items noted for "Further Reading" at the end of this chapter, such as the "SD-Access Design Guide" noted.

Now that you have seen how to define all the basics for your network access—your site hierarchy and sites, critical services, IP subnets, and devices—let's begin to delve into the design of various network policies within the Policy workflow in Cisco DNA Center. This is illustrated in Figurer 19-35.

Initially, you land on a dashboard for the Policy workflow in Cisco DNA Center, showing an overview of the various polices already defined. This example already has a total of 6 virtual networks defined, a total of 10 group-based access control policies (leveraging

SGACLs), and a total of 45 Scalable Groups (using SGTs), along with various other network policies for IP-based groupings and traffic copy policies.

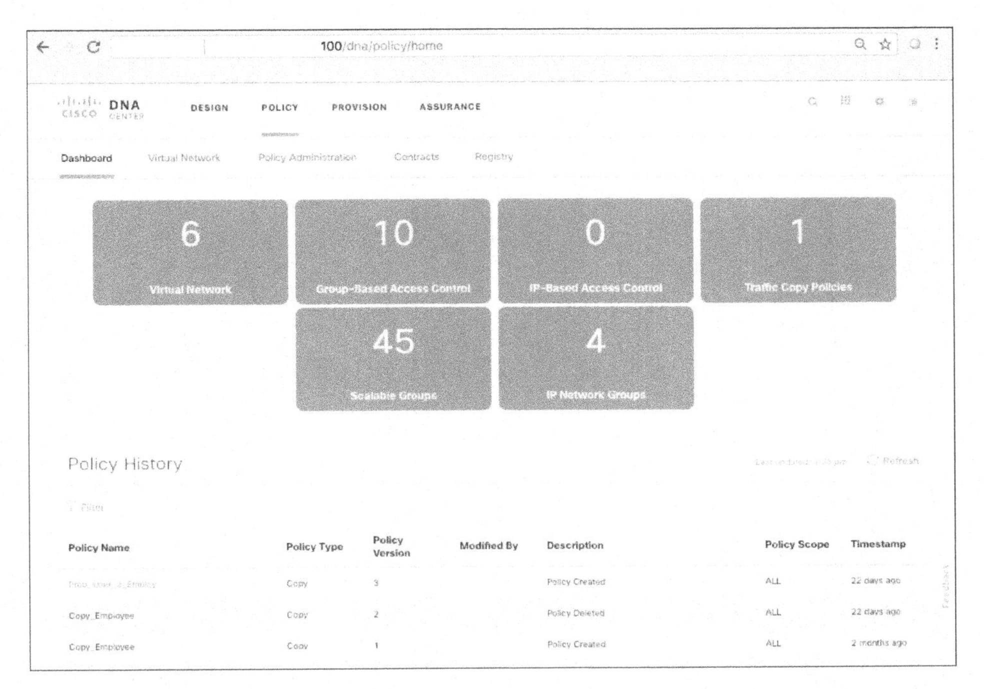

Figure 19-35 *Cisco DNA Center Policy Workflow: Dashboard*

You can also see a summary of the history of the policies that were created or modified in Cisco DNA Center, including the type of policy, the version and scope, a description of what action was taken with regard to each policy, and the time that this action took place. This is very valuable for keeping track of which policies were created or modified, when, and by whom.

First, let's zoom over into the Virtual Network area and see what is defined for VNs currently, as shown in Figure 19-36.

Here, you see on the left side of the screen all six of the VNs currently defined. Initially, as indicated by the arrow, you are viewing the Default VN (DEFAULT_VN). This VN always exists in a fabric, and is the VN into which users, devices, and things are mapped by default if no other VN is chosen. The groups shown on the far right side are already mapped into this VN, meaning that any user or device that attaches and is assigned to one of these groups is mapped into the Default VN. The groups shown on the left side are available to assign into this VN if desired. This is done merely by dragging and dropping these groups into the right-side pane and clicking Save.

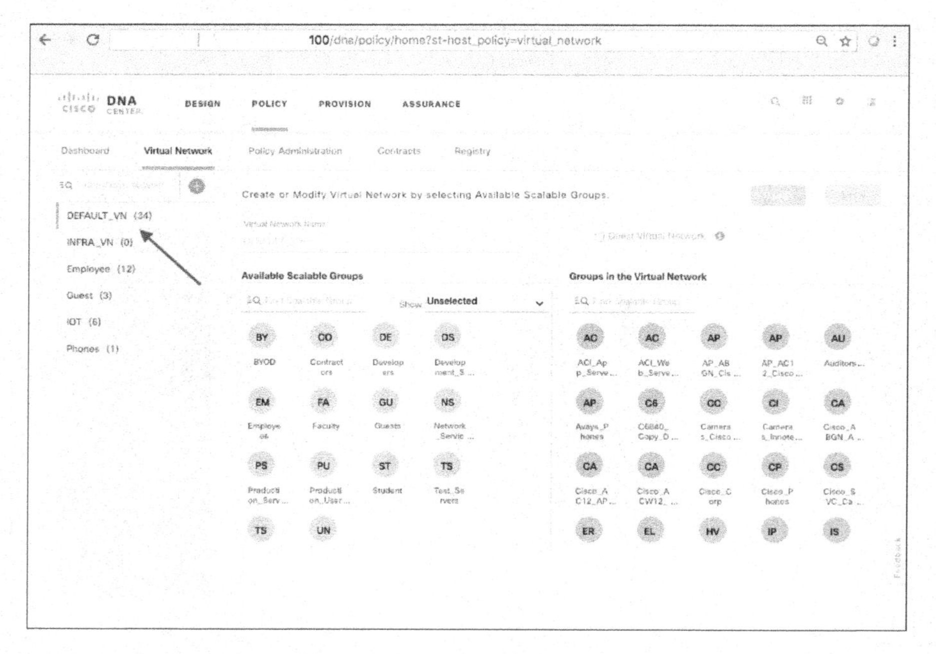

Figure 19-36 *Policy Workflow: Virtual Network*

Now, you may ask yourself, where do all of these groups come from? Most commonly, the groups are created within Cisco ISE and then imported into Cisco DNA Center when ISE is integrated with Cisco DNA Center as its assigned AAA server. In turn, ISE may have obtained these groups from an outside source such as Active Directory (assuming the organization involved has ISE and AD integration configured).

Another VN that you can observe in the list is the INFRA_VN. This is a VN that "infrastructure" devices such as access points and extended nodes are mapped into. This VN is somewhat "special" in that users are never mapped into this VN—it is reserved for infrastructure devices only. The INFRA_VN is also special in that it is not mapped into a VRF instance like other VNs are—it is mapped into the Global Routing Table (GRT) in the underlay, but with a LISP instance in the GRT (i.e., VRF 0) to keep track of these infrastructure devices and their locations. This provides maximum simplicity of operation for these devices, as such devices (for example, APs) often need to contact their related services (such as a WLC, for example) located outside of the fabric, and locating these devices in the underlay GRT allows for simplified configuration at the fabric border to facilitate such connectivity.

The other VNs in the list (Employee, Guest, IOT, and Phones) were created by the network manager. In this example, these are the VNs associated with a university deployment. Each of these VNs is mapped into a corresponding VRF in the fabric overlay.

Creating a new VN is very simple. Simply click the blue plus sign icon, as shown in Figure 19-37.

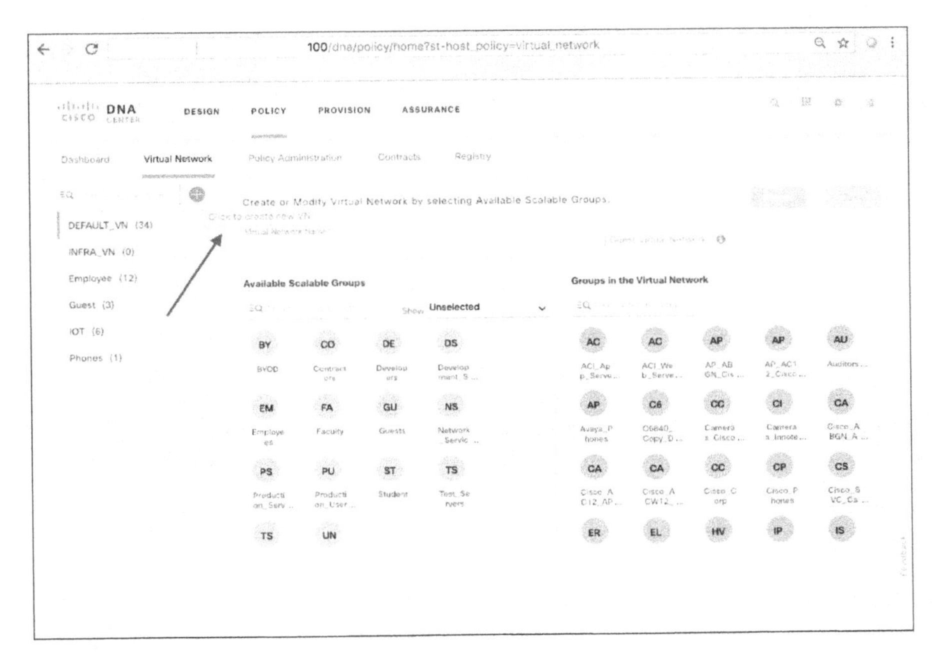

Figure 19-37 *Policy Workflow: Adding a New Virtual Network*

After selecting to add a new VN, simply type in the new name and click Save. This triggers Cisco DNA Center to provision the VN into all of the associated devices within the fabric, creating all of the VRFs, Route Distinguishers, Route Targets, and other ancillary components necessary to set up the VN for operation.

Figure 19-38 shows how to set up a new VN called Cameras, into which you could place IP-based security cameras. After setting up the new VN, you can assign groups into it simply by dragging and dropping them, as shown on the right in Figure 19-38.

In this case study, the IP-based cameras were not yet unboxed and ready to plug into the network, so the configuration was not saved. It's important to note that none of the changes you make in Cisco DNA Center are deployed until you click Save, thus providing ample opportunity to explore the interface without actually making any network changes.

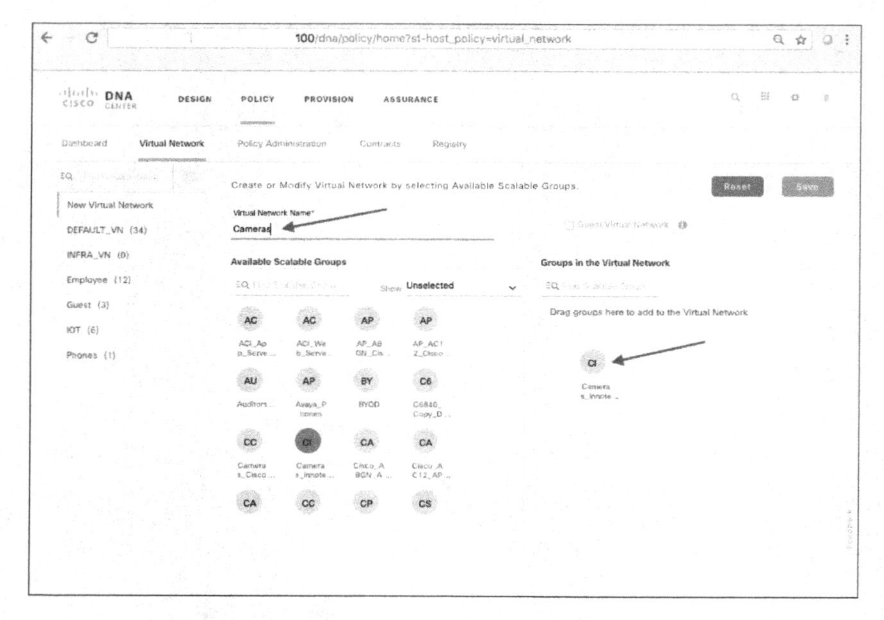

Figure 19-38 *Policy Workflow: Assigning Groups to a New Virtual Network*

Now that you have explored VNs, click the Policy Administration tab to see how to work with groups and group-based policies in Cisco DNA Center. Figure 19-39 shows a quick summary of all the various group-based policies that are currently defined for the fabric infrastructure in the example.

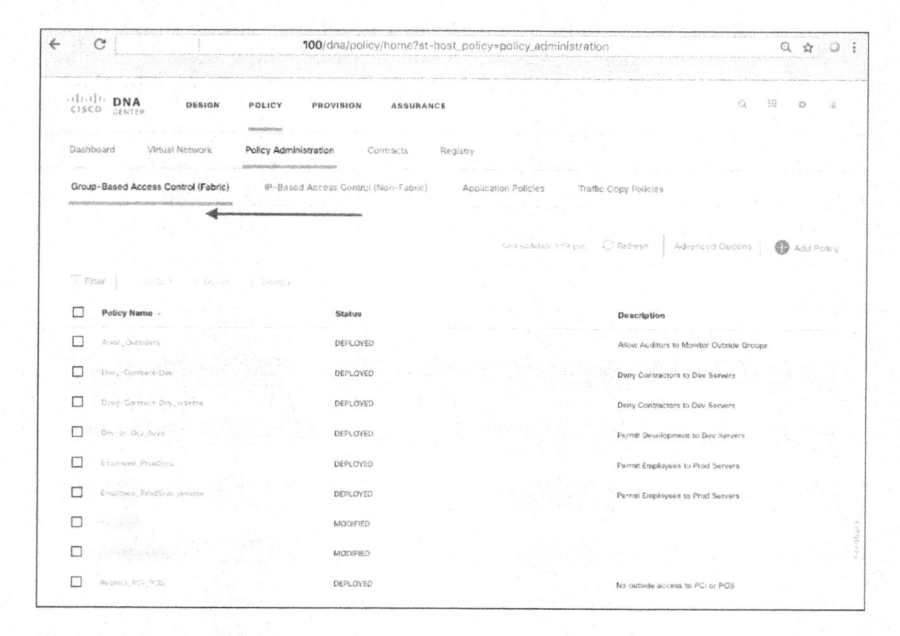

Figure 19-39 *Policy Workflow: Policy Administration, Group-Based Access Control (Fabric) Tab*

From here, you see all the policies that currently exist. Let's explore the one named Employee_ProdSrvs. Clicking its name opens the Details dialog box shown in Figure 19-40. This policy is intended to provide employees with access to production servers and services via the fabric.

Here, you can observe that the policy is defined to allow two groups, Employees and Contractors, access to (permit) any server or service in the group Production_Servers. Any user or device authenticating into either of these source groups is allowed access to any server or service mapped into this destination group, based on this policy as shown.

At this point, you are just viewing the policy. Figure 19-41 shows what happens if you click the Edit button for this policy.

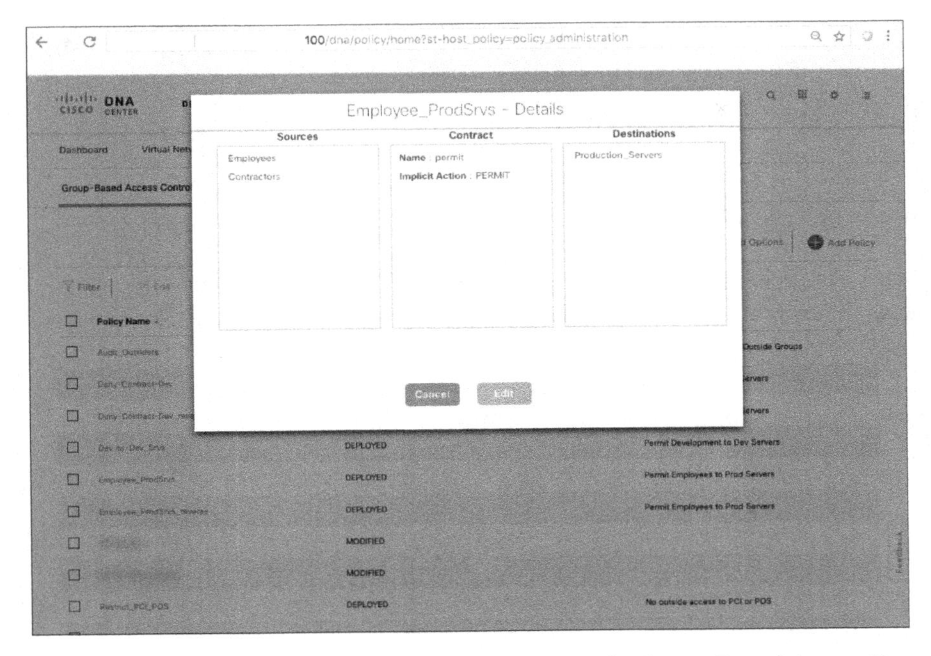

Figure 19-40 *Reviewing an Individual Policy via the Group-Based Access Control (Fabric) Tab*

Creating or editing a policy basically consists of three steps: defining the source group(s), defining the destination group(s), and creating a contract between them that specifies how the groups involved can interact, or the action to be taken on their traffic flows. Here, you see all the components defined that allow for the desired policy involved in this example—namely, a source of Employees or Contractors, a destination of Production_Servers, and an action of Permit.

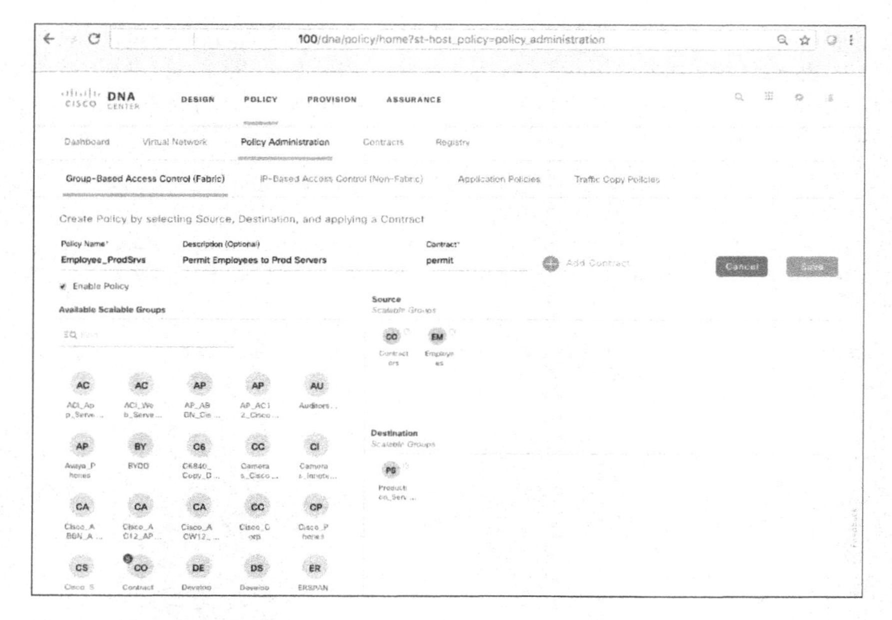

Figure 19-41 *Editing a Policy via the Group-Based Access Control (Fabric) Tab*

Let's say a request had just come through to allow an Auditors groups within the university access to these same servers and services. Figure 19-42 shows how to accommodate this request.

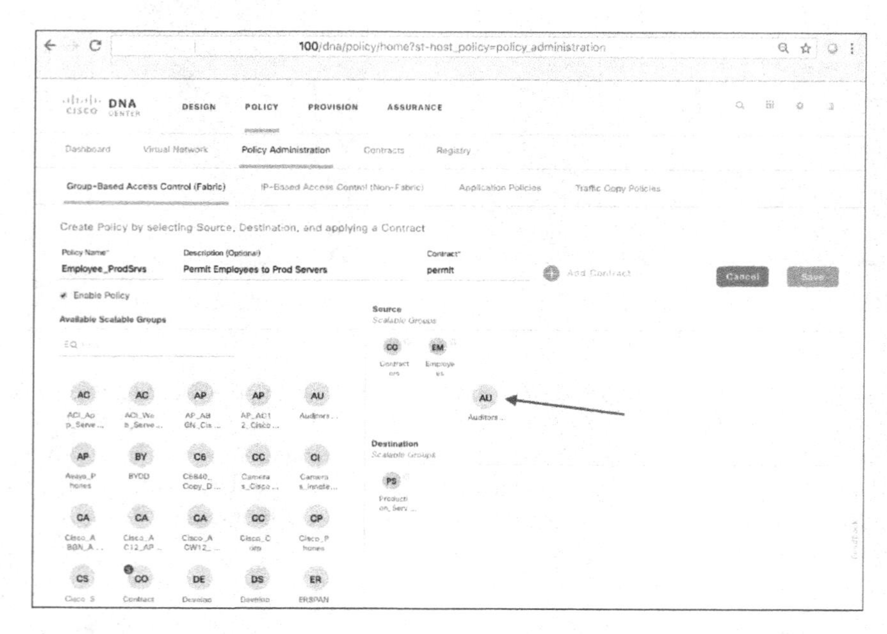

Figure 19-42 *Assigning a New Group to a Policy via the Group-Based Access Control (Fabric) Tab*

Here, you would simply drag the assigned group (Auditors) into the source area for Scalable Groups assigned to the policy. And that's it! It's really that simple. But remember, nothing is committed until you click Save. Figure 19-43 shows the policy being saved.

Cisco DNA Center sanity-checks the policy and, once done, creates the necessary policy configurations and pushes the policy so created over to ISE. ISE in turn deploys the updated group-based policy to all the appropriate devices within the fabric. All of this happens seamlessly and without further need for intervention by the network operator.

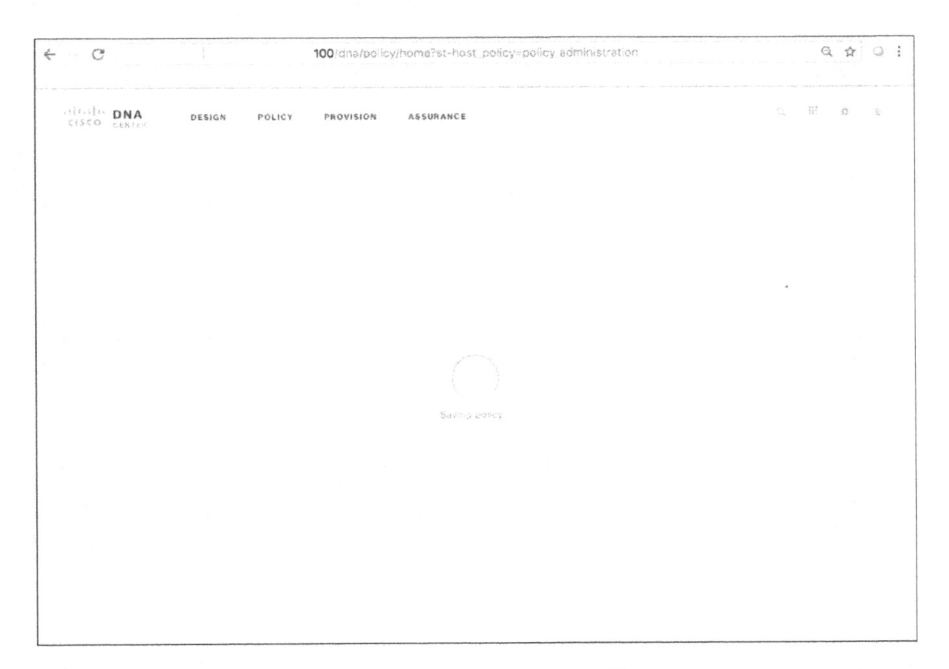

Figure 19-43 *Cisco DNA Center—Saving Policy Changes*

To provide a positive indication that these changes took place, the pop-up message shown in Figure 19-44 briefly appears within Cisco DNA Center to indicate the success of the policy change.

Now that we have explored policy configuration and alteration, let's delve into provisioning the fabric itself. Switching to the Provision workflow in Cisco DNA Center again presents the Device Inventory, as shown in Figure 19-45.

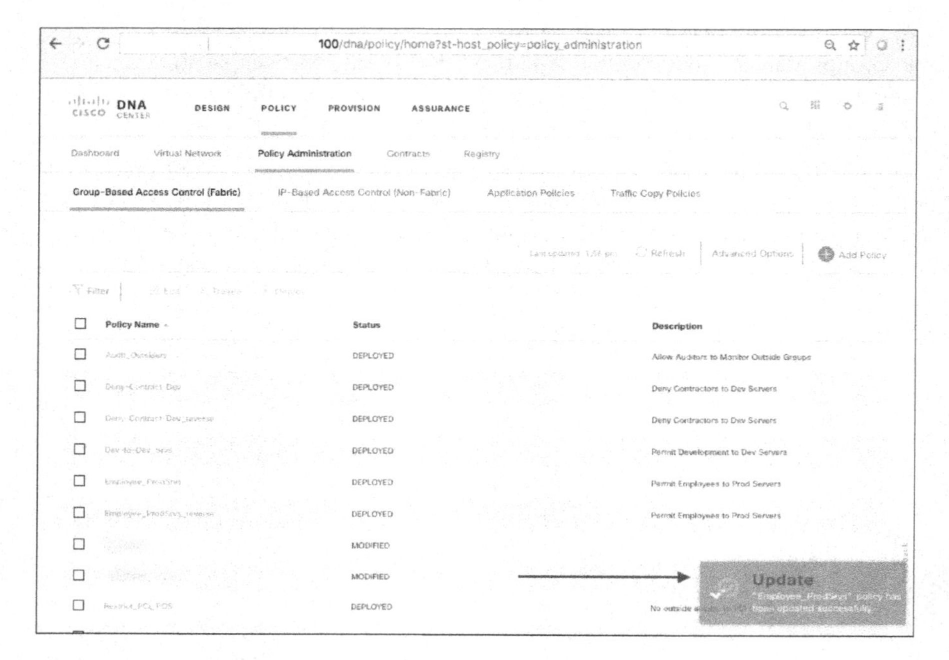

Figure 19-44 *Successful Policy Change*

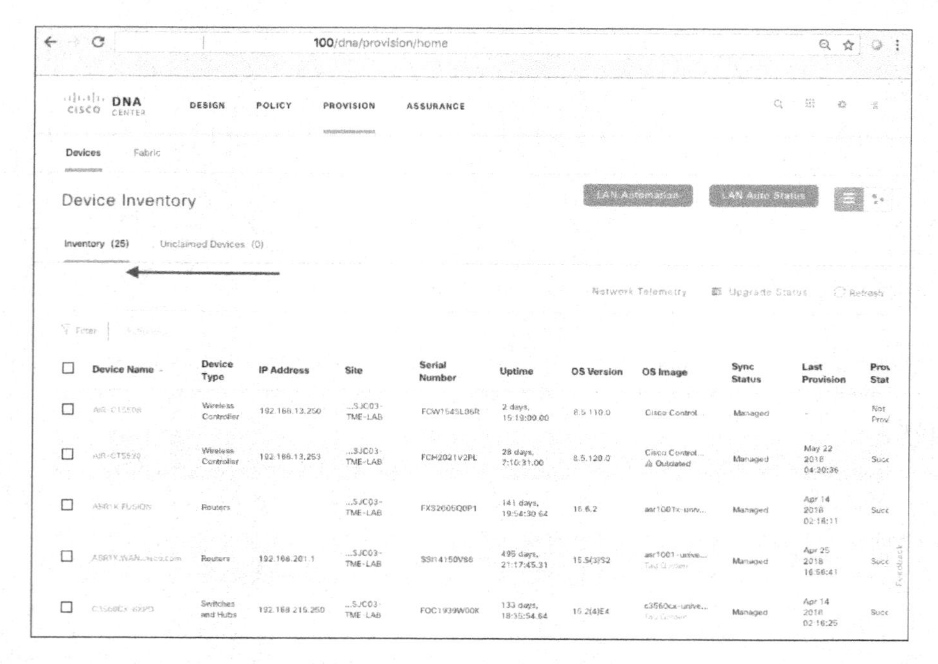

Figure 19-45 *Cisco DNA Center Provision Workflow: Device Inventory*

On the Inventory tab, you can assign to sites the devices that you discovered and added to your inventory, and you can provision them to prepare them for the various roles that they will take on within the fabric. Again, you can review OS images, check the provisioning status, and check the sync status (indicating whether Cisco DNA Center has obtained the necessary copy of the device's configuration).

Since you are interested in building out a fabric, click the Fabric tab. This brings you to a screen such as the one illustrated in Figure 19-46.

In this screen, you see a summary of all the various fabrics set up so far. In this example there are four: the Default LAN Fabric, along with three others, New York, Raleigh, and San Jose—locations where the university has campuses. Adding a new fabric is as a simple as clicking the blue plus sign icon and assigning the appropriate name and site type. However, in this example, let's explore an existing fabric and see how to assign new devices to an existing deployment.

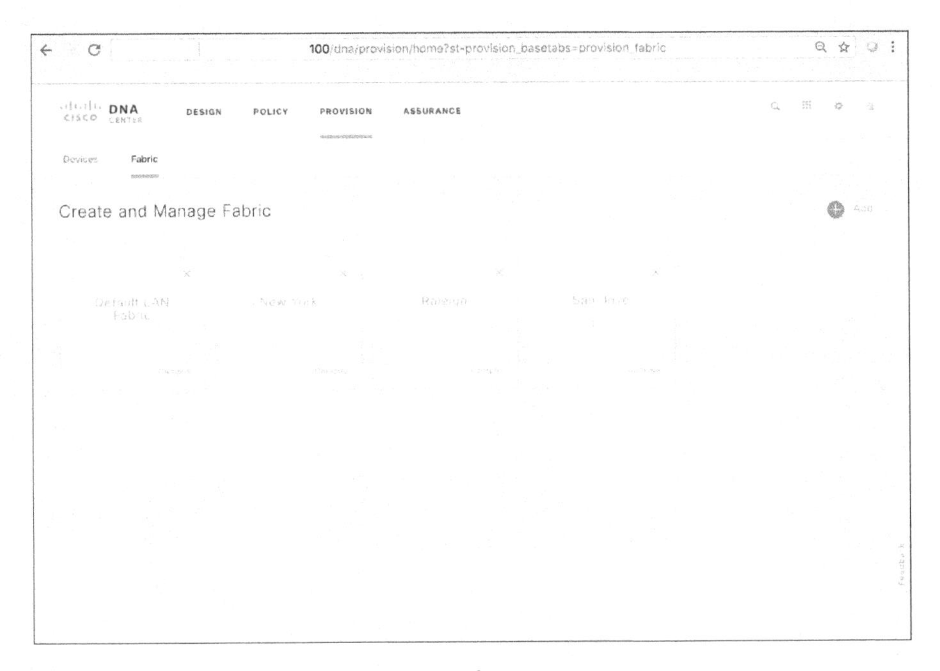

Figure 19-46 *Provision Workflow: Fabric*

Figure 19-47 shows the screen presented after selecting the San Jose fabric.

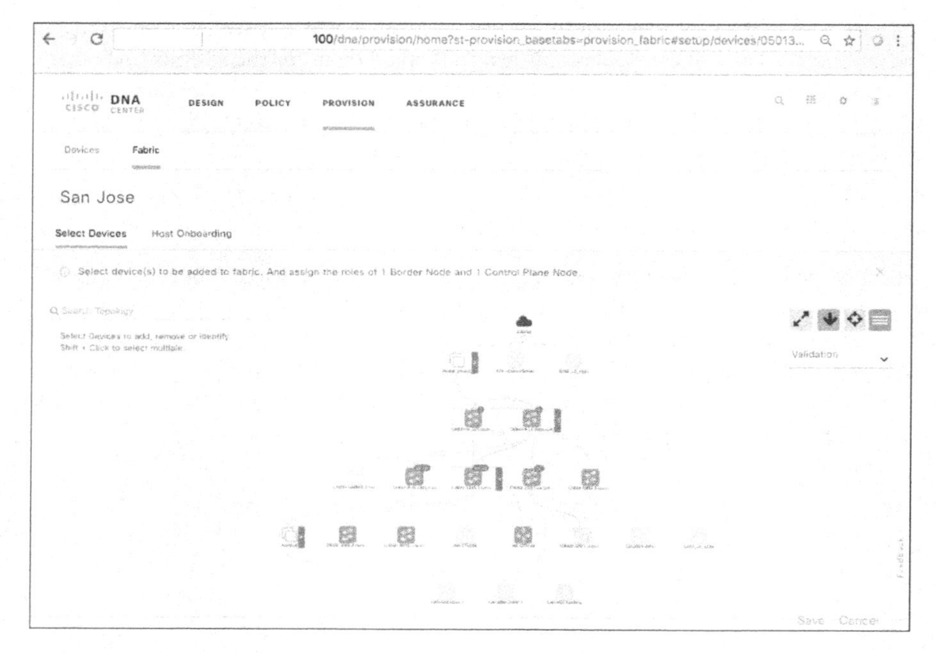

Figure 19-47 *Provision Workflow: Editing a Fabric Site*

There's quite a bit going on here, so take your time and explore it. First, notice that you need to assign at least a border node and a control plane node to build out the fabric. The example topology shown actually has four border nodes: two defined on a pair of Catalyst 6800s (a 6807 and a 6880), one defined on a Catalyst 6840, and one defined on a Catalyst 9500. The topology also has a single control plane node, as defined on a second Catalyst 9500. Most networks actually have two control plane nodes deployed for redundancy, but this example is still early in the deployment cycle and so only has one defined. This is shown "zoomed in" in Figure 19-48, for greater clarity. Please note that all devices that are currently added to and participating in the fabric are shown in a blue color (non-fabric or underlay-only devices are shown in gray).

As you can see, border nodes are clearly marked with a "B" and the control plane node is indicated with a "CP." Again, this example has a total of four borders and only one control plane node, as shown in Figure 19-48.

Another item of note is that two of the nodes acting as borders are also marked with "RP," indicating these nodes are acting as Rendezvous Points for the multicast deployment within the fabric. As per standard multicast operation, the RPs are where the multicast sources are joined to the appropriate destinations, using Protocol Independent Multicast (PIM) as the control plane for operation of the multicast system.

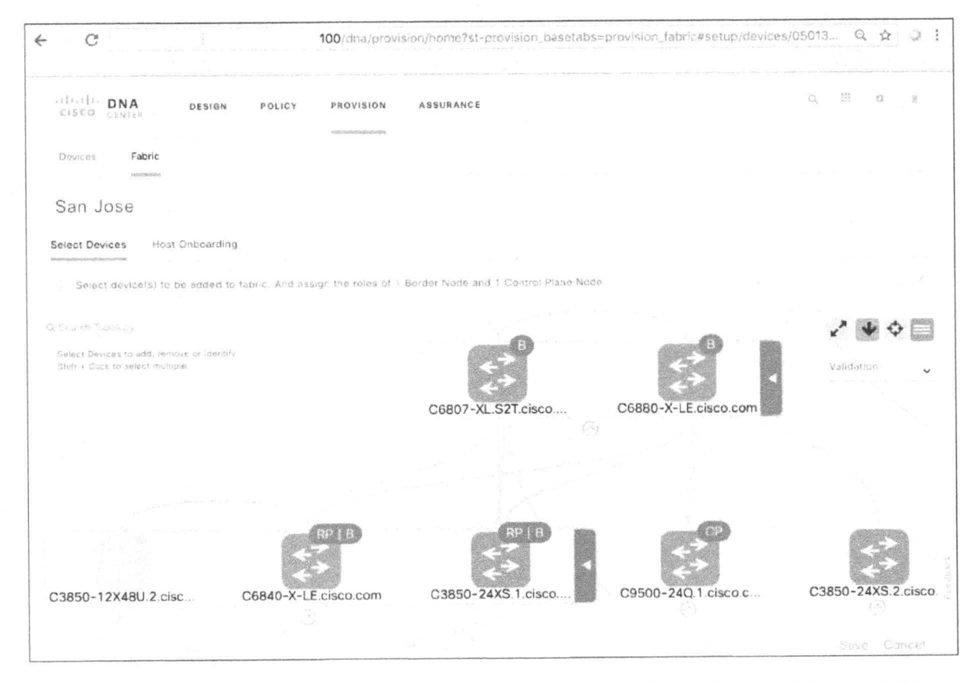

Figure 19-48 *Editing a Fabric Site, Zoomed-In View of Borders and Control Planes*

It is worth noting that the default mode of operation for multicast within the fabric environment is via head-end replication—meaning that all multicast packets for the overlay network are replicated at the ingress node (typically, an edge switch) and sent as individual unicast-VXLAN-encapsulated packets to each egress switch, which then decapsulates the unicast VXLAN outer header, exposing the inner user multicast packet, which then undergoes local multicast replication for delivery to any receivers for that multicast group at the egress node.

Although this mode of operation is not as efficient as true underlay multicast replication is, it does have the beneficial property of not requiring the underlay network itself to be multicast-enabled—a very important consideration for many existing enterprise networks that may desire to have multicast available for use by fabric-based overlay applications but never have gone to the time and effort of enabling multicast network-wide on their existing (underlay) network infrastructures. If multicast is in fact available in the underlay, a future revision to the SD-Access solution is currently planned to enable the underlay multicast system to be leveraged for distributed multicast replication.

The San Jose fabric also has a number of edge switches defined, based on Catalyst 3650s and other switches, as shown in Figure 19-49.

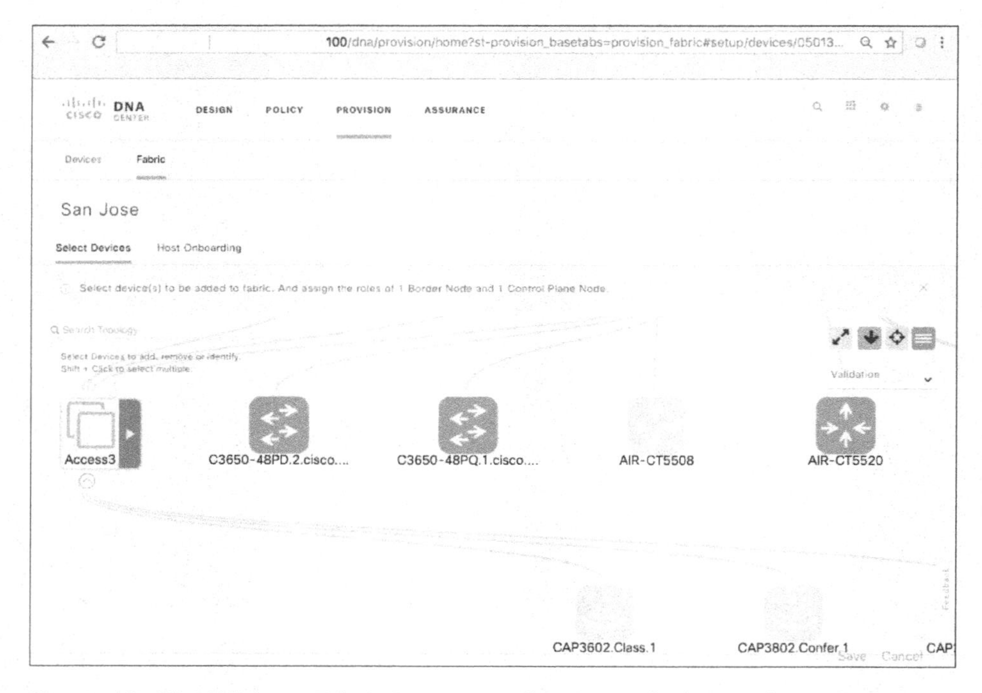

Figure 19-49 *Editing a Fabric Site, Zoomed-In View of Edges and Wireless Devices*

Notice the close-up view of the various edge switches added to the fabric, along with wireless devices (APs and WLCs). As shown, San Jose already has two Catalyst 3650s added to the fabric, along with a WLC 5520 and a number of APs (note, the 3602 AP shown is not fabric-capable, but the 3802 AP is). You know that these are fabric edge switches because they are shown in a blue color (thus added to fabric), but they do not have any tag on them as the border or control plane switches have. Any devices so colored but untagged are edge switches as shown in the topology.

One interesting item also shown here is the access grouping called Access3. For additional clarity, Cisco DNA Center allows devices shown in the topology view to be collapsed together for simplified viewing. In this case, clicking the triangle symbol expands this device group, as shown in Figure 19-50.

Figure 19-50 reveals that this device group contains a Catalyst 4503 edge switch already added to the fabric, along with a Catalyst 3850 switch that has not been added.

Let's see how to add a switch into the fabric. The result of selecting a Catalyst 9300 24-port switch, clicking it in the topology, and selecting Add to Fabric is illustrated in Figure 19-51.

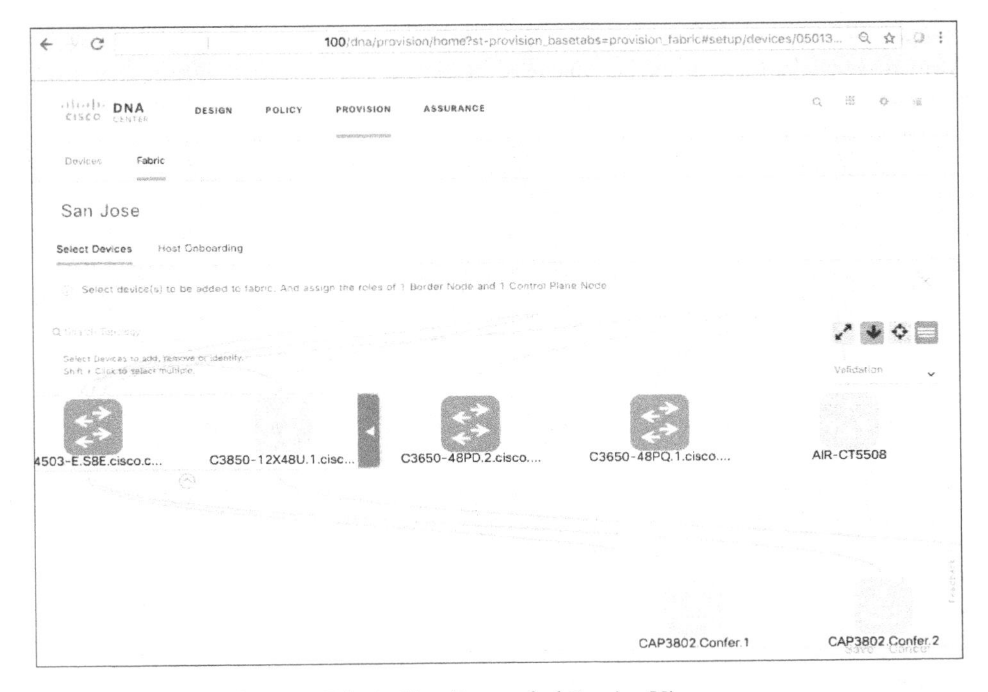

Figure 19-50 *Editing a Fabric Site, Expanded Device View*

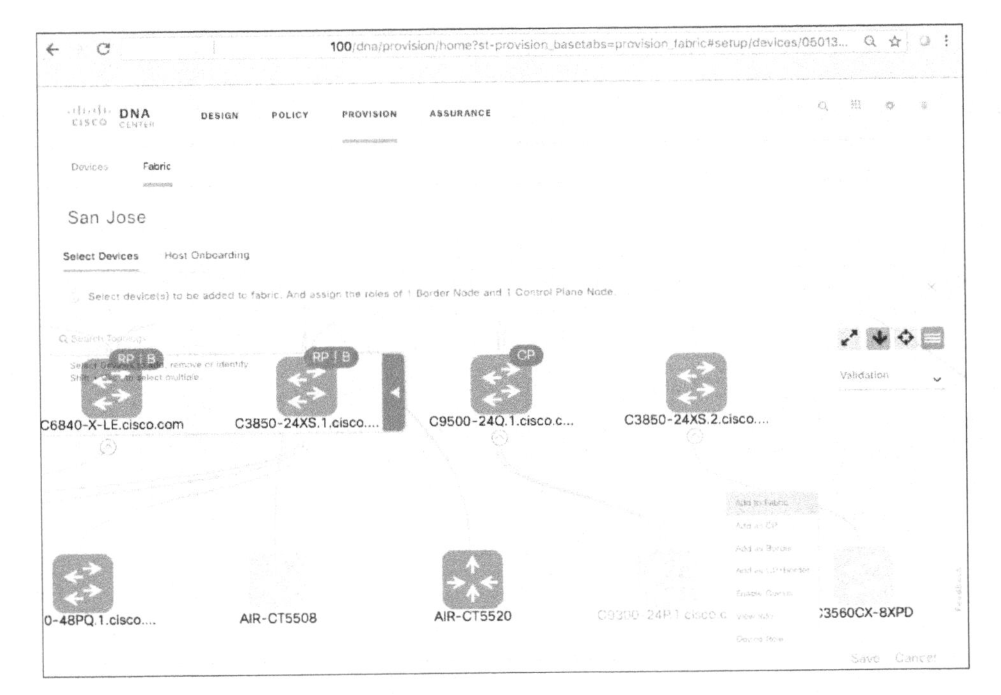

Figure 19-51 *Editing a Fabric Site, Adding a Fabric Edge Switch*

Because the device is not being added as a border or control plane, it is by default added as an edge switch. Right-clicking the name of the device and choosing Add to Fabric (and zooming back out a bit for clarity on the entire topology) opens a screen similar to that shown in Figure 19-52.

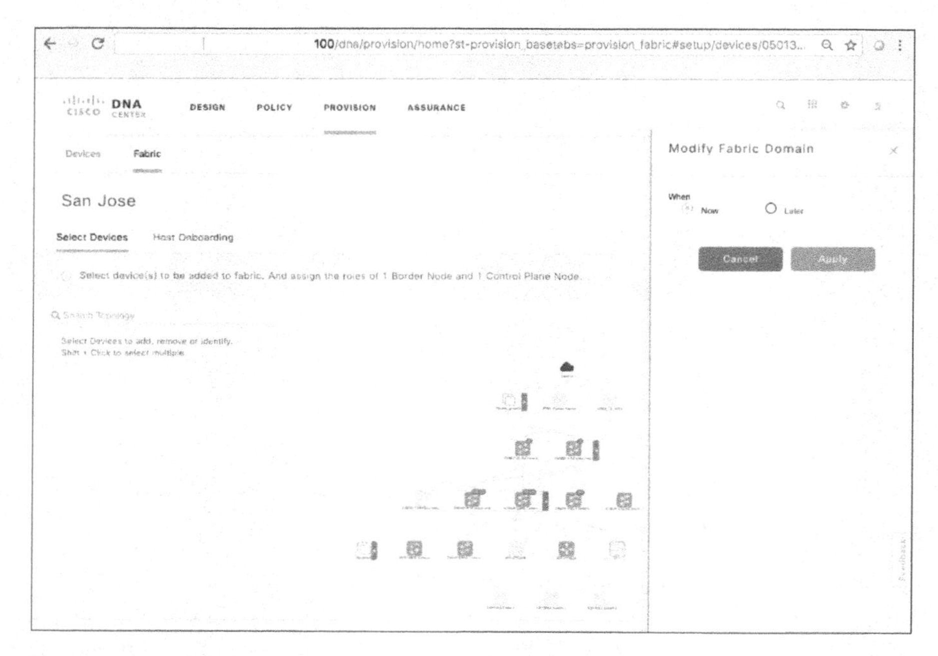

Figure 19-52 *Editing a Fabric Site, Adding a Fabric Edge Switch, Now or Later Option*

Because converting a switch to be a fabric edge involves fairly substantial changes to the switch's configuration—adding a LISP instance, configuring VRFs and new IP subnets, pointing it to the fabric's control planes and default border elements, and much more—the choice is given to deploy this configuration immediately or defer it to a later (scheduled) time. In this case study, the switch was deployed immediately, launching the update screen shown in Figure 19-53.

At this point, all the necessary switch configurations are created by Cisco DNA Center, deployed to the switch or switches involved (because many devices can be deployed at once by the network manager), and checked for proper deployment. Once the configuration is verified as correct, the network icon on the map changes from gray to blue. Success! A new edge switch was added to the fabric.

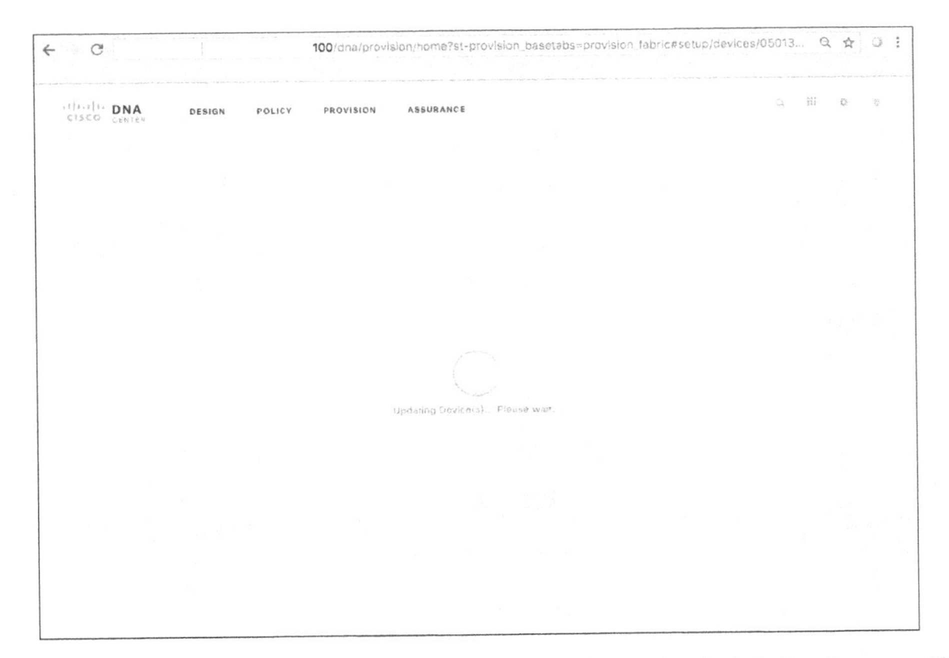

Figure 19-53 *Editing a Fabric Site, Adding a Fabric Edge Switch, Deployment Phase*

Adding a WLC to the fabric is accomplished in much the same way, with APs continuing to be deployed and managed via the WLC as always—but now operating in a distributed mode using local VXLAN tunnels to drop off user data directly at the edge switch, leveraging the distributed anycast default gateway, stretch subnets, and VN/SGT-based policies for wireless traffic just as is done for wired traffic. In this example, the WLC 5520 and any compatible APs are deployed in a fabric mode of operation.

Finally, let's take a closer look at assigning IP host pools (subnets) to VNs, and defining how users and devices are mapped into these host pools at the network edge. Figure 19-54 shows the Host Onboarding tab within the Fabric area with the Employees VN open for editing to examine its configuration.

Notice on the left side of the screen that various authentication types exist. These include 802.1X Closed Mode, 802.1X Open Mode, Easy Connect, and No Authentication. NoAuth is just what it sounds like—for this port type, no authentication is performed, and users attaching to each port are simply mapped by the port's static configuration to a given IP host pool, VN, and SGT. The 802.1X modes are more sophisticated, in that they actually perform strong authentication (username/password) for an attached host using the 802.1X protocol, with an option to fall back to an open authentication mode should the 802.1X auth fail if so chosen.

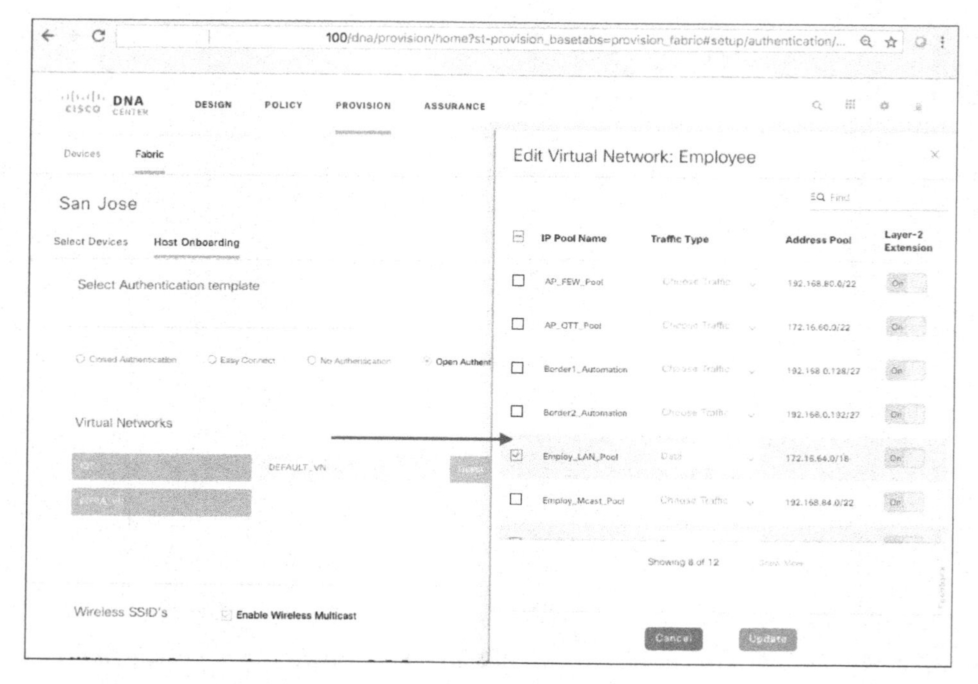

Figure 19-54 *Host Onboarding, VN and IP Host Pool Configuration*

Many devices today (most modern operating systems, and many end devices) support 802.1X, and this choice is obviously more secure than a static authentication option, and should be used if possible (as one of the major benefits of SD-Access is integrated segmentation, based on user/device identity). In this case, the user/device identity is authenticated by the edge switch with the AAA server (ISE), as defined earlier in the Cisco DNA Center setup.

The Easy Connect option is an interesting one; it leverages a capability within ISE to authenticate end devices using their Active Directory login and, based on this, to assign the endpoint into the appropriate network segment, similarly as if they had used an 802.1X supplicant (but without having to have an 802.1X supplicant necessarily deployed). This is useful in cases where AD may be in use, and an 802.1X rollout may not have already been done by the organization involved.

Next, remember the process for setting up the various IP host pools in the Design workflow? Here is where you would attach those subnets to the appropriate VNs, so that when users and devices attach to the fabric and get authenticated as a member of a particular VN, they would then also be dropped into the appropriate IP host pool (subnet) to receive their IP address (typically via DHCP). It is worth noting that if you were to connect to any edge switch within the fabric (say, via SSH), you would see that each switch has a local VLAN created on it, mapped into each address pool as shown, with all edge switches sharing the same virtual default gateway IP address and virtual MAC address for that subnet (thus enabling the distributed anycast default gateway capability for attached endpoints).

Now, you may again ask yourself, if all of the edge switches share the same virtual IP address (and you may have many, many edge switches deployed within a given fabric), how does DHCP work? In other words, when the DHCP relay function on the switch picks up the user's initial DHCP_REQUEST packet and forwards this to the DHCP server, how does the DHCP server know which of the many edge switches to send the response back to? Normally this is done by referencing the Gateway IP Address (GIADDR) field in the relayed packet to both pick the appropriate subnet for IP address assignment to the host and return the packet offering this address—the DHCP_OFFER—to the client using the DHCP relay node. In other words, when the GIADDR is not unique, but is shared across many edge switches, how does DHCP operate? Good question. Let's explore that for a bit.

In SD-Access, the initial edge switch to which the user or device is attached inserts an extra bit of information into the relayed DHCP packet that is sent up to the DHCP server. Specifically, it inserts an Option 82 field with its own unique loopback IP address inserted in this option, along with the actual user subnet inserted as usual in the GIADDR field. The receiving DHCP server then serves up an IP address to the user, as selected from the GIADDR subnet (i.e., the host pool into which the user is mapped), and returns the DHCP_OFFER packet to this address (which is not unique, but which is part of the fabric).

Importantly, the Option 82 information is simply reflected back in this DHCP_OFFER packet, unaltered (and thus including the information about which actual edge switch initially relayed the request). Once this packet arrives back at the fabric border, this DHCP Option 82 data is extracted by the border device and is used to determine which actual edge switch to send the DHCP_OFFER packet back to, after which this packet is dispatched on its way with this updated information—and the end host user or device gets its IP address. In this way, it is not necessary to update or modify the DHCP server, and yet operation of the DHCP service with a distributed anycast default gateway deployment is transparently accommodated. All of the necessary configurations to enable the appropriate handing of this operation for DHCP Option 82 are configured by Cisco DNA Center to the border devices when these borders are added to the fabric.

As you can see, there is a lot that goes on "under the hood" of the fabric deployment—but maintaining the simplicity of fabric configuration, operation, and use is always paramount as new capabilities are added to the fabric.

When you switch over to examining the wireless configuration for IP host pools, you see something similar, as shown in Figure 19-55.

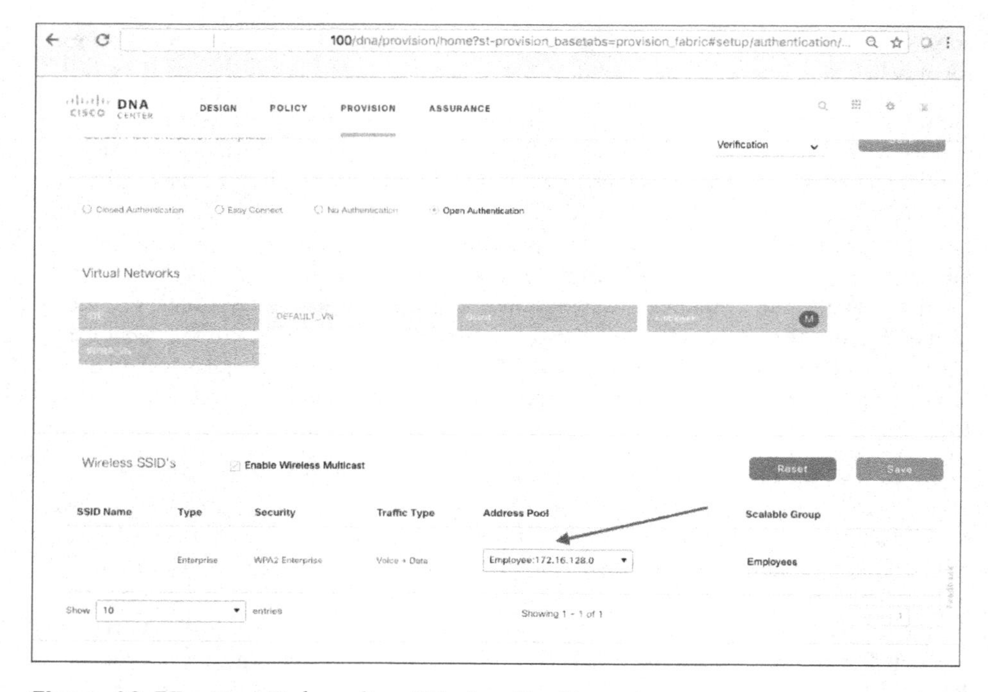

Figure 19-55 *Host Onboarding, Wireless Configuration*

Here, you can see the defined fabric-enabled SSID (again, obscured for security reasons), along with the type of wireless security mode deployed, the traffic types involved, and the IP host pool mapped to this SSID. Also note that users in this SSID are by default mapped into the Employees group, and that wireless multicast is enabled.

Finally, let's examine configurations all the way down to individual fabric switches and switch ports, as shown in Figure 19-56.

On the left side, we can observe individual switches within the fabric deployment, and as shown you can select into any individual switch and choose to view and configure all of the ports on the switch, or any individual port or group of ports, to be assigned to a particular host pool (mapped to VN), group (SGT), or authentication type (Closed Auth, Open Auth, Easy Connect, or No Auth). In this way, you have fine-grained control all the way down to the individual port level to determine how endpoints are able to attach to the fabric network, what security method they will use when they do attach, and where and how they will be mapped into the fabric network (statically via port assignment, or dynamically via AAA-delivered attributes associated with the end-point's login).

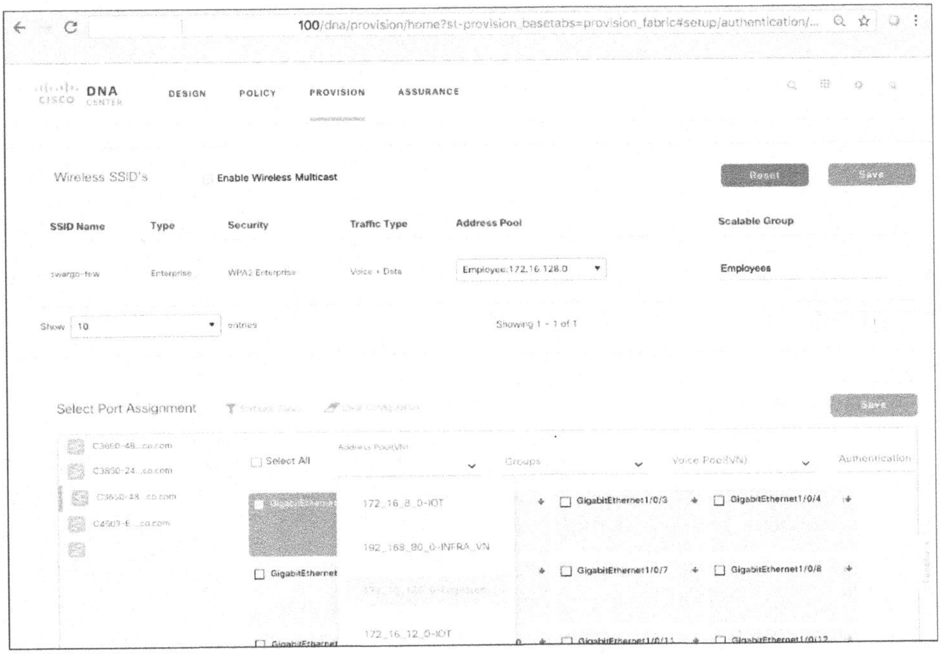

Figure 19-56 *Host Onboarding, Wired Configuration*

SD-Access Case Study, Summing Up

There are so many areas to explore within SD-Access and Cisco DNA Center that going through them all here would be an entire book in and of itself! However, hopefully this case study served to at least briefly outline how the concepts introduced earlier in this chapter—fabric overlays and underlays, the various node types (border, control plane, and edge), host pools, distributed anycast default gateways, and the like—come together and are provisioned and managed as a single, cohesive, and simple system using Cisco DNA Center.

In the "Further Reading" section, you will find a number of excellent references that will allow you to dive deeper into both Software-Defined Access and Cisco DNA Center and examine in even greater detail how SD-Access can be defined, provisioned, deployed, and managed to meet the existing—and future—goals of your organization for network segmentation, security, and simplification.

Summary

This chapter covered the following:

- The challenges of enterprise networks today
- An overview of Software-Defined Access as a fabric for the enterprise

- A detailed examination of the capabilities and benefits of Software-Defined Access
- An SD-Access case study illustrating how these capabilities can be deployed in practice

To recap, the Cisco Software-Defined Access solution introduces many key new features that, taken together, serve as a foundation for a revolution in how enterprise networks are designed, deployed, and operated. SD-Access addresses both wired and wireless deployments and, working with Cisco DNA Center and ISE, provides a solution that seamlessly integrates security, segmentation, and group-based policy enforcement in a fully automated way and with powerful monitoring and assurance capabilities.

Figure 19-57 summarizes some of the key elements and aspects of SD-Access.

By leveraging Cisco DNA Center for simplified automation and sophisticated analytics and assurance capabilities, SD-Access provides a true next-generation set of network capabilities and forms the underpinning for an entirely new approach to enterprise networking—one that supports the requirements of modern organizations for speed, simplicity, and sophisticated, secure functionality.

As much ground as was covered in this chapter, you have only begun to scratch the surface of what SD-Access offers. If you'd like to dig deeper, a good place to start is with the items noted in the "Further Reading" section that follows.

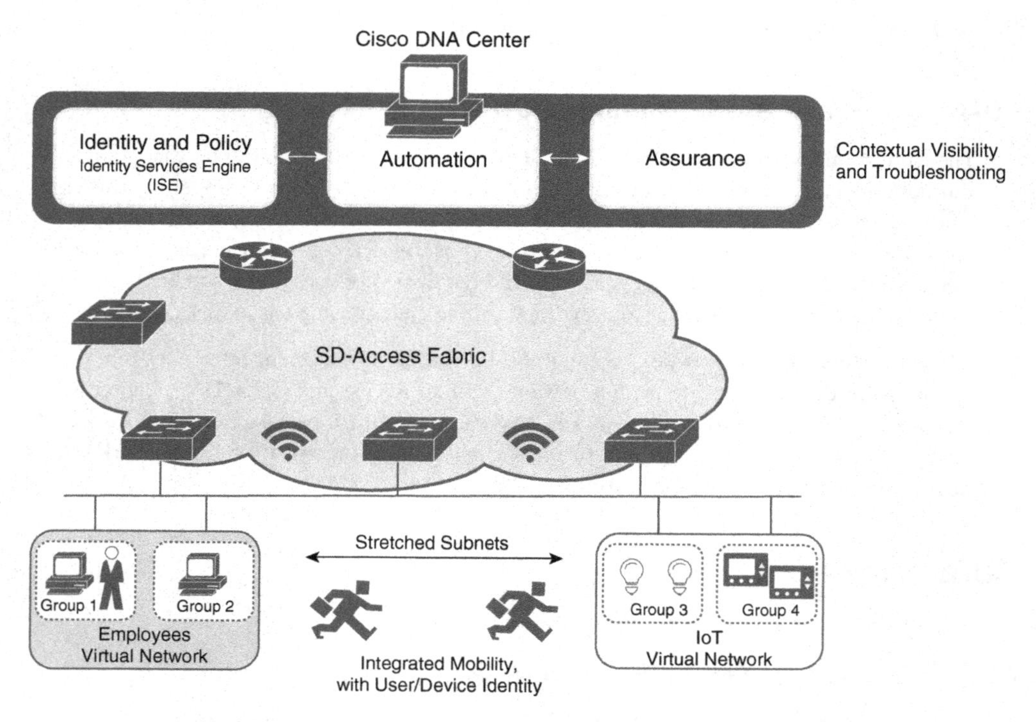

Figure 19-57 *Software-Defined Access Solution Summary*

Also note that SD-Access as a solution is continuing to evolve—and to evolve rapidly. Accordingly, there are many new functions and capabilities that, by the time you read this text, may already have been introduced for SD-Access and may be available for your use. This chapter focused mainly on the core functionality of SD-Access, items that are part of the base level of the solution and are fundamental to understand as you consider implementing SD-Access in your own network.

However, be sure to keep a sharp lookout for these new capabilities as they appear, as many of them will serve to extend the reach, functionality, and depth of the Software-Defined Access solution in exciting new ways. We are only at the beginning of the SD-Access lifecycle!

As you move on from SD-Access to the next topic area, keep your eye on SD-Access! It will continually evolve for quite some time to come, helping to drive many more new and useful innovations in the area of enterprise networking.

Further Reading

Cisco Systems Software-Defined Access portal: https://www.cisco.com/c/en/us/solutions/enterprise-networks/software-defined-access/index.html.

As noted in the chapter summary, SD-Access as a solution is only at the beginning of its lifecycle, and many new and advanced capabilities are being added to the solution constantly. Bookmark this URL and check it frequently to keep abreast of the latest developments.

Hill, C., et al. *Cisco Software-Defined Access: Enabling Intent-Based Networking.* Cisco Systems eBook. https://www.cisco.com/c/dam/en/us/products/se/2018/1/Collateral/nb-06-software-defined-access-ebook-en.pdf

This is a comprehensive, yet concise, introduction to SD-Access capabilities and benefits and a deeper dive into the details of SD-Access design, deployment, and operation, created by some of the same authors of this book but published in an e-book format.

Cisco Validated Design Guides

Cisco Validated Design (CVD) guides for all aspects of system design, including Cisco DNA and Cisco SD-Access, are available at the Cisco Design Zone: https://www.cisco.com/c/en/us/solutions/design-zone.html. CVDs provide authoritative Cisco guidance for best practice deployments and serve as a valuable reference as you delve deeper into the Software-Defined Access solution.

Cisco DNA–specific CVDs and other resources are available at the following URL: https://www.cisco.com/c/en/us/solutions/design-zone/networking-design-guides/digital-network-architecture-design-guides.html

The following are CVDs specific to SD-Access (as of this writing):

Software-Defined Access Design Guide (August 2018) https://www.cisco.com/c/dam/en/us/td/docs/solutions/CVD/Campus/CVD-Software-Defined-Access-Design-Guide-2018AUG.pdf

SD-Access Segmentation Design Guide (May 2018) https://www.cisco.com/c/dam/en/us/td/docs/solutions/CVD/Campus/CVD-Software-Defined-Access-Segmentation-Design-Guide-2018MAY.pdf

Software-Defined Access Deployment Guide (April 2018) https://www.cisco.com/c/dam/en/us/td/docs/solutions/CVD/Campus/CVD-Software-Defined-Access-Deployment-Guide-2018APR.pdf

Chapter 20

Cisco DNA Application Policy

Today's enterprises have thousands of applications on their networks, with hundreds of applications hiding within encrypted flows. Many of these applications directly contribute to business objectives; however, many more do not.

As such, few network operators are even aware of *how much* traffic is traversing their infrastructure by application, let alone *how well* these applications are being treated across their network. Even fewer operators have aligned their business objectives with end-to-end application policies deployed across their networks. This is primarily due to the intrinsic complexity of implementing such policies across various places in the network, as tools, mechanisms, and syntax often vary from platform to platform.

Cisco DNA provides a comprehensive architecture to monitor, manage, provision, and troubleshoot applications. Specifically, Cisco DNA provides powerful hardware and software infrastructure capabilities to support granular application recognition—of even encrypted applications—as well as flexible and detailed application treatment capabilities. Additionally, Cisco DNA includes Application Policy, which automates the deployment of intent-based application policies in an end-to-end manner over both brownfield and greenfield networks. Complementing this, Cisco DNA also includes application assurance (which is discussed in detail in Chapter 21, "Cisco DNA Analytics and Assurance") to monitor, report, and remediate (when necessary) how applications are being treated across the network.

This chapter discusses Cisco DNA Application Policy, which provides operators a simple user interface to express their business intent of how their applications are to be treated across their networks. However, this chapter also "lifts the hood" to detail the inner workings of Application Policy, as well as the underlying network infrastructure hardware and software mechanisms that deliver application policy treatment and reporting. This chapter explains the following:

- How applications are managed within Cisco DNA Center
- How intent-based policies for application policies can be configured and deployed from within Cisco DNA Center
- How Cisco DNA programmable infrastructure implements and delivers these application policies for
  - Routers
  - Switches
  - Wireless access points and controllers

Managing Applications in Cisco DNA Center

Cisco DNA Center is the single pane of glass to design, provision, and assure your network. This also includes managing applications and application policy, as will be the focus of this chapter.

There are four tools within Cisco DNA Center to manage applications:

- **Application Registry:** To provide and to customize individual applications details
- **Application Sets:** To provide groupings of applications to simplify policy administration
- **Application Policy:** To specify and deploy the business intent for application treatment
- **Application Assurance:** To report on the treatment of applications

The first three of these tools are discussed in this chapter, and application assurance is discussed in Chapter 21.

Application Registry

The Application Registry contains all the details of the known applications in the enterprise; these include over 1400 default applications (to which more are added every month), as well as any custom applications, as shown in Figure 20-1.

Figure 20-1 *Cisco DNA Center Application Registry*

Note All screenshots are current as of the time of writing and are based on Cisco DNA Center 1.2.5 release; however, these are subject to change for subsequent releases.

Applications are viewed either by their names or grouped by standards-based traffic classes. Operators are not expected to know these traffic classes, but these are explained for reference. These traffic classes, based on IETF RFC 4594, "Configuration Guidelines for DiffServ Service Classes,"[1] are summarized as follows:

- **Control:** This traffic maintains infrastructure availability—directly or indirectly—and is further broken down as follows:
  - **Network Control:** This traffic class is intended for network control plane traffic, which is required for reliable operation of the enterprise network. Example traffic includes Enhanced Interior Gateway Routing Protocol (EIGRP), Open Shortest Path First (OSPF) routing protocol, Border Gateway Protocol (BGP), Hot Standby Router Protocol (HSRP), Internet Key Exchange (IKE) protocol, etc.
  - **Signaling:** This traffic class is intended for signaling traffic that supports IP voice and video telephony overlay infrastructures. Example traffic includes Skinny Call Control Protocol (SCCP), Session Initiation Protocol (SIP), H.323, etc.
  - **Operations/Administration/Management (OAM):** This traffic class is intended for network operations, administration, and management traffic. This class is critical to the ongoing maintenance and support of the network. Example traffic includes Secure Shell (SSH), NetFlow, Simple Network Management Protocol (SNMP), syslog protocol, etc.

1 https://tools.ietf.org/html/rfc4594

- **Voice:** This traffic class is intended for audio traffic (only). Example traffic includes G.711 and G.729a codecs, as well as the audio components of multimedia conferencing applications, such as Cisco Jabber, WebEx, and Spark, Microsoft Skype for Business, etc.
- **Video:** This traffic may be broken down further, depending on whether the video streams are unidirectional or bidirectional and whether the flows adapt to network congestion (i.e., are "elastic," per RFC 4594 terminology) or not:
  - **Broadcast Video:** This traffic class is intended for unidirectional, inelastic video streams, such as for broadcast TV, live events, video surveillance flows, and similar video flows. Example traffic includes live Cisco Enterprise TV streams and Cisco IP Video Surveillance.
  - **Real-Time Interactive:** This traffic class is intended for inelastic, bidirectional (i.e., interactive) video applications. Example traffic includes Cisco TelePresence, immersive gaming apps, etc.
  - **Multimedia Conferencing:** This traffic class is intended for elastic, bidirectional multimedia collaboration applications. Note: Whenever possible, audio, signaling, and data media subcomponents of this class should be separated out and assigned to their respective traffic classes. Example applications include Cisco Jabber, WebEx, and Spark, Microsoft Skype for Business, etc.
  - **Multimedia Streaming:** This traffic class is intended for elastic, unidirectional (i.e., streaming) video applications. Example applications include Cisco Digital Media System Video on Demand (VoD) streams, e-learning videos, YouTube, etc.
- **Data:** Data traffic, from an application treatment perspective, can be broken down into two main subgroups, depending on whether the applications are user-interactive or not:
  - **Transactional Data:** This traffic class is intended for user-interactive data applications, also known as "foreground" applications. Users of these foreground applications are waiting for a response—via the network—before they can proceed with their tasks. As such, any delays or losses incurred on these flows directly impact user productivity. Example applications include data components of multimedia collaboration applications, enterprise resource planning (ERP) applications, customer relationship management (CRM) applications, database applications, etc.
  - **Bulk Data:** This traffic class is intended for non-user-interactive data applications, also known as "background" applications. These background applications are typically machine-to-machine flows, thus any losses incurred on these flows do not really slow down users (furthermore, any packet losses are automatically corrected by Transmission Control Protocol [TCP] retransmissions). Example applications include email, backup operations, File Transfer Protocol (FTP)/Secure FTP (SFTP), video and content distribution, etc.

Traffic classes are a standards-based method of grouping applications together, but they are not the only method. Additional grouping flexibility is provided via Application Sets, which are described in the following section.

However, before discussing Application Sets, two additional points bear mentioning relating to the Application Registry.

The first is that details on any given application can be viewed from within the Application Registry, as shown in Figure 20-2.

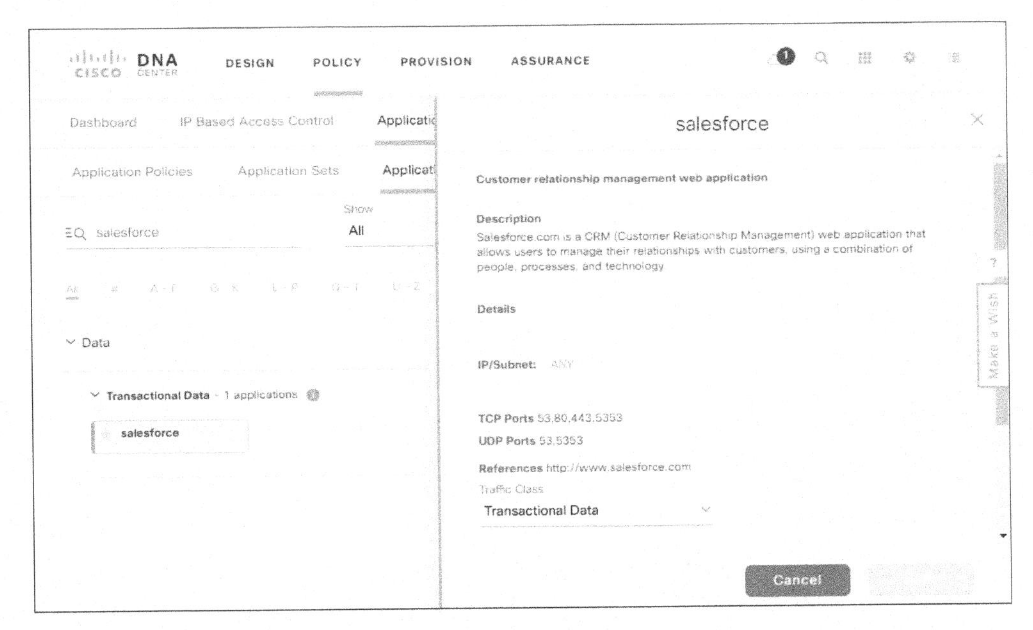

Figure 20-2 *Cisco DNA Center Application Registry—Application Details*

The second point is that you, as the operator, can define custom applications within the Application Registry simply by clicking the Add Application button (shown previously in Figure 20-1). This introduces a sliding panel that enables you to define the new custom application, as illustrated in Figure 20-3. Within this panel, you provide a name for the application, define how to identify it (e.g., by URL or by IP/port-level specifics), and specify how to treat the application. When it comes to defining treatment, you have two choices:

- If you are familiar with the standards-based traffic classes (already defined), click the Traffic Class radio button and simply select the appropriate traffic class to service the application.
- Click the Similar To radio button and select any application from the registry (of 1400+ apps) that your custom app is similar to; the custom application then receives the same treatment as the specified (similar) app.

Figure 20-3 *Cisco DNA Center Application Registry—Adding a Custom Application*

Application Sets

To simplify policy administration, it is helpful to group applications with similar policy requirements together; otherwise you need to set policy on an application-by-application basis, which doesn't scale well, especially when starting from an application library of over 1400 apps.

As previously mentioned, grouping by traffic classes is a standards-based method of combing applications with similar policy requirements together. This method is particularly suited to provisioning quality of service (QoS) policies to applications. However, although QoS is a foundational and primary use case of application policy, it is not the only type of policy that can be extended to an application. Additional types of application policy include

- Performance routing
- Traffic engineering
- Security
- Encryption
- Switched Port Analyzer (SPAN)/Encapsulated Remote SPAN (ERSPAN)
- Packet captures

Thus, any given method of grouping applications together that serves one of these use cases may not necessarily serve another. For example, while traffic classes may well suit QoS policy, they may not meet the needs of performance routing and traffic-engineering policies, etc. As such, the manner in which applications are grouped together needs to be flexible and customizable. This is the purpose of Application Sets, as shown in Figure 20-4.

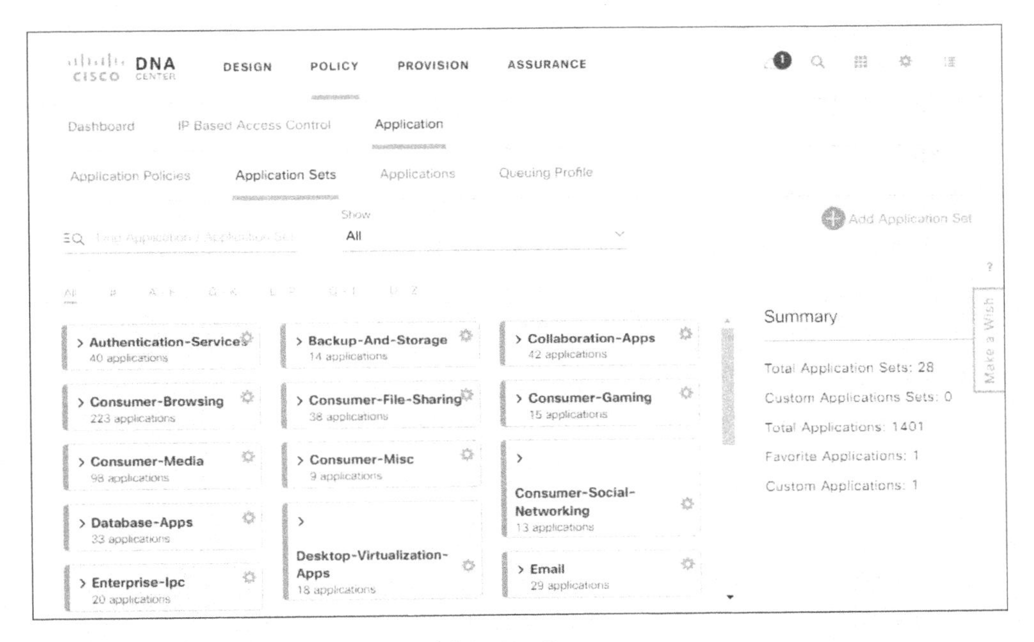

Figure 20-4 *Cisco DNA Center Application Sets*

Application Sets describe groupings of applications in common business-level language, such as

- Backup-and-Storage
- Email
- File-Sharing
- SaaS Apps
- Software-Updates

As such, you do not have to familiarize yourself with technical terminology (such as was the case in the previous exercise of defining traffic classes, which included becoming familiar with terms such as "elastic," "foreground," "background," etc.).

Click the Add Application Set button (shown in Figure 20-4) to create custom application sets, into which you can then drag and drop individual applications to meet your specific application policy requirements.

Application Policy

With applications organized into sets, it becomes very quick and easy to express intent-based policies for applications. In fact, there are only four simple steps required to deploy an end-to-end application policy across the enterprise network:

Step 1. Click Add Policy and enter a name for the policy.

Step 2. Select a Site Scope to which the policy is to be applied.

Step 3. Assign the business intent for the applications.

Step 4. Choose when to deploy the policy (immediately or at a future time).

These steps are illustrated in Figures 20-5 through 20-9.

Required Steps

The process begins by clicking Add Policy, as shown in Figure 20-5.

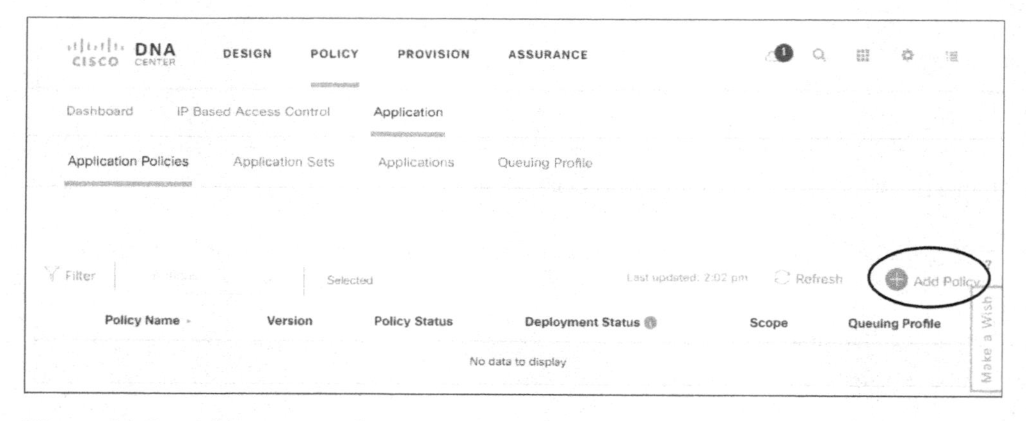

Figure 20-5 *Adding an Application Policy*

Next, you need to name the policy and choose its site scope, as shown in Figure 20-6.

Click Site Scope to view a sliding panel that enables you to select which site(s) the application policy is to be applied to, as shown in Figure 20-7. Sites are presented in a hierarchal manner, and may be selected at any level of the hierarchy. The policy may also be applied globally (by checking the Global box).

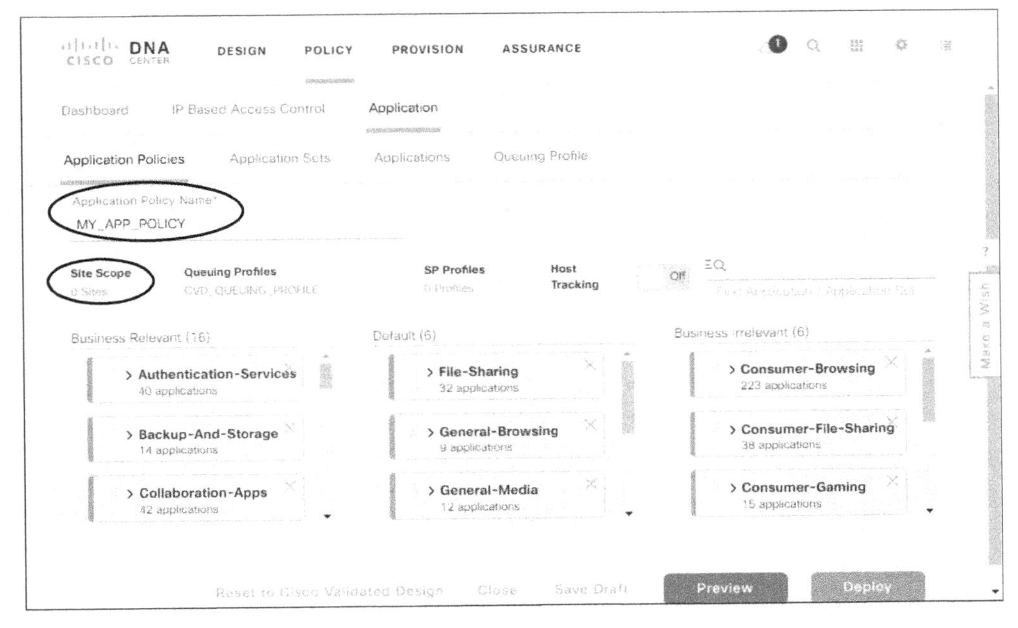

Figure 20-6 *Naming the Application Policy and Choosing a Site Scope*

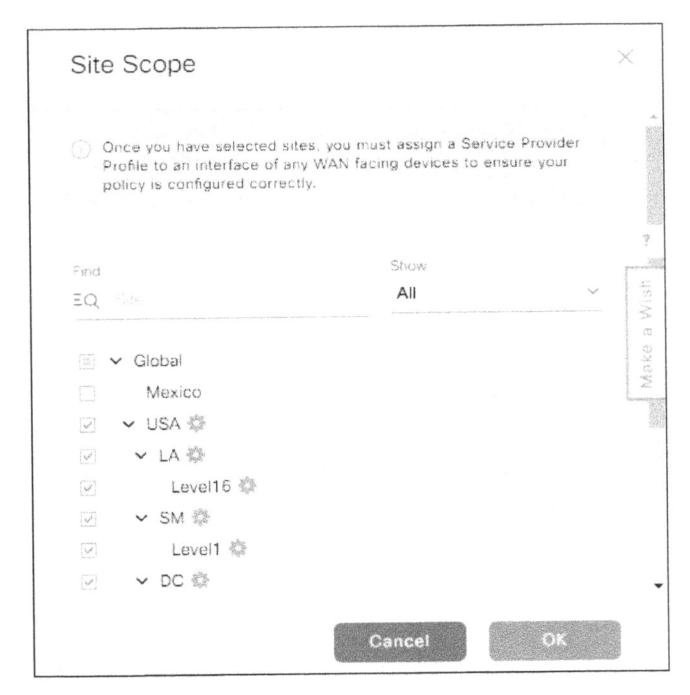

Figure 20-7 *Selecting the Site Scope for the Application Policy*

The third step is to assign business intent to applications. This is expressed by simply dragging and dropping application sets to the appropriate business-relevance bucket.

There are three levels of business relevance:

1. **Business Relevant:** These applications are *known to contribute to the business objectives* of the organization. Applications assigned as business relevant receive *preferential treatment* across the network infrastructure. Example business-relevant application sets include: Backup-And-Storage, Collaboration-Apps, Database-Apps, Email, Network-Control, Network-Management, Signaling, etc.

2. **Default:** These applications *may or may not contribute to business objectives, or there is no business reason to justify explicit policy treatment—whether preferential or deferential—for these applications.* As such, these applications remain treated exactly as they were prior to any application policy being deployed, which is commonly referred to as a "best effort" treatment and represents *neutral treatment* (i.e., neither preferential nor deferential). General-Browsing is an example of an application set that sometimes may contribute to business objectives but other times may not.

3. **Business Irrelevant:** These applications are *known to have no contribution to business objectives*, as these are often consumer- and/or entertainment-oriented in nature. Applications assigned as business irrelevant receive *deferential treatment* across the network infrastructure. Example business-irrelevant application sets include Consumer-Gaming, Consumer-Media, Consumer-Social-Networking, etc.

Application sets are auto-assigned to given business-relevant buckets, but these are very much intended to be modified to suit specific business objectives. For example, by default the Software-Updates application set is assigned to the Default bucket. However, some companies have found these software updates to be disruptive to their business operations and have chosen instead to assign them to the Business Irrelevant bucket, as illustrated in Figure 20-8.

After you have finished expressing business intent, you have the option to click Preview (shown at the bottom of Figure 20-6) or proceed directly to deployment by clicking Deploy. If you click Preview, then the Policy Preview Configurations side panel shown in Figure 20-9 opens.

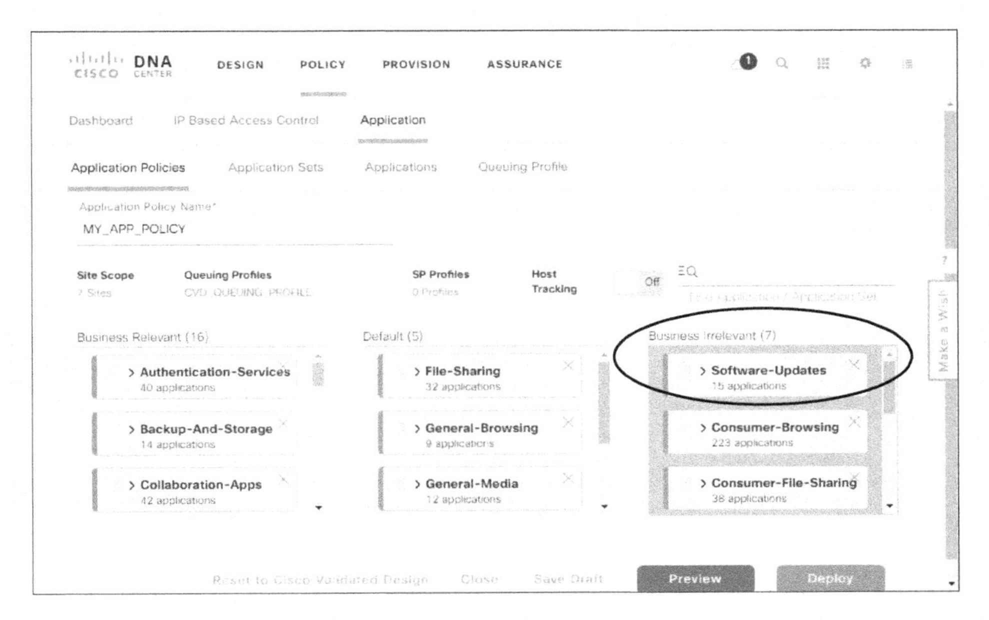

Figure 20-8 *Expressing Business Intent for Applications*

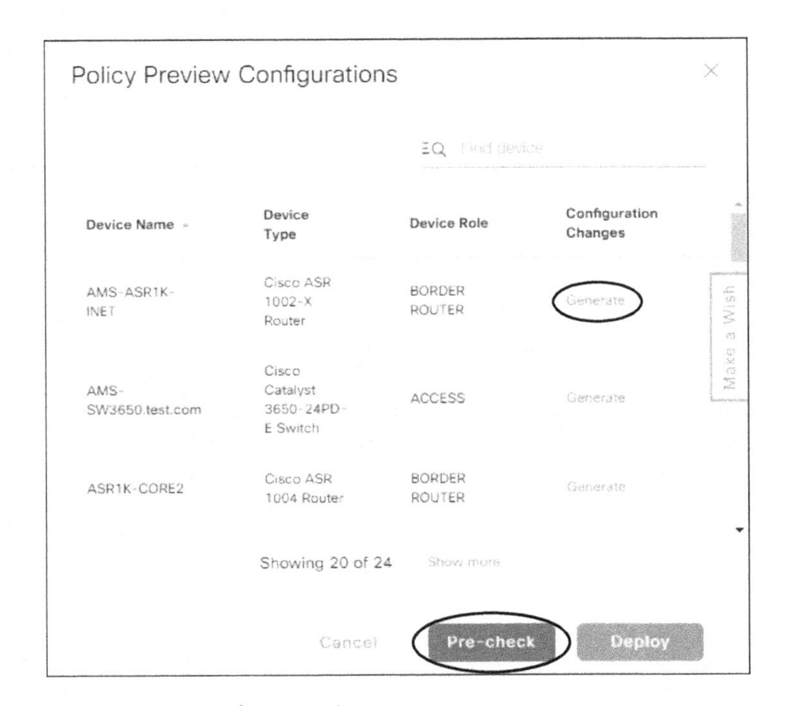

Figure 20-9 *Policy Preview*

From the Policy Preview side panel, you can click Pre-check to check network device software versions, licensing, and configurations to ensure that when the application policy is deployed, no issues will prevent it from being successful. Example output from clicking Pre-check is illustrated in Figure 20-10.

Note No configurations are pushed to the devices by clicking Pre-check.

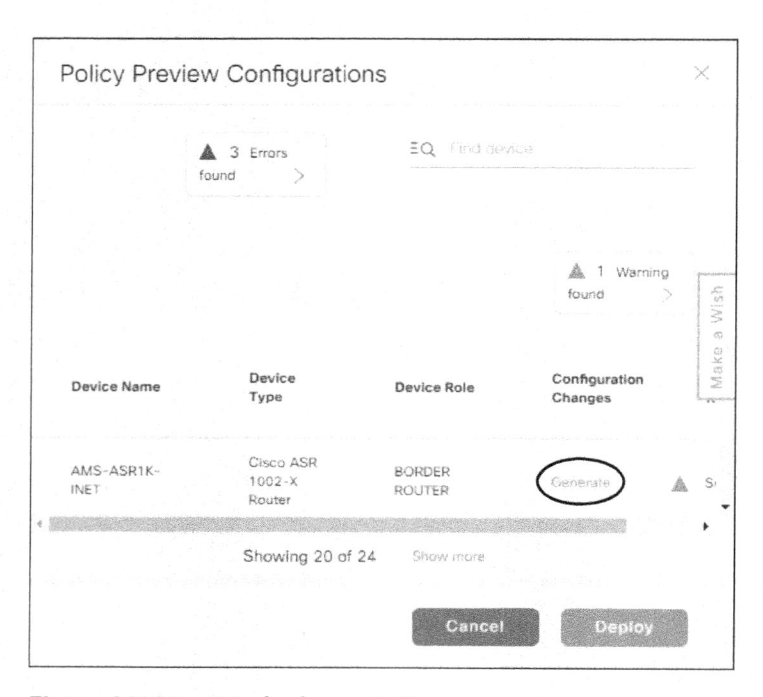

Figure 20-10 *Pre-checking a Policy*

Additionally, you can click the Generate link next to any device (shown in Figures 20-9 and 20-10) to generate the device configuration. This produces the list of all configuration commands that are sent to the device when the policy is deployed. When the configuration is generated, the Generate link is replaced by a View link, which you can click to display the device configuration to be pushed out at deployment, as illustrated in Figure 20-11.

The final required step is to deploy an application policy across the enterprise network. When you click Deploy, a sliding panel presents the option to Run Now or to Schedule Later, as displayed in Figure 20-12.

Note No configurations are pushed to the devices by clicking Generate or View.

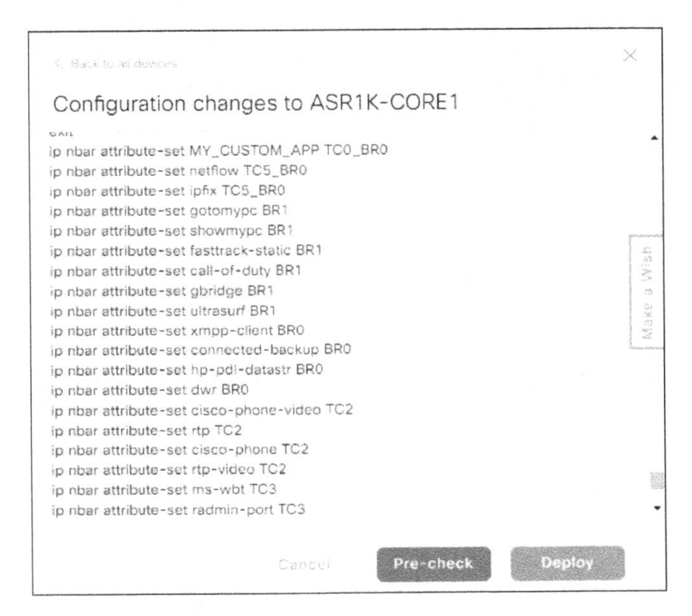

Figure 20-11 *Previewing Device Configurations*

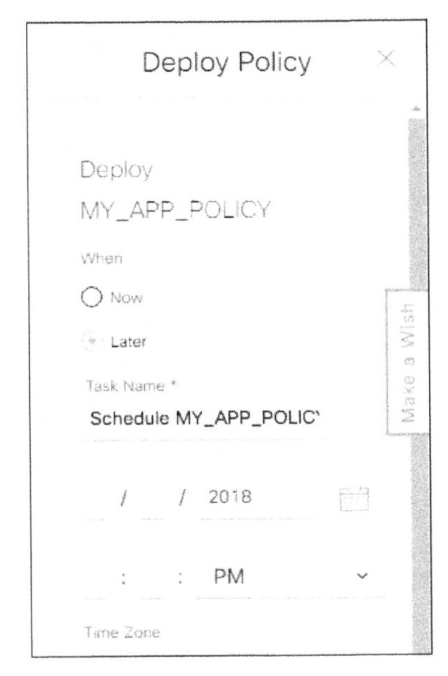

Figure 20-12 *Choosing When to Deploy*

That's it. That's all it takes to deploy end-to-end application policies across routers, switches, and wireless platforms in the enterprise network.

Customers have shared with Cisco that deployments of such policies have taken four to six months and cost as high $1 million per deployment. Some customers have even reported having to repeat the process only a few months later in response to evolving business requirements. Now, instead of taking months, comprehensive application policies tightly aligned to evolving business objectives are deployed in a matter minutes!

Optional Steps

While completing the preceding four steps is all that's required to deploy policies, Application Policy also supports a few optional steps that may be taken to customize application policies to a specific business environment. These optional steps include customizing the

- Queuing profile
- Marking profile
- Service provider profile

The following sections discuss each of these customizable profile options in turn.

Queuing Profile

The queuing profile (selected by clicking the Queuing Profiles link, as shown earlier in Figure 20-8) allows an advanced administrator to assign custom bandwidth allocations to traffic classes, as illustrated in Figure 20-13.

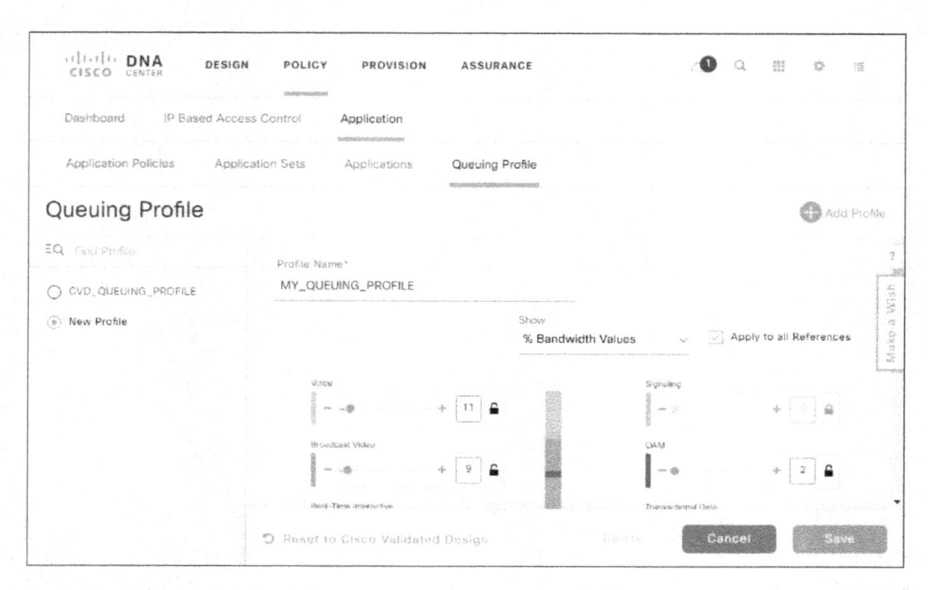

Figure 20-13 *Cisco DNA Center Application Policy—Customizing a Queuing Profile*

Bandwidth is increased to a traffic class by clicking the + icon for the class; similarly, bandwidth is decreased from a traffic class by clicking the – icon for the class. When bandwidth is added (or subtracted) from a traffic class, it has to come from somewhere, and as such the other classes are subtracted from (or added to). Thus, at some point you may elect to *lock* the bandwidth allocation to a traffic class, which you do by clicking the lock icon; at this point, bandwidth may not be added to, nor subtracted from, this traffic class. To comply with best-practice recommendations, some traffic classes are locked by default (such as the Network Control, Signaling, etc.); however, these may be overridden and unlocked, according to business requirements.

Marking Profile

Not only bandwidth can be modified, but also the Differentiated Services Code Point (DSCP) markings used by Application Policy. Although these DSCP markings are standards based (originating from RFC 4594), you may choose to use different DSCP markings, either to accommodate legacy environments or to support migrations. In either case, you can change DSCP marking profiles from the same Queuing Profiles sliding panel by choosing DSCP Values (instead of Bandwidth Values) from the Show drop-down list, as illustrated in Figure 20-14.

Figure 20-14 *Cisco DNA Center Application Policy—Customizing a DSCP-Marking Profile*

Service Provider Profile

Because enterprise QoS policies have to align to service provider QoS profiles, the details of these profiles must be entered into Cisco DNA Center. You create SP profiles within the Cisco DNA Center Design workflow by choosing Network Settings and clicking the SP Profiles tab, as shown in Figure 20-15.

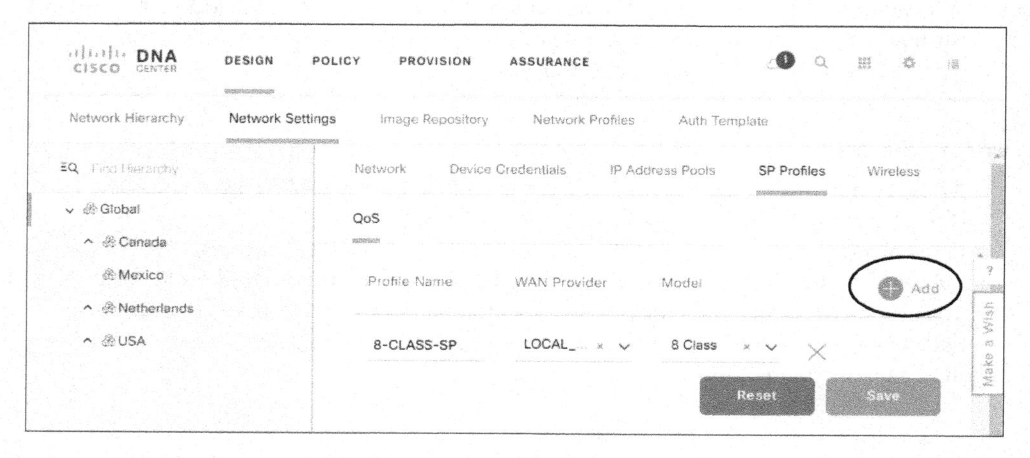

Figure 20-15 *Creating a Service Provider Profile*

Similar to queuing and marking profiles, you can also customize SP profiles, in this case to modify and optimize enterprise-to-service provider QoS. To customize an SP profile, first select the profile from within the Application Policy, as shown in Figure 20-16.

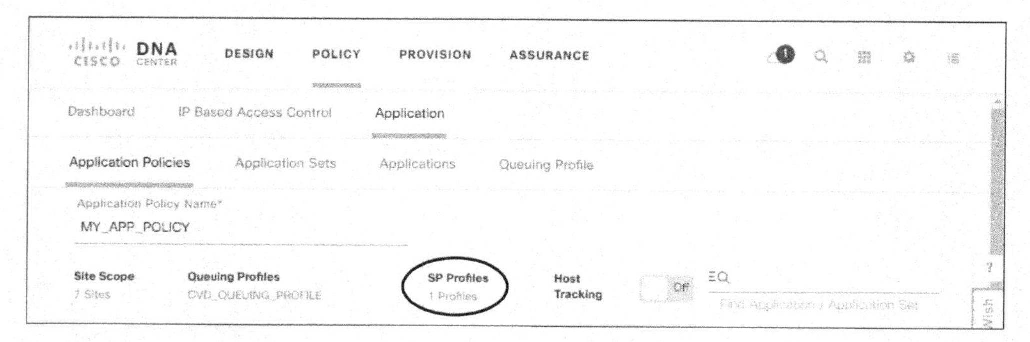

Figure 20-16 *Selecting a Service Provider Profile to Customize*

Once the service provider profile is selected, you can fully customize the profile to reflect your service provider's QoS model, as shown in Figure 20-17.

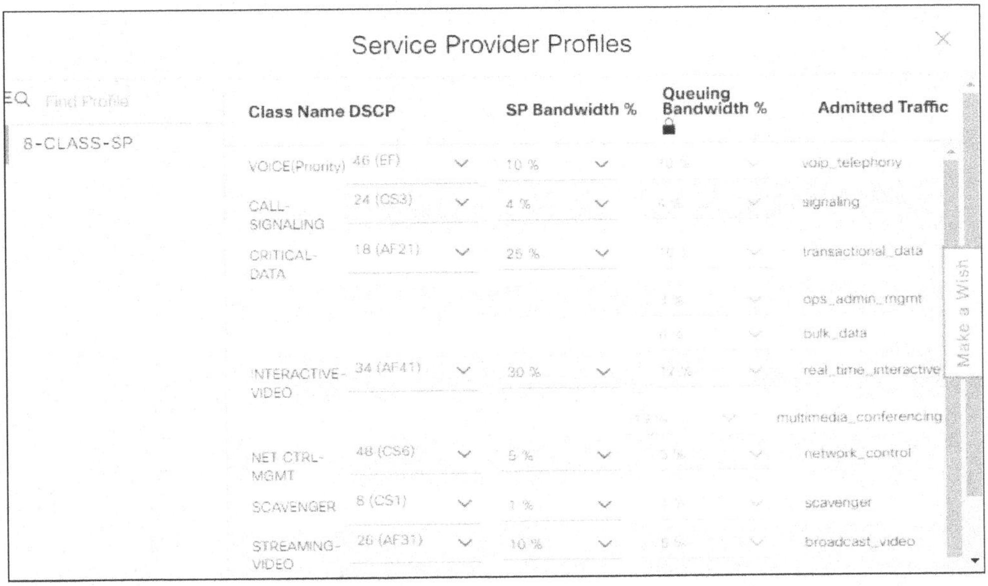

Figure 20-17 *Customizing a Service Provider Profile*

These required and optional steps to manage application policies may seem relatively simple and straightforward, which is very much intended. However, it may be of interest to you to gain a deeper understanding into the inner workings of Application Policy, as well as the underlying hardware and software infrastructure tools and technologies that are leveraged to deliver these application policy treatments. Providing that deeper understanding is the purpose of the next section.

What Happens "Under the Hood"?

Application Policy has its roots in the Cisco Application Policy Interface Controller Enterprise Module (APIC-EM) EasyQoS application, which was one of the industry's first expressions of intent-based networking in the enterprise. Being so revolutionary and different, it typically elicited one of two strong responses from customers:

- Some customers loved the simplification; they no longer had to pore through 1000-page Cisco Validated Design (CVD) guides and got to their end result with a simple, turnkey approach; they just started using the app to meet their business objectives and never looked back.
- Other customers immediately pressed for all the details of the inner workings the product team was trying their best to abstract, wanting to know all the specifics on questions such as: How did it work? What would it do in this situation? And what would it do in that one? What exactly would be configured on a given network device?

Therefore, to answer the questions of the latter group, Cisco produced a comprehensive CVD on the EasyQoS solution itself. Ironically, this CVD itself quickly swelled to over 300 pages, and became the very kind of document the product team didn't want to burden the customers with having to read. However, with all these inner workings fully documented, at least any and all who wanted these details have access to them. The overall aim behind this CVD is to instill confidence in even advanced and experienced network administrators that the tool implements all the tested and validated, standards-based, best-practice designs that they have come to expect from Cisco. (The URL for the EasyQoS CVD is in the "Further Reading" section at the end of this chapter.)

The balance of this chapter is devoted to the same goal, namely to increase confidence in intent-based networking for application policy, and to highlight how an architectural approach to application policy is significantly greater than any sum-of-the-parts approach. To this end, let us consider the following:

- The inner logic of how Application Policy translates business intent into device-level policy configurations
- Powerful network infrastructure software solutions like Network Based Application Recognition 2 (NBAR2) and Software-Defined Application Visibility and Control (SD-AVC)
- Platform-specific technologies within routers, switches, and wireless controllers and access points
- The internal workings of Unified Access Data Plane (UADP) and Quantum Flow Processor (QFP) ASICS, which ensure that even *within* the ASICs all data paths are aligned to deliver on the expressed business-level intent of application packet flows

Translating Business Intent into Application Policy

The Application Policy solution abstracts QoS policy by using a declarative model as opposed to an imperative model.

A *declarative* model focuses on the intent, or WHAT is to be accomplished, without describing HOW it is to be accomplished. For example, you may express that an application such as Cisco WebEx is business relevant—meaning that it is to be treated with the appropriate service—but not specify the details of how the QoS/QoE policies are to be configured in order to achieve this intent.

In contrast, an *imperative* model focuses on the execution of the intent (describing in detail HOW the objective is to be realized). For example, an imperative policy may include assigning Cisco WebEx to a hardware priority queue with a given bandwidth allocation percentage on a specific network switch interface.

The user interface screens that were reviewed thus far are the means of soliciting your declaration of intent. In these screens you specified

- Which applications contribute to business objectives (i.e., are business relevant)
- Which applications are known to detract from business objectives (i.e., are business irrelevant)
- Which applications have a neutral impact on business objectives (i.e., are default business relevant)

Because the UI presents only these three options (for the sake of maximizing the simplicity of soliciting business intent), some people have mistakenly concluded that only three levels of service are provisioned across the network; however, what actually happens under the hood is that 12 standards-based classes of service are provisioned across the network, as summarized in Figure 20-18.

	Application Class	Per-Hop Behavior	Queuing & Dropping	Application Examples
Business-Relevant	VoIP Telephony	EF	Priority Queue (PQ)	Cisco IP Phones (G.711, G.729)
	Broadcast Video	CS5	(Optional) PQ	Cisco IP Video Surveillance/Cisco Enterprise TV
	Real-Time Interactive	CS4	(Optional) PQ	Cisco TelePresence
	Multimedia Conferencing	AF4	BW Queue + DSCP WRED	Cisco Jabber, Cisco WebEx
	Multimedia Streaming	AF3	BW Queue + DSCP WRED	Cisco Digital Media System (VoDs)
	Network Control	CS6	BW Queue	EIGRP, OSPF, BGP, HSRP, IKE
	Signaling	CS3	BW Queue	SCCP, SIP, H.323
	Ops/Admin/Mgmt (OAM)	CS2	BW Queue	SNMP, SSH, Syslog
	Transactional Data	AF2	BW Queue + DSCP WRED	ERP Apps, CRM Apps, Database Apps
	Bulk Data	AF1	BW Queue + DSCP WRED	E-mail, FTP, Backup Apps, Content Distribution
Default	Default Forwarding	DF	Default Queue + RED	Default Class
Business-Irrelevant	Scavenger	CS1	Min BW Queue (Deferential)	YouTube, Netflix, iTunes, BitTorrent, Xbox Live

Figure 20-18 *(RFC 4594-based) Application Classification, Marking, Queuing, and Dropping Policies*

Figure 20-18 illustrates the following:

- If you assign an application as Business Relevant, then the application is further classified according to the traffic class that the application belongs to (based on the logic discussed earlier in this chapter in the "Application Sets" section), including
  - Voice
  - Broadcast Video
  - Real-Time Interactive

- Multimedia Conferencing
- Multimedia Streaming
- Network Control
- Signaling
- Operations/Administration/Management (OAM)
- Transactional Data
- Bulk Data

- If you assign an application as Default, the application is marked to Default Forwarding (DF) and treated with what is commonly called "best effort" service.
- If you assign an application as Business Irrelevant, the application is marked to DSCP Class Selector 1 (CS1), commonly known as Scavenger, and treated with a "less than best effort" service, as specified in RFC 3116.

At this point Application Policy has

- Captured the expressed business intent for the application policy
- Mapped this business intent into a
  - Standards-based marking scheme for all the traffic classes of applications (which may be customized, as discussed in the "Marking Profile" section)
  - Standards-based queuing and dropping scheme for all the traffic classes of applications (which again, may be customized, as discussed earlier in the "Queuing Profile" section)

Thus, the next set of requirements to implementing this policy across the infrastructure consists of the following:

1. Identifying the applications on the network
2. Grouping these applications into the same traffic classes
3. Expressing the operator-selected business relevance for the applications
4. Marking the traffic end to end across the network
5. Consistently queuing the traffic end to end across the network (including internally, when necessary)

Powerful application-recognition software technologies such as NBAR2 and SD-AVC meet the first three requirements. An abstracted cross-platform policy meets the fourth requirement. And hardware platform-specific implementations meet the last of these requirements. The following sections discuss each in turn.

Cisco DNA Infrastructure Software Requirements for Application Policy

Cisco DNA infrastructure requires powerful application recognition capabilities, especially considering that the majority of applications traversing today's enterprise networks are encrypted. Additionally, application recognition engines should be extensible (so as to easily provide support for new applications), consistent (so as to provide compatible policy enforcement, regardless of platform), and efficient (so as not to place excessive burdens on the network infrastructure). To meet these requirements, Cisco developed two key cross-platform software technologies, NBAR2 and SD-AVC.

NBAR2

NBAR2 is a completely different technology than the predecessor it happens to share its name with (i.e., original NBAR). NBAR2 technology was developed by a startup named P-Cube and so impressed Cisco that it quickly snapped it up for $200 million back in 2004. Other than a shared configuration syntax, NBAR2 has absolutely no resemblance to original NBAR technology.

NBAR2 is currently one of the best deep packet inspection (DPI) engines in the industry, providing stateful classification for enterprise business applications, cloud applications, and hundreds of consumer applications. NBAR2 actually includes thousands of stateful signatures that look into patterns inside packet payload, correlate flows and state, and use sophisticated supplementary mechanisms for identifying applications, including

- Statistical classification
- Behavioral classification
- Domain Name Service (DNS) snooping
- Secure Sockets Layer (SSL) snooping
- Machine learning of applications, services, and servers
- Signature customization

As such, NBAR2 can classify more than 90 percent of encrypted traffic on enterprise networks, as the following example demonstrates. In 2017 at Cisco Live Las Vegas, NBAR2 was enabled on the network to classify all the user traffic from the over 28,000 users in attendance, who over the course of five days generated over 65 TB of network traffic, a summary of which is displayed in Figure 20-19.

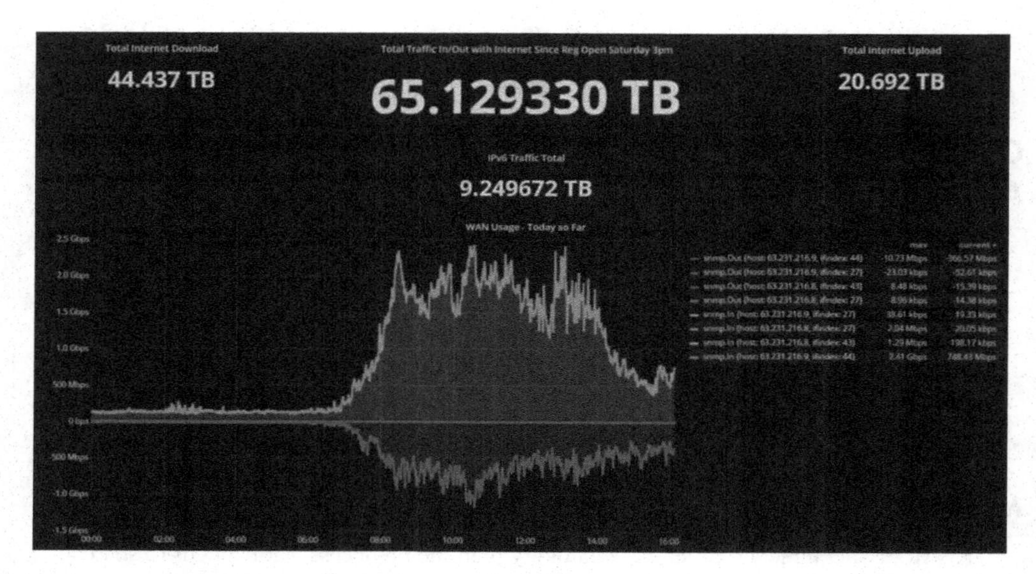

Figure 20-19 *Total Network Traffic Generated by 28K Attendees at Cisco Live Las Vegas 2017*

Note that approximately 72 percent of traffic generated at Cisco Live Las Vegas 2017 was encrypted, as illustrated in Figure 20-20.

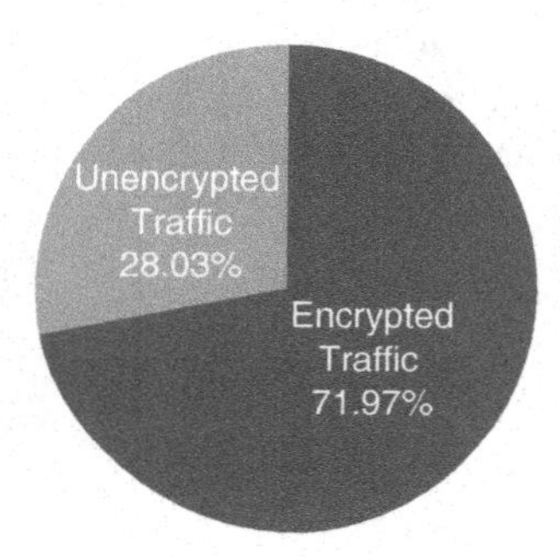

Figure 20-20 *Encrypted Versus Unencrypted Breakdown of 65 TB of User Traffic from 28K Attendees at Cisco Live Las Vegas 2017*

As such, a normal DPI engine would be expected to classify only about 28 percent of the traffic (i.e., the unencrypted part). However, NBAR2 was actually able to classify over 99 percent of all application traffic, recognizing over 570 applications, as illustrated in Figure 20-21.

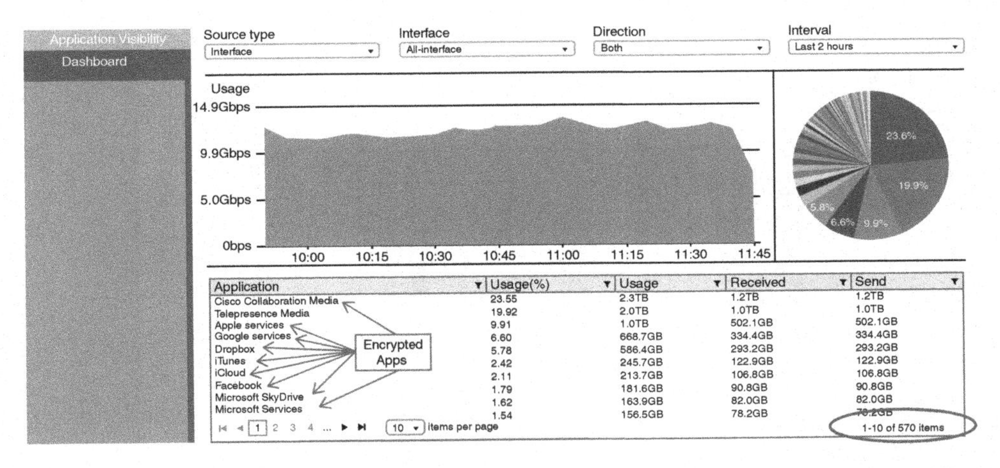

Figure 20-21 *NBAR2 Recognizing 99.14 Percent of Application Traffic at Cisco Live Las Vegas 2017 (570 Apps)*

The total amount of unrecognized application was less than 1 percent; specifically:

- 0.52 percent of Hypertext Transfer Protocol Secure (HTTPS) traffic
- 0.34 percent of SSL traffic

However, note that NBAR2 signatures are being developed and added to the common library every month. Even these outstanding flows are being analyzed for new application signatures.

> **Note** The latest NBAR2 Protocol Packs can be downloaded from http://www.cisco.com/c/en/us/td/docs/ios-xml/ios/qos_nbar/prot_lib/config_library/nbar-prot-pack-library.html.

Before taking a look at how NBAR2 accomplishes such detailed and comprehensive application recognition, let's briefly examine performance impact.

Some administrators have expressed reluctance to enable NBAR2 on their network platforms because of performance-impact concerns (which sometimes were attributed to experiences with original NBAR technology). Continuing the prior example, when NBAR2 was enabled on an ASR1001-HX router at Cisco Live Las Vegas 2017, classifying over 500 applications at 10-Gbps line rates for five days straight, it never exceeded 14 percent CPU utilization, as shown in Figure 20-22.

Let's now take a brief look at how NBAR2 achieves these impressive and efficient application-recognition feats, by examining its internal operation.

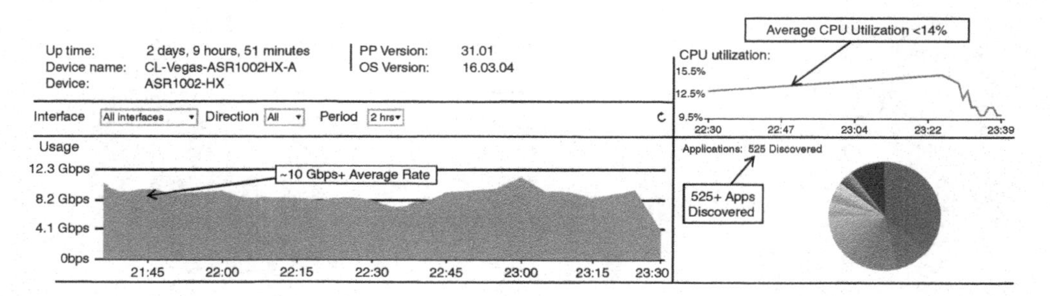

Figure 20-22 *NBAR2 Performance While Recognizing 500+ Apps at 10-Gbps Speeds (With Less Than 14 Percent CPU Impact)*

NBAR2 Operation

NBAR2 internal operation is represented in Figure 20-23.

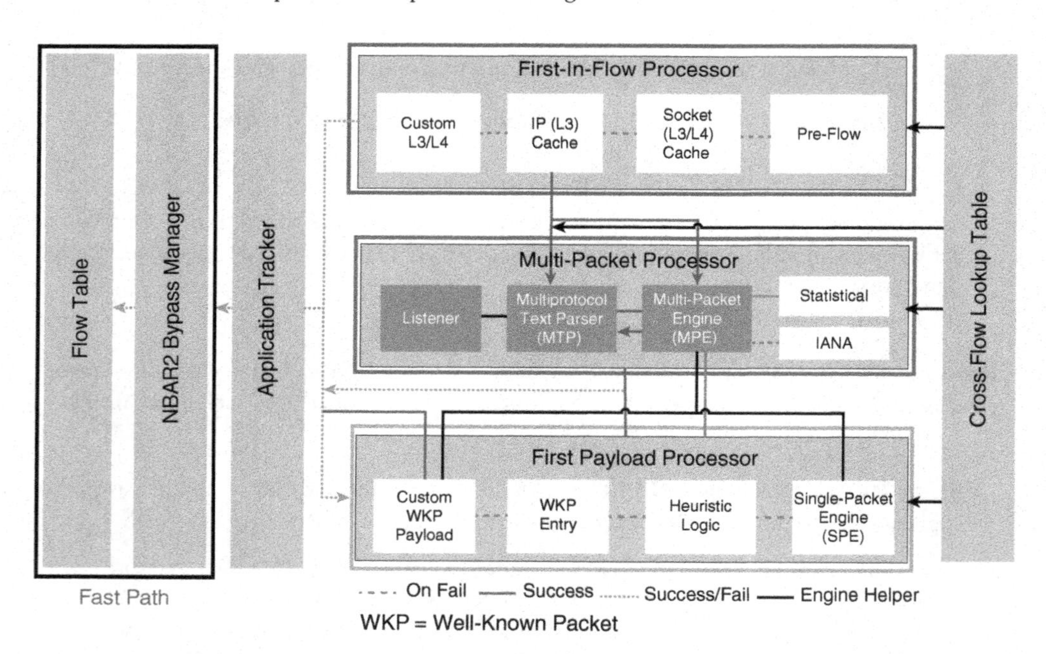

Figure 20-23 *NBAR2 Internal Architecture and Operational Flows*

NBAR2 has been tuned such that both internal testing and testing with customer traffic samples show that less than 5 percent of all packets need to be processed by the NBAR2 engine on an average customer network. This is because the engine must analyze only the first (or first few) packets of a flow to recognize the application generating the flow. After the engine makes a classification decision, it caches the result in the Flow Table (shown at the far left of Figure 20-23). Thus the remaining (95 percent+) packets of the flow are already recognized and bypass all NBAR2 engines (this decision is managed by the NBAR2 Bypass Manager). The combination of the Flow Table and the NBAR2 Bypass Manager constitutes a "fast path" of application classification, which is highly optimized and can even be implemented in hardware (as discussed later in this chapter).

Also, when an application is recognized, then the classification details are cached to the Application Table. In this manner, when a new application flow is initiated, then full classification processing does not need to take place; rather, recent application recognition decisions are leveraged to make a faster and more efficient classification decision of these new application flows.

Of the 5 percent of packets needing additional processing to reach a classification decision, there are three main engines that are utilized by NBAR2 to achieve this:

- **First-in-Flow Processor:** Recognizes approximately 40 percent of the packets requiring advanced classification, which it does by leveraging a combination of the following:
    - **Custom and/or authoritative (L3 and/or L4) information:** You may have defined custom IP and/or L4 protocol and port combinations to identify your apps. Additionally, technologies such as DNS as an Authoritative Source (DNS-AS), which includes application metadata in DNS records (which are thus considered an "authoritative source"), may be used for such classification. Similarly, SD-AVC (which is discussed later in this chapter) also provides authoritative information to identify applications via L3/L4 details.
    - **Socket (L3/L4) cache information:** By way of review, sockets are combinations of L3 IP addresses, an L4 protocol (TCP/UDP), and an L4 Port; for example, (10.1.1.1:80 TCP) represents a socket (in this case a web server). When an application server is identified, such as in a previous operation, then its details are cached to expedite the classification of new client flows to the same application server.
    - **Pre-flow information:** For example, a signaling packet may provide information of a Real-time Transport Protocol (RTP) flow that is being initialized. Similarly, FTP control packets can be snooped to identify FTP-Data flows that are to follow. Such details are used to pre-position NBAR2 to be ready for an immediate classification decision on the subsequent flow, without having to perform additional processing.
- **First-Payload Processor:** Recognizes the next 50 percent (approximately) of the packets requiring advanced classification, which it does by leveraging a combination of the following:
    - **Custom well-known port payload:** When you define a custom protocol, which includes payload details, then this custom definition is checked against the packet.
    - **Well-known packet entry:** Some applications are bound to "well-known ports" and are identified from such.

- **Heuristic logic:** Runs heuristics, based on port indicators or regular expressions, seeking to understand which engine in the Multi-Packet Processor block should try to handle this traffic and be invoked. So, for example, if the port is 80 it invokes the Multiprotocol Text Parser (which parses HTTP) to process the packet payload.
- **Single-packet engine:** An advanced engine to identify packets by advanced analysis of the payload.

- **Multi-Packet Processor:** The remaining 10 percent of packets requiring advanced classification are passed on to the Multi-Packet Processor, which leverages the following:
  - **Listener:** Looks for clues in the setup of the session so as to identify the application.
  - **Multiprotocol text parser:** Examines textual protocols (such as HTTP, SSL, DNS, SIP, etc.) to identify the application
  - **Multi-Packet engine:** Examines binary protocols, such as RTP, to identify the application.
  - **Statistical machine learning:** Provides machine-learning capabilities and behavioral analysis to identify the application.
  - **IANA library:** Identifies standards-based protocols.

And finally, all these engines utilize a common Cross-Flow Look-Up Table, which shares information from previous decisions to further expedite the application classification process.

Once applications are recognized, NBAR2 checks them against the intent-based policies that specify how these are to be treated, which is discussed next.

QoS Attributes

As previously mentioned, the NBAR2 library has over 1400 applications; however, IOS XE supports only 32 **match** statements per class map. Although it's true that class maps can be nested within each other (for two levels only), this provision would still only allow 1024 applications to be matched in a given policy (32 apps per class map × 32 nested class maps); furthermore, such a configuration would require over 1052 lines of CLI. In such a scenario, only a maximum of 75 percent of the protocols in the NBAR2 library could be leveraged for a policy and the resulting policy would be extremely lengthy, complex, and unwieldy. Furthermore, every time a new business-relevant application is added to a new NBAR2 Protocol Pack, such a policy would have to be modified on all network devices where it was deployed.

However, as an alternate approach, NBAR2 groups applications by attributes so as to simplify policy configuration. The attributes of an application are viewed in the NBAR2 Protocol Pack documentation or from the command line by using **show ip nbar**

protocol-attribute. An example of application attributes is illustrated in Example 20-1, where the NBAR2 attributes of Airbnb are presented.

Example 20-1 *Displaying NBAR2 Protocol Attributes*

```
Router# show ip nbar protocol-attribute airbnb
encrypted              encrypted-no
tunnel                 tunnel-no
category               browsing
sub-category           Other
application-group      Other
p2p-technology         p2p-tech-no
traffic-class          transactional-data
business-relevance     business-irrelevant
```

As of Cisco IOS 15.5(3)M and IOS XE 3.16S, every application in the NBAR2 library was assigned two QoS attributes:

- **Traffic-class:** Based on RFC 4594 application classification logic
- **Business-relevance:** Based on customer usage and operator input

These QoS attributes for Airbnb are highlighted in Example 20-1.

The default settings for business-relevance are based on customer-telemetry data. Specifically, from the telemetry data that customers have elected to share with Cisco (from over a quarter-million network devices), Cisco identifies which applications are commonly considered business relevant, business irrelevant, and default. As such, the NBAR2 business-relevance attribute is pre-populated to match. This is why Example 20-1 shows that Airbnb is most commonly identified as a "business-irrelevant" application, as it is consumer-oriented in nature (for the most part).

That being said, the NBAR2 Business-Relevant QoS attribute is very much intended to be customized by individuals to suit their specific business objectives. For example, let's consider a travel agency that commonly uses Airbnb for its business transactions. To the travel agency, Airbnb is not considered a "business-irrelevant" application, but rather a "business-relevant" one. Such a change is easily made via an attribute map, as shown in the following snippet:

```
Router(config)# ip nbar attribute-map ATTRIBUTE_MAP-RELEVANT attribute
  business-relevance business-relevant
Router(config)# ip nbar attribute-set airbnb ATTRIBUTE_MAP-RELEVANT
```

All three options of business-relevance mapping are as follows:

```
Router(config)# ip nbar attribute-map ATTRIBUTE_MAP-RELEVANT attribute
  business-relevance business-relevant
Router(config)# ip nbar attribute-set APPLICATION-NAME ATTRIBUTE_MAP-
  RELEVANT
```

```
Router(config)# ip nbar attribute-map ATTRIBUTE_MAP-DEFAULT attribute
  business-relevance default
Router(config)# ip nbar attribute-set APPLICATION-NAME ATTRIBUTE_MAP-
  DEFAULT
Router(config)# ip nbar attribute-map ATTRIBUTE_MAP-IRRELEVANT attribute
  business-relevance business-irrelevant
Router(config)# ip nbar attribute-set APPLICATION-NAME ATTRIBUTE_MAP-
  IRRELEVANT
```

Any subsequent applications that need to change the default attribute settings for business relevancy only need a single line to do so (e.g., **ip nbar attribute set** *APPLICATION-NAME ATTRIBUTE_MAP_NAME.*

"Holy Grail" Classification and Marking Policy

The addition of Traffic-Class and Business-Relevance QoS attributes to NBAR2 allows for the expression of intent-based classification and marking policies to be reduced from 1600+ lines to just 57 lines (a 96 percent reduction in configuration complexity!) This policy was dubbed the "Holy Grail" classification and marking policy by the Cisco DNA Architecture team, and is shown in Example 20-2.

Example 20-2 *NBAR2 "Holy Grail" Classification and Marking Policy*

```
class-map match-all VOICE-NBAR2
   match protocol attribute traffic-class voip-telephony
   match protocol attribute business-relevance business-relevant

class-map match-all BROADCAST_VIDEO-NBAR2
   match protocol attribute traffic-class broadcast-video
   match protocol attribute business-relevance business-relevant

class-map match-all REALTIME_INTERACTIVE-NBAR2
   match protocol attribute traffic-class real-time-interactive
   match protocol attribute business-relevance business-relevant

class-map match-all MULTIMEDIA_CONFERENCING-NBAR2
   match protocol attribute traffic-class multimedia-conferencing
   match protocol attribute business-relevance business-relevant

class-map match-all MULTIMEDIA_STREAMING-NBAR2
   match protocol attribute traffic-class multimedia-streaming
   match protocol attribute business-relevance business-relevant

class-map match-all NETWORK_CONTROL-NBAR2
   match protocol attribute traffic-class network-control
   match protocol attribute business-relevance business-relevant
```

```
class-map match-all SIGNALING-NBAR2
   match protocol attribute traffic-class signaling
   match protocol attribute business-relevance business-relevant

class-map match-all NETWORK_MANAGEMENT-NBAR2
   match protocol attribute traffic-class ops-admin-mgmt
   match protocol attribute business-relevance business-relevant

class-map match-all TRANSACTIONAL_DATA-NBAR2
   match protocol attribute traffic-class transactional-data
   match protocol attribute business-relevance business-relevant

class-map match-all BULK_DATA-NBAR2
   match protocol attribute traffic-class bulk-data
   match protocol attribute business-relevance business-relevant

class-map match-all SCAVENGER-NBAR2
   match protocol attribute business-relevance business-irrelevant

policy-map MARKING
 class VOICE-NBAR2
  set dscp ef
 class BROADCAST_VIDEO-NBAR2
  set dscp cs5
 class REALTIME_INTERACTIVE-NBAR2
  set dscp cs4
 class MULTIMEDIA_CONFERENCING-NBAR2
  set dscp af41
 class MULTIMEDIA_STREAMING-NBAR2
  set dscp af31
 class NETWORK_CONTROL-NBAR2
  set dscp cs6
 class SIGNALING-NBAR2
  set dscp cs3
 class NETWORK_MANAGEMENT-NBAR2
  set dscp cs2
 class TRANSACTIONAL_DATA-NBAR2
  set dscp af21
 class BULK_DATA-NBAR2
  set dscp af11
 class SIGNALING-NBAR2
  set dscp cs1
 class class-default
  set dscp default
```

Note If for some reason, you need to change the marking values for this policy, do so, as discussed in the "Marking Profile" section.

Note The "-NBAR2" suffix was added to the class-map names, to differentiate these NBAR2-based class maps from the DSCP-based class maps that are also required to support egress queuing policies, as shown later in Example 20-3.

The logic of this "Holy Grail" policy is as follows:

- Every class of traffic uses a **match all** logical operator (a logical AND function), indicating that *both match statements need to be true* in order for the traffic to match the class.
  - The first match statement matches on the (RFC 4594-based) traffic class.
  - The second match statement matches on whether the operator has indicated that the specific application in the traffic class is relevant to their business objectives (or not).
- Any applications that were indicated to be business irrelevant are assigned to the Scavenger class.
- Any applications that were not explicitly assigned a preferential or deferential treatment are treated in the default class.

The benefits of this policy include

- As this "Holy Grail" policy is based on abstraction, it significantly simplifies the complexity of configuration—and by extension, monitoring and troubleshooting—of application policies.
- This policy is cross-platform and modular, as QoS attributes were also introduced on (UADP-based) Catalyst switches in IOS XE 16.8.1, and on Elastic Wireless LAN controllers (eWLC) platforms in IOS XE 16.10.
- Once configured, this policy never has to be changed—even as new applications are added to NBAR2 Protocol Packs; this saves significant operational complexity, while simultaneously allowing businesses to be agile in supporting new applications on an ongoing basis.

At this point, the first four challenges of application policy were met (specifically, recognizing, grouping, classifying, and marking applications). Before addressing the final challenge (of platform-specific queuing), let's briefly discuss one additional architectural enhancement that improves the operation of these first four challenges. This enhancement to NBAR2 is SD-AVC.

SD-AVC

SD-AVC (which at the time of writing is being proposed to be dubbed Cisco DNA-based Application Recognition or DBAR) was born of the requirement to classify traffic in asymmetric routing scenarios, common in software-defined wide-area networking (SD-WAN) environments.

As previously discussed, a minority of packets requires multi-packet processing, but in asymmetric routing scenarios (as illustrated in Figure 20-24), only one side of the conversation is available for such analysis and processing, and as such, a classification decision is not always possible.

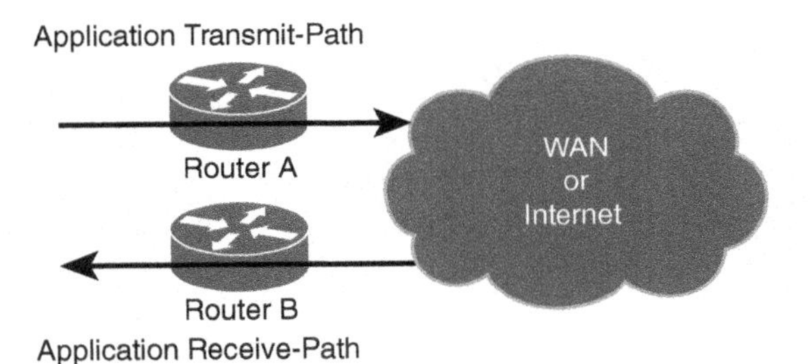

Figure 20-24 *NBAR2 Multi-Packet Processing Limitation on Asymmetric Routing Environments*

To solve this issue, the NBAR2 engineering team began investigating how classification information could be shared not just between the classification engines on a single device (as described in the "NBAR2 Operation" section), but even between multiple devices, such as between Router A and Router B in Figure 20-24. As such, application flow information could be "stitched" together for analysis, despite traversing independent network devices. The work done to solve this specific scenario evolved into SD-AVC.

SD-AVC consists of two basic components:

- A centralized SD-AVC network service (which is hosted in Cisco DNA Center as a micro service)
- An SD-AVC Agent component running on each SD-AVC-enabled device in the network

Basic SD-AVC operation is illustrated in Figure 20-25.

As NBAR2 identifies application flows on the network, it shares the results of these application decisions with a centralized network service (the SD-AVC service within Cisco DNA Center). These classification results are then distributed and shared with all other network devices running SD-AVC. Thus, SD-AVC offers a controller-based solution to application-recognition that operates network-wide. Additionally, it serves as an efficient vehicle for centralized deployment of NBAR2 Protocol Pack updates.

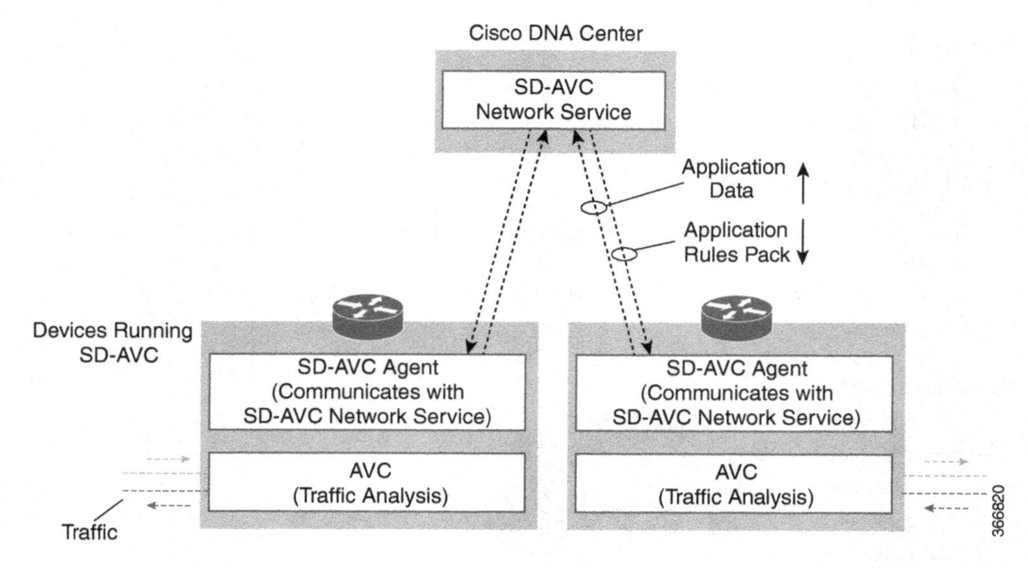

Figure 20-25 *Basic SD-AVC Operation*

Furthermore, the centralizing of application classification information provides even more performance gains in application recognition, as well as the ability to leverage network-wide analytics and "wisdom." For example, SD-AVC supports day-zero support in the field by automatically generating application recognition based on observed traffic behavior and patterns.

Additionally, SD-AVC connects to trusted external sources for even more application information. For instance, SD-AVC communicates via APIs to

- Microsoft Office 365 RSS feeds, to learn the latest servers worldwide
- Infoblox, to ingest DNS-AS application metadata
- Cisco Advanced Storage Implementation (CASI) Cloudlock security database, which contains over 12,000 SaaS applications

Finally, SD-AVC even shares classification decisions with devices that do not have full NBAR2 capabilities. For example, access switches and wireless access points could simply run a "consumer mode" of SD-AVC, where they do not perform any application classification, but rather simply ingest the classification decisions that were made elsewhere in the network and, using the results, mark and treat application flows according to defined policy. Figure 20-26 illustrates the SD-AVC architecture.

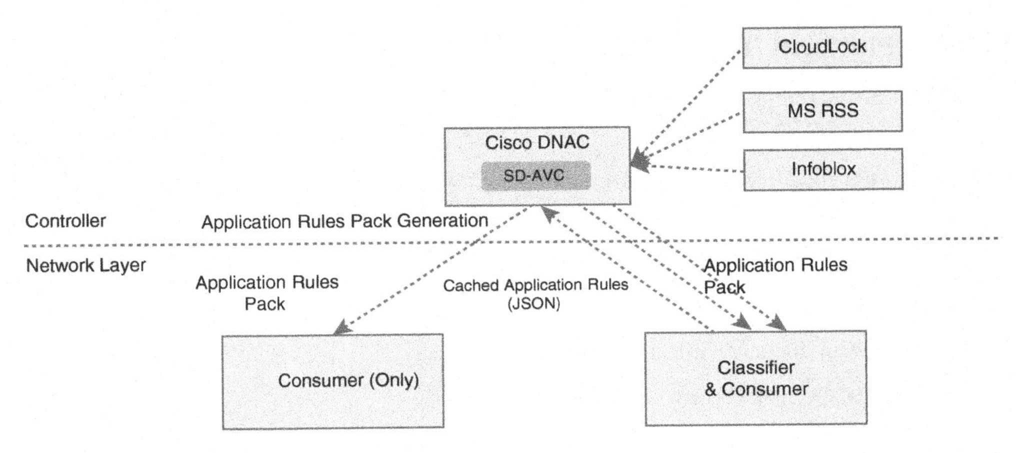

Figure 20-26 *SD-AVC Architecture*

To summarize, SD-AVC accomplishes the following:

- Solves application classification in asymmetric routing environments
- Significantly increases the number of applications that are recognized, via
  - Network-wide (versus device-level) analytics
  - API integration with authoritative sources
- Improves the overall performance of the network by sharing classification decisions (versus requiring every network node to arrive at these independently)
- Benefits devices that do not even support NBAR2
- Improves the breadth of the application policy, as applications can be identified by any access device supporting SD-AVC

Now let's examine the platform-specific elements of Application Policy.

Cisco DNA Infrastructure Platform-Specific Requirements for Application Policy

In addition to common infrastructure software technologies, like NBAR2 and SD-AVC, routing, switching, and wireless platforms also have unique platform-specific requirements to suit their roles in the enterprise network.

Routing Platform Requirements

The following policy elements are required for application treatment on Cisco WAN/branch Aggregation Services Router (ASR) and Integrated Switch Router (ISR) routers:

- Ingress classification and marking policies, on both the LAN edges and the WAN edges
- Egress queuing policies on the WAN edges
- Enterprise-to-service provider mapping
- Hardware queuing (ASR platforms only)
- Internal QoS (ASR platforms only)

Note More commonly the egress queuing policies on the WAN edges are hierarchical shaping-with-nested-queuing policies, to be discussed later in this section.

Application Classification and Marking Policies

"Holy Grail" classification and marking policies, as shown previously in Example 20-2, are applied on all interfaces, both LAN and WAN, in order to classify traffic flows in both directions, as shown in Figure 20-27.

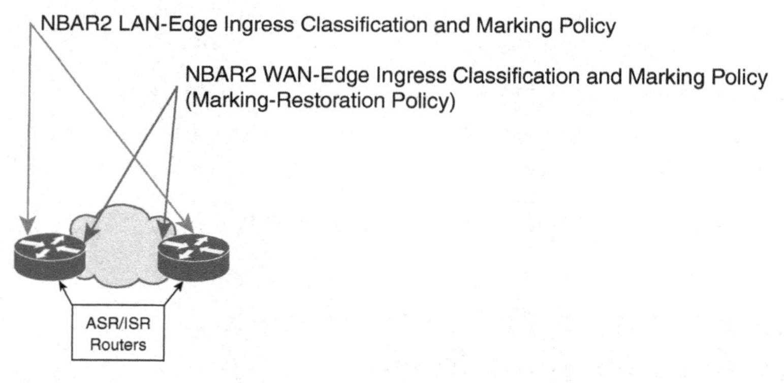

Figure 20-27 *WAN/Branch Ingress Classification and Marking Policies*

Ingress classification and marking policies are required at the LAN edges to ensure that applications sourced from campus or branch networks and destined over the WAN are properly classified and marked, both for QoS treatment and for performance routing (in the case of Cisco Intelligent WAN [IWAN] and Software-Defined WAN [SD-WAN]).

However, these classification and marking policies are also required on the WAN edges on ingress, as markings may have been changed when interfacing or transiting service provider networks (as discussed in more detail later).

Queuing and Dropping Policies

Cisco offers generic best-practice recommendations when it comes to queuing application traffic, including

- Not provisioning more than 33 percent of a link's bandwidth for strict priority traffic classes (otherwise non-priority traffic has widely varying application-response times, depending on whether priority traffic is present/absent)
- Provisioning at least 25 percent of a link's bandwidth for the default queue (recognizing that this queue represents traffic from hundreds, if not thousands, of applications, and as such should be adequately provisioned)
- Assigning Scavenger traffic to a minimum bandwidth queue (so as to aggressively starve these business-irrelevant traffic flows during congestion scenarios to minimize their impact on business-relevant traffic flows)
- Enabling congestion avoidance mechanisms, such as Weighted Random Early Detect (WRED) thresholds to optimize throughput within the queue
- Enable flow-based fair-queuing pre-sorters for each queue, so that no single flow dominates the bandwidth assigned to a queue

An example policy based on the preceding recommendations is illustrated in Figure 20-28.

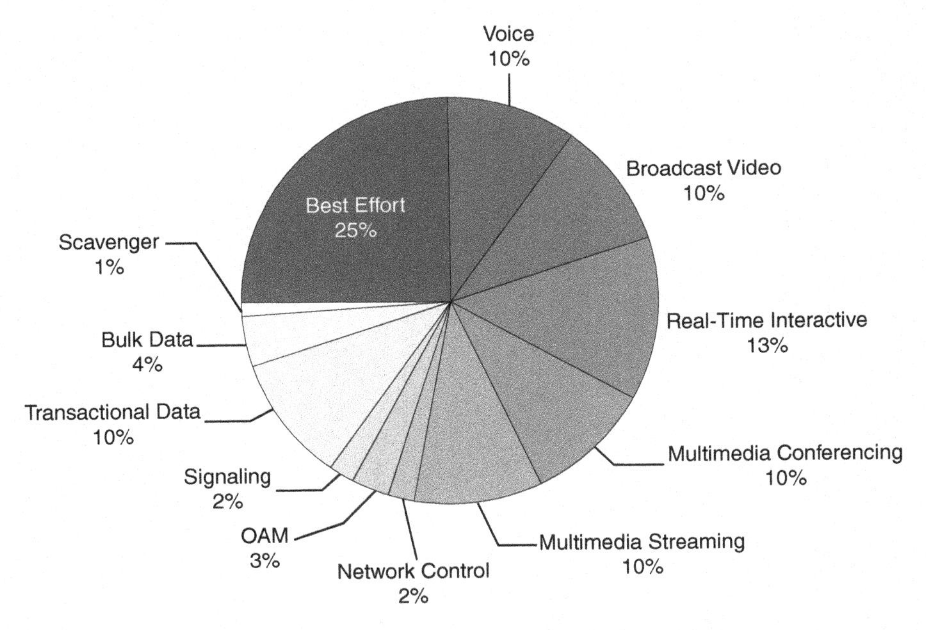

Figure 20-28 *CVD-based WAN/Branch Queuing Policies*

Note It bears repeating that if you wish, you can customize these bandwidth allocations to suit your specific business objectives, as discussed earlier in the "Queuing Profile" section.

The configuration for such a WAN/branch queuing policy is shown in Example 20-3.

Example 20-3 *CVD-based WAN/Branch Queuing Policy*

```
class-map match-all VOICE-DSCP
   match dscp ef
class-map match-all BROADCAST_VIDEO-DSCP
   match dscp cs5
class-map match-all REALTIME_INTERACTIVE-DSCP
   match dscp cs4
class-map match-all NETWORK_CONTROL-DSCP
   match cs6
class-map match-all SIGNALING-DSCP
   match cs3
class-map match-all NETWORK_MANAGEMENT-DSCP
   match cs2
class-map match-all MULTIMEDIA_CONFERENCING-DSCP
   match dscp af41
class-map match-all MULTIMEDIA_STREAMING-DSCP
   match dscp af31
class-map match-all TRANSACTIONAL_DATA-DSCP
   match dscp af21
class-map match-all BULK_DATA-DSCP
   match dscp af11
class-map match-all SCAVENGER-DSCP
   match dscp cs1

policy-map QUEUING-OUT
 class VOICE-DSCP
  police rate percent 10
  priority
 class BROADCAST_VIDEO-DSCP
  police rate percent 10
  priority
 class REALTIME_INTERACTIVE-DSCP
  police rate percent 13
  priority
 class NETWORK_CONTROL-DSCP
  bandwidth remaining percent 3
 class SIGNALING-DSCP
```

```
  bandwidth remaining percent 3
 class NETWORK_MANAGEMENT-DSCP
  bandwidth remaining percent 5
 class MULTIMEDIA_CONFERENCING-DSCP
  bandwidth remaining percent 15
  fair-queue
  random-detect dscp-based
 class MULTIMEDIA_STREAMING-DSCP
  bandwidth remaining percent 15
  fair-queue
  random-detect dscp-based
 class TRANSACTIONAL_DATA-DSCP
  bandwidth remaining percent 15
  fair-queue
  random-detect dscp-based
 class BULK_DATA-DSCP
  bandwidth remaining percent 6
  fair-queue
  random-detect dscp-based
 class SCAVENGER-DSCP
  bandwidth remaining percent 1
 class class-default
  bandwidth remaining percent 37
  fair-queue
  random-detect dscp-based
```

Note The "-DSCP" suffix was added to the class-map names to differentiate these DSCP-based class maps from the NBAR2-based class maps used in the "Holy Grail" classification and marking policy, shown in Example 20-2.

Sub-Line Rate Hierarchical QoS Policies

WAN connectivity to a service provider–managed service offering may involve sub-line rate bandwidth provisioning—meaning that the provisioned bandwidth is below the physical interface of the ISR or ASR router platform. For example, it is common to provision a managed-service offering in which the physical connectivity between the customer edge router and the provider edge router is a Gigabit Ethernet connection. However, the contracted rate between the service provider and the organization may only be provisioned for 50 Mbps or 100 Mbps of bandwidth.

Because queuing policies only engage when physical links congest, a two-part policy is required to accommodate sub-line rate handoffs:

1. A policy that shapes to the sub-line rate
2. A queuing policy that prioritizes traffic *within* the sub-line rate

A sub-line rate interface is identified and tagged as such within Cisco DNA Center. For instance, Example 20-4 shows an interface that was identified as a 50-Mbps sub-line rate circuit within its interface description (i.e., containing the string **#WAN#50M#**) and was provisioned as such with the appropriate hierarchical shaping-with-nested-queuing policy.

Example 20-4 *CVD-based Hierarchical Shaping-and-Queuing Policy for a 50-Mbps Sub-Line Rate Link*

```
policy-map HQOS-50M-OUT
 class class-default
  shape average 50M
  service-policy QUEUING-OUT
…
interface GigabitEthernet0/2
 description AT&T Circuit from SJ-13-12 to RTP-Ridge-7 #WAN#50M#
 service-policy output HQOS-50M-OUT
```

Enterprise-to-Service Provider Mapping

Service providers offer their own QoS models for customers to map into. These profiles need to be expressed within Cisco DNA Center so that efficient and effective mappings can be automatically provisioned at customer edges. These mappings may involve remarking DSCP values (to direct the application traffic into the appropriate SP class of service) as well as adjusting bandwidth allocation so as to match the SP model.

An example of a 12-class enterprise QoS model being mapped into an 8-class service provider model is presented in Figure 20-29.

As shown in Figure 20-29, maximizing compatibility between this 12-class enterprise model and this 8-class service provider model requires:

- Broadcast Video traffic to be remarked to AF31
- Real-Time Interactive traffic to be remarked to AF41
- Network Management traffic to be remarked to AF21
- Bulk Data traffic to be remarked to AF21

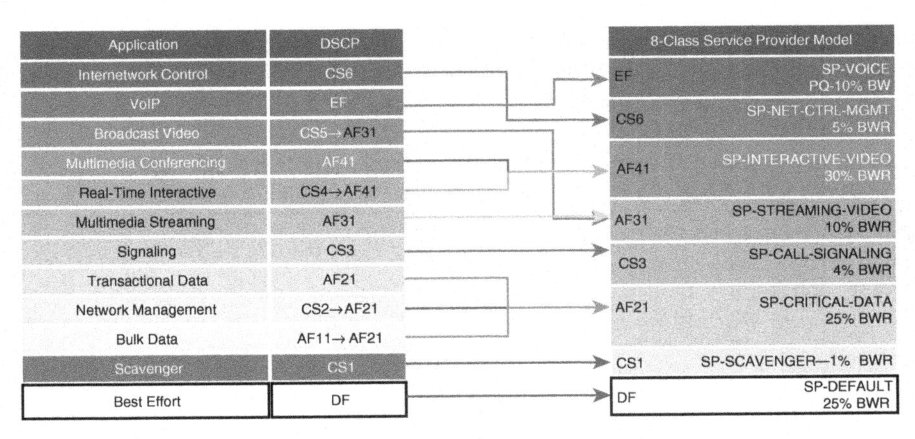

Figure 20-29 *CVD-based Mapping of a 12-Class Enterprise QoS Model to an 8-Class Service Provider Model*

Additionally, the CE edge bandwidth allocations need to be aligned between the enterprise and service provider QoS models, as illustrated in Figure 20-30.

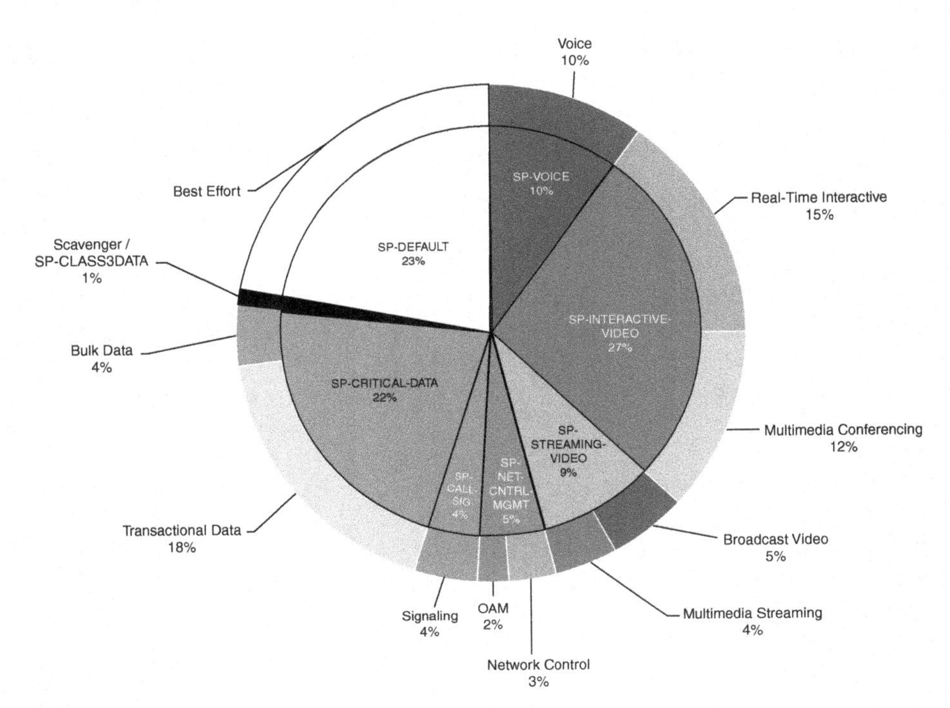

Figure 20-30 *CVD-based Bandwidth Allocation Alignment Between a 12-Class Enterprise QoS Model and an 8-Class Service Provider Model*

The resulting enterprise-to-service provider mapping policy configuration is shown in Example 20-5, where the queuing model presented in Example 20-3 was amended to align to an example service provider profile named SPP-8-CLASS.

Example 20-5 *CVD-based Hierarchical Shaping-and-Queuing Policy for a 50-Mbps Sub-Line Rate Link with Mapping to an 8-Class Service Provider QoS Model*

```
policy-map QUEUING-SPP-8CLASS-OUT
 class VOICE-DSCP
  police rate percent 10
  priority
  set dscp ef
 class BROADCAST_VIDEO-DSCP
  police rate percent 5
  priority
  set dscp af31
 class REALTIME_INTERACTIVE-DSCP
  police rate percent 15
  priority
  set dscp af41
 class MULTIMEDIA_CONFERENCING-DSCP
  bandwidth remaining percent 17
  fair-queue
  random-detect dscp-based
  set dscp af41
 class MULTIMEDIA_STREAMING-DSCP
  bandwidth remaining percent 6
  fair-queue
  random-detect dscp-based
  set dscp af31
class NETWORK_CONTROL-DSCP
  bandwidth remaining percent 4
  set dscp cs6
class SIGNALING-DSCP
  bandwidth remaining percent 6
  set dscp cs3
 class NETWORK_MANAGEMENT-DSCP
  bandwidth remaining percent 3
  set dscp cs6
class TRANSACTIONAL_DATA-DSCP
  bandwidth remaining percent 26
  fair-queue
  random-detect dscp-based
  set dscp af21
class BULK-DATA-DSCP
```

```
  bandwidth remaining percent 6
  fair-queue
  random-detect dscp-based
  set dscp af21
class SCAVENGER-DSCP
  bandwidth remaining percent 1
  set dscp cs1
 class class-default
  bandwidth remaining percent 31
  fair-queue
  random-detect dscp-based
  set dscp default
…
policy-map HQOS-50M-SPP-8CLASS
 class class-default
  shape average 50M
  service-policy QUEUING-SPP-8CLASS-OUT

…
interface GigabitEthernet0/2
 description AT&T Circuit from SJ-13-12 to RTP-Ridge-7 #WAN#50M#SPP-8CLASS#
 service-policy output policy-map HQOS-50M-SPP-8CLASS
```

Note The DSCP-based class maps for the enterprise-to-service provider mapping policy are the same as the class maps used in Example 20-3, but for the sake of minimizing redundancy, these are not repeated in Example 20-5.

Hardware Queuing

Integrated Switch Router (ISR) platforms implement QoS policies, including queuing, in software. This is appropriate and economical for branch environments, for which these platforms are positioned. Platform data sheets provide scaling recommendations for specific ISR models.

However, Aggregation Services Router (ASR) platforms are intended (as their name clearly expresses) for aggregation, and as such have significantly higher scalability requirements that extend beyond the efficient capabilities of software. Therefore, these platforms have dedicated hardware to perform queuing operations, as illustrated in Figure 30-31.

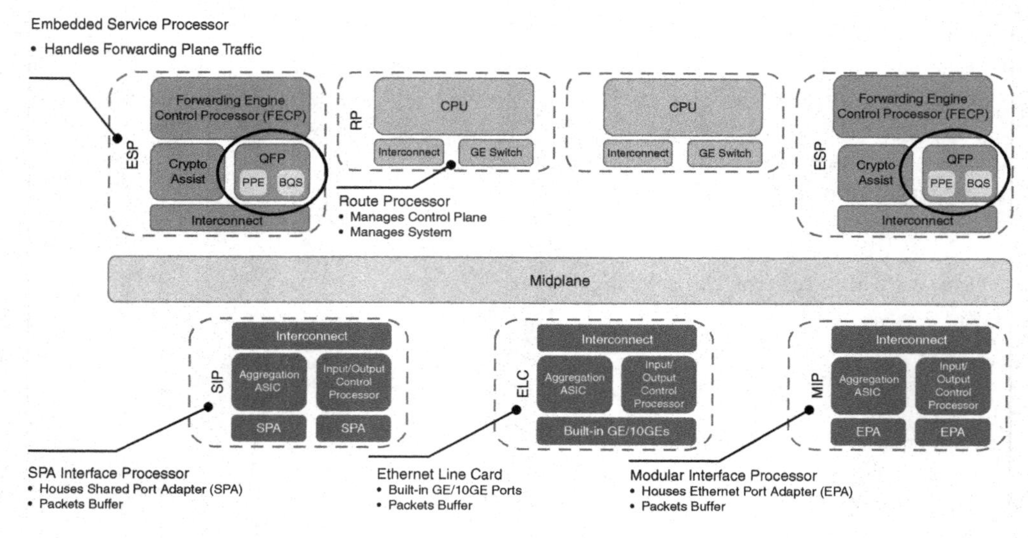

Figure 20-31 *ASR Internal Architecture*

The main ASIC in the ASR architecture is the QuantumFlow Processor (QFP), which was discussed in detail in Chapter 7, "Hardware Innovations." Specific to QoS, the QFP has two internal components:

- Packet Processing Engines (PPEs), each of which performs application classification and marking and policing and WRED (prior to enqueuing packets)
- Buffering and Queuing System (BQS), which performs shaping and scheduling

The relationships between these complimentary subsystems are illustrated in Figure 20-32.

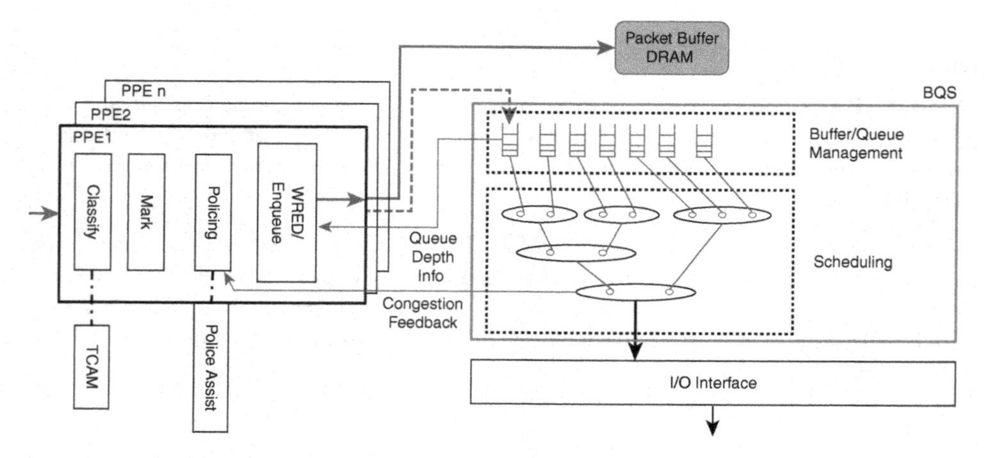

Figure 20-32 *ASR QFP PPE and BQS Subsystems*

As shown in Figure 20-32, the Packet Processing Engines perform classification (including NBAR2/SD-AVC) and marking. These engines also perform policing, with input from BQS; this input is needed so as to indicate when implicit policers need to be invoked for traffic offered to the Low Latency Queues (LLQs). WRED is also implemented in the PPEs, as any WRED drops that need to be made must occur prior to enqueuing within BQS (as no packets are dropped once handed over to BQS); as such, this Enqueuing/WRED sub-subsystem also needs feedback from BQS, specifically it requires knowledge of the instantaneous queue depths.

After all PPE QoS functions are complete, the packet is put in packet buffer memory and a packet handle (which is effectively a pointer to the packet's memory location) is sent to BQS.

Once a packet handle is presented to BQS, it performs all shaping and queuing operations. BQS boasts the following powerful capabilities:

- Multilayer hierarchies (five layers in total, as illustrated in Figure 20-33)
  - Shared Port Adaptor (SPA) Interface Processing (SIP) scheduling
  - Interface scheduling
  - + Up to three layers of queuing configured with Modular QoS Command-Line Interface (MQC) QoS
- Two levels of priority traffic (1 and 2)
- Strict and conditional priority rate limiting
- Priority Propagation to ensure no loss priority forwarding via minimum parameter
- Three-parameter scheduler:
  - **Minimum Rate:** Configured with the **bandwidth** MQC command
  - **Maximum Rate:** Configured with the **shaping** MQC command
  - **Excess Weight:** Configured with the **bandwidth remaining** MQC command

Such a flexible and multilevel scheduling architecture even support highly complex use cases, such as:

- Shaping to SIP rates, while
- Shaping to sub-line circuit rates, while
- Shaping logical tunnels to remote branch ingress rates, while
- Queuing traffic per application business intent, while
- Pre-queuing application traffic per tier of user

Thus, with such powerful hardware architecture, ASR platforms handle complex, granular, and discrete application policies at scale.

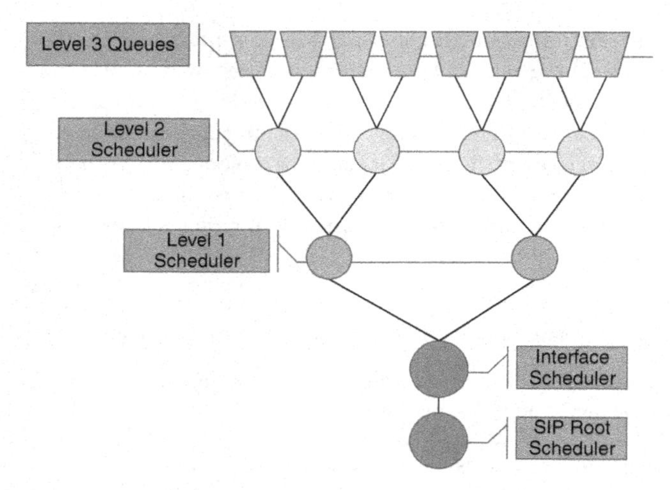

Figure 20-33 *ASR QFP BQS Scheduling Levels*

Internal System QoS

One final requirement that needs to be addressed is internal QoS, to ensure critical application traffic doesn't get bottlenecked *within* a system.

There are three places within the ASR architecture where potential internal system congestion can occur:

- BQS (which has already been discussed)
- SIP ingress, shown as Circle 1 in Figure 20-34
- SIP egress, shown as Circle 2 in Figure 20-34

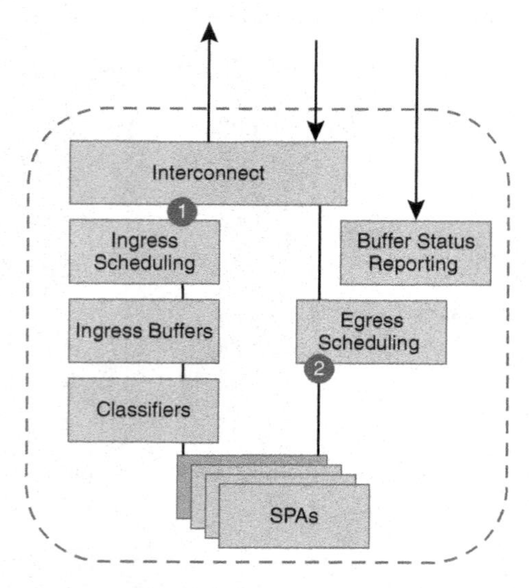

Figure 20-34 *ASR SIP Ingress and Egress Internal System QoS*

SIP internal QoS classification is based on

- 802.1p
- IPv4/IPv6 DSCP
- Multiprotocol Label Switching (MPLS) Traffic Class (formerly known as Experimental [EXP] bits)

SIP internal QoS, configurable on a per-port or per-VLAN basis, supports two queues:

- High-priority queue (a strict-priority queue)
- Low-priority queue

By default, all ports have a weight proportional to the interface bandwidth, with bandwidth being shared; additionally, excess weight is configurable on a per-port basis.

As such, these internal mechanisms ensure that applications are treated according to business priority not only end to end but also *within* the system.

Cisco DNA Application Policy not only configures hardware and software queuing systems to align to business priority, but automatically does the same for these internal QoS systems.

Switching Platform Requirements

The following policy elements are required for application treatment on campus Catalyst switches:

- Ingress classification and marking policies, on the access edge switch ports
- Egress hardware queuing policies on all switch ports
- Internal QoS

Application Classification and Marking Policies

One of the incredible advantages of the Unified Access Data Plane (UADP) ASIC is that it is programmable (as was discussed in Chapter 7). As such, it could be reprogrammed, via software updates, to support new protocols and features in hardware. One such new feature that UADP switching platforms now support, primarily in hardware, is NBAR2.

NBAR2 became available on UADP Catalyst switching platforms beginning with the IOS XE 16.3 software release. In this implementation, the "Fast Path" of NBAR2 (called out earlier in Figure 20-23) is implemented entirely in hardware, which provides application recognition for over 95 percent of packets.

Of the remaining packets, a copy is made of each packet, which is then punted to the CPU for deeper analysis (as previously described in the "NBAR2 Operation" section of this chapter). This is very important to understand, *for at no time does packet forwarding ever get interrupted or delayed on these switches when NBAR2 is utilized* for application recognition.

Before we review the current performance numbers of NBAR2 operation on Catalyst 9300 Series access switches, consider that the last time Cisco implemented stateful DPI capabilities in hardware was back in 2007 on a Catalyst 6500 daughter card called the Programmable Intelligent Services Accelerator (PISA) module, and it supported 90 protocols at a maximum throughput of 2 Gbps.

By way of comparison, NBAR2 performance on a 48-port Catalyst 9300 switch is as follows:

- Protocols supported: 1400+ (with new applications being added monthly)
- Total number of unique connections per second: up to 4900
  - which equates to over 100 new connections per second per switch port
- Total number of application flows: 20,000 for each set of 24 ports
- Maximum CPU utilization: 50 percent

Note CPU utilization is deliberately limited by the architectural implementation of NBAR2.

From these numbers, notice that NBAR2 scales very well on Cisco DNA switching platforms.

Additionally, NBAR2 QoS attributes were added to UADP-based Catalyst platforms beginning with IOS XE 16.8.1. As such, the "Holy Grail" application classification and marking policy (shown earlier in Example 20-2) can be used on these switches, *with completely identical syntax*.

Now let's discuss hardware queuing on the UADP Catalyst switches.

Hardware Queuing Policies

Gigabit/Multigigabit campus speeds require queuing to be performed in hardware. And because traditional fixed-configuration hardware varies according to platform role and price points, hardware queuing capabilities likewise vary. As such, over the years, Cisco produced dozens of different hardware queuing models across its many switching platforms, some of which are summarized in Table 20-1 (specifically, Table 20-1 summarizes all of the brownfield Catalyst queuing models that are supported by Cisco DNA Application Policy).

Incidentally, hardware queuing models are expressed as combinations of

- *x*P, where *x* represents the number of priority queues supported
- *y*Q, where *y* represents the number of non-priority queues supported
- *z*T, where *z* represents the number of supported drop thresholds per non-priority queue

Table 20-1 *Cisco Brownfield Hardware Queuing Models Supported by Cisco DNA Application Policy*

Platform	Ingress Queuing Model(s)	Egress Queuing Model(s)
Catalyst 2960	N/A	1P3Q3T
Catalyst 3560	1P1Q3T	1P3Q3T
Catalyst 3750	1P1Q3T	1P3Q3T
Catalyst 4500	N/A	1P7Q1T
Catalyst 6500	1Q8T	1P3Q8T
	2Q4T	1P3Q4T
	2Q8T	1P7Q4T
	8Q4T	1P7Q8T
	8Q8T	2P6Q4T
	1P7Q2T	
	2P6Q4T	

UADP-based Catalyst platforms (such as the Catalyst 3650/3850 and 9000 series switches) support the following hardware queuing models:

- **8Q3T:** All eight hardware queues are non-priority
- **1P7Q3T:** A single strict-priority queue can interrupt the servicing of the remaining seven non-priority queues
- **2P6Q3T:** Where:
  - Priority Queue 1 can interrupt the servicing of any queue
  - Priority Queue 2 can interrupt the servicing of any non-priority queue

Note The second priority queue was added to UADP as a result of customers who wanted a way to treat loss-sensitive high-definition business video without interfering with voice. This example again illustrates the flexibility of UADP, as new queuing structures are simply programmed into the hardware via software updates (where, in contrast, this is impossible to do on fixed-configuration hardware).

As UADP continues to pervade Cisco's campus portfolio of switching platforms, a massive simplification of campus QoS is taking place, which enables the convergence of the many queuing models shown in Table 20-1 into a single recommended queuing model (2P6Q3T) at multiple layers of the campus.

The CVD best practice queuing recommendation for the 2P6Q3T hardware queuing model is shown in Figure 20-35.

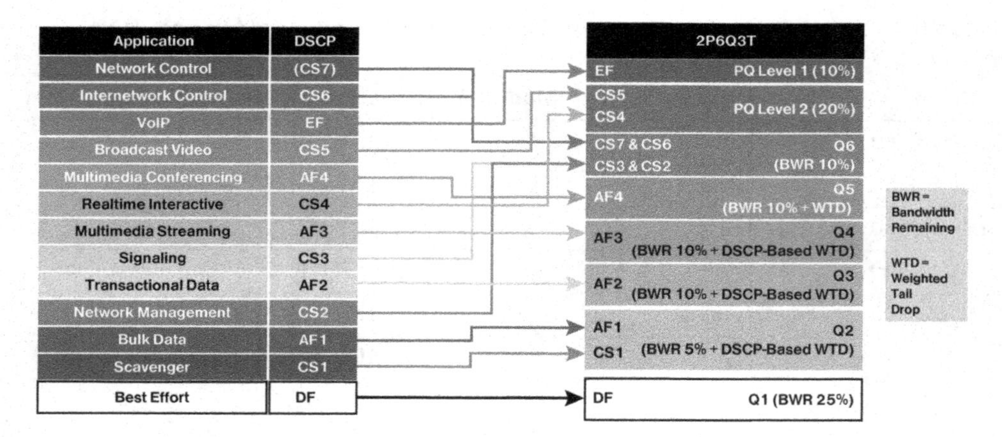

Figure 20-35 *CVD 2P6Q3T Queuing Model*

The corresponding CVD configuration for the 2P6Q3T queuing model is shown in Example 20-6.

Example 20-6 *CVD-based 2P3Q3T Queuing Model*

```
class-map match-any VOICE-PQ1
 match dscp ef
class-map match-any VIDEO-PQ2
 match dscp cs4
 match dscp cs5
class-map match-any CONTROL-MGMT-QUEUE
 match dscp cs7
 match dscp cs6
 match dscp cs3
 match dscp cs2
class-map match-any MULTIMEDIA-CONFERENCING-QUEUE
 match dscp af41
 match dscp af42
 match dscp af43
class-map match-any MULTIMEDIA-STREAMING-QUEUE
 match dscp af31
 match dscp af32
 match dscp af33
class-map match-any TRANSACTIONAL-DATA-QUEUE
 match dscp af21
 match dscp af22
 match dscp af23
class-map match-any SCAVENGER-BULK-DATA-QUEUE
 match dscp cs1
 match dscp af11
```

```
 match dscp af12
 match dscp af13

policy-map 2P6Q3T
 class VOICE-PQ1
  priority level 1
  police rate percent 10
 class VIDEO-PQ2
  priority level 2
  police rate percent 20
 class CONTROL-MGMT-QUEUE
  bandwidth remaining percent 10
  queue-buffers ratio 10
 class MULTIMEDIA-CONFERENCING-QUEUE
  bandwidth remaining percent 15
  queue-buffers ratio 10
  queue-limit dscp af42 percent 90
  queue-limit dscp af43 percent 80
 class MULTIMEDIA-STREAMING-QUEUE
  bandwidth remaining percent 15
  queue-buffers ratio 10
  queue-limit dscp af32 percent 90
  queue-limit dscp af33 percent 80
 class TRANSACTIONAL-DATA-QUEUE
  bandwidth remaining percent 15
  queue-buffers ratio 10
  queue-limit dscp af22 percent 90
  queue-limit dscp af23 percent 80
 class SCAVENGER-BULK-DATA-QUEUE
  bandwidth remaining percent 10
  queue-buffers ratio 10
  queue-limit dscp values af12 percent 90
  queue-limit dscp values af13 cs1 percent 80
 class class-default
  bandwidth remaining percent 35
  queue-buffers ratio 25
…
interface range GigabitEthernet 1/0/1-48
 service-policy output 2P6Q3T
```

Note Catalyst 3650 and 3850 switches support only Weighted Tail Drop (WTD) for congestion avoidance, as shown in Example 20-6. However, Catalyst 9000 series platforms support both WTD and Weighted Random Early Detect (WRED), the latter of which is deployed by Cisco DNA Application Policy as of Release 1.2.8.

Internal System QoS

The internal architecture of UADP is shown in Figure 20-36.

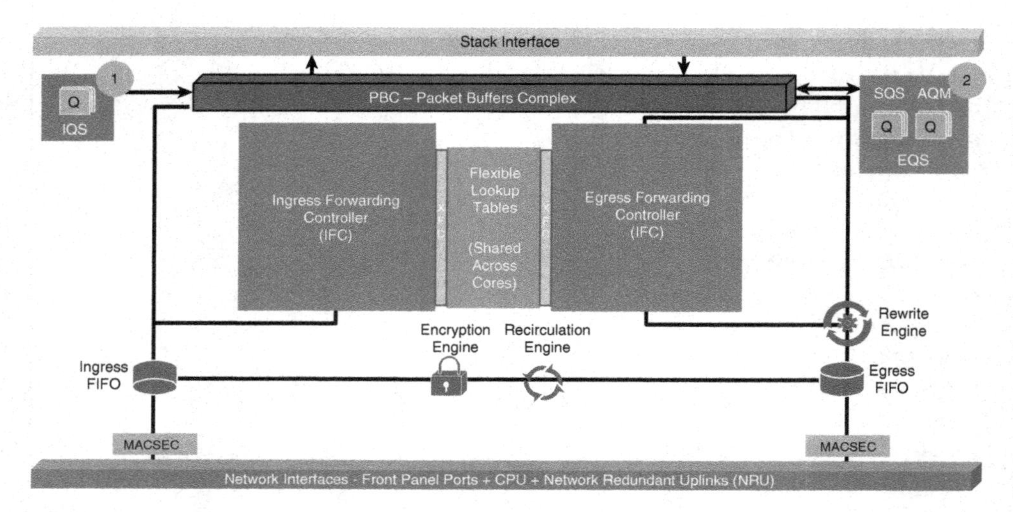

Figure 20-36 *UADP 2.0 Core Architecture*

As shown in Figure 20-36, there are two places within the UADP architecture where potential internal system congestion occurs:

- **Ingress Queuing Scheduler (IQS):** The IQS manages arbitration for packets contending to access the switch stack, in the event that the stack interface is busy.
- **Egress Queuing Scheduler (EQS):** The EQS manages congestion for packets exiting the stack interface (as well as from other paths, discussed shortly); the EQS is actually composed of multiple subsystems, including
  - Stack Queuing and Scheduling (SQS)
  - Active Queue Management (AQM)

An important point to make before discussing how these individual mechanisms manage internal congestion is that none of these internal queuing systems actually queue *packets*, but rather queue only *packet descriptors* (metadata pointers to the packet location within the buffer complex). Once a packet is received by UADP, it is copied and stored in the Packet Buffers Complex (PBC), with only packet descriptors queued within these internal queuing mechanisms. Furthermore, the contents of a packet are copied out of the PBC only when one of these internal queuing and scheduling systems decides that the packet is to be sent out an interface (or over the stack or even dropped).

Let's now consider these internal queuing and scheduling systems in turn, beginning with IQS.

IQS includes two sets of queues, each with up to 8000 configurable queue entries per queue; these queue sets include

- Eight queues for network data packets
- Eight queues for CPU-bound packets

Additionally, IQS hardware supports Weighted Tail Drop (WTD) or Weighted Random Early Detect (WRED) with configurable common pool and reserved pool buffer allocations for each queue, including

- Three configurable common buffer thresholds
- Three configurable reserved buffer thresholds

Note Not all IQS hardware functionality is software enabled at the time of writing.

The default software-enabled IQS queuing model is illustrated in Figure 20-37.

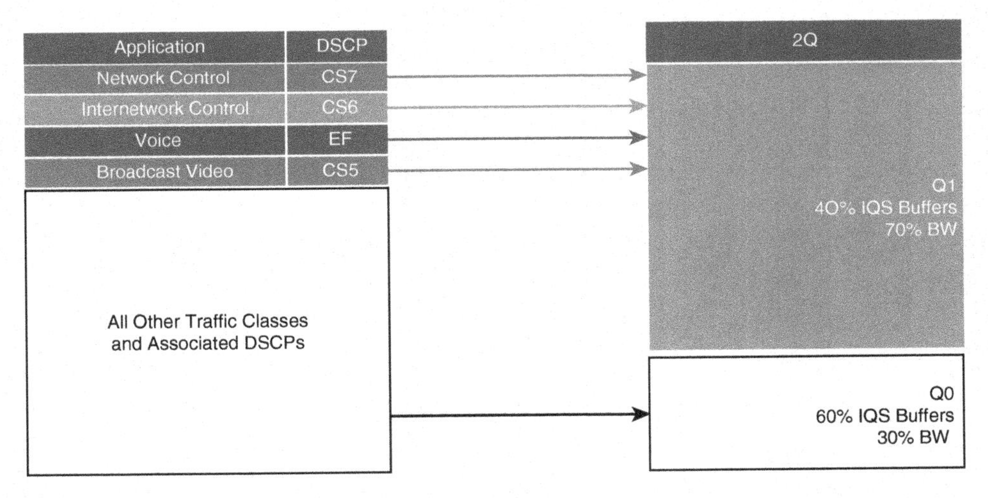

Figure 20-37 *UADP IQS (Default) Queuing Model*

In turn, on the egress side of the stack interface, the EQS system manages traffic received from

- **Within the local UADP core:** In the case where packets are sourced from a given switch port and destined to another switch port within the local 24-port group (as there is one UADP core per 24 switch ports).
- **The sister UADP core:** In the case where packets are sourced from a switch port on an adjacent 24-port group of a 48-port switch and are destined to a local switch port (note that these packets do not traverse the stack interface).

- **The stack interface:** In the case where packets are sourced from a switch port on another stack member and are destined to a switch port on the local 24-port group.
- **Recirculating packets within the local UADP core:** UADP supports up to 16 recirculations.

These queues are managed by the SQS subsystem of EQS, and are illustrated in Figure 20-38.

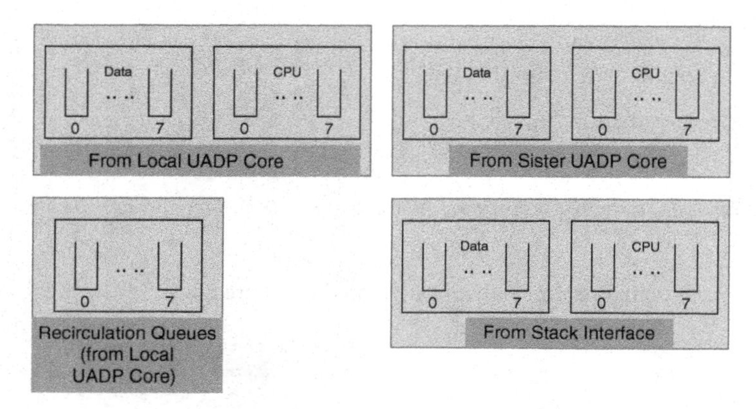

Figure 20-38 *UADP SQS Queues*

The default queuing model for SQS is shown in Figure 20-39.

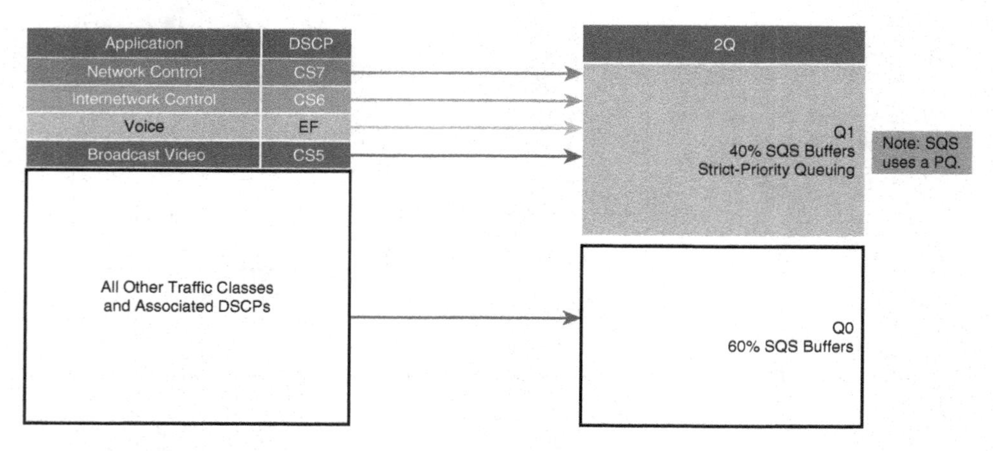

Figure 20-39 *UADP SQS (Default) Queuing Model*

A second subsystem within EQS is the AQM subsystem. AQM assigns the packets to their designated queues and decides which packets to enqueue and which to drop. AQM also deals with inter-port replication. Additionally, the AQM subsystem also includes the Dynamic Threshold and Scaling (DTS) sub-subsystem, which dynamically manages the queue sizes from a common pool of buffers. And within DTS are sub-sub-subsystems as well.

Peter Jones, a Cisco Distinguished Engineer who led UADP development, summarized this state of affairs very well: "When it comes to ASICs, there is no bottom. And if you try to reach the bottom, you'll only drown."

Therefore, rather than drowning in all the data that the 10,000+ page engineering specs of UADP contain, the point of this brief discussion was simply to illustrate that achieving business-level objectives for application treatment extends all the way down to even the internal ASIC level of network infrastructure hardware.

Wireless Platform Requirements

The following policy elements are required for application treatment on wireless LAN controllers and access points:

- Application classification and marking policies
- DSCP-to-UP mapping
- Internal QoS

Each of these required elements are now discussed within the context of AireOS Wireless LAN Controllers (WLCs).

Application Classification and Marking Policies

NBAR2-based application classification and marking is supported on AireOS WLCs via Cisco Application Visibility and Control (AVC) Profiles that are applied to individual service set identifiers (SSID). However, note a few of the limitations:

- Only 32 applications per AVC Profile are supported.
- AireOS uses older NBAR2 classification engines (and thus older Protocol Packs) as compared to other infrastructure platforms; as such, some newer application signatures may not be available on these wireless platforms.
- Application classification and marking takes place on the WLC in centralized deployment models, but at the AP in FlexConnect deployment models.

The gating limit of only 32 applications within an AVC Profile is significant, considering that hundreds of applications can be assigned for preferential/deferential policy treatment within the abstracted QoS attribute-based "Holy Grail" model (presented earlier in Example 20-2).

Note Cisco eWLC, released in IOS XE 16.10, supports the QoS attribute-based "Holy Grail" QoS model.

To provide network operators a method to work within these platform-specific limitations, Cisco DNA Application Policy includes a concept of "Favorite" applications. From within the Application Registry, any given application(s) can be tagged as a Favorite by clicking the star that appears to the left of the application name, as shown in Figure 20-40, where cisco-collab-audio, cisco-collab-video, and cisco-collab-control have all been tagged as Favorites.

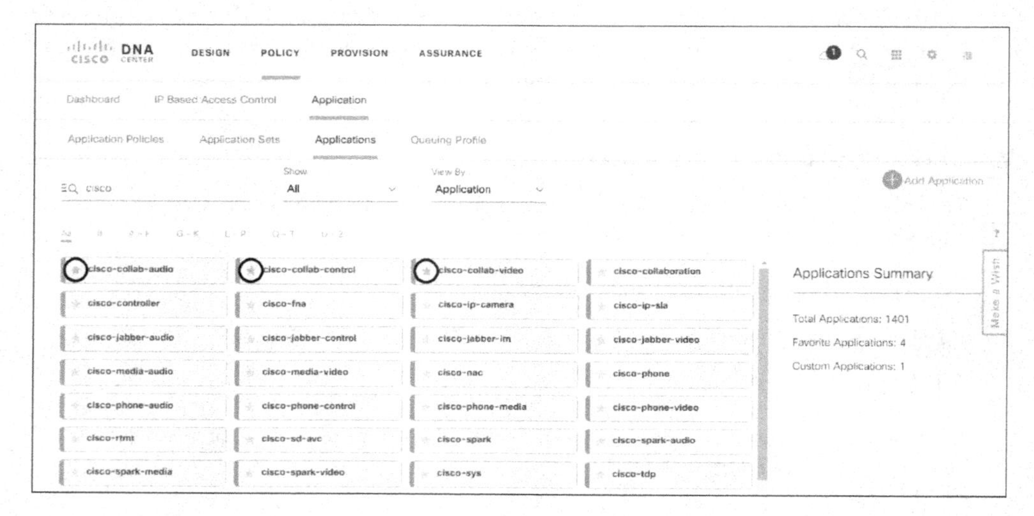

Figure 20-40 *Cisco DNA Center Application Registry—Tagging an Application as a "Favorite"*

Applications that were tagged as Favorite are (among other Cisco DNA Center operations) programmed into the platform application policy configuration ahead of all other applications, which, in the example illustrated in Figure 20-40, means that cisco-collab-audio, cisco-collab-video, and cisco-collab-control are programmed first into an AireOS AVC profile, leaving room for 29 other applications to also be programmed.

Incidentally, if fewer than 32 applications were tagged as Favorite—which is typically the case in most enterprise deployments—then the AVC Profile is populated by other applications that were assigned to the Business Relevant bucket, in an order that is determined by popularity (that is, which applications are most commonly deployed). As previously discussed, thousands of customers shared telemetry data with Cisco, and based on this data Cisco ranked applications within its library by how commonly these are deployed.

DSCP-to-UP Mapping

Wireless access points present a unique challenge to application policy because they represent a transition of media. The majority of the network is Ethernet, whereas enterprise wireless media is defined in IEEE 802.11.

Furthermore, wireless presents significant challenges to application policy because wireless media

- Is typically slower
- Is half-duplex

- Is shared
- Is non-deterministic
- Does not support priority servicing
- Does not support bandwidth guarantees
- Supports only four levels of service (via Access Categories)

As such, it is vital to do everything possible to optimize application flows on wireless media.

Because application servicing is a function of the Layer 2 802.11 User Priority (UP) marking, these markings must be present. Furthermore, it is these UP marking values alone that determine the Access Category that the traffic is serviced in as it contends for the wireless media. These UP-to-Access Category markings and mappings are summarized in Table 20-2.

Table 20-2 *IEEE 802.11 UP Values and Access Categories*

802.11 UP Value	802.11 Access Category	WMM Designation	Cisco AireOS WLC Designation
7	AC_VO	Voice	Platinum
6	AC_VO	Voice	Platinum
5	AC_VI	Video	Gold
4	AC_VI	Video	Gold
3	AC_BE	Best Effort	Silver
0	AC_BE	Best Effort	Silver
2	AC_BK	Background	Bronze
1	AC_BK	Best Effort	Bronze

Not only do UP markings need to be present in order to provide preferential/deferential services to applications over the wireless media, but these markings must be compatible with the intended treatment of the application, which is not always the case by default. This incompatibility is primarily due to the fact that two different standards bodies administer QoS for wired versus wireless networks. Specifically, the IETF defines standards for IP QoS networks, and the IEEE specifies the standard for wireless networks, and their respective recommendations do not always align.

For example, consider the example of a voice packet, recommended to be marked as EF DSCP (46) on the IP wired network (per RFCs 4594 and 3246, and as shown earlier in Figure 20-18). By default, most APs take the first three bits of the DSCP marking to generate a UP value. The binary notation of 46 is 101110, and thus in such a case, a UP value of 5 (101) is generated for this voice packet. However, as shown in Table 20-2, an 802.11 frame marked with a UP value of 5 is treated as video over the wireless network, and not as voice.

Recognizing this, some of the Cisco DNA architects at Cisco undertook an exercise to align Diffserv QoS with 802.11, with the result of this exercise being summarized in Figure 20-41. These mappings are automatically enabled in all Cisco APs as part of an Application Policy deployment.

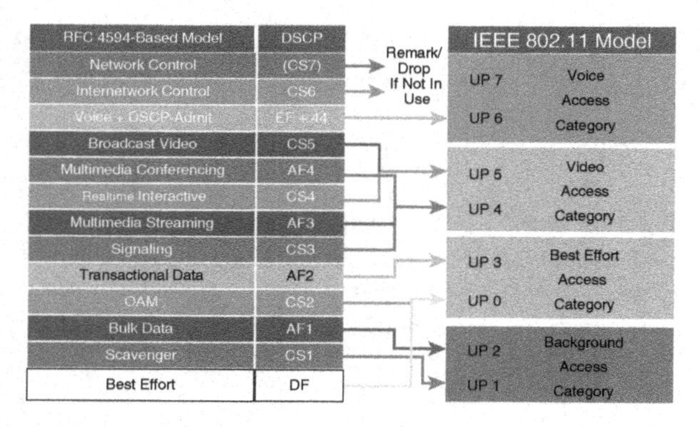

Figure 20-41 *CVD Recommended DSCP-to-UP Mapping*

Additionally, Cisco shared these DSCP-to-UP mapping recommendations with the IETF and in early 2018 these were formalized in a standards-track RFC: RFC 8325, "Mapping Diffserv to IEEE 802.11."[2]

Hardware QoS

The key QoS function that access points perform is the IEEE 802.11 Enhanced Distribution Coordination Function (EDCF), also referred to as the Hybrid Coordination Function (HCF). This function not only provides Carrier Sense Multiple Access/Collision Avoidance (CSMA/CA) over the wireless media, but also provides four levels of QoS, called Access Categories (AC). These QoS treatments for these wireless access categories are achieved by delaying frame transmission via fixed and variable delay timers.

The fixed delay timers are referred to as Arbitration Inter Frame Spaces (AIFS); these vary by access category, as detailed in Table 20-3.

Table 20-3 *Arbitration Inter Frame Spaces by Access Category*

Access Category	Designative (informative)	AIFS (Slot Times)
AC_VO	Voice	2
AC_VI	Video	2
AC_BE	Best Effort	3
AC_BK	Background	7

2 https://tools.ietf.org/html/rfc8325

The variable timers are referred to as Contention Windows (CW); Contention Windows include explicitly set minimum and maximum values (abbreviated to CWmin and CWmax, respectively); these CW values are also defined on a per-access-category basis, as shown in Table 20-4.

Table 20-4 *Contention Windows by Access Category*

Access Category	Designative (Informative)	CWmin (Slot Times)	CWmax (Slot Times)
AC_VO	Voice	3	7
AC_VI	Video	7	15
AC_BE	Best Effort	15	1023
AC_BK	Background	15	1023

Note Both the AIFS and CW are defined in "slot times." The slot time is the basic unit of time measure on which all other IEEE 802.11 timers are based. The slot-time duration varies with the different generations of data rates and performances. For example, IEEE.802.11-2016[3] specifies the slot time to be 20 microseconds.

When a station transmits a frame, it must first wait until the medium is clear, and then further wait for a period that includes both the fixed timer (AIFS) and the variable timer (CW).

The CW value is initially a random value between 0 and CWmin. However, if a collision occurs during this initial transmission attempt, then a retransmission attempt is made, but the range of the CW doubles. Put another way, during the first retransmission attempt, the CW is a random number between 0 and 2 × CWmin.

If further collisions occur, then this process repeats until the CWmax is reached. At this point, retransmissions may still be attempted, but the range of the CW will not increase.

When the fixed and randomly generated timers are added together on a per-access-category basis, then traffic assigned to the Voice Access Category (i.e., traffic marked to UP 6 or 7) receives a statistically superior service relative to traffic assigned to the Video Access Category (i.e., traffic marked UP 5 and 4), which, in turn, receives a statistically superior service relative to traffic assigned to the Best Effort Access Category traffic (i.e., traffic marked UP 3 and 0), which finally receives a statistically superior service relative to traffic assigned to the Background Access Category traffic (i.e., traffic marked to UP 2 and 1). This statistical favoring of access categories is illustrated in Figure 20-42.

3 https://standards.iee'e.org/findstds/standard/802.11-2016.html

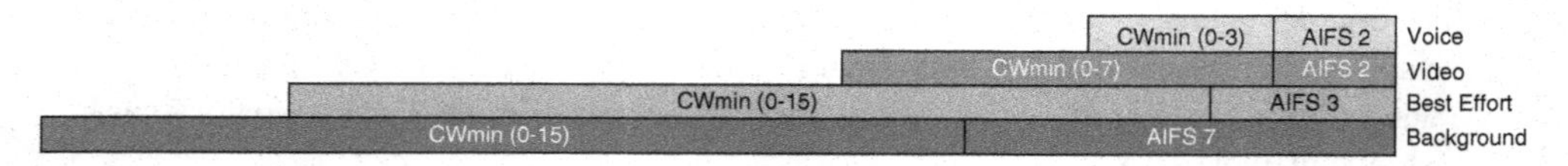

Figure 20-42 *IEEE 802.11 Access Categories Fixed and Variable Delay Timers (AIFS + CWs)*

Note For a technical overview of IEEE 802.11 QoS, refer to IETF 8325 Section 6. For full details, refer to IEEE 802.11-16.

IEEE 802.11 EDCA/HCF is performed in hardware, on both the APs and the clients.

Internal System QoS (Wireless Access Points)

Wireless access points are the most pervasively deployed network infrastructure components in an enterprise. These units are typically deployed in an unassuming manner; more often with the intent of "blending in" (versus standing out). As such, it's easy to assume that these devices have very humble QoS capabilities; however, with Cisco access points, this is hardly the case.

To maximize QoS flexibility, granularity, and fairness, Cisco APs complement the hardware Hybrid Coordination Function with extensive, hierarchical software queuing, which is performed on a

- per-User Priority basis, and on a
- per-client basis, and on a
- per-SSID basis

Let's discuss this hierarchical AP software queuing model.

To complement the intent of IEEE 802.11 User Priority, wireless frames are assigned to software queues on a per-User Priority basis, as illustrated in Figure 20-43.

To ensure fairness between wireless clients, each client within a given SSID is provisioned with an individual set of eight UP queues, as is shown in Figure 20-44. As SSIDs support up to 200 clients, provisioning such treatment requires 1600 queues per SSID.

And finally, to ensure fairness (or to manage unfairness) between SSIDs, airtime is scheduled between SSIDs. Up to 16 SSIDs are supported by a single radio, and as such, provisioning such treatment requires 25,600 software queues (8 UPs per client × 200 clients per SSID × 16 SSIDs per radio), as shown in Figure 20-45.

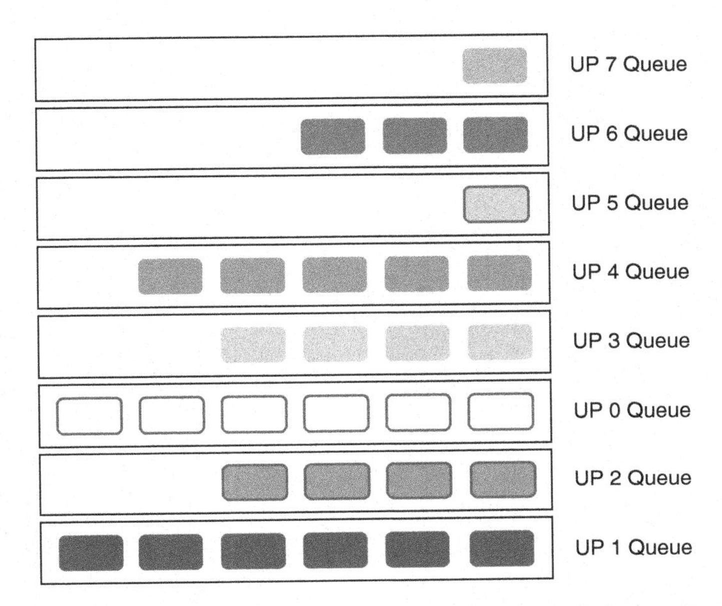

Figure 20-43 *Cisco AP Internal QoS—Per-UP Software Queuing*

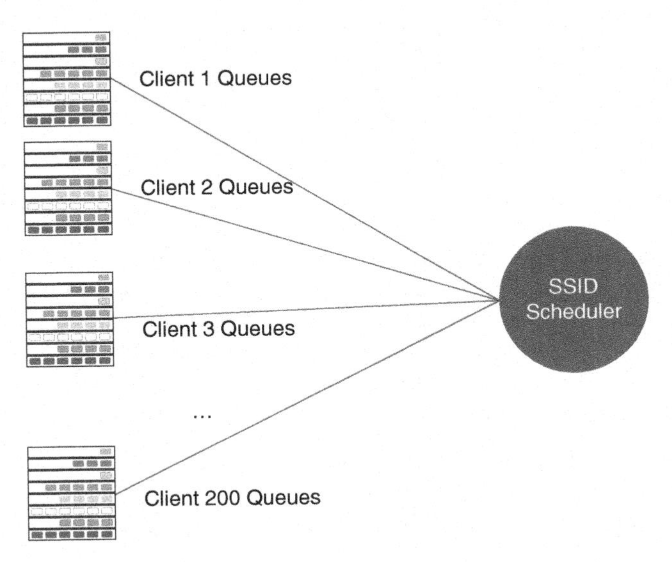

Figure 20-44 *Cisco AP Internal QoS—Per-Client, Per-UP Software Queuing*

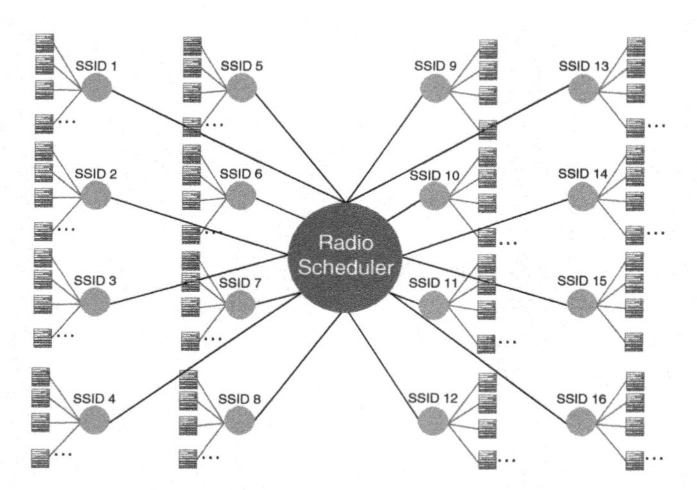

Figure 20-45 *Cisco AP Internal QoS—Per SSID, Per Client, Per UP Software Queuing*

Note For more details on ASR/ISR router, Catalyst switch, WLC, or access point QoS architecture, operation, and configuration, refer to the Cisco Press book *End-to-End QoS Network Design: Quality of Service for Rich-Media & Cloud Networks*, Second Edition or the Cisco Live breakout sessions: "Enterprise QoS Design 5.0" and "The Blood and Guts and Gore of QoS," all of which are referenced in the "Further Reading" section of this chapter.

Summary

This chapter introduced Cisco DNA Center Application Policy, which provides operators a simple user interface to express their business intent regarding how their applications are to be treated across their enterprise networks. The goal of this chapter was to show both how simple it is for operators to deploy intent-based application policies with Cisco DNA Center, and how powerful and complex the underlying programmable infrastructure is that enforces and delivers these application policies.

The discussion began with an overview of the basic steps of creating and deploying Application Policy within Cisco DNA Center. Additionally, the optional steps of customizing a Queuing Profile, a Marking Profile, and a Service Provider Profile were presented.

Next, this chapter "lifted the hood" to detail the inner workings of Application Policy, as well as the underlying network infrastructure hardware and software mechanisms that deliver application policy treatment and reporting.

The inner workings of Cisco DNA Application Policy were explained to show how it uses a declarative model (versus an imperative model) to translate business intent into application classification, marking, queuing, and dropping specifics, all per a standards-based 12-class model.

Next, this chapter discussed the powerful cross-platform network infrastructure software solutions Network Based Application Recognition 2 (NBAR2) and Software-Defined Application Visibility and Control (SD-AVC), showing how these can identify over 90 percent of encrypted traffic in the enterprise, as well as share these classification decisions with devices that do not have these advanced application recognition capabilities.

Next, platform-specific technologies within routers, switches, and wireless controllers were discussed in detail. For routers, the QFP ASIC was detailed, showing how this ASIC provisions up to 128,000 hardware queues—in five levels of hierarchy—so as to meet highly complex business requirements for application treatments. Similarly, for switches, the inner workings of the UADP ASIC were also shown, highlighting how this flexible and programmable hardware supports NBAR2, as well as advanced internal QoS mechanisms (including IQS and EQS).

Finally, wireless platforms were also discussed to highlight how these to map QoS markings between Layer 3 DSCP and Layer 2 UP in a compatible and consistent manner. Additionally, the hardware Hybrid Coordination Function (HQF) was introduced (as well as complementary internal software queuing models within Cisco APs) that provisions up to 25,600 queues to deliver expressed intent for application traffic.

Further Reading

Cisco Systems. *Cisco EasyQoS Solution Design Guide APIC-EM Release 1.6.* Dec. 2017. https://www.cisco.com/c/en/us/td/docs/solutions/CVD/Dec2017/APIC-EM-EasyQoS-DesignGuide-Dec2017.pdf.

Keinan, G. "Optimizing Enterprise Networks through SD-AVC." Cisco Live Barcelona 2018 BRKCRS-2502. https://www.ciscolive.com/global/on-demand-library/?search=brkcrs-2502#/session/1498024635316001CZfF.

RFC 3662. "A Lower Effort Per-Domain Behavior (PDB) for Differentiated Services." Dec. 2003. https://tools.ietf.org/html/rfc3662.

Szigeti, T., C. Hattingh, R. Barton, and K. Briley, Jr. *End-to-End QoS Network Design: Quality of Service for Rich-Media & Cloud Networks*, Second Edition. Indianapolis: Cisco Press; 2014.

Szigeti, T. "Enterprise QoS Design 5.0." Cisco Live Melbourne 2017 BRKCRS-2501. https://www.ciscolive.com/global/on-demand-library/?search=szigeti#/session/1475057169922001dbEy.

Szigeti, T. "The Blood and Guts and Gore of QoS." Cisco Live US 2016 BRKRST-3057. https://www.ciscolive.com/global/on-demand-library/?search=szigeti#/session/14502096283830017a6q.

Chapter 21

Cisco DNA Analytics and Assurance

Most networking departments today are bogged down by operations and are spending the majority of their time manually troubleshooting their networks. However, network analytics can significantly free up such IT time and resources and allow these to be more effectively reallocated to driving strategic projects, and thus digital transformation.

This chapter discusses the role of analytics within the enterprise network architecture and introduces Cisco DNA Center Assurance, a powerful network monitoring and troubleshooting application that allows network operators to "go back in time" to solve network issues.

This chapter discusses how Cisco DNA Assurance monitors and remediates the health of

- Clients
- Network devices
- Applications

Introduction to Cisco DNA Assurance

According to a 2016 study by McKinsey sponsored by Cisco, companies spend over $60B in network operations, with 75 percent of network OPEX being spent on visibility and troubleshooting.

These statistics are hardly surprising when considering that most enterprises have thousands of users, thousands of applications, and often tens of thousands of network-enabled devices. Furthermore, IP traffic is projected to more than double from 2016 to 2020; additionally, 10 billion more Internet of Things (IoT) devices are expected to come online within the same timeframe.[1]

1 https://spectrum.ieee.org/tech-talk/telecom/internet/popular-internet-of-things-forecast-of-50-billion-devices-by-2020-is-outdated

Managing network operations manually is becoming increasingly untenable for IT departments, a challenge that is exacerbated by the myriad of inconsistent and incompatible hardware and software systems and devices in the enterprise. Furthermore, troubleshooting network, client, or application issues is a complex end-to-end problem, which can often involve over 100 points of failure between the user and the application, as illustrated in Figure 21-1.

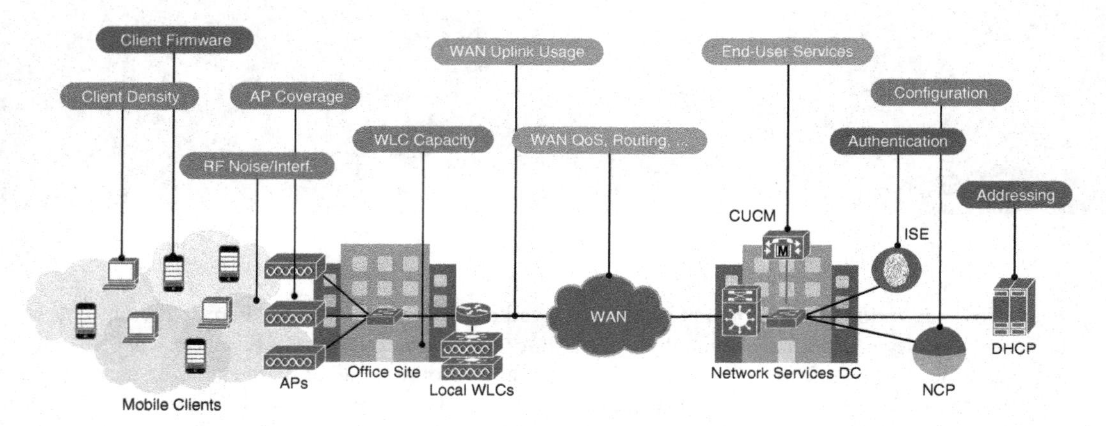

Figure 21-1 *Points of Failure That Can Impact User Experience*

Network troubleshooting challenges include the following:

- **Data collection challenge:** Network operators spend four times more time *collecting* data than analyzing/troubleshooting based on the insights revealed by the collected data.
- **Replication challenge:** It's impossible for you as a network operator to troubleshoot issues that are not manifest at the same time you begin troubleshooting (which may be minutes, hours, or even days after the reported event); unless you can detect and/or replicate the issue, you are simply unable to investigate it any further.
- **Time to resolution:** Most network quality issues take hours (or even longer) to find the root cause and to ultimately resolve.
- **The network is to blame by default:** Per customer data (as discussed in Chapter 3, "Designing for Humans"), the network is often blamed first as the cause of any given problem, but in the majority of instances, this is incorrect; as such, you spend considerable cycles simply proving the network's innocence.

Companies that can get a handle on the skyrocketing operational costs of running their networks stand to gain considerable profitability and advantage. The key? Digital analytics. Digital analytics yield considerable productivity gains. For example, a 2017 study by McKinsey projects 20 percent productivity rises for enterprises leveraging digital analytics to streamline their operations.

This is where the closed loop of Cisco Digital Network Architecture really comes into play, as illustrated in Figure 21-2.

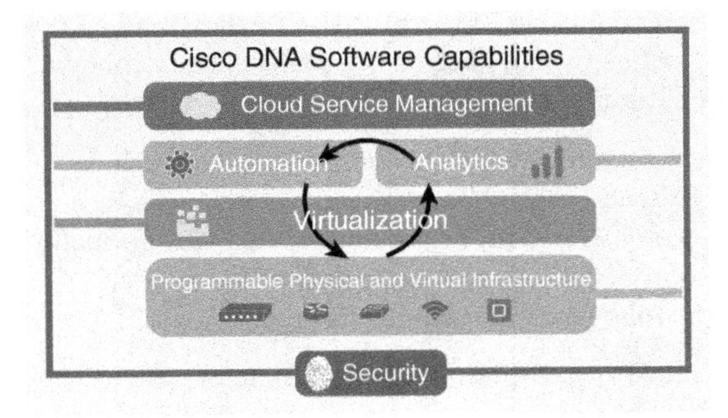

Figure 21-2 *Cisco DNA: A Closed-Loop Architecture*

The primary purpose of the automation platform in Cisco DNA is to "talk" to the network; in other words, to take the expressed business intent and translate this into optimal platform-specific configurations on the network devices, and deploy these across the network at scale. In a complementary manner, the primary role of the analytics platform is to "listen" to the network, specifically to gather, process, and make sense of all the network telemetry generated by network devices, correlating this data with the expressed business intent.

Additionally, the analytics platform closes the loop by either

- Providing quantitative data *proving* that the intent has been delivered
- *Alerting* the controller of the need to take a remediation action to deliver the intent

Cisco DNA Assurance closes this loop by providing two key functions of the network intuitively: context and learning (which are discussed in the following sections).

Context

It's often said that "context is key," and this is certainly true in network analytics. To understand why, it is beneficial to review a more familiar, verbal example of how context is key to gaining insights, and then compare this to a networking example.

A number of years ago in an advertisement for a Broadway play, the producers of the play quoted a theatre critic as saying "By all means go and see this play." However, what the theatre critic actually wrote in his critique was "If triviality is what you happen to be wanting, by all means go and see this play." The advertised partial quote is a classic example of taking things out of context. Specifically, the producers exhibited bias in their data-selection process by carefully and deliberately editing what the critic had actually said. A common result of taking things out of context is being led to a wrong conclusion.

For example, a reader of the advertisement may readily conclude that, based on the theatre critic's reputation, the play is entertaining and worthwhile; however, this will likely lead the reader to a disappointing experience. However, an individual that compared multiple data points—such as reading several reviews of the play, and perhaps reading the full and unedited review by the quoted critic—would likely arrive at the correct context and thus make a more informed decision, leading to a better conclusion.

Similarly in networking, context plays a vital role in understanding what is happening. Context is key to gaining accurate insights, and to implementing correct actions to remediate issues. Accurate context, as demonstrated in the previous example, is optimally provided by correlating multiple data sources (akin to multiple points of view) of an object or event in question. Consider the following networking example.

In this example, a user has called in to the IT help desk and is complaining of poor application performance for WebEx. You, the analyst receiving the call, have no idea if this is a network issue or an application issue, nor where the root cause of the issue may be. However, by correlating multiple sources of information, you may be able to zero in on the root cause efficiently and effectively. The following series of figures shows the incremental context and insights that correlating multiple related data sources via an analytics engine provides for troubleshooting such an issue.

As a starting point, because the user's identity is known, consult the policy engine, specifically the Identity Services Engine (ISE), for details of the user and which device(s) he is using, as shown in Figure 21-3.

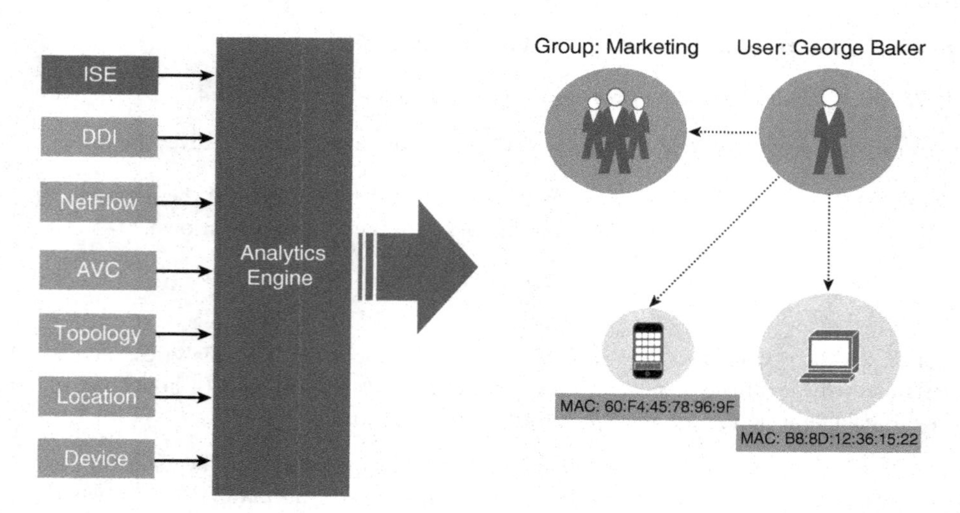

Figure 21-3 *Contextual Correlation Example—Part 1: Identifying the User and His Device(s)*

Next, the analytics engine correlates the Media Access Control (MAC) address of the user's device(s) with data provided by the Domain Name System (DNS), Dynamic Host

Configuration Protocol (DHCP), and IP Addressing and Management (IPAM) systems, to identify the IP address of the device experiencing the issue, as shown in Figure 21-4.

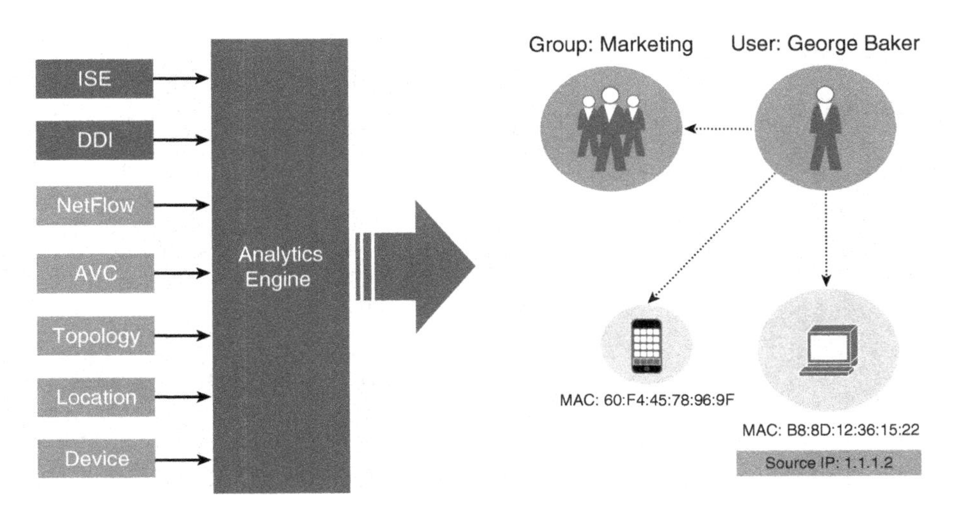

Figure 21-4 *Contextual Correlation Example—Part 2: Identifying the Client IP Address*

Following this, the analytics engine filters all the collected NetFlow records by the source IP address of the client device, as shown in Figure 21-5.

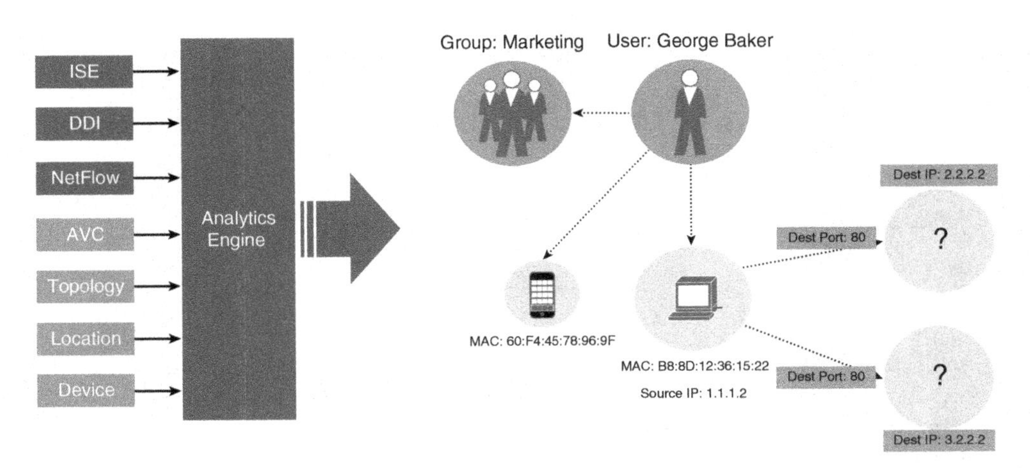

Figure 21-5 *Contextual Correlation Example—Part 3: Filtering the NetFlow Records*

The question now becomes: Which flow (or flows) represents the WebEx application that the user was having issues with? Basic NetFlow records do not include details of which application generated the flow; however, this information is inserted into NetFlow records via Cisco Application Visibility and Control (AVC) technologies. Now the flow records can be matched to their respective applications, with the WebEx flow being clearly identified, as shown in Figure 21-6.

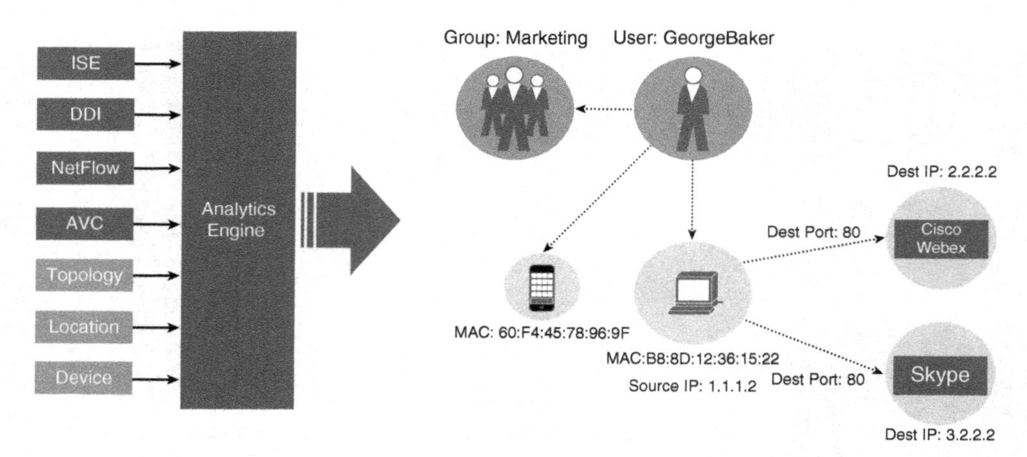

Figure 21-6 *Contextual Correlation Example—Part 4: Identifying the Application Flow(s)*

Next the analytics engine correlates the network topology that the flow traversed, beginning with the attachment point of the client, as shown in Figure 21-7.

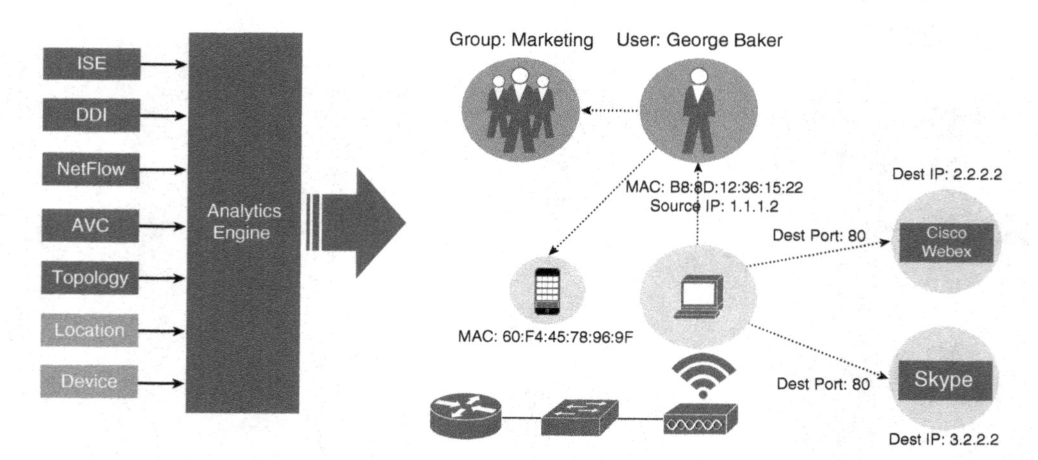

Figure 21-7 *Contextual Correlation Example—Part 5: Identifying the Network Attachment Point and Network Topology*

Geographical location may also be correlated, as shown in Figure 21-8, as sometimes issues are local to specific buildings and sites.

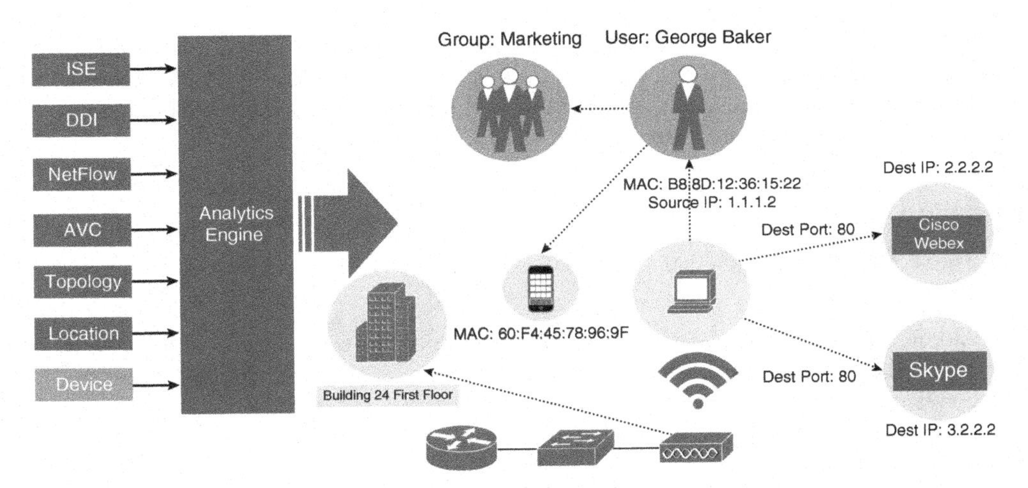

Figure 21-8 *Contextual Correlation Example—Part 6: Correlating Location Information*

Following this, device information, including key performance indicators (KPI), policy metrics, configuration details, syslogs, etc., can all be included in the correlation exercise so as to identify the root cause of the network issue, as shown in Figure 21-9.

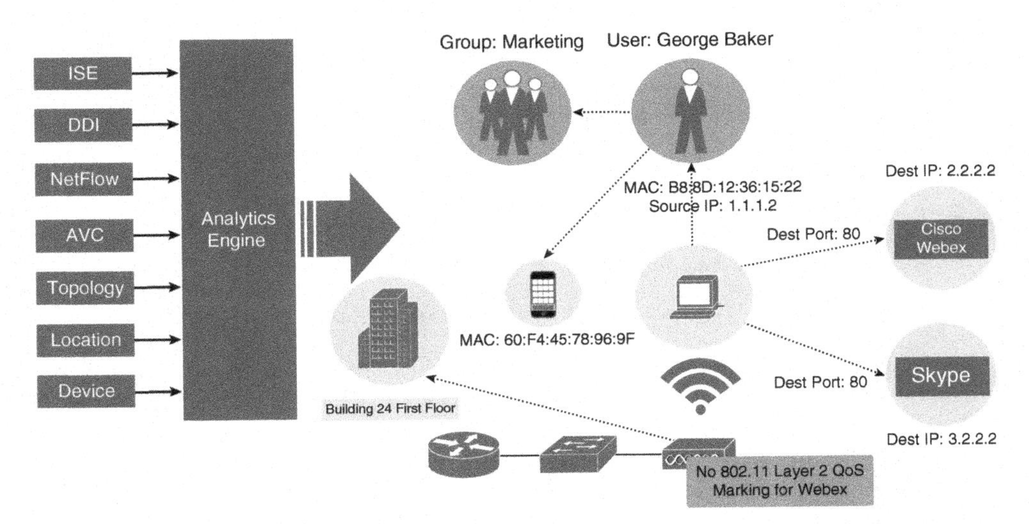

Figure 21-9 *Contextual Correlation Example—Part 7: Correlating Network Device Data*

In this specific example, a comprehensive contextual correlation exercise accurately identified the root cause of the poorly performing application to be a lack of quality of service (QoS) marking and treatment on the wireless LAN.

However, arriving at a root-cause insight is not enough: the remediation should be actionable. Continuing the example, at this point a remedial action could be presented to you, such as enabling the Fastlane for iOS feature on George Baker's iPhone and including WebEx as one of the whitelisted applications to benefit from this treatment. This recommended remedial action could then be implemented via a single click and (in the future, ultimately) automated.

Learning

The second core function that Cisco DNA Assurance provides you with (in addition to context) is learning.

Although analytics engines provide valuable insights by the contextual correlation of data, these engines must be explicitly programmed to choose which data points to correlate and analyze. As previously noted in this chapter, in enterprise networking there could be over 100 points of failure between users and their applications; as such, the permutations of all possible data-point correlations become rapidly beyond a human's ability to identify, understand, and ultimately program into an analytics engine. For example, with 100 points of failure, the number of potential combinations that could produce that failure is 4950 [(100 × (100 – 1) / 2)].

Enter machine learning (ML). Machine learning is an application of artificial intelligence (AI) that enables systems to automatically learn and improve from experience without being explicitly programmed to do so. The primary aim is to allow these systems to learn automatically with minimal (or no) human intervention.

The process of machine learning begins with observations of data and looking for patterns within the data so as to make increasingly better correlations, inferences, and predictions. For example, there may be

- No pattern between data points
- A pattern between data points that may be attributable to pure coincidence
- A pattern between data points indicative of a correlation
- A pattern between data points that is the result of causation

When patterns indicating correlation are identified, then similar patterns can be searched for to identify root causes. For example, if a correlation is identified between a particular client operating system and several instances of high wireless roaming rates, then this pattern can be searched against for all clients having that operating system, potentially identifying the root cause of poor roaming experience to be in the client OS. However, it is also possible that the correlation may not necessarily be causation, as the root cause may in fact be something else. For instance, the root cause may in fact turn out to be hardware drivers that happened to be released around the same time as the particular OS version for the client.

Identifying such root causes of issues is the function of *cognitive analytics*. However, once these root causes are identified, cognitive analytics extends into the realm of *predictive analytics*, in other words, foreseeing imminent issues before they actually occur, with the goal of taking data-driven actions to prevent such from ever occurring.

For example, consider a case where causation was identified between the memory consumption of a device and its crashing. By identifying this causation, and by carefully monitoring the memory consumption of the family of devices, the system could redirect or prune processes to prevent a system crash before these ever happen.

Machine learning applied to enterprise networking is illustrated in Figure 21-10.

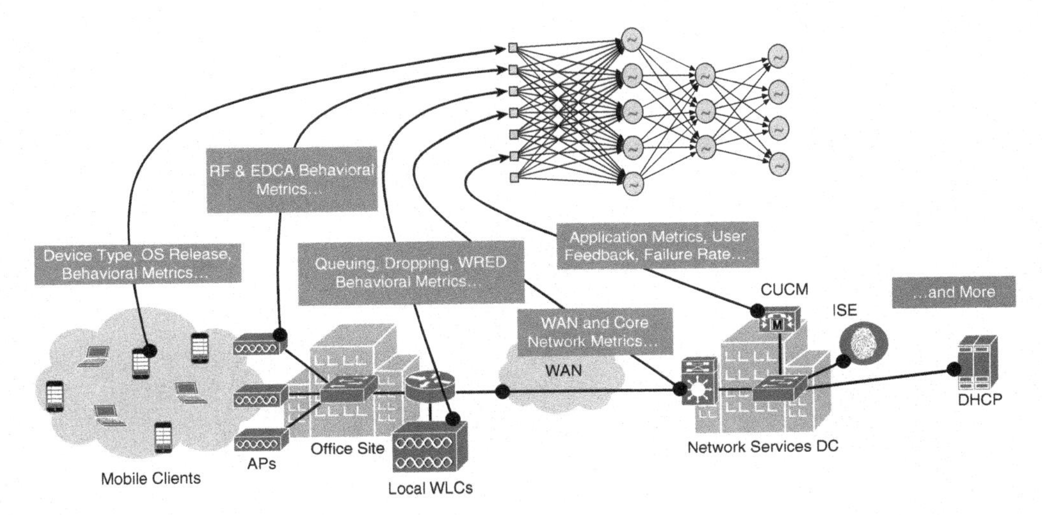

Figure 21-10 *Machine-Learning Algorithms Applied to Enterprise Networking Example*

The Architectural Requirements of a Self-Healing Network

The strategic vision for intent-based networking is to create a self-learning, self-defending, and self-healing network. Although the concept of a self-healing network may seem more like science fiction than reality, if looked at architecturally, it may seem a little closer to reality than perhaps initially thought.

While Cisco DNA Center is the platform that introduces automation and analytics into the enterprise network, an entire *architecture* is required to deliver intent-based networking, with the ultimate goal of the self-healing network. In other words, while Cisco DNA Assurance provides the user interface to visualize network analytics data, a tremendous amount of functionality is required of the infrastructure hardware, software, and protocols—in addition to the analytics platform—to deliver this complex solution. Combined, these architectural functions include

- Instrumentation
- On-device analytics
- Telemetry

- Scalable storage
- Analytics engine
- Machine learning
- Guided troubleshooting remediation
- Automated troubleshooting and remediation

Let's examine these architectural requirements.

Instrumentation

You cannot monitor, report, analyze, correlate, and learn from something that hasn't first been measured. As such, instrumentation is the first architectural requirement of a self-remediating network, as shown in Figure 21-11.

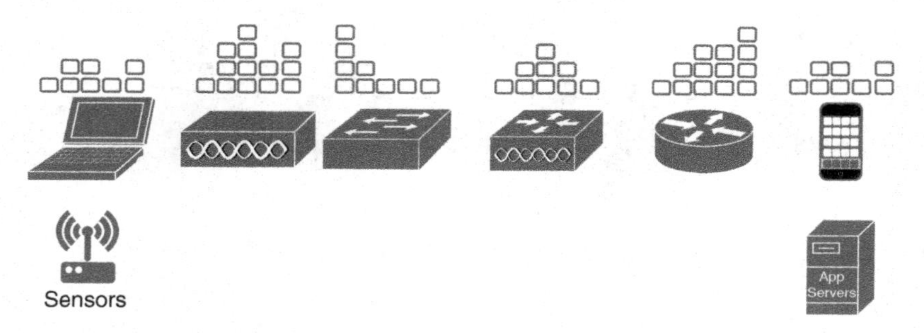

Figure 21-11 *Self-Healing Network—Architectural Requirement #1: Instrumentation*

To this end, Cisco introduced unprecedented instrumentation in its Cisco DNA-ready network devices, such as the Cisco Catalyst 9000 Series switches, which are built on the Unified Access Data Plane (UADP) 2.0 ASIC. As previously discussed, each UADP 2.0 ASIC supports 384,000 flexible counters, which are used to instrument virtually any event within the chip, in addition to the 128,000 NetFlow records that each ASIC can store in its tables.

That being said, it bears pointing out that not only the network requires instrumentation. For example, to accurately capture user quality of experience (QoE), it is critical to not only instrument network QoS metrics (such as loss, latency, and jitter), but also include relevant performance metrics from all elements affecting the flow, including hardware and software elements operating beyond the network, such as client endpoints, sensors, application servers, etc.

Clients can also be instrumented. A compelling example of client instrumentation for analytics is Apple/Cisco iOS Analytics, where Apple devices share their view of the network with Cisco DNA Assurance, including the wireless access points (APs) that they see (complete with signal levels and noise ratios), as well sharing the reasons with the analytics engine as to why these devices disassociated from the network (e.g., the device going idle, a user-triggered disassociation, a proprietary failure, etc.).

Another valuable example of instrumenting clients is to gain insight into adaptive application behavior. For instance, many multimedia applications leverage rate-adaptive video codecs. These codecs raise or lower resolution and/or frame rates, depending on network conditions. Consider the example where an adaptive video codec detects network congestion and, to compensate, lowers video resolution from Full-HD (1920×1080 pixels) to VGA (640×480 pixels) and video frame rates from 24 frames per second (fps) to 5 fps—the combination of which represents a 97 percent degradation in video quality. After such an adjustment, the network service level attributes of loss, latency, and jitter may all be within the highest levels; however, these network metrics alone do not reflect the significantly degraded user experience. As such, a more holistic approach is required to accurately reflect end-user experience, by instrumenting relevant KPIs from beyond the network, such as from clients and/or application servers.

Another manner in which beyond-the-network metrics are instrumented is via sensors. For example, wireless sensors may be deployed throughout the enterprise to proactively and continually test and report on onboarding experience, the availability and performance of network services (like authentication, authorization, and accounting [AAA], DHCP, DNS, etc.), as well as specific applications.

Distributed On-Device Analytics

The wealth of data to be instrumented on network devices and other devices generates the challenge of deciding which KPIs are more critical than others, so that appropriate actions are taken in each case. For example, if each of the 384,000 flexible counters on each UADP 2.0 ASIC were equally important and required specific action(s) to be taken, this could easily flood CPU and/or network resources to accommodate.

To offset such a scenario, on-device analytics is recommended. In this manner, critical metrics are identified and immediately acted on, while other, noncritical metrics are still retained for informational purposes or for advanced troubleshooting scenarios, which is discussed later. On-device analytics serves to make the architecture not only more efficient (by distributing analytics and processing), but also more responsive (as the device may self-analyze a problem and immediately remediate, without having to send telemetry to an external analytics engine and await a response). On-device analytics is illustrated in Figure 21-12.

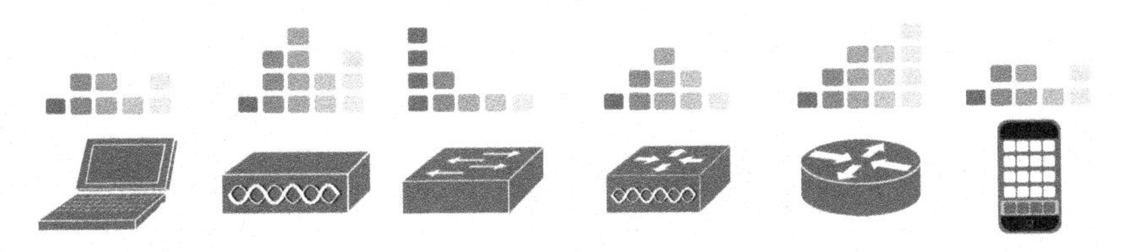

Figure 21-12 *Self-Healing Network—Architectural Requirement #2: On-Device Analytics*

Telemetry

The next challenge is getting data off the device, which requires telemetry. Telemetry has existed in many forms for many years, including legacy protocols such as Simple Network Management Protocol (SNMP), syslog, etc. However, some of these protocols, SNMP in particular, have serious shortcomings in a Cisco Digital Network Architecture. For example, SNMP is primarily poll based, and as such, if a critical KPI was measured on a device, the collector likely wouldn't know about it until the next polling interval. Furthermore, often the entire Management Information Base (MIB) would need to be read in to the collector, even if only a single data point was required. Finally, if multiple receivers wanted this information, SNMP info would have to be unicast to each receiver. These restrictions make SNMP slow and inefficient, and also presents scalability limitations for today's programmable infrastructures.

On the other hand, model-based streaming telemetry provides significant improvements in getting data off a device. First, data can be "pushed" off a device at any time (rather than "pulled" at given polling intervals). Additionally, individual metrics can be streamed (rather than entire MIBs). For example, if you were interested in whether a particular application was being dropped on a router, rather than pulling in the entire CISCO-CBQOS-MIB (which includes all stats and counters displayed from a **show policy-map interface** command) and searching for the relevant queue and then searching for drops in that queue, you can configure the router to push an alert whenever a drop for that specific application is counted. Furthermore, information can be streamed on a message bus, so that any/all interested parties to the data can receive it immediately and efficiently. Figure 21-13 shows critical metrics being pushed off devices to a collector via model-based streaming telemetry.

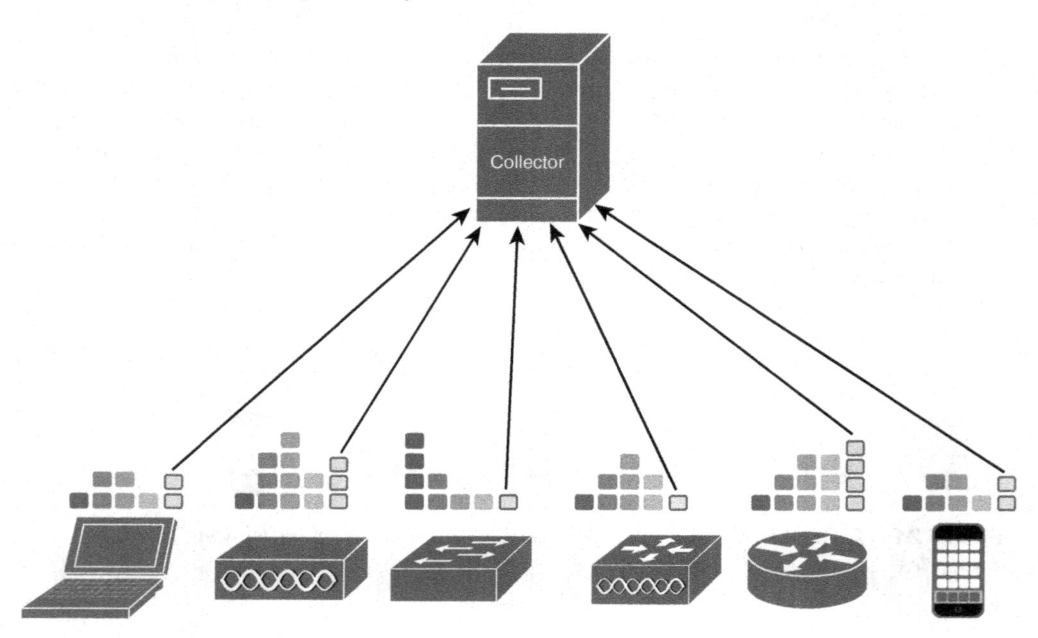

Figure 21-13 *Self-Healing Network—Architectural Requirement #3: Telemetry*

Due to the dynamic nature of digital networks, including their need to make decisions in real time, streaming telemetry is the key to solve these network monitoring and troubleshooting challenges, including reducing (or ultimately eliminating) preventable network outages and detecting urgent situations and automating immediate actions.

Scalable Storage

The sheer volume of data that a network generates—in typical cases about 5 TB of data per day—requires adequate provisioning for scalable storage. Scalable storage may take the form of

- **Centralized collectors:** Simpler to deploy, but are the least scalable of the options
- **Distributed collectors:** Allow for greater scalability, but come at the cost of complexity
- **Cloud-based collectors:** Allow for the greatest scalability and are simple to operate, but typically entail ongoing expenses from cloud service providers

These storage options are illustrated in Figure 21-14.

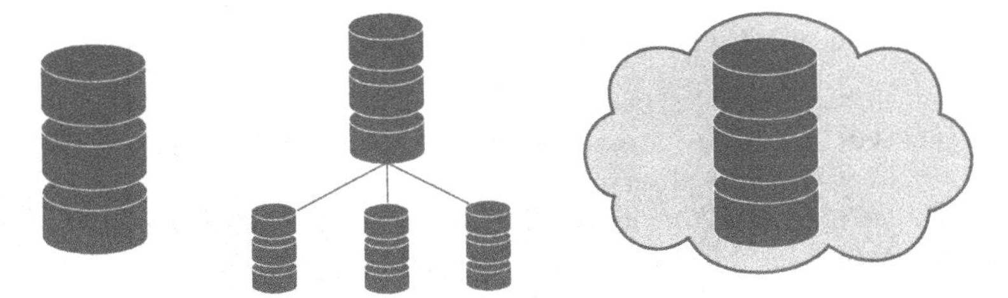

Figure 21-14 *Self-Healing Network—Architectural Requirement #4: Scalable Storage*

Whatever option(s) you choose, you will sooner or later have to deal with the questions of how much data needs to be stored and for how long it needs to be stored. None of these scalable storage solutions provide infinite and ongoing capacity (at least, not without significant cost). As such, raw data is typically aggregated after defined time intervals. For example, you may decide that after 30 days, only averages, along with minimum and maximum outliers, are required to be stored (as opposed to all raw data points). The time interval at which granular data is processed to a coarser level depends on enterprise policy, regulatory requirements, capacity trending and planning requirements, etc.

Analytics Engine

After the data is collected from the network into a central, distributed, or cloud-based storage system, it is now ready to be analyzed by the analytics engine. One of the first analytical operations is to baseline; that is, to trend what is "normal" (or at least normal for a given enterprise network). Once a baseline is established, identify anomalies (i.e., significant deviations from the baseline) and trigger further actions, as shown in Figure 21-15.

Figure 21-15 *Self-Healing Network—Architectural Requirement #5: Analytics Engine*

Machine Learning

As previously noted, analytics engines must be programmed to compare specific data points with other data points. However, the sheer number of permutations of enterprise network data points is completely overwhelming for any programmer to identify, let alone program. Therefore, machine-learning algorithms complement traditional analytics engines in searching for and identifying previously unknown correlations and causations.

Machine learning is done in either a guided or an unguided manner (also referred to as supervised and unsupervised). In a guided manner, the ML presents observations to you and you provide input as to whether the observations are interesting or not. If the observation is deemed interesting, then AI adjusts its learning pattern to look for similar relationships. In Cisco DNA Assurance, the machine-learning algorithm operates in a guided manner and you can tag an observation as interesting by clicking a thumbs-up icon; alternatively you can click a thumbs-down icon if the observation is deemed uninteresting. Benefits of machine learning are presented in Figure 21-16.

Figure 21-16 *Self-Healing Network—Architectural Requirement #6: Machine Learning*

Guided Troubleshooting and Remediation

Analytics and machine learning help identify an issue or potential issue, but often additional troubleshooting procedures are needed to achieve root-cause analysis.

These procedures typically begin with pulling in additional information from the suspected devices. This is similar to opening a case with Cisco Technical Assistance Center (TAC), where typically the first step in troubleshooting a reported issue is to supply the TAC engineer with a **show tech** command output from the device, which reports on virtually every monitored metric.

Following this, generally a divide-and-conquer approach is required to isolate the problem area, making it smaller and smaller until the root cause is clearly identified. This may include running troubleshooting tests, where the output of one test determines what the next test should be.

However, zeroing in on a root cause is not the end of the troubleshooting exercise; it's not enough just to know what the cause of the current problem is. You need to present specific remediation action(s). You should be able to quickly enable the recommended action via the automation platform, which pushes out the recommended action(s) to the network device(s). Guided troubleshooting and remediation is illustrated in Figure 21-17.

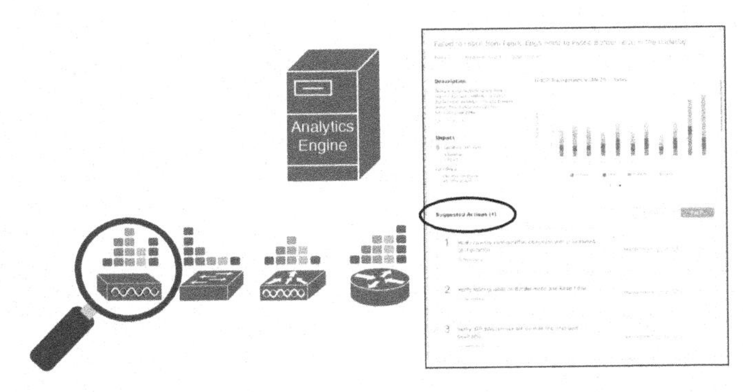

Figure 21-17 *Self-Healing Network—Architectural Requirement #7: Guided Troubleshooting and Remediation*

Automated Troubleshooting and Remediation

The guided troubleshooting system needs to monitor its own effectiveness. Sometimes the recommended action does not, in fact, remediate the root cause. In such cases, the guided troubleshooting algorithm needs to learn and adapt its troubleshooting approach. Perhaps the system may even present its self-measured effectiveness, stating something along the lines of "93 percent of the time action X solved this problem."

Over time, and as the effectiveness score increases, you may wish to disengage from your manual role in the process (i.e., explicitly clicking the button to take the recommended action) and prefer instead for the system to simply "always take the recommended action" when this problem is manifest, as shown in Figure 21-18. At this point, the goal of a self-healing network is realized.

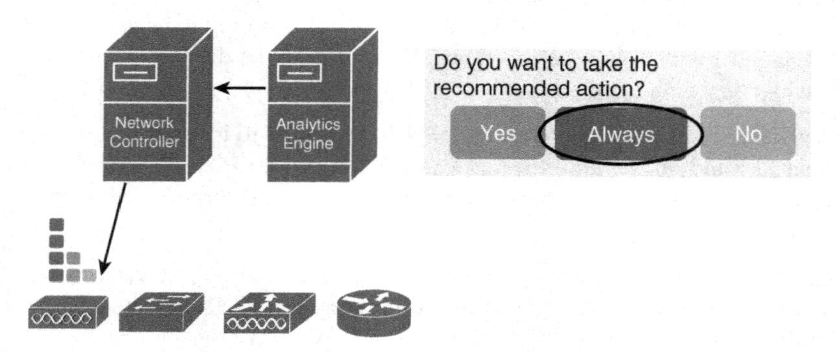

Figure 21-18 *Self-Healing Network—Architectural Requirement #8: Automated Troubleshooting and Remediation*

Although it's unlikely that every last issue is addressable by a self-healing workflow, the most common and recurring issues definitely are addressable. And the number of addressable issues can be added to over time, via both manual programming and machine learning.

An important observation to make here is that this final architectural requirement not only involves a technical challenge (i.e., a self-learning troubleshooting algorithm), but also presents a confidence challenge.

To illustrate this challenge of confidence, consider the self-driving car analogy. Some automobile manufacturers (such as Tesla Motors, for example) produce vehicles that include self-driving capabilities. However, even though these technical capabilities exist, many drivers prefer not to enable them, as they haven't yet gained sufficient confidence in them.

Similarly with networking. Network administrators are responsible for the state of their network. You should only allow machines to fix machines when you have developed adequate confidence and trust in the capabilities of your automated systems. As such, it is important to have maximum transparency of the underlying processes so you don't view the system as a mysterious black box, but rather as a predictable, deterministic system that you can gradually trust.

Returning to the self-driving car example, if a driver understands that dozens of cameras are continually monitoring every area around the car, in addition to radar, lasers, redundant systems, etc., the driver's confidence in her vehicle's autonomous abilities likely will increase, thus increasing the likelihood the driver will utilize these features.

> **Note** At the time of writing (October 2018), five of these eight distinct architectural requirements to realize the goal of a self-healing network have already been delivered, with a sixth expected within a few months' time. Thus, even though a self-healing network may seem an ambitious goal, it may in fact not be an overly distant one.

Cisco DNA Center Analytics and Assurance

As previously discussed, Cisco DNA Center is a single pane of glass for designing a network, provisioning the network, administering policy for the network, and assuring the network.

To achieve this end, the Cisco DNA Center appliance includes key software components that align to the Cisco DNA architecture, including

- **Network Controller Platform (NCP):** The automation component of Cisco DNA
- **Network Data Platform (NDP):** The analytics component of Cisco DNA

Additionally, like most platforms, Cisco DNA Center includes some built-in applications. One of these applications is Cisco DNA Assurance, which is discussed in detail in this chapter.

The relationship between NCP, NDP, and Cisco DNA Assurance within Cisco DNA Center is illustrated in Figure 21-19.

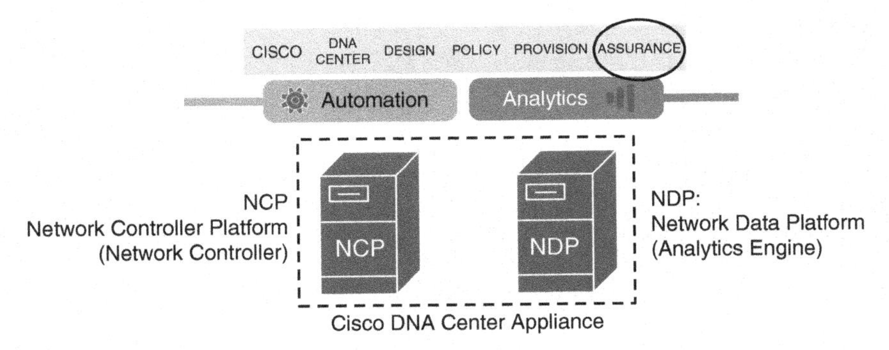

Figure 21-19 *Cisco DNA Center—NCP, NDP, and Cisco DNA Assurance*

However, before taking a look at Cisco DNA Assurance, first consider the underlying analytics engine: the Network Data Platform.

Network Data Platform

Monitoring and troubleshooting the enterprise network end to end in a proactive and predictive manner requires the collection of numerous sources of data from various siloed systems via multiple methods of telemetry, which are then ingested and integrated in massive volumes, so as to be inspected, correlated, and ultimately analyzed. Very quickly, it becomes apparent that the network monitoring and troubleshooting challenge is a big data problem.

This big data problem is broken down into four challenge areas:

- **Volume:** Terabytes (even petabytes) of data are generated on a daily basis.
- **Velocity:** Streaming telemetry at multigigabit network speeds and push/pull/message-bus models present a firehose stream of data to the analytics engine.
- **Variety:** Data may be structured, semistructured, or unstructured and represented in a variety of protocols, including SNMP, syslog, NetFlow, Network Configuration Protocol (NETCONF) modeled with Yet Another Next Generation (YANG), etc.
- **Veracity:** Some sources of instrumentation are more accurate than others; for instance, both Cisco IOS IP Service Level Agreement (IP SLA) and interface counters measure packet loss, but the former method is based on sampled active probing, and as such could easily miss events such as packet drops due to micro-bursting (which is very common in campus networks); such relative veracity must also be factored into correlation in order to accurately reconcile differing measured values.

The goal of network analytics is to transform data into actionable insights; as such, each step of data processing generates incremental business value, as shown in Figure 21-20.

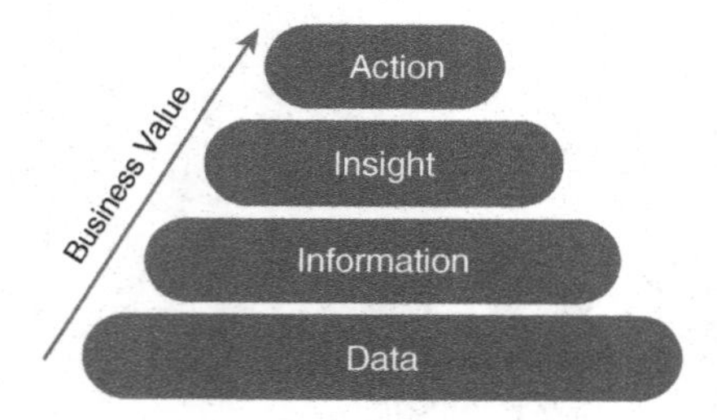

Figure 21-20 *Transforming Network Data into Actionable Insights*

The role of the analytics engine is to apply a set of principles and methodologies to process and analyze big data using mathematical algorithms and statistical models, with the goal of extracting meaningful insights. Streaming analytics, also called event stream processing, is the analysis of large, in-motion data called event streams. These streams are composed of events that occur as the result of an action or a set of actions. The Cisco DNA analytics engine—the Network Data Platform—processes data in (near) real time with the objective of delivering operational insights at the right time and right place, thus triggering the right action to be taken. Let's take a closer look at NDP.

NDP is the network industry's first network analytics engine for a Cisco Digital Network Architecture. NDP broadly integrates various network telemetry and adjacent data sets, and delivers the following key capabilities:

- Contextual correlation and time machine
- Complex event processing
- Time series analysis

Each of these capabilities of NDP will now be discussed in turn. Following this discussion, we will examine the NDP architecture, operation, and extensiblity.

NDP Contextual Correlation and Time Machine

Contextual correlation provides the ability to slice and dice network data according to the desired context. For example, data can be pivoted around any of the following:

- A specific user's perspective (e.g., what has George Baker's network experience been like today?)
- A group of users' perspective (e.g., what has been the experience for guests on our network today?)
- A specific client-device's perspective (e.g., what has been the experience for George Baker when using his iPad today?)
- A group of client-devices (e.g., what has been the experience of Android users today?)
- A specific network device's perspective (e.g., how has this router/switch/wireless LAN controller/access point performed today?)
- A group of devices (e.g., how has the San Jose building 24 network performed today?)
- A specific application's perspective (e.g., how has WebEx performed today?)
- A group of applications' perspective (e.g., how are all collaboration applications performing on our network today?)

Additionally, correlated contextual data inherently includes the notion of time. NDP provides contextual correlation by continuously enriching, aggregating, correlating, and analyzing data in (near) real time and saving the contextual relationship in a patented temporal graph database; therefore, NDP understands the past and current relationships and interactions of the network entities, understand the health of these entities, and allows NDP users to go "back in time" to visually compare dynamic network behavior.

To achieve this, NDP is constantly taking snapshots of the network and saving these snapshots in NDP's temporal graph database. As such, you can go back in time to check the network entity relationships and the health of the entities at any previous point in time, similar to using the reverse button on a digital personal video recorder (PVR).

Time machine functionality is key to solving the replication challenge discussed at the outset of this chapter. You no longer have to rely on a network issue being manifest at the time that you begin troubleshooting, but rather you can go back in time to the period where the issue was manifest and troubleshoot what went wrong at any specific moment in time.

NDP Complex Event Processing

Complex event processing (CEP) provides the ability to identify meaningful patterns, trends, and data relationships among multiple streams of events to derive second-order insights that empower businesses to be agile, resilient, and responsive while using network data. For example, such insights may include application policy and bandwidth utilization relationships that are used to avoid traffic congestion on critical WAN links.

CEP combines data from multiple sources to infer events or patterns. NDP users declaratively define business-relevant input streams, and then patterns derived from these streams, complete with descriptive analytics, trigger immediate notifications for anomalies, which can be further analyzed with extended processing or combined with batch-analytics insights, before rendering these to a user interface. The goal of CEP is to identify meaningful events and respond to them as quickly as possible.

NDP Time Series Analysis

Time series analysis refers to the analysis of time series data with a view to extrapolating and predicting future scenarios, while comparing historical deviations in data sets. Phrased another way, time series analysis is the ability to look at the past and apply lessons learned with a view to predicting the future.

Time series is a set of observations collected at equally spaced time intervals for a KPI. NDP supports time series analysis with built-in aggregation functions, statistical models, and window aggregates. Streaming analytics applications built on top of NDP leverage these built-in capabilities to track KPIs, establish baselines, identify anomalies, form trending lines, and predict future performance.

NDP Architecture

NDP is designed from the ground up, based on a best-of-breed open source technology stack, including Apache Kafka, Apache Flink, Apache Beam, etc.

While performing stream processing, scanning, and analyzing data in motion, NDP can also send a copy of the curated and anonymized data to a batch analytics system running in the cloud for machine learning. For example, the Cisco DNA Assurance user can leverage Cisco DNA Assurance dashboards to view the combined insights of the local analytics engine, as well as machine-learned insights from batch processing performed in the cloud.

NDP is deployed on an infrastructure service layer that provides cloud provider–agnostic services including cluster management, tenant management, etc. A high-level overview of the NDP architecture is illustrated in Figure 21-21.

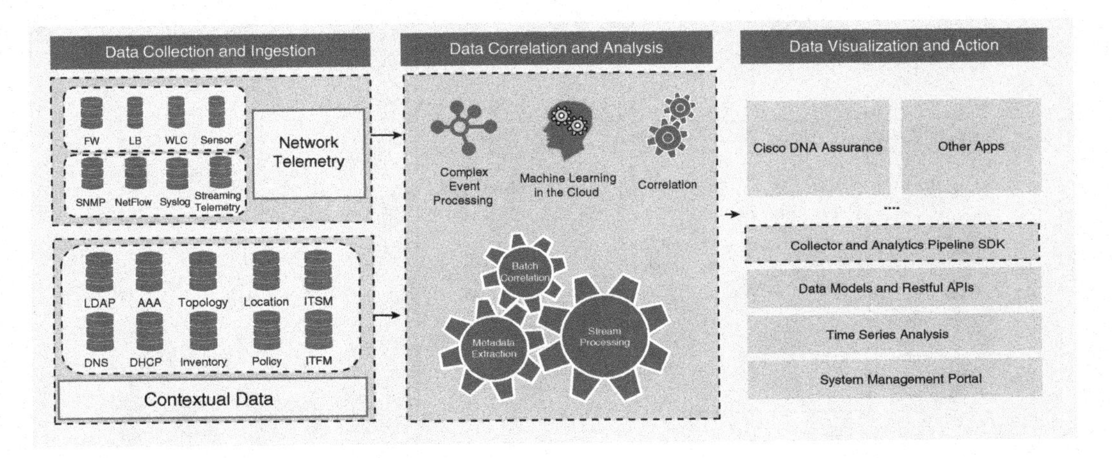

Figure 21-21 *NDP Architecture*

NDP consists of the following three architectural layers:

- **Data collection and ingestion:** As shown in Figure 21-21, NDP offers a wide collection of built-in collectors (e.g., SNMP, NetFlow, Syslog, Streaming Telemetry, DNS, DHCP, AAA, etc.). These high-performance collectors ingest network telemetry, system metrics, and contextual data from a variety of data sources before streaming the data to the core analytics engine. Each data type has a corresponding collector, which is configured and deployed as microservices and scaled horizontally. All collectors are developed using the collector software development kit (SDK) and monitored by the NDP collection framework once deployed.
- **Data correlation and analysis:** This layer is where contextual correlation, complex event processing, and time series analysis happen. NDP leverages analytics pipelines to continuously enrich, aggregate, correlate, and analyze data in real time (or near real time). The analytics pipelines run inside distributed analytics runtimes to enable high-speed data processing.
- **Data visualization and action:** NDP provides multiple storage options to address different analytics use cases. For example, Elastic is used to store syslog and system logs, InfluxDB is used to host time series data, and Redis is the storage for contextual cache, etc. This layer also supports various export pipelines for sharing raw or incrementally processed data with external systems.

NDP Operation

NDP collects and processes network data as illustrated in Figure 21-22. Collectors are set up to use the onboard instance or are deployed closer to a specified network segment (in the latter case, the collector is referred to as a satellite).

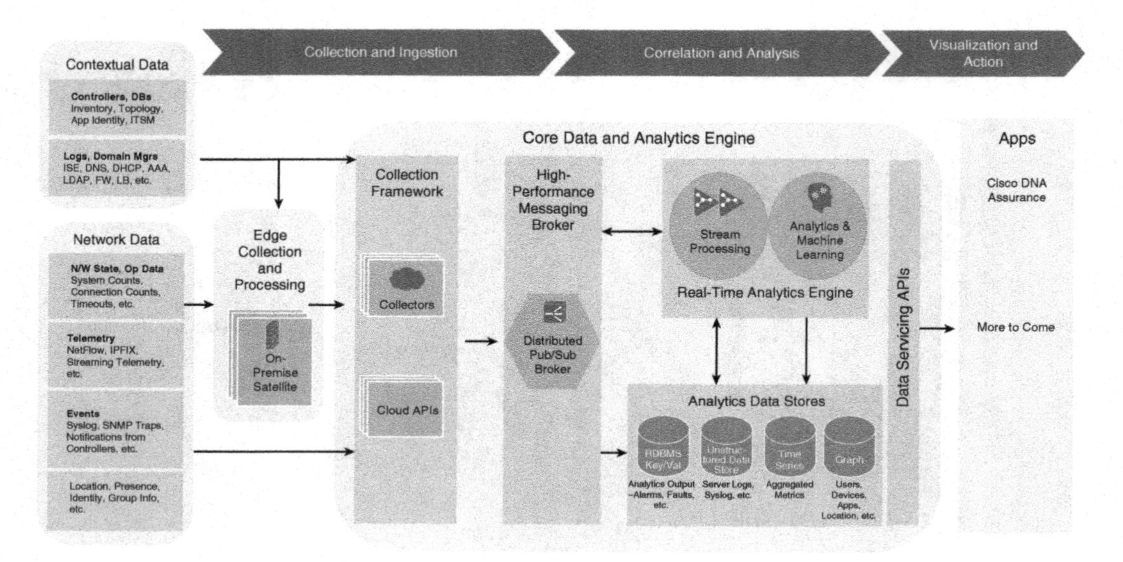

Figure 21-22 *NDP Operation*

The end-to-end process includes the following steps:

Step 1. Devices generate the telemetry (in specified formats).

Step 2. Collectors de-duplicate and clean the data.

Step 3. The Ingestion process publishes the data to the pub/sub messaging broker, delivering the data to the proper pipeline for further analysis.

Step 4. The Correlation and Analysis process represents the core processing capability and consists of both a stream processing channel and a micro-batch processing channel.

Step 5. The Visualization and Action process presents the data in application-specified UI formats.

NDP's unique approach to ensuring a high level of data quality consists of three distinct tiers of operation:

1. The first tier reduces data noise so that the enterprise enables minimal telemetry data but gains the maximum visibility for analysis. The term "reducing data noise" refers to identifying relevant data from the irrelevant. An example of data noise was

provided earlier in this chapter when discussing SNMP; specifically, it is usually the case that an entire MIB needs to be ingested for just a few (or one) data points. In such a case, identifying the relevant data point(s) within the MIB and discarding the rest would occur at this tier.

2. The second tier builds context-aware data graphs and makes them available through APIs. Based on historical data and machine-learning algorithms, NDP quickly identifies abnormal patterns and trends depending on the use case.

3. The third tier offers model-driven metadata and analytical pipeline management APIs to further extend the platform to integrate with external applications.

NDP Extensibility

NDP provides the appropriate query APIs for northbound access to the underlying data. This includes Representational State Transfer (REST) APIs for on-demand querying capabilities as well as a streaming API to receive data in a publisher/subscriber fashion. These APIs allow access to backend data stores as well as a native Graph Query Language that enables developers to traverse NDP's domain-specific data models. Furthermore, NDP provides access to a Natural Language Search (NLS) engine that translates common vernacular English-language terms to the relevant search query structure.

These metadata and analytical extensibility options allow customers to

- Go vertical, by enabling new analytics applications
- Go deep, by collecting proprietary network telemetry for broader device integration
- Go wide, by adding more contextual sources or providing complementary analytics

With these extensibility options, NDP significantly increases the business value potential of network data.

Cisco DNA Assurance

Cisco utilized a top-down approach to designing Cisco DNA Assurance to meet the user requirements manifest during the Design Thinking process (outlined in Chapter 3 "Designing for Humans"), including

- Being proactive, not reactive
- Accurately representing the overall health of all clients, network devices, and applications
- Displaying both wide (end-to-end) visibility and deep ("360-degree") visibility for any client, network device, or application

- Being network aware with machine-learning capabilities
- Using contextual correlation to deliver actionable insights
- Being flexible and programmable
- Providing microservices based on agile streaming telemetry
- Supporting open interfaces and a rich partner ecosystem
- Supporting a hyper-distributed, multitenant, and cloud-ready architecture
- Providing guided remediation, with the north-star goal of fully automating the remediation process

Key capabilities of Cisco DNA Assurance thus include

- End-to-end network visibility, achieved by continually learning from the network devices and the clients attached to the network
- Actionable insights to proactively identify and respond to events before users begin complaining
- Guided remediation actions for over 150 insights
- The ability to "travel back in time" (by viewing historical data) and troubleshoot network issues that occurred in the past
- Increased network visibility and faster time to resolution by visualizing real-time application traffic flow
- Proactive troubleshooting capabilities to discover the root cause of issues ahead of time and with more granular details

Cisco DNA Assurance monitors the enterprise using three distinct dimensions of health:

- Network Health
- Client Health
- Application Health

In the current version of the Cisco DNA Assurance (at the time of writing), only Network and Client health have tiles assigned to them on the landing page (as shown in Figure 21-23); however, if the Health link is selected (at the top left), all three health dimensions are available to the operator.

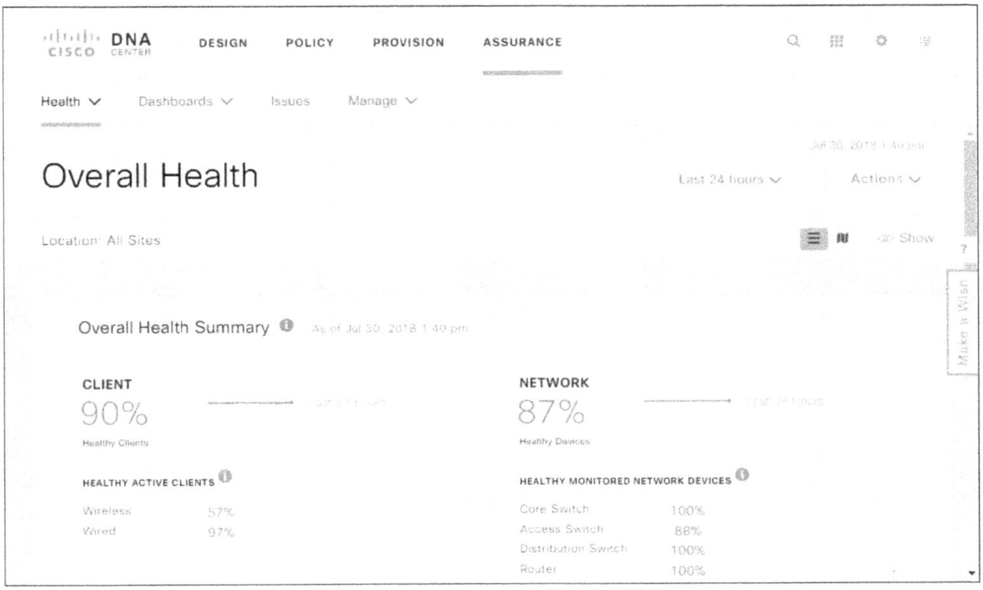

Figure 21-23 *Cisco DNA Assurance—Landing Page*

These health dimensions are each discussed in detail next, in turn. Incidentally, additional health dimensions are planned for the future.

Network Health

The Cisco DNA Network Health page allows you to very easily identify problem areas in your global network. The Network Health page is accessible by clicking on the Network Health tile from the landing page (or by selecting HEALTH > NETWORK).

The first element of every Health page in Cisco DNA Assurance is the timeline, as shown in Figure 21-24.

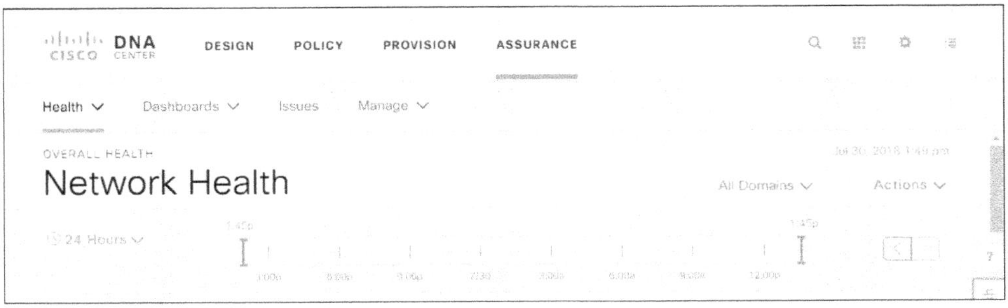

Figure 21-24 *Network Health—Part 1: Timeline*

The timeline specifies the period of interest and sets the context for all data displayed on the page. By default, the timeline specifies the past 24 hours, but it can be adjusted to accommodate any time interval you are interested in, as is shown in Figure 21-25.

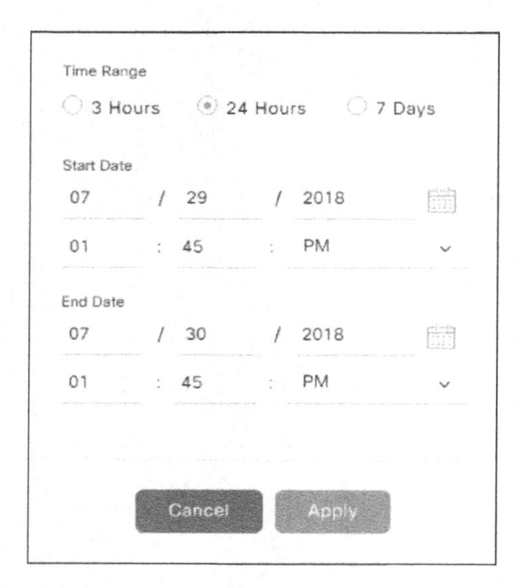

Figure 21-25 *Network Health—Part 2: Time Range Options*

You can choose how you want to view the network by switching among three different views, the icons for which are located to the left of Show. Clicking the rightmost icon displays a geographic map view, as shown in Figure 21-26.

Figure 21-26 *Network Health—Part 3: Map View*

Each site (or building, depending on the zoom scale) is represented by a colored dot that corresponds to its health score. The color legend is:

- Green = Good Health
- Orange = Fair Health
- Red = Poor Health
- Dark-gray = Unmonitored

Thus, with a quick glance, you can identify problem areas in this enterprise network.

You can also choose to view the network in a topological view, as shown in Figure 21-27.

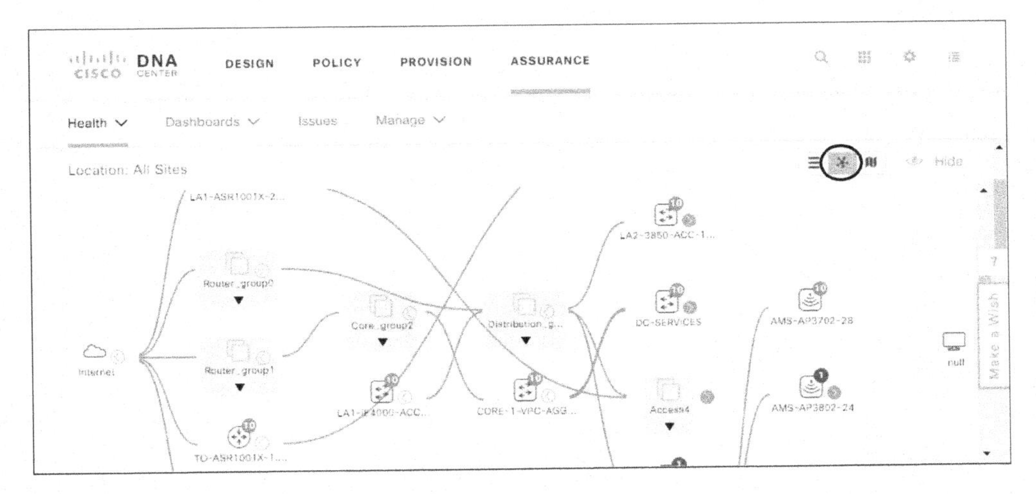

Figure 21-27 *Network Health—Part 4: Topology View*

The overall health of the network is summarized by device roles (as shown in Figure 21-28), including

- Access switches
- Distribution switches
- Core switches
- Routers
- Wireless (includes both APs and Wireless LAN Controllers)

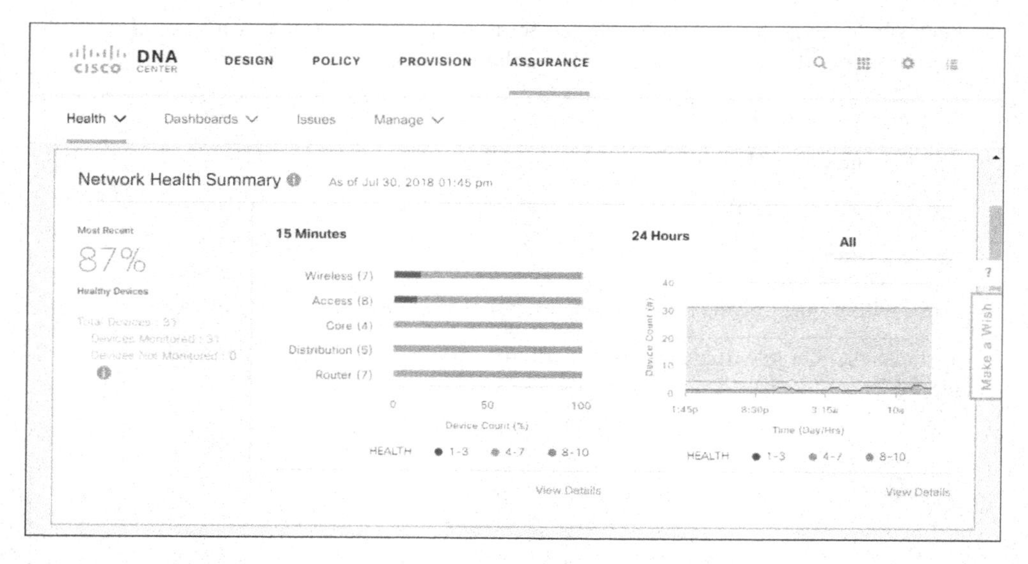

Figure 21-28 *Network Health—Part 5: Network Health Summary*

Additional details are shown for each of these network device roles, as shown in Figure 21-29.

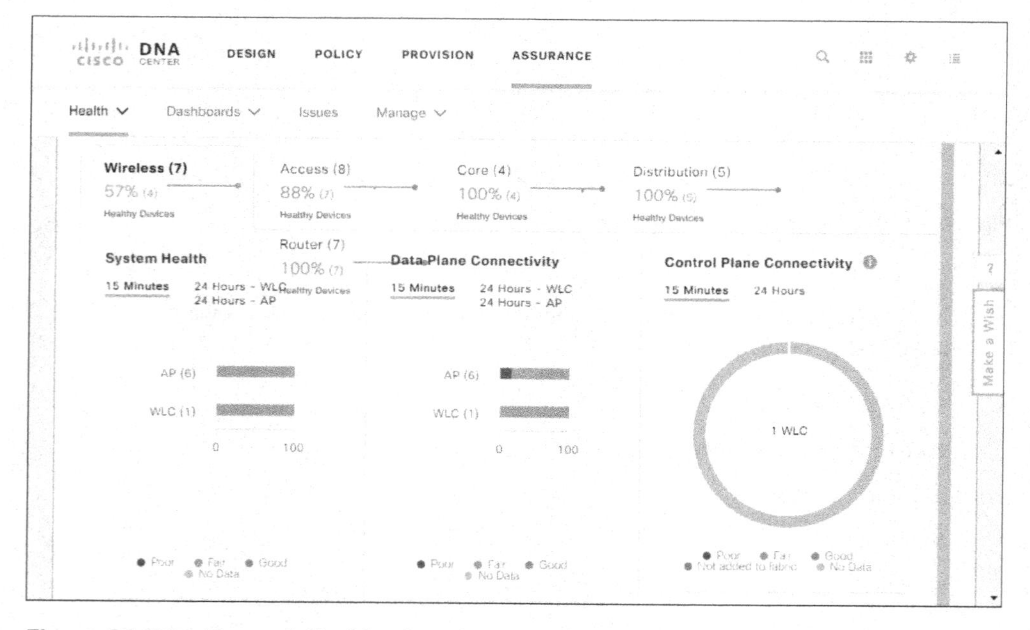

Figure 21-29 *Network Health—Part 6: Network Health by Device Role*

And finally, each network device is listed—or filtered—with its individual health statistics summarized in a tabular form, as shown in Figure 21-30.

Figure 21-30 *Network Health—Part 7: Network Device Table*

Each network device is hyperlinked to the most detailed view—which in Cisco DNA Assurance is called a "Device 360" view. Network devices, clients, users, and applications all have their own 360 view pages in Cisco DNA Assurance.

Thus, every network device has its own Device 360 view page, displaying a timeline of health, any known issues, neighbor topology, and monitored KPI details (including CPU, memory, temperature, control plane and data plane stats, etc.). Specifically, a Device 360 view displays

- Device Health (over time)
- Issues
- Physical Neighbor Topology
- Path Trace
- Device Info

The top of a Device 360 view shows the health of the device over the selected time period, as shown in Figure 21-31.

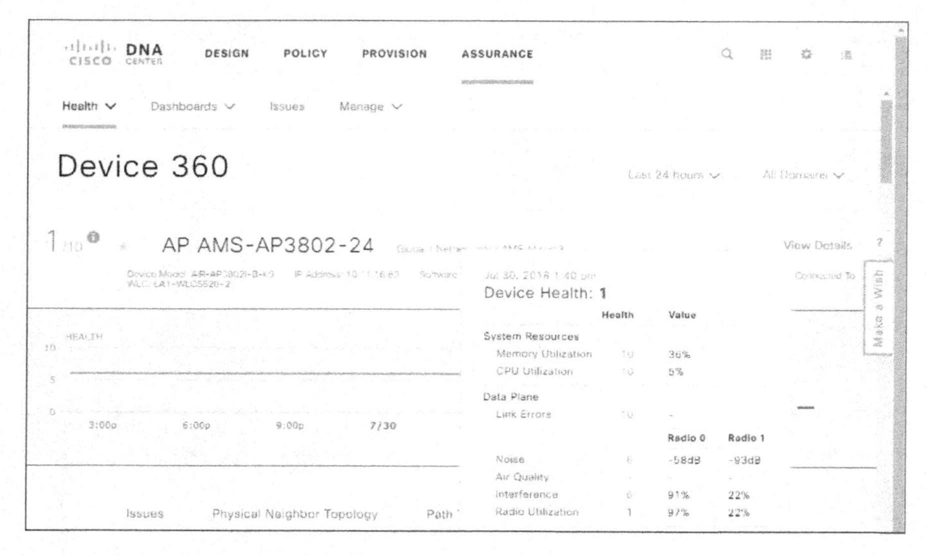

Figure 21-31 *Device 360—Part 1: Device Health Timeline*

Device health is a composite metric, composed of KPIs, including CPU and memory utilization, data plane availability, link errors, and control plane reachability. Over time, additional metrics are added to the health score computation for additional comprehensibility.

Next, each Device 360 page summarizes any issues that the device, user, client, or application is experiencing, as shown in Figure 21-32.

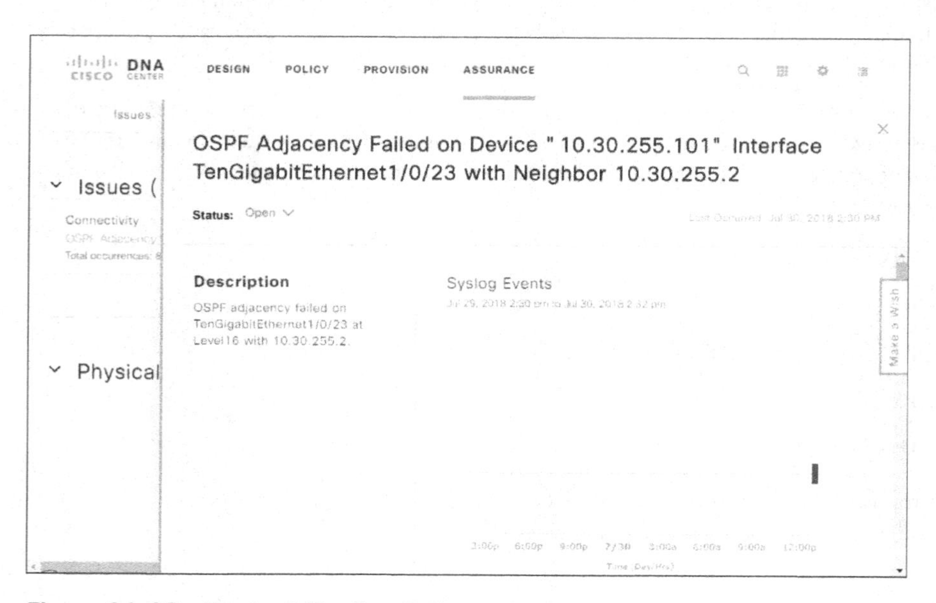

Figure 21-32 *Device 360—Part 2: Issues*

In addition to reporting detected issues, Cisco DNA Assurance also provides step-by-step guided troubleshooting of known issues. Furthermore, the suggested command is run with a single click from within Cisco DNA Assurance, saving you from having to begin a new Secure Shell (SSH) session with the device, log in, find the appropriate interface or process to test, and run the recommended commands. Guided remediation is shown in Figure 21-33.

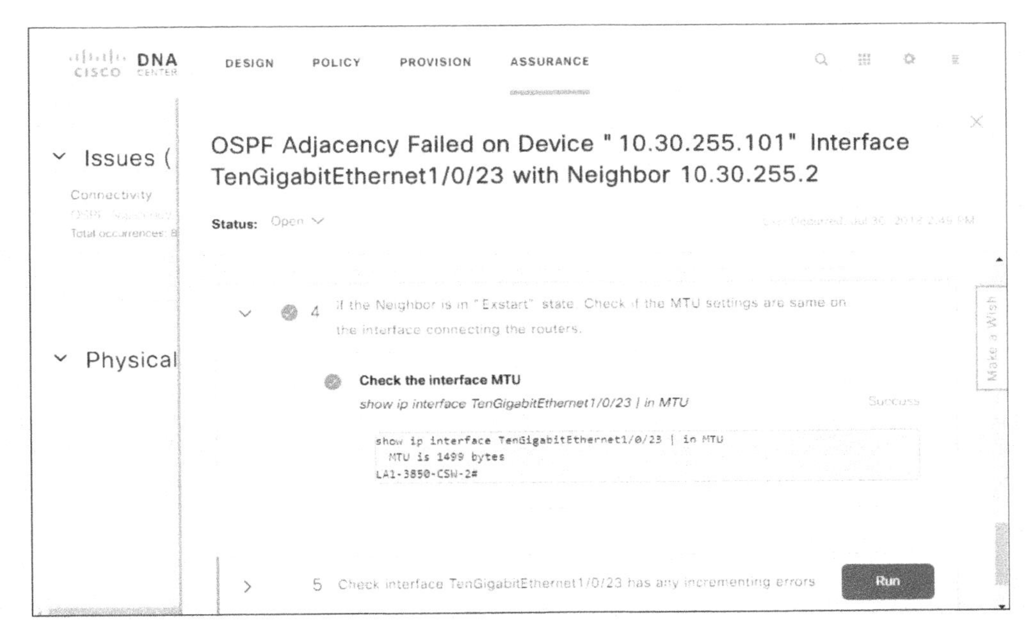

Figure 21-33 *Device 360—Part 3: Guided Remediation*

The physical network topology is displayed, as shown in Figure 21-34, showing the device with all adjacent neighbor devices. Also, a downstream client list can be optionally displayed, detailing which clients may be affected by any issues that the device is experiencing.

At the bottom of the Device 360 pages are the full details about the network device, including

- Device Name
- IP Address
- Device Model
- MAC Address
- Software Version
- Uptime

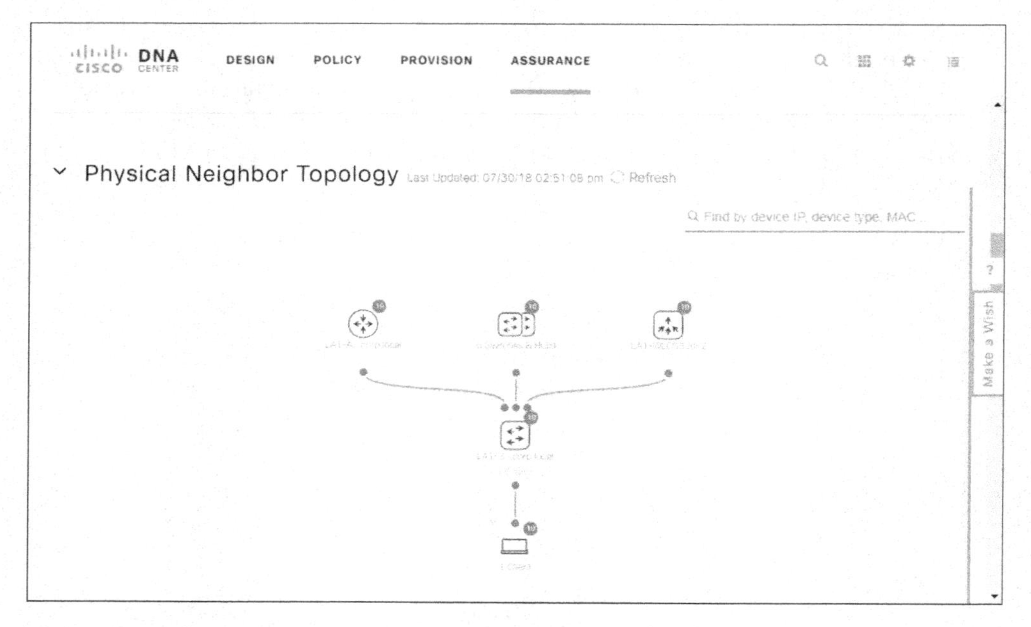

Figure 21-34 *Device 360—Part 4: Physical Topology*

And finally, detailed graphs of all KPIs being monitored on the device, which collectively comprise the device health score, are presented, as shown in Figure 21-35.

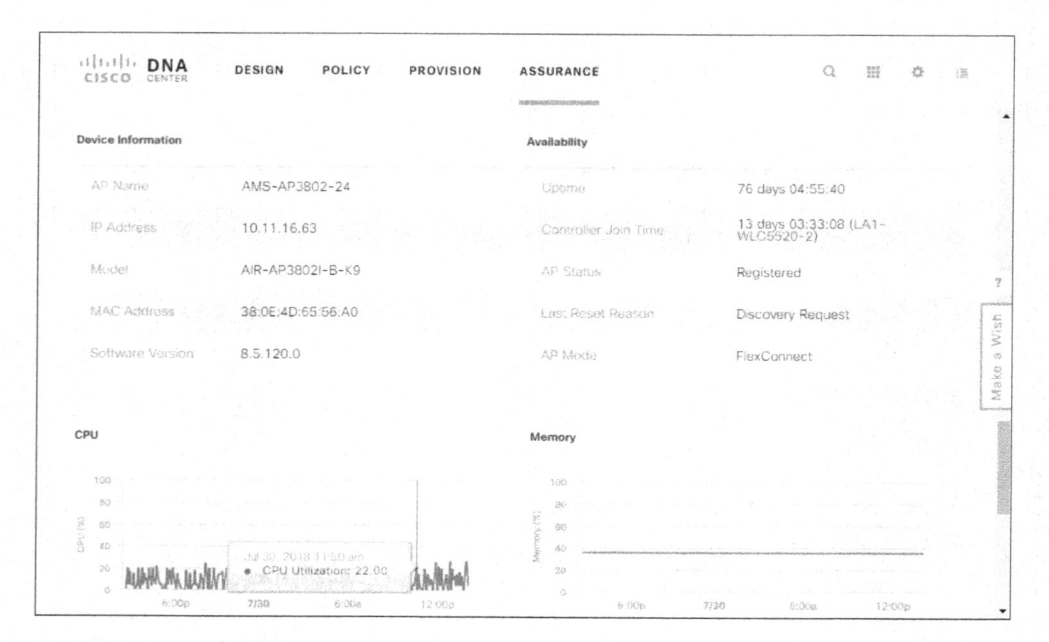

Figure 21-35 *Device 360—Part 5: Device Detailed Information*

Client Health

One of the key requirements of efficient network management is the ability to rapidly assess the state of not only network devices, but also individual endpoint clients. A *client* is any endpoint device detected by the network infrastructure. The client can be actively connected to the network or even simply attempting to connect.

In most scenarios, you need to know about three different and complementary categories of information elements:

- **The state of a given client attempting to connect to the network:** This requirement is typically associated to network testing or troubleshooting, and aims at answering concerns such as "Can the client successfully join the network with the current infrastructure configuration?" or "Why can't this particular client join the network successfully?"
- **The condition of a particular client already connected to the network and sending or receiving traffic:** This requirement is typically related to performance, and aims at answering concerns about quality of experience. The concept of quality of experience covers different meanings and is detailed later in this section.
- **The state or conditions of clients as an aggregate:** This requirement is typically associated to site performance or troubleshooting and aims at determining if a particular region of the network is performing as designed, or if a particular group of clients is receiving the expected quality of experience.

Cisco DNA Assurance provides visibility into each of these three categories. Providing such visibility implies monitoring multiple values over time for each client and each network element. Displaying these values unfiltered through a collection of graphs or table is of limited value, because such process transfers the complexity of the analysis to you, the network operator.

For this reason, Cisco DNA Center Assurance was designed to absorb the complexity and expose meaningful conclusions about the computed condition of each client. This result is reported under the "Client Health" value. This value is representative of the ability of a client to connect, as well as the quality of the client's connection to the network. More KPIs are also planned to be added to the client health score, with the goal of making it fully customizable by operators.

When hundreds or thousands of clients are present in the network at any time, providing a view to each client is often considered as noise. You need to know the general state of the clients, which includes visibility into the number of clients that are in good health and an intuitive way to determine which clients' health has degraded and requires attention. On the Client Health page, shown in Figure 21-36, the main graph shows the relative proportion of clients with good health (score of

8 or more), fair health (4 to 7), poor health (1 to 3), or inactive. Incidentally, the screenshot was taken at Cisco Live Orlando in June 2018 and illustrates Cisco DNA Assurance monitoring the collective health of 17,310 real-user wireless clients.

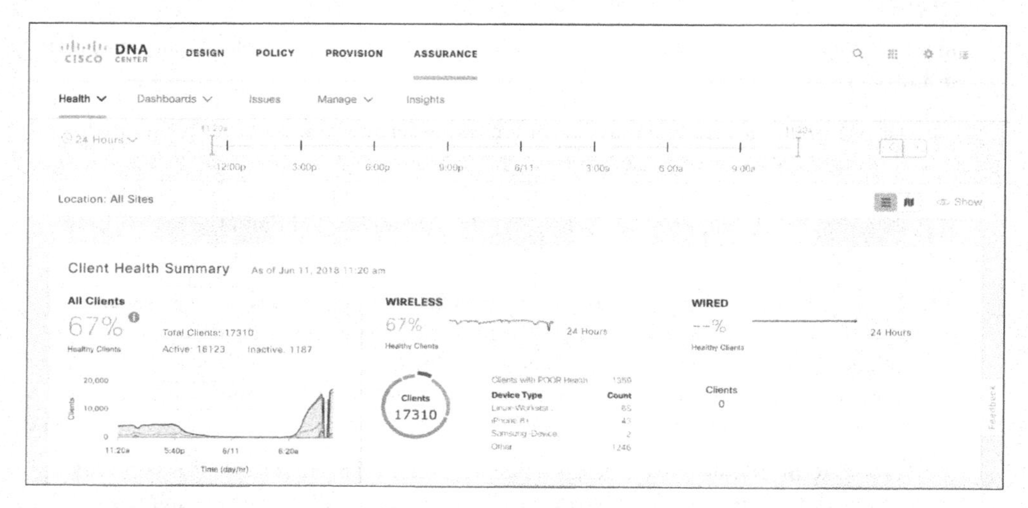

Figure 21-36 *Client Health—Part 1: Client Health Summary*

A graph of the global score variation over the monitored period is also displayed to help you evaluate whether the current score is normal. The graph makes obvious any change in the global score, and provides an efficient way to determine if the overall client health has degraded (or improved) over the monitored period.

A separate donut chart is available for wireless and wired clients, showing in a compact format the total client count of each type, and the relative proportion of clients in bad, fair, and good health. For increased efficiency, the clients in poorest health are counted and listed by operating system. In many scenarios, this representation provides an immediate view into commonalities (e.g., in the example shown in Figure 21-36, most clients in poor health are Linux wireless workstations, which indicates immediately that the common form factor and operating system may be the first parameter to examine in order to understand the root cause of the issue).

Additional details relating to the aggregate experience of clients on the network are next displayed, as shown in Figure 21-37. These include average onboarding times, Received Signal Strength Indicators (RSSIs), Signal to Noise Ratios (SNRs), etc.

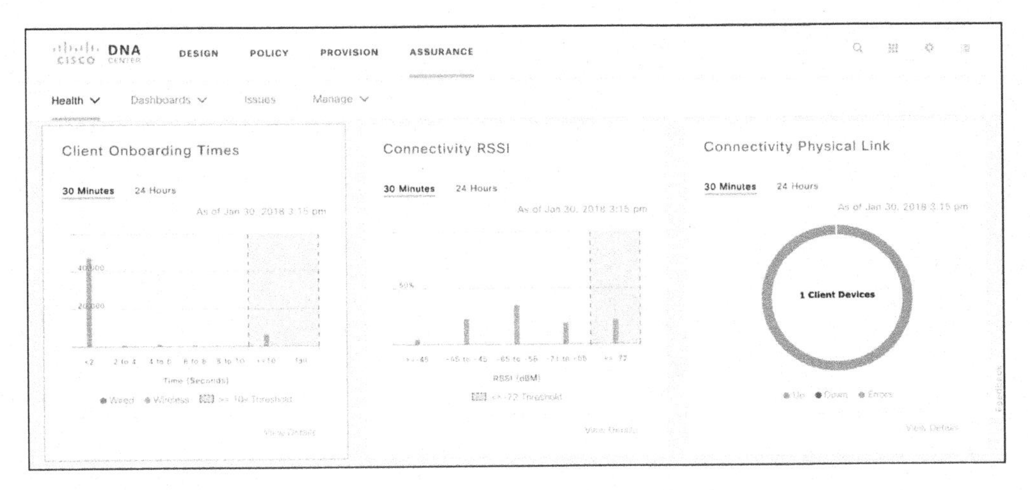

Figure 21-37 *Client Health—Part 2: Client Health Details*

For instance, as can be seen in Figure 21-37, which was incidentally taken from Cisco Live 2018 Barcelona, the vast majority of clients (that onboarded in the 30-minute period during which this sample was taken) were onboarded in less than 2 seconds (over 40,000 events in total), with only a very few requiring more than 10 seconds, and there were no onboarding failures. Such valuable aggregate data helps filter out whether reported issues were truly indicative of the overall user experience or simply outlying anomalous events.

Below these views, and as with Network Health, a tabular view of all client devices can be displayed, filtered by any desired parameter.

Similarly, as with network devices, each client device is hyperlinked to its Client 360 view, as shown in Figures 21-38 to 21-43. Client 360 views include:

- Client Health
- Issues
- Onboarding
- Events
- Path Trace
- Application Experience
- Detail Information

Client 360 views begin with showing the health of a client device over the designated time period, as illustrated in Figure 21-38 for a 24-hour period.

Figure 21-38 *Client 360—Part 1: Client Health Timeline and Events*

Figure 21-38 illustrates a common scenario where a user has multiple devices that may be on the network at a given time; in this particular case, a user named Daphne Blake has an iPad, a PC, and an iPhone on the network. However, at this particular instant (as represented by the two dotted vertical lines on the timeline), her PC is not connected to the network, which is why its health score is shown as 1.

For any client, healthy conditions represent sets of parameters whereby the user performs the tasks at hand without perception of failure or difficulty. Rather than displaying all possible variables in graphs and tables, leaving you the task to estimate if all elements together are constitutive of acceptable conditions, Cisco DNA Assurance groups parameters into the following main categories:

- Onboarding
- Connected experience
- Roaming

The first step for a client is to join the network, which is also known as *onboarding*. For a wireless client, this phase includes 802.11 association, authentication (Open, Pre-Shared Key [PSK], or AAA based), and IP address assignment (typically DHCP). A wired client does not typically include the 802.11 phase, but also goes through the other steps. Data from hundreds of thousands of networks showed that each of these phases is fast, but with large variability. For example, most clients may complete 802.11 associations within a few hundreds of milliseconds, but some isolated clients may suddenly get stuck in a retry cycle for more than a second. However, an onboarding event (including all phases until DHCP completes) within 10 seconds is perceived as "normal" by most users, and 10 seconds is the threshold below which onboarding normality is measured. A global onboarding that completes successfully but takes more than 10 seconds or an individual subphase (e.g., AAA or DHCP) that completes successfully but takes more than 5 seconds is flagged as slow. Successful onboarding is the condition of having an acceptable network experience. Successful onboarding provides 3 points on the individual client health scale.

Once a client is connected, its ability to exchange traffic at optimal speed is a good measure of the connection conditions. For a wired client, this ability is easily achieved if the switch port configuration is correct. This condition is measured by the quantity of link errors on the client port. Less than 1 percent error is expected to provide a perfect score of 10. For a wireless client, that same ability depends on the client radio frequency (RF) distance to its connecting access point. Clients at the edge of the cell may suffer from a degraded service because the AP signal is weak. For this reason, the 7 other points of a wireless client health score are determined by the signal (RSSI) to the AP. Any client actively benefiting from the minimum RSSI values recommended for dynamic cells supporting real time applications (–67 dBm at the edge) receive 7 full health points. Clients with weaker signals receive between 0 and 6 additional points, resulting in an overall health ranging from 3 (connected, poor signal) to 10 (connected, –67 dBm or better signal).

Fundamentally, there is not much difference between onboarding and roaming, however, roaming adds an element of signal degradation, a time of disconnection and discovery of the next access point, and a phase of onboarding. All these elements are measured during onboarding. It is often said that roaming is a form of onboarding, but for an already known client. With this approach in mind, the elements of roaming are integrated into the client health score as onboarding events.

Cisco DNA Assurance provides a compact, easy-to-leverage, yet multilevel view into the network. Because onboarding time, signal level (for wireless clients), and physical link connectivity (for wired clients) are key components of the client network experience, it is critical for you to have a view of the "normality" level or baseline for each of these components. What is the usual onboarding time? Is the onboarding time increasing? How many clients are within the standard range, and how many exceed the normality thresholds? Having immediate access to this type of information makes the difference between easy planning with proactive troubleshooting and reactive panic.

Below the Client Health score timeline, any issues that the client is experiencing are presented (in a manner similar to Device 360s). Below this, the onboarding experience of clients is also graphically summarized, as shown in Figure 21-39.

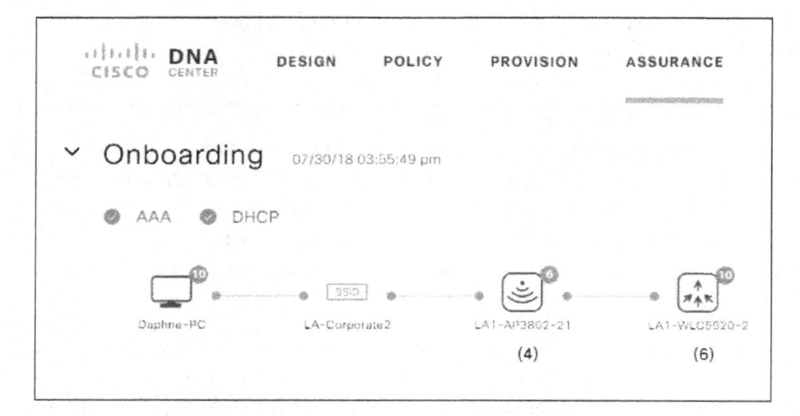

Figure 21-39 *Client 360—Part 2: Onboarding Experience*

Below onboarding in a Client 360 view, a powerful troubleshooting tool is presented: Path Trace (which is also available in Network and Application 360 views). Path Trace is discussed in more detail in its own section later in the chapter.

Next, the Client 360 view displays the Application Experience of the client's apps, as shown in Figures 21-40 and 41.

CISCO DNA CENTER DESIGN POLICY PROVISION ASSURANCE

Application Experience BETA As of Jul 30, 2018 4:13 pm Refresh

Business Relevant Business Irrelevant Default

Application (5) Export

Filter Find

Name	Host Name	Health: Most Recent	Health: Last 24 Hours	Usage	Average Throughput	Average Bandwidth Utilization (%)	Traffic Class	Packet Loss (%): Max	Packet Loss (%): Average	Latency: Max	Latency: Ave
ssh	--	4	View	905.54 MB	87.92 Kbps	0.12	ops-admin-mgmt	100	33	4 min	
cifs	--	1	View	948.06 MB	92.05 Kbps	0.13	bulk-data	100	17	58 sec	

Figure 21-40 *Client 360—Part 3: Application Experience*

Each individual application that the client is running from any given device is monitored—not only in terms of quantitative metrics (i.e., how much application traffic is being generated?) but also in terms of qualitative metrics (i.e., how well is the application being treated over the network?). As with other health scores, Application Health is a composite metric, composed of several KPIs, including latency, jitter, loss, application delay (i.e., server delay), etc. These individual KPI details are also displayed, as shown in Figure 21-41.

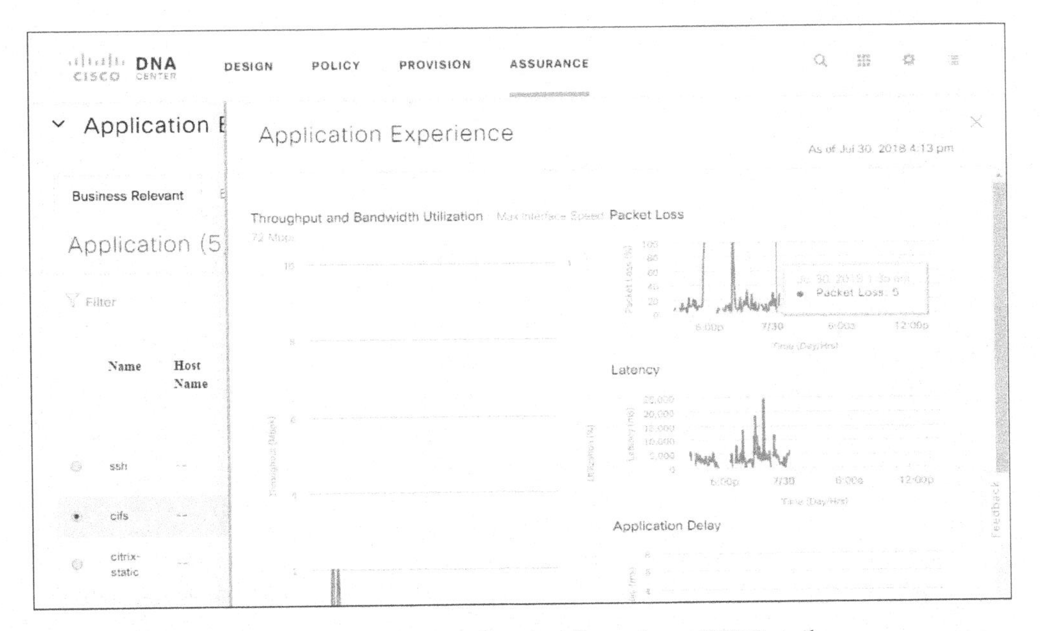

Figure 21-41 *Client 360—Part 4: Application Experience KPI Details*

The final section of a Client 360 view shows all the details pertaining to the device. These include static information, such as:

- User name
- Host name
- MAC Address
- IP Address
- Device Type
- Operating System
- Virtual LAN (VLAN) ID
- Band
- Spatial Streams
- Channel Width

However, the device Detail Information section also presents dynamic details, such as RF KPIs, as illustrated in Figure 21-42.

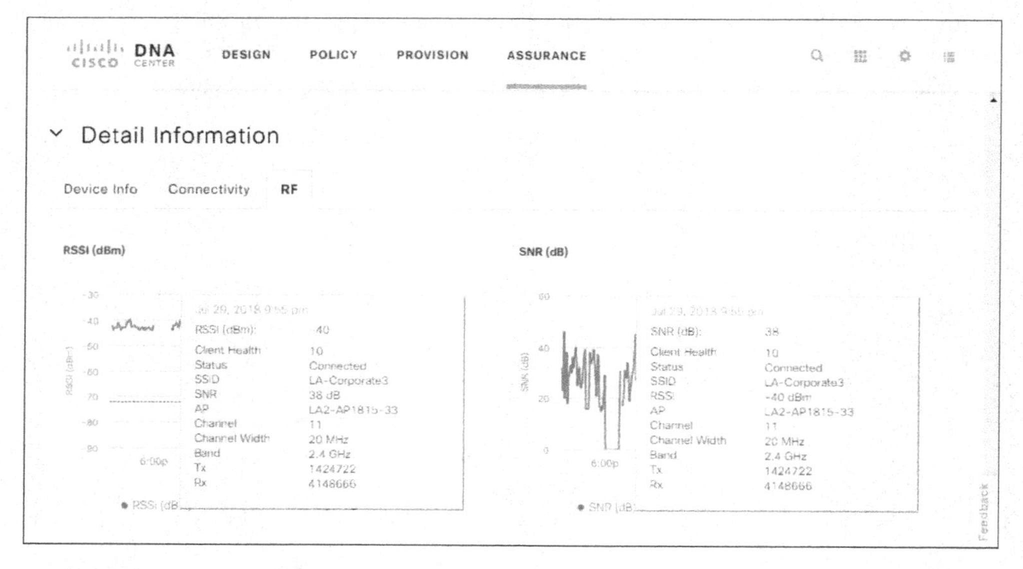

Figure 21-42 *Client 360—Part 5: RF Details*

One last view that bears explicit mentioning is exclusive to Apple iOS devices, as it is a result of the Apple/Cisco partnership. Apple devices can share their perspective of the network with Cisco DNA Assurance, including any/all APs they see, complete with relative signal Received Signal Strength Indicator (RSSI) and Signal to Noise Ratios (SNRs), but also the reasons that a client disconnected from the network (such as device idle, user-triggered disassociations, failures, etc.), as shown in Figure 21-43.

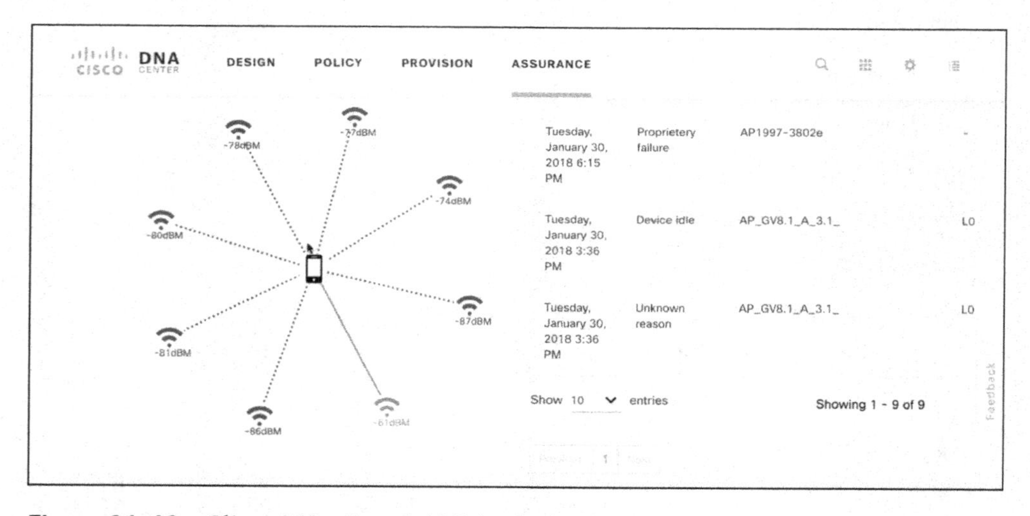

Figure 21-43 *Client 360—Part 6: iOS Analytics*

Application Health

Once users have onboarded onto the network, it is not uncommon that they immediately begin taking the network for granted...that is, until they experience issues with their applications. As such, Cisco DNA Assurance also monitors the health of the applications on the network.

The Application Health page shows a graphical summary of the health of the applications on the network, as illustrated in Figure 21-44.

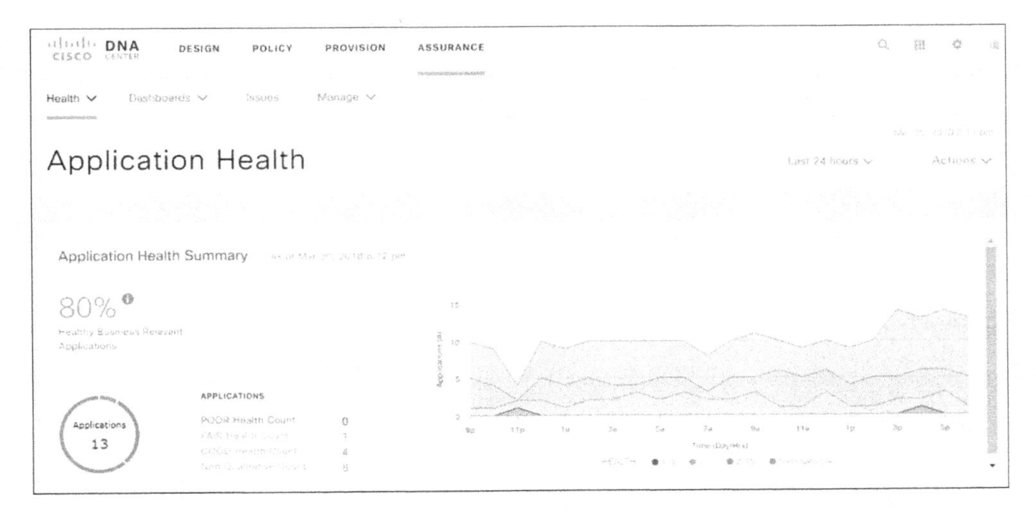

Figure 21-44 *Application Health—Application Health Summary*

Below this summary, as with the network and Client Health pages, is a tabular listing of all applications and their individual health metrics, from which users can select any application by its hyperlink to view the application's 360 page, as shown in Figures 21-45 through 21-47.

The Application 360 page consists of:

- Overall Application Health score timeline and details, as shown in Figure 21-45
- Application Experience table (by region), as shown in Figure 21-46
- Application Experience KPI details, as shown in Figure 21-47

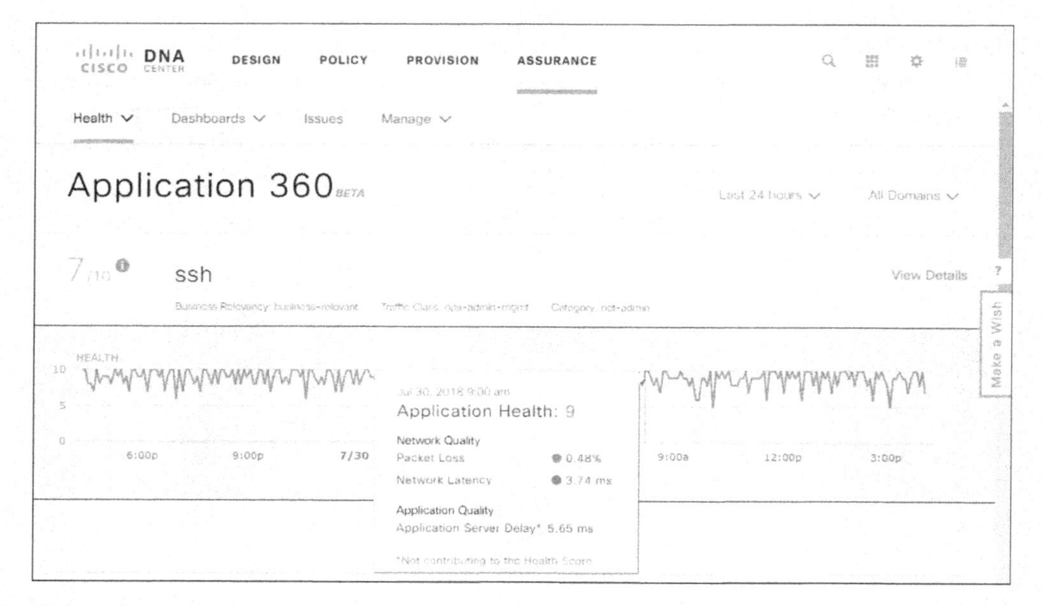

Figure 21-45 *Application 360—Application Health Timeline*

CISCO DNA CENTER DESIGN POLICY PROVISION ASSURANCE

Application Experience

Filter Export Find

Source Location	Health		Clients	Usage	Average Throughput	Average Bandwidth Utilization (%)	DSCP		Packet Loss (%)		Latency (ms)	
	Most Recent	Last 24 Hours					Marking	Preservation	Max	Average	Max	Average
USA	10	View	3	1.45 GB	140.53 Kbps	0.01	CS2	No	50	0.17	102	5
USA/LA	4	View	1	33.88 MB	3.21 Kbps	0	CS2	No	100	55	154858	2681
USA/SM	1	View	1	310.38 MB	29.43 Kbps	0	CS2	No	100	37	306643	11593

Figure 21-46 *Application 360—Application Experience Table (by Region)*

Two important questions to address at this point are how these application metrics are measured and how a health score is calculated from these measurements, as discussed next.

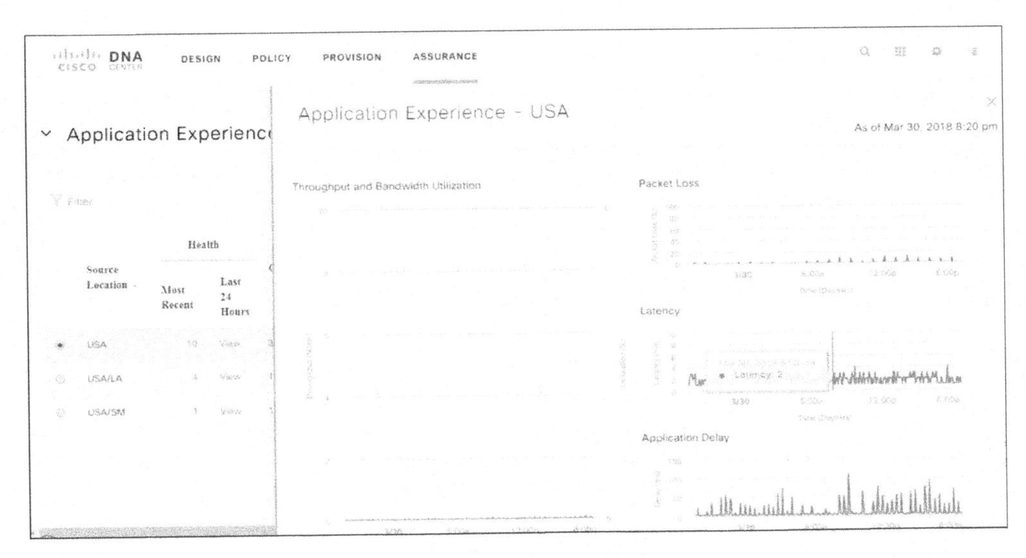

Figure 21-47 *Application 360—Application Experience KPI Details*

The answer to the first question is that a variety of tools can be used, including

- **Cisco IOS Flexible NetFlow (FNF) with Application Visibility and Control (AVC):** Measures application traffic quantity (i.e., how many bytes/packets per application flow)
- **Cisco Performance Monitor (PerfMon):** Measures latency and loss of Real-Time Protocol (RTP) applications, like voice and video
- **Application Response Time (ART) Monitor:** Measures network and application latency, as well as loss (as reflected by Transmission Control Protocol [TCP] retransmissions) for TCP applications
- **Cisco Class-based Quality-of-Service MIB:** Measures packets matched, transmitted, dropped, etc. on a per-interface queue basis
- **Cisco IOS IP Service Level Agreement (IP SLA):** A proactive monitoring tool that uses probes to test (among other metrics) loss, latency, and jitter
- APIs to application servers, clients, and/or agents

Let's consider a couple of these tools in a bit more depth. First, let's take a look at PerfMon.

PerfMon takes a close look at the RTP headers of voice and video packets and makes performance calculations on the metadata contained therein, as shown in Figure 21-48.

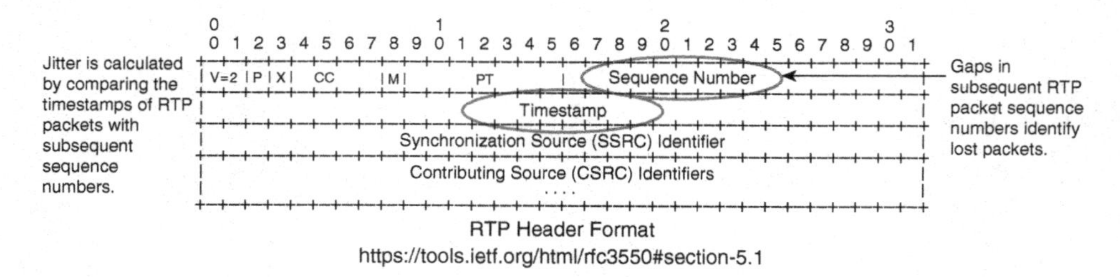

Figure 21-48 *Calculating Jitter and Loss from RTP Metadata*

Figure 21-48 highlights that within every RTP packet there is a sequence number and a timestamp. As packets flow through a network device, gaps in sequence numbers are noted and identified as packet drops. Similarly, when the timestamps of these packets are compared on a packet-by-packet basis with the time they are received by a network device (such as a router), then induced jitter can also be calculated.

These maximum, minimum and average loss and jitter values are then exported (along with other flow details) in FNF to a NetFlow collector (in this case, NDP).

But what about TCP-based applications? Although it's true that TCP contains a sequence number, from which retransmissions are detected (inferring packet loss), it does not contain any timestamp metadata. So how can latency be measured for TCP?

The answer lies in understanding the TCP operations and measuring the gaps between various signals, as shown in Figure 21-49, which illustrates Application Response Time (ART) operation.

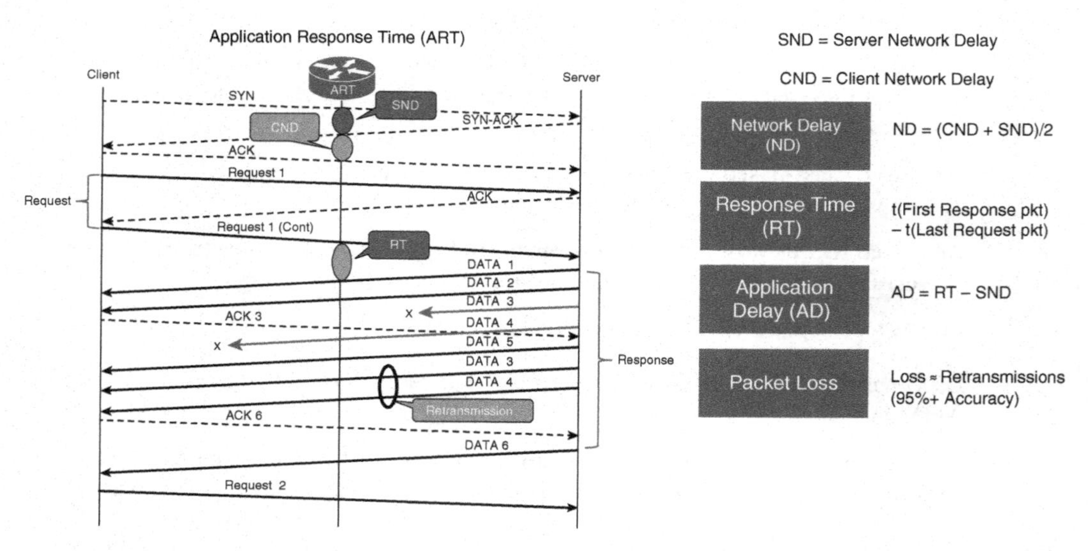

Figure 21-49 *Calculating Network and Application Delay and Loss from TCP Flows Using Application Response Time*

Specifically, ART calculates

- The time delta from the initial TCP segment with the Synchronize (SYN) bit set, as compared to the TCP segment with the Synchronize and Acknowledge (SYN-ACK) bits set, which represents the Server Network Delay (SND); that is, the network delay on the server side of the router.
- The time delta from the initial SYN-ACK to the initial ACK as Client Network Delay (CND), which represents the network delay on the client side of the router.
- Adding these two delay components together provides total Round Trip Time (RTT); one-way Network Delay (ND) divides this result by 2, specifically ND = (CND + SND) / 2.

Note Establishing a TCP session via this three-way handshake does not require any application processing; as such, it provides a baseline of network-only delay.

- Response Time (RT) is measured by calculating the time delta between the first response packet and the last request packet.
- When the Server Network Delay is removed from the Response Time result, you have an accurate indication of how long the application took to process the request, which is called the Application Delay (AD).

As with PerfMon, ART include all these metrics in the FNF export of the application flow to NDP, which performs further analysis and converts these metrics into Application Health scores.

Application Health scores are primarily comprised of two main components:

- **Network Quality of Service (QoS):** Network QoS is a reflection of how well the application is transported across the network, and is composed of three primary service level attributes, per the industry de facto standard, IETF RFC 4594:[2]
  - Loss
  - Latency
  - Jitter
- **Application Quality of Experience (QoE):** Application QoE is a reflection of the end-to-end user experience, which includes not only the network transport, but also the client and/or server experience. As a previously discussed example illustrated, a video application client can adjust resolution and/or frame rates to achieve good results for QoS, but the user experience is downgraded in the process. As such, this downgrading of user experience is not being captured by QoS statistics; similarly, operations, issues, or errors occurring on application clients and servers may likewise compromise user experience but are not reflected by QoS statistics.

2 "Configuration Guidelines for DiffServ Service Classes," https://tools.ietf.org/html/rfc4594.

Therefore, Cisco DNA Assurance monitors both sets of metrics and accurately reflects each in overall application health.

> **Note** At the time of writing, only Cisco routers support PerfMon and ART. However, Cisco engineers are currently scoping the addition of these functions to UADP-based switches and to Elastic Wireless LAN Controllers (eWLC).

The next step in accurately representing application health is to normalize these metrics into scores to be compared (and weighted) against each other. For example, if the network reports a value of 213 ms for WebEx latency, is this Good? Fair? Bad? What about a measurement of 83 ms for WebEx jitter?

To normalize such KPIs, Cisco has applied standards-based guidance in its Application Health score calculations. For example, in the case of latency, ITU-T G.114[3] provides scales that express quality scores for increasing latency thresholds, as shown in Figure 21-50.

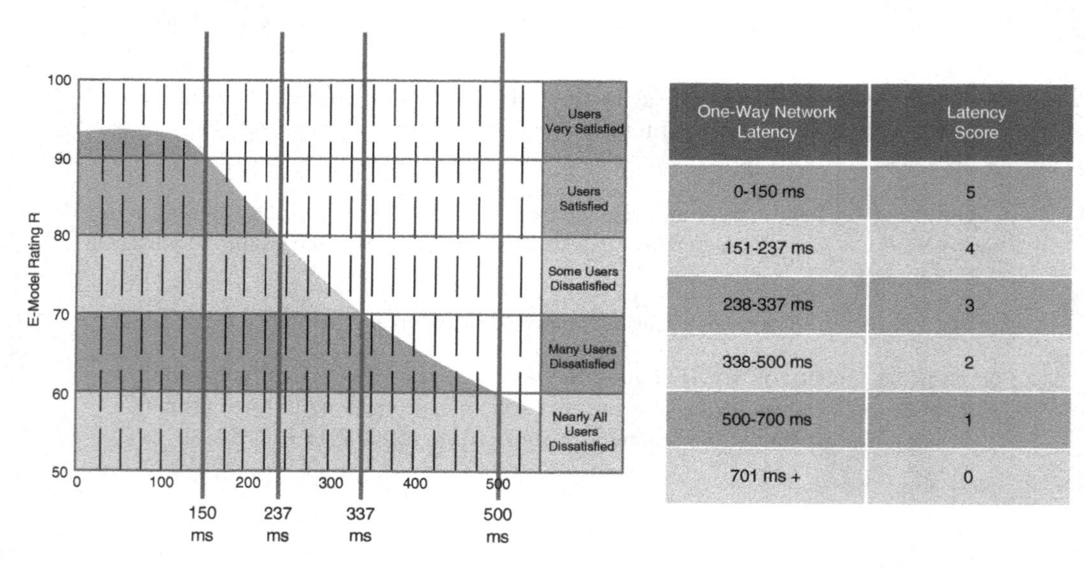

One-Way Network Latency	Latency Score
0-150 ms	5
151-237 ms	4
238-337 ms	3
338-500 ms	2
500-700 ms	1
701 ms +	0

Figure 21-50 *Converting Application KPIs into Scores—ITU-T G.114 Latency Example*

Similar exercises were done for jitter and loss, based on guidance found in ITU-T Y.1541.[4]

Because not every application is equally sensitive to loss, latency, and/or jitter, an appropriate weighing was made on a per-service-class and per-SLA basis. To make this weighing, again relevant standards were consulted; specifically the guidance found in RFC 4594 was applied, as summarized in Table 21-1.

---

3 "One-way transmission time," https://www.itu.int/rec/T-REC-G.114-200305-I/en.

4 "Network performance objectives for IP-based services," https://www.itu.int/rec/T-REC-Y.1541-201112-I/en.

Table 21-1 *RFC 4594 Service Class Characteristics Table (RFC 4594 Figure 2)*

Service Class Name	Traffic Characteristics	Tolerance to Loss	Tolerance to Delay	Tolerance to Jitter
Network Control	Variable size packets, mostly inelastic short messages, but traffic can also burst (BGP)	Low	Low	Yes
Telephony	Fixed-size small packets, constant emission rate, inelastic and low-rate flows	Very Low	Very Low	Very Low
Signaling	Variable size packets, somewhat bursty short-lived flows	Low	Low	Yes
Multimedia Conferencing	Variable size packets, constant transmit intervals, rate adaptive, reacts to loss	Low – Medium	Very Low	Low
Real-Time Interactive	RTP/UDP streams, inelastic, mostly variable rate	Low	Very Low	Low
Multimedia Streaming	Variable size packets, elastic with variable rate	Low – Medium	Medium	Yes
Broadcast Video	Constant and variable rate, inelastic, non-bursty flows	Very Low	Medium	Low
Low-Latency Data	Variable rate, bursty short-lived elastic flows	Low	Low – Medium	Yes
OAM	Variable size packets, elastic & inelastic flows	Low	Medium	Yes
High-Throughput Data	Variable rate, bursty long-lived elastic flows	Low	Medium – High	Yes
Standard	A bit of everything	Not Specified	Not Specified	Not Specified
Low-Priority Data	Non-real-time and elastic	High	High	Yes

Voice, video, and application experts, both Cisco-internal and customers, were consulted in setting default scoring thresholds for these metrics.

With such an approach, Application Health scores provide a composite metric as to how an application is performing, without overwhelming you with data (and in some cases, noise) that you have to interpret. All underlying metric data are included in 360 views, as previously shown.

In addition to using network-measured KPIs, Application Health scores also include data from external sources via APIs. Such integrations help you "see" into areas that were traditionally blind spots, as illustrated in Figure 21-51.

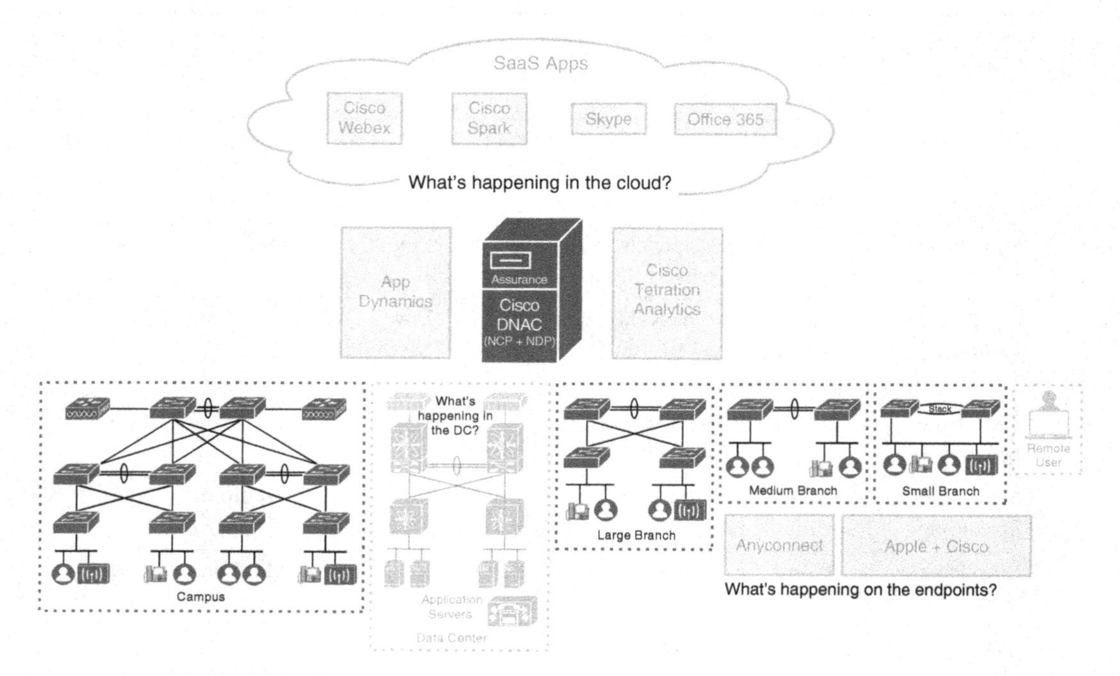

Figure 21-51 *Enterprise Networking "Blind Spots"*

Two such integration examples relating to Application Health include AppDynamics integration and Microsoft Skype for Business integration, each of which is discussed in turn.

> **Note** At the time of writing, Cisco DNA Assurance integration with AppDynamics is in the Proof-of-Concept stage (i.e., *not* a shipping feature); coverage is included here for the sake of illustrating the flexibility and power of integrations with applications/ application agents.

AppDynamics Integration

Application issues are particularly challenging to solve, as they often involve finger pointing between the network team and the application teams, as illustrated in Figure 21-52.

Figure 21-52 *Application Issue Triage Decision: Is It a Network Issue or an Application Issue?*

The Cisco DNA Assurance/AppDynamics integration primary use case is to address the critical application experience triage question: is it an application issue or a network issue? Networking and app teams are typically very independent and lack visibility into each other's domains; however, troubleshooting application issues generally requires the cooperation of both teams, as sharing insights across the enterprise and data center domains is valuable to both teams.

AppDynamics software includes a concept very similar to Cisco DNA Assurance Application Health scores, namely the Transaction Scorecard, as shown in Figure 21-53.

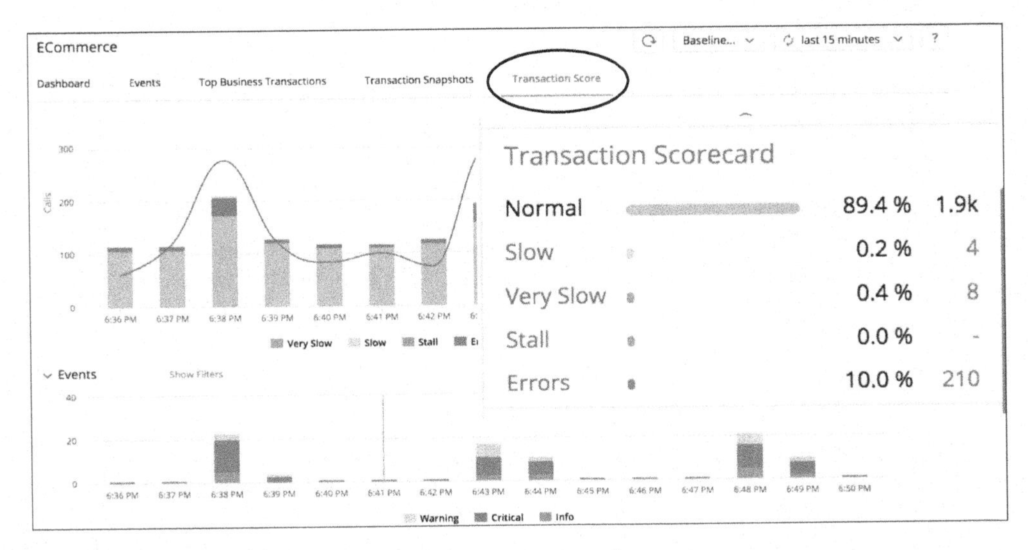

Figure 21-53 *AppDynamics Transaction Scorecard*

Like the Cisco DNA Assurance Application Health score, the AppDynamics Transaction Scorecard is a composite metric composed of several KPIs relating to application performance, albeit in a data center/runtime environment (as opposed to an enterprise network environment).

As such, the Cisco DNA Assurance and AppDynamics engineering teams developed APIs to exchange information between these systems, so that the AppDynamics Transaction Scorecard is ingested by Cisco DNA Assurance. The Transaction Scorecard is used not only as part of the overall Application Health calculation (in addition to Network Quality KPIs), but also to make explicit on "which side of the fence" the application issue is occurring (i.e., over the enterprise network or within the data center, or even possibly in both places). A screenshot of Cisco DNA Assurance featuring AppDynamics integration is shown in Figure 21-54.

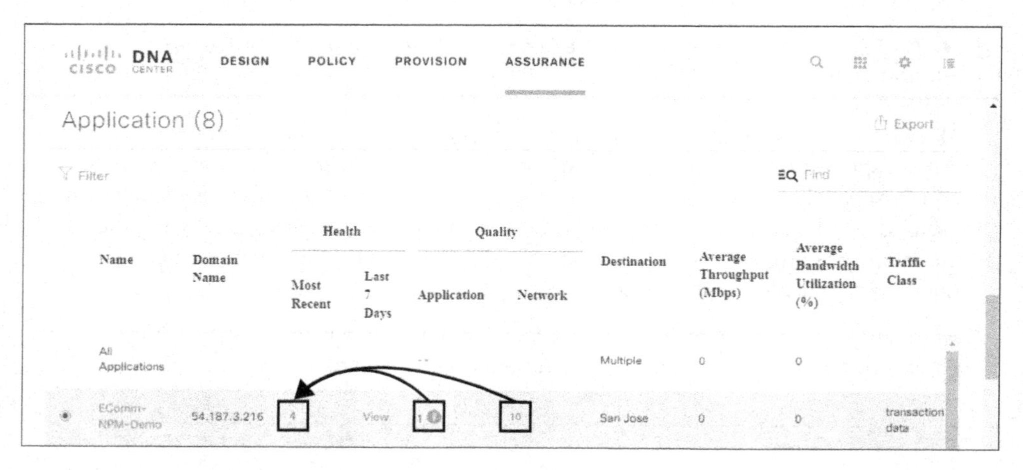

Figure 21-54 *Cisco DNA Assurance/AppDynamics Integration—Part 1: (External) Application Quality Metrics Integration into Application Health Scores*

As shown in Figure 21-54, external data (in this case the data comprising the AppDynamics Transaction Scorecard) was ingested and included (along with Network Quality data) into the Application Health score calculation. In this example, the overall Application Health score for the EComm-NPM-Demo application is 4, but is composed of two parts:

- The Application Quality score (sourced from AppDynamics), which is 1
- The Network Quality score, which is 10

As such, with a quick glance, even a Tier 1 analyst can make a confident triage decision: this is an *application* issue (and the network is innocent!).

Additionally, hovering over the "information" icon next to the Application Quality score displays the AppDynamics Transaction Scorecard, as shown in Figure 21-55, providing at a quick glance some additional details pertaining to this application's performance within the data center.

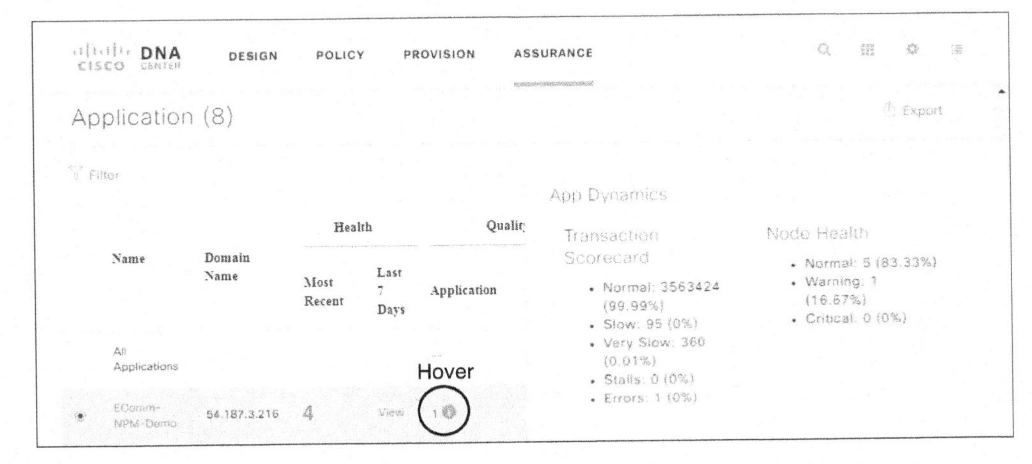

Figure 21-55 *Cisco DNA Assurance/AppDynamics Integration—Part 2: AppDynamics Transaction Scorecard Details*

Additionally, to facilitate a troubleshooting workflow, the integration supports contextual cross-launch. For example, if you want to dig deeper, simply click the Application Quality score and you are cross-launched directly into AppDynamics Controller to the specific application's Transaction Scorecard page, as shown in Figure 21-56.

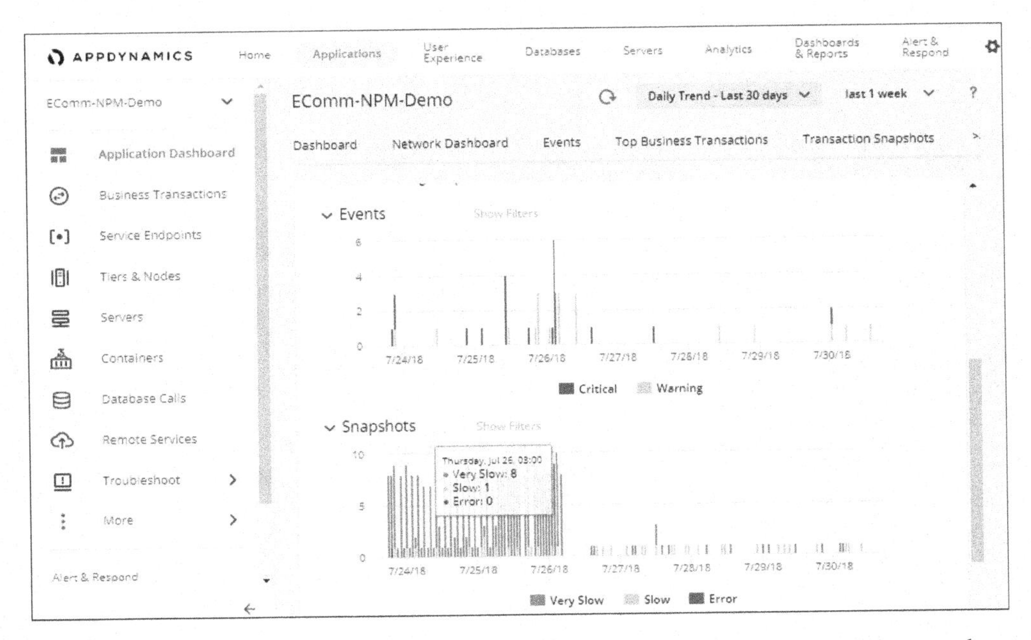

Figure 21-56 *Cisco DNA Assurance/AppDynamics Integration—Part 3: Contextual Cross-Launch into AppDynamics*

From within AppDynamics, even Tier 1 analysts "trained to look for red lights" can quickly zero in on root-cause issues, such as data center network issues, server issues, or even code issues. As shown in Figure 21-57, a critical issue has been flagged for the business transaction health (indicating a code issue), and also a server issue was flagged (albeit as a warning).

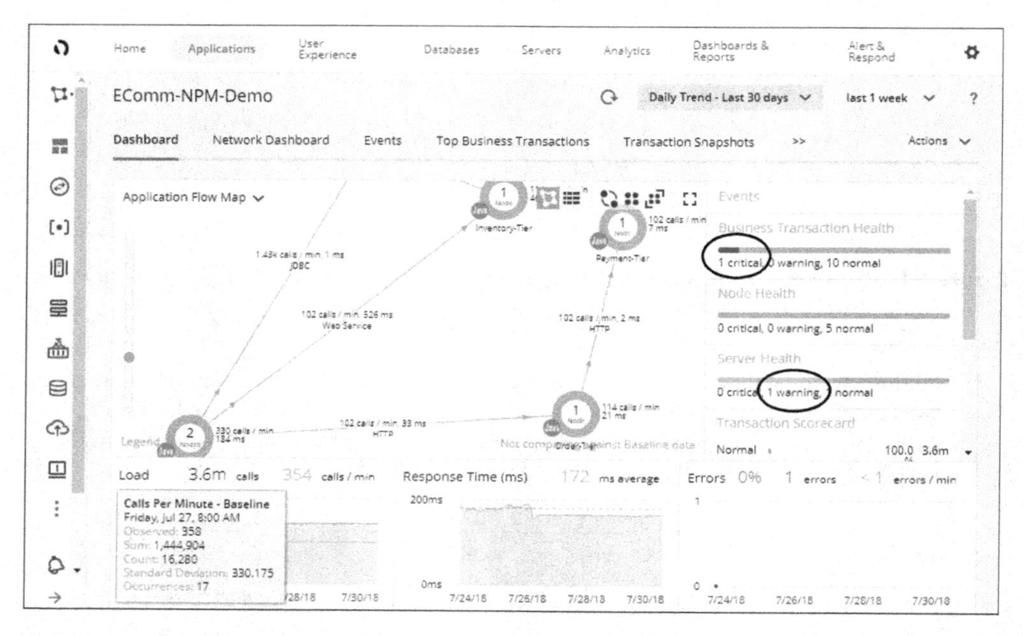

Figure 21-57 *Cisco DNA Assurance/AppDynamics Integration—Part 4: AppDynamics Dashboard Indicating Transaction and Server Issues*

Zooming into these respective issues leads you to the root-cause details. For example, as shown in Figure 21-58, the business transaction health critical error is the result of excessive execution times of the /json/cart/.GET transaction.

Drilling down even further gets to the specific call and reasons for the error(s), as shown in Figures 21-59 and 21-60.

AppDynamics also monitors server resources so that problems can be obviated. In this example, AppDynamics has noted that the server that this app is executing on is running out of disk space, as shown in Figure 21-61.

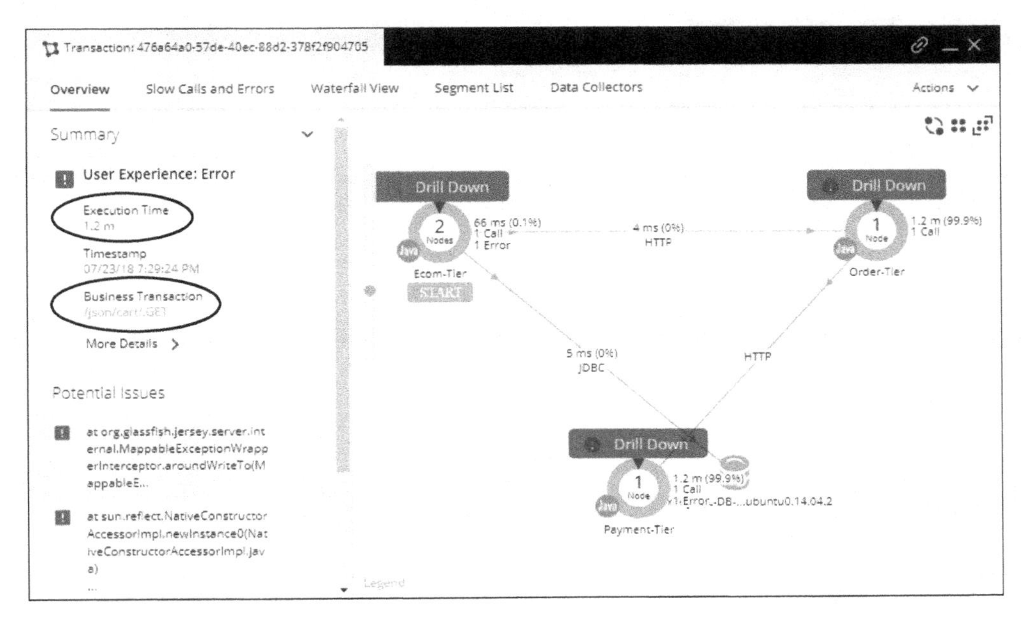

Figure 21-58 *Cisco DNA Assurance/AppDynamics Integration—Part 5: Identifying Root-Cause Issues in Code*

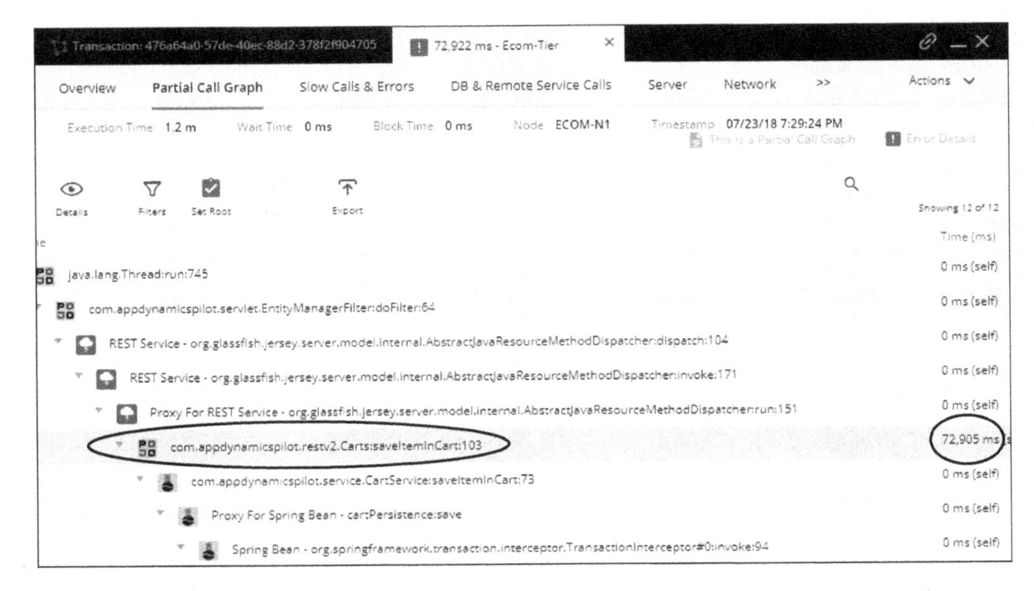

Figure 21-59 *Cisco DNA Assurance/AppDynamics Integration—Part 6: Identifying Root-Cause Issues in Code (continued)*

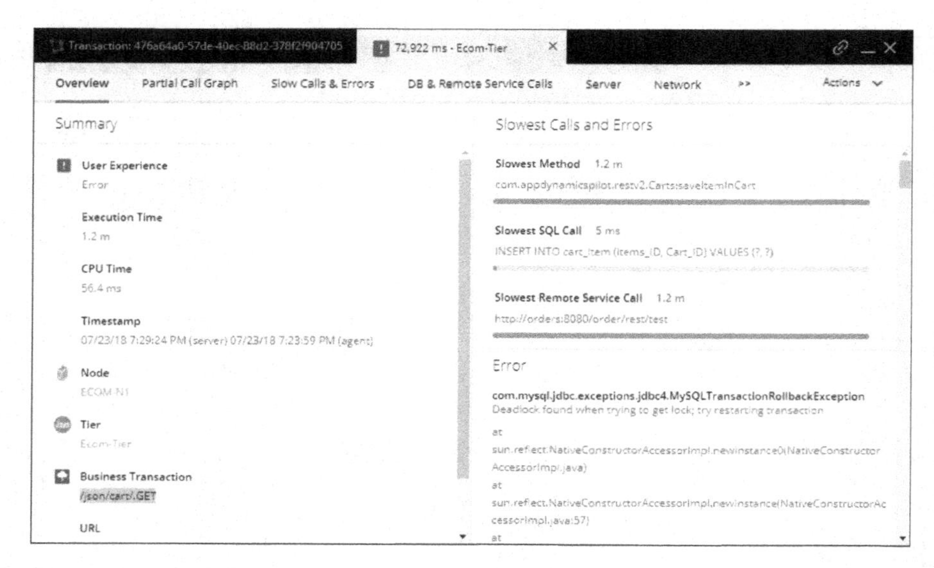

Figure 21-60 *Cisco DNA Assurance/AppDynamics Integration—Part 7: Identifying Root-Cause Issues in Code (continued)*

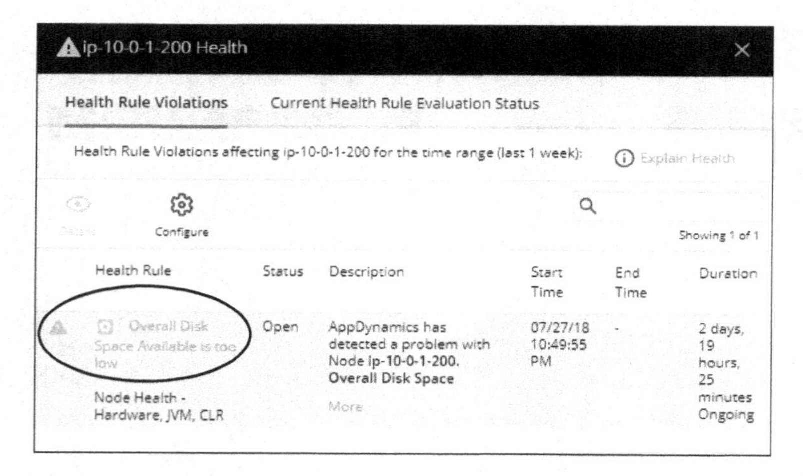

Figure 21-61 *Cisco DNA Assurance/AppDynamics Integration—Part 8: Identifying Resource Limitation Root-Causes*

The goal of the Cisco DNA Assurance and AppDynamics integration is not only to ingest Transaction Scorecard data to generate a more holistic and representative Application Health score, but also to share issues between these two systems so that network operators are alerted to specific issues happening in the data center (and vice versa). Additionally, Cisco DNA Center supports integration with IT Service Management (ITSM) applications, like ServiceNow. As such, when a ticket for an application issue is generated, both network data (sourced from Cisco DNA Center) and application data (sourced from AppDynamics) are logged to the same ticket, to prevent the "IT routing loop" referenced earlier in Figure 21-52.

Note The Cisco DNA Assurance/AppDynamics integration is (at the time of writing) in its early stages; significant additional integration use cases are also planned.

Microsoft Skype for Business Integration

Cisco DNA is an open, extensible, and developer-friendly architecture; as such, many integrations of Cisco DNA Assurance are being researched including

- Integrating directly with applications, such as Microsoft Skype for Business (S4B), Cisco WebEx, Cisco Unified Call Manager (CUCM), Cisco Jabber, Microsoft Office 356, etc.
- Integrating with peer analytics systems, such as Cisco Tetration, Meraki, and vAnalytics.
- Integrating with Cisco AnyConnect Network Visibility Module for additional visibility into client health
- Evolving the Cisco/Apple strategic partnership to provide additional analytics solutions

One of the first of these integrations pursued was to integrate with Microsoft Skype for Business (S4B) because it already publishes several key application QoE KPIs via its APIs, including

- S4B Voice KPIs:
  - Call Volume
  - Average Mean Opinion Score (MOS) Scores
  - Poor Call Percentage
  - Round-Trip Times
  - Packet Loss
  - Jitter
  - Master Concealed Ratio
  - Master Stretched Ratio
  - Master Compressed Ratio
- S4B Video KPIs:
  - Call Volume (Total/Wireless/VPN/External)
  - Poor Call Percentage
  - Average Bit-Rates
  - Low Bit-Rates

    - Outbound Packet Loss
    - Outbound Average Frame Rates
    - Inbound Average Frame Rates
    - Client Health
- S4B Application Sharing KPIs:
    - Call Volume (Total/Wireless/VPN/External)
    - Poor Call Percentage
    - Jitter
    - Average Relative One-Way Delay
    - Average Tile Processing Latency
    - Total Spoiled Tile Percentage

Perhaps you may wonder: Why ingest performance metrics from applications like Skype for Business when (as discussed earlier in this section) the network can measure application performance? There are, in fact, two key reasons to do so:

- Network measurements for KPIs such as loss, latency, and jitter are made midstream; if these KPIs are induced downstream from the network-measurement point, then these are not reported to Cisco DNA Assurance, as shown in Figure 21-62. As such, measuring and reporting these KPIs from application endpoint devices serves to augment network data and provide a more accurate report of network QoS.
- The network can measure and report on quality of service (QoS), but not quality of experience (QoE), as illustrated in Figure 21-63. Today's video codecs can react to network congestion by lowering frame rates and/or resolution levels to the point where packet flows may look perfect from the network QoS perspective, even during periods when the user experience may be significantly degraded due to video quality downgrading. As such, combining network data with application data provides a more holistic view of the user's application experience.

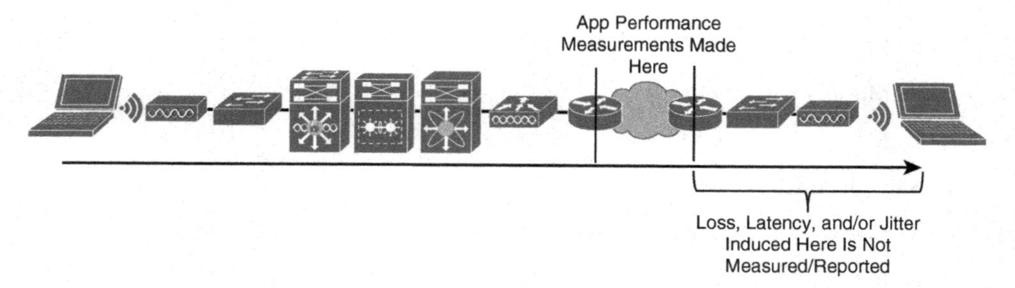

Figure 21-62 *Loss, Latency, or Jitter Induced Downstream from Network Measurement Points for RTP Apps Is Not Reported to Cisco DNA Assurance*

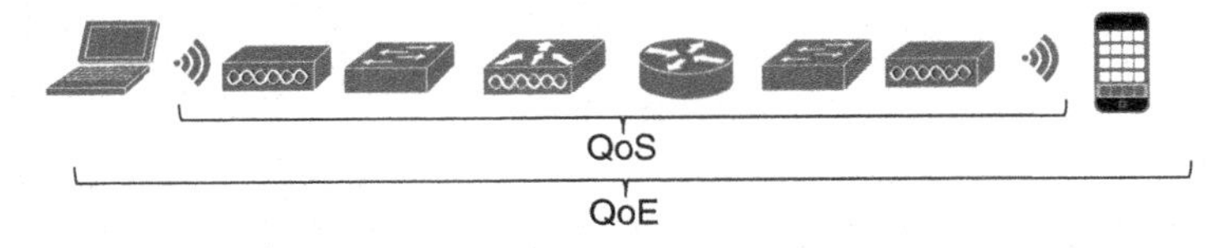

Figure 21-63 *Network Can Measure QoS but Not Application QoE*

As such, Cisco DNA Assurance integration with Skype for Business combines network-sourced KPIs with application (S4B) reported KPIs and presents these in a consolidated view, as shown in Figure 21-64 (this view expands on the Client 360 Application Experience—KPI Details side-panel view shown earlier in Figure 21-41).

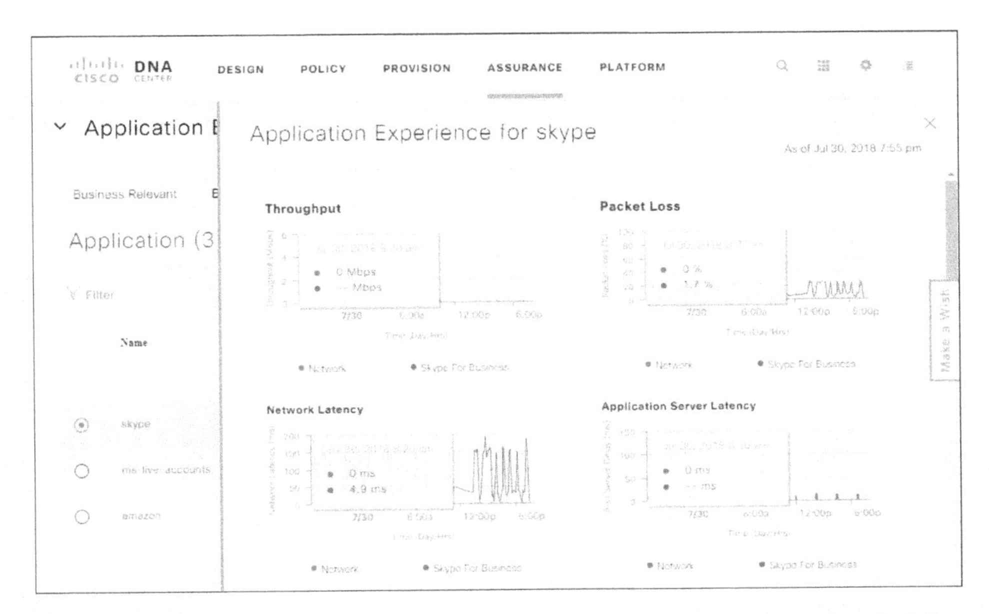

Figure 21-64 *Cisco DNA Assurance/Skype for Business Integration—Part 1: S4B-Reported KPIs Augmenting Network-Reported KPIs*

As shown in Figure 21-64:

- The network reported 0 ms of latency, but S4B endpoints reported 4.9 ms of latency (as these endpoints are measuring latency end to end, rather than to/from a midstream point, like a router).
- The network reported packet loss of 0 percent, but evidently loss was induced downstream from this network measurement point, as the endpoints have reported loss of 1.7 percent.

This example serves to illustrate how application data can serve to complement and augment network data, providing a more accurate and holistic report of user application experience. Additionally, comparing and contrasting network measurements with endpoint measurements serves also to isolate the problem domain (e.g., answers whether the problem is occurring upstream or downstream from the network measurement point).

Scrolling further down, MOS scores are also reported by S4B clients. MOS is a QoE metric that cannot be measured by the network on a per-flow basis (although it can be estimated by tools such as IP SLA for synthetic flows). The (color-coded) MOS scores for all calls made by the client within the specified time period are reported, as shown in Figure 21-65.

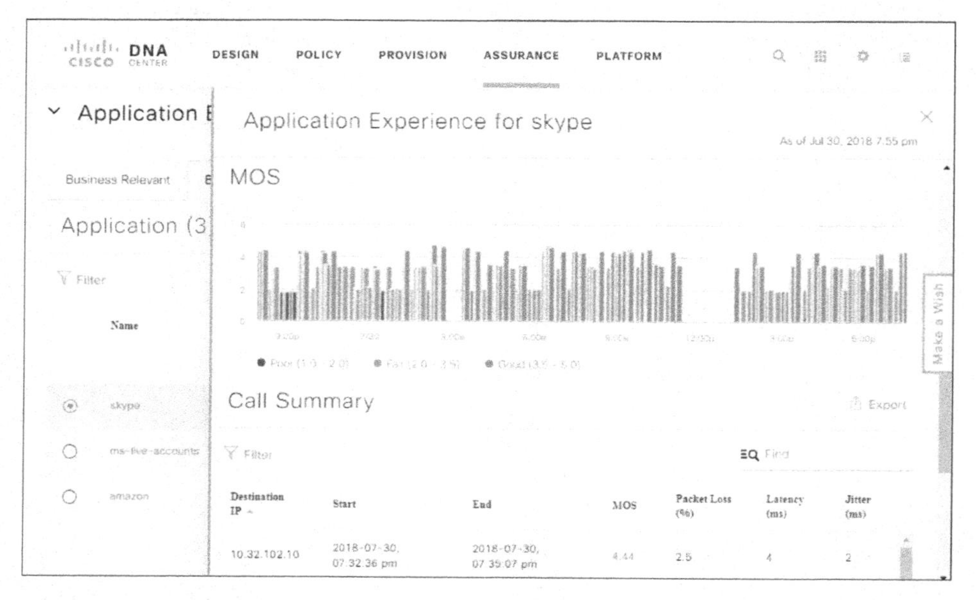

Figure 21-65 *Cisco DNA Assurance/Skype for Business Integration—Part 2: Skype for Business Call Quality Details*

> **Note** Similar application integrations for Cisco collaboration applications, such as WebEx, WebEx Teams, Jabber, etc., are also being researched and developed.

Path Trace

Based on extensive customer interviews, Cisco has determined that a typical workflow for troubleshooting a network, client, or application issue occurs as follows:

Step 1. A network analyst receives a report of a poorly performing network device (or client or application) and wants to either root-cause a network issue or rule out the network as the cause of the issue (at which point the analyst will likely punt the case over the fence to the app team).

Step 2. The analyst asks the client for the IP address of his device and default gateway.

Step 3. The analyst looks up the IP address of the end device (or application server) that the client is having issues with.

Step 4. The Tier 1 analyst (or possibly a T2 or T3 network engineer, in the event the issue was escalated) logs into the default gateway and performs a traceroute to the end device's IP address.

Step 5. The analyst/engineer iteratively pings each device in the path to test for reachability and to approximate latency, etc.

Step 6. The analyst/engineer iteratively logs into each device in the path and executes **show** commands to check for errors (syslog messages, interface errors, queue drops, etc.).

Step 7. The analyst/engineer possibly finds device issues/errors, but cannot always definitively associate them with any particular flow or application (she can only infer). Furthermore, analyst/engineer cannot always correlate these to having occurred at the time that the issue was originally manifest.

Step 8. If the network is suspected, then the engineer tries to replicate the problem

Step 9. If the issue can be replicated, then the case is likely routed to a T3/4 architect, who decides how to remediate (i.e., check access control lists [ACL] and access control entries [ACE] and modify as needed, change routing parameters or filters or redistribution policies, assign more bandwidth or deeper buffers to application queues, etc.); however, if nothing remarkable is found, then the issue is often bounced to the app team.

A few things become apparent when reviewing this application-issue troubleshooting process:

- Many steps are involved.
- Many people become involved.
- It relies on primary troubleshooting tools (ping, traceroute, **show** commands) that are 30+ years old.
  - Furthermore, tools like ping and traceroute only show the Layer 3 routing infrastructure; these do not reveal the Layer 2 wireless or switching underlay, nor any logical overlay (such as tunnels, virtual private networks [VPN], etc.).
- Unless the issue is manifest during re-creation (Step 8), it is likely not root-cased and remediated.

To significantly streamline application troubleshooting, Cisco DNA Assurance provides integrated troubleshooting tools, notably Path Trace. Path Trace allows even Tier 1 analysts to perform the first seven of the preceding steps with just a few clicks.

Path Trace is included in Device 360 and Client 360 pages, as shown in Figure 21-66. Also, Path Trace output is available via northbound APIs (to external applications).

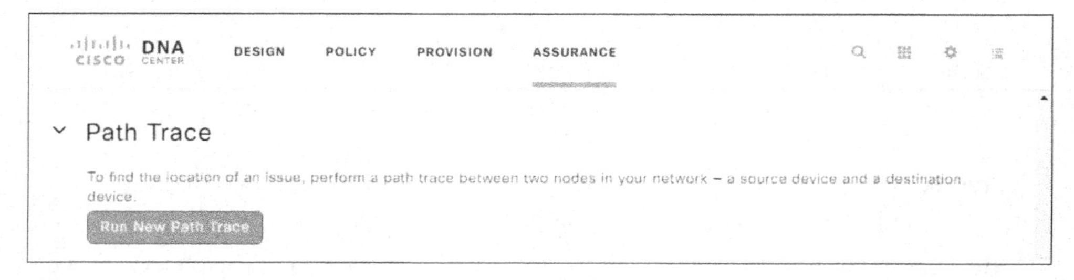

Figure 21-66 *Cisco DNA Assurance—Path Trace*

The source IP of the Path Trace is auto-populated (as this option is presented in the Device or Client 360 pages, the starting point is known). You can then enter a destination IP and optionally specify

- Source Port
- Destination Port
- Layer 4 Protocol (TCP/UDP)

You are also presented with several options, displayed in Figure 21-67, in which you may select whether to

- Refresh the trace every 30 seconds or not
- Include ACL trace (discussed shortly)
- Include device statistics
- Include interface statistics
- Include QoS statistics

To better appreciate the power of Path Trace, let's consider an example. A user has called into the help desk and reported that she is unable to print from her PC to the local printer. The Tier 1 analyst can quickly troubleshoot this issue by initiating a Path Trace from the client's PC to the printer on the TCP ports that are in use (let us assume this is run over the common printing port; that is, TCP port 9100), as illustrated in Figure 21-67.

Example output from such a Path Trace with these options selected is displayed in Figure 21-68. Note the circle around "ACL" on the second-to-last switch (on the right). For a person trained to look for red lights, the problem becomes immediately obvious. However, let's circle back to this after looking at some of the details that Path Trace has provided.

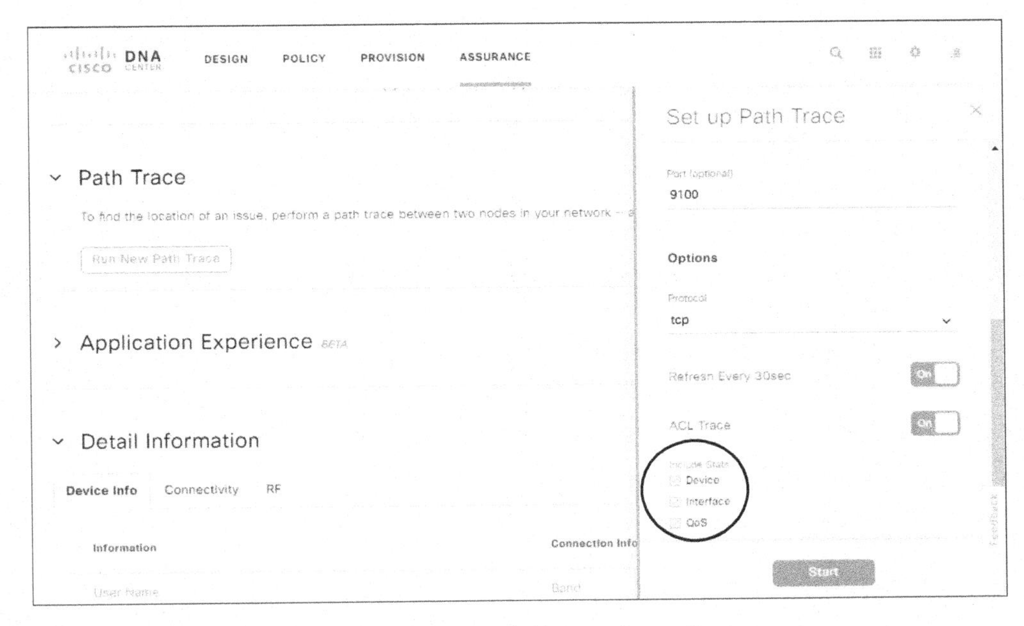

Figure 21-67 *Cisco DNA Assurance—Path Trace—Setup Options*

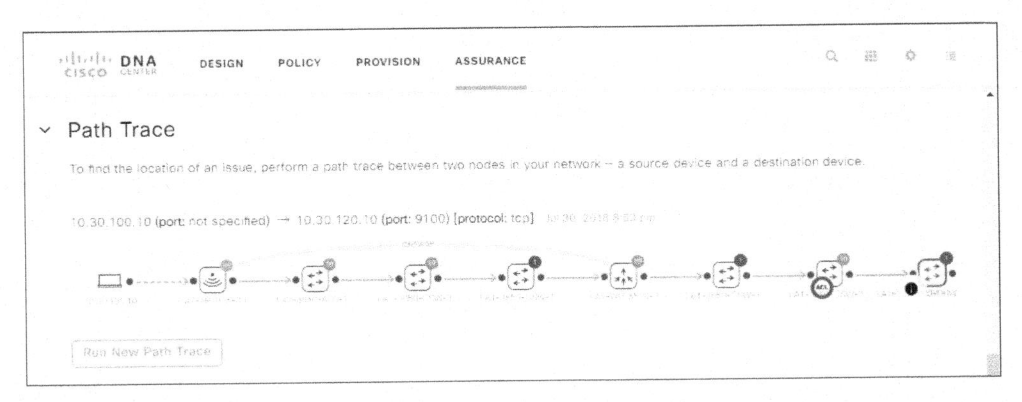

Figure 21-68 *Cisco DNA Assurance—Path Trace—Part 1: Basic Path Trace*

As illustrated in Figure 21-68, Path Trace does not just report the Layer 3 hops in the path (i.e., the routers), but also reports

- Layer 2 wireless network details, such as SSIDs
- Layer 2 wired network details, such as switched network links
- Layer 4 overlays, such as Control and Provisioning of Wireless Access Points (CAPWAP) or Virtual Extensible Local Area Network (VXLAN)

Additionally, Path Trace provides the following detailed information for a given trace:

- **Device Details:** Information regarding all the network devices along the path, with a pointer to the Device 360 page to get further detailed information. This includes the device name, IP address, etc.
- **Link Information Source:** For all the links along the application flow path trace, the link information source is displayed. Some examples for this particular field include
  - **Routing protocols (Open Shortest Path First [OSPF], Border Gateway Protocol [BGP], etc.):** The link is based on the routing protocol table.
  - **Equal Cost Multipath (ECMP):** The link is based upon a Cisco Express Forwarding load-balancing decision.
  - **NetFlow:** The link is based upon NetFlow cache records collected on the device.
  - **Static:** The link is based on a static routing table.
  - **Wired and wireless:** Type of end client (in case the source or destination is a client device).
  - **Switched:** The link is based on Layer 2 VLAN forwarding information.
  - **Traceroute:** The link is based on information collected by the traceroute app.
  - **Tunnels:** Visualization of the overlay tunnels present along the application flow path. Examples include CAPWAP, VXLAN, etc.

Yet further details provided by Path Trace include, as shown in Figure 21-69 through 21-71, the following:

- **Device Statistics:** Device health (and optional CPU and memory statistics) for every network device along the path, as shown in Figure 21-69.

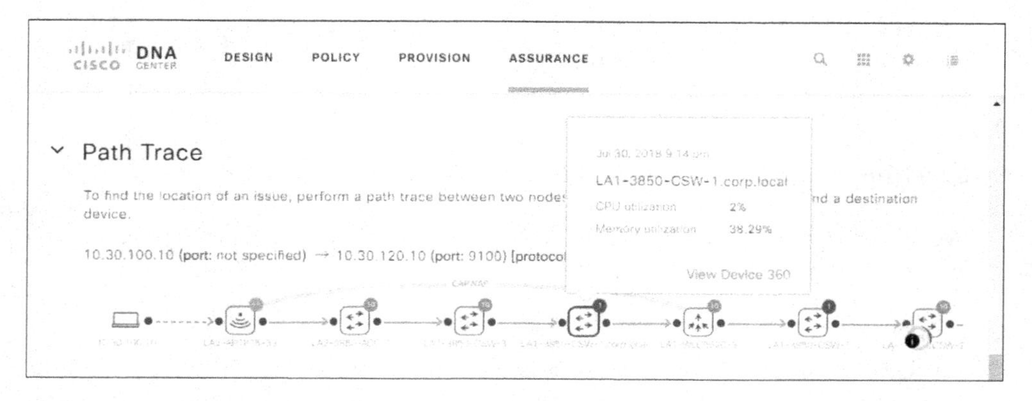

Figure 21-69 *Cisco DNA Assurance—Path Trace—Part 2: Device Details*

- **Interface Details:** Ingress and Egress interface on the devices for the application flow path. Some of the other optional information provided by Path Trace includes
  - **Interface Statistics:** Detailed statistics for every interface along the path. This includes data such as VLAN information, packet drop counters, packet rate counters, operational state, etc., as shown in Figure 21-70.

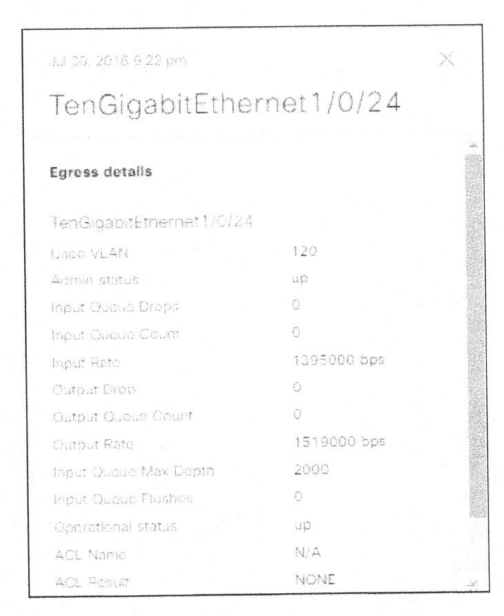

Figure 21-70 *Cisco DNA Assurance—Path Trace—Part 3: Interface and QoS Statistics*

  - **QoS Statistics:** QoS statistics for each interface, including input/output packet rates, maximum queue depths, and drops, as shown in Figure 21-70.
  - **ACL Trace:** The Cisco DNA Assurance Path Trace function looks for ACLs on all the relevant interfaces along the flow path and determines if any of the ALEs in these ACLs might have an impact on the application flow (permit or deny). This impact is highlighted in Path Trace with the ability to further look into the ACL details as part of the interface details, as illustrated in Figure 21-71.

ACL Name	120
ACL Result	DENY
Matching ACE Rule	50 deny ip any any
Matching ACE Result	DENY

Figure 21-71 *Cisco DNA Assurance—Path Trace—Part 4:ACL Trace Details*

Thus, to conclude our troubleshooting example, the ACL trace details confirm that the reason the user is unable to print is that her print-job traffic is being denied by ACE entry 50 under ACL 120 on the TenGigabitEthernet interface 1/0/24 of switch LA1-3850-CSW-2. Take a moment to think about how long such an issue would have taken to troubleshoot via the manual/traditional workflow outlined at the beginning of this section. With Path Trace, the Tier 1 analyst can identify the root cause of this problem in about 10 seconds.

Now, let's look at how the flow path is calculated for a given application defined by a 2-5 tuple combination. To review, flow tuples include

- Source IP address (SA)
- Destination IP address (DA)
- Layer 4 protocol (typically TCP/UDP)
- Source port
- Destination port

The minimum information required to perform a trace is a source and destination IP address (SA + DA); however, optional Layer 4 information makes the flow more specific to the application.

The Cisco DNA Center Network Information Base (NIB) periodically collects the device, client, and routing table information for all the network elements. This information includes Cisco Discovery Protocol (CDP), Link Layer Discovery Protocol (LLDP), and Internet Protocol Device Tracking (IPDT) information; link state information; VLAN and Spanning Tree Protocol (STP) data; Hot-Standby Router Protocol (HSRP), OSPF, Intermediate System to Intermediate System (IS-IS), Enhanced Interior Gateway Protocol (EIGRP), BGP, and static route data; and so forth.

For any given 2-5-tuple input, Cisco DNA Center initially tries to calculate the path using the information stored in the Cisco DNA NIB. In certain scenarios, the Cisco DNA Center Path Trace function queries the network on demand to obtain the most accurate path information, including

- **ECMP along the application flow path:** Cisco DNA Center queries the network device to get the exact egress interface for the given application flow. Note: It is important to provide the 5-tuple information for the application flow for accurate path trace results.
- **Unknown or unsupported device along the path:** Cisco DNA Center uses traceroute to get the best possible path.
- **Source and destination IP address are on different sites:** To determine which border router actually received the application flow for the path trace, Cisco DNA Center looks at the NetFlow cache records on all the border routers in the destination site network.

Path Trace sources of information are illustrated in Figure 21-72.

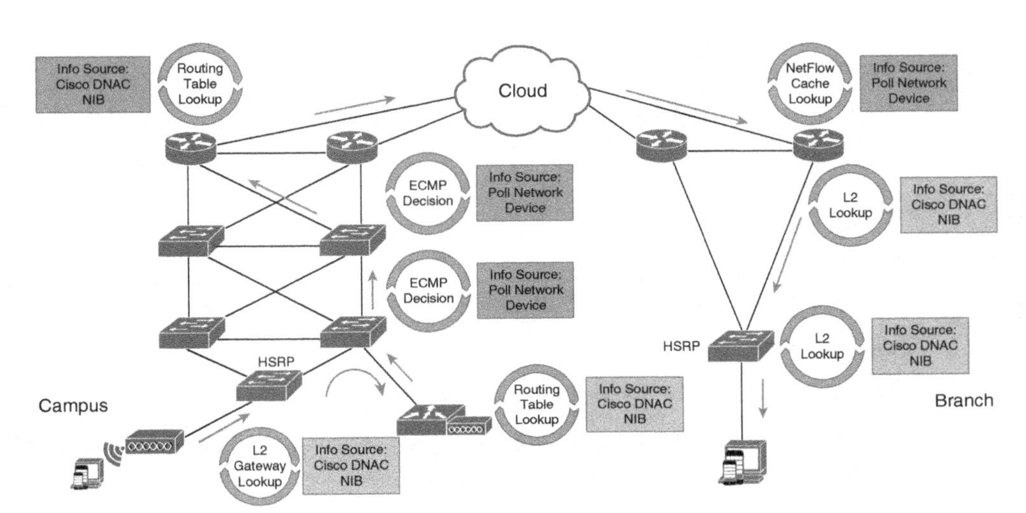

Figure 21-72 *Cisco DNA Assurance—Path Trace—Sources of Information*

Sensor-Driven Tests

Client health is also optionally augmented by configuring and running sensor-driven tests. Sensor tests are run from:

- Dedicated sensors (such as the Cisco 1800 Series sensors)
- APs used as dedicated sensors (such as the Cisco 1815, 1830, 1850, 2800, 3800, and 4800 APs)

Sensors represent clients in times or locations where clients are not present, or test services that clients are not currently using. A great strength of Cisco sensors is their flexibility: Specialized sensors are deployed throughout the network. These specialized access points are positioned near floor level, where users are located. The sensors then connect to Cisco DNA Assurance using Ethernet or a wireless link through the active access points.

Wireless sensors perform and report on the following type of tests:

- Onboarding tests
  - 802.11 Association
  - 802.11 Authentication & Key Exchange
  - IP Addressing DHCP (IPv4)

- Network tests
  - DNS (IPv4)
  - RADIUS (IPv4)
  - First Hop Router/Default gateway (IPv4)
  - Intranet Host
  - External Host (IPv4)
- Application tests
  - Email: Outlook Web Access (IPv4), IMAP, POP3
  - File Transfer: FTP (IPv4)
  - Web: HTTP & HTTPS (IPv4)

Sensor-driven tests are configured, managed, and reported on from within Cisco DNA Assurance, as illustrated in Figure 21-73.

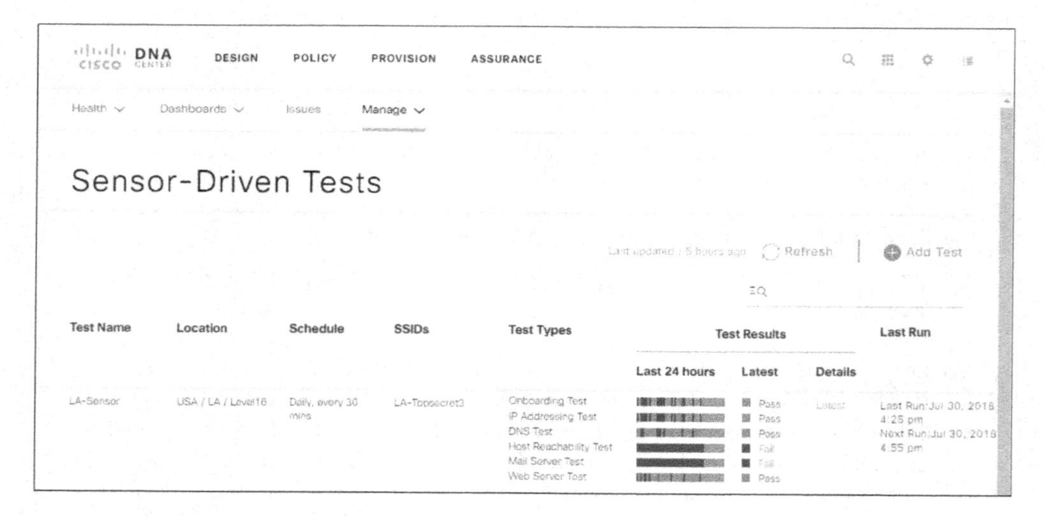

Figure 21-73 *Cisco DNA Assurance—Managing Sensor-Driven Tests*

Clicking the Latest link under Details on the Test Results tab displays the detailed results of individual tests, as illustrated in Figure 21-74.

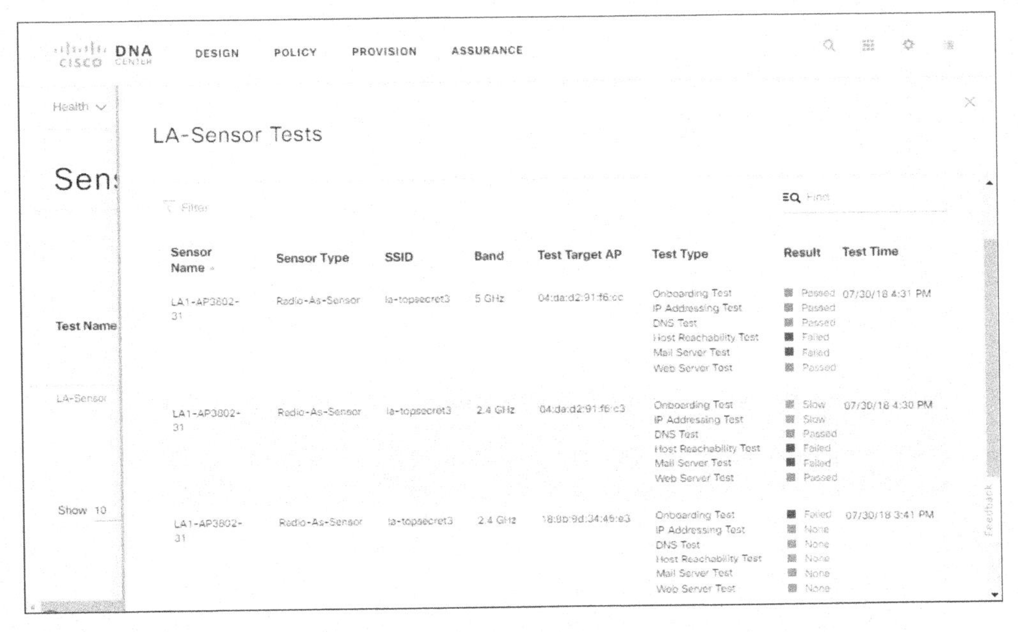

Figure 21-74 *Cisco DNA Assurance—Sensor-Driven Test Details*

Intelligent Capture

When it comes to monitoring and troubleshooting a network, there are at least three broad levels of underlying tools, which are summarized as follows:

- High-level monitoring tools
  - Purpose: Watchdog function
  - Answers: Do I have a potential issue on my network?
  - Granularity of data: Coarse
  - Frequency of use: Always on
  - Performance impact: Low
  - Examples: Streaming Telemetry, Flexible NetFlow, SNMP, syslog, etc.
- Mid-level monitoring/troubleshooting tools
  - Purpose: Isolate problem domain
  - Answers: Where/when is the issue occurring on my network?
  - Granularity of data: Medium
  - Frequency of use: Sampled, periodic, and/or on demand

  - Performance impact: Low
  - Examples: Sensor-driven tests, Path Trace, IP SLA, etc.
- Low-level troubleshooting tools
  - Purpose: Root-cause analysis
  - Answers: What is causing the issue on my network?
  - Granularity of data: Fine
  - Frequency of use: On demand
  - Performance impact: High
  - Examples: Intelligent Capture, packet captures, etc.

Intelligent Capture is a new tool that belongs in the low-level, on-demand troubleshooting toolset. Intelligent Capture complements and extends Cisco DNA Assurance troubleshooting capabilities for wireless networks. Specifically, it leverages the Flexible Radio in Cisco 4800 Series Access Points to provide wireless packet captures (complete with Layer 2 headers) and analyzes these packet captures in near real time (~5-second increments).

Intelligent Capture is seamlessly integrated into Cisco DNA Assurance from Client 360 views (for wireless clients associated to Cisco 4800 APs) as an On-Demand Tool, as shown in Figure 21-75.

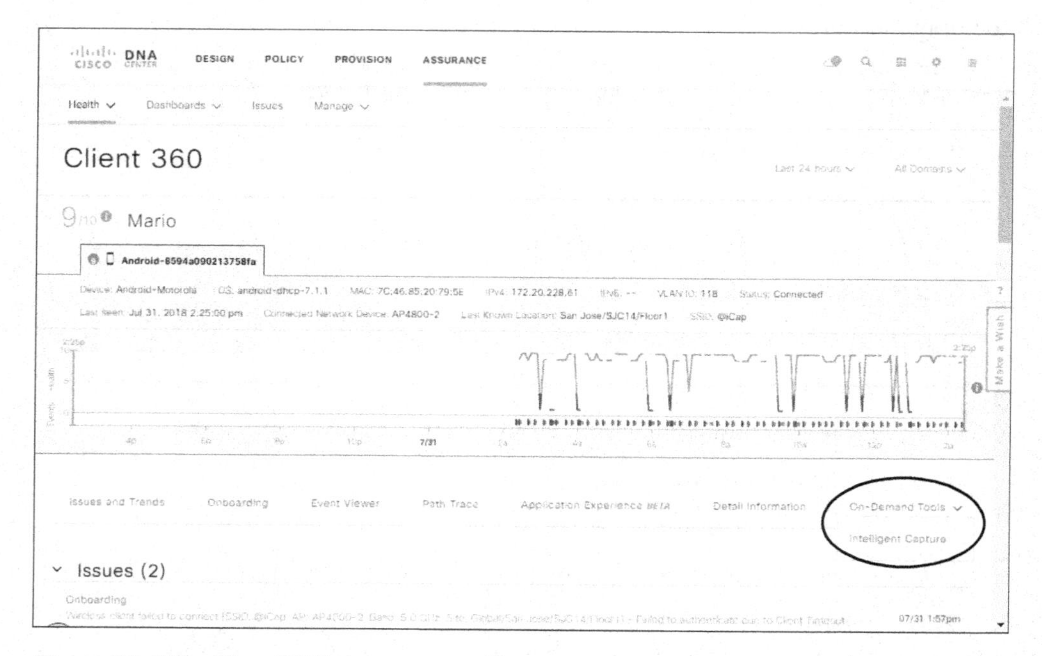

Figure 21-75 *Cisco DNA Assurance—Client 360 On-Demand Tools: Intelligent Capture*

Taking a packet capture of a wireless client's traffic becomes as easy as a single click, as shown near the top of Figure 21-76. Even this simple function saves considerable troubleshooting time and effort, for without it, you have one of two unattractive options for obtaining the same information:

- Dispatching a technician to the location where the client is having the issue (which may happen significantly after the fact), and having the technician take the packet capture
- Taking a nearby AP out of service—temporarily—and using this AP to take a packet capture

Both options have considerable drawbacks, and as such, you rarely get the benefit of having wireless packet captures available to analyze issues.

However, Intelligent Capture goes significantly beyond the basic ability to capture packets by also providing near-real-time analysis of these packets in the following areas:

- Real-time Client Tracking (shown in Figure 21-76), which allows operators to track users' Wi-Fi experience in 5-second intervals, providing real-time updates of their
  - Location
  - RSSI
  - SNR
  - Data Rates
  - Throughout
  - Packet Drop Rate
- Auto Packet Analyzer (shown in Figure 21-78)
- Application Analysis (shown in Figure 21-79)
- Real-time RF Stats (shown in Figure 21-81)

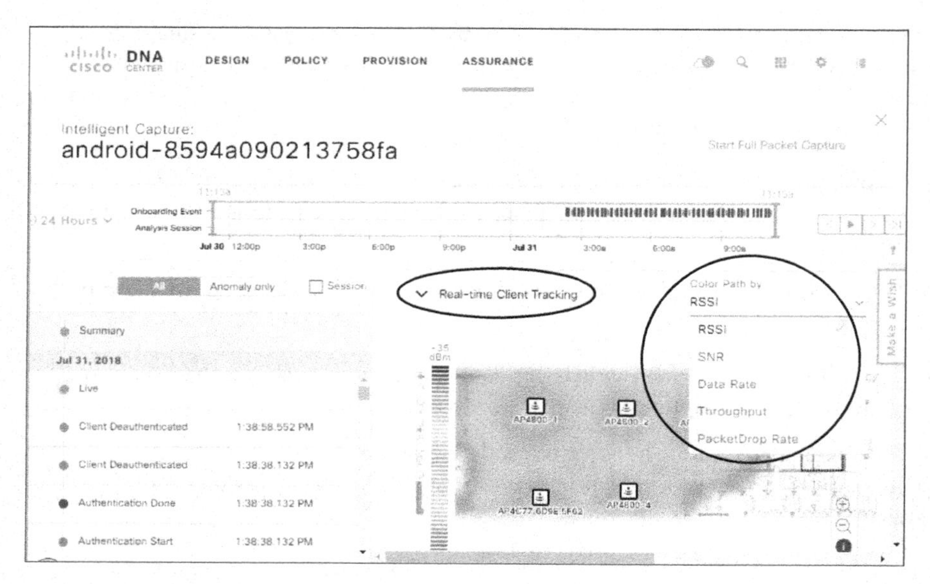

Figure 21-76 *Cisco DNA Assurance—Client 360 On-Demand Tools: Intelligent Capture—Real-Time Client Tracking*

Packet captures are taken on both the wired and wireless interfaces of the Cisco 4800 AP, and may be downloaded directly to the operator's PC, as shown in Figure 21-77.

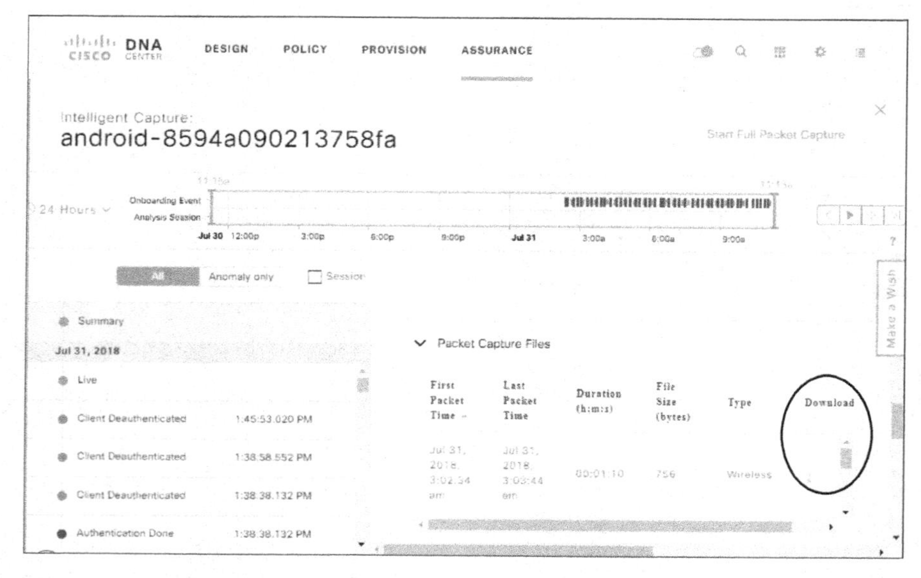

Figure 21-77 *Cisco DNA Assurance—Client 360 On-Demand Tools: Intelligent Capture—Packet Capture Download*

However, rather than just downloading a raw capture, *Intelligent* Capture lives up to its name by providing auto-analysis of the packets. For example, Intelligent Capture can analyze the onboarding process and color-code the packets according to whether the particular operation was successful or failed. For example, as shown in Figure 21-78, Auto Packet Analyzer is summarizing an onboarding event, detailing which packets were

- Sent from the Client to the AP (as represented by a right-side-up triangle)
- Sent from the AP to the Client (as represented by an upside-down triangle)
- Probes
- For IEEE 802.1x Authentication
- For Association
- For Extensible Authentication Protocol (EAP)
- For DHCP
- Data packets

This allows you to quickly identify the packets of interest (versus manually sifting through dozens or hundreds of packets one-at-a-time).

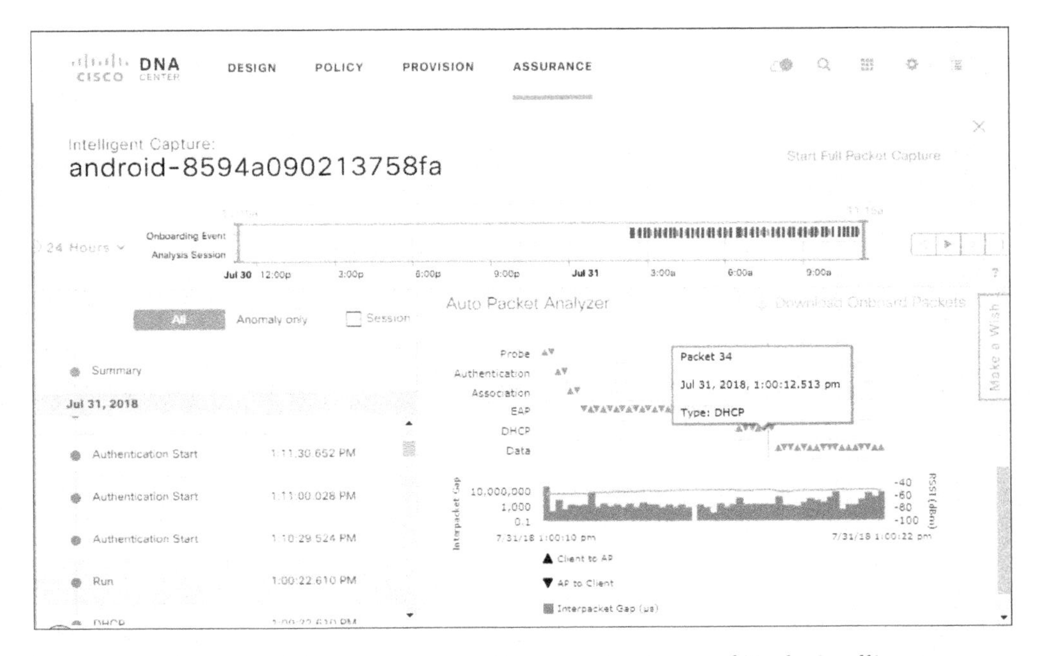

Figure 21-78 *Cisco DNA Assurance—Client 360 On-Demand Tools: Intelligent Capture—Packet Capture: Auto Packet Analyzer*

The wireless LAN is the second most likely place (after the WAN edge) in the enterprise network for application traffic to experience quality issues, due to induced latency, jitter, and loss. Wireless is a particularly challenging media for QoS, as it is shared, half duplex, and nondeterministic. Another major challenge with wireless QoS is that there's often little or no visibility to verify the performance of application traffic over the WLAN—that is, until Intelligent Capture.

Intelligent Capture can perform Application Analysis, as shown in Figure 21-79, to confirm if the Layer 2 QoS markings are set correctly. These include both of the following:

- IEEE 802.11 User Priority (UP) markings (also known as Wireless Multi-Media [WMM] markings)
- IP Differentiated Services Code Point (DSCP) markings

Additionally, Application Analysis will report on the loss, latency, and jitter that the frames are experiencing over the wireless media between the client and the access point.

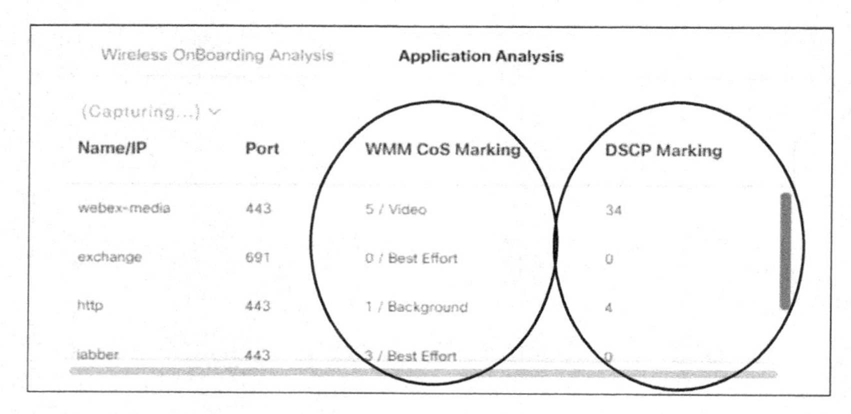

Figure 21-79 *Cisco DNA Assurance—Client 360 On-Demand Tools: Intelligent Capture—Packet Capture: Application Analysis*

There are several other use cases that are supported via Intelligent Capture, including

- Client and app real-time forensics
- Monitoring anomalous flows in real time
- Hyperlocation client pinpointing (to within 3 meters of accuracy)
- On-demand RF scanner (to identify coverage holes)
- VIP client service assurance (e.g., ensuring wireless quality in a hospital environment for critical healthcare monitors)

Intelligent Capture is not only an on-demand tool accessible from Client 360 views, but is also available as an on-demand tool from Device 360 views for Cisco 4800 Access Points, as shown in Figure 21-80.

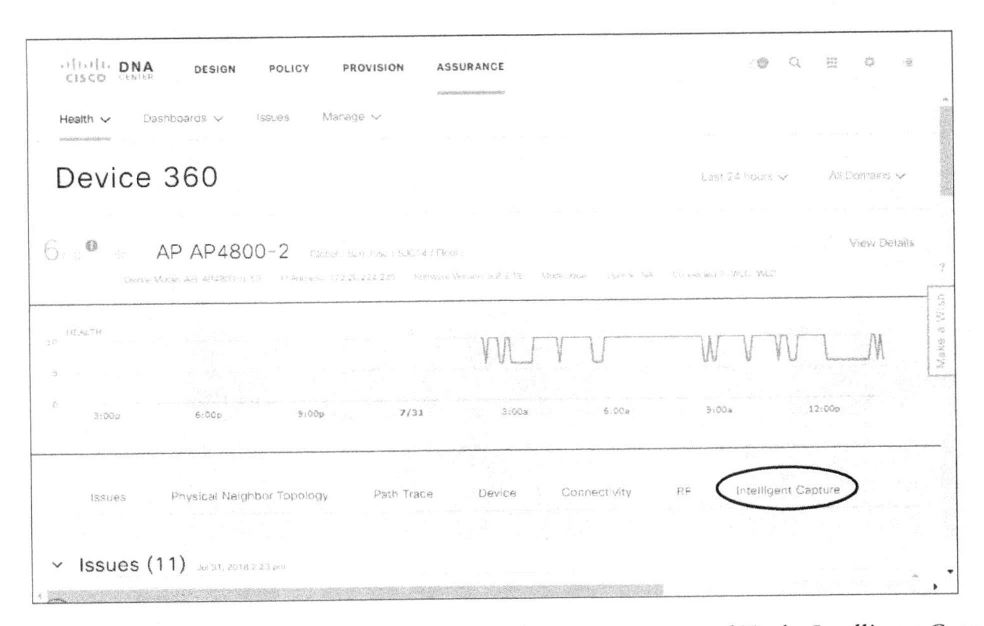

Figure 21-80 *Cisco DNA Assurance—Device 360 On-Demand Tools: Intelligent Capture*

Intelligent Capture provides an array of additional RF statistics not available to other APs, as shown in Figure 21-81.

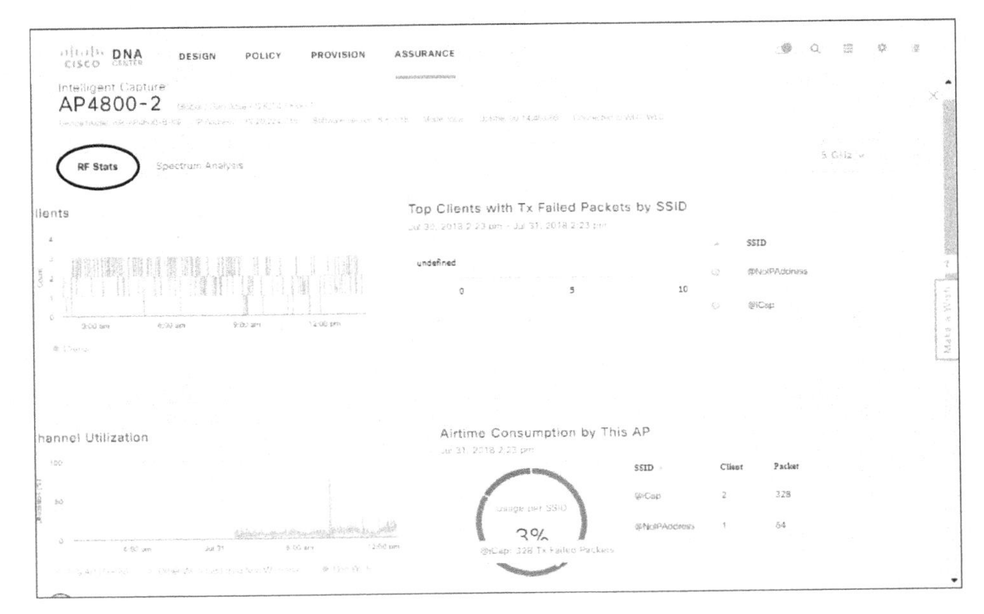

Figure 21-81 *Cisco DNA Assurance—Device 360 On-Demand Tools: Intelligent Capture RF Stats*

And finally, Intelligent Capture even provides an on-demand Spectrum Analysis from the AP location, as illustrated in Figure 21-82.

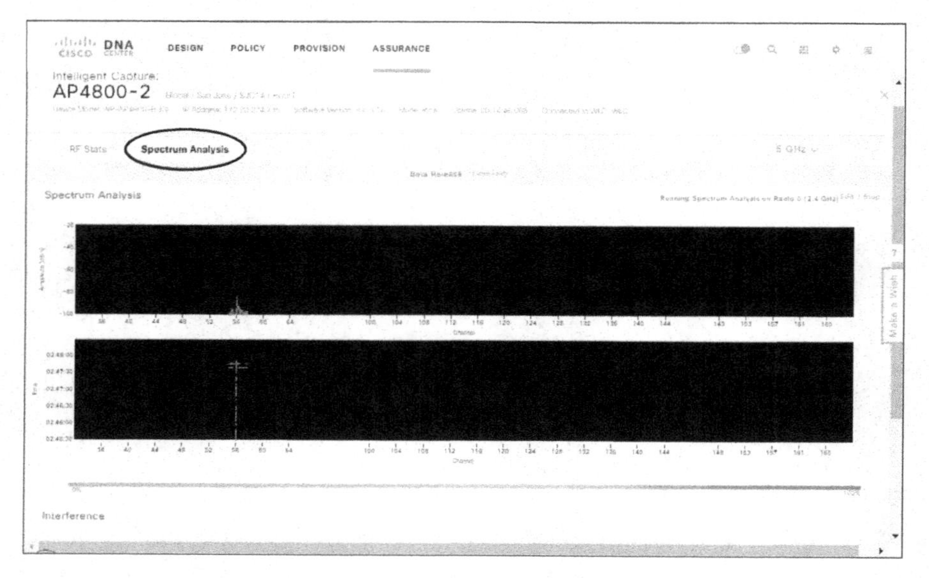

Figure 21-82 *Cisco DNA Assurance—Device 360 On-Demand Tools: Intelligent Capture Spectrum Analysis*

In summary, it cannot be overemphasized that for the majority of network administrators, Intelligent Capture provides net-new visibility and insight and assists in rapidly and effectively troubleshooting wireless issues in the enterprise.

Machine Learning

This chapter previously discussed the role and value that machine learning brings to analytics, and to this end Cisco is introducing a cloud-based machine-learning architecture to Cisco DNA Assurance. This ML solution supports

- **Cognitive Analytics:** To extract behavioral patterns in the network
- **Predictive Analytics:** To predict expected network and user experience
- **Trending Analytics:** For capacity planning purposes and what-if scenario modeling

The use of ML algorithms allows for understanding complex network dynamics to identify potential issues, ease troubleshooting and root-cause analysis, perform what-if scenarios, and even predict issues before they happen, all using the same Cisco DNA Assurance user interface. Specifically, ML enhances the "Issues" that are reported within Cisco DNA Assurance, as shown in Figures 21-83 through 21-86.

In Figure 21-83, ML has identified a Radio Throughput issue. This issue is presented within the Cisco DNA Assurance UI in the same manner as any other issue. The issue summary includes predictive analytics, as represented by a green band where the throughput levels are predicted to be (based on network baselining), and flags times when the actual measured value was outside of this predicted window.

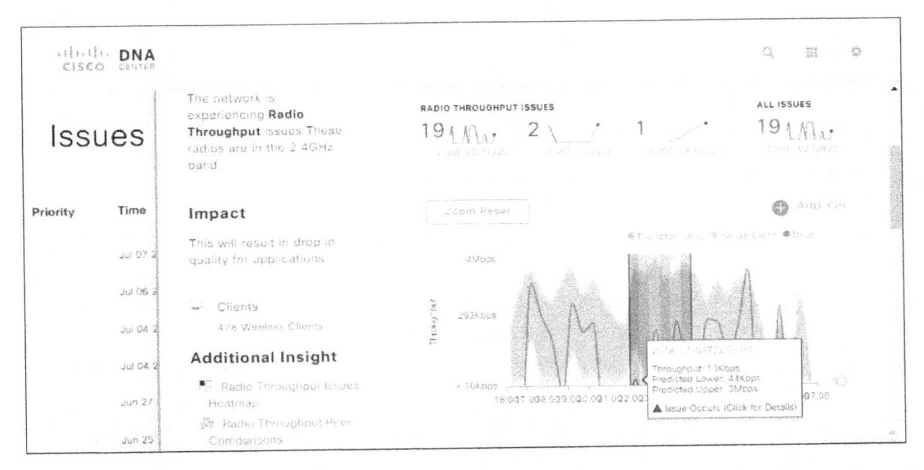

Figure 21-83 *Cisco DNA Assurance—Machine Learning—Radio Throughput Issue*

Machine learning goes beyond simply identifying an issue; it also shows all the monitored variables that exhibited similar patterns, or common traits, and presents these to the advanced administrator as potential correlations or causations. This Common Traits view is shown in Figure 21-84. In this particular instance, the client count shows a strong correlation to the decrease in radio throughout (significantly more so than interference levels and MAC packet retries/second).

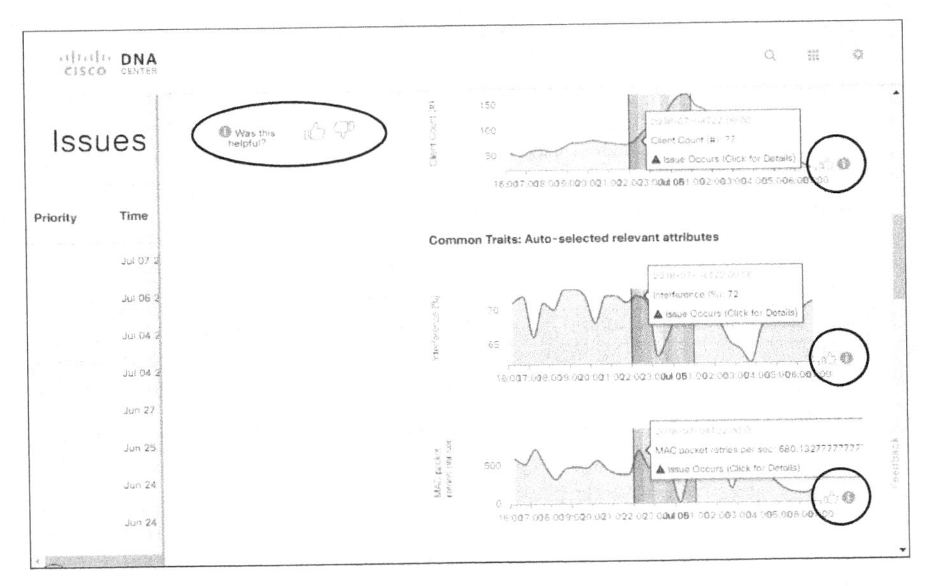

Figure 21-84 *Cisco DNA Assurance—Machine Learning—Common Traits*

Additionally, Figure 21-84 illustrates the user inputs for supervised machine learning. Specifically, you can select if the inclusion of a given variable exhibiting common traits was "helpful" or not. In this particular example, radio throughput is abnormally low and several variables are presented, including

- Client counts
- Interference
- MAC packet retries

As it turns out, this particular issue was traced back to abnormally high client counts; as such, the ML algorithm is guided by you giving a "thumbs-up" to the inclusion of "Client Count" as being helpful. Such supervised feedback trains the algorithm to look for more of these types of correlations, present interference at the top of the list of common traits, and filter out (or relegate) other variables that were identified as "not helpful."

Machine learning also presents a battery of big-data variables in network heatmap views and visually displays patterns such as when (day/week/month) issues arise and on what these devices such issues are manifest the most. Such a network heatmap view is presented in Figure 21-85, which summarizes interference patterns, highlighting:

- When the most interference has been observed (identifying July 6, 2018 as the most disrupted day)
- Where the most interference has been observed (by AP)
- The frequency that interference has been observed by the AP (the daily average being reported as 49 observed occurrences of interference)
- The severity of the interference (as indicated by the red bars)

And finally, ML provides insights to the question "How does my network compare to my peers' networks?" All information sent to Cisco's cloud-based machine-learning architecture is encrypted via a one-way hash, so as to fully anonymize source details. Nonetheless, this collective information allows for peer comparisons, as illustrated in Figure 21-86.

The Cisco cloud-based ML engine gathers data from various sources to compute ML-based models. This allows for ongoing learning of advanced patterns in the network, an unlimited source of highly valuable insights on network behaviors. This approach supports predictive analytics, thus anticipating issues, optimizing the user experience, easing troubleshooting, and performing root-cause analysis, to mention a few key advantages of such an approach.

Data collection is performed using a variety of data feeds and telemetry, and processed by a centralized ML engine (which makes use of NDP for data collection, processing, and storage before being converted into a common data intelligence YANG model). Advanced models are computed by the ML Kernel component on this data, while ensuring strong privacy (e.g., anonymized datasets) in order to perform advanced analytics on networking data.

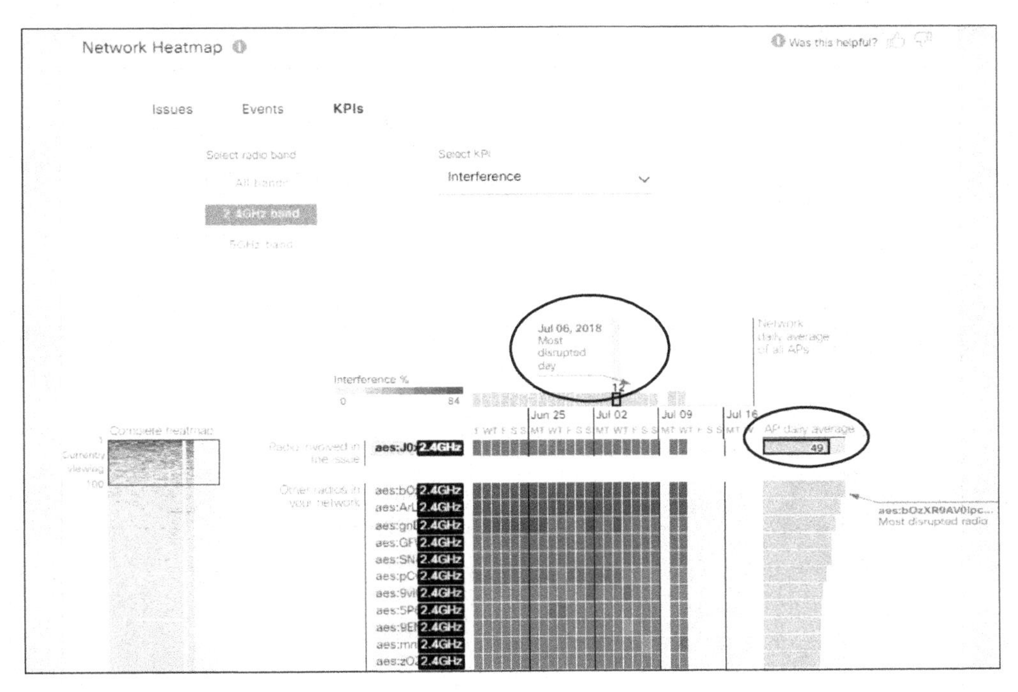

Figure 21-85 *Cisco DNA Assurance—Machine Learning—Network Heatmap*

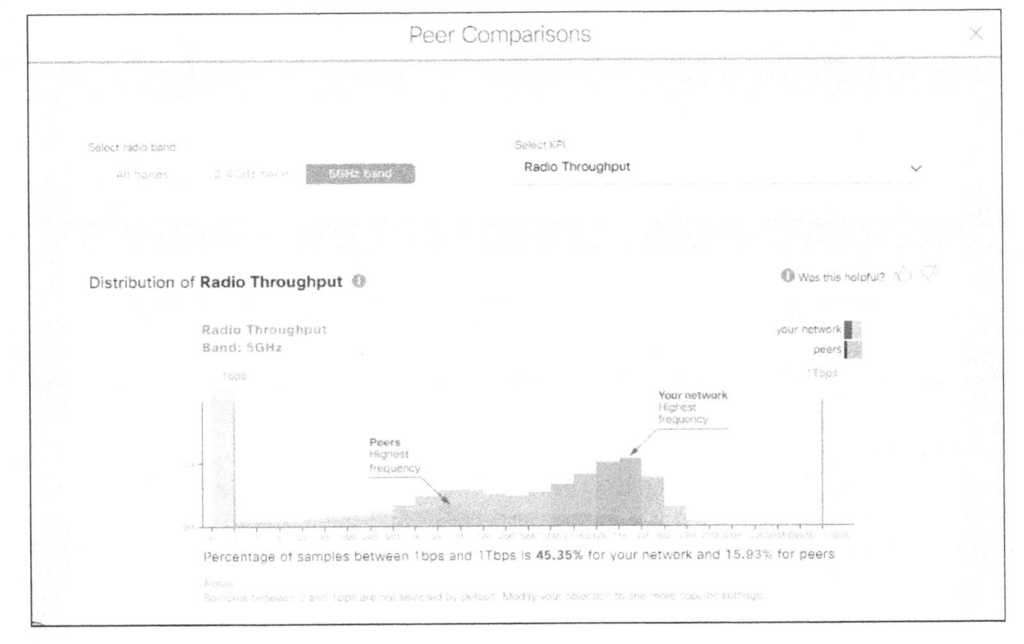

Figure 21-86 *Cisco DNA Assurance—Machine Learning—Peer Comparisons*

Cognitive Analytics

The aim of cognitive analytics is to find behavioral patterns in complex and unstructured datasets.

For the sake of illustration, for wireless networks ML extracts

- Patterns of Wi-Fi roaming in the network
- Roaming behaviors, such as
  - Sticky clients
  - "Ping-pong" clients
  - The number of visited APs
  - Roaming triggers
- Device details
  - Hardware
  - OS
  - Drivers
- Network device details (AP and WLC)
  - Hardware
  - Software
  - Configurations
- Geographic place in the network
- Time of day
- Routing topology
- Network metrics
- Roaming failure rates

In the case of throughput, ML will be able to identify areas where the offered throughput is abnormally low compared to expectation for a given location, time of day, and device type, as well as offer potential root-cause analysis.

Predictive Analytics

Predictive Analytics is a central component of ML that enables the prediction of the network and user experiences, representing a true paradigm shift from reactive approaches.

For example, in a Wireless network, ML will be able to build predictive models for various wireless parameters such as

- Noise
- Utilization
- Roaming failure rates, by taking into account hundreds of parameters, including
  - RF variables
  - Time of day
  - Number of clients
  - Traffic load
  - DHCP/DNS/Radius response times
  - AP/WLC utilization levels
  - WAN utilization levels

These advanced models can even predict the network throughput and then detect issues *before* they happen.

Furthermore, when possible, the ML system will be able to identify root causes of potential network outages as they develop, with the goal of preemptively remediating these *before* a network outage event occurs.

In yet another example, predictive models for voice/video quality using network variables will be built where ML will predict the actual user experience (e.g., 1 to 5 stars application ranking from Skype-for-Business, WebEx, etc.) as function of the network state, a much superior approach than metrics such as the Mean Opinion Score (MOS), a rudimentary metric that has been used to reflect user experience for the past few decades.

Such prediction of user experience may be provided to the network architect and (potentially in real time) to the end device for closed-loop control. Imagine a cloud-based architecture capable of signaling to an iPhone or IoT healthcare device that better QoS will be provided if re-roaming to a different AP (or conversely request to not roam because QoS would be affected for the said device).

Trending Analytics

Last but not least, ML will be able to perform what-if scenarios to assess the user and network performance when adjusting variables (e.g., What if the number client increases by 20 percent? What if the application rate decreases by 30 percent?).

Trends using multivariate models will be forecasted by ML to predict states of the network in the future, thus separating noise from actual trends. This approach could be used for capacity planning and other more-advanced what-if scenarios.

Note At the time of writing, the cloud-based machine-learning component of Cisco DNA Assurance is in customer field trials.

Summary

This chapter focused on Cisco DNA Analytics and Assurance. It began by outlining the value of context and learning within an intent-based networking architecture. Next, it provided an overview of the following architectural requirements of a self-healing network:

- Instrumentation
- Distributed on-device analytics
- Telemetry
- Scalable storage
- Analytics engine
- Machine learning
- Guided and automated troubleshooting and remediation

The majority of these requirements are already delivered in Cisco DNA, with Cisco DNA Center providing the analytics, machine-learning, and troubleshooting functional requirements.

An overview of the relationship between Cisco DNA Assurance and the underlying analytics platform, the Network Data Platform (NDP), was presented. Additionally, key features of the NDP were introduced, including contextual correlation, complex event processing, and time series analysis. The architecture, operation, and extensibility options of NDP were also reviewed.

Next, the discussion shifted to the Cisco DNA Assurance application, which leverages the functionality provided by NDP for monitoring and troubleshooting enterprise networks, clients, and applications. Health pages and 360 views for network devices, clients, and applications were detailed, as were supplemental tools and technologies, including Path Trace, sensor-driven tests, machine learning, and Intelligent Capture.

Further Reading

Cisco Systems. "Cisco Visual Networking Index: Forecast and Methodology, 2016–2021." Updated September 15, 2017. https://www.cisco.com/c/en/us/solutions/collateral/service-provider/visual-networking-index-vni/complete-white-paper-c11-481360.html.

Mercedes, G., P. Radtke, K. Speicher, and R. Westinner. "Ops 4.0: Fueling the Next 20 Percent Productivity Rise with Digital Analytics." McKinsey&Company. April 2017. https://www.mckinsey.com/business-functions/operations/our-insights/ops-4-0-fueling-the-next-20-percent-productivity-rise-with-digital-analytics.

RFC 3550. "RTP: A Transport Protocol for Real-Time Applications." July 2003. https://tools.ietf.org/html/rfc3550.

Chapter 22

Cisco DNA Encrypted Traffic Analytics

This chapter examines an important and exciting new area of security innovation within Cisco Digital Network Architecture—namely, Encrypted Traffic Analytics (ETA).

Cisco ETA provides two very important capabilities for enterprises wishing to enhance their security posture, as depicted in Figure 22-1:

- **Encrypted malware detection:** Today, more threats than ever that lurk on the enterprise network are leveraging encryption in an effort to avoid detection. ETA provides the capability to distinguish malicious from benign flows in encrypted traffic streams, without having to decrypt the traffic flows.
- **Cryptographic compliance:** Many enterprises have policies regarding how encryption is supposed to be deployed within their organizations. However, assessing how cryptography is actually rolled out in applications running across the network is difficult. ETA addresses this shortcoming and allows enterprises to more easily audit their deployment of encryption policies.

Figure 22-1 *Primary Benefits of Encrypted Traffic Analytics*

This chapter explores these capabilities in detail by

- Defining the challenges that ETA helps to solve
- Outlining how ETA functions
- Explaining the benefits that ETA provides

When examining encrypted traffic to determine whether or not it contains malware, several important considerations must be examined. End-to-end confidentiality must be preserved (thus, no decryption of data can occur at a midpoint in the network). The integrity of the confidential encrypted channel must be maintained. And, it is necessary to be able to adapt as encryption standards themselves change, as they do from time to time. When examining cryptographic compliance, it is necessary to determine how much of the organization's digital business is using strong encryption—and to audit for Transport Layer Security (TLS) policy violations, as well as passively detect possible cipher suite vulnerabilities as these become identified. All of these are capabilities that ETA provides and areas of operation that it supports.

In short, there is a lot to what ETA offers. Let's dive in to examine the issue of malware detection in encrypted traffic flows, and see how ETA provides a powerful, innovative new solution to this critical requirement for enterprise network security.

Encrypted Malware Detection: Defining the Problem

In today's network, many types of malware lurk. These malicious applications are looking to perform any number of deleterious actions, including (but not limited to) the following:

- Encrypting the hard disk storage of a user or server, then demanding a ransom to unlock and recover the encrypted data (for which only the malware owner holds the key)
- Wiping the hard disk storage of a user or server, permanently deleting the data and causing havoc
- Executing a denial of service (DoS) attack and crippling an organization's network infrastructure, possibly leveraging a distributed set of internal or external compromised resources (botnets)
- Surreptitiously exfiltrating confidential data from an organization, and subsequently leveraging this data for competitive advantage, financial gain, or invasion of privacy

Of course, this only scratches the surface of what malicious software, deployed across the network, is capable of. However, even this short list of possible malicious activities is enough to keep a network manager up at night, considering the various ways that such malicious activities impact any organization, public or private.

A troubling trend in recent times, as outlined in Figure 22-2, is that many such malware threats are beginning to leverage encryption as a way to hide their activities—and even their presence—within enterprise networks.

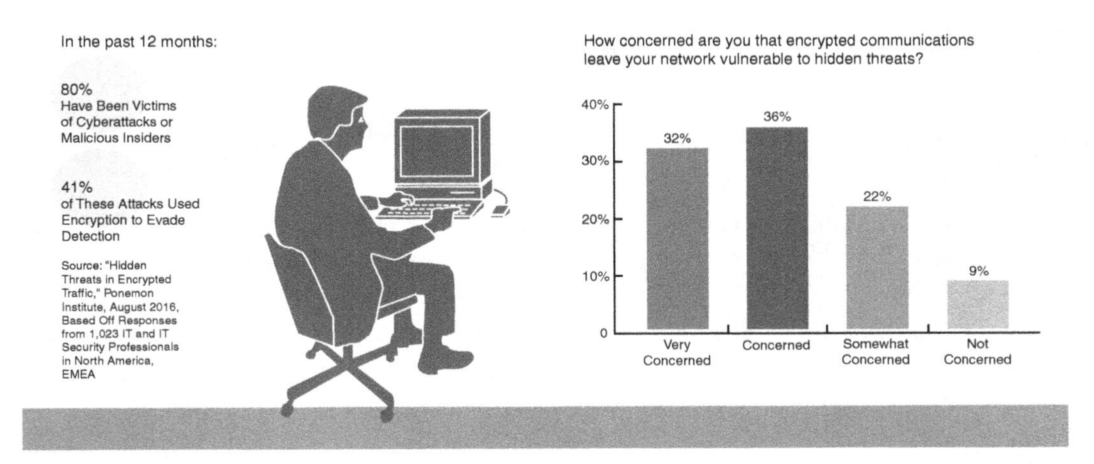

Figure 22-2 *Network Threats Are Changing to Leverage Encryption*

Many organizations are concerned that such threats exist, and are growing in terms of both scale and potential impact to the organization. And yet, what can be done to address such threats? If the malware is encrypted, how can you spot it?

Disabling encryption across the enterprise network is not possible as a response. Many, if not most, legitimate enterprise applications use encryption for their own purposes, such as to protect confidential data in flight and to provide privacy and authentication for users and things, and their associated data flows.

And yet, encryption is encryption. Its purpose is to hide data by effectively scrambling it—making data appear as noise. Unfortunately, the same encryption methods that protect sensitive data in transit for legitimate purposes are also leveraged by malicious actors to ensure that traditional methods of malware detection are rendered inoperable.

So how do you solve this problem? How can you tell "good noise" (benign encrypted applications) from "bad noise" (encrypted malware) within the network?

Until recently, this was considered an impossible problem to solve. However, the efforts of a few key Cisco engineers began the movement toward solving this critical problem—a solution that ultimately became the Cisco Encrypted Traffic Analytics capability.

An important contribution was a paper submitted to the Association for Computing Machinery (ACM) in 2016 by two Cisco engineers, Blake Anderson and David McGrew, entitled "Identifying Encrypted Malware Traffic with Contextual Flow Data."[1] This paper

1 https://dl.acm.org/citation.cfm?id=2996768

outlined methods which could be used to determine which flows in a network might be malicious in intent versus other flows that are benign—even when both types of flows are encrypted—and without having to decrypt any of the data.

Expanding on this idea, Cisco crafted the Encrypted Traffic Analytics solution. Let's explore how the solution works and the benefits it provides.

Encrypted Malware Detection: Defining the Solution

To begin with, let's tackle the obvious question up front: Why not just decrypt the traffic in the network and run traditional methods of malware detection on the then-decrypted flows?

Two major challenges render this option impractical.

The first challenge is performance and resource requirements. Encryption of data is hard work to begin with, and decryption of data without access to the encryption key is massively difficult and time consuming, and requires extensive amounts of computing power. This makes such an approach completely impractical at the network edge—the place closest to the user, where you would typically like to be able to detect this issue first—and would be very expensive and difficult at any place in the network where high data rates are involved (and they almost always are in networking).

The second challenge is more subtle perhaps, but no less real. Users, devices, and applications leverage encryption for legitimate purposes, to encode data and protect confidential assets as well as individual privacy. Midstream decryption of data to search for encrypted malware that may be hiding within the data risks exposing all of the other benign, but encrypted, applications involved to additional risk to the compromise of their legitimate data, and may be prohibited by corporate policies or legal protections for such data flows.

But without decrypting the data in flight, you are back to the same problem. How can you tell the difference between legitimate encrypted data flows and encrypted malware? How can you tell "good noise" from "bad noise"?

Enter two key capabilities of Encrypted Traffic Analytics: Initial Data Packet (IDP) inspection, and examination of the Sequence of Packet Lengths and Times (SPLT). Each of these are examined in turn in the following text.

ETA: Use of IDP for Encrypted Malware Detection

Encrypted Traffic Analytics takes advantage of the fact that the setup of any new encrypted flow always includes a few unencrypted packets as the encrypted session is established.

By inspecting these Initial Data Packets (IDP), it is possible to a fairly high degree of accuracy to determine many important characteristics of the flow—including (but not limited to) the application or browser types in use, the TLS types being used, what cipher suites are being asked for and agreed upon by the two endpoints involved, whether a self-signed certificate or a certificate signed by a known root certificate authority is being employed, and many other aspects of the subsequent encrypted session that is being set up. This is illustrated in Figure 22-3.

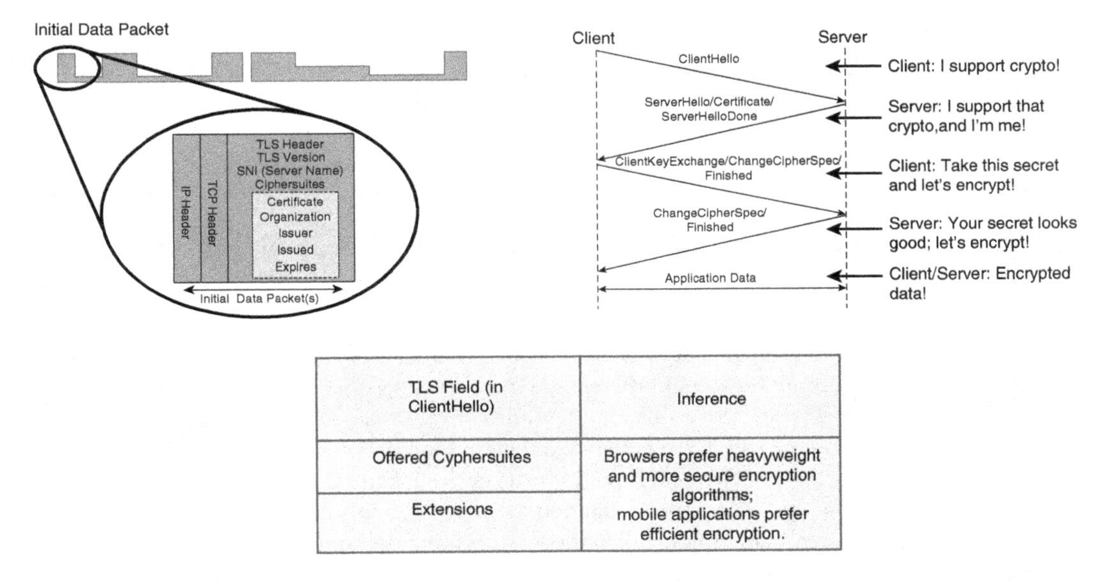

TLS Field (in ClientHello)	Inference
Offered Cyphersuites	Browsers prefer heavyweight and more secure encryption algorithms; mobile applications prefer efficient encryption.
Extensions	

Figure 22-3 *Initial Data Packet Exchange*

By examining these IDPs in the cryptographic exchange, a set of reference points can be determined to begin to assist with the identification of the encrypted flow that follows. By itself, this is not indicative of the presence of malware—however, when used in conjunction with additional data, as you will see, identification of malicious encrypted flows versus benign flows begins to emerge. Let's examine this further to see how this is accomplished.

ETA: Use of SPLT for Encrypted Malware Detection

By combining the data extracted from observing the IDP exchange (which takes place within the first several packets of a given encrypted flow) with an examination of the subsequent packets in a flow—specifically, the sequence of encrypted packets, their length in terms of bytes, and the spacing of the packets in terms of time delays and inter-packet gaps—it is possible to further "fingerprint" the flows, identifying the patterns that begin to emerge that can signal the presence of encrypted malware.

The use of SPLT (Sequence of Packet Lengths and Times) is outlined in Figure 22-4.

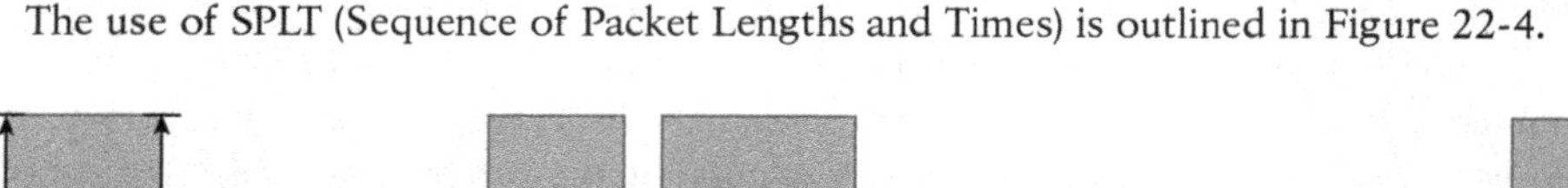

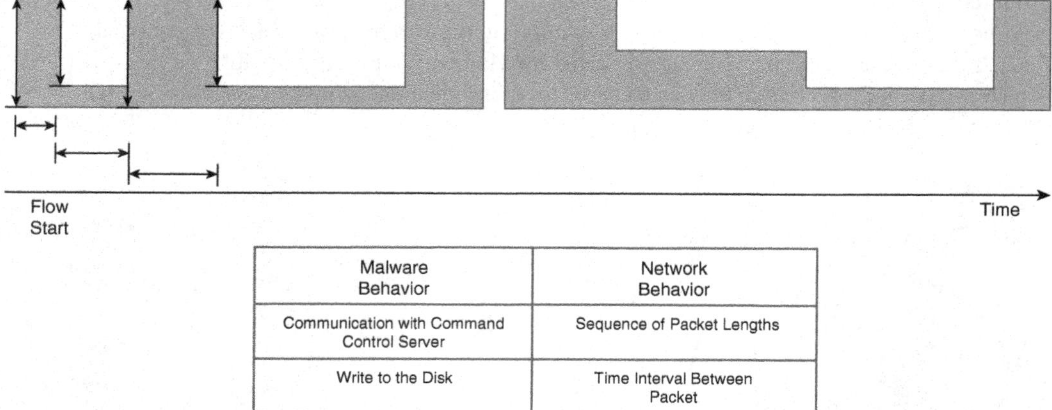

Malware Behavior	Network Behavior
Communication with Command Control Server	Sequence of Packet Lengths
Write to the Disk	Time Interval Between Packet

Figure 22-4 *Sequence of Packet Lengths and Times (SPLT)*

The combination of IDP and SPLT data provides sufficient indicators for ETA to detect encrypted malware flows and differentiate them from benign encrypted flows—without having to decrypt any of the data in flight. Effectively, this provides a "fingerprint" for the encrypted flow within the network, a fingerprint that, when combined with knowledge of many thousands of encrypted flow types supplied via a cloud-based database, allows for a highly accurate determination to be made as to whether a given encrypted flow contains malware or not—all without decrypting the traffic flows involved.

Sounds intriguing? Let's review an example of how this works to gain more insight into the operation of ETA.

Encrypted Malware Detection: The Solution in Action

To begin with, let's examine an encrypted transaction over the network that is benign in nature. For this example, let's review a user executing a Google search.

As a common practice, Google now encrypts all transactions using HTTPS, rendering them opaque to the network infrastructure, as well as to anyone in between the client using a web browser for the search and Google's own servers. As you examine what this Google search looks like on the wire (again, without decrypting any of it), the pattern shown in Figure 22-5 emerges—essentially, a "digital fingerprint" of the Google search itself.

In the figure, the source for the Google search (the user) is shown on the left and the destination (a Google server) is shown on the right. The horizontal line running across the middle denotes the direction of traffic flow—everything above the line is user-to-server traffic and everything below the line is server-to-user traffic.

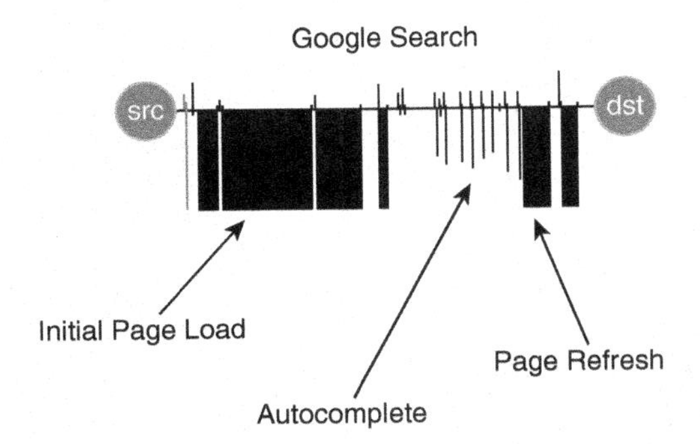

Figure 22-5 *Benign Encrypted Transaction Fingerprint: Google Search*

Initially, you see a certificate exchange (the line on the far left), followed quickly by a burst of data as Google serves up the initial Google search splash page. Then you see a number of small back-and-forth packet flows as the user types her query one character at a time, which is transmitted back in real time to Google's servers, which attempt to provide auto-completion for the query as it is typed (every character typed by the user is a back-and-forth packet exchange with the Google server). Finally, the user submits her query, and a further burst of data signals the arrival of Google's query results to the user.

You cannot decrypt any of the data—nor do you necessarily need to. Any Google query can differ in terms of what is looked for; however, they all produce a characteristic fingerprint that resembles the pattern shown in Figure 22-5, simply by the nature of how such a query operates. The data varies, and it is all encrypted and secure end to end, but the basic packet exchange pattern remains the same, and can be observed via ETA.

Now, compare this benign encrypted transaction to one that is more threatening.

For this example, let's examine the fingerprint shown in Figure 22-6. This fingerprint is associated with a banking Trojan known as Bestafera. The purpose of this malware is to extract data from the user's machine without the user's knowledge or consent—possibly including confidential data related to the user's banking account access or financial transactions.

In this fingerprint, notice several elements that may trigger suspicion. First, a self-signed certificate is in use. This is not necessarily incriminating in and of itself, but serves as a red flag that may warrant further inspection. Second, observe that almost no data is sent from the server to the user—but rather, a large amount of data is very quickly extracted from the client to the server (this might include the user's contacts info or other important data, such as user keystrokes). Finally, after this data is exfiltrated, an ongoing command and control (C2) channel is established between the malicious actor's remote server and the local client, possibly allowing further data to be exfiltrated in the future, or allowing other methods of compromise to be undertaken. Again, ETA observes and records all of this data at the switch level.

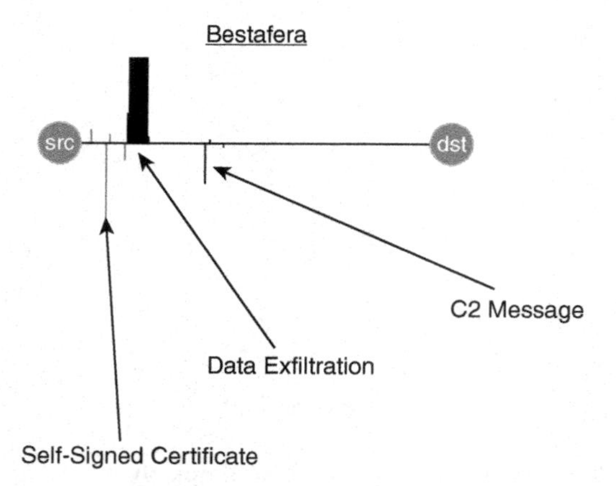

Figure 22-6 *Malicious Encrypted Transaction Fingerprint: Bestafera*

After recording all of this data for a given encrypted flow on the Catalyst 9000 Series switch, the data is packaged up in a NetFlow record associated with that encrypted flow, and exported to the Stealthwatch system. Stealthwatch is a Cisco security management platform that, among its other uses, is used to receive these NetFlow records containing ETA information, extract the necessary data, and compare this against a cloud-based database of known malicious traffic flow fingerprints.

The use of NetFlow is key because this not only allows the ETA-specific data as noted (IDP and SPLT) to be extracted for a given flow, but also allows the complete IP information about the flow to be included. This in turn allows the destination IP addresses involved to be compared against known malicious hosts, or specific regions or countries, which may serve as higher risk points for malware. In addition, the ability to inspect the initial data packets for a given flow allows for certain fields commonly used by malware in self-signed certificates to be inspected and this data exported for analysis. By leveraging NetFlow to extract this data, the maximum amount of information possible from the switch can be provided to Stealthwatch for analysis.

In both cases examined here by ETA's IDP and SPLT capabilities, none of the data is decrypted—nor does it need to be. When looked at from this perspective, the differences between the benign Google search flow and the Bestafera banking Trojan flow are starkly apparent. These differences serve as a foundational analytical component of the Cisco Encrypted Traffic Analytics solution.

It is worth noting that ETA, by its nature of comparing encrypted traffic fingerprints to a cloud-based database system, is inherently focused on traffic flows from inside the organization going to locations outside the organizational boundaries (typically, to locations on the Internet). In other words, ETA focuses on flows that can be broadly observed and for which a malicious traffic fingerprint database can be constructed and maintained, rather than monitoring encrypted flows of traffic within the organization itself.

Encrypted Malware Detection: Putting It All Together

In ETA, each element within the network has an important and distinct role to play.

First, the flow must be detected, and the traffic within it gathered for analysis. This is done in the Catalyst 9300 and 9400 switches—platforms that sit directly adjacent to the users within the network infrastructure and thus are ideally placed to gather this data (because they always see both directions of the traffic flow, not being subject to asymmetrical routing that might otherwise interfere with the traffic analysis).

This is illustrated in Figure 22-7, which outlines the complete sequence of events for the ETA analysis of a flow.

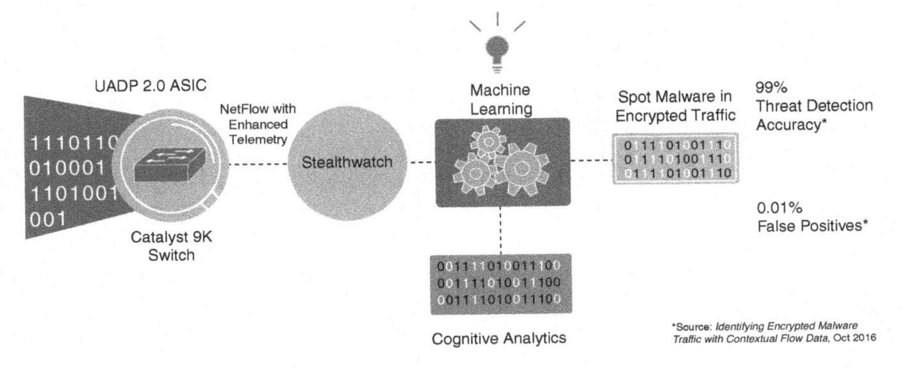

Figure 22-7 *Encrypted Traffic Analytics: Solution Overview*

Leveraging the UADP ASIC in the Catalyst 9300/9400 switch platforms, along with the powerful, multicore Intel CPU that these platforms also employ, Encrypted Traffic Analytics gathers the IDP and SPLT data for any new encrypted flow. This data is then exported via Flexible NetFlow up to the Cisco Stealthwatch collector. Again, the use of NetFlow from the access switch is key because this allows a number of important additional elements to be extracted concerning the flow, along with the critical elements of data gathered by ETA itself (IDP and SPLT).

In turn, Stealthwatch compares all of this data against Cisco's cloud-based Cognitive Threat Analytics solution, which leverages an extensive data set from Cisco's vast Talos security database. By applying machine-learning techniques, it is possible to identify malicious encrypted flows with this supplied data to a level of detection accuracy exceeding 99 percent, with a very low false-positive rate.

And so, ETA enables you to achieve what seemed impossible at first: without needing to decrypt anything, you are able to positively identify malicious traffic flows within the network, in close to real time, and differentiate them from benign encrypted flows.

Can you tell "good noise" from "bad noise"? It turns out that you can. By leveraging the unique and powerful capabilities of Cisco's premier access switching platforms, and combining them with Cisco's industry-leading cloud-based security capabilities and throwing in a dash of machine learning, Encrypted Traffic Analytics enables a new generation of sophisticated threat detection.

Stealthwatch analysis also enables organizations to monitor their compliance with cryptographic security policies by reporting even on benign flows via the Stealthwatch management console, and allowing network and security managers to be alerted (for example) if older, less-secure cipher suites are in use. Because encryption standards change periodically (with new ciphers being introduced and older, less-secure methods being deprecated), being able to passively audit the security protocols in use within the organization for non-malicious flows, and report on any deviations from the organization's defined security best practices, is an important additional use case for ETA.

And so, ETA serves as an important new weapon in the arsenal of network and security managers everywhere in the ongoing battle to secure the enterprise network. While ETA is just one component in a much broader array of security tools and capabilities (which typically include firewalls, intrusion detection and prevention systems, and much more), it serves as an important complement to these systems, and assists to solve an important problem that is otherwise very difficult to address.

Enterprises everywhere can benefit from the powerful new, industry-leading, network-integrated security capability that Encrypted Traffic Analytics offers—an excellent proof point of the power of Cisco Digital Network Architecture.

Summary

This chapter introduced and explored the following:

- The challenges that ETA helps to solve
  - Addressing encrypted malware in the network, without decrypting it
  - Allowing organizations to provide auditing for cryptographic compliance
- How ETA functions
  - IDP analysis of initial packet exchanges between encryption endpoints
  - SPLT analysis of packet sequences, lengths, and times
  - NetFlow export of these and other data points to Stealthwatch for further analysis
- The benefits that ETA provides

Keep your eye on this space! ETA is an evolving solution, and one that shows the power of network-integrated security to solve challenges that are otherwise difficult, if not impossible, to address. As you explore the possible uses of ETA within your own organization, you will no doubt gain better insights as to how to better secure your own network environment, now and into the future.

Chapter 23

Cisco DNA Evolution

Cisco DNA is Cisco's long-term strategy for enterprise networking architecture. As such, the platforms, technologies, and solutions described in this book are all in a state of rapid evolution and development, and therefore these should not be taken as the fixed and final expression of this architecture; if anything, consider these as merely the beginning of Cisco's DNA journey.

To accurately reflect this dynamic and progressive state, and to appropriately conclude this book, the authors (all of whom serve as Cisco DNA architects) wanted to share some of their thoughts on how they see Cisco DNA evolving over the next few years.

Prognostication is always a risky business, and becomes even more so when you have to guard and limit expressions of thought leadership due to the stringent confidentiality requirements of a highly competitive industry. Nonetheless, this brief chapter summarizes a few of these expressions to give a sense of where Cisco DNA is heading, without giving away strategic implementation details.

The following list summarizes some thoughts by the authors on the future direction of Cisco DNA, arranged by technologies:

- **Programmable hardware:** The Unified Access Data Plane (UADP) ASIC demonstrates the phenomenal agility, flexibility, capabilities, and performance that programmable ASICs bring to the network infrastructure devices; as such, expect to see programmable hardware pervasively embedded throughout the enterprise network infrastructure.
- **Software innovations:** All enterprise platforms (routing, switching, wireless) will converge on a single network operating system: IOS XE. This will maximize feature modularity, syntax consistency, and operational simplicity, as well as accelerate feature development (as currently, a major part of the engineering efforts of a new feature is the porting of it across platforms; with IOS XE, such resources can be reallocated to developing, rather than merely transporting).

- **Protocol innovations:** At Layer 2, expect to see wireless speeds continuing to increase (beyond 802.11ac, such as 802.11ax and beyond), with the same expectations for wired Multigigabit Ethernet (with the latter reaching 25GE and 100GE in the near future); at Layer 4+, look for extensions to protocols such as Virtual Extensible Local Area Networking (VXLAN) protocol that will enable greater policy flexibility, as well as support valuable metadata that could potentially be leveraged for richer network analytics.
- **Programmable interfaces:** More platforms and functions will be supported via programmable interfaces; similarly, more sources of instrumentation will become available via model-based streaming telemetry. Software Development Kits (SDKs) will also enable third-party products supporting model-based programmable interfaces to be supported and managed with Cisco DNA Center.
- **Virtualization:** Look for more end-to-end service chaining (rather than local-only), extending virtual network functions from the access layer of the campus all the way through to the data center and/or cloud; expect automation to spin up virtual machines and containers on demand. Also anticipate an increasing number of third-party partners developing applications to be hosted within IOS XE containers on Cisco devices; such applications complement core networking functions in a variety of manners, and as such, Cisco is encouraging developers to use this platform for their applications, thus delivering maximum options to our customers.
- **Enterprise fabric:** Expect Software-Defined Access (SD-Access) to extend beyond the campus, fully integrating with all the best features of software-defined wide-area networking (SD-WAN), from Cisco's Viptela acquisition. The building blocks have already been laid to enable end-to-end segmentation, policy-driven application treatment, and comprehensive analytics; all that remains is the cohesive integration of these blocks to collectively make enterprise fabric a reality in the near future, and this entire enterprise fabric will be centrally managed from within Cisco DNA Center.
- **IoT (Internet of Things):** Although not discussed at length in this book, expect to see extended Cisco DNA integration with IoT devices, technologies, and services.
- **Analytics:** Look for analytics to become more distributed (rather than centralized). Also keep an eye out for more application programming interface (API) integrations with data sources beyond the enterprise network, including peer analytics systems (as this industry—and the offerings within it—is just exploding). Further, expect to see completely autonomous self-remediating workflows for common network issues in the near future.
- **Machine learning:** Machine learning will be applied to an extended number of use cases (beyond wireless). Look for a greater emphasis on predictive analytics (versus cognitive); look also for applications of machine reasoning for troubleshooting and remediation.

- **Cisco DNA Center:** Cisco DNA Center will become the integration point between the network and the rest of IT; the APIs being developed today to support a fixed set of use cases will be the foundational building blocks that will allow IT to leverage the enterprise network as a single, cohesive, programmable entitiy (and vice versa); additionally, Cisco is actively developing an ecosystem of partners to use Cisco DNA Center as a platform, on which they can port (or build) their best-of-breed solutions, alleviating them of all the platform-specific complexity of integrating directly with network devices.
- **Cross-domain orchestration:** As intent-based networking extends beyond the enterprise, policy and analytics orchestration must similarly span across domains, so as to integrate with Cisco Application Centric Infrastructure (ACI), Tetration, Network Assurance Engine (NAE) in the data center, Cisco Network Services Orchestrator (NSO), and Platform for Network Data Analytics (PaNDA) in the service provider, etc.; such orchestration will heavily depend on the definition of common policy language(s) across such domains to express intent, as well as common methods of correlating analytics data to the expressed intent.
- **Cloud integration:** Cisco DNA Center and supporting technologies will allow the enterprise to extend its reach into the cloud for policy, automation, and assurance of their applications. Further, Cisco DNA Center will leverage the cloud to augment and extend its on-premises capabilities; while solutions in this space are nascent at the time of writing, exciting innovations are being developed to extend Cisco DNA Center capabilities via its cloud-tethered connection.

Finally, consider not only the future of the network, but also the future of the network administrator. It cannot be overemphasized that now, more than ever, with these major evolutionary changes occurring in the enterprise network, you need to remain current or, better yet, be ahead of the curve. Expand your lower-level skills, such as configuring network devices via the command-line interface (CLI), to include programming skills (which can be acquired by taking advantage of resources like Cisco DevNet). Also, as the lines between NetOps, DevOps, and SecOps are all expected to blur, it is highly recommended to expand awareness and skillsets into these adjacent technology areas. Furthermore, aim not only to broaden your technology skillsets, but also to raise them. This means developing a deeper understanding of the business-level requirements of your company, always looking for ways to marry such organizational objectives to specific technologies that can deliver them. The more you can understand and speak the language of the CIO, the more impact and influence you will bring to your company, remaining a valuable (and not replaceable) employee during this disruptive transition to intent-based networking in the enterprise.

Again, it bears repeating that these are simply predictions by the authors at the time of writing of where they think Cisco DNA is heading. How Cisco DNA ultimately evolves will be primarily driven by customer demand as well as marketplace pressures.

In summary: Cisco's DNA journey is just beginning, and is already proving itself to be a bold and dynamic ride, with possibilities that are wide open and very exciting!

Are you ready?

Index

Numbers

10GBASE-T, 232
25G Ethernet, 234
40-Gbps Ethernet, 226–227

A

abstractions, leveraging to deliver intent-based networking, 372–375
ACLs (access control lists), 262
actionable insights, 26
"Adventure Series" scanner, 32
advertising, digital transformation in, 3
aggregation, 432
Ahrendts, Angela, 8
Air France, digitally transforming employee experience, 12–13
analytics. *See also* Analytics Engines; Telemetry
"big data," 407, 424
cognitive, 708
Cognitive Threat Analytics, 719
context, 633–638
correlation, 406
defining, 397–398
distributed network analytics, 408–411
distributed on-device analytics, 641
ETA, 711–712
Instrumentation, 407–408
learning, 638–639
NDP, 647–649
architecture, 650–651
CEP, 650
contextual correlation and time machine, 649–650
extensibility, 653
operation, 652–653
network analytics, 398–399
history of, 400–401
role of in Cisco DNA, 402–403
opportunities and challenges of, 399–400
predictive, 708–709
proactive, 401
quality of data, 440–441

reactive, 401
reasons for, 401–402
role of the cloud for, 82, 420–421
Telemetry, 352–353, 411–412
traditional approach, 416–418
trending, 709–710
Analytics Engine, 416, 423–424, 427–428, 643–644. *See also* **Cisco Tetration Analytics; NDP (Cisco Network Data Platform)**
application development simplification, 420
Cisco Tetration Analytics, 439–440
analytics layer, 445–446
benefits of, 446–448
data center visibility, 442–444
data collection layer, 444–445
enforcement layer, 446
visualization layer, 446
data scalability, 419
efficiency, 419–420
NDP, 428–430
architecture components, 433–435
architecture layers, 431–433
architecture principles, 430–431
cloud deployments, 437–438
collectors, 432, 435
data store function, 433
data visualization function, 433
on-premises deployment, 436–437
security and high availability, 438–439
TQ, 430
need for, 418–419
reasons for, 425–427
analytics layer (Cisco Tetration Analytics), 445–446
analytics platform, 77, 112
the cloud, 319–322
data collection, 77, 113
data export, 114–115
data ingestion, 114
data reporting, 78
data sources, 405–407
Cisco DNA analysis, 78–79
feedback and control, 79–80
leveraging the cloud for, 118–120
Ansible, 355–356
Anycast Default Gateway, 529
APIC-EM (Cisco Application Policy Interface Controller Enterprise Module), 222, 585
APIs, 83–84
open APIs, 26–27, 460–461
AppDynamics, 678–685
application classification and marking policies, 602, 621–622
Application Health page (Cisco DNA Assurance), 671–678
application hosting, 357–358
Cisco IOS XE, 205–206
in the cloud, 116–118
Application Policy, 569–570
deploying end-to-end application policies, 576–582
marking profile, 583
NBAR2, 589–591
engines, 593–594
"Holy Grail" classification and marking policy, 596–598
internal operation, 592–594
QoS attributes, 594–596
SD-AVC, 599–601

queuing profile, 582–583
routing platform requirements, 602
application classification and marking policies, 602
enterprise-to-service provider mapping, 606–609
hardware queuing, 609–611
internal system QoS, 612–613
queuing and dropping policies, 603–605
sub-line rate hierarchical QoS policies, 605–606
service provider profile, 584–585
switching platform requirements, 613
hardware queuing policies, 614–617
internal system QoS, 618–621
translating business intent into application policy, 586–589
wireless platform requirements, 621
application classification and marking policies, 621–622
hardware QoS, 624–626
internal system QoS, 626–628
Application Registry, 570–574
application details, viewing, 573
custom applications, defining, 573–574
traffic classes, 571–572
Application Sets, 574–576
applications, role of the cloud for in Cisco DNA, 81–82
archetypes
experts, 45–47
firefighters, 44
front-line engineers, 42–43
planners, 48–49
architectural benefits of NFV, 271–272
architectural principles
cloud integration, 65
extensibility, 62
of NDP, 430–431
openness, 61
policy-based networking, 63
programmability, 62–63
security, 63–64
software driven, 64–65
architectural requirements of self-healing networks, 639–647
analytics engine, 643–644
distributed on-device analytics, 641
instrumentation, 640–641
machine learning, 644
scalable storage, 643
telemetry, 642–643
architecture layers of NDP, 431–433, 650–651
ASICs (application-specific integrated circuits), 131, 136. *See also* flexible silicon
BGA, 143
densities, 143
designing and building, 136–143
EARL series, 146–147
faulty chip design, 145–146
flexible silicon, 152–154
floor planning, 141
functional validation, 141–142
impurities in silicon wafers, 144–145
network ASICs, packet processing, 149–150
packaging, 143
photomasking, 141

QFP, 173–174
architecture, 176–177
key attributes of, 174–176
packet processing, 177–179
QoS, 180
TCAM and memory resources, 179
use in platforms, 180–181
SDNs, 148–149
synthesis process, 140
UADP
on-chip micro engines, 161–162
common denominator across variants, 171–172
EFC, 158
FlexParser, 156–158
IQS, 158
model comparison, 166
NetFlow, 163
recirculation, 159–160
stacking interface, 160–161
use cases, 163–165
versions 2.0 and 3.0, 165–171

assigning IP host pools to VNs, 561–564

assurance workflow in Cisco DNA Center, 514

attacks
ensuring device identity, 220–221
IOS modification, 215–216
mitigation, 216
mitigation techniques
image validation and signing, 217
runtime defenses, 217–218
Secure Boot, 218

automated troubleshooting and remediation, 645–647

automation, 73
centralized systems, 331
controllers, 73–74, 330
relationship with service definition and orchestration layer, 110–111
current impediments to, 364–367
device programmabiity, 337
CLI automation, 338–340
encoding, 345–346
model-based data, 340–341
protocols, 344–345
SNMP, 340
YANG, 341–344
in Cisco DNA Center, 377
domain controllers, 375–377
imperative versus declarative control, 331–332
increasing importance of, 362
infrastructure and Cisco DNA service automation, 368–369
lowering risk through, 326
moving faster with, 328
network controller, 333–334
network programmability, 332–333
orchestrators, 75–76, 334–335
reasons for, 325–326
reducing errors in the network, 363
reducing TCO, 326–327
reducing time to execute operations, 363–364
role of controllers in, 371–372
role of the cloud for in Cisco DNA, 82
scaling your infrastructure, 328–329
and SDN, 330

security, 364
simplifying with, 330
standard and nonstandard tasks, 369–371
standardization, 382–383
standardized settings for supporting network functions, 384
thinking "out of the box," 329
AVC (Cisco Application Visibility and Control), 74

B

BC Hydro, digitally transforming business operations, 16
benefits
of Cisco Tetration Analytics, 446–448
of NFV, 268
architecture, 271–272
CAPEX, 268–269
OPEX, 270–271
of public cloud adoption, 309–310
of SMUs, 212
Bestafera, 717
BGA (ball grid array), 143
BGP (Border Gateway Protocol), 239
"big data," 407, 424, 648
Boeing, digitally transforming business operations, 14–15
boot sequence attacks, 218–220
Secure Boot, 218
border nodes, 519, 523–524
fabric border nodes, 524–525
fabric default border nodes, 525–526
supported devices, 526–527
branch virtualization
Cisco DNA Center, 478–485
NFV use case, 274–275
orchestration, 473
SAE, 488–489
building blocks, 492–493
motivation for, 489–492
building blocks of SD-Access, 512
Cisco DNA Center, 514–515
Burberry, digitally transforming customer experience, 8–9
business intent
relationship with Cisco DNA policy services, 92–93
translating into application policy, 586–589
business operations, digital transformations in
BC Hydro, 16
Boeing, 14–15
Codelco, 15–16
business requirements
cost reduction, 25–26
of Cisco DNA
actionable insights, 21–22
cost reduction, 20
intent-based networking, 23–24
risk mitigation, 20–21, 26
businesses, digital transformation in, 7–8

C

cabling, Ethernet, 230–234
capabilities of SD-Access
IP host pools, 515–516
scalable groups, 506–508, 517–518
stretched subnets, 508–512
VNs, 505–506, 516–517

CAPEX, benefits of NFV, 268–269
CAPWAP (Control and Provisioning of Wireless Access Points), 300
case studies
SD-Access
adding a WLC to the fabric, 561
assigning IP host pools to VNs, 561–564
Cisco DNA Center, 542–555
editing a fabric site, 555–560
Catalyst 5000 switch, 192–193
Catalyst 6500 switch, 193
CatOS, 193
CEF (Cisco Express Forwarding), 191
centralized systems, 331
CEP (Complex Event Processing), 650
challenges
of cloud computing, 310–311
of enterprise networks, 497–499
of network analytics, 425–427
of troubleshooting, 632–633
changing needs of networks, 126–127
characteristics of Cisco DNA fabric, 69–70
on-chip micro engines, 161–162
chips. *See also* **ASICs (application-specific integrated circuits); flexible silicon**
on-chip micro engines, 161–162
CPUs, 150–151
design drivers and density, 143–145
EARLs, 146–147
faulty design, 145–146
Cisco, digitally transforming employee experience, 13–14
Cisco Adaptive Security Virtual Appliance, 464
Cisco Aironet 4800, 183
FRA, 183–185
Intelligent Capture, 185
Cisco Collaboration Tools, 14
Cisco CSR 1000V, 316–318
Cisco Design Thinking Framework, 34–35
Define phase, 37–39
for Cisco DNA, 49–53
Discovery phase, 35–37
for Cisco DNA, 41
Explore phase, 39–40
for Cisco DNA, 53
Opportunity Statement, 36–37
Problem To Be Solved Statement, 38–39
VNFs, 67
Cisco DNA. *See* **Cisco DNA (Cisco Digital Network Architecture)**
Cisco ENCS Series hardware, 457–459
Cisco Firepower NGFWv, 464
Cisco Integrated Services Virtual Router, 463–464
Cisco IOS
CLI automation, 338–340
control plane, evolution of, 194–195
data plane, evolution of, 191–194
management plane, evolution of, 195–196
Cisco IOS XE, 198, 199–202
application hosting, 205–206
benefits of SMUs, 212
cold patches, 211
container framework, 205–206
database, 203–204

hot patches, 211
IOS modification attacks, 215–216
platform support, 212–213
RAFA, 207–208
running virtualized applications and VNFs inside, 493–495
single release train, 209
SMUs, installing, 211–212
software maintenance upgrades, 209–210
subsystems, 202–203
Cisco IT network change requests, Q2-Q4 FY2016, 49–50
Cisco Prime vNAM (Virtual Network Analysis Module), 465
Cisco strategy for virtualization in the enterprise, 452–453
Cisco Tetration Analytics, 439–440
analytics layer, 445–446
benefits of, 446–448
data center visibility, 442–444
data collection layer, 444–445
enforcement layer, 446
visualization layer, 446
Cisco TrustSec solution, 301
Cisco UCS E-Series hardware, 455–456
Cisco vWAAS (Virtual Wide Area Application Services), 465
Cisco vWLC (Virtual Wireless LAN Controller), 465–466
classes of traffic, 571–572
CLI automation, 338–340
Client Health page (Cisco DNA Assurance), 663–670
cloud integrated functionality of Cisco DNA, 65
the cloud, 308
adoption of, 307–308
advantages of adopting, 309–310
for analytics, 319–322
application hosting, 116–118
for automation, 318–319
challenges of, 310–311
Cognitive Threat Analytics, 719
deployment models, 312–313
for Cisco DNA, 315–316
IaaS, 312
"IDC CloudView," 313
leveraging for Cisco DNA controllers and analytics, 118–120
multicloud strategy, 313–314
PaaS, 311–312
on-premises and off-premises agnosticism, 115–116
role of for analytics, 420–421
role of in Cisco DNA, 80–81
for analytics, 82
for applications, 81–82
for automation and management, 82
SaaS, 117, 311
service models, 311–312
cloud-enabled requirements for Cisco DNA, 60
Codelco, digitally transforming business operations, 15–16
cognitive analytics, 708
Cognitive Threat Analytics, 719
cold patches, 211
collectors, 432, 435
commands, NFVIS host configuration, 485–488
communication protocols, 225. *See also* **networking protocols**

communications, digital transformation in, 4
comparing UADP models, 166
complexity and cost, Cisco DNA requirements for reducing, 57–58
compliance, Cisco DNA requirements for, 58–59
compression, 432
ConfD, 354
configuration management, CLI automation, 338–340
configuring NFVIS hosts, 485–488
construction of ASICs, 136–143
container framework, Cisco IOS XE, 205–206
context, 633–638
context collectors, 432
continuity, need for in next-generation networks, 129
control plane,101, 191
- in Cisco IOS, evolution of, 194–195
- LISP as next-generation overlay control plane, 257
- segmentation, 302
  - *multihop path isolation techniques, 302–303*
  - *single-hop path isolation techniques, 303–304*
- simplified wireless control plane, 534–538
- virtualization, NFV use case, 272–274

control plane nodes, 519, 520–522
- supported devices, 522–523

control plane protocols, relationship with domain controllers, 375–377
controllers, 73–74, 330. ***See also*** **automation**
- automating transport and network functions infrastructure, 99
- Cisco vWLC, 465–466
- in the DC, 328
- domains, 102–105
- EFC, 158
- instantiating and maintaining Cisco DNA services, 100–101
- leveraging the cloud for, 118–120
- maintaining view of infrastructure functions and connected endpoints, 100
- relationship with service definition and orchestration layer, 110–111
- role in automation, 371–372
- WLC, 519

correlation, 406, 638–639
- contextual, 634–638

cost, Cisco DNA requirements for reducing, 57–58
CPUs, 150–151
Craigslist, 3
current impediments to automation, 364–367
custom applications, defining, 573–574
customer experience, digital transformations in
- Burberry, 8–9
- digitally transforming, 8
- Starbucks, 9–10
- UPS, 11

customers, pain points, 52

D

data collection, 77, 113
data collection layer (Cisco Tetration Analytics), 444–445
data export, 114–115
data extraction, 113

data ingestion, 114
data plane, 69–70, 190
in Cisco IOS, evolution of, 191–194
optimized wireless, 538–539
data reporting, 78
data sources of analytics, 405–407
quality of data, 440–441
database, Cisco IOS XE, 203–204
DC (data center), controllers, 328
declarative control, 331–332
deduplication, 432
Define phase for Cisco DNA, 49–53
Define phase of Cisco Design Thinking Framework, 37–39
definition of analytics, 397–398
deployment models
for the cloud, 312–313
NDP
cloud deployments, 437–438
on-premises deployment, 436–437
VNFs, 293
design of ASICs, 136–143
design thinking, 31–32. ***See also*** **Cisco Design Thinking Framework**
Cisco Design Thinking Framework, 34–35
principles, 33–34
design workflow in Cisco DNA Center, 514
device programmabiity, 337. ***See also*** **devices**
CLI automation, 338
encoding, 345–346
model-based data, 340–341
protocols, 344–345
SNMP, 340
YANG, 341–344
devices
border node support, 526–527
control plane node support, 522–523
edge node support, 530–531
ensuring identity of, 220–221
fabric enabled, 99
in SD-Access, 518–520, 541
digital advertising, 3
digital disruption
threat of, C01.001700-C01.1727
WhatsApp, 127
"Digital Vortex: How Digital Disruption Is Redefining Industries," 126
Digital Vortex report, 128
digitally transforming industries
advertising, 3
in business operations
BC Hydro, 16
Boeing, 14–15
Codelco, 15–16
communications, 4
in customer experience
Burberry, 8–9
Starbucks, 9–10
UPS, 11
in employee experience
Air France, 12–13
Cisco, 13–14
RehabCare, 13
finance, 4
with IOT, 16–17
media and entertainment, 3–4
transportation services, 5–7
Discovery phase of Cisco Design Thinking Framework, 35–37
for Cisco DNA, 41

distributed analytics, 408–411
Distributed Anycast Default Gateway, 510
distributed forwarding, 192
distributed on-device analytics, 641
distributed systems, 331
DMZ, evolution of, 116–118
Cisco DNA (Cisco Digital Network Architecture), 124–125
abstractions, leveraging to deliver intent-based networking, 372–375
analytics, 77, 112
"big data," 407, 424
data collection, 77, 113
data export, 114–115
data ingestion, 114
data reporting, 78
data sources, 405–407
definition, 397–398
feedback and control, 79–80
Instrumentation, 407–408
opportunities and challenges of, 399–400
proactive, 401
reactive, 401
reasons for, 401–402
role of the cloud for, 420–421
traditional analytics approach, 416–418
Analytics Engines, 423–424, 427–428
application development simplification, 420
data scalability, 419
efficiency, 419–420
reasons for, 425–427
APIs, 83–84
application, user, and device awareness, 59
application policy, 569–570
Application Registry, 570–574
application details, viewing, 573
custom applications, defining, 573–574
traffic classes, 571–572
Application Sets, 574–576
architectural principles
cloud integration, 65
extensibility, 62
openness, 61
policy-based networking, 63
programmability, 62–63
security, 63–64
software-driven, 64–65
automation, 73
controllers, 73–74
imperative versus declarative control, 331–332
lowering risk through, 326
moving faster with, 328
network controller, 333–334
network programmability, 332–333
orchestrators, 75–76, 334–335
reasons for, 325–326
reducing TCO, 326–327
role of controllers in, 371–372
and SDN, 330
business requirements
actionable insights, 21–22
cost reduction, 20
intent-based networking, 23–24
risk mitigation, 20–21

business value of, 24–25
the cloud, 315–316
  for analytics, 319–322
  for applications, 316–318
  for automation, 318–319
  leveraging for Cisco DNA controllers and analytics, 118–120
cloud-enabled requirements, 60
control plane, 871
control plane-based segmentation, 302
  multihop path isolation techniques, 302–303
  single-hop path isolation techniques, 303–304
controllers
  automating transport and network functions infrastructure, 99
  domains, 102–105
  instantiating and maintaining Cisco DNA services, 100–101
  maintaining view of infrastructure functions and connected endpoints, 100
data plane, 69–70
Define phase, 49–53
design thinking, 31–32
Discovery phase, 41
distributed network analytics, 408–411
ETA, 711–712
evolution of the DMZ, 116–118
expert archetype, 45–47
Explore phase, 53
firefighters, 44
flexible silicon, 152–154
front-line engineer archetypes, 42–43
future direction of, 721–723
infrastructure, 66–67
  domains, 67–69
  network fabrics, 69–70, 98–99
  policy, 72–73
  supporting network functions, 96–97
  transport, 94–96
  virtualization, 70–72
infrastructure solutions
  flexible hardware, 130–131
  flexible software, 131–132
  new and evolving protocols, 132
intelligent feedback mechanism, 59
interfaces, 105–107
key outcome of the Cisco DNA approach, 84–85
network analytics, role of, 402–403
network segmentation architecture
  network access control, 298
  network services edge, 299
  network virtualization, 298–299
packet transport, 94–96
planner archetype, 48–49
policies, 905
policy services, relationship with business intent, 92–93
policy-based path segmentation, 299–302
on-premises and off-premises agnosticism, 115–116
requirements
  to increase operational flexibility, 58–60
  to reduce complexity and cost, 57–58

role of the cloud in, 80–81
for analytics, 82
for applications, 81–82
for automation and management, 82
SAE, 117–118
security and compliance requirements, 58–59
service definition and orchestration layer, 107–109
relationship with controllers, 110–111
services, 88–90
policy, 91–92
transport, 90
technology scopes, 102–105
Telemetry, 79–80
MDT (Model-driven Telemetry), 414–416
UNI, 90
virtualization, 267–268
transport virtualization, 296–297

Cisco DNA Assurance, 631–633, 653–655
AppDynamics integration, 678–685
Application Health, 671–678
Client Health, 663–670
context, 633–638
Intelligent Capture, 697–704
learning, 638–639
Microsoft Skype for Business Integration, 685–688
ML, 704–708
Network Health page, 655–662
Path Trace, 688–695
sensor-driven tests, 695–697

Cisco DNA Center, 377–380, 512, 514–515, 519, 542–555
Application Policy
application classification and marking policies, 602, 621–622
deploying end-to-end application policies, 576–582
enterprise-to-service provider mapping, 606–609
hardware QoS, 624–626
hardware queuing, 609–611
hardware queuing policies, 614–617
internal system QoS, 612–613, 618–621, 626–628
marking profile, 583
NBAR2, 589–591
queuing and dropping policies, 603–605
queuing profile, 582–583
routing platform requirements, 602
service provider profile, 584–585
sub-line rate hierarchical QoS policies, 605–606
switching platform requirements, 613
translating business intent into application policy, 586–589
automating the deployment of network elements and functions, 390–394
automation, 377
characterizing wireless LAN profiles, 386–387
device credentials, automating, 384–385

device discovery, inventory, and topology, 380–382
lifecycle operations, automating, 394–395
network design standardization, 388–390
reserving and managing IP address pools, 385–386
standardized settings for supporting network functions, 384
standarized service provider QoS profiles, 386–387
workflows, 514

DNS-AS (DNS as Authoritative Source), 74

domain controllers, relationship with control plane protocols, 375–377

domains, 67–69, 102–105

E

EARLs (Encoded Address Recognition Logic), 146–147

EasyQoS, 585–586

edge nodes, 519, 527–530
supported devices, 530–531

editing a fabric site, 555–560

EFC (Egress Forwarding Controller), 158

EGR (Egress Global Resolution), 168–169

EIGRP (Enhanced Interior Gateway Routing Protocol), 239

emergence of virtualization, 133

employee experience, digital transformations in
Air France, 12–13
Cisco, 13–14
RehabCare, 13

encapsulation, 243. ***See also*** **packet encapsulation**

encoding, 345–346

encrypted malware detection, 719–720
Bestafera, 717
defining the problem, 712–713
IDP, 714–715
solution for, 714, 716–718
SPLT, 715–716

ENCS (Cisco Enterprise Network Compute System), 451

end-to-end application policies, deploying, 576–582

enforcement layer (Cisco Tetration Analytics), 446

ENFV (Cisco Enterprise Network Functions Virtualization), 453–455. ***See also*** **NFVIS (Cisco Enterprise Network Function Virtualization Infrastructure Software)**
configuring NFVIS hosts, 485–488
NFVIS, 459–463
platform options
Cisco ENCS Series hardware, 457–459
Cisco UCS E-Series hardware, 455–456
VNFs
Cisco Adaptive Security Virtual Appliance, 464
Cisco Integrated Services Virtual Router, 463–464
Cisco Prime vNAM, 465
Cisco vWAAS, 465
Cisco vWLC, 465–466
NGFWv, 464
sample packet flow, 470–471

service chaining, 468–469, 471–472

third-party support, 466–468

ENFV (Enterprise Network Functions Virtualization), 451

enterprise networks. ***See also*** **ENFV (Cisco Enterprise Network Functions Virtualization)**

challenges of, 497–499

fabrics, 500–501

network segmentation, 503

overlay networks, 503

reasons for using, 501–505

simplification through, 504–505

underlay networks, 503

enterprise-to-service provider mapping, 606–609

ETA (Encrypted Traffic Analytics), 711–712

encrypted malware detection, 719–720

defining the problem, 712–713

solution for, 714, 716–718

IDP, 714–715

SPLT, 715–716

Stealthwatch, 719–720

ETAB (Enterprise Technical Advisory Board), 41

Ethernet, 226–227

10-Gbps, 231

25G, 234

cabling, 230–232

frame format, 227

mGig, 231–233

applications, 232–233

speeds, 231–232

performance, 226

PoE, 227–230

future of, 230

wireless standards, 233

evolution

of Cisco IOS, 190–191

control plane, 194–195

data plane, 191–194

management plane, 195–196

of Cisco IOS XE, 198

of Cisco networking software, 196–198

of the DMZ, 116–118

of networking software, 189–190

experts, 45–47

Explore phase of Cisco Design Thinking, 39–40

for Cisco DNA, 53

extended nodes, 531–532

extensibility, 62

NDP, 653

F

fabric border nodes, 524–525

fabric default border nodes, 525–526

fabric edge nodes, 527–530

supported devices, 530–531

fabrics, 98–99, 102–105, 500–501

editing, 555–560

IP host pools, 515–516

network segmentation, 503

overlay networks, 503

reasons for using, 501–505

simplification through, 504–505

underlay networks, 503

Fast PoE, 229

faulty chip design, 145–146

feedback and control, 79–80
filtering, 432
finance, digital transformation in, 4
firefighter archetypes, 44–45
first-hop reachability protocols, HSRP, 237–238
flexibility, Cisco DNA support for, 58
flexible hardware in Cisco DNA, 130–131
flexible lookup tables, 167
flexible silicon
microcode update, 153
QFP, 173–174
architecture, 176–177
key attributes of, 174–176
packet processing, 177–179
QoS, 180
TCAM and memory resources, 179
use in platforms, 180–181
UADP, 154–163
on-chip micro engines, 161–162
common denominator across variants, 171–172
EFC, 158
FlexParser, 156–158
IQS, 158
model comparison, 166
NetFlow, 163
recirculation, 159–160
stacking interface, 160–161
use cases, 163–165
versions 2.0 and 3.0, 165–171
flexible software, 131–132
FlexParser, 156–158
floor planning of ASICs, 141
FPGAs (field-programmable gate arrays), 131, 151–152
FRA (Flexible Radio Assignment), 183–185
frame format, Ethernet, 227
front-line engineer archetypes, 42–43
functional validation of ASICs, 141–142
future direction of Cisco DNA, 721–723
future of PoE, 230

G

group-based policies, SGT, 261–263
gRPC (Google Remote Procedure Call), 351–352
gRPC Telemetry, 353–354
GUI, for NFVIS, 473–478
guided troubleshooting and remediation, 645

H

hardware
ASICs
BGA, 143
floor planning, 141
photomasking, 141
synthesis process, 140
for ENFV, Cisco UCS E-Series hardware, 455–456
faulty chip design, 145–146
importance of, 135–136
QoS, 624–626
queuing, 609–611, 614–617
validating integrity of, 221
health dimensions in Cisco DNA Assurance
Application Health, 671–678

Client Health, 663–670
Network Health, 655–662
high availability, NDP, 438–439
history of network analytics, 400–401
"Holy Grail" classification and marking policy, 596–598
horizontal-run cabling, installing, 230
host mobility, LISP, 252
hot patches, 211
HSRP (Hot Standby Routing Protocol), 237–238
hybrid cloud, 313
hypervisor scheduling, NFV, 281–282

I

IaaS (infrastructure as a service), 312
"IDC CloudView," 313
IDP (Initial Data Packets) for encrypted malware detection, 714–715
IEEE 802.3, 226. *See also* Ethernet
IGR (Ingress Global Resolution), 168–169
image validation and signing, 217
imperative versus declarative control, 331–332
impurities in silicon wafers, 144–145
increasing importance of automation, 362
industries under threat of digital disruption, 2
infrastructure. *See also* virtualization
automating transport and network functions infrastructure, 99
network fabrics, 98–99
scaling, 328–329
supporting network functions, 96–97
transport functions, 94–96
infrastructure component of Cisco DNA, 66–67
network fabrics, 69–70
policy, 72–73
virtualization, 70–72
infrastructure domains, 67–69
infrastructure solutions of Cisco DNA
flexible hardware, 130–131
flexible software, 131–132
new and evolving protocols, 132
innovation
Cisco DNA support for, 58
application, user, and device awareness, 59
flexibility, 58
intelligent feedback mechanism, 59
FRA, 183–185
Intelligent Capture, 185
in wireless mobility, 182–183
input/output technologies for virtualization, 283–288
installing
horizontal-run cabling, 230
SMUs, 211–212
instantiating and maintaining Cisco DNA services, 100–101
Instrumentation, 407–408
instrumentation, 640–641
integrity, validating, 221
Intelligent Capture, 185, 697–704
intelligent feedback mechanism, 59
intent-based networking, 23–24, 372–375
translating business intent into application policy, 586–589

interfaces, NNIs, 105–107
intermediate nodes, 519
internal operation of NBAR2, 592–594
internal system QoS, 612–613, 618–621, 626–628
intuitive networking, 222–223
IOS modification attacks, 215–216
IOT (Internet of Things), digitally transforming industries with, 16–17
IP address
  functions of, 258
  stretched subnets, 508–512
IP host pools, 515–516
  assigning to VNs, 561–564
ISE (Identity Services Engine), 512, 519
IS-IS (Intermediate System to Intermediate System), 249
iTunes, 3

K

key outcome of the Cisco DNA approach, 84–85
KVM (Kernel-based Virtual Machine), 459

L

Lancope's Stealthwatch, 79
Layer 2 protocols
  STP, 235–236
  tunneling over Layer 3, 241–242
  VLANs, 236–237
Layer 3 protocols
  HSRP, 237–238
  tunneling, 241–242
learning, 638–639
  ML, 704–708
leveraging the cloud for Cisco DNA controllers and analytics, 118–120
lifecycle operations, automating in Cisco DNA Center, 394–395
lighting, PoE, 229
limitations of Telemetry protocols, 413–414
LISP (Location/ID Separation Protocol), 249–251
  control plane nodes, 520–522
  map-servers/resolvers, 273
  need for host mobility, 252
  need for host scale, 252–253
  as next-generation overlay control plane, 257
  roaming operation, 255–257
logic of "Holy Grail" policy, 598
lowering risk through automation, 326

M

maintaining
  Cisco DNA services, 100–101
  view of infrastructure functions and connected endpoints, 100
management, role of the cloud for in Cisco DNA, 82
management plane, 191
  evolution of, 195–196
managing applications in Cisco DNA, Application Registry, 570–574
Map-Registration, 251
map-servers/resolvers, 273

markets of Cisco networking software, 196–198

marking profile, 583

MDT (Model-driven Telemetry), 411, 414–416

media and entertainment, digital transformation in, 3–4

memory

NUMA, 281–282

QFP, TCAM and memory resources, 179

TCAM, 194

metadata, data extraction, 113

MFMT (multi-feature multi-tenant) VNFs, 293

MFST (multi-feature single-tenant) VNFs, 293

mGig (Multigigabit Ethernet), 233–234

10GBASE-T, 232

applications, 232–233

speeds, 231–232

microcode update, 153

Microsoft Skype for Business Integration, 685–688

ML (machine language), 638–639, 644, 704–708

model-based data, 340–341

modern network, picturing, 124–125

Moore's law, 143

moving faster with automation, 328

MPLS (Multiprotocol Label Switching), 241

use cases, 208

MRI (magnetic resonance imaging), 32

redesign for children, 33

multicast, SD-Access support for, 542

multicloud strategy, 313–314

multihop path isolation techniques, 302–303

MyStarbucks app, 9–10

N

NBAR2, 589–591

engines, 593–594

"Holy Grail" classification and marking policy, 596–598

internal operation, 592–594

QoS attributes, 594–596

SD-AVC, 599–601

NCC, 354

Ncclient, 354

NDP (Cisco Network Data Platform), 428–430, 647–649

architectural principles, 430–431

architecture, 650–651

architecture components, 433–435

architecture layers, 431–433

CEP, 650

cloud deployments, 437–438

collectors, 432, 435

contextual correlation and time machine, 649–650

data store function, 433

data visualization function, 433

extensibility, 653

operation, 652–653

on-premises deployment, 436–437

security and high availability, 438–439

TQ, 430

needs and motivators

of experts, 47

of firefighters, 44–45

of front-line engineers, 43
of planners, 48–49
NETCONF, 347–350
NetFlow, 163
for encrypted malware detection, 718
network access control, 298
network analytics, 398–399. *See also* **Analytics Engines; ETA (Encrypted Traffic Analytics)**
"big data," 407
challenges of, 425–427
data sources, 405–407
distributed network analytics, 408–411
ETA, 711–712
encrypted malware detection, 712–713, 714
history of, 400–401
Instrumentation, 407–408
NDP, 647–649
architecture, 650–651
CEP, 650
contextual correlation and time machine, 649–650
extensibility, 653
operation, 652–653
phase 1.0, 400
phase 2.0, 400
phase 3.0, 400–401
reasons for, 401–402
role of in Cisco DNA, 402–403
role of the cloud for, 420–421
Telemetry, 411–412
network ASICs, packet processing, 149–150
network controller, 333–334
network fabrics, 69–70, 98–99, 102–105, 500–501
reasons for using, 501–505
network functions, supporting, 96–97
Network Health page (Cisco DNA Assurance), 655–662
network programmability, 332–333
network services edge, 299
network virtualization, 298–299
networking, 148–149. *See also* **networking protocols**
context, 633–638
CPUs, 150–151
flexible silicon, 152–154
FPGAs, 151–152
Intelligent Capture, 185
intuitive, 222–223
IOS modification attacks, 215–216
markets, 196–198
wireless, SD-Access integration, 532–538
networking protocols, 225–226, 242. *See also* **routing protocols; VXLAN (Virtual Extensible LAN)**
encapsulation, 243
Ethernet, 226–227
25G, 234
cabling, 230–232
frame format, 227
performance, 226
PoE, 227–230
wireless standards, 233
gRPC, 351–352
HSRP, 237–238
IS-IS, 249

LISP, 249–251

need for host mobility, 252

need for host scale, 252–253

roaming operation, 255–257

NETCONF, 347–350

overlay networks, 244–245

PVRST+, 236

PVST+, 236

RESTCONF, 350–351

STP, 235

underlay networks, 244

VLANs, 236–237

VRRP, 237–238

VXLAN, 243–247

networking software, evolution of, 189–190

new and evolving protocols, 132

Newmark, Craig, 3

next-generation networks, 264

continuity, need for, 129

need for change, 126–127

simplicity, need for, 128–129

speed, need for, 127–128

NFV (Network Function Virtualization), 267–268. ***See also*** **ENFV (Cisco Enterprise Network Functions Virtualization)**

benefits of, 268

architecture, 271–272

CAPEX, 268–269

OPEX, 270–271

ENFV, 453–455

hypervisor scheduling and NUMA, 281–282

input/output technologies for virtualization, 283–288

optimizing server configurations, 290–291

oversubscribing the physical hardware resources, 290

performance, 289–290

selecting the right I/O technique, 291–292

system architecture, 278–281

transport virtualization, 296–297

use cases, 272

branch virtualization, 274–275

control plane virtualization, 272–274

virtualization of multicloud exchanges, 276–277

virtualization to connect applications in VPCs, 275–276

NFVIS (Cisco Enterprise Network Function Virtualization Infrastructure Software), 133, 454, 459–463

default internal network connectivity, 462–463

device management, 461

functional building blocks, 461–462

GUI, 473–478

host configuration and monitoring, 485–488

lifecycle management and health monitoring, 460

open APIs, 460–461

service chaining, 460

and standard Linux operating system, 461

VNF requirements, 466–468

web server, 461

ZTP, 459–460

NGFWv (NGFW Virtual), 464

NNIs (network-to-network interfaces), 105–107

nodes

border, 519, 523–524

fabric border nodes, 524–525

fabric default border nodes, 525–526

supported devices, 526–527

control plane, 519, 520–523

edge, 519, 527–530

supported devices, 530–531

extended, 531–532

intermediate, 519

nonstandard automation tasks, 369–371

NSO (Cisco Network Services Orchestrator), 357

NUMA (Non-uniform Memory Access), 281–282

O

open APIs, 26–27, 460–461

openness, 61

operational flexibility

Cisco DNA support for, 58

application, user, and device awareness, 59

flexibility, 58

intelligent feedback mechanism, 59

OPEX (operational expenses)

benefits of NFV, 270–271

reducing, 57–58

opportunities and challenges of analytics, 399–400

Opportunity Statement, 36–37

experts, 47

firefighters, 45

front-line engineers, 43

planners, 49

optimized wireless data plane, 538–539

optimizing server configurations for VNF, 290–291

orchestration in branch infrastructure, 473

orchestrators, 75–76, 334–335

origins

of Cisco IOS, 190–191

control plane, 194–195

data plane, 191–194

management plane, 195–196

of Cisco IOS XE, 198

of Cisco networking software, 196–198

OSPF (Open Shortest Path First), 239

OTT (Over-the-Top) deployment mode, 540

outcome of the Cisco DNA approach, 84–85

overlay networks, 244–245, 503

LISP, 249–251. *See also* LISP (Location/ID Separation Protocol)

oversubscribing VNF physical hardware resources, 290

P

PaaS (platform as a service), 311–312

packaging ASICs, 143

packet encapsulation

in VXLAN, 246–247

scalable group tag support, 248

UDP, 247

virtual network support, 248

packet processing, QFP, 177–179

packet transport in Cisco DNA, 94–96
pain points
of customers, 52
for experts, 47
for firefighters, 45
for front-line engineers, 43
for planners, 49
Path Trace, 688–695
PEPs, 911
performance
of Ethernet, 227
of NFV, 289–290
Perpetual PoE, 229
PFC (Policy Feature Card), 193
phases
of Cisco Design Thinking
Define phase, 37–39
Discovery phase, 35–37
Explore phase, 39–40
philosophy of design thinking, 33–34
photomasking, 141
picturing the modern network, 124–125
planner archetype, 48–49
PoE (Power over Ethernet), 227–229
Fast PoE, 229
future of, 230
Perpetual PoE, 229
policies, 72–73, 905
hardware queuing, 614–617
“Holy Grail” classification and marking policy, 596–598
reporting, 91
security, 91
SGT, 257–264
end-to-end transport across the network, 263–264
for group-based policies, 261–263
policy services, 91–92
policy workflow in Cisco DNA Center, 514
policy-based networking, 63
policy-based path segmentation, 299–302
polling, 411
predictive analytics, 708–709
on-premises and off-premises agnosticism, 115–116
on-premises deployment (NDP), 436–437
principles, of design thinking, 33–34
private cloud, 313
proactive analytics, 401
Problem To Be Solved Statement, 38–39
programmability, 62–63
protocols, 344–345
provision workflow in Cisco DNA Center, 514
public bike sharing, 7
public cloud, 313
advantages of, 309–310
Puppet, 356
PVRST+ (Per-VLAN Rapid Spanning Tree), 236
PVST+ (Per-VLAN Spanning Tree), 236
Pyang, 354

Q

QFP (Cisco QuantumFlow Processor), 173–174
architecture, 176–177
key attributes of, 174–176
packet processing, 177–179

QoS, 180
TCAM and memory resources, 179
use in platforms, 180–181
QoS
attributes, 594–596
internal system QoS, 618–621, 626–628
QFP, 180
UADP, 164
quality of data, 440–441
queuing and dropping policies, 603–605
queuing profile, 582–583

R

RAFA (Run Any Feature Anywhere), 207–208
reactive analytics, 401
recirculation, 159–160
reducing
complexity and cost, Cisco DNA requirements for, 57–58
TCO, 326–327
regular expressions, 339–340
RehabCare, digitally transforming employee experience, 13
relationship between Cisco DNA policies and business intent, 92–93
release trains, Cisco IOS XE, 209
reporting policies, 91
requirements
of Cisco Design Thinking, to increase operational flexibility, 58–60
of Cisco DNA, to reduce complexity and cost, 57–58
of next-generation networks
continuity, 129
need for change, 126–127
simplicity, 128–129
speed, 127–128
responsibilities
of experts, 46
of firefighters, 44
of front-line engineers, 42
of planners, 48
RESTCONF, 350–351
RFID (radio-frequency identification), 6, 9, 14
RIP (Routing Information Protocol), 238
roaming, LISP, 255–257
routed service chaining, 471–472
routing, 191
routing platform requirements for Application Policy, 602
application classification and marking policies, 602
enterprise-to-service provider mapping, 606–609
hardware queuing, 609–611
internal system QoS, 612–613
queuing and dropping policies, 603–605
sub-line rate hierarchical QoS policies, 605–606
routing protocols, 521. ***See also*** **virtual routing**
BGP, 239
EIGRP, 239
OSPF, 239
RIP, 238
VRFs, 240–241
RRs (route reflectors), 273
runtime defenses, 217–218

S

SaaS (software as a service), 117, 311

SAE (Secure Agile Exchange), 117–118, 451, 488–489

building blocks, 492–493

motivation for, 489–492

scalability

of Analytics Engines, 419

need for host scale, 252–255

scalable groups, 506–508, 517–518

tag support in VXLAN, 248

scalable storage, 643

SD-Access, 499–500

Anycast Default Gateway, 529

border nodes, 523–524

fabric default border nodes, 525–526

supported devices, 526–527

building blocks, 512

Cisco DNA Center, 514–515

capabilities

scalable groups, 506–508, 517–518

stretched subnets, 508–512

VNs, 505–506, 516–517

case study

adding a WLC to the fabric, 561

assigning IP host pools to VNs, 561–564

Cisco DNA Center, 542–555

control plane nodes, 520–522

supported devices, 522–523

device roles, 518–520

Distributed Anycast Default Gateway, 510

extended nodes, 531–532

fabric edge nodes, 527–530

supported devices, 530–531

fabric sites, editing, 555–560

fabrics, 500–501

IP host pools, 515–516

network segmentation, 503

overlay networks, 503

reasons for using, 501–505

simplification through, 504–505

underlay networks, 503

multicast support, 542

wireless integration, 532–534

optimized wireless data plane, 538–539

OTT wireless support, 540

simplified wireless control plane, 534–538

supported devices, 541

SD-AVC, 599–601

SDN (software-driven networking), 148–149, 330

Secure Boot, 218–220, 221

security, 63–64

automation, 364

Cisco DNA requirements for, 58–59

ISE, 512

NDP, 438–439

policies, 91

self-healing networks, architectural requirements, 639–647

analytics engine, 643–644

distributed on-device analytics, 641

instrumentation, 640–641

machine learning, 644

scalable storage, 643

telemetry, 642–643

sensor-driven tests, 695–697
service chaining, 468–469
sample packet flow, 470–471
transparent versus routed, 471–472
service definition and orchestration layer, 107–109
relationship with controllers, 110–111
service provider profile, 584–585
services, 88–90
policy, 91–92
transport, 90
SFMT (single-feature multi-tenant) VNFs, 293
SFST (single-feature single-tenant) VNFs, 293
SGACLs, 262
SGTs (Scalable Group Tags), 257–264, 517–518
end-to-end transport across the network, 263–264
for group-based policies, 261–263
silicon wafers, impurities in, 144–145
simplicity, need for in next-generation networks, 128–129
simplified wireless control plane, 534–538
single release train, Cisco IOS XE, 209
single-hop path isolation techniques, 303–304
SMUs (software maintenance upgrades)
benefits of, 212
Cisco IOS XE, installing, 211–212
SNMP (Simple Network Management Protocol), 340
polling, 411
software. *See also* Cisco IOS; SD-Access
CatOS, 193
Cisco IOS
CLI automation, 338–340
origins and evolution of, 190–191
Cisco IOS XE, 198, 199–202
application hosting, 205–206
benefits of SMUs, 212
cold patches, 211
database, 203–204
hot patches, 211
platform support, 212–213
RAFA, 207–208
single release train, 209
software maintenance upgrades, 209–210
subsystems, 202–203
VNFs, running, 493–495
networking, evolution of, 196–198
validating integrity of, 221
software-driven functionality of Cisco DNA, 64–65
solution for encrypted malware detection, 716–718
speeds, mGig, 231–232
SPLT (Sequence of Packet Lengths and Times), for encrypted malware detection, 715–716
stacking interface, 160–161
standard automation, 369–371
Stanford d.school, 32
Starbucks, digitally transforming customer experience, 9–10
Stealthwatch, 79, 719–720
STP (Spanning Tree Protocol), 236

stretched subnets, 508–512
sub-line rate hierarchical QoS policies, 605–606
subsystems of Cisco IOS XE, 202–203
SUDI (Secure Unique Device Identifier), 220–221
supporting network functions, 96–97
switching, 192–194
Application Policy platform requirements, 613
hardware queuing policies, 614–617
internal system QoS, 618–621
SXP (SGT Exchange Protocol), 263
system architecture, NFV, 278–281

T

TAm (Trust Anchor module), 221
TCAM, 194
TCO (total cost of ownership), reducing, 326–327
technical requirements of Cisco DNA
cloud-enabled requirements, 60
operational flexibility, 58–59
security and compliance requirements, 60
technology
design thinking, 32
Cisco Design Thinking Framework, 34–35
principles, 33–34
Moore's law, 143
networking, 148–149
technology scopes, 102–105
Telemetry, 352–353, 411–412, 642–643
data extraction, 113
gRPC, 353–354
MDT, 414–416
reasons for, 412
third-party support of VNFs, 466–468
TQ (Telemetry Quotient), 430
traditional analytics approach, 416–418
traffic
classes, 571–572
classifying, 599–601
handling
CPUs, 150–151
FPGAs, 151–152
transistors. *See also* **ASICs (application-specific integrated circuits); flexible silicon**
densities, 143
EARLs, 146–147
faulty chip design, 145–146
impurities in silicon wafers, 144–145
Moore's law, 143
translating business intent into application policy, 586–589
transparent service chaining, 471–472
transport functions of Cisco DNA infrastructure, 94–96
transport segmentation architecture
network access control, 298
network services edge, 299
network virtualization, 298–299
transport services, 90
transport virtualization, 296–297
transportation services, digital transformation in, 5–7

trending analytics, 709–710

troubleshooting

automated troubleshooting and remediation, 645–647

challenges of, 632–633

guided troubleshooting and remediation, 645

Intelligent Capture, 697–704

Path Trace, 688–695

sensor-driven tests, 695–697

trustworthy systems, 214–215

attack mitigation, 216

image validation and signing, 217

runtime defenses, 217–218

Secure Boot, 218–220

SUDI, 220–221

tunneling, 241–242

U

UADP (Unified Access Data Plane)

on-chip micro engines, 161–162

common denominator across variants, 171–172

EFC, 158

FlexParser, 156–158

internal architecture, 618–621

IQS, 158

model comparison, 166

NetFlow, 163

QoS, 164

recirculation, 159–160

stacking interface, 160–161

use cases, 163–165

versions 2.0 and 3.0, 165–171

Uber, 5–7

UDP (User Datagram Protocol), encapsulation in VXLAN, 247

underlay networks, 244, 503

IS-IS, 249

UNIs (user-to-network interfaces), 90, 105–107

untrusted domains, virtualizing connectivity to, 488–489

UP (User Priority) values, 623

upgrades, Cisco IOS XE software upgrades, 209–210

UPS, digitally transforming customer experience, 11

use cases

for MPLS, 208

for NFV, 272

branch virtualization, 274–275

control plane virtualization, 272–274

virtualization of multicloud exchanges, 276–277

virtualization to connect applications in VPCs, 275–276

UADP, 163–165

user experience, points of failure impacting, 632

V

validating integrity of software/hardware, 221–222

viewing

application details in Application Registry, 573

NBAR2 protocol attributes, 595

virtual network support in VXLAN, 248

virtual routing, 240–241

MPLS, 241

virtualization, 70–72, 267–268, 459. *See also* **NFV (Network Function Virtualization)**
branch virtualization
Cisco DNA Center, 478–485
orchestration, 473
connecting applications in VPCs, NFV use case, 275–276
emergence of, 133
ENFV, 453–455
Cisco ENCS Series hardware, 457–459
Cisco UCS E-Series hardware, 455–456
in the enterprise, 452–453
of multicloud exchanges, NFV use case, 276–277
NFVIS, 459–463
default internal network connectivity, 462–463
SAE, 488–489
building blocks, 492–493
motivation for, 489–492
visualization layer (Cisco Tetration Analytics), 446
VLANs, 236–237
VNFs (virtualized network functions), 67, 133, 267
Cisco Adaptive Security Virtual Appliance, 464
Cisco Integrated Services Virtual Router, 463–464
Cisco Prime vNAM, 465
Cisco vWAAS, 465
Cisco vWLC, 465–466
deployment models, 293
footprint considerations, 292–293
input/output technologies for virtualization, 283–288
multi-tenancy and multi-function, 293–296
NGFWv, 464
optimizing server configurations, 290–291
orchestration, 473
running in Cisco IOS XE, 493–495
selecting the right I/O technique, 291–292
service chaining, 468–469
sample packet flow, 470–471
transparent versus routed, 471–472
third-party support, 466–468
VNs (virtual networks), 505–506, 516–517
assigning IP host pools to, 561–564
VoIP (Voice over Internet Protocol), 4
VPNs, MPLS, 241
VRF-lite, 240
VRFs (virtual routing and forwarding), 240–241
VRRP (Virtual Router Redundancy Protocol), 237–238
VXLAN (Virtual Extensible LAN), 67, 875, 130, 132, 243–249
overlay networks, 245
packet encapsulation, 246–247
scalable group tag support, 248
UDP, 247
virtual network support, 248
reasons for, 248–249

W

websites, Ethernet Alliance, 235

WhatsApp, 4, 127, 127

wireless Ethernet, 233

wireless mobility, 182–183

FRA, 183–185

wireless networking

SD-Access integration, 532–538

multicast support, 542

optimized wireless data plane, 538–539

OTT wireless support, 540

simplified wireless control plane, 534–538

supported devices, 541

wireless platform requirements for Application Policy

application classification and marking policies, 621–622

hardware QoS, 624–626

internal system QoS, 626–628

WLC (wireless LAN controllers), 273, 519

adding to fabric, 561

workflows in Cisco DNA Center, 514

Y

YANG (Yet Another Next Generation), 59, 74, 341–344, 415–416

NETCONF, 347–350

RESTCONF, 350–351

YANG Catalog, 355

YANG-explorer, 355

YDK (Yang Development Kit), 356

yield, 145

Z

ZBFW (zone-based firewall), 317

Zipcar, 6

ZTP (Zero-Touch Provisioning), 459–460